Lecture Notes in Computer Science 6688

Commenced Publication in 1973
Founding and Former Series Editors:
Gerhard Goos, Juris Hartmanis, and Jan van Leeuwen

Editorial Board

Anders Heyden Fredrik Kahl (Eds.)

Image Analysis

17th Scandinavian Conference, SCIA 2011
Ystad, Sweden, May 2011
Proceedings

Springer

Volume Editors

Anders Heyden
Centre for Mathematical Sciences
Lund University, Lund, Sweden
E-mail: heyden@maths.lth.se

Fredrik Kahl
Centre for Mathematical Sciences
Lund University, Lund, Sweden
E-mail: fredrik@maths.lth.se

ISSN 0302-9743 e-ISSN 1611-3349
ISBN 978-3-642-21226-0 e-ISBN 978-3-642-21227-7
DOI 10.1007/978-3-642-21227-7
Springer Heidelberg Dordrecht London New York

Library of Congress Control Number: Applied for

CR Subject Classification (1998): I.4, I.5, I.3

LNCS Sublibrary: SL 6 – Image Processing, Computer Vision, Pattern Recognition, and Graphics

Typesetting: Camera-ready by author, data conversion by Scientific Publishing Services, Chennai, India

Printed on acid-free paper

Springer is part of Springer Science+Business Media (www.springer.com)

Preface

This volume contains the papers presented at the Scandinavian Conference on Image Analysis, SCIA 2011, which was held at Ystad Saltsjöbad, Ystad, Sweden, May 23–27.

SCIA 2011 was the 17th in the biennial series of conferences, which has been organized in turn by the Scandinavian countries Sweden, Finland, Denmark, and Norway since 1980. The event itself has always attracted participants and author contributions from outside the Scandinavian countries, making it an international conference.

The conference included a full day of tutorials and five keynote talks provided by world-renowned experts. The program covered high-quality scientific contributions within image analysis, segmentation, multiple view geometry, categorization and classification, structure from motion and SLAM, medical and biomedical applications, 3D shape, and medical imaging. For the first time in the SCIA history, we used a two-stage reviewing system with the ten Program Committee members serving as Area Chairs, each responsible for about 15 papers. The papers were carefully selected based on three reviews and a consolidating report and acceptance/rejection recommendation from the responsible Area Chair. Among 140 submissions 74 were accepted, leading to an acceptance rate of 53%.

SCIA has a reputation of having a friendly environment, in addition to high-quality scientific contributions. We focused on maintaining the reputation, by designing a technical and social program that we hope the participants found interesting and inspiring for new research ideas and network extensions. We also hope that the relaxed and nice atmosphere at Ystad Saltsjöbad also contributed.

We thank the authors for submitting their valuable work to SCIA. This is of course of prime importance for the success of the event. However, the organization of a conference also depends critically on a number of volunteers. We are sincerely grateful for the excellent work done by the reviewers and the Program Committee members, which ensured that SCIA maintained its reputation of high quality. We thank the keynote and tutorial speakers for their enlightening lectures. And finally, we thank the local Organizing Committee and all the other volunteers that helped us in organizing SCIA 2011.

We hope that all participants had a joyful stay in Ystad, and that SCIA 2011 met its expectations.

March 2011

Anders Heyden
Fredrik Kahl

Organization

scia 2011

SCIA 2011 was organized by the Centre for Mathematical Sciences, Lund Univeristy, Sweden, on behalf of the Swedish Society for Automated Image Analysis.

SVENSKA SÄLLSKAPET FÖR AUTOMATISERAD BILDANALYS
SWEDISH SOCIETY FOR AUTOMATED IMAGE ANALYSIS
MEMBER OF THE INTERNATIONAL ASSOCIATION FOR PATTERN RECOGNITION

Executive Committee

Conference Chair	Anders Heyden (Lund University, Sweden)
Program Chairs	Fredrik Kahl (Lund University, Sweden) Anders Heyden (Lund University, Sweden)

Program Committee

Magnus Oskarsson	Lund University, Sweden
Magnus Borga	Linköping University, Sweden
Rasmus Larsen	Denmark Technical University, Denmark
Arnt-Børre Salberg	Norwegian Computing Center, Norway
Matti Pietikäinen	University of Oulu, Finland
Adrien Bartoli	Université d'Auvergne, France
Gabriella Sanniti di Baja	Istituto di Cibernetica "Eduardo Caianiello", Italy
Sylvia Pont	Delft University of Technology, The Netherlands
Rene Vidal	The Johns Hopkins University, USA
Akihiro Sugimoto	National Institute of Informatics, Japan

Invited Speakers

Richard Hartley	Australian National University and NICTA, Australia
Kyros Kutulakos	University of Toronto, Canada
Tinne Tuytelaars	KU Leuven, Belgium
Ghassan Hamarneh	Simon Fraser University, Canada
Tomas Akenine-Möller	Lund University, Sweden

Tutorials

Alvaro Guevara	Goethe Universität, Frankfurt am Main
Rudolf Mester	Goethe Universität, Frankfurt am Main
Björn Gottfried	Unviersity of Bremen
Michael Haindl	Academy of Sciences of the Czech Republic
Jiří Filip	Academy of Sciences of the Czech Republic
Lourdes Agapito	Queen Mary University of London
Adrien Bartoli	Université d'Auvergne
Alessio Del Blue	Italian Institute of Technology

Reviewers

H. Aanaes
L. Agapito
J. Ahlberg
F. Albregtsen
F. Anton
H. Ardö
D. Ariu
I. Austvoll
A. Berge
M. Björkman
M. Brown
A. Bruhn
M. Byröd
U. Castellani
E. Castelli
S. Chambon
T. Chateau
M. de Bruijne
M. De Marsico
C. De Stefano
A. del Blue
J.-D. Dorou
L. Eikvi
J.-O. Eklundh
T. Eltoft
E. Emilsson
B. Ersbøll
I. Farup
M. Felsberg
P. Fite-Georgel
R. Fjörtoft
F. Fontanella
P.-E. Forssen
M. Freschini
A. Fusiello
R. Gallea
O.-C. Granmo
I.Y.-H. Gu
T. Haavardsholm
A. Hadid
J.Y. Hardeberg
S. Hauberg
J. Hedborg
J. Heikkilä
F. Huang
A.C. Jenssen
R. Jenssen
H. Kalviainen
J. Kamarainen
K. Kanatani
J. Kannala
S. Karlsson
R. Kawakami
S. Keller
Y. Kita
H. Kjellström
P. Kontschieder
M. Koskela
N. Kruger
V. Kruger
M. La Cascia
J. Laaksonen
S. Larsen
F. Larsson
M. Lecca
R. Lenz
A. Linderhed
M. Loog
J. Lundström
C. Madsen
M. Magnusson
A. Maki
F. Malmberg
R. Mester
T. Moeslund
Y. Mukaigawa
L. Mussi
M. Nappi
J. Nilsen
S. Nobuhara
K. Nordberg
I. Nyström
T. Oigard
T. Oshi
T. Okabe
T. Okatani
C. Olsson
H. Palm
T. Paquet
J. Parkkinen
R. Paulsen
K. Pedersen
G. Percannella
A. Petrosino
G. Pirlo
D. Pizarro

E. Rahtu
G. Ramella
A. Rizzi
A. Robert-Inacio
J. Röning
J. Rydell
C. Samir
R. Sara
L. Sarry
T. Schoenemann
T. Seppånen
I.-M. Sintorn
M. Sjöberg
K. Skretting
Ö. Smedby
L. Snidaro
S. Solbö
Y. Song
C. Spampinato
J. Sporring
R. Strand
J. Sullivan
S. Svensson
J. Thielemann
T. Ueshiba
M. Vento
V. Viitaniemi
N. Wadströmer
E. Wernersson
Z. Yang
F. Åström
K. Åström
K. Öfjäll

Sponsoring Institutions

SVENSKA SÄLLSKAPET FÖR AUTOMATISERAD BILDANALYS
SWEDISH SOCIETY FOR AUTOMATED IMAGE ANALYSIS
MEMBER OF THE INTERNATIONAL ASSOCIATION FOR PATTERN RECOGNITION

CELLAVISION

COGNIMATICS

LUND UNIVERSITY

IAPR

Table of Contents

Multiple View Geometry

Segmentation

Poster Session I

Image Analysis I

Categorization and Classification

Structure from Motion and SLAM

Medical and Biomedical Applications

3D Shape

Medical Imaging

Poster Session II

Image Analysis II

Camera Self-calibration with Parallel Screw Axis Motion by Intersecting Imaged Horopters

Ferran Espuny[1], Joan Aranda[2], and José I. Burgos Gil[3]

[1] Dépt. Images et Signal, GIPSA-Lab, Grenoble-INP
Ferran.Espuny@gipsa-lab.grenoble-inp.fr
[2] Dept. of Automatic Control and Computing Engineering, UPC
Joan.Aranda@upc.edu
[3] Instituto de Ciencias Matemáticas, CSIC-UAM-UCM-UC3
jiburgosgil@gmail.com

Abstract. We present a closed-form method for the self-calibration of a camera (intrinsic and extrinsic parameters) from at least three images acquired with parallel screw axis motion, i.e. the camera rotates about parallel axes while performing general translations. The considered camera motion is more general than pure rotation and planar motion, which are not always easy to produce. The proposed solution is nearly as simple as the existing for those motions, and it has been evaluated by using both synthetic and real data from acquired images.[1]

1 Introduction

We say that a camera follows a *parallel screw axis* motion when it rotates about axes parallel to a fixed *screw direction*, while translating in any direction neither orthogonal nor parallel to that direction. We consider in this paper the self-calibration problem from three or more images acquired by a camera with unchanging internal parameters undergoing a parallel screw axis motion.

By *self-calibration*, we mean the calibration of a camera without any knowledge on the scene or the camera pose (location and orientation) [11,6].

A scene can be reconstructed up to a projective ambiguity (*projective reconstruction*) by using two views of the scene. This can be done by using the fundamental matrices between pairs of views, or, alternatively, multiple view tensors. We will follow a *stratified approach* for self-calibration, consisting in looking first for an *affine reconstruction*, and then upgrading it to a Euclidean reconstruction. We can achieve the affine level by determining the relative infinite homographies, and the Euclidean one through the calibration of the camera.

The most simple methods for the Euclidean self-calibration of a camera correspond to particular camera motions: pure rotations [9] and planar motion [1,7,12,5]. However, since the camera centre is not visible, the assumption of pure rotation of a camera is only plausible for distant scenes. The assumption of planar motion requires in turn the relative translations of the camera to be orthogonal to a fixed screw direction. We relax the previous motion constraints,

[1] Research supported by the Spanish MICINN project MTM2009-14163-C02-01.

A. Heyden and F. Kahl (Eds.): SCIA 2011, LNCS 6688, pp. 1–12, 2011.

by allowing the camera to translate in more general directions (for three views, one relative planar motion will yet be allowed).

The parallel screw axis camera motion is known to be degenerate for direct self-calibration methods [17]: there exists a uni-parametric family of possible conics consistent with the displacements of the camera. The existing general stratified self-calibration methods could be used with this camera motion, but some require the performance of a 3-dimensional search [10,13,15], and the closed-form ones [14,16,8] do not guarantee the uniqueness of the solution, having all of them a high degree of complexity. In contrast, we give in this paper a simple closed-form (unique) solution to the stratified self-calibration problem with parallel screw axis camera motion.

The horopter curve of two images is the set of space points projecting onto two points of identical coordinates in both images. Under general motion, the horopter is a twisted cubic that projects on a non-degenerate conic, given by the symmetric part of the fundamental matrix. Horopter curves have already been used for camera self-calibration with general [15] and planar [1,7,5] motions.

The intersection of the imaged horopters corresponding to three views will allow us to determine: the *apex* (image of the screw axis direction) and the image of the two *circular points*, which give the metric on the planes orthogonal to the screw axes. Similarly to planar motion, the scene can be recovered up to a 1-D affinity in the screw direction. To resolve this ambiguity, some assumptions on the camera pixel geometry can be made that lead us to a complete camera calibration (zero-skew constraint, known image aspect ratio or known principal point); the screw direction conditions the necessary additional assumptions [20,2].

In Section 2 we state the basis for understanding our method and give a characterisation of the apex, which we will use for the self-calibration in some particular cases. In Section 3 we formulate the problem and deduce the constraints used for its resolution. We detail our stratified solution in Section 4: the affine step consists of a closed-form solution with an optional iterative refinement, and the linear Euclidean upgrade uses the knowledge of the apex and imaged circular points. Finally, experimental results and conclusions are given.

Notation. We will use $\simeq$ to denote an equality up to scale factor, $\cdot$ for the matrix-vector and matrix-matrix products, $\times$ for the cross product of 3-vectors, and $[u]_\times$ for the matrix associated to a 3-vector u so that $[u]_\times \cdot v = u \times v$, $\forall v$.

2 Background

The general contents of this section can be found in [6,11]; extra references are given in the text. Let us consider a set of two images of a rigid scene acquired from different locations and with different orientations by a camera with intrinsic parameters given by a *calibration matrix*

$$K = \begin{pmatrix} \alpha_u & s & u_0 \\ & \alpha_v & v_0 \\ & & 1 \end{pmatrix} = \begin{pmatrix} fk_u & -fk_u \cot\varphi & u_0 \\ & fk_v/\sin\varphi & v_0 \\ & & 1 \end{pmatrix} , \tag{1}$$

being f the *focal length*, (u_0, v_0) the image *principal point*, k_v/k_u the *aspect ratio*, s the *skew parameter*, and φ the angle between the camera sensor axes.

The affine knowledge of the scene, codified by the plane at infinity π_∞, allows us to recognise parallel lines and to compute affine ratios of aligned points. The Euclidean knowledge of the scene, codified by the *absolute conic* Ω_∞, allows us to compute distances up to scale and angles. We denote by $\begin{pmatrix} R & t \\ 0^T & 1 \end{pmatrix}$ the *relative displacement*, taking the second camera to the first one. We assume that the relative angle of rotation θ satisfies $0 < \theta < \pi$ and that the relative translation satisfies $t \neq 0$ (we exclude pure translations and pure rotations). We denote by I, J, r the three fixed points of the relative displacement (eigenvalues of R), which span the plane at infinity. The *circular points* $I, J \in \Omega_\infty$ are orthogonal to r, and codify the metric of the planes orthogonal to r. We denote by $\tilde{I}, \tilde{J}, v$ the images of those three points: $\tilde{I} \sim K \cdot I$, $\tilde{J} \simeq K \cdot J$, $v \simeq K \cdot r$.

2.1 Stratified Self-calibration

A *reconstruction* of the scene and cameras is called *projective*, *affine* or *Euclidean* when it corresponds with the real scene and cameras via a projectivity, affinity or similarity, respectively.

The *fundamental matrix* F represents the *epipolar map* assigning to a point on the first image the *epipolar line* of possible corresponding points on the second image; F^T represents the epipolar map in the inverse image order. These maps are not defined in the *epipoles* e, e', right an left null-spaces of F, respectively. The fundamental matrix is determined in general by seven or more correspondences. Its knowledge is equivalent to knowing a projective reconstruction.

The *infinite homography* H_∞ is the homography between the two images induced by the plane at infinity π_∞. The matrix F can be decomposed as:

$$F \simeq [e']_\times \cdot H_\infty \ . \tag{2}$$

The knowledge of H_∞ allows us to upgrade a projective reconstruction to an affine one. In fact, the fixed points of the infinite homography are the apex v and the imaged circular points $\tilde{I}, \tilde{J}$, which are image of three points on the plane at infinity. By construction, we have that $H_\infty \simeq K \cdot R \cdot K^{-1}$ or, equivalently:

$$H_\infty \simeq \left(\tilde{I} \; \tilde{J} \; v \right) \cdot \operatorname{diag}\left(\exp(-i\theta), \exp(i\theta), 1\right) \cdot \left(\tilde{I} \; \tilde{J} \; v \right)^{-1} \ . \tag{3}$$

The *image of the absolute conic*, denoted by ω_∞, is a conic on the image plane codifying, up to scale, the metric on this plane. We denote by ω_∞^* its dual. Both conics are equivalent to the camera calibration, since $\omega_\infty \simeq \left(K \cdot K^T\right)^{-1}$, $\omega_\infty^* \simeq K \cdot K^T$, and allow us to upgrade a projective reconstruction to a Euclidean one. It follows from $H_\infty \simeq K \cdot R \cdot K^{-1}$ and $\omega_\infty \simeq \left(K \cdot K^T\right)^{-1}$ that ω_∞ is invariant under the infinite homography H_∞. In fact, using (3), we obtain that, for some $\lambda \neq 0$, it holds [20]:

$$\omega_\infty^* \simeq (\tilde{I} \cdot \tilde{J}^T + \tilde{J} \cdot \tilde{I}^T) + \lambda v \cdot v^T \ . \tag{4}$$

In conclusion, we can follow a *stratified approach* to camera calibration from the fundamental matrix F: first, we determine the infinite homography H_∞ (*affine self-calibration*); then, we linearly determine ω_∞, the image of the absolute conic, which is invariant under that homography (*Euclidean self-calibration*).

2.2 Horopter Curves

The *horopter curve* of two images is the set of space points that project onto points of identical (i.e. proportional) coordinates in both images. The horopter curve passes through the camera centres and through the fixed points of the relative displacement, which include r, the point at infinity of the rotation axis, and the circular points I, J. For a general camera motion, it is a proper (irreducible) twisted curve. It decomposes as three lines when t is parallel to r, and as a circle plus a line (screw axis), when t is orthogonal to r (*planar motion*).

The image of the horopter is a conic, non-degenerate a for general camera motion and degenerate (two lines) otherwise. Since the image of the horopter is the locus of corresponding points with identical coordinates, it is a conic with matrix given by the symmetric part of the fundamental matrix:

$$F_{sym} := \frac{1}{2}(F + F^T) . \tag{5}$$

This conic will contain the apex v and $\tilde{I}$, $\tilde{J}$, the image of the circular points.

The ratios of intersection of the horopter curves with the plane at infinity have been exploited for the self-calibration with general camera motion in [15]. We will use a similar constraint for an auxiliary characterisation of the apex:

Lemma 1. *If F_{sym} is non degenerate and μ is a scalar such that*

$$F \cdot \tilde{I} = \mu \exp(-i\theta) e' \times \tilde{I} , \tag{6}$$

then the apex is the only point $v \in F_{sym}$ satisfying

$$F \cdot v = \mu e' \times v . \tag{7}$$

Proof. Both equations follow from (3) and (2). If we had $v' \neq v$ satisfying (7) then, for every $\lambda \in \mathbb{R}$ we would have $F \cdot (v + \lambda v') = \mu e' \times (v + \lambda v')$, and thus $(v + \lambda v')^T \cdot F \cdot (v + \lambda v') = 0$. Hence, the conic F_{sym} would contain the line $v \times v'$ and it would be degenerate. □

3 Problem Statement and Constraints

Remember that we say that a camera follows a parallel screw axis motion when it rotates about axes parallel to a screw direction while translating in any direction neither orthogonal nor parallel to that direction. Assume that we know three fundamental matrices $F^{i,j}, 1 \leq i < j \leq 3$ corresponding to three images acquired from different orientations by a camera with unchanging internal parameters undergoing a parallel screw axis motion. We are interested in solving the stratified self-calibration of the camera, as explained in Section 2.

Accordingly, we want to determine three points in the image: the apex v and the imaged circular points $\tilde{I}, \tilde{J}$, which are common to the three views:

Theorem 1 (Intersection of the Imaged Horopters). *Under parallel screw axis camera motion, the three different imaged horopters (conics represented by the symmetric parts of the fundamental matrices) intersect at the images $\tilde{I}, \tilde{J}$ of the circular points (which are complex conjugate points) and the (real) apex v. A fourth real intersection point can exist under particular camera motions.*

Proof. The screw direction r of the rotation axes and the circular points I, J are common to all the camera relative displacements. Therefore, their images belong to the imaged horopters. Five or more intersection points can not exist for the three imaged horopters, since then these conics would be coincident, and the relative displacements would be all the same. In particular, the intersection can not contain a fourth non-real intersection point (and its conjugate). □

Observe that the three fundamental matrices $F^{i,j}$ corresponding to three views of a common scene satisfy three compatibility constraints [6,11]:

$$(e^{2,3})^T \cdot F^{1,2} \cdot e^{1,3} = (e^{3,2})^T \cdot F^{1,3} \cdot e^{1,2} = (e^{3,1})^T \cdot F^{2,3} \cdot e^{2,1} = 0 \,. \quad (8)$$

Using the infinite homographies $H_\infty^{i,j}$ to parametrise the fundamental matrices, these constraints reduce to a single one:

Theorem 2 (Three-View Affine Compatibility). *Consider the infinite homographies $H_\infty^{i,j}$, epipoles $e^{i,j}$ and fundamental matrices $F^{i,j}$ such that*

$$F^{i,j} \simeq [e^{j,i}]_\times \cdot H_\infty^{i,j} \,, \quad (9)$$

$$e^{j,i} \simeq H_\infty^{i,j} \cdot e^{i,j} \,, \quad (10)$$

$$H_\infty^{2,3} \simeq H_\infty^{1,3} \cdot (H_\infty^{1,2})^{-1} \,. \quad (11)$$

The three compatibility equations (8) are satisfied if, and only if, any of the following set of points is linearly dependent:

$$\{e^{1,2} \,, e^{1,3} \,, (H_\infty^{1,2})^{-1} \cdot e^{2,3}\} \subset \mathcal{R}_1 \,, \quad (12)$$

$$\{e^{2,1} \,, e^{2,3} \,, H_\infty^{1,2} \cdot e^{1,3}\} \subset \mathcal{R}_2 \,, \quad (13)$$

$$\{e^{3,1} \,, e^{3,2} \,, H_\infty^{2,3} \cdot e^{2,1}\} \subset \mathcal{R}_3 \,, \quad (14)$$

where $\mathcal{R}_i$ denotes the i-th image plane.

Proof. By (10) and (11), the sets (13) and (14) are the result of applying $H_\infty^{1,2}$ and $H_\infty^{1,3}$, respectively, to the set (12). Hence, the linear dependence of any of those sets is equivalent to the linear dependence of all of them. The direct substitution of the parametrisation (9) into (8) gives directly two of the linear dependency conditions; for instance, the first term in (8) is

$$(e^{2,3})^T \cdot F^{1,2} \cdot e^{1,3} \overset{(9)}{\simeq} (e^{2,3})^T \cdot [e^{2,1}]_\times \cdot H_\infty^{1,2} \cdot e^{1,3} ,$$

which is zero if, and only if, the vectors in (13) are linearly dependent. □

4 Self-Calibration Method

We will solve the affine self-calibration problem by intersecting the imaged horopters (Theorem 1), given by the symmetric part of the fundamental matrices $F^{i,j}$, $1 \le i < j \le 3$. We propose a two-step method for computing this intersection: a closed-form solution is obtained and further refined using Theorem 2. We also revisit the upgrading step from affine to Euclidean self-calibration.

4.1 Affine Self-calibration by Intersecting the Imaged Horopters

Given the three fundamental matrices $F^{i,j}$, $1 \le i < j \le 3$, we can compute the imaged horopters. To intersect them, we will follow a least squares approach, which we obtain by adapting the method in the Appendix of [3] to our constraints: the conics intersect in three points, one real and two complex conjugate.

General Intersection. Assume that we have a pair of conics C, C' with coefficients in $\mathbb{R}$, intersecting in $\tilde{I}, \tilde{J}$ (complex-conjugate pair) and v, P (two points with coordinates in $\mathbb{R}$). Each of the three degenerate conics (zero determinant) in the family $C + \mu C'$ is a pair of lines joining two points in the intersection of C with C'. The only lines with real coefficients will be $\tilde{I} \times \tilde{J}$ and $v \times P$. Therefore, if we tale $\mu \in \mathbb{R}$ such that $D = C + \mu C'$ has $\det D = 0$, then D consists of the line joining the imaged circular points plus a line passing through the apex.

Using the three imaged horopters, we can compute three degenerate conics D^k following the described procedure. The apex v will be the unique point in the intersection of the D^k, and the imaged circular points can be obtained by averaging the intersection of the common line of the three D^k with each of the conics (see Figure 1). Note that both computations can be integrated in a least-squares estimation process in presence of noise, and/or if more than three images are available. Once we have an estimation for the apex v and the imaged circular points $\tilde{I}$, $\tilde{J}$, the relative rotation angles $\theta^{i,j}$ can be computed using (6).

The previous estimations can be optionally refined by minimising the sum of squares of distances of the image points to the epipolar lines obtained using the fundamental matrices parametrised as follows. By (9), we can use 13 parameters to describe the three fundamental matrices: we can take one coordinate of $\tilde{I}$ to be one (4 dof for $\tilde{I}$, $\tilde{J}$), 2 parameters for the relative rotation angles (since $\theta^{2,3} = \theta^{1,3} - \theta^{1,2}$), unitary vectors for the apex v and the epipoles $e^{j,1}$ (6 dof), and 1 parameter for $e^{3,2}$ satisfying (14).

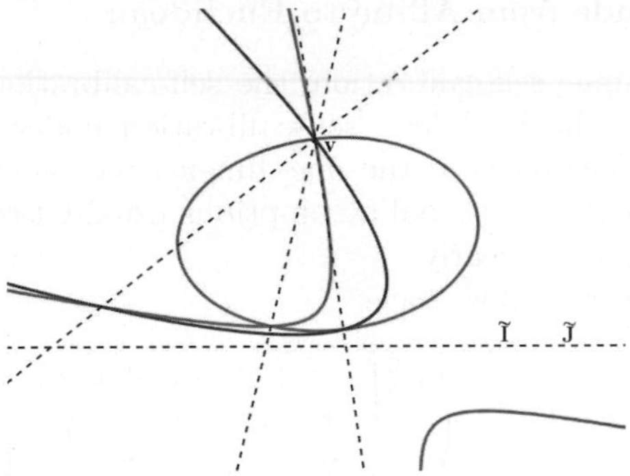

Fig. 1. Imaged horopters corresponding to a general parallel screw axis motion. The discontinuous lines represent the real degenerate conics from each pair-wise linear family of conics. The apex v can be obtained by intersecting the lines not containing $\tilde{I}$, $\tilde{J}$.

Particular Cases. We excluded in our assumptions the cases of pure translation and planar motion. However, it could happen that the relative displacements are close to these degenerate motions. In the first case, the fundamental matrix is practically anti-symmetrical, and the computation of the imaged horopter is badly conditioned. In the second case, the imaged horopter is degenerate. This is not a problem if only happens for one relative displacement (see Fig. 2, left); otherwise, a planar motion self-calibration method should be used.

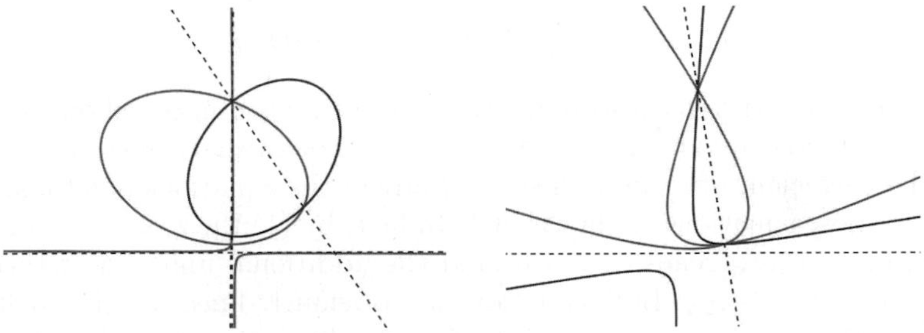

Fig. 2. Left: if one relative displacement is (close to being) planar, the image of the horopter is degenerate (coordinate hyperbola in the picture). Right: an example of three conics intersecting in two real and two complex conjugate points.

As we said in Theorem 1, the three imaged horopters can intersect in four points for particular camera motions. The characterisation of these motions is out of the scope of this paper. In this case, the pair-wise real degenerate conic will be the same for any pair of imaged horopters (see Fig. 2, right). The four intersection points can be obtained by averaging the intersection of such degenerate conic with each imaged horopter. The imaged circular points will be the non-real points, while the apex will be the real point satisfying Lemma 1.

4.2 Linear Upgrade from Affine to Euclidean

Once we know the affine self-calibration, the self-calibration equations are not enough to determine the Euclidean self-calibration under parallel screw axis camera motion: all the conics in the one-dimensional family (4) satisfy those equations. We revisit the additional assumptions usually taken on ω^*_∞, showing that they can be imposed linearly.

Observe that by Section 2 we have:

$$\omega^*_\infty \simeq K \cdot K^T = \begin{pmatrix} \alpha_u^2 + s^2 + u_0^2 & s\alpha_v + u_0 v_0 & u_0 \\ s\alpha_v + u_0 v_0 & \alpha_v^2 + v_0^2 & v_0 \\ u_0 & v_0 & 1 \end{pmatrix} , \tag{15}$$

being the coefficients of K denoted as in (1). If the rotation direction r has non zero x and y components, the *zero skew assumption* ($s = 0$) determines uniquely the conic ω^*_∞ as that ω^* in (4) satisfying

$$\omega^*_{1,2}\omega^*_{3,3} - \omega^*_{1,3}\omega^*_{3,2} = 0 , \tag{16}$$

where $\omega^*_{i,j} = \omega^*_{j,i}$ denotes the element in the i-th row and j-th column of a matrix representing ω^*.

However, if the rotation direction r has zero x or y components, then the zero skew constraint (16) is satisfied by every conic in the family (4) [20,2]. In this case, if the rotations are not about axes parallel to the z axis, assuming zero skew, $s = 0$, and *unit aspect ratio*, $\alpha_u = \alpha_v$, determines uniquely ω^*_∞. The equation to impose is the *square pixel constraint*:

$$\omega^*_{1,1}\omega^*_{3,3} - \left(\omega^*_{1,3}\right)^2 = \omega^*_{2,2}\omega^*_{3,3} - \left(\omega^*_{2,3}\right)^2 . \tag{17}$$

Apparently, the last two constraints (16) and (17), when imposed on the family (4), give equations quadratic in λ. We observe though that, since $(w \cdot w^T)_{i,j} = w_i w_j$, the coefficient of λ^2 in both sides of any of the equations is zero, and consequently those equations are linear in λ. In fact, by (1) the zero skew constraint imposed on $\omega = \omega_\infty$ reads $\omega_{1,2} = 0$, and the additional unit aspect ratio constraint reads $\omega_{1,1} = \omega_{2,2}$. Both equations are obviously linear on the coefficients of ω_∞ and therefore equivalent to those for ω^*_∞. An optional bundle adjustment step [4] could be used to refine the Euclidean self-calibration.

5 Experiments

We conducted experiments with both synthetic and real data in order to evaluate the performance of the self-calibration method of Section 4. We used simulated data to study the behaviour of the method with respect to the pitch and roll angles of the camera for different levels of noise in the initial image correspondences used for the computation of the fundamental matrices. Finally, we applied the method to a set of real images, comparing our results with a ground truth given by the calibration from pattern method in [18,19].

Synthetic Data In our simulations, we generated a cloud of 100 points uniformly distributed inside a 3-D sphere. We placed in the space three random cameras related by a parallel screw axis motion in such a way that each camera could view at least half of the sphere. The calibration matrix of the cameras was

$$K = \begin{pmatrix} 1000 & 0 & 320 \\ 0 & 1000 & 240 \\ 0 & 0 & 1 \end{pmatrix} .$$

In the Euclidean frame associated to the first camera, the screw direction had coordinates

$$r = \big(\sin\alpha \sin\beta \,, \, -\cos\alpha \sin\beta \,, \, \cos\beta \big) \,, \tag{18}$$

where β was the *pitch angle*, considered as the angle between the principal axis of the camera (the z axis) and the screw direction, and α was the *roll angle*, understood as the angle of rotation of the camera about the z axis. The relative rotation angles, relating any pair of cameras, varied randomly between 10 and 120 degrees. We added Gaussian noise (with deviation σ ranging from 0 to 3 pixels) to the projection of the 3-D points and used the noisy image points as initial data for the self-calibration method. For each combination of values α, β and σ we simulated 1000 times different 3-D points, camera poses and image points; we applied the proposed self-calibration method to each simulation and computed the mean of the obtained errors.

In a first experiment (Figure 3), we fixed the roll angle α to be zero and varied the pitch angle β. Since r had no x component, we used the unit aspect ratio constraint to achieve a Euclidean reconstruction (Section 4). We observed that

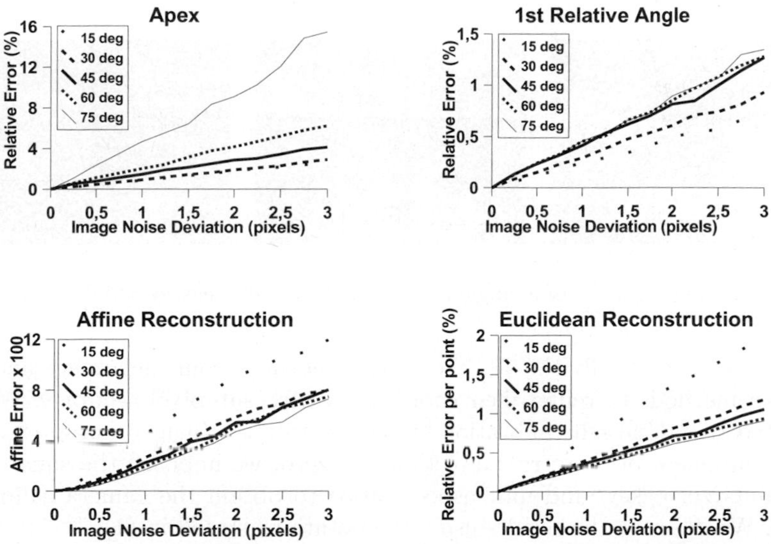

Fig. 3. Errors for roll angle $\alpha = 0$ and different values of β (degs) and σ (pixels)

the closer the cameras were to being parallel to the screw direction (β small), the more exact was the apex and relative angles computation but the more inexact was the estimation of the image of the circular points and, consequently, the worst were the obtained affine and Euclidean reconstructions.

In a second experiment (Figure 4), we fixed $\beta = 60$ degrees and varied the roll angle α from 0 to 45 degrees. According to Section 4, the zero skew constraint was sufficient for the values of $\alpha \neq 0$ in order to upgrade the affine reconstruction to a Euclidean one. We observed that the bigger the angle α was, the better were the estimations of the apex and image of the circular points and, consequently, the better were the obtained affine and Euclidean reconstructions.

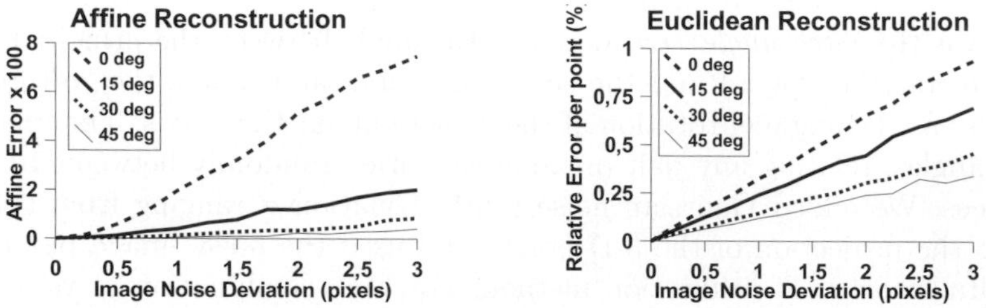

Fig. 4. Errors for $\beta = 60$ degs and different values of α (degs) and σ (pixels)

Real Images. The images shown in Figure 5 are part of a 5-image sequence (768 $\times$ 576 pixels) acquired by a camera mounted on an articulated robotic arm. The screw direction (rotation axis) had no x component and the angle between this direction and the z axis of the camera was approximately equal to 60 degrees.

Fig. 5. Image sequence of a single pattern with $\beta = 60$ degs, $\alpha = 0$ degs (aprox.)

We selected manually the 48 "chessboard" corners from each image and used standard methods to refine their coordinates with sub-pixel accuracy. We first computed the affine self-calibration by intersecting the imaged horopters. Since the x component of the screw direction was zero, we imposed the square pixel constraint (zero skew and unit aspect ratio) to obtain the camera calibration matrix. We describe the results using the notations stated in (1):

Table 1. Results with the 5 real images, being $\alpha = \alpha_u = \alpha_v$. First: least-square solution using the 10 imaged horopters. Next: mean, median and deviation of the closed-form solution applied to each of the 10 triplets of images.

	value	mean	median	deviation
α	863.07	864.01	862.36	38.03
u_0	355.65	374.24	369.63	51.78
v_0	233.76	255.71	270.06	34.32

In order to obtain the ground truth values, we applied the calibration from pattern method in [18,19], using all the "chessboard" patterns in the five images. The ground truth angle between the sensor axes was $\theta = 89.42$ degrees, and the ground truth aspect ratio was $k_v/v_u = 1.01$. Therefore, the assumption of unit aspect ratio can be considered as valid for the camera. The ground truth parameters of the focal lengths α_u, α_v and the camera centre (u_0, v_0) were:

$$\alpha_u = 856.33 \ , \ \alpha_v = 865.86 \ , \ u_0 = 385.24 \ , \ v_0 = 273.22 \ .$$

We observe that, even if the square pixel assumption was not completely correct for the actual camera, the obtained calibration was close to its ground truth.

6 Conclusion

We have shown that the parallel screw axis camera motion can be used in order to obtain image sequences easy to self-calibrate, being this motion a possible substitute or complement to planar camera motions. Our method complexity is not higher than cubic: after finding the unique real root of certain univariate cubics, two linear steps are performed to achieve the camera self-calibration.

The proposed stratified self-calibration method has been demonstrated to give good results on both synthetic and real data. Experiments on synthetic images have shown that better results are obtained when the camera is oriented far from being parallel to the screw direction. The addition of a roll angle to the camera also improves the estimation of the affine and Euclidean reconstructions.

The study of the resilience of the method to deviations from the assumption of parallel rotation axes could be a further topic of research. An algebraic characterisation of those camera motions leading to imaged horopters intersecting in four points has been omitted in this paper, due to lack of space; its geometric interpretation is missing and would also be desirable.

References

1. Armstrong, M., Zisserman, A., Hartley, R.I.: Self-calibration from image triplets. In: Buxton, B.F., Cipolla, R. (eds.) ECCV 1996. LNCS, vol. 1065, Springer, Heidelberg (1996)

2. Demirdjian, D., Csurka, G., Horaud, R.: Autocalibration in the presence of critical motions. In: Proc. BMVC (1998)
3. Demirdjian, D., Zisserman, A., Horaud, R.: Stereo autocalibration from one plane. In: Vernon, D. (ed.) ECCV 2000. LNCS, vol. 1843, pp. 625–639. Springer, Heidelberg (2000)
4. Engels, C., Stewénius, H., Nistér, D.: Bundle adjustment rules. In: PCV (2006)
5. Espuny, F.: A new linear method for camera self-calibration with planar motion. J. Math. Imag. Vis. 27(1), 81–88 (2007)
6. Faugeras, O., Luong, Q.T., Papadopoulou, T.: The Geometry of Multiple Images: The Laws That Govern The Formation of Images of A Scene and Some of Their Applications. MIT Press, Cambridge (2001)
7. Faugeras, O., Quan, L., Sturm, P.: Self-calibration of a 1D projective camera and its application to the self-calibration of a 2D projective camera. In: Burkhardt, H.-J., Neumann, B. (eds.) ECCV 1998. LNCS, vol. 1406, p. 36. Springer, Heidelberg (1998)
8. Habed, A., Boufama, B.: Camera self-calibration: A new approach for solving the modulus constraint. In: Proc. ICPR (2004)
9. Hartley, R.I.: Self-calibration from multiple views with a rotating camera. In: Eklundh, J.-O. (ed.) ECCV 1994. LNCS, vol. 801, Springer, Heidelberg (1994)
10. Hartley, R.I., de Agapito, L., Reid, I.D., Hayman, E.: Camera calibration and the search for infinity. In: Proc. ICCV (1999)
11. Hartley, R.I., Zisserman, A.: Multiple View Geometry in Computer Vision, 2nd edn. Cambridge University Press, Cambridge (2004)
12. Knight, J., Zisserman, A., Reid, I.: Linear auto-calibration for ground plane motion. In: Proc. CVPR (2003)
13. Manning, R.A., Dyer, C.R.: Stratified self calibration from screw-transform manifolds. In: Heyden, A., Sparr, G., Nielsen, M., Johansen, P. (eds.) ECCV 2002. LNCS, vol. 2353, pp. 131–145. Springer, Heidelberg (2002)
14. Pollefeys, M., Van Gool, L., Oosterlinck, A.: The modulus constraint: A new constraint for self-calibration. In: Proc. ICPR (1996)
15. Ronda, J.I., Valdés, A., Jaureguizar, F.: Camera autocalibration and horopter curves. Int. J. Comput. Vis. 57(3), 219–232 (2004)
16. Schaffalitzky, F.: Direct solution of modulus constraints. In: Proc. ICVGIP (2000)
17. Sturm, P.: Critical motion sequences for monocular self-calibration and uncalibrated Euclidean reconstruction. In: Proc. CVPR (1997)
18. Sturm, P., Maybank, S.J.: On plane-based camera calibration: A general algorithm, singularities, applications. In: Proc. CVPR (1999)
19. Zhang, Z.: Flexible camera calibration by viewing a plane from unknown orientations. In: Proc. ICCV (1999)
20. Zisserman, A., Liebowitz, D., Armstrong, M.: Resolving ambiguities in autocalibration. Phil. Trans. Roy. Soc. Lond. Math. Phys. Sci. 356(1740), 1193–1211 (1998)

Triangulating a Plane

Carl Olsson[1] and Anders Eriksson[2]

[1]Centre for Mathematical Sciences, Lund University, Sweden
[2]School of Computer Science, University of Adelaide, Australia

Abstract. In this theoretical paper we consider the problem of accurately triangulating a scene plane. Rather than first triangulating a set of points and then fitting a plane to these points, we try to minimize the back-projection errors as functions of the plane parameters directly. As this is both geometrically and statistically meaningful our method performs better than the standard two step procedure. Furthermore, we show that the error residuals of this formulation are quasiconvex thereby making it very easy to solve using for example standard local optimization methods.

1 Introduction

The use of planes and their homographies has become increasingly important since the introduction of graph cuts for dense stereo reconstruction [3]. Since then a number of methods building on this work has been proposed (e.g. [22,13,5]), all working in a similar fashion. Typically a family of planes are used to represent the scene, and using α-expansion each pixel is classified as belonging to one of the planes in the family. The cost of assigning a pixel to a plane is computed using back-projection between the two cameras via plane-induced homography (see [8]). If a pixel, back-projected from one camera to the other, looks similar to the corresponding pixel in the second camera then the cost of assigning that pixel to the current plane is low. Furthermore, to obtain smooth classifications a standard regularization term is added [3].

In this paper we investigate the problem of determining the family of planes accurately. The typical way of determining a scene plane from stereo correspondences is by first triangulating the image points (using for example [7]) and then fitting a plane to the 3D-points (see [8]). There are two downsides to this approach. First, when we are triangulating the points we are not using the knowledge that all the points are lying on the same plane. Second, and perhaps more importantly, when fitting the plane we are measuring distances in 3D. Hence, we are optimizing a quantity that we cannot observe in our data and therefore may be inaccurate. The latter is a problem in particular if the baseline is small. On the other hand fitting problems with a small baseline is very important since descriptors such as SIFT usually perform much better in this case.

Instead we propose to estimate the plane by minimizing the back-projection errors of the plane-induced-homography. We will show that this method gives a good estimation of the plane. Direct estimation (without computing the 3D points) of a scene plane has been considered before. For example in [11,10] two iterative methods are presented. There are however no guarantees of convergence to the global optimum. In [1] both structure and motion is estimated. Here 3D points are constrained to fulfill co-planarity

A. Heyden and F. Kahl (Eds.): SCIA 2011, LNCS 6688, pp. 13–23, 2011.

constraints exactly, and a bundle adjustment process is employed. In this paper we assume that the cameras are known, but a similar approach (optimizing reprojection error with the points constrained to lie on the unknown plane) can of course be used. Such a method would however have to rely on triangulation of the 3D points for initialization and would only be locally convergent.

In contrast, we show in this paper that when minimizing back-projection errors of the plane-induced-homography, the problem can be globally optimized using convex optimization. In particular we show that the error residuals are affine functions composed with a projection. It was shown in [9] that this type of functions are examples of quasiconvex functions. Since quasiconvexity is preserved under the max-operation these problems exhibit no local minima when we minimize the max-norm of the errors. More recently minimizing the least squares error, using standard Levenberg-Marquardt type procedures, was addressed in [6,19]. It was shown that for the vast majority of problems from this class it is possible to use use local methods and verify that the solution is in fact globally optimal. Furthermore, in [21,14,16,17] systematic ways for handling outliers in the data was given.

1.1 Quasiconvex Optimization

In this section we very briefly recall the definition and basic properties of quasiconvex functions. A much more detailed treatment can be found in [18].

When dealing with optimization problems convexity is a very useful property. For example, when minimizing a convex function we are guaranteed that local methods converge to globally optimal solutions. Unfortunately, convexity does hardly ever occur in multiple view geometry problems because projections are in general not convex. More commonly occurring is the slightly weaker notion of quasiconvexity.

Definition 1. *A function f is called quasiconvex on a convex set C if its sublevel sets*

$$S_\mu(f) = \{\, x \in C; f(x) \leq \mu \,\} \tag{1}$$

are convex for all $\mu \in \mathbb{R}$.

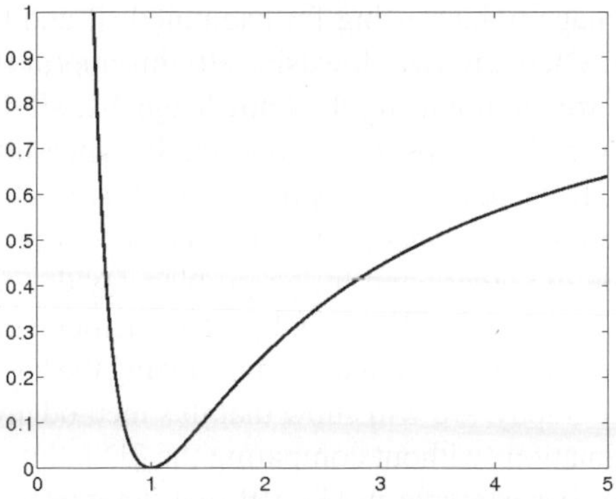

Fig. 1. A quasiconvex but not convex function

Figure 1 shows a function that is quasiconvex. It is not convex since it is possible to draw a line between two points on graph, such that the function is above the line. Quasiconvexity is not preserved under addition. It is, however, preserved under the max operation. That is minimizing the maximal error (see equation (4)) is a quasiconvex problem if all the error residuals are quasiconvex. The simplest, and perhaps the most common way of solving such problems is to employ a bisection method. Checking whether there is an x such that $f(x) \leq \mu$ for a fixed μ is a convex problem. Hence, by solving a sequence of convex problems one can find an optimal μ (see [9,12,18]). In [6,19] it was shown that in the vast majority of cases it is also possible to solve the least squares formulation (see equation (7)) using local methods.

2 3D-Plane Triangulation

Next we consider the problem of determining a scene plane from two images. We assume that the image data is given as two sets of corresponding points in the two images that are known to be projections of points located on the 3D-plane. Let $P_1 = [R_1\ t_1]$, $P_2 = [R_2\ t_2]$ be the two known (calibrated) camera matrices, $\{x^i\}$, $\{y^i\}$ be the image coordinates and p the unknown scene plane. When dealing with points, we will use lower case letters to denote points in euclidean coordinates and capital letters to denote its homogeneous coordinates. Hence $\{X^i\}$ and $\{Y^i\}$ are the homogeneous coordinates of $\{x^i\}$ and $\{y^i\}$ respectively.

It is well known that (in a noise free system) there is a homography H_{21} from image 1 to image 2 such that

$$Y^i \sim H_{21} X^i. \tag{2}$$

(Here $\sim$ denotes equality up to an unknown scale factor.) And similar for the inverse homography $H_{12} = H_{21}^{-1}$ from image 2 to image 1

$$X^i \sim H_{12} Y^i. \tag{3}$$

Now, suppose that the system is not noise free. We would like to find the plane (or homography) that gives the smallest back-projection errors in both images. Therefore we formulate the following minimization problem

$$\min_p \max_i R_i(p) \tag{4}$$

where

$$R_i(p) = \max(||x^i - \Pi(H_{21}Y^i)||^2, ||y^i - \Pi(H_{21}^{-1}X^i)||^2) \tag{5}$$

and $\Pi : \{(x_1, x_2, x_3) \in \mathbb{R}^3; x_3 > 0\} \rightarrow \mathbb{R}^2$ is the projection mapping given by

$$\Pi(x) = \begin{pmatrix} x_1/x_3 \\ x_2/x_3 \end{pmatrix}. \tag{6}$$

The constraint $x_3 > 0$ reflects the fact that visible points in the image should be located in front of the cameras. The residual errors are similar to what is used in homography estimation with the $\mathbb{L}_\infty$ norm [9,12], note however that the homography H_{21} depends on the plane p. In homography estimation it is not possible to use back-projection errors in both images since the inverse of H_{21} cannot be parameterized linearly in terms of the elements in H_{21}, and therefore does not yield a quasiconvex problem. However in this setting this is not a problem, since, as we will show, both H_{21} and its inverse can be parameterized linearly by the plane parameters p.

In (4) and (5) we have used the maximum (squared) residual error as is traditionally done in the $\mathbb{L}_\infty$-framework. However, recent results (see [6,19]) show that solving the least squares formulation using local methods also works well for the same framework. In both cases we need to parameterize H_{21} and its inverse linearly. The least squares formulation of our problem is

$$\min_p \sum_i R_i(p) \tag{7}$$

where

$$R_i(p) = ||x^i - \Pi(H_{21}Y^i)||^2 + ||y^i - \Pi(H_{21}^{-1}X^i)||^2. \tag{8}$$

In this paper we will use both formulations. The latter is solved using local methods with initialization from the former.

2.1 Homography from a Plane

In this section we derive the expression for the homographies H_{12} and H_{21}. For simplicity let us first assume that the camera matrices are of the form $P_1 = [I\ 0]$ and $P_2 = [R\ t]$, and the plane parameters are $p = (a^T, b)^T$ where $a \in \mathbb{R}^3$ and $0 \neq b \in \mathbb{R}$.

Lemma 1. *If $P_1 = [I\ 0]$ and $P_2 = [R\ t]$ then the homography H_{21} can be written*

$$H_{21} = Rb - ta^T. \tag{9}$$

The special case $b = 1$ is proven in [8] and our proof is just a simple extension. It is however essential, since without it, it is not possible to use both H_{12} and its inverse in the error residual, which would prevent us from using symmetric error residuals.

Let x and y be the projections of the point z belonging to p. Then

$$X = P_1 Z = [I\ 0]Z, \tag{10}$$

which implies that $Z = (X^T,\ d)^T$ for some $d \geq 0$. Since z belongs to p we have $0 = p^T Z = a^T X + bd$. And therefore

$$d = -\frac{a^T X}{b}. \tag{11}$$

Now, since Z is the homogeneous coordinates for z we may we multiply Z with the scale factor b, assuming b is positive, without changing anything. The fact that this assumption is no restriction will be motivated later on. Therefore we obtain

$$Z = \begin{pmatrix} bX \\ -a^T X \end{pmatrix} \tag{12}$$

Projecting z into image 2 now gives

$$Y = P_2 Z = [R\, t] \begin{pmatrix} bX \\ -a^T X \end{pmatrix} = (Rb - ta^T)X, \tag{13}$$

which proves the statement.

Now for the general case we use a transformation to prove the following.

Corollary 1. *If* $P_1 = [R_1\ t_1]$, $P_2 = [R_2\ t_2]$ *then the homography* H_{21} *can be written*

$$H_{21} = (b - t_1^T R_1 a) R_2 R_1^T + (R_2 R_1^T t_1 - t_2)(R_1 a)^T. \tag{14}$$

Let

$$T = \begin{bmatrix} R_1^T & -R_1^T t_1 \\ 0 & 1 \end{bmatrix}. \tag{15}$$

Changing coordinates using T we get in the new coordinate system

$$\tilde{P}_1 = P_1 T = [I\ \ 0] \tag{16}$$

$$\tilde{P}_2 = P_2 T = [R_2 R_1^T\ \ -R_2 R_1^T t_1 + t_2] \tag{17}$$

$$\tilde{p} = T^T p = \begin{bmatrix} R_1 a \\ b - t_1^T R_1 a \end{bmatrix}. \tag{18}$$

Substituting (16), (17) and (18) into (9) now yields (14). A similar expression for $H_{21}^{-1} = H_{12}$ is of course obtained by exchanging P_1 and P_2. Hence H_{21} depends linearly on the plane parameters p and we will write $H_{21}(p)$ to indicate this dependence. Furthermore, we let H_{21}^i denote the i'th row of H_{21}.

To prove that the error residual $||x^i - \Pi(H_{21}(p)Y^i)||^2$ is a quasiconvex function on the set $C = \{p;\, H_{21}^3(p)Y^i > 0\}$ we need to prove that the sublevel set

$$\{p \in (C);\, ||x^i - \Pi(H_{21}(p)Y^i)||^2 \leq \mu^2,\ \forall i\} \tag{19}$$

is convex for a fixed μ (see Definition 1, Section 1.1). However since $H_{21}^3(p)Y^i > 0$ it is easy to see that (19) is equivalent to

$$||(ap, bp)|| \leq \mu cp, \tag{20}$$

where

$$ap = (x_1^i H_{21}^3(p) - H_{21}^1(p))Y^i, \tag{21}$$

$$bp = (x_2^i H_{21}^3(p) - H_{21}^2(p))Y^i, \tag{22}$$

$$cp = H_{21}^3(p)Y^i. \tag{23}$$

and x_j^i denotes the j'th coordinate of x^i. Since (21)-(23) are linear functions (20) will be a second order cone constraint (see [2]) which is convex. Hence the error residuals are quasiconvex functions (H_{12} is handled in the same way), and the theory from [9,12,21,14,6,19,16,20] extends to this problem as well.

2.2 Chirality

In the proof of lemma 1 we did not motivate b being positive. It is easy to see that if $b < 0$ then there will be a sign change when multiplying X with b, and hence X might not have positive depth in the second camera. Similarly when using 1 we want the quantity $b - R_1^T t_1$ to be positive. This can always be ensured unless the cameras are located on opposite sides of the plane. Let $P_1 = [R_1\, t_1]$, $P_2 = [R_2\, t_2]$ and $p = (a^T, b)^T$ as previously. We then have

$$b - a^T R_1^T t_1 = p^T \begin{bmatrix} c_1 \\ 1 \end{bmatrix} \tag{24}$$

$$b - a^T R_2^T t_2 = p^T \begin{bmatrix} c_2 \\ 1 \end{bmatrix} \tag{25}$$

where c_1 and c_2 are the camera centers. Now it is easy to see that if one of these are negative then c_1 and c_2 cannot be on the same side of the plane.

Since the cameras need to see the same points the sign of b is normally not a problem in practice. However, note that in case we for some reason would like to solve a problem where this is not fulfilled one simply multiplies X with $-b$ instead and the same result holds. If we do not know anything about the relative locations of the cameras and the plane we have to test both possibilities. Similar to other multiple view geometry problems (see [9]), it is easily shown that for each choice there is a local minimum.

3 Experiments

In this section we perform some simple experiments to verify the theory and evaluate the quality of the proposed methods. In equation (14) the homography H_{21} is written as a linear expression in a and b. However as 3 parameters is enough for specifying a plane we will choose b to be 1 in all our implementations. Note that we still need to use (14). It is not possible to parameterize both H_{21} and H_{12} linearly using only (9) (with b=1).

3.1 Stability of the Proposed Formulation

As we have mentioned before the standard way of fitting a scene plane to image data, is to first compute 3D-points using triangulation and then fit a plane to these points. In our first experiment we compare this approach to the two proposed formulations on synthetically generated data. We use synthetic data since we would like to know the true parameters of the plane that generated the measurements. The setup is as follows: First we placed 30 points randomly on the plane $z = 0$, within the box $-1 \leq x \leq 1$, $-1 \leq y \leq 1$. Then we placed two cameras at a distance roughly 4 from the origin with camera centers fulfilling $z \leq -2$. We then added noise with standard deviation 0.0025 to the image coordinates. Figure 2 shows a typical example of the generated images. We also selected a maximal value for the baseline, that is, the camera centers was placed closer to each other than this maximal value. Figure 3 shows the results for a number of different values of the maximal baseline. To the left is the back-projection error when

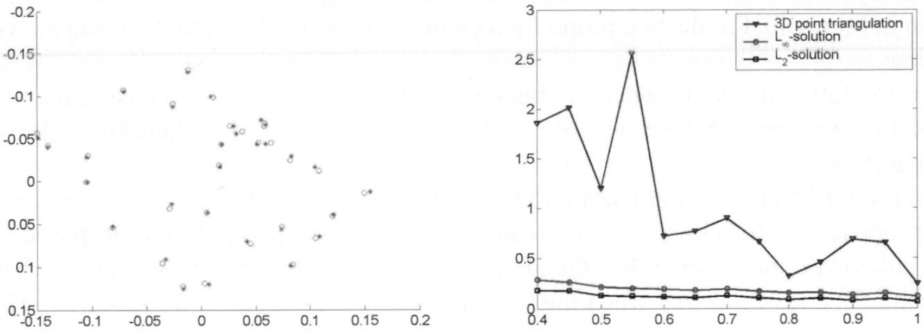

Fig. 2. Left: An example image used in the synthetic experiments. x - the exact image point, o - image point perturbed by noise (noise with std. dev. 0.0025 as in Figure 3).
Right: Same result as in Figure 3 (right panel) using the mean instead of the median.

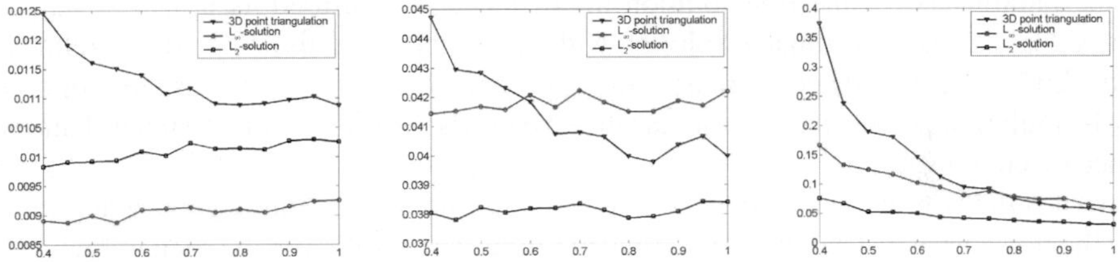

Fig. 3. Results of the synthetic experiments for the three methods. Left: The max-norm back-projection error (5) versus the maximal baseline. Middle: The $\mathbb{L}_2$-norm back-projection error (8) versus the maximal baseline. Right: The distance to the true (noise less) solution.

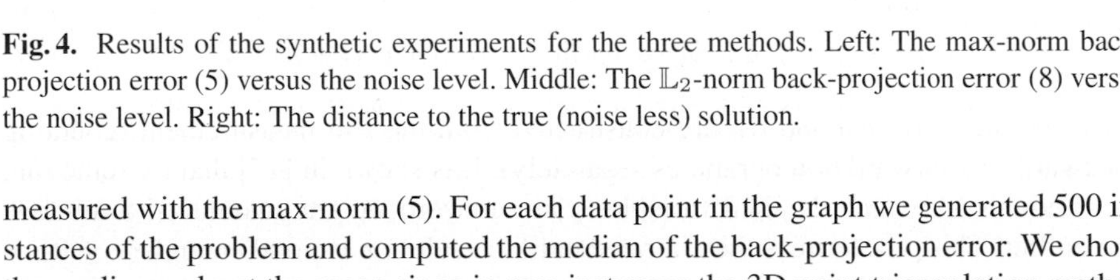

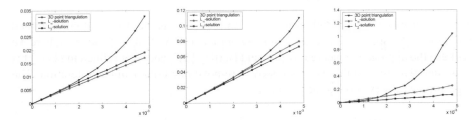

Fig. 4. Results of the synthetic experiments for the three methods. Left: The max-norm back-projection error (5) versus the noise level. Middle: The $\mathbb{L}_2$-norm back-projection error (8) versus the noise level. Right: The distance to the true (noise less) solution.

measured with the max-norm (5). For each data point in the graph we generated 500 instances of the problem and computed the median of the back-projection error. We chose the median and not the mean since in rare instances the 3D point triangulation method produces a plane that is almost perpendicular to the true plane, resulting in extremely large back-projection errors. Even though we are averaging over a large number of experiments this gives a noisy graph which is difficult to interpret, therefore we use the median instead (for comparison we plotted one of the graphs obtained when using the mean in Figure 2). For the two proposed formulations the median and the mean are very similar.

To the left is the result when the back-projection error is measured using the max-norm (4). As expected the proposed $\mathbb{L}_\infty$ formulation performs best here (regardless of the baseline).

In the middle is the result when the error is measured with the $\mathbb{L}_2$-norm (8). Here the proposed $\mathbb{L}_2$ formulation is the winner. Somewhat surprisingly the proposed $\mathbb{L}_\infty$ formulation performs better than the 3D-point triangulation approach when the baseline is small. The reason is that when the baseline is small distances in the direction of the depth is difficult to observe accurately in the cameras. Hence, the position of the 3D-points in this direction is uncertain. Therefore, using distances in 3D instead of back-projection errors results in a more unstable procedure.

To the right is perhaps the most interesting graph. Here we have plotted the median of the distance from the computed solutions to the true (noiseless solution). If $(a_{true}, 1)$ is the parameters for the true solution the distance is measured as $||a_{true} - a_{est}||_2$ where $(a_{est}, 1)$ is the estimated solution with one of the methods. When the baseline is sufficiently large the 3D point triangulation approach is almost as good as the proposed $\mathbb{L}_2$ formulation however when the baseline becomes smaller it is less stable than the other two methods.

To test the stability with respect to noise we also plotted the same figures when varying the noise level instead of the maximal baseline. The results cam be seen in Figure 4. Here the maximal baseline was set to 0.5 and the noise level was varied between 0 and 0.005. The proposed formulations appear to exhibit roughly linear growth in the errors whereas the triangulation approach seem to grow faster.

3.2 Outlier Removal and Estimation

Next we evaluate our method on real data. In real settings the data is often corrupted by outliers. A popular method for removing outliers is RANSAC [4], however, here we will use the approach pioneered by Sim and Hartley [21], and later refined in [17]. This is an iterative method that is guaranteed to remove one outlier in each iteration. The algorithm works by solving the problem

$$\min s \tag{26}$$

$$\text{s.t. } ||(a_i p + a_{i0}, b_i p + b_{i0})|| \leq \mu(c_i p + c_{i0}) + s, \quad \forall i, \tag{27}$$

where $a_i, b_i, c_i, a_{i0}, b_{i0}$ and c_{i0} are constructed from the i'th measurement (counting backward and forward homographies separately). It is shown in [17] that by removing the residuals for which the dual variables y are nonzero we are guaranteed to remove one outlier. This procedure is then iterated until the solution is good enough ($s \leq 0$).

We ran the algorithm on the stereo pair seen in Figure 5. Since the posters located on the wall has similar texture we obtained a lot of mismatches where points on one of the poster matches to points on the other. Using SIFT [15] we determined 678 point correspondences. In order to find a solution with all errors less than 10 pixels 112 iterations was needed. In total 241 image points where discarded. Manual inspection reveals

Fig. 5. Resulting estimation for the office stereo pair. Read points - outliers, blue points - inliers.

that almost all the discarded cases is either a mismatch or a point not belonging to the dominant plane.

4 Conclusions

In this theoretical paper we have proposed a procedure for triangulating a scene plane. Our method is based on the framework of quasiconvex optimization making it easy to solve with guaranteed optimality. Furthermore, since we have shown that our problem belongs to this class, all the previously developed theory naturally applies to this problem as well. Since the formulation is based on back-projection which is a geometrically meaningful quantity it is also stable with respect to noise and geometry.

Acknowledgments

This work has been funded by the European Research Council (GlobalVision grant no. 209480), the Swedish Research Council (grant no. 2007-6476), the Swedish Foundation for Strategic Research (SSF) through the program Future Research Leaders and the Australian Research Council's Discovery Projects funding scheme (project DP0988439).

References

1. Bartoli, A., Sturm, P.: Constrained structure and motion from multiple uncalibrated views of a piecewise planar scene. International Journal of Computer Vision 52(1) (2003), 13
2. Boyd, S., Vandenberghe, L.: Convex Optimization. Cambridge University Press, Cambridge (2004), 17
3. Boykov, Y., Veksler, O., Zabih, R.: Fast approximate energy minimization via graph cuts. IEEE Trans. Pattern Analysis and Machine Intelligence 23(11), 1222–1239 (2001), 13
4. Fischler, M.A., Bolles, R.C.: Random sample consensus: a paradigm for model fitting with application to image analysis and automated cartography. Commun. Assoc. Comp. Mach. 24, 381–395 (1981), 20
5. Furukawa, Y., Curless, B., Seitz, S.M., Szeliski, R.: Reconstructing building interiors from images. In: Proc. Int. Conf. on Computer Vision, Kyoto, Japan (2009), 13
6. Hartley, R., Seo, Y.: Verifying global minima for L_2 minimization problems. In: Conf. Computer Vision and Pattern Recognition, Anchorage, USA (2008), 14, 15, 16, 17
7. Hartley, R., Sturm, P.: Triangulation. Computer Vision and Image Understanding 68(2), 146–157 (1997), 13
8. Hartley, R.I., Zisserman, A.: Multiple View Geometry in Computer Vision. Cambridge University Press, Cambridge (2004), 13, 16
9. Kahl, F., Hartley, R.: Multiple view geometry under the L_1-norm. IEEE Trans. Pattern Analysis and Machine Intelligence 30(9), 1603–1617 (2008) 14, 15, 17, 18
10. Kanatani, K., Niitsuma, H.: Optimal two-view planar scene triangulation. In: Kimmel, R., Klette, R., Sugimoto, A. (eds.) ACCV 2010, Part II. LNCS, vol. 6493, pp. 242–253. Springer, Heidelberg (2011), 13
11. Kanazawa, Y., Kenichi, K.: Direct reconstruction of planar surfaces by stereo vision. IEICE Transactions on Information and Systems, E78-D(7) (1995), 13

12. Ke, Q., Kanade, T.: Quasiconvex optimization for robust geometric reconstruction. IEEE Trans. Pattern Analysis and Machine Intelligence 29(10), 1834–1847 (2007), 15, 17
13. Kolmogorov, V., Zabih, R.: Multi-camera scene reconstruction via graph cuts. In: Heyden, A., Sparr, G., Nielsen, M., Johansen, P. (eds.) ECCV 2002. LNCS, vol. 2352, pp. 82–96. Springer, Heidelberg (2002), 13
14. Li, H.: A practical algorithm for L_∞ triangulation with outliers. In: Conf. Computer Vision and Pattern Recognition, Minneapolis, USA (2007), 14, 17
15. Lowe, D.: Distinctive image features from scale-invariant keypoints. Int. Journal Computer Vision (2004), 20
16. Olsson, C., Enqvist, O., Kahl, F.: A polynomial-time bound for matching and registration with ouliers. In: Conf. Computer Vision and Pattern Recognition, Anchorage, USA (2008), 14, 17
17. Olsson, C., Eriksson, A., Hartley, R.: Outlier removal using duality. In: Conf. Computer Vision and Pattern Recognition, San Francisco, USA (2010), 14, 20
18. Olsson, C., Kahl, F.: Generalized convexity in multiple view geometry. J. Math. Imaging Vis. 38(1), 35–51 (2010), 14, 15
19. Olsson, C., Kahl, F., Hartley, R.: Projective least-squares: Global solutions with local optimization. In: Conf. Computer Vision and Pattern Recognition, Miami, USA (2009), 14, 15, 16, 17
20. Seo, Y., Hartley, R.: A fast method to minimize L_∞ error norm for geometric vision problems. In: Int. Conf. Computer Vision, Rio de Janeiro, Brazil (2007), 17
21. Sim, K., Hartley, R.: Removing outliers using the L_∞-norm. In: Conf. Computer Vision and Pattern Recognition, New York City, USA, pp. 485–492 (2006), 14, 17, 20
22. Woodford, O., Torr, P., Reid, I., Fitzgibbon, A.: Global stereo reconstruction under second order smoothness priors. Proc. IEEE Trans. Pattern Analysis and Machine Intelligence 31, 2115–2128 (2009), 13

Human 3D Motion Computation from a Varying Number of Cameras

Magnus Burenius, Josephine Sullivan, Stefan Carlsson, and Kjartan Halvorsen*

KTH CSC/CVAP, S-100 44 Stockholm, Sweden
http://www.csc.kth.se/cvap

Abstract. This paper focuses on how the accuracy of marker-less human motion capture is affected by the number of camera views used. Specifically, we compare the 3D reconstructions calculated from single and multiple cameras. We perform our experiments on data consisting of video from multiple cameras synchronized with ground truth 3D motion, obtained from a motion capture session with a professional footballer. The error is compared for the 3D reconstructions, of diverse motions, estimated using the manually located image joint positions from one, two or three cameras. We also present a new bundle adjustment procedure using regression splines to impose weak prior assumptions about human motion, temporal smoothness and joint angle limits, on the 3D reconstruction. The results show that even under close to ideal circumstances the monocular 3D reconstructions contain visual artifacts not present in the multiple view case, indicating accurate and efficient marker-less human motion capture requires multiple cameras.

Keywords: Motion Capture, 3D Reconstruction, Monocular, Bundle Adjustment, Regression Splines.

1 Introduction

This paper addresses the challenging computer vision problem of precise marker-less human motion capture from video sequences. It focuses on measuring its feasibility and achievable accuracy with respect to the number of cameras used. This is of interest to anyone who wants to acquire the accurate 3D motion of people performing interesting actions from real video footage. These questions have been partially explored for the standard actions of walking and jogging using the HumanEva dataset [6]. It, however, has primarily been used to compare the accuracy of reconstruction algorithms as opposed to investigating if and when computer vision can be used for accurate human motion capture.

Our motivation is that we want to reconstruct, in real time, the 3D motion of a football player during a real game to augment the video broadcast and enhance the viewer's experience. Presently, the most effective and reliable way to achieve this would be to map image measurements to 3D motions [7]. However, learning

* Royal Institute of Technology, School of Technology and Health, Stockholm, Sweden.

A. Heyden and F. Kahl (Eds.): SCIA 2011, LNCS 6688, pp. 24–35, 2011.

such mappings, as they are poor at extrapolation, requires a large amount of relevant training data and unfortunately large databases of football motion capture data are not available. And perhaps, even more pertinently, the complete repertoire of football actions cannot be replicated in a motion capture studio. Thus we need to create training data from footage of players in real games.

In the absence of significant training data, there are two distinct approaches taken. One is based on tracking: given the 3D pose in the first frame tracking is used to compute the most likely poses for the subsequent frames [11] using either Kalman or particle filters[13]. The initialization is typically done manually and visual features of the images are matched to those hypothesized by the state of the 3D model. These methods can produce nice results, especially with multi-camera footage, however, they are slow and brittle and potentially require manual re-initialization when applied to fast extended motions.

The other approach is the direct geometrical solution that can be used if the image positions of the joints are known and the skeleton is assumed to be a kinematic chain [1,2,3,4,5]. These algorithms can be adopted to both monocular and multi-camera data, although the monocular case is a decidedly more difficult. This type of approach is appealing as it is simple and fast to implement and there is a large scope for (semi-)automating the localization of the joints in the images and depth estimation. However, it is unclear if the precision of their reconstructions, even with manually clicked image joint positions, is good enough especially from monocular footage.

In this paper we explore what is the achievable accuracy for these methods given manually estimated joint locations and known camera calibrations. Thereby we estimate a lower bound for any future automated process. We also compare the accuracy of monocular reconstructions with stereo and three-view reconstructions [12]. Our experiments rely on a data set consisting of video from multiple cameras synchronized with ground truth 3D motion. The motions are football actions performed by a professional player in a motion capture studio. We also present a new bundle adjustment procedure for imposing temporal smoothness, link length and joint angle constraints on the 3D reconstruction. This algorithm imposes the weakest possible priors on the resulting reconstruction and reduces the errors due to the noise in the estimated joint positions. The results indicate that even under close to ideal circumstances the monocular 3D reconstructions show visual artifacts not present in the multiple view case. While the latter are visually identical to the ground truth. Thus, precise reconstructions for large amounts of data is not feasible from monocular data.

The rest of the paper is organized as follows. Section 2 describes how to create an initial 3D reconstruction from measurements of image joint positions. Both the monocular and multiple camera case is mentioned. To reduce the effect of measurement noise we impose weak prior constraints on the reconstruction in section 3. Section 4 describes the new data set of motion capture synchronized with video recordings. The data set is used to test the new algorithm and the accuracy of reconstructions from varying number of cameras. In section 5 we discuss our conclusions and possible future work.

2 Initial 3D Reconstruction

The human is modeled as a kinematic chain consisting of joints and links. We assume that we are given image measurements, from one or multiple calibrated cameras, of the human joint positions shown in figure 1, for all time frames. These may have been computed fully automatically, or completely manually, or somewhere in between. The joints are chosen as rotation centers to have a well defined position. Two auxiliary joints that are not rotation centers, neck and pelvis, are added so that all joints form a kinematic chain. These two joints are not measured explicitly but computed from the measurements of the other joints. The neck is defined to be the mean of the shoulders. The pelvis is defined to be the mean of the hips. Note that we do not include the hands, feet or head in our model. These body parts are not well represented by one rigid link. Their 3D reconstruction could be obtained by alternative methods, e.g. they could have standard offsets relative the other joints, or be reconstructed by a volumetric model. Given the image positions of the joints their position in 3D can be reconstructed. Two particular scenarios are examined.

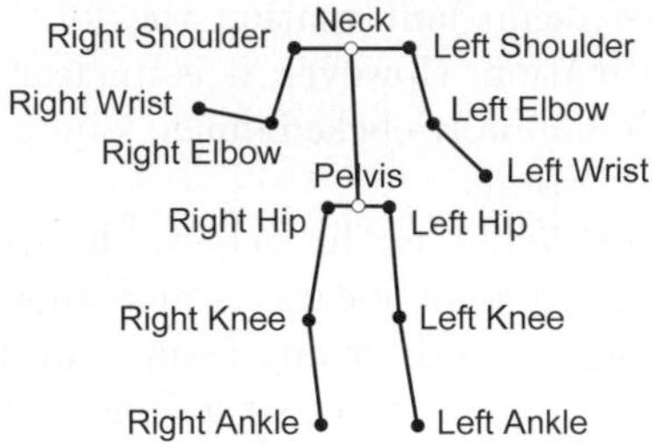

Fig. 1. Joint positions

Multiple Camera Case. When considering the joint positions from several cameras, triangulation is used to give initial reconstruction of the points in 3D [12]. Each point at each frame is reconstructed independently of the other points. The points are not treated as a kinematic chain but as a simple point cloud.

Monocular Camera Case. In contrast when we consider measurements from just one camera the reconstruction process, due to the depth ambiguities, is more involved. The reconstruction method implemented, following previous work in this area [1,2,3,4,5], makes several assumptions. These are that the skeleton is a kinematic chain with known link lengths, the depth of the root joint (required for a projective camera) and the *flip* of each link is known. The flip tells which end of a link that is closest to the camera. These quantities can be estimated automatically, though with difficulty [5]. This further degrades the accuracy of the obtained reconstructions is not considered within this paper. In summary, the skeltal kinematic chain is reconstructed in 3D, by starting at the root joint and reconstructing each link in turn.

3 Imposing Weak Priors on the Initial Reconstruction

Due to measurement noise the initial reconstruction might not look sufficiently good. This is especially true for monocular reconstruction. Figure 2 shows examples of measured image joint positions and the corresponding monocular 3D reconstructions from another view. Even though the measurements seems to be close to the ground truth in the camera view, the 3D reconstruction typically differs more if viewed from another angle. Also since the initial reconstruction is done independently for each frame it is not guaranteed to be continuous over time. An example of this is shown in the third and fourth examples of figure 2, which displays the reconstruction of two consecutive frames.

To improve the initially estimated reconstruction we need a stronger model of what we are reconstructing. By relying more on a prior model the influence of measurement noise can be reduced. We are trying to reconstruct a human performing some arbitrary action. Therefore we do not want to restrict the prior to just model specific actions. The model should fit (almost) all possible human motions. It is just the completely unnatural motions that should be constrained. In section 3.1 we describe how to impose link length and joint angle constraints. In fact the link length constraints are already fulfilled by the initial monocular reconstruction but it should be imposed on the multiple view reconstruction as well. In section 3.2 we describe how to also impose temporal smoothness.

3.1 Link Length and Joint Angle Constraints

As a first step constraints can be imposed on the link lengths and joint angles to reduce the effect of measurement noise. The joints of the human skeleton cannot rotate freely. For instance the knee and elbow angles have a range smaller than 180°. This is one thing that makes the initial monocular estimation look weird. If these types of constraints are not imposed the arms and legs may be twisted in unnatural ways. These are the constraints typically applied in human reconstruction methods. They are used by e.g. [1,5], although they do not mention the details of their parametrization.

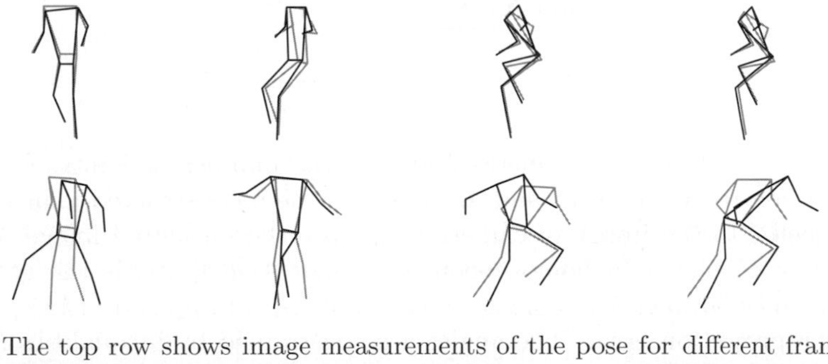

Fig. 2. The top row shows image measurements of the pose for different frames. The measurements are black and the ground truth is grey. The bottom row shows the corresponding initial monocular 3D reconstructions viewed from another direction. The reconstruction errors are significantly larger in this new view.

To implement the constraints we let a human pose be defined by a set of joint angles and the Cartesian position of one root joint which we define to be the pelvis. The rotation of the root is not constrained and has three degrees of freedom (DOF). The elbows and knees are modeled with a single rotation DOF with upper and lower bounds. The rotation of left and right hip and shoulder have three DOF, but they should be constrained to not allow the arms and legs to be twisted unnaturally. We use the twist-swing parametrization [9,10] to deal with this and constrain the twist parameter with to be within $[-\pi/2, \pi/2]$. The swing component is unconstrained. This is a good approximation of the true constraints for humans [9,10].

These are the parameters that are used to define a pose: 6 for the root, 3 for each shoulder and hip, and 1 for each elbow and knee, giving a total of $A = 22$ parameters. This is a reduced set of parameters compared to using three Cartesian coordinates for each joint giving a total of 36 parameters. More formally let $a = (a_1, a_2, \ldots, a_A)$ be the generalized joint coordinates. The constraints are then expressed by linear vector inequalities, where the elements are infinite for the unconstrained components:

$$a_{min} \le a \le a_{max} \tag{1}$$

The length of all links are assumed to be known and fixed. The fixed link length constraints are fulfilled by construction in this parametrization. Let $r = (r_1, r_2, \ldots, r_J)$ where r_j is the homogeneous coordinates of the position of joint j. Denote the mapping from joint angles to the position of the joints in homogeneous coordinates as f:

$$r = f(a) \tag{2}$$

A Bundle Adjustment Implementation. We now formulate an optimization problem that can be solved iteratively to get a refined estimate by imposing constraints on joint angles and link lengths. The initial reconstruction of section 2 is used as an initial guess and the joint angles a are optimized to minimize the reprojection error:

$$\begin{aligned} \min_a \quad & \sum_{c=1}^{C} \sum_{j=1}^{J} d(M_c r_j, z_{c,j})^2 \\ \text{s.t.} \quad & a_{min} \le a \le a_{max} \\ & r = f(a) \end{aligned} \tag{3}$$

where C is the number of cameras and J is the number of joints. M_c is the projection matrix of camera c and $M_c r_j$ is thus the reconstructed joint position r_j reprojected to the image of camera c. $z_{c,j}$ are the measured image position in camera c of joint j in homogeneous coordinates. $d(p_1, p_2)$ is the geometric image distance between the homogeneous points p_1 and p_2 and $d(M_c r_j, z_{c,j})$ is thus the reprojection error. The angles are constrained by inequalities (1) and the link length constraints are fulfilled by construction (equation 2). Given the initially estimated reconstruction the local minimum of the constrained minimization problem gives the refined reconstruction. The constrained nonlinear least squares problem is solved iteratively using the trust-region-reflective algorithm [17,18,19], which is implemented by the MATLAB function `lsqnonlin`. Note that this refinement step works the same way no matter how many cameras we use.

3.2 Temporal Smoothness, Link Length and Joint Angle Constraints

Both the initial estimate and the refined estimate, imposing link length and joint angle constraints, have so far been computed independently for each frame. Due to this the reconstructed animation can look jittery and unnatural, since it is not forced to be continuous. This is especially true for the monocular reconstruction. The reasonable assumption of finite muscle forces implies finite joint accelerations and continuous velocities. In this section we describe how to also impose constraints on temporal smoothness.

Interpolation. A standard way to impose temporal continuity on the reconstruction is to use interpolation. Some frames are selected as key-frames and the reconstruction is interpolated between them. Often the joint angles are interpolated linearly, using SLERP [8] for the joints having three rotational DOF. However, using linear interpolation the joint velocities will not be continuous at the key-frames and the reconstruction will look a bit stiff. To get a smoother reconstruction splines can be used [16]. We use natural cubic splines to do this leading to continuity in the second derivative at all key-frames/knots (figure 3). One drawback of interpolation is that the values at the knots are fixed. We interpolate between them but do not try to improve the values at the knots. If we have measurements taken between the knots, then those are not taken into account.

Regression Splines. The drawbacks of interpolation can be fixed by the use of smoothing splines, e.g. regression splines [16]. The idea is to let the values at the knots be variables of an optimization problem and find the ones that gives a spline that minimizes the difference to all measurements. In this way the spline that best fit the measurements can be computed (figure 3). We use equidistantly distributed knots. The smoothness is then controlled by a single parameter which is the distance between knots. The larger distance the smoother estimate. The measurements of all time frames are considered simultaneously, in a batch procedure, as opposed to standard Kalman or particle filters [13] which proceeds chronologically.

New Bundle Adjustment Algorithm. We formulate a new algorithm to perform 3D reconstruction while imposing temporal smoothness in addition to the constraints on link lengths and joint angles. The reprojection error is minimized while imposing our prior model. The difference is that now we express each angle parameter i as a function of time t by a regression spline:

$$a_{i,t} = P(t, \alpha_i) \tag{4}$$

where $a_{i,t}$ is the interpolated joint angle at time t given its values at all knots α_i. Let the values for all angles and knots be stored in $\alpha = (\alpha_1, \alpha_2, \ldots, \alpha_A)$.

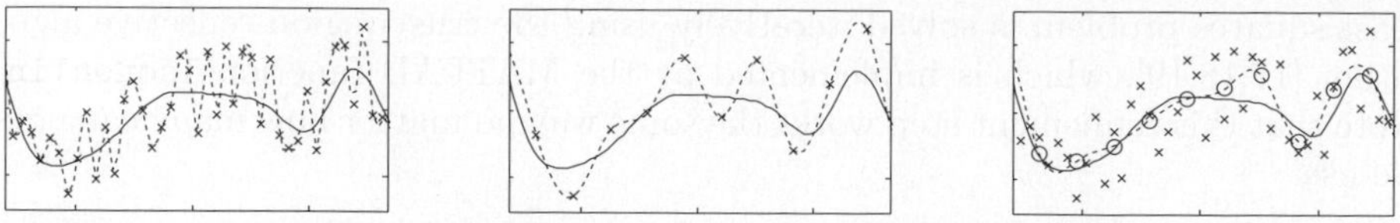

Fig. 3. The difference between interpolation and regression splines. The full line is the ground truth, the crosses are the measurements and the dashed line is the estimation. The left image shows interpolation between all measurements. The center image shows interpolation between every fourth measurement. The right image shows regression splines with a knot at every fourth measurement. Knots are drawn as circles.

The distance between knots is a variable the user may choose manually and control the smoothness of the reconstruction. It is considered to be fixed in the optimization. The initial value of all parameters at the knots are taken from the initially estimated reconstruction, described in section 2. The values at the knots are then optimized to minimize the reprojection error:

$$\begin{aligned} \min_{\alpha} \sum_{c=1}^{C}\sum_{j=1}^{J}\sum_{t=1}^{T} d(M_c r_{j,t}, z_{c,j,t})^2 & \\ \text{s.t.} \quad \alpha_{min} \leq \alpha \leq \alpha_{max} & \\ a_{i,t} = P(t, \alpha_i) & \\ r_t = f(a_t) & \end{aligned} \tag{5}$$

In contrast to the previous bundle adjustment in section 3.1 all frames (T) are considered simultaneously. The variables we optimize over are the joint angle parameters at all knots. Given the initial reconstructions at all knots, the local minimum to the constrained minimization problem gives the refined reconstruction. The solution is found iteratively just as in section 3.1.

4 Results

To evaluate the accuracy of the monocular and multiple view reconstructions we obtained 3D motions of a professional footballer, using a commercial off the shelf motion capture system with passive markers. It provided the ground truth at a frequency of 200 Hz. We used 35 markers which were not placed at the joint positions (figure 1), but from the markers the rotation centers defining the joint positions could be computed. The player was also recorded at 25 Hz by three regular video cameras at a resolution of 1920x1080 pixels (figure 4). A total of 30 sequences of different football actions were recorded (17 minutes of data). The videos were calibrated and synchronized to the ground truth.

Using these videos the joint image positions in the three cameras were estimated manually for seven different action instances: receiving and passing the ball, receiving ball on chest and passing, free kick, pass, defending, running plus a sharp change of direction, a contested jumping header. This corresponds in total to 16 s. Note that since the markers used by the motion capture system

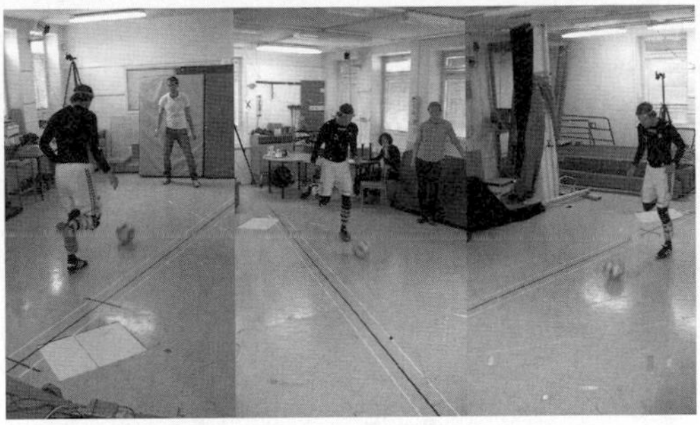

Fig. 4. A motion capture studio was used to capture ground truth animations corresponding to video from three cameras

did not correspond to the joints, the markers were not used to aid the manual joint estimation in the videos. This is important since the algorithm is intended to be used in situations outside the motion capture studio without the use of markers. These measurements were used to reconstruct the actions in 3D and the results were compared to the ground truth provided by the motion capture system. Each reconstruction was calculated using the four different algorithms described in section 2 & 3:

1. **Initial Estimate**. Independent reconstruction for each frame.
2. **Limb Length & Joint Angle Constraints**. Initial estimate refined independently for each frame.
3. **Limb Length & Joint Angle Constraints Interpolated**. Reconstruction (2) is computed for each key-frame and interpolated in-between.
4. **Limb Length, Joint Angle & Temporal Smoothness Constraints**. Initial estimate refined by the new bundle adjustment algorithm, using regression splines in a batch process.

Note that the algorithms work on both monocular and multiple view reconstruction. Each algorithm was tested on several different camera combinations. For the initial monocular reconstruction we assumed known link lengths, flips and the depth of the root joint. This was obtained from the ground truth. Also note that the calibrated cameras were static and that the videos had little motion blur and no occlusion by any other objects. These assumptions and the fact that we did manual joint measurements in high resolution images makes it possible to compute a lower error bound under ideal conditions. In a real situation outside the motion capture studio the reconstruction will be worse.

Evaluation of the algorithms and comparison between monocular and multiple view reconstruction requires a quantitative measure of the reconstruction error. This measure should correspond to the perceived error. The most disconcerting part of a reconstruction is if the joint angles are unnatural. We therefore look at the mean joint angle error:

$$\frac{1}{TA}\sum_{t=1}^{T}\sum_{i=1}^{A}|a_{i,t} - \hat{a}_{i,t}| \tag{6}$$

However, it might not be appropriate to combine the angles describing 1D rotations and the ones describing 3D rotations by the twist-swing decomposition. For this reason we also define an error measure that only takes the mean over the 1D angles, describing the knees and elbows.

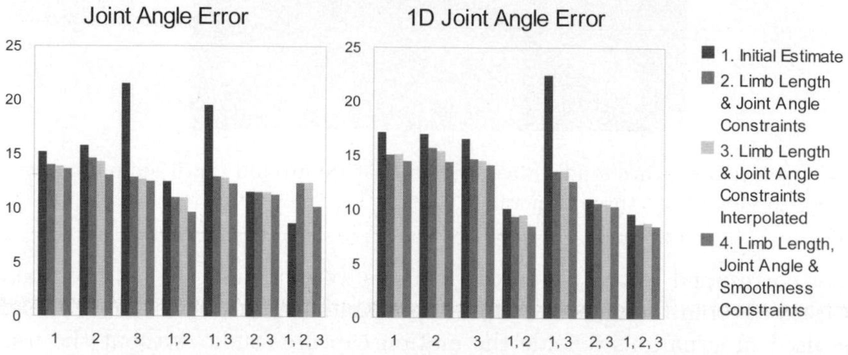

Fig. 5. The mean reconstruction error in degrees, vertical axis, resulting from different camera configurations, horizontal axis. Four different methods of reconstruction are evaluated. The errors are the mean taken over seven different motions with a total duration of 16 s.

Figure 5 show these mean reconstruction errors over all mesured sequences, for different algorithms and camera configurations. The 1D joint angle error shows a big difference between the monocular and multiple view cases. The error is almost twice as large for the monocular case. As expected the initial estimate (1) has the largest error and our new algorithm based on regression splines (4) has the lowest, while algorithm (2) and (3) are somewhere in-between. However, except the initial estimate the difference between the algorithms are not that big in these measures, especially not between algorithm (2) and (3). Nevertheless, in the monocular case the smooth reconstructions produced by algorithms (3) and (4) looks much nicer than the jittery reconstructions produced by (1) and(2). In this sense the perceived error is not captured well by these error measures. One would likely need an error measure involving derivative approximations to capture this aspect. Disregarding the nice appearance of temporal smoothness the new algorithm (4) still performs best even with this simple error measure.

Figure 6 shows monocular and stereo reconstructions compared to the ground truth for four different frames (one per quadrant). The reconstructions is viewed from each camera. In this figure camera 1 is used for monocular reconstruction and camera 1 and 2 for stereo reconstruction. In the view of camera 2 it can clearly be seen that the monocular reconstruction does not give the same accuracy as the stereo reconstruction. The two frames at the bottom are consecutive and show that the initial monocular reconstruction is not consistent over time.

Looking at the reconstructions in motion our subjective opinion is that for the three camera case the initial estimate always looks good. For our measurement accuracy the bundle adjustments does not give a visible improvement in this

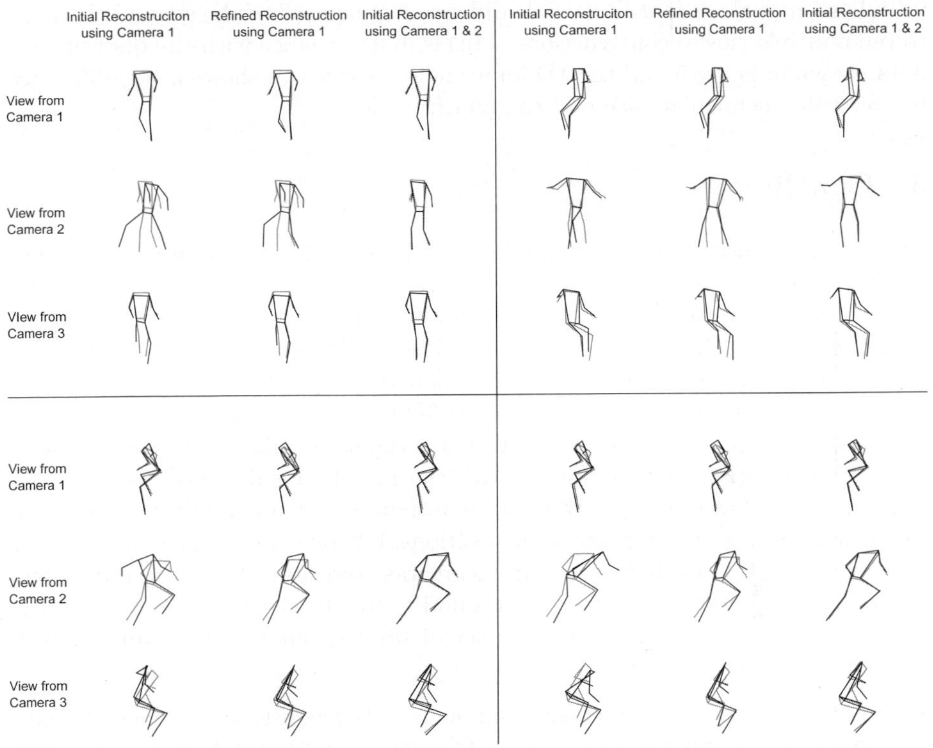

Fig. 6. Each quadrant shows the 3D reconstruction (black) and the ground truth (gray) for a single frame. The first column shows the initial monocular 3D reconstruction obtained from camera 1. The second column shows the refined monocular reconstruction, imposing constraints on joint angles and temporal smoothness. The third column shows the stereo reconstruction obtained from camera 1 & 2. Each row shows the reconstructions in one of the three cameras. The view from camera 2 is the interesting one since the monocular reconstruction looks significantly worse than the stereo reconstruction from this view. Camera 3 is almost facing camera 1 and for this reason both reconstructions look all right in it, although the stereo reconstruction looks slightly better.

case. For the two camera case the initial estimate mostly looks good. It looks a little bit wobbly sometimes. In those cases the reconstruction by algorithm (4) gives a small but visible improvement. The reconstruction from camera 1 & 3 looks much worse than the reconstructions from camera 1 & 2 or camera 2 & 3. This is since camera 1 & 3 are almost facing each other. For the bad reconstructions from camera 1 & 3 algorithm (4) gives a big improvement. This improved reconstruction looks about the same as the reconstructions from camera 1 & 2 and camera 2 & 3. In the monocular case the initial estimate generally looks bad. It does not improve that much by just imposing the joint angle constraints of algorithm (2). Imposing the smoothness of algorithm (3) or (4) gives a bigger improvement. The reconstruction of algorithm (4) looks slightly better than that of (3). However, even if this refined reconstruction looks much better than the initial estimate there is still a visible difference compared to the ground truth, or to the multiple view reconstructions. This is in accordance with the quantitative data shown in figure 5 and the 1D joint angle error which shows a big difference between the monocular case and the multiple view.

5 Conclusion

By imposing constraints on the link lengths, joint angles, and temporal continuity, the refined estimate created by the bundle adjustment algorithm generally looks better then the initial estimate. However, in the monocular case the improvement is not big enough. Even under close to ideal conditions the monocular reconstruction looks significantly worse than the multiple view reconstruction. For our final application of reconstructing 3D motion from a real football game, we can expect even worse accuracy. To make the monocular reconstruction look good it is necessary to manually tweak the measurements until the 3D pose looks correct. However, then the 3D reconstruction is not really created from the measurements of the image joint positions, but rather constructed manually in this feedback loop. If two or three cameras were used both the initial and refined estimate look similar to the ground truth. In the two camera case the initial estimate looks bad for a small set of frames, but those are improved in the refinement step.

Future Work. We conclude that monocular 3D reconstruction does not give the accuracy our application requires. The next step is then to try to use multiple cameras to accurately reconstruct the 3D motion of a player, outside the motion capture studio. For our football application we would like to deal with multiple uncalibrated rotating and zooming cameras. Affine factorization [14] and auto-calibration [15] can then be used to get the initial reconstruction and the bundle adjustment algorithm could be extended to also impose smoothness on the camera calibration. It would also be of interest to explore to what extent the joint localization can be automatized given the accuracy requirements.

Acknowledgment

This work was supported by the EU project "Free-viewpoint Immersive Networked Experience" and The Swedish Foundation for Strategic Research and the Knowledge Foundation in the project "Large Scale Visualization of Human Action". The authors would also like to thank Tracab for arranging the motion capture session and Per Karlsson (AIK) for being the subject in our experiments.

References

1. Lee, H.J., Chen, Z.: Determination of 3D human body postures from a single view. Computer Vision, Graphics, and Image Processing 30(2), 148–168 (1985) ISSN 0734-189X, doi:10.1016/0734-189X(85)90094-5

2. Taylor, C.J.: Reconstruction of articulated objects from point correspondences in a single uncalibrated image. In: Proceedings of IEEE Conference on Computer Vision and Pattern Recognition, vol. 1, pp. 677–684 (2000)
3. Eriksson, M., Carlsson, S.: Monocular reconstruction of human motion by qualitative selection. In: Proceedings of Sixth IEEE International Conference on Automatic Face and Gesture Recognition, May 17-19, pp. 863–868 (2004)
4. Parameswaran, V.: View independent human body pose estimation from a single perspective image. In: CVPR (2004)
5. Wei, X.K.: Jinxiang Chai: Modeling 3D human poses from uncalibrated monocular images. In: 2009 IEEE 12th International Conference on Computer Vision, September 29-October 2, pp. 1873–1880 (2009)
6. Sigal, L., Balan, A., Black, M.: HumanEva: Synchronized Video and Motion Capture Dataset and Baseline Algorithm for Evaluation of Articulated Human Motion. International Journal of Computer Vision 87(1), 427 (2010)
7. Bo, L., Sminchisescu, C., Kanaujia, A., Metaxas, D.: Fast Algorithms for Large Scale Conditional 3D Prediction. In: IEEE International Conference on Computer Vision and Pattern Recognition (June 2008)
8. Shoemake, K.: Animating rotation with quaternion curves. SIGGRAPH (1985)
9. Baerlocher, P., Boulic, R.: Parametrization and Range of Motion of the Ball-and-Socket Joint (2000)
10. Grassia, F.S.: Practical parameterization of rotations using the exponential map. Journal of Graphics Tools 3, 29–48 (1998)
11. Sidenbladh, H., Black, M.J., Fleet, D.J.: Stochastic tracking of 3D human figures using 2D image motion. In: Vernon, D. (ed.) ECCV 2000. LNCS, vol. 1843, pp. 702–718. Springer, Heidelberg (2000)
12. Hartley, R., Zisserman, A.: Multiple View Geometry in Computer Visio., 2nd edn. Cambridge University Press, Cambridge (2004)
13. Thrun, S., Burgard, W., Fox, D.: Probabilistic Robotics. MIT Press, Cambridge (2005)
14. Tomasi, C., Kanade, T.: Shape and motion from image streams under orthography: a factorization method. International Journal of Computer Vision 9, 137–154 (1992)
15. Quan, L.: Self-calibration of an Affine Camera from Multiple Views. International Journal of Computer Vision 19, 93–105 (1994)
16. de Boor, C.: A Practical Guide to Splines. Springer, Heidelberg (1978)
17. Coleman, T.F., Li, Y.: An Interior, Trust Region Approach for Nonlinear Minimization Subject to Bounds. SIAM Journal on Optimization 6, 418–445 (1996)
18. Coleman, T.F., Li, Y.: On the Convergence of Reflective Newton Methods for Large-Scale Nonlinear Minimization Subject to Bounds. Mathematical Programming 67(2), 189–224 (1994)
19. Dennis Jr., J.E.: Nonlinear Least-Squares. In: Jacobs, D. (ed.) State of the Art in Numerical Analysis, pp. 269–312. Academic Press, London (1977)

Generalized Hard Constraints for Graph Segmentation

Filip Malmberg, Robin Strand, and Ingela Nyström

Centre for Image Analysis, Uppsala University,
Uppsala, Sweden
{filip,robin,ingela}@cb.uu.se

Abstract. Graph-based methods have become well-established tools for image segmentation. Viewing the image as a weighted graph, these methods seek to extract a graph cut that best matches the image content. Many of these methods are *interactive*, in that they allow a human operator to guide the segmentation process by specifying a set of hard constraints that the cut must satisfy. Typically, these constraints are given in one of two forms: *regional constraints* (a set of vertices that must be separated by the cut) or *boundary constraints* (a set of edges that must be included in the cut). Here, we propose a new type of hard constraints, that includes both regional constraints and boundary constraints as special cases. We also present an efficient method for computing cuts that satisfy a set of generalized constraints, while globally minimizing a graph cut measure.

Keywords: Image segmentation, Graph cuts, Regional constraints, Boundary constraints.

1 Introduction

In recent years, several efficient methods for image segmentation have been formulated in the framework of *edge weighted graphs*. Common for these methods is that they seek to extract a *cut* from a *pixel adjacency graph*, i.e., a graph whose vertex set is the set of image elements, and whose edge set is given by an adjacency relation between the image elements. Informally, a cut in a connected graph is a set of edges such that if they are removed, the graph is separated into two or more connected components.

Generally, the goal of these methods is to find a cut that best matches some criterion based on image content, e.g., a cut that coincides with high contrast regions in the image. In interactive (or supervised) methods, the cut is additionally required to satisfy a set of *hard constraints*. These constraints may be specified by a human user in an interactive setting, or by an automated procedure. Typically, the constraints are given in one of two forms.

Regional constraints. The cut is required to separate all elements in a specified subset of the graph vertices.

A. Heyden and F. Kahl (Eds.): SCIA 2011, LNCS 6688, pp. 36–47, 2011.

Boundary constraints. The cut is required to include a specified subset of the graph edges.

Computing cuts with respect to regional constraints is a well-studied problem, and many efficient algorithms have been proposed for this purpose. See, e.g., [2, 15,6,9,4]. A unified theoretical framework, incorporating many of these methods, was recently proposed by Couprie et al. [3].

The most prominent example of image segmentation with respect to boundary constraints is the Live-wire method [7]. In its original form, this method is restricted to 2D image segmentation. Many attempts have been made to extend this paradigm to 3D, see, e.g., [12] and references therein. In general, these methods, unlike the 2D Live-wire method, do not guarantee optimality of the resulting segmentation. A notable exception is [10], where a method is presented for computing globally minimal discrete surfaces with prescribed boundary.

Here, we propose a new type of hard constraints for supervised graph segmentation. Informally, a generalized constraint is a pair of distinct vertices that any feasible cut must separate. We show that both boundary constraints and regional constraints may be viewed as special cases of the proposed generalized constraints. Moreover, we present an efficient method for finding cuts that satisfy a set of generalized constraints, and for which the maximal edge weight in the cut is globally minimal.

2 Preliminaries

In this Section, we present basic definitions of edge weighted graphs, graph cuts and vertex labelings. Moreover, we introduce the notion of graph cut segments.

2.1 Edge Weighted Graphs

We define a (undirected) *graph* as a pair $G = (V(G), E(G))$ where $V(G)$ is a set and $E(G)$ is composed of unordered pairs of distinct elements in V, i.e., E is a subset of $\{\{v, w\} \subseteq V \mid v \neq w\}$. The elements of V are called *vertices* of B, and the elements of E are called *edges* of G. In order to simplify the notation, the vertices and edges of a graph will be denoted V and E instead of $V(G)$ and $E(G)$ whenever it is clear from the context which graph they belong to. An edge spanning two vertices v and w is denoted $e_{v,w}$. If $e_{v,w}$ is an edge in E, the vertices v and w are *adjacent*. For the remainder of this paper, G denotes a graph (V, E), such that $|V|$ is finite.

We assign to each edge $e \in E$ a non-negative real value $W(e)$, called a *weight*. The weight represents vertex affinity, i.e., two adjacent vertices are closely related if the weight of the edge connecting them is high. A common task in image segmentation applications is to segment an image into regions of homogeneous intensity. To this end, we may define edge weights as, e.g.,

$$W(e_{v,w}) = I_{max} - |I(v) - I(w)| , \tag{1}$$

where $I(v)$ is the intensity of the image element corresponding to the vertex v, and I_{max} is the maximum intensity value present in the image. The method proposed here is *contrast invariant*, i.e., applying a strictly monotonic transformation to the edge weights does not change the output of the method.

2.2 Graph Partitioning

A partitioning of a graph is commonly represented either as a *vertex labeling* or as a *graph cut*. The two representations are closely related, and the choice of one representation over the other is largely a matter of preference. Here, we use the graph cut representation in Sections 3 and 4 to derive our theoretical results. In Section 5, we switch to the vertex labeling representation, in order to formulate a practical algorithm for the proposed method. In this Section, we provide formal definitions of both representations, and clarify the relation between them.

A *path* in G is an ordered sequence of vertices $\pi = \langle v_1, v_2, \ldots, v_k \rangle$ such that $e_{v_i,v_{i+1}} \in E$ for all $i \in [1, k-1]$. Two vertices v and w are *linked* in G if there exists a path in G that starts at v and ends at w. The notation $v \underset{G}{\sim} w$ will here be used to indicate that v and w are linked on G. If all pairs of vertices in a graph are linked, then the graph is *connected*, otherwise it is *disconnected*. For the remainder of this paper, we assume that the graph G is connected.

If G and H are graphs such that $V(H) \subseteq V(G)$ and $E(H) \subseteq E(G)$, then H is a *subgraph* of G. If H is a connected subgraph of G and $v \underset{G}{\not\sim} w$ for all vertices $v \in H$ and $w \notin H$, then H is a *connected component* of G.

Definition 1. *Let $S \subseteq E$, and $G' = (V, E \setminus S)$. If, for all $e_{v,w} \in S$, it holds that $v \underset{G'}{\not\sim} w$, then S is a* (graph) cut *on G.*

If S is a non-empty cut on G, then the removal of S from G separates G into two or more connected components. Note that E is a cut on G.

Definition 2. *A* (vertex) labeling *$\mathcal{L}$ of G is a map $\mathcal{L} : V \to L$, where L is an arbitrary set of* labels.

In the following, we assume that $|L| \geq |V|$. The *boundary*, $\partial\mathcal{L}$, of a vertex labeling $\mathcal{L}$ is defined as the edge set $\partial\mathcal{L} = \{e_{v,w} \in E \mid \mathcal{L}(v) \neq \mathcal{L}(w)\}$. The relation between labelings and cuts is summarized in Theorem 1.

Theorem 1. *For any graph $G = (V, E)$ and set of edges $S \subseteq E$, the following statements are equivalent:*

1. *There exists a labeling $\mathcal{L}$ of G such that $S = \partial\mathcal{L}$.*
2. *S is a cut on G.*

A proof of Theorem 1 can be found in [11]. Next, we introduce the concept of *graph cut segments*, which is central to the development of the proposed method in Section 4.

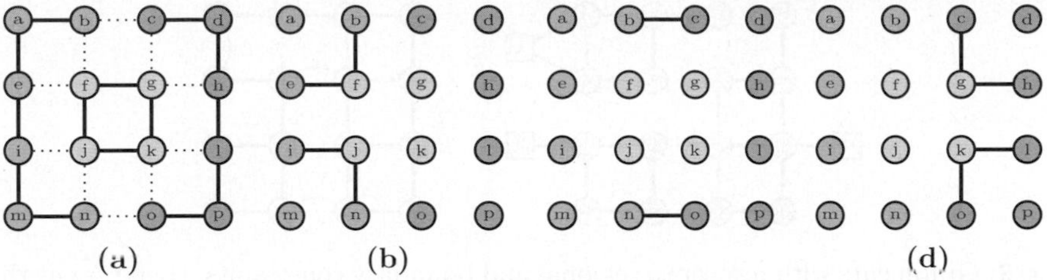

Fig. 1. Graph cut segments. (a) A graph cut, shown as dotted lines. The cut separates the graph into three connected components, shown in red, green, and blue. (b-d) The segments of the cut.

Definition 3. *Let S be a cut on G, let $e \in S$, and let $G' = (V, E \setminus (S \setminus \{e\}))$. The* segment S_e *of S corresponding to e is defined as*

$$S_e = \{e_{v,w} \mid e_{v,w} \in S,\ v \underset{G'}{\sim} w\} . \tag{2}$$

Any cut $S \neq \emptyset$ consists of one or more segments. From Definition 3, it follows that $e_{v,w} \in S_{e_{x,y}} \Leftrightarrow e_{x,y} \in S_{e_{v,w}}$, and thus a segment can be uniquely identified by any of its constituent edges. Figure 1 illustrates the concept of graph cut segments.

3 Constrained Graph Cuts

In this Section, we introduce the proposed generalized hard constraints, hereinafter referred to as *constraints*.

Definition 4. *A* constraint *on G is an unordered pair of distinct elements in V, i.e., a constraint is an element in the set $\{\{v, w\} \subseteq V \mid v \neq w\}$.*

Note that while the definition of constraints is identical to the definition of graph edges in Section 2.1, we do not generally require a constraint to be an element of E. To differentiate between constraints and edges, a pair of vertices $\{v, w\}$ that represents a constraint is denoted $c_{v,w}$.

Definition 5. *Let $S \subseteq E$ and let C be a set of constraints. We say that S* satisfies C *if*

$$\forall c_{v,w} \in C, v \underset{(V,E \setminus S)}{\not\sim} w \tag{3}$$

and

$$\forall e \in S, \exists c_{v,w} \in C \text{ such that } \underset{(V,E \setminus (S \setminus \{e\}))}{v \sim w} . \tag{4}$$

If $S \subseteq E$ does not satisfy (3) then S is an *under-segmentation* with respect to C. If S does not satisfy (4), then S is an *over-segmentation* with respect to C. In

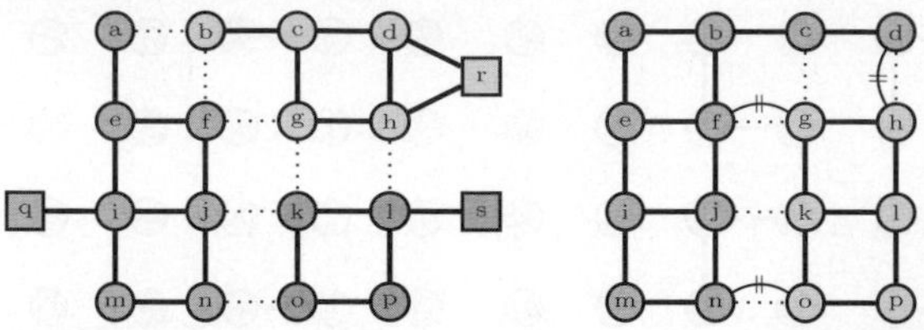

Fig. 2. Graph cuts with respect to regional and boundary constraints. (Left) A cut that satisfies the regional constraints $\{q, r, s\}$. The cut (dotted lines) separates the graph into three connected components. (Right) A cut that satisfies the boundary constraints $\{e_{d,h}, e_{f,g}, e_{n,o}\}$. The cut separates the graph into two connected components.

other words, a set of edges S satisfies the constraints C if it is neither an over- nor an under-segmentation with respect to C.[1]

Theorem 2. *Let C be a set of constraints and let $S \subseteq E$ such that S satisfies C. Then S is a cut on G.*

Proof. Let $G' = (V, E \setminus S)$. If S satisfies C, then for each edge $e_{v,w} \in S$ there exists a constraint $c_{x,y} \in C$ such that either $x \underset{G'}{\sim} v$ and $y \underset{G'}{\sim} w$ or $x \underset{G'}{\sim} w$ and $y \underset{G'}{\sim} v$. From (3), it thus follows that $v \underset{G'}{\not\sim} w$. □

In the remainder of this Section, we show that the proposed definition of constraints includes both boundary constraints and regional constraints as special cases.

3.1 Regional Constraints

A *regional constraint* on G is a vertex in V. Informally, a cut S satisfies the set of regional constraints $C_r \subseteq V$ if each connected component of $(V, E \setminus S)$ contains exactly one element in C_r. This is formalized in Definition 6.

Definition 6. *Let $C_r \subseteq V$ be a set of regional constraints and let $S \subseteq E$. We say that S* satisfies *C_r if*

$$\forall v, w \in C_r, v \underset{(V,E\setminus S)}{\not\sim} w \tag{5}$$

and

$$\forall e \in S, \exists v, w \in C_r \text{ such that } v \underset{(V,E\setminus(S\setminus\{e\}))}{\sim} w . \tag{6}$$

When regional constraints are used in image processing applications, the pixel adjacency graph is usually augmented with a set of *terminal vertices* that

[1] A similar definition of over- and under-segmentation was proposed by Felzenszwalb and Huttenlocher [8], in the context of unsupervised segmentation.

constitute the regional constraints [2]. Each terminal vertex represents an object category (e.g., object or background), and a vertex that is adjacent to a terminal vertex is called a *seed-point.* In this way, an object may be segmented from an image by specifying one or more seed-points corresponding to that object. See Figure 2.

From Definitions 5 and 6, it becomes clear that regional constraints are a special case of the generalized hard constraints proposed here. For any set of regional constraints C_r there exists a set of constraints C, namely $C = \{c_{v,w} \mid v, w \in C_r\}$, such that $S \subseteq E$ satisfies C if and only if it satisfies C_r.

3.2 Boundary Constraints

A boundary constraint on G is an edge in E. Intuitively, a cut S satisfies the set of boundary constraints $C_b \subseteq E$ if $C_b \subseteq S$. This definition, however, is clearly not sufficient, since the cut $S = E$ satisfies this condition for any C_b. Instead, we propose the following definition.

Definition 7. *Let $C_b \subseteq E$ be a set of boundary constraints and let S be a cut on G. If $C_b \subseteq S$ and each segment of S contains at least one element of C_b, then we say that S* satisfies *C_b.*

From Theorem 3 and its Corollary below, it follows that Definition 7 coincides with Definition 5 in the special case that $C \subseteq E$. In this sense, boundary constraints are a special case of the proposed generalized constraints. See Figure 2.

Theorem 3. *Let $C \subseteq E$ be a set of constraints and let, $S \subseteq E$ such that S satisfies C. Then $C \subseteq S$.*

Proof. Assume to the contrary that S is a cut with respect to $C \subseteq E$ and $C \not\subseteq S$. Then there exists an edge $e_{v,w} \in C \setminus S$, and thus $v \underset{G'}{\sim} w$, where $G' = (V, E \setminus S)$. This contradicts the assumption that S is a cut with respect to C. □

Corollary 1. *Let $C \subseteq E$ be a set of constraints, let $S \subseteq E$ such that S satisfies C. For all $e \in S$, there exists a constraint $c \in C$ such that $c \in S_e$.*

Proof. Let $e_{v,w} \in S$. Since S satisfies C, there exists a constraint $c_{x,y} \in C$ such that $x \underset{(V,E \setminus (S \setminus \{e_{v,w}\}))}{\sim} y$. By Theorem 3 it holds that $c_{x,y} \in S$. Therefore $c_{x,y} \in S_e$. □

4 Strategies for Computing Constrained Graph Cuts

In this Section, we consider the problem of computing a cut that satisfies a set of constraints. We start by defining a general strategy for computing such cuts. Based on this general strategy, we show that for any set of constraints on G, there exists one or more cuts on G that satisfies the constraints. Additionally, we show that any such cut can be computed using the general strategy. Thereafter, we present a particular instance of the general strategy, that produces cuts such that the maximum edge weight in the cut is globally minimal.

4.1 A General Strategy for Computing Constrained Graph Cuts

If $S \subseteq E$ is a cut on G and $G' = (V, E \setminus S)$, then each segment of S forms a boundary between exactly two connected components of G'. Therefore, the removal of a segment from a cut is called a *merging operation.*

Definition 8. *Let S be a cut on G and let $e \in S$. The* merging operation $S \oslash e$ *is defined as*

$$S \oslash e = S \setminus S_e \, . \tag{7}$$

Note that merging operations preserve cuts, i.e., $S \oslash e$ is a cut on G.

Definition 9. *Let C be a set of constraints and let S be a cut on G. An edge $e \in S$ is* mergeable *with respect to C if $S \oslash e$ is not an under-segmentation with respect to C.*

The set of edges in S that are mergeable with respect to C is denoted $M_C(S)$.

Lemma 1. *Let C be a set of constraints and let S be a cut on G such that S is not an under-segmentation with respect to C. Then the following statements are equivalent:*

1. *S is an over-segmentation with respect to C.*
2. *$M_C(S) \neq \emptyset$.*

Proof. S is an over-segmentation with respect to $C \Leftrightarrow \exists e \in S$ such that $\forall c_{v,w} \in C, \; v \underset{(V,E\setminus(S\setminus\{e\}))}{\not\sim} w \Leftrightarrow \exists e \in S$ such that $\forall c_{v,w} \in C, \; v \underset{(V,E\setminus(S\oslash e))}{\not\sim} w \Leftrightarrow \exists e \in M_C(S) \Leftrightarrow M_C(S) \neq \emptyset$. □

Definition 10. *Let S be a cut on G, and let $\sigma = \langle e_1, e_2, \ldots, e_k \rangle = \langle e_i \rangle_{i=1}^k$ be a sequence of edges in S. If $e_{n+1} \in S \oslash e_1 \oslash e_2 \oslash \ldots \oslash e_n$ for all $n \in [1, k-1]$, then σ is a* merging sequence *for S.*

If $\sigma = \langle e_i \rangle_{i=1}^k$ is a merging sequence for S, we define $S \oslash \sigma$ as

$$S \oslash \sigma = S \oslash e_1 \oslash e_2 \oslash \ldots \oslash e_k \, . \tag{8}$$

If C is a set of constraints and $e_{n+1} \in M_C(S \oslash \langle e_i \rangle_{i=1}^n)$ for all $n \in [1, k-1]$, then σ is *valid* with respect to C. If $M_C(S \oslash \sigma) = \emptyset$ then σ is *complete* with respect to C. If σ_1 and σ_2 are merging sequences for S, we denote by $\sigma_1 \cdot \sigma_2$ the concatenation of the two sequences. If σ_2 is a merging sequence for $S \oslash \sigma_1$, it holds that $\sigma_1 \cdot \sigma_2$ is a merging sequence for S and $S \oslash (\sigma_1 \cdot \sigma_2) = S \oslash (\sigma_2 \cdot \sigma_1)$.

Theorem 4. *Let C be a set of constraints, let S be a cut on G such that S is not an under-segmentation with respect to C, and let σ be a complete valid merging sequence for S with respect to C. Then $S \oslash \sigma$ satisfies C.*

Proof. Since $M_C(S \oslash \sigma) = \emptyset$, it holds by Lemma 1 that $S \oslash \sigma$ is not an over-segmentation with respect to C. Since S is not an under-segmentation with respect to C, it follows from the definition of mergeable edges that $S \oslash \sigma$ is also not an under-segmentation with respect to C. □

If S is a cut on G such that S is not an under-segmentation with respect to a set of constraints C, then there exists a merging sequence σ for S such that σ is valid and complete with respect to C. In particular, we can construct such a σ using the following procedure:

1. Let σ be an empty sequence
2. While $M_C(S \oslash \sigma) \neq \emptyset$, append an element from $M_C(S \oslash \sigma)$ to σ.

Thus, it follows from Theorem 4 that if S is a cut on G such that S is not an under-segmentation with respect to C, there exists one or more $S' \subseteq S$ such that S' satisfies C. We define the set $\Sigma(S, C)$ as

$$\Sigma(S, C) = \{S' \subseteq S \mid S' \text{ satisfies } C\} . \tag{9}$$

Note that if S satisfies C, then $\Sigma(S, C) = \{S\}$.

Theorem 5. *Let C be a set of constraints, let $S \subseteq E$ be a cut on G such that $\Sigma(S, C) \neq \emptyset$, and let $S' \in \Sigma(S, C)$. Then there exists a (possibly empty) merging sequence σ for S' such that $S' = S \oslash \sigma$ and σ is valid with respect to C.*

Proof. Consider the following procedure:

1. Let σ be an empty sequence
2. While $S \oslash \sigma \setminus S' \neq \emptyset$, append an element from $S \oslash \sigma \setminus S'$ to σ.

Since S' is a cut on G, it holds that $S' \subseteq S \oslash \sigma$ at each step of this procedure. In particular, this holds when the procedure terminates. By then it also holds that $S \oslash \sigma \setminus S' = \emptyset$, and so $S \oslash \sigma = S'$. The validity of σ follows from the fact that S' satisfies C. □

Any cut S on G is, by definition, a subset of E. Thus it follows from Theorem 5 that if S satisfies a set of constraints C, then $S = E \oslash \sigma$ for some merging sequence σ, i.e., any cut that satisfies C may be obtained by repeatedly performing merging operations on mergeable edges in E.

4.2 An Optimal Strategy for Computing Constrained Graph Cuts

In Section 4.1, we established that for any set of constraints C, there exists one or more cuts that satisfy C. In this Section we are interested in finding cuts, among all cuts that satisfy C, that represent "good" partitionings of the graph. Commonly, the goodness of a cut is measured by some function of the weight of the edges in the cut, i.e., the sum of the edge weights [2], the normalized sum of the edge weights [14], or the maximum edge weight [13]. Here, we define the *weight* $W(S)$ of a cut S as the latter, namely

$$W(S) = \max_{e \in S}(W(e)) . \tag{10}$$

A cut S is considered to be good if it has a low weight. The relevance of this criterion for image segmentation has previously been demonstrated by others. For example, the popular *fuzzy connectedness* method has been shown to optimize the same criterion in the presence of regional constraints [13]. If S is a cut that is not an under-segmentation with respect to a set of constraints C, we define $\Sigma^*(S, C)$ as

$$\Sigma^*(S, C) = \operatorname*{argmin}_{S' \in \Sigma(S,C)} (W(S')) . \tag{11}$$

Since all cuts in $\Sigma^*(S, C)$ have the same (minimal) weight, $W(\Sigma^*(S, C))$ is well defined even if $|\Sigma^*(S, C)| > 1$. We now present a strategy for finding a merging sequence σ such that $E \oslash \sigma \in \Sigma^*(E, C)$, i.e., finding a cut $S = E \oslash \sigma$ for which $W(S)$ is globally minimal.

Lemma 2. *Let C be a set of constraints, let S be a cut on G such that S is not an under-segmentation with respect to C, and let $e \in M_C(S)$. If $W(e) = \max_{e' \in M_C(S)} (W(e'))$, then $W(\Sigma^*(S \oslash e, C)) = W(\Sigma^*(S, C)))$.*

Proof. Assume to the contrary that there exists a $S' \in \Sigma(S, C)$ such that $W(S') < W(\Sigma^*(S \oslash e, C))$. If $W(e) = \max_{e' \in M_C(S)} (W(e'))$, then $W(S') < W(e)$ and so $e \notin S'$. By Theorem 5, S' can thus be written as $S' = S \oslash \sigma$, where σ is a merging sequence of the form $\sigma_1 \cdot \langle e \rangle \cdot \sigma_2$. Since $S \oslash \sigma_1 \cdot \langle e \rangle \cdot \sigma 2 = S \oslash \langle e \rangle \cdot \sigma_1 \cdot \sigma_2$ it holds that $S' \in \Sigma(S \oslash e, C)$. This contradicts the assumption that $W(S') < W(\Sigma^*(S \oslash e, C))$. □

Definition 11. *Let S be a cut on G, let C be a set of constraints, and let $\sigma = \langle e_i \rangle_{i=1}^k$ be a merging sequence for S such that σ is valid with respect to C. If*

$$W(e_{n+1}) = \max_{e \in M_C(S \oslash \langle e_i \rangle_{i=1}^n)} (W(e)) \tag{12}$$

for all $n \in [1, k-1]$, then σ is maximal *with respect to C.*

Following the procedure for constructing a complete valid merging sequence in Section 4.1, it is straightforward to show that a complete maximal merging sequence exists for any S and C. From Lemma 2 it follows by induction that if σ is a merging sequence for S such that σ is maximal with respect to C, then $S \oslash \sigma \in \Sigma^*(S, C)$. Thereby, Theorem 6 follows.

Theorem 6. *Let C be a set of constraints, and let S_1 and S_2 be cuts that satisfy C. If $S_1 = E \oslash \sigma$, where σ is a maximal sequence with respect to C, then $W(S_1) \leq W(S_2)$.*

5 A Practical Algorithm

In this Section, we re-formulate the approach presented in Section 4.2 in terms of a practical algorithm, listed in pseudo-code in Algorithm 1. Given a set of constraints C, the algorithm computes a vertex labeling $\mathcal{L}$ such that $\partial\mathcal{L} \in \Sigma^*(E, C)$. The algorithm is based on the observation that, given a vertex labeling such that each component has a unique label, a merging operation between two adjacent components is equivalent to replacing all labels in one component with the label of the other component.

The computational efficiency of Algorithm 1 depends on a number of implementational choices. Below, we highlight some implementational details that we have found greatly improves the speed of the algorithm.

Pre-sorting edges. At each step of the outermost loop of Algorithm 1, an edge with maximum weight is selected (line 4). This can be implemented efficiently by pre-sorting all edges of the graph in a non-increasing order by weight. If the edge weights are integer valued, this can be performed in $\mathcal{O}(|E|)$ operations using count sorting. In interactive segmentation applications, this sorting step need only be performed once, prior to user interaction.

Efficient region merging. A naive implementation of the region merging step of Algorithm 1 (lines 6–7) involves updating the label of all elements for which $\mathcal{L}(z) = \mathcal{L}(v)$. This becomes prohibitively slow even for modestly sized images. Instead, we have used a look-up table to keep track of the label of each region. This table maps the initial, unique, label of each vertex to its label in the final segmentation. Thus, lines 6–7 of Algorithm 1 is replaced by an operation that can be performed in constant time.

With the above techniques implemented, the most computationally expensive operation within the outermost loop of Algorithm 1 is to check the existence of a constraint that makes $e_{v,w}$ non-mergeable (line 5). In our current implementation, this check is performed by iterating over all constraints in C. The outermost loop is repeated $|E|$ times and so, in total, the algorithm requires $\mathcal{O}(|E||C|)$ operations.

Algorithm 1: Computing minimum weight cuts satisfying generalized hard constraints.

Input: A weighted graph $G = (V, E)$ and a set C of constraints.
Output: A vertex labeling $\mathcal{L}$ such that $\partial\mathcal{L} \in \Sigma^*(E, C)$.
Auxiliary: A set of edges E'.

1 Initialize $\mathcal{L}$ so that each vertex has a unique label;
2 Set $E' \leftarrow E$;
3 **while** $E' \neq \emptyset$ **do**
4   Select an edge $e_{v,w} \in E'$ such that $W(e_{v,w})$ is maximal;
5   **if** $\mathcal{L}(v) \neq \mathcal{L}(w)$ *and* $\nexists c_{x,y} \in C$ *s. t.* $\mathcal{L}(v) = \mathcal{L}(x)$ *and* $\mathcal{L}(w) = \mathcal{L}(y)$ **then**
6   **foreach** $z \in V$ *s.t.* $\mathcal{L}(z) = \mathcal{L}(w)$ **do**
7   Set $\mathcal{L}(z) \leftarrow \mathcal{L}(v)$;
8   Set $E' \leftarrow E' \setminus \{e_{v,w}\}$;

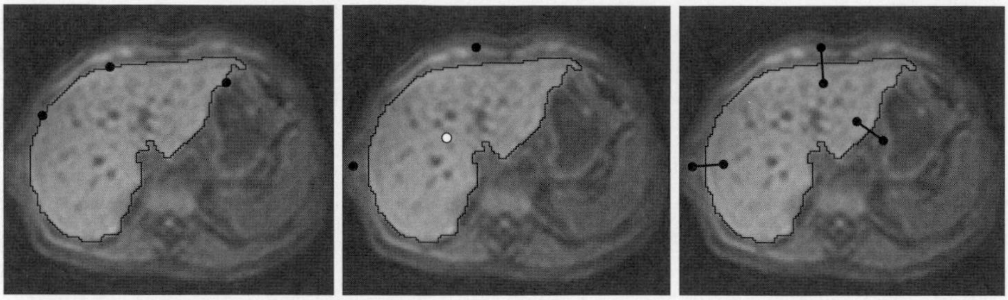

Fig. 3. Interactive segmentation of the liver in a slice from an MR volume image, using three different interaction paradigms. All segmentations were computed using Algorithm 1. (Left) Segmentation using boundary constraints. The black dots indicate graph edges that must be included in the segmentation boundary. (Middle) Segmentation using regional constraints. Black and white dots indicate background and object seeds, respectively. (Right) Segmentation using generalized constraints. Each constraint is displayed as two black dots connected by a line. [MRI data courtesy of Dr. Olof Dahlqvist-Leinhard at CMIV, Linköping University, Sweden.]

6 Conclusions

We have defined graph cuts with respect to generalized hard constraints, and shown that this new type of constraints include boundary constraints and regional constraints as special cases. In previous work on supervised graph segmentation, different computational strategies have typically been required to compute cuts that satisfy regional and boundary constraints, respectively. This work unifies and generalizes the two paradigms. Figure 3 illustrates the ability of Algorithm 1 to handle different types of constraints. We emphasize that while this example shows segmentation of a 2D image, our results are derived for arbitrary undirected graphs and thus directly applicable to images of any dimension.

All interactive segmentation methods are subject to variations in user input. It is therefore desirable for a segmentation method to be invariant to "small" changes in the set of constraints [1]. Initial experiments indicate that Algorithm 1 indeed satisfies such a property. Note, e.g., that all three segmentations shown in Figure 3 are identical, despite being computed from different sets of constraints. In future work, the precise nature of this robustness property will be investigated.

In Section 5, we presented a practical algorithm for computing minimum weight cuts that satisfy a set of constraints. In future work, we intend to explore further the computational aspects of the proposed method. In particular, *differential* algorithms are of interest [5].

References

1. Audigier, R., Lotufo, R.A.: Seed-relative segmentation robustness of watershed and fuzzy connectedness approaches. In: Falcão, A.X., Lopes, H. (eds.) Proceedings of the 20th Brazilian Symposium on Computer Graphics and Image Processing, pp. 61–68. IEEE Computer Society, Los Alamitos (2007)

2. Boykov, Y., Jolly, M.-P.: Interactive graph cuts for optimal boundary & region segmentation of objects in N-D images. In: Proceedings of the 8th IEEE International Conference on Computer Vision (ICCV), vol. 1, pp. 105–112 (2001)
3. Couprie, C., Grady, L., Najman, L., Talbot, H.: Power watersheds: A unifying graph-based optimization framework. IEEE Transactions on Pattern Analysis and Machine Intelligence 99(PrePrints) (2010), doi:10.1109/TPAMI.2010.200.
4. Cousty, J., Bertrand, G., Najman, L., Couprie, M.: Watershed cuts: Thinnings, shortest path forests, and topological watersheds. IEEE Transactions on Pattern Analysis and Machine Intelligence 32(5), 925–939 (2010)
5. Falcão, A.X., Bergo, F.P.: Interactive volume segmentation with differential image foresting transforms. IEEE Transactions on Medical Imaging 23(9), 1100–1108 (2004)
6. Falcão, A.X., Stolfi, J., Lotufo, R.A.: The image foresting transform: Theory, algorithms, and applications. IEEE Transactions on Pattern Analysis and Machine Intelligence 26(1), 19–29 (2004)
7. Falcão, A.X., Udupa, J.K., Miyazawa, F.K.: An ultra-fast user-steered image segmentation paradigm: Live wire on the fly. IEEE Transactions on Medical Imaging 19(1), 55–62 (2000)
8. Felzenszwalb, P.F., Huttenlocher, D.P.: Efficient graph-based image segmentation. International Journal of Computer Vision 59(2) (2004)
9. Grady, L.: Random walks for image segmentation. IEEE Transactions on Pattern Analysis and Machine Intelligence 28(11), 1768–1783 (2006)
10. Grady, L.: Minimal surfaces extend shortest path segmentation methods to 3D. IEEE Transactions on Pattern Analysis and Machine Intelligence 32(2), 321–334 (2010)
11. Malmberg, F., Lindblad, J., Sladoje, N., Nyström, I.: A graph-based framework for sub-pixel image segmentation. Theoretical Computer Science (2010), doi:10.1016/j.tcs.2010.11.030.
12. Malmberg, F., Vidholm, E., Nyström, I.: A 3D live-wire segmentation method for volume images using haptic interaction. In: Kuba, A., Nyúl, L.G., Palágyi, K. (eds.) DGCI 2006. LNCS, vol. 4245, pp. 663–673. Springer, Heidelberg (2006)
13. Miranda, P.A., Falcão, A.X.: Links between image segmentation based on optimum-path forest and minimum cut in graph. Journal of Mathematical Imaging and Vision 35(2), 128–142 (2009)
14. Shi, J., Malik, J.: Normalized cuts and image segmentation. IEEE Transactions on Pattern Analysis and Machine Intelligence 22(8), 888–905 (2000)
15. Udupa, J.K., Saha, P.K., Lotufo, R.A.: Relative fuzzy connectedness and object definition: Theory, algorithms, and applications in image segmentation. IEEE Transactions on Pattern Anaysis and Machine Intelligence 24(11), 1485–1500 (2002)

Highly Consistent Sequential Segmentation*

Michael Donoser[1], Martin Urschler[2,1],
Hayko Riemenschneider[1], and Horst Bischof[1]

[1] Institute for Computer Graphics and Vision
Graz University of Technology, Austria
{donoser,urschler,hayko,bischof}@icg.tugraz.at
[2] Ludwig Boltzmann Institute for Clinical Forensic Imaging
Graz, Austria

Abstract. This paper deals with segmentation of image sequences in an unsupervised manner with the goal of getting highly consistent segmentation results from frame-to-frame. We first introduce a segmentation method that uses results of the previous frame as initialization and significantly improves consistency in comparison to a single frame based approach. We also find correspondences between the segmented regions from one frame to the next to further increase consistency. This matching step is based on a modified version of an efficient partial shape matching method which allows identification of similar parts of regions despite topology changes like merges and splits. We use the identified matched parts to define a partial matching cost which is then used as input to pairwise graph matching. Experiments demonstrate that we can achieve highly consistent segmentations for diverse image sequences, even allowing to track manually initialized moving and static objects.

1 Introduction

Unsupervised segmentation is one of the fundamental tasks in computer vision and is an important step for many high-level tasks including tracking, object recognition and 3D reconstruction. Despite the tremendous progress in the field of segmentation [5,9,1,8], image segments have not been a popular choice as underlying representation in most areas of computer vision. This is due to the fact that segmentation is an ill-posed problem and results for images acquired under slightly different conditions (such as different lighting properties, viewpoint changes or movement in the scene) differ significantly. Mostly minor changes in image gradients lead to multiple splits and merges of neighboring regions and therefore most segmentation methods fail to provide consistent regions.

Analyzing region correspondences between two segmented images allows to improve the consistency [12] but since no a-priori information about the scene is used, results are still far from being acceptable for most vision tasks. The main issue is that shape and appearance of regions change significantly for images of

* This work was supported by the Austrian Research Promotion Agency (FFG) project FIT-IT CityFit (815971/14472-GLE/ROD).

A. Heyden and F. Kahl (Eds.): SCIA 2011, LNCS 6688, pp. 48–58, 2011.

scenes obtained from different viewpoints, therefore matching regions in such images is a highly ill-posed problem.

In this paper we focus on the much easier problem of efficiently segmenting a sequence of images with the main goal of providing consistent segmentations throughout the sequence. This has many potential applications in computer vision like tracking, background substitution, object recognition or video editing. Please note, that we do not want to directly segment outlines of moving or static objects in the sequence, since we are not including any high-level cues or a priori information. The results are solely intended to serve as pre-processing step for subsequent high-level vision applications.

In general there are two different directions of research for improving segmentation consistency in image sequences in the literature. First, using interest point tracks to find region matches and second, composite clustering of pixels from all frames in the sequence.

Feature-point based approaches use trajectories of interest points to merge regions with similar motions. Wills et al. [18] detected feature points using the Foerstner operator and matched them by comparing high-dimensional descriptors obtained by repeated filtering steps. The feature tracks are used to find similar motion layers in videos. In [11] feature points were tracked and grouped together by using a variant of the Expectation-Maximization method mainly for the task of video editing. Common to all these approaches is that interest point tracks do not directly define the spatial cohesiveness of the underlying objects. Mostly heuristics have to be applied to assign tracks to regions and strong assumptions on the scene have to be made to get reasonable results.

Clustering based approaches take all pixels from all frames at once and find the most appropriate spatial grouping. Each pixel is represented in the (x, y, t) space and compared to all others by analyzing local descriptors. For example in [6] the well known Mean Shift approach is used for hierarchical clustering, analyzing features consisting of color and motion cues. In [17] the video was represented as a graph and motion profiles were used to define the edge weights. Connected segments are found by a standard normalized cut method. Recently a hyper-graph cut method for video object segmentation was proposed [13], which allows to define more complex edge weights (beyond the pairwise setting) in graph matching, achieving promising results. But there are two major issues in these approaches. First, it is difficult to relate the spatial and temporal domain. Setting a suitable tradeoff between spatial and temporal changes again requires some knowledge about the scene, for example the amount and size of moving objects. Second, computation time is also a weak point since clustering in high-dimensional feature spaces becomes infeasible even for relatively short sequences.

We propose a method that achieves highly consistent segmentation results for image sequences by repeatedly matching regions between subsequent frames overcoming the aforementioned limitations. Our method can be applied online on a live stream from a camera, since we do not need to perform any post-processing over the entire sequence. Our work has three major contributions. First, we propose a segmentation method for image sequences which provides highly consistent segmentations by using the result of frame t as initialization for segmenting frame $t+1$. The method makes use of a fast and accurate geodesic active contour algorithm formulated in the weighted total variation framework and significantly improves over single image consistency. Our second contribution is an adaption of a recently proposed partial shape matching method which can be used to obtain partial match costs between regions of subsequent frames. We propose a novel descriptor analyzing angles between chords connecting sampled points and corresponding horizontal lines. Finally, we show how to use the obtained partial matching costs in a spectral graph matching formulation. Graph matching returns a list of many to many correspondences between segments in consecutive frames and this list is used to merge and split segments. In such a way we obtain even more consistent results. This step is formulated in a general manner, and can therefore be applied to improve any of the available single image segmentation methods.

The most related work to ours is from Brendel and Todorovic [3] who recently proposed a video object segmentation method where the results of single frame segmentation were improved by also analyzing a partial match cost between segments. But there are some major differences to our work. First, they only use a single frame segmentation method like mean shift as input and neglect any analysis about how to improve the main segmentation consistency. For defining the partial match cost, they apply a partial matching method denoted as cyclic dynamic time warping which has a runtime of $200\,ms$. In our setup finding the partial match cost only requires a few milliseconds. Finally, for analysis of the identified costs for region matching they do a final clustering of all regions from the sequence by relaxation labeling which requires the entire sequence to be provided in advance and prevents online processing.

2 Consistent Image Sequence Segmentation

Unsupervised segmentation is one of the most intensively researched topics in computer vision and many different segmentation methods have been proposed achieving excellent results on reference data sets like Berkeley [5,9,1,8]. But most of the methods are very sensitive to slight changes in image conditions and do not provide consistent segments.

The straightforward idea for obtaining image sequence segmentation is to apply any of the available segmentation methods independently to every frame. Of course, such an approach neglects that subsequent frames have many similarities that can be exploited to improve segmentation consistency. Another fundamental idea for image sequence segmentation is to use the segmentation of frame t as initialization for segmenting the frame $t+1$. Unfortunately, it is often rather hard or even impossible to apply such a scheme to state-of-the-art segmentation approaches. Our approach utilizes this straight-forward idea and exploits a recently proposed segmentation method [8] which perfectly supports the initialization concept.

In [8] an unsupervised segmentation method was introduced which was based on the main idea of obtaining the final segmentation as a composition of several differently focused sub-segmentations. In a first step salient regions are extracted which highlight the main color and texture distributions of the image. Then, each of the salient regions is passed to a weighted total variation segmentation method (TV-Seg), that provides an accurate figure/ground segmentation for each salient region. Total variation segmentation minimizes a convex energy functional [4] and therefore returns a global optimal solution. It has proven to be one of the most accurate figure/ground segmentation methods available. Since each salient region provides one figure/ground segmentation, these results have to be merged to one composite image (see [8] for more details).

We extend this concept for segmentation of image sequences. Instead of applying a salient region detector to obtain the different initializations for the TV-Seg method, we use results of the previous frame. Each segmented region of frame t is mapped to the frame $t+1$. In our experiments described in Section 4 this mapping is just a copy of the segment location from frame t to $t+1$, but of course any motion model can be incorporated here. Each of the mapped segments is then used as salient region input to the total variation segmentation method for providing a figure/ground segmentation. One important property of the method proposed in [8] is that, after performing the segmentations for every salient region, the still unassigned areas in the image are automatically passed to TV-Seg to also get accurate segmentations in these areas. In such a way, for example newly appearing objects in the image sequence become also correctly segmented. Experiments demonstrate that these frame-to-frame segmentation approach improves the consistency compared to a single image based approach.

3 Frame-to-Frame Segment Matching

To further increase consistency in the sequences we additionally apply segment matching between subsequent frames. Finding such correspondences between regions allows to handle the frequently occurring splits and merges of regions as it is illustrated in Figure 1. Since the global properties of segments change drastically if merges and splits happen, they cannot be used directly for obtaining reliable matches.

Similar to [12] we compare similarities between segments in subsequent frames only in the portions that are common to the segments. To be able to identify the common parts of the two segments we exploit the properties of image sequences, assuming that the shape of object outlines does not change significantly from one frame to the next. Therefore, we use a partial shape matching method to identify the common parts between two segments. The goal of partial shape matching in this context is to find all boundary fragments that match between the segments, i. e. possess a high shape similarity. Please note, that for an entire sequence we have to compare a lot of different segments, therefore very high efficiency is required in this step.

This requirement prevents the use of most of the state-of-the-art shape matching methods like [2,15,10] since they require several hundreds of milliseconds per match. For example, the top performing shape matching method [10] on the well known MPEG-7 shape retrieval data set requires half a second per match which would be too inefficient for our scenario.

This was also outlined in the closely related video object segmentation framework of Brendel and Todorovic [3]. They therefore proposed a cyclic dynamic time warping (CDTW) method for obtaining the partial matches with quadratic complexity. The authors state that their method, excluding the segmentation itself, requires several seconds to process a frame, with a matching time of $200ms$ per segment pair despite using a C implementation. This runtime still seems to be too slow for an application like image sequence segmentation.

For efficient shape matching we adapt a recently proposed method [7] for this purpose. This paper introduced a partial shape matching method which uses sampled contour points as underlying representation and solves an order preserving assignment problem. Integral images are used as efficient underlying data structure which enables partial matching within a few milliseconds. This approach was designed for similarity transformation invariant matching, which is not directly applicable in our scenario, since the invariance properties lead to frequent unnecessary confusions in segment matches.

In [7] each shape with N sampled contour points is described by an $N \times N$ descriptor matrix containing angles between chords connecting the sampled points. The invariance of angles to translation and rotation leads to the aforementioned properties. To make the approach sensitive to rotation (which is desired in our scenario), one has to find a novel $N \times N$ descriptor. The rest of the method stays exactly the same (see [7] for details).

We propose a novel descriptor for matching which uses angles between sampled points on the segment outline and a hypothetical horizontal line. Let a segment outline sampled with N points be denoted as $B = b_1, b_2, \ldots b_N$. Our descriptor Ω is an $N \times N$ matrix where every entry ω_{ij} is defined by the angle between a line connecting the points b_i and b_j and a hypothetical horizontal line through b_j. Thus, the descriptor matrix Ω consists of angles computed by

$$\omega_{ij} = \sphericalangle \left(\overline{b_i\, b_j}\, ,\, \overline{b_j\, h_j}\right) \quad \forall i, j = 1, \ldots, N\,, \tag{1}$$

where h_j is the hypothetical horizontal line through b_j. For each segment these angles are calculated over all possible point combinations. The resulting descriptor matrix is non-symmetric, translation invariant and encodes the rotational orientation, which is strongly in contrast to the descriptor of [7]. Based on this descriptor, we can apply the same, highly efficient matching scheme with encoded orientation information.

We now apply this method to obtain the partial matches between the segments. We use equidistantly sampled points along the segment boundaries as underlying representation. Since we only want rough partial matches between segments, it is not necessary to consider all boundary points for matching as it is also illustrated in the experiments. Matching returns a set of correspondences, where it is possible that several, not necessarily connected, boundary fragments are returned as result. Using the provided correspondences we can estimate any type of transformation (e. g. a thin-plate spline transformation) between the matched regions which allows to register the segments to each other. Because we have an ordered sequence of boundary points, we can easily identify the areas of the boundaries that are not matched and estimate a connected region by just drawing a line between the endpoints of the fragments. In such a way we get the matched parts between the segments for both frames t and $t+1$ and can now easily estimate accurate partial match costs between the segments, for example by analyzing the color similarity. This step is also illustrated in Figure 1.

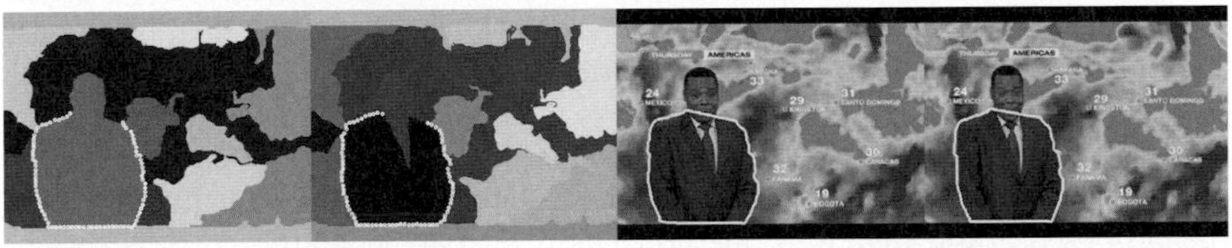

Fig. 1. First two columns show segmentation results in subsequent frames with occurring splits. Segments are matched by comparing shape, where matched parts are highlighted by white sampled points. Last two columns show partial match areas highlighted with yellow boundary, which are used to calculate the partial matching cost.

We use the obtained partial match cost to identify many to many correspondences between the segments in a graph matching scenario where we exploit unary (partial match cost) and pairwise (edge length) potentials.

Each segment is considered as a node of a graph, and neighboring regions are connected by an edge. Matching regions now equals to finding a binary assignment vector $\mathbf{x}^*$ of length $N_1 N_2$ where each entry x_{ia} should be one if segment i of the frame t matches to a segment a of the frame $t+1$ and N_1 and N_2 are the number of segments of frame t and $t+1$ respectively. The assignment vector is found in a quadratic assignment optimization procedure by maximizing

$$\mathbf{x}^* = \underset{\mathbf{x}}{\operatorname{argmax}} \left(\mathbf{x}^T \mathbf{A} \mathbf{x}\right) = \underset{\mathbf{x}}{\operatorname{argmax}} \sum A_{ia,jb}\, x_{ia}\, x_{jb}\,, \tag{2}$$

where A is a provided $N_1 N_2 \times N_1 N_2$ affinity matrix describing how well a pair of segments (i,j) in frame t agrees in terms of local descriptors and geometry with a pair of segments (a,b) in frame $t+1$. The affinity matrix A mainly contains the pairwise potentials and the unary potentials are placed in the main diagonal. Many different methods have been proposed to solve this NP-hard problem approximately, mostly by relaxing the discrete problem to the continuous domain and we apply a spectral method [14] for finding the principal eigenvector of the affinity matrix A to obtain the solution $\mathbf{x}^*$.

The most important step to obtain a reasonable matching result is the definition of an appropriate affinity matrix, containing the compatibilities of segments in subsequent frames. This segment compatibility is based on the identified partial matches between the segments. We define the entries of the affinity matrix as a combination of unary potentials measuring the color similarity and pairwise potentials measuring the difference in edge lengths by

$$A_{ia,jb} = e^{-\left(w_1\,\epsilon(c_i,c_a)+w_2\,\epsilon(c_j,c_b)+w_3\,\frac{d_{ij}-d_{ab}}{d_{ij}+d_{ab}}\right)}, \qquad (3)$$

where c_i is a color descriptor of segment i, d_{ij} is the distance between the center points of the matched segments and w_1,w_2 and w_3 are manually selected weight parameters. We use n-dimensional color histograms as segment descriptor. Since the two segments to be compared are of approximately the same size after mapping, we do not need any normalization and can directly use a histogram intersection distance ϵ to define the unary potentials.

Graph matching returns a list of many to many correspondences and this list is used to merge and split segments in subsequent frames. Experiments prove that this step further improves segmentation consistency. Please note further, that the proposed graph matching method based on partial match costs is totally independent of the underlying segmentation method and can therefore improve any single image segmentation results.

4 Experiments

Experiments focus on demonstrating the improved consistency of our proposed method in comparison to the state-of-the-art. In Section 4.1 we first show the improved consistency by using our proposed image sequence segmentation methods in comparison to three state-of-the-art segmentation methods. In Section 4.2 we show that the proposed method is also applicable for tracking static and moving objects through sequences, based on a manual initialization of the object in the first frame.

In all experiments we used the same parameters as outlined in [8] for the total variation segmentation method TV-Seg. The distance between sampled points for partial shape matching was fixed to 10 and the graph matching weights w_1 to w_3 were all set to the same value 1/3. We implemented the proposed method in Matlab which enables segmenting an image in a few seconds independent of the type of initialization. All required frame-to-frame partial segment matches and the graph matching optimization together only require about 180ms per frame. Thus, the main computational bottleneck is the segmentation method, but it has to be pointed out that as e.g. shown by Pock et al. [16] it is possible to implement Total Variation methods on GPUs, thereby significantly reducing computation time.

4.1 Evaluating Consistency

Our first experiment shows the improved consistency of our proposed method in comparison to three state-of-the-art segmentation methods: Mean Shift [5], a graph based approach [9] and a saliency driven method [8]. We focused on single image methods because we are not aware of any publicly available approach for segmenting whole image sequences. Unfortunately, also for the two most related

Table 1. Comparison of image sequence consistency scores $f(S)$ on different test sequences. Best result per video is shown in bold

Video / Method	GB [10]	MS [5]	Sal [8]	OurSeq	+ GM
Video News	70.23%	82.91%	84.96%	86.60%	**88.12%**
Video Flower Garden	57.64%	62.81%	60.51%	61.45%	**64.04%**
Video Daria Jack	54.52%	82.14%	92.66%	**96.88%**	**96.88%**
Video Dynamic Texture	52.50%	57.79%	76.83%	76.79%	**78.98%**
Video Cartoon	57.64%	72.59%	76.55%	81.07%	**82.06%**

methods [3,12] no code is available. We selected five diverse image sequences for comparison: the well-known flower garden with a moving camera, a static camera news messenger sequence, a video from an action recognition data set, a dynamic texture example and a cartoon sequence.

For quantitative comparison of the obtained results we calculate a frame-to-frame consistency score $O(R,Q)$ by

$$O(R,Q) = \frac{1}{A} \sum_{R_a} \max_{Q_i} \frac{R_a \cap Q_i}{R_a \cup Q_i}, \tag{4}$$

where R and Q are two segmentation results in subsequent frames, and R_a and Q_i are the corresponding segments, i. e. the consistency score is the mean overlap score between the segments, assuming R to be the reference segmentation. For a segmentation of an entire image sequence S it is possible to provide an overall score $f(S)$ by measuring the mean frame consistency score over the entire sequence. Of course, such an evaluation neglects the quality of the segmentations itself, for example always segmenting each image in one region would yield a perfect consistency score. Therefore, we parameterized all algorithms to provide approximately the same number of regions and as can be seen e. g. in Figure 2 all methods return reasonable segmentation results.

Table 1 summarizes the results on the five test sequences for Mean Shift (MS), Graph Based (GB), Saliency Segmentation (Sal), our extended segmentation method described in Section 2 (OurSeq) and the results for additionally activated graph matching (OurSeqGM) as described in Section 3. Results show that the saliency driven segmentation method [8] yields the most stable segments. Adding our initialization concept as described in Section 2 improves results on average about 2%. Additionally, activating graph matching as described in Section 3 provides another improvement of one percent. Although this quantitative improvement seems to be small, several wrong splits and merges are corrected, as it is also demonstrated in the tracking application presented in Section 4.2. Figure 2 furthermore shows selected frames from the news messenger sequence for the compared methods. Each segment is mapped to its mean RGB value to be able to identify wrong merges and splits easily. As can be seen the improved consistency using our proposed approach is visually much more appealing.

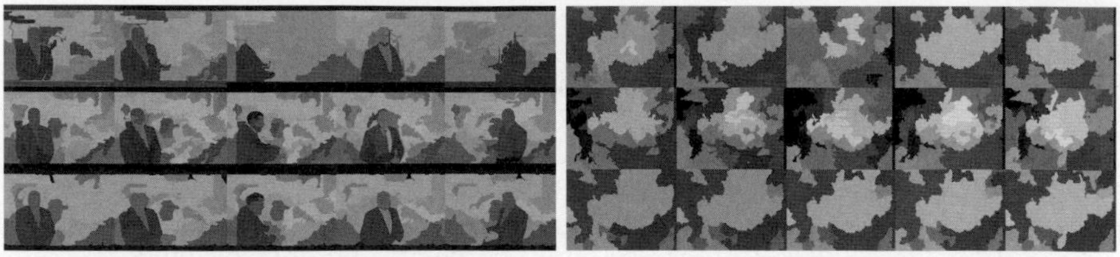

(a) News messenger sequence (b) Dynamic texture sequence

Fig. 2. Direct comparison of image sequence segmentation results using Felzenszwalb's method [9] (first row), Mean Shift [5] (second row) and results of our proposed method (last row). Each obtained segment is mapped to its mean RGB color to be able to visually demonstrate improved consistency (best viewed in color).

Table 2. Comparison of image sequence consistency scores $f(S)$ on different test sequences. GM denotes activation of the proposed graph matching step which merges and splits several regions to improve consistency.

Video / Method	GB [10]	+ GM	MS [5]	+ GM	OurSeq	+ GM
Video News	70.23%	70.99%	82.91%	83.72%	**86.60%**	**88.12%**
Video Flower Garden	57.64%	60.82%	**62.81%**	63.71%	61.45%	**64.04%**
Video Daria Jack	54.52%	56.04%	80.99%	82.96%	**96.88%**	**96.88%**
Video Dynamic Texture	52.50%	54.19%	57.79%	60.03%	**76.79%**	**78.98%**
Video Cartoon	57.64%	59.78%	72.59%	74.71%	**81.07%**	**82.06%**

The graph matching approach presented in Section 3 is independent of the underlying segmentation. Therefore, we also made experiments concerning possible improvements using other underlying segmentations. These results are shown in Table 2 and again demonstrate improved consistency.

Since we only apply a frame-to-frame segment correspondence analysis, drifting might be an important problem. We do not notice severe drifting problems in our tested image sequences. A simple test to verify this visual insight is to apply our method also on the image sequence in reversed order (starting at the last frame) and compare the segmentation differences between the results for standard and reversed ordering. For quantitative evaluation we calculated the frame-to-frame consistency score as explained in Equation 4, this time comparing the segmentations of the same frame obtained in standard versus reversed ordering. On average we get a consistency score of 84.48%, which illustrates that no severe drifting effects take place.

4.2 Object Tracking

We further demonstrate the benefit of the proposed partial matching cost based graph matching step by using our method in a tracking scenario. We initialize a tracker by segmenting the first frame of the sequence and by manually merging regions that belong to the object-to-be-tracked.

Using this initialization as input, we apply the same methods as described in the previous sections, but this time constraining the graph matching to one-to-many matches. Our method finds the combination of segments in the subsequent frame that best fits to the initialization, which allows tracking the defined object throughout the sequence. To avoid major drifting effects we only update our reference segmentation when the graph matching step improves the frame-to-frame consistency.

Such a tracking approach enables quantitative evaluation of the segmentation accuracy by comparing obtained results to ground truth. We use the publicly available Weizmann database, which is commonly used to evaluate action recognition methods. This data set provides binary segmentations per frame for all videos. We selected three videos showing different actions and initialized our tracker in the first frame manually. On average, segmentation accuracy was 48.44% for Mean Shift [5], 53.37% for Felzenszwalb's method [9] and 70.12% for our proposed graph matching approach. The performance gain of approximately 20% comes from the fact that in single image based segmentation often the upper body part, the face and the legs are split which are correctly merged by our proposed method. In Figure 3 we directly compare results to the two most related image sequence segmentation methods of [12,3] showing improved results due to our proposed graph matching verification. Further results and exemplary videos can be found at our homepage[1].

(a) Input Image (b) Brendel [3] (c) Hedau [12] (d) Proposed

Fig. 3. Direct comparison on Weizmann sequence to most related methods of [12,3]

5 Conclusion

This paper introduced an unsupervised method for segmenting image sequences. We first described a method obtaining highly consistent segments exploiting the similarities between subsequent frames. A second contribution showed that efficient partial shape matching exploiting a novel angle based descriptor allows finding similar parts between segments and the definition of a partial match cost. These costs are used to find correspondences between segments in subsequent frames in a pairwise graph matching step for handling the repeatedly occurring splits and merges of segments. This graph matching extension is formulated in a general way and can be applied to any available segmentation method, improving the overall sequence consistency. Experimental evaluation demonstrated the improved performance on diverse videos and an application for tracking manually initialized objects through sequences.

[1] `http://vh.icg.tugraz.at`

References

1. Arbelaez, P., Maire, M., Fowlkes, C., Malik, J.: From contours to regions: An empirical evaluation. In: Proc. of Conf. on Comp. Vision and Pattern Recognition, CVPR (2009)
2. Belongie, S., Malik, J., Puzicha, J.: Shape matching and object recognition using shape contexts. Trans. on Pattern Analysis and Machine Intelligence (PAMI) 24(4), 509–522 (2002)
3. Brendel, W., Todorovic, S.: Video object segmentation by tracking regions. In: Proc. of International Conf. on Comp. Vision, ICCV (2009)
4. Bresson, X., Esedoglu, S., Vandergheynst, P., Thiran, J.P., Osher, S.J.: Fast global minimization of the active contour/snake model. Journal of Mathematical Imaging and Vision 28(2), 151–167 (2007)
5. Comaniciu, D., Meer, P.: Mean shift: a robust approach toward feature space analysis. Trans. on Pattern Analysis and Machine Intelligence (PAMI) 24(5), 603–619 (2002)
6. DeMenthon, D., Megret, R.: Spatio-temporal segmentation of videos by hierachical mean shift analysis. In: Proc. of Conf. on Comp. Vision and Pattern Recognition, CVPR (2002)
7. Donoser, M., Riemenschneider, H., Bischof, H.: Efficient partial shape matching of outer contours. In: Zha, H., Taniguchi, R.-i., Maybank, S. (eds.) ACCV 2009. LNCS, vol. 5994, pp. 281–292. Springer, Heidelberg (2010)
8. Donoser, M., Urschler, M., Hirzer, M., Bischof, H.: Saliency driven total variation segmentation. In: Proc. of International Conf. on Comp. Vision, ICCV (2009)
9. Felzenszwalb, P., Huttenlocher, D.: Efficient graph-based image segmentation. International Journal of Comp. Vision (IJCV) 59 (2004)
10. Felzenszwalb, P., Schwartz, J.D.: Hierarchical matching of deformable shapes. In: Proc. of Conf. on Comp. Vision and Pattern Recognition, CVPR (2007)
11. Goldman, D.B., Gonterman, C., Curless, B., Salesin, D., Seitz., S.M.: Video object annotation, navigation, and composition. In: Proceedings of ACM Symposium on User Interface Software and Technology, UIST (2008)
12. Hedau, V., Arora, H., Ahuja, N.: Matching images under unstable segmentations. In: Proc. of Conf. on Comp. Vision and Pattern Recognition, CVPR (2008)
13. Huang, Y., Liu, Q., Metaxas, D.: Video object segmentation by hypergraph cut. In: Proc. of Conf. on Comp. Vision and Pattern Recognition, CVPR (2009)
14. Leordeanu, M., Hebert, M.: A spectral technique for correspondence problems using pairwise constraints. In: Proc. of International Conf. on Comp. Vision, ICCV (2005)
15. Ling, H., Jacobs, D.W.: Using the inner-distance for classification of articulated shapes. In: Proc. of Conf. on Comp. Vision and Pattern Recognition (CVPR), vol. 2, pp. 719–726 (2005)
16. Pock, T., Unger, M., Cremers, D., Bischof, H.: Fast and exact solution of total variation models on the gpu. In: CVPR Workshop on Visual Computer Vision on GPUs, pp. 1–8 (2008)
17. Shi, J., Malik, J.: Motion segmentation and tracking using normalized cuts. In: Proc. of International Conf. on Comp. Vision, ICCV (1998)
18. Wills, J., Agarwal, S., Belongie, S.: What went where. In: Proc. of Conf. on Comp. Vision and Pattern Recognition, CVPR (2003)

Improved Video Segmentation by Adaptive Combination of Depth Keying and Mixture-of-Gaussians

Ingo Schiller and Reinhard Koch

Multimedia Information Processing (MIP)
Institute of Computer Science, University of Kiel, Germany
{ischiller,rk}@mip.informatik.uni-kiel.de
http://www.mip.informatik.uni-kiel.de

Abstract. Video segmentation or matting, the separation of foreground objects from background in video sequences, is a demanding task and is needed for a broad range of applications. The most widespread method for video segmentation is chroma-keying using a known background color for which a controlled environment is required. Recently a different method of keying fore-and background has been proposed in which the chroma-keying is replaced by depth-keying using a Time-of-Flight (ToF) camera. The current ToF-cameras suffer from noise and low resolution sensors, which results in unsatisfying segmentation results. We propose to combine the segmentation of dynamic objects in depth with a segmentation in the color domain using adaptive background models. We weight the two measures depending on the actual depth values using either the variance of the depth images of the ToF-camera or the amplitude image of the ToF-camera as reliability measure. We show that both methods significantly improve the segmentation results.

1 Introduction

Today, television content as well as movie content contains a significant amount of artificially composed scenes. To generate such scenes with a mixture of real and artificial content the real foreground objects have to be separated from the background. The most common and reliable method for this segmentation task is to use chroma-keying techniques with a known background color as described in [6]. Wang and Cohen [8] give a very good overview of the field of matting and segmentation for still images and extend the discussion to video streams. In their survey they discuss many different approaches such as Poisson Matting, Graph Cut Matting, Baysian Matting, Random Walk matting and others. A combined segmentation approach based on depth from stereo and color using Mixture-of-Gaussians was presented by Gordon et al. in [4], in which all pixels detected by either color or depth are considered foreground. The usage of active distance measurement devices providing interactive frame-rates for segmentation has first been introduced by Gvili et al. in [5] and was extended in [1] to segment dynamic objects with a Time-of-Flight (ToF)-camera [10]. Crabb et al. [2] propose the generation of a Trimap from ToF-depth and use Cross-Bilateral filtering for segmentation. They

A. Heyden and F. Kahl (Eds.): SCIA 2011, LNCS 6688, pp. 59–68, 2011.

however miss to show results of more challenging scenes so that a real evaluation is not possible. Zhu et al. [11] use a combination of stereo and ToF-camera for video matting which shows promising results. The complexity of the approach however does not allow real-time usage. Gong et. al [3] very recently extended the Poisson Matting approach for the usage of additional ToF-depth images using Trimaps. In contrast to their work and most other recently proposed methods, no Trimaps are required in our proposed segmentation algorithm.

The use of a ToF-camera that delivers depth for each pixel facilitates object segmentation, because depth is invariant to changing scene illumination and object shadows. However, ToF depth images typically have low resolution compared to color CCD images, hence a combination of depth and color segmentation is desirable. In our system we combine a ToF-camera (204×204 pixel) with a color CCD-camera (1600×1200 pixel) (see figure 1 (a)) by warping the depth data into the CCD video stream using the approach described in [1]. We propose to combine segmentation of depth measurements by a ToF-camera with the foreground detection by Mixture-of-Gaussians (MoG). We adaptively weight the two modalities dependent on the current reliability of the depth measurement. To determine the reliability of depth measurements we compare the usage of the depth variance and amplitude image. We argue that the two methods mutually improve the deficits of the other and with the proposed weighting it is possible to significantly improve the segmentation results.

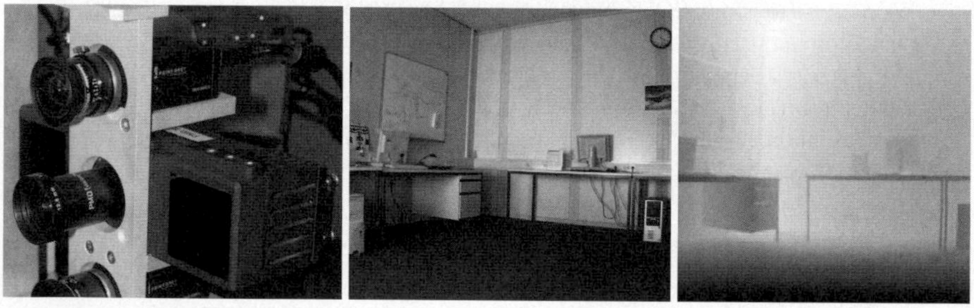

(a) (b) (c)

Fig. 1. The capturing system (a) with a CCD camera above a PMDTec CamCube ToF-camera. Averaged background CCD- (b) and depth- image (c). Brighter values indicate bigger distances.

2 Segmentation

In this section we discuss the segmentation of foreground objects using depth thresholding and the Mixture-of-Gaussians method which we also extend to a forth depth channel. Finally we introduce our proposed method which adaptively weights color and depth clues.

2.1 Segmentation by Depth Keying

The most obvious way to detect moving objects is to compare a background depth image of the scene and the current depth image delivered by the ToF-camera. The background depth can be created by averaging several ToF-images (see figure 1). In the segmentation phase the depth $z(x)$ of every pixel x of a ToF-image is compared to the background image pixel's depth $z_b(x)$ and if: $z(x) < z_b(x) - \tau$ the pixel x is classified as foreground or moving object (τ is a threshold).

The keying is executed on the GPU using shaders in the domain of the CCD-camera. Figure 2 shows the depth- (a) and corresponding CCD-image (b) with a person in the scene. Image (c) shows the keying result on the depth image and (d) shows the corresponding color result. This simple keying approach has one main limitation: the segmentation is not very precise at object boundaries due to noise and the low depth resolution. Therefore an improved segmentation at object boundaries is needed.

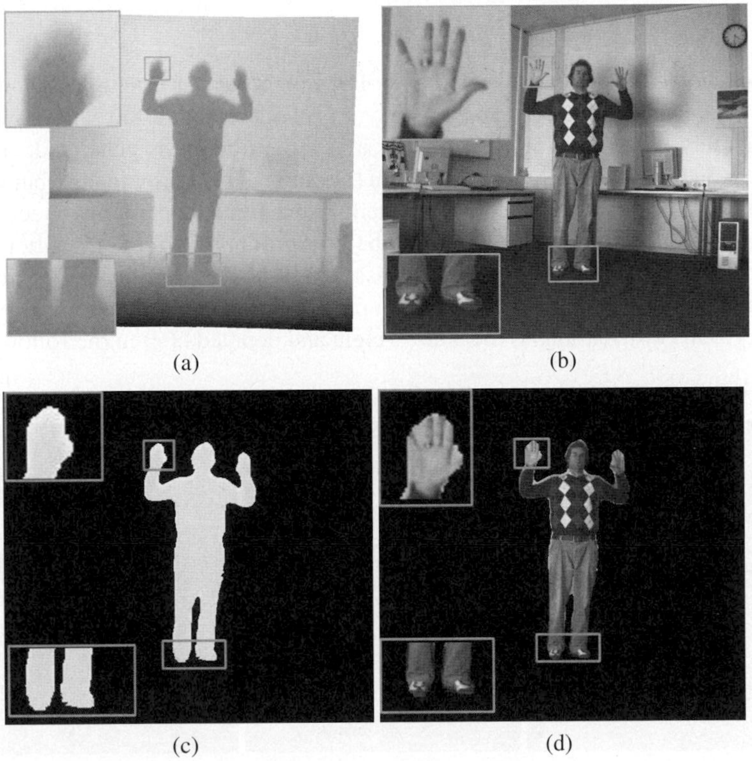

Fig. 2. Warped depth image with person (a), Corresponding CCD image (b), depth segmented image (c) and corresponding CCD image (d)

2.2 Segmentation by Mixture-of-Gaussians

A well-known method for segmentation is Mixture-of-Gaussians (MoG). The detection of dynamic objects in a scene using an adaptive background mixture model relates to the work of Xu et al. [9] and Stauffer et al. [7]. They describe a method that uses multiple Gaussian distributions to model each pixel of an image. An intensity image is defined by the three color channels in RGB space $F = (F_R, F_G, F_B)$. Assuming that no channel is saturated this representation can be transformed into a normalized form $f = (f_r, f_g, f_b)$ with e.g. : $f_r = F_R/\sqrt{F_R^2 + F_G^2 + F_B^2}$. It is concluded that it is appropriate to model each $f_k \in f$ using a Gaussian distribution and the probability of observing a value $f_t = (f_{r,t}, f_{g,t}, f_{b,t})$ at a pixel at time t is therefore given by:

$$P(f_t) = \sum_{i=1}^{N} \omega_{i,t} \frac{1}{\sqrt{2\pi}\sigma_{i,t}} e^{-\frac{(f_t - \mu_{i,t})^2}{2\sigma_{i,t}^2}} \tag{1}$$

where N is the number of distributions, $\omega_{i,t}$ is a weighting factor for each distribution, $\sigma_{i,t}^2$ are the variances and $\mu_{i,t}$ the mean of the Gaussian distributions. Initial values for variance $\sigma_{0,0}^2$ and mean $\mu_{0,0}$ are determined over a small image region Δx. A pixel is classified as belonging to a distribution i if:

$$||f_t - \mu_{i,t-1}|| < c\sigma_{i,t-1}, (c \approx 3) \tag{2}$$

and the parameters are updated accordingly. The weights $\omega_{i,t}(x)$ are increased while the weights of the not matched distributions $\omega_{j,t}(x)$ are decreased. If the current pixel does not match any of the existing distributions a new distribution is generated, and if the number of distributions exceeds a maximum (we allow 3 background distributions), the distribution with the lowest weight is deleted. In our implementation we record about 50 images of the empty scene and build the background distributions. After that the update of the background distributions is disabled and only the distances (see equation (2)) to the background distributions are computed. The average distance of a pixel x to the background distributions is the color weight and denoted $c(x)$ in the following.

(a) Depth (b) MoG (rgb) (c) MoG+Depth (rgbd)

Fig. 3. MoG segmentation result: The color segmentation easily under- or over-segments foreground objects (a), (b). MoG with depth as fourth channel improves the result, but borders remain erroneous (c).

Figure 3 (a) and (b) shows a segmentation result if only the Mixture-of-Gaussian on color is used as segmentation clue. It can be seen that the algorithm tends to either under- or over-segment the person, especially if a challenging scene is chosen with many shadows and colors similar to the background.

2.3 Combining Color and Depth

From the results of the depth- and MoG- segmentation we conclude that a combination of the two approaches will improve the segmentation. The crucial decision is, which segmentation is more likely to be correct and if the two approaches deliver different results which one to trust. The first intuitive possibility is to add the depth information as forth channel to the MoG on color images. The vector on which the distributions are defined is then formed by the three color channels in rgb space and the depth value d as combined rgbd space: $f = (f_r, f_g, f_b, d)$. Figure 3 (c) shows that this can compensate some of the shortcomings of the pure MoG segmentation, but the borders of the foreground person are still erroneous.

Therefore we propose to use a reliability measure for depth information in the segmentation. We evaluate two different approaches as reliability measure. The first (method A) is the usage of the variance in depth and the second (method B) is the usage of the amplitude information provided by the ToF-camera. The amplitude image quantifies the amount of light that is reflected from the object to the camera. The higher the values the more reliable is the measurement. At object discontinuities less light is reflected due to scattering effects. Therefore we use the inverse of the amplitude image to enable its usage in the same way as the variance image.

Discontinuities in method A are detected by analyzing the variance in the original depth image. High variances are marked as shown in figure 4 (a). To be able to compare the different modalities they have to be normalized. The current depth difference $d(x) = z(x) - z_b(x)$ is normalized between the minimum d_{min} and the maximum depth difference d_{max} in that image and in the same way the weight of the color foreground pixels $c(x)$ is normalized between the minimum and maximum color weights c_{min} and c_{max}:

$$\hat{d}(x) = \frac{d(x) - d_{min}}{d_{max} - d_{min}} \qquad \hat{c}(x) = \frac{c(x) - c_{min}}{c_{max} - c_{min}} \tag{3}$$

The variance and inverted amplitude values are also normalized between zero and one to be comparable to the other measurement weights $\hat{d}(x)$ and $\hat{c}(x)$, and denoted the normalized uncertainty $\hat{v}(x)$. In areas in which the depth uncertainty is high, the depth measurement is considered unreliable. Therefore we weight the normalized depth difference $\hat{d}(x)$ with the uncertainty $\hat{v}(x)$, resulting in an uncertainty filtered depth $\hat{dv}(x)$ which is scaled between zero and one dependent on the uncertainty. In contrast to that is the color more reliable if the depth uncertainty is high. Therefore the color weight $\hat{c}(x)$ is multiplied with the depth uncertainty $\hat{v}(x)$ and added to the color weight. The result is that if the depth uncertainty is high the color weight is weighted even higher while at the same time the uncertainty filtered depth is weighted lower. To consider all measures in an adequate manner the following equations are proposed:

$$\hat{dv}(x) = (1 - \hat{v}(x))\hat{d}(x) \tag{4}$$

$$\hat{cv}(x) = (1 + \hat{v}(x))\hat{c}(x) \tag{5}$$

$$\hat{s}(x) = \frac{1}{2}(\hat{dv}(x) + \hat{cv}(x)) \tag{6}$$

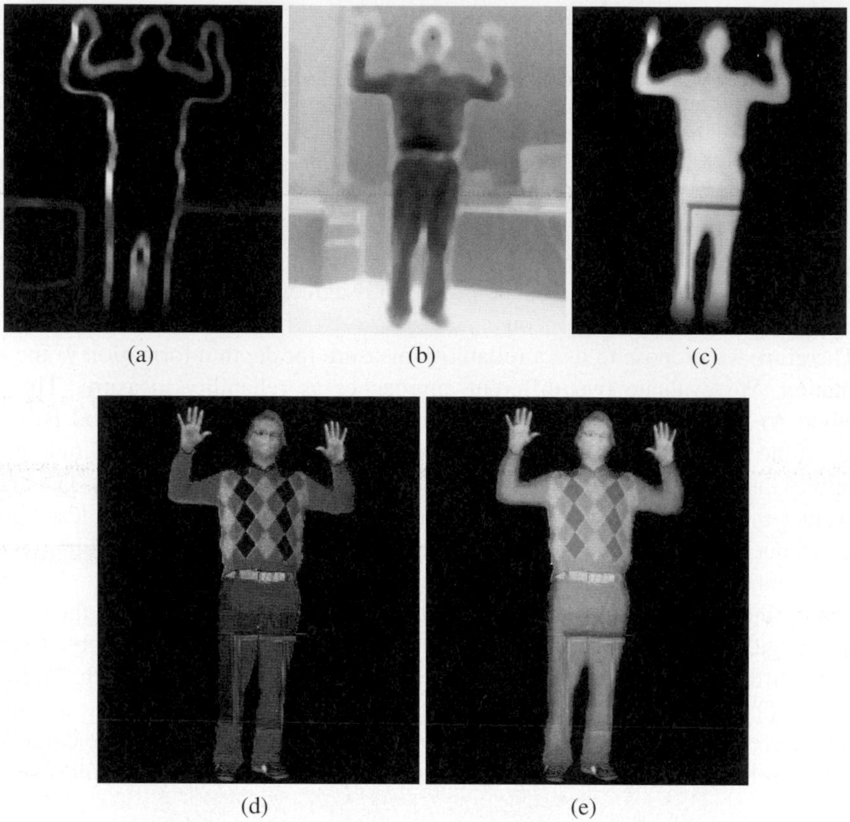

Fig. 4. Weighting images:(a)+(b) variance weight image and amplitude image (uncertainty) $\hat{v}(x)$, (c) variance weighted depth difference $\hat{dv}(x)$, (d) MoG weight $\hat{c}(x)$ and (e) combined weight image $\hat{s}(x)$

Figure 4 shows the weighting images of the proposed approaches. Image (b) shows the inverted normalized amplitude image, (c) the normalized variance weighted depth image, (d) the weighting image of the MoG and the combined weighting image $\hat{s}(x)$. Brighter values indicate higher weights. It is clearly visible that the color segmentation gains more importance on fine structures such as the hands and the feet of the person. For finally composing the image C (see images in figure 7), we use blending between foreground F and background color B with $\hat{s}(x)$ the matting alpha:

$$C = \hat{s}(x)F + (1 - \hat{s}(x))B \tag{7}$$

3 Results

The approaches are evaluated with the depth maps warped to the domain of the color camera. Two images have been labeled by hand (see figure 5 (a) and (b)) to allow quantitative evaluation. We chose challenging examples in which colors of the background

(a) (b) (c)

Fig. 5. Manually labeled silhouette images for quantitative evaluation in tables 1 (a) and 2 (b). (c) shows the to (b) corresponding color image and (a) corresponds to the images in figure 2.

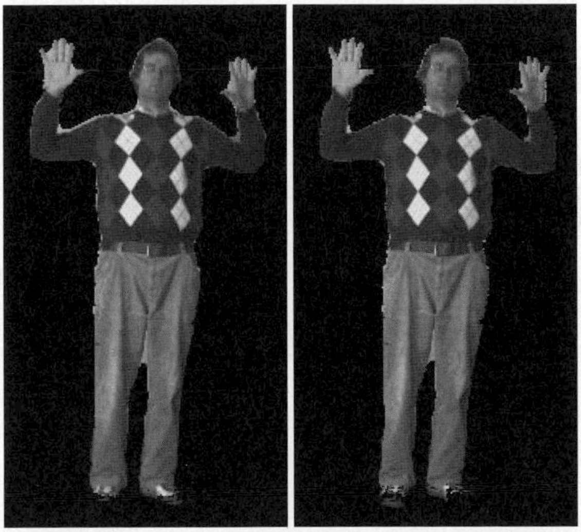

(a) MoG with variance weighted depth (b) MoG with amplitude weighted depth

Fig. 6. Segmented images, corresponding to table 1: (a) Proposed method A, (b) proposed method B. Note the increased segmentation quality at the borders, especially at the top of the person.

are also present in the foreground and in which we try to distinguish a person from the floor it is standing on. Tables 1 and 2 show the evaluation results of the segmentation for the different approaches. The tables compare the number (#) of matching pixel, which describes how many pixel have been correctly identified as fore-or background, how many false positives (detected as foreground, but belonging to background) and how many false negatives are produced by the different approaches. The computed matte values $\hat{s}(x)$ have been thresholded for this purpose to obtain a binary segmentation result with $\hat{s}(x) > 0.1$. Percentages of matching pixel are relative to the number of pixel, percentages of false positives, false negatives and the total error are given relative to the number of foreground pixel.

Table 1. Segmentation evaluation for image (a) of figure 5. The image consists of 225000 pixel of which 18087 have been manually selected as foreground.

Approach	Matching pixel #/%	False positives #/%	False negatives #/%	Total error #/%
Depth	223125 / 99.167	1542 / 8.287	333 / 1.79	1875 / 10.076
MoG	221207 / 98.314	2320 / 12.468	1473 / 7.916	3793 / 20.384
MoG+Depth	222098 / 98.710	2680 / 14.402	222 / 1.193	2902 / 15.595
Proposed Method A	223782 / 99.459	599 / 3.219	619 / 3.327	1218 / 6.546
Proposed Method B	223782 / 99.471	561 / 3.015	630 / 3.386	1191 / 6.4

Figure 7 shows the segmentation results of the combined approach. At some particular difficult points, in this example the shoes of the person, the segmentation is not entirely correct, because the similarity between the white shoes and the gray floor is too high after color normalization. The improved segmentation is clearly visible at hands,

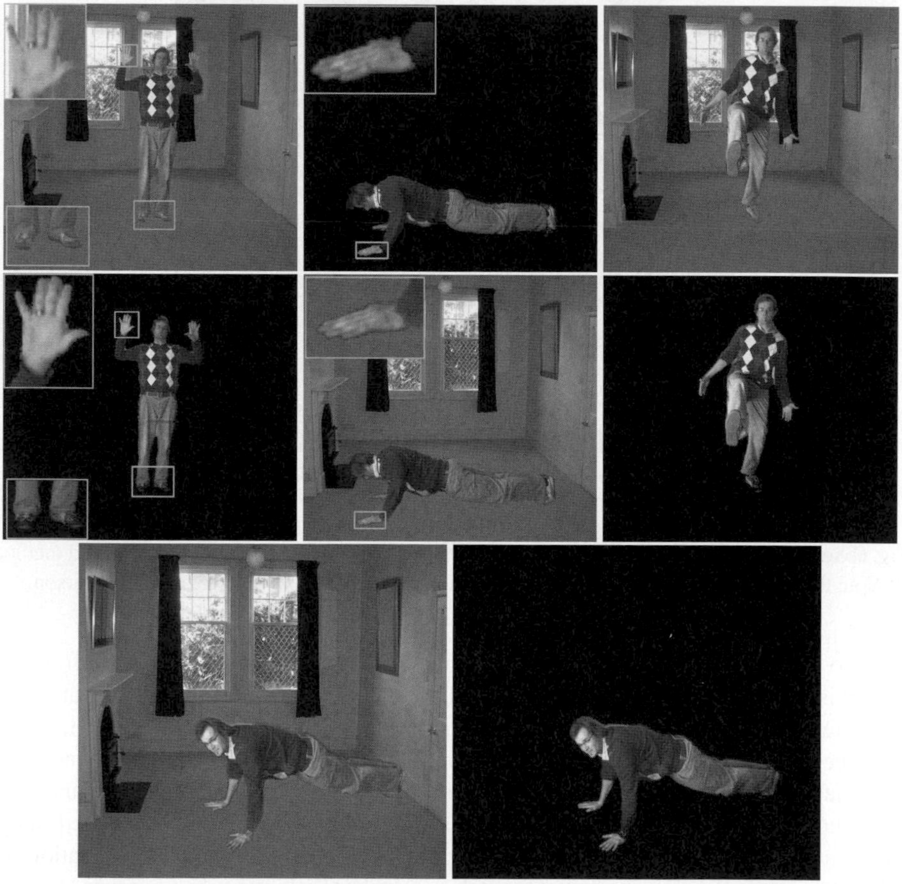

Fig. 7. Final results blended with background image and with black background using equation 7. Some of the improved regions are marked and enlarged.

Table 2. Segmentation evaluation for image (b) of figure 5. The image consists of 225000 pixel of which 20859 have been manually selected as foreground.

Approach	Matching pixel #/%	False positives #/%	False negatives #/%	Total error #/%
Depth	221054 / 98.246	3512 / 16.837	434 / 2.081	3946 / 18.918
MoG	221128 / 98.280	1944 / 9.320	1928 / 9.243	3872 / 18.563
MoG+Depth	221522 / 98.454	3300 / 15.821	178 / 0.853	3478 / 16.674
Proposed Method A	222704 / 98.980	1955 / 9.372	341 / 1.635	2296 / 11.007
Proposed Method B	223297 / 99.243	1375 / 6.592	328 / 1.572	1703 / 8.164

hair, the silhouette and feet of the person. Tables 1 and 2 show a quantitative evaluation of the different approaches. It can be clearly seen that our proposed method outperforms the other methods. The proposed method B, which utilizes the amplitude images of the ToF-camera as reliability measure, performs better than the proposed method A.

Our current implementation is not optimized for speed, but to quantify the possibilities we will give some numbers of the current implementation. The current algorithm operates at 7 Hz on a standard Intel Core i7 PC. Warping the depth to the CCD image takes $\approx$ 20ms, applying MoG to a color image takes $\approx$ 140ms and segmenting the image on the GPU takes $\approx$ 20ms including uploading the images to textures and readout of textures to images. At the moment we use two shader passes which can be reduced to one. MoG, the limiting factor, is currently executed on the CPU, parallel to the final segmentation. Transferring it to the GPU will significantly speed up the process.

4 Conclusions

We proposed a combined color and depth segmentation approach using a ToF-camera for depth- and Gaussian-Mixture-Models for color segmentation. Our contribution is the combination of the two approaches using the amplitude image of the ToF-camera or the depth variance as reliability measure for the depth measurements which significantly reduces segmentation errors on fine structures and image areas in which fore- and background meet. The approach is real-time capable as the depth segmentation and the evaluation of the combined weighting function is processed on the GPU. The refined segmentation requires, unlike other methods, no user interaction such as the selection of a coarse outlining of the foreground object. With these qualities the approach is well-suited for a variety of applications such as Mixed Reality approaches, teleconferencing systems or virtual studios.

Acknowledgment

This work has partially been funded by the "Zukunftsprogramm Schleswig-Holstein (2007-2013)" with funds from the European Commission (EFRE) and Land Schleswig-Holstein, Germany, as part of the Initiative KoSSE, project 122-09-048.

References

1. Bartczak, B., Schiller, I., Beder, C., Koch, R.: Integration of a time-of-flight camera into a mixed reality system for handling dynamic scenes, moving viewpoints and occlusions in real-time. In: Proceedings of the 3DPVT Workshop, Atlanta, GA, USA (June 2008)
2. Crabb, R., Tracey, C., Puranik, A., Davis, J.: Real-time foreground segmentation via range and color imaging. In: IEEE Computer Society Conference on Computer Vision and Pattern Recognition Workshops (CVPRW), pp. 1–5 (June 2008)
3. Gong, M., Wang, L., Yang, R., Yang, Y.H.: Real-time video matting using multichannel poisson equations. In: Proceedings of Graphics Interface (GI), pp. 89–96. Canadian Information Processing Society, Toronto (2010), `http://portal.acm.org/citation.cfm?id=1839214.1839231`
4. Gordon, G., Darrell, T., Harville, M., Woodfill, J.: Background estimation and removal based on range and color. In: IEEE Computer Society Conference on Computer Vision and Pattern Recognition (CVPR), vol. 2, pp. 458–464 (1999)
5. Gvili, R., Kaplan, A., Ofek, E., Yahav, G.: Depth keying, vol. 5006, pp. 564–574. SPIE (2003), `http://link.aip.org/link/?PSI/5006/564/1`
6. Smith, A.R., Blinn, J.F.: Blue screen matting. In: SIGGRAPH 1996: Proceedings of the 23rd Annual Conference on Computer Graphics and Interactive Techniques, pp. 259–268. ACM, New York (1996)
7. Stauffer, C., Eric, W., Grimson, L.: Adaptive background mixture models for real-time tracking. In: IEEE Computer Society Conference on Computer Vision and Pattern Recognition (CVPR), pp. 2246–2252 (1999)
8. Wang, J., Cohen, M.F.: Image and video matting: a survey. Foundations and Trends in Computer Graphics and Vision 3(2), 97–175 (2007)
9. Xu, M., Ellis, T.: Illumination-invariant motion detection using colour mixture models. In: British Machine Vision Conference (BMVC), pp. 163–172 (2001)
10. Xu, Z., Schwarte, R., Heinol, H., Buxbaum, B., Ringbeck, T.: Smart pixel - photonic mixer device (PMD). In: International Conference on Mechatronics and Machine Vision in Practice (M2VIP), Nanjing, p. 259–264 (1998)
11. Zhu, J., Liao, M., Yang, R., Pan, Z.: Joint depth and alpha matte optimization via fusion of stereo and time-of-flight sensor. In: IEEE Computer Society Conference on Computer Vision and Pattern Recognition (CVPR), pp. 453–460. IEEE, Los Alamitos (2009)

Sparse Similarity-Based Fisherfaces

Jens Fagertun[1], David D. Gomez[2], Mads F. Hansen[1], and Rasmus R. Paulsen[1]

[1] DTU Informatics, Image Analysis & Computer Graphics
Lyngby, Denmark
[2] Carlos III University, Department of Signal Theory and Communications
Madrid, Spain

Abstract. In this work, the effect of introducing Sparse Principal Component Analysis within the Similarity-based Fisherfaces algorithm is examined. The technique aims at mimicking the human ability to discriminate faces by projecting the faces in a highly discriminative and easy interpretative way. Pixel intensities are used by Sparse Principal Component Analysis and Fisher Linear Discriminant Analysis to assign a one dimensional subspace projection to each person belonging to a reference data set. Experimental results performed in the AR dataset show that Similarity-based Fisherfaces in a sparse version can obtain the same recognition results as the technique in a dense version using only a fraction of the input data. Furthermore, the presented results suggest that using SPCA in the technique offers robustness to occlusions.

Keywords: Face recognition, Sparse Principal Component Analysis, Fisher Linear Discriminant Analysis, Biometrics, Multi- Subspace Method.

1 Introduction

Recognizing a face is an important everyday task for human interaction. It is a skill we acquire before we can walk, and we are able to perform it with high accuracy using little or no effort. Due to the importance of this skill, machine aided face recognition is one of the most researched fields in image analysis. However, results reported in literature suggest that facial recognition still lacks the performance that a human operators can achieve.

In the last two decades, as advanced spectral techniques have emerged, there have been a gradual shift of the research on face recognition from geometrical towards spectral analysis. Such methods include the unsupervised method Eigenfaces [1,2] and the supervised method Fisherfaces [3]. Later on, related techniques have been proposed aiming at obtaining better classification results by developing more discriminative projections [4,5]. Most supervised methods in the literature today try to project the face representation into a subspace where a measure of global separation is maximized. However, the proposed algorithm in this paper tries to project the face representation into a series of one-dimensional subspaces where one person (class) is discriminated from all others in the population.

A. Heyden and F. Kahl (Eds.): SCIA 2011, LNCS 6688, pp. 69–78, 2011.

By solving the problem in a series of subspaces, this algorithm makes the enrollment or removal of a person easy. It is not needed to recalculate all of the existing individual subspaces when changes to the population are made. When a new person is introduced, simply a new individual subspace is added. If a person has to be removed from the database, it is only needed to remove the corresponding individual subspace.

In this article the algorithm of Similarity-based Fisherfaces proposed in [7] is extended by introducing Sparse Principal Component Analysis (SPCA) into the recognition algorithm. The terms *dense* and *sparse* will be used to differentiate between standard Principal Component Analysis (PCA) and SPCA.

The structure of the paper is as follows. Section 2 describes the algorithm to construct the sparse similarity-based face representation. Section 3 presents results that show the discriminative power of using SPCA versus PCA in Sparse Similarity-based Fisherfaces and its ability to discover the individuals most discriminative characteristics. Section 4 gives a discussion and conclusion for Sparse Similarity-based Fisherfaces.

2 Algorithm Description

The proposed algorithm builds upon SPCA [10] and Fisher Linear Discriminant Analysis (FLDA) [3].

However, unlike traditional FLDA, which maximizes a global measure of class separation[1], it obtains a one-dimensional individual linear subspace for each person (class) enrolled in a training database. The value of the projection of each sample (face representation) projected into this subspace aims at measuring the similarity of the sample with respect to that person for whom the subspace was created. Following, the proposed algorithm is briefly described. For a better understanding, Fig. 1 displays a diagram of the algorithm.

2.1 Obtaining the Texture Formulation

Face Recognition can be conducted using several types of features such as geometrical and textural[2]. In this work, visible texture features are used. The texture features are obtained by a piece-wise affine warp based on the Delaunay triangulation of the mean shape. Hereafter, the texture is normalized to zero mean and unit variance.

When the facial feature representations has been obtained, these are projected into a SPCA feature space to remove redundancy. There are different ways to formulate the SPCA objective function [9,10]. In this study the generalized power method for SPCA formulation is used as described in [10]

$$\phi_{\ell_0}(\gamma) = \max_{x \in S^P} \sum_{i=1}^{n} [(a_i^T x)^2 - \gamma]_+. \quad (1)$$

[1] In a subspace of dimensionality "Number of classes" minus one.

[2] Textural features can be recovered from any spectral range (E.g. visible or infrared).

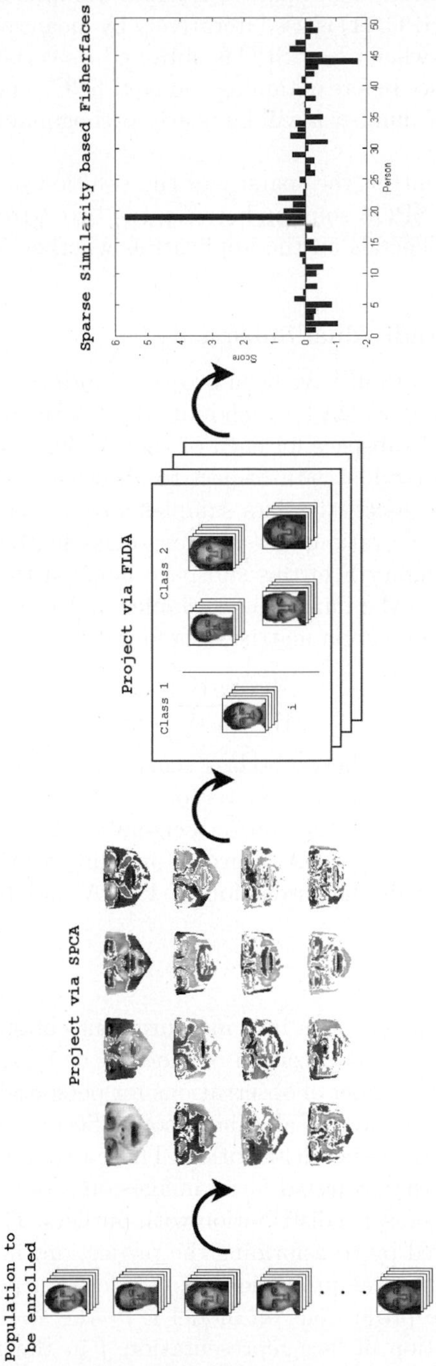

Fig. 1. Algorithm overview. SPCA and FLDA is used in turn on the population to be enrolled, in order to obtain the Sparse Similarity-based Fisherface representations.

Formulation (1) yields a single Sparse Principal Component (SPC). In order to obtain more than one SPC, (1) is used iteratively by means of deflation. Deflation is obtained as follows: when a new SPC is obtained its variation is removed from the populations variance before obtaining the next SPC. The advantage of this is that the resulting SPC number k will be nearly orthogonal to the $k-1$ previous computed SPC.

The γ parameter controls the sparsity of the solution in such a way that the size of γ will move the SPCA solution between the two extremes: a full PCA and the zero solution. It depends on the application whether sparsity or explained variance is valued.

2.2 Creating the Individual Subspaces

After the face representations have been projected into the SPCA feature space, a second projection using FLDA for each individual in the database is conducted to build a personalized subspace for each of them. This subspaces are obtained discriminating each individual with respect to all others.

A standard FLDA projects the data samples into an F-dimensional subspace so that, it maximizes the ratio of the between-class scatter to the within-class scatter. The dimensionality F of this subspace is equal to the minimum of n - 1 and m - 1, where n is the number of variables and m is the total number of people (classes). The projection matrix W is found by maximizing the ratio

$$\frac{W^T S_B W}{W^T S_W W}, \tag{2}$$

where S_B and S_W are the between-class scatter and the within class scatter matrices, respectively. The projection vectors of this matrix W correspond to the eigenvectors associated to the non-zero eigenvalues of the matrix $S_W^{-1} S_B$.

In this case of two classes FLDA returns a one dimensional subspace for each individual. For a more formal discussion of FLDA and Individual Subspaces see [7].

2.3 Classification

To turn the obtained projections into measurements of similarity a standardization is applied. The standardization of model $i = 1, \ldots, m$ is based on two assumptions. First, the number of observations for person i is much smaller than the number of the observations of all other people. Second, the projection of the other people follows a Gaussian distribution. These two assumptions imply that the distribution of all the projected facial images on a particular discriminative individual model is a Gaussian distribution with outliers. The standardization of model i is then achieved by transforming the projections into a standard Gaussian distribution, keeping the projections of the person i positive. Formally, let $\bar{x}_i$ be the mean of the projections on model i, σ_i the standard deviation, and let $x_{i,j}$ be the projection of face representation j in the ith subspace. These projections are standardized by

$$\hat{x}_{i,j} = (x_{i,j} - \bar{x}_i)/\sigma_i. \tag{3}$$

If the standardized projection for the images corresponding to person i are negative, then $\hat{x}_{i,j}$ are replaced by $-\hat{x}_{i,j}$ for all projections. This causes the projection of the images corresponding to person i to be positive and far from the mean of the gaussian.

Once the model i is standardized, the probability of a projected image to belong to person i is given by the value of the standard normal cumulative function in the projected value. This fact is used to classify a given image. If it is assumed that the image belongs to a person from the data set, the image is projected by all the models and classified as belonging to the model that gives the largest probability. Moreover, it is also statistically possible to decide if a given person belongs to the data set or it is unknown. This can be achieved by comparing the largest projection obtained in all the models with a probabilistic threshold. For example if a 99.9% of probability is required, a given image will only be considered as belonging to the database if the projection in one of the individual models is higher than 3.1 standard deviations.

3 Experimental Results

In this article two experiments are presented. The first experiment aims at determining classification rates of sparse vs. dense versions of Eigenfaces, Fisherfaces and Similarity-based Fisherfaces, together with a visualization of Sparse Principal Components. The second experiment analyzes and visualizes which are the most discriminating pixels in a face image based on the algorithm for Sparse and Dense Similarity-based Fisherfaces.

3.1 Classification Accuracy

This experiment aims at comparing the performance of SPCA and PCA in the proposed method with respect to Fisherfaces and Eigenfaces method in terms of false classification rates. Both PCA and SPCA versions of Fisherfaces and Eigenfaces will be used in this experiment.

As data set for this study 50 persons (25 male and 25 female) was randomly selected from the AR face database [8]. The database is composed of two independent sessions recorded 14 days apart (Only images without occlusions is used). An example of the selected images for two persons is displayed in Fig. 2. All the images were manually annotated with 22 landmarks.

The data set was divided into two sets. The images of the first session were used to train the algorithms, whereas the images from the second session were subsequently used to test the performance. In order to obtain the texture representation of each face in the training set, the different images were warped with respect to the mean shape, represented by 41339 pixels. These representations was normalized to zero mean and unit variance.

In the Fisherface and the Eigenface algorithms the Nearest-Neighbor algorithm with Euclidean metric was used as classifier. In the proposed method the classification is performed in such a way; that a given face image is recognized as the person associated to the subspace that yields the highest probability.

Fig. 2. The AR data set: (A) The seven images without occlusions from first session, (B) The seven images without occlusions from the second session.

The test was repeated a second time changing the roles of the training and the test sets: session two was used as training data and session one as test data.

Determine γ for Use in SPCA. Considering the formulation for SPCA (1) it can be determined that as γ goes to zero the SPCA goes to a full PCA solution. As described before, the process of choosing γ is not trivial and depends on the problem at hand, whether a more dense or sparse solution to SPCA is wanted. After performing exploratory experiments with different values of γ the value of $\gamma = 0.003$ was chosen as a good value for this problem. It is beyond the scope of this paper to analyze methods for determining an optimal γ for a given problem. The value of $\gamma = 0.003$ is used for the experiments in this study.

The false classification rates for the different techniques are shown in Fig. 3, where these rates are plotted as a function of using the first i PC/SPC. The figure shows rates up to the first one hundred PC/SPC.

To analyze the effect of the light variance, another test was conducted where the three pictures containing extreme light of each person in the test and training set was removed. This reduces the inner class variance, due to lighting noise. Any method for postprocessing could be used for removing light variation.

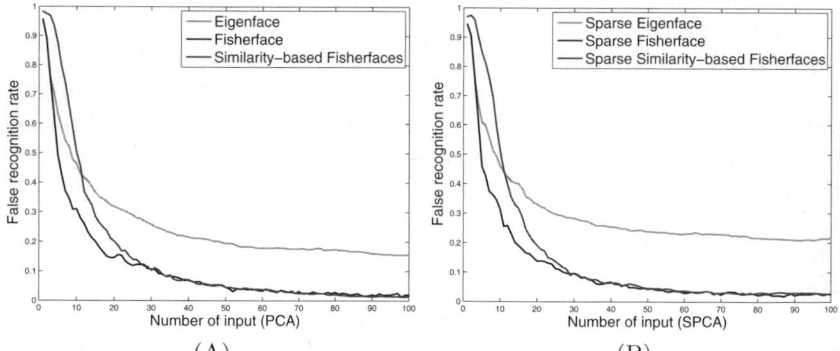

Fig. 3. False classification rates for Eigenfaces, Fisherfases and Similarity-based Fisherfaces with extreme light variation. (A) displays the Dense versions, (B) displays the Sparse versions. The rates are plotted as a function of using the first i PC/SPC, $i = 1 \dots 100$.

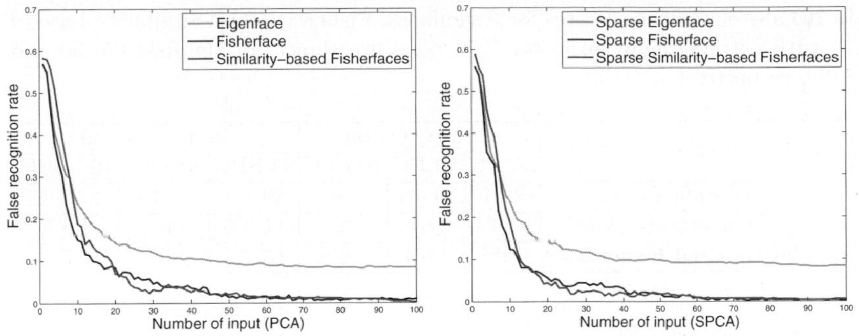

(A) (B)

Fig. 4. False classification rates for Eigenfaces, Fisherfases and Similarity-based Fisherfaces without extreme light variation. (A) displays the Dense versions, (B) displays the Sparse versions. The rates are plotted as a function of using the first i PC/SPC, $i = 1 \ldots 100$.

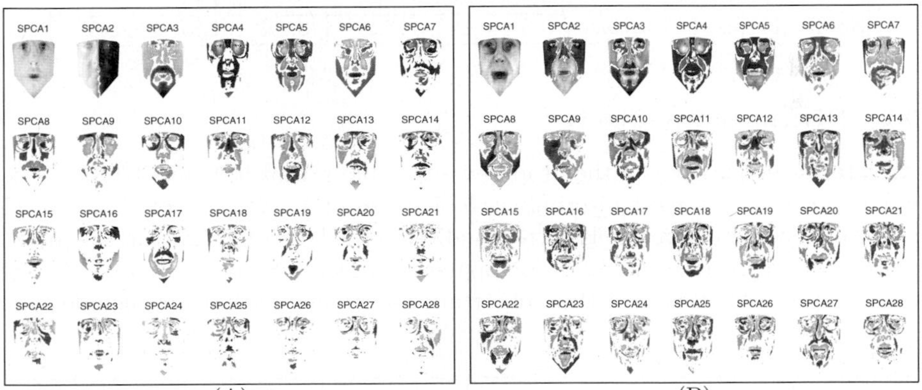

(A) (B)

Fig. 5. Visualization of the first 28 Sparse Principal Components from the experiment (A) with extreme light variation (B) without extreme light variation.

However, for simplicity the images are simply removed in this study. The new false classification rates for the different techniques are shown in Fig. 4. The SPC can be seen in Fig. 5 for the two experiments with and without extreme light, respectively.

From Fig. 3 it can be seen that the Sparse versions of Fisherfaces and Similarity-based Fisherfaces obtain similar recognition results as the Dense versions with only using a fraction of the input data. In Fig. 4 it can be seen that Sparse Similarity-based Fisherfaces preforms even better than the Dense version when large variance in the sample population due to inner class variance noise is minimized (removing light variation). The false classification rates for the first 25, 50 and 100 PC/SPC in Table 1 and Table 2 for the different techniques with and without extreme lighting, respectively.

Table 1. False classification rates for Eigenfaces, Fisherfases and Similarity-based Fisherfaces with extreme light variation. The rates are shown for the first 25, 50 and 100 PC/SPC, respectively.

Method	Dense version			Sparse version		
	25 PC	50 PC	100 PC	25 SPC	50 SPC	100 SPC
Eigenfaces	29%	19,4%	15,6%	29,7%	23,9%	21,7%
Fisherfases	11,9%	4,6%	2%	11,3%	4,6%	2,6%
Similarity-based Fisherfaces	14%	4,6%	1,4%	13,7%	4,3%	2,7%

Table 2. False classification rates for Eigenfaces, Fisherfases and Similarity-based Fisherfaces without extreme light variation. The rates are shown for the first 25, 50 and 100 PC/SPC, respectively.

Method	Dense version			Sparse version		
	25 PC	50 PC	100 PC	25 SPC	50 SPC	100 SPC
Eigenfaces	13%	9,4%	8,4%	12,4%	9,8%	8,4%
Fisherfases	5,8%	1,4%	1%	3,6%	1,8%	0,2%
Similarity-based Fisherfaces	3,8%	2%	0,2%	3,2%	1,8%	0,6%

3.2 Discriminative Pixels

An interesting property of the proposed algorithm is that it is possible to determine which are the most discriminative features of a given person. The 10, 15 and 25% discriminative pixels corresponding to the highest weights in the model are displayed (in red) in Fig. 6 for Sparse and Dense Similarity-based Fisherfaces respectively. It is clear that important discriminating features include eyes,

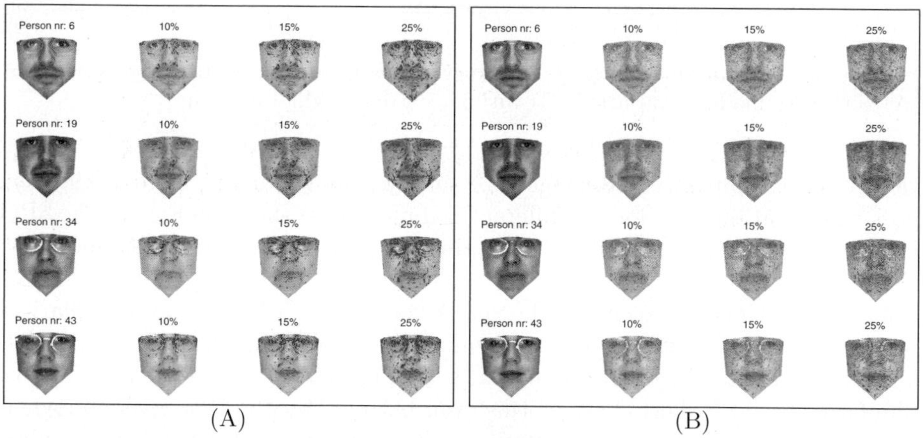

Fig. 6. The 10, 15 and 25% discriminative pixels displayed in red for (A) Similarity-based Fisher and (B) Sparse Similarity-based Fisherfaces

noses, glasses, moles and beards. Notice that the Dense algorithm detects the glasses and the mole of person 43 in Fig. 6 as discriminative features, whereas the Sparse algorithm does not do this to the same degree. This suggests that the Sparse method will be more robust giving the same result no matter if the person is wearing glasses in one picture and contact lenses in another.

4 Discussion and Conclusion

In this work, the effect of introducing Sparse Principal Component Analysis within the Similarity-based Fisherfaces algorithm are examined. Both the dense and sparse version of Similarity-based Fisherfaces aims at being a precise and robust algorithm that can be incorporated into biometrical security systems.

Experimental results in this study have shown that the technique in a sparse version can obtain the same recognition results as the technique in a dense version (presented in [7]) with only a fraction of the input data.

Furthermore, the presented results suggest that using SPCA in the technique offers robustness to occlusions. The discriminative pixels are not primarily fixed on naturally occurring occlusions in the face (Glasses, molds etc.), whereas for the dense version of the algorithm they are. This point needs to be examined in detail in future work.

Moreover, just as the dense version, the sparse version also allows for a simple interpretation of the results in the final one-dimensional individual subspace.

Another interesting property of the proposed algorithm is that by solving the problem in a series of subspaces, this algorithm makes the enrollment or removal of a person easy. It is not needed to recalculate all of the existing individual subspaces when changes to the population are made. When a new person is introduced, simply a new individual subspace is added. If a person has to be removed from the database, it is only needed to remove the corresponding individual subspace.

References

1. Kirby, M., Sirovich, L.: Application of the Karhunen-Loeve procedure for the characterization of human faces. IEEE Transactions on Pattern Analysis and Machine Intelligence 12, 103–108 (1990)
2. Turk, M., Pentland, A.: Eigenfaces for Recognition. Journal of Cognitive Neuroscience 3, 71–86 (1991)
3. Belhumeur, P.N., Hespanha, J.P., Kriegman, D.J.: Eigenfaces vs. Fisherfaces: Recognition using class specific linear projection. IEEE Transactions on Pattern Analysis and Machine Intelligence 19, 711–720 (1997)
4. Cevikalp, H., Neamtu, M., Wilkes, M., Barkana, A.: Discriminative common vectors for face recognition. IEEE Transactions on Pattern Analysis and Machine Intelligence 27, 4–13 (2005)
5. Liu, Q., Huang, R., Lu, H., Ma, S.: Face recognition using Kernel-based Fisher discriminant analysis. In: 2002 Proceedings: Fifth IEEE International Conference on Automatic Face and Gesture Recognition, pp. 197–201 (2002)

6. Baddeley, A.D.: Essentials of Human Memory. Psychology Press, Taylor and Francis (1999)
7. Gomez, D.D., Fagertun, J., Ersbll, B., Sukno, F.M., Frangi, A.F.: Similarity-based Fisherfaces. Pattern Recognition Letters 30(12), 1110–1116 (2009)
8. Martinez, A.M., Benavente, R.: The AR Face Database. Technical Report, Computer Vision Center Purdue University (1998)
9. Zou, H., Hastie, T., Tibshirani, R.: Sparse Principal Component Analysis. Journal of Computational and Graphical Statistics 15, 265–286 (2006)
10. Journee, M., Nesterov, Y., Richtarik, P., Sepulchre, R.: Generalized Power Method for Sparse Principal Component Analysis. The Journal of Machine Learning Research 11, 517–553 (2010)

Accumulation of Different Visual Feature Descriptors in a Coherent Framework

Jeppe Barsøe Jessen[1], Florian Pilz[2], Dirk Kraft[1], Nicolas Pugeault[3], and Norbert Krüger[1]

[1] Mærsk Mc-Kinney Møller Institute, University of Southern Denmark, Odense, Denmark
http://www.mmmi.sdu.dk/covig/
[2] Department of Architecture, Design & Media Technology, Aalborg University, Denmark
[3] Centre for Vision, Speech and Signal Processing, University of Surrey, United Kingdom

Abstract. We present a temporal accumulation scheme which disambiguates different kinds of visual 3D descriptors within one coherent framework. The accumulation consists of a twofold process: First, by means of a Bayesian filtering outliers become eliminated and second, the precision of the extracted information becomes enhanced by means of an unscented Kalman filtering process. It is a particular property of our algorithm to be able to deal with different kinds of visual descriptors by the very same mechanism. We show quantitative and qualitative results.

1 Introduction

This article proposes a novel on-line method for learning representations of objects' shape based on probabilistic tracking of a family of heterogeneous local descriptors over time, in 2D and 3D. We present a unified method that allows the temporal filtering of such different visual descriptors using a common approach. This approach allows a robotic system to learn autonomously representations of objects by manipulating them. Having internal representations of object shapes is required by state-of-the-art robotic grasping and manipulation approaches, and it is often provided as prior knowledge (e.g., as CAD models). The capacity for a robotic system to learn on-line an internal representation enabling object interaction and manipulation is an important goal for cognitive robotics [8]. In this work, we describe an object using a combination of local descriptors that are accumulated over time while the robot manipulates the object. Here, we will describe objects using a combination of edges, junctions and texture patches. The object representation is based on an Early Cognitive Vision (ECV) framework that has been presented in [16].

Visual descriptions of objects and scenes can be constituted from a variety of feature types, like point features [9,10], edge-like features ([16,1]) or texture descriptors in terms of patchlets [11]) carrying complementary information. Some feature types can be shown to have different relevance for different tasks, and

A. Heyden and F. Kahl (Eds.): SCIA 2011, LNCS 6688, pp. 79–90, 2011.

previous work has outlined these limitations and the benefits of using a combination of descriptors to alleviate these limitations (e.g., for the case of motion estimation, [13]). In the ECV system described in [16], these different image structures are distinguished and represented by different kinds of symbolic descriptors which parameterize the content of the local patches according to the semantic content of the local patch (see figure 1). In addition to geometric properties such as position and orientation, these features also possess appearance information. It has been shown (see, e.g., [13]) that it is advantageous to make use of these different aspects of visual information depending on the task and the actual context.

When using 3D information in visual representations, we face three problems: Firstly, wrong correspondences in (stereo) matching result in outliers in the representation. Secondly, occlusion lead to incomplete representations. Thirdly, 3D information is subject to uncertainties evolving in the reconstruction process. All three problems can be reduced by merging information across different object views. For this purpose, a number of methods have been developed (SFM, SLAM, bundle adjustment). These methods have been designed mainly for point features (see, e.g., [2,12]), although some work also exists on line features [4,15].

In this paper, we describe an algorithm that is designed such that it can be applied to different feature types *jointly* allowing for the accumulation of rich and disambiguated scene and object representations. This flexibility is achieved through a generic three stage scheme, which 1) makes use of Bayesian filtering for outlier removal based on confidences associated to the different feature types, 2) extends the representation by novel scene or object aspects and 3) reduces the uncertainties by an unscented Kalman filtering approach. A particular property of our approach is that all three stages of our scheme can deal with the different kinds of descriptors by the very same machinery.

The algorithm was introduced in [15] and includes the use of an Unscented Kalman Filter (UKF) [5] to track the distribution in the whole feature space, instead of only considering the position of the feature. This includes the semantic interpretation of each individual descriptor allowing us to keep track of the relative reliability of different components of the feature vector by their altered cross modality variance. Furthermore the algorithm incorporates probabilistic matching of features based on both geometric and appearance information. Moreover it uses temporal re-evaluation of a feature's confidence according to tracking success, including a mechanism for deletion and preservation of descriptors over time. This work extends the described approach to be able to cope seamlessly with different feature descriptors. Appropriate parameterizations for the different feature types are discussed.

The accumulation of the symbolic representation is an important disambiguation mechanism of the ECV system and has been applied for object learning and recognition [8] in the context of line features. The work introduced in this paper will allow for the extension of such work to richer representations realizing even more efficient and stable pose estimation, recognition and grasping.

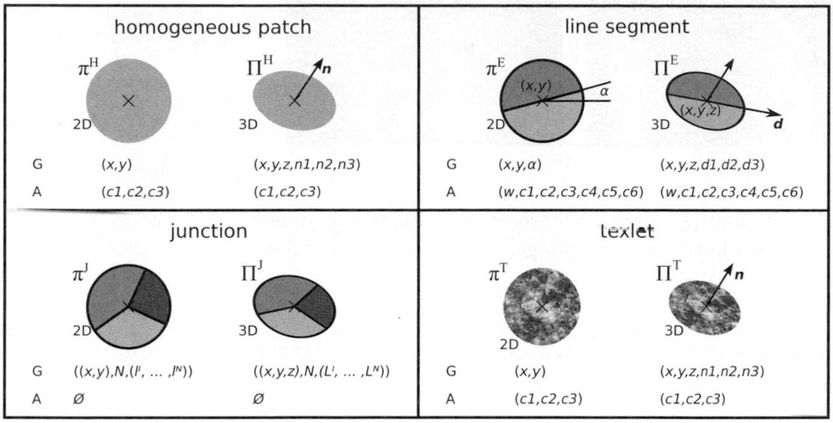

Fig. 1. Four different image structures in 2D and 3D and their parameterization. We distinguish between four different kinds of local image structures: *homogeneous patches*, *edges*, *junctions* and *textured patches*. All four structures need to be represented by local symbolic descriptors covering appearance as well as geometric information, both in 2D and 3D. The semantic content is very different for the different kinds of structure.

2 Feature Descriptors

The differentiation in feature type is achieved by making use of the concept of intrinsic dimensionality of the local image signal [3]. When we talk about a specific kind of descriptor Π^K, as shown in figure 1, we indicate this by a superscript $K \in \{H, E, J, T\}$ denoting homogeneous patches, edges, junctions and texture patches respectively.

The 3D feature descriptors $\Pi^K = (G^K, A^K, \Sigma_G^K, \Sigma_A^K, B)$ illustrated in figure 1 together with their 2D equivalent π^K, are parameterized by five terms representing geometric information G^K, appearance information A^K, corresponding uncertainty estimates Σ_G^K and Σ_A^K and a confidence $B \in [0, 1]$. The confidence B represents the system's current belief that the given descriptor is a correctly extracted primitive representing a feature in the physical scene. The first four terms depend on the feature type itself and will be defined below.

Tracking the different feature types using an UKF requires a state vector representing the current state of a primitive. Thus, for each primitive type K we define the state vector $S^K = \mathbf{state}(\Pi^K) = (G^K, A^K)$ which also allows for a straightforward update of the primitive when a new state has been estimated. The exact parameterization of the descriptors as well as the associated initial covariance matrices are defined in the following subsections. Note that we do not discuss homogeneous primitives here since our system is based on stereo processing which can not be initialized at homogeneous areas.[1]

[1] However, note that the accumulation scheme could also be used on data extracted by sensors not having this problem, such as, e.g., laser sensors.

(a) Left (b) Right (c) Stereo model

Fig. 2. (a) and (b) shows a stereo pair from the sequence. (c) is the extracted stereo primitives projected onto an image. Some features are labeled to illustrate the difference in visualization.

Edge Primitives. have an orientation that can be reliably computed. Their position is on a one-dimensional manifold (aperture problem). The local structure can also be determined from local filter responses [7], allowing to differentiate between step edges (e.g., transition from dark to bright) and line structures (e.g., bright line on darker background). This structure is taken into consideration when extracting and encoding the color information [16]. An appropriate geometric representation of the edge or line segment primitive carries a full 6D pose in 3D. First we have the 3D position and second there is a vector $\mathbf{d}$ pointing in the direction of the line. The appearance information of the line segment consist of two color triplets defining the color on the left and right side of the edge (and one possibly on the edge for a line structure), and a phase ω defining the color transition. Formally, we have $G^E = (\mathbf{t}, \mathbf{r}) = (x, y, z, d_1, d_2, d_3)$, $A^E = (\omega, c_1^l, c_2^l, c_3^l, c_1^r, c_2^r, c_3^r)$. The covariance of the edge primitive is $\Sigma_{G,0}^E \in \mathbb{R}^6 \times \mathbb{R}^6$ for the geometry and $\Sigma_{A,0}^E = I_6$ for the appearance (where I_n is the identity matrix of dimension $n \times n$).

Junction Primitives. are intersections of edges and have a complex 2D geometry covering the intersection point as well as half–lines extending from it. Because of this complexity, a large degree of ambiguity can be expected in the computation of the junction parameters and appearance information is not reliable enough for matching. The complex geometry extends to the 3D domain where an important distinction is whether the lines intersecting in 2D also intersect in 3D. We represent the geometric information of the junction primitive as the 3D position where the lines intersect. A list of the intersecting lines of the junction is also maintained as a list of links L to line segment primitives. These line segments are accumulated using the normal procedure for lines with the added constraint that they can only be matched with line segments that belongs to matching junctions. Color information is contained in the line segments. Formally, we have $G^J = \{(x, y, z), n, (L_1^E, ..., L_n^E)\}$. Appearance information is disregarded for junctions. The covariance for the junction primitive is $\Sigma_{G,0}^J \in \mathbb{R}^3 \times \mathbb{R}^3$ for the geometry.

Texture Primitives. are characterized by an intrinsic complexity which is difficult to characterize in 2D [14]. This complexity however allows in general for the computation of reliable correspondences for stereo and optic flow processing. A reasonable 3D interpretation is a 3D surface patch, which in contrast to homogeneous patches, can be computed reliably by stereo matching. However, also irregular structures (e.g., trees) in 3D create 2D textures. Hence a 3D representation of the geometric information probably also requires at least two different descriptors for surface patches and irregular structures as outlined in [6] to which we also refer to for further details. The texture primitive, also denoted texlet because of the similarities with the patchlet introduced in [11], is defined by a full 6D pose in 3D. For now the only appearance information computed for the texlet is the mean color. Formally, we have $G^T = (x, y, z, n_1, n_2, n_3)$, $A^T = (c_1, c_2, c_3)$. The covariance for the texture primitive is $\Sigma^T_{G,0} \in \mathbb{R}^6 \times \mathbb{R}^6$ for the geometry and $\Sigma^T_{A,0} = I_3$ for the appearance.

3 The Accumulation Algorithm

In this chapter we describe a framework which makes use of the spatial representation by computing the different image descriptors at a given frame (see [16]) and (already available or estimated) Rigid Body Motion (RBM) information in order to predict a representation for the next frame, compare it with the actual representation extracted in the next frame and finally merge the two representations.

Some notation must be introduced to describe the generic use of unscented Kalman filtering of motion and Bayesian confidence update. Every primitive that has been extracted from the image is an *observed* primitive in the Kalman filtering domain and we denote this Π. An accumulated primitive $\tilde{\Pi}$ on the other hand is an abstract entity, which most likely has never been observed in its exact form in any image. It is the result of interpolation between matches over multiple frames. From the abstract primitives in the accumulated representation we compute predictions $\hat{\Pi}$ by applying a RBM. These predictions can then be matched with the extracted primitives of the next frame.

When a 3D primitive is represented by its corresponding state vector we denote this accordingly, meaning that S is the extracted state, $\tilde{S}$ is the accumulated state and $\hat{S}$ is the predicted state. Uncertainties can also be denoted according to the primitive it belongs to, i.e., Σ, $\tilde{\Sigma}$, $\hat{\Sigma}$. We use the notation $\Pi^K_{i,t}$ to indicate the i–th primitive in a set of primitives of type K belonging to the t–th frame. Similarly we have $S^K_{i,t}$ for the state vectors.

All primitives have an associated confidence. The confidence $B^K_{i,t}$ indicates the system's belief at time t whether this descriptor corresponds to an object structure. For the newly extracted ones we use a prior confidence depending on the type of primitive, the confidence of an accumulated abstract primitive is estimated using Bayesian filtering and the predicted primitive will have a confidence identical to the originating abstract primitive.

In the following subsections the individual parts of the accumulation algorithm will be described in further detail based on the state vector representation of the primitive. The first three steps are basically Kalman filtering involving a prediction, matching and correction step. The final step is Bayesian filtering, which updates the confidences according to primitive state and matching history.

3.1 Kalman Filtering

The RBM can be formulated in generic terms applying for all primitives defined as state vectors. It will affect geometric information only as the appearance ideally would stay constant.

$$\hat{S}^K_{t+1} = \mathbf{state}(\hat{\Pi}^K_{t+1}) = \mathbf{state}(\mathbf{RBM}^{(T,R)}(\tilde{\Pi}^K_t)) \quad (1)$$

We make use of the Scaled Unscented Transform (SUT) to estimate the new covariance $\hat{\Sigma}^K_{t+1}$ of the predicted state $\hat{S}^K_{t+1}$. The SUT allows for the prediction of the transformation of a normal distribution by a non-linear process f. This is done by selecting a specific set of sample points from the distribution, and transforming them according to $f(S)$ as described in [15].

The transformation of the primitive under a RBM includes a transition of the geometric information in the current state to the Special Euclidean group of dimension 3, $SE(3)$. In this work we use dual quaternions when representing $SE(3)$. We will not go into further detail on the theory of dual quaternions here but instead guide the interested reader to [15]. Both the feature pose and Rigid Body Motions (RBMs) are well described by dual quaternions, which then allows for a compact formulation of a pose transformation under a RBM (with T, R being the translation and rotation parameters of the RBM):

$$\mathbf{RBM}^{(T,R)}(\tilde{\Pi}^K_t) = \hat{\Pi}^K_{t+1} \,. \quad (2)$$

We indicate that a predicted primitive $\hat{\Pi}$ has been matched with an observed primitive Π at time t by $\mu_t(\hat{\Pi}, \Pi)$.

Having computed the predicted representation, the next step of the filtering is to compare this model with the observed features. A newly observed 3D–primitive Π_j is matched with a predicted 3D–primitive $\hat{\Pi}_i$ if their associated states are matched according to a χ^2 criterion applied to their Mahalanobis distance:

$$(\hat{S}^K_{i,t+1} - S^K_{j,t+1})^\top (\hat{\Sigma}^K_{i,t+1} + \Sigma^K_{j,t+1})^{-1} (\hat{S}^K_{i,t+1} - S^K_{j,t+1}) < \chi^2_{k=N^K, p=0.05} \,. \quad (3)$$

In this equation $\chi^2_{k=N^K, p=0.05}$ indicates the $p = 0.05$ value in the χ^2 distribution of dimension N^K. By definition of the Mahalanobis distance, this implies that 95% of the correct matches will satisfy this criterion. In this case, the likelihood of the match μ_t in each projected frame is evaluated using a normal distribution centered on the predicted primitive. By that we define the binary match function $\mu_t(\tilde{\Pi}_i)$ which is 1 when an abstract primitive was matched at time t or 0 elsewise.

It may happen that several observed features match an accumulated one, notably when the accumulated feature's covariance is large. This will happen for example when an object is moved closer to the camera: the predicted covariance will be large, and cover several newly observed features. In this case, the most likely match (according to Eq. (4)) is preserved in a winner–take–all fashion.

$$p\left[\mu_t(\hat{\Pi}_i, \Pi_j)\right] = \frac{\exp\left[-\frac{1}{2}(\hat{S}_i - S_j)^\top \hat{\Sigma}_t^{-1} (\hat{S}_i - S_j)\right]}{(2\pi)^{n/2}\sqrt{|\hat{\Sigma}_t|}} \quad (4)$$

If the χ^2 criterion is not met, we define that $p\left[\mu_t(\hat{\Pi}_i, \Pi_j)\right] = 0$. Once the matching is done, the set of predicted model features $\hat{\Pi}_t$ can be corrected from the newly observed features Π_t using a straightforward Kalman filtering approach as outlined in [15] for line features.

3.2 Accumulation of Confidence

We define the tracking history of an abstract primitive $\tilde{\Pi}_i$ from its emergence at time 0 until time t as:

$$\boldsymbol{\mu}_t(\tilde{\Pi}_i) = \left(\mu_t(\tilde{\Pi}_i), \mu_{t-1}(\tilde{\Pi}_i), \cdots, \mu_0(\tilde{\Pi}_i)\right)^T \tag{5}$$

thus, applying Bayes formula

$$p\left[\Pi_i|\boldsymbol{\mu}_t(\tilde{\Pi}_i)\right] = \frac{p\left[\boldsymbol{\mu}_t(\tilde{\Pi}_i)|\Pi_i\right] p\left[\Pi_i\right]}{p\left[\boldsymbol{\mu}_t(\tilde{\Pi}_i)|\Pi_i\right] p\left[\Pi_i\right] + p\left[\boldsymbol{\mu}_t(\tilde{\Pi}_i)|\neg\Pi_i\right] p\left[\neg\Pi_i\right]} \tag{6}$$

where $p\left[\Pi\right]$ is the prior likelihood that a primitive of a specific type has been correctly extracted and $p\left[\neg\Pi\right]$ is the prior likelihood that it has been erroneously extracted. $p\left[\boldsymbol{\mu}_t(\tilde{\Pi}_i)|\Pi\right]$ is the likelihood of a primitive tracking history $\boldsymbol{\mu}(\tilde{\Pi}_i)$ given that the primitive Π is correctly extracted.

According to [15], if we rewrite Eq. 6 and assume independence between successive observations we have: [2]

$$p\left[\Pi_i|\boldsymbol{\mu}_t(\tilde{\Pi}_i)\right] = \left(1 + \frac{\prod_t p\left[\mu_t(\tilde{\Pi}_i)|\neg\Pi_i\right] p\left[\neg\Pi_i\right]}{\prod_t p\left[\mu_t(\tilde{\Pi}_i)|\Pi_i\right] p\left[\Pi_i\right]}\right)^{-1} . \tag{7}$$

The computed likelihood is used as feature confidence B. This allows both for elimination of entities with confidence below a minimum threshold and to freeze entities with confidence above an acceptance threshold. Eliminated features are removed from the representation as a result of poor matching or matching quality. Frozen features have their confidence locked, but are still updated with the Kalman filter when matching is possible.

4 Results

To evaluate the accumulation framework we apply the system in two different scenarios. First, an artificial image sequence is generated using a simple cube rendered in OpenGL for perfectly known motion, shape and pose. This is ideal for quantitative verification of pose correction and Bayesian confidence update

[2] Note that a particular issue of this formulation is the requirement to record the entire matching history $\boldsymbol{\mu}_t(\tilde{\Pi}_i)$. Therefore we use a recursive formulation derived from equation (7) introduced in [15], which is more practical for an on-line algorithm.

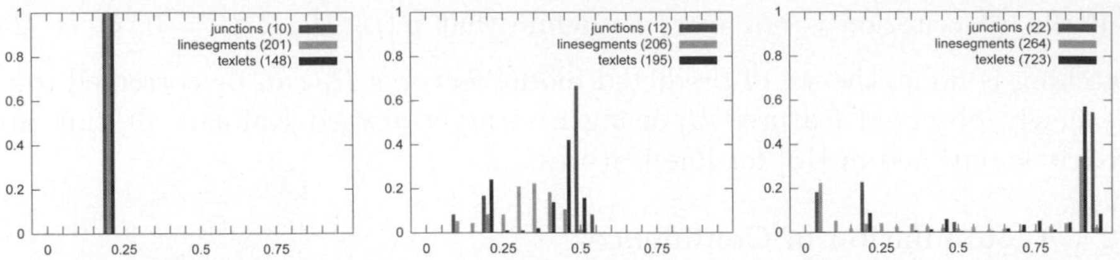

(a) frame 0 (b) frame 1 (c) frame 10

Fig. 3. Confidence histograms including eliminated features

based on matching quality and history. Second, we grasp a series of objects using a robot and record natural scene images while the objects are subject to motion. This is used for qualitative evaluation of the ability to build object models.

Artificial sequence: Figure 2 shows an example of a stereo pair of images. We use a simple object with the shape of a cube. Our cube has four faces of uniform colors, one face of marble texture and one face with a simple pattern of four colors. Inside the faces of uniform colors we do not expect to extract (homogeneous) features since stereo cannot generate correspondences at such structures. At the edges of the cube we expect to extract lines in two categories. Either the faces of the cube are visible on both sides of the edge and the extracted edge feature will contain colors of the object only, or the edge represents a depth discontinuity with the color of the face of the cube on one side and the background color on the other side. The face with a simple pattern of four colors, on the other hand, provides unambiguous edges, with stable appearance. At the corners of the cube the edges meet and we expect to extract junctions. At the textured face we primarily expect textured patches, but could also encounter areas that will be classified as edges or junctions.

Figure 3 shows the distribution of confidences in some early iterations. After 10 iterations we see the characteristic three–modal distribution in figure 3(c). The leftmost peak represents the eliminated features which will be removed from the set and thus no longer updated; in general they originate from wrong stereo matches. The second peak represents newly observed features that could not be matched with existing ones and thus are added to the representation with a confidence that equals the prior probability of a correctly observed feature. The rightmost peak represents the permanently accepted features. It is an important observation that the majority of the primitives are distributed by confidence into one of the three groups. This indicates that after a few frames most primitives are either discarded or accepted as a result of the matching quality.

A ground truth model of the cube geometry is necessary to compute the distribution of errors in position and orientation for the set of features. It is straightforward to obtain for the outer geometry such as the edges, corners and faces. The internal structure of the texture is more complicated in terms of ground truth, as it contains edges and junctions depending on scale. To avoid complications, we use a special extraction procedure when we want to compute the error distribution. First we extract edges and junctions on a cube without

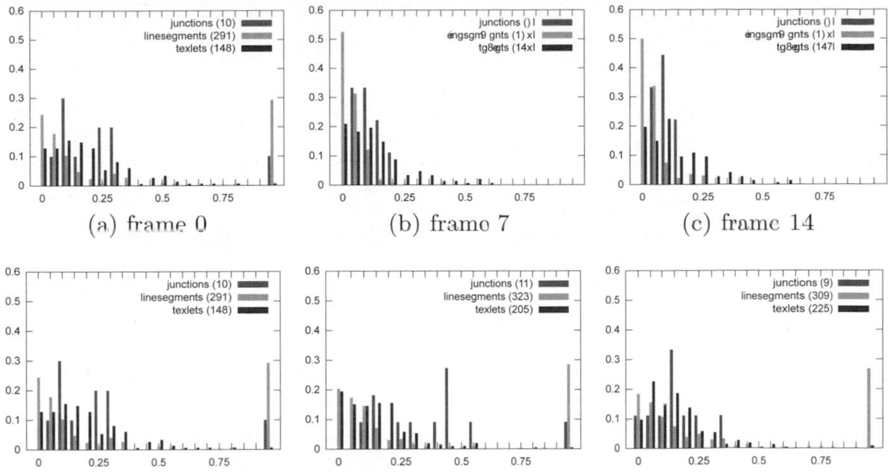

(a) frame 0 (b) frame 7 (c) frame 14

(d) frame 0 (e) frame 7 (f) frame 14

Fig. 4. (a)-(c): Position error histogram of corrected features, where no new hypotheses are added after first frame. (d)-(f): Position error of features extracted at corresponding single frames.

texture. Then we add the texture and extract textured patches. In this way we avoid the need for hand labeling features extracted within the textured surface. For each extracted feature we compute the shortest distance in 3D to a corresponding geometric element in the ground truth model, which is then the error in position. Having found the nearest element in the ground truth model we can also compute the error in orientation.

In figure 4 we show the development of position error on an accumulated model. The features are extracted at the first frame and will afterwards only be updated and not extended with new hypotheses during accumulation in order to compare the corrected representation to the stereo representation extracted at the single frames. In figures 4(a) to 4(c) we show the distribution of position errors for the accumulated representation at different stages. The single frame stereo representation extracted at the actual frame are shown in figures 4(d) to 4(f) for comparison. Features with an error out of range on the x-axis are gathered in the rightmost bar of the histogram. These high-error features disappear during accumulation when outliers are removed and the total number of features decreases. In general the small corrections lead to a shift towards smaller errors for the entire representation. Note that figures 4(a) and 4(d) are identical, as the accumulated representation after the first frame is exactly the extracted stereo.

Figure 5 shows the mean error for each of the feature types in each frame. We notice how it is reduced by outlier removal and pose correction. Also here, no new features are added after the first frame, which makes it easy to see this development.

In figure 6 we compare the accumulated heterogeneous feature model of the cube from two viewpoints at different stages in the process. The green blobs

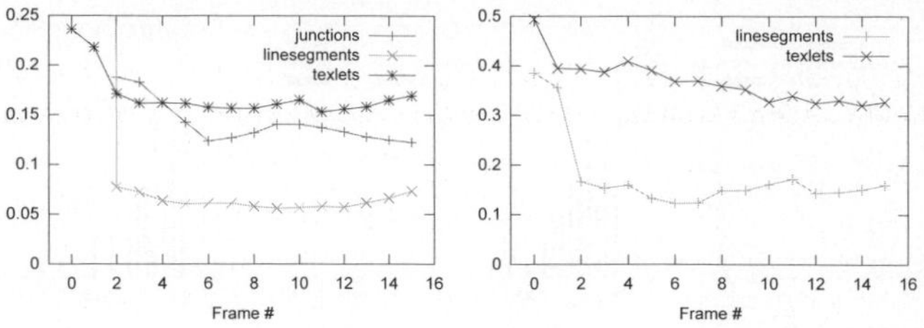

(a) Mean position error (b) Mean orientation error

Fig. 5. Correction of features added in first frame. Junctions have no orientation in this context.

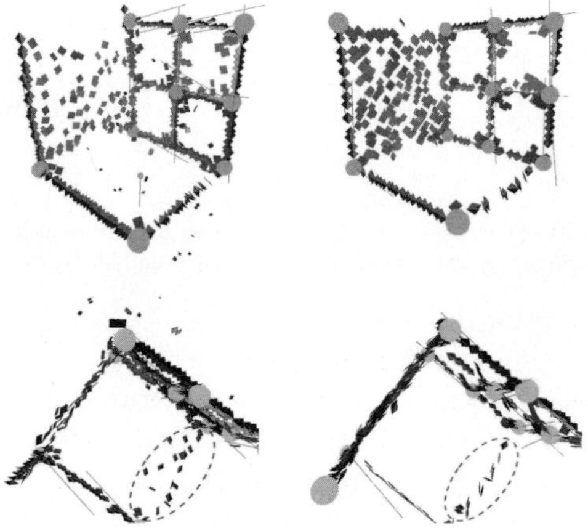

(a) 1 iteration (b) 15 iterations

Fig. 6. Cube represented by accumulated set of heterogeneous 3D features

indicate junctions, single colored squares represents textured patches and dual colored squares represents line segments. Multiple viewpoints are chosen to give an idea of the 3D information. Figure 6(a) shows the model after one iteration and here we see a number of outliers and inaccurate reconstructions caused by the noise we apply to the artificial image and wrong stereo matches. After fifteen iterations we observe two significant changes to the model, which is shown in figure 6(b). First, the outliers has been removed or corrected in position, as seen e.g. in the 'difficult' lines marked with a red ellipse at the bottom. This side of the cube are all the time close to horizontal in the image sequence and hence the reconstructed primitives are very noisy. Note also how the noisy line appear very nice from one viewpoint (in the top) but a lot worse from another (in the bottom). Second, the model is now more complete, seen e.g. in the number of textured patches on the textured face of the cube, the good descriptions of correctly positioned lines and the occurrence of two additional junctions.

Real world scene. Figure 7 shows objects in a real scene and their accumulated model after 10 frames. Rotational motion is applied to the object using the robot between each frame. We use motion estimation [13] to capture the motion

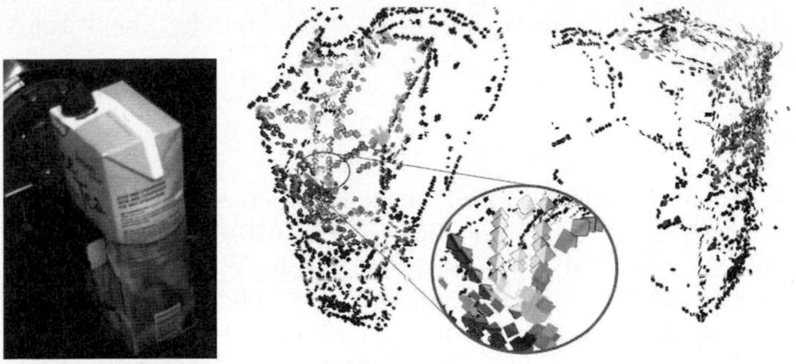

(a) Ice tea (b) Multiple viewpoints of accumulated model

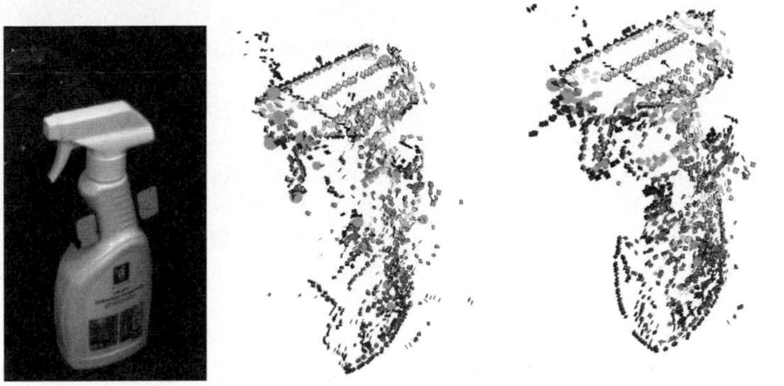

(c) Spray (d) Single stereo model (e) Accumulated model

Fig. 7. Real scene objects rotated by robot. The object models are accumulated over 10 frames.

information required for prediction. We see that the two objects are described by line segments at the contours. Junctions are extracted where the lines meet and the surface in between contour lines is nicely represented by texlets and also some line segments. The robot gripper is shown as a part of the object model as it of course shares the same motion as the object. The gripper can easily be removed because of known geometry. Figure 7(b) shows the accumulated model of an ice tea from two different viewpoints. The surface facing the camera is represented by numerous texlets and line segments and only few outliers exist. Figure 7(d) and 7(e) compares a single stereo model with the confidence thresholded accumulated model. As expected, we see that the accumulated model is indeed more complete and has fewer outliers.

5 Conclusion

We have introduced an accumulation framework that is able to disambiguate object representations consisting of different visual descriptors in a coherent way using the same machinery for all descriptors. By this we have extended the work in [15] on line segments to generic visual descriptors which will provide richer and more powerful representations for a variety of tasks as being addressed in the early cognitive vision system [16].

Acknowledgement. This work has been supported by the IntellAct project (FP7-ICT-269959).

References

1. Canny, J.: A computational approach to edge detection. IEEE Transactions on Pattern Analysis and Machine Intelligence 8(6), 679–698 (1986)
2. Dissanayake, M., Newman, P., Clark, S., Durrant-Whyte, H., Csorba, M.: A solution to the simultaneous localization and map building (SLAM) problem. IEEE Transactions on Robotics and Automation 17(3), 229–241 (2001)
3. Felsberg, M., Kalkan, S., Krüger, N.: Continuous dimensionality characterization of image structures. Image and Vision Computing 27, 628–636 (2009)
4. Isard, M., Blake, A.: Condensation — conditional density propagation for visual tracking. International Journal of Computer Vision (IJCV) 29(1), 5–28 (1998)
5. Julier, S., Uhlmann, J., Durrant–Whyte, H.: A new approach for the nonlinear transformation of means and covariances in linear filters. IEEE Transactions on Automatic Control (1996)
6. Kalkan, S., Wörgötter, F., Krüger, N.: Statistical analysis of local 3D structure in 2D images. In: IEEE Computer Society Conference on Computer Vision and Pattern Recognition (CVPR), vol. 1, pp. 1114–1121 (2006)
7. Kovesi, P.: Image features from phase congruency. Videre: Journal of Computer Vision Research 1(3), 1–26 (1999)
8. Kraft, D., Pugeault, N., Başeski, E., Popović, M., Kragic, D., Kalkan, S., Wörgötter, F., Krüger, N.: Birth of the Object: Detection of Objectness and Extraction of Object Shape through Object Action Complexes. International Journal of Humanoid Robotics 5(2), 247–265 (2008)
9. Lowe, D.G.: Robust model-based motion tracking through the integration of search and estimation. International Journal of Computer Vision (IJCV) 8(2), 113–122 (1992)
10. Mikolajczyk, K., Schmid, C.: A performance evaluation of local descriptors. IEEE Transactions on Pattern Analysis and Machine Intelligence 27(10), 1615–1630 (2005)
11. Murray, D., Little, J.J.: Patchlets: Representing stereo vision data with surface elements. In: IEEE Workshop on Applications of Computer Vision, vol. 1, pp. 192–199 (2005)
12. Nistér, D.: Preemptive RANSAC for live structure and motion estimation. Machine Vision and Applications 16(5), 321–329 (2005)
13. Pilz, F., Pugeault, N., Krüger, N.: Comparison of Point and Line Features and Their Combination for Rigid Body Motion Estimation. In: Cremers, D., Rosenhahn, B., Yuille, A.L., Schmidt, F.R. (eds.) Statistical and Geometrical Approaches to Visual Motion Analysis. LNCS, vol. 5604, pp. 280–304. Springer, Heidelberg (2009)
14. Portilla, J., Simoncelli, E.: A parametric texture model based on joint statistics of complex wavelet coefficients. International Journal of Computer Vision (IJCV) 40(1), 49–71 (2000)
15. Pugeault, N., Krüger, N.: Temporal accumulation of oriented visual features. Journal of Visual Communication and Image Representation 22(2), 153–163 (2011)
16. Pugeault, N., Wörgötter, F., Krüger, N.: Visual primitives: Local, condensed, semantically rich visual descriptors and their applications in robotics. International Journal of Humanoid Robotics 7(3), 379–405 (2010)

Person Re-identification by Descriptive and Discriminative Classification

Martin Hirzer[1], Csaba Beleznai[2], Peter M. Roth[1], and Horst Bischof[1]

[1] Institute for Computer Graphics and Vision
Graz University of Technology, Austria
{hirzer,pmroth,bischof}@icg.tugraz.at
[2] Austrian Institute of Technology, Austria
csaba.beleznai@ait.ac.at

Abstract. Person re-identification, i.e., recognizing a single person across spatially disjoint cameras, is an important task in visual surveillance. Existing approaches either try to find a suitable description of the appearance or learn a discriminative model. Since these different representational strategies capture a large extent of complementary information we propose to combine both approaches. First, given a specific query, we rank all samples according to a feature-based similarity, where appearance is modeled by a set of region covariance descriptors. Next, a discriminative model is learned using boosting for feature selection, which provides a more specific classifier. The proposed approach is demonstrated on two datasets, where we show that the combination of a generic descriptive statistical model and a discriminatively learned feature-based model attains considerably better results than the individual models alone. In addition, we give a comparison to the state-of-the-art on a publicly available benchmark dataset.

1 Introduction

Due to ceaseless advances in the research in semi-conductor, communications, and image sensors there is an increasing number of public areas that are subject to video surveillance. Thus, it becomes infeasible to analyze the ever growing amount of data – automatic systems are required. This especially applies for person re-identification, a central task in many surveillance scenarios, which can be described as recognizing an individual in different locations across a network of non-overlapping cameras. Besides of specific re-identification scenarios, e.g., tracking criminals over multiple cameras, typical tasks also include anonymous applications such as crowd analysis by identifying single instances. In general, this task has to be considered very challenging. Typical problems that have to be handled are extremely varying appearances of a person across the camera network (due to changing lighting conditions, different viewpoints, varying poses, etc.), people occluding each other, or a high number of very similar instances. Thus, motivated by the large number of practical applications and still unresolved problems there has been a considerable scientific interest within the last years.

For instance, Gheissari et al. [6] fit a triangulated graph to each individual to account for pose variations. However, the approach is only applicable for similar viewpoints. The same applies for the approach of Wang et al. [22], who segment an image of a

A. Heyden and F. Kahl (Eds.): SCIA 2011, LNCS 6688, pp. 91–102, 2011.

person into regions and capture their color spatial structure by a co-occurrence matrix. A more flexible approach was presented by Farenzena et al. in [4] exploiting perceptual principles relying on symmetry and asymmetry. They first run a segmentation step to obtain a person's silhouette and then accumulate the feature responses of color and texture features to a signature. Bird et al. [2] propose to segment the query image in equally spaced horizontal segments and extract the median HSL color of the foreground pixels of each of these segments.

In contrast, instead of designing specific features by hand, other methods aim to learn a suitable feature set or to directly generate a ranking model. Bak et al. [1] run a person detector and estimate a visual signature using Haar-like features that have been selected for each individual using AdaBoost. A similar but more sophisticated approach was presented by Gray and Tao [8]. They also select the most relevant features (color and texture) using AdaBoost but additionally estimate a likelihood ratio test for comparing corresponding features providing a similarity function. Lin et al. [13] and Schwartz et al. [18] propose to learn pairwise dissimilarities which can be applied for classification. Both approaches, however, require a training stage and labeled samples. Prosser et al. [16] formulate the person re-identification problem as a ranking problem. They introduce Ensemble RankSVM, which allows to learn a subspace where the potential true match gets the highest rank.

To further improve the classification results additional cues can be exploited. Makris et al. [14] and Rahimi et al. [17] simplify the problem by temporal reasoning on the spatial layout of the observed environment. Javed et al. [10] learn transitions between cameras to cope with problems such as illumination changes. Zheng et al. [23] enrich the description of persons by contextual visual information coming from the surrounding people.

These approaches can mainly be subdivided in two groups: (a) methods which employ a representation of descriptive statistics of the human appearance (using hand crafted features) [22,6,4,17] and (b) approaches that are based on discriminative learning [8,13,18,16,3]. Thus, to take advantage of these complementary information cues, we apply the two strategies in parallel. First, we estimate a generic covariance-based description and calculate a similarity measure yielding a rank model. For examples that can not be classified in this way we compute a more specific discriminative model using boosting for feature selection. Moreover, we introduce a new covariance-based descriptor and adopt covariance features for the usage within a boosting framework. In the experimental results, we demonstrate the benefits of the proposed approach on two different datasets. In particular, we show that using a descriptive and discriminative model in parallel clearly improves the person re-identification capability. Additionally, we give a comparison to the state-of-the-art showing competitive results.

2 Person Re-identification System

Given two camera views observing different locations of a scene, the goal of person re-identification is to select a certain person in one view and to recognize it in the other view. In the work on hand, we assume that we have already detected the persons in both views and we will refer the image of the selected person to as the *probe image* and

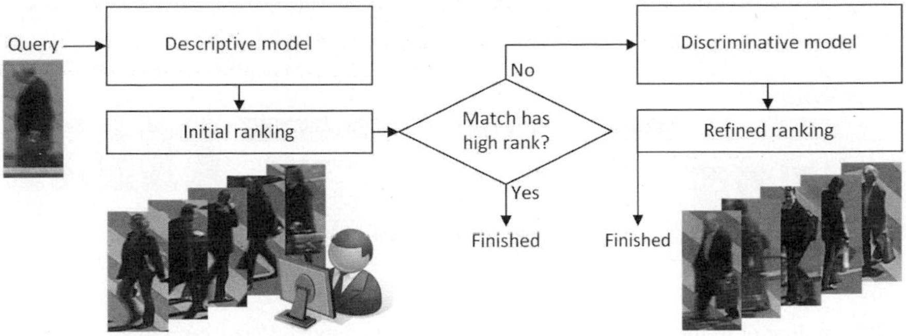

Fig. 1. Overview of the proposed system. After applying a descriptive model to obtain an initial ranking, a discriminative model can be used to refine the result.

the images searched through the *gallery images* [7]. In particular, our system, which is illustrated in Figure 1, consists of a descriptive person model (see Section 3) and a discriminative person model (see Section 4), which are run consecutively.

For each probe image we first apply the descriptive person model to get an initial ranking of all gallery images. The first 50 images of this ranking are shown to a human operator, who then decides whether the searched person has been found or not. If not, we run the second stage, i.e., learn and evaluate the discriminative person model and rank the samples according to their confidence values. Since this model captures different aspects of an individual, focusing on details best separating it from others, there is a good chance that it can improve the ranking.

The descriptive model is based on a hand designed feature representation, hence, it can be estimated for any given single image. The discriminative model, however, is learned for each instance requiring positive and negative training data. Since we focus on person re-identification in a surveillance scenario, where multiple images of a person (multi-shot scenario) are available, we can use these images as training samples. If just one probe image is available (single-shot scenario), we can generate virtual samples using geometrical transformations and displacements. Hence, obtaining positive training samples is not much of a problem.

Though, for the negative training samples a more sophisticated sampling mechanism is required. For this purpose we use our descriptive model as starting point. As described before, applying this model already generates an initial ranked list of person images. Thus, we sample the negative images from the end of the list. Assuming that the descriptive person model provides a "good" ranking those images should be most dissimilar to the searched person. The overall principle is illustrated in Figure 2.

3 Descriptive Person Model

In the first stage of our person re-identification system we generate a descriptive statistical model which encodes visual appearance information. Considering the given task, the employed representation must meet requirements of specificity, invariance and computational efficiency. It implies that on the one hand the visual description must encompass

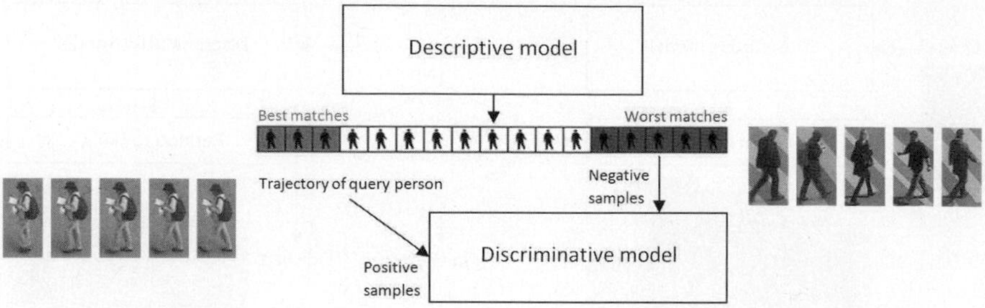

Fig. 2. Sampling of training images for the discriminative model. Positive samples are obtained from the trajectory of the query person, negative samples are drawn from the worst matches of the initial ranking provided by the descriptive model.

discriminating visual information. On the other hand it must remain mostly unaffected in presence of photometric, view and pose changes. Moreover, for practical applicability the representation should be computed and matched rapidly at small memory requirements.

For our purpose we employ the region covariance descriptor of Tuzel et al. [20], which meets these criteria quite well. The descriptor is capable to combine multiple complementary cues, easy to compute and generates a compact signature. Since the descriptor aggregates several visual features, structural information of human visual appearance – such as the brightness relationship between upper and lower body halves – is represented only to a limited extent. In order to enhance the structural specificity of the representation, we use a set of covariance descriptors computed from multiple horizontal stripes covering the area of an image patch. This strategy is similar to the multiple region scheme used by [20] and to the principal axis histogram signature employed by [9].

For a given bounding box R with dimensions $W \times H$ a set of region covariance descriptors is computed in the following manner: The image within the bounding box $I_R(x, y)$ is used to compute a set of features, which represent intensity, color and texture. In order to capture spatial, color and gradient information, in our case the employed set of visual features comprises of

$$\{\mathbf{f}\} = \left[\mathbf{y}, \mathbf{L}, \mathbf{a}, \mathbf{b}, \left|\frac{\partial \mathbf{L}}{\partial \mathbf{x}}\right|, \left|\frac{\partial \mathbf{L}}{\partial \mathbf{y}}\right|\right], \tag{1}$$

i.e., the $\mathbf{y}$ pixel coordinate vector, the $\mathbf{L}$, $\mathbf{a}$, $\mathbf{b}$ color channels and the horizontal and vertical derivatives of the luminosity channel, respectively. The x-component of pixel coordinates is excluded from the feature set, thus allowing some invariance with respect to view variations when the person is seen from various sides.

The bounding box R is divided into N ($N = 7$ in our experiments) equally large horizontal stripes $\{S_l\}_{l=1..N}$ and within each stripe the covariance descriptor is computed as

$$C^l = \frac{1}{z-1} \sum_{k=1}^{z} (\mathbf{f}_k - \mu)(\mathbf{f}_k - \mu)^T, \tag{2}$$

where C^l denotes the covariance matrix computed over z feature values within the l-th stripe and μ represents the vector of mean values computed on the individual features of the feature set.

The obtained set of covariance matrices $\{C^l\}_{l=1..N}$ defines a compact descriptor which encodes the interdependence between individual features computed inside the region of interest. A coarse structural information is captured using the set of covariances from multiple horizontal regions and by the weak spatial dependence given by the only slightly specific variation within the y-coordinate feature.

Similarity computation between two human appearances is performed by estimating the distance between two covariance matrices [5] in pairwise manner by

$$\rho\left(C^l_i, C^l_j\right) = \sqrt{\sum_{k=1}^{d} \ln^2 \lambda_k \left(C^l_i, C^l_j\right)}, \tag{3}$$

where C^l_i and C^l_j are computed for two different images i and j, but using the same stripe element with index l. λ_k denotes the generalized eigenvalues of C^l_i and C^l_j, and d is the number of features within the employed feature set ($d = 6$ in our case).

The covariance-based distance between two human appearances is defined as

$$\bar{d}_{ij} = \frac{1}{N} \sum_{l=1}^{N} \rho\left(C^l_i, C^l_j\right), \tag{4}$$

where $\bar{d}_{ij}$ is the mean covariance distance measure obtained from N stripe-versus-stripe comparisons. When a specific probe image is used as query, the probe image is compared to all gallery images and a set of distances is obtained. This set of distances is used to generate a ranking for every image in the gallery with respect to the probe.

4 Discriminative Person Model

In the second stage of our system we apply a discriminative model, which is estimated by Boosting for Feature Selection [19, 21]. Thus, similar to [8, 1] the goal is to select the most discriminant features for a specific instance from an over-complete feature set. However, unlike these methods, our approach does not involve any labeling of training data by hand. Moreover, the goal is not to learn a similarity function between image pairs but similar to [16] to finally generate a ranking of all gallery images. In particular, we train a model for each probe image and evaluate it on all gallery images. Those are then sorted according to their confidence values: a higher confidence results in a higher rank.

4.1 Estimating Ranks by Boosting for Feature Selection

Given a training set of positive and negative samples $\mathcal{S} = \{(\mathbf{x}_1, y_1), ..., (\mathbf{x}_L, y_L)\}$, where $\mathbf{x}_l \in \mathbb{R}^m$ is a sample and $y_l \in \{-1, +1\}$ is the corresponding label, a set of possible features $\mathcal{F} = \{f_1, ..., f_M\}$, a learning algorithm $\mathcal{L}$, and a weight distribution

D, that is initialized uniformly by $D(l) = \frac{1}{L}$. Then, the main idea of boosting for feature selection is that each feature f_j corresponds to a single weak classifier h_j and that boosting selects an informative subset of N features. In each iteration n, $n = 1, ..., N$ all features $f_j, j = 1, \ldots, M$ are evaluated on all samples $(\mathbf{x}_l, y_l), l = 1, \ldots, L$ and hypotheses are generated by applying the learning algorithm $\mathcal{L}$ with respect to the weight distribution D over the training samples. The best hypothesis is selected and forms the weak classifier h_n. The weight distribution D is updated according to the error of the selected weak classifier.

The process is repeated until N features are selected, i.e., N weak classifiers are trained (N = 20 in our experiments). Finally, we estimate a confidence measure[1] C according to a weighted linear combination of all weak classifiers h_n:

$$C(x) = \sum_{n=1}^{N} \alpha_n h_n(x). \tag{5}$$

4.2 Features

Due to the popularity various different features, e.g., Haar-like [21], Edge Orientation Histograms [12], or boundary fragments [15] have been introduced for the application with boosting for feature selection. Such features mainly capture generic visual object properties and have shown excellent performance for object recognition/detection and tracking. However, for the re-identification task they are often not discriminative enough. In particular, as also discussed in Section 5.1, we found that the most important information queues are intensity changes between the upper and lower body of a person and color. Thus, for our application we use a combination of horizontally divided Haar features and covariance features. Moreover, to avoid that too much background information is modeled by the (local) features we prohibit features that are placed close to the image borders.

Since Haar features are well known in the context of boosting (e.g., [21]) in the following we focus on the discussion on the covariance features capturing the essential color information. As described in Section 3, covariance matrices, in general, provide an elegant way of integrating various different feature channels, in our case RGB color channels, into one compact representation. They capture the variance of these channels and the correlation between them. However, since the space of covariance matrices does not form a Euclidean space they cannot directly be used in a boosting framework. To overcome this limitation, we follow the approach described in [11], allowing to describe the covariance matrices in a Euclidean vector space. In particular, for the d-dimensional case a set of $2d + 1$ specific vectors $\mathbf{s}_i \in \mathbb{R}^d$, called *Sigma Points*, is constructed as follows:

$$\mathbf{s}_0 = \mu \qquad \mathbf{s}_i = \mu + \alpha(\sqrt{C})_i \qquad \mathbf{s}_{i+d} = \mu - \alpha(\sqrt{C})_i, \tag{6}$$

with $i = 1 \ldots d$, μ and C being the data's mean vector and covariance matrix respectively, and $(\sqrt{C})_i$ being the i-th column of the covariance matrix square root. The scalar α is a constant weighting for the elements in the covariance matrix and is set to $\alpha = \sqrt{2}$

[1] If required a strong classifier H can be estimated by $H(x) = sign\,(C(x))$.

for Gaussian data. The points $\mathbf{s}_i$ accurately capture the statistics of the original covariance matrix up to third order for Gaussian and up to second order for non-Gaussian data. The final feature representation is built by concatenation of all *Sigma Points* into one vector. Hence, *Sigma Points* provide a very powerful representation that is capable of integrating various different feature channels into one compact feature vector.

With this representation we are now able to efficiently capture local color information in our boosting algorithm. As for Haar features, we use a rectangular shaped region for extracting color information (RGB) from an image. All pixels within the covariance feature's region are used to calculate the mean vector μ, covariance matrix C and finally the *Sigma Points* representation. This enables us to capture very discriminative, local color features of a person (e.g., red bag), as opposed to the descriptive statistical model described in Section 3, which extracts color and gradient information from regular stripe regions laid over the person image. As weak learner h_j we apply a Bayesian decision criterion for the Haar features and a multidimensional nearest neighbor classifier for the *Sigma Points*. Haar and covariance features are illustrated in Figure 3.

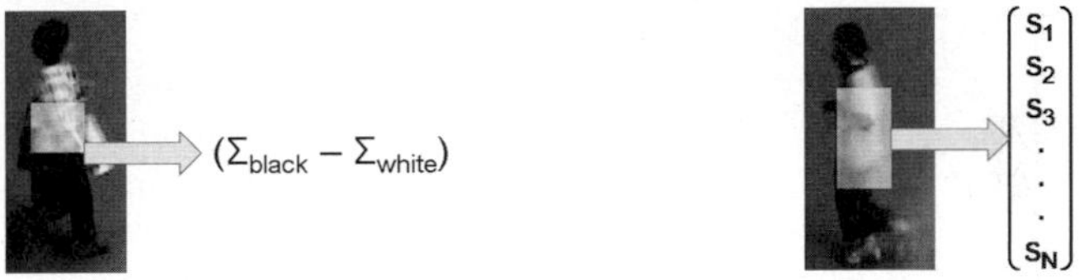

(a) (b)

Fig. 3. Applied features: (a) Haar features mainly capture intensity changes between the upper and lower body of a person, (b) covariance features extract local color information in form of vectors of *Sigma Points*

5 Experimental Results

We evaluated our approach on two datasets[2], the public VIPeR dataset [7] (single-shot scenario) and our own person re-identification dataset[3] (multi-shot scenario). Examples of both are shown in Figure 4. As performance measure we use Cumulative Matching Characteristic (CMC) curves [22], which represent the expectation of the true match being found within the first n ranks.

5.1 VIPeR Dataset

The VIPeR dataset consists of 632 person image pairs taken from two different camera views. Most of the example pairs contain a viewpoint change of about 90 degrees as well as significant changes in pose and illumination, making person re-identification very challenging. To compare our method to other approaches, we followed the evaluation

[2] Other benchmarks have been proposed (e.g., [4,1,16]), however, since either no annotations are available or the datasets are not uniquely defined, we did not used them for our experiments.

[3] Available at http://lrs.icg.tugraz.at/downloads.php

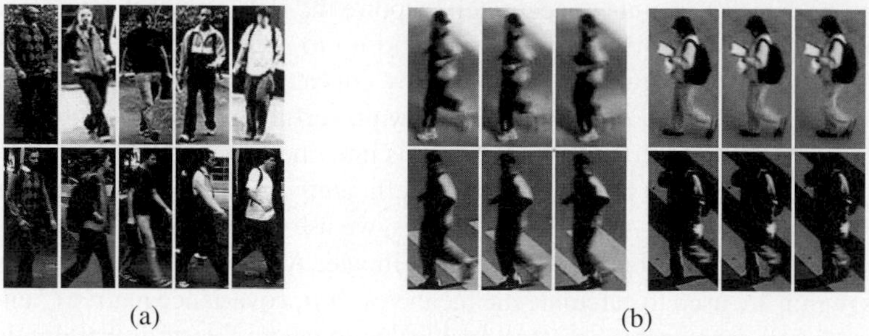

Fig. 4. Example image pairs from the VIPeR dataset (a) and example trajectory images from our multi-frame dataset (b). Upper and lower row correspond to different camera views.

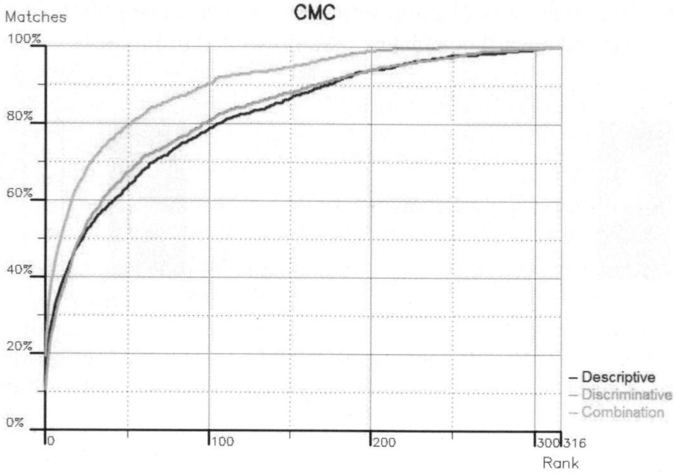

Fig. 5. CMC curves of our approach on the VIPeR dataset. The blue curve shows the descriptive and the green curve shows the discriminative person model. The combination of both models is depicted in cyan color.

procedure described in [8, 4]. The authors split the set of 632 image pairs randomly into two sets of 316 image pairs each, one for training and one for testing, and build the average over several runs. Since we do not need a training set, we evaluate our algorithm on a subset of 316 randomly selected image pairs and also average the results of several runs. Considering images from one camera as the probe set, and images from the other camera as the gallery set, we match each probe image with all images from the gallery set.

When applying our discriminative person model we need positive and negative training samples for the boosting step. In our scenario positive training samples are extracted from person trajectories, and negative training samples are drawn from the gallery images that received the lowest ranks in the initial, descriptive ranking step. However, the VIPeR dataset does not provide trajectories, just image pairs. Thus, we generate virtual

Table 1. Matching rates for ELF, SDALF, ERSVM and our algorithm on the VIPeR dataset

Rank	ELF	SDALF	ERSVM	Our Approach
1	12%	20%	13%	19%
10	43%	50%	50%	52%
25	66%	70%	71%	69%
50	81%	85%	85%	80%

positive training images from the probe image by randomly applying slight geometric distortions and smoothing. Figure 5 and Table 1 show the average results of our approach on the VIPeR dataset of 5 runs on randomly selected subsets of 316 image pairs.

As one can see, the descriptive and discriminative person model have similar performance. However, since they describe different aspects of a person, taking into account both models yields a significant improvement. This is shown by a third curve that is generated using the model returning the higher match rank for each probe image, simulating the human operator decision described in Section 2. Moreover, in Table 1 we compare the performance of our approach on the range relevant for our approach, i.e., the first 50 ranks, to state-of-the-art methods [8, 4, 16]. As can be seen we obtain competitive results, especially, for rank 1. Even though in contrast to [8, 16] we do not need any (hand) labeling of data and unlike [4] we do not use a foreground-background segmentation. However, we expect that using a segmentation step will improve our results notably, especially in cases of great pose variations, e.g., varying leg postures.

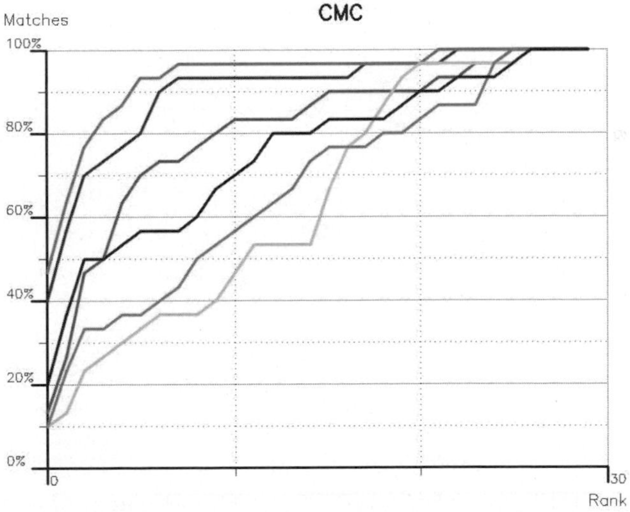

Fig. 6. Different feature types evaluated on the first 30 image pairs of the VIPeR dataset: Haar (red), HOG (green), LBP (cyan), Covariance (blue), Haar + Covariance (magenta), combination of all types (black)

As discussed in Section 4, we apply only Haar and covariance features for our re-identification task. In the following, we illustrate that exactly these features are best suited for our task by evaluating different features on the first 30 image pairs of the VIPeR dataset: Haar-like, histograms of oriented gradients (HOGs), local binary patterns (LBPs), covariance features using RGB channels, as well as their combinations. The obtained results in form of CMC curves are depicted in Figure 6. It can clearly be seen that color (captured by covariance features) is the strongest cue, followed by Haar-like features, which particularly capture intensity changes between the upper and lower body of a person. HOGs and LBPs, on the other hand, perform rather poorly, since they concentrate on finer structures that are often not visible in the gallery image due to viewpoint changes. In fact, the best performance was achieved using a combination of Haar-like and covariance features.

5.2 Multi-shot Dataset

Since the intended use case for the proposed method was to apply person re-identification on surveillance data, we generated a multi-shot dataset. It consists of images extracted from multiple person trajectories recorded from two different static surveillance cameras. Images from these cameras contain a viewpoint change and a stark difference in illumination, background and camera characteristics (e.g., green cast). Since images are extracted from trajectories, several different poses per person are available in each camera. We have recorded 475 person trajectories from one camera and 753 from the other one, with 245 persons appearing in both views. Thus, each of the 245 persons in the probe set is searched in a gallery set of 753 individuals. Each trajectory consists of approximately 100 to 150 images, depending on the walking speed of an individual. For the gallery set we equidistantly extracted 5 images per trajectory. The maximum rank returned by these 5 images defines the rank of a person.

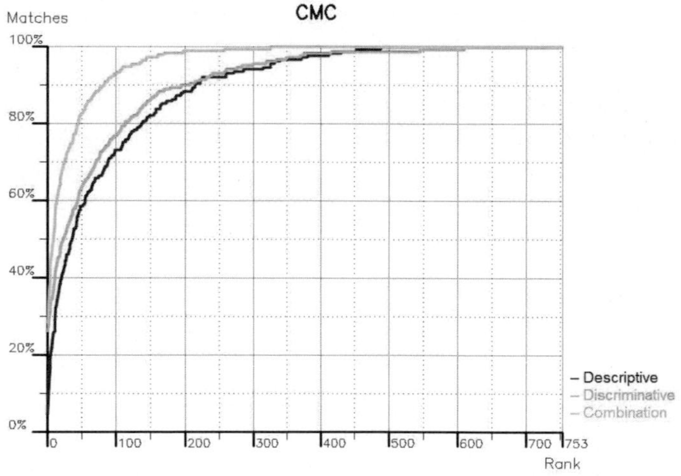

Fig. 7. CMC curves of the proposed algorithm on our multi-frame dataset. The blue curve shows the descriptive and the green curve shows the discriminative person model. The combination of both models is depicted in cyan color.

On this dataset, positive samples for the boosting step can easily be extracted from the trajectory of the searched person. To get some additional variation into the positive training set, we also generate a few virtual samples, as for the VIPeR dataset. To acquire negative training samples we again use the ranked list of gallery images provided by our descriptive model. For the features used in the boosting step we use the same setup as for the VIPeR dataset.

Figure 7 shows the average results of our approach on this dataset after 3 runs. As shown by the curves, in contrast to the VIPeR image pairs, the discriminative model slightly outperforms the descriptive model. This can be explained by greater variability captured if positive training samples are extracted from a whole trajectory. Thus, an overfitting to the small number of positive samples can be prevented. Finally, like on the VIPeR dataset, taking into account descriptive and discriminative information leads to superior performance.

6 Conclusion

Typical approaches for person re-identification either estimate a visual signature describing the appearance of a query sample or train a discriminative model. In this paper we took advantage of both approaches and introduced a system combining descriptive and discriminative models. We first run an appearance-based matcher using a covariance description, which has shown to be a considerable trade-off between speed and accuracy. For examples where this representation exhibits low specificity in a second stage a discriminative model is estimated by boosting for feature selection. In particular, we found that two types of features describing intensity transitions and color information (i.e., Haar features and *Sigma Points*) are best suited for the given task. The experimental results demonstrated that compared to the single cues using the proposed approach significatly better results can be obtained. In addition, we gave a comparison to state-of-the-art methods on a publicly available dataset. Even though avoiding any labeling and having only a limited amount of training data we can report competitive results.

Acknowledgments. This work has been supported by Siemens AG Österreich, Corporate Technology (CT T CEE), Austria, and the project SECRET (821690) under the Austrian Security Research Programme KIRAS.

References

1. Bak, S., Corvee, E., Brémond, F., Thonnat, M.: Person re-idendification using Haar-based and DCD-based signature. In: Workshop on Activity Monitoring by Multi-Camera Surveillance Systems (2010)
2. Bird, N.D., Masoud, O., Papanikolopoulos, N.P., Isaacs, A.: Detection of loitering individuals in public transportation areas. IEEE Trans. Intelligent Transportation Systems 6(2), 167–177 (2005)
3. Chapelle, O., Keerthi, S.S.: Efficient algorithms for ranking with SVMs. Information Retrieval 13(3), 201–215 (2010)

4. Farenzena, M., Bazzani, L., Perina, A., Murino, V., Cristani, M.: Person re-identification by symmetry-driven accumulation of local features. In: Proc. CVPR(2010)
5. Förstner, W., Moonen, B.: A metric for covariance matrices. Technical report, Department of Geodesy and Geoinformatics, Stuttgart University (1999)
6. Gheissari, N., Sebastian, T.B., Hartley, R.: Person reidentification using spatiotemporal appearance. In: Proc. CVPR (2006)
7. Gray, D., Brennan, S., Tao, H.: Evaluating appearance models for recognition, reacquisition, and tracking. In: Proc. PETS (2007)
8. Gray, D., Tao, H.: Viewpoint invariant pedestrian recognition with an ensemble of localized features. In: Forsyth, D., Torr, P., Zisserman, A. (eds.) ECCV 2008, Part I. LNCS, vol. 5302, pp. 262–275. Springer, Heidelberg (2008)
9. Hu, M., Lou, J., Hu, W., Tan, T.: Multicamera correspondence based on principal axis of human body. In: Proc. ICIP (2004)
10. Javed, O., Shafique, K., Shah, M.: Appearance modeling for tracking in multiple non-overlapping cameras. In: Proc. CVPR (2005)
11. Kluckner, S., Mauthner, T., Roth, P.M., Bischof, H.: Semantic classification in aerial imagery by integrating appearance and height information. In: Zha, H., Taniguchi, R.-i., Maybank, S. (eds.) ACCV 2009. LNCS, vol. 5995, pp. 477–488. Springer, Heidelberg (2010)
12. Levi, K., Weiss, Y.: Learning object detection from a small number of examples: The importance of good features. In: Proc. CVPR (2004)
13. Lin, Z., Davis, L.S.: Learning pairwise dissimilarity profiles for appearance recognition in visual surveillance. In: Advances Int'l Visual Computing Symposium (2008)
14. Makris, D., Ellis, T., Black, J.: Bridging the gaps between cameras. In: Proc. CVPR (2004)
15. Opelt, A., Axel Pinz, A.Z.: A boundary-fragment-model for object detection. In: Leonardis, A., Bischof, H., Pinz, A. (eds.) ECCV 2006. LNCS, vol. 3952, pp. 575–588. Springer, Heidelberg (2006)
16. Prosser, B., Zheng, W.-S., Gong, S., Xiang, T.: Person re-identification by support vector ranking. In: Proc. BMVC (2010)
17. Rahimi, A., Dunagan, B., Darrell, T.: Simultaneous calibration and tracking with a network of non-overlapping sensors. In: Proc. CVPR (2004)
18. Schwartz, W.R., Davis, L.S.: Learning discriminative appearance-based models using partial least squares. In: Proc. Brazilian Symposium on Computer Graphics and Image Processing (2009)
19. Tieu, K., Viola, P.: Boosting image retrieval. In: Proc. CVPR (2000)
20. Tuzel, O., Porikli, F., Meer, P.: Region covariance: A fast descriptor for detection and classification. In: Leonardis, A., Bischof, H., Pinz, A. (eds.) ECCV 2006. LNCS, vol. 3952, pp. 589–600. Springer, Heidelberg (2006)
21. Viola, P., Jones, M.J.: Rapid object detection using a boosted cascade of simple features. In: Proc. CVPR (2001)
22. Wang, X., Doretto, G., Sebastian, T.B., Rittscher, J., Tu, P.H.: Shape and appearance context modeling. In: Proc. ICCV (2007)
23. Zheng, W.S., Gong, S., Xiang, T.: Associating groups of people. In: Proc. BMVC (2009)

On Inferring Image Label Information Using Rank Minimization for Supervised Concept Embedding

Dmitriy Bespalov[1], Anders Lindbjerg Dahl[2], Bing Bai[3], and Ali Shokoufandeh[1]

[1] Department of Computer Science, Drexel University
[2] DTU Informatics, Technical University of Denmark
[3] NEC Labs America

Abstract. Concept-based representation — combined with some classifier (e.g., support vector machine) or regression analysis (e.g., linear regression) — induces a popular approach among image processing community, used to infer image labels. We propose a supervised learning procedure to obtain an embedding to a latent concept space with the pre-defined inner product. This learning procedure uses rank minimization of the sought inner product matrix, defined in the original concept space, to find an embedding to a new low dimensional space. The empirical evidence show that the proposed supervised learning method can be used in combination with another computational image embedding procedure, such as bag-of-features method, to significantly improve accuracy of label inference, while producing embedding of low complexity.

1 Introduction

Inferring label information from image data has a wide range of applications in computer vision and image processing. A common approach to tackle this problem is to first build a descriptor for every image, for instance bag-of-features (BOF) histogram, followed by the label inference formulated as classification or regression analysis problem. Computationally, this process is congruent to embedding of every image to multi-dimensional vector space. The vector space defined by the embedding is sometimes referred to as the *concept space*, and the embedding itself is said to give rise to *concept-based representation* of the data.

Concept-based representation is a popular approach in information retrieval community. The representation describes an item — e.g., text document, image, etc — using sparse vectors of concepts. Construction of the item's concept-based representation can be viewed as category labeling procedure, and corresponding concept set as collection of categories. Furthermore, weights associated with every concept relates information content of the item with the concept's category. Intuitively, two related items should receive similar category labels and formally, relatedness between two items is computed with cosine similarity (i.e., cosine of the angle between two vectors) in the concept space. Naturally, it may be desirable to control concept weights to suit specific category labeling task. We refer to this process as computing *context* for concept-based representation. The context controls which concepts are promoted during construction of the item's concept-based representation.

A. Heyden and F. Kahl (Eds.): SCIA 2011, LNCS 6688, pp. 103–113, 2011.

In this paper, we propose supervised learning procedure that finds an embedding to concept space with the inner product operator tuned for the specific label inference task. Our procedure can be used in conjunction with another label inference method to improve its accuracy. Among all possible concept spaces that can describe a training set, the proposed method estimates the one of lowest dimensionality. The labels from the training data are used to construct "ground truth" similarity matrix, which in turn will be used to compute the inner product operator that defines the embedding. Our method requires concept-based representation for the input data. Hence, it can be applied to any popular unsupervised image embedding procedure used for label inference. The proposed supervised learning framework is applied to the concept space obtained with a variant of unsupervised embedding, the so-called bag-of-features representation. We show that significant improvements in accuracy of label inference is achieved over the original embedding, when supervised learning is used. In addition, the dimensionality of the new concept space is much lower than the original.

Classical examples of linear concept space embedding include Singular Value Decomposition (SVD) based methods, Principal Component Analysis (PCA) [13] and Latent Semantic Indexing (LSI) [6]. LSI finds orthogonal loading vectors that minimizes the reconstruction error of the matrix of interest. These methods have been very successful in pattern recognition and information retrieval. In recent years, different criteria or constraints have been proposed to address specific needs. For instance, Independent Component Analysis (ICA) enforces statistical independence of loading vectors, and sparse coding (SC) promotes sparse components. These methods are unsupervised and consequently independent of the classification task. This can result in unnecessary information loss in the feature extraction stage. Therefore, a large effort has been put into generating the loading vectors directly from the targeted task, using supervised learning. A well known example is supervised metric distance learning [16]. Recently, applications of such methods were reported on large scale problems like information retrieval [1] and image annotations [17]. These supervised methods usually achieve better performance when training labels are available.

A common problem to concept-based representation is selecting the dimensionality of the concept space (i.e., the correct number of concepts). The dimensionality can affect performance of computational tasks in that concept space. Hence, it is usually desirable to find a concept space of low dimensionality. Most methods that achieve this require expensive validation or experience, which might not be available. Components can be ranked in methods like PCA or LSI, but this ranking is not necessarily optimal for the targeted task. Rank Minimization (RM) [10] on the other hand, when combined with the optimization for the supervised embedding, can estimate the optimal dimensionality for the specific label inference task.

In this paper we use supervised learning with RM to obtain concept space embedding tuned for the specific label inference task. We show that our method can significantly improve accuracy of a label inference procedure that uses concept-based representation of images. We experiment with several label inference tasks relating images with meat spoilage, defined on a set of hyper-spectral images of minced meat. The improved accuracy is demonstrated on meat spoilage measured as bacterial count (regression analysis) and sensor panel assessment (classification). In addition only few features are selected, which is highly relevant for interpretation of the obtained result.

2 Related Work

Using embedding into concept spaces has a long history in information retrieval. The first and perhaps most well-known method is Latent Semantic Indexing (LSI) [6]. LSI applies SVD on term-document matrix, and simultaneously computes loading and document embedding vectors. Unseen documents can be represented in the concept space by projecting to the loading factors. LSI create an index structure for the documents using concepts instead of "terms", thus can match documents with "synonyms", which was absent in term-based indexing models. LSI is considered the pioneering work that inspired methods such as probabilistic LSI (pLSI) [11] and Latent Dirichlet Allocation (LDA) in a probabilistic framework [2]. There are also alternative methods for generating concepts directly from labeled data. Such approaches have been applied to conceptual embedding and learning in a variety of information retrieval tasks such as link prediction, cross-lingual retrieval, and image annotations [1,17]. Despite their success these methods suffer from lack of clear strategy for setting the dimensionality of embedding space.

Concept space embedding has also been successfully used in pattern recognition: e.g., simple clustering approach to obtain BOF [5,15] for images or video. Compared to raw feature matching used in early work [12,14], the BOF represents an image as a histogram of "visual words", giving rise to image embedding to a vector space where retrieval or classification can take place.

Furthermore, observe that RM is a generalization of sparse representation for matrices. Various pursuit methods for minimizing the L_0 norm attain remarkable results within problems such as image denoising, compression, inpainting and upscaling [4,9]. In addition, RM methods have found a number of successful applications for problems such as visual tracking [8] and video inpainting [7].

3 Method

Assume, we are given a set of Q training items $d_i \in \mathbb{R}^M, i \in [1, Q]$ arranged in columns of matrix $D \in \mathbb{R}^{M\times Q}$. Each element in d_i can be a raw feature or a concept, which can be viewed as an extracted feature. Let $\tilde{S} \in \mathbb{R}^{Q\times Q}$ denote the "Ground-truth Similarity matrix (GSM)" of D. That is, $\tilde{S}_{i,j}$ is assigned with "ground truth" similarity for the corresponding items d_i and d_j. The GSM can be generated in different ways from labeled data, or from unsupervised learning, depending on the task of interest. For example, in classification tasks, we can have

$$\tilde{S}_{i,j} = \begin{cases} 1 & \text{items } i \text{ and } j \text{ in same category,} \\ -1 & \text{otherwise.} \end{cases}$$

In inferring continuous measurement values, we can have element

$$\tilde{S}_{ij} = 1 - 2|c_i - c_j|/R,$$

where c_i and c_j are measurement values for items i and j, respectively; $R = r_1 - r_2$ and r_1 and r_2 are maximum and minimum values of the measurement.

We then define "Contextualized Similarity Matrix"(CSM) $S = D^\top W D$, where W is what we call "Context Matrix". Every element $S_{ij} = d_i^\top W d_j$ describes the "Contextualized Similarity" between sample d_i and d_j. The formulation of contextualized similarity was used in [1] for the problem of text retrieval. Intuitively speaking, the element W_{ij} models the relevance of the i-th element of d_1 and j-th element of d_2.

Note that the CSM S is not necessarily $D^T D$, in which $W = I$ and no learning is required.

In this paper, we try to find the optimal context matrix W that minimizes the reconstruction error: $\|S - \tilde{S}\|$. From a supervised learning point of view, the W will catch the essential information that best describes our target task.

We observe that W should be a symmetric matrix, so the similarity within the context maintains the commutative property. Moreover, W will be diagonally dominant matrix, since each item should be ranked most similar to itself. As a result, we obtain that W is a positive semi-definite matrix, so it defines an inner product in concept space. In addition, W gives rise to new concept space embedding. Indeed, since W is positive semi-definite, we obtain $W = P^T P$ where $P \in \mathbb{R}^{r \times M}$ and $r = \text{rank}(W)$. Matrix P transforms any item $d \in \mathbb{R}^M$ defined in the original concept space, to the new concept space $Pd \in \mathbb{R}^r$. Among all possible solutions W to the norm minimization, selecting the one with minimum rank, describes the new concept space with the least number of concepts. Clearly, if we minimize the rank of W so that $r < M$, we also obtain a lower-dimensional embedding of the original concept space. It should also be noted that rank minimization can be considered a generalization of vector sparsity for matrices [10]. Indeed, minimizing a rank of a diagonal matrix is equivalent to minimizing number of non-zero elements of the diagonal vector.

The problem of *learning minimum rank context embedding* W for the given set of training items D can be formulated as optimization problem (1):

$$\begin{aligned} &\min_W \|D^T W D - \tilde{S}\| + \gamma \,\text{rank}(W) \\ &s.t. \quad W \succeq 0. \end{aligned} \tag{1}$$

Here, γ is regularization parameter. In general, optimizations with rank(.) can not be solved directly. However, Fazel *et al.* [10] showed that approximate solution to (1) can be obtained by replacing rank(W) objective by its smooth surrogate function $\log\det(W + \delta I)$. This results in the following iterative method for approximating rank(W):

$$W_{k+1} = \underset{W \in \mathcal{C}}{\text{argmin}} \,\text{Trace}(W_k + \delta I)^{-1} W \tag{2}$$

where $\mathcal{C}$ is a set of optimization constraints from (1). Computing each iteration of W_{k+1} requires solving a semi-definite program (SDP), and its initial estimate W_0 can be obtained with another SDP: e.g., replacing rank(W) objective with Trace(W) (the so-called trace heuristic). Empirical evidence in [10] suggests that $\log\det$ heuristic produces better approximations of rank(W) (i.e., lower rank solutions can be found) than trace heuristic. Our procedure, detailed in Algorithm 1, uses $\|D^T W D - \tilde{S}\|$ objective to find W_0 followed by few iterations of (2). The value for parameter γ was empirically chosen to ensure the rank is not optimized at the expense of the norm $\|D^T WD - \tilde{S}\|$ minimization. Parameter β ensures the low rank solution W results in the norm value very close to the minimum.

Algorithm 1. Minimum Rank Context Embedding

Input: $\{d_i\}$, set of training items
$D \in \mathbb{R}^{M \times Q}$, concept based representation for d_i arranged in columns

Output: P, minimum rank embedding for learned context W

$\gamma = 0.0001$
$\beta = 1 + 10^{-6}$
$\tilde{S} = \text{getGSM}(\{d_i\})$ # build Ground-truth Similarity Matrix
$W_0 = \arg\min_{W \in \mathcal{C}} \|D^T WD - \tilde{S}\|$ # Initialize W_0 (solve SDP)
$\kappa = \|D^T W_0 D - \tilde{S}\|$
$\mathcal{C} = \left\{ \begin{array}{l} W \succeq 0 \\ \|D^T WD - \tilde{S}\| \leq \beta\kappa \end{array} \right\}$ # create set of constraints
for $k = 1$ to 3 **do**
  $W_k = \arg\min_{W \in \mathcal{C}} \left[\|D^T WD - \tilde{S}\| + \gamma \, \text{Trace}(W_{k-1} + \delta I)^{-1} W \right]$
end for # log det approx. (solve 3 SDPs)
decompose $W_3 = P^T P$
return P

Due to high complexity of SDP solvers, the size of problems that can be handled is very limited. On the other hand, a large number of concepts Q is needed to describe even moderately sized datasets (e.g., tens to hundreds of thousands). Hence, handling optimizations of that size by Algorithm 1 is impractical. We employ Latent Semantic Indexing [6] (LSI), a well known dimensionality reduction technique that is widely used in information retrieval community for efficient document indexing and retrieval. For the given set of training items $\{d_i\}$ and their concept-based descriptors arranged in columns of D, SVD of $D = U\Sigma V^T$ is computed using SlepC library[1]. Matrix $\Sigma_l^{-1} U^T$ forms an embedding for every concept-based item descriptor in l-dimensional space, where Σ_l is a matrix formed with l most significant singular values of D. Computing $\hat{D} = \Sigma_l^{-1} U^T D$ yields low dimensional (e.g., $15 \leq l \leq 100$) representation of training items, and matrix $\hat{D}$ is passed to Algorithm 1 for learning minimum rank context embedding.

Alternatively, one may choose to use first-order method described in [18] and [19] to approximate optimization (1) using convex relaxation. Each iteration of their method requires only a SVD, that can handle large matrices (on the order of hundreds of million non-zero entries) using efficient libraries such as Slepc. Using such an approximation to (1) in Algorithm 1 will enable learning context embedding for larger datasets described in higher dimensional concept spaces. As a result, no dimensionality reduction such as LSI or PCA will be required.

[1] http://www.grycap.upv.es/slepc/

The primary objective of this work was to empirically validate the viability of the proposed framework, described in Algorithm 1, to improve the accuracy of label inference and reduce dimensionality of concept space. The results of our empirical validations are presented in Section 4. Having obtained initial validation for the minimum rank context embedding framework, the most prominent direction of our future work is re-formulating optimization (1) so a first order approximation method can be used instead of SDP.

4 Experiments

Non-destructive methods for food inspection is important in industrial manufacturing, and image processing can be one way of measuring such quality parameters. We present results for label inference experiments on multi-spectral images of minced meat with ground truth labels for storage degradation. The rest of this section is organized as follows. Section 4.1 describes dataset of meat images used in our empirical validations. Algorithm 1 assumes the input data is represented in concept space. Hence, Section 4.2 presents a variant of popular BOF-based image representation used to embed images to a concept space. Finally, results of label inference experiments performed in both concept spaces, can be found in Section 4.3.

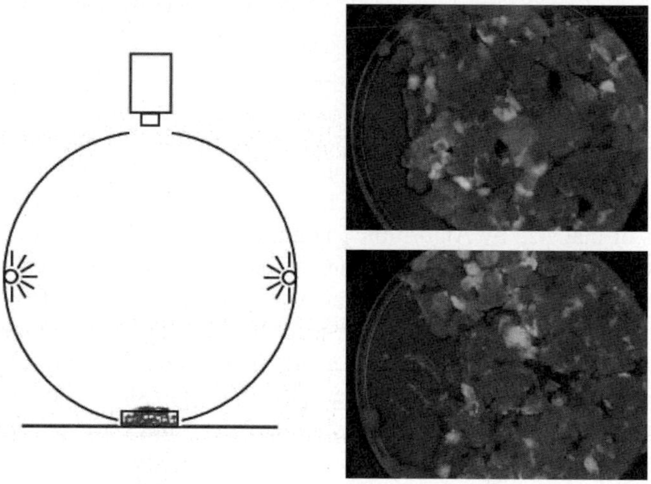

(a) (b)

Fig. 1. Principle sketch of the VideometerLab integrating sphere (a), with camera at the top, LED's along the equatorial rim, and a petri dish at the bottom. The wavelengths are 405, 435, 450, 470, 505, 525, 570, 590, 630, 645, 660, 700, 850, 870, 890, 910, 940 and 970 nm. Image examples in a petri dish (b). Top is a fresh meat sample and bottom is a sample stored for 67 hours at 20°C. Note the black spots of bacteria growth on the bottom sample. Color images are made from three spectral band (R – 630nm, G – 525nm, and B – 450nm).

4.1 Data

Our multi-spectral images are acquired from device called VideometerLab[2], which employs wavelength specific LED illumination placed in an integrating sphere, see Figure 1. Hereby the meat sample is illuminated by narrow spectral bands of diffuse light spanning the spectrum at 18 wavelengths from 405 – 970 nm. An image is acquired from each spectral band using a normal CCD camera. The resolution of the sample images is 1280 × 960 pixels. The minced meat samples have been stored at different temperature and under different package conditions, and the spoilage has been assessed with six bacteria count methods and a sensory panel assessment into three categories – *fresh* (F), *semi-fresh* (SF), and *spoiled* (S). Figure 1 shows an example of the image data, and Table 1 gives an overview of the measured parameters.

Table 1. Data parameters. Bacteria is measured by blending the meat sample and placing it on an agar medium and counting the number of bacteria colonies after an incubation period.

Storage				
AIR (normal atmosphere)		MAP (modified atmosphere)		
Temperature				
0°C	5°C	10°C	15°C	20°C
Storage time				
0 – 590 hours				
Incubation methods for bacteria count				
PCA (Plate Count Agar – 30°C for 48 hours)				
PAB (Pseudomonas Agar Base – 30°C for 48 - 72 hours)				
STAA (Streptomycin Thallous Acetate-Actidione Agar – 25°C for 72 hours)				
RBC (Rose Bengal Chloramphenicol Agar – 25°C for 72 hours)				
VRBGA (Violet Red Bile Glucose Agar – 37°C for 18 - 24 hours)				
MRS (Man-Rogosa-Sharp medium – 30°C for 48 hours)				
Acidity measurement				
pH				
Sensory panel				
F – fresh		*SF* – semi-fresh		*S* – spoiled

4.2 Explicit Unsupervised Feature Extraction

The proposed *concept-based representation for images* treats each image as a collection of *terms;* i.e., pre-defined descriptors for extracted image features. Given a set of images, we construct their concept-based representation as follows. First, a subset of images is randomly selected and all of their terms are recorded as *concepts*. Then, the remaining images are interpreted in terms of these concepts. Every term associated with an image votes for k nearest concepts that are identified using approximate nearest neighbor data structure. A histogram bin, associated with every concept, accumulates

[2] http://www.videometer.com/

weights received from each term. The weight $\chi(t,q)$ between term t and concept q is computed using

$$\chi(t,q) = \begin{cases} 1 - \|t-q\| & \text{when } \|t-q\| \leq 1 \\ 0 & \text{otherwise} \end{cases},$$

where $\|t - q\|$ is Euclidean distance between term t and concept q. Once all terms are processed, histogram bins are normalized to form concept-based descriptor for the image. Formal overview of this procedure is presented in Algorithm 2.

Algorithm 2. Concept-based Image Interpretor

Input: $q_i \in \mathbb{Q}$, concepts terms
$t_j \in \mathbb{I}$, image terms
k, nearest neighbor parameter

Output: d, concept-based representation of image $\mathbb{I}$

```
d = 0
for all t_j ∈ I do
    {q_{n_i}} = kNN(Q, t_j, k)                 # select k closest concepts q_{n_i} for term t_j
    for all {q_{n_i}} do
        d[q_{n_i}] = d[q_{n_i}] + χ(t_j, q_{n_i})   # accumulate weight for concept q_{n_i}
    end for
end for
d = d/||d||                                    # normalize concept-based image descriptor
return d
```

Note that the aforementioned method is a variant of well-known bag-of-features representation. However, it does not perform any clustering or other feature quantization when concepts are created. In the spirit of recent empirical evidence presented by Boiman *et al.* [3], we decided against feature quantization.

Images of minced meat samples contain intensities in 18 spectral bands. Image features that are used as terms in the proposed concept-based representation are defined as follows. The proposed image feature descriptor combines histograms of intensity changes in neighboring spectral bands. Each feature descriptor is constructed for a rectangular image window. For every band b_i, we compute the difference of intensity values with the two neighboring bands b_{i-1} and b_{i+1}. Then, each pixel in band b_i is characterized with the angle formed by the two corresponding changes in intensities. A normalized orientation histogram is computed for each of the 16 bands (two extrema bands are not used), and the orientation histograms are concatenated to form a feature descriptor for the rectangular window. We use 9 orientation bins, which results in $9 \times 16 = 144$ dimensional feature descriptors. Image features are computed for 17×17 pixel windows, sampled every 11 pixels.

We extract image features for regions that depict minced meat only, while ignoring regions that depict plate or table. Mask for minced meat region is computed for every sample image. The mask is constructed by training a foreground-background classifier from one hand-labeled image. From the training image a random subset of pixels was

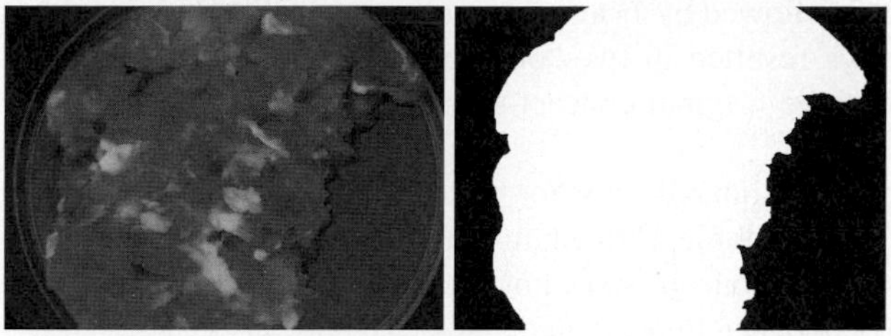

Fig. 2. Illustration of minced meat region mask

selected and clustered to 30 clusters using k-means algorithm. Each cluster was labeled foreground or background, depending on the majority of the labels of the pixels in the cluster. For an unknown image the nearest cluster center was found, using Euclidean distance, and the pixel was labeled with the label of the cluster. Finally, morphological opening and closing was applied to smooth the result, using 11 pixels squared structuring element. Only features residing entirely within the meat region are selected as terms for the sample. Please refer to Figure 2 for the illustration of a minced meat region mask.

We now present findings for label inference experiments using the aforementioned concept-based representation for meat samples. We measure accuracy of SVM classifier and linear regression, trained in concept space computed with Algorithm 2. We then use Algorithm 1 to obtain embedding to new concept space, and compare label inference performance in the new space with the original.

4.3 Label Inference Results

We collected a total of 141 pork meat samples. In all of the experiments, 10 meat samples were randomly selected as terms, while 30 samples were used for training, and the rest of the samples were used for testing. Every experiment was repeated 100 times and average prediction accuracy (or error) was recorded. We retained 15 most significant singular values in LSI procedure and used them in the construction of matrix $\hat{D}$, that is then passed to Algorithm 1. Inferring sensory panel scores is a classification problem, since only three labels (fresh, semi-fresh and spoiled) are available. However, predicting bacteria count values for the meat samples requires regression analysis, since the bacteria count values are continuous. We used LibSVM tool[3] for both classification and regression problems: SVM classifier with linear kernel and parameter $C = 32$, and linear regression with parameters $C = 32$ and $\epsilon = 0.1$ (used in loss function). The choice of linear kernel was motivated by the formulation of the proposed supervised embedding. We performed a limited set of classification experiments using RBF kernel, that showed no clear advantage of using non-linear kernel for the supervised embedding with RM.

For inference of sensory panel score, the average classification accuracy for unsupervised embedding (Algorithm 2) was 69.2%[4], while for supervised embedding with

[3] `http://www.csie.ntu.edu.tw/~cjlin/libsvm/`

[4] The best accuracy using RBF kernel ($C = 2.0, \gamma = 0.5$) was 71.3%. The parameters were estimated for the training data using LibSVM's grid-search tool.

RM (Algorithm 2 followed by 1) average accuracy was 73.6%[5]. In addition, supervised embedding always resulted in two- or three- dimensional concept spaces, while the dimensionality of the original concept space obtained with unsupervised BOF-based embedding was 15.

The average mean squared error for predicting six various bacteria count measurements can be found in Table 2. In addition to significant improvement in accuracy, the dimensionality of the concept space, obtained with the supervised embedding procedure, was always between two and five.

Table 2. Predicting bacteria counts. Mean squared error.

Method	PCA	PAB	STAA	RBC	VRBGA	MRS
Algorithm 2	1.28	2.32	1.19	3.72	3.55	1.34
Algorithm 2 followed by 1	0.44	0.74	0.38	0.70	0.99	0.46
Measurement min	5.1	4.9	3.7	2.3	2.2	3.2
Measurement max	9.9	9.9	8.2	6.8	8.8	8.1

5 Conclusion

We presented a supervised learning procedure to compute embedding in concept space, where inner product operator is tuned for specific task. We show that the proposed framework can significantly improve label inference performance of prior art methods that rely on concept-based representation. However, current formulation of the procedure (i.e. Algorithm 1) requires solving several SDP's, which significantly limits the complexity of the problems that can be tackled. Our imminent goals for future work is to introduce first-order approximation method for (1). Another promising direction for future work is introduction of novel image features used as terms in Algorithm 2 that can improve label inference on the meat dataset.

Acknowledgments

The first and fourth authors of this work are supported by National Science Foundation grant #0803670 under the IIS Division, and Office of Naval Research grant ONR-N000140410363. The second was financed by the Centre for Imaging Food Quality project which is funded by the Danish Council for Strategic Research (contract no 09-067039) within the Programme Commission on Health, Food and Welfare.

References

1. Bai, B., Weston, J., Collobert, R., Grangier, D., Sadamasa, K., Qi, Y., Chapelle, O., Weinberger, K.: Supervised semantic indexing. In: Proceeding of the 18th ACM Conference on Information and Knowledge Management, pp. 187–196. ACM, New York (2009)

[5] The best accuracy using RBF kernel ($C = 2.0, \gamma = 0.5$) was 73.4%.

2. Blei, D.M., Ng, A.Y., Jordan, M.I.: Latent dirichlet allocation. The Journal of Machine Learning Research 3, 993–1022 (2003)
3. Boiman, O., Shechtman, E., Irani, M.: In defense of nearest-neighbor based image classification. In: IEEE Conference on Computer Vision and Pattern Recognition, pp. 1–8. IEEE, Los Alamitos (2008)
4. Bruckstein, A.M., Donoho, D.L., Elad, M.: From sparse solutions of systems of equations to sparse modeling of signals and images. SIAM review 51(1), 34–81 (2009)
5. Csurka, G., Dance, C., Fan, L., Willamowski, J., Bray, C.: Visual categorization with bags of keypoints. In: Workshop on Statistical Learning in Computer Vision, ECCV, vol. 1, p. 22. Citeseer (2004)
6. Deerwester, S., Dumais, S.T., Furnas, G.W., Landauer, T.K., Harshman, R.: Indexing by latent semantic analysis. Journal of The American Society for Information Science 41(6), 391–407 (1990)
7. Ding, T., Sznaier, M., Camps, O.I.: A rank minimization approach to video inpainting. In: IEEE International Conference on Computer Vision, pp. 1–8 (2007)
8. Ding, T., Sznaier, M., Camps, O.I.: Receding horizon rank minimization based estimation with applications to visual tracking. In: Proceedings of the 47th IEEE Conference on Decision and Control, CDC 2008, Cancún, México, December 9-11, pp. 3446–3451 (2008)
9. Elad, M.: Sparse and Redundant Representations: From Theory to Applications in Signal and Image Processing. Springer, Heidelberg (2010)
10. Fazel, M., Hindi, H., Boyd, S.P.: Log-det heuristic for matrix rank minimization with applications to hankel and euclidean distance matrices. In: Proceedings American Control Conference, pp. 2156–2162 (2003)
11. Hofmann, T.: Probabilistic latent semantic indexing. In: Proceedings of the 22nd annual international ACM SIGIR Conference on Research and Development in Information Retrieval, pp. 50–57. ACM Press, New York (1999)
12. Lowe, D.G.: Distinctive image features from scale-invariant keypoints. International Journal of Computer Vision 60(2), 91–110 (2004)
13. Pearson, K.: On lines and planes of closest fit to systems of points in space. Philosophical Magazine 2(6), 559–572 (1901)
14. Schmid, C., Mohr, R.: Local grayvalue invariants for image retrieval. IEEE Transactions on Pattern Analysis and Machine Intelligence 19(5), 530–535 (1997)
15. Sivic, J., Zisserman, A.: Video google: Efficient visual search of videos. In: Ponce, J., Hebert, M., Schmid, C., Zisserman, A. (eds.) Toward Category-Level Object Recognition. LNCS, vol. 4170, pp. 127–144. Springer, Heidelberg (2006)
16. Weinberger, K.Q., Blitzer, J., Saul, L.K.: Distance metric learning for large margin nearest neighbor classification. In: NIPS. MIT Press, Cambridge (2006)
17. Weston, J., Bengio, S., Usunier, N.: Large scale image annotation: Learning to rank with joint word-image embeddings. Machine learning 81(1), 21–35 (2010)
18. Yang, J., Yuan, X.: An Inexact Alternating Direction Method for Trace Norm Regularized Least Squares Problem. Report, Department of Mathematics, Nanjing Uinversity (2010)
19. Yuan, X.: Alternating Direction Methods for Sparse Covariance Selection. In: 20th International Symposium of Mathematical Programming, ISMP (2009)

Saliency in Spectral Images

Steven Le Moan[1,2], Alamin Mansouri[1], Jon Hardeberg[2], and Yvon Voisin[1]

[1] Laboratoire Le2i, BP16, 89010 Auxerre Cédex, France
[2] Colorlab, Gjøvik University College, P.O. Box 191, N-2802 Gjøvik, Norway

Abstract. Even though the study of saliency for color images has been thoroughly investigated in the past, very little attention has been given to datasets that cannot be displayed on traditional computer screens such as spectral images. Nevertheless, more than a means to predict human gaze, the study of saliency primarily allows for measuring informative content. Thus, we propose a novel approach for the computation of saliency maps for spectral images. Based on the *Itti* model, it involves the extraction of both spatial and spectral features, suitable for high dimensionality images. As an application, we present a comparison framework to evaluate how dimensionality reduction techniques convey information from the initial image. Results on two datasets prove the efficiency and the relevance of the proposed approach.

1 Introduction

Visual attention modeling is the study of the human visual interpretation of a given scene. In other words, which objects/features will first draw attention and why ? This notion is closely linked to the analysis of saliency. Yet, the latter is a much broader concept in that it can be seen as a way of measuring informative content for any kind of data.

Following early influential work by Treisman *et al.* [1] and Koch & Ullman [2], Itti *et al.* [3] proposed a general visual attention model allowing for the computation of so-called saliency maps, which purpose is to predict human gaze given a certain scene. This model involves center-surround comparisons and combinations of three main feature channels, namely colors, intensity and orientations. More recent work involve for instance the use of graph theory [4], spectral residual [5], information theory [6], or face recognition [7].

Yet, only a few studies have extended the concept of saliency to objects which cannot be entirely displayed on traditional computer screens. Among them, it is worth mentioning the pioneer work by Lee *et al.* [8] on 3D mesh saliency. This paper does not tackle such objects but follows however the same idea of measuring prominent features (in a general way) for non-displayable objects, that is, multi- or hyperspectral images.

Spectral imaging consists of acquiring the same scene at several different ranges of wavelengths, usually several dozens. Since multispectral display devices are yet rare, most of today's popular display hardware is based on the three-stimulus paradigm [9]. Thus, in order to visualize spectral images, a dimensionality reduction step is required so that only three channels (Red, Green

A. Heyden and F. Kahl (Eds.): SCIA 2011, LNCS 6688, pp. 114–123, 2011.

and Blue) can contain most of the visual information. Such methods involve PCA [10,11], band selection [12], Color Matching Functions [13], and are based on a maximization of the informative content of the reduced dataset. However, assessing the quality of a dimensionality reduction technique is very challenging and application-dependent. When it comes to the task of visualization, one usually aims at displaying as much information as possible while easing interpretation by preserving natural colors and contrasts [14].

Even though visual attention has already been used in the context of spectral images for dimensionality reduction purposes [15], the computation of an actual saliency map from the entire high-dimensional image has not been tackled so far to our knowledge. In this paper, we propose a simple method to compute such a map, based on the extraction of both spectral and spatial features. It involves a spectrum segmentation for a local analysis of the reflectance curves. By extending the concept of saliency outside the scope of human visual attention and considering it as a measure of information, the proposed approach can be used for images ranging outside the visible wavelengths (400-700nm), especially since, in many cases, considering for instance the near Infra Red (nIR) allows to enhance the discrimination between materials and objects of a scene. Consequently, we have derived a simple technique to measure the efficiency of dimensionality reduction techniques to convey informative content from the initial spectral image.

In the following, we make a step-by-step description of the saliency map computation by explaining the feature extraction, the spectral center-surround comparisons and the creation of the final map. In a second section, results are shown on two spectral datasets and an evaluation framework involving one PCA-based band transformation approach and two band selection techniques is presented. Eventually, results are discussed and conclusions are drawn.

2 Saliency for Multispectral Images

We propose a simple and efficient method for saliency map computing for spectral images. It is based on the *Itti* model of which we have modified the feature maps computation in order to make it suitable for high dimensional reflectance vectors. Figure 1 gives the synopsis of the proposed approach.

2.1 Channels Computation

Visual attention modeling usually involves the analysis of three main features, namely Color, Intensity and Orientation from which several sets of channels are created (e.g. two for color oppositions, one for intensity and four different orientations). Each set is in fact a gaussian pyramid of an initial channel at several different spatial scales (typically nine). The purpose of these channels is to allow for a straight-forward center-surround comparison by means of a simple across-scale difference. However, if computing color and intensity channels from RGB images is quite easy, it becomes much more challenging when it comes to create such channels from reflectance data. As stated in the introduction, many band

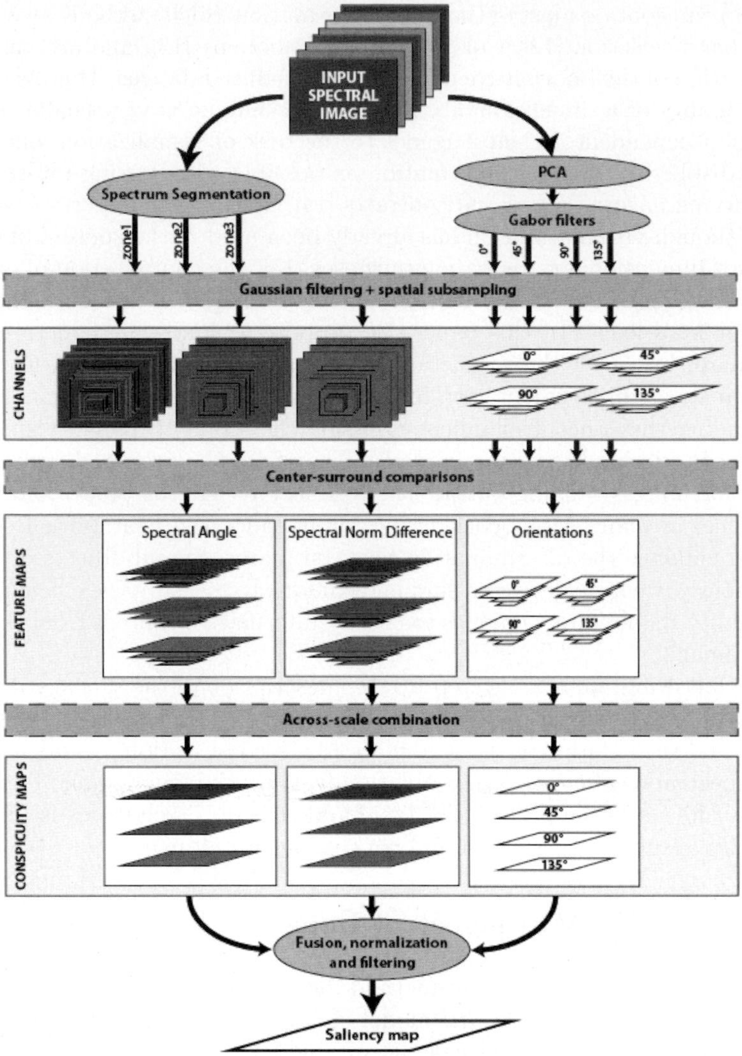

Fig. 1. Synopsis of the proposed approach

transformation and band selection methods exist at this aim, all of them producing different results, and each of them being suitable for a given task such as automatic classification, visualization, compression, noise reduction, etc. In this paper however, we aim at analyzing saliency in the high-dimensional space, therefore no dimensionality reduction must be involved at this point. Nevertheless, we propose to divide the spectrum into three regions, roughly corresponding to the blue, green and red wavelength ranges, in order to allow for a local analysis of the reflectance spectra. For images ranging outside the visible wavelengths (400-700nm), we suggest to add spectrum segments for the Ultra-Violet and near Infra-Red ranges. However, in the remaining of this paper, we will consider only visible-ranging images. Consequently, three subset of the initial image are obtained and nine spatial scales are created for each of them (from $1 : 2^0$, the initial scale, to $1 : 2^8$, the coarser one). As for the creation of orientation channels, we have assumed that differences of orientations being relatively small from one spectral band to another, it would make sense to compute one orientation map for the whole set of spectral bands. Therefore, we have applied Principal Components Analysis (PCA) to the spectral dataset and applied four Gabor filters (at 0°, 45°, 90° and 135°) to the first Principal Component (PC), which usually contains more than 95% of the data energy. Eventually, we obtain one set of three spectral cubes, each one of them at nine different spatial scales, as well as four sets of nine orientation channels, also at nine different spatial scales. From this point, the later four sets have been processed exactly the same way as in the *Itti* model.

2.2 Center-Surround Comparisons

While RGB-based saliency analysis involves the extraction of color and intensity channels prior to the center-surround differences computation, we propose to decouple color from intensity during this latter step, by means of relevant comparison metrics:

- Spectral Angle (SA) allows for an intensity-decoupled comparison of reflectance spectra. For a given couple of pixels with respective spectra being noted s_1 and s_2,the SA is given by the following formula:

$$SA(s_1, s_2) = \frac{s_1}{\|s_1\|} \cdot \frac{s_2}{\|s_2\|}$$

- Spectral Norm Difference (SND) depicts the difference, in terms of amount of reflected light, between two spectra. It is given by the following formula:

$$SND(s_1, s_2) = abs(\|s_1\| - \|s_2\|)$$

The substitution of across-scale difference by these metrics allows for the comparison of spectra without dimensionality reduction. Therefore, visual attention is analyzed all over the spectrum. In the common case of spectral images ranging outside the visible wavelengths (400-700nm), one can no longer talk about visual attention, but we believe this study to be relevant nonetheless, since its first aim is to provide a measure of informative content.

Figure 2 gives an example of three reflectance spectra extracted from the dataset presented in the next section. By applying the aforementioned metrics, we obtain the results given in the table in Figure 2. These results confirm that the SND allows for a discrimination between highly and poorly reflecting objects while the SA achieves a comparison in terms of the shape of the curves.

By means of these metrics, we have computed 6 maps by feature, corresponding to the comparison between scales $c \in \{2, 3, 4\}$ and $c + \delta$, $\delta \in \{3, 4\}$. An across-scale fusion at scale four (1:8) allows then for the creation of ten conspicuity maps

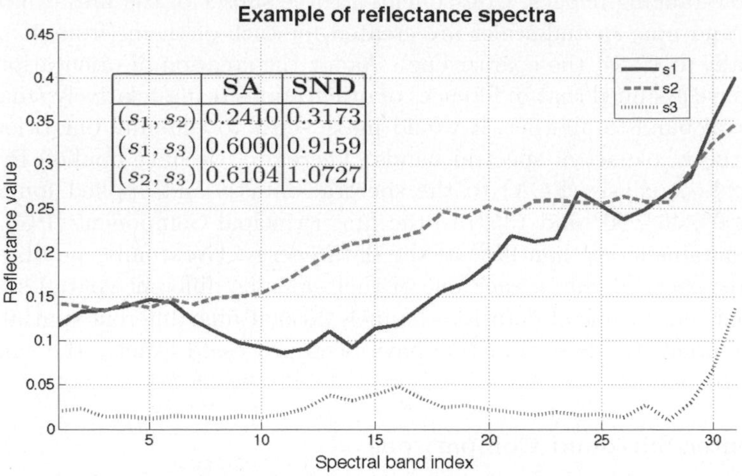

Fig. 2. Example of three different spectra s_1 (red plain), s_2 (grey dashed) and s_3 (blue dotted)

(3 SA, 3 SND and 4 Orientations) which are then respectively averaged in order to obtain one conspicuity map by mode. They are then fused into one single saliency map, here again averaging appears to be the best option considering the heterogeneity of the features. The map is then normalized (division by its global maximum) in order to reduce the number of salient locations and blurred (gaussian filtering) to avoid tiny salient spots and increasing global smoothness.

3 Experiments and Results

3.1 Data Sets

For our experiments, we used two calibrated multispectral datasets of 31 bands, ranging in the visible spectrum (400-700 nm):

- "Flowers" represents a natural scene with flowers, leaves and a background. It comes from a database presented in [16].
- "MacBeth" is the well-known MacBeth CC color calibration target.

Only raw reflectance has been used (no illuminant). Each dataset have been preprocessed so that bands with average reflectance value below 2% and those with low correlation (below 0.8) with their neighboring bands have been removed, as suggested in [17].

3.2 Saliency Map

Figures 3 and 4 represent the final conspicuity maps for both datasets. The depicted maps are actually averages of the three conspicuity maps corresponding

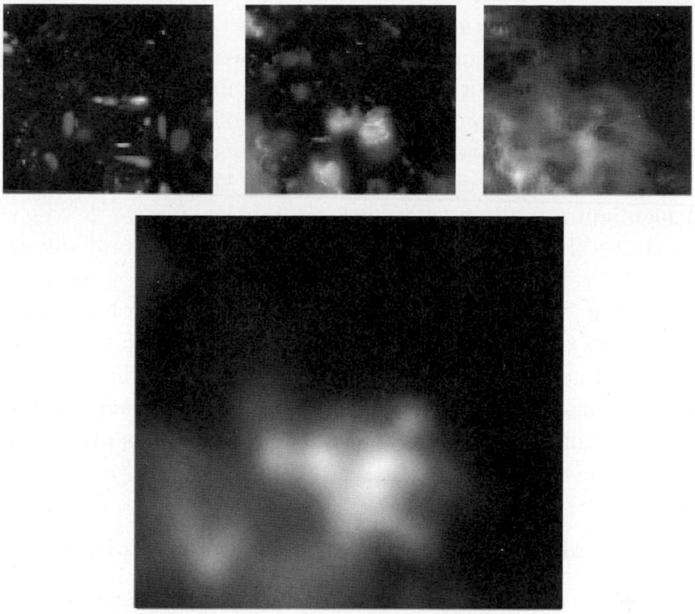

Fig. 3. Conspicuity and final saliency maps for the "Flowers" image. From left to right: SA, SND and Orientations.

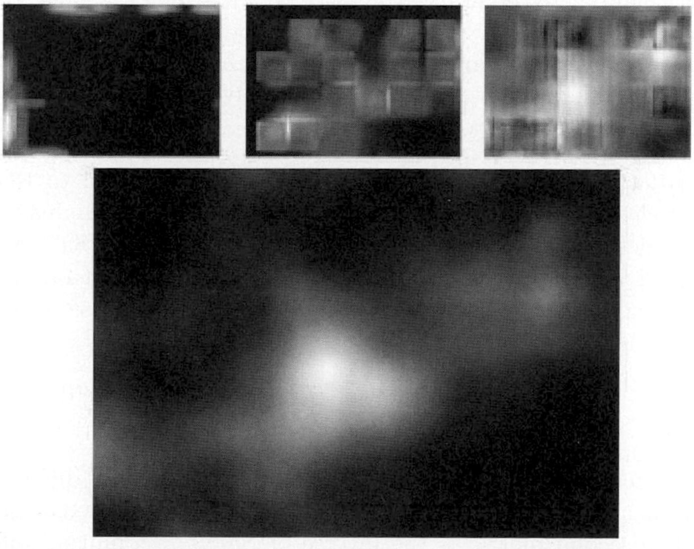

Fig. 4. Conspicuity and final saliency maps for the "Macbeth" image. From left to right: SA, SND and Orientations.

to each segment of the spectrum (for the SA and SND features) and of the four angles maps (for the orientation).

As explained before, these maps depict which locations are the most prominent in terms of SA, SND and orientations, *i.e.* the flowers in the first image and the white patch in the second one. The effect of normalization and filtering yields high contrast and smoothness, which allows for an easier interpretation by highlighting a restrained number of relatively large areas. On the "Flowers" image, SA highlights small areas of background through the leaves while SND mainly emphasizes the flowers. Both metrics find very different salient locations, hence their relative independence and the relevance to use both in the whole process. As for the "MacBeth" target, while the orientation-related saliency is meaningless due to the regular structure of the image, the orientation appears to be the most influential feature in the computation of the final map. This is due to the fact that, in this image, the orientation maps have the highest mean values. Moreover, this also induces that very few locations are salient in terms of colors, barely the white patch.

3.3 Evaluation of Dimensionality Reduction Techniques

We propose to illustrate one application of the spectral saliency map on the evaluation of dimensionality reduction techniques. At this aim, we have computed tri-stimulus representations of both datasets by means of one band transformation and two band selection methods:

- PCA_{rgb} is the traditional Principal Components Analysis of which components are mapped to the RGB color space ($PC1 \rightarrow R; PC2 \rightarrow G; PC3 \rightarrow B$).
- LP-based band selection has been proposed by Du *et al.* [12] and consists of progressively selecting bands by maximizing their respective orthogonality.
- Entropy-based band selection (ENT) is a naive method selecting the three bands with maximal entropy.

For the two latter techniques, resulting channels are mapped to RGB by descending wavelengths. In order to compare the different tri-stimulus composites, we have considered two simple metrics that we will refer to as Saliency Discrepancy number 1 and 2, respectively ($SD1$ and $SD2$). The first one is based on a point-by-point difference, summed along both spatial dimensions and divided by the total number of pixels:

$$SD1(im_1, im_2) = \frac{\sum\limits_{i=1:sizeX} \sum\limits_{j=1:sizeY} smap(im_1(i,j)) - smap(im_2(i,j))}{sizeX * sizeY}$$

with im_1 and im_2 any two images of same size but potentially different number of spectral channels and *smap*(.) an operator computing the saliency map of its input. The second metric is the inverse of *Shannon*'s mutual information, normalized by the sum of entropies:

$$SD2(im_1, im_2) = \frac{H(smap(im_1)) + smap(im_2))}{MI(smap(im_1));smap(im_2))}$$

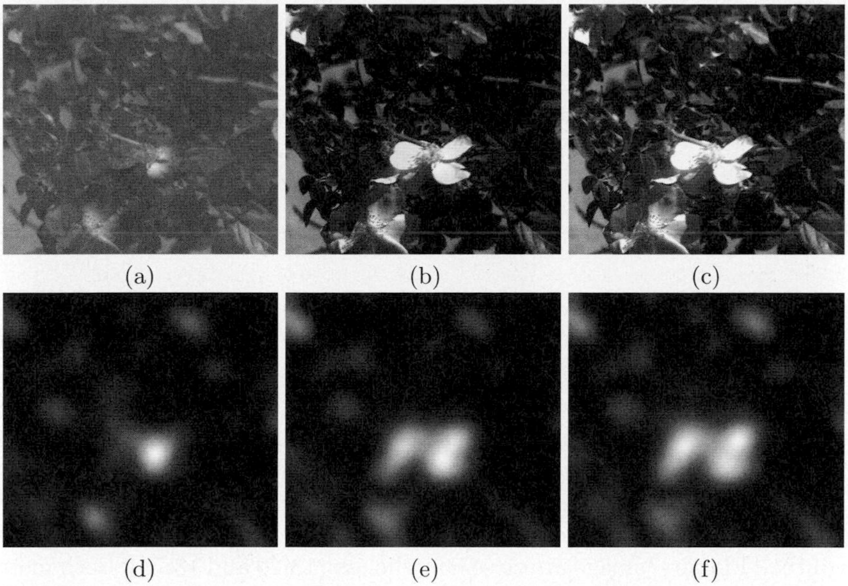

Fig. 5. Results from the dimensionality reduction techniques: (a) PCA (b) LP (c) Entropy and their associated saliency maps (d-f)

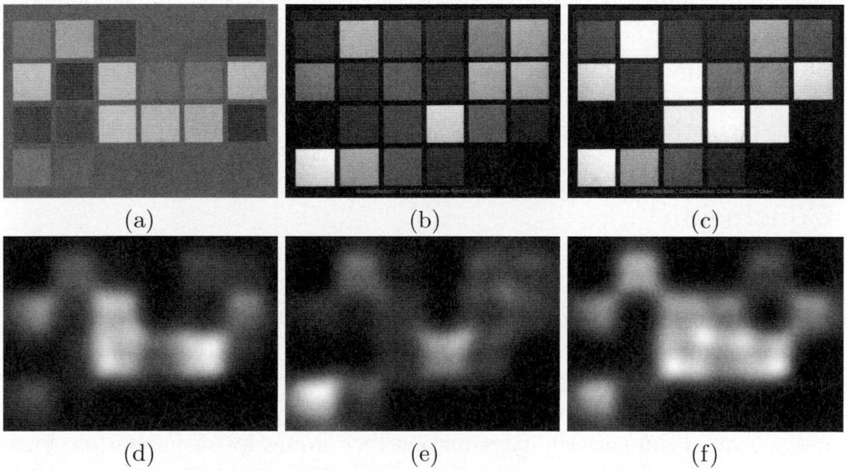

Fig. 6. Results from the dimensionality reduction techniques: (a) PCA (b) LP (c) Entropy and their associated saliency maps (d-f)

with $H(.)$ and $MI(.;.)$ being respectively the entropy and mutual information operators. Figures 5 and 6 depict the resulting tri-stimulus representations by means of the aforementioned techniques as well as their associated saliency maps.

Table 1. Saliency Discrepancies between the spectral images and their respective tri-stimulus composites

		PCA_{rgb}	LP	ENT
SD1	"Flowers"	**13.20**	18.73	19.72
	"MacBeth"	23.95	**16.07**	33.74
SD2	"Flowers"	19.41	**10.78**	12.31
	"MacBeth"	12.01	**10.61**	10.90

Table 1 gives the results of the *SD* metrics. One must notice that the resulting tri-stimulus composites are very different from each other in terms of color and consequently in terms of saliency. Different regions are highlighted and this reflects the variety of manners to conveys information from the spectral image. Consequently, we observe large fluctuations of *SD* between the initial datasets and their tri-stimulus composites. As expected, we observe that the *SD* is independent from the overall visual appeal of the image. Indeed, images with very different hues such as the ones from PCA compared to the results from LP in the case of the "Flowers" image are close nonetheless (13.20 and 18.73). Both metrics are in accordance to elect LP as the most suitable method for the visualization of the "MacBeth" target. However, $SD1$ ranks ENT as the worst method for both images while $SD2$ gives PCA_{rgb} as the method conveying the less saliency. This divergence is due to the fact that Figures 5d and 6d have respectively lower entropies than Figures 5f and 6f, a property that is conveyed by the normalization in $SD2$. For this, we believe that $SD2$ is more efficient and accurate than $SD1$ in measuring discrepancies. *In fine*, PCA is globally outperformed by the two band selection techniques in retaining saliency from the input dataset and the LP is the method giving best results.

4 Conclusion

We have presented a new method to create saliency maps for spectral images. It is based on the extraction of both spectral and spatial features and involves a spectrum segmentation for a better handling of local variations of the reflectance curves. Further than the single scope of visual attention, it is meant to be a way of measuring informative content. An example of application has been given on the comparison of dimensionality reduction techniques for visualization. Further study will investigate the use and influence of different spectrum segmentation techniques as well as means to use saliency as a criterion for dimensionality reduction, in order to control the visual features of a tri-stimulus composite.

Acknowledgements

The author wish to express their gratitude to the Regional Council of Burgundy for supporting this work.

References

1. Treisman, A., Gelade, G.: A feature-integration theory of attention. Cognitive Psychology 12, 97–136 (1980)
2. Koch, C., Ullman, S.: Shifts in selective visual attention: towards the underlying neural circuitry. Hum. Neurobiol. 4, 219–227 (1985)
3. Itti, L., Koch, C., Niebur, E.: A model of saliency-based visual attention for rapid scene analysis. IEEE Trans. on Pattern Analysis and Machine Intelligence 20, 1254–1259 (1998)
4. Harel, J., Koch, C., Perona, P.: Graph-based visual saliency. Advances in Neural Information Processing Systems 19, 545 (2007)
5. Hou, X., Zhang, L.: Saliency detection: A spectral residual approach. In: IEEE Conference on Computer Vision and Pattern Recognition, CVPR 2007, pp. 1–8. IEEE, Los Alamitos (2007)
6. Bruce, N., Tsotsos, J.: Saliency, attention, and visual search: An information theoretic approach. Journal of Vision 9 (2009)
7. Cerf, M., Harel, J., Einhäuser, W., Koch, C.: Predicting human gaze using low-level saliency combined with face detection. Advances in Neural Information Processing Systems 20, 241–248 (2008)
8. Lee, C., Varshney, A., Jacobs, D.: Mesh saliency. In: ACM SIGGRAPH 2005 Papers, p. 666. ACM, New York (2005)
9. Grassmann, H.: On the theory of compound colors. Phil. Mag. 7, 254–264 (1854)
10. Jia, X., Richards, J.: Segmented principal components transformation for efficient hyperspectral remote-sensing image display and classification. IEEE Trans. on Geoscience and Remote Sensing 37, 538–542 (1999)
11. Tyo, J., Konsolakis, A., Diersen, D., Olsen, R.: Principal-components-based display strategy for spectral imagery. IEEE Trans. on Geoscience and Remote Sensing 41, 708–718 (2003)
12. Du, Q., Yang, H.: Similarity-based unsupervised band selection for hyperspectral image analysis. IEEE Geoscience and Remote Sensing Letters 5, 564–568 (2008)
13. Poldera, G., van der Heijdena, G.: Visualization of spectral images. In: Proc. SPIE., vol. 4553, p. 133 (2001)
14. Jacobson, N., Gupta, M.: Design goals and solutions for display of hyperspectral images. IEEE Trans. on Geoscience and Remote Sensing 43, 2684–2692 (2005)
15. Zhang, H., Peng, H., Fairchild, M., Montag, E.: Hyperspectral image visualization based on a human visual model. In: Proceedings of SPIE, vol. 6806, p. 68060N (2008)
16. Nascimento, S., Ferreira, F., Foster, D.: Statistics of spatial cone-excitation ratios in natural scenes. Journal of the Optical Society of America A 19, 1484–1490 (2002)
17. Cai, S., Du, Q., Moorhead, R.: Hyperspectral imagery visualization using double layers. IEEE Trans. on Geoscience and Remote Sensing 45, 3028–3036 (2007)

Mixed-State Particle Filtering for Simultaneous Tracking and Re-identification in Non-overlapping Camera Networks

Boris Meden[1], Patrick Sayd[1], and Frédéric Lerasle[2,3]

[1] CEA, LIST, Laboratoire Vision et Ingénierie des Contenus, Point Courrier 94, F-91191 Gif-sur-Yvette, France
[2] CNRS; LAAS; 7 avenue du Colonel Roche, F-31077 Toulouse Cedex 4, France
[3] Université de Toulouse; UPS, INSA, INP, ISAE; UT1, UTM, LAAS; F-31077 Toulouse Cedex 4, France
{boris.meden,patrick.sayd}@cea.fr, lerasle@laas.fr

Abstract. This article presents a novel approach to person tracking within large-scale indoor environments monitored by non-overlapping field-of-view camera networks. We address the image-based tracking problem with distributed particle filters using a hierarchical color model. The novelty of our approach resides in the embedding of an already-seen-people database in the particle filter framework. Doing so, the filter performs not only position estimation but also does establish identity probabilities for the current targets in the network. Thus we use online person re-identification as a way to introduce continuity to track people in disjoint camera networks. No calibration stage is required. We demonstrate the performances of our approach on a 5 camera-disjoint network and a 16-person database.

Keywords: re-identification, tracking, camera network, non-overlapping fields of view, particle filtering.

1 Introduction

The problem of estimating the trajectory of an object as it moves in an area of interest, known as tracking, is one of the major topics of research in computer vision (see a comprehensive survey in [14]). That becomes even more challenging with multiple objects tracking (MOT), aiming to maintain identities of tracks. MOT has been tackled by supervised approaches [13], but also with distributed particle filters [12] [1]. However, it is usually not feasible to completely cover large areas with cameras having overlapping views due to economic and/or computational reasons. Thus, in realistic scenarii, the system should be able to handle multiple cameras with non-overlapping fields of view (NOFOV). Beyond the intra-camera tracking problem, the crucial difficulty resides in the transitions between cameras and the problem of maintaining targets' identities at the network level. The differences in target appearances are mainly due to different poses of cameras and different colorimetric responses.

A. Heyden and F. Kahl (Eds.): SCIA 2011, LNCS 6688, pp. 124–133, 2011.

That jump between cameras, known as the re-identification problem, can be seen as twofold with on the one hand the robustness of the descriptor and on the other hand the specific strategy to match identities. As most approaches, Gray *et al.* [4] focus on the target descriptor to achieve the best frame to frame re-identification rate. They propose the VIPeR dataset, composed of pedestrian images taken for two cameras with different viewpoints and illuminations. Prosser *et al.* used a similar approach in [11]. Rather than choosing which cues to use, these works let a meta-algorithm provide a descriptor highlighting the invariant cues of pedestrian silhouette relatively to a learning database. The limitations here are the great number of samples needed. Other works, also on the descriptor level, try to project their color descriptors on the same subspace, putting the focus on the color consistency issue and resorting to color calibration. Thus, Javed *et al.* in [6] compute a subspace based color brightness transfer function. That transfer function is estimated over a set of training samples seen in the network. Bowden *et al.* in [3] go further into the learning of that transfer function as they compute it incrementally. Again here, the limitations reside in the training phase which takes processing time and is biased as the sample target set cannot be exhaustive.

The different aforementioned approaches consider all a frame to frame comparison strategy. Cong *et al.* in [2] propose a more enhanced process in matching not only single images of the target but whole tracking sequences. They perform a spectral analysis of the graph Laplacian of the matrix of two sequences. The number of clusters in the matrix (*i.e.* the number of similar descriptors) is directly linked to the eigenvalues. With SVM classification in the reduced eigenspace, the decide whether the sequences belong to the same target or not. The inter-camera re-identification is achieved through the RGB Greyworld normalization and an elaborated strategy over the sequences. However the comparison is only done for two sequences at the same time. To bridge the gap between cameras, Makris *et al.* in [8] learn spatiotemporal transitions to infer re-appearance time of targets evolving in a blind spot of the network. With the same goal, Lim *et al.* in [7] propose a two-behavior particle filter: when the tracked target is visible, usual tracking is performed, when it is in a blind spot, particles evolve in the metric map of the building, dividing the current group in two at each intersection. Re-identification is achieved when a detection in a camera coincide with particles in the metric map. Limitations of these approaches resides clearly in the multiple objects configurations.

In this paper, we see the tracking in NOFOV networks as an extension of the multiple objects tracking (MOT) in mono- or multi-ocular sequences [13] [12]. To do so, we propose to embed re-identification within the particle filter framework. Thus we estimate not only relative position in a given camera but also the identity of the target in respect to an *a priori* learned person database (people that have entered the building where the network is set). Moreover, we use distributed filters, which implies low complexity and enable the approach to be extended to large networks. This strategy is an enhanced frame to frame comparison as the filter introduce temporality, but still produce a re-identification result at each new frame. As there is no public dataset treating about extended camera networks, we tested our algorithms on our private 5-camera network composed of a 34-meter long corridor, a meeting room and a building outdoor entrance with a total 16 pedestrians are wandering in it.

In the following, Section 2 first presents how we learn the identities that we will track in the other cameras and build a target-database. Section 3 details the particle filter adaptation. Section 4 introduces a supervisor notion for the network monitoring. And finally Section 5 presents the way we evaluated the approach.

2 Learning Identities to Re-identify and Track

2.1 Target Representation

To avoid any camera geometrical calibration problem, the tracking is conducted in the image plane. We use a rectangular geometric model as Region Of Interest (ROI). The descriptor is hierarchical: the ROI is sliced into regular horizontal stripes and each stripe is described by its color distribution. Color histograms have proven to be robust to appearance changes [9] with their global aspect. The addition of spatial constraints in the signature localizes the colors and increases the discrimination power. It has been successfully used for tracking purpose by Pérez *et al.* [10] as well as for re-identification purpose by Cong *et al.* [2]. Moreover that type of descriptor (termed Hand Localized Histogram) was part of the evaluations conducted by Gray *et al.* in [4] and also achieved good results in frame to frame comparison. We use color histograms in the RGB color space with 8 bins per channel for tracking computing time, and we tuned the number of stripes using [4] evaluation. As they did, we computed Cumulative Matching Characteristic (CMC) curves over the VIPeR dataset, for different numbers of stripes from 1 to 30 and kept the best curve, corresponding to the 5-stripe descriptor. Associated to a normalization process explained in subsection 3.2, large bins allow us to handle color discrepancy between cameras.

2.2 Reducing the Database to Key Frames

Before recognizing people we have to see them a first time. We propose to do a learning of identities in a first camera seen as an entrance point in the network (*e.g.* the hall of a building, and Site 0 in the figure 4). Then we will treat the network as a closed system with a collection of identities walking in it. First we run a traditional CONDENSATION[1] particle filter on the learning sequence. We extract a view of the target for each frame. Then, we reduce offline this collection of descriptors to key ones. To select an appropriate number of key frame to retain the same amount of variation for each identity, we perform a spectral analysis of the tracking sequences. Our approach is inspired by [2] but here limited to a single person. Thus we focus on the variations of the target descriptor for the

[1] For Conditional Density Propagation.

same target to extract the main representative descriptors of the sequence. To do so, we build the similarity matrix of each tracking sequence taken from the learning camera as $W_{ij} = \exp(-K \cdot \sum_{k=1}^{N_c} d^2(s_i(k), s_j(k)))$, where $d(.,.)$ is the discrete Bhattacharyya Distance, $s_i(k)$ (*resp.* $s_j(k)$) is k-th color distribution of target i (*resp.* j), N_c the number of color distributions per target and K a normalization constant. We apply spectral clustering method to that similarity matrix calculating its un-normalized Graph Laplacian $\Delta = D - W$ where D is the diagonal matrix of the horizontal sums of W elements: $D_{ii} = \sum_j W_{ij}$. We then diagonalize the Graph Laplacian. The eigenvalues present an eigengap when the number of clusters is reached [2]. In a one person sequence, the gap may not be obvious, so just put a threshold on the eigenvalues and perform k-means clustering in the reduced space of the k first eigenvectors, k being the number of eigenvalues lesser than the threshold. Thus we summarize a tracking sequence to key frames that retain the main variability in terms of appearance. Figure 1 shows some of the tracking boxes and the chosen key frames. Out of 100 tracking boxes, we extract between 4 and 10 key frames.

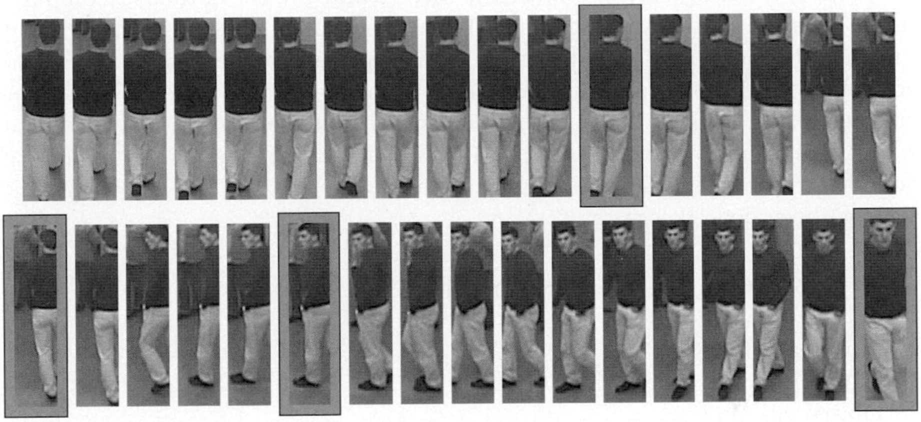

Fig. 1. Some boxes part of a tracking sequence (scaled to have the same height for design purpose). The green frame highlights the four key frames selected by the k-means algorithm to represent that identity. These key frames capture the biggest variation of the target appearance in the tracking sequence.

3 Embedding Re-identification into the Tracking Process

3.1 Particle Filter Framework

A bayesian tracking filtering process begins with the choice of a reference region in an image, and then proceed to a recursive search of similar regions in the remaining of the sequence. Given the identity database, we have got here another reference descriptor to compare with. We use the Mixed State CONDENSATION particle filter framework [5], to estimate our Mixed State vector composed by continuous parameters (the target's image coordinates $\mathbf{x}$) and also a discrete parameter (the target's identity y) in the filter loop, namely

$$\mathbf{X} = (\mathbf{x}, y)^\mathsf{T}, \ \mathbf{x} \in \mathbb{R}^4, \ y \in \{1, \ldots, N_{id}\}$$

In our case, we track in the image plane with a rectangular geometric model. We have $\mathbf{x} = [x_c, y_c, h_x, r]^\mathsf{T}$, where $(x_c, y_c)^\mathsf{T}$ are the coordinates of the box center, h_x is the half width of the box, and r is the width-height ratio which is assumed constant, and where N_{id} is the cardinal of the identity database, and N the number of particles. Given that extended state, the sampling process density at frame t can be written as in [5]:

$$p(\mathbf{X}_t|\mathbf{X}_{t-1}) = T(\mathbf{X}_t, \mathbf{X}_{t-1}) \cdot p(\mathbf{x}_t|\mathbf{x}_{t-1})$$

where $T(\mathbf{X}_t, \mathbf{X}_{t-1})$ is a transition probability matrix which will sample the discrete ID parameter, and $p(\mathbf{x}_t|\mathbf{x}_{t-1})$ is the sampling on the continuous part of the state. The transition matrix $T = [t_{ij}]$ is built over the key frame set. The element t_{ij} is the similarity between identities i and j in the database, computed using equation (1) between the most distant key frames of each identity.

The difference with [5] resides in the discrete parameter meaning. They used it to include different motion models into the filter and to have it decide which one fits the best. For us, and this is the main novelty of that paper, this parameter refers to an identity in our already-seen-person database and allows us to perform simultaneous tracking and re-identification. To the best of our knowledge this has not been done before.

3.2 Estimating the Identity and the Position

After the sampling stage, the new positions of the particles are evaluated relatively to the new image $\mathbf{Z}_t$. The traditional temporal likelihood $p(\mathbf{Z}_t|\mathbf{x}_t^{(n)})$ is estimated as:

$$w_{Temp}^{(n)}(t) = \exp\{-K \cdot \sum_{j=1}^{N_c} d^2\left(s_t^{(n)}(j), s_{model}(j)\right)\}, \ \forall\, n = 1, \ldots, N$$

where N_c is as previously the number of color distributions per target, $s_{model}(.)$ the set of color distributions of the tracking reference model (*i.e.* the initial box of a tracking process, that we do not update during the process), $s_t^{(n)}(.)$ the set of color distributions of the current particle, and N is the number of particles.

The Mixed-State CONDENSATION framework adapted to re-identification provides an additional likelihood, weighting the particle relatively to its identity, $p(\mathbf{Z}_t|\mathbf{x}_t^{(n)}, y_t^{(n)})$:

$$w_{Id}^{(n)}(t) = \exp\{-K \cdot \min_{i \in N_y} \sum_{j=1}^{N_c} d^2\left(s_t^{(n)}(j), s_{identity}(j, y_t^{(n)}, i)\right)\}, \ \forall\, n = 1, \ldots, N \quad (1)$$

where N_y is the cardinal of the key frame class of identity $y_t^{(n)}$ ($y_t^{(n)}$ being the identity assigned to the n-th particle at time t), N_c the number of color distributions per target, $s_{identity}(., y_t^{(n)}, i)$ is the set of color distributions of the i-th keyframe of identity $y_t^{(n)}$ in the database, $s_t^{(n)}(.)$ is the set of color distributions of the current particle, and N is the number of particles. Figure 2 sum up the principle of these two likelihoods per particle. Each particle is evaluated relatively to the reference of tracking (w_{Temp}), but also (w_{Id}) relatively to its identity (described by a collection of key frames).

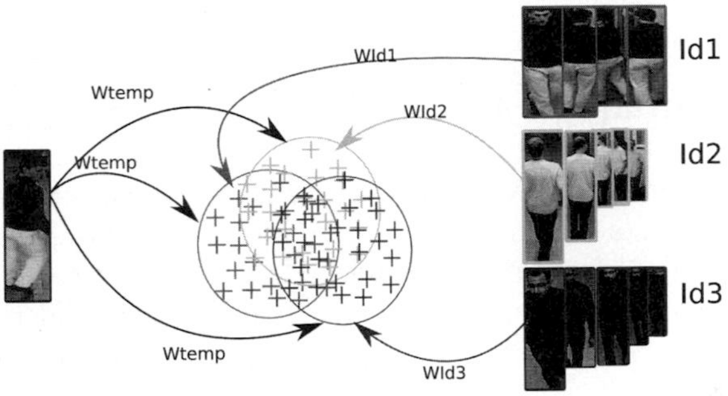

Fig. 2. Illustration of our mixed state particle filter in the case of a database of cardinal of 3. The particle cloud is divided into three subcloud, identically distributed at the initialisation of the filter (as displayed in the figure). Then the strongest identity will take the lead, because of the combined likelihood and the transition matrix T. Mixed state particles share the same temporal tracking reference (left), but a different identity in the database (right, with the key frames).

As these two types of likelihood do not share the same order of magnitude, we normalize them over the set of particles before the resampling stage. That way, we guarantee the jump between two cameras, known as re-identification. Here, we do not favor any bins in the histograms, as [6] and [3] do with the computation of a transfer function. We assume a linear transformation between the cameras colorimetric responses, adopt a rather large bin quantization to absorb that transformation and apply that normalization. Moreover, unlike color calibration, this approach is independent of the pair of cameras considered. We note the normalized likelihood w_{Id}^* and w_{Temp}^*. If w_{Temp}^* is greater than a threshold (*i.e.* if the particle is relevant, otherwise we just use the low temporal similarity as the combined one), we combine both of these similarities to obtain our likelihood formulation which will be injected into the particle weighting stage:

$$\pi_t^{(n)} = \alpha \cdot w_{Temp}^{*(n)}(t) + (1 - \alpha) \cdot w_{Id}^{*(n)}(t),\ \forall\, n = 1, \ldots, N.$$

Doing so, we give weight to the particles that moved into the right place, assuming that they hold the right identity. The state estimation is then a two-stage process. First we need to compute the MAP on the discrete parameter, *i.e.* a partial re-identification.

$$\hat{y}_t = \arg\max_j P(y_t = j|\mathbf{Z}_t) = \arg\max_j \sum_{n\in\mathbf{\Upsilon}_j} \pi_t^{(n)}, \text{ where } \mathbf{\Upsilon}_j = \left\{n|s_t^{(n)} = (\mathbf{x}_t^{(n)}, j)\right\} \quad (2)$$

The continuous state components are then estimated on the subset of particles that have the strongest identity (equation (3)).

$$\hat{\mathbf{x}}_t = \sum_{n\in\hat{\mathbf{\Upsilon}}} \pi_t^{(n)} \cdot \mathbf{x}_t^{(n)} / \sum_{n\in\hat{\mathbf{\Upsilon}}} \pi_t^{(n)}, \text{ where } \hat{\mathbf{\Upsilon}} = \{n|s_t^{(n)} = (\mathbf{x}_t^{(n)}, \hat{y}_t)\} \quad (3)$$

4 The Non-ubiquity Constraint

Our distributed approach provides a strategy for re-identification. Instead of comparing one query image to every entries in the database, we let our mixed-state particle filter perform the decision, allowing identity concurrency in the process. The drawback of the approach resides in the fact that there is no interactions between filters, which means that nothing constrain filters from choosing the same identity.

Thus we add to the approach a light supervising procedure that gather re-identification probabilities thanks to the online identity characterization and assign each filter its most likely identity respectively to the other filters. For a multiple targets configuration supervised, equation 2 transforms to equation 4.

$$\hat{y}_t(f) = \arg\max_j P(y_t = j|\mathbf{Z}_t, f) = \arg\max_j \sum_{n\in\mathbf{\Upsilon}_j(f)} \pi_t^{(n)}(f), \quad (4)$$
$$\text{where } \mathbf{\Upsilon}_j(f) = \left\{n|s_t^{(n)}(f) = (\mathbf{x}_t^{(n)}(f), j)\right\}, \ \forall f = 1 \dots N_{filters}$$

where $(s_t^{(n)}(f), \pi_t^{(n)}(f))$ is the n-th particle and its likelihood, of the f-th filter, and $N_{filters}$ is the number of particle filters currently running. When a filter receive an identity, this identity becomes no more available for the remaining filters. That way, we avoid having the same identity for two separate targets.

5 Evaluations

5.1 Evaluation Network Setup

We used a five-camera network presenting non-overlapping fields of view (Figure 4). The camera 0 is the one we used to learn offline the database. Then, we let 16 pedestrians wandering in the network. Figure 3 shows a key frame per identity of the database.

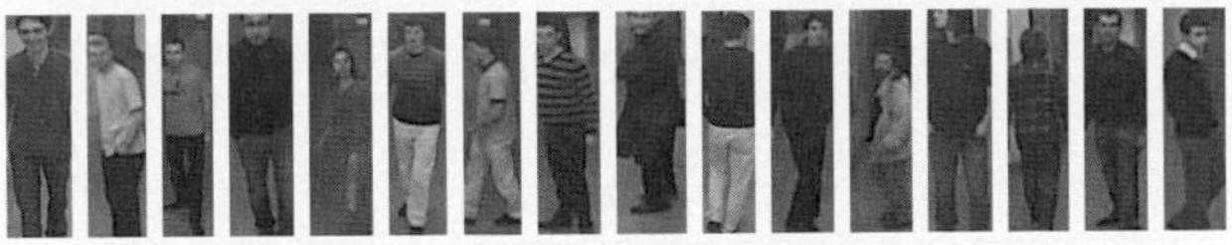

Fig. 3. Our private 16-pedestrian database for experiments

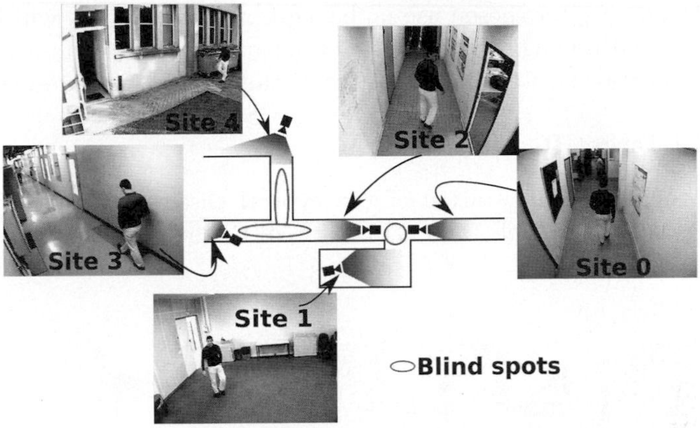

Fig. 4. Overview of the testing network composed of one 34-meter long corridor, one meeting room and one outside area

5.2 Re-Identification Efficiency

As we explained in Section 1 , our mixed-state approach provides a new strategy for the re-identification problem. First we provide a thorough comparison of that strategy to the state of the art one, considering the case of the single target tracking. We compute re-identification results of all the 16 database identities for all cameras, for a frame to frame strategy and for ours. In both cases we use the same descriptor (as we evaluate only the strategy), and initializations of tracking are provided by a configuration file hand-made. A complete system would resort to a detector. For the frame to frame, we run the tracking process with no identity feedback, and compare the estimated position to each entry in the database, at each time step. Evaluated with identity ground truth, both strategies produce binary answers at each time step for each target. For each camera, we sum the results, which true gives re-identification rates per frame, and then we average them over the overall sequence. The rates are also averaged over five runs of each tracking sequence due to the stochastic nature of Particle Filters. Table 1 summarize these results.

We observe different re-identification rates depending on the camera considered. The site #0 is where the identities have been learned, so descriptors are really similar, hence the almost 100% rate. However, sites #1 and #4 are rather different in terms of camera pose and background colors (site #4 being moreover

Table 1. Re-identification rates for camera to camera comparison of the trivial approach and Mixed State one

Approach	Site #0 to #0	Site #0 to #1	Site #0 to #2	Site #0 to #3	Site #0 to #4
Track then ID	0.96	0.40	0.66	0.65	0.30
Track + ID	0.98	0.46	0.81	0.71	0.34

outside). The descriptor chosen use no background subtraction, which is an explanation to the dropping rates. Still, for each camera, the simultaneous tracking and re-identification strategy performs better than the frame to frame one.

5.3 Multi-Target Re-identification

Figure 5 provides an illustration of the typical case where the non-ubiquity constraint is useful: multiple targets evolving in the network. Quantitative evaluations are being studied.

Fig. 5. Tracking 5 targets in the network: four in site #2 and one in site #3. Re-identification results are reported on a map of the network.

6 Conclusion and Perspectives

We have proposed a new approach for people tracking in NOFOV camera networks, which does not require any *a priori* knowledge on the network. Here we see person re-identification as a means to bring continuity between tracking sequences from different cameras. The main novelty of that paper is to embed re-identification into the particle filter framework to estimate simultaneously the target's position and its ID within the camera network. Rather than focusing on the descriptor, we propose here an enhanced matching strategy, introducing temporal filtering in the re-identification process. We have proved by a thourough comparison over every sites of our private network and every identities considered that our mixed-state particle filtering strategy outperforms the usual frame to frame comparison. Moreover, our approach is theoretically independent of the cameras number as the filters are distributed. And we also provide a way to constrain ubiquity of identities between the filters in case of multiple targets tracking.

Further work will investigate on an online construction and updating procedure of the identity database. Moreover, adding interaction forces between filters as proposed in [12] would reinforce the multi-targets mono-camera tracking. Finally, while our approach only uses 2D information, additional knowledge about the scene (*e.g.*, a ground plane to improve targets' size estimation), or about the network (*e.g.*, a topology map to infer some unlikely positions in the network) would be beneficial.

References

1. Breitenstein, M., Reichlin, F., Leibe, B., Koller-Meier, E., Van Gool, L.: Robust tracking-by-detection using a detector confidence particle filter. In: Proceedings of the International Conference on Computer Vision (2010)
2. Cong, D.N.T., Khoudour, L., Achard, C., Meurie, C., Lezoray, O.: People re-identification by spectral classification of silhouettes. Signal Processing (2009)
3. Gilbert, A., Bowden, R.: Tracking objects across cameras by incrementally learning inter-camera colour calibration and patterns of activity. In: Leonardis, A., Bischof, H., Pinz, A. (eds.) ECCV 2006. LNCS, vol. 3952, pp. 125–136. Springer, Heidelberg (2006)
4. Gray, D., Tao, H.: Viewpoint invariant pedestrian recognition with an ensemble of localized features. In: Forsyth, D., Torr, P., Zisserman, A. (eds.) ECCV 2008, Part I. LNCS, vol. 5302, pp. 262–275. Springer, Heidelberg (2008)
5. Isard, M., Blake, A.: A mixed-state condensation tracker with automatic model-switching. In: Proceedings of the International Conference on Computer Vision (1998)
6. Javed, O., Shafique, K., Shah, M.: Appearance modeling for tracking in multiple non-overlapping cameras. In: Proceedings of the International Conference on Computer Vision and Pattern Recognition (2005)
7. Lim, F., Leoputra, W., Tan, T.: Non-overlapping distributed tracking system utilizing particle filter. The Journal of VLSI Signal Processing (2007)
8. Makris, D., Ellis, T., Black, J.: Bridging the gaps between cameras. In: Proceedings of the International Conference on Computer Vision and Pattern Recognition (2004)
9. Nummiaro, K., Koller-Meier, E., Van Gool, L.: An adaptive color-based particle filter. Image and Vision Computing (2003)
10. Perez, P., Vermaak, J., Blake, A.: Data fusion for visual tracking with particles. Proceedings of the IEEE (2004)
11. Prosser, B., Zheng, W., Gong, S., Xiang, T., Mary, Q.: Person Re-Identification by Support Vector Ranking. In: Proceedings of the British Machine Vision Conference (2010)
12. Qu, W., Schonfeld, D., Mohamed, M.: Distributed bayesian multiple-target tracking in crowded environments using multiple collaborative cameras. EURASIP J. Appl. Signal Process. (2007)
13. Smith, K., Gatica-Perez, D., Odobez, J.: Using particles to track varying numbers of interacting people. In: Proceedings of the International Conference on Computer Vision and Pattern Recognition (2005)
14. Yilmaz, A., Javed, O., Shah, M.: Object tracking: A survey. Acm Computing Surveys (CSUR) 38(4), 13 (2006)

Smoothing-Based Submap Merging in Large Area SLAM

Anders Karlsson, Jon Bjärkefur, Joakim Rydell, and Christina Grönwall

Swedish Defence Research Agency
Linköping, Sweden
http://www.foi.se/

Abstract. This paper concerns simultaneous localization and mapping (SLAM) of large areas. In SLAM the map creation is based on identified landmarks in the environment. When mapping large areas a vast number of landmarks have to be treated, which usually is very time consuming. A common way to reduce the computational complexity is to divide the visited area into submaps, each with a limited number of landmarks. This paper presents a novel method for merging conditionally independent submaps (generated using e.g. EKF-SLAM) by the use of smoothing. By this approach it is possible to build large maps in close to linear time. The approach is demonstrated in two indoor scenarios, where data was collected with a trolley-mounted stereo vision camera.

1 Introduction

Simultaneous localization and mapping (SLAM) refers to techniques for estimating the trajectory along which a person or robot moves in an unknown environment, while also creating a map of the surrounding area. Many SLAM methods are based on observing and recognizing landmarks present in the environment, and the created map consists of the estimated positions of these landmarks. Sensors commonly used for SLAM include visual cameras, laser range finders, sonar and radar.

Apart from feature extraction and data association, a successful SLAM implementation needs to tackle three major issues; loop closing, large numbers of landmarks, and consistency. Loop closing shall occur when the sensor revisits a previously seen area and the result should be an updated and improved map. In the loop closure the current state of the sensor is also updated. The SLAM algorithm must be able to handle large maps, i.e., a large number of landmarks. The major problem with many landmarks is that they are usually time consuming to calculate. Executions times proportional to n^2, where n is the number of landmarks, are common. Furthermore, the resulting map needs to be consistent, i.e., correct. Inconsistency is usually related to linearization problems, which cause the uncertainty about landmark positions and sensor position and orientation to be underestimated.

The submap SLAM approach that is presented in this paper handles loop closing, can treat large sets of landmarks in close to linear time, and is consistent. Examples using stereo camera data is shown.

A. Heyden and F. Kahl (Eds.): SCIA 2011, LNCS 6688, pp. 134–145, 2011.

2 Background and Related Work

2.1 SLAM Algorithms

One of the most well-known SLAM methods is EKF-SLAM, which, as the name implies, is based on the extended Kalman filter. The filter state $\mathbf{X}$ contains all information about the sensor pose as well as the position of all landmarks in the map. Assuming that the landmarks are stationary and that a constant velocity and angular velocity model is used for the sensor motion,

$$\mathbf{X} = (\mathbf{t}, \dot{\mathbf{t}}, \mathbf{r}, \dot{\mathbf{r}}, \mathbf{l}_1, \ldots, \mathbf{l}_n)^T,$$

where $\mathbf{t}$ and $\dot{\mathbf{t}}$ denote the sensor position and velocity, respectively, $\mathbf{r}$ and $\dot{\mathbf{r}}$ denote the orientation and angular velocity (using e.g. Euler angles or a quaternion representation), $\mathbf{l}_i$ denotes the ith landmark position and n is the number of landmarks in the map. Obviously, the state dimensionality grows with the number of landmarks. The dimensionality of $\mathbf{X}$ is $12 + 3n$ if the orientation and angular velocity are represented using Euler angles and landmarks are represented using their coordinates in $\mathbb{R}^3$.

Since the EKF explicitly models the covariance between all landmarks, the SLAM algorithm does not need additional logic to handle loop closures. However, due to linearization errors EKF-SLAM tends to underestimate the covariances. This may cause inconsistent estimates of the trajectory, and may preclude successful loop closures. Another disadvantage of EKF-SLAM is that the covariance matrix grows with the square of the number of landmarks in the map. This quickly causes the computational complexity to become prohibitively large.

A number of alternative algorithms, which address one or both of these disadvantages, have been proposed. Information form methods use the information matrix instead of the covariance matrix. The information matrix is “almost sparse”, i.e., many elements in this matrix are very close to zero. By removing weak links between landmarks in a controlled manner, the information matrix is made sparse, which improves the computational performance. This sparsification can be performed in several ways. In the Sparse Extended Information Filter (SEIF) [12] the approximation causes the method to produce overconfident estimates (worse than EKF-SLAM), while the Exactly Sparse Extended Information Filter (ESEIF) [13] breaks links in such a way that more conservative estimates are obtained. However, in these methods the landmark covariances are not immediately available, which makes data association more computationally expensive.

Another SLAM method is FastSLAM [7] (or FastSLAM 2.0 [8]), where the sensor pose uncertainty is represented by a particle filter. Since the landmark positions are conditionally independent given the sensor pose, and since each particle represents one (completely certain) pose hypothesis, the covariance between different landmark positions is zero in this formulation. Hence the uncertainty about each landmark can be modeled by a separate covariance matrix of size 3×3, thereby elimininating the quadratic growth rate. On the other hand, a large number of particles may be needed.

2.2 Smoothing and Mapping

The algorithms mentioned above, like most other SLAM algorithms, perform *filtering*, i.e., compute the new sensor pose and updates the map whenever a new measurement is available, but retain the previous sensor pose trajectory without modification. This is obviously suboptimal. In the Smoothing and Mapping (SAM) [3] algorithm, *smoothing* is used instead of filtering. This essentially means that the entire map and sensor pose trajectory are computed using all measurements. Hence, all parameters are recomputed whenever a new measurement becomes available.

SAM solves the least squares problem given by

$$\boldsymbol{\Theta}^* = \arg\min_{\boldsymbol{\Theta}} \left\{ \sum_{i=1}^{N} \|f_i(\mathbf{X}_{i-1}, \mathbf{u}_i) - \mathbf{x}_i\|^2_{\boldsymbol{\Lambda}_i} + \sum_{k=1}^{K} \|h_k(\mathbf{X}_{i_k}, \mathbf{l}_{j_k}) - \mathbf{z}_k\|^2_{\boldsymbol{\Sigma}_k} \right\},$$

where $\boldsymbol{\Theta}^*$ is a parameter vector containing the trajectory and map information, K and N are the number of observations and positions along the trajectory, respectively, and $\boldsymbol{\Lambda}$ and $\boldsymbol{\Sigma}$ are the process and measurement noise covariances. f and h are functions defining the the process and measurement models. Further, $\mathbf{z}$ represents actual measurements and $\mathbf{u}$ is the odometry information (the estimated motion in the submap).

By linearizing f and h, $\boldsymbol{\Theta}^*$ can be obtained by solving a standard linear least squares problem of the form

$$\delta^* = \arg\min_{\delta} \|\mathbf{A}\delta - \mathbf{b}\|^2.$$

Here δ^* is the optimal adjustment of the linearization point $\boldsymbol{\Theta}$ (the previous estimate). $\mathbf{A}$ contains Jacobians of the process and measurement model, evaluated at the current linearization point, while $\mathbf{b}$ contains the odometry and measurement prediction errors. The details of the SAM algorithm, including how to construct $\mathbf{A}$ and $\mathbf{b}$ are omitted here in order to conserve space; a very nice presentation is available in [3]. Nevertheless, two important points should be noted here: 1) The system of equations rapidly becomes very large. However, $\mathbf{A}$ is sparse since most landmarks are only observed along a short part of the sensor trajectory. By rearranging the columns of $\mathbf{A}$ (and the rows of δ^*) this sparsity can be exploited, greatly reducing the computational complexity of the algorithm. 2) Since the entire trajectory and map are updated and the problem is relinearized in every iteration using the current state estimate, SAM does not suffer from inconsistent solutions due to linearization errors.

2.3 Submaps

One way to cope with rapidly growing computational complexity of SLAM methods is to divide the environment into smaller areas, or *submaps*. In addition to reducing the computational cost, submapping techniques may also improve the consistency of the globally estimated map [1]. In Conditionally Independent Divide and Conquer SLAM [11] a chain of submaps is created, and the submaps are merged by back-propagating information. Loop closure is performed by adding landmarks common to the current and previous submap at the loop closure location. Conditionally Independent Graph SLAM [10] is similar, but maintains a spanning tree making it possible to transmit information between submaps. Tectonic SAM [9] is based on the smoothing and mapping concept described above, and is similar to the method presented in this paper. However, Tectonic SAM utilizes all observations of landmarks which are shared between different submaps. Also, Tectonic SAM creates the submaps *and* merges them using SAM-like approaches.

3 Method

As stated in the previous section, EKF-SLAM works relatively well in very small environments, but produces inconsistent maps and is computationally expensive when the map grows and linearization errors arise. SAM, on the other hand, does not suffer from inconsistency problems. However, its computational complexity grows rapidly with the number of landmark measurements and with the number of poses in the sensor trajectory. We therefore propose a method where small submaps are created using EKF-SLAM and merged using an approach similar to Tectonic SAM. Compared to Tectonic SAM, our approach uses only one measurement per submap, creates the submaps using EKF-SLAM and merges them using smoothing. In the merging step, each submap is considered just one measurement and one position along the sensor trajectory. Hence, in the SAM step, only a skeleton of the entire trajectory is considered. This submapping approach reduces the computational complexities of both the EKF-SLAM and the SAM steps, while also alleviating the consistency issues of EKF-SLAM.

Section 3.1 presents our approach for creating conditionally independent submaps using EKF-SLAM. Section 3.2 describes the merging process, which we refer to as Submap Joining Smooting and Mapping (SJSAM).

3.1 Conditionally Independent Submaps

Conditionally independent submaps are created with EKF-SLAM in a way very similar to [11]. A new submap is initiated when the sensor has moved a user-specified distance from the start of the current submap. Each submap is locally referenced, i.e., the sensor position is set to the origin and the orientation to a default rotation matrix. The covariance for the new pose is zero. The velocity of the sensor is initiated with the velocity of the sensor in the previous submap, rotated to compensate for resetting the sensor orientation.

The landmarks that were matched in the last step of the previous submap are copied to the new submap and used as its initial landmarks. Their positions are also compensated for the orientation reset. The covariance of the landmark positions is calculated from the previous submap by marginalization of the previous uncertainty about sensor pose:

$$\mathbf{P}_{l,l} = \mathbf{P}_{l,l} - \mathbf{P}_{l,c}\mathbf{P}_{c,c}^{-1}\mathbf{P}_{c,l},$$

where $\mathbf{P}_{l,l}$ is the covariance matrix for all landmark positions in the submap, $\mathbf{P}_{c,c}$ is the covariance of the sensor pose and $\mathbf{P}_{l,c} = \mathbf{P}_{c,l}^T$ is the cross covariance. The resulting covariance matrix is finally rotated to compensate for the orientation reset within the new submap.

3.2 Submap Merging

In the original SAM approach, the state vector contains all sensor poses along the trajectory. This means that the state vector grows with time, even if no new landmarks are observed. Additionally, all landmark observations are stored in the matrix $\mathbf{A}$, which defines the equation system to be solved in each iteration. If 20 3D landmarks are observed in every frame, a frame rate of 10 Hz corresponds to $20 \times 3 \times 10 = 600$ additional rows in $\mathbf{A}$ every second. While these rows are sparse, this still causes the computational complexity to increase rapidly, particularly since each observation increases the relinearization workload in the algorithm.

In SJSAM, actual landmark observations are not used within the SAM framework. Instead, these observations are used to create submaps using EKF-SLAM. Submaps are then merged using SAM, treating each submap as just *one combined measurement*. Similarly, instead of considering each sensor pose along the trajectory, the entire estimated motion within each submap is treated as *one sample* of odometry data to be used in SAM. This approach results in that only a skeleton of the sensor trajectory is maintained in the SAM state vector. Hence both the dimensionality of the state vector in SAM and the number of equations corresponding to measurements are reduced significantly.

Measurement equation. In SJSAM, the landmarks of a submap are considered relative measurements from the origin of the submap. Each measurement consists of the relative displacement between the landmark and the sensor in three dimensions (Δx, Δy and Δz). The measurement equation is

$$\mathbf{z} = (\Delta x \quad \Delta y \quad \Delta z)^T = h(\mathbf{x}_c, \mathbf{l}) = \mathbf{T}(\mathbf{l} - \mathbf{x}_c)$$

where $\mathbf{z}$ is the measurement, $\mathbf{x}_c$ is the sensor pose (in this context: the global coordinates of the first position in the current submap), $\mathbf{l}$ is the position of the observed landmark (also in global coordinates) and $\mathbf{T}$ is a rotation matrix transforming from global to submap-specific coordinates. The covariances of the landmarks in the submaps are used as measurement noise in SJSAM.

System dynamics. The last position in each submap is considered as odometry information in the prediction part of the SJSAM merging algorithm. This gives an initial estimate of the sensor state and the linearization points needed in

SAM. The equation for predicting a new sensor pose given the previous pose estimate and the odometry information is the following:

$$\mathbf{x}_i = \begin{pmatrix} x_i \\ y_i \\ z_i \\ \phi_i \\ \theta_i \\ \psi_i \end{pmatrix} = f(\mathbf{x}_{i-1}, \mathbf{u}_{i-1}) = \begin{pmatrix} x_{i-1} \\ y_{i-1} \\ z_{i-1} \\ \phi_{i-1} \\ \theta_{i-1} \\ \psi_{i-1} \end{pmatrix} + \begin{pmatrix} \mathbf{T}^{-1} \begin{pmatrix} \Delta x \\ \Delta y \\ \Delta z \end{pmatrix} \\ \Delta\phi \\ \Delta\theta \\ \Delta\psi \end{pmatrix},$$

where the pose of the robot in the end of a locally referenced submap is Δx Δy Δz $\Delta\phi$ $\Delta\theta$ $\Delta\psi$, i.e., the odometry input given by the final pose in the submap. The covariance of the final robot pose in the submap is used as process noise in SJSAM.

Algorithm. For each submap, a number of steps are carried out, see Algoritm 1. First, the linearization points corresponding to the estimates of the sensor state in sample i and $i-1$ are retrieved. The linearization point in $i-1$ is found in the last rows of the state vector. The linearization point for i is calculated using the process equation using the state in $i-1$ and the odometry information of the previous submap.

The second step is data association. The measurements in a sample correspond to the landmarks of one submap. For reasons of computational complexity, the data association is performed using nearest neighbor calculation with Euclidean distances. For each landmark a SURF descriptor [2], representing the appearance of the surrounding area in the image, is stored. This descriptor is used as a validity check in the data association.

In the third step the measurement matrix **A** is augmented with three rows for each landmark in the submap. The odometry data is also appended to **A** and the new data about measurement and odometry prediction errors is appended to the vector **b**. Complete details of how to structure **A** and **b** are available in [3].

SJSAM will incrementally find better estimates of the linearization points used in the past. Hence **A**, which depends on the linearization points, needs to be recalculated once in a while. This is called relinearization and is performed whenever data from a new submap (odometry and measurements) is processed by the SAM framework. During relinearization the entire **A** matrix and the vector **b** are traversed.

SJSAM then solves the least squares problem using Q-less QR-factorization with the sparse **A** matrix and the vector **b**. Solving the resulting QR-factorization gives δ^* with information of how much to change each variable in the current state vector $\mathbf{\Theta}$ (see Section 2.2).

The exact sensor state covariance estimates can be retrieved efficiently from the QR-factor R using back-substitution [6]. Conservative estimates of the landmark covariances can be retrieved efficiently using the sensor covariance and the measurement noise used when the landmark was initiated. Exact estimates are more costly to access.

Algorithm 1. Submap Joining Smoothing and Mapping (SJSAM)

Data: Submaps $\mathbf{s}_i = (\mathbf{x}_i \; \mathcal{L}_i)^T \in \mathcal{S}$ created with e.g. EKF-SLAM. $\mathbf{x}_i$ is the last state of the camera in submap i, and $\mathcal{L}_i$ is the landmarks in submap i

Result: A state vector $\mathbf{\Theta}^* = (\hat{\mathbf{x}} \; \hat{\mathbf{m}})^T$, where $\hat{\mathbf{x}}$ is a skeleton trajectory and $\hat{\mathbf{m}}$ is the map

begin
    forall *submaps* $\mathbf{s}_i \in \mathcal{S}$ **do**
        1. Retrieve the linearization points
        if $i = 1$ **then**
            Initiate $\hat{\mathbf{x}}_1$ with zeros
        else
            $\hat{\mathbf{x}}_{i-1}$ is the last camera state estimate in $\mathbf{\Theta}$
            $\hat{\mathbf{x}}_i = f(\hat{\mathbf{x}}_{i-1}, \mathbf{u}_{i-1})$ where $\mathbf{u}_{i-1}$ is the odometry information from $\mathbf{s}_{i-1}$
        end
        2. Data association
        Find all $\mathbf{l}_j \in \mathcal{L}_i$ that match a previously seen landmark
        Find all $\mathbf{l}_n \in \mathcal{L}_i$ that have not been seen before
        3. Measurement update
        forall *reobservations* $\mathbf{l}_j$ **do**
            Compute measurement Jacobians with respect to landmark positions and camera state
            Add measurement Jacobians to $\mathbf{A}$ (3 rows)
            Add measurement prediction errors to $\mathbf{b}$ (3 rows)
        end
        forall *new observations* $\mathbf{l}_n$ **do**
            Compute an initial estimate for the landmark using the measurement
            Add initial estimate to $\mathbf{\Theta}$ (3 rows)
            Compute measurement Jacobians with respect to landmark positions and camera state
            Add measurement Jacobians to $\mathbf{A}$ (3 rows, 3 columns)
            Add measurement prediction errors to $\mathbf{b}$ (3 rows)
        end
        4. Time update
        if $i = 1$ **then**
            Add identity matrix to $\mathbf{A}$ (6 rows, 6 columns)
            Add process prediction errors to $\mathbf{b}$ (3 rows)
        else
            Compute the process model Jacobian
            Add Jacobian and identity matrix to $\mathbf{A}$ (6 rows, 6 columns)
            Add process model prediction errors to $\mathbf{b}$ (6 rows)
        end
        Add $\hat{\mathbf{x}}_\mathbf{i}$ to $\mathbf{\Theta}$ (6 rows)
        5. Relinearization
        Recompute all the elements of $\mathbf{A}$ and $\mathbf{b}$ that were created during sample $1 \ldots (i-1)$, using the new linearization points
        6. Solve the least squares problem
        Solve $\mathbf{A}\delta^* = \mathbf{b}$ using Q-less QR-factorization
        $\mathbf{\Theta} = \mathbf{\Theta} + \delta^*$
    end
end

Similar work. The Sparse Local Submap Joining Filter (SLSJF) [4] is similar to SJSAM in that it uses a hierarchical submap approach. SLSJF also stores each start/end pose of the submaps in the state vector. However, SLSJF uses an Extended Information Filter (EIF) representation for the submap merging instead of the SAM representation. SLSJF and I-SLSJF [5] retrieves the state vector from the information matrix by solving a least squares problem. This is similar to SJSAM. However, I-SLSJF only recomputes the measurement matrix and vector somtimes, while SJSAM performs this step in each sample. Additionally, I-SLSJF does not use a specific prediction step.

4 Examples

We have evaluated the idea with SJSAM on several data sets. Two of them will be presented here. Both sets are collected in indoor environments with a stereo camera mounted horizontally on a trolley. The trolley was moved at roughly constant speed throughout the data collections.

4.1 Implementation Details

Both the EKF-SLAM- and SJSAM-algorithm are implemented in MATLAB and are currently not capable of real-time processing. The main reason for this is the feature extraction. We divide the map creation process into four essential steps:

1. Data acquisition.
2. Feature extraction with SURF [2].
3. Creation of submaps using EKF-SLAM.
4. Merging of submaps with SJSAM.

There are currently two different methods for submap creation. The first method is to use the traveled distance as the bounding limit for each submap, e.g., a new submap is initiated when the camera has moved more than one meter since the start of the submap. The other method uses the number of landmarks the submap contains as the condition to start a new submap, e.g., a new submap is created when the current submap contains more than 100 landmarks. This later approach gives a more predictable time complexity but the traveled distance approach gives more evenly spread out submaps. In the experiments below we use a maximum travel distance of one meter for each submap, to test the algorithm's handling of several submaps.

4.2 Small Area Experiment

The first experiment was conducted in a small conference room. During this experiment the trolley moved a total path of approximately 15 m which gives a total of 15 submaps and 358 landmarks. Figure 1 shows the result from the submap generation, colored dots represent landmarks and black dots correspond to the trajectory. The black squares mark the start of each submap and those points will be used as input to the SJSAM algorithm.

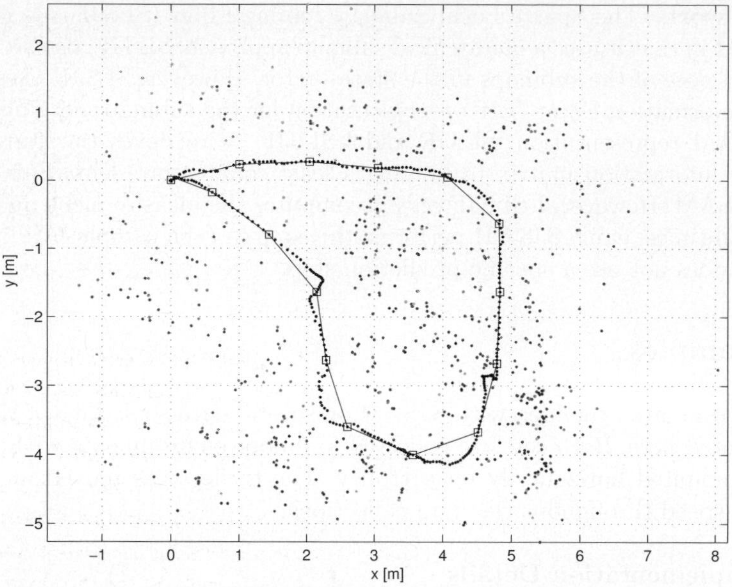

Fig. 1. Submaps from the small area. The start of each submap is marked with a square. The thin lines represent a skeleton map created only from the start of each submap. Axes in meters.

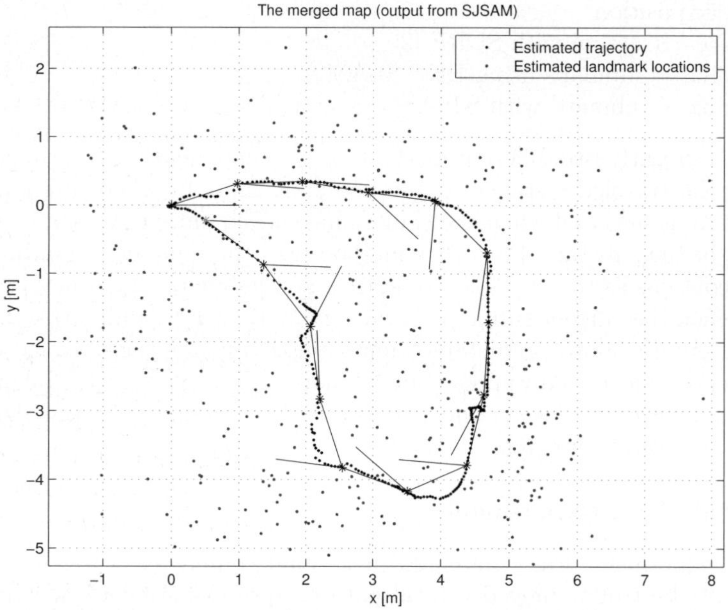

Fig. 2. Submaps from the small area processed with the SJSAM algorithm. The short lines represents the camera's orientation at the start of each submap. In total there are 358 landmarks in the map. Axes in meters.

Since this is a fairly small data set it could also be processed with standard EKF-SLAM for computational comparison. The total processing time for this data set with EKF-SLAM was about 6.5 s and with submaps the same data set can be processed in 3.8 s indicating that the use of submaps significantly reduces the computational complexity.

Processing the submaps with the SJSAM algorithm yields the map depicted in Figure 2. It is hard to see any significant improvement but the figure clearly shows that the algorithm has performed loop-closure and that the trolley has returned almost exactly to its original position.

4.3 Large Area Experiment

The second experiment was conducted in a dining room connected to a conference room by a normal doorway, a total path of approximately 34 meters. The trolley was moved through the dining room, into the conference room, and then back to the initial position. This results in a trajectory that is eight-shaped.

Figure 3 shows the resulting trajectory using EKF-SLAM. The figure shows that the trolley not has returned to its original position. This kind of behavior occurs due to drift and the lack of loop-closure between the submabs. The complete map consists of 34 submaps and the total processing time is about 26 s.

The previously created submaps can be processed by SJSAM algorithm. By sequential merging of the submaps and re-linearization of the whole problem in each sample we get the map presented in Figure 4, left. This map consists of 1275 landmarks and the merging time is 3 seconds. It can be seen from the figure that loop closure has occurred. This can also be seen in the sparse measurement

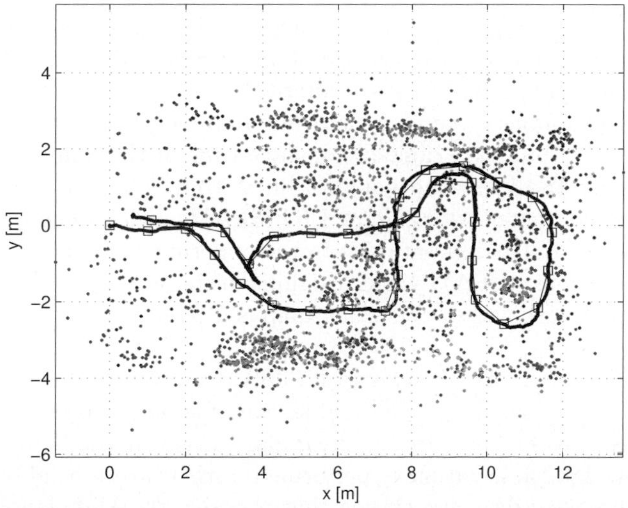

Fig. 3. The large area experiment, the trajectory consisting of 34 submaps. Processed using EKF-SLAM. Axes in meters.

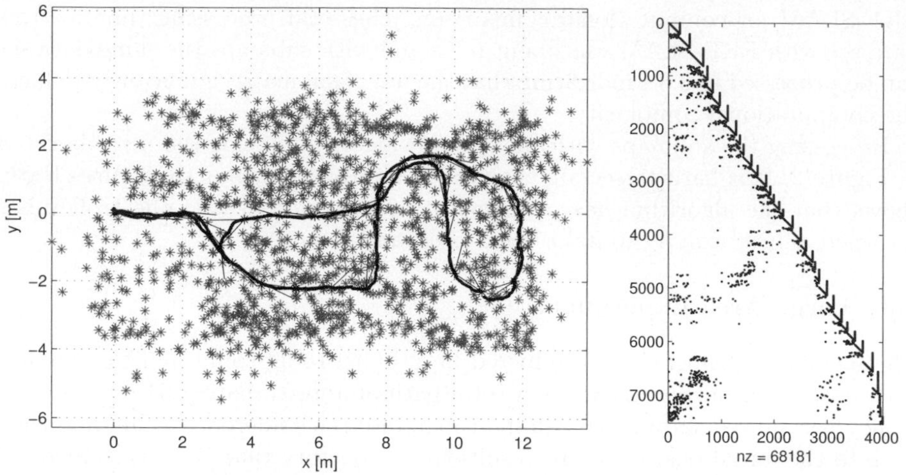

Fig. 4. The large area experiment. Left: the trajectory after merging the 34 submaps using SJSAM. Axes in meters. Right: the sparse measurement matrix **A** illustrating loop closure. The dots illustrates non-zero elements in **A**. Axes represents the position of the elements in the matrix.

matrix **A** in Figure 4, right, by looking at the lower triangular part of the matrix: elements that are non-zero and not close to the diagonal represent landmarks that have been seen before and recognized.

5 Conclusions

We have presented an approach for merging of submaps using smoothing and mapping. The approach is called Submap Joining Smoothing and Mapping.

The approach is illustrated in two examples using data from a stereo vision camera. In both examples we can see that a submap-based approach is successful. The generation of submabs is done in constant time in the number of submaps and merging with SJSAM is done in almost linear time. This is in a relatively low time complexity compared to standard EKF-SLAM, which makes this method suitable for intermediate sized data sets.In the experiment with a larger data set (large area experiment) SJSAM yields a significant improvement. SJSAM is able to perform loop-closure and the resulting map is a large improvement compared to using only submaps.

This paper shows our first results with SJSAM and in the future the performance need to be evaluated. The optimal length of submaps needs to be studied and SJSAM needs to be compared with similar SLAM methods. In the current implementation data association is performed with nearest neighbor. Extending the algorithm with data association that uses e.g. the Mahalanobis distance may lead to improved performance and less sensitivity to drift. It may also be necessary to use picture comparison techniques, such as tree-of-words.

References

1. Bailey, T., Nieto, J., Guivant, J., Stevens, M., Nebot, E.: Consistency of the EKF-SLAM algorithm. In: 2006 IEEE/RSJ International Conference on Intelligent Robots and Systems, pp. 3562–3568 (2006)
2. Bay, H., Tuytelaars, T., Van Gool, L.: Surf: Speeded up robust features. In: Leonardis, A., Bischof, H., Pinz, A. (eds.) ECCV 2006. LNCS, vol. 3951, pp. 404–417. Springer, Heidelberg (2006)
3. Dellaert, F., Kaess, M.l.: Square root sam: Simultaneous localization and mapping via square root information smoothing. Int. J. Rob. Res. 25(12), 1181–1203 (2006)
4. Huang, S., Wang, Z., Dissanayake, G.: Sparse local submap joining filter for building large-scale maps. IEEE Transactions on Robotics 24(5), 1121–1130 (2008)
5. Huang, S., Wang, Z., Dissanayake, G., Frese, U.: Iterated SLSJF: A sparse local submap joining algorithm with improved consistency. In: 2008 Australiasan Conference on Robotics and Automation, Citeseer (2008)
6. Kaess, M., Ranganathan, A., Dellaert, F.: iSAM: Incremental smoothing and mapping. IEEE Transactions on Robotics 24(6), 1365–1378 (2008)
7. Montemerlo, M.: FastSLAM: A Factored Solution to the Simultaneous Localization and Mapping Problem with Unknown Data Association. PhD thesis, Robotics Institute, Carnegie Mellon University, Pittsburgh, PA (July 2003)
8. Montemerlo, M.l., Thrun, S., Roller, D., Wegbreit, B.: Fastslam 2.0: an improved particle filtering algorithm for simultaneous localization and mapping that provably converges. In: Proceedings of the 18th International joint Conference on Artificial Intelligence, San Francisco, CA, USA, pp. 1151–1156 (2003)
9. Ni, K., Steedly, D., Dellaer F.: Tectonic sam: exact, out-of-core, submap-based slam. In: Proc. IEEE International Conference on Robotics and Automation, pp. 1678–1685 (2007)
10. Piniés, P., Paz, L.M., Tardós, J.D.: CI-Graph: An efficient approach for Large Scale SLAM. In: IEEE International Conference on Robotics and Automation (2009)
11. Piniés, P., Tardós, J.D.: Large-scale slam building conditionally independent local maps: Application to monocular vision. IEEE Transactions on Robotics 24(5), 1094–1106 (2008)
12. Thrun, S., Liu, Y., Koller, D., Ng, A.Y., Ghahramani, Z., Durrant-Whyte, H.: Simultaneous Localization and Mapping with Sparse Extended Information Filters. The International Journal of Robotics Research 23(7-8), 693–716 (2004)
13. Walter, M.R., Eustice, R.M., Leonard, J.J.: Exactly sparse extended information filters for feature-based SLAM. The International Journal of Robotics Research 26(4), 335 (2007)

Watermark Recovery from a Dual Layer Hologram with a Digital Camera

Anu Pramila*, Anja Keskinarkaus, Esa Rahtu, and Tapio Seppänen

Department of Electrical and Information Engineering,
University of Oulu, P.O. Box 4500, FIN 90014 University of Oulu
Tel.: +358-8-553-2797; Fax: +358-8-553-2534
{anu.pramila,anja.keskinarkaus,esa.rahtu,tapio.seppanen}@ee.oulu.fi
http://www.cse.oulu.fi

Abstract. In this paper we present a method for reading a watermark from a dual layer hologram image with a digital camera. Here the base of the hologram out of which the hologram was designed is a binary image. The hologram obtained is placed on a planar surface and an image is captured from the hologram by setting up a light source and a digital camera on appropriate distances and angles relative to the hologram. The captured image is corrected from affine distortions and a saliency detector based segmentation is performed for the image. The watermark is read from the resulting reconstructed binary image. The obtained results show that the watermark can be recovered perfectly from a dual layer hologram with a proper setting of the camera and light sources.

Keywords: Digital watermarking, watermarking holograms, print-cam process.

1 Introduction

Holograms and watermarking have both been considered as safety measures against copying. In this paper, these two techniques are combined and a method for recovering a watermark from a dual layer hologram is introduced. This adds another level of security to the holograms.

Wang et al. [1] proposed a method for watermarking a dot matrix hologram. For embedding the watermark they used a modified halftoning technique exclusively designed for dot matrix color hologram. When extracting the watermark, the hologram was photographed by carefully selecting a high resolution digital camera and proper lighting conditions.

However, there are many hologram techniques available and here a dual layer hologram as shown in Fig. 1 was manufactured and used instead of a dot matrix hologram as in [1]. The hologram consists of a background image and foreground image layers. The frame and the pseudorandom pattern on the hologram background were considered only as artistic features.

* The financial support from the Academy of Finland and Graduate school of is gratefully acknowledged. Hologram by courtesy of Starcke Ltd.

A. Heyden and F. Kahl (Eds.): SCIA 2011, LNCS 6688, pp. 146–155, 2011.

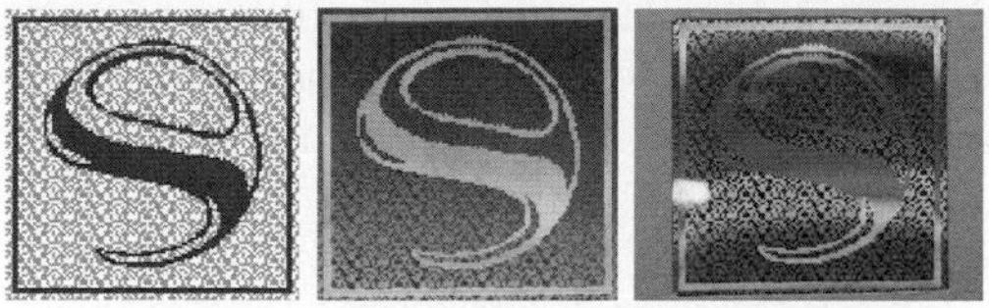

Fig. 1. a) A design for the hologram. b) The obtained hologram. c) The phase change in the hologram background and foreground.

When reading a watermark from a printed image with a digital camera, the watermark should be robust against 3 dimensional distortions, rotation, scaling, and translation [2,3,4]. In addition, there may be variations in the environment, such as lighting and reflections. The camera itself inflicts various attacks to the watermark, for example, JPEG-compression and lens distortions [5,6].

When reading a watermark from a hologram, the problems to be solved are increased. The hologram surface is often mirror like and the watermarked image may not be visible in all directions or with all light sources. Source and direction of the light affects the way the hologram is seen. Due to the rainbow effect on the surface of the hologram, the color and intensity changes across the watermarked image when the hologram is tilted relative to the light source. However, it can be assumed that the color varies in the background of the image in different phase to that of the foreground as illustrated in Fig. 1.

In this paper, based on the notion of locally different colors on the background and foreground, the hologram image is segmented and the watermark read. Original unwatermarked image is employed in the process. The segmentation method used in the process is based on a method by Rahtu et al. [9]. The segmentation process is explained with more detail in Section 2.2.

Here the hologram is created from a binary image. Due to the reflective nature of the hologram, it is difficult to detect single separate pixels and thus pattern matching methods were used to modify the method by Tseng et al. [8]. The watermarking method is explained with more detail in Section 2.1. The experiments were made and the test set-up and results are shown in Chapter 3.

2 Methods

In this chapter, the method applied is explained in detail. First the watermarking method which was applied is explained, then the correction of geometrical distortions and finally image segmentation algorithm is described.

2.1 Watermarking Method

Pan et al. [7] proposed a data hiding method for binary images. Tseng et al. [8] later identified some image quality issues and improved the method. In this paper we have modified the method by Tseng et al. by applying patten matching methods in order to better adapt the method for our application. Below is a review of the method by Tseng et al. and afterwards the modifications are explained.

In the methods by Pan et al. [7] and Tseng et al. [8] the main idea is to use a secret key and a weight matrix to protect the hidden data. It is shown that for each $m \times n$ block in the host binary image I, $r \leq \lfloor \log_2(mn+1) \rfloor - 1$ bits of data can be embedded by changing at most 2 bits in the block.

In the following, K is a key, a randomly selected binary matrix of size $m \times n$. W is a weight matrix which is an integer matrix of size $m \times n$. Here, $[W]_{i,j}$ denotes the element of W at row i and column j. W satisfies the condition that $\{[W]_{i,j} | i = 1...m, j = 1...n\} = \{1, 2, ..., 2^{r+1} - 1\}$ and each 2×2 sub-block contains at least one odd element. [8]

Tseng et al. [8] aimed to improve the method by Pan et al. [7] by introducing a distance measure in order to ensure that the modified bit is adjacent to another bit with the same value. The distance matrix was calculated with

$$[dist(I)]_{i,j} = \min_{\forall x,y} \{ \sqrt{|i-x|^2 + |j-y|^2} \mid [I]_{i,j} \neq [I]_{x,y} \} , \quad (1)$$

where $[dist(I)]_{i,j}$ is the distance from $[I]_{i,j}$ to the closest element $[I]_{x,y}$ such that the complement of $[I]_{i,j}$ is equal to $[I]_{x,y}$.

A bit stream $b_1 b_2 ... b_r$ is embedded into each non-black and non-blank host block I_i by first computing following set for each $w = 1..2^{r+1} - 1$:

$$\begin{aligned} T'_w = \{(j,k) | [([W]_{j,k} = w) \wedge ([I_i \oplus K]_{i,j} = 0) \wedge ([dist(I)]_{j',k'} \leq \sqrt{2})] \\ \vee [([W]_{j,k} = 2^{r+1} - w) \wedge ([I_i \oplus K]_{i,j} = 1) \wedge ([dist(I)]_{j',k'} \leq \sqrt{2})]\} , \end{aligned} \quad (2)$$

where $[dist(I)]_{j',k'}$ is for the bit corresponding to $[I_i]_{i,j}$ in block I_i. $\oplus$ means bitwise exclusive or of two binary matrices. Here each bit has 8 neighbors and thus the distance $\leq \sqrt{2}$. [8]

Second, a weight difference is defined ($\otimes$ means pairwise multiplication of two matrices and SUM means the sum of all elements in a matrix)

$$d' \equiv (b_1 b_2 ... b_r 0) - SUM((I_i \oplus K) \otimes W) \ (mod\ 2^{r+1}) . \quad (3)$$

If $d' = 0$, there is no need to change I_i. Otherwise [8]:

if(there exists an $h \in \{0, 1, ..., 2^r - 1\}$ such that $T'_{hd'} \neq \emptyset$ and $T'_{-(h-1)d'} \neq \emptyset$)
  Randomly pick an h which satisfies the above condition;
  Randomly pick a (j,k) $\in T'_{hd'}$ and complement the bit $[I_i]_{j,k}$;
  Randomly pick a (j,k) $\in T'_{-(h-1)d'}$ and complement the bit $[I_i]_{j,k}$;
else
  if($SUM((I_i \oplus K) \otimes W)\ mod\ 2 = 1$)
    Keep I_i intact;
  else
    Select a (j,k) such that $[W]_{j,k}$ is odd and its corresponding $[dist(I)]_{j',k'}$ is the smallest and complement the bit $[I_i]_{j,k}$;
  end
end

If the resulting modified image block I'_i is completely black or blank, the data hiding is regarded as invalid. The same bit sequence $b_1 b_2 ... b_r$ is hidden to the next block if applicable. [8]

The receiver computes the hidden data from each block with $(SUM((I'_i \oplus K) \otimes W))/2$, if I'_i is not completely black or blank and $SUM((I'_i \oplus K) \otimes W)$ is even. Otherwise, I'_i contains no hidden information. [8]

The method by Tseng et al. [8] guarantees that each modified bit is neighboring a bit that is equal to the new value of the modified bit. Authors focus on 8-neighborhood which, however, results in sporadic pixels such as in Fig. 2.

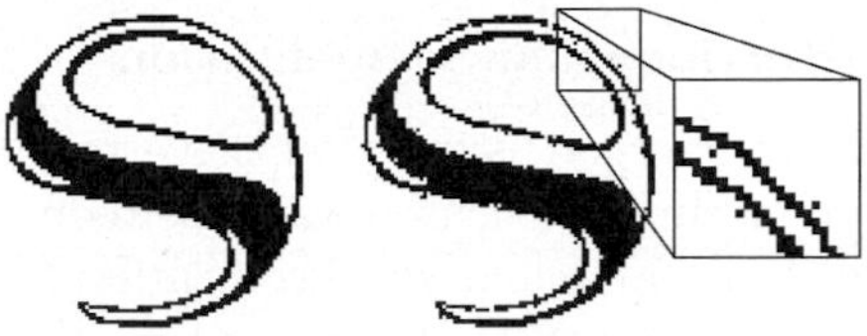

Fig. 2. Original image and a watermarked image with the method by Tseng et al.

In holograms, the shiny surface inflicts spreading of the pixels in the captured image. Therefore, sporadic pixels may be difficult to detect reliably. In order to minimize the possibility for sporadic pixels due to the watermarking method, we modify the method by Tseng et al. [8] by applying pattern matching methods to determine possible locations for the watermarked pixels. The watermark is embedded only in those predetermined locations on such a way that the reading method of the watermark is not affected. The patterns used are in Fig. 3.

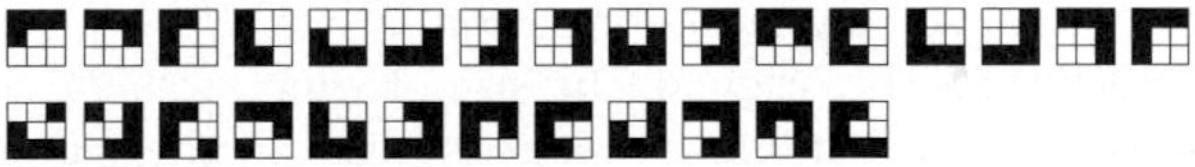

Fig. 3. Patterns used for watermark embedding

Each pixel neighborhood is compared with each of the patterns. If a mach is found the pixel is marked as a possible location for a watermark bit. Therefore T'_w becomes

$$\begin{aligned} T''_w = \{(j,k) | [([W]_{j,k} = w) \wedge ([I_i \oplus K]_{i,j} = 0) \\ \wedge ([dist(I)]_{j',k'} \leq 1)] \vee [([W]_{j,k} = 2^{r+1} - w) \\ \wedge ([I_i \oplus K]_{j,k} = 1) \wedge ([dist(I)]_{j',k'} \leq 1)] \wedge ([M]_{j,k} = 1)\} \,, \end{aligned} \tag{4}$$

where M is a matrix, containing obtained results of the pattern matching. The $\sqrt{2}$ is changed to 1 because we are interested only of 4-neighborhood. The watermark is read as in the method by Tseng et al. [8] and the final watermarked image can be seen in Fig. 4.

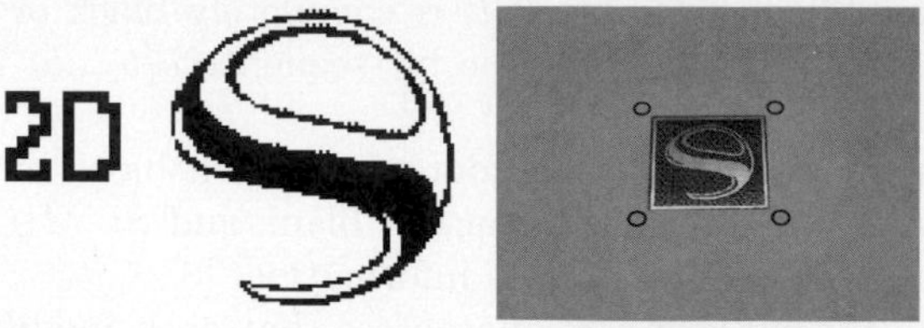

Fig. 4. a) Watermark message as an image. b) Watermarked binary image. c) Final hologram and synchronization markings.

2.2 Correcting Distortions and Segmentation

The binary watermarking method is very sensitive to geometrical distortions and as was noted in [10] accurate synchronization is required so that the binary image can be restored. Here a circular synchronization template, as illustrated in Fig. 4 is placed on each corner of the image and the user is prompted to select these templates from the captured image through a user interface before the captured image is processed and the watermark read. The exact locations of the circles are known and thus the distortions can be calculated and corrected with the following affine transformation.

$$x' = \frac{a_1 x + b_1 y + c_1}{a_0 x + b_0 y + 1}, \; y' = \frac{a_2 x + b_2 y + c_2}{a_0 x + b_0 y + 1}, \tag{5}$$

where (x', y') are the original picture positions, (x, y) are the camera picture positions and a, b and c are coefficients calculated from the circle locations.

In order to recover the watermarked binary image, the captured and corrected hologram image is segmented. The segmentation is done for a significantly larger image than the original so that no information is lost. Here we used an image size five times larger than the original, the size of which was 94×90 pixels.

The original unwatermarked binary image is given to the segmentation algorithm as an initial assumption. However, because the color varies in the background of the hologram in different phase to that of the foreground, it is advantageous work with RGB color space instead of grayscale images. By experimenting, it was discovered that the segmentation algorithm operates best if the binary image is not copied to each of the channels but instead roughly divided among each of the channels by first calculating approximately which channels hold most of the information corresponding to the binary image. This is done by calculating for each channel c

$$g_i(c) = \frac{\sum_j^N \sum_k^L U_i(c) B_i}{\sum_j^N \sum_k^L U_i(c)(1 - B_i)}, \tag{6}$$

where U_i is ith block on the corrected and captured image U, B is the original binary image and M and L the size of the image block. It is assumed that the colors run horizontally on the image and thus a horizontal block with width of that of the image and height of 30 was used here. Now, the binary template B' is calculated with

$$\begin{aligned} B_i'(c_1) &= B_i \\ B_i'(c_2) &= B_i \; if \; g_i(c_1) - g_i(c_2) < 0.4 \, , \end{aligned} \tag{7}$$

where c_1 is the channel where g_i is the largest and c_2 is the channel where g_i was the second largest.

The segmentation is based on a method by Rahtu et al. [9] and detects visually salient areas. The method applies a sliding window approach where a window is moved across the image and the saliency of a point in the window is estimated by determining the conditional probability of a pixel to be realized from the distribution estimated inside the window compared to the distribution of the surrounding area.

In the following, a rectangular window U_w' is divided into an inner kernel and an outer border, based here on the binary template. F contain feature values, i.e. here we used the RGB values as features. Two hypotheses are defined, H_0: point x is not salient, and H_1: point x is salient. Corresponding priori probabilities are $P(H_1)$ $P(H_0) = 1 - P(H_1)$. The initial assumption is that H_1 is valid for points in the kernel and H_0 is valid for points in the border. The conditional feature distributions $p(F(x)|H_1)$ and $p(F(x)|H_0)$ are estimated from the feature values F in kernel and border. Then with Bayes theorem [9]

$$P(H_1|F(x)) = \frac{p(F(x)|H_1)P(H_1)}{p(F(x)|H_0)P(H_0) + p(F(x)|H_1)P(H_1)} \, , \; x \in \Re^2 \, . \tag{8}$$

The saliency measure $S(x)$ is thus defined as $S(x) = P(H_1|F(x))$.

A window $U_w'(i)$ is slid over the image U' using a step s_w and measure $S_i(x)$ is calculated at each window position i. The step s_w is defined such that windows do overlap and the final saliency value of a pixel is defined as maximum [9]

$$S(x) = \max_j \{S_j(x)|x \in U_w'(j)\} \, , \tag{9}$$

The final salient objects were segmented from the background by thresholding $S(x)$. The threshold corresponds to the lowest probability which is allowed for a salient pixel to have for hypotheses H_1. Further, all 4-connected sets that cover less than 0.1 percent of the image area were removed and a morphological closing was performed with disk of radius $0.01 * min\{w_{U'}, h_{U'}\}$ where $w_{U'}$ and $h_{U'}$ are the image width and height respectively. the prior probability was set as $P(H_1) = 0.25$. For RGB image, the measure was calculated independently for each channel and maximum was taken as the final saliency value. [9]

In a hologram image the color varies across the image depending on the alignment of the hologram in relation to the light source. A red area might be background in one part of the image and foreground in the other part of the image. The sliding window size is here selected experimentally to be smaller than assumed color variation but big enough to lead to a reliable segmentation. It is assumed that the light source is aligned horizontally to the hologram and thus the window size was selected here such that $w_{U'_w} = 150$ and $h_{U'_w} = 50$ with step size $s_{U'_w} = 20$, for image size $w_{U'} = 470$ and $h_{U'} = 450$. However, due to the properties of the binary image, 8-connected sets that cover less than 0.01 percent of the image area were removed instead of 4-connected sets.

The segmentation method does not take into account the fact that the pixel size in the corrected image is a multiple of the pixel size in the original image. Therefore, while segmenting just before thresholding, the image is divided into blocks of size $a \times a$, where a is the multiple. All the pixels in a block are given the mean value of the center pixels of the block. The thresholded and segmented binary image is then scaled to its original size 94×90 and the watermark is read.

3 Experiments

Due to the high cost involved in hologram manufacturing, we were restricted in using only one hologram. The test setting is depicted in Fig. 5. The hologram was placed on a plane, the angle of which could be changed. A camera (Canon G7, 10 MP) was placed on a tripod and set in front of the hologram. The pedestal was set initially 10cm away from the hologram plane. The test were conducted by varying the angle of the hologram plane and directing the camera accordingly as well as varying the camera pedestal distance from 10cm to 15cm and 20cm.

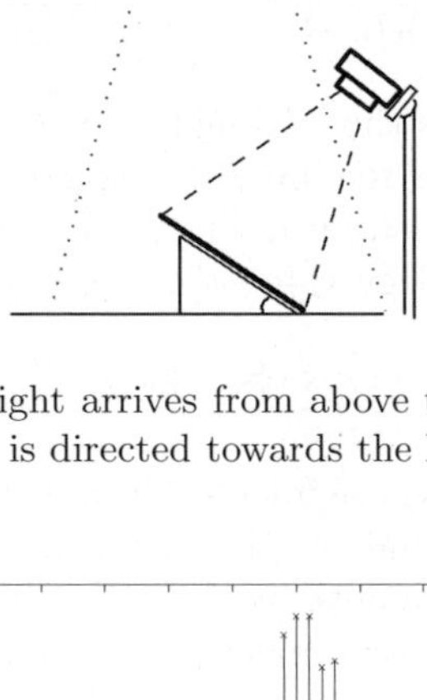

Fig. 5. The test setting. The light arrives from above the hologram which is set on a plane at an angle. The camera is directed towards the hologram.

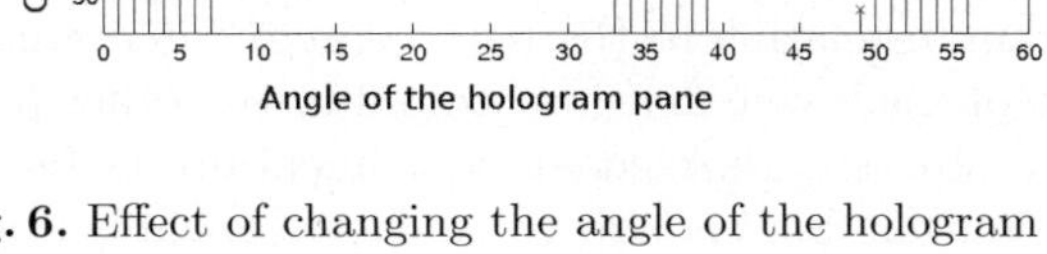

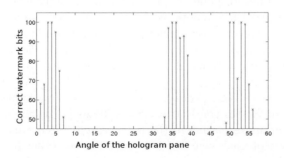

Fig. 6. Effect of changing the angle of the hologram plane

The experiments were conducted by first holding the camera still and turning the hologram plane from 0 to 59 degrees, a degree at a time. The results were collected to Fig. 6 in which y-axis shows the amount of correct watermark message bits relative to the angle, 100 being the maximum. It can be seen from the image, that there are three locations at which the watermark was fully extracted and the segmentation successful. At these locations the watermarked image was lit fully, and the color and intensity of the background were locally different relative to the foreground. At the other locations, the watermark recovery is not possible due to the hologram properties; The logo is not fully lit and properly visible. No error correction coding was applied.

The results in the three locations are further illustrated in Fig. 7 and Fig. 8 a) and b). In Fig. 7 are the original image, corrected image, segmented image and the obtained watermark message respectively. In the Fig. 8 the original captured images are left out.

Next, the experiments were conducted by moving the camera away from the hologram. The angle was incremented from 49 to 59 degrees and the camera pedestal was moved from 10cm to 15cm and 20cm. The height of the pedestal was increased accordingly so that the view to the hologram stayed the same. The results are illustrated in Fig. 7 and Fig. 9 a) and b).

Together the experimental results show that the most important factor in watermark recovery reliability is not distance of the camera but the angle of the hologram relative to the camera and light source. Perfect recovery of the watermark was attained with certain angles of the hologram and correct photographing set-up.

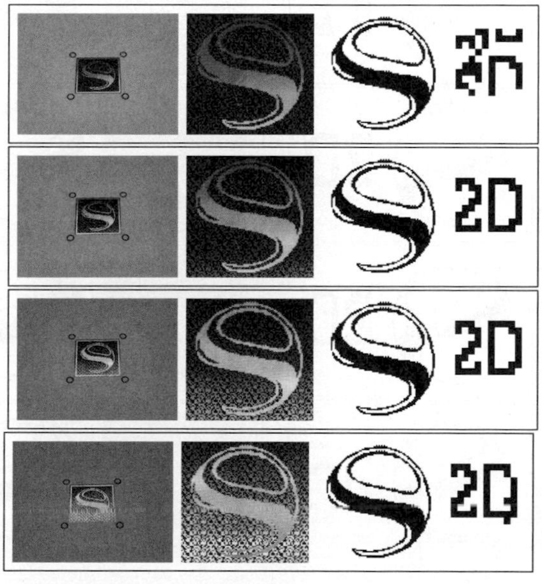

Fig. 7. Captured images with angles 2 to 5 and with distance 10cm

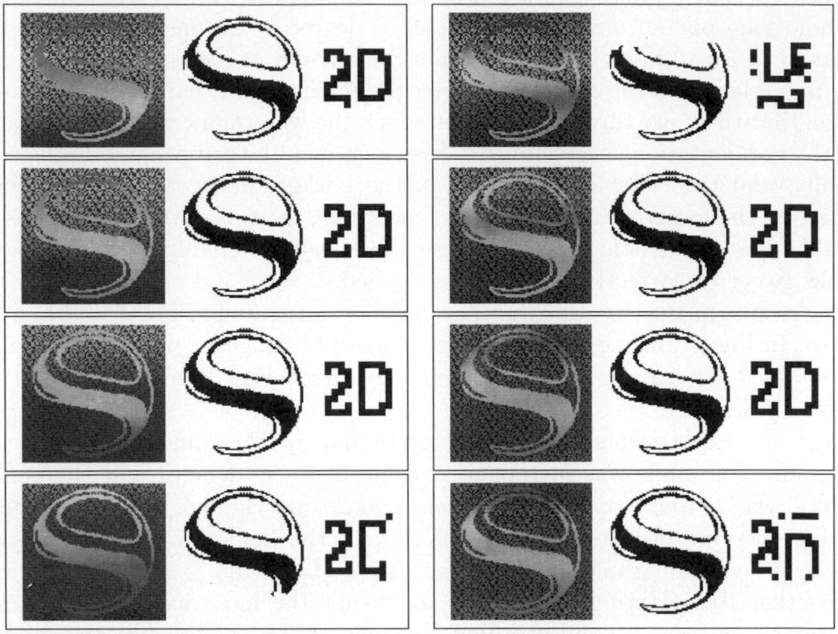

Fig. 8. Captured images with distance 10cm and with angles a) 34 to 37 and b) 49 to 52

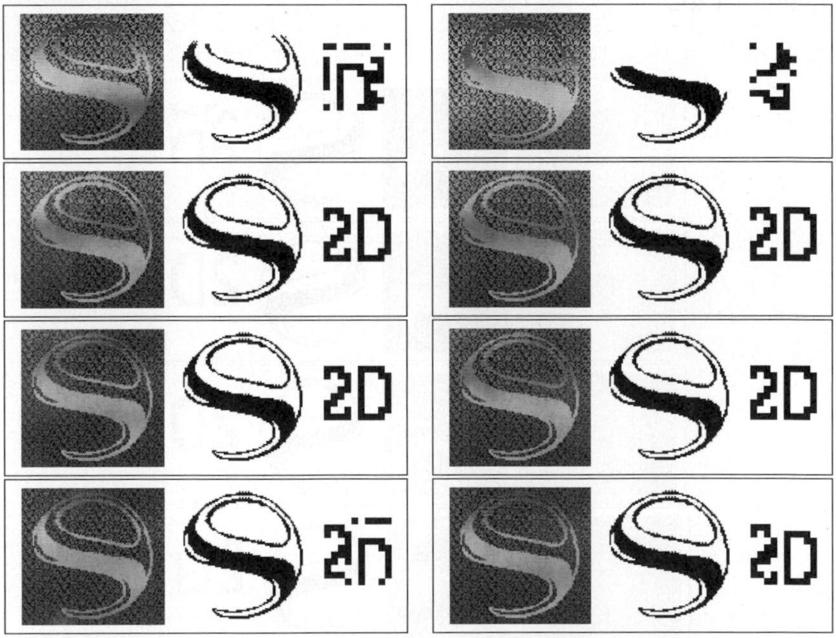

Fig. 9. Captured images with angles 49 to 52 and with distance a) 15 cm b) 20 cm

4 Conclusion

A method for reading a watermark from a dual layer hologram with a digital camera is presented in this paper. With correct set-up, the watermark was reconstructed perfectly. The recovery of the watermark from a hologram requires robustness against 3D distortions, color variations and reflections. The binary image needs to be reconstructed perfectly pixel by pixel in order to be able to read the watermark. The method was based on inversion of the distortions by applying synchronization markings around the image and segmenting the corrected image. In the future work, the aim is to remove the synchronization markings as well as take better into account the unique properties of the hologram.

References

1. Wang, H.-C., Wang, W.-C.: Data hiding in a hologram by modified digital halftoning techniques. In: Khosla, R., Howlett, R.J., Jain, L.C. (eds.) KES 2005. LNCS (LNAI), vol. 3683, pp. 1086–1092. Springer, Heidelberg (2005)
2. Lin, C.Y., Chang, S.F.: Distortion modeling and invariant extraction for digital image print-and-scan process. In: International Symposium on Multimedia Information Processing Taiwan (1999)
3. He, D., Sun, Q.: A practical print-scan resilient watermarking scheme. In: IEEE International Conference on Image Processing (ICIP), vol. 1, pp. I-257–I-260 (2005)
4. Solanki, K., Madhow, U., Manjunath, B.S., Chandrasekaran, S.: Estimating and Undoing Rotation for Print-scan Resilient Data Hiding. In: IEEE International Conference on Image Processing (ICIP), vol. 1, pp. 39–42 (2004)
5. Perry, B., MacIntosh, B., Cushman, D.: Digimarc MediaBridge - The birth of a consumer product, from concept to commercial application. In: Proc. of SPIE Security and Watermarking of Multimedia Contents IV, San Jose, CA, USA, vol. 4675, pp. 118–123 (2002)
6. Stach, J., Brundage, T.J., Hannigan, B.T., Bradley, B.A., Kirk, T., Brunk, H.: On the use of web cameras for watermark detection. In: Proc. of SPIE Security and Watermarking of Multimedia Contents IV, San Jose, CA, USA, vol. 4675, pp. 611–620 (2002)
7. Pan, H.-K., Chen, Y.-Y., Tseng, Y.-C.: A secure data hiding scheme for two-color images. In: Fifth IEEE Symposium on Computers and Communications, pp. 750–755. IEEE Press, Los Alamitos (2000)
8. Tseng, Y.-C., Pan, H.-K.: Secure and invisible data hiding in 2-color images. In: 10th Annual Joint Conference of the IEEE Computer and Communications Societies, vol. 2, pp. 887–896. IEEE Press, Los Alamitos (2001)
9. Rahtu, E., Heikkilä, J.: A simple and efficient saliency detector for background subtraction. In: IEEE Intl. Workshop on Visual Surveillance, Kyoto, Japan, pp. 1137–1144 (2009)
10. Pramila, A., Keskinarkaus, A., Seppänen, T.: Reading watermarks from printed binary images with a camera phone. In: Ho, A.T.S., Shi, Y.Q., Kim, H.J., Barni, M. (eds.) IWDW 2009. LNCS, vol. 5703, pp. 227–240. Springer, Heidelberg (2009)

Point Pattern Matching for 2-D Point Sets with Regular Structure

Tapio Manninen[1], Risto Rönkkä[1], and Heikki Huttunen[2]

[1] DropAim Oy, Tampere, Finland
[2] Tampere University of Technology, Tampere, Finland

Abstract. Point pattern matching (PPM) is a widely studied problem in algorithm research and has numerous applications, e.g., in computer vision. In this paper we focus on a class of brute force PPM algorithms suitable for situations where the state-of-the-art methods do not perform optimally, e.g., due to point sets with regular structure. We discuss of an existing algorithm, which is optimal in the sense of brute force testing of different point pairings. We propose a parameter choosing scheme that minimizes the memory consumption of the algorithm. We also present a modified version of the algorithm to overcome issues related to its implementation and accuracy. Due to its brute force nature, the algorithm is guaranteed to return the best possible result.

Keywords: Point Pattern Matching, Computer Vision, Printed Electronics.

1 Introduction

Point pattern matching (PPM) is a method for finding a one-to-one correspondence and the related transformation between two point sets. What makes finding the right transformation in PPM a non-trivial problem in practice are things like noise in the point locations, unknown correspondence between the points in both of the sets, and possible missing or extra points in either one of the sets. In this paper, we focus on a special PPM case typical of applications in image analysis and computer vision, i.e., finding the optimal similarity transformation (scaling, rotation, and translation) between two sets of points P and Q in $\mathbb{R}^2$.

Good reviews of state-of-the-art PPM algorithms have been written by Li et al. [8] and van Wamelen et al. [14]. Different methods include, e.g., relaxation [11], graph-based approaches [7,5,4,2], iterative approaches [1], and clustering [13,12,3]. The choice of the PPM algorithm depends significantly on the application at hand.

In our earlier papers, we have used point pattern matching as a part of a correction system for printed electronics manufacturing [9]. The problem is to estimate translations of electronic components, and the connectors of the integrated circuits serve as registration points. The related matching problem, however, is slightly different from the usual in that the patterns are man-made and thus regular, as seen in Figure 1. This means that the connectors typically

A. Heyden and F. Kahl (Eds.): SCIA 2011, LNCS 6688, pp. 156–165, 2011.

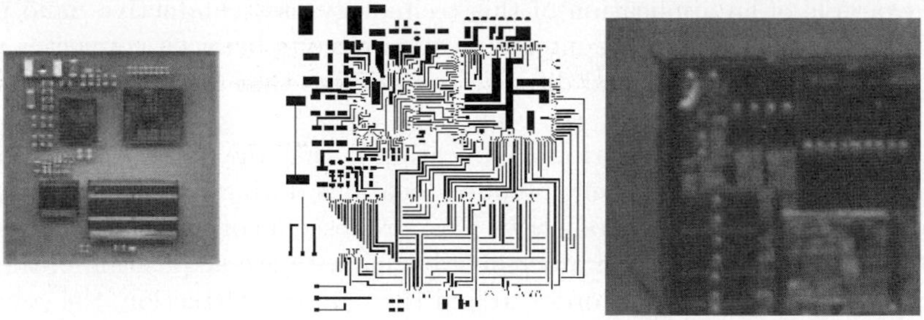

Fig. 1. A sample multi-IC module (left) ready for printing the connections (center). A zoom into the upper left corner is shown in the right.

reside equidistantly on a straight line, which means that several well matching subset pairs can be found. In Section 2, there is a brief description of this kind of application area for PPM.

The most efficient PPM algorithms for the general point pattern matching problem take advantage of the randomness and uniqueness of the patterns in a way that make them unsuitable for our case. Due to the shape of the point sets, the only applicable methods are those using exhaustive search to guarantee the optimal solution even in the presence of good local optima. In this paper, we consider PPM algorithms following the general idea of *alignment* (see Section 3). In the alignment approach, different pairings between the matched point sets are tested to find the best match.

There exists an alignment based PPM algorithm by Chang et al. [3], which will work as a basis for this paper. The algorithm is briefly described in Section 3 where we also show that the Chang's method has an optimal time complexity of $O(m^2n^2)$ among all PPM methods based on the alignment of two sets having m and n points, respectively. However, there are major problems in the algorithm details that can lead to failing of the algorithm or difficulties in the implementation. These problems relate to the two-dimensional accumulator array used in the algorithm to collect scale-rotation pairs created by different alignments of the point sets. The accumulator array is discussed in more detail in Section 4.

In Section 5, we propose a modification of Chang's method that fixes the problems related to the accumulator array. Our solution replaces the array with a search algorithm in continuous space. In Section 6, we discuss more about the practical limitations of the Chang's original algorithm and give an example case where the modified algorithm is necessary. Section 7 concludes the paper.

2 Printed Electronics

The application area, where the need for an efficient point pattern matching method for regular patterns arises is *inkjet printed electronics*. Printed electronics is an additive process and a relatively new area of research, which uses traditional printing devices for interconnecting or manufacturing components.

An example of an application of this technology uses conductive nano particle and dielectric inks to create interconnection circuits between connector pads of integrated circuits (ICs) and discrete components that have been molded onto the background surface [10], see Figure 1.

The problem in the described application is that the embedded components tend to drift away from their intended locations during and after the molding process. In our earlier papers [9], we have proposed a computer vision system to overcome this problem. The processing begins with the acquisition of the image of the distorted module. In order to find the required correction, the connectors of the ICs and their locations are detected from the image by means of automated image analysis. After detection, the problem is to search for a transformation between the two coordinate sets (i.e., to combine the knowledge where the objects are with the knowledge where they should be). The transformation is found using PPM, for which we propose a method in this paper. After the transformation and correspondence between the point sets are available, the wiring is redrawn to match the true situation.

3 Point Pattern Matching

Consider a two-dimensional point set $P = \{\mathbf{p}_k \in \mathbb{R}^2 \mid k = 1, \ldots, m\}$ that is to be matched with the point set $Q = \{\mathbf{q}_k \in \mathbb{R}^2 \mid k = 1, \ldots, n\}$, where $m \leq n$. The aim is to find the parameters of a similarity transformation, i.e., scale $s \in \mathbb{R}^+$, rotation $\theta \in [0, 2\pi)$ of the rotation matrix $\mathbf{R}_\theta$, and translation $\mathbf{t} = (t_x, t_y) \in \mathbb{R}^2$, which maximize the number of matching pairs between sets P and Q. Points $\mathbf{p} \in P$ and $\mathbf{q} \in Q$ are said to match if $||\mathbf{q} - \mathbf{p}'|| < d$, where $d \in \mathbb{R}^+$ is the allowed point distortion and $\mathbf{p}' = s\mathbf{R}_\theta\mathbf{p} + \mathbf{t}$ is the transformed version of $\mathbf{p}$. The resulting transformation should also minimize the sum of the squared errors between the points in Q and the corresponding points in the transformed version of P.

The PPM problem can be divided into two parts. First, we find the best possible pairing of the two points sets P and Q and discard the outlier points in both sets. Second, we find the parameters of the optimal transformation between the paired points. We are only interested in the former problem, because closed form optimal solutions are available for the latter one.

In this paper, we focus on brute force PPM methods based on a general and intuitive idea of *alignment*. In the alignment approach, the point sets are aligned such that points $\mathbf{p}_i$ and $\mathbf{p}_j$ from set P exactly match the points $\mathbf{q}_u$ and $\mathbf{q}_v$ from set Q and then the total number of matching pairs is calculated over the whole sets. In a naive solution, the best match is found by looping each of the $mn(m-1)(n-1)/4$ alignments and calculating the number of matching pairs by finding a nearest neighbor for each point.

Chang's PPM method [3] re-arranges the calculation in the alignment approach such that the number of matching pairs can be calculated in constant time. The best point pairing is found by clustering of scale-rotation pairs achieved by calculating scales and rotations between each possible pair of point pairs $(\mathbf{p}_i, \mathbf{p}_j)$ and $(\mathbf{q}_u, \mathbf{q}_v)$. Pairs with true correspondence tend to cluster around the same region in the scale-rotation space, while non-matching pairs distribute more randomly. The average scale and rotation of the detected cluster is approximately the scale and rotation of the transformation between the two sets.

After determining the parameters of an approximate transformation that transforms set P into set Q, the actual point correspondence is determined by transforming P with the approximate transformation and pairing each point to the closest point in Q. If no pair is found within a given distance, the point is considered an outlier and discarded. Unlike in the naive case, the nearest neighbors are needed to be found only once.

What makes Chang's algorithm effective is that it uses an accumulator array with size independent of the number of points. The array is used to collect each scale-rotation pair after which the element of the accumulator array with the most hits is found. While efficient, the discrete accumulator array is also the weakest part of the algorithm for several reasons. The main reason is that for point sets with points both relatively close and relatively far from each other, there exists multiple alignment transformations that have very little deviation in their scale and rotation but still result in different point pairing. In this case, the accumulator array has to be very dense in order for the right cluster not to mix with false hits. Unfortunately, large arrays create problems in implementation. In addition, too dense an array increases the possibility of the borders of the array bins to split the target cluster in half, which can make the algorithm to fail. In the original paper, they do not discuss about choosing a proper size for the accumulator. In the next section, we propose a method for choosing the array size in Chang's algorithm such that the total array size is minimized.

4 Choosing Accumulator Array Size for Chang's Method

In the original paper of Chang et al. [3], the authors do not discuss about choosing the dimensions of the accumulator array used for collecting the scale-rotation pairs calculated between each point pair in P and each point pair in Q. However, the size and density of the accumulator array has a significant impact on the performance of the algorithm and it also sets restrictions concerning the implementation of the algorithm.

Like mentioned in the previous section, a single accumulator array bin has to be small enough such that scale-rotation pairs originating from one point set alignment cannot get mixed with the scale-rotation cluster of the alignment that will result from another point pairing. In this section, we will propose a method for determining the largest possible size of the array bin that minimizes the accumulator array memory consumption while preserving adequate resolution for detection of the target cluster.

Consider two points $\mathbf{q}_a$ and $\mathbf{q}_b$ chosen from set Q such that the points are located on distance d_{ab} from each other. Also consider a third point $\mathbf{q}_c \in Q$ with a distance of d_{bc} from point $\mathbf{q}_b$ in direction determined by angle $\phi \in [0, \pi]$. Together with points $\mathbf{p}_i$ and $\mathbf{p}_j$ from set P, we form two different alignments: first, between point pairs $(\mathbf{p}_i, \mathbf{p}_j)$ and $(\mathbf{q}_a, \mathbf{q}_b)$ and, second, between point pairs $(\mathbf{p}_i, \mathbf{p}_j)$ and

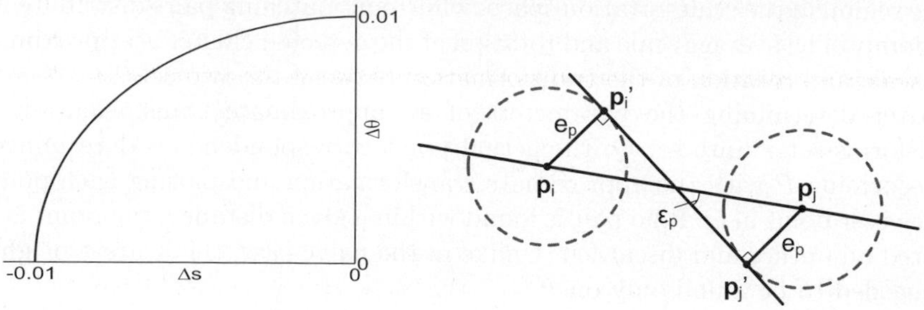

Fig. 2. Left: A curve representing a lower bound for the difference between scales and rotations of two different alignments of sets P and Q. Right: Given the maximum error e_p that the observed points $\mathbf{p}_i'$ and $\mathbf{p}_j'$ can have with respect to their true locations $\mathbf{p}_i$ and $\mathbf{p}_j$, this figure illustrates the maximum error ε_p that can occur in the observed orientation of the point pair.

$(\mathbf{q}_a, \mathbf{q}_c)$. Depending on ϕ, the difference between the scale and rotation of these two alignments can be defined as

$$\Delta s = \frac{d_{ac} - d_{ab}}{d_p} \quad \text{and} \quad \Delta\theta = \arccos\left(\frac{d_{ac}^2 - d_{bc}^2 + d_{ab}^2}{2 d_{ac} d_{ab}}\right), \tag{1}$$

where $d_p = ||\mathbf{p}_i - \mathbf{p}_j||$ and $d_{ac} = ||\mathbf{q}_a - \mathbf{q}_c|| = \sqrt{d_{bc}^2 - 2 d_{bc} d_{ab} \cos(\phi) + d_{ab}^2}$. Here we have used the cosine rule.

Let d_{max} and d_{min} be the largest and smallest distances between any two points in Q, respectively. Intuitively, by setting $d_{ab} = d_{max}$ and $d_{bc} = d_{min}$ we get a lower bound for Δs and $\Delta\theta$. Additionally, by denoting $r = d_{min}/d_{max}$, $s = d_{ab}/d_p$, and $r_e = d_{ac}/d_{max} = \sqrt{r^2 - 2r\cos(\phi) + 1}$, we can write these lower bounds for equations (1) as

$$\Delta s = s(r_e - 1) \quad \text{and} \quad \Delta\theta = \arccos\left(\frac{r_e^2 - r^2 + 1}{2 r_e}\right), \tag{2}$$

respectively. We restrict further investigation on the interval $\phi \in [0, \phi_{max}]$ where $\phi_{max} = \arccos(r/2)$. This is because the values $\phi \in (\phi_{max}, \pi]$ give $d_{ac} > d_{max}$, which is not desired as d_{max} was chosen as the largest of any two point distances. Equations (2) give us a parametric representation of a lower bound for minimum difference between two different alignments. In Figure 2 (left), we have plotted this lower bound with respect to varying ϕ when $s = 1$ and $r = 1/100$.

The problem is to choose the accumulator array bin dimensions such that two scale-rotation pairs from two different alignments cannot occur in the same bin. Simultaneously, the bin area should be as large as possible implying a small number of bins needed to cover the entire scale-rotation space. An optimization scheme is proposed based on Figure 2 (left): maximize the area of a rectangle (representing an accumulator array bin) confined between the coordinate axis and the $(\Delta s, \Delta\theta)$ curve.

Both Δs and $\Delta\theta$ are monotonically increasing on $\phi \in [0, \phi_{max}]$. As an implication, the maximum area rectangle we are looking for is amongst those rectangles that have one corner in the origin and the opposing corner on the $(\Delta s, \Delta\theta)$ curve. The area of such a rectangle is

$$a(\phi) = |\Delta s||\Delta\theta| = s(1 - r_e) \arccos\left(\frac{1 - r\cos(\phi)}{r_e}\right). \tag{3}$$

The maximization problem of $a(\phi)$ doesn't depend on s. In addition, it isn't necessary to apply any kind of normalization for Δs or $\Delta\theta$ to make sure that we are maximizing a valid type of area because this wouldn't change the location of the optimum. Thus, we can equivalently maximize function

$$J(\phi; r) = \left(1 - \sqrt{r^2 - 2r\cos(\phi) + 1}\right) \arccos\left(\frac{1 - r\cos(\phi)}{\sqrt{r^2 - 2r\cos(\phi) + 1}}\right). \tag{4}$$

Here we have emphasized by substituting r_e from above that there is only one parameter that we need to know beforehand. This parameter is r, i.e., the ratio of the distances between the two closest and two most distant points in Q.

We use numerical methods to solve the maximum point of $J(\phi; r)$ with a given r. After this, we can calculate the accumulator array bin size by using Equations (2). However, Δs still depends on the unknown s, which is the scale of the alignment transformation. This suggests that we shouldn't use a uniform scale axis in our accumulator array. Instead, we need to choose a bin width that increases linearly as the scale gets larger.

The final issue concerning the size of the accumulator array are the truncation points for the scale axis. The optimal scale range for the given point sets P and Q is such that the first scale bin in the array equals to the smallest possible alignment scale $s_{min} = d_{min}/\delta_{max}$ and the last bin equals to the largest possible scale $s_{max} = d_{max}/\delta_{min}$. Here we use δ_{max} and δ_{min} to denote the distance between the two most distant and two closest points in P, similarly to d_{max} and d_{min} that we use for Q. The dimensions of the accumulator array are now determined by the following equations:

$$N_s = \left\lceil \frac{\log(s_{max}/s_{min})}{\log(2 - r_e)} \right\rceil \quad \text{and} \quad N_\theta = \left\lceil \frac{2\pi}{|\Delta\theta|} \right\rceil. \tag{5}$$

To achieve N_s we have summed together widths $|\Delta s|$ of N_s bins starting from $s = s_{min}$ and then set this sum equal to $s_{max} - s_{min}$.

To conclude, the entire procedure for choosing the accumulator array size in Chang's PPM method is described in the following steps:

1. Loop through each point pair in P and find δ_{min} and δ_{max}.
2. Loop through each point pair in Q and find d_{min} and d_{max}.
3. Calculate r, ϕ_{max}, s_{min}, and s_{max}.
4. Find $\phi \in [0, \phi_{max}]$ that maximizes $J(\phi; r)$.
5. Divide accumulator rotation axis $[0, 2\pi]$ into bins with equal size of $|\Delta\theta|$.
6. Divide accumulator scale axis $[s_{min}, s_{max}]$ into bins with variable size of $|\Delta s|$.

5 Modified Method without Discrete Accumulator Array

An improved version of the Chang's PPM method [3] is now proposed to overcome the problems related to using a discrete accumulator array. The basic idea is for each scale-rotation pair to individually form a *rectangle* defining the error bounds for that particular scale-rotation pair. The target cluster is then considered as the area where most rectangles intersect each other in the *continuous* scale-rotation space. Dimensions for each rectangle are derived from the given error bounds of each point in the following manner.

Consider point pairs $(\mathbf{p}_i, \mathbf{p}_j)$ and $(\mathbf{q}_u, \mathbf{q}_v)$ from sets P and Q, respectively. Also let $i \neq j$ and $u \neq v$. Assume that, when observed, we can only have the noisy point locations $\mathbf{p}'_i = \mathbf{p}_i + \mathbf{n}_i$, $\mathbf{p}'_j = \mathbf{p}_j + \mathbf{n}_j$, $\mathbf{q}'_u = \mathbf{q}_u + \mathbf{n}_u$, and $\mathbf{q}'_v = \mathbf{q}_v + \mathbf{n}_v$, where $\mathbf{n}_i, \mathbf{n}_j, \mathbf{n}_u, \mathbf{n}_v \in \mathbb{R}$ are random noise terms with arbitrary distributions.

Let's assume that we are provided with constant quantities $e_p, e_q \in \mathbb{R}^+$ that indicate—with a certain confidence level that depends on the distribution of the noise—the maximum error the points in P and Q are assumed to have, respectively. It follows that the distance d_p between the points $\mathbf{p}_i$ and $\mathbf{p}_j$ is now somewhere between the limits $||\mathbf{p}'_i - \mathbf{p}'_j|| - 2e_p \leq d_p \leq ||\mathbf{p}'_i - \mathbf{p}'_j|| + 2e_p$ and, similarly, distance d_q between the points $\mathbf{q}_u$ and $\mathbf{q}_v$ is somewhere between the limits $||\mathbf{q}'_u - \mathbf{q}'_v|| - 2e_q \leq d_q \leq ||\mathbf{q}'_u - \mathbf{q}'_v|| + 2e_q$. From these inequalities it follows that the true scale parameter $s = d_q/d_p$ is somewhere on the interval

$$\frac{||\mathbf{p}'_i - \mathbf{p}'_j|| - 2e_p}{||\mathbf{q}'_u - \mathbf{q}'_v|| + 2e_q} \leq s \leq \frac{||\mathbf{p}'_i - \mathbf{p}'_j|| + 2e_p}{||\mathbf{q}'_u - \mathbf{q}'_v|| - 2e_q}. \tag{6}$$

This gives the worst case error bounds for the scale parameter of the alignment defined by the point pairs $(\mathbf{p}_i, \mathbf{p}_j)$ and $(\mathbf{q}_u, \mathbf{q}_v)$.

Bounds for the rotation parameter θ can be established in a similar manner. Figure 2 (right) illustrates the worst case scenario from the rotation point of view. Both of the measured points $\mathbf{p}'_i$ and $\mathbf{p}'_j$ have the maximum error e_p in their locations. The direction of the error is such that the angle $\varepsilon_p \in [0, \pi/2]$ is maximized. The true orientation θ_p of the line traveling from point $\mathbf{p}_i$ to point $\mathbf{p}_j$, i.e., the angle between the line and the x-axis, is obviously somewhere between the limits $\theta'_p - \varepsilon_p \leq \theta_p \leq \theta'_p + \varepsilon_p$, where θ'_p is the orientation of the line from $\mathbf{p}'_i$ to $\mathbf{p}'_j$ and $\varepsilon_p = \arctan\left(2e_p||\mathbf{p}'_i - \mathbf{p}'_j||^{-1}\right)$. Similarly, for set Q we get $\varepsilon_q = \arctan\left(2e_q||\mathbf{q}'_u - \mathbf{q}'_v||^{-1}\right)$. From these error bounds, we can derive the limits for the true rotation parameter $\theta = \theta_q - \theta_p$:

$$(\theta'_q - \theta'_p) - (\varepsilon_p + \varepsilon_q) \leq \theta \leq (\theta'_q - \theta'_p) + (\varepsilon_p + \varepsilon_q). \tag{7}$$

Given now a scale-rotation pair, instead of accumulating a corresponding bin in a discrete accumulator array, we construct a rectangle, whose dimensions are given by equations 6 and 7. The closer the points $\mathbf{p}'_i$ and $\mathbf{p}'_j$ or the points $\mathbf{q}'_u$ and $\mathbf{q}'_v$ are to each other, the more dominant the error terms e_p and e_q become, thus, resulting in larger rectangles. In calculating ε_p and ε_q we assume that $||\mathbf{p}'_i - \mathbf{p}'_j|| > 2e_p$ and $||\mathbf{q}'_i - \mathbf{q}'_j|| > 2e_q$. This is reasonable as this would otherwise allow the noise to be so powerful that some of the points in the sets would be able to change places. No point pattern matching method could survive that.

The final step in the improved algorithm is to find the scale-rotation cluster. As the scale-rotation pairs now each form a rectangle indicating its error bounds, the problem—instead of finding the maximum from an accumulator array—becomes finding the area where most rectangles intersect. This can be done by using a sweep line algorithm, familiar, e.g., from computer graphics (*scanline rendering* [15]). The principle of the sweep line algorithm is simple: The scale-rotation space is scanned with a horizontal sweep line that moves in y-direction simultaneously keeping track on rectangles, which intersect the line. The area where most rectangles intersect at the same time is stored in the memory.

Replacing Chang's accumulator array with a sweep line algorithm takes care of the memory issues. However, it also results in increased computational complexity, which we will now discuss a bit more. There are $mn(m-1)(n-1)/4$ different alignments of the two point sets P and Q in the general alignment approach for solving the PPM problem. Thus, the time complexity of any PPM algorithm based on the alignment approach is $O(m^2n^2k)$, where k depends on the complexity of calculating the matching pairs. A naive solution calculates the number of matching pairs by finding the nearest neighbors for each point with a given alignment. Nearest neighbors can be found in $O(m \log n)$ time giving the naive solution a total complexity of $O(m^3n^2 \log n)$.

In Chang's PPM algorithm [3], the number of matching pairs is calculated in constant time. This makes the algorithm optimal in the alignment sense with time complexity of $O(m^2n^2)$. In the improved algorithm proposed in this paper, the optimality is lost as finding the best scale-rotation cluster depends on the number of points. However, there exists an optimal sweep line based solution with time complexity of $O(k \log k)$ for finding the largest possible subset of intersecting rectangles from a set of k rectangles [6]. Thus, the complexity of the improved algorithm is $O(m^2n^2 \log n)$, where the additional logarithmic term is fortunately quite marginal compared to the optimal solution.

6 Example Case

The main problem in Chang's original PPM algorithm is the high memory consumption in cases where the characteristics of the point sets require large accumulator arrays. In Figure 3, we have experimented with the total accumulator array memory consumption with respect to $1/r$, i.e., the ratio between the two most distant and two closest points in Q. To be able to calculate the number of bins in the scale axis for arbitrary point sets, we have assumed $r = \delta_{min}/\delta_{max} = d_{min}/d_{max}$. This results in $s_{max}/s_{min} = r^{-2}$, i.e., the number of scale axis bins (Equation (5)) is independent of s_{min} and s_{max}. In Chang's algorithm, there are at most $m-1$ scale-rotation pairs from a single alignment per iteration. Our accumulator array design guarantees that there cannot be more hits than this in a single array bin. Thus, we have used 16 bit accumulator array bin, which is adequate with all reasonable size point sets.

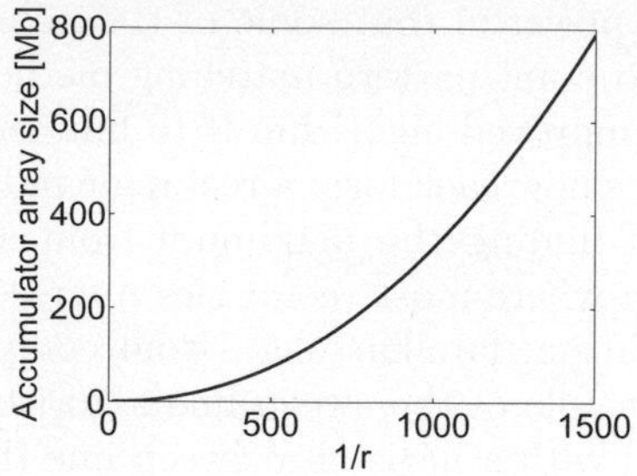

Fig. 3. Memory consumption of a 16 bit accumulator array with respect to the ratio between the distance of the two most distant points and two closest points

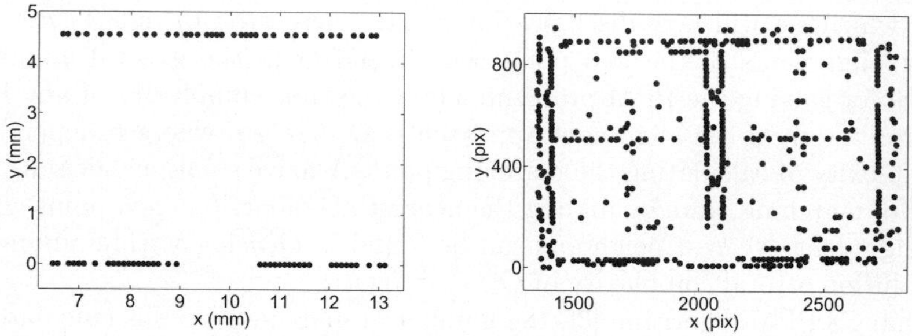

Fig. 4. Left: Locations of IC connector pads according to design data. Right: Locations of connector pad candidates detected from an image.

To provide a real life example, consider the IC registration case presented in Section 2 and the printed electronics module shown in Figure 1. In Figure 4 (left) there are the locations of the connector pads given by the design data of the IC on the lower right corner of the module. Figure 4 (right) shows connector pad candidates of the same IC detected from an image. To be able to find the exact position of the IC in the image, we plan to run Chang's PPM algorithm to find the transformation between the two point sets. However, there exists extremely close points in both of the sets, namely, $d_{min} = 1\,\text{pix}$, $d_{max} = 1636\,\text{pix}$, $\delta_{min} = 97.9\,\mu\text{m}$, and $\delta_{max} = 7894\,\mu\text{m}$. According to Equations (5), we would need an accumulator array of size 27283×14535, which requires 756 MB of memory. Unfortunately, we don't have that much contiguous memory available in the printing lab PC. However, by using the improved algorithm proposed in this paper, we only need to store coordinates of $(m-1) \cdot (n-1)$ rectangles per iteration. In this case this results in extra memory usage of just 4.5 MB.

7 Conclusions

In this paper we have proposed a modified version of the point pattern matching algorithm by Chang et al. [3]. The original method is optimal among all PPM methods that are based on brute force testing of different alignments, which is the only way to guarantee success in case of regular point sets.

Despite the optimality, Chang's method has some problems, e.g., a high demand for memory when matching point sets with clustered points. We have proposed a method for choosing the accumulator array size that minimizes the memory consumption. In addition, we have proposed an improved version of the original algorithm that overcomes the issues related to using a discrete accumulator array. To the best of our knowledge, these result have not been discovered earlier.

References

1. Besl, P., McKay, H.: A method for registration of 3-D shapes. IEEE Trans. Pattern Anal. Machine Intell. 14(2), 239–256 (1992)
2. Carcassoni, M., Hancock, E.: Point pattern matching with robust spectral correspondence. In: Proc. IEEE Conf. on Comp. Vis. Pattern Recogn. vol. 1, pp. 649–655 (2000)
3. Chang, S., Cheng, F., Hsu, W., Wu, G.: Fast algorithm for point pattern matching: Invariant to translations, rotations and scale changes. Pattern Recogn. 30, 311–320 (1997)
4. Chui, H., Rangarajan, A.: A new point matching algorithm for non-rigid registration. Comp. Vision and Image Understanding 89(2-3), 114–141 (2003)
5. Grimson, W.E.L., Lozano-Pérez, T.: Localizing overlapping parts by searching the interpretation tree. IEEE Trans. Pattern Anal. Machine Intell. 9(4), 469–482 (1987)
6. Imai, H., Asano, T.: Finding the connected components and a maximum clique of an intersection graph of rectangles in the plane. Journal of Algorithms 4(4), 310–323 (1983)
7. Lavine, D., Lambird, B.A., Kanai, L.N.: Recognition of spatial point patterns. Pattern Recogn. 16(3), 289 (1983)
8. Li, B., Meng, Q., Holstein, H.: Point pattern matching and applications-a review. In: IEEE Intern. Conf. on Syst., Man and Cybern., vol. 1, pp. 729–736 (2003)
9. Manninen, T., Pekkanen, V., Rutanen, K., Ruusuvuori, P., Rönkkä, R., Huttunen, H.: Alignment of individually adapted print patterns for ink jet printed electronics. J. Imag. Sci. and Tech. 54(5), 050306 (2010)
10. Miettinen, J., Pekkanen, V., Kaija, K., Mansikkamäki, P., Mäntysalo, J., Mäntysalo, M., Niittynen, J., Pekkanen, J., Saviauk, T., Rönkkä, R.: Inkjet printed system-in-package design and manufacturing. Elsevier Microelectr. J (2008)
11. Ranade, S., Rosenfeld, A.: Point pattern matching by relaxation. Pattern Recogn. 12(4), 269–275 (1980)
12. Stockman, G.: Object recognition and localization via pose clustering. Comp. Vision, Graph. and Image Process. 40(3), 361–387 (1987)
13. Stockman, G., Kopstein, S., Benett, S.: Matching images to models for registration and object detection via clustering. IEEE Trans. Pattern Anal. and Mach. Intell. PAMI-4, 229–241 (1982)
14. Wamelen, P.B.V., Li, Z., Iyengar, S.S.: A fast expected time algorithm for the 2-d point pattern matching problem. Pattern Recogn. 37(8), 1699–1711 (2004)
15. Wylie, C., Romney, G., Evans, D., Erdahl, A.: Half-tone perspective drawings by computer. In: Proc. Fall Joint Comp. Conf., pp. 49–58. ACM, New York (1967)

Real Time Surface Registration for PET Motion Tracking

Jakob Wilm[1], Oline V. Olesen[1,2,3], Rasmus R. Paulsen[1], Liselotte Højgaard[2], Bjarne Roed[3], and Rasmus Larsen[1]

[1] Informatics and Mathematical Modelling, Technical University of Denmark
Richard Petersens Plads, Building 321, DK-2800 Kgs. Lyngby, Denmark
http://imm.dtu.dk/

[2] Department of Clinical Physiology, Nuclear Medicine & PET, Rigshospitalet, Copenhagen University Hospital, University of Copenhagen

[3] Siemens Healthcare, Siemens A/S, Denmark

Abstract. Head movement during high resolution Positron Emission Tomography brain studies causes blur and artifacts in the images. Therefore, attempts are being made to continuously monitor the pose of the head and correct for this movement. Specifically, our method uses a structured light scanner system to create point clouds representing parts of the patient's face. The movement is estimated by a rigid registration of the point clouds. The registration should be done using a robust algorithm that can handle partial overlap and ideally operate in real time. We present an optimized Iterative Closest Point algorithm that operates at 10 frames per second on partial human face surfaces.

Keywords: motion tracking, registration, ICP.

1 Introduction

High resolution medical imaging modalities are highly sensitive to patient movement during image acquisition. The effect of patient movement during a dynamic Positron Emission Tomography (PET) recording is shown in Fig. 1. Acquisition times vary from several minutes to a few hours.

Since the invention of PET in the 1970's [1], resolution has been ever increasing. Our motion tracking method is targeted at the Siemens High Resolution Research Tomograph (HRRT), which features a spatial resolution below 2 mm [2]. This is well below the average drift that is observed in healthy subjects during a 45 min period [3]. The problem of patient movement is often mitigated by the use of thermoplastic head restraints or vacuum pillows. However, it is not possible to completely avoid motion using these methods [4].

A popular method for real time motion tracking is the use of an optical tool tracker such as Polaris Vicra [5]. The difficulty with such systems is to keep the optical tool well attached to the patients head, and in the field of view (FOV) of the tool tracker. This is particularly cumbersome in the narrow gantry of the HRRT PET scanner.

A. Heyden and F. Kahl (Eds.): SCIA 2011, LNCS 6688, pp. 166–175, 2011.

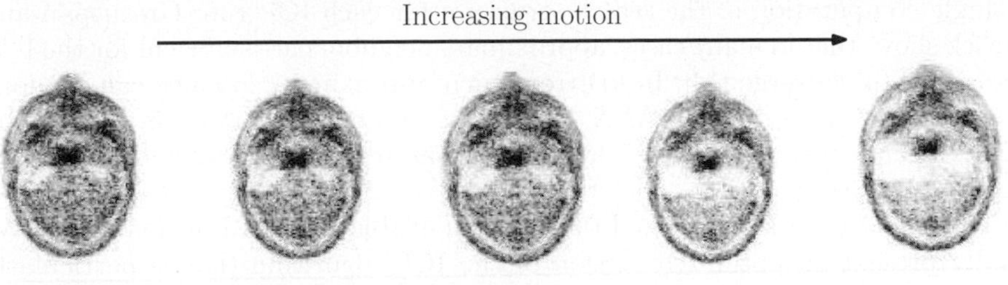

Fig. 1. A simulation of the effect of patient movement on a dynamic PET recording with radioactive tracer [11-C] Verapamil. Notice the white regions of no diagnostic value that appear with increased motion. Modified from [6].

We have previously presented a structured light system for motion tracking [7]. In contrast to the optical tool tracker, our method 1) does not need any optical tool and preparation of the subject, 2) fits into the narrow gantry of the HRRT PET scanner and 3) can potentially be built into future medical scanners.

In this paper, we focus on the registration of surfaces emerging from the current system. Ideally such registrations should be performed in real time, enabling online motion correction. In a clinical PET environment, this has many advantages over post processing, in that it allows for interventions based on the results, and improves clinical work flow.

The standard framework for rigid registration of point clouds is the Iterative Closest Point (ICP) algorithm. It was introduced by Chen and Medioni [8] and in a similar version by Besl and McKay [9]. It has gained wide spread popularity due to its simple formulation and low complexity. Besl and McKay use a point to point error metric. They also propose an extrapolation scheme to reduce the number of necessary iterations.

Several authors have proposed enhancements to the speed and robustness of the algorithm. Most of these are usage specific. An overview of ICP variants is given by Rusinkiewicz and Levoy in [10]. In the same paper they introduce the concept of normal space sampling to emphasize feature rich regions of the surfaces. This paper demonstrates the usefulness of such feature extraction methods.

For partial surfaces, Turk and Levoy suggested to reject point pairs that match to a mesh boundary [11]. A similar effect might be achieved by rejecting point pairs that are far apart [10]. In most real world situations, including our own, one of these techniques is necessary, because the algorithm would otherwise create correspondences between points that are not present in both surfaces.

As several authors have noted, the determination of nearest neighbors is by far the most time consuming step in the algorithm. Different acceleration structures are employed to reduce computation time. These can be grouped into space partitioning structures such as quad-trees [12], kD-trees [13] or Voronoi diagrams and data partitioning like Elias algorithm and bucket sorting into a uniform grid. Using these methods, the complexity of nearest neighbor searches can be reduced from the $O(N^2)$ of brute force searching to an expected $O(N \log N)$ in kD-trees [13] and $O(N)$ for the uniform grid. They do, however necessitate a single computation of the search structure for each ICP run. Greenspan and Yurick show, that in many cases, approximate neighbors are sufficient for the ICP algorithm to converge [14]. In kD-trees such approximate lookups can be done using the highly optimized ANN library by Mount and Arya [15]. A caching kD-tree implementation by Nüchter et al. was reported to halve computation times in ICP [16].

The use of both kD-trees and the uniform grid is discussed in this paper. We finally present an optimized version of the ICP algorithm that is particularly well suited for fast and robust registration of human face scans.

2 Methods

Our structured light scanner uses two cameras and a Pico projector that are mounted just above the patient tunnel. The setup is shown in Fig. 2. A sequence of patterns is projected onto the patient's face. Based on the distortion of these patterns, and using a Phase Shifting Interferometry (PSI) algorithm, point clouds are created. The scanner's FOV is set to cover the region around the eyes, which in most cases is free of soft tissue deformations during image acquisition.

The system creates point cloud representations of a part of the patient's face. These are reconstructed to surfaces and inter frame motion is estimated using a rigid registration with the ICP algorithm.

We process our data to create a single polygonal surface from the input of the two cameras. The reconstruction and merging of the two point clouds is done in one step using the Markov Random Field surface reconstruction algorithm [17]. This reconstruction method extracts an isosurface from a regularized distance field, and has been shown to be particularly well suited for human surface scans [18]. We call one such reconstructed surface a single frame. The frames contain approximately 50 k triangles and 30 k points

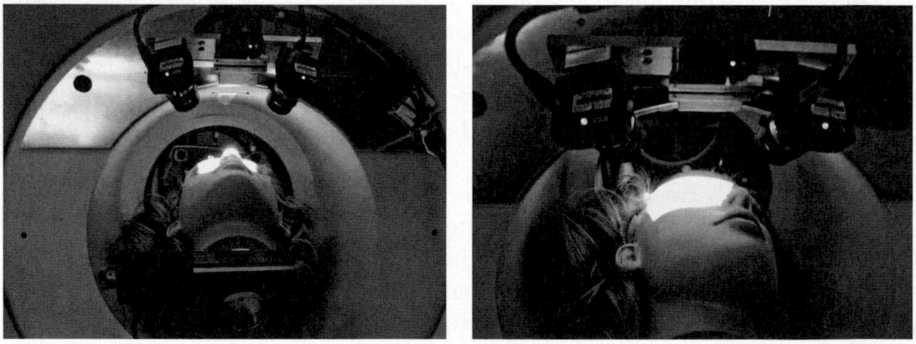

Fig. 2. Photographs of a mannequin head inside the HRRT PET scanner with the SL system in the front mounted to the gantry

To perform motion tracking, every frame must be registered to some reference frame. To evaluate our algorithm, we use the simulated registration problem shown in Fig. 3. It shows a surface resembling part of a mannequin head and it was preprocessed as described above. We transform the same surface using known parameters and add Gaussian noise individually to the target and reference. This way, we know the correct point correspondences, and we evaluate the registration results objectively as they are compared to ground truth, instead of the value of the objective function. For some experiments we remove parts of both surfaces, as shown, to create partial overlap.

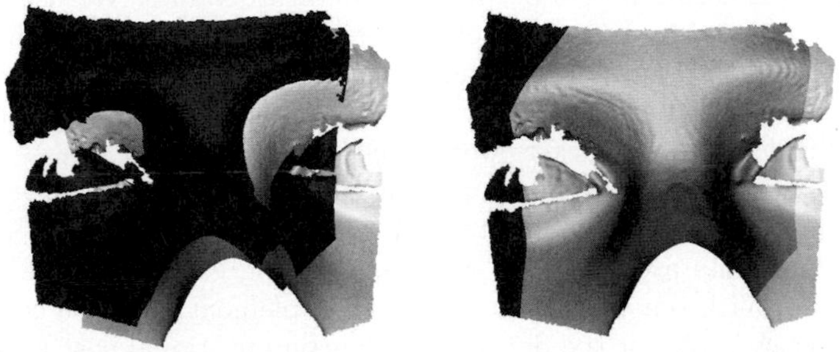

Fig. 3. A simulated registration scene with a mannequin head. There are approximately $N = 30\,\text{k}$ points on each surface. The left side shows the situation before registration, the right side after. We have used a known transformation. Parts of both surfaces were removed to simulate the effect of partial overlap.

We state the problem of aligning the point set $\mathbf{P} = \{p_i\}$ for $i = 1 \ldots N_p$, to another point set, $\mathbf{Q} = \{q_j\}$ for $j = 1 \ldots N_q$, where individual point correspondences are not known.

In order to address the issue of missing point correspondence, the ICP algorithm iteratively performs the following steps until convergence

1. Matching: every data point in $\mathbf{P}$ is matched to a point in the model point set $\mathbf{Q}$ to form the nearest neighbor pair $(p_i, \hat{q}_i)$.
2. Minimization: the error metric is minimized.
3. Transformation: data points are transformed using the minimization result.

The point to point error metric is

$$E = \sum_{i=1}^{N} \|\mathbf{R}p_i + \boldsymbol{T} - \hat{q}_i\|^2 \ , \tag{1}$$

where $\mathbf{R}$ is an orthogonal rotation matrix and $\boldsymbol{T}$ is a translation vector.

The minimization of E has several closed form solutions, using either quaternions [19], orthonormal matrices [20] or the singular value decomposition (SVD) [21]. We use the SVD because it results in the fewest calculations.

We consider sub sampling of the surfaces for two reasons. Firstly, it reduces the overall computational cost of ICP registration. Most time is spend on nearest neighbor searches with a complexity of at most $O(N^2)$ for the brute force approach, and we expect that halving the number of points can quarter computation times at best. The other reason is, that an appropriate sampling strategy will improve ICP convergence.

By bucketing the points according to their normal direction, and sampling across these buckets, the relative sampling density in feature rich regions is increased. A reasonable choice is to divide the unit sphere into 27 equally sized regions to obtain the normal buckets. A similar exploitation of differential properties is sampling across points of different curvature values. We use a method for curvature estimation on point clouds due to Pauly et al. [22]. The authors demonstrate, that the variance in a point's neighborhood can be used to approximate the surface mean curvature. For our surfaces a local neighborhood size of 100 points divided into 10 buckets works well.

For point clouds that have only partial overlap, point pairs involving the border of the target might be rejected [11]. This is illustrated conceptually in Fig. 4. Border points are identified as those defining edges that are only part of one triangle. With our data, this is easy to implement, because connectivity information is available for the data. Also, the computational cost is very low.

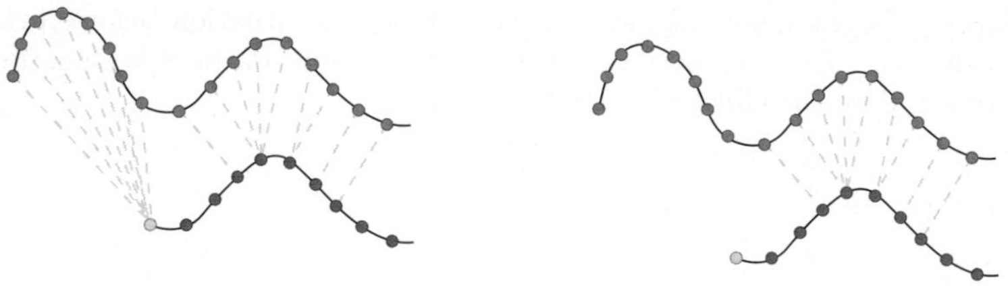

Fig. 4. In surfaces with partial overlap, many erroneous matches to the border of the target might occur. In border rejection, these pairs are discarded. Modified from [10].

Statistical approaches to remove erroneous matches require no triangulation of the target. Albeit, we don't consider them as robust as the border point rejection, because the latter will let surfaces *slide in place* even if the degree of overlap is small.

An important observation concerning the algorithm is that, in many iterations, it will make small updates in approximately the same direction. This will in some cases allow us to extrapolate the results of preceding iterations to move quicker.

Using unit quaternions to represent the current rotation, the transformation may be represented by a seven dimensional vector with six degrees of freedom:

$$\boldsymbol{q} = [q_w \; q_x \; q_y \; q_z \; T_x \; T_y \; T_z]^{\mathrm{T}}$$

Letting $\boldsymbol{q}_k$ denote the total transformation state vector at the kth iteration, one may define the change in every iteration as

$$\Delta_k = \boldsymbol{q}_k - \boldsymbol{q}_{k-1}$$

The angle between the last two directions is

$$\theta_k = \operatorname{acos}\left(\frac{\Delta_k \cdot \Delta_{k-1}}{\|\Delta_k\| \, \|\Delta_{k-1}\|}\right)$$

If the angles θ_k and θ_{k-1} are small, extrapolation might be considered. It is noteworthy that the computational overhead of extrapolation is insignificant and that, it can be combined with all other ICP modifications presented here. Details of the technique are described in the paper of Besl and McKay [9].

As noted before, the most time consuming part of ICP is the determination of nearest neighbors. The points on the reconstructed surfaces are close to equally spaced, which is the result of re-meshing in our surface reconstruction. For this reason, we consider bucket sorting the points into a uniform grid as an alternative to the popular kD-tree approach. Naturally, bucketing works best, when the data points are distributed uniformly such that every cell is occupied by exactly one point, in which case the algorithm provides $O(N)$ complexity. Point matches are made by spiraling out from the query point cell and calculating the distances to all points encountered. When the closest point so far is closer than all unvisited cells, the search is terminated. It should be noted that the performance of bucketing can rapidly decrease in the case of outliers, which cause the data bounding box to grow. For our data, this does not present an issue, because the Markov Random Field surface reconstruction removes outliers in the data.

3 Results and Discussion

Results for uniform sampling, normal-space sampling and curvature sampling are shown in Fig. 5. For this evaluation the scene shown in Fig. 3 is used with full overlap. Therefore the results converge towards zero. It is seen, that normal space and curvature space sampling perform well and yield faster convergence than normal uniform sampling. Because normal sampling requires fewer computations in our case, we use it in our implementation.

We compare the border rejection scheme with dynamic rejection of all pairs whose distance is either in the upper 10% or more than 2.0 times the standard deviation. Here we use the scene depicted in Fig. 3 in which model and data have only partial overlap. The results of using these rejection methods are seen in Fig. 6. It is observed, that for this scene, a rejection strategy is absolutely necessary. Whilst the border rejection converges slower than the statistical methods we consider it more robust because of its parameter independence.

The result of using quaternion extrapolation on our registration problem is shown in Fig. 7. Extrapolation occurs at several instances throughout the registration, and it reduces the number of iterations significantly. Because extrapolation introduces basically no overhead, we use it in our implementation.

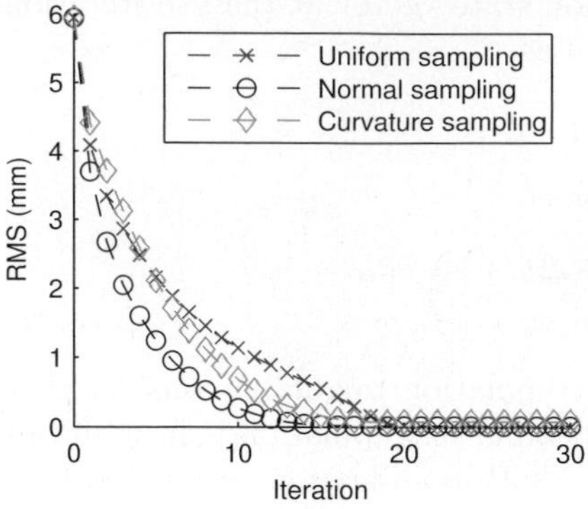

Fig. 5. Convergence for different sampling strategies. The surfaces with full overlap were used. In all cases, 1/4 of the available points were used.

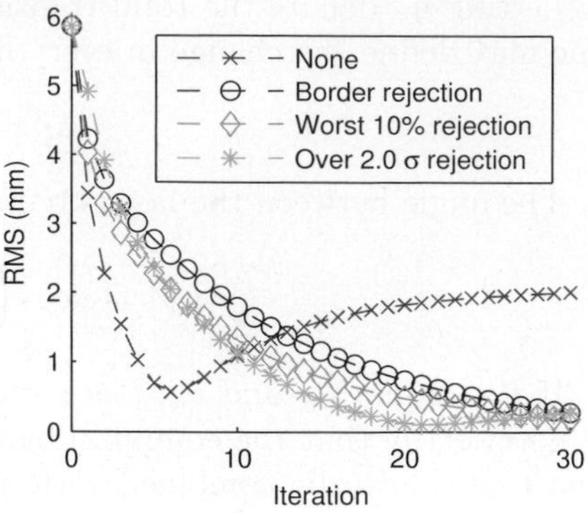

Fig. 6. Convergence for different rejection strategies on the surfaces with partial overlap

Nearest neighbor search methods are compared in Fig. 8. We use the ANN library by Arya and Mount for exact kD-tree searches. Both target and reference contain the full surfaces. It is seen that bucketing in a uniform grid results in nearest neighbor search times lower than what is achieved with the highly optimized ANN library. Both methods are much faster than the brute force approach.

Our custom registration algorithm builds upon the preceding discussion and results of sampling, border rejection and extrapolation. It samples 1/4 of the points from across 27 normal buckets. Point pairs involving the model border

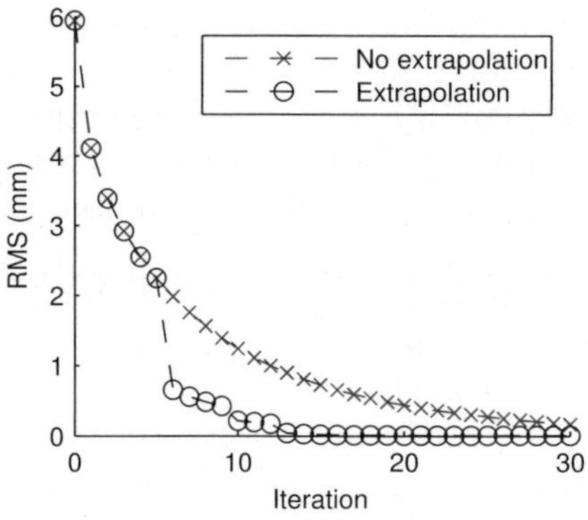

Fig. 7. Convergence behaviour for the test scene with and without extrapolation in transformation space

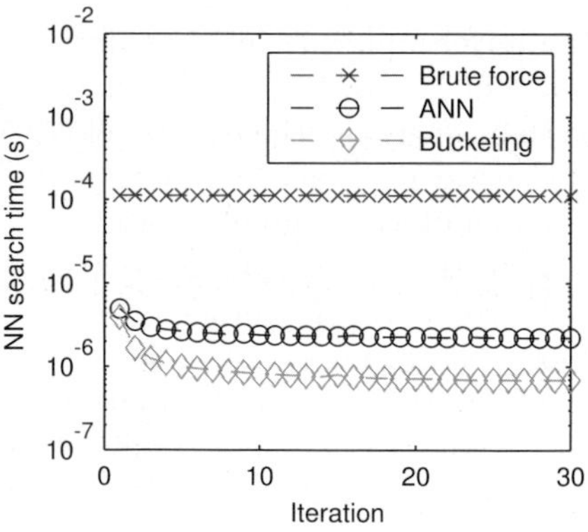

Fig. 8. Nearest neighbor search times versus iteration count for the test scene with $N = 29,678$ points in both model and data

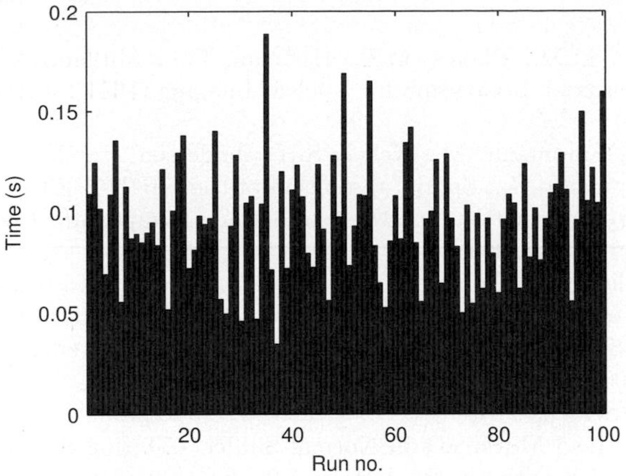

Fig. 9. Alignment times for 100 runs of our robust ICP algorithm with different random transformations. The measurements have mean 0.1 s and standard deviation 0.03 s.

are rejected. Extrapolation in quaternion space is performed to speed up the algorithm. Matching is done using bucketing in a uniform grid. The custom registration algorithm is run 100 times with different transformations. In every run, the rotation axis and angle are drawn from a uniform distribution. Rotation angles vary from −5 to +5 degrees. Translations are also uniformly distributed in the interval −5 mm to +5 mm. In every run, the algorithm is terminated when the change in RMS value is below 1 μm. Measurements are performed on a 2.16 GHz machine. The results are seen in Fig. 9.

The registration times have mean 0.1 s and standard deviation 0.03 s. This makes our implementation suitable for real time motion tracking in our PET application.

4 Conclusion

We have presented a method for motion tracking during PET scans. It builds upon a structured light system, surface reconstruction and a highly optimized version of the ICP algorithm. The algorithm is specifically designed for fast alignment of facial scans. Quantitative experiments show that it is able to run at approximately 10 fps. This makes our implementation suitable for real time motion tracking in a clinical situation. In the future, this will result in much fewer artifacts on high resolution PET. Our system may be easily adapted to other imaging modalities in which motion artifacts are a major source of error. For the optimized ICP algorithm, we see many other applications that reach beyond the medical imaging field.

References

1. Ter-Pogossian, M.M., Phelps, M.E., Hoffman, E.J., Mullani, N.A.: A Positron-Emission Transaxial Tomograph for Nuclear Imaging (PETT). Radiology 114, 89–98 (1975)
2. Olesen, O.V., Sibomana, M., Keller, S.H., Andersen, F., Jensen, J., Holm, S., Svarer, C., Højgaard, L.: Spatial resolution of the HRRT PET scanner using 3D-OSEM PSF reconstruction. In: Nuclear Science Symposium Conference Record 2009, pp. 3789–3790 (2009)
3. Dinelle, K., Blinder, S., Cheng, J.C., Lidstone, S., Buckley, K., Ruth, T.J., Sossi, V.: Investigation of Subject Motion Encountered During a Typical Positron Emission Tomography Scan. In: Nuclear Science Symposium Conference Record 2006, pp. 3283–3287 (2006)
4. Green, M.V., Seidel, J., Stein, S.D., Tedder, T.E., Kempner, K.M., Kertzman, C., Zeffiro, T.A.: Head Movement in Normal Subjects During Simulated PET Brain Imaging with and without Head Restraint. Journal of Nuclear Medicine 35(9), 1538–1546 (1994)
5. Rahmim, A.: Advanced Motion Correction Methods in PET. Iranian Journal of Nuclear Medicine 13(24), 1–17 (2005)
6. Anton-Rodriguez, J.M., Sibomana, M., Walker, M.D., Huisman, M.C., Matthews, J.C., Feldmann, M., Keller, S.H., Asselin, M.: Investigation of Motion Induced Errors in Scatter Correction for the HRRT Brain Scanner (to appear)
7. Olesen, O.V., Jørgensen, M.R., Paulsen, R.R., Højgaard, L., Roed, B., Larsen, R.: Structured Light 3D Tracking System for Measuring Motions in PET Brain Imaging. In: Proceedings of SPIE 7625 76250X (2010)
8. Chen, Y., Medioni, G.: Object Modeling by Registration of Multiple Range Images. In: 1991 IEEE International Conference on Robotics and Automation, vol. 3, pp. 2724–2729 (1991)
9. Besl, P.J., McKay, N.D.: A Method for Registration of 3-D Shapes. IEEE Transactions on Pattern Analysis and Machine Intelligence 14(2), 239–256 (1992)
10. Rusinkiewicz, S., Levoy, M.: Efficient Variants of the ICP Algorithm. In: Third International Conference on 3-D Digital Imaging and Modeling, p. 145 (2001)
11. Turk, G., Levoy, M.: Zippered Polygon Meshes from Range Images. In: ACM SIGGRAPH 1994, pp. 311–318 (1994)
12. Finkel, R.A., Bentley, J.L.: Quad Trees A Data Structure for Retrieval on Composite Keys. Acta Informatica 4(1), 1–9 (1974)
13. Friedman, J.H., Bentley, J.L., Finkel, R.A.: An Algorithm for Finding Best Matches in Logarithmic Expected Time. ACM Transactions on Mathematical Software 3(3), 209–226 (1977)
14. Greenspan, M., Yurick, M.: Approximate K-D Tree Search for Efficient ICP. In: Fourth International Conference on 3-D Digital Imaging and Modeling, 3DIM 2003, pp. 442–448 (2003)
15. Arya, S., Mount, D.: ANN: A Library for Approximate Nearest Neighbor Searching. In: 2nd CGC Workshop on Computational Geometry (1997)
16. Nüchter, A., Lingemann, K., Hertzberg, J.: Cached k-d tree search for ICP algorithms. In: Sixth International Conference on 3-D Digital Imaging and Modeling, 3DIM 2007, pp. 419–426 (2007)
17. Paulsen, R.R., Larsen, R.: Anatomically Plausible Surface Alignment and Reconstruction. In: Proceedings of Theory and Practice of Computer Graphics 2010, Eurographics UK (2010)

18. Paulsen, R.R., Bærentzen, J.A., Larsen, R.: Markov Random Field Surface Reconstruction. IEEE Transactions on Visualization and Computer Graphics, 636–646 (2009)
19. Horn, B.K.P.: Closed-form solution of absolute orientation using unit quaternions. Journal of the Optical Society of America A 4(4), 629–642 (1987)
20. Horn, B.K.P., Hilden, H.M., Negahdaripour, S.: Closed-form solution of absolute orientation using orthonormal matrices. Journal of the Optical Society of America A 5(7), 1127–1135 (1988)
21. Arun, K.S., Huang, T.S., Blostein, S.D.: Least-Squares Fitting of Two 3-D Point Sets. IEEE Transactions on Pattern Analysis and Machine Intelligence 9(5), 698–700 (1987)
22. Pauly, M., Gross, M., Kobbelt, L.P.: Efficient Simplification of Point-Sampled Surfaces. In: IEEE Visualization, VIS 2002, pp. 163–170 (2002)

Image Reconstruction by Prioritized Incremental Normalized Convolution

Anders Landström, Frida Nellros, Håkan Jonsson, and Matthew Thurley

Department of Computer Science, Electrical and Space Engineering,
Luleå University of Technology, 971 87 Luleå, Sweden
{andlan,frinel,hj,mjt}@ltu.se
http://www.csee.ltu.se

Abstract. A priority-based method for pixel reconstruction and incremental hole filling in incomplete images and 3D surface data is presented. The method is primarily intended for reconstruction of occluded areas in 3D surfaces and makes use of a novel prioritizing scheme, based on a pixelwise defined confidence measure, that determines the order in which pixels are iteratively reconstructed. The actual reconstruction of individual pixels is performed by interpolation using normalized convolution.

The presented approach has been applied to the problem of reconstructing 3D surface data of a rock pile as well as randomly sampled image data. It is concluded that the method is not optimal in the latter case, but the results show an improvement to ordinary normalized convolution when applied to the rock data and are in this case comparable to those obtained from normalized convolution using adaptive neighborhood sizes.

Keywords: image reconstruction, hole filling, normalized convolution.

1 Introduction

There are many ways in which an image can be incomplete. Image sensors can be faulty, 3D surface image data can contain areas of missing data due to surface reflectance properties and occlusion [9] or image pixels can be lost or distorted during transmission of data.

As an example of missing data, including sensor occlusion, consider Fig. 6 (on page 183) showing two grayscale images depicting 3D surface data of a rock pile where missing pixels are marked in black. The image to the right shows the rows of range data as measured by a structured lighting sensor [9]. To simplify later analysis of the measurements, we consider how these missing pixels can be reconstructed.

While many techniques deal with reconstruction of randomly missing pixels [3, 6, 7, 8], there is also a potential benefit from being able to reconstruct missing regions within an image. This particular kind of image reconstruction is known as *hole filling* and can be summarized into three broad categories.

A. Heyden and F. Kahl (Eds.): SCIA 2011, LNCS 6688, pp. 176–185, 2011.

Inpainting describes the technique where an artist reconstructs missing sections in a painting. This process can be formalized into solvable mathematical problems with the aim of producing visually pleasing images [1, 2].

Geometric methods are typically used when image data comprises a surface of 3D points, or it is appropriate to represent image pixels in this way. Points are triangulated into a mesh, upon which the reconstruction is based. Holes appear as non-triangulated parts of the mesh. These methods fill each hole by computing a suitable patch that fits in seamlessly within the close proximity of the hole. The patch is then sampled to get values for the missing points [5].

Kernel regression methods are commonly used for reconstruction of images based on sparse sets of irregularly sampled pixels, but can also be applied to whole regions of missing pixels. These methods are based on a foundation of linear algebra and use basis expansions of local neighborhoods to improve or fill in the data of a pixel [8]. The neighborhoods are weighted by an applicability function so the key point in these methods is how to choose the neighborhood size, shape and applicability. More recently, methods that adapt the neighborhood size according to the density of sampled points in the neighborhood and the shape of the applicability function to shapes of edges surrounding the neighborhood have been presented [7, 8].

In this paper we present a Prioritized Incremental algorithm using Normalized Convolution (PINC) for reconstruction of missing regions in incomplete images and 3D surface data. Specifically, when applied to surface data of piled particles (e.g. rocks) the presented method seeks to reconstruct the data in a way that preserves local topological variation and particle distinctness. The method makes use of a novel prioritizing scheme, based on a pixelwise defined confidence measure, that determines the order in which pixels are iteratively reconstructed. The actual reconstruction is performed by interpolation using the kernel regression method known as normalized convolution [6].

2 Method

At any time during the reconstruction process for an image, every pixel can be sorted into one of the three following classes:

1. *Valid* pixels, where the original image contains data.
2. *Unfilled* pixels; non-valid pixels where no value has been assigned.
3. *Filled* pixels; non-valid pixels that have been assigned an interpolated value.

The presented method reconstructs holes (regions of *unfilled* pixels) in a data set by interpolation of *unfilled* pixels in an order such that those with more "reliable data" in their proximity are processed before those with less. In order to achieve this reconstruction, a prioritizing strategy needs to be defined. Such a prioritization can be achieved by using a measure of the "validity" of the neighbors of an *unfilled* pixel.

Let $d(\boldsymbol{x})$ denote the 2D Euclidean distance from the pixel $\boldsymbol{x}$ to the closest pixel containing *valid* data. A pixelwise confidence measure can then be defined as

$$w_c(\boldsymbol{x}) = \begin{cases} 1 & \text{if } \boldsymbol{x} \text{ contains } \textit{valid} \text{ data,} \\ 0 & \text{if } \boldsymbol{x} \text{ contains } \textit{unfilled} \text{ data,} \\ \frac{1}{d(\boldsymbol{x})+1} & \text{if } \boldsymbol{x} \text{ contains } \textit{filled} \text{ data .} \end{cases} \tag{1}$$

As *unfilled* pixels are filled, their confidence measure is changed according to (1). Pixel confidence values for *filled* data thus monotonically decrease from 1 at the border of valid data towards 0 in the unfilled pixels.

Consider an *unfilled pixel* $\boldsymbol{x}$ with a surrounding $n \times n$ neighborhood $N_{\boldsymbol{x},n}$ containing pixels $\boldsymbol{x}_{N,1}, \boldsymbol{x}_{N,2}, \ldots, \boldsymbol{x}_{N,n^2}$. By summing up the confidence of the pixels in $N_{\boldsymbol{x},3}$, a priority measure $p(\boldsymbol{x})$ based on the confidence in the immediate neighborhood of $\boldsymbol{x}$ can then be defined as

$$p(\boldsymbol{x}) = \sum_{k=1}^{9} w_c(\boldsymbol{x}_{N,k}) \,. \tag{2}$$

Since $d(\boldsymbol{x}) \geq 0$, $0 \leq w_c(\boldsymbol{x}) \leq 1$ and $0 \leq p(\boldsymbol{x}) \leq 8$. For example, if $\boldsymbol{x}$ is a *unfilled* pixel entirely surrounded by *valid* data, $p(\boldsymbol{x})$ would be 8 and that pixel should consequently be filled in before a pixel with fewer *valid* neighbors. The range of $p(\boldsymbol{x})$ depends on $w_c(\boldsymbol{x})$, and will thus change if another confidence measure is selected. The idea is that w_c should be chosen so that holes are filled inwards from their perimeters.

The order of reconstruction is thus determined by prioritizing pixels using the defined confidence measure. *Unfilled* pixels of equal priority are processed in the same step. Knowledge of data set restrictions can be included where values are known to be within a certain interval. This is accomplished by truncating each assigned value within the interval limits directly after the interpolation step.

The PINC algorithm is a combination of a strategy for selecting the order for filling-in missing data and a method for assigning values to the *unfilled* pixels. It can be summarized as follows:

```
While unfilled pixels remain, do:
   Select the set X of pixels with highest priority.
   For each pixel x in X:
      Obtain coefficients for a local polynomial expansion
       around x.
      Approximate and constrain the value at x.
   Update the confidences of X and recalculate priorities.
```

2.1 Local Polynomial Expansion: Assigning Values

Let $\boldsymbol{x}$ denote an *unfilled* pixel and f the pixelwise signal values of the data set. The value of $\boldsymbol{x}$, $f(\boldsymbol{x})$, can be approximated by the constant-term coefficient for a best-fit local expansion in a selected basis (for instance, consider the constant term in a Taylor expansion). In this work a polynomial basis is used.

Expressing the data values for $N_{\boldsymbol{x},n}$ by the signal vector

$$\boldsymbol{f} = \boldsymbol{f}(N_{\boldsymbol{x},n}) = \left(f(\boldsymbol{x}_{N,1}), f(\boldsymbol{x}_{N,2}), \ldots, f(\boldsymbol{x}_{N,n^2})\right)^T \in \mathbb{R}^{n^2} \quad (3)$$

and letting $\{\boldsymbol{b}_1, \boldsymbol{b}_2, \ldots, \boldsymbol{b}_m\}$ constitute a set of $m < n^2$ linearly independent bases spanning a subspace S of $\mathbb{R}^{n^2}$, it is possible to approximate $\boldsymbol{f}$ by its projection $\boldsymbol{f}_S$ onto S. By letting $\boldsymbol{B} = (\boldsymbol{b}_1, \boldsymbol{b}_2, \ldots, \boldsymbol{b}_m)^T$ denote the basis matrix and $\boldsymbol{c} = \{c_1, c_2, \ldots, c_m\}$ represent the corresponding coefficients for $\boldsymbol{f}_S$, we can write $\boldsymbol{f}_S = \boldsymbol{Bc}$. The coefficients contained in $\boldsymbol{c}$ are given by

$$\arg \min_{\boldsymbol{c} \in \mathbb{R}^m} \|\boldsymbol{f}_S - \boldsymbol{f}\| = \arg \min_{\boldsymbol{c} \in \mathbb{R}^m} \|\boldsymbol{Bc} - \boldsymbol{f}\| , \quad (4)$$

which can be recognized as a least squares problem.

However, an adjustment of the influences of the different pixels in $N_{\boldsymbol{x},n}$ is desired so that pixels closer to $\boldsymbol{x}$ have a greater impact on the result than those further away. Care should also be taken to the reliability of the values in the neighborhood pixels. These desired objectives of pixelwise influence and reliability can be achieved by using normalized convolution with the diagonal matrices for applicability and certainty given by

$$\boldsymbol{W_a} = \begin{pmatrix} w_a(\boldsymbol{x}_{N,1}) & \cdots & 0 \\ \vdots & \ddots & \vdots \\ 0 & 0 & w_a(\boldsymbol{x}_{N,n^2}) \end{pmatrix} \text{ and } \boldsymbol{W_c} = \begin{pmatrix} w_c(\boldsymbol{x}_{N,1}) & \cdots & 0 \\ \vdots & \ddots & \vdots \\ 0 & 0 & w_c(\boldsymbol{x}_{N,n^2}) \end{pmatrix}$$

respectively. For all pixels in the neighborhood $N_{\boldsymbol{x},n}$, $w_a(\boldsymbol{x}_{N,k})$ is a Gaussian mask providing applicability weights and $w_c(\boldsymbol{x}_{N,k})$ is the corresponding confidence mask, where $k = 1, 2, \ldots, n^2$. Following the outline provided by Farnebäck [4], influences of the neighborhood pixels in (4) are assigned weights by a matrix $\boldsymbol{W}$, implicitly defined by $\boldsymbol{W}^2 = \boldsymbol{W}_a \boldsymbol{W}_c$ (Fig. 1). A vector $\boldsymbol{c_W}$, representing the basis coefficients for the weighted neighborhood, can then be obtained from

$$\arg \min_{\boldsymbol{c_W} \in \mathbb{R}^m} \|\boldsymbol{WBc} - \boldsymbol{Wf}\| . \quad (5)$$

The solution to this problem is then given by

$$\boldsymbol{c_W} = (\boldsymbol{B}^T \boldsymbol{W}_a \boldsymbol{W}_c \boldsymbol{B})^{-1} \boldsymbol{B}^T \boldsymbol{W}_a \boldsymbol{W}_c \boldsymbol{f} , \quad (6)$$

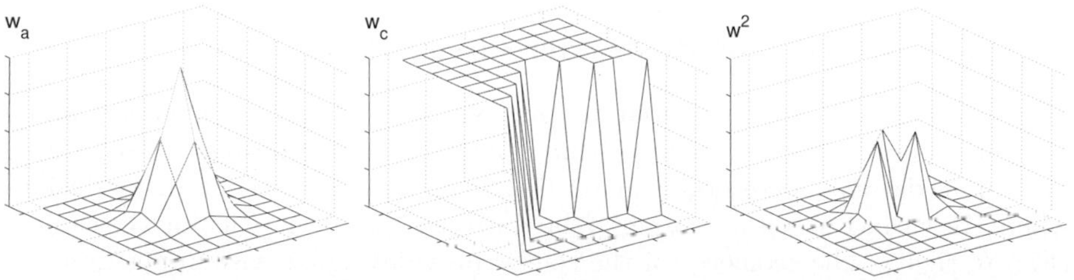

Fig. 1. Example of neighborhood weights corresponding to values of W_a (*left*), W_c (*center*) and W^2 (*right*) for $N_{\boldsymbol{x},9}$

which can be efficiently solved [4]. Once the coefficients in $\boldsymbol{c_W}$ have been calculated, the coefficient corresponding to the constant base function can be retrieved, providing the approximation of the pixel value $f(\boldsymbol{x})$.

3 Experiments and Results

Three different data sets were reconstructed by both ordinary normalized convolution (NC) and the PINC algorithm:

1. A gray-scale image, corrupted by randomly removing 90% of the pixels.
2. The same image as in 1, with holes of three different shapes.
3. 3D surface data for a pile of rocks, where data is partially missing.

3.1 Reconstruction of Randomly Removed Data

Figure 2 shows an original image and a version with 90% of the pixels randomly removed. Reconstructions were performed using a neighborhood size for coefficient extraction of 15×15 and a Gaussian mask with $\sigma = 1.5$ as the applicability function. The original image is restricted to values in the range $\mathbb{R}\,[0,\,1]$, wherefore these limits were chosen as constraints for the reconstruction. Results of the NC and PINC algorithms, using zeroth and second order polynomials, are presented in Fig. 3. It should be noted that the PINC algorithm provides a less detailed result, but shows a more stable behavior for higher order polynomials where ordinary normalized convolution returns small regions of extreme values (Fig. 3, upper right).

3.2 Reconstruction of Holes

Figure 4 shows the same image as in the previous section (Sec. 3.1), now artificially corrupted by creating holes. The resulting reconstructed images, obtained by using the same parameter setup as in the previous section, are presented in Fig. 5. Differences between the two reconstruction algorithms are visible, especially in the row of circles crossing the face region. Black and white defects remain in the lower section of the reconstructions performed by ordinary normalized convolution, especially for higher order polynomial expansions.

3.3 Reconstruction of Missing 3D Surface Data

3D surface data from a structured lighting sensor [9] comprising a camera and a projector was used to test the algorithm. The data consists of spatially separated rows of 3D data points recorded on a 256×256 image grid and contains occlusions where the surface structure obscures the reflected light from reaching the camera (Fig. 6, right). The geometry of the sensor provides a pixelwise upper limit for the reconstruction of the occluded data, in the form of a linear interpolation between the measured pixels.

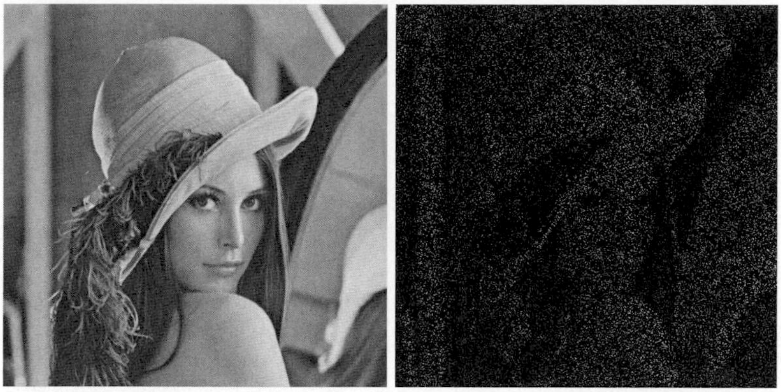

Fig. 2. The original image (*left*) and the version with 90% randomly removed data (*right*)

Fig. 3. Reconstructions of the right image in Fig. 2 using NC (*first row*) and PINC (*second row*). Order of polynomials used for interpolation are 0 (*left*) and 2 (*right*).

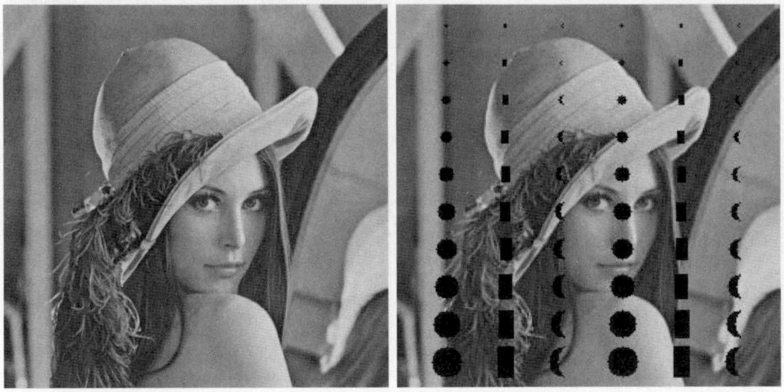

Fig. 4. The original image (*left*) and a version with holes (*right*)

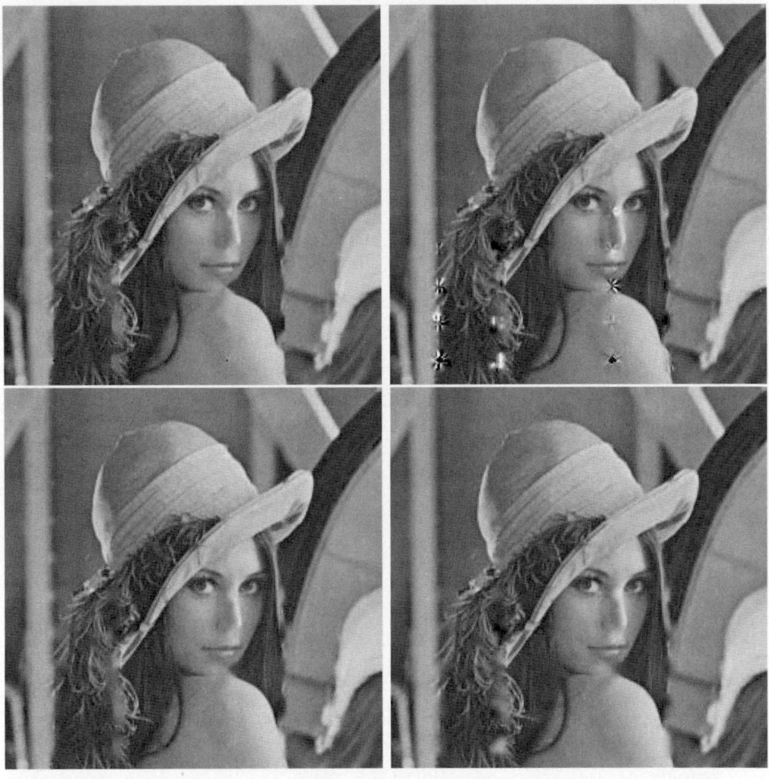

Fig. 5. Reconstructions of the right image in Fig. 4 using NC (*first row*) and PINC (*second row*). Order of polynomials used for interpolation are 0 (*left*) and 2 (*right*).

Fig. 6. 3D surface data of a rock pile: Combined information from all six measurements (*left*) and from one measurement only (*right*)

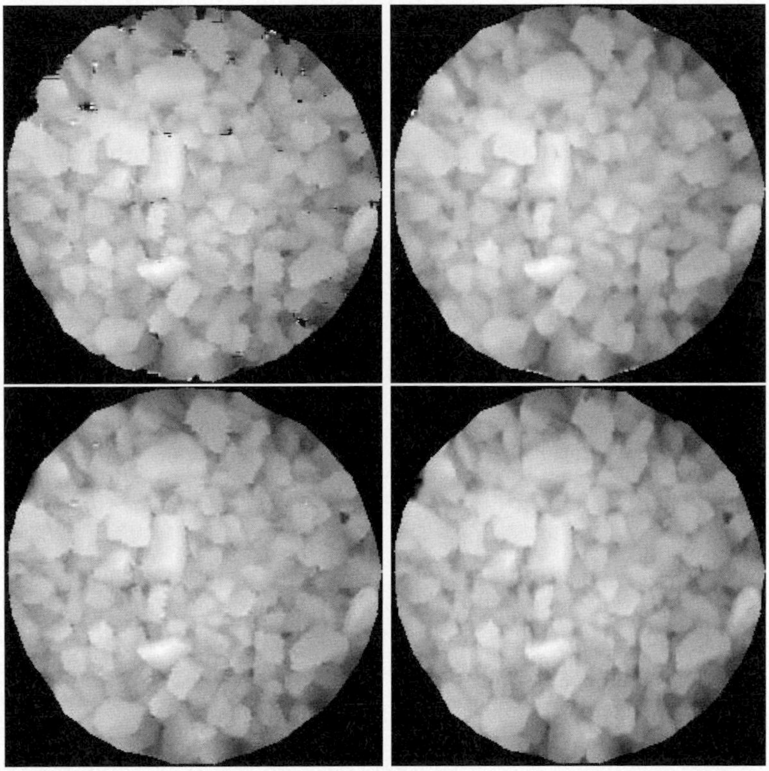

Fig. 7. Reconstructions of 3D surface data (Fig. 6, right) using 9 × 9 neighborhood NC (*upper left*), 15 × 15 neighborhood NC (*upper right*), adaptive neighborhood NC (*lower left*), and 9 × 9 neighborhood PINC (*lower right*). Order 2 polynomials were used, giving RMSE values 0.055, 0.031 0.030 and 0.029 respectively.

The performance of the PINC algorithm was measured by calculating Root Mean Squared Error (RMSE) values between the interpolated data and a second data set comprising six overlapping measurements (Fig. 6, left), rescaling the data sets to gray scale images of range $\mathbb{R}[0, 1]$. For comparison, the surface was also reconstructed by three different NC approaches. First, a neighborhood of the same size as used for the PINC algorithm, 9×9 pixels, was applied. Secondly, the neighborhood was extended to 15×15 to avoid the type of holes visible in the NC results presented in Fig. 5 (upper right). Thirdly, the NC algorithm was used with adaptive neighborhoods, where for each pixel the smallest surrounding neighborhood containing at least 25% *valid* data was used for interpolation. Results for second order polynomials are presented in Fig. 7. For the 9×9 neighborhood NC reconstruction, the RMSE value for the resulting data is 0.055. It should be noted that in this case the small neighborhood does not bridge the regions of missing data, giving a potential large error for those pixels. The 15×15 neighborhood NC reconstruction fills in the holes, providing an RMSE value of 0.031. NC reconstruction using an adaptive neighborhood gives a lower RMSE value, 0.030. Finally, the suggested PINC algorithm gives the RMSE value 0.029.

4 Discussion

As can be seen in Fig. 3, the PINC algorithm does not reconstruct fine details as effectively as NC on 90% randomly distributed missing data. The reconstruction by growing property of PINC can result in image structure from a location with a local cluster of pixels, spreading over the image and influencing the reconstruction around more isolated pixels. However, while the presented incremental method is less likely to capture small details in the randomly sampled data, it is less sensitive to extreme values when using higher order polynomials.

From Fig. 5, it is clear that the suggested incremental approach fills in missing data where ordinary normalized convolution does not. This is because the chosen neighborhood is too small to bridge the largest holes. The problem can be approached by using adaptive neighborhoods, as described in [7, 8]. Also, the result from the PINC algorithm is in general more pleasant to the eye than the NC reconstructed image.

Presented results for 3D range data shows that our method gives the best RMSE value for the tested data. Also, as expected, we see that NC needs a larger neighborhood to cover the missing regions. The use of locally adaptive neighborhoods partially solves this problem, but demands more computational power due to the unconstrained size of the neighborhoods when available pixels become very sparse. However, since the PINC algorithm currently reaches the same performance as NC with adaptive neighborhood sizes, it should be possible to improve PINC by incorporating the techniques that adapt to their surroundings such as neighborhood and applicability presented in [7, 8].

Even though the NC reconstruction with a 15×15 neighborhood here produces an RMSE value that is comparable to PINC and adaptive NC, this is not something we can expect to be true in the general case. The images used in this work are at quite low resolution and all occluded regions are roughly of the same magnitude which in this case makes the 15×15 neighborhood suitable for all regions. When having occluded regions of different size, this means that for using NC we would have to use neighborhoods that bridges the largest occluded region, something that would introduce smoothing in the smaller cavities.

5 Conclusion

By measuring RMSE values between a reconstructed partially occluded 3D rock pile surface and its true topology, we conclude that the suggested image reconstruction by prioritized incremental normalized convolution (PINC) performs better than ordinary normalized convolution (NC). To adapt the size of neighborhoods seem to be another possible approach of improving the performance of NC, but we have shown that a comparable result can be achieved using smaller neighborhoods.

The presented hole filling and reconstruction of randomly sampled data (Figs 5 and 3, respectively) highlights the differences between PINC and NC algorithms. The PINC algorithm is not adapted for reconstruction of data sets where most data is randomly removed, but is useful for its purpose; filling holes in 3D surface data.

References

[1] Averbuch, A., Gelles, G., Schclar, A.: Fast hole-filling in images via fast comparison of incomplete patches. In: Gunsel, B., Jain, A.K., Tekalp, A.M., Sankur, B. (eds.) MRCS 2006. LNCS, vol. 4105, pp. 738–744. Springer, Heidelberg (2006)

[2] Bertalmio, M., Sapiro, G., Caselles, V., Ballester, C.: Image inpainting. In: Proceedings of the 27th Annual Conference on Computer Graphics and Interactive Techniques, SIGGRAPH 2000, pp. 417–424. ACM Press, New York (2000)

[3] Faille, F., Petrou, M.: Invariant image reconstruction from irregular samples and hexagonal grid splines. Image and Vision Computing 28(8), 1173–1183 (2010)

[4] Farnebäck, G.: Polynomial Expansion for Orientation and Motion Estimation. PhD thesis, Linköping University, Sweden (2002)

[5] Ju, T.: Fixing geometric errors on polygonal models: A survey. Journal of Computer Science and Technology 24, 19–29 (2009)

[6] Knutsson, H., Westin, C.-F.: Normalized and differential convolution. In: Proceedings of IEEE Computer Society Conference on Computer Vision and Pattern Recognition, CVPR 1993, pp. 515–523 (June 1993)

[7] Pham, T.Q., van Vliet, L.J., Schutte, K.: Robust fusion of irregularly sampled data using adaptive normalized convolution. EURASIP J. Appl. Signal Process. 2006, 236–236 (2006)

[8] Takeda, H., Farsiu, S., Milanfar, P.: Kernel regression for image processing and reconstruction. IEEE Transactions on Image Processing 16(2), 349–366 (2007)

[9] Thurley, M.J., Ng, K.C.: Identifying, visualizing, and comparing regions in irregularly spaced 3D surface data. Computer Vision and Image Understanding 98(2), 239–270 (2005)

Forming Different-Complexity Covariance-Model Subspaces through Piecewise-Constant Spectra for Hyperspectral Image Classification

Are Charles Jensen[1] and Marco Loog[2]

[1] Department of Informatics, University of Oslo, Norway
[2] Pattern Recognition Laboratory, Delft University of Technology, The Netherlands

Abstract. A key factor in classifiers based on the normal (or Gaussian) distribution is the modeling of covariance matrices. When the number of available training pixels is limited, as often is the case in hyperspectral image classification, it is necessary to limit the complexity of these covariance models. An alternative to reducing the complexity uniformly over the whole feature space, is to form orthogonal subspaces and reduce the model complexity within them separately, e.g., forming full-complexity within-class, or interior-class, subspace models, and reduced-complexity exterior-class subspace models. We propose to use subspaces created by forming fewer and wider spectral bands, instead of the more general principal component analysis transform (PCA), in an attempt to exploit a-priori knowledge of the data to create more generalizable subspaces. We investigate the resulting classifiers by studying their performances on four hyperspectral data sets. On each data set, experiments where run using different training set sizes. The results indicate that the classifiers seem to benefit from using this more data-specific approach to forming subspaces.

1 Introduction

A recurring challenge in supervised classification of hyperspectral image data is that of handling the high number of per-object, or per-pixel, measurements (i.e., spectral bands) in combination with the often low number of samples available for training the classifiers. Typically we have about 100 to 200 spectral measurements per pixel, making the space in which we operate quite large and, usually, very sparsely sampled. As a result, when trying to build a statistical classifier, we most often have to resort to extremely simple models to avoid *overfitting* the training data. Even simple probability density functions (pdfs) like the normal distribution quickly turn out to be too complex, and, generally, we have to turn to dimensionality reduction, further restrictions of our model or other types of regularization, all preferably guided by some appropriate a-priori knowledge of the specific problem or data itself. The fewer samples we have available to train the classifiers, the more we rely on creating suitable restraints on our models to be able to harvest the spectral richness.

A. Heyden and F. Kahl (Eds.): SCIA 2011, LNCS 6688, pp. 186–195, 2011.

Many classifiers are based on modeling normal distributions, although differing greatly in how they impose a-priori stricture. In this paper we will focus on the approach of separating the feature space, principally differently for each class, into a *primary* and *secondary* orthogonal subspace, in which the complexity of how we model the two spaces differs. The primary space is meant to model a class' interior, or within, variance, while the secondary space models the exterior-class, or between-class, variance. The idea of such a separation for spectral data dates back to the work by Wold et al.[8] and Frank [2] in their SIMCA and DASCO approaches. If we choose the secondary space to cover a large part of the full feature space and let it be more simply modeled, we reduce the overall model complexity and hence limit the chance of overfitting.

In SIMCA, DASCO and common derivatives [7], the division of the feature space is based on an eigenvalue-decomposition (PCA) of the covariance matrix. A certain number of the eigenvectors corresponding to the highest eigenvalues are used to form the primary space, while the rest of the space is assumed to have equal variance in all directions, i.e., the remaining eigenvalues are set to their average value. By an eigenvalue-decomposition of the covariance matrix to form the primary space, we get the linear subspace containing the highest fraction of the total variance of the data, or, put another way, the subspace that can best represent the data in a squared error sense. However, there are no constraints or links to the data-generating process when the linear subspace is formed. This, in turn, could lead to an overfitting of the training samples, in the sense that it could make the primary space fail to represent the more generalizable within-class variance and give an artificially low variance in the secondary space.

In this paper, we suggest to replace the very general eigenvalue-decomposition with a more application-specific, or data-specific, approach to forming the primary and secondary subspaces. In particular, we propose to form primary spaces by finding the low-dimensional linear subspaces that, like the PCA, can best represent the data in a squared error sense, but with the restrictions that each basis vector corresponds to a single, wider spectral band, and that they together cover the whole spectrum. By enforcing this restriction, based on a-priori knowledge of the data, i.e., that they stem from samples of *continuous* curves, we should be able to obtain within-class subspaces that are less prone to overfitting.

In section 2 we recount the general normal distribution-based classifier, specify the feature-space separation formulation and give details of our proposed choices of how to define these subspaces. Details about the experiments, their results and a discussion on the findings can be found in section 3. Finally, section 4 gives some concluding remarks.

2 Model Formulation

Before we look at the specific models that we will investigate, we start by recapitulating the general formulation of the normal distribution-based classifiers.

2.1 Discriminant Analysis

Let $\mathbf{y}$ be a column vector containing the spectral band values of a single pixel. Now, by our assumption that each class follows a normal distribution, we end up with the following discriminant functions if we want to minimize the Bayes error [1]:

$$g_c(\mathbf{y}) = -\frac{1}{2}\log|\Sigma_c| - \frac{1}{2}(\mathbf{y}-\mu_c)'\Sigma_c^{-1}(\mathbf{y}-\mu_c) + \log \pi_c, \tag{1}$$

where μ_c, Σ_c^{-1} and π_c are the mean vector, the inverse covariance matrix (also called the precision matrix) and a-priori probability for class c, respectively. That is, a new sample (pixel) $\mathbf{y}^*$ will be classified to the class c giving the highest value of $g_c(\mathbf{y}^*)$.

In practice, neither the mean vectors nor the covariance matrices are available and hence they have to be estimated from the (very limited) amount of available data. When there are no constraints on the estimates, the maximum likelihood solutions for the means and covariance matrices are the sample means and the sample covariance matrices, denoted by $\tilde{\mu}_c$ and $\tilde{\Sigma}_c$, respectively:

$$\tilde{\mu}_c = \frac{1}{N_c}\sum_{i=1}^{N_c}\mathbf{y}_i, \tag{2}$$

$$\tilde{\Sigma}_c = \frac{1}{N_c}\sum_{i=1}^{N_c}(\mathbf{y}_i-\tilde{\mu}_c)(\mathbf{y}_i-\tilde{\mu}_c)', \tag{3}$$

where N_c is the number of samples in class c. In this paper we will not be altering the mean-value estimates, but focus on putting restraints on the harder-to-estimate covariance matrices.

2.2 Primary and Secondary Subspaces

The models that we focus on are based on separating the feature space into orthogonal *primary* and a *secondary* subspaces. The primary subspace is meant to capture the essential within-class variance, and the "richness" in the probability density modeling within this space is retained, while the secondary space, containing the exterior-class variance, is modeled using a spherical pdf.

To be more specific, let m be the total number of features in the full space (number of spectral bands) and let m_p and m_s be the dimensionality of the primary and secondary spaces, respectively, making $m = m_p + m_s$. Now, letting P_c be the projection matrix for the primary space for class c and $P_{\perp c} = I - P_c$ the corresponding matrix projecting onto the secondary space, we form new covariance matrices like this:

$$\begin{aligned}\hat{\Sigma}_c &= P_c\tilde{\Sigma}P_c + \alpha_c P_{\perp c} I P_{\perp c}\\ &= P_c\tilde{\Sigma}P_c + \alpha_c P_{\perp c},\end{aligned} \tag{4}$$

where the constant α_c is set to $\frac{1}{m_s}\mathrm{tr}\{P_{\perp c}\tilde{\Sigma}_c P_{\perp c}\}$ to ensure that the overall variance is retained, i.e., $\mathrm{tr}\{\hat{\Sigma}_c\} = \mathrm{tr}\{\tilde{\Sigma}_c\}$. Although put a bit loosely, we can say that the variance in the primary space is retained, while the remaining variance is spread spherically, or uniformly, in the secondary space. These covariance estimates, together with the sample means, $\tilde{\mu}_c$, are plugged into the discriminant functions in (1) to form the classifier.

2.3 Subspace Modeling Using PCA

The original SIMCA approach and its derivatives form the primary-secondary space separation by eigenvalue decompositions of the sample covariance matrices. That is, letting V_p^{pca} be an $m \times m_p$ matrix containing the m_p eigenvectors corresponding to the highest eigenvalues and V_s^{pca} the rest of the eigenvectors of $\tilde{\Sigma}_c$ in (3), we choose $P_c = V_p^{pca} V_p^{pca\prime}$. When we use such a P_c, we of course have $\tilde{\Sigma}_c = P_c\tilde{\Sigma}_c P_c + P_{\perp c}\tilde{\Sigma}_c P_{\perp c}$, meaning that there is no (sample) variance across the two spaces. This equality will generally not hold for other choices of P_c.

A slightly different model can be achieved if we do not subtract the class mean when we calculate the sum of outer products constituting $\tilde{\Sigma}_c$, and then eigenvalue-decompose that matrix to get the P_c projection matrix, i.e., we set $\tilde{\mu}_c = 0$ and eigenvalue-decompose (3). By doing this, we include some of the information that is found in the class' mean value when deciding on the primary, or within-class, subspace. When we form the primary space this way, we have $\tilde{\Sigma}_c \neq P_c\tilde{\Sigma}_c P_c + P_{\perp c}\tilde{\Sigma}_c P_{\perp c}$ since there is actual variance across the subspaces which we by our modeling enforce to be zero.

A related approach is that of choosing exactly the same projection matrix for every class. Again we can use the eigenvalue decomposition, although one would make use of the total scatter matrix. This is very similar to the general PCA approach used as a dimensionality reducer, although in (4) we keep the secondary space, i.e., we retain the full dimensionality. Setting $\alpha_c = 0$ for all classes c in (4), on the other hand, would reduce it to the classical PCA approach if the zero-valued eigenvalues were ignored (cf. use of pseudo inverses) in the discriminant function (1).

2.4 Subspace Modeling Using Wider Spectral Bands

In trying to include more domain-specific information into the reduction of model complexity, we propose to form the primary and secondary space separation based on a linear dimensionality reduction technique specifically designed for (continuous) spectral data. Stated more explicitly, we propose to use the dimensionality reduction approach described in [5], which finds the optimal, in a squared-error representation sense, cuts of the spectral curves when forming fewer, but wider, spectral bands. An example of a spectral curve represented with different numbers of wider spectral bands can be seen in Figure 1. Now, by running the algorithm separately with sample sets from the different classes, we get a different set of spectral bands for each class, i.e., each class has its own

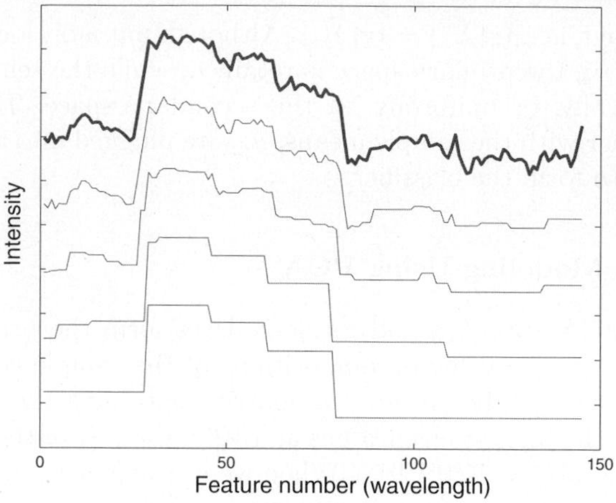

Fig. 1. An example of a spectral curve from the KSC data set represented using different numbers of segments, i.e., using different numbers of primary-subspace dimensions. From top to bottom; using 5, 10, 37, 73 and 145 (maximum, shown in bold) dimensions. The curves are vertically shifted for visual clarity.

linear subspace representing as much of the variance as possible. The idea is that the data-specific restrictions placed on how we form the within-class subspaces make them more generalizable.

Let us say that V is the $m \times m_p$ matrix transforming the data from m to m_p dimensions, or from m to m_p spectral bands, that one obtains using the training samples of a certain class c as input to the just mentioned algorithm. We then obtain the matrix projecting onto the primary space by $P_c = V(V'V)^{-1}V'$, which is then used in (4) to obtain the reduced-complexity covariance estimate used in the discriminant function (1).

Of course, analogous to keeping or ignoring the per-class mean values when we do an eigenvalue decomposition to form the primary subspaces, we can also choose whether or not to remove the per-class means before we run the dimensionality reduction algorithm that finds the new, broader spectral bands. Furthermore, we can use a common projection matrix for all our classes, again analogous to that of the eigendecomposition case described in section 2.2.

2.5 Primary-Subspace Size

What is left to be decided is the dimensionality of the primary subspace for each class. There are several criteria that could be deployed, but in our case we focus on rather small numbers of training samples, and we want to minimize the number of free parameters, hence we choose an equal size for all the classes' primary subspaces. In our experiments, this shared primary-space dimensionality is chosen through crossvalidation on the classification error.

3 Experiments

3.1 Data Sets

To evaluate the classification performance of the discussed approaches we have performed experiments on four hyperspectral images of various sceneries captured using different sensors.

The first image, Pavia [3], is of an urban scene taken by an airborne sensor. It has 71 bands, a pixel size of 2.6 m and the ground truth consists of nine classes. The second image, DC Mall [6], is again from an airborne sensor and also contains urban type data. It is divided into five classes, has a pixel size of 3 m, and has 150 bands. The third and fourth images, Botswana and Kennedy Space Center (KSC), are intended for vegetation inventory [4]. The former was captured by the Hyperion sensor aboard the NASA EO-1 satellite over the Okavango Delta, Botswana on May 31st, 2001. The image has a pixel size of 30 m, the labeled data consists of 14 classes, and the number of raw radiance bands used is 145. The latter data set was captured by an airborne sensor over Kennedy Space Center (KSC) at Cape Canaveral, Florida on March 23rd, 1996. It has a pixel size of about 20 m, has 171 bands, and the ground truth consists of 13 classes. All the above data sets are well known, and the listed references are publications where the data sets are used with various classification algorithms.

3.2 Experiment Details

We compare the classification performance of the normal distribution-based classifier (1) using the covariance matrix estimate of (4) with the six different choices of choosing the primary space projection matrix, P, discussed in section 2. That is, there are three projection matrix schemes found using PCA; not subtracting the class means before calculating the scatter matrices, subtracting the class-means first, and having a common projection matrix for all the classes based on the full scatter matrix, and we have the three proposed corresponding projection matrices using the dimensionality reduction transforms that is based on forming fewer and wider spectral bands.

Furthermore, we also report results using the PCA and the other approach that seeks wider spectral bands to reduce the number of dimensions explicitly, i.e., the same as having a common projection matrix for the classes and ignoring the secondary space completely.

For each of the discussed approaches, the number of dimensions, shared by all classes, of the primary spaces is found using tenfold crossvalidation on the classification error rate. We define the error rate to be the average of the classes' individual error rates.

Each data set was divided into two equally sized, spatially separate, and mostly disjoint training and test sets. We are interested in how the performance varies with training sample size, and hence we have chosen to report results where the total number of training samples are 0.5, 1, 2, 4 and 8 times the dimensionality of each data set. For each training sample size, the experiments were repeated five times, randomly drawing the selected number of samples from the training set. All data sets were normalized by subtracting the total mean and rescaling the mean within-class variances to one before fitting the models and doing the classification.

3.3 Results

Tables 1 to 4 show the average error rates over the five experiments run for the different training set sizes and for the different data sets. The numbers in parenthesis are the numbers of times the particular classifier gave a lower classification error on the test data than did the other corresponding classifier.

From these numbers we can see that, as expected, the classification error generally decreases with an increased number of training samples. More interestingly, when comparing the proposed way of finding subspaces with that of PCA, we see that the proposed approach seems to dominate at least when modeling each class separately. In the case of a common primary-secondary space separation for all the classes, the proposed approach still performs better than the traditional approach, although not quite as dominantly. When ignoring the secondary spaces, i.e., performing dimensionality reduction, there is no significant difference between the two approaches.

For all data sets, there is a noticeable difference between the results we get when we keep the full dimension of the space and the ones we get when we do a dimensionality reduction. When the number of training samples is very low, about equal to, or lower than, the number of original spectral bands, keeping the full-dimensional feature space gives better results than when doing a dimension reduction. When increasing the number of training samples, the error rates of the two techniques approach each other.

In Figure 2 we show error-rate curves from the Botswana data set when changing the number of dimensions in the primary space. In both the very low training-sample case and where there are quite some more training samples available, we see that there are wider intervals of primary space dimensions that gives acceptable classification errors when applying the proposed approach to finding subspaces. Similar results (not shown) are found using the other data sets.

3.4 Discussion

The way that the proposed approach finds the subspaces is much more restricted than that using PCA, as the proposed approach is based on finding a linear basis that consists of the average of contiguous original spectral bands instead of allowing any linear combination of the original bands. The results seem to indicate that we are capable of modeling the within-class variance properly, while avoiding overfitting the training data.

The dimensionality of the primary space is found through crossvalidation and it seems like a lot of the success of the proposed approach stems from the wider range of such primary-space dimensions that give acceptable results. That is, there is a greater number of choices of primary-space dimensions that give good

Table 1. Mean classification errors on the 5 experiments per training set size using the DC Mall data set. On the left of the slash we show results based on the proposed way to find subspaces, on the right the traditional PCA-based one. In parenthesis one can find the number of "wins" (out of the 5 repeated experiments) for the classifier.

Train-set size	Mean included	Mean excluded	Common P	Dim. reduction
0.5	13.7 (5) / 25.1 (0)	14.9 (5) / 26.4 (0)	14.1 (3) / 15.6 (2)	20.7 (0) / 18.2 (5)
1.0	12.5 (5) / 26.8 (0)	10.6 (5) / 23.5 (0)	10.0 (5) / 12.0 (0)	17.2 (3) / 15.3 (2)
1.5	9.5 (5) / 22.0 (0)	9.4 (5) / 19.7 (0)	9.7 (5) / 11.0 (0)	11.1 (4) / 11.3 (1)
2.0	11.4 (5) / 19.0 (0)	9.8 (5) / 19.6 (0)	10.6 (4) / 13.9 (1)	13.3 (2) / 13.2 (3)
4.0	13.0 (5) / 20.7 (0)	10.3 (5) / 20.5 (0)	9.5 (3) / 10.5 (2)	10.3 (1) / 8.6 (4)
8.0	8.9 (5) / 16.3 (0)	8.9 (5) / 15.9 (0)	9.2 (2) / 9.5 (3)	7.8 (4) / 8.5 (1)

Table 2. Data set: Pavia. For explanation, see the caption of Table 1.

Train-set size	Mean included	Mean excluded	Common P	Dim. reduction
0.5	24.7 (5) / 31.8 (0)	23.6 (4) / 32.4 (1)	29.3 (2) / 30.2 (3)	54.2 (2) / 50.8 (3)
1.0	16.6 (4) / 22.3 (1)	22.6 (2) / 20.1 (3)	15.2 (5) / 24.1 (0)	28.3 (2) / 23.8 (3)
1.5	11.7 (5) / 22.2 (0)	13.2 (5) / 17.7 (0)	12.1 (5) / 21.2 (0)	20.9 (2) / 19.9 (3)
2.0	11.0 (5) / 16.3 (0)	12.4 (5) / 16.1 (0)	9.6 (5) / 15.2 (0)	15.7 (2) / 15.7 (3)
4.0	9.4 (4) / 21.6 (1)	11.3 (4) / 13.1 (1)	10.1 (5) / 13.5 (0)	12.7 (5) / 13.6 (0)
8.0	8.1 (5) / 11.8 (0)	9.0 (5) / 12.7 (0)	7.0 (5) / 11.0 (0)	10.3 (4) / 11.6 (1)

Table 3. Data set: KSC. For explanation, see the caption of Table 1.

Train-set size	Mean included	Mean excluded	Common P	Dim. reduction
0.5	34.4 (5) / 42.9 (0)	37.8 (5) / 92.3 (0)	32.8 (4) / 32.4 (1)	62.3 (3) / 63.1 (2)
1.0	28.2 (4) / 30.4 (1)	26.7 (5) / 30.0 (0)	29.1 (2) / 30.0 (3)	34.8 (1) / 34.8 (4)
1.5	23.6 (5) / 30.5 (0)	21.4 (5) / 28.5 (0)	22.6 (5) / 26.1 (0)	29.4 (1) / 26.3 (4)
2.0	21.3 (5) / 29.6 (0)	19.6 (5) / 25.4 (0)	20.7 (5) / 24.8 (0)	23.5 (2) / 23.5 (3)
4.0	20.0 (5) / 29.6 (0)	19.2 (5) / 26.1 (0)	19.1 (2) / 18.7 (3)	19.0 (2) / 19.2 (3)
8.0	17.0 (5) / 29.8 (0)	16.7 (5) / 27.6 (0)	16.1 (0) / 14.7 (5)	15.4 (3) / 16.1 (2)

Table 4. Data set: Botswana. For explanation, see the caption of Table 1.

Train-set size	Mean included	Mean excluded	Common P	Dim. reduction
0.5	25.2 (5) / 32.1 (0)	22.7 (5) / 33.0 (0)	25.5 (3) / 28.4 (2)	38.8 (5) / 41.5 (0)
1.0	15.8 (5) / 28.8 (0)	16.0 (4) / 20.6 (1)	14.2 (5) / 23.0 (0)	22.8 (2) / 22.1 (3)
1.5	14.9 (3) / 19.9 (2)	13.2 (5) / 21.1 (0)	16.8 (4) / 18.3 (1)	19.4 (2) / 19.1 (3)
2.0	14.3 (4) / 17.6 (1)	10.8 (5) / 18.7 (0)	11.1 (4) / 13.0 (1)	15.6 (0) / 13.5 (5)
4.0	9.9 (5) / 18.7 (0)	10.1 (5) / 17.7 (0)	10.4 (2) / 9.2 (3)	8.9 (3) / 9.1 (2)
8.0	8.9 (5) / 19.1 (0)	8.3 (5) / 17.4 (0)	7.6 (4) / 8.2 (1)	7.8 (3) / 8.8 (2)

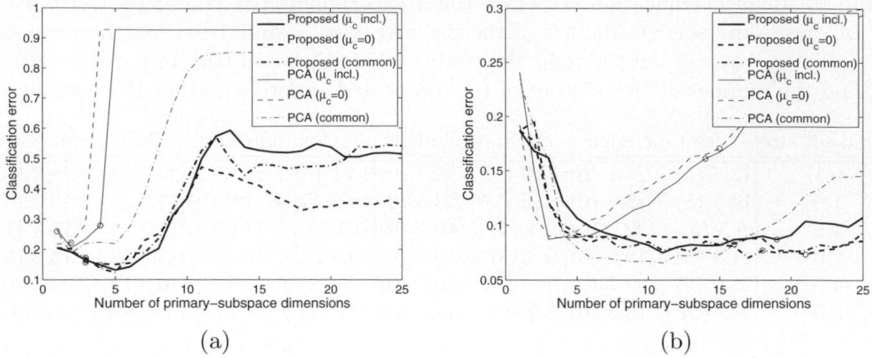

Fig. 2. Classification error rates when varying the size of the primary subspace for the Botswana data set. Training set sizes are (a) about equal to the number of original spectral bands and (b) about 8 times as many. Note how quickly the error rates for the PCA-based approaches increase with added dimensions, making it hard for any crossvalidation technique to choose a good primary-space size. Subspace sizes chosen by crossvalidation for these particular training sets are marked by 'o's.

classification results using the proposed approach than there are choices giving good results using PCA. After adding a few PCA-dimensions to the primary space, the whole sample variance is captured, leaving us with an artificial, or overfitted, primary space, while at the same time there is no variance left to "spread out" over the secondary space.

Especially in the case of a very limited set of training samples, it seems to be a good idea to avoid doing a "crisp" dimensionality reduction, but rather keep the secondary space, although with a simpler pdf model. When there are very few training samples, it is important to try to keep as much as possible of the space that they span, while at the same time avoid overfitting. Modeling the "surplus" space using a simpler model, rather then ignoring it, seems to be a good compromise.

4 Conclusion

Modeling the covariance is a key factor in normal distribution-based classifiers. When there is a need to restrict the complexity of such models, one rather flexible approach is to form orthogonal subspaces of the feature space, and let the variance in each of them be modeled with a different complexity. In this paper we have studied the classifier performance on hyperspectral image data when applying different approaches to forming these subspaces. In particular, we have proposed to use subspaces created by forming fewer and wider spectral bands instead of the more general PCA. The results indicate that the classifiers seem to benefit from using this more data-specific approach.

References

1. Duda, R.O., Hart, P.E., Stork, D.G.: Pattern Classification, 2nd edn. Wiley Interscience, Hoboken (2000)
2. Frank, I.E.: Dasco: a new classification method. Chemometrics and Intelligent Laboratory Systems 4(3), 215–222 (1988)
3. Gamba, P.: A collection of data for urban area characterization. In: Proc. IEEE Geoscience and Remote Sensing Symposium (IGARSS 2004), pp. 69–72 (2004)
4. Ham, J., Chen, Y., Crawford, M.M., Ghosh, J.: Investigation of the random forest framework for classification of hyperspectral data. IEEE Trans. Geosci. Remote Sensing 43(3), 492–501 (2005)
5. Jensen, A.C., Solberg, A.S.: Fast hyperspectral feature reduction using piecewise constant function approximations. IEEE Geoscience and Remote Sensing Letters 4(4), 547–551 (2007)
6. Landgrebe, D.A.: Signal Theory Methods in Multispectral Remote Sensing. Wiley Interscience, Hoboken (2003)
7. Næs, T., Indahl, U.: A unified description of classical classification methods for multicollinear data. Journal of chemometrics 12(3), 205–220 (1998)
8. Wold, S.: Pattern recognition by means of disjoint principal components models. Pattern Recognition 8(3), 127–139 (1976)

Mobile Visual Search from Dynamic Image Databases

Xi Chen and Markus Koskela

Department of Information and Computer Science
Aalto University School of Science, Espoo, Finland
{xi.chen,markus.koskela}@aalto.fi

Abstract. Mobile phones with integrated digital cameras provide new ways to get access to digital information and services. Images taken by the mobile phone camera can be matched to a database of objects or scenes, which enables linking of digital information to the physical world. In this paper, we describe our method for mobile image recognition, which is a part of a pilot system for linking of magazine page images to additional digital content. Such magazine databases are highly dynamic, so the recognition method needs to support addition and deletion of images without rebuilding the whole database. Meanwhile we significantly reduce the memory cost in the system without sacrificing retrieval accuracy. We present recognition results with two different databases.

Keywords: image recognition, mobile visual search, mobile augmented reality.

1 Introduction

Mobile augmented reality, i.e. augmenting the user's perception of her surroundings using a mobile device, is a relatively new field of research, which has been invigorated by the current prevalence of capable mobile computing devices. These devices are becoming increasingly small and inexpensive, and they allow us to use various computing facilities while roaming in the real world. In particular, ordinary mobile phones with integrated digital cameras are ubiquitous, and already they can provide new ways to get access to digital information and services. The images or video captured by the mobile phone can be analyzed to recognize the objects [3] or scenes [18,5] appearing in the recordings.

Consequently, the research on applicable image matching algorithms has recently been very active (e.g. [17,10,12,13]), and the current state-of-the-art methods can handle recognition from databases containing millions of images. A mobile image matching algorithm should be robust against variations in illumination, background clutter, viewpoint, and scale. Mobile applications should work with stringent bandwidth, memory and computational requirements. This requires the optimization of the performance and memory usage. For example, it is possible to perform feature extraction directly on the mobile client [19], which may reduce the system latency and provide better system scalability.

A. Heyden and F. Kahl (Eds.): SCIA 2011, LNCS 6688, pp. 196–205, 2011.

In this paper, we describe our image recognition engine which is a part of a pilot system aimed at linking of images taken with a mobile phone to interactive, contextual, and short-term mobile services [4]. This kind of technologies can be used for various purposes: possible application areas include outdoor advertising, magazine and newspaper advertising, tourist applications, and shopping. We focus here on a use case with a magazine publisher as the content provider.

The rest of the paper is organized as follows. We first review briefly some relevant related work and discuss the differences to our method in Section 2. In Section 3, we describe our method for image recognition from dynamic image databases. In Section 4, we present results from experiments with two different databases. Conclusions and plans for future work are discussed in Section 5.

2 Related Work

Image and object recognition based on extracting image patches, describing each patch with a high-dimensional descriptor, and comparing the descriptors has become extremely popular and successful [10]. In particular, the *visual words* paradigm, where the descriptors are first clustered and each descriptor is then represented by a cluster identity has made it possible to recognize images from very large databases [17,12,13]. The visual words are however relatively noisy, as the quantization is an additional error source, so direct pair-wise matching can provide more accurate results [14], especially with very few query descriptors.

Using mobile phones to retrieve additional information related to the users' interests has been studied in a number of research projects. Many systems, such as the Nokia's MARA [9] are based on the camera's various sensors, i.e. GPS receiver, accelerometer, and magnetometer. Recently, applications based on image analysis using the mobile phone camera have also been presented. An outdoors augmented reality system for mobile phones is described in [18], where GPS location data is used to prune the image data prior to the image matching stage.

The recognition of various objects with mobile phone cameras has also raised considerable research and commercial interest. For example, an application to recognize book and CD covers from live video on mobile phones is presented in [3]. One of the most popular commercial applications with similar functionalities has been launched by Amazon / SnapTell[1]. After taking a photo with the mobile and sending it to Amazon, corresponding information about the products appearing in the photo or similar products will be sent back to the user if the object is on sale in Amazon. Further examples of similar commercial applications are *Google Goggles*[2], *kooaba*[3], and Nokia's *Point and Find*[4].

In comparison to the above applications, we present in this paper a system for retrieving extended magazine content for mobile phones. Due to page limitations, printed magazines can not include all related information on some comprehensive

[1] `http://www.a9.com/`

[2] `http://www.google.com/mobile/goggles/`

[3] `http://www.kooaba.com/`

[4] `http://www.pointandfind.nokia.com/`

or interesting topics, or advertisements. This information can, however, be made accessible on the internet. The focus of the application is not on the recognition of magazine covers or other full pages, but on the varying articles and other items within the page layout in the magazines. Therefore, the photos the users submit are not limited to whole pages, but can be of small images or details in the articles, or of some advertisements. The active database consists of a certain number of latest issues only, but is highly dynamic as new issues are constantly appearing and are added to the database. Also, the system has to work with the mainstream of mobile phones currently in use, not just with the high-quality cameras included in the high end phones. This can result e.g. in highly blurred and out-of-focus input images with very few local features due to the difficulty of the mobile phone cameras to autofocus on macro distances. Therefore, we use in this work the direct pair-wise matching of local features as our starting point and aim for real-time matching with high accuracy in this setup.

3 Mobile Image Matching from Dynamic Databases

Our mobile visual searching system [4] is divided into two parts: the mobile client and the server backend. The user takes photos of interest using the client software, which then sends the image to the server for recognition. From the user point of view the system architecture is a quite ordinary web service accessible with any kind of relatively modern mobile phone equipped with a camera and an internet connection. In some applications, the local descriptors are extracted directly on the phone and sent to the server for matching [19], which is only meaningful when the size of the descriptors are significantly smaller than the original images. However, the size of standard descriptors (e.g. SIFT [10] or SURF [1]) with normal parameter settings is often about three times the size of the original images, unless some algorithm can be applied to select the useful descriptors, which means even more computational burden on the phone. Therefore, in our current application, we resize the query images on the client to 640×480 pixels (about 25–50 kB in size) and send the resized images to the server. The scale of the query image is an important parameter for both matching accuracy and speed, and even a query image smaller than this is often sufficient for recognition. In this work, we extract and use SURF descriptors for the matching.

3.1 Sub-linear Indexing

A practical method for image recognition and matching must support sub-linear indexing, i.e. it has to match the query image to the database images with complexity that does not grow linearly with the size of the database. With methods that explicitly compare the query to each item in the database, the response time will at some point be unacceptable. This is crucial especially for methods that describe the images with non-global descriptions, such as using sets of local features for each image. Standard methods for sub-linear indexing include hashing [8] and tree-based approaches [11].

The classical kd-tree algorithm [7] splits the data from the median in the dimension which has the largest variance of data among the dimensions, but fails to provide any speed-up with high-dimensional spaces. Therefore, a common approach is to use some approximate algorithm, such as Best-Bin-First [10], multiple randomized kd-trees [16], or hierarchical k-means [12].

Recently, Silpa-Anan and Hartley proposed an approximate version of kd-tree which uses multiple randomized kd-trees [16]. A randomized kd-tree selects the dimension to split the data randomly from the first M dimensions with the greatest variance in the data, and in their method N_t such trees are constructed. When searching, a single priority queue is maintained for the N_t trees so that the search can be ordered by distance to each bin boundary. The degree of approximation is determined by examining a fixed number of leaf nodes, at which point the search is terminated and the best candidates returned. In the following, we refer to the multiple randomized kd-trees as a *randomized kd-forest*.

Neither the kd-tree nor the randomized kd-tree can be modified after construction, i.e. new branches or nodes cannot be added or deleted from the tree without rebuilding. The time to build the tree is also relatively long when the dataset is large. If new data is continuously added and old data is removed from the database, it is infeasible to constantly keep rebuilding the tree. Therefore, in order to handle the constant changes in a dynamic database, we use multiple forests of randomized kd-trees. When a new batch of descriptors is added to the database, these descriptors form a separate randomized kd-forest. Similarly, when a certain batch of data is removed, we can just remove the corresponding forest. This multiple forests approach facilitates also parallel processing, which can further speed up the searching, increase accuracy, and enable query-time restrictions to the database (cf. Section 3.3).

In our current project, the image database consists of a set of recently published issues of a certain magazine or magazines from a publisher. When a new magazine issue is published, it is added to the database with each page as a separate image, a new randomized kd-forest is built for the magazine issue, and the forest is added to the database index. Similarly, the outdated magazine issues are removed from the database by removing the corresponding randomized kd-forests from the index.

3.2 Descriptor Pruning

A common method for limiting the number of descriptors extracted from images is to reduce the resolution of the images. This can also be combined with restricting the number of image-wise descriptors based on some magnitude criterion. E.g. the SURF feature adopts a fast multi-scale Hessian keypoint detector for the extraction of the keypoints, and the number of descriptors can be restricted using a threshold for the Hessian.

In the setup of this paper, the magazine pages we are considering are quite different from common images, as there are large portions of text on many pages, which is common cause of wrong matches, and we cannot reduce the resolution of the images too much as the system has to be able to recognize also small details

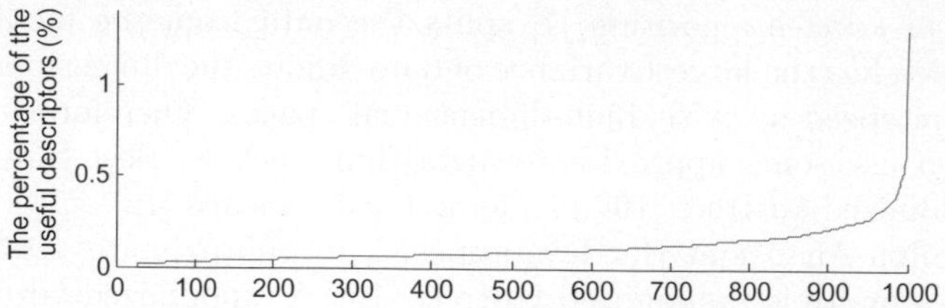

Fig. 1. The percentage of survived nearest neighbors in the clusters

from the pages. As a result, with default parameter settings and a sufficient resolution, each magazine page can generate over 10 000 descriptors.

Since each page generates a large number of descriptors, many of them ineffective, it is advantageous to study if and how much we can reduce the number of descriptors without compromising the search accuracy. Two straightforward approaches for accomplishing this are to increase the Hessian threshold and to randomly sample the keypoints. A third approach proposed in this paper is to classify the keypoints based on their estimated probability of matching. For this, we use a clustering-based classification method.

As the training data set for the clustering, we selected one magazine outside of the testing database, extracted SURF descriptors from each magazine page, and build a randomized kd-forest for all the descriptors. The full set of descriptors, 650 000 in total, was then clustered using k-means with 1000 clusters. We collected a total of 100 images taken with a mobile phone as query images, used the recognition engine to find the matching magazine pages, and recorded all the query descriptors that were matched correctly. We then assigned each matching descriptor from the data set to its cluster, recorded the number of matches for each cluster, and sorted the clusters according to their total sums of matches. The relationship between the clusters in sorted order and the percentage of matched descriptors is depicted in Fig. 1.

From Fig. 1, we can observe that the last 20% of the clusters contain more than half of the matched keypoints in the data set, which suggests that it could be feasible to remove a large portion of the clusters and associated descriptors with marginal effect to the matching performance. We can utilize these sorted clusters to prune descriptors from other data sets as well, by removing the descriptors associated to clusters below a certain cluster threshold.

3.3 Matching with Multiple Indices

The recognition of query images received from the mobile clients is implemented using a two-stage algorithm described in this section. Assume we are matching a query image q to N_f randomized kd-forests. The first stage begins after d_q descriptors have been extracted from q. The N_n nearest neighbors of each query descriptor are returned from each randomized kd-forest. We thus obtain a total of $N_f N_n d_q$ descriptors, each associated with a certain database item. We calculate for each item the total number of its descriptors that belong to this set. Finally, the N_c best-scoring magazine pages are selected as candidates for the second stage.

On the second stage, for the N_c candidates, we do a full pair-wise matching of the d_q query descriptors as in [10] to find the overall best matching pages. At this stage, we only accept nearest neighbors whose distance is less than τ of the distance of the second nearest neighbor. The approximate nearest neighbor algorithm typically results in a substantial number of wrong pair-wise correspondences. In the studied application domain, especially the body text on the magazines produces incorrect matches. Therefore, to exclude the wrong matches from further analysis, we estimate a homography between the point correspondences for the N_c candidates using RANSAC [6] and remove the outliers.

4 Experiments

In this section, we describe our experiments with two databases: a collection of nine issues from three different magazines and the publicly available ZuBuD Zurich Buildings database [15]. The latter is used to validate and compare our method to other published results, as the Magazines database is not public. We use the OpenCV implementation of randomized kd-trees from the Fast Library for Approximate Nearest Neighbors (FLANN) [11], which uses a fixed $M = 5$ and constructs a set of N_t randomized kd-trees to be searched in parallel. We use the parameter values $N_t = 4$, $N_n = 1$, $N_c = 5$, and $\tau = 0.6$ in these experiments.

4.1 Magazines Database

In the Magazines data set, a total of $N_f = 9$ issues are included from three different magazines, each containing about 80–130 pages. The size of each page image is 771×1024 pixels, and a total of 6.5 million descriptors are extracted. The three descriptor pruning approaches are applied before building the randomized kd-forests as described in Section 3.2.

For testing the recognition accuracy, we took a total of 300 query images from three issues, each from a different magazine. The images were taken by a Nokia E71 phone camera and resized to 640×480 pixels. The images were taken of such content that could be potentially interesting to the readers of the magazines and mostly contain only a small portion of whole page. Some of the query images are illustrated in Fig. 2. In the server, the query images are first resized with a scale of 0.5, that is to 320×240 pixels, as we have observed in our initial experiments that size to work well both in accuracy and speed.

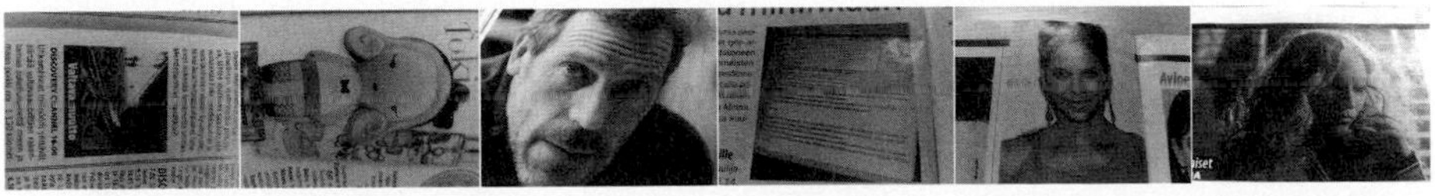

Fig. 2. A random sample of the query images in the Magazines data set

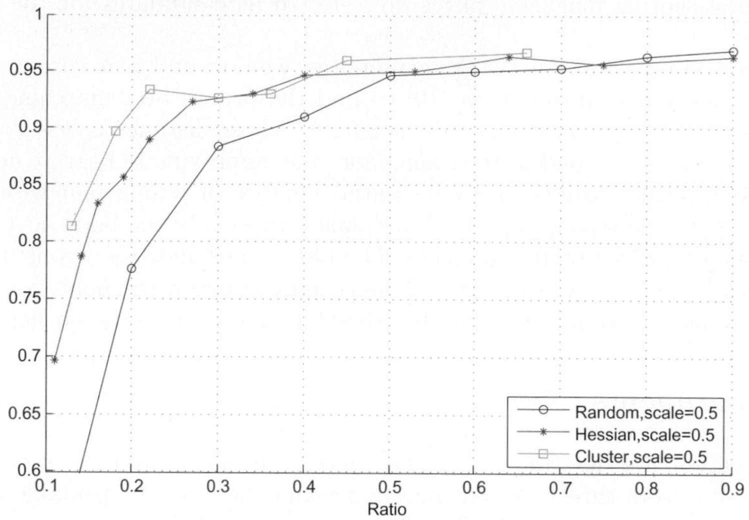

Fig. 3. A comparison for the recognition accuracies of the three descriptor pruning methods, using a fixed scale of $s = 0.5$

In the extraction of the SURF descriptors, the Hessian threshold is initially set to the default value of 500 of the OpenCV implementation, and the three proposed descriptor pruning methods are then applied. As the name implies, the *random method* samples the descriptors randomly from each page before forming the *k*d-forests. In these experiments, the random descriptor sample varies from 10% to 90% with 10% intervals. In the *Hessian pruning method*, we sort the descriptors from each page according to their Hessian values, use page-wise thresholds between 800 and 8000 descriptors, and remove the surplus descriptors. With the *clustering-based descriptor classification method*, we prune the descriptors mapped to 40%–90% of the clusters with the lowest fractions of matching descriptors as shown in Fig. 1. The results of these experiments are shown in Fig. 3, from where we can observe that the matching accuracy of the clustering-based classification method is somewhat higher than the other two methods, especially when the size of the *k*d-forests is only a small fraction of the whole database. In particular, the matching accuracy remains over 0.9 with only 18% of the whole database remaining. The average matching time is about 500 ms.

The SURF descriptor is well known for multiscale matching due to the generation of descriptors using multi-scale scanning. However, the size of the query image determines the number of descriptors and in practice has a notable effect on the recognition accuracy. In the above experiments, the query image was scaled to 0.5 of the original size, which seems to work well overall, but also results in some failed recognitions. Thus, in the following experiments we use a multi-scale approach, where the matching is initially done with the scale of 0.5 and if no match was found, again with scales of 0,67, 0.8, and 1.0. The same

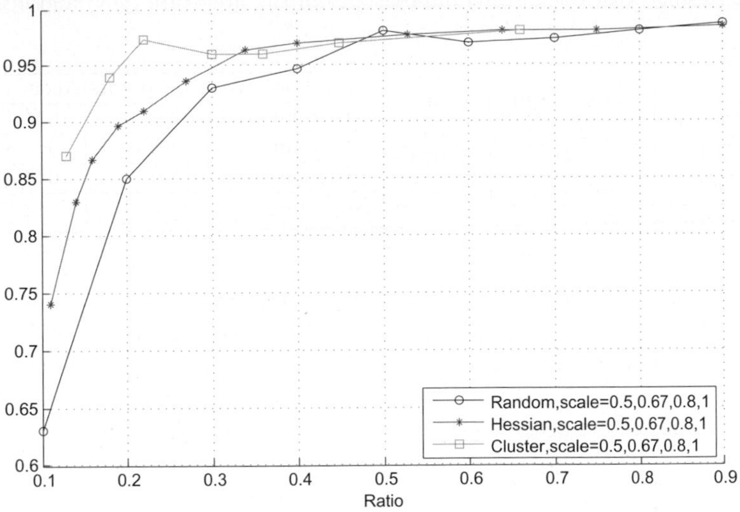

Fig. 4. A comparison for the recognition accuracies of the three descriptor pruning methods, using multiple scales $s \in \{0.5, 0.67, 0.8, 1.0\}$

experiments for the random, Hessian and clustering-based methods are performed with the multiple-scale approach, and the matching accuracy is shown in Fig. 4.

Comparing the two figures, the multiple-scale matching attains slightly better results than the single scale of 0.5, with the accuracy remaining near 0.95 with only 18% of the database used. Furthermore, since most of the query images are matched correctly with the initial scale, only a small portion of the images are processed with multiple scales, so the multiple-scale approach decreases the average response time only slightly while increasing the system accuracy.

4.2 ZuBuD Database

We have also experimented with a publicly available image database to compare our method and our recognition results with results published in previous works. The ZuBuD database contains color images of 201 buildings in the city of Zurich. There are a total of 1005 images as each building is represented by five shots, taken from different viewpoints and in different lighting conditions. In addition, there are 115 query images included, each having a correct answer among the 201 buildings in the database. The database is relatively easy, as many works report high average accuracies, and it is small enough so that exhaustive pairwise image matching can be used.

Table 1 shows recognition results from two sources, [20,2], which both use exhaustive matching and report accuracies of over 0.95. With this database, we used $N_f = 10$, Hessian pruning with different thresholds, and multiple scales of the query images. The results are shown in Table 1, which shows that our

Table 1. Results with the ZuBuD database; from the literature (left) and our results (right)

Method	# of keypoints	Accuracy
[2] (SIFT)	600	0.956
[2] (CHoG)	600	0.974
[20]	unknown	0.965

Method	# of keypoints	Accuracy
Hessian	600	0.974
Hessian	400	0.948
Hessian	300	0.921
No homog.	600	1.0

method is able to reach similar performance with sub-linear matching. The average matching time is about 300 ms. It can be noted that with 600 keypoints, as in [2], we get only three failed recognitions, and that these failures are due to a missing homography. If in this case we accept the image that is most often selected for the second stage as the recognition result, we get accuracy of 1.0.

5 Conclusions

In the project described in this paper, we maintain a dynamic image database with magazines from a publishing company. As the database is constantly updated by adding new issues and removing old ones, the separate randomized kd-forest for each magazine fulfills the requirements for the high flexibility, and facilities the use of multiple threads to speed up the matching. Due to the demand for high matching accuracy with query images that are often of poor quality, we use direct matching of descriptors instead of visual words. The magazine pages usually contains a large number of descriptors due to high resolution and large amounts of text. In order to reduce the size of the kd-forests while preserving the matching accuracy, a clustering-based descriptor classification method is applied to the descriptor database. By keeping the descriptors only from the selected clusters, the matching accuracy can reach 0.9 with only 15% of the descriptors. Therefore, the proposed method significantly reduces the memory consumption while retaining a high matching accuracy.

References

1. Bay, H., Tuytelaars, T., Van Gool, L.: SURF: Speeded up robust features. In: Leonardis, A., Bischof, H., Pinz, A. (eds.) ECCV 2006. LNCS, vol. 3951, pp. 404–417. Springer, Heidelberg (2006)
2. Chandrasekhar, V., Chen, D.M., Lin, A.L., Takacs, G., Tsai, S.S., Cheung, N.M., Reznik, Y., Grzeszczuk, R., Girod, B.: Comparison of local feature descriptors for mobile visual search. In: IEEE International Conference on Image Processing (ICIP). Hong Kong (September 2010)
3. Chen, D., Tsai, S., Vedantham, R., Grzeszczuk, R., Girod, B.: Streaming mobile augmented reality on mobile phones. In: Proceedings of International Symposium on Mixed and Augmented Reality (ISMAR 2009). Orlando, Florida (October 2009)

4. Chen, X., Koskela, M., Hyväkkä, J.: Image based information access for mobile phones. In: Proceedings of 8th International Workshop on Content-Based Multimedia Indexing, Grenoble, France (June 2010)
5. El Choubassi, M., Nestares, O., Wu, Y., Kozintsev, I., Haussecker, H.: An augmented reality tourist guide on your mobile devices. In: Boll, S., Tian, Q., Zhang, L., Zhang, Z., Chen, Y.-P.P. (eds.) MMM 2010. LNCS, vol. 5916, pp. 588–602. Springer, Heidelberg (2010)
6. Fischler, M.A., Bolles, R.C.: Random sample consensus: a paradigm for model fitting with applications to image analysis and automated cartography. Communications of the ACM 24(6), 381–395 (1981)
7. Friedman, J.H., Bentley, J.L., Finkel, R.A.: An algorithm for finding best matches in logaritmic expected time. ACM Transactions on Mathematical Software 3(3), 209–226 (1977)
8. Gionis, A., Indyk, P., Motwani, R.: Similarity search in high dimensions via hashing. In: Proceedings of 25th International Conference on Very Large Data Bases (VLDB 1999), pp. 518–529. Edinburgh, Scotland, UK (September 1999)
9. Kähäri, M., Murphy, D.: MARA – Sensor based augmented reality system for mobile imaging. In: Proceedings of International Symposium on Mixed and Augmented Reality (ISMAR 2006), Santa Barbara, CA (October 2006)
10. Lowe, D.G.: Distinctive image features from scale-invariant keypoints. International Journal of Computer Vision 60(2), 91–110 (2004)
11. Muja, M., Lowe, D.G.: Fast approximate nearest neighbors with automatic algorithm configuration. In: Proceedings of International Conference on Computer Vision Theory and Applications (VISAPP 2009), Lisboa, Portugal (February 2009)
12. Nistér, D., Stewénius, H.: Scalable recognition with a vocabulary tree. In: Proceedings of IEEE CVPR 2006, vol. 2, pp. 2161–2168 (2006)
13. Philbin, J., Chum, O., Isard, M., Sivic, J., Zisserman, A.: Object retrieval with large vocabularies and fast spatial matching. In: Proceedings of the IEEE Conference on Computer Vision and Pattern Recognition (June 2007)
14. Philbin, J., Isard, M., Sivic, J., Zisserman, A.: Descriptor learning for efficient retrieval. In: Daniilidis, K. (ed.) ECCV 2010, Part III. LNCS, vol. 6313, pp. 677–691. Springer, Heidelberg (2010)
15. Shao, H., Svoboda, T., van Gool, L.: ZuBuD - Zurich buildings database for image based recognition. Tech. Rep. 260, ETH Zurich (April 2006)
16. Silpa-Anan, C., Hartley, R.: Optimised KD-trees for fast image descriptor matching. In: IEEE Computer Society Conference on Computer Vision and Pattern Recognition (2008)
17. Sivic, J., Zisserman, A.: Video Google: A text retrieval approach to object matching in videos. In: Proc. of ICCV 2003, vol. 2, pp. 1470–1477 (October 2003)
18. Takacs, G., Chandrasekhar, V., Gelfand, N., Xiong, Y., Chen, W.C., Bismpigiannis, T., Grzeszczuk, R., Pulli, K., Girod, B.: Outdoors augmented reality on mobile phone using loxel-based visual feature organization. In: Proceeding of the 1st ACM International Conference on Multimedia Information Retrieval (MIR 2008), Vancouver, British Columbia, Canada, pp. 427–434 (2008)
19. Tsai, S.S., Chen, D., Chandrasekhar, V., Takacs, G., Cheung, N.M., Vedantham, R., Grzeszczuk, R., Girod, B.: Mobile product recognition. In: ACM Multimedia (ACM MM), Florence, Italy (October 2010)
20. Zhang, W., Kosecka, J.: Hierarchical building recognition. Image and Vision Computing 25(5), 704–716 (2007)

Histogram-Based Description of Local Space-Time Appearance*

Karla Brkić[1], Axel Pinz[2], Siniša Šegvić[1], and Zoran Kalafatić[1]

[1] Faculty of Electrical Engineering and Computing, University of Zagreb, Croatia
[2] Graz University of Technology, Austria

Abstract. We introduce a novel local spatio-temporal descriptor intended to model the spatio-temporal behavior of a tracked object of interest in a general manner. The basic idea of the descriptor is the accumulation of histograms of an image function value through time. The histograms are calculated over a regular grid of patches inside the bounding box of the object and normalized to represent empirical probability distributions. The number of grid patches is fixed, so the descriptor is invariant to changes in spatial scale. Depending on the temporal complexity/details at hand, we introduce "first order STA descriptors" that describe the average distribution of a chosen image function over time, and "second order STA descriptors" that model the distribution of each histogram bin over time. We discuss entropy and χ^2 as well-suited similarity and saliency measures for our descriptors. Our experimental validation ranges from the patch- to the object-level. Our results show that STA, this simple, yet powerful novel description of local space-time appearance is well-suited to machine learning and will be useful in video-analysis, including potential applications of object detection, tracking, and background modeling.

1 Introduction

Recent development of powerful detectors and descriptors has led to a tremendous boost of the success of computer vision algorithms to recognize, detect, and localize events in images. Most of these algorithms, for instance keypoint detection (DoG [11], Kadir and Brady saliency [5], MSER [13]), local scale or affine covariant description (SIFT [11], affine Harris/Laplace [14], LAF [15]), and object detection [2] are applied *at the image level*, i.e. in the 2D spatial domain. When *temporal* information (video) is available, we find that the same algorithms are still applied at a 2D image level, and the temporal aspect is often just covered by simple tracking of these 2D detections/descriptions over time.

* This research has been funded by the Croatian Science Foundation and IPV Zagreb. We also acknowledge the support by OeAD and the Croatian Ministry of Science, Education and Sports for bilateral Austrian-Croatian exchange.

A. Heyden and F. Kahl (Eds.): SCIA 2011, LNCS 6688, pp. 206–217, 2011.

A principled manner to treat the *description of local spatio-temporal events in video sequences* is still missing[1].

In this paper, we present a histogram-based descriptor for capturing the local spatio-temporal behavior of an "object" of interest. Having a description of spatio-temporal behavior at the object level opens the door for a wide variety of potential applications. Applications depend on how we view the "object" in question: is it a neighborhood of an interest point, is it a fixed rigid object with apparently moving background, such as a traffic sign seen from a moving observer, or is it a highly complex object with moving parts such as a human? Depending on the "object", we can elegantly utilize existing building blocks – for instance, a mean-shift tracker for tracking regions of interest, the Viola-Jones detector for traffic sign detection [1] or a HOG descriptor for detecting humans – to track an object of interest over time. In summary, we depart from existing 2D image-based detection and track salient events over time using existing tracking algorithms. We show a novel, principled manner to describe the local spatio-temporal behavior of objects in videos.

The benefit of having a descriptor of local spatio-temporal behavior is manyfold. At the level of interest points, consider the problem of "Multibody Structure and Motion" (MSaM [16]) analysis that requires the sparse 3D reconstruction of stationary background and a factorization of the foreground into independently moving objects. To avoid the need for many background points to be tracked, it would be very useful to identify a few, sparsely distributed "good features to track" [18] in the stationary background. At the level of fixed, rigid objects, an illustrative example comes from traffic sign detection. A traffic sign viewed from a moving car is a rigid object with a distant, moving background. But stickers that look like speed limit signs are sometimes glued to the back of a truck. A system for traffic sign detection relying solely on appearance could report such a sticker as a valid traffic sign. By modeling the local spatio-temporal behavior, however, it could be inferred that the detected object is glued to a fixed, unchanging background, so it must be a false positive. At the level of complex objects (for instance human actions, pedestrian detection and tracking), available research strongly favors the use of spatio-temporal information – be it motion trajectories, spatio-temporal volumes, or temporal HOG.

2 Related Work

The majority of work in spatio-temporal analysis concerns some type of dynamic behavior, most commonly human actions. Laptev and Perez [9] study automatic recognition of human actions in scenes taken from real movies. Their framework for detection and recognition is based on boosted window classifiers which use histogram-based spatio-temporal features. Two types of histograms are used: (i)

[1] There are a few exceptions to this observation, including the elegant extension from 2D spatial scale space theory [10] to scale in space and time [8]. But their contribution mostly covers the *detection* of local, salient space-time events at their characteristic scale, not a principled way to *describe* such events.

a HOG with four bins, to model local appearance and (ii) optical flow histograms with five bins (four orientations and one bin to represent the lack of optical flow), to model motion. Each feature is defined by the space-time cuboid on which it is calculated, by the type of the histogram used for calculation and by the mode of calculating the feature. Depending on the mode of calculation, a histogram is either calculated on the entire spatio-temporal cuboid, or the cuboid is divided into smaller parts for which individual histograms are calculated. To enable detection and recognition of actions using the proposed features, an AdaBoost classifier is trained, with Fisher Discriminants as weak learners. This classifier is combined with a purely 2D appearance classifier, which works better than any of both classifiers individually.

Ke et al. [6] focus on event detection using volumetric (i.e. spatio-temporal) features. Inspired by the success of the Viola-Jones detector, they generalize the notion of 2D rectangular features used by Viola and Jones to 3D box features. Viola and Jones themselves proposed a temporal extension of their detector intended for pedestrian detection [19], but their extension employed the differences between just two consecutive frames. The volumetric features of Ke et al., however, can span through multiple frames. The authors suggest computing the features on the optical flow of the video.

Luo et al. [12] present a learning method for human action detection in video sequences. They introduce a descriptor set named local motion histograms. Motivated by Laptev [9], they use Fisher Discriminants as weak learners on the descriptor set and then train a Gentle AdaBoost action classifier. An action is contained within a spatio-temporal volume. This volume is divided into "basic blocks" in different configurations, similar to Laptev and Perez [9]. Within each block the local motion histograms are calculated, using the magnitude and the orientation of the optical flow. Three types of histograms are defined, differing in the manner in which they are calculated (either using raw optical flow or variants of differential flow).

Dollar et al. [3] develop a framework for generic behavior detection and recognition from video sequences. Their idea is to represent a behavior by using spatio-temporal feature points, which they define as short, local video sequences such as, for instance, an eye opening or a knee bending. They propose an interest point detector intended to react to periodic motions and to spatio-temporal corners. At the interest points found by the detector they extract spatio-temporal cuboids. Each cuboid is represented by a descriptor in one of the following ways: (i) by simply flattening the cuboid into a vector, (ii) by histogramming the values in the cuboid or (iii) by dividing the cuboid into a number of regions, constructing a local histogram for each region and then concatenating all the histograms. Authors suggest histogramming either normalized pixel values, the brightness gradient, or windowed optical flow. The proposed descriptors are used in action classification by constructing a library of cuboid prototypes. A histogram of cuboid types is calculated at the level of the entire video, and is used as the behavior descriptor.

Kläser et al. [7] introduce a local descriptor for video sequences based on histograms of oriented 3D spatio-temporal gradients. The descriptor is a generalization of the well-known HOG descriptor to spatio-temporal data. The gradients become three-dimensional as they are calculated within spatio-temporal volumes using regular polyhedra. The gradient vector is positioned in the center of a regular polyhedron, and the side to which the vector points determines the histogram bin in which the vector will be placed. In their experiments, they represent video sequences as bags of words using the described spatio-temporal HOG generalization. To classify the action type, they use histograms of visual word occurences (similar to Dollar et al.) with a non-linear SVM with a χ^2 kernel.

All the approaches outlined above are intended for video analysis *once the entire video sequence is available.* In this paper, we propose a descriptor capable of harnessing spatio-temporal information on a per-frame basis, not assuming that the entire video is available. Such a descriptor can easily be used in an online setting. The descriptor is based on accumulating histograms through time. Our descriptor is not intended exclusively for action recognition – rather, it aims to model the spatio-temporal behavior of an object in a general manner.

3 Building the Spatio-temporal Appearance Descriptor

To build the spatio-temporal appearance (STA) descriptor, we require a tracked object of interest. The descriptor is calculated in every frame using the current frame information and the information from previous frames. Tracking can be achieved either by detection, or by using a standard tracker such as meanshift or KLT [17]. The algorithm for descriptor calculation assumes that a bounding box around the object of interest is available in every frame. In order to compute the descriptor, the bounding box around the object is divided into a regular grid of patches. The size of the grid is a parameter of the algorithm. For each patch, a histogram is calculated and normalized so it represents an empirical probability distribution. The value being histogrammed is a parameter of the descriptor. Possible values include hue, gradient, grayscale intensity, normalized grayscale intensity, optical flow or any other image measurement. By normalizing the histogram, i.e. representing the histogram as an empirical probability distribution, we minimize the influence of scale on the descriptor. If the histogram were absolute-valued, patches of a larger scale would have more weight. In every frame, the empirical probability distribution of each patch is updated with new measurements. The descriptor is constructed by concatenating the empirical probability distributions of all patches into a feature vector. The advantage of such an approach is that we obtain a fixed-length spatio-temporal appearance descriptor of the object in question, regardless of the spatial or temporal scale of the object. By using a grid of patches, we compensate for the possibly inaccurate object localization.

We propose two variants of the spatio-temporal appearance descriptor that differ in the level of detail in which they describe spatio-temporal behavior: (i) spatio-temporal appearance descriptor of the first order (first-order STA descriptor), and (ii) spatio-temporal appearance descriptor of the second order (second-order STA descriptor).

3.1 Spatio-temporal Appearance Descriptor of the First Order

In the spatio-temporal appearance descriptor of the first order, each patch of the bounding box grid is represented with a single histogram, which shows the distribution of some image measurement (e.g. hue, gradient) through time.

To construct the descriptor, the bounding box around the object is in each frame divided into a regular grid of $r \times s$ patches. The n-bin histogram of the patch (u, v) is a set of bins paired with their respective relative frequencies:

$$H_{u,v} = \{(b_i, p(b_i))\}, \quad i = 1 \ldots n \tag{1}$$

This histogram estimates an empirical probability distribution, where $p(b_i)$ is the *a posteriori* probability of the bin b_i. We propose integrating the histograms of an individual patch over time to obtain the first-order spatio-temporal appearance histogram (STA histogram) of the patch:

$$H_{u,v}^{(t)} = \left\{ \left(b_i, \sum_{\theta=1}^{t} \alpha_\theta p^{(\theta)}(b_i) \right) \right\} = \{(b_i, p_t(b_i))\}, \quad i = 1 \ldots n \tag{2}$$

Here, we introduce the notation $p_t(b_i)$ which denotes the average empirical probability of the bin b_i in time t. The probability of bin b_i in time θ is denoted as $p^{(\theta)}(b_i)$. Parameters α_θ describe the influence of the histogram in frame θ on the overall histogram. The simplest choice for α_θ is

$$\alpha_\theta = \frac{1}{t} \tag{3}$$

which can be interpreted as histograms from all previous frames contributing equally to the final histogram. This is a good choice when we consider all the detections of the object equally valuable, regardless of *when* they were obtained. Whether all detections are considered equally valuable will depend on the nature of the problem – for instance, in the case of the observer moving towards the object, the later detections would probably be more valuable, as they would have a larger scale than the early detections. One possible way of giving more weight to the newer detections is that the integrated histogram for a given frame is equal to the average of the histogram in the current frame and the integrated histogram for all previous frames. In this case, it can be shown that the parameters α_θ are:

$$\begin{aligned} \alpha_1 &= \alpha_2 = \tfrac{1}{2^{t-1}} \\ \alpha_\theta &= \tfrac{1}{2^{t-\theta+1}} \qquad 2 < \theta \leq t \end{aligned} \tag{4}$$

assuming that the sequence has more than one frame, i.e. $t \geq 2$. The final first-order STA descriptor for an individual frame is a concatenation of the first-order STA histograms of all patches in the grid:

$$\delta^{(t)} = \left[H_{u,v}^{(t)} \right]^T, \quad u = 1 \ldots r, \ v = 1 \ldots s \tag{5}$$

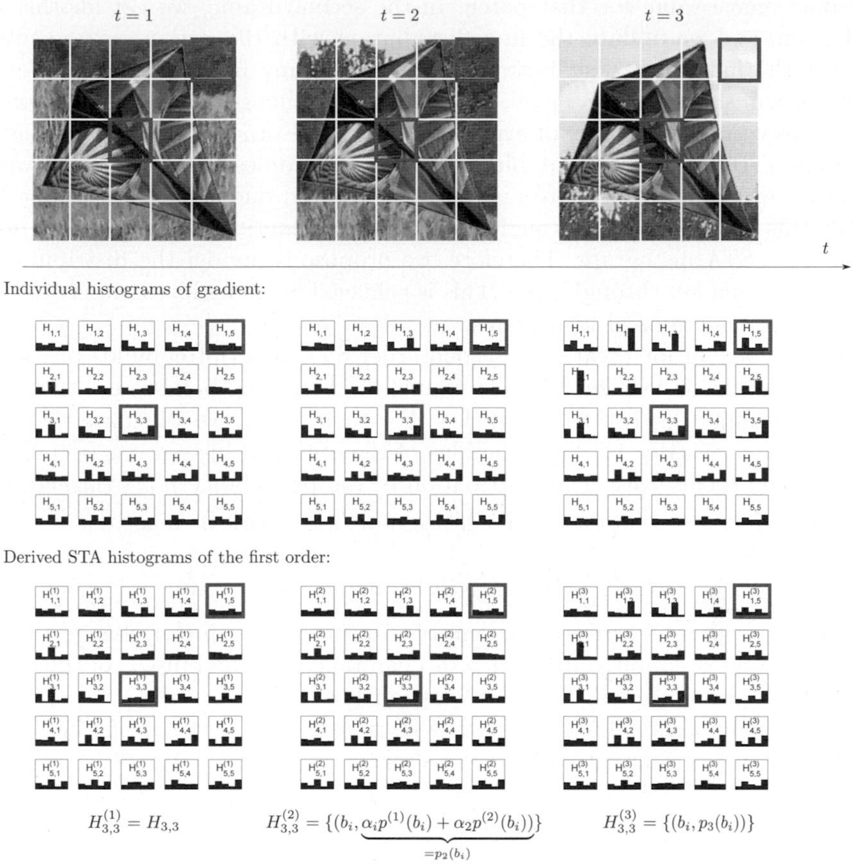

Fig. 1. Constructing the first order STA histograms for a sequence of three frames. Two patches are highlighted in red: a patch which lies in the background and a patch which lies on the object. Notice how the STA histograms of the object patch are constant through time, while the STA histograms of the background patch change.

By expanding $H^{(t)}_{u,v}$, we get:

$$\delta^{(t)} = [\underbrace{p_t(b_1)\ p_t(b_2) \ldots p_t(b_n)}_{u=1,v=1}\ \underbrace{p_t(b_1)\ p_t(b_2) \ldots p_t(b_n)}_{u=1,v=2}\ \ldots\ \underbrace{p_t(b_1)\ p_t(b_2) \ldots p_t(b_n)}_{u=r,v=s}]^T \tag{6}$$

An illustration of constructing a first order STA descriptor is shown in Fig. 1.

3.2 Spatio-temporal Histogram Descriptor of the Second Order

The first-order STA descriptor describes the distributions of some image value over a regular grid of patches through time. For simplicity, consider the behavior of the descriptor for a single patch. In the first frame, we get the distribution of some image value for that patch. In the second frame, we get another distribution, and we update the first distribution with the new measurements so we get the integrated distribution. Therefore, in any frame our first-order descriptor will show the *average* distribution of some image value measured on the patch over time. The value of every bin of the first-order STA histogram is the average of the values of that bin in all elapsed frames (see Fig. 1). However, when considering only the average value of the bin one cannot determine how much this bin had varied through time. That information is not available in the first-order STA histogram. Therefore, we propose to model the distribution of *each histogram bin* through time. This is achieved by using histograms of second order, i.e. histograms of histograms.

The algorithm for creating a second-order STA descriptor builds on the descriptors of the first order. In every frame, the bounding box around the object is divided into a grid of $r \times s$ patches. For each patch, we calculate the patch histogram, as in (Eq. 1). Now, the bins of the obtained histograms become histogrammed themselves. The distribution of the probability $p(b_i)$ through time is modeled by a second-order STA histogram $H'^{(t)}_{u,v,i}$ with m bins β_j:

$$H'^{(t)}_{u,v,i} = \{(\beta_j, p(p_t(b_i) \in \beta_j))\}\,,\; j = 1 \ldots m \tag{7}$$

This histogram describes how empirical probabilities $p_t(b_i)$ change through time. As the maximum value that $p_t(b_i)$ can take is 1, the bins β_j of the second order STA histogram will have the width of $1/m$.

The second-order STA descriptor is obtained by concatenating the second-order STA histograms into a feature vector:

$$\delta'^{(t)} = \left[H'^{(t)}_{u,v,i}\right]^T,\; u = 1 \ldots r,\; v = 1 \ldots s \tag{8}$$

As explained in Subsection 3.1, the first-order STA descriptor describes the average appearance of an object through time. In contrast, the second-order descriptor encodes both the object appearance and the change of that appearance.

4 Learning from the STA Descriptor

Having built a spatio-temporal appearance descriptor, it is interesting to review possible saliency measures which can be applied to the descriptor to distinguish different kinds of space-time behavior. Both variants of the STA descriptor $\delta^{(t)}$ are a concatenation of histogram probabilities. We simplify the notation and denote every element of the histogram descriptor d_k. Hence, the STA descriptor of the first order is:

$$\delta^{(t)} = [d_1\; d_2 \ldots\; d_k]^T,\quad k = r \times s \times n \tag{9}$$

while the STA descriptor of the second order is:

$$\delta'^{(t)} = [d_1\; d_2 \ldots\; d_k]^T,\quad k = r \times s \times n \times m \tag{10}$$

4.1 Entropy

Because every element of our descriptor originates in a histogram and estimates a probability, we can calculate the total entropy of the descriptor by:

$$E(\delta^{(t)}) = -\sum_k d_k \log d_k \tag{11}$$

which is essentially the sum of entropies of histograms which were concatenated into the descriptor[2]. The formula is valid for first and second order descriptors.

Entropy of the STA descriptor conveys important information about the behavior of the object through time. Consider the case of the first-order STA descriptor. If a patch changes a lot through time, its first-order STA histogram will approach a uniform distribution – because if the patches were changing completely randomly, every bin of the histogram would be equally likely. On the other hand, if the patch remains fairly constant through time, we expect a stable and constant histogram. As entropy is a measure of randomness, a larger entropy will indicate a distribution closer to uniform. Therefore, using entropy, we can distinguish between patches that vary and patches that stay the same. There is, however, one problem: by measuring the entropy of the first-order STA histogram, we cannot distinguish between a patch which is constant through time, but has an appearance resulting in a uniform histogram, and a patch whose appearance varies a lot through time. Both cases lead to a uniform first-order STA histogram. To address this, one can measure the total entropy of the second-order STA descriptor. As the STA histogram of the second order models the *change* in the first-order STA histogram, the entropy we obtain will be invariant to the object appearance.

We envision two uses for the entropy measure. First, at the level of a single object, knowing the parameters of the descriptor and having a training set of descriptors $\delta^{(t)}$ one can find which patches inside the grid of the object bounding box are temporally stable – i.e., which patches are likely to describe the object, and which patches are likely to describe the background. Second, at the level of multiple objects, one can compare total entropies of two different objects to find which object is more stable through time. This has proved to be especially useful in finding good features to track (see the experimental section).

4.2 The χ^2 Measure

The spatio-temporal behavior of an object can also be investigated using the χ^2 measure. This measure shows whether some empirical probability distribution matches with the theoretically expected distribution. In a general experiment, the χ^2 measure is calculated as

$$\chi^2 = \sum_{i=1}^{n} \frac{(O_i - E_i)^2}{E_i} \tag{12}$$

[2] We denote entropy by E, because H is already in use for histograms.

with O_i being the observed frequency and E_i being the expected frequency. In the context of our histograms, we can use the χ^2 measure to determine how much a patch changes through time (similarly to the entropy measure). Suppose that we wish to determine whether a patch changes a lot. If it were changing a lot, we would expect its first-order STA histogram to be fairly uniform. Hence, we choose a null hypothesis that the part of the descriptor corresponding to the histogram of one patch represents a uniform distribution.

Mathematically, assume that the descriptor is given by Eq. 6. For patch $u = 1$, $v = 1$, the observed values are $p_t(b_i)$, $i = 1 \dots n$, while the expected values correspond to a uniform distribution and thus are $\mu(p_t(b_i)) = 1/n$. Then, the χ^2 measure of similarity of the patch (u, v) with a uniform distribution is:

$$\chi^2_{u,v} = \sum_{i=1}^{n} \frac{(p_t(b_i) - 1/n)^2}{p_t(b_i)} \tag{13}$$

Using this measure, we can determine the similarity of the observed distribution with a uniform distribution, which might provide an important clue to whether a patch is changing or not.

4.3 Using the STA Descriptor in Machine Learning

The STA descriptor can be used directly as a feature vector in any machine learning algorithm. The descriptor length is a constant, regardless of the number of frames through which the object spans or the scale of the object. At the same time, the descriptor is richer in information than a single image of an object, because it includes the temporal dimension as well. Instead of using the descriptor directly, one can first transform it by applying one of the mentioned saliency measures on the elements of the descriptor which correspond to STA histograms of individual patches. In case of the first-order STA descriptor this means applying the saliency measures on the histograms of patch appearance, while in case of the second-order STA this means applying them on the histograms of such histograms. Using the descriptor as a feature vector, we can train a classifier that discriminates between various classes of objects. Depending on the desired level of complexity, we will use either the first-order or the second-order descriptor. The training set is constructed by tracking the objects through time and calculating the descriptors in frames of interest. Depending on the application, one might choose to calculate the descriptor of the object in every frame, and thus obtain more training samples, or to calculate the descriptor in several selected frames, or perhaps just in the last frame. An important constraint to keep in mind is the dimensionality of the descriptor, which can be quite large, especially for the second-order descriptor (if we assume a grid of 5×5 patches, and $m = n = 5$, then the dimensionality of the second order descriptor will be $r \times s \times m \times n = 5^4 = 625$). In order to train a classifier which uses such a descriptor, one needs a large number of training samples. Possible classifiers which might be suitable include neural networks, support vector machines, k-NN classifiers, tree-based classifiers, variants of boosting etc.

5 Illustrative Experiments

To present the benefits of using the STA descriptor, we chose three illustrative examples: discriminating between true and false positives, discriminating between static and dynamic background and finding good features to track.

5.1 Discriminating between True and False Positives

Object detectors, when applied to large amounts of data such as videos, inevitably produce false positive detections. To deal with that, one usually trains additional classifiers exploiting different classification cues. Here, we analyze the benefit of training one such classifier on STA descriptors of the object over training it on object images without the temporal component. Our positive samples are triangular traffic signs tracked using a combination of the Viola-Jones detector and the KLT tracker. For negatives, we choose two variants: (i) artificial false positives – background patches which are randomly selected and then tracked and (ii) real false positives obtained as the responses of the Viola-Jones detector trained on traffic signs [1]. To build the training set, we calculate the first-order STA descriptor of the object in every frame, and add the descriptor to the set with the corresponding label (object / non-object). Hence, for every frame in which the object appears we obtain one training sample. In calculating the descriptor, we use a grid of 5×5 patches and 10 histogram bins. The value being histogrammed is hue. For the classifier, we use a random forest of 10 trees. When using real false positives, the total number of training samples is 17806, while the total number of testing samples is 1978. When using artificial false positives, the total number of training samples is 25370, while the number of testing samples is 2818. Results summarized in Table 1 show that by using the first-order STA descriptor we reduce the number of false positives and obtain much better ROC curves than when working with raw data.

Table 1. Results of discriminating objects (traffic signs) and non-objects (false positives) using different types of false positives (artificial examples or examples obtained by the Viola-Jones detector), different operators (hue, gradient) and different feature vectors (raw pixels / HOG vs first-order STA). The employed classifier is a random forest. We show true positive (TP), false positive (FP), true negative (TN) and false negative (FN) rates for the decision threshold of .5.

negatives	function	feature vector	TP	FN	FP	TN	AuROC
artificial	hue	raw pixels	0.994	0.006	0.172	0.828	0.903
artificial	hue	first-order STA	0.981	0.019	0.018	0.982	0.989
Viola-Jones	hue	raw pixels	0.843	0.157	0.168	0.832	0.898
Viola-Jones	hue	first-order STA	0.840	0.160	0.101	0.899	0.947
Viola-Jones	gradient	raw HoG	0.851	0.149	0.336	0.664	0.831
Viola-Jones	gradient	first-order STA	0.868	0.132	0.080	0.920	0.960

5.2 Distinguishing between a Static and a Moving Background

Using the proposed saliency measures and the second-order STA descriptor, we can train a classifier which distinguishes between objects of the same class that are glued to a static background and objects which have a moving, distant background. To illustrate this fact, we created an artificial training set consisting of tracked triangular signs on a static background and tracked triangular signs with a moving background. An image of a sign is first selected from a database of 2000 real traffic sign images and masked to remove its background. Then the artificial background is randomly selected from a set of available backgrounds. We simulate the tracking of the sign through time by enlarging the sign and the background by a plausible random value until the sign reaches some predefined scale limit. For the class of signs with the moving background, we also simulate background motion. Additionally, we simulate localization noise by randomly offsetting the bounding box around the sign. In every frame, we create the second-order STA descriptor of the object. The descriptor is calculated over a grid of 5×5 patches and 10 histogram bins are used both for the first-order and the second-order histogram. The value being histogrammed is gradient orientation. We calculate the entropy of each second-order histogram and form a feature vector by concatenating all the calculated entropies. The dimensionality of the feature vector is then equal to the dimensionality of the first-order STA descriptor: 250. We use around 40000 training samples and around 10000 testing samples. To allow motion to develop, we include only the descriptors of the frames after frame 3 of the object. The trained random forest classifier achieves a true positive rate of 0.999 and a false positive rate of 0.125, which shows that the proposed descriptor successfully models change.

5.3 Finding Stable Features to Track

Finally, we collected first experimental evidence regarding the benefit of our novel STA descriptors for the problem of finding good features to track in the background of complex Multibody Structure and Motion (MSaM) scenes. We analyzed a recent MSaM secquence by Holzer and Pinz [4], where their original algorithm detects and tracks about 200 point features in the scene. Typically, 150-180 of these points are located in stationary background. We harvested the most salient background features by ordering all the points by the entropy of their first-order STA descriptors in every frame and selecting the top 20 points. These points can be seen as a sparse reconstruction of the stationary background and can be used in terms of "good features to track" [18] the camera pose.

6 Conclusion and Outlook

The main contribution of this paper certainly is a fundamental one: we have introduced STA - a novel spatio-temporal appearance descriptor based on histograms. We believe that STA will be widely used and highly successful in many applications of video processing due to its simplicity and general applicability. The descriptor combines spatial and temporal information into a fixed-length feature vector, independent of spatial or temporal scale of an object. Our proposed saliency measures are helpful in analyzing the space-time behavior of the object further. We have illustrated how the descriptor can be applied in different use cases, from discriminating between objects to finding good features to track.

In our future work, we plan to use STA descriptors for the analysis of complex Multibody Structure and Motion (MSaM) scenes, and for the learning and discrimination of category specific motion patterns.

References

1. Brkić, K., Pinz, A., Šegvić, S.: Traffic sign detection as a component of an automated traffic infrastructure inventory system. In: Proc. 33rd ÖAGM Workshop, Stainz, Austria (May 2009)
2. Dalal, N., Triggs, B.: Histograms of oriented gradients for human detection. In: Proc. CVPR (2005)
3. Dollár, P., Rabaud, V., Cottrell, G., Belongie, S.: Behavior recognition via sparse spatio-temporal features. In: VS-PETS (October 2005)
4. Holzer, P., Pinz, A.: Mobile surveillance by 3d-outlier analysis. In: Proc. ACCV Workshop on Visual Surveillance (2010)
5. Kadir, T., Brady, M.: Scale, saliency and image description. Int. J. Computer Vision 45(2), 83–105 (2001)
6. Ke, Y., Sukthankar, R., Hebert, M.: Efficient visual event detection using volumetric features. In: Proc. ICCV, vol. 1, pp. 166–173 (October 2005)
7. Kläser, A., Marszałek, M., Schmid, C.: A spatio-temporal descriptor based on 3d-gradients. In: British Machine Vision Conference, pp. 995–1004 (September 2008)
8. Laptev, I., Lindeberg, T.: Space-time interest points. In: Proc. ICCV (2003)
9. Laptev, I., Perez, P.: Retrieving actions in movies. In: Proc. ICCV, pp. 1–8 (2007)
10. Lindeberg, T.: Scale Space theory in Computer Vision. Kluwer, Dordrecht (1994)
11. Lowe, D.: Distinctive image features from scale-invariant keypoints. Int. J. Computer Vision (2), 91–110 (2004)
12. Luo, Q., Kong, X., Zeng, G., Fan, J.: Human action detection via boosted local motion histograms. Mach. Vision Appl. 21, 377–389 (2010)
13. Matas, J., Chum, O., Urban, M., Pajdla, T.: Robust wide baseline stereo from maximally stable extremal regions. In: Proc. 13th BMVC, pp. 384–393 (2002)
14. Mikolajczyk, K., Schmid, C.: A performance evaluation of local descriptors. IEEE Transactions on Pattern Analysis & Machine Intelligence 27(10), 1615–1630 (2005)
15. Obdržálek, S., Matas, J.: Object recognition using local affine frames on distinghuished regions. In: Proc. 13th BMVC, pp. 113–122 (2002)
16. Ozden, K., Schindler, K., van Gool, L.: Multibody structure-from-motion in practice. IEEE PAMI 32(6), 1134–1141 (2010)
17. Šegvić, S., Remazeilles, A., Chaumette, F.: Enhancing the point feature tracker by adaptive modelling of the feature support. In: Leonardis, A., Bischof, H., Pinz, A. (eds.) ECCV 2006. LNCS, vol. 3952, pp. 112–124. Springer, Heidelberg (2006)
18. Shi, J., Tomasi, C.: Good features to track. In: Proc. CVPR, pp. 593–600 (1994)
19. Viola, P., Jones, M.J., Snow, D.: Detecting pedestrians using patterns of motion and appearance. Int. J. Computer Vision 63, 153–161 (2005)

Content Based Detection of Popular Images in Large Image Databases

Martin Solli and Reiner Lenz

Media and Information Technology (MIT),
Department of Science and Technology (ITN), Linköping University,
SE-601 74 Norrköping, Sweden
{martin.solli,reiner.lenz}@liu.se
http://www.itn.liu.se/mit, http://diameter.itn.liu.se/

Abstract. We investigate the use of standard image descriptors and a supervised learning algorithm for estimating the popularity of images. The intended application is in large scale image search engines, where the proposed approach can enhance the user experience by improving the sorting of images in a retrieval result. Classification methods are trained and evaluated on real-world user statistics recorded by a major image search engine. The conclusion is that for many image categories, the combination of supervised learning algorithms and standard image descriptors results in useful popularity predictions.

1 Introduction

The motivation for this research is the basic need of every image search engine to show popular images in the search result, especially within the first images shown. In a typical real-life image retrieval task, the user queries a search interface with a keyword, for instance the name of an object. To satisfy the user the list of images that is returned should contain images of the desired object or scene. But what else makes an image popular? Here we investigate if ordinary image descriptors, together with supervised learning algorithms, can be used for estimating the popularity of images. The intended application is in large scale image search engines, where the proposed approach can improve the sorting of images in a retrieval result, and thereby enhancing the user experience. Either we can boost popular images, or do the opposite with non-popular images. We emphasize that in the current study we want to explore how far we can reach by using statistical measurements of image content only. The use of other relevance feedback tools, such as image click statistics, is not included in this paper. In a real-life application, however, the method can function as a complement to already implemented feedback methods. In the proposed approach we don't need to consider *why* an image is popular. Knowing that the image *is* popular is sufficient. We will train our system using two sub-sets of images, the most popular images, and remaining ones, in this paper referred to as non-popular images. Sub-sets are created based on recorded user behaviors in the Picsearch image search engine. Moreover, since the intended application is as a complement to

A. Heyden and F. Kahl (Eds.): SCIA 2011, LNCS 6688, pp. 218–227, 2011.

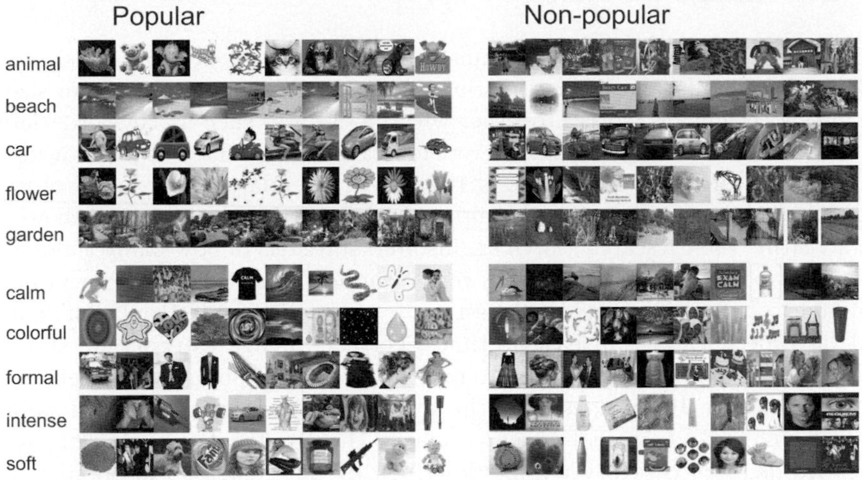

Fig. 1. Examples of popular and non-popular images from different keyword categories

other methods, we don't need to label every possible image. We will only label images that have a high probability, meaning that they are strong candidates for the popular or non-popular class.

Content based image retrieval has been an active research field for many years now. See for instance [12][3][9] for recent developments within image indexing and relevance feedback. The topic of estimating image popularity from statistical measurements of image content has not been addressed in the literature before. Instead we mention two papers by Datta et al. [1][2]. They use images from a photo sharing web page, peer-rated in two qualities, *aesthetics* and *originality*. Numerous visual or aesthetical image features, like Exposure, Depth-of-field, etc., are extracted. The relationship between features and observer ratings are explored through Support Vector Machines and classification trees, with the goal to build a model that can predict the quality of an image. A few other papers related to photo quality or aesthetics are Ke et al. [5] and Liu et al. [6][7]. We also mention Cohen-Or et al. [8] presenting a method that enhances the harmony among colors of a given image. There are however important differences between the references mentioned above, and the work presented here. First, since the standard approach for displaying image retrieval results is to display image thumbnails, we will only work with small images (maximum size 128 pixels). Earlier work typically use images of much larger size. Secondly, for many methods predicting photo quality, numerous specialized image descriptors are developed. Here we prefer to start our investigations using common image descriptors, with the advantage that they are already computed in many image retrieval systems.

2 The Image Database

Our database is collected from the image search engine[1] belonging to Picsearch AB (publ). The database contains thumbnail images, with a maximum size of 128 pixels (height or width), together with meta-data, such as keywords/labels and user statistics. Original images were crawled from public web pages using 20 different keywords, given in Table 1. 10 of them are related to ordinary objects, and 10 are based on emotional properties. Image thumbnails were shown to users visiting the Picsearch search engine, and statistics of how many times each image has been viewed and clicked were recorded. The ratio "number of clicks / number of views" is used as an estimate of popularity, but only for images that have been viewed at least 50 times. For each image category we start by splitting the images into two sub-groups, the 1000 most popular, and remaining ones. We sample 100 images from the remaining ones, and save them as non-popular images. As popular images we save the 100 most popular images. In other words, each category will be described by 200 images, 100 popular, and 100 non-popular. To illustrate the database, the 10 most popular, and 10 non-popular images, for examples of categories, are plotted in Fig. 1. Each image category in our database typically contains several thousand images, so it may sound strange that only 100+100 images are used from each category. The reason is that the popularity score declines quite rapidly for many image categories, making it risky to include more than 100 images in the popular class.

Table 1. The keywords used in the experiments. 1-10 are representing objects (or scenes), and 11-21 are related to emotions.

1:	animal	5:	garden	9:	food	13:	formal	17:	cold
2:	beach	6:	cat	10:	lion	14:	intense	18:	warm
3:	car	7:	dog	11:	calm	15:	soft	19:	pure
4:	flower	8:	doll	12:	colorful	16:	vivid	20:	quiet

3 Image Descriptors

There is a huge number of image descriptors that can be applied in the following experiments. However since a comprehensive comparison of image descriptors is beyond the scope of this study, we will limit ourselves to two local and two global image descriptors. As local descriptors we use bag-of-features (or bag-of-words) models, known as state-of-the-art solutions in object and scene classification. These are compared to global histogram descriptors. The descriptors are:

RGB-histogram: 512 ($8 \times 8 \times 8$) bins RGB-histogram, with equally sized bins.

[1] http://www.picsearch.com/

Bags-of-emotions: A color-based emotion-related image descriptor proposed by Solli and Lenz [15]. The descriptor is based on an emotion metric derived in psychophysical experiments, and the assumption that color emotions in images are mainly affected by homogenous regions, and transitions between regions. Emotion scores are derived for found regions, and transitions between regions, and values are saved in a *bag-of-emotions*, which is a 112 bins histogram. The result is a single histogram, and not a collection of histograms as in ordinary bag-of-features models.

SIFT: Scale Invariant Feature Transform, a standard tool in image processing and computer vision, proposed by Lowe [13]. We use a SIFT implementation by Andrea Vedaldi[2], both for interest point detection, and descriptor extraction. The result is a 128 bins histogram describing each interest point.

OpponentSIFT: The recommended descriptor in the evaluation of color descriptors carried out by van de Sande et al. [14]. In OpponentSIFT, all three channels in the opponent color space are described by the SIFT descriptor. One of the channels contains the intensity information, whereas the others contain color information invariant to changes in light intensity. The descriptor is included in a software package by van de Sande[3].

In the following we will refer to the above descriptors as "RGB", "ebags", "SIFT" and "OSIFT". The average number of found interest points per thumbnail (for SIFT/OSIFT) is 125, which is believed to be sufficient for the intended application. For SIFT and OSIFT, we adopt the common procedure for bag-of-features models and perform clustering in the descriptor space (also known as codebook generation), followed by vector quantization to obtain the distribution over cluster centers (the distribution over codewords). For clustering we use k-means, with 500 cluster centers, and 10 iterations, each with a new set of initial centroids. Then we search for the iteration that returns the minimum within-cluster sums of point-to-centroid distances. Clustering is carried out with 10 000 descriptors (1000 descriptors randomly selected from each of the keywords 1-5 and 11-15). State-of-the-art solutions in image classification are often using codebooks of even greater size. But since our experiments focus on thumbnail images, where the number of found interest points is relatively low, we find it appropriate to limit the size to 500 cluster centers. Preliminary experiments with an increased codebook size did not result in increased performance. Similar conclusions about the size of the codebook can for instance be found in van Gemert et al. [4]. The ebags histogram has 112 dimensions (bins), whereas SIFT and OSIFT have 500 (after vector quantization), and RGB has 512 bins. For an easier and fair comparison, we use Principal Component Analysis to reduce the number of dimensions of the RGB, SIFT and OSIFT histograms, leaving the 112 dimensions with the highest variance.

---

[2] http://www.vlfeat.org/~vedaldi/

[3] http://www.colordescriptors.com/

Table 2. The overall classification accuracy for different descriptors, different sets of images (objects and/or emotions), and two different values on the threshold t

t	Images	RGB	ebags	SIFT	OSIFT	mean
0	all	0.57	0.58	0.55	0.56	0.57
0	objects	0.60	0.61	0.58	0.61	0.60
0	emotions	0.55	0.56	0.53	0.54	0.55
0.25	all	0.52	0.70	0.69	0.71	0.66
0.25	objects	0.68	0.77	0.72	0.74	0.73
0.25	emotions	0.43	0.58	0.50	0.65	0.54
mean		0.56	0.63	0.60	0.64	

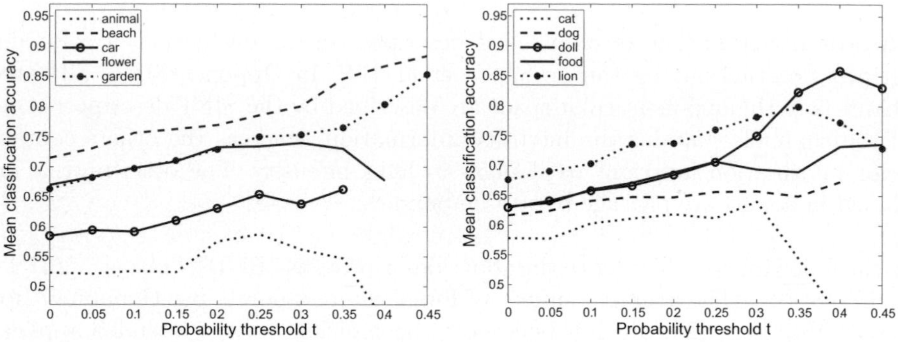

(a) Image categories 1-5 (objects) (b) Image categories 6-10 (objects)

Fig. 2. The mean classification accuracy over descriptors RGB, ebags, and OSIFT, for different object categories and varying values of t

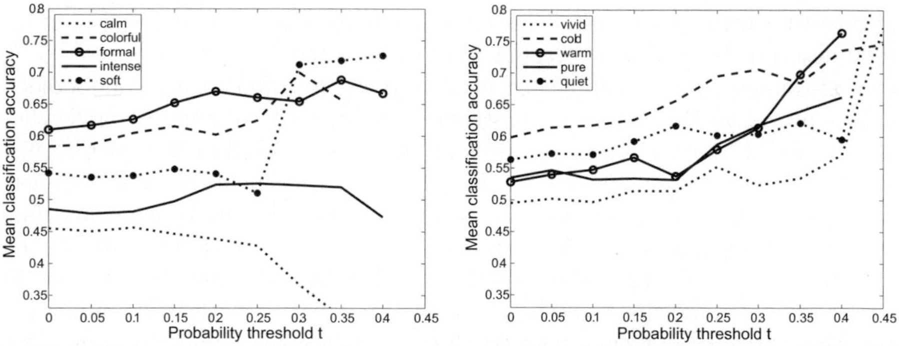

(a) Image categories 11-15 (emotions) (b) Image categories 16-20 (emotions)

Fig. 3. The mean classification accuracy over descriptors RGB, ebags, and OSIFT, for different emotion categories and varying values of t

4 Classification

With database images separated into popular and non-popular images, the goal is to be able to predict what class an unknown image belongs to. Our classification experiments are based on a stratified 10-fold cross-validation procedure. The original image set of 200 images belonging to each category is partitioned into 10 subsets, each containing the same number of popular and non-popular images (10 + 10). The cross-validation process is repeated K times, where $K-1$ subsets are used for training the classifier, and the remaining subset is used for validating the model. After K training runs, each image in the category has received a classification score, and obtained scores are used for deriving the overall classification accuracy. An advantage with this kind of cross-validation is that all images are used for both training and validation, which is useful when the number of images is limited. A disadvantage, however, is that we obtain 10 classification models for each category. Depending on the final application, we might need to combine the result from all models.

A common method for solving a two-class problem is to utilize a supervised learning algorithm, for instance a Support Vector Machine. Here we use *SVM-light* by Thorsten Joachims [10]. For simplicity, and to ensure reproducibility, all experiments are carried out with default settings. Obtained classification scores are translated to probabilities using the method proposed by Lin et al. [11]. For the intended application, it is not crucial that every single image is labeled with popular or non-popular. As an alternative, we only label images that have a probability estimate close to 1 or 0, meaning that they are strong candidates for the popular and non-popular class respectively. For image i, with probability estimate p_i, we define a probability threshold t. Image i will only be classified if p_i lies outside the interval $\{0.5 - t \leq p_i \leq 0.5 + t\}$.

5 Results

The classification accuracy for different descriptors, different sets of images, and two different thresholds t, can be seen in Table 2. Here the classification model was trained and tested on merged image sets, containing images from all emotion categories, or all object categories, or a large set containing both emotions and objects. The classification accuracy is given by the proportion of correctly labeled images (e.g. 0.8 means that 80% of the images were labeled correctly). Obtained scores indicate that it is harder to predict popularity in emotion categories than in object categories. Since the SIFT descriptor usually performs poorer than OSIFT, we will exclude the SIFT descriptor from the remaining experiments. The overall performance for all descriptors is rather poor (an accuracy close to 0.5 is equivalent to a random classification). When we, however apply the learning algorithm on individual categories, we notice large differences in accuracy between different categories. The result for different object categories can be seen in Fig. 2. The plot shows the relationship between the mean classification accuracy over descriptors RGB, ebags and OSIFT, and different

Table 3. The classification accuracy for the best performing image categories, and three different descriptors. (t=0.3)

Image category	RGB	ebags	OSIFT
beach	0.82	0.82	0.77
flower	0.77	0.76	0.69
garden	0.80	0.73	0.72
doll	0.78	0.70	0.77
food	0.70	0.72	0.67
lion	0.80	0.81	0.74
colorful	0.68	0.70	0.72
formal	0.76	0.57	0.63
soft	1.00	0.61	0.53
cold	0.72	0.71	0.69
warm	0.72	0.63	0.49
mean	0.78	0.70	0.67

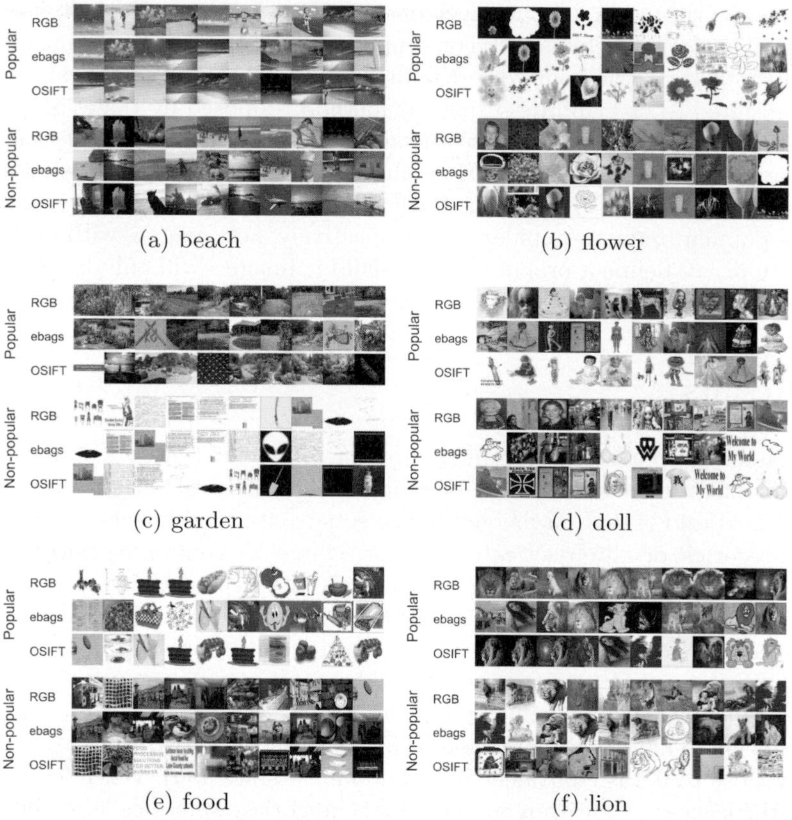

(a) beach (b) flower (c) garden (d) doll (e) food (f) lion

Fig. 4. Classification examples for the best performing object categories

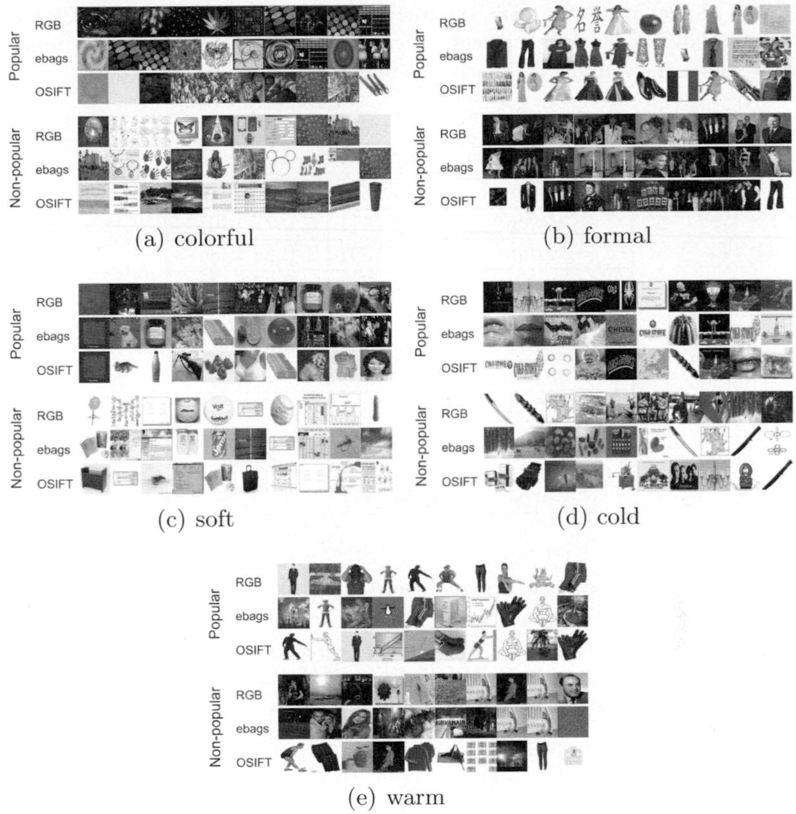

(a) colorful (b) formal (c) soft (d) cold (e) warm

Fig. 5. Classification examples for the best performing emotion categories

values on the probability threshold t. Similar plots for the emotion categories can be seen in Fig. 3. For some categories, a raised probability threshold eventually results in an empty class, shown as a terminated curve in the figure. We see that for object categories *beach*, *flower*, *garden*, *doll*, *food* and *lion*, the accuracy is relatively high, and shows consistency for an increased t value. The same holds for the emotion categories *colorful*, *formal*, *soft*, *cold* and *warm*. Remaining categories, especially the remaining emotion categories, show poor performance. The classification accuracy for the best performing categories, for different image descriptors, can be seen in Table 3. We find a value of $t = 0.3$ appropriate. The RGB histogram performs best, followed by ebags and OSIFT.

We illustrate the classification result by plotting examples of classified images. For each image category, and the descriptors RGB, ebags and OSIFT, the 10 images that obtained the highest probability score (most popular) are plotted together with the 10 images that obtained the lowest score. Plots for the object categories *beach*, *flower*, *garden*, *doll*, *food* and *lion* are shown in Fig. 4, and plots for the emotion categories *colorful*, *formal*, *soft*, *cold* and *warm* are shown in Fig. 5. As we might expect, for some of the categories, especially *cold* and

Table 4. The mean classification accuracy (over RGB, ebags, OSIFT) for different categories and different image subsets: only popular, or only non-popular images. The table also shows the number of images belonging to each subset. (t=0.3)

	Accuracy (Nr of images)	
Image category	popular	non-popular
beach	0.79 (57)	0.82 (54)
flower	0.72 (41)	0.77 (39)
garden	0.63 (39)	0.84 (38)
doll	0.62 (33)	0.84 (41)
food	0.67 (35)	0.72 (34)
lion	0.82 (43)	0.74 (44)
colorful	0.70 (25)	0.72 (23)
formal	0.72 (37)	0.43 (22)
soft	0.69 (18)	0.39 (20)
cold	0.67 (33)	0.74 (34)
warm	0.60 (27)	0.64 (23)

warm, the popularity of the images seem to have very little in common with emotional color properties.

In our final experiments we derive the mean classification accuracy (over descriptors RGB, ebags and OSIFT) for subsets containing popular and non-popular images only. The result is shown in Table 4, including the average number of images that were classified to belong to each subset. Subsets are rather small due to the threshold t (here $t = 0.3$). However, since many users only look at the first few images in a search result, a popular subset of only 20-30 images is often sufficient. And depending on the application, we can of course use the probability estimate to rank all images in a category, not only the popular or non-popular ones. We notice that it is usually easier to classify non-popular images than popular ones (even if it is completely the opposite in a few categories), but there is no general relationship between the classification accuracy and the number of images in each subset.

6 Summary and Conclusions

We have investigated the use of standard image descriptors, both local and global, for estimating the popularity of thumbnail images. The intended application is in large scale image search engines, where the estimate of popularity can be used (in conjunction with other methods) to improve the ordering of images in a retrieval result, and thereby enhancing the user experience. The topic is crucial for any large scale image search engine. In the experiments, a Support Vector Machine was used in a 10-fold cross-validation procedure to distinguish between popular and non-popular images. To our surprise, the best performing descriptor is a global descriptor, the traditional RGB histogram, followed by Bags-of-emotions, and OpponentSIFT. The classification accuracy, however, varies significantly between different image categories. In the current experiments, the popularity estimate was proven to be useful in 11 out of 20 image categories. By using earlier recorded user statistics for individual image categories, one can easily decide which categories the proposed approach can be applied to. The overall conclusion is that for many image categories, the combination of supervised learning algorithms and standard image descriptors results in useful popularity predictions. An advantage of using standard descriptors is that these are often already included in many image databases. The next step would be to explore how to combine the result with other types of features, for instance real-time user feedback based on image click statistics.

References

1. Datta, R., Joshi, D., Li, J., Wang, J.Z.: Studying aesthetics in photographic images using a computational approach. In: Leonardis, A., Bischof, H., Pinz, A. (eds.) ECCV 2006. LNCS, vol. 3953, pp. 288–301. Springer, Heidelberg (2006)
2. Datta, R., Li, J., Wang, J.: Learning the consensus on visual quality for next-generation image management. In: 15th ACM Int. Conf. on Multimedia, MM 2007, Augsburg, pp. 533–536 (2007)
3. Datta, R., Joshi, D., Li, J., Wang, J.: Image retrieval: Ideas, influences, and trends of the new age. ACM Comput. Surv. 40(2) (2008)
4. van Gemert, J.C., Veenman, C.J., Smeulders, A.W., Geusebroek, J.-M.: Visual word ambiguity. IEEE TPAMI 32, 1271–1283 (2010)
5. Ke, Y., Tang, X., Jing, F.: The design of high-level features for photo quality assessment. In: IEEE Comp. Soc. Conf. on Computer Vision and Pattern Recognition, vol. 1, pp. 419–426 (2006)
6. Liu, L., Chen, R., Wolf, L., Cohen-Or, D.: Optimizing photo composition. Computer Graphics Forum (Proceedings of Eurographics) 29, 469–478 (2010)
7. Liu, L., Jin, Y., Wu, Q.: Realtime aesthetic image retargeting. In: Proc. of Eurographics WS on Computational Aesthetic in Graphics, Visualization, and Imaging, pp. 1–8 (2010)
8. Cohen-Or, D., Sorkine, O., Gal, R., Leyvand, T., Xu, Y.-Q.: Color harmonization. In: ACM SIGGRAPH 2006, vol. 25, pp. 624–630 (2006)
9. Huang, T.S., Dagli, C.K., Rajaram, S., Chang, E.Y.: Active Learning for Interactive Multimedia Retrieval. Proceedings of the IEEE 96(4), 648–667 (2008)
10. Joachims, T.: Making large-scale support vector machine learning practical. In: Advances in Kernel Methods: Support Vector Learning, pp. 169–184 (1999)
11. Lin, H.T., Lin, C.J., Weng, R.C.: A note on platt's probabilistic outputs for support vector machines. Mach. Learn. 68(3), 267–276 (2007)
12. Liu, Y., Zhang, D., Lu, G., Ma, W.-Y.: A survey of content-based image retrieval with high-level semantics. Pattern Recogn. 40(1), 262–282 (2007)
13. Lowe, D.G.: Distinctive image features from scale-invariant keypoints. International Journal of Computer Vision 60(2), 91–110 (2004)
14. van de Sande, K.E., Gevers, T., Snoek, C.G.: Evaluating color descriptors for object and scene recognition. IEEE TPAMI 32, 1582–1596 (2010)
15. Solli, M., Lenz, R.: Color based bags-of-emotions. In: Jiang, X., Petkov, N. (eds.) CAIP 2009. LNCS, vol. 5702, pp. 573–580. Springer, Heidelberg (2009)

Unscented Kalman Filtering for Articulated Human Tracking

Anders Boesen Lindbo Larsen, Søren Hauberg, and Kim Steenstrup Pedersen

Department of Computer Science
University of Copenhagen
{abll,hauberg,kimstp}@diku.dk
http://diku.dk/

Abstract. We present an articulated tracking system working with data from a single narrow baseline stereo camera. The use of stereo data allows for some depth disambiguation, a common issue in articulated tracking, which in turn yields likelihoods that are practically unimodal. While current state-of-the-art trackers utilize particle filters, our unimodal likelihood model allows us to use an unscented Kalman filter. This robust and efficient filter allows us to improve the quality of the tracker while using substantially fewer likelihood evaluations. The system is compared to one based on a particle filter with superior results. Tracking quality is measured by comparing with ground truth data from a marker-based motion capture system.

1 Introduction

Articulated human motion tracking is the process of estimating the human body configuration over time from a series of sensor inputs [1]. Motion tracking has a wide variety of uses ranging from computer gaming and film making to medical applications. Currently, the most accurate methods are based on physical markers attached to the human body that can be tracked in three dimensions using multiple calibrated cameras. These methods have serious drawbacks since they are cumbersome to set up and too intrusive to be used easily outside laboratory settings, e.g. in private homes. Therefore, an accurate markerless tracking method based solely on input from a camera is needed for a vast array of non-laboratory applications.

To alleviate this need, much research has gone into markerless articulated tracking. The most common solution is to use a nonlinear filter with a likelihood model based on monocular images. Due to the lack of depth information from such data, these likelihood models are inherently multimodal, which has forced researchers to perform the inference using very general techniques such as particle filters [2,3,4,5,6]. However, recent boosts in computational power has made consumer stereo cameras possible, see e.g. the Bumblebee[1] or the Microsoft

[1] http://www.ptgrey.com/products/bumblebee2/

A. Heyden and F. Kahl (Eds.): SCIA 2011, LNCS 6688, pp. 228–237, 2011.

Kinect[2] camera. Using such cameras allows us to construct approximately unimodal likelihood models. This, in turn, allows us to perform the inference using the more constrained *Unscented Kalman Filter (UKF)* [7,8]. These constraints allow for a more robust estimation using fewer computational resources compared to a particle filter. Both these features are sorely needed in practical applications.

The objective of articulated tracking is to estimate joint angles of a skeleton model in each frame of an image sequence. The most common approach is to infer these joint angle from monocular images using a particle filter, see e.g. [2,3,4,5,6].

Due to the flexibility of the human body, the skeleton model needs to exhibit many degrees of freedom. Robust estimation of joint angles then requires many samples in the particle filter, rendering the approach computationally very demanding. A commonly used approach to deal with this problem is to reduce the degrees of freedom in the model by confining the set of legal joint angles to some (often nonlinear) subspace of the angle space. It seems that most researchers taking this route focus on simple low-dimensional motions, such as *walking* [9,10,11,12], *golf swings* [11,12], *tennis playing* [13] etc. This approach can be both robust and computationally efficient, but suffers from the main drawback that the resulting trackers only work with very specific motions.

The need for particle filters stems from the fact that the used likelihood models often are multimodal, making the posterior distribution of the joint angles multimodal as well. The multimodality of the likelihood comes from the use of monocular images that makes depth ambiguities an inherent part of the problem. Examples of such likelihoods include a combination of edge strength and horizontal flow [14], silhouettes extracted using background subtraction [5] and texture models for each limb [2]. One way of making the largest mode of the likelihood easier to locate is to use multiple calibrated cameras, as was done by Deutscher et al. [3]. The need for several calibrated cameras, however, makes the approach hard to use outside the laboratory. One compromise is to use a single pre-calibrated stereo camera as suggested by Hauberg et al. [6]. This is also the approach we will be taking as it will allow us to infer the joint angles using an unscented Kalman filter.

Unscented Kalman filters have seen little use in articulated tracking as the likelihood models have usually been multimodal which does not fit with the Gaussian assumptions of this filter. One notable exception is the work of Ziegler et al. [15] whose approach shares many similarities with ours. Using four stereo cameras placed at a 90° angle from each other, they are able to track a human upper body reliably using the UKF. This is also to be expected as data from the four stereo cameras should be sufficient to avoid any observational ambiguities. Another example of articulated tracking with the UKF is found in [16], where a hand is tracked. Here, the likelihood is based on edges in a monocular image, so there is little reason to believe that the likelihood actually is unimodal. Further-

[2] `http://www.xbox.com/kinect`

more, it seems that they only conduct experiments on image sequences of hands where the articulation of the fingers remains unchanged for the entire sequence.

In this work we make the following contributions.

- We show that unimodality of the human pose distribution can be assumed when working with data from a single, narrow-baseline stereo camera.
- We apply the unscented Kalman filter for articulated tracking and achieve superior results in terms of accuracy and realism of body movements. Furthermore, UKF gives us the benefit of requiring significantly fewer likelihood evaluations resulting in a lower computational complexity.

This paper is organized as follows. In the next section we describe the general nonlinear filtering framework and two possible implementations: the UKF and the particle filter. This is then specialized to articulated tracking in Sec. 3. Results are presented in Sec. 4 and the paper is concluded in Sec. 5.

2 Nonlinear Filtering

The articulated tracking of human motion can be formulated as a nonlinear estimation problem modelled by the two difference equations

$$\boldsymbol{x}_t = f(\boldsymbol{x}_{t-1}, \boldsymbol{v}_{t-1}) \tag{1}$$

$$\boldsymbol{y}_t = h(\boldsymbol{x}_t, \boldsymbol{n}_t) \tag{2}$$

where $\boldsymbol{x_t} \in \mathbb{R}^{n_x}$ denotes the state of the system at time t and $\boldsymbol{y}_t \in \mathbb{R}^{n_y}$ the observation. With our motion tracking, the system state corresponds to the pose of a human body while the observation is a stereo image of the human. The function f models the transition between system states over time while h relates the hidden state space to the observation space. Both f and h are deterministic. $\boldsymbol{v}_t$ and $\boldsymbol{n}_t$ are random variables representing process noise and measurement noise respectively.

2.1 The Unscented Kalman Filter

Below follows a very brief introduction to the UKF, we refer to [7,8] for a thorough presentation.

The UKF provides a sequential estimation of the posterior density $p(\boldsymbol{x}_t|\boldsymbol{y}_{1:t})$ where $\boldsymbol{y}_{1:t} = \{\boldsymbol{y}_1, \boldsymbol{y}_2, \ldots, \boldsymbol{y}_t\}$. This is achieved by updating the posterior density recursively. In each time step, UKF selects a set of $2n_x + 1$ sample points $\boldsymbol{\mathcal{X}}_i$, $i = 0, 1, \ldots, 2n_x$ that completely captures the mean and covariance of the state distribution $p(\boldsymbol{x})$. These sample points (called *sigma points*) are then updated according to the state prediction function f and propagated through the observational model h into observation space. In observation space, their deviation from the observation is measured by the likelihood model $p(\boldsymbol{y}|\boldsymbol{\mathcal{X}}_i)$. From the likelihood of all sigma points, the Kalman gain $\boldsymbol{K}$ is updated. $\boldsymbol{K}$ is then used to update the state estimate $\boldsymbol{x}$ as well as the state distribution $p(\boldsymbol{x})$.

2.2 The Particle Filter

The particle filter works by generating a set of n weighted random sample points $\boldsymbol{\mathcal{X}}_i$, $i = 1, 2, \ldots, n$ from the prior distribution $p(\boldsymbol{x}_t|\boldsymbol{x}_{t-1})$. Like with the sigma points of UKF, each of these sample points are projected into observation space where their likelihood $p(\boldsymbol{y}|\boldsymbol{\mathcal{X}}_i)$ is quantified and weights assigned accordingly. The new pose estimate $\boldsymbol{x}_t$ becomes the mean of $p(\boldsymbol{x}_t|\boldsymbol{y}_{1:t})$. A more comprehensive description of the particle filter is presented in [17].

3 Filtering for Articulated Tracking

3.1 The State Model

The articulated human body model is built from a kinematic skeleton consisting of rigid bones connected by joints with up to three degrees of freedom depending on the joint type (e.g. an elbow joint has one degree of freedom and a shoulder joint has three). This approach is common within articulated tracking [1,3]. The set of joint angles of the kinematic skeleton constitutes our state model vector $\boldsymbol{x}$. In this work we limit our tracker to consider only a human body from the hip and up as depicted in Fig. 1. Furthermore, we assume that the human is standing still and only moving the upper body parts. Notice however, that it is trivial to extend the model to include full body motion.

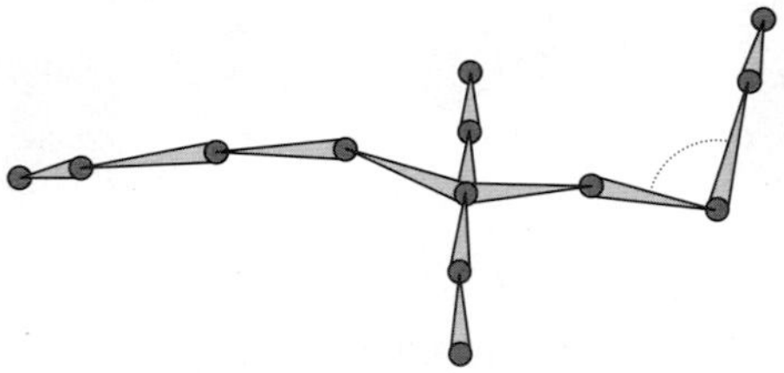

Fig. 1. The kinematic skeleton of the upper human body that we wish to track

As joints of the human skeleton cannot move freely due to physical constraints, we enforce similar angular constraints on our model. More specifically, we limit each angle to some interval $[l, u]$ where l and u denote the lower and upper bound. These box constraints are applied to both the sigma points and the samples in the particle filter to ensure that the prediction does not consider illegal joint angles. However, we do not handle self-intersections between body parts.

We initialize the first state $\boldsymbol{x}_0$ manually so that it matches the actual state as close as possible. We also provide a probability density estimate $p(\boldsymbol{x}_0)$ of the initial state. The state is propagated in time by adding zero mean Gaussian noise to each joint angle independently, i.e.

$$p(\boldsymbol{x}_t|\boldsymbol{x}_{t-1}) = \mathcal{N}(\boldsymbol{x}_t|\boldsymbol{x}_{t-1}, \boldsymbol{\Sigma}) \tag{3}$$

where $\boldsymbol{\Sigma}$ is a diagonal matrix. In our experience, it is not worthwhile to perform prediction of the state transition between frames as the changes are too small. Therefore, we perform no actual state transition between frames by letting function f from Eq. 1 be the identity function. The above model has, among others, been applied by Sidenbladh et al. [10], Balan et al. [18] and Bandouch et al. [19].

3.2 The Observation Model

The stereo camera provides us with a set of three-dimensional points in each frame. We perform a simple but efficient segmentation of the input image by removing points that are further away than a certain background threshold. If the remaining points contain any outliers (points far away from the body), we translate these points to bring them within a given Euclidean distance of their nearest limb. This final set of points constitutes the input observation vector $\boldsymbol{y}$. An example of an observation along with a human pose estimate is shown in Fig. 2.

Fig. 2. (a) A segmented stereo image of a human body. (b) A human skeleton estimate projected on the image data.

We use the observational model presented in [6]: For each time step t we generate a set of sample points $\boldsymbol{\mathcal{X}}$ of which each sample $\boldsymbol{\mathcal{X}}_i$ is to be compared with the observation in order to compute the likelihood $p(\boldsymbol{y}|\boldsymbol{\mathcal{X}}_i)$. For this, we use the nonlinear mapping h (Eq. 2) constructed as follows. Given a state vector $\boldsymbol{\mathcal{X}}_i$ and an input observation $\boldsymbol{y}$, we want to represent the state $\boldsymbol{\mathcal{X}}_i$ in observation space. The state is composed of all joint angles in a kinematic skeleton. To each bone in this skeleton we assign a cylinder with a radius corresponding to the thickness of the limb; these will serve as our skin model. We then project all points from $\boldsymbol{y}$ onto the nearest cylinder of the stick figure. As we are working with cylinders, these projections can be performed trivially. By projecting the points of $\boldsymbol{y}$ onto skeleton $\boldsymbol{\mathcal{X}}_i$ we obtain a new observation vector $\boldsymbol{\mathcal{Y}}_i$ that is comparable to $\boldsymbol{y}$ since they both have the same dimensionality and the points in the vectors correspond to each other. Thus, the likehood model can be expressed as

$$p(\boldsymbol{y}|\boldsymbol{\mathcal{X}}_i) = \mathcal{N}(\boldsymbol{y}|\boldsymbol{\mathcal{Y}}_i, \lambda^2 \boldsymbol{I}) \ , \tag{4}$$

where λ^2 is a variance parameter.

3.3 Computational complexity

The computational complexity of the tracker depends on the filtering method used. For the particle filter, the computational complexity is $O(n(n_y + \log(n)))$ with n being the number of particles sampled and n_y the dimensionality of the observation space. For the UKF, the computational complexity is $O(n_x^2 n_y^2)$ due to a singular value decomposition of a $\mathbb{R}^{n_y \times n_x}$ matrix. In our experience, the performance of UKF is very competitive with that of the particle filter since $n >> n_x$.

4 Results and Evaluation

To measure the performance of the particle filter vs. the UKF we apply both filters on two image sequences of 300 frames each. Examples of the results are shown in Fig. 3. The videos are available from `http://humim.org/scia2011`. We see that the UKF provides smoother and visually more accurate results compared to the particle filter. Only when the particle filter sampling is dense (1500 particles), the quality is somewhat close visually to that of the UKF. In the first image sequence, both filters are able to track the motion reasonably. The second sequence is harder to track as body parts move close to each other and self-occlusions occur. The particle filter fails on several occasions during sequence 2. UKF proves more robust than the particle filter as it misestimates the human pose on only one occasion where an arm passes by the head closely. We believe that most of these problems are caused by our simple skin model and our observational model that for each point in the observation makes a projection onto the nearest cylindrical limb. This is very likely to cause problems when limbs are positioned close to each other.

Overall, the unimodal assumption seems to hold since the observational model is strong enough to favorize the single, correct pose by a large margin. It is possible, however, to imagine special cases in which unimodality cannot be assumed, e.g. if an entire arm is hidden behind a person's back. In this case, when updating the Kalman gain $\boldsymbol{K}$, the variance of the kinematic joints related to the arm will automatically be adjusted to reflect this uncertainty. Thus, when the variance goes up for certain joints, the tracker should try to estimate these joints differently, e.g. by relying on a predictive model.

4.1 Accuracy

To obtain a more precise basis for comparison, the tracked person is wearing physical markers that are tracked in 3D using a high precision motion capture system. These will serve as our ground truth data. In total, there are eight markers placed on the human; three markers on each arm and two on the shoulders.

Fig. 3. The human skeleton estimated by the different filters is superimposed over selected frames from two videoes. The images in the upper two rows comes from video 1 while the two bottom rows are taken from video 2. The full videoes are available at `http://humim.org/scia2011`. Both particle filters have visible difficulties tracking the motion in the sequence as they seem less prone against self-occlusions and closely positioned body parts (which happens more often in sequence 2 than in sequence 1).

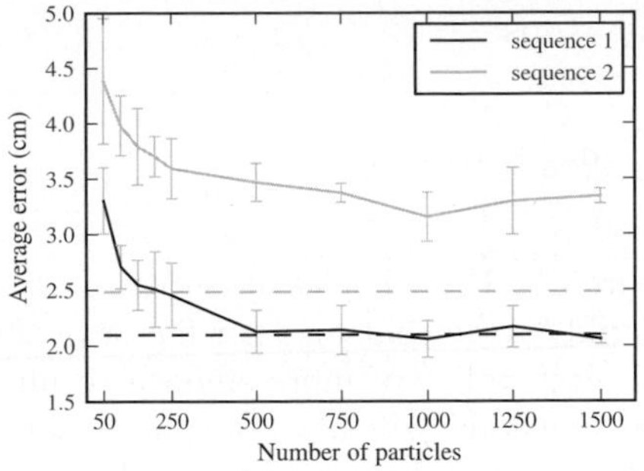

(a)

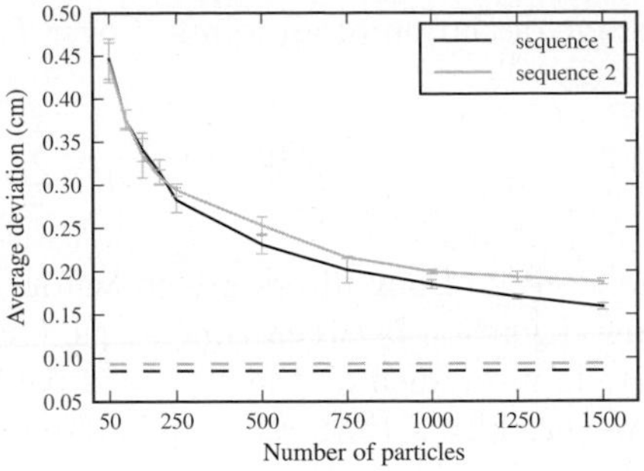

(b)

Fig. 4. (a) Average error of the tracking filters. The particle filter is represented by the solid lines and the UKF by the dashed lines. The vertical error bars represent two times the standard deviation caused by the Monte Carlo sampling. The deviation is measured over several trials of the particle filter. (b) Smoothness of the filters measured by the average deviation of absolute joint positions between time steps. Low values indicate smooth trajectories. The solid lines represent the particle filter and the dashed lines represent the UKF.

To quantify the tracking quality we measure how well the markers fit with the estimated poses. For each marker, we make a projection onto the nearest limb; just as we did in the observational model. The Euclidean distance between the projection $\boldsymbol{o}$ and the marker point $\boldsymbol{m}$ can then be used as error measure. To determine the error from all eight markers of a state $\boldsymbol{x}$ over all time steps T, we calculate the average error:

$$\mathcal{E}(\boldsymbol{x}_{1:T}) = \frac{1}{8T} \sum_{t=1}^{T} \sum_{j=1}^{8} ||\boldsymbol{m}_{t,j} - \boldsymbol{o}_{t,j}|| \ . \tag{5}$$

The resulting average error for the different filters are shown in Fig. 4a. It is clear that the UKF performs just as good or better than particle filters with a dense sampling. Furthermore, it is noteworthy that the monte carlo sampling of the particle filter results in significant deviations in accuracy when repeating the tracking. In this regard, the deterministic algorithm of the UKF offers more reliable results.

4.2 Motion Smoothness

When looking at the image sequences, it becomes clear that the UKF tracking produces smoother and more realistic motions whereas the skeleton generated by the particle filter tends to shake between time steps. To quantify this smoothness, we introduce the following measure. For each time step t we take the absolute position $\boldsymbol{a}_{t,j}$ of each joint j in the human skeleton and measure the movement from the previous time step. The smoothness measure is then calculated as the average deviation of all joints J over T time steps.

$$\mathcal{S}(\boldsymbol{x}_{1:T}) = \frac{1}{TJ}\sum_{t=1}^{T}\sum_{j=1}^{J}||\boldsymbol{a}_{t,j} - \boldsymbol{a}_{t-1,j}|| \tag{6}$$

The results of our filters are shown in Figure 4b. UKF is clearly superior with a low deviation between time steps. One could image that another flavor of the particle filter such as the annealed particle filter will give more smooth results. However, filters that rely on Monte Carlo methods will always exhibit some jittering. This reveals another advantage of using the deterministic UKF.

5 Conclusion

In this paper we have shown that not only is the unscented Kalman filter applicable for articulated tracking, it also provides superior results in terms of accuracy and smoothness compared to the particle filter using substantially fewer likelihood evaluations. For this to be possible it is, however, essential that the likelihood model is mostly unimodal. For general monocular situations this is not the case, but it seems to be a reasonable assumption when working with stereo data. This observation makes practical articulated tracking systems much more plausible.

In this paper we used a simple likelihood model based on a simple skin model. For particle filters, this simplicity is essential as we need to be able to evaluate the likelihood fast due to the vast number of particles required. When using UKF, more involved likelihood models are possible as we only need to evaluate it a few times due to the low number of sigma points. Thus, in the future, we will consider more realistic skin models in the observational model. Other future work includes an automatic initialization of the tracker as well as an extension of the implementation to work with full body models as this will extend the use of the tracking system. Finally, we need a more elaborate evaluation of the tracker on more sequences of varied complexity.

References

1. Poppe, R.: Vision-based human motion analysis: An overview. Computer Vision and Image Understanding 108, 4–18 (2007)
2. Hauberg, S., Lapuyade, J., Engell-Nørregård, M., Erleben, K., Steenstrup Pedersen, K.: Three dimensional monocular human motion analysis in end-effector space. In: Cremers, D., Boykov, Y., Blake, A., Schmidt, F.R. (eds.) EMMCVPR 2009. LNCS, vol. 5681, pp. 235–248. Springer, Heidelberg (2009)
3. Deutscher, J., Blake, A., Reid, I.: Articulated body motion capture by annealed particle filtering. In: Proceedings IEEE Conference on Computer Vision and Pattern Recognition, vol. 2, pp. 126–133. IEEE Comput. Soc, Los Alamitos (2000)

4. Bandouch, J., Beetz, M.: Tracking humans interacting with the environment using efficient hierarchical sampling and layered observation models. In: IEEE International Workshop on Human-Computer Interaction, vol. 2 (2009)
5. Kjellström, H., Kragić, D., Black, M.J.: Tracking people interacting with objects. In: CVPR 2010: Proceedings of the 2010 IEEE Computer Society Conference on Computer Vision and Pattern Recognition (2010)
6. Hauberg, S., Sommer, S., Pedersen, K.S.: Gaussian-like spatial priors for articulated tracking. In: Daniilidis, K., Maragos, P., Paragios, N. (eds.) ECCV 2010. LNCS, vol. 6311, pp. 425–437. Springer, Heidelberg (2010)
7. Julier, S., Uhlmann, J.: A new extension of the Kalman filter to nonlinear systems. In: Int. Symp. Aerospace/Defense Sensing, Simul. and Controls, vol. 3, p. 26 (1997)
8. Wan, E., Van Der Merwe, R.: The unscented Kalman filter for nonlinear estimation. In: Proceedings of Symposium, pp. 153–158 (2000)
9. Lu, Z., Carreira-Perpinan, M., Sminchisescu, C.: People Tracking with the Laplacian Eigenmaps Latent Variable Model. In Platt, J., Koller, D., Singer, Y., Roweis, S., eds.: Advances in Neural Information Processing Systems 20. MIT Press, Cambridge, MA (2008) 1705–1712
10. Sidenbladh, H., Black, M.J., Fleet, D.J.: Stochastic tracking of 3D human figures using 2D image motion. In: Vernon, D. (ed.) ECCV 2000. LNCS, vol. 1843, pp. 702–718. Springer, Heidelberg (2000)
11. Elgammal, A.M., Lee, C.S.: Tracking People on a Torus. IEEE Transaction on Pattern Analysis and Machine Intelligence 31, 520–538 (2009)
12. Urtasun, R., Fleet, D.J., Hertzmann, A., Fua, P.: Priors for people tracking from small training sets. In: Tenth IEEE International Conference on Computer Vision, ICCV 2005, vol. 1, pp. 403–410 (2005)
13. Loy, G., Eriksson, M., Sullivan, J., Carlsson, S.: Monocular 3D reconstruction of human motion in long action sequences. In: Pajdla, T., Matas, J(G.) (eds.) ECCV 2004. LNCS, vol. 3024, pp. 442–455. Springer, Heidelberg (2004)
14. Sminchisescu, C., Triggs, B.: Kinematic Jump Processes for Monocular 3D Human Tracking. In: IEEE International Conference on Computer Vision and Pattern Recognition, pp. 69–76 (2003)
15. Ziegler, J., Nickel, K., Stiefelhagen, R.: Tracking of the articulated upper body on multi-view stereo image sequences. In: CVPR 2006: Proceedings of the 2006 IEEE Computer Society Conference on Computer Vision and Pattern Recognition, pp. 774–781. IEEE Computer Society, Washington, DC, USA (2006)
16. Stenger, B., Mendonca, P.R.S., Cipolla, R.: Model-based hand tracking using an unscented kalman filter. In: Proc. British Machine Vision Conference, vol. I, pp. 63–72 (2001)
17. Cappé, O., Godsill, S., Moulines, E.: An overview of existing methods and recent advances in sequential Monte Carlo. Proceedings of the IEEE 95, 899–924 (2007)
18. Balan, A.O., Sigal, L., Black, M.J.: A Quantitative Evaluation of Video-based 3D Person Tracking. In: Proceedings of the 14th International Conference on Computer Communications and Networks, pp. 349-356. IEEE Computer Society, Los Alamitos (2005)
19. Bandouch, J., Engstler, F., Beetz, M.: Accurate human motion capture using an ergonomics-based anthropometric human model. In: Proc. of the 5th Int. Conf. on Articulated Motion and Deformable Objects, pp. 248–258. Springer, Heidelberg (2008)

Using Fourier Descriptors and Spatial Models for Traffic Sign Recognition

Fredrik Larsson and Michael Felsberg

Computer Vision Laboratory, Linköping University,
SE-581 83 Linköping, Sweden
{larsson,mfe}@isy.liu.se

Abstract. Traffic sign recognition is important for the development of driver assistance systems and fully autonomous vehicles. Even though GPS navigator systems works well for most of the time, there will always be situations when they fail. In these cases, robust vision based systems are required. Traffic signs are designed to have distinct colored fields separated by sharp boundaries. We propose to use locally segmented contours combined with an implicit star-shaped object model as prototypes for the different sign classes. The contours are described by Fourier descriptors. Matching of a query image to the sign prototype database is done by exhaustive search. This is done efficiently by using the correlation based matching scheme for Fourier descriptors and a fast cascaded matching scheme for enforcing the spatial requirements. We demonstrated on a publicly available database state of the art performance.

Keywords: Traffic sign recognition, Fourier descriptors, spatial models, traffic sign dataset.

1 Introduction

Traffic sign recognition is important for the development of driver assistance systems and fully autonomous vehicles. Even though GPS navigator systems work well for most of the time, there will always be situations when no GPS-signal is available or when the map is invalid, temporary sign installations near road works just to mention one example. In these cases, robust vision based systems are required, preferably making use of monochromatic images.

1.1 Related Work

Many different approaches to traffic sign recognition have been proposed and there are commercial vision based systems available, for example in Volkswagen Phaeton [4], Saab 9-5 [3] and in the BMW 5 and 7 series [1].

One common approach is to threshold in a carefully chosen color space, e.g. HSV [5], HSI [14] or CBH [18], in order to obtain a (set of) binary image(s). This is then followed by detection and classification using the authors favorite choice

A. Heyden and F. Kahl (Eds.): SCIA 2011, LNCS 6688, pp. 238–249, 2011.

of classifier, e.g. support vector machines [12] or Neural networks [5,14]. Another common approach is to consider an edge map using e.g. Fourier descriptors [10], Hough transform [6] or distance transforms [7]. For an excellent overview of existing approaches see [14].

One thing that most published methods have in common is that they report excellent results on their own data sets. Typically they achieve more than 95% recognition rate with very few false positives. However, there are unfortunately no publicly available database for comparing different road sign recognition systems. Meaning that most authors report results on their own dataset and do not provide any means of comparing against their method. One of the main contributions of this paper is to provide a labeled database of more than 20 000 frames captured while driving 350 km on highways and in city environment.

It was recently announced that a dataset of patches containing German traffic signs will be released [2]. The patches contains a traffic sign and an additional border of 10 % around the actual sign. The dataset used in this paper contains the entire image, meaning that both detection and recognition have to be solved. Not only recognition.

1.2 Main Contribution

The main contributions of this paper are:

1. Extending the work [10] with an implicit star-shaped object model, leading to improved performance.
2. Removing the need for a region-of-interests detector used in [10], leading to a fully automatic system.
3. Releasing a database with more than 20 000 frames, 20% being hand labeled, containing a total of 3488 traffic signs.

2 Methods

The proposed method consists of three steps: extraction of Fourier descriptors (FDs), matching of FDs, and matching of previously acquired prototypes with spatial models.

2.1 Fourier Descriptors

The Fourier descriptor (FD) of a shape/contour is created by applying the Fourier transform to a periodic representation of the contour, which results in a shape descriptor in the frequency domain.

Adopting the notation in [8], the closed contour c with coordinates x and y is parameterized as a complex valued periodic function

$$c(l) = c(l + L) = x(l) + iy(l), \tag{1}$$

where L is the contour length.[1] The Fourier coefficients C are obtained by taking the 1D Fourier transform of c,

$$C(n) = \frac{1}{L}\int_{l=0}^{L} c(l)\exp(-\frac{i2\pi nl}{L})\,dl \quad n = 0, ..., N, \tag{2}$$

where $N \leq L$ is the descriptor length.

Each coefficient has a clear physical meaning making FDs easy to interpret. Using only a few of the low frequency coefficients is equivalent to using a smoothed version of the contour, see fig. 1 where a pedestrian outline is reconstructed starting with two low frequency coefficients and gradually using more and more high frequency components.

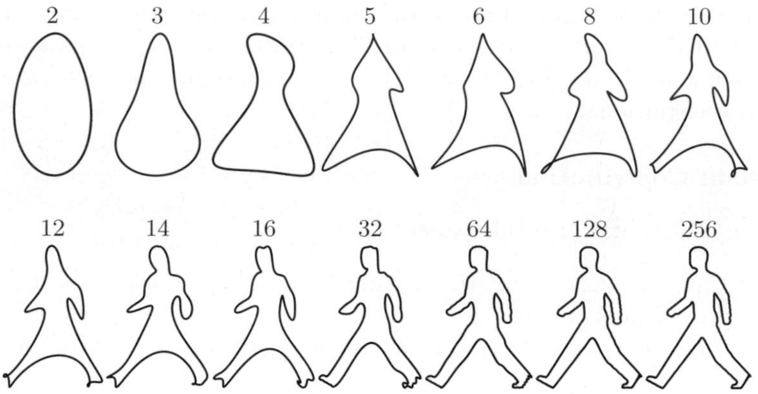

Fig. 1. Reconstruction of a detail from a Swedish pedestrian crossing sign using increasing number (shown above respective contour) of Fourier coefficients

The main reason for the popularity of FDs is their behavior under common geometric transformations, such as translation, scaling and rotation. The DC component $C(0)$ is the only one that is affected by translations c_0 of the curve $c(l) \mapsto c(l) + c_0$. By disregarding this coefficient, the remaining $N-1$ coefficients are invariant under translation. Scaling of the contour, i.e. $c(l) \mapsto ac(l)$, affects the magnitude of the coefficients and the FD can thus be made scale invariant by normalizing with the energy (after $C(0)$ has been removed). Without loss of generality, we assume that $\|C\|^2 = 1$ ($\|\cdot\|^2$ denotes the quadratic norm) and $C(0) = 0$ in what follows.

Rotating the contour c with ϕ radians counter clockwise corresponds to multiplication of (1) with $\exp(i\phi)$, which adds a constant offset to the phase of the Fourier coefficients

$$c(l) \mapsto \exp(i\phi)c(l) \qquad \Rightarrow \qquad C(n) \mapsto \exp(i\phi)C(n) \ . \tag{3}$$

[1] We treat contours as continuous functions here, where the contour samples can be thought as of impulses with appropriate weights.

Furthermore, if the index l of the contour is shifted by Δl, a linear offset is added to the Fourier phase, i.e. the spectrum is modulated

$$c(l) \mapsto c(l - \Delta l) \qquad \Rightarrow \qquad C(n) \mapsto C(n) \exp(-\frac{i2\pi n \Delta l}{L}) \ . \tag{4}$$

Note that in what follows, the term translation refers to spatial translation of the entire contour while shift refers to a shift of the start point for sampling the contour.

2.2 Matching of FDs

Rotation and index-shift result in modulations of the FD and it has been suggested to neglect the phase in order to be invariant to these transformations. However, most of the information is contained in the phase and simply neglecting it means to throw away potentially useful information [15].

According to (3) and (4), the phase of each FD component is modified by a rotation of the corresponding trigonometric basis function, either by a constant offset or by a linear offset. Considering the magnitudes only can be seen as finding the optimal rotation of all different components of the FD independently. Given a FD of length $N-1$, matching the magnitudes only corresponds to finding $N-1$ different rotations instead of estimating two degrees of freedom (constant and slope). Due to the removal of $N-3$ degrees of freedom, two contours can be very different even though the magnitude in each FD component is the same.

Recently, a new efficient correlation based matching method for FDs was proposed by Larsson et al. [10]. This approach is partly similar to established methods such as [9,17], but differs in some respects: Complex FDs are directly correlated to find the relative rotation between two FDs without numerically solving equation systems. Let $\mathcal{T}$ denote a transformation corresponding to rotation and index-shift. Let c_1 and c_2 denote two normalized contours, then

$$\min_{\mathcal{T}} \|c_1 - \mathcal{T}c_2\|^2 = 2 - 2\max_{l} |r_{12}(l)| \tag{5}$$

where $|\cdot|$ denotes the complex modulus and the cross correlation r_{12} is computed between the Fourier descriptors C_1 and C_2 according to [16], p. 244–245,

$$r_{12}(k) = (c_1 \star c_2)(k) \doteq \int_0^L \bar{c}_1(l) c_2(k+l)\, dl = \mathcal{F}^{-1}\{\bar{C}_1 \cdot C_2\}(k) \ . \tag{6}$$

In particular, if c'_1 and c'_2 denote two contours so that $c'_2 = \mathcal{T}'c'_1$, where $\mathcal{T}'$ denotes a transformation covering scaling, translation, rotation and index-shift, then

$$\min_{\mathcal{T}} \|c'_1 - \mathcal{T}c'_2\|^2 = 2 - 2\max_{l} |r_{12}(l)| = 0 \tag{7}$$

where the correlation r_{12} is computed after the FDs have been normalized with respect to scale and translation. The parameters of the transformation $\mathcal{T}$ that minimize (7) are given as

$$\Delta l = \arg\max_l |r_{12}(l)| \qquad \phi = \arg r_{12}(\Delta l) \tag{8}$$

$$s = \frac{(\sum_{n=1}^{\infty} |C_1'(n)|^2)^{\frac{1}{2}}}{(\sum_{n=1}^{\infty} |C_2'(n)|^2)^{\frac{1}{2}}} \qquad t = C_1'(0) - C_2'(0) \ . \tag{9}$$

It is also shown in [10] that considering the maximum of the real part instead of the absolute value in (7), corresponds to not compensating for the rotation, i.e. rotation variant matching is given according to

$$\min_{T/R} \|c_1' - c_2'(\Delta l)\|^2 = 2 - 2\max_l \operatorname{Re}\{r_{12}(l)\} \ . \tag{10}$$

2.3 Sign Prototypes

A traffic sign prototype is created from a synthetic image of the traffic sign, see first row in fig. 5. The synthetic image is low-pass filtered before local contours are extracted using Maximally Stable Extremal Regions (MSER)[13]. Each extracted contour $\mathbf{c}_k$ is described by its Fourier descriptor $\mathbf{C}_k$.

In order to describe the spatial relationships between the local features an extra component $\mathbf{v}_k$ is added, creating a pair $(\mathbf{C}_k, \mathbf{v}_k)$ where the first component captures the local geometry (contour) and the second component the global geometry of the sign. This second component $\mathbf{v}_k$ is simply the vector from the center of the local feature to the center of the object, see fig. 2. This can be seen as a simple implicit star-shaped object model [11] where each local feature is connected to the center of the object. The combination of FDs and corresponding spatial vectors gives the final traffic sign prototype as

$$P = \{(\mathbf{C}_k, \mathbf{v}_k)\} \quad k = 1..K \tag{11}$$

where K is the total number of contours for the sign prototype.

These spatial components effectively remove the need for a region-of-interests detector as a first step. Even though each $\mathbf{C}_k$ might give matches not corresponding to the actual sign, it is unlikely that multiple matches vote for the same position if they not belong to the actual traffic sign.

2.4 Matching Sign Prototypes

J contours $\mathbf{q}_j$ are extracted from a query image and represented by their FDs $\mathbf{Q}_j$, see top row in fig. 3. For each sign prototype, all prototype contours $\mathbf{C}_k$ are compared to all extracted contours $\mathbf{Q}_j$. Since traffic signs have a well defined orientation, we use the rotation variant matching score:

$$e_{jk} = 2 - 2\max_l \operatorname{Re}\{\mathcal{F}^{-1}\{\bar{\mathbf{Q}}_j \cdot \mathbf{C}_k\}(l)\} \ . \tag{12}$$

This results in the binary matrix $\mathbf{M} = (m)_{jk}$ of matched contours with

$$m_{jk} = \begin{cases} 1 & e_{jk} \leq \theta_k \\ 0 & e_{jk} > \theta_k \end{cases} \tag{13}$$

Fig. 2. Extracted local features (green contours) and corresponding vectors (red arrows) pointing towards the center of the traffic sign

Fig. 3. Upper left: Query image. Upper right: Extracted contours. Lower left: Contours that matched any of the contours in the pedestrian crossing prototype are shown in a non-yellow color. Lower right: The final result after matching against all sign prototypes.

where θ_k is a manually selected threshold for each prototype contour k, see fig. 3 lower left for an example of matched contours.

The next step is to verify which combinations of matched contours $\mathbf{Q}_j$ fit to the spatial configuration of the sign prototype. This is done by a cascaded matching scheme. For each individual match m_{jk}, we obtain by means of (9) the parameters s_k and t_k and compute an estimate $\mathbf{v}'_{jk} = s_{jk}\mathbf{v}_k + t_{jk}$.

The vector $\mathbf{v}'_{j1}$ defines a hypothesized prototype center. We then go through all prototype contours $k = 2 \dots K$ and verify for all $m_{ik} \neq 0$, $i \neq j$, that s_{ik}/s_{j1} is sufficiently close to 1 and that $\mathbf{v}'_{ik}$ is sufficiently close to the hypothesized prototype center. These contours are consistent with respect to scale and location and if only if sufficiently many contours are consistent, a detection of the corresponding sign is flagged, see fig. 3 lower right.

2.5 Dataset

A dataset has been created by recording sequences from over 350 km of Swedish highways and city roads. A 1.3 mega-pixel color camera, a Point-Grey Chameleon, was placed inside a car on the dashboard looking out of the front window. The camera was pointing slightly to the right, in order to cover as many relevant signs as possible. The lens had a focal length of 6.5mm, resulting in approximately 41 degrees field of view. Typical speed signs on motorways are about 90 cm wide, which corresponds to a size of about 50 pixel if they are to be detected at a distance of about 30 m.

A human operator started the recording whenever a traffic sign was visible and stopped the recording when no more signs were visible. In total, in over 20 000 frames have been recorded of which every fifth frame has then been

Fig. 4. Examples from the database

manually labeled. The label for each sign contains sign type (pedestrian crossing, designated lane right, no standing or parking, priority road, give way, 50 kph, or 30 kph), visibility status (occluded, blurred, or visible) and road status (whether the signs is on the road being traveled or on a side road), see fig 4 for examples. The entire database including ground truth is available at `http://www.cvl.isy.liu.se/research/traffic-signs-dataset`.

3 Experiments

Synthetic images of Swedish road signs, see bottom row of fig. 5, were used for creating models according to the methodology described in Sec. 2.3. The sign models were then matched against real images from two datasets. The first dataset, denoted *Manually ROIs dataset*, is the one used in [10] which is using patches from bounding boxes of 200x200 pixels, see fig. 5. The second evaluation was done on the the newly collected dataset, denoted *Summer dataset*, see Sec. 2.5. All processing is done frame wise not using temporal clues.

Note that the evaluation was done using grey scale images and thus do not use the distinct colors occurring in the signs as a descriptor. The images used correspond to the red channel of a normal color camera. This is easily achieved by placing a red-pass filter in front of an ordinary monochromatic camera. Using normal grey-scale conversion would be problematic since some of the signs are isoluminant, e.g. sign (c) in fig. 5. The reason for not using colors is that color cameras have lower frame rates given a fixed bandwidth and resolution. High frame rates are crucial for cameras to be used within the automotive industry. Higher frame rates mean for example higher accuracy when estimating the velocity of approaching cars.

3.1 Results Manually ROIs Dataset

The first dataset is used in order to compare to the reported results in [10] and contains 316 regions-of-interests (ROIs) of 200x200 pixels, see fig. 5. The

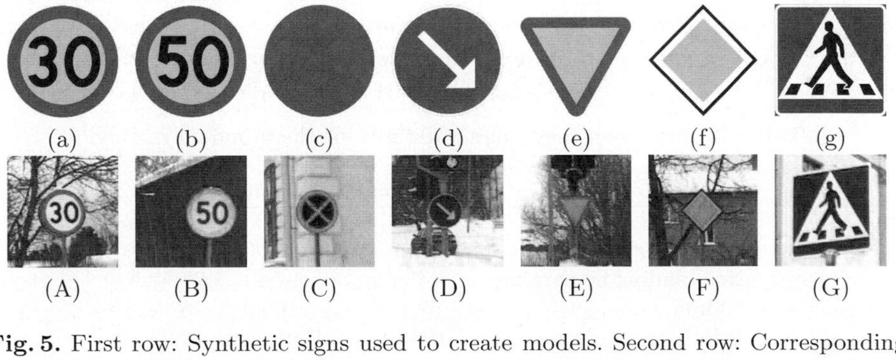

Fig. 5. First row: Synthetic signs used to create models. Second row: Corresponding real world examples.

Table 1. Performance on the Manually ROIs dataset for the method presented in [10] and the proposed algorithm

	Proposed method		[10]	
Sign type	Recall%	#FP	Recall%	#FP
Pedestrian crossing	98.0	0	98.0	1
Designated lane right	95.8	0	95.8	2
No standing or parking	100.0	0	96.6	1
50 kph	91.7	2	91.7	2
30 kph	95.8	1	95.8	1
Priority road	95.7	0	95.7	1
Give way	94.7	0	94.7	2

ROIs were manually extracted around 216 signs and 100 non-signs. The result is summarized in table 1. This dataset is fairly simple and the proposed method increases the already good performance of [10]. Using constraints on the spatial arrangement of contours removes some of the false positives (FPs) while keeping the same recall level or increasing it by allowing for less strict thresholds on the individual contours. The classes *Priority road* and *Give way* are unaffected since they consist of a single contour each, thus not benefiting from the added spatial constraints.

3.2 Results Summer Dataset

The second evaluation is done on the new Summer dataset, see Sec. 2.5 for details regarding the dataset. The evaluation was limited to include signs for the road being traveled on with a bounding box of at least 50x50 pixels, corresponding to a sign more than 30 m from the camera. Table 2 contains the results for the same sign classes that was used in the Manually ROIs dataset, with one exception. The class 30kph was removed since only 11 instances of the sign were visible, not giving sufficient statistics. The entire image was giving as query without any ROIs.

All classes except from *Give Way* show excellent precision. The recall rates for the *Pedestrian crossing* and *Designated lane right* classes are above 90% while the *50 kph, Priority road* and *No standing or parking* classes show recall over 70%. The *Giveway* class shows less impressive performace, recall rate under

Table 2. Results on the Summer dataset for the proposed method

Sign type	Total Signs	Precision%	Recall%
Pedestrian crossing	158	96.03	91.77
Designated lane right	107	100.00	95.33
No standing or parking	44	97.14	77.27
50 kph	67	100.0	76.12
Priority road	198	98.66	74.24
Give way	67	59.26	47.76

Fig. 6. The first three rows show examples of correctly detected signs. Bottom left shows an example of a missed detection and bottom right shows an example of a false positive, classified as a Give way sign.

50% combined with poor precision. The *Giveway* class contains only one single contour and thus can not benefit from the spatial model. Increasing the recall rate for the *Giveway* class is possible but would also lead to a dramatic increase in the number of FPs. Using [10] on this dataset resluts in a high recall rate but in the order of 2000 FPs for all classes giving precision rates of less than 10%, showing the dependency of ROIs. The three top rows in fig. 6 show examples of correctly detected and recognized traffic signs.

The FPs produced are always due to the contour extraction going awry, see bottom left in fig. 6 for an example of a missed sign. The contour extraction algorithm were not able to extract sufficient contours from this image resulting in a missed *Designated lane right* sign. The bottom right image in fig. 6 shows a false positive of the *Give way* class. It is shown in order to illustrate the problems induced when using a single contour.

4 Conclusions

A method for using locally extracted contours in combination with an implicit star-shaped object model was presented. The presented method works fully automatically on query images with no need for regions-of-interests. It is shown that the presented method performs well for traffic signs that contain multiple distinct contours, such as the Swedish pedestrian crossing sign. For traffic signs with few or a single contour, such as the Swedish give way sign, the method still needs improvement.

A major contribution is the release of the first publicly available large traffic sign database not only containing small patches around traffic signs, thus allowing for evaluation of detection and recognition not only recognition. The database contains over 20 000 frames with 20% being labeled. The database will in the future be extended to include different ambient conditions, such as night and rain, and also to include signs from different countries.

Acknowledgments

This work has been supported by the Swedish Research Council under the frame project grant *Extended Target Tracking* and by the Swedish Government through ELLIIT, the Strategic Area for ICT research.

References

1. BMW Automobiles (2010), `http://www.bmw.com/`
2. German Traffic Sign Recognition Benchmark (2010), `http://benchmark.ini.rub.de/`
3. Saab (2010), `http://www.saab.com/`
4. VW Media Services (2010), `https://www.volkswagen-media-services.com/`

5. Fleyeh, H., Dougherty, M., Aenugula, D., Baddam, S.: Invariant Road Sign Recognition with Fuzzy ARTMAP and Zernike Moments. In: 2007 IEEE Intelligent Vehicles Symposium, pp. 31–36 (2007)
6. Garcia-Garrido, M., Sotelo, M., Martin-Gorostiza, E.: Fast Road Sign Detection Using Hough Transform for Assisted Driving of Road Vehicles. In: Moreno Díaz, R., Pichler, F., Quesada Arencibia, A. (eds.) EUROCAST 2005. LNCS, vol. 3643, pp. 543–548. Springer, Heidelberg (2005)
7. Gavrila, D., Philomin, V.: Real-time object detection for ldquo;smart rdquo; vehicles. In: The Proceedings of the Seventh IEEE International Conference on Computer Vision, vol. 1, pp. 87–93 (1999)
8. Granlund, G.H.: Fourier Preprocessing for Hand Print Character Recognition. IEEE Trans. on Computers C–21(2), 195–201 (1972)
9. Kuhl, F.P., Giardina, C.R.: Elliptic Fourier features of a closed contour. Computer Graphics and Image Processing 18, 236–258 (1982)
10. Larsson, F., Felsberg, M., Per-Erik, F.: Correlating Fourier Descriptors of Local Patches for Road Sign Recognition. IET Computer Vision (2011) (accepted for publication)
11. Leibe, B., Leonardis, A., Schiele, B.: Robust Object Detection with Interleaved Categorization and Segmentation. International Journal of Computer Vision 77(1), 259–289 (2008), `http://dx.doi.org/10.1007/s11263-007-0095-3`
12. Maldonado-Bascon, S., Lafuente-Arroyo, S., Gil-Jimenez, P., Gomez-Moreno, H., Lopez-Ferreras, F.: Road-sign detection and recognition based on support vector machines. IEEE Trans. on Intelligent Transportation Systems 8(2), 264–278 (2007)
13. Matas, J., Chum, O., Urban, M., Pajdla, T.: Robust wide baseline stereo from maximally stable extremal regions. In: BMVC. pp. 384–393 (2002)
14. Nguwi, Y.Y., Kouzani, A.Z.: Detection and classification of road signs in natural environments. Neural Comput. Appl. 17, 265–289 (2008)
15. Oppenheim, A., Lim, J.: The importance of phase in signals. Proc. of the IEEE 69(5), 529–541 (1981)
16. Papoulis, A.: The Fourier Integral and its Applications. McGraw-Hill, New York (1962)
17. Persoon, E., Fu, K.S.: Shape discrimination using fourier descriptors. IEEE Transactions on Systems, Man and Cybernetics 7(3), 170–179 (1977)
18. Zhang, Q., Kamata, S.: Automatic road sign detection method based on Color Barycenters Hexagon model. In: ICPR 2008 (2008)

Multichannel Segmentation Using Contour Relaxation: Fast Super-Pixels and Temporal Propagation

Rudolf Mester[1,2], Christian Conrad[1], and Alvaro Guevara[1]

[1] VSI Lab*, Computer Science Dept., Goethe University, Frankfurt, Germany
[2] Computer Vision Laboratory, Dept. EE, Linköping University, Sweden

Abstract. The contribution describes a statistical framework for image segmentation that is characterized by the following features: It allows to model scalar as well as multi-channel images (color, texture feature sets, depth, ...) in a region-based manner, including a Gibbs-Markov random field model that describes the spatial (and temporal) cohesion tendencies of 'real' label fields. It employs a principled target function resulting from a statistical image model and maximum-a-posteriori estimation, and combines it with a computationally very efficient way ('contour relaxation') for determining a (local) optimum of the target function. We show in many examples that even these local optima provide very reasonable and useful partitions of the image area into regions. A very attractive feature of the proposed method is that a reasonable partition is reached within some few iterations even when starting from a 'blind' initial partition (e.g. for 'superpixels'), or when — in sequence segmentation — the segmentation result of the previous image is used as starting point for segmenting the current image.

1 Motivation

The term 'image segmentation' is used in a very large variety of meanings; in the ideal case it denotes the process of subdividing images into 'meaningful' regions; however, what the term 'meaningful' means is hard to pinpoint. For recent reviews, see e.g. [16,5]. If we use the term 'segmentation' in the following, we intend to refer to the computation of a division of a given image into parts that are homogeneous from a signal perspective, that is: homogeneous w.r.t. a statistical model of color, gray value, depth or similar 'features' that can be associated with a pixel, or pixel *cell*, on the image grid. We present an approach that is able to compute such an 'over-segmentation', particularly for the case of multichannel data (color, or gray value plus other features). As Veksler et al [17] state, the idea of operating on atomic, homogeneously colored or textured regions is old (see for instance [11] as only one example), whereas the now popular

* This work was funded by the German Federal Ministry of Education and Research (BMBF) in the project Bernstein Fokus Neurotechnologie – 01GQ0841, and in parts supported by the ELLIIT programme funded by the Swedish Government.

A. Heyden and F. Kahl (Eds.): SCIA 2011, LNCS 6688, pp. 250–261, 2011.

term 'superpixels' has been coined recently [12] and is a very active research area [7,9,1,17]. We consider it to be the main characteristics of our approach that it is statistically principled and offers a really quick transition from a 'bad' partition (that could be 'guessed' or determined by some heuristic) into a very good over-segmentation.

2 The Region-Based Generative Image Model for Multi-channel Data

A region-based image model assumes that the structure of each image is dominated by regions. The complete image area is subdivided into a *partition* $\mathcal{Q}$ consisting of regions $R_i, i = 1, \ldots, N_R$. Each site on the image grid is associated with a measurable entity, for instance a gray value, or an RGB color value. It might also be that additional entities which are not directly measurable are associated with the individual grid sites, for instance a motion vector, a disparity vector, a depth value, or combinations of such entities. Finally, a region could also be filled by values which are determined from intermediate computations, e.g. the output of a set of texture operators. In the interest of a compact presentation, we denote all these variants as the (region-specific) *texture signal.*

Besides that each measurement may be single channel or vectorial (= multichannel), measurements can be organized in cells (see Fig. 2), for instance for implementing multi-resolution segmentation algorithms. We do not discuss cells here due to limited space; the mathematical generalization is straightforward.

It is important that a probability measure can be associated with each realization of the texture signal, that is: it is considered as a realization of a random process. These region-specific random processes share the same functional structure all over the image, but each region is associated with an individual region-specific parameter vector $\boldsymbol{\theta}_i$ (see Fig. 1). So only the *numerical values* of these parameters vary from region to region.

In the experiments performed in this paper, we make two assumptions which drastically simplify the appearing expressions and reduce the computational effort, being fully aware that both these assumptions are not true for real image material. However, we show that even these drastic approximations do not prevent the resulting procedures from yielding very useful results. It has been confirmed in a very large number of experiments that even a very shallow, incomplete description of region texture signals is most of the time sufficient for differentiating such textures. These approximations are:

- A1: The feature values at different *pixel sites* obey the same distribution inside of a region, but they are statistically independent of each other.
- A2: The feature values in the different *feature channels* at each pixel site are statistically independent of each other.

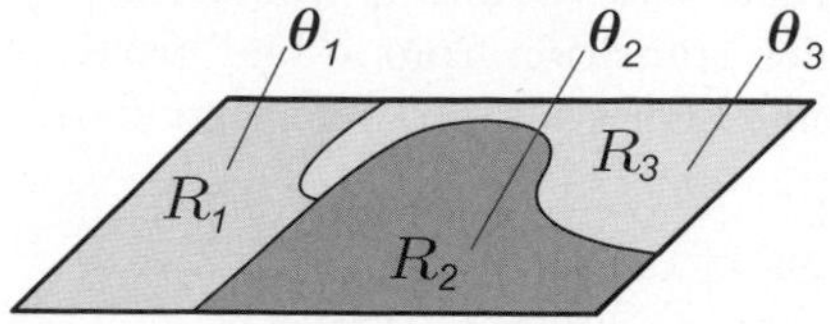

Fig. 1. Region-based image model, associating one parameter vector $\boldsymbol{\theta}_i$ to each region R_i. The values at each pixel site can be vector-valued (=multi-channel).

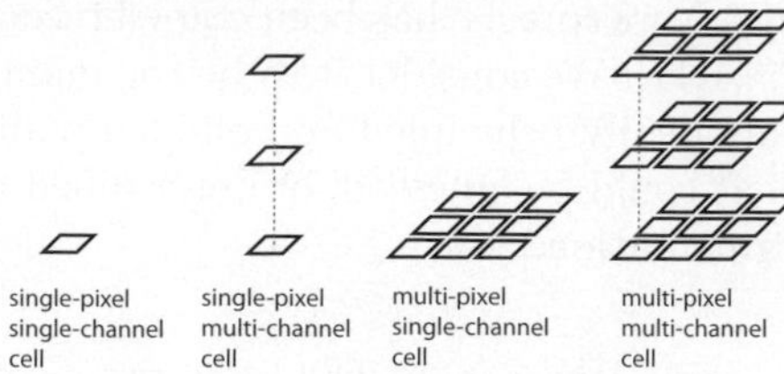

Fig. 2. Measurements are organized in cells which may include a single measurement or several ones; each measurement may be single channel or vectorial (= multi-channel)

3 Segmentation as a Maximum-a-Posteriori (MAP) Estimation Problem

We proceed by formulating the segmentation task as an estimation problem, as this deduces an 'energy function' to be optimized from first principles. Corresponding approaches can already be found in early publications on image segmentation such as [15,14,4,6,11].

Let $\boldsymbol{z}$ be the vector of measurements (a 2D array of vectors) on the image array and let $\mathcal{Q} = \{R_1, R_2, \dots R_n\}$ be a partition of the image array. We assume that the measurements *inside* of each region have been generated by a region-specific stochastic process. Each of these processes is characterized by a set of *parameters*. Thus, to each region R_i of the partition, a stationary stochastic process with an individual model parameter vector $\boldsymbol{\theta}_i = \boldsymbol{\theta}(R_i)$ is assigned.

The ensemble $\{\boldsymbol{\theta}\} = \{\boldsymbol{\theta}_1, \boldsymbol{\theta}_2, \dots \boldsymbol{\theta}_n\}$ of model parameter vectors $\boldsymbol{\theta}_i$ represents, together with the partition $\mathcal{Q}$, a complete, piecewise stationary[1] model for the image process. We denote the combination of a partition $\mathcal{Q}$ and the parameter ensemble $\{\boldsymbol{\theta}\}$ as the 'array state' $\mathcal{S}$. For each completely specified array state $\mathcal{S}$, we can provide a conditional probability density for the total ensemble of random variables $\boldsymbol{z}$, conditioned on $\mathcal{Q}$ and $\{\boldsymbol{\theta}\}$. With prior distributions for the partition $\mathcal{Q}$ and the parameter set $\{\boldsymbol{\theta}\}$, we can turn this into a joint distribution $p(\boldsymbol{z}, \mathcal{Q}, \{\boldsymbol{\theta}\}) = p(\boldsymbol{z}, \mathcal{S})$.

Based on this formulation, the segmentation task now consists in finding a likely (hidden) array state $\mathcal{S}$ as the cause for an observed image vector $\boldsymbol{z}$.

In maximum-a-posteriori (MAP) segmentation, we consider the specific combination of a partition $\mathcal{Q}$ and the corresponding model parameters $\{\boldsymbol{\theta}_1, \boldsymbol{\theta}_2, \dots \boldsymbol{\theta}_n\}$ as the sought estimate of the array state $\mathcal{S}$ if it maximizes the posterior distribution

$$p(\mathcal{S} \mid \boldsymbol{z}) = p(\mathcal{Q}\ ,\ \{\boldsymbol{\theta}_1, \boldsymbol{\theta}_2, \dots \boldsymbol{\theta}_n\} \mid \boldsymbol{z}). \tag{1}$$

[1] We can deviate from stationarity by assuming a smooth deterministic parametric function to be overlaid by a stationary process, but this is not done here.

This posterior is, as always, linked by Bayes' theorem with the prior and the conditional observation density:

$$p(\mathcal{S} \mid \boldsymbol{z}) = p(\boldsymbol{z} \mid \mathcal{S}) \cdot p(\mathcal{S})/p(\boldsymbol{z}). \tag{2}$$

Since the observed image vector $\boldsymbol{z}$ is a fixed realization of a random process, $p(\boldsymbol{z})$ is merely a normalization constant. Thus the MAP segmentation is given by the particular array state $\mathcal{S}$ which maximizes

$$p(\boldsymbol{z} \mid \mathcal{S}) \cdot p(\mathcal{S}) = p(\boldsymbol{z},\, \mathcal{S}) = p(\boldsymbol{z} \mid \mathcal{Q}, \boldsymbol{\theta}) \cdot p(\boldsymbol{\theta} \mid \mathcal{Q}) \cdot p(\mathcal{Q}) \quad \rightarrow \max \quad . \tag{3}$$

This way we try to find the 'most probable cause' for the generation of the given image. Now we have to specify the conditional densities for $\boldsymbol{z}$, given the individual region model processes, and also the prior distribution $p(\mathcal{Q})$ for the partitions $\mathcal{Q}$. Gibbs random fields (GRF) relate $p(\mathcal{Q})$ to the *clique potentials* $V_c(c_i)$ defined on pairs of neighboring sites on the label array. These 'potentials' depend on whether the label values in such a clique are identical or not. The sought distribution is built from the clique potentials as

$$p(\mathcal{Q}) = \frac{1}{Z} \cdot \exp(-\sum_{c_i} V_c(c_i)). \tag{4}$$

Fortunately, the 'partition function' Z in Eq. 4 is not needed in our algorithm.

The remaining entity to be specified are the region-specific model parameter vectors $\boldsymbol{\theta}$. They are considered as unknown 'deterministic parameters', that is: there is no non-uniform prior on their value range. With that assumption, we can write

$$p(\mathcal{S}) = p(\boldsymbol{\theta}, \mathcal{Q}) = k \cdot p(\mathcal{Q}). \tag{5}$$

The model parameters $\boldsymbol{\theta}$ are obtained by a region-specific maximum likelihood estimation: the partition $\mathcal{Q}$ is kept fixed, and the term $p(\boldsymbol{z} \mid \mathcal{S})$ is maximized with respect to the parameter $\boldsymbol{\theta}$

$$\begin{aligned} p(\boldsymbol{z}, \mathcal{S}) &= p(\boldsymbol{z} \mid \mathcal{S}) \cdot p(\mathcal{S}) \\ &= k \cdot p(\boldsymbol{z} \mid \mathcal{Q}, \{\hat{\boldsymbol{\theta}}^{ML}(\mathcal{Q})\}) \cdot p(\mathcal{Q}). \end{aligned}$$

We assume the texture processes of the individual regions to be 'pairwise statistically independent'; this denotes a situation where the knowledge of the complete texture signal inside region R_i does not provide *any* information on the texture signal inside region $R_j, j \neq i$. Under this assumption, the joint probability density of observing *all* the texture signals — in other words: the complete vector-valued image $\boldsymbol{z}$ — can be factorized in

$$p(\boldsymbol{z} \mid \mathcal{Q}) = \prod_{R_i} \prod_{k} p(\boldsymbol{z}_{ik} \mid \hat{\boldsymbol{\theta}}_i^{ML}), \tag{6}$$

where index i enumerates the regions, and index k runs over the feature channels. The simple structure of eq. 6 does of course result from the assumed region-to-region and inter-feature channel independences stated in assumptions A1 and A2.

4 The Contour Relaxation

With the target function to be maximized being defined by the preceding section, we proceed now to present the mere optimization method. We begin with an initial partition Q_0 and improve it by a constrained variation of pixel labels. We regard only those grid points x_0 that are located on the contour of a region — thus the notion 'contour relaxation' —, and check whether certain changes of the point's region label yields an increase of criterion (3). If so, that particular label change is executed. However, only the current label $q(x_0)$, and the labels of the eight nearest neighbours of x_0 are allowed for x_0. Since the labels of all other pixels are kept fixed in each step, only those 8 cliques that include x_0 have to be taken into account, as only their potentials depend on the label of x_0. Thus, the 'label image term' $p(\mathcal{Q})$ (Eq. 4) can be written as

$$p(\mathcal{Q}) = k_1 \cdot \exp(-n'_B B - n'_C C) \,. \tag{7}$$

Here, k_1 is a constant, and B and C are the costs for inhomogeneous horizontal/vertical, and diagonal cliques, respectively. The exponential term implicitly varies with the choice of the label for x_0: the numbers of inhomogeneous cliques in the regarded clique subset for different choices of $q(x_0)$ are expressed by the values n'_B and n'_C.

Correspondingly, the conditional likelihood of the image data $\boldsymbol{z}$ given the partition $\mathcal{Q}$ can be expressed as the product of a constant term and a variable term that depends on $q(x_0)$:

$$p(\boldsymbol{z} \mid \mathcal{Q}) = k_2 \cdot \prod_{\{\mathcal{R}_j\}} p\big(\boldsymbol{z}(\mathcal{R}_j) \mid \boldsymbol{\theta}(\mathcal{R}_j)\big). \tag{8}$$

Note that the product on the rhs comprises only those regions R_j that are neighbors to site x_0, or directly include contour pixel x_0. It is important that the ML estimates of the region parameters change depending on the choice of the label chosen for x_0. This all boils down to evaluating the expression

$$p(\boldsymbol{z}, \mathcal{Q}) = k_1 \cdot k_2 \cdot \exp(-n'_B B - n'_C C) \cdot \prod_{\{\mathcal{R}_j\}} p\big(\boldsymbol{z}(\mathcal{R}_j) \mid \boldsymbol{\theta}(\mathcal{R}_j)\big), \tag{9}$$

for all the (few) legal choices of $q(x_0)$. Grid point x_0 obtains the specific label that maximizes expression (9). In a practical implementation, the negative logarithm of equation (9) is minimized, which directly yields an energy function that has been constructed from 'first principles'.

A simple, though efficient optimization scheme is obtained by scanning the image several times, with systematically varying the scan direction each time. Since the presented optimization operation needs only to be executed for those grid points that are located on the boundary of a region, computational costs are low. The values of the parameters B and C of the Gibbs model are far from being critical; in our experiments, B had values between 0.3 and 1.5 (typically 0.7) and $C = B/\sqrt{2}$. The relaxation may be stopped as soon as a scan over the whole image yields only few label changes. In general, about 2-4 iterations are required.

5 Likelihood Expressions for Region-Oriented Segmentation Approaches

Under different pdf models (Gaussian, Laplacian, unilateral exponential...), the maximum likelihood estimates of the pdf parameters only depend on some few simple functions of the observables z_j that need to be updated continuously:

- $N \stackrel{def}{=} \sum_j 1$, the number of measurements in the cell.
- $S \stackrel{def}{=} \sum_j z_j$, the sum of all measurement values.
- $Q \stackrel{def}{=} \sum_j z_j^2$, the sum of the squares of all measurement values.
- $A \stackrel{def}{=} \sum_j |z_j|$, the sum of the absolute values of all measurement values.

For a given region, and assuming that the measurement values are uncorrelated between channels, only these numbers have to be computed (per feature channel), and only these numbers are needed for the computation of the likelihood terms appearing in eq. (8) and (9). Since, under a given pdf assumption, these numbers fully represent all the necessary information contained in a set of measurement values, these numbers are denoted as *'sufficient statistics'*.

5.1 The Data Likelihood Term for a Set of Measurements under the Gaussian Assumption

The value of the pdf for N statistically independent scalar measurements z_j from the same Gaussian distribution is

$$p_z(\boldsymbol{z}) = \left(\frac{1}{\sqrt{2\pi}}\right)^N \cdot \left(\frac{1}{\sigma}\right)^N \cdot \exp\left(-\frac{1}{2}\sum_j \frac{(z_j - m_i)^2}{\sigma^2}\right) . \tag{10}$$

Estimating the parameters and finding the likelihood value. For the parameters m and σ^2, we assume their maximum likelihood estimates are determined from the given data set. We obtain

$$\hat{m} = S/N; \qquad \hat{\sigma}^2 = \frac{Q}{N} - \left(\frac{S}{N}\right)^2 . \tag{11}$$

With these estimates, the exponent in eq. 10 is

$$\frac{1}{2\sigma^2}\sum_j (z_j - \hat{m})^2 = \frac{N}{2} .$$

Inserting this into eq. 10, we obtain

$$p_z(\boldsymbol{z}) = \left(\frac{1}{\sqrt{2\pi}}\right)^N \cdot \left(\frac{N^2}{NQ - S^2}\right)^{N/2} \cdot \exp\left(-\frac{N}{2}\right) . \tag{12}$$

Taking the logarithm of this expression, we obtain

$$\ln p_z(z) = \frac{N}{2} \cdot \left(-\ln(2\pi) + \ln\left(\frac{N^2}{NQ - S^2}\right) - 1 \right) . \tag{13}$$

Data likelihood terms for other pdf models, e.g. Laplacian can be determined easily and used in exactly the same way.

Fig. 3. Original images used within the experiments: (left to right) *Baboon*, *Starfish*, *Venus*, *Tsukuba*, *Tiger* and *Teddy*

6 Experimental Results

In the following we present experimental results obtained for multi-channel contour relaxation applied to single images and to a stream of images. We show results obtained when the initial segmentation is given by (i) a blind segmentation or (ii) a sparse segmentation, i.e., in the simplest case provided as several strokes in the image marking the desired foreground and background. Figure 4 (top left) and Fig. 7 (bottom left) visualize exemplary initial segmentations for both cases.

For images with a resolution of 640×480 pixels, 4 passes of a C/C++ version of the contour relaxation on the three color channels takes about 150 milliseconds on an Intel Xenon 2.8GHz processor. Note that this implementation is only single threaded and unoptimized.

6.1 Contour Relaxation Applied to Single Images

In this section, we show segmentation results obtained when multi channel contour relaxation is applied to single images. We use several well known images from the Middlebury web site [8] and the Berkeley segmentation database [10] (cf. Fig. 3).

Automatic Initialization by a Blind Segmentation. A blind segmentation is generated by subdividing the input image into non-overlapping regions of $n \times n$ pixels, where $n = 32$ throughout the experiments. The clique costs are set to 0.3 and $\frac{0.3}{\sqrt{2}}$ for inhomogenous horizontal or vertical and diagonal cliques, respectively. Then, contour relaxation is applied to the initial segmentation where first the sufficient statistics of each region on each of the three image channels

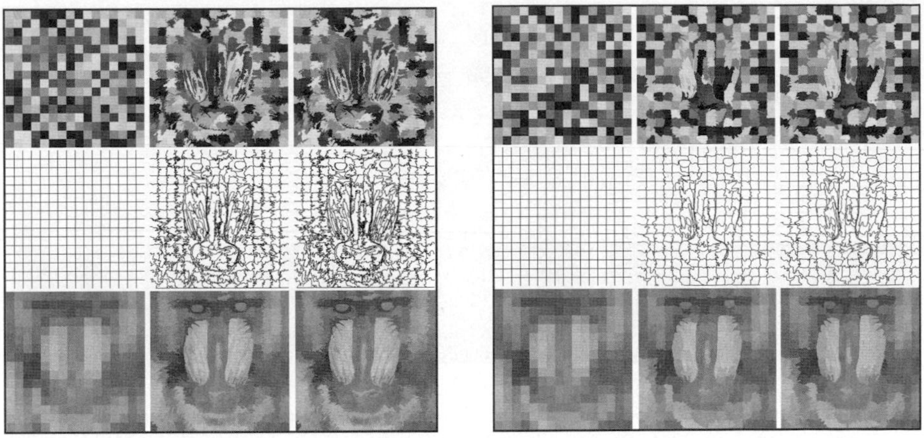

Fig. 4. Segmentation results for image *'Baboon'*: (left) low clique costs, (right) high clique costs. Upper row: label images after 0, 4 and 8 runs of contour relaxation. Middle row: contour images; lower row: region mean images. Best viewed in color.

(Y, U, V)[2] are computed. Then the relabeling of pixels along the region contours is performed as described in Sec. 4. We perform 4 passes of contour relaxation, where each pass is subdivided into 4 sub-passes, that is, within the relabeling algorithm, pixels are visited from (i) left-right, up-down, (ii) left-right, down-up, (iii) right-left, up-down and (iiii) right-left, down-up. The purpose of this scheme, also known as using *coding sets*, is to bias the results as little as possible with respect to the used pixel visiting scheme. For all presented results, at latest after 4 passes of contour relaxation have been performed, the segmentation remained stable, e.g., no further significant change of the labeling could be observed.

Figures 4 to 6 show the results for the data sets *Baboon*, *Venus*, *Tsukuba*, *Cones* and *Teddy*. Here, we display the label arrays, the contour images and the region mean images after 0, 4 and 8 sub-passes of contour relaxation have been performed. The region mean images are generated by filling a region of the label array with the color mean value of all pixels assigned to that specific label (cf. Sec. 5).

The result figures show that our approach typically produces an over-segmentation in the sense of a super-pixel representation of the input image. That is, the image is subdivided into many regions (super-pixels), where all pixels in one region are similar with respect to their color value. Here, it is of utmost importance that a single super-pixel does not contain different objects within the image, such as foreground and background, and that the super-pixels are aligned with the object boundaries. Depending on the number of labels (i.e., the number of regions R_n) within the initial blind segmentation, the amount of over-

[2] The Y channel encodes the luminance, U and V the chrominance of each pixel. This color space is in reasonable accordance to the assumption of statistically independent feature channels, since it decorrelates the (strongly correlated) RGB color values.

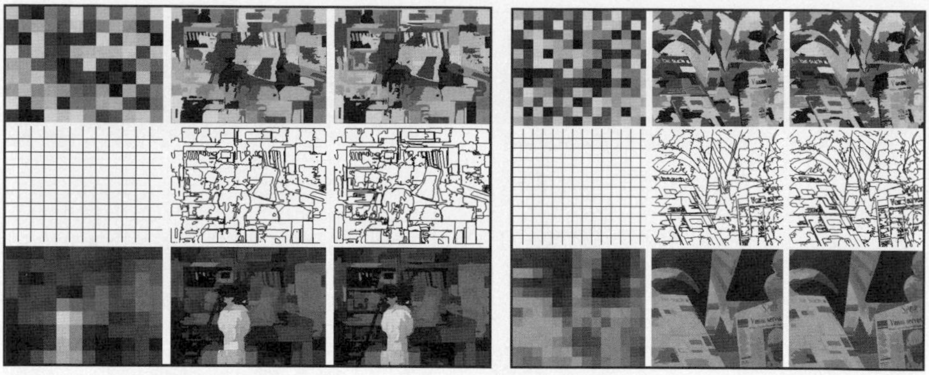

Fig. 5. Segmentation results for image *'Tsukuba'* (left) and image *'Venus'* (right): Upper row: label images after 0, 4 and 8 runs of contour relaxation. Middle row: contour images; lower row: region mean images. Best viewed in color.

segmentation can be controlled. However, as long as only low-level information, such as the pixel color value, is available, in general no segmentation on an object level can be computed, as typically mid-level information, such as motion or depth, or high-level object knowledge are decisive.

Throughout Fig. 4 to Fig. 6 it can be seen that the super-pixels are aligned with the object boundaries, such as the head in the *Tsukuba* image, the posters and newspaper in the *Venus* image, the tail of the tiger within the *Tiger* image (cf. with the results obtained in [3]) and the cuddly toys within the *Teddy* image. Note that also fine-grained details, such as the characters on the newspaper within *Venus*, or the *Baboons* whiskery, are captured as well. For the *Baboon* image we also show the influence of different clique costs on the resulting segmentation. In Fig. 4 (right) the costs for inhomogeneous cliques are doubled. Therefore the segmentation appears to be more block-like, whereas in the case for lower clique costs (Fig. 4 (left)), the segmentation adapts more to the fine-grained details. This can also be seen within the contour images for both cases, where the contour image in the case of higher clique costs has a much less 'ragged' appearance.

Manual Initialization by a Given Sparse Segmentation. The results presented so far have been obtained in a completely unsupervised manner, where the initial segmentation was generated 'automatically'. For a typical task such as foreground/background segmentation, often some kind of user input is available, where parts of the foreground and parts of the background are explicitly labeled. Such user input can be given by several line strokes within the input image, marking the different textures (or objects) to be segmented out. Figure 7 shows an example for the *Starfish* image, where the background is marked by a blue stroke and the foreground object by a red stroke. All other pixels remain initially unlabeled. We use the same initial segmentation as in [13].

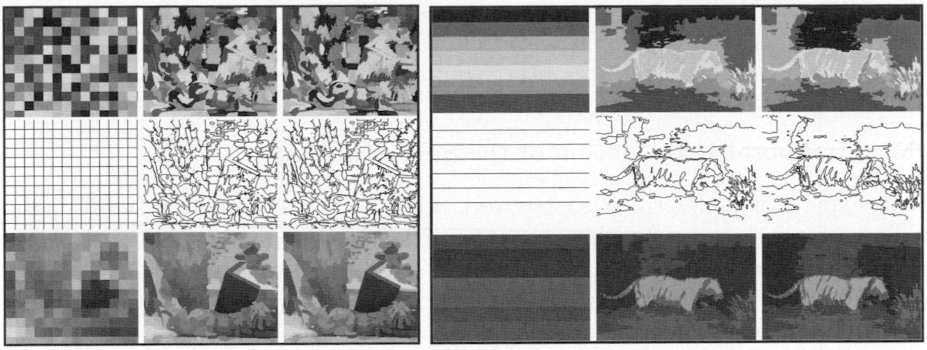

Fig. 6. Segmentation results for image *'Teddy'* (left) and *'Tiger'* (right): Upper row: label images after 0, 4 and 8 runs of contour relaxation. Middle row: contour images; lower row: region mean images. Best viewed in color.

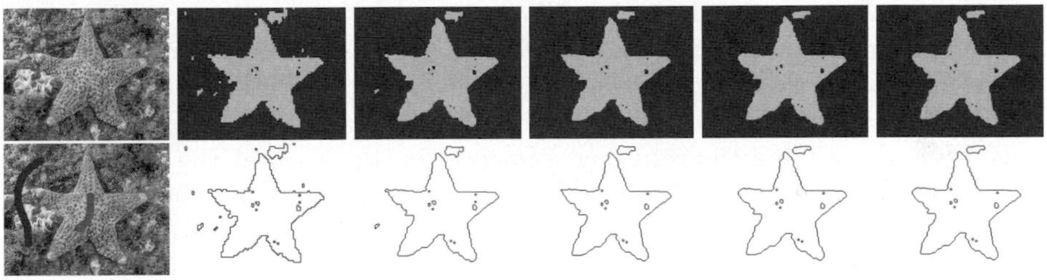

Fig. 7. Segmentation of the *'Starfish'*. First column shows the original image and the user strokes. Second column shows the result of a maximum likelihood classification, columns 3 to 6 show results after 2, 4, 8 and 12 passes of contour relaxation, where row 1 is the label image and row 2 the contour image. Best viewed in color.

We obtain a full segmentation as described in Sec. 4 by a maximum likelihood classification of all unlabeled pixels to either foreground or background. Such maximum likelihood labeling is then subject to several passes of contour relaxation, to remove false classifications and to smooth the label image. The second column of Fig. 7 shows the maximum likelihood classification result for the *Starfish* image and the corresponding contour image. This yields a label array where the contours of the foreground object are already well captured. However, several pixels which lie in the background are classified as foreground and vice versa. Columns 3 to 6 in Fig. 7 visualize how the segmentation is adapted by applying several passes of multi channel contour relaxation. We are aware of the fact that optimum solutions to such two-class labeling problems are available [13,2]. However, we would like to stress that the contour relaxation gives results which are virtually indistinguishable from these optimum ones, even for multi-class problems, at much lower complexity of the procedure and lower computational effort. It can be seen that a small amount of pixels in the upper right are still marked as foreground. This is caused by the fact that the statistics of the three color channels for this specific region and the foreground object are nearly identical. Resolving this issue requires higher level information.

6.2 Temporal Propagation of the Segmentation

The experiments described so far were applied to single images only. In the following, we show briefly that our approach can be applied to image sequence segmentation as well.

In order to let image sequence segmentation be efficient it is crucial to exploit prior knowledge obtained during the processing of the previous images. At time t, such prior knowledge is, e.g., the segmentation result obtained at time $t-1$. In our framework, the segmentation result from time $t-1$ will therefore be the initialization of the segmentation to be computed for the image at time t. This significantly decreases the computational effort. Furthermore the labelings of the images are to a very large extent coherent over time, i.e., a single object will almost always maintain its label from image to image. Figure 8 shows the segmentation results obtained for a cluttered office scene, where a person is moving in front of the camera. The segmentation was automatically initialized with a blind segmentation as described earlier. Then, 4 passes of contour relaxation have been applied and the resulting segmentation was used as the initialization for the next frame to be processed. Again, the label and the contour images show the desired feature of super-pixels being well aligned with object boundaries. Fine grained object structures such as the table legs, or the lamp are well preserved. Furthermore, the labeling remains largely consistent over time.

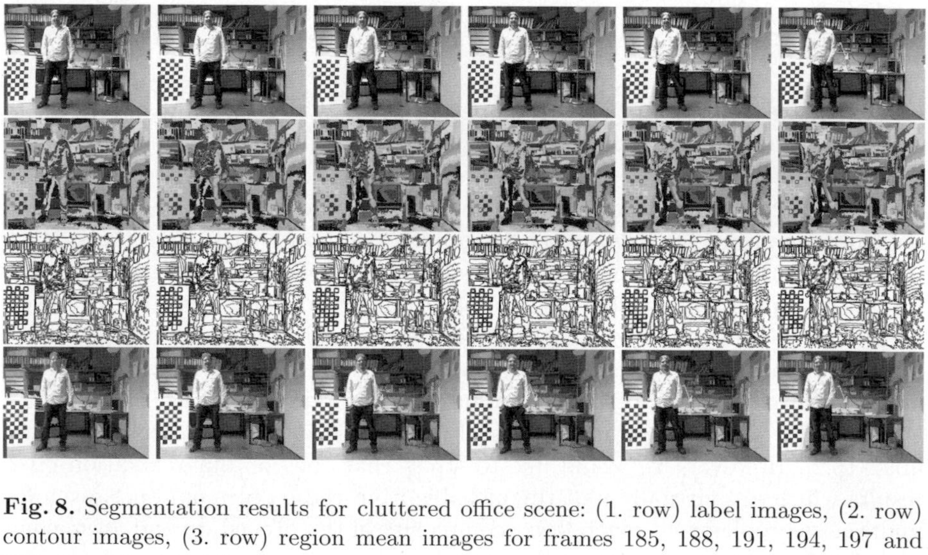

Fig. 8. Segmentation results for cluttered office scene: (1. row) label images, (2. row) contour images, (3. row) region mean images for frames 185, 188, 191, 194, 197 and 200 where the label images are propagated. Best viewed in color and upscaled.

7 Conclusions

We have demonstrated the performance of the combination of a region-based stochastic model with the 'contour relaxation' optimization which very efficiently yields a 'superpixel' segmentation. Even though we are fully aware that no guarantees concerning achieving a globally optimum solution can be given, the various application examples hopefully conveyed the very 'benign' performance and the versatile applicability of the scheme. The generalization of the approach to texture, or using depth and/or motion is obviously a promising next goal.

References

1. Achanta, R., Shaji, A., Smith, K., Lucchi, A., Fua, P., Suesstrunk, S.: SLIC Superpixels. Tech. Rep. Nr. 149300, EPFL, Lausanne (CH) (June 2010)
2. Boykov, Y., Veksler, O., Zabih, R.: Fast approximate energy minimization via graph cuts. IEEE Trans. PAMI 23(11), 1222–1239 (2002)
3. Brox, T., Cremers, D.: On local region models and a statistical interpretation of the piecewise smooth Mumford-Shah functional. IJCV 84(2), 184–193 (2009)
4. Chellappa, R., Chatterjee, S.: Classification of textures using Gaussian Markov random fields. IEEE Trans. ASSP 33(4), 959–963 (1985)
5. Cremers, D., Rousson, M., Deriche, R.: A review of statistical approaches to level set segmentation: integrating color, texture, motion and shape. International Journal of Computer Vision 72(2), 195–215 (2007)
6. Derin, H., Cole, W.: Segmentation of textured images using Gibbs random fields. Computer Vision, Graphics, and Image Processing, pp. 72–98 (1986)
7. Felzenszwalb, P., Huttenlocher, D.: Efficient graph-based image segmentation. IJCV 59(2), 167–181 (2004)
8. http://vision.middlebury.edu:
9. Levinshtein, A., Stere, A., Kutulakos, K., Fleet, D., Dickinson, S., Siddiqi, K.: Turbopixels: Fast superpixels using geometric flows. PAMI 31(12), 2290–2297 (2009)
10. Martin, D., Fowlkes, C., Tal, D., Malik, J.: A database of human segmented natural images and its application to evaluating segmentation algorithms and measuring ecological statistics. In: Proc. ICCV 2001, vol. 2, pp. 416–423 (2001)
11. Mester, R., Franke, U.: Statistical model based image segmentation using region growing, contour relaxation and classification. In: Proc. SPIE Visual Communications and Image Processing, Cambridge, MA, pp. 616–624 (1988)
12. Ren, X.R., Malik, J.: Learning a classification model for segmentation. In: Proc. ICCV, vol. 1, pp. 10–17. IEEE Computer Society Press, Los Alamitos (2003)
13. Rother, C.: Tutorial on map inference in discrete models. In: ICCV (2009)
14. Sclove, S.L.: Application of the conditional population-mixture model to image segmentation. IEEE Trans. PAMI 5, 428–433 (1983)
15. Therrien, C.W.: An estimation-theoretic approach to terrain image segmentation. Computer Vision, Graphics, and Image Processing 22(3), 313–326 (1983)
16. Unnikrishnan, R., Pantofaru, C., Hebert, M.: Toward objective evaluation of image segmentation algorithms. IEEE Trans. PAMI, 929–944 (2007)
17. Veksler, O., Boykov, Y., Mehrani, P.: Superpixels and supervoxels in an energy optimization framework. In: Daniilidis, K., Maragos, P., Paragios, N. (eds.) ECCV 2010. LNCS, vol. 6315, pp. 211–224. Springer, Heidelberg (2010)

Color Persistent Anisotropic Diffusion of Images

Freddie Åström, Michael Felsberg, and Reiner Lenz

Linköping University, SE-581 83 Linköping, Sweden
{freddie.astrom,michael.felsberg}@itn.liu.se, reiner.lenz@itn.liu.se

Abstract. Techniques from the theory of partial differential equations are often used to design filter methods that are locally adapted to the image structure. These techniques are usually used in the investigation of gray-value images. The extension to color images is non-trivial, where the choice of an appropriate color space is crucial. The RGB color space is often used although it is known that the space of human color perception is best described in terms of non-euclidean geometry, which is fundamentally different from the structure of the RGB space. Instead of the standard RGB space, we use a simple color transformation based on the theory of finite groups. It is shown that this transformation reduces the color artifacts originating from the diffusion processes on RGB images. The developed algorithm is evaluated on a set of real-world images, and it is shown that our approach exhibits fewer color artifacts compared to state-of-the-art techniques. Also, our approach preserves details in the image for a larger number of iterations.

Keywords: non-linear diffusion, color image processing, perceptual image quality.

1 Introduction

In this paper we consider the problem of anisotropic diffusion of color images. By decorrelating the RGB color space we derive an improved color diffusion scheme which exhibits fewer color artifacts compared to state-of-the-art techniques. Moreover, using different edge-stopping functions for each decorrelated channel yields a diffusion tensor that does not effect structures in other color channels.

Diffusion filtering is based on partial differential equations (PDEs). In image enhancement applications a diffusion scheme is called anisotropic if the filter-process is adapted according to the image structure. On the other hand, if the diffusion scheme does not take into account the underlying structure, it is called isotropic diffusion. Perona and Malik [8] were first to propose a PDE-based anisotropic diffusion scheme

$$\partial_t u = \mathrm{div}(g(|\nabla u|^2)\nabla u) \ , \tag{1}$$

with diffusivity function $g(|\nabla u|) = (1 + (|\nabla u|/K)^2)^{-1}$ where K is a contrast parameter and ∇u is the image gradient. In the terminology of Weickert [17], the

A. Heyden and F. Kahl (Eds.): SCIA 2011, LNCS 6688, pp. 262–272, 2011.

Perona-Malik diffusivity is non-linear scalar diffusion and anisotropic diffusion denotes methods that use a diffusion tensor

$$D = \sum_i g(\lambda_i)\mathbf{e}_i\mathbf{e}_i^T \ , \tag{2}$$

where λ_i are the eigenvalues and $\mathbf{e}_i$ the eigenvectors of the structure tensor [3]

$$T = \int w \begin{pmatrix} \partial u_x \partial u_x & \partial u_x \partial u_y \\ \partial u_y \partial u_x & \partial u_y \partial u_y \end{pmatrix} dxdy \ . \tag{3}$$

w is typically a Gaussian weight function. The diffusion equation now takes the form

$$\partial_t u = \mathrm{div}(D\nabla u) \ . \tag{4}$$

If the eigenvalues of the structure tensor is $\lambda_i = \lambda_{i+1}, \forall i$ the anisotropic diffusion equation reduces to isotropic (scalar) diffusion. The presented diffusion process is applicable for scalar (gray-valued) images [1, 10, 12].

1.1 Related Work

Several PDE based approaches to suppress noise in color images [2, 5, 15, 9, 18, 14, 13] have been suggested in the past. Despite the progress in the field of color PDE filtering, the most frequently occurring drawback of the existing methods is the generation of color artifacts near edges. This problem will be referred to as a lack of color persistency. The reason for this type of artifact is that an edge (or noise) in one channel may not be present in the same location in another channel.

A relatively straightforward extension from gray image diffusion to color image diffusion is to use the same diffusion tensor for each of the color channels. This standard approach is described by Weickert [18] where the diffusion tensor is computed from the weighted average sum of the structure tensors for each RGB channel. An alternative approach was taken by Tang et al. [14] who map the RGB color vector space to two separate components, the direction (chromaticity) and the magnitude (brightness). Thereafter, they perform the diffusion process separately on these two channels. An important point made in their work is filtering the chromaticity channel can introduce color artifacts. Sochen et. al [13], have perhaps taken the most general approach to deriving the diffusion process. They view a two-dimensional (2D) image as a surface in 3D space and a color image as 2D surfaces in a 5D space. According to these mappings they define a metric and derive what they call the Beltrami flow.

1.2 Main Contribution

In this work we propose a color diffusion method based on a PCA-like technique to decorrelate the RGB color space, derived by Lenz and Carmona [7]. Furthermore, we compare our diffusion approach with the standard approach described in [18] on real-world natural images and standard test images. Also, the proposed diffusion scheme is compared to the color space derived from decorrelating the RGB channels using standard principal component analysis and the Beltrami flow [13]. The experiments show that our approach is in general more color persistent in comparison with these state-of-the-art techniques.

2 Methods

2.1 Standard Approach to Color Image Diffusion

What we call the standard approach is to sum the structure tensors of the RGB channels [18]

$$T = \sum_i w_i T_i = \sum_i w_i \sum_j \lambda_{ij} \mathbf{e}_{ij} \mathbf{e}_{ij}^T \ , \tag{5}$$

where i is the indices of the color channels and $\sum_i w_i = 1$ is a weight. The diffusion function used in this work to compute the diffusion tensor is $g(\lambda) = \exp(-\lambda/K)$ [4].

2.2 Color Model

The RGB color space channels are correlated [11]. However, the noise that may exist in an image may not be correlated across channels. This can introduce color artifacts if the RGB space is not decorrelated prior to applying the diffusion filtering process. In an attempt to decorrelate the R,G and B channels, Lenz and Carmona [7] introduced the transformation matrix

$$P = \frac{1}{\sqrt{3}} \begin{pmatrix} 1 & 1 & 1 \\ \sqrt{2} & \sqrt{2}\cos(2\pi/3) & \sqrt{2}\cos(4\pi/3) \\ 0 & \sqrt{2}\sin(2\pi/3) & \sqrt{2}\sin(4\pi/3) \end{pmatrix} \ . \tag{6}$$

This transformation is derived from the assumption that permutations of the three RGB channels are on average equally probable. Using tools from the representation theory of the permutation group S(3) it can be shown that the result is a decorrelation of the original RGB variables into a one-dimensional intensity, I, and a two-dimensional color-opponent component. In cases where the assumption of equally probable permutations is satisfied it can be shown that the rows of this matrix are the eigenvectors of the correlation matrix computed from the RGB vectors and that the color-opponent components belong to a two-dimensional eigenspace belonging to the same eigenvalue.

2.3 New Approach to Color Image Diffusion

In this work we propose a new approach to color image diffusion, with the aim to reduce color artifacts. The proposition is to first transform the RGB color space onto the irreducible representation (6) and to compute the diffusion tensors D_1, D_2 and D_3, one for each component in the transformed color space

$$D = \begin{pmatrix} D_1 & 0 & 0 \\ 0 & D_2 & 0 \\ 0 & 0 & D_3 \end{pmatrix} . \tag{7}$$

$D_i = \sum_j g_i(\lambda_{ij})\mathbf{e}_{ij}\mathbf{e}_{ij}^T$ allows for different diffusivity functions $g_i(\cdot)$ to be used in different channels. However, in order to enable a comparative evaluation of the two filtering techniques, the diffusion function described in section 2.1 will be used to compute all diffusion tensors, although with different contrast factors K.

3 Experiments

3.1 Data Set

To evaluate the two approaches to color diffusion, the algorithms are applied to real-world RGB color images obtained from a data set of road signs. The test images have been used with the permission of the authors of [6]. The images were taken in an urban environment. The camera was mounted in the cabin of a car behind the windscreen. Appropriate regions were cropped from the full images (1280×960 pixels) which are of JPEG format. Hence, color artifacts introduced by the JPEG-compression are already present in the images. Regions of interest are edges with different color tone and intensity. Images `image00756.jpg` and `image00312.jpg` from the data set were used to extract regions S1 and S2 of size 512×512 pixels seen in Fig. 3 and Fig. 4. Regions of size 56×56 pixels were zoomed in S1 and S2 seen in the same figures. Standard test images used are the Mandrill and Lena (512×512 pixels) seen in Fig. 1 and Fig. 2. Regions of interest of size 56×56 pixels were extracted from both images, in order to illustrate color artifacts.

3.2 Tested Methods

Four diffusion filtering methods are compared with respect to color persistency. The first method is the standard approach where the structure tensor is summed and weighted equally. The second, proposed approach, is based on decorrelating the standard RGB color space using (6) prior to computing the structure tensors. The diffusion processes were implemented using a finite-difference approximation and yield the iterative update scheme

$$u_{t+1} = u_t + \tau(\nabla D \nabla u_t + D\nabla^2 u_t) \ , \tag{8}$$

where the index t is current iteration. τ is a step parameter and should not be selected too large, as the diffusion process will then violate the scale-space properties stated in [17], for a stable diffusion process as $t \to \infty$. The stopping time

t_{MAX} was determined such that all algorithms terminated when a negative slope of their error curve was observed. The negative exponential diffusion function described in section 2.1 was used for all components in all diffusion schemes. For the experiments, the contrast parameter K was set to 10^{-3} in the standard approach and in the intensity channel I of the proposed approach. For the two color balance channels in the new approach, K was set to 10^{-1}. The third method used is decorrelation of the RGB color space using standard principal component analysis (PCA). Eigenvectors are computed from the average of all test images to enable a fair comparison between the proposed method and the PCA decomposition. In this case the contrast parameter was set to 10^{-3}. The final and fourth method, is the state-of-the-art Beltrami flow, which for images Baboon, S1 and S2 used a contrast parameter of 10^{-3} and for the Lena image we used 10^{-2}. All parameter values were set empirically.

The step length was set as follows, in the Baboon image all implementations used steplength 10^{-1} except for the Beltrami flow which used 10^{-3}. For the Lena image step length was set to 10^{-1} for all implementations. In images S1 and S2 all algorithms were set to use a step length of 1/5 except the Beltrami flow, which used a steplength of 10^{-3}.

3.3 Performance Evaluation

Since color artifacts are primarily introduced around edges, these regions are zoomed in order to visually get an understanding of the color distortion. Quantitative measurements are often given by the peak-signal-to-noise ratio (PSNR) in the literature. However, the structural similarity index (SSIM) has been shown to be a more accurate measurement when determining image similarities [16]. Parameters of the index were set to the default values as recommended by the author [16]. The source code to compute the MSSIM is available online (`http://www.ece.uwaterloo.ca/~z70wang/research/ssim/`). To apply the SSIM index to the RGB color space, we have chosen to apply the SSIM measure to each individual color component and average the result. This approach was chosen since there is, to be best of our knowledge, no previously published work on the effect of applying the SSIM measurement to individual color components in the RGB color space.

4 Results

The four diffusion filtering approaches were tested and compared as described in section 3.2. Figures are organized as follows: from left to right and up to down: original image and zoomed region, noisy image, output after maximum number of iterations of our approach, sum of tensors, PCA and finally the Beltrami flow. Each of the algorithms has a corresponding zoomed region to their right of the corresponding full image. First a perceptual analysis based on the visual impression of the filtering outputs will be done, thereafter an quantitative analysis is made based on the SSIM index. Figures are best viewed in color.

Gaussian noise of zero mean and 0.01 standard-deviation has been applied to the Mandrill and Lena images seen in Fig. 1 and Fig. 2. A subjective assessment of the diffusion process is that as the number of iterations increase, high-frequency components in the Mandrill image become more blurred in the standard approach. Visual inspection reveal that the structure in the Mandrill's zoomed region is preserved longer before becoming blurred in our method compared to the standard approach. The result of the PCA approach is competitive with our proposed color space, but visual inspection of the zoomed regions in Fig. 1 show that color artifacts have been introduced in the high-frequency regions. The Beltrami flow cannot handle the noise level and does introduce color artifacts. A similar result is seen in Fig. 2, but after 200 iterations it is recognized that there is no perceptual difference between our proposed approach and diffusion in the decorrelated PCA color space. However, the standard approach experience excessive blurring not seen in any other method.

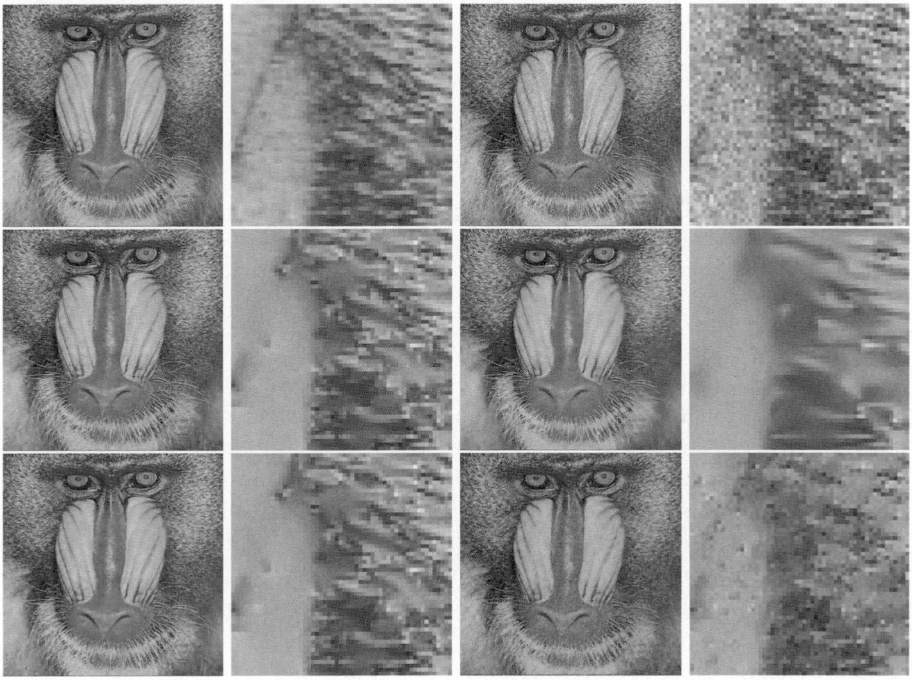

Fig. 1. Mandrill with zero mean and $\sigma = 0.01$ Gaussian noise. Results are shown after 100 iterations. See text for details.

Image S1 is shown in Fig. 3, interesting parts of the zoomed region is the gable of the building. Total number of iterations for this image was set to 200. In the standard approach and the Beltrami flow the white gable is severely blurred and color artifacts has been introduced around the frame of the window. Diffusion in our proposed color space preserves the gable and no color artifact is introduced

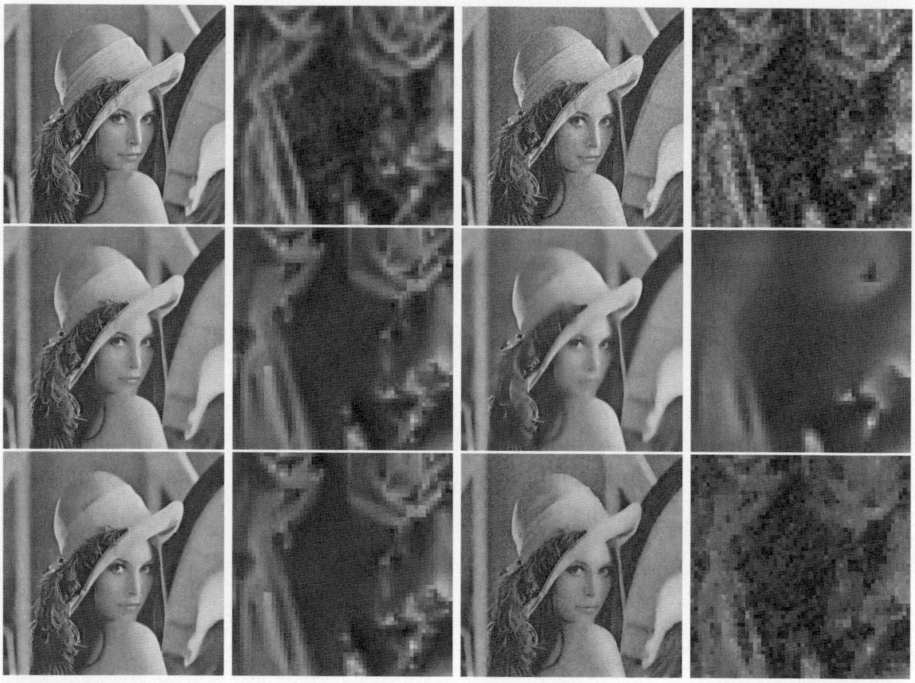

Fig. 2. Lena with zero mean and $\sigma = 0.01$ Gaussian noise. Results are shown after 200 iterations. See text for details.

around the frame of the window as seen in the PCA color space. Image S2 is run for 100 iterations. It is seen in this test image that our method does perform slightly worse than the PCA on the edge of the road sign, but considering the trunk of the branch in the zoomed image a color artifact was introduced in the PCA not seen in our approach. Furthermore, the standard filtering and the Beltrami flow is considerably worse than the other two diffusion schemes.

A quantitative measurement of the two diffusion approaches was made based on the SSIM index. Performance of the tested images can be seen in Fig. 5. A higher MSSIM value (maximum value is 1) indicate that the structure of the filtered image is more similar to the noise free image. Comparing the proposed and other methods in Fig. 5, it can be seen that the overall result for all the images are significantly better for the proposed filtering method.

An observation with regards to the Mandrill error graph is that for iterations 100 the PCA performs better than our proposed method. However, in Fig. 1 it is visible that, our approach produces perceptually more similar results to the ground truth compared to the PCA approach. Furthermore, considering the slope of the error curves, it is obvious that the standard approach and the Beltrami flow will continue to degrade the image quality to a larger extend than our method.

Fig. 3. S1 with zero mean and $\sigma = 0.01$ Gaussian noise. Results are shown after 200 iterations. See text for details.

Fig. 4. S2 with zero mean and $\sigma = 0.01$ Gaussian noise. Results are shown after 100 iterations. See text for details.

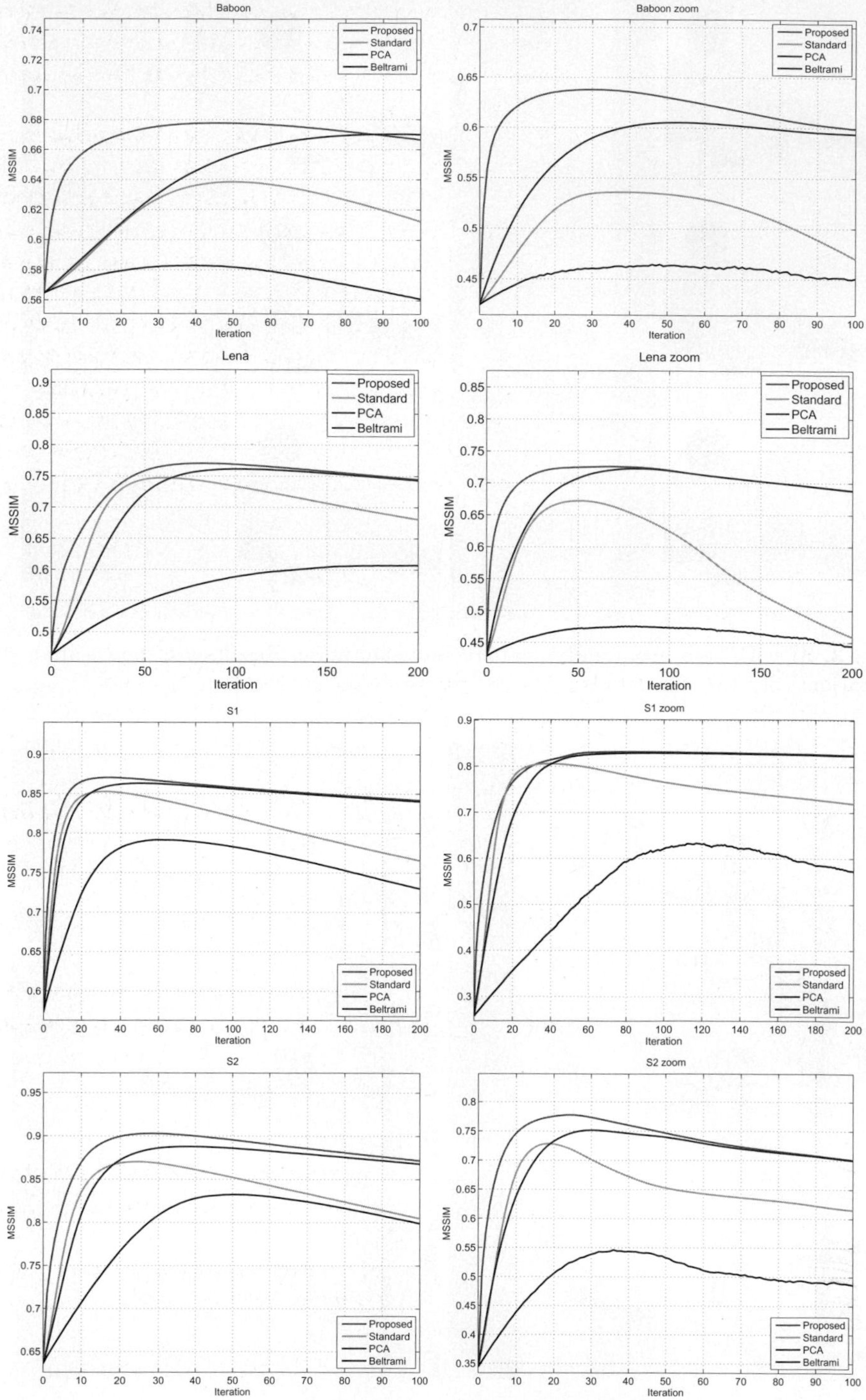

Fig. 5. MSSIM-values for proposed and implemented diffusion filtering methods

5 Conclusion

In this work a novel color image diffusion method is introduced, where the standard euclidean RGB color space is transformed to a non-euclidean representation. The basis of the new color space represents the color vector intensity and color balance. It has been shown that non-linear diffusion in the proposed color space introduces fewer color artifacts compared to standard state-of-the-art diffusion techniques. The findings are supported quantitatively by a higher structural similarity index.

Acknowledgement

This research has received funding from the The Swedish Research Council through a grant for the project *Non-linear adaptive color image processing*, from the EC's 7th Framework Programme (FP7/2007-2013), grant agreement 247947 (GARNICS), and by ELLIIT, the Strategic Area for ICT research, funded by the Swedish Government.

References

[1] Black, M.J., Sapiro, G., Marimont, D.H., Heeger, D.: Robust anisotropic diffusion. IEEE Transactions on Image Processing 7(3), 421–432 (1998)

[2] Chambolle, A.: Partial differential equations and image processing. In: Proceedings of the IEEE International Conference Image Processing, ICIP 1994, vol. 1, pp. 16–20 (November 1994)

[3] Felsberg, M.: On the relation between anisotropic diffusion and iterated adaptive filtering. In: Rigoll, G. (ed.) DAGM 2008. LNCS, vol. 5096, pp. 436–445. Springer, Heidelberg (2008)

[4] elation-Driven Diffusion Filtering. IEEE Transactions on Image Processing (2011), doi:10.1109/TIP.2011.2107330

[5] Kimmel, R., Malladi, R., Sochen, N.: Images as embedded maps and minimal surfaces: Movies, color, texture, and volumetric medical images. International Journal of Computer Vision 39, 111–129 (2000)

[6] Larsson, F., Felsberg, M., Forssen, P.E.: Patch contour matching by correlating fourier descriptors. In: Digital Image Computing: Techniques and Applications, DICTA 2009, pp. 40–46 (December 2009)

[7] Lenz, R., Carmona, P.L.: Hierarchical s(3)-coding of rgb histograms. In: Selected Papers from VISAPP 2009, vol. 68, pp. 188–200. Springer, Heidelberg (2010)

[8] Perona, P., Malik, J.: Scale-space and edge detection using anisotropic diffusion. IEEE Transactions on Pattern Analysis and Machine Intelligence 12, 629–639 (1990)

[9] Renner, A.I.: Anisotropic Diffusion in Riemannian Colour Space. Ph.D. thesis, Ruprecht-Kars-Universitt, Heidelberg (2003)

[10] Scharr, H., Black, M.J., Haussecker, H.W.: Image statistics and anisotropic diffusion. In: Proceedings of the Ninth IEEE International Conference on Computer Vision, pp. 840–847 (October 2003)

[11] Sharma, G.: Digital Color Imaging Handbook. CRC Press, Inc., Boca Raton (2002)
[12] Sochen, N., Kimmel, R., Bruckstein, A.: Diffusions and confusions in signal and image processing. Journal of Mathematical Imaging and Vision 14, 195–209 (2001)
[13] Sochen, N., Kimmel, R., Malladi, R.: A general framework for low level vision. IEEE Transactions on Image Processing 7(3), 310–318 (1998)
[14] Tang, B., Sapiro, G., Caselles, V.: Color image enhancement via chromaticity diffusion. IEEE Transactions on Image Processing 10, 701–707 (2002)
[15] Tschumperle, D., Deriche, R.: Diffusion pdes on vector-valued images. IEEE Signal Processing Magazine 19(5), 16–25 (2002)
[16] Wang, Z., Bovik, A., Sheikh, H., Simoncelli, E.: Image quality assessment: from error visibility to structural similarity. IEEE Transactions on Image Processing 13(4), 600–612 (2004)
[17] Weickert, J.: Anisotropic diffusion in image processing (1996)
[18] Weickert, J.: Coherence-enhancing diffusion of colour images. Image and Vision Computing 17(3-4), 201–212 (1999)

Analysis of Seed Sorting Process by Estimation of Seed Motion Trajectories

Ole Thomsen Buus[1], Johannes Ravn Jørgensen[1], and Jens Michael Carstensen[2]

[1] Aarhus University, Faculty of Agricultural Sciences, Department of Genetics and Biotechnology, 4200 Slagelse, Denmark
{Ole.Buus,Johannes.Jorgensen}@agrsci.dk
[2] Informatics and Mathematical Modelling, Technical University of Denmark, Building 321, DK-2800 Lyngby, Denmark
jmc@imm.dtu.dk

Abstract. Seed sorting is a mechanical process in which the goal is to achieve a high level of purity and quality in the final product. Prediction and control of such processes are generally considered very difficult. One possible solution is a systems identification approach in which the seeds and their movement are directly observed and data about important process parameters extracted. Image analysis was used to extract such data from the internal sorting process in one particular seed sorting device - the so-called "indented cylinder". Twenty high speed image sequences were recorded of the indented cylinder in action, sorting a batch of barley with both whole and broken kernels. The motion trajectories and angle of escape for each seed in each frame were estimated. Motion trajectories and frequency distributions for the angle of escape are shown for different velocities and pocket sizes. A possible linear relationship is shown to exist between velocity and the angle. The temporal stability of certain parameters in the sorting process were also analysed and is shown to be quite stable for lower velocities.

Keywords: Seed sorting, indented cylinder, system identification, motion trajectories, image analysis.

1 Introduction

When seeds are harvested from fields they contain a number of larger impurities (for example stones, leaves, branches, insects) that need to be removed. When these impurities have been removed using various preprocessing machinery all that remains are particles of generally the same size. If necessary this relatively clean seed material can now be processed further. This later step is known as *seed sorting* and is the industrial application that we have focused on in this work. In seed sorting the task is to further sort or *divide* the preprocessed seed material into at least two individual sets of particles.

Different types of seed sorting machines are used in the industry today. By physically manipulating the seed material in a way that takes advantage of various individual physical distinguishing characteristics of the seeds (usually one

A. Heyden and F. Kahl (Eds.): SCIA 2011, LNCS 6688, pp. 273–284, 2011.

for each type of machine) these machines are able to sort the material. Typical examples of such characteristics are (1) *mass* (density), (2) surface *texture* (friction with surfaces), (3) *length*, (4) general *size*, and (5) *shape* (for example round, prolonged, egg-shaped, flat).

The *prediction* and *control* of the process in these machines is generally considered very difficult. This is primarily due to the biological variations in the physical characteristics of the individual seeds. This is where the application of image analysis becomes relevant. There is a need for a systems identification approach wherein (parts of) the mechanical particle manipulation process is directly observed and useful information about important process parameters extracted. Image analysis is a natural tool for this.

In this paper we show results from experiments wherein image analysis was used to extract information from the internal process in the *indented cylinder* (laboratory scale). The indented cylinder is a *length* sorter that divides the incoming seed material into two subsets: (1) *long* and (2) *short* seeds. This is necessary for some seed species for which sorting based on other characteristics is not possible. The machine consists of a rotating cylinder lying down. The seed material is fed from one side. The inner surface of this cylinder is equipped with small pockets (indented into the metal). Due to the rotation of the cylinder these pockets carry the seeds up to a certain angle. This angle is dependent on the individual length of the seeds. In principle: Shorter seeds will be carried further than longer seeds. A catch-pan mounted at the centre of the cylinder will catch the shorter seeds while the longer seeds fall down to the bottom of the cylinder again. Due to a small tilt of the cylinder itself the longer seed material advances to the other side due to gravity. The shorter material is advanced using vibration of the catch-pan. Most of these basic principles are also depicted graphically in Figure 1(a).

Berlage et al. [2,3,4] are some of the earliest examples on the use of image analysis to analyse and improve seed sorting using prototypical machines (not indented cylinders). Dell'Aquila [7] is an example of a recent review on the subject of automated inspection of seed sorting for quality testing. On the modelling aspect again early work by Berlage et al. [1] and Churchill et al. [6] are mentionable. The analysis, modeling and simulation of the flow of particles in rotating cylinders has been done to great extent. But mostly for use in chemical, pharmaceutical, and matallurgical industries. Positron emission particle tracking (PEPT) [10,11] and particle image velocimetry (PIV) [5] are examples of specialised technologies which have been applied for various purposes. Sandidi et al. [12] used a CCD camera for analysing the flow in a rotating drum used for coating tablets. Lastly we mention the summarised work in Grochowich [8] – one of the earliest full analyses of various types of seed sorting machines and their inherent complexity.

In this work we have specifically focused on deducing the *angle of escape* θ (with horizontal) of the individual seeds from recordings of the indented cylinder during an actual sorting process. The distribution of this important process

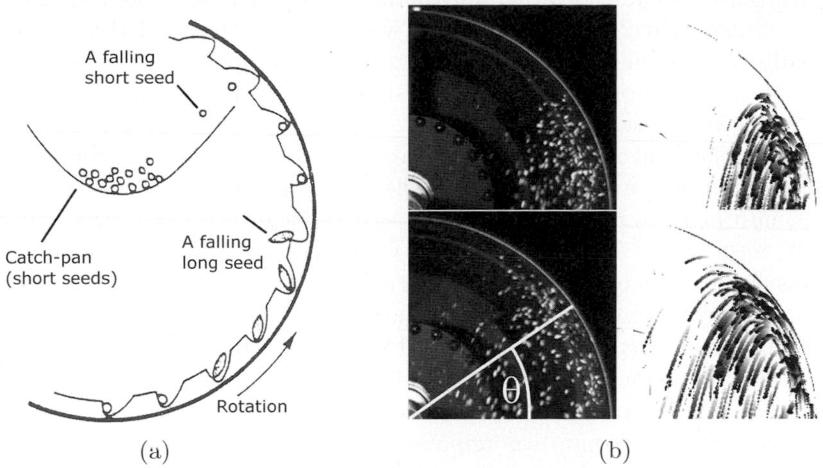

Fig. 1. A graphic and four examples of frames from the imaging data. Figure 1(a): The basic principles of the sorting process in the indented cylinder (modified from [9]). Figure 1(b): Four examples on frames acquired in the experiments. The two rows each show a situation from two different angular velocities of the cylinder (top: 26 rpm [revolutions per minute], bottom: 34 rpm). To the left we see the original version and to the right we see examples on accumulated seed segmentations (accumulated of over 10 frames starting from the one on the left). The *angle of escape* θ is shown graphically in the lower left original version.

parameter over time says something about the machines current ability to process and sort the material given to it.

We placed a colour CCD camera in front of the active cylinder (it was in motion with material in it) with the catch-pan removed. Each image frame (taken at 260 frames/sec) was then segmented and the (approximate) location of each seed (or particle) in the image plane was extracted. Using a combination of these locations and the laws of motion (no drag included) we were able to deduce the most likely parabolic escape trajectories and thus also an estimate for the angle of escape θ for each particle. Figure 1(b) shows two examples of the images recorded for two different rotational speeds of the cylinder.

Section 2 describes in more detail the experiments, seed material (barley), and the acquired data (20 image sequences). Section 3 explains the basic methods used for extracting the seed locations and for estimating the angle of escape θ. Section 4 presents the results and Section 5 concludes.

2 Materials and Data

2.1 Experimental Setup

We used a laboratory-sized indented cylinder (Westrup L-AT *LAT-0801*) that supports cylinders with a radius of 200 mm and a depth of 500 mm. The cylinder had a (fixed) inclination with horizontal of 0.7°. A CCD colour camera (Point Grey Grasshopper *GRAS-03K2C-C*) was placed in front of the cylinder with the direction of sight aligned with the plane containing the cylinder's axis of rotation. The end of the cylinder closest to the camera was slightly lower due to the small inclination angle.

It was placed at a distance such that the width of the image corresponded to the apparent width of the cylinder. The monofocal lens used had a focal length of 25 mm and a horizontal and (deduced) vertical angle of view of 10.97° and 8.24°, respectively. The camera was also rotated 180° to use sub-sampling of the sensor lines and achieve a higher framerate. Using these parameters, the correct camera-to-cylinder distance was estimated to be 2.7 m.

Illumination was provided by a 150 W halogen modelling light (*SOLO 1600 B*) placed between camera and cylinder. The angle of light was such that all the seed material inside the cylinder received the same amount of illumination. Note that the catch-pan was removed to give room for visual inspection with the camera.

2.2 The Seed Material

The seed material used was barley (*Hordeum vulgare L.*). The indented cylinder is particularly suitable for filtering *broken* (usually half) non-useful barley kernels from *whole* useful barley kernels.

The barley used was filtered manually using the indented cylinder. This allowed us to create a modelled seed batch with a known per particle distribution of whole and broken kernels. The modelled batch consisted of 50 % whole and 50 % broken barley kernels. The mixed batch had a total mass of 2 kg which was more than enough for the experiments.

2.3 Experiments and Acquired Data

The cylinder was fed with the modelled seed batch and configured to run with different settings of two important system variables. These were: (1) the cylinder rotational speed and (2) the diameter of the pockets in the cylinder. We recorded the sorting process of the cylinder for *ten* different rotational speeds and for *two* different pocket diameters. The speed was sampled in the range from 26 rpm (*revolutions per minute*) to 49 rpm with an average step of 2.56 rpm (corresponding to angular frequencies of 2.73 rad/s to 5.14 rad/s with an average step of 0.27 rad/s). We used two different cylinders with pocket diameters of 6.0 mm and 7.0 mm.

A total of $2 \times 10 = 20$ image sequences were recorded at approximately 260 frames/sec for a total of ten seconds. After recording all sequences were temporarily synchronized such that the position of the cylinder circumference was the same in the first frame. This resulted in *five* seconds (1300 frames) of useful data in all 20 sequences (26000 frames in total). Each frame is of active dimensions 240×240 pixels and contains the *upper right quadrant* of the imaged cylinder circumference.

Let $K = 1300$ be the number of frames in each sequence, $V = 10$ the number of velocity steps, and $D = 2$ the number of pocket diameters. One can then define integer indexes $k = 1, \ldots, K$, $v = 1, \ldots, V$, and $d = 1, \ldots, D$ (where $d = 1$ and $d = 2$ corresponds to pocket diameter 6.0 mm and 7.0 mm, respectively). Any frame in any of the 20 sequences can now be described as a matrix $\mathbf{F}^{(k)}_{(v,d)} \in \mathbb{R}^{N \times N}$, where $N = 240$. Each sequence has also been given a mathematical name: $\mathcal{S}_{(v,d)} \in \mathbb{R}^{N \times N \times K}$. Finally, the following shorthand notations are defined: $\mathbf{F}^{(k)}$ is the k'th frame in any sequence $\mathcal{S}_{(v,d)}$ and $\mathbf{F}$ is any frame in any sequence. One final sequence exists: $\mathcal{B}$. This is a background sequence with no seeds in the scene – just the empty cylinder ($d = 2$) rotating at velocity step $v = 5$.

3 Methods

3.1 Estimation of Seed Locations

Figure 2 shows the 11 image processing steps used to extract the locations of the seeds in each frame $\mathbf{F}^{(k)}_{(v,d)}$. The average $\mathbf{B}_{ref}$ of sequence $\mathcal{B}$ is the static background frame mentioned in step 5. This is used for background subtraction to acquire a global segmentation and to remove certain problematic areas of the image. The resulting absolute difference map was scaled to range $[0, 1]$ and

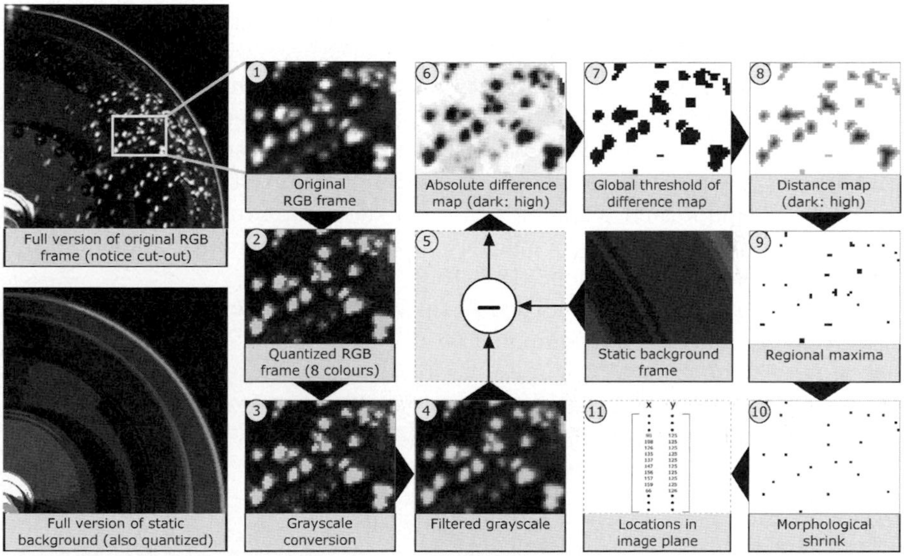

Fig. 2. The 11 image processing steps used to extract the seed locations (in the image plane). In the top-left part an example of a full frame is seen (cylinder velocity is 36 rpm [revolutions per minute]). Step 10 mentions the process of "morphological erosion". It is a continued erosion that shrinks objects without holes to single points (holes in objects are removed prior to the operation).

a global threshold (step 7) of 0.4 was used (everything above that level was considered part of foreground/seed). Various morphological tools are then used to produce binary map containing approximate seed locations in the image plane. Finally these locations in the image plane are transformed to a 2-dimensional *world space* in $\mathbb{R}^2$ by a linear interpolation.

3.2 Estimating the Angle of Escape θ

We have estimated the angle of escape θ and calculated the corresponding parabolic trajectory for all twenty configurations of the indented cylinder. Figure 3 show six such "trajectory plots" for rotational speeds v = 1, 2, 5, 6, 9, and 10; and for both pocket sizes d = 1 and 2. Note the visible difference in trajectories due to change in speed. The points shown are the ones extracted from the recorded frames using the methods described above.

The estimation of θ was done for all points extracted from all frames $\mathbf{F}$ using the processing steps just described (one estimate per point). To minimize data representation complexity, the seed locations from every 10 frames were combined into a single set of points. That is, for any sequence $\mathcal{S}_{(v,d)}$ we generate $L = K/10 = 1300/10 = 130$ *accumulated* point sets $A^{(l)}$ containing $I^{(l)}$ points $(x_i, y_i) \in \mathbb{R}^2$. These accumulated point sets are then analysed for $l = 1, \ldots, L$ resulting in a solution set $\Theta^{(l)}$ containing $I^{(l)}$ scalars $\theta_i \in \mathbb{R}$.

The specific number of points $I^{(l)}_{(v,d)}$ available in each $A^{(l)}_{(v,d)}$ varies only slightly over l but expectedly varies more over index v and d. Especially for d since the 1 mm difference in pocket diameter has the effect that different amounts of seeds are caught by the pockets.

During sorting, a seed or particle moves with the cylinder up to a certain angle θ. This angle is dependent on the radius r and current angular frequency ω of the indented cylinder. We model the movement of each such particle as a point (x_i, y_i) moving in $\mathbb{R}^2$ in its own local time domain, starting at time $t_i = 0$ when a force equilibrium (explained in great detail in Grochowich [8, Chp. 7]) accelerates the particle off the cylinder wall and (in our model, influenced now only by gravity) into a parabolic trajectory.

At that time the particle modelled as the point (x_i, y_i) will have the following *initial* velocity and position components:

$$
\begin{aligned}
\dot{x}_0(\theta, \omega, r) &= -r\omega \sin\theta \\
\dot{y}_0(\theta, \omega, r) &= r\omega \cos\theta \\
x_0(\theta, r) &= r\cos\theta \\
y_0(\theta, r) &= r\sin\theta \ .
\end{aligned}
\tag{1}
$$

The parabolic time-dependent motion of a single particle (x_i, y_i) is described by components:

$$x_i(t, \theta, \omega, r) = \dot{x}_0(\theta, \omega, r)t_i + x_0(\theta, r) \tag{2a}$$

$$y_i(t, \theta, \omega, r) = -(g/2){t_i}^2 + \dot{y}_0(\theta, \omega, r)t_i + y_0(\theta, r) \ , \tag{2b}$$

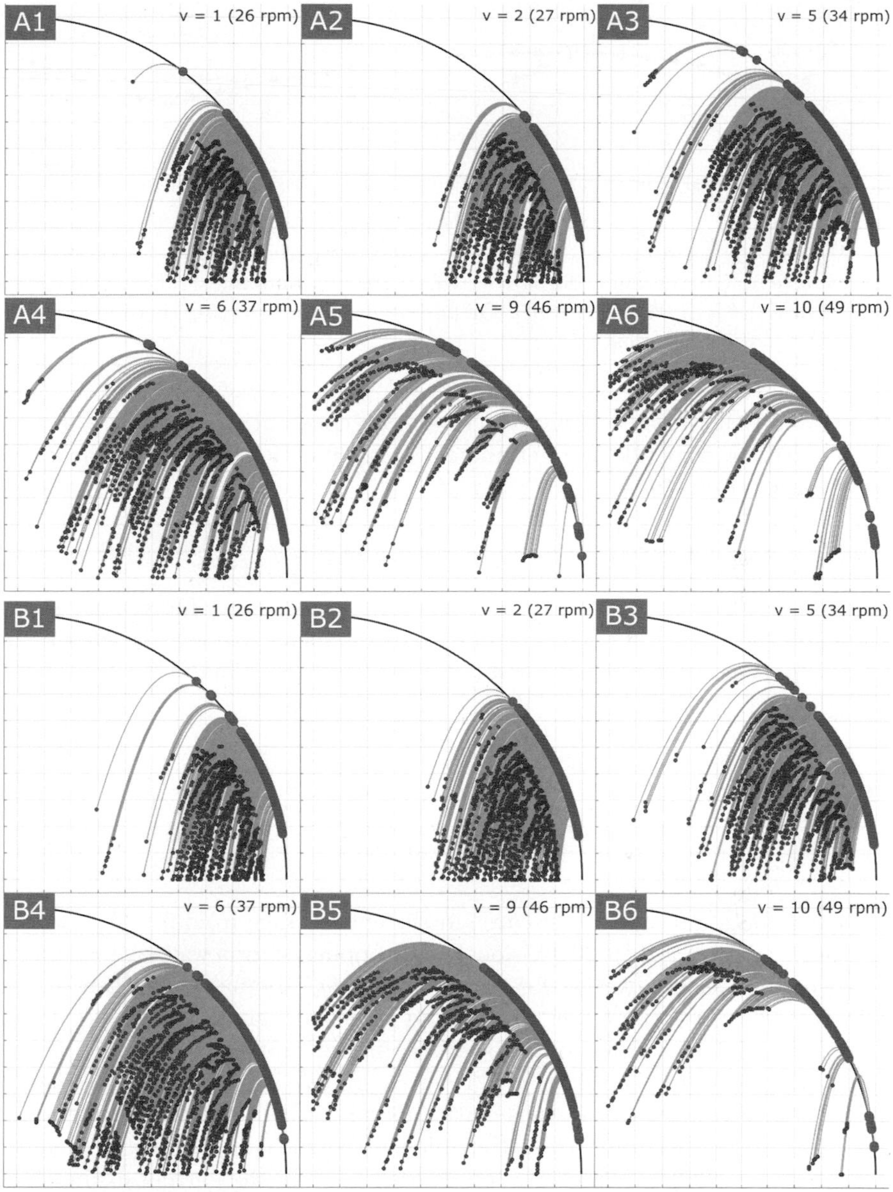

Fig. 3. Twelve "trajectory plots": In the top part (markings "A1" to "A6") they are shown for six velocities $v = 1, 2, 5, 6, 9,$ and 10; for pocket size d = 1 (6.0 mm). In the lower part (markings "B1" to "B6") they are shown for the same velocities but for pocket size $d = 2$ (7.0 mm). The points shown correspond to the extracted point locations in $\mathbb{R}^2$. The markings on the circumference depict the estimated θ values.

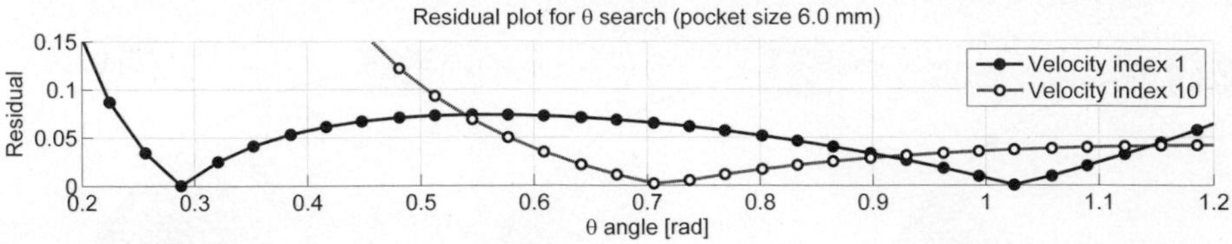

Fig. 4. Two residual curves for two distinct points: (x_{100}, y_{100}) from $A^{(65)}_{(1,1)}$ and (x_{160}, y_{160}) from $A^{(65)}_{(10,1)}$. That is, for both the slowest rotational speed $v = 1$ ("Velocity index 1") and the fastest $v = 10$ ("Velocity index 10"), though only for one pocket diameter $d = 1$. On the curve for $v = 1$ there are two minima at (1) $\theta = 0.29$ rad [16.49°] and (2) $\theta = 1.03$ rad [58.83°]. On the other curve ($v = 10$) there is only one minima at $\theta = 0.71$ rad [40.90°].

where $g = 9.82\ \text{m/s}^2$ is the gravity acceleration constant. Solving for t in (2a) and substituting into (2b) we get the following function (dropping the point index i for generality):

$$\tilde{y}_{\omega,r}(\theta, x) = G_\omega \frac{1}{r^2} \csc^2\theta [r\cos\theta - x]^2 + \cot\theta\, [r\cos\theta - x] + r\sin\theta \ , \tag{3}$$

where the constant $G_\omega = -(g/2)\omega^{-2}$ is the only factor involving gravity acceleration constant g and ω. The problem is now to solve (3) for θ for each point (x_i, y_i). This was done numerically. First we defined a residual function:

$$e_{\omega,r}(\theta, x_i, y_i) = |\tilde{y}_{\omega,r}(\theta, x_i) - y_i| \ , \tag{4}$$

which naturally makes it a minimization problem in $\mathbb{R}$:

$$\theta_i = \arg\min_\theta e_{\omega,r}(\theta, x_i, y_i) \ . \tag{5}$$

We chose to do a full numerical search in the entire range from 0 to $\pi/2$ with a step size of $h = 10^{-3}\pi/2$ (1000 divisions). No stopping criteria was used, resulting in a list of 1000 residual values for each point (x_i, y_i) to analyse further.

Figure 4 shows two plots for the residual value calculated for two points for the slowest and fastest rotational speed (see figure caption for details). When looking at the residual curve for $v = 1$, there are two solutions for the angle θ (two minima exist). This is a mathematical detail easily dealt with. For current point (x, y) only θ values for which the following is true can possibly be member of the solution set Θ_l: $\theta < \arccos(x/r)$, where $x \leq r$. In the current example we have $x = 0.17$, meaning that the upper θ limit is $\arccos(0.17/0.2) = 0.56$ rad [31.90°]. Thus only the lower θ value in the current example would be considered. Finally, we notice that for the residual from motion at velocity step $v = 10$ there is only one minima at a higher angle than for the $v = 1$ curve.

4 Results and Discussion

The methods presented in Section 3 made it possible to analyse for what angle with horizontal the seeds are thrown off the cylinder wall. For each solution set Θ_l available at each time index l in any sequence, we created a frequency distribution h_l over θ and estimate a normal fit with parameters μ_l and σ_l. Beyond this, all distributions h_l for each sequence were also summed and a normal density fitted as well. This made it possible to statistically describe the behaviour of θ for each full sequence using only two parameters (we refer to it specifically as the *summed* distribution).

In Figure 5 we see examples of the summed frequency distributions with the corresponding normal fit superimposed. They are specifically shown for three

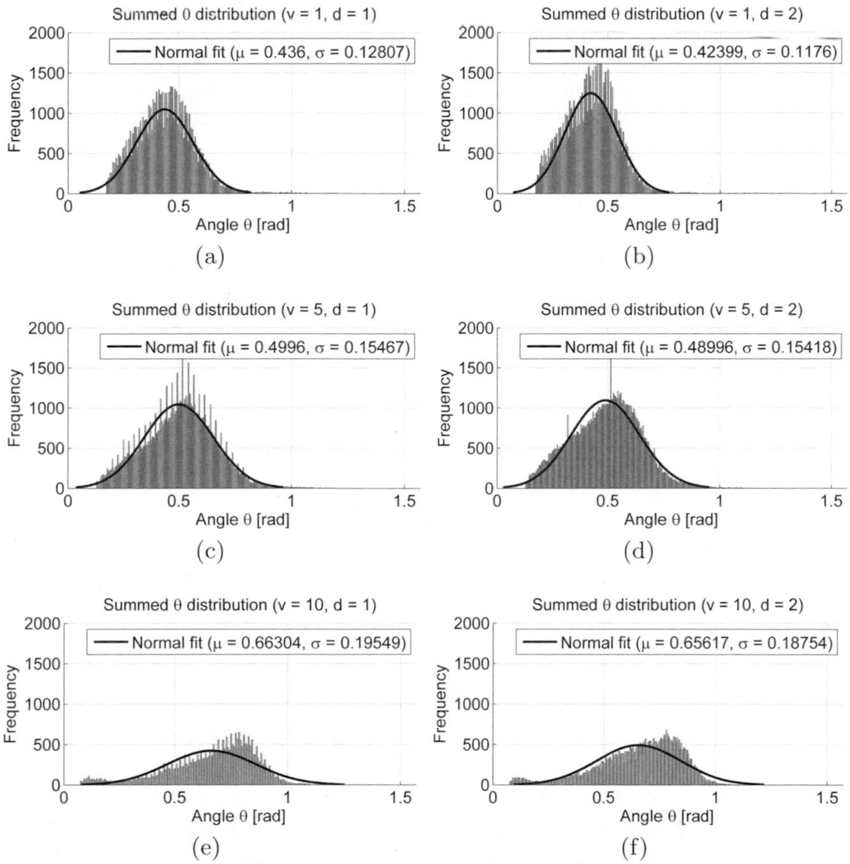

Fig. 5. Six θ frequency distributions with fitted normal density superimposed. Fig. 5(a), 5(c) and, 5(e) show the distributions and normal fit for velocities $v = 1$, 5, and 10; for pocket diameter $d = 1$ (6.0 mm). Fig. 5(b), 5(d) and, 5(f) show the distributions and normal fit for the same three velocities, but now instead for pocket diameter $d = 2$ (7.0 mm).

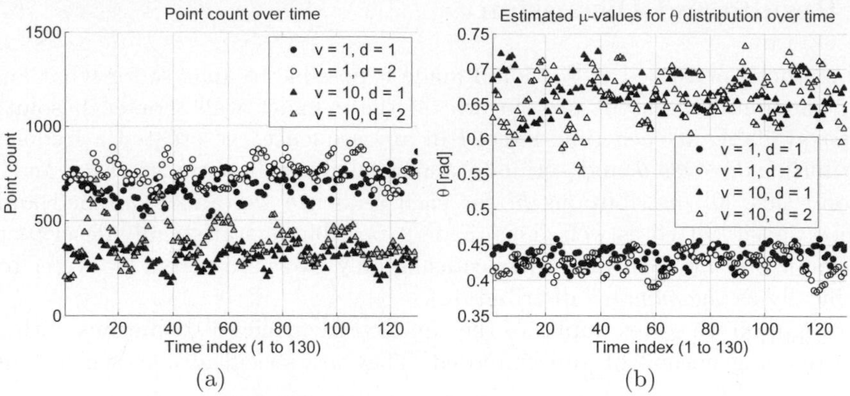

Fig. 6. Two scatter plots showing different variables gathered over time: Figure 6(a) shows a scatter plot of point counts $I_{(d,v)}^{(l)}$ over $l, \ldots, L$ for $v = 1, 10$ and $d = 1, 2$. In other words: The number of points accumulated for every ten frames, for the slowest and fastest velocity and for both pocket sizes. Figure 6(b) shows a scatter plot of estimated normal μ-parameter from frequency distributions generated from solution sets Θ_l over the same index ranges as in Figure 6(a).

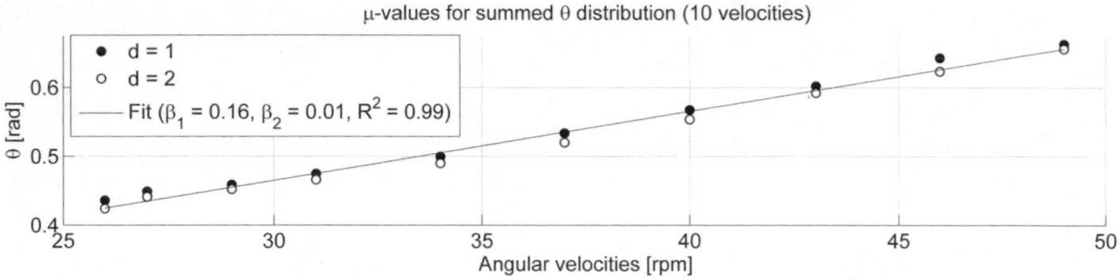

Fig. 7. Scatter plot and a linear regression fit of the μ-parameter estimated from the summed (accumulated over time) frequency distributions under the assumption that the distribution is normal. The data are shown for all ten angular velocities and for both pocket sizes. The linear fit was done using all 20 data points (with rpm values as predictors).

velocity steps: (1) slowest, middle ($d = 5$), and fastest; for both pocket sizes. Not much difference in appearance of the distribution over pocket sizes can be observed directly – mostly the difference is within changes in rotational speed. Generally, for a higher speed there seems to be a higher probability for larger values of θ. Also, for the highest speed the distribution also seems to become slightly multi-modal. Two modes are observable in figures 5(e) and 5(f) and also in the trajectories plotted in Figure 3 (for that particular rotational speed).

Figure 6(a) show a scatter plot of number of points available in each time step l. The values are shown for both slowest and fastest velocity step, as well as for both pocket sizes. The system seems to have some stability over time. It is also evident that for the fastest velocity step, fewer seeds are extracted than for the slowest velocity step. Figure 6(b) show for the same velocity steps and pocket sizes the estimated μ_l parameter for the frequency distributions generated over time. Again we observe stability. On top of this, we observe that θ is generally larger for the fastest velocity step than for the slowest velocity step. Also, the number of points extracted is fewer for the fastest velocity step than for the slowest.

Figure 7 show the estimated μ-parameter for the summed frequency distributions over all ten rotational speeds and for both pocket sizes. The regression fit indicates the possibility of a linear relationship between the rotational speed of the indented cylinder and the angle of escape θ.

5 Conclusions

In this work we have experimentally verified a certain behaviour of the sorting process in the indented cylinder. First and foremost, at least for the 5 seconds of recording that we have dealt with, we show that the process has some stability (but mostly for the lower velocity steps). Secondly, we show a linear relation between rotational speed and angle of escape θ. As mentioned in the introduction there is a need for a systems identification approach in where the indented cylinder is analysed to acquire information about important parameters. Thus a third results is a more tentative one: We have shown that image analysis can be used for flow analysis of particles moving in an indented cylinder. This is a novel step toward the goal of predicting and controlling the sorting process in these machines.

One final important remark: Our choice of using a seed batch with 50 % whole and 50 % broken barley kernels will undoubtedly have had an impact on the distribution of the angle of escape θ. Had the kernel size distribution been more realistic, for instance, with 10 % broken, and 90 % whole or opposite, then we would likely have observed a multi-modal frequency destribution of θ. That would be interesting to try in the future.

Acknowledgements

We would very much like to acknowledge the support and guidance received from Westrup A/S, Denmark.

References

1. Berlage, A.G., Bilsland, D.M., Brandenburg, N.R., Cooper, T.M.: Experimental indent cylinder for separating seeds. Transactions of the American Society of Agricultural Engineers 27(2), 358–361 (1984)
2. Berlage, A.G., Churchill, D.B., Cooper, T.M., Bisland, D.M.: The application of new technologies to seed conditioning. Journal of Agricultural Engineering Research 42(3), 193–202 (1989)
3. Berlage, A.G., Cooper, T.M., Aristazabal, J.F.: Machine vision identification of diploid and tetraploid ryegrass seed. Transactions of the American Society of Agricultural Engineers 31(1), 24–27 (1988)

4. Berlage, A.G., Cooper, T.M., Carone, R.A.: Seed sorting by machine vision. Agricultural Engineering 65(10), 14–17 (1984)
5. Buchhave, P.: Particle image velocimetry–status and trends. Experimental Thermal and Fluid Science 5(5), 586 (1992), special Issue on Experimental Methods in Thermal and Fluid Science
6. Churchill, D.B., Berlage, A.G., Bilsland, D.M., Cooper, T.M.: Decision-support system development for conditioning seeds with indent cylinder. Transactions of the American Society of Agricultural Engineers 32(4), 1395–1398 (1989)
7. Dell'Aquila, A.: Towards new computer imaging techniques applied to seed quality testing and sorting. Seed Science and Technology 35(3), 519–538 (2007)
8. Grochowicz, J.: Machines For Cleaning And Sorting Of Seeds. Department of Agriculture (1980) (translated from polish)
9. Lampeter, W.: Die Saatgutaufbereitung. VEB Deutscher Landwirtschaftsverlag, Berlin (1965)
10. Parker, D.J., Dijkstra, A.E., Martin, T.W., Seville, J.P.K.: Positron emission particle tracking studies of spherical particle motion in rotating drums. Chemical Engineering Science 52(13), 2011–2022 (1997)
11. Pianko-Oprych, P., Nienow, A., Barigou, M.: Positron emission particle tracking (pept) compared to particle image velocimetry (piv) for studying the flow generated by a pitched-blade turbine in single phase and multi-phase systems. Chemical Engineering Science 64(23), 4955 – 4968 (2009)
12. Sandadi, S., Pandey, P., Turton, R.: In situ, near real-time acquisition of particle motion in rotating pan coating equipment using imaging techniques. Chemical Engineering Science 59(24), 5807–5817 (2004)

Improving Particle Segmentation from Process Images with Wiener Filtering

Lauri Laaksonen, Nataliya Strokina, Tuomas Eerola, Lasse Lensu, and Heikki Kälviäinen

Machine Vision and Pattern Recognition Laboratory (MVPR)
Department of Information Technology
Lappeenranta University of Technology (LUT)
P.O. Box 20, FI-53851 Lappeenranta, Finland
firstname.lastname@lut.fi
http://www2.it.lut.fi/mvpr

Abstract. While there is growing interest in in-line measurements of paper making processes, the factory environment often restricts the acquisition of images. The in-line imaging of pulp suspension is often difficult due to constraints to camera and light positioning, resulting in images with uneven illumination and motion blur. This article presents an algorithm for segmenting fibers from suspension images and studies the performance of Wiener filtering in improving the sub-optimal images. Methods are presented for estimating the point spread function and noise-to-signal ratio for constructing the Wiener filter. It is shown that increasing the sharpness of the image improves the performance of the presented segmentation method.

Keywords: pulp suspension, fiber segmentation, Wiener filtering, machine vision, image processing and analysis.

1 Introduction

The paper industry has recently shown increasing interest in the in-line measurements as they could provide information on the state of the process on-line, making it possible to control the process while the product is still forming. Reliable on-line estimates could be used for process optimization, automation and avoiding breaks and delays in the process. However, accurate on-line measurements are difficult to obtain due to restrictions to camera and illumination, low contrast of many of the measured particles and the execution times required for timely measurements.

There are methods for obtaining certain measures related to the papermaking process and the quality of the end-product. Sitholé and Filion compare quality measurements of recycled pulp [12]. Wang and Hubbe [13] propose a method for measuring the electrical properties of fiber surfaces [13] and Saarela et al. [11] use a streak camera for measuring the fines content of pulp with unknown consistency. These methods, however, tend to be specific for a certain measurement and are often performed on pulp sheets in laboratory conditions.

A. Heyden and F. Kahl (Eds.): SCIA 2011, LNCS 6688, pp. 285–294, 2011.

Among the most important factors affecting the quality of the end product are the properties and formation of the fiber web. The characteristics of the fibers have a significant effect on the quality of the pulp and the end product. For example, the length and coarseness of fibers affect the flocculation (the forming of mass concentrations within the suspension) and the mobility of the fibers, both of which are factors in the uniformity of the suspension and the extent the suspension uniformity can be altered. [10]

Before it is possible to make measurements of the fiber characteristics, the fibers need to be segmented from the suspension images. The low contrast and varying intensity values of the pixels depicting fibers cause thresholding and traditional edge detection methods to perform poorly.

This article presents an approach for fiber segmentation from pulp suspension images, which is a part of a fully automated system of pulp flow analysis for the inline measurements. Wiener filtering for image restoration is presented. The estimation of the Wiener filter parameters is discussed. An algorithm for segmenting fibers is proposed and its feasibility as a part of on-line measurements is studied. Experiments concerning the effect of the Wiener filtering on the performance of the segmentation algorithm are presented and discussed.

2 Imaging and Image Processing

The images of flowing low-consistency pulp used in this article were taken from within a pilot process in LUT FiberLaboratory in Savonlinna. The camera used was a Guppy F-046B, manufactured by Allied Vision Technologies. The 8.3 µm × 8.3 µm CCD-cells of the camera could produce a maximum of 780 × 582 pixel images with a framerate up to 49.4 frames per second [1]. As the in-line environment of papermaking process offers limited or no accessibility for a camera with a normal lens, the camera was fitted to a Richard Wolf borescope with a video lense from the same manufacturer.

To improve the contrast of the fibers, they were processed with an agent that radiated fluorescent light. One of the pulp images for testing the fiber segmentation algorithm is presented in Fig. 4.

2.1 Wiener Filtering

Wiener filtering is an inverse filtering method that takes the statistical characteristics of image noise into account. Both the image and image noise are considered as random variables and the undistorted image f is estimated by minimizing the mean square error between the undistorted image and estimated image. [5]

The error measure for the mean square error is calculated from

$$e^2 = E\{(f - \tilde{f})^2\}, \qquad (1)$$

where e^2 is the squared error, $\tilde{f}$ the estimate of the undistorted image and $E\{\cdot\}$ is the expected value of the argument [5]. The degraded image is defined as

$g = h(f + N)$, where h is the point spread function and N the additive noise in the image.

The noise-to-signal ratio (NSR) required for the filtering is rarely known, but it can be approximated by a constant [9]. Replacing NSR with constant γ, the frequency representation of $\tilde{f}$ minimizing the error function in Eq. 1 is gained from

$$\tilde{F}(u,v) = \left[\frac{1}{H(u,v)} \frac{|H(u,v)|^2}{|H(u,v)|^2 + \gamma}\right] G(u,v), \tag{2}$$

where H is the frequency domain representation of the point spread function of the whole system and G the frequency domain representation of the degraded image. [5] The parameters required for the filtering are now reduced to point spread function H and the constant estimating the noise-to-signal ratio γ.

Estimation of point spread function. The point spread function of a camera can be estimated from images with a sharp edge [8]. The location of the edges present in an image is derived by performing Canny edge detection [3] and performing connected component analysis on the found edges.

To find a proper estimate for the edge, RANSAC (Random Sample Concensus) [4] is used to find the line represented by the edge pixels. A number of edge profiles are taken along the line, five pixels from both sides of the edge. The mean edge profile is calculated and normalized between [0 1] by

$$Z_i = \frac{p_i - p_{min}}{p_{max} - p_{min}}, \tag{3}$$

where p_i is the i:th intensity value of the mean edge profile, p_{max} is the maximum value of the mean profile, p_{min} the minimum and Z_i the normalized profile value.

The normalized values are compared to an ideal, infinitely sharp edge p_{ideal}, positioned at the center of the normalized profile. The ideal edge depicts an instant transition between the edge and non-edge pixels. In practice, the ideal edge cannot be achieved for normal or high-resolution cameras as it would require alignment of the edge target and the camera CCD-cells, and perfect illumination conditions. Thus, this method of estimation always yields some amount of point spread.

The directional point spread estimates e_x and e_y are calculated as $|p_x - p_{ideal}|$ and $|p_y - p_{ideal}|$, respectively. The point spread function matrix M_{psf} is calculated from the column vectors e_x and e_y by

$$M_{psf} = \frac{e_y^T \times e_x}{\sum(e_y^T \times e_x)}. \tag{4}$$

Estimation of noise-to-signal ratio. Murphy et al. [7] present two suitable methods to estimate the noise in an image. Taking a large uniform area of the image, the noise can be measured as the standard deviation of the intensity values of the area. Another approach is to take two images of the same target, subtract one image from the other and calculating the standard deviation of the difference. This method can be improved by increasing the number of images taken and subtracting the mean image from each of the original ones.

With the statistical characteristics of the noise known, an estimation of the mean noise-to-signal ratio (NSR) can be calculated for the images from

$$NSR = \frac{\sigma(n)}{\sigma(u)}, \tag{5}$$

where $\sigma(u)$ is the standard deviation of the undistorted image (i.e. the mean image of the set) and $\sigma(n)$ is the standard deviation of the noise [2].

As the environmental conditions are expected to remain constant for the duration of image acquisition and the noise is assumed to be caused mainly by characteristics of the camera, the NSR is expected to remain approximately the same regardless of the imaged target. However, as temperature and other environmental factors may change over time in the process environment, re-estimation of the noise model may be required from time to time.

Estimation result. The sharp edges for estimating the PSF were produced in the image with two thin razors imaged from the distance of 380 mm (see Fig. 1). It was assumed that the thin edges can be accurately represented by straight lines to the accuracy of 780 × 582 pixels captured by the camera. Fig. 2 shows the estimated edge profiles. A visual representation of the PSF estimated from the given images is shown in Fig. 3.

Fig. 1. Image for estimating the edge spread function

The noise caused by the camera, measured over ten images, was normally distributed (see Fig. 3) with zero mean and standard deviation of 0.0032. The Lilliefors test [6], a statistic test for determining if data is normally distributed when the mean and variance must be estimated from the sample, was performed on the noise model of each image. The test suggested that the models are normally distributed with the probability of 99.9 %.

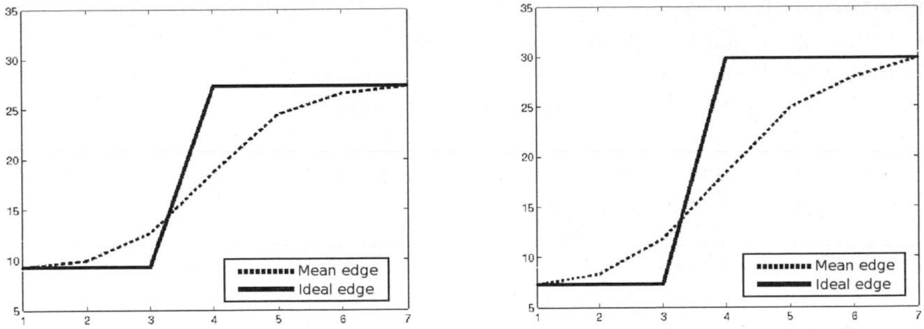

(a) (b)

Fig. 2. Mean edge profiles: (a) Horizontal; (b) Vertical

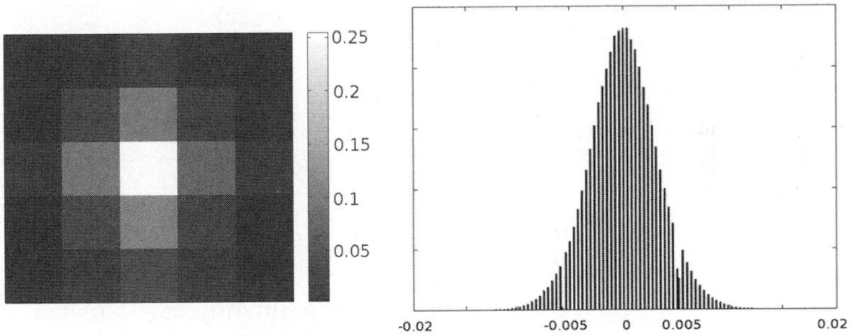

(a) (b)

Fig. 3. Camera noise: (a) Visual presentation of the PSF; (b) Distribution of the noise.

2.2 Fiber Segmentation

The approach for detecting the fibers is summarized in Algorithm 1. Due to poor performance of standard edge detection filters, the initial segmentation of fibers is done by a set of filters designed specifically for the images in Fig. 4. The filter assumes the fibers to manifest as long, thin objects in the images, with intensity higher than the background. While there is a loss of generality due to the resolution dependency of the filter set, the designed filters supercede the traditional edge detection filters in performance.

The filter set is generated by rotating the filter

$$M = \begin{bmatrix} -2 & -1 & 0 & 1 & 4 & 1 & 0 & -1 & -2 \\ -2 & -1 & 0 & 1 & 4 & 1 & 0 & -1 & -2 \\ -2 & -1 & 0 & 1 & 4 & 1 & 0 & -1 & -2 \end{bmatrix}$$

by 45° both clockwise and counter-clockwise to produce the filters for diagonally positioned fibers, and by rotating M by 90° for detecting horizontal fibers.

Algorithm 1: Fiber segmentation

1: Filter the image for initial detection of fibers.
2: Integrate above average responses from the filters.
3: Form objects by connected component labeling.
4: Remove objects with area below threshold t_1.
5: Remove branching points to disconnect overlapping objects.
6: Give remaining objects individual labels.
7:

```
for object endpoints do
    if endpoint with a different label found near the current endpoint then
        for endpoints of different label do
            Fit a polynomial of degree n to all the points of both labels.
            Calculate the STD of error between the points and the polynomial.
        end for
        Choose the polynomial with lowest error.
        if error between points and curve < threshold t2 then
            Give the segments the same label.
        end if
    end if
end for
```

8: Remove labels with area below threshold t_3.

Before integrating the filter responses, any response below the mean intensity of the image is removed to reduce false responses. Connected component analysis is performed on the remaining responses to form objects depicting the fiber segments. Objects with area below t_1 are removed as noise (Step 4).

Binary thinning, i.e. the iterative removal of the outer edge pixels of an object, is performed in Step 5. The segments with a width of single pixel are disconnected by removing any branch point on the single pixel wide path of a fiber segment. This results in a number of objects with an area of only one or few pixels. These objects are considered as noise and removed, while the remaining segments are given individual labels.

The area around the endpoints of each labeled segment is investigated. If an endpoint with a different label is found, a polynomial curve of degree n is fit to all pixels of both labels. The standard deviation of the error between the datapoints and the fitted curve is calculated. If the error is below a threshold t_2 the segments are considered to belong to the same fiber and are given the same label.

In the case of multiple nearby labels, the curve is fit to the segment containing the investigated endpoint and to the pixels of all the labels in turn, and the curve between the label with least error in the fit is tested against the threshold. Objects with pixel area remaining below t_3 after connecting the segments are removed. The segmented fibers, can be seen in Figures 5.

3 Experiments and Discussions

The presented segmentation method was applied to the set of 6 images, one of which is presented in Fig. 4. Using the first image the following parameters of the algorithm were defined: $t_1 = 40$, $t_2 = 5$, $t_3 = 30$ and $n = 3$. The method correctly classified reasonably difficult cases. In Fig. 6d a closer look is taken at several typical situations the method faces when deciding if segments close to each other should be classified as one fiber.

Fig. 6a shows a simple case of joining the segments of a straight fiber. In Fig. 6b the mean interpolation error of the curve fit to the pixels of the two long segments is too large and the segments are classified as separate fibers. A more difficult case is shown in Fig. 6c, where the segments of the two straight fibers are connected, while the two fibers are classified as separate and the segments of one fiber are not classified as a part of the other. One of the most difficult cases is shown in Fig. 6d, where a straight fiber in several segments is overlapped by a curved fiber in two segments. For this instance, the method correctly classifies the overlapping fibers.

The effect of edge sharpening by the Wiener filter on the performance of the fiber segmentation method was tested on the same set of six suspension images. The output of the segmentation algorithm was referenced to a visual estimation of the correct fibers in the image. While the visual estimation was done by a non-expert, the fibers in the used pulp images are salient enough to assume a reasonable accuracy for the estimation.

The results of the segmentation were divided in to three categories: detected fibers (det.) with most of the fiber segments were found and correctly labeled, partly detected fibers (par.) with a part of the fiber detected, but missing segments, and incorrect (inc.) with wrong segments joined or noise segmented as fiber segment. The number of fibers (num.) was manually estimated for each image to provide ground truth for the segmentation result.

Filtering the image with Wiener filter resulted in an increase of detected segments in all categories. The amount of complete fibers detected was significantly increased along with the amount of the more obscure fibers partially found. While there was some increase in the false filter responses detected as fiber segments, most of the final false segments were relatively small and could be removed by pixel area based thresholding, although at the cost of small true segments.

The results of the segmentation are shown in Tab. 1. The Matlab implementation of the segmentation algorithm was tested on a desktop computer with two Intel Pentium 3.00 GHz processors and 2.0 GB of memory. On the average, the method performed the segmentation for the unfiltered images in approximately 0.56 seconds. When performing the algorithm on filtered images the segmentation took approximately 0.88 seconds due to increased number of detections (both real segments and noise)

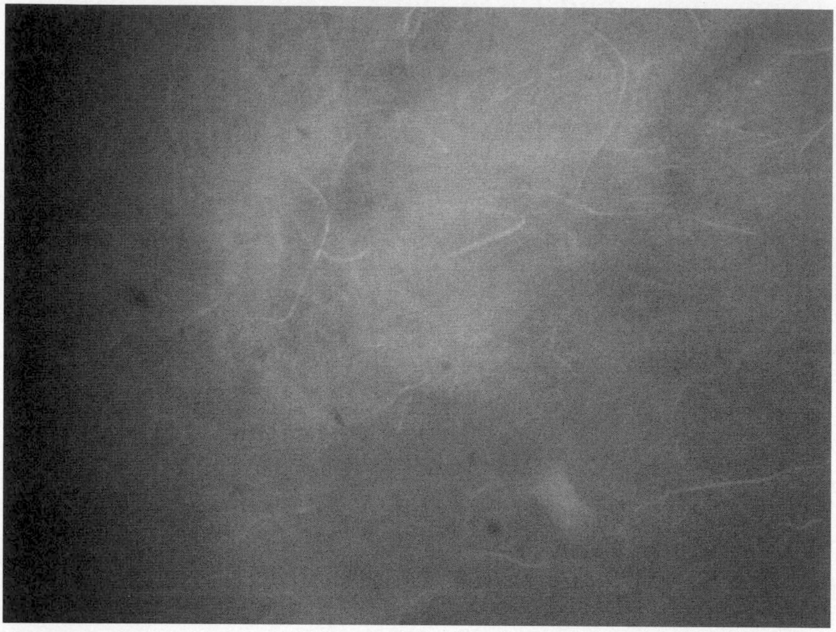

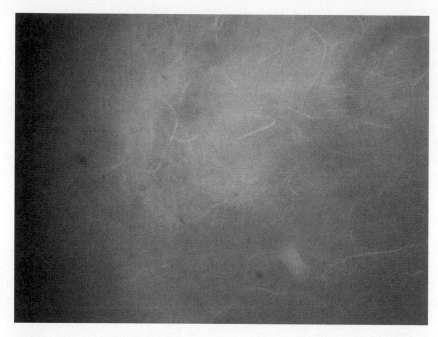

Fig. 4. An example of the test images for the fiber segmentation algorithm

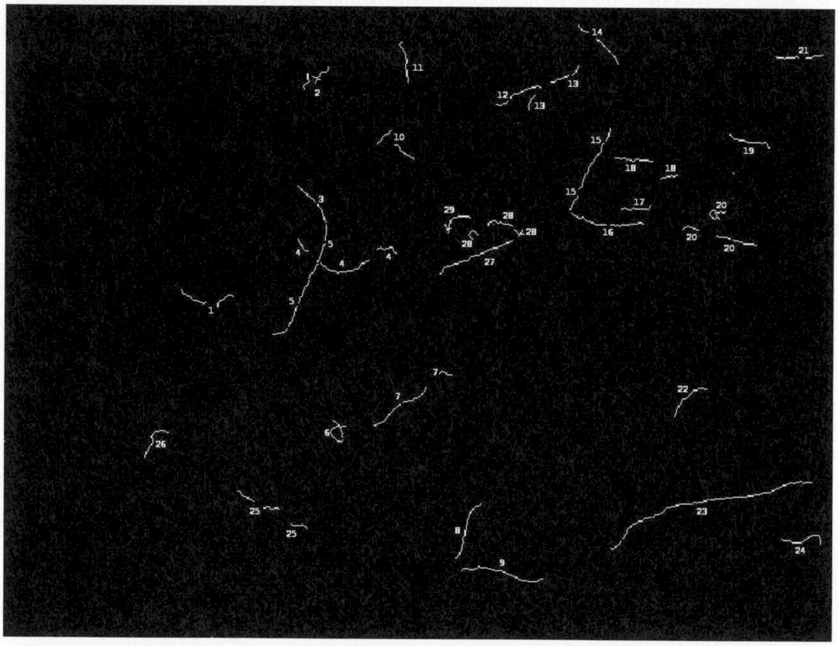

Fig. 5. Segmented fibers with small segments removed

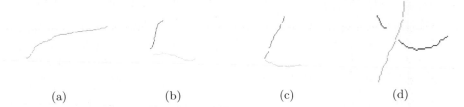

(a) (b) (c) (d)

Fig. 6. Closer examination of segment joining results: (a) Segments recognized as a straight fiber; (b) Segments recognized as separate fibers; (c) Segments recognized as two separate straight fibers; (d) Segments from overlapping fibers recognized as a straight and a curved fiber

Table 1. Effect of Wiener filtering on fiber segmentation. (det.) correctly detected, (par.) partially detected, (inc.) noise segmented or segments joined incorrectly, (num.) estimated number of fibers.

	Filtered image			No filtering			
	det.	par.	inc.	det.	par.	inc.	num.
Image 1	9	7	5	4	9	0	19
Image 2	6	1	4	4	0	2	11
Image 3	7	4	4	3	5	0	16
Image 4	2	5	1	0	2	0	12
Image 5	2	4	1	2	1	0	14
Image 6	1	6	1	0	1	0	9

3.1 Future Work

The segmentation of the fibers is the first step in in-line measurements. There is still demand for tracking the fibers to determine the flow, classification of the fibers and further study of the process based on the measurements. Methods for studying the formation and behaviour of the fiber web are also of interest.

4 Conclusion

While the in-line measurements of paper making process are difficult due to restrictions to the location of the camera and positioning of the light, the benefits are significant. In this work, a method for segmenting fibers from pulp suspension images was presented, along with methods for estimating the point spread function and the noise-to-signal ratio for constructing the Wiener filter. The improved sharpness of the image after Wiener filtering significantly improved the performance of the fiber segmentation algorithm.

Acknowledgements

The research was carried out in the "PulpVision" project (TEKES project 70010/10) funded by the European Union and the participating companies. The authors wish to acknowledge the FiberLaboratory in LUT for cooperation and providing the pulp images used in the article.

References

1. Allied Vision Technologies. Guppy Techical Manual (2009)
2. Buades, A., Coll, B., Morel, J.M.: A review of image denoising algorithms, with a new one. Multiscale Modeling and Simulation 4, 490–530 (2005)
3. Canny, J.: A computational approach to edge detection. IEEE Transactions of Pattern Analysis and Machine Intelligence 8, 679–698 (1986)
4. Fischler, M.A., Bolles, R.C.: Random sample consensus: a paradigm for model fitting with applications to image analysis and automated cartography. Communications of the ACM 24, 381–395 (1981)
5. Gonzales, R.C., Woods, R.E.: Digital Image Processing, 3rd edn. Pearson Prentice Hall, London (2008)
6. Lilliefors, H.W.: On the kolmogorov-smirnov test for normality with mean and variance unknown. Journal of the American Statistical Association 62, 399–402 (1967)
7. Murphy, B.W., Carson, P.L., Ellis, J.H., Zhang, Y.T., Hyde, R.J., Chenevert, T.L.: Signal-to-noise measures for magnetic resonance imagers. Magnetic Resonance Imaging 2, 425–428 (1993)
8. Szeliski, R., Joshi, N., Kriegman, D.J.: Psf estimation using sharp edge prediction. In: IEEE Conference on Computer Vision and Pattern Recognition, CVPR (2008)
9. Pang, M.-C.: A novel blind super-resolution technique based on the improved poisson maximum a posteriori algorithm. International Journal of Imaging Systems and Technology 12, 239–246 (2002)
10. Robertson, G., Olson, J., Allen, P., Chan, B., Seth, R.: Measurement of fiber length, coarseness, and shape with the fiber quality analyzer. Tappi Journal 82, 93–98 (1999)
11. Saarela, J., Törmänen, M., Myllylä, R.: Measuring pulp consistency and fines content with a streak camera. Measurement Science and Technology 14, 1801–1806 (2003)
12. Sitholé, B., Filion, D.: Assessment of methods for the measurement of macrostickies in recycled pulps. Progress in Paper Recycling 17 (2008)
13. Wang, F., Hubbe, M.: Development and evaluation of an automated streaming potential measurement device. Colloids and Surfaces A: Physicochemical and Engineering Aspects 194, 221–232 (2001)

Efficient Hyperelastic Regularization for Registration

Sune Darkner[1], Michael Sass Hansen[2], Rasmus Larsen[2], and Mads F. Hansen[2]

[1] eScience Center, Department of Computer Science, University of Copenhagen
Universitetsparken 1, DK-2100 Copenhagen, Denmark
[2] DTU Informatics, Technical University of Denmark
Richard Petersens Plads, DK-2800 Lyngby, Denmark
darkner@diku.dk, {msh,rl,mfh}@imm.dtu.dk

Abstract. For most image registration problems a smooth one-to-one mapping is desirable, a diffeomorphism. This can be obtained using priors such as volume preservation, certain kinds of elasticity or both. The key principle is to regularize the strain of the deformation which can be done through penalization of the eigen values of the stress tensor. We present a computational framework for regularization of image registration for isotropic hyper elasticity. We formulate an efficient and parallel scheme for computing the principal stain based for a given parameterization by decomposing the left Cauchy-Green strain tensor and deriving analytical derivatives of the principal stretches as a function of the deformation, guaranteeing a diffeomorphism in every evaluation point. Hyper elasticity allows us to handle large deformation without re-meshing. The method is general and allows for the well-known hyper elastic priors such at the Saint Vernant Kirchoff model, the Ogden material model or Riemanian elasticity. We exemplify the approach through synthetic registration and special tests as well as registration of different modalities; 2D cardiac MRI and 3D surfaces of the human ear. The artificial examples illustrate the degree of deformation the formulation can handle numerically. Numerically the computational complexity is no more than 1.45 times the computational complexity of Sum of Squared Differences.

1 Introduction

Registration has been the subject of intense research as it forms the basis for most quantitative methods for analyzing and tracking morphological changes. It is well known that image registration is an ill-posed problem and to obtain a meaningful solution the problem has to regularized. Simple regularizers include re-sampling and re-gridding or diffusion and linear elasticity which penalize deformation directly upon the elements of the displacement gradient. It is desirable to use a proper rotation-invariant measure such as the strain tensor. Frequently used regularization approaches are volume preservation, parameter constraints through subspace projection, or more advanced methods such as the methods we describe based on strains e.g. Riemanian elasticity. These more advanced regularizers are based on physical models such as viscosity or elasticity. The elasticity model is

A. Heyden and F. Kahl (Eds.): SCIA 2011, LNCS 6688, pp. 295–305, 2011.

attractive as it is invariant to local translation and rotation assuring meaningful regularization through the use of principal stretches; the eigen value of the left and right stretch tensor. The use of this type of regularizer is computational expensive. However, as we show very efficient computations through analytical expressions can be made including their derivatives. The resulting scheme is 1.45 times the computational cost of SSD for tedrahedra in 3D. This enables the use of gradient based methods, with fast convergence. Furthermore, this provides the local scaling (the determinant of the stretch) such that the non-linearity in the transformation can be accounted for in the similarity measure. We present a registration framework that simplifies the implementation of these constraints. The framework is based on the left Cauchy-Green strain tensor and its eigen values (squared principal stretches). We form analytical derivatives of the eigen values with respect to the parameters, independent of the parameterization. This is essential for easy and fast implementation. Through the chain-rule it is possible to easily change bases and elasticity model. We illustrate the method on synthetic data, 2D MRI data and 3D surface registration of Human ear canals. We model the deformation and exemplify some derivations with tetrahedra and B-splines as the bases to illustrate the approach and implementation.

2 Previous Work

Registration is an area of continuous research because of its importance in creating a basis for further analysis. The problem is generally ill-posed, so it needs a prior or regularization to obtain meaningful results. In most registration schemes, a regularizer is applied to ensure a valid spatial deformation which is smooth and preserves topology. The majority of regularization approaches find their motivation in continuum mechanics. Linear elastic body forces was initially proposed by [1] to regularize the deformation. This was later adapted into a registration algorithm in [2]. Riemannian elasticity was introduced by [3] which, in contrast to linear elasticity, is rotation-invariant and therefore capable of capturing much larger deformations. Elastic image registration by incorporating volume-preserving soft constraints in registration of pre- and post-contrast MRIs of the female breast was essentially performed in [4] and [5]. Similarly, [6] used volume-preserving hard constraints together with linear elasticity to register pre- and post-contrast MRIs. [7] proposed diffusive regularization, which is the squared Fröbenius norm of the displacement gradient. The use of viscous-fluid priors was introduced in [8] which regularize the flow of the deformation rather than the relative spatial displacements. Fluid registration has become widely popular in the neuro-imaging community [8, 9] because of its ability to model large deformations. Rueckert et al. [10] reduced the dimensionality of the image registration problem and ensured a smooth deformation field by using B-splines to describe the deformations between images. Many research groups have since adapted this approach [11, 12]. Other typical parameterizations of the deformation field are the cosine kernel proposed by [13] and different kinds of radial basis functions [14]. The focus of this work is on generalization of non-linear strain and we exemplify using

Riemannian elasticity, with a formulation that allows for easy exchange of the regularizer to other forms such as the Ogden material model [15]. The reminder of this paper is organized as follows: In section 3 we briefly review registration, in section 4 we briefly discuss similarity measures and derive the first order structure for SSD as an example. In section 5 we present the regularization framework and present our approach to evaluate the regularization functional and the first order structure. In section 6 we discuss two different commonly used bases, B-splines and tetrahedra. In section 7 we present experimental results, discuss the method in 8 and draw our conclusion in section 9.

3 Registration

We formulate the registration problem as follows: Find a transformation $\boldsymbol{\phi}$ which maps $\boldsymbol{R}$ to $\boldsymbol{I}$ minimizing the similarity measure $\mathcal{D}$. This is an ill-posed problem, so we add a regularization term $\mathcal{S}$ to the function $\boldsymbol{\phi}$. This can be written as the following objective function

$$\mathcal{F}[I, R, \boldsymbol{\phi}] = \mathcal{D}[R, I \circ \boldsymbol{\phi}] + \alpha \mathcal{S}[\boldsymbol{\phi}], \tag{1}$$

where $\boldsymbol{\phi}$ is the deformation. Most registration schemes are formulated numerically and the influence of local scaling which occur for non-rigid transformations are left out. Some schemes compensate for this through re-gridding. However when dealing with large deformation as non-linear hyper elasticity a decision about local scaling has to be made, one is to take scaling into account or to consider the problem as re-sampling. For the minimization of $\mathcal{F}$ we use the gradient-based methods, in particular LBFGS [16]

4 Similarity Measure and Image Function

The image forces which drive the registration are derived from the similarity between the reference and the deformed template image. The natural choice is sum of squared differences (SSD), however, this requires images where the values are directly comparable without major bias, gradients etc. To counter these effects, several other similarity measures exist. The most important include: mutual information [17], normalized mutual information [18], normalized gradient fields [19], cross correlation [1] and correlation ratio [20]. For surfaces, the choice is often SSD on a signed distance field or point-to-point distance (Iterated Closes Point ICP) [21].For first order structure of the similarity measure SSD, we write

$$\mathcal{D}[I, R, \boldsymbol{\phi}] = \int_{\Omega} (R(\boldsymbol{x}) - I \circ \boldsymbol{\phi}(\boldsymbol{x}; \boldsymbol{p}))^2 d\boldsymbol{x}. \tag{2}$$

Differentiating with respect to the parameters p and using the chain rule we get

$$\frac{\partial \mathcal{D}}{\partial \boldsymbol{p}} = \frac{1}{2} \int_{\Omega} (R(\boldsymbol{x}) - I \circ \boldsymbol{\phi}(\boldsymbol{x}; \boldsymbol{p})) \frac{\partial I(\boldsymbol{x})}{\partial \tilde{\boldsymbol{x}}} \frac{\partial \boldsymbol{\phi}(\boldsymbol{x}; \boldsymbol{p})}{\partial \boldsymbol{p}} d\boldsymbol{x} \tag{3}$$

where $\tilde{\boldsymbol{x}} = \boldsymbol{\phi}(\boldsymbol{x}; \boldsymbol{p})$. Images are considered to be smooth functions ensured by using cubic B-spline interpolation, which is C_2-continuous.

5 Regularization

We formulate the regularization energy upon $\boldsymbol{\phi}$ as the integration of an energy density function r, i.e.

$$\mathcal{S}[\boldsymbol{\phi}] = \int_{\Omega} r[\boldsymbol{\phi}](\boldsymbol{x})d\boldsymbol{x}, \tag{4}$$

We prefer the elasticity-based regularizers as they allow for large deformation because of rotation-invariance. Any isotropic elasticity energy density function can be formulated as a function of the eigen values of the left Cauchy-Green strain tensor.

$$\mathbf{E}(\boldsymbol{x}) = \nabla\boldsymbol{\phi}(\boldsymbol{x})\nabla\boldsymbol{\phi}(\boldsymbol{x})^T. \tag{5}$$

Among these elasticity-based regularizers are volume preservation, Riemanian elasticity and St. Venant Kirchoff elasticity. The density functions are

$$r_{vol}[\boldsymbol{\phi}] = (\prod_i \epsilon_i - 1)^2, \tag{6}$$

$$r_{rie}[\boldsymbol{\phi}] = \frac{\mu}{4}\sum_i \log^2 \epsilon_i + \frac{\lambda}{8}\left(\sum_i \log \epsilon_i\right)^2, \tag{7}$$

$$r_{svk}[\boldsymbol{\phi}] = \frac{\mu}{4}\sum_i (\epsilon_i - 1)^2 + \frac{\lambda}{8}\left(\sum_i (\epsilon_i - 1)\right)^2 \tag{8}$$

where $\boldsymbol{\epsilon}$ is the eigen values of the left Cauchy-Green strain tensor. The regularizer must be differentiated with respect to the parameters which, as we propose, can be achieved using the chain rule. The purpose is to derive an expression for

$$\frac{\partial r[\boldsymbol{\phi}]}{\partial p} = \sum_i \frac{\partial r[\boldsymbol{\phi}]}{\partial \epsilon_i}\frac{\partial \epsilon_i}{\partial p}. \tag{9}$$

It is straight forward to compute $\frac{\partial r[\boldsymbol{\phi}]}{\partial \epsilon}$ i.e. for Riemanian elasticity

$$\frac{\partial r_{rie}[\boldsymbol{\phi}]}{\partial \epsilon_i} = \frac{\mu}{2}\frac{1}{\epsilon_i}\log \epsilon_i + \frac{\lambda}{4}\frac{1}{\epsilon_i}\sum_i \log \epsilon_i \tag{10}$$

Thus, our concern is to find a way to compute $\frac{\partial \epsilon_i}{\partial p}$, the derivatives of the eigen values w.r.t. the deformation parameters.

5.1 Eigen Values and Derivatives

We regularize the strain of the deformation through the eigen values of the strain tensor which can be decomposed as $\mathbf{E} = \mathbf{U}\boldsymbol{\Lambda}\mathbf{U}^T$. $\mathbf{E} = \nabla_x\boldsymbol{\phi}(\boldsymbol{x})\nabla_x\boldsymbol{\phi}(\boldsymbol{x})^T$ a positive definite symmetric matrix, assuming diffeomorphism. We want to take the derivative with respect to the eigen values Λ. For eigen values of a symmetric matrix with multiplicity of one it holds

$$\mathbf{E} = \mathbf{U}\boldsymbol{\Lambda}\mathbf{U}^t \Leftrightarrow \frac{\partial \epsilon_i}{\partial p} = \mathbf{u}_i^T\frac{\partial \mathbf{E}}{\partial p}\mathbf{u}_i \tag{11}$$

The change in the strain can be written as

$$\frac{\partial \mathbf{E}}{\partial p_j} = \frac{\partial \nabla_x \boldsymbol{\phi}(\boldsymbol{x};\boldsymbol{p})}{\partial p_j} \nabla_x \boldsymbol{\phi}(\boldsymbol{x};\boldsymbol{p})^T + \nabla_x \boldsymbol{\phi}(\boldsymbol{x};\boldsymbol{p}) \frac{\partial \nabla_x \boldsymbol{\phi}(\boldsymbol{x};\boldsymbol{p})^T}{\partial p_j} \tag{12}$$

Combining eq. 12 and eq. 11 the change in eigen values can be written as

$$\frac{\partial \epsilon_i}{\partial p_j} = \mathbf{u}_i^T \left(\frac{\partial \nabla_x \boldsymbol{\phi}(\boldsymbol{x};\boldsymbol{p})}{\partial p_j} \nabla_x \boldsymbol{\phi}(\boldsymbol{x};\boldsymbol{p})^T + \nabla_x \boldsymbol{\phi}(\boldsymbol{x};\boldsymbol{p}) \frac{\partial \nabla_x \boldsymbol{\phi}(\boldsymbol{x};\boldsymbol{p})^T}{\partial p_j} \right) \mathbf{u}_i \tag{13}$$

For multiplicity greater than one, no unique eigen vector exist however the derivatives are easily dealt with as follows. As we assume diffeomorphism the multiplicity simply indicates isotropy on a hyper plane. Thus, orthogonal to the distinct eigen vectors we find a hyper plane on which the stretch is the same in any direction. We can therefore freely choose the vectors in this hyper plane since all will be eigen vectors, thus the directions of the derivatives are free within this plane due to isotropy. These special cases can be dealt with easily in the implementation. Alternatively explicit derivatives exist for the SVD [22].

6 Choice of Basis Functions

The choice of function for $\boldsymbol{\phi}$ has a huge impact on performance, so both interpolating and non-interpolating functions can be used. We formulate the problem for a general basis function for $\boldsymbol{\phi}$ which models the local neighborhood transformation and is evaluated at a single point $\boldsymbol{x}$. The local transformation of $\boldsymbol{x}$ can be written as follows.

$$\boldsymbol{\phi}(\boldsymbol{x};\boldsymbol{p}) = \boldsymbol{x} + \boldsymbol{B}(\boldsymbol{x})\boldsymbol{p} \tag{14}$$

where $\mathbf{p}$ is the parameters of $\boldsymbol{\phi}(\boldsymbol{x},\boldsymbol{p})$. $\boldsymbol{\phi}$ characterizes the local deformation at $\boldsymbol{x}$. The Jacobian $\boldsymbol{\nabla}\boldsymbol{\phi} = \boldsymbol{J}$ can then be written as

$$\begin{aligned} \nabla_x \boldsymbol{\phi}(\boldsymbol{x};\boldsymbol{p}) &= \boldsymbol{I} + \\ &\qquad [\boldsymbol{B}_1(\boldsymbol{x})\boldsymbol{p} \ \ldots \ \boldsymbol{B}_N(\boldsymbol{x})\boldsymbol{p}], \qquad (15) \\ \nabla_p \boldsymbol{\phi}(\boldsymbol{x};\boldsymbol{p}) &= \boldsymbol{B}(\boldsymbol{x}), \qquad (16) \end{aligned}$$

where $\boldsymbol{B}_i(\boldsymbol{x}) = \frac{\partial \boldsymbol{B}(\boldsymbol{x})}{\partial x_i}$. Several choices of basis functions exist and the above formulation does not limit the choice. For bases such as tensor product B-splines as used in [10], cosine basis as used in [23] or polyhedra it is fast and straight forward.

6.1 Basis Examples

As examples we formulate the problem with tetrahedra and B-splines as the basis function which models the local neighborhood. Tetrahedra models an affine transformation, and we represent this by a single point $\boldsymbol{x}$, the barycenter [24] of the tetrahedra for deformation constraint, and the points as the parameters

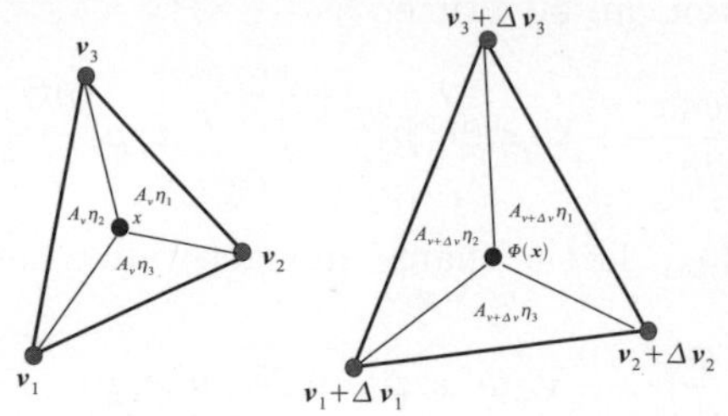

Fig. 1. Illustration of the linear/affine transformation from triangle $\mathbf{v_1}, \mathbf{v_2}, \mathbf{v_3}$ to $\mathbf{v_1} + \mathbf{\Delta v_1}, \mathbf{v_2} + \mathbf{\Delta v_2}, \mathbf{v_3} + \mathbf{\Delta v_3}$

in the transformation i.e. a free form deformation for all sample points with a constraint formulated for the barycenter. Figure 1 shows the a deformation based on triangles in $\mathbf{x}$ can be written as a linear combination of the vertices $\boldsymbol{V}$ in the tetrahedra$\boldsymbol{x} = [\boldsymbol{v_1}, \ldots, \mathbf{1_n}]\boldsymbol{\eta} = \boldsymbol{V\eta}$ thus $\boldsymbol{\eta} = \boldsymbol{V}^{-1}\begin{bmatrix}\boldsymbol{x}\\1\end{bmatrix} = [\boldsymbol{D\eta}^0]\begin{bmatrix}\boldsymbol{x}\\1\end{bmatrix}$ where $\boldsymbol{\eta}$ is the barycentric coordinates of $\boldsymbol{x}$. Thus by choosing polyhedra as the basis, the analytical derivations of the objective function and its first order derivative becomes feasible. By first splitting the position of $\boldsymbol{x}$ up we write $\boldsymbol{x} = \boldsymbol{x}_0 + \boldsymbol{\Delta x}$, the deformation and the Jacobian $\boldsymbol{\nabla\phi} = \boldsymbol{J}$ can then be written as

$$\boldsymbol{\phi(x)} = \mathbf{x} + \mathbf{\Delta P}\eta = \boldsymbol{x} + \boldsymbol{\Delta P}[\boldsymbol{D\eta}_0]\begin{bmatrix}\boldsymbol{x}\\1\end{bmatrix} \quad \boldsymbol{\nabla_x\phi(x)} = \boldsymbol{I} + \boldsymbol{\Delta PD} \tag{17}$$

Similarly for B-splines the derivatives can be derived. As B-splines are tensor product basis function we restrict ourselves to the 1-dimensional case. The basis polynomials and derivatives are given by:

$$\boldsymbol{B}(t) = \begin{Bmatrix} -t^3 + 3t^2 - 3t + 1 \\ 3t^3 - 6t^2 + 4 \\ -3t^3 + 3t^2 + 3t + 1 \\ t^3 \end{Bmatrix}, \boldsymbol{\Delta B}(t) = \begin{Bmatrix} -3t^2 + 6t - 3 \\ 9t^2 - 12t \\ -9t^2 + 6t + 3 \\ 3t^2 \end{Bmatrix}, \quad 0 \leq t < 1 \tag{18}$$

thus we write $\boldsymbol{\phi}(t) = t_0 + \boldsymbol{B}(t)\boldsymbol{p}$ where p are the parameters and $\nabla_t\boldsymbol{\phi} = 1 + \boldsymbol{\Delta B}(t)\boldsymbol{p}$. The extension to ND is straight forward.

7 Experiments

Two types of experiments have been conducted. One type is on synthetic data to illustrate the ability to handle large deformations. We use 2D registration with B-splines and a 3D simulation using tetrahedra. For the real data we apply correlation ratio (CR) for MRI as distance measures and the SSD of a signed distance map for the ears. For all real data experiments a scale space approach has been used in a coarse to fine manner for the deformation, thus propagating the deformation field to a set of basis functions with higher resolution.

7.1 Synthetic Data

Several experiments on synthetic data are presented to illustrate the properties of the elasticity in this formulation for large-scale deformation. 2D experiments with 3rd degree B-splines and 3D using tetrahedra.

Large deformations. To test the regularization and its ability to capture large-scale deformation we have performed three experiments. We register a square to a disc, a C to a disc and a disc to a C (figure 2). The experiments are performed in 2D with a uniform B-spline basis as parameterization of the deformation ϕ and cubic B-spline image interpolation.For the first experiment we use a resolution of 10 pixels between each node in the B-spline on the images with resolution 300×300 pixels. The number of samples are uniformly 100×100 in each direction. As figure 2(a) show, we can register a square to a circle obtaining smooth deformation fields that is diffeomorphic by definition. Registration of a C to a disc and vice versa is a difficult task and the success heavily depends on the right choice of scale for the basis functions. In this experiment we use 60 pixels between nodes 30, 8, 4, and 2 to obtain the desired result without falling into a local minimum. As figure 3(b) and figure 3(c) shows, we obtain deformation fields for both C to disc and disc to C with very large deformations. The obtained deformation fields are guaranteed to be diffeomorphic. To obtain symmetric solution such as in figure 3(a) all of the basis functions at each resolution must be placed exactly symmetric and the problem must be exactly symmetric. Otherwise the solution will be slightly asymmetric, emphasizing slightly.

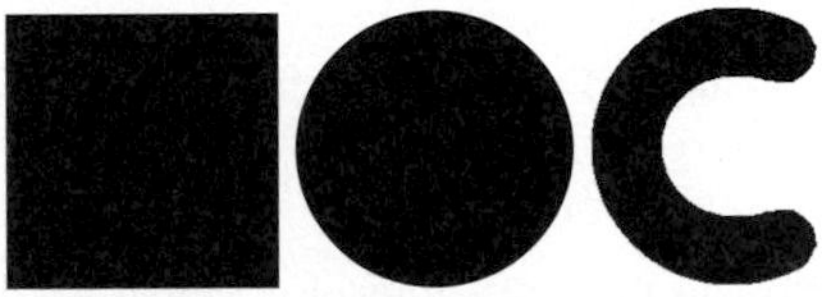

(a) Square (b) Disk (c) C

Fig. 2. The square (a) and the C (c) have been registered to the disc (b)

Tetrahedra. To show the efficiency of the model and its ability to handle large deformations we have deformed a 3d cube of 6000 tetrahedra under constant force. The result in figure 4(b) is obtained without numerical instability and handles as can be seen very large deformations. Over 80 evaluations we compared the hyper elastic energy and SSD which gave a ratio of computational time of HE/SSD=1.45 which shows the efficiency of the algorithm.

7.2 Cardiac Data

This data is a part of a cardiac data set of patients with a serious heart condition. The data consists of 2D slices from different patients which we co-register using CR and B-spline parameterization of ϕ. The slices are not obtained in exactly

(a) Square to disc (b) C to disc (c) Disc to C

Fig. 3. (a)The deformation field for the registration of the square registered using Riemanian elasticity and B-spline.(b) The deformation field of the C registered to the disc using Riemanian elasticity and B-spline. (c) The deformation field of the disc registered to the C using Riemanian elasticity and B-spline.

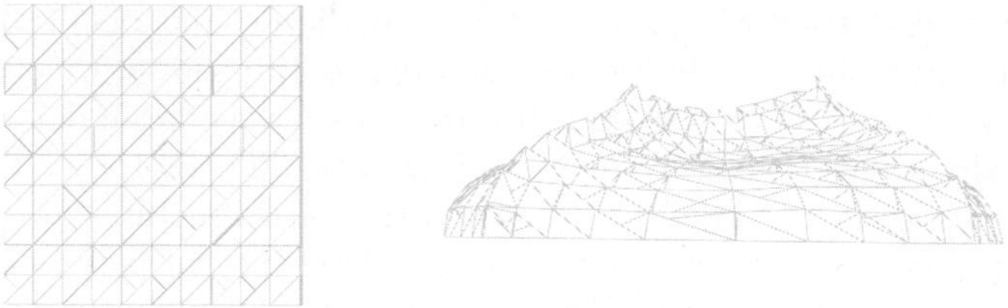

(a) (b)

Fig. 4. (a)The un-deformed cube (b) the deformed cube. The transformation to **b** from **a** is guaranteed to be diffeomorphic.

the same angle relative to the patient. Therefore most of the background in the images has been removed for demonstration purposes. The classes for the CR is based on a reference image segmented by hand. Figure 5 show a registration results, the transformation, the residual and the segmentation difference. The results show that the elasticity forces help move the papillary muscles into place as we know that they are considered a part of the myocardium by the CR due to the segmentation.

7.3 Ear Data

In addition we register 80 3D surfaces representing ear impression using 3D hyper elastic prior. This data was presented in [25] and was obtained to analyze the shape changes induced in the ear canal by movement of the mandible. The resulting average shape and a random deformation field is shown in figure 6.

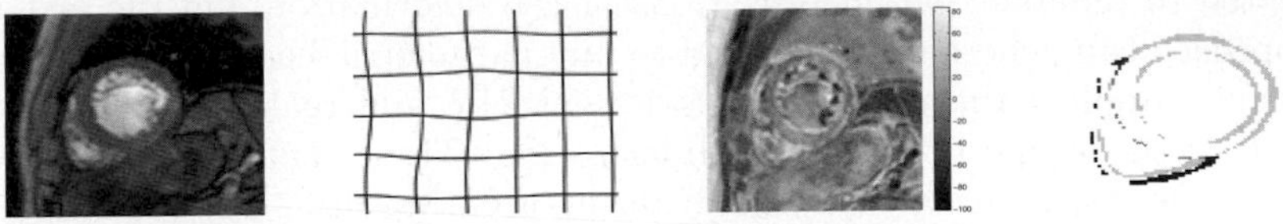

(a) Reference (b) Transformation (c) Residual (d) Dice image

Fig. 5. (a) The reference image. (b) The transformation. (c) The intensity residual showing that the papillary muscles are registered correctly. (d) The difference in segmentations after registration.

(a) Average ear (b) Deformation field

Fig. 6. (a) The average ear from 80 ears. (b) A 3D deformation field from registration of 2 ears.

8 Discussion

The method described in this paper can be implemented in parallel and offers due to the chain rule an easy way of switching between different kinds of elasticity. The performance in highly dependent on the parameterization ϕ e.g. a B-spline in 3D will have 192 parameters where as the tetrahedra only has 12 from which the strain tensor is computed. Thus, one should when solving a specific problem carefully select the appropriate parameterization such that speed, accuracy and performance suit the given task.

9 Summary and Conclusion

We have presented an efficient way of implementing hyper elastic regularization based on the chain rule and the derivatives of the eigen values of the left Cauchy-Green strain tensor. The method is illustrated on Riemanian Elasticity but it is in no way limited to this. We have shown in practice how the methodology is adapted to different parameterizations of the deformation and the fact that the approach can generally be adapted to any parametric base. Finally we have successfully applied the method to both synthetic and real data, in so doing illustrating the properties of the regularization. These include the ability to capture large deformation such as registering a C to a disc. The regularization can also capture more subtle deformation such as the deformation between ears in a population and it can capture very small local deformations such as the MRI data. Finally we have illustrated the effectiveness of the approach by comparing it to the computational complexity of SSD. The results were very convincing and only 1.45 times as computational expensive as SSD using B-spline interpolation.

References

1. Broit, C.: Optimal Registration of Deformed Images. PhD thesis, University of Pennsylvania (1981)
2. Bajscy, R., Lieberson, R., Reivich, M.: A computerized system for the elastic matching of deformed radiographic images to idealized atlas images. Computer assisted Tomography 5, 618–625 (1983)
3. Pennec, X., Stefanescu, R., Arsigny, V., Fillard, P., Ayache, N.: Riemannian Elasticity: A Statistical Regularization Framework for Non-linear Registration. In: Duncan, J.S., Gerig, G. (eds.) MICCAI 2005. LNCS, vol. 3750, p. 943. Springer, Heidelberg (2005)
4. Rohlfing, T., Maurer Jr., C., Bluemke, D., Jacobs, M.: Volume-preserving nonrigid registration of MR breast images using free-form deformation with an incompressibility constraint. IEEE Transactions on Medical Imaging 22(6), 730–741 (2003)
5. Tanner, C., Schnabel, J., Degenhard, A., Castellano-Smith, A., Hayes, C., Leach, M., Hose, D., Hill, D., Hawkes, D.: Validation of Volume-Preserving Non-rigid Registration: Application to Contrast-Enhanced MR-Mammography. In: Dohi, T., Kikinis, R. (eds.) MICCAI 2002. LNCS, vol. 2488, pp. 307–314. Springer, Heidelberg (2002)
6. Haber, E., Modersitzki, J.: Numerical methods for volume preserving image registration. Inverse Problems 20(5), 1621–1638 (2004)
7. Fischer, B., Modersitzki, J.: Fast diffusion registration. AMS Contemporary Mathematics, Inverse Problems, Image Analysis, and Medical Imaging 313, 117–129 (2002)
8. Christensen, G.: Deformable shape models for anatomy. Electrical Engineering D. Sc. Dissertation, Washington University, St. Louis, Missouri (1994)
9. Cardenas, V., Studholme, C., Gazdzinski, S., Durazzo, T.C., Meyerhoff, D.J.: Deformation-based morphometry of brain changes in alcohol dependence and abstinence. NeuroImage 34, 879–887 (2007)
10. Rueckert, D., Sonoda, L.I., Hayes, C., Hill, D.L.G., Leach, M.O., Hawkes, D.J.: Nonrigid registration using free-form deformations: application to breast MR images. IEEE Transactions on Medical Imaging 18(8), 712–721 (1999)
11. Studholme, C., Constable, R., Duncan, J.: Accurate alignment of functional EPI data to anatomical MRI using aphysics-based distortion model. IEEE Transactions on Medical Imaging 19(11), 1115–1127 (2000)
12. Vester-Christensen, M., Erbou, S.G., Darkner, S., Larsen, R.: Accelerated 3D image registration. In: SPIE Medical Imaging 2007 (2007)

13. Cootes, T., Twinning, C., Taylor, C.: Diffeomorphic Statistical Shape Models. In: British Machine Vision Conference, vol. 1, pp. 447–456 (2004)
14. Bookstein, F.L.: Principal warps: thin-plate splines and the decomposition of deformations. IEEE Transactions on Pattern Analysis and Machine Intelligence 11(6), 567–585 (1989)
15. Ogden, R.W.: Large Deformation Isotropic Elasticity-On the Correlation of Theory and Experiment for Incompressible Rubberlike Solids. Proceedings of the Royal Society of London. Series A, Mathematical and Physical Sciences (1934-1990) 326(1567), 565–584 (1972)
16. Liu, D.C., Nocedal, J.: On the limited memory BFGS method for large scale optimization. Mathematical programming 45(1), 503–528 (1989)
17. Wells, W., Viola, P., Atsumi, H., Nakajima, S., Kikinis, R.: Multi-modal volume registration by maximization of mutual information. Medical Image Analysis 1(1), 35–51 (1996)
18. Studholme, C., Hill, D., Hawkes, D.: An overlap invariant entropy measure of 3D medical image alignment. Pattern Recognition 32(1), 71–86 (1999)
19. Haber, E., Modersitzki, J.: Intensity Gradient Based Registration and Fusion of Multi-modal Images. Methods of Information in Medicine 46(3), 292 (2007)
20. Roche, A., Malandain, G., Pennec, X., Ayache, N.: The Correlation Ratio as a New Similarity Measure for Multimodal Image Registration. In: Wells, W.M., Colchester, A.C.F., Delp, S.L. (eds.) MICCAI 1998. LNCS, vol. 1496, pp. 1115–1124. Springer, Heidelberg (1998)
21. Besl, P., McKay, N.: A method for registration of 3-D shapes. IEEE Transactions on Pattern Analysis and Machine Intelligence 14(2), 239–256 (1992)
22. Papadopoulo, T., Lourakis, M.: Estimating the Jacobian of the Singular Value Decomposition: Theory and Applications. In: Vernon, D. (ed.) ECCV 2000. LNCS, vol. 1842, pp. 554–570. Springer, Heidelberg (2000)
23. Cootes, T., Marsland, S., Twining, C., Smith, K., Taylor, C.: Groupwise diffeomorphic non-rigid registration for automatic model building. In: Pajdla, T., Matas, J(G.) (eds.) ECCV 2004. LNCS, vol. 3024, pp. 316–327. Springer, Heidelberg (2004)
24. Möbius, A.F.: Der barycentrische Calcul: ein neues Hülfsmittel zur analytischen Behandlung der Geometrie: mit 4 Kupfertafeln, JA Barth (1827)
25. Darkner, S., Larsen, R., Paulsen, R.: Analysis of deformation of the human ear and canal caused by mandibular movement. In: Proceedings of the 10th International Conference on Medical Image Computing and Computer-Assisted Intervention, pp. 801–808. Springer, Heidelberg (2007)

Degradation Based Blind Image Quality Evaluation

Ville Ojansivu[1], Leena Lepistö[2], Martti Ilmoniemi[2], and Janne Heikkilä[1]

[1] Machine Vision Group, University of Oulu, Finland
firstname.lastname@ee.oulu.fi
http://www.cse.oulu.fi/MVG
[2] Nokia Corporation, Tampere, Finland
{leena.i.lepisto,martti.ilmoniemi}@nokia.com

Abstract. In this paper, we propose a novel framework for blind image quality evaluation. Unlike the common image quality measures evaluating compression or transmission artifacts this approach analyzes the image properties common to non-ideal image acquisition such as blur, under or over exposure, saturation, and lack of meaningful information. In contrast to methods used for adjusting imaging parameters such as focus and gain this approach does not require any reference image. The proposed method uses seven image degradation features that are extracted and fed to a classifier that decides whether the image has good or bad quality. Most of the features are based on simple image statistics, but we also propose a new feature that proved to be reliable in scene invariant detection of strong blur. For the overall two-class image quality grading, we achieved ≈ 90% accuracy by using the selected features and the classifier. The method was designed to be computationally efficient in order to enable real-time performance in embedded devices.

Keywords: image artifacts, blur, exposure, no-reference, quality measurement.

1 Introduction

In this paper, we propose a method for automatic image quality evaluation based on different types of image degradations such as blur, under or over exposure, saturation, or lack of meaningful information which are illustrated in Figure 1. The method does not need the original image as a reference, but the evaluation is done solely based on the features extracted from the degraded image. Our method is designed to be fast to compute so that it can be applied on-line. The method could be applied, for example, to assist photographer by prompting to capture new image, maybe with different camera parameters, if the obtained image quality is poor. Another application could be classifying gallery images based on quality and placing the poor quality images into a trash-folder.

Most of the current image and video quality evaluation methods are aimed for detecting quality reduction due to lossy compression or transmission errors [7]. Part of these methods use original non-degraded image as a reference and

A. Heyden and F. Kahl (Eds.): SCIA 2011, LNCS 6688, pp. 306–316, 2011.

Fig. 1. Examples of typical image degradations

perform the evaluation relative to this image. Others are no-reference or blind methods. Typical degradations are blur, noise, and block-based artifacts due to compression. The blind quality evaluation independent of image content is a much more difficult task for a computer although it may be simple for humans. The distinction between image details and impairments may be difficult [4]. For example, the measurements of blur and noise correlate typically heavily with the image content [7]. To our knowledge, there are not many methods for evaluating the overall image quality based on the degradations due to exposure and blurring. The different degradations are measured typically separately before image capture to adjust the imaging parameters. For example, under or over exposure and saturation might be measured for optimal exposure control. On the other hand, there are methods for measuring blur to achieve optimal focus. These methods typically compare the metric between multiple images from the same scene i.e. they make the evaluation relative to a reference. In [5], the authors have taken different approach to image quality evaluation by classifying images as professional vs. snapshots based also on the composition of the image.

We are interested in the overall perceived quality of the image due to multiple factors which include, in addition to blur, also saturation of pixels, incorrect exposure, and information content of the image. The last property means that we consider accidentally captured images representing, for example, floor as poor quality. So, instead of evaluating the technical quality traditionally, we are interested in the overall quality perceived by human. We perform the evaluation without any reference information and independent on the scene content.

Figure 2 presents our framework for image quality evaluation which consists of three steps: preprocessing, feature extraction, and classification. In the preprocessing step, the images are low-pass filtered and resized to the VGA size. This is followed by feature extraction. We used seven scalar features each reflecting the amount of single degradation present in the image. These features are described in more detail in Section 2 and summarized in Table 1. The features are fed to a binary classifier which has been trained based on subjective evaluations of the training images. Classification is described in more detail in Section 3. The features as well as the classifier are selected carefully so that they can be implemented efficiently on-line. For this purpose we tested various methods for feature extraction as well as for classification. We also developed a completely new feature for detecting strong blur.

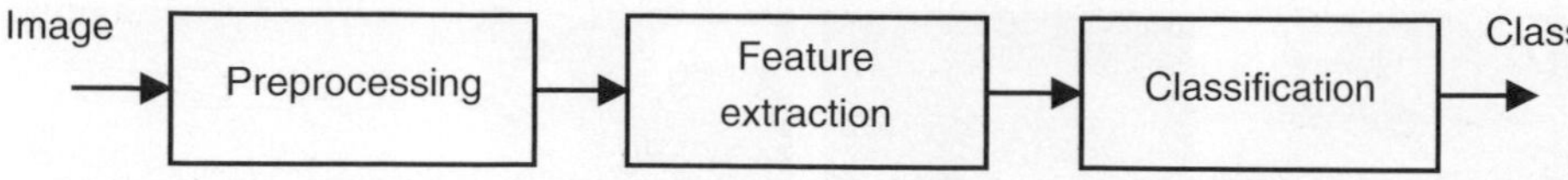

Fig. 2. Framework for blind image quality evaluation

2 Features for Detecting Degradations

We used seven separate features for detecting different impairments: blur, under or over exposure, saturation, and lack of information. These features are presented in the following with possible discussion of alternatives. Notice that the amount of noise can be typically predicted based on the exposure parameters and therefore it is not considered in this work.

Blur. In this work, the aim was to measure global blur caused by sudden camera motion or defocus of the lens system without any reference information. Different approaches for blur measurement are shortly reviewed next, before presenting the method we used.

A lot of earlier research exists on blur measurement in few different contexts. Traditionally, blur has been measured using metrics based on variance of image pixels, autocorrelation, image derivatives, estimation of edge widths, investigation of frequency spectrum, or histograms of pixels values or DCT coefficients. All these methods are based on the fact that blurring fades out image details and edges which corresponds to attenuation of the high frequency components of the image spectrum [4]. Image noise often disturbs these measures as it brings more variation to image which may be interpreted as sharp details.

Many of the existing blur measurement methods are targeted for autofocusing systems. In these systems, blur of the same image is measured with different focus settings. These methods can also work with motion blur. The only criterion for the measure is that it behaves monotonically when the amount of blur changes. If these blur measures are applied to images of different scenes, such as in Figure 4(a)-4(c), the results are not comparable as the amount of details in the image also affects to the measure. There are also methods which are targeted for quality evaluation of JPEG coded images. These methods measure the blurring caused by quantization or deblocking filter and are not suitable for our purpose [7].

Another group of blur metrics, which attempts to measure the amount of blur independent of the image content, is based on edge detection followed by estimation of the average edge width in the gradient direction or just horizontally [4]. These methods divide images into blocks and use only blocks containing edges. When the blur is strong [9] or images noisy [3] it may be however difficult to find edges reliably. A bigger obstacle is that these methods are suitable only for defocus blur. In motion blurred images, the sharpest edges are in opposite direction of the motion which makes the results incorrect. There is also a method which estimates partially blurred images with different scenes [6]. The method divides images into blocks and compares blur metrics between these blocks and the whole image to detect blurred/sharp blocks corresponding to foreground objects. The method does not work for global blur.

Absolute blurriness between completely different scenes is very difficult to measure reliably because the image content affects sometimes even more to the metric than the blurring. From our tested methods, the most consistent blur measurements between different scenes gave a method proposed by Crete et al. [1]. The method is based on comparison of the x and y gradients of a blurred and re-blurred image. The method uses the assumption that re-blurring already blurred image does not change the image derivatives as much as blurring of a sharp image.

When the approach of Crete is used, there is another problem in the case of strong blur: noise added into the smooth image after blurring appears as false texture lowering measured blur level. This can be alleviated by suppressing noise using low pass filtering. In addition, we propose another method for detecting especially strong blur, which is presented next.

Strong Blur. The feature for strong blur detection is computed by average normalized difference d_α between observed image $g_{\mathbf{n}}$ and an artificially blurred image $b^\alpha_{\mathbf{n}}$, namely

$$d_\alpha = \sum_{\mathbf{n}} \frac{|g_{\mathbf{n}} - b^\alpha_{\mathbf{n}}|}{g_{\mathbf{n}} + \delta} , \qquad (1)$$

where α is the motion blur angle used to blur the observed image, $\mathbf{n}$ denotes pixel location, and δ is a small real number. For an observed image $g_{\mathbf{n}}$, which already contains defocus blur d_α is small for all angles α of artificial blur, and for an image containing motion blur, d_α will be small for angle α corresponding to the motion blur direction in observed image $g_{\mathbf{n}}$. For this reason, minimum of results d_α is selected as the final blur feature d, namely

$$d = \min\{d_{\alpha_i}\} . \qquad (2)$$

Blur to the observed image is generated by a 1×9 averaging filter which is rotated into angles $\alpha = \{0, 45, 90, 135\}$ degrees. The main difference between the proposed and Crete's [1] method is that we do not use image gradient for computing the feature.

Under or Over Exposure. Under and over exposure is measured using the mean of the image pixel values, which ranges from 0 to 255. It is assumed that value 128 corresponds to a well exposed image. Smaller values correspond to under exposure and larger values over exposure. We used separate features for under and over exposure. Using two separate features enables to weight them differently in the classification step to better correspond to the subjective evaluation of the image quality.

Saturation. The saturation features are based on amount of saturated pixels in saturated areas which are larger than 50 pixels. These are supposed to correspond disturbing highlighted areas in image. So, single saturated pixels are not counted. Saturation is detected separately in 1/3 top image and 2/3 bottom image. This

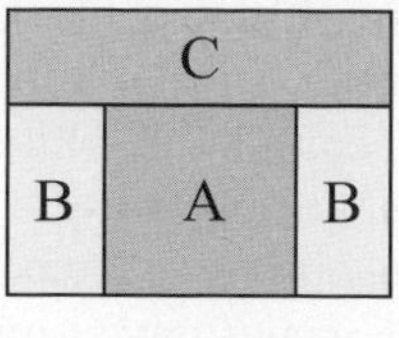

Fig. 3. Saturation is detected separately for areas A, B, and C

Table 1. Features used to measure artifacts for image quality evaluation

Feature	Range	Based on	Time sec.
1. blur	0...1	Difference of derivates of image and blurred image	0.18
2. strong blur	0...1	Difference of image and blurred image	0.10
3. under exposure	0...1	Mean value of image pixels	0.0010
4. over exposure	0...1	Mean value of image pixels	incl. to 3.
5. no-information	0...1	Entropy of image	0.011
6. top saturation	0...1	Saturated pixels in top 1/3 area of image	0.023
7. bottom saturation	0...1	Saturated pixels in bottom 2/3 area of image	0.024

Range: 0 = no artifact
1 = strong artifact

is due to the fact that most of the saturation in natural images appears in top area including sky, sun, lights etc. This top image saturation cannot be avoided in many situations, and on the other hand, top image saturation is perceived as more natural and not so disturbing. Top-saturation feature is computed from area C in Figure 3.

Bottom image saturation feature is computed from areas A and B. It is assumed that saturation of image is most disturbing in the central area A. For this reason the area A has double weight compared to area B in computation of the bottom-saturation. The algorithm assumes that the image orientation is known.

No-Information. Some images do not contain any meaningful information. These images may be captured accidentally, for example, toward the floor. The image entropy is used as a feature to measure the lack of information in the image.

All the features are normalized logarithmically into scale [0,1] so that feature value 0.5 corresponds approximately to the threshold between good and bad images in subjective quality. The features with their ranges, basis techniques, and approximate computation times are summarized in Table 1. Times are based on computation of the features for a VGA image using non-optimized Matlab implementations and 3 GHz Intel Core 2 Duo E8400 CPU with 4 GB RAM.

3 Classifier for Quality Evaluation

We compared different classifiers for quality evaluation of the images. What we need is a binary classifier which takes the seven features characterizing the degradations as input and gives the class good/bad quality as output. The quality cannot be classified simply by using a concatenation the features, because single strong artifact destroys the image quality even if the other features indicate good quality. It seems that the dominant degradation in the image will indicate quite well the subjective image quality.

Based on the previous discussion we first tried to use classifier which bases the classification only on single dominant degradation. This means that the classifier selects the largest artifact feature value to represent image quality. This value is compared to a threshold. During training with subjectively labeled data the relative weights of the features are selected by increasing or decreasing them iteratively to best reflect the subjective evaluations. This method, referred hereafter as *MaxFeature* classifier, produced relatively good results as shown in the experiment section and the method is also very fast to compute.

We tested also AdaBoost and support vector machine (SVM) classifiers. Both of these methods are well known classifiers for a two-class classification problem. For SVM we used the radial basis function (RBF) kernel, which is in general a good choice when the relation between the classes and features is nonlinear.

4 Experimental Results

Test Images and Preprocessing. As test images, we used 508 5 Mpix images photographed using Nokia N95 mobile phone. These images contain degradations caused by real imaging situation including blur, noise, under or over exposure, saturation of pixel values caused by over exposure or bright sky, sun, lights etc., and also accidentally captured images with random content. Figures 1, 6, and 8 show examples of the test images.

This data set is challenging since the images are photographed in various situations resulting also in images containing no meaningful information ("no-information"). Many of the images contain multiple degradations at the same time. Most common artifact is blur due to motion or out of focus. All images contain also substantial amount of noise. Many images are saturated in part but at the same time in part under exposed. Saturation appears especially in the images depicting gray sky.

Before computing the artifact features we preprocessed the 5 Mpix image as follows. We first low-pass filtered the images to suppress noise, which is essential for the blur detection, although the image is at the same time blurred slightly. Filtering was done using a 5-by-5 uniform filter, which can be implemented very efficiently but still resulted in similar results as a Gaussian filter. Subsequently the images were resized to the VGA size (640×480) to reduce the computation in the feature extraction step.

Subjective Evaluation. For training and testing of the classifiers, the image quality of the 508 images was evaluated subjectively. This was done by inspecting the original images on a 19 inch screen. The images were given one of the grades $\{0, 1, 2, 3\}$, ranging from good to useless quality, with respect to the attainable quality range of a mobile phone camera. For the blur measurement experiment the images were evaluated similarly but taking into account only the perceived blur artifact.

4.1 Features for Detecting Blur

In this section, we present results with blur measurement algorithms. The selection of blur features for overall image quality evaluation was based on these results. In the first experiment, we compared methods for detecting blur in images containing completely different types of scenes, shown in Figure 4(a)-4(c), because blur feature should be invariant to the scene content. As blurring appears as smoothing of the image, the blur detection algorithms often rate image containing more texture, such as Figure 4(a), as sharper than image containing smoother regions, such in Figure 4(c).

We compared our proposed method and the Crete's method [1] for which there is a Matlab implementation available online[1]. Additionally we compared the following methods. Method by Erasmus and Smith [2] is based on the variance of the image. This method is targeted for autofocusing and illustrates how this kind of methods are dependent on the image content. The method of Tsomko et al. [8] computes variances of horizontal derivative image blocks and uses the maximum variance as a measure of blurriness. The method by Zhu and Milanfar [10] is a more complicated method which attempts to measure noise and blur simultaneously. It is included only for demonstration because the Matlab implementation is available online[2].

Diagrams in Figures 4(d)-4(f) and 4(g)-4(i) illustrate the results of blur estimation with different methods in case of increasing the extent of artificial circular or horizontal motion blur, respectively. In both cases, it can be noticed that the Crete's method and the proposed method behave most consistently between the three different scenes. The least consistent results are obtained with Erasmus' method, which mainly reflects the amount of texture in the image instead of blur. Zhu's method is nearly as inconsistent between the scenes and in addition does not behave monotonically. Tsomko's method is better, but not among the best. Based on these results we selected the proposed and Crete's method for further experiments.

Next we applied the selected features for the 508 test images. For detecting two highest blur levels $\{2, 3\}$ out of possible levels $\{0, 1, 2, 3\}$ we obtain the receiver operating characteristics (ROC) curves illustrated in Figure 5(a). Curves show the true positive rate (TPR) of detecting blur as a function of false positive rate (FPR) when the thresholds for the different features are lowered. As can be seen, Crete's method gives slightly better results than the proposed method. However, a combination of the methods, which selects the larger of the single features, gives clearly the best results. (Area under curve (AUC): Crete 0.902, proposed 0.870, and combined 0.943.) In the other case, illustrated by ROC curves in Figure 5(b), we investigated detection of the strongest blur level $\{3\}$.

---
[1] `www.mathworks.com/matlabcentral/fileexchange/24676-image-blur-metric`
[2] `http://users.soe.ucsc.edu/~xzhu/doc/metricq.html`

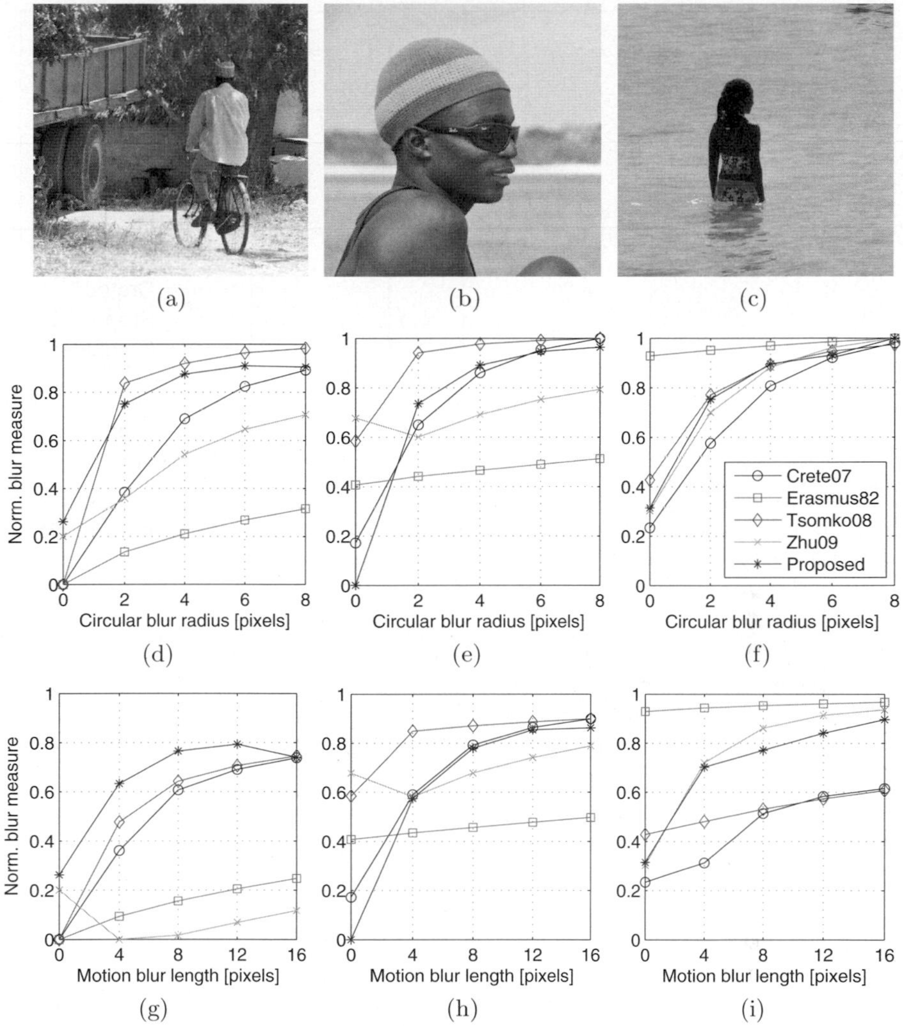

Fig. 4. Blur estimation results using different methods for different types of scenes (a-c) when blur level is increased: circular blur (d-f) and horizontal motion blur (g-i)

As can be seen, the proposed method can detect the strongest blur better than Crete's method while the combined method is superior in this sense. (AUC: Crete 0.826, proposed 0.911, and combined 0.974.) It seems that Crete's method, based on image gradients, is more sensitive to remaining noise in the image which appears as false texture in strongly blurred, smooth, images. Figure 6 illustrates some examples of images, containing strong blur, which can be detected by the combination of the proposed and Crete's feature but are missed with Crete's feature alone.

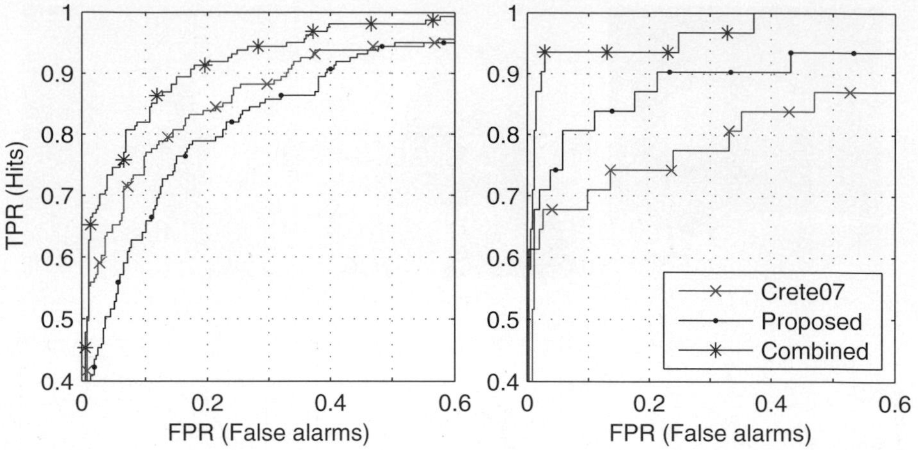

(a) (b)

Fig. 5. ROC curves for detecting blurred images with different methods: detection of blur levels {2,3} (a) and only strongest level {3} (b)

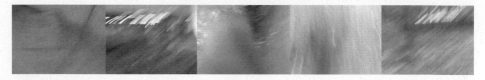

Fig. 6. Examples of strongly blurred images which can be detected with the combination of the proposed and Crete's feature but not by Crete's feature alone. (Corresponds to operating point FPR=0.09 in Figure 5(a).)

4.2 Image Quality Classification

For the classification step, we tested three methods: Support Vector Machine (SVM) with the RBF kernel[3], Real AdaBoost[4] with single branch weak learners, and our own MaxFeature classifier using only single dominant artifact feature. The classifiers are trained/tested using leave-one-out cross validation. This means that one image at time is picked for testing and the classifier is trained using the remaining 507 images. This gives largest amount of training data without using the test sample for training.

Figure 7 shows the ROC curves for classification using different classifiers. True/false (T/F) correspond to bad/good quality images with labels {3,4}/{0,1}, respectively. The ROC curves show TPR and FPR when the threshold for the score of the classifier is lowered gradually. As can be seen in Figure 7, SVM gives the best result followed by quite similar MaxFeature and AdaBoost

[3] `www.csie.ntu.edu.tw/~cjlin/libsvm`

[4] `graphics.cs.msu.ru/ru/science/research/machinelearning/adaboosttoolbox`

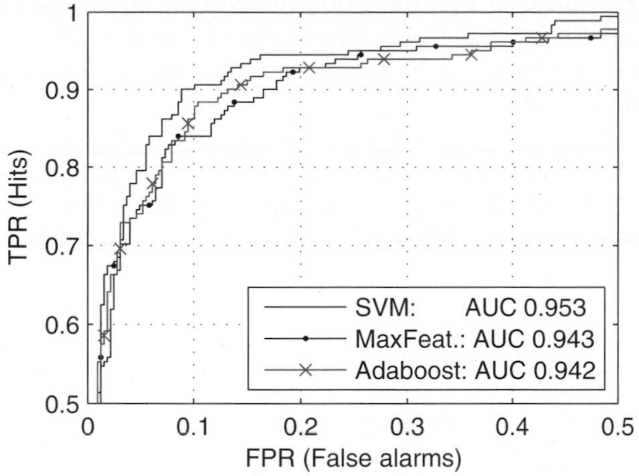

Fig. 7. ROC curves for detecting bad quality images with different classifiers

Fig. 8. Examples of classification results. Bad quality (top row) and good quality (bottom row).

classifiers. Although, the MaxFeature classifier is fastest to compute, we chose to use SVM classifier in operating point corresponding to the threshold 0: TPR 0.812 (147/181), FPR 0.055 (18/327), and total accuracy 89.76. Figure 8 shows some examples of classification results. It is noteworthy that in this operating point there was no $\{0\}$ labels in FP samples and only four $\{3\}$ labels among FN samples. So, none of the best quality images would be thrown away, which is important.

5 Conclusions

In this study, we proposed a method for blind image quality evaluation based on different types of image degradations. Evaluation was done using features extracted from the image which are subsequently fed to a SVM classifier. Also a completely new feature for detecting strong blur was proposed. According to the experiments, the most reliable detection of the blur is achieved by using both an existing and the proposed blur measurement features. For the overall two-class image quality grading, we achieved ≈ 90% accuracy by using the selected features and the classifier.

The proposed method is designed to be fast to compute so that it can be applied on-line and also with mobile devices. The applications could include, for example, assisting photographer by warning about low quality results or removing low quality gallery images.

References

1. Crete, F., Dolmiere, T., Ladret, P., Nicolas, M.: The blur effect: Perception and estimation with a new no-reference perceptual blur metric. In: Proc. SPIE, vol. 6492 (2007)
2. Erasmus, S.J., Smith, K.C.A.: An automatic focusing and astigmatism correction system for the sem and ctem. Journal of Microscopy 27, 185–199 (1982)
3. Ferzli, R., Karam, L.J.: No-reference objective wavelet based noise immune image sharpness metric. In: IEEE International Conference on Image Processing, pp. 405–408 (2005)
4. Ferzli, R., Karam, L.J.: A no-reference objective image sharpness metric based on the notion of just noticeable blur (JNB). IEEE Trans. Image Processing 18(4), 717–728 (2009)
5. Ke, Y., Tang, X., Jing, F.: The design of high-level features for photo quality assessment. In: IEEE Conference on Computer Vision and Pattern Recognition, New York, NY, pp. 419–426 (June 2006)
6. Liu, R.T., Li, Z.R., Jia, J.Y.: Image partial blur detection and classification. In: IEEE Conference on Computer Vision and Pattern Recognition, pp. 1–8 (2008)
7. Sheikh, H.R., Bovik, A.C., Cormack, L.: No-reference quality assessment using natural scene statistics: JPEG 2000. IEEE Trans. Image Processing 14(11), 1918–1927 (2005)
8. Tsomko, E., Kim, H.J., Paik, J., Yeo, I.K.: Efficient method of detecting blurry images. Journal of Ubiquitous Convergence Technology 2(1), 27–39 (2008)
9. Varadarajan, S., Karam, L.J.: An improved perception-based no-reference objective image sharpness metric using iterative edge refinement. In: IEEE International Conference on Image Processing, pp. 401–404 (2008)
10. Zhu, X., Milanfar, P.: A no-reference sharpness metric sensitive to blur and noise. In: International Workshop on Quality of Multimedia Experience, pp. 64–69 (2009)

Evaluation of Image Quality Metrics for Color Prints

Marius Pedersen[1,2], Yuanlin Zheng[1,3], and Jon Yngve Hardeberg[1]

[1] Gjøvik University College, Gjøvik, Norway
[2] Océ Print Logic Technologies S.A., Creteil, France
[3] Xi'an University of Technology, Xi'an Shaanxi, China

Abstract. New technology is continuously proposed in the printing technology, and as a result the need to perform quality assessment is increasing. Subjective assessment of quality is tiresome and expensive, the use of objective methods have therefore become more and more popular. One type of objective assessment that has been subject for extensive research is image quality metrics. However, so far no one has been able to propose a metric fully correlated with the percept. Pedersen et al. (J Elec Imag 19(1):011016, 2010) proposed a set of quality attributes with the intention of being used with image quality metrics. These quality attributes are the starting point for this work, where we evaluate image quality metrics for them, with the goal of proposing suitable metrics for each quality attribute. Experimental results show that suitable metrics are found for the sharpness, lightness, artifacts, and contrast attributes, while none of the evaluated metrics correlate with the percept for the color attribute.

Keywords: Image quality, metrics, print quality, quality attributes, color printing.

1 Introduction

Image Quality (IQ) assessment is an important part in the printing industry. The introduction of new technology and products require assessment of quality to see if the quality is improved over the current technology. When observers judge IQ they base their decision a number of quality attributes, such as colorfulness, contrast, and sharpness. Many researchers have been investigating the importance of different quality attributes and their influence on IQ [14,20,19,24,23]. Knowledge about the importance of quality attributes can be used to achieve an optimal reproduction of an image [8]. However, evaluating all quality attributes in the literature is not practical, therefore most researchers evaluate a subset of quality attributes. A subset of quality attributes helps reduce the complexity of IQ, and the strengths and weaknesses of a system can be modeled using only a few parameters. Recently, Pedersen et al. [24,23] proposed a set of six Color Printing Quality Attributes (CPQAs) for the evaluation of print quality:

- The **color** CPQA contains aspects related to color such as hue, saturation, and color rendition, except lightness.
- The **lightness** CPQA is considered so perceptually important that it is beneficial to separate it from the color CPQA. Lightness ranges from light to dark.

A. Heyden and F. Kahl (Eds.): SCIA 2011, LNCS 6688, pp. 317–326, 2011.

- The **contrast** CPQA can be described as the perceived magnitude of visually meaningful differences, global and local, in lightness and chromaticity within the image.
- The **sharpness** CPQA is related to the clarity of details and definition of edges.
- The **artifacts** CPQA includes noise, contouring, and banding. In color printing, some artifacts can be perceived in the resulting image. These artifacts can degrade the quality of an image if they are detectable.
- The **physical** CPQA contains all physical parameters that affect quality, such as paper properties and gloss.

These were proposed with the intention of being used in both subjective and objective evaluation of quality. Validation of the CPQAs showed that they were suitable to evaluate IQ [24,26]. Not long ago, Pedersen et al. [25,27] evaluated IQ metrics for each CPQA. Their evaluation indicated that metrics based on structural similarity gave good results for the sharpness, contrast, and lightness CPQAs, but for the other CPQAs the results were inconclusive. The conclusion was that further evaluation was needed in order to find suitable metrics to assess the quality of the CPQAs. We continue this work and evaluate IQ metrics for the CPQAs, with the intention of proposing suitable metrics for each CPQA. This work is considered as a part of our long term goal to be able to assess quality without being dependent on human observers.

The remainder of the paper is organized as follows: in the next section we introduce the experimental setup, before we evaluate a set of metrics against the perceptual data from the experiment. Finally we conclude and propose future work.

2 Experimental Setup

We want to investigate the relationship between the percept of the CPQAs and IQ metrics. In order to do this we have carried out an experiment where human observers judge the quality of the CPQAs on a set of printed images.

2.1 Test Images

Ten images (Figure 1) were selected from the ISO standards [12,13]. The number of images follow the recommendation by Field [9], who recommend between five and ten images, and the CIE [5], who recommend at least four images. The images were selected to cover a wide range of characteristics, such as lightness from low to high levels, saturation from low to high levels, contrast from low to high levels, hue primaries, fine details, memory colors as skin tones. These different characteristics will ensure evaluation of many different aspects of IQ.

Fig. 1. The ten test images used in the experiment. Each reproduced with four different settings.

2.2 Printing Workflow

Firstly, the color space of all the images was changed to sRGB to define the reference images . Secondly, then the color space was changed to CMYK using the output profile that was generated using a TC3.5 CMYK test target, measured with a GretagMacbeth Eye-One Pro spectrophotometer and generated with ProfileMaker Pro 5.0.8. Finally the CMYK images were printed by a HP DesignJet 10ps printer with the HP software RIP v2.1.1 using four different modes: the best print mode, with the resolution of 1200x1200, and the perceptual intent (abbr. BP), the best mode and relative colorimetric intent (abbr. BR), normal print mode, with the resolution of 600x600 and the perceptual intent (abbr. NP), and the last with normal print mode and relative colorimetric intent (abbr. NR). This resulted in the ten images having four different reproductions, giving a total of 40 images for the observers to judge.

2.3 Observers

Ten observers participated in the experiment, all had normal vision without visual deficits. There were 3 females and 7 males with an average age of 23 years.

2.4 Viewing Conditions

The observers were presented with a reference image on an EIZO ColorEdge CG224 at a color temperature of 6500 K and luminance level of 80 cd/m2. The image set was rendered for sRGB display, and therefore a monitor capable of displaying the sRGB gamut was the most adapted reproduction device for the set of images. A hood was fitted to the monitor to prevent glare. The printed images were presented randomly in a controlled viewing room at a color temperature of 5200 K, an illuminance level of 450 $\pm$75 lux and a color rendering index of 96. The observers viewed the reference image and the printed image simultaneously from a distance of approximately 60 cm. The experiment followed the CIE guidelines [5] as closely as possible.

2.5 Experiment Procedure

The observers were asked to compare one image selected from the ten images at random to its four prints. Sharpness quality, color quality, lightness quality, contrast quality, artifacts quality, and the quality of the main characteristics were evaluated on a five step scale, where 1 indicated best quality and 5 the worst quality. The physical CPQA was not evaluated since no physical parameter was changed.

3 Experimental Results

From the experiment z-scores were calculated using the color engineering toolbox [10], which indicated the perceived differences between the four reproductions. These z-scores were calculated for each CPQA and the main characteristics, both image-wise and for the complete dataset.

It has been suggested in the literature that some regions of the image is more important than others [30,18,43]. In order to investigate the relationship between the CPQAs and different regions of the image, we have calculated the Pearson correlation coefficients [15] between the main characteristics and the CPQAs. This analysis would reveal if the quality of the CPQAs are related to the quality of main characteristics (region-of-interest). From Table 1 we can see that in the different reproductions the main characteristics have varying correlation coefficients with the CPQAs. This indicates that the quality of the CPQAs are not directly linked with main characteristics, but that other characteristics are important for the impression of quality of most CPQAs. However, for some CPQAs and printing modes we see a high correlation between the main characteristics and the CPQAs, this might indicate that IQ metrics performing a weighting of regions could be more suitable than those assigning equal weight to the entire image.

Table 1. Pearson correlation between z-scores of the main characteristics and the z-scores of the CPQAs for each printing mode and for all modes

	CPQAs				
Mode	Color	Lightness	Sharpness	Contrast	Artifacts
BP	0.85	0.47	0.55	0.92	0.28
BR	0.72	0.45	0.48	0.78	0.55
NP	-0.02	0.60	0.30	0.61	0.71
NR	0.31	0.29	0.31	0.88	0.60
All	0.79	0.77	0.71	0.89	0.77

4 Evaluation of Image Quality Metrics

Our long term goal is to be able to automatically evaluate IQ through the CPQAs, more specifically using IQ metrics. In this part we evaluate a set of IQ metrics for each CPQA against the perceptual data from the experiment.

4.1 Preparation of the Printed Images

The printed images cannot be directly used with IQ metrics, since the metrics require a digital input. Because of this the images need to be digitized. To perform this we have adopted the framework by Pedersen and Amirshahi [22]. First the images were scanned at a resolution of 600 dpi using an HP ScanJet G4050. The scanner was characterized with the same test target as used to generate the printer profile. Since the experiment was carried out under mixed illumination, the CIECAM02 chromatic adaptation transform [6] was used to ensure consistency in the calculations for the metrics. The CIE guidelines were followed [6], using the measured reference white point of the monitor and the media were used as input to the adaptation transform.

4.2 Selected Image Quality Metrics

There are a number of IQ metrics proposed in the literature [31]. We cannot evaluate all of these, and because of this we have made a selection based on previous

Table 2. Selected IQ metrics for the evaluation of CPQAs

Metric \ CPQA	Sharpness	Color	Lightness	Contrast	Artifacts
ABF [38]		X	X		X
Busyness [21]	X		X		
blurMetric [7]	X				
Cao [3]	X				X
CW-SSIM[40]	X		X	X	X
ΔLC [2]	X		X	X	X
IW-SSIM [39]	X		X	X	X
LinLab [16]		X	X		X
MS-SSIM [42]	X		X	X	X
M-SVD [34]	X		X		X
PSNR-HVS-M[32]	X		X		X
PSNR-HVS [32]	X		X		X
RFSIM [44]	X		X	X	X
RRIQA [41]	X		X	X	X
S-CIELAB [45]		X	X		X
S-DEE [35]		X	X		X
SHAME [29]		X	X		X
SHAME-II [29]		X	X		X
SSIM [37]	X		X	X	X
VIF [33]	X		X	X	X
VSNR [4]	X		X		X
WLF [36]				X	X
YCXCzLab [17]		X	X		X

evaluations [1,11,22,25,27], the criteria on which the metrics were created, guidelines for metrics for CPQAs [27], and their popularity. Since many of the metrics are designed to account for specific aspects, only the ones suitable for a given CPQA is evaluated. An overview of the 23 metrics selected for the evaluation and the CPQAs they evaluate is found in Table 2.

4.3 Evaluation Method

Three different methods were adopted for the evaluation of the IQ metrics. In order to evaluate all aspects of the metrics we will investigate the performance of the IQ metrics both image by image, and the overall performance over the entire set of images. The Pearson correlation [15] is used for the image-wise evaluation, comparing the calculated quality and observed quality. The mean of the correlation for each image in the dataset and the percentage of images with a correlation above 0.6 is used as a measure of performance. Overall performance is also an important aspect, and for this evaluation we will use the rank order method [28], where the correlation between the z-scores from the observers and the z-scores of the metric is the indication of performance. With only four data points it is important to carry out visual inspections of the z-scores to validate the correlation values.

4.4 Evaluation Results

Due to many IQ metrics and several CPQAs we will only show the results of the best performing metrics for each CPQA.

Sharpness. For sharpness the Structural SIMilarity (SSIM) based metrics perform well (Table 3). The Multi-Scale SSIM (MS-SSIM) has the highest mean correlation with 0.73 and the highest number of images with a correlation above 0.6. It also performs among the best for the rank order correlation. The results show that metrics based on structural similarity are well-suited to measure perceived sharpness quality. However, other approaches as the ΔLC and the Riesz-transform based Feature SIMilarity metric (RFSIM) have very good performance, indicating that these might be suitable as well.

Table 3. Evaluation of IQ metrics for the sharpness CPQA

Metric	Mean correlation	Above 0.6	Rank order Correlation	Rank order p-value
CW-SSIM	0.66	70	0.94	0.06
ΔLC	0.43	50	1.00	0.00
IW-SSIM	0.56	70	0.89	0.11
MS-SSIM	0.73	80	0.94	0.06
RFSIM	0.61	70	0.97	0.03
SSIM	0.66	80	0.96	0.04

Table 4. Evaluation of metrics for the color CPQA. $_{\text{Color}}$ indicates the color part of the metric.

Metric	Mean correlation	Above 0.6	Rank order Correlation	Rank order p-value
ABF	0.07	0	0.23	0.77
LinLab	-0.09	0	0.04	0.96
SCIELAB	-0.27	0	-0.24	0.76
S-DEE$_{\text{Color}}$	-0.38	0	-0.35	0.65
SHAME	0.01	10	0.10	0.90
SHAME$_{\text{Color}}$	0.05	20	0.12	0.88
SHAMEII	0.23	30	0.27	0.73
YCxCzLab	0.24	30	0.33	0.67

Color. For the color CPQA none of the evaluated metrics perform well (Table 4). It should be noted that all of these metrics are based on color differences, and this might be an indication that using only the color difference from the original is not enough to predict perceived color quality. The color CPQA had a fairly high correlation for all modes between the main characteristic and perceived IQ (Table 1), which might indicate that metrics giving more importance to certain regions, such as SHAME and SHAME-II, could perform better than the metrics that equally weight the entire image. The experimental results in Table 4 shows that these metrics do not outperform other metrics.

Lightness. The SSIM based metrics perform very well for the lightness attribute (Table 5), the Complex Wavelet SSIM (CW-SSIM) has a mean correlation 0.86 and all images have a correlation above 0.6. However, other metrics also perform well, such as the RFSIM, ΔLC, Spatial-DEE with only the lightness part (S-DEE$_{\text{Lightness}}$) and Adaptive Bilateral Filter with only the lightness part (ABF$_{\text{Lightness}}$). The results indicate that any of these are appropriate to measure lightness quality. These metrics take different approaches to measure lightness quality, indicating that different strategies are suitable.

Table 5. Evaluation of metrics for the lightness CPQA. $_{\text{Lightness}}$ indicates the lightness part of the metric.

Metric	Mean correlation	Above 0.6	Rank order Correlation	p-value
$ABF_{Lightness}$	0.69	80	0.87	0.13
CW-SSIM	0.86	100	0.93	0.07
ΔLC	0.69	80	0.99	0.01
IW-SSIM	0.85	80	0.95	0.05
MS-SSIM	0.82	90	0.93	0.07
RFSIM	0.86	90	1.00	0.00
$S\text{-}DEE_{Lightness}$	0.80	90	0.89	0.11
SSIM	0.63	70	0.98	0.02

Table 6. Evaluation of metrics for the contrast CPQA

Metric	Mean correlation	Above 0.6	Rank order Correlation	p-value
CW-SSIM	0.72	90	1.00	0.00
IW-SSIM	0.59	70	0.94	0.06
MS-SSIM	0.72	80	1.00	0.00
RFSIM	0.67	80	0.96	0.04
SSIM	0.65	70	0.99	0.01

Contrast. Many metrics perform well for the contrast CPQA (Table 6). The SSIM based metrics all have a correlation above 0.6 in more than 70% of the images, they also have a high mean correlation and excellent rank order correlation. The RFSIM has a similar performance to the SSIM based metrics. All of these metrics would be appropriate for measuring contrast. One should notice that all of the well performing metrics for contrast are based on lightness, and none of them take color information into account. This might make them inappropriate to measure contrast in images where color strongly contributes to the impression of contrast.

Table 7. Evaluation of metrics for the artifacts CPQA

Metric	Mean correlation	Above 0.6	Rank order Correlation	p-value
CW-SSIM	0.83	90	0.97	0.03
ΔLC	0.72	70	0.94	0.06
IW-SSIM	0.83	90	0.99	0.01
MS-SSIM	0.77	90	0.97	0.03
RFSIM	0.82	90	0.99	0.01
SSIM	0.60	70	1.00	0.00

Artifacts. The performance for the artifacts CPQA (Table 7) follow the results of many of the other CPQAs. The SSIM based metrics perform well together with ΔLC and RFSIM. There are only minor differences between these, and any of them seem to be suitable to measure artifacts. However, artifacts can vary significantly and to measure specific artifacts specially designed metrics might be required.

5 Conclusion and Future Work

In this research we focused on quality attributes for automatic assessment of print quality. We evaluated a set of image quality metrics for a set of quality attributes, with the intention of proposing suitable metrics for each attribute. The experimental results show that structural similarity based metrics perform well for the sharpness, contrast, and artifacts attributes, but for the color attribute none of the evaluated metrics correlated with the percept, and for the lightness attribute many different metrics perform well.

Future work should include further investigation of the color attribute in order to find a suitable metric. Another important issue is how to combine the results from the attributes to obtain one number representing overall image quality.

Acknowledgments

The author hereof has been enabled by Océ-Technologies B.V. to perform research activities which underlies this document. This document has been written in a personal capacity. Océ-Technologies B.V. disclaims any liability for the correctness of the data, considerations and conclusions contained in this document.

References

1. Ajagamelle, S.A., Pedersen, M., Simone, G.: Analysis of the difference of gaussians model in image difference metrics. In: 5th European Conference on Colour in Graphics, Imaging, and Vision (CGIV), pp. 489–496. IS&T, Joensuu (2010)
2. Baranczuk, Z., Zolliker, P., Giesen, J.: Image quality measures for evaluating gamut mapping. In: Color Imaging Conference, pp. 21–26. IS&T/SID, Albuquerque (2009)
3. Cao, G., Pedersen, M., Baranczuk, Z.: Saliency models as gamut-mapping artifact detectors. In: 5th European Conference on Colour in Graphics, Imaging, and Vision (CGIV), pp. 437–443. IS&T, Joensuu (2010)
4. Chandler, D., Hemami, S.: VSNR: A wavelet-based visual signal-to-noise ratio for natural images. IEEE Transactions on Image Processing 16(9), 2284–2298 (2007)
5. CIE: Guidelines for the evaluation of gamut mapping algorithms. Tech. Rep., CIE TC8-03 (156:2004) ISBN: 3-901-906-26-6
6. CIE: Chromatic adaptation under mixed illumination condition when comparing softcopy and hardcopy images. Tech. Rep., CIE TC8-04 (162:2004) ISBN: 3-901-906-34-7
7. Crete, F., Dolmiere, T., Ladret, P., Nicolas, M.: The blur effect: perception and estimation with a new no-reference perceptual blur metric. In: Rogowitz, B.E., Pappas, T.N., Daly, S.J. (eds.) Proceedings of SPIE Human Vision and Electronic Imaging XII, vol. 6492, p. 64920I (March 2007)
8. Fedorovskaya, E.A., Blommaert, F., de Ridder, H.: Perceptual quality of color images of natural scenes transformed in CIELUV color space. In: Color Imaging Conference, pp. 37–40. IS&T/SID (1993)
9. Field, G.G.: Test image design guidelines for color quality evaluation. In: Color Imaging Conference, pp. 194–196. IS&T, Scottsdale (1999)
10. Green, P., MacDonald, L. (eds.): Colour Engineering: Achieving Device Independent Colour. John Wiley & Sons, Chichester (2002)

11. Hardeberg, J., Bando, E., Pedersen, M.: Evaluating colour image difference metrics for gamut-mapped images. Coloration Technology 124(4), 243–253 (2008)
12. ISO: ISO 12640-2: Graphic technology - prepress digital data exchange - part 2: XYZ/sRGB encoded standard colour image data (XYZ/SCID) (2004)
13. ISO: ISO 12640-3 graphic technology - prepress digital data exchange - part 3: CIELAB standard colour image data (CIELAB/SCID) (2007)
14. Keelan, B.W.: Handbook of Image Quality: Characterization and Prediction. Marcel Dekker, New York (2002)
15. Kendall, M.G., Stuart, A., Ord, J.K.: Kendall's Advanced Theory of Statistics: Classical inference and relationship, 5th edn., vol. 2. A Hodder Arnold Publication (1991)
16. Kolpatzik, B., Bouman, C.: Optimized error diffusion for high-quality image display. Journal of Electronic Imaging 1(3), 277–292 (1992)
17. Kolpatzik, B., Bouman, C.: Optimal universal color palette design for error diffusion. Journal of Electronic Imaging 4(2), 131–143 (1995)
18. Larson, E.C., Chandler, D.M.: Unveiling relationships between regions of interest and image fidelity metrics. In: Pearlman, W.A., Woods, J.W., Lu, L. (eds.) Visual Communications and Image Processing. SPIE Proceedings, vol. 6822, pp. 68222A–68222A–16. SPIE, San Jose (2008)
19. Lindberg, S.: Perceptual determinants of print quality. Ph.D. thesis, Stockholm University (2004)
20. Norberg, O., Westin, P., Lindberg, S., Klaman, M., Eidenvall, L.: A comparison of print quality between digital, offset and flexographic printing presses performed on different paper qualities. In: International Conference on Digital Production Printing and Industrial Applications, pp. 380–385. IS&Ts (May 2001)
21. Orfanidou, M., Triantaphillidou, S., Allen, E.: Predicting image quality using a modular image difference model. In: Farnand, S.P., Gaykema, F. (eds.) Image Quality and System Performance V. SPIE Proceedings, vol. 6808, pp. 68080F–68080F–12. SPIE/IS&T, San Jose, USA (2008)
22. Pedersen, M., Amirshahi, S.: A modified framework the evaluation of color prints using image quality metrics. In: 5th European Conference on Colour in Graphics, Imaging, and Vision (CGIV), pp. 75–82. IS&T, Joensuu (2010)
23. Pedersen, M., Bonnier, N., Hardeberg, J.Y., Albregtsen, F.: Attributes of a new image quality model for color prints. In: Color Imaging Conference, pp. 204–209. IS&T, Albuquerque (2009)
24. Pedersen, M., Bonnier, N., Hardeberg, J.Y., Albregtsen, F.: Attributes of image quality for color prints. Journal of Electronic Imaging 19(1), 011016–1–13 (2010)
25. Pedersen, M., Bonnier, N., Hardeberg, J.Y., Albregtsen, F.: Estimating print quality attributes by image quality metrics. In: Color and Imaging Conference, pp. 68–73. IS&T/SID, San Antonio (2010)
26. Pedersen, M., Bonnier, N., Hardeberg, J.Y., Albregtsen, F.: Validation of quality attributes for evaluation of color prints. In: Color and Imaging Conference, pp. 74–79. IS&T/SID, San Antonio (2010)
27. Pedersen, M., Bonnier, N., Hardeberg, J.Y., Albregtsen, F.: Image quality metrics for the evaluation of print quality. In: Gaykema, F., Farnand, S. (eds.) Image Qualtiy and System Performance. Proceedings of SPIE. SPIE, San Francisco (2011)
28. Pedersen, M., Hardeberg, J.Y.: Rank order and image difference metrics. In: 4th European Conference on Colour in Graphics, Imaging, and Vision (CGIV), pp. 120–125. IS&T, Terrassa (2008)
29. Pedersen, M., Hardeberg, J.Y.: A new spatial hue angle metric for perceptual image difference. In: Trémeau, A., Schettini, R., Tominaga, S. (eds.) CCIW 2009. LNCS, vol. 5646, pp. 81–90. Springer, Heidelberg (2009)

30. Pedersen, M., Hardeberg, J.Y., Nussbaum, P.: Using gaze information to improve image difference metrics. In: Rogowitz, B., Pappas, T. (eds.) Human Vision and Electronic Imaging VIII, San Jose, CA, USA. SPIE Proceedings, vol. 6806, p. 680611 (January 2008)
31. Pedersen, M., Hardeberg, J.: Survey of full-reference image quality metrics. Høgskolen i Gjøviks rapportserie 5, The Norwegian Color Research Laboratory (Gjøvik University College) (June 2009) ISSN: 1890-520X
32. Ponomarenko, N., Silvestri, F., Egiazarian, K., Carli, M., Astola, J., Lukin, V.: On between-coefficient contrast masking of DCT basis functions. In: Third International Workshop on Video Processing and Quality Metrics for Consumer Electronics VPQM 2007, Scottsdale, Arizona, USA, pp. 1–4 (January 2007)
33. Sheikh, H.R., Bovik, A.C.: Image information and visual quality. IEEE Transactions on Image Processing 15(2), 430–444 (2006)
34. Shnayderman, A., Gusev, A., Eskicioglu, A.M.: An SVD-based grayscale image quality measure for local and global assessment. IEEE Transactions On Image Processing 15(2), 422–429 (2006)
35. Simone, G., Oleari, C., Farup, I.: Performance of the euclidean color-difference formula in log-compressed OSA-UCS space applied to modified-image-difference metrics. In: 11th Congress of the International Colour Association (AIC), Sydney, Australia (October 2009)
36. Simone, G., Pedersen, M., Hardeberg, J.Y., Rizzi, A.: Measuring perceptual contrast in a multilevel framework. In: Rogowitz, B.E., Pappas, T.N. (eds.) Human Vision and Electronic Imaging XIV, vol. 7240. SPIE, San Jose (2009)
37. Wang, Z., Bovik, A.C., Sheikh, H.R., Simoncelli, E.P.: Image quality assessment: from error visibility to structural similarity. IEEE Transactions on Image Processing 13(4), 600–612 (2004)
38. Wang, Z., Hardeberg, J.Y.: An adaptive bilateral filter for predicting color image difference. In: Color Imaging Conference, pp. 27–31. IS&T/SID, Albuquerque, NM, USA (2009)
39. Wang, Z., Li, Q.: Information content weighting for perceptual image quality assessment. IEEE Transactions on Image Processing (2010)
40. Wang, Z., Simoncelli, E.: Translation insensitive image similarity in complex wavelet domain. In: IEEE International Conference on Acoustics, Speech and Signal Processing, vol. 2, pp. 573–576 (2005)
41. Wang, Z., Simoncelli, E.P.: Reduced-reference image quality assessment using a wavelet-domain natural image statistic model. In: Human Vision and Electronic Imaging X. Proceedings of SPIE, vol. 5666, pp. 149–159. SPIE, San Jose (January 2005)
42. Wang, Z., Simoncelli, E.P., Bovik, A.C.: Multi-scale structural similarity for image quality assessment. In: Proceedings of the 37th IEEE Asilomar Conference on Signals, Systems and Computers, pp. 1398–1402 (November 2003)
43. Wang, Z., Bovik, A.C., Lu, L.: Wavelet-based foveated image quality measurement for region of interest image coding. In: International Conference on Image Processing, pp. 89–92. IEEE, Los Alamitos (2001)
44. Zhang, L., Zhang, L., Mou, X.: RFSIM: A feature based image quality assessment metric using riesz transforms. In: Internatonal Conference on Image Processing, Hong Kong, pp. 321–324 (September 2010)
45. Zhang, X., Farrell, J., Wandell, B.: Application of a spatial extension to CIELAB. In: Very high resolution and quality imaging II, San Jose, CA, USA. SPIE Proceedings, vol. 3025, pp. 154–157 (February 1997)

Supercontinuum Light Sources for Hyperspectral Subsurface Laser Scattering

Applications for Food Inspection

Otto Højager Attermann Nielsen[1], Anders Lindbjerg Dahl[1], Rasmus Larsen[1], Flemming Møller[2], Frederik Donbæk Nielsen[3], Carsten L. Thomsen[3], Henrik Aanæs[1], and Jens Michael Carstensen[1]

[1] DTU Informatics, Technical University of Denmark
[2] DANISCO A/S
[3] NKT Photonics A/S

Abstract. A materials structural and chemical composition influences its optical scattering properties. In this paper we investigate the use of subsurface laser scattering (SLS) for inferring structural and chemical information of food products. We have constructed a computer vision system based on a supercontinuum laser light source and an Acousto-Optic Tunable Filter (AOTF) to provide a collimated light source, which can be tuned to any wavelength in the range from 480 to 900 nm. We present the newly developed hyperspectral vision system together with a proof-of-principle study of its ability to discriminate between dairy products with either similar chemical or structural composition. The combined vision system is a new way for industrial food inspection allowing non-intrusive online process inspection of parameters that is hard with existing technology.

1 Introduction

The properties of a suspended materials or colloids are affected by the particle size distribution. Knowledge about particle size distribution is especially relevant for many products in the food industry, for example fat and protein particles suspended in water. The size and density distribution of particles influences parameters such as "mouth feel" and shelf life, which are important quality parameters in the food industry. In this paper we address the problem of inferring information about particle size distribution based on subsurface laser scattering (SLS). The subsurface scattering of light is affected by both the chemical and structural composition of a material [8]. Based on these properties we have designed a vision system consisting of a hyperspectral laser and a CCD camera for measuring subsurface scattering. We provide a proof-of-principle for inferring information about particle size distribution demonstrated on a number of dairy products. This system allows an opportunity for effective online monitoring of food products as well as real time process inspection, based on a non-intrusive system.

A. Heyden and F. Kahl (Eds.): SCIA 2011, LNCS 6688, pp. 327–337, 2011.

Related work

Other methods exist for measuring parameters affected by particle size distribution, for example rheology based on a measurement of the consistency and flow of the food product [5]. Another approach is based on measuring the scattering of a water diluted sample [14]. However the water dilution can alter the particle composition of the food product. A vision system avoids the intrusive nature of these methods yet being fast and objective.

Many vision based techniques have been developed for industrial food inspection, and especially multispectral and hyperspectral methods have been successful [3,4,15]. The present system is based on a supercontinuum lightsource, filtered by and AOTF and light delivered through a single mode fiber. Together with a camera, as illustrated in Figure 1, the setup becomes a highly flexible vision system. Our setup follows the work of [1], where an SLS-system[1] devised with laser diodes is demonstrated. In their work SLS-features are correlated with the composition of milk and rheology of yoghurt. Our system is extended with multiple wavelengths.

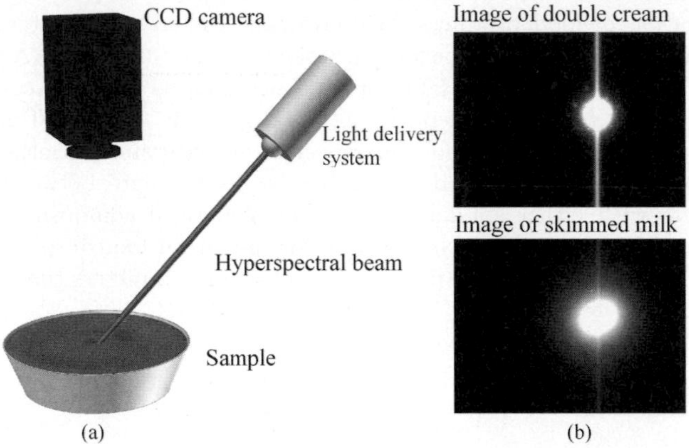

Fig. 1. **(a)** Illustration of our hyperspectral vision system for probing a samples SLS properties. **(b)** Image examples of the SLS properties of two diary products measured at 630 nm. Both structural and chemical properties affect the appearance of the laser spot.

Hyperspectral imaging was originally developed for geology and mining based on remote sensing [11,16] and many hyperspectral analysis techniques have been developed from these problems like spectral unmixing. But hyperspectral imaging has many other useful applications including food analysis where these techniques is widely employed in both research and industry [7,10,15].

Hyperspectral images can be acquired by point scanning, line scanning, area scanning and single shot acquisition [15]. In the point and line scanning the acquisition device or the sample, needs to be moved to obtain a hyperspectral

[1] `http://www.videometer.com/products/products.html`

image, which potentially is a source of error [7,13]. In the area scanning, multiple exposures are acquired from the same geometry, whereas the single shot acquires the full hyperspectral information at one exposure. Single shot has clear advantages for speed and robustness, but hyperspectral single shot technology is still under development and not ready for industrial inspection [18]. The narrow spectrum for hyperspectral images are typically obtained by filtering in front of the imaging device [15], whereas we perform light filtering based on an AOTF allowing a precise control of the wavelength. In this setup we take advantage of the stable geometry with a fixed camera. The tradeoff is the need for multiple exposures – one at each wavelength. Our aim is to construct a setup where a few relevant wavelengths can be identified and subsequently used for constructing an industrial inspection system.

A very simple approach for obtaining hyperspectral images is to use a filter wheel [2], but this is restricted to a limited number of spectral bands. Tunable filters has a clear advantage in providing a flexible control of the wavelengths, but until now the use of tunable filters for food inspection has been limited [15,17]. There are some examples tunable filters for quality control of food including the estimation of fruit firmness in [12] and rot of mandarins in [6] based on a LCTF (liquid crystal tunable filter). The LCTF is placed in front of the camera lens to filter the light into the camera, in contrast to our setup where the light source is filtered. The LCTF technology is capable of covering a similar spectral range as the AOTF. We have chosen the AOTF because it is appropriate with the laser beam setup that we employ.

The main contributions of this paper are:

1. A SLS computer vision setup based on a CCD camera and a hyperspectral laser obtained with an AOTF in front of a supercontinuum laser.
2. A proof-of-principle that particle size distribution can be inferred from the SLS measurements.
3. A platform for future development of hyperspectral SLS.

In the following section we will provide details of the vision system and describe how we extract relevant features. After that we show our experimental validation, and finally we discuss the obtained results.

2 Method

The purpose of the SLS technique is to correlate the observed image response with material properties of the measured samples. This involves design choices for the vision setup, extraction of relevant features and statistical analysis of the robustness of the measurements.

Vision system

The hyperspectral analysis is based on images acquired from the vision system shown in Figure 1 and 2. The system components are described in Table 1. The systems ability to perform hyperspectral imaging is imposed by changing

Table 1. Hardware used in the SLS vision system

System	Device
Supercontinuum light source	SuperK Power from NKT Photonics
AOTF	SpectraK Dual from NKT Photonics
Camera	Grasshopper CCD camera from Point Grey

the wavelength of the illumination light. The illumination system is based on a supercontinuum white light laser producing a quasi continues output in the range from 470 nm to 2400 nm. The output is delivered in a microstructured optical fiber to an AOTF for spectral filtering of the beam. Currently the spectral filtering is supported in the range from 480 nm - 850 nm with a spectral width growing linearly from 3.5 nm to 14 nm. The final beam power output of the combined system varies as a function of wavelength from around 0.4 to 2.5 mW, but the output is very stable over time. The AOTF is controlled by a direct digital synthesizer (DDS) which enables a fast computer controlled frequency change up to 10 times per second with an accuracy of 0.1 nm.

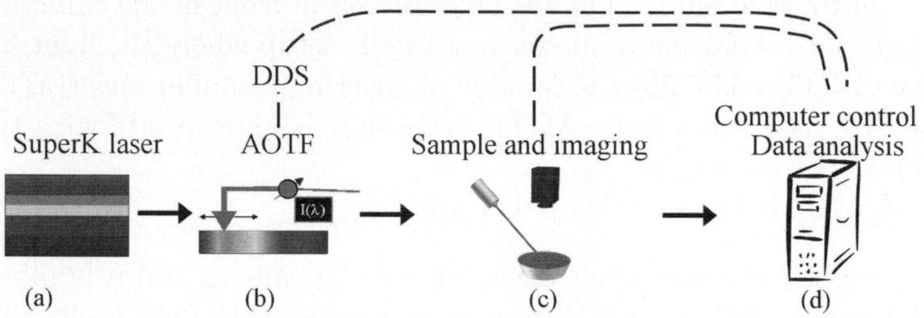

Fig. 2. Schematic illustration of the system interfaces and the scheme for generating the hyperspectral illumination system. The supercontinuum laser (a) delivers white collimated light to the AOTF, which is controlled by the DDS (b). A focused laser beam is illuminating the sample and an image is captured with a normal CCD camera (c). The entire setup is computer controlled (d).

The scattering distribution monitored from the sample will be a convolution of the scattering profile with the beams profile on the surface. Therefore, it is preferred to have a small simple beam profile. The final light delivery from the AOTF to the food sample is performed using a LMA-5 photonic-crystal fiber. The beam is collimated after the fiber using a 5 mm focal length lens. Simultaneously the scattering center for the hyperspectral visions system remains fixed because the LMA-5 fiber support light delivery in the full spectral range covered by the AOTF.

The scattering profile is imaged using a 16 bit CCD camera with a spatial resolution of 1600 × 1200 pixels. The current camera connection reduces the frame rate to 4 Hz, resulting in a total acquisition time of about 3 min for a hyperspectral characterization of a sample with images from 480 nm to 850 nm with a spectral resolution of 5 nm.

Characterization of SLS features

The images are characterized by analysing a single profile through the scattering distribution. We have adopted a model from [1] to characterize the distributions, based on taking the logarithm to the distribution and fitted with a linear curve. An example of the data analysis is presented in Figure 3.

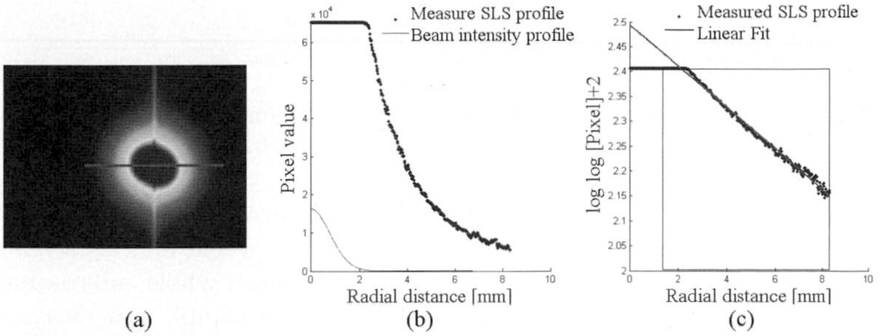

Fig. 3. Illustration of the data produced with the new vision system and the data analysis from the loglog model. (**a**) An image of the SLS profile in whole milk, the red trace is used in the analysis of the scattering profile (red pixels have is high intensities and blue have low). (**b**) Intensity through the scattering profile together with the beam profile. (**c**) loglog model for the scattering profile together with the linear fit. The black box indicate the range of data for the analysis.

The image from Figure 3 (**a**) shows a typical example of the scattering profile. It is vaguely elongated along the vertical-axis due to the beam being non orthogonal to the samples surface. In addition the images are suffering from a vertical smearing because of the heavy overexposure of the center pixels. An example of a scattering profile used and the loglog analysis of the image is presented in Figure 3. The scattering profile shows two different regimes previously presented by [9]. The interval closest to the scattering center is dominated by single scattering or diffuse reflection. In this regime the resulting scattering profile is almost proportional to the beam profile projected on the samples surface. Light rays in this part of the image have not undergone multiple scattering and do not give much information on the samples properties. The scattering pattern, which exceeds the size of the beam width, have undergone multiple scattering events and can to some extend be modeled as a diffusion process. In this range, the data with higher intensity than the background noise of the camera is fitted with a linear slope. The trace analyzed with this method results in two parameters, a slope and an offset. The offset of the loglog curve, which represents the amplitude of the SLS profile at the image center, is very system dependent. It may be possible to make the value independent of the system by calibrating the signal strength on the CCD camera. The slope of the loglog curve describes the rate of descend and is therefore a combination of the scattering properties of the sample and its absorption spectrum. A high value of the loglog slope corresponds to a narrow scattering profile.

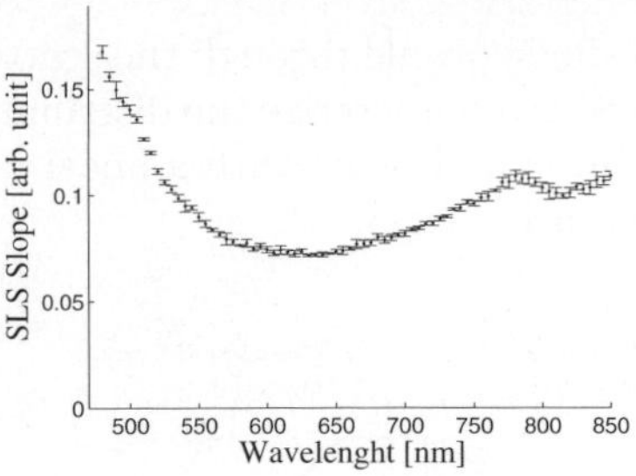

(a) Measurement of the same sample repeated four times.

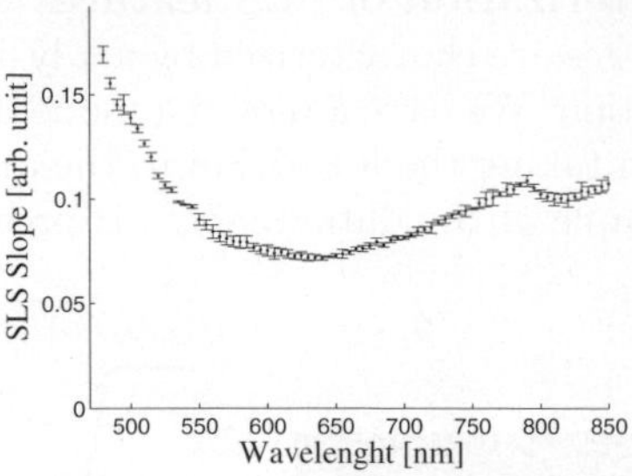

(b) Measurement of the whole procedure repeated four times.

Fig. 4. Average value and standard deviation showing the loglog slope of the scattering distribution in four measurements on the same sample of whole milk as a function of the spectral band. The figures are almost identical because whole milk is measured in both experiments – the difference is that the same milk sample was measured four times in (a) whereas four different samples were used in (b).

This form of characterization will be referred to as the loglog model. It only makes use of a limited amount of image information close to the scattering centre. The loglog model is not motivated by a physical understanding of the scattering process, but it gives a robust method that previously has been shown to correlate well with the structure of the sample [1].

Reproducability

The measurements are performed by first filling up a measuring cup to a specific height, then conduct a measurement. This procedure has two major uncertainty elements, the reproducibility of characterizing the same sample, which is a combined effect of the vision system, and a simpler uncertainty element in the way the sample and cup is positioned in the vision system. The beam is not perfectly collimated so the spot size of the laser beam may vary as a function of the samples height in the cup. A variation of the samples height will also change the size of the scattering profile measured by the camera, which is focused to fixed depth below the camera.

To estimate the vision systems robustness against variations in the characterization of a given sample, the same sample was depicted four times and analyzed with the loglog model as shown in Figure 4. The resulting average values and standard deviation is presented in Figure 4(a). Similarly the reproducibility of the measurements procedure was estimated by performing the parameters of the same product four times. The whole milk was poured into the measurement cup and analyzed with the vision system, and the results are presented in Figure 4(b). The standard deviation of the sample characterization is generally much smaller than both the amplitude and the range spanned by the slope of the full spectrum that have been analyzed.

3 Experiments

Here we present the results of experiments that demonstrate the vision systems capabilities of discriminating chemical and structural variation. These measurements are the first presentation of hyperspectral characterization of the SLS properties of a material. As a proof-of-principle study a set of commercially available diary product where measured and characterized using the loglog model.

Chemical composition

The first three measurements focus on products with different chemical contents. We have chosen cream products with different fat percentage to be characterized using the SLS vision system. The different fat contents will affect the scattering profile because it increases the number of scattering centers in the sample, and thus the slope and offset of the profile. The measured profiles are presented in Figure 5 showing a generally increasing slope as a function of the fat contents.

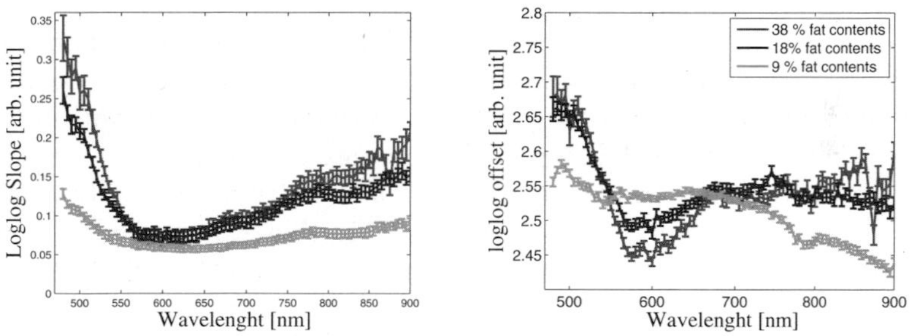

(a) Slope parameter (b) Offset parameter

Fig. 5. Experiment showing the hyperspectral response for cream products differing by fat content. The fat content is especially distinguishable for low and high wavelengths for the slope parameter, whereas there is also information in the mid rage of the offset parameter.

The measurements of the scattering slope using the loglog model indicate that the largest discriminative power is found at the long and short wavelengths. The slope curves collapse in the spectral range from ~ 530 nm to ~ 700 nm. It is seen that the changes in the slope occurs on a length scale of one hundred nanometer in this spectral range. With the new hyperspectral vision system we are able to verify this trend. However the offset still discriminates between the samples in this interval.

Structural variation

Another important parameter, that we intend to measure is the particle sizes of different components in the sample. As a first indication of this, the SLS properties of reduced fat milk was performed on conventional milk and a organic product.

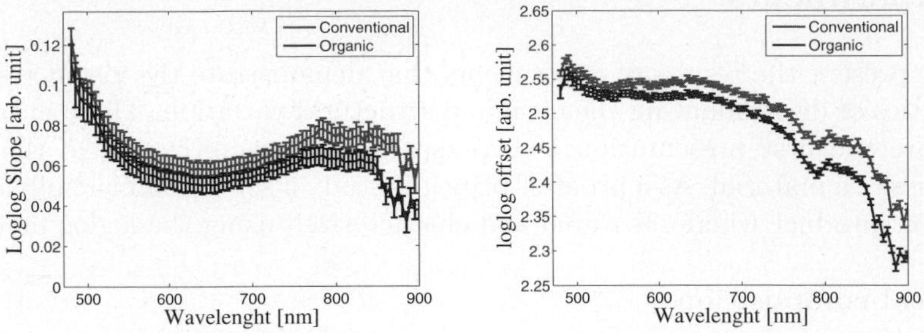

(a) Slope parameter (b) Offset parameter

Fig. 6. Experiment showing the hyperspectral response for reduced fat milk differing by particle size and distribution. The organic product is unhomogenized whereas the conventional is homogenized. The homogenization process alters the size and distribution of the fat particles. Note that the difference is primarily a scale change of the SLS parameters.

These products have different particle size distributions due to the homogenization of the conventional milk, which reduces the particle size. Consequently the conventional milk has a higher density of scattering centers, but with a smaller average size. The resulting SLS response is presented in Figure 6.

The gain of hyperspectral analysis is small, but from the analysis we can choose the most discriminative wavelengths. This allows a simple but powerful method for discriminating between these products that only differ by homogenization process.

To illustrate the diversity of samples that can be examined using the new hyperspectral SLS vision system, the scattering profiles of a high particle density cream is compared to the scattering profile of fat reduced milk and yoghurt. The measured profiles are presented in Figure 7(a).

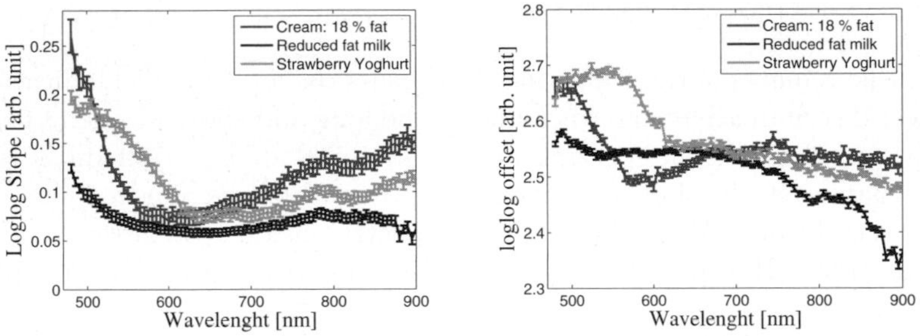

(a) Slope parameter (b) Offset parameter

Fig. 7. Experiment showing the hyperspectral response for a diverse collection of products. This illustrates the large amount of information in hyperspectral SLS measurements.

4 Discussion

We have demonstrated hyperspectral SLS on a number of samples and shown that we can uniquely characterize a sample using SLS parameters. Repeated studies show that the parameters only vary slightly when the data acquisition is performed several times, indicating that the system is stable over time. This is very encouraging in relation to industrial inspection of food products based on this technique.

We chose to demonstrate the hyperspectral SLS on dairy products because they contain suspended particles causing the subsurface scattering. Also a large variety of dairy products are easily available making it a good choice for demonstrating the SLS system. But the SLS technique can be used for measuring many other products – especially biological samples have subsurface scattering, making the technique widely applicable to a range of food products including meat and vegetables.

We measure a parameter based on the logarithm of the measured pixel intensity taken twice ($log(log(I))$, where I is the image intensity), which is adopted from [1]. Empirical studies have shown that this map becomes linear, which allows a characterization based on two parameters – the slope and the intercept of the profile. The simplicity of this approach is very attractive, because it has shown to be robust and it is easy to measure. The only problem is the parameters dependence of the system, and to overcome this we need to include a calibration procedure in a future system. Further research should address the parameters characterizing a sample. One interesting application would be to directly infer particle size and distribution and another would be to measure refractive properties.

Results are reported for a single profile, so at the moment we are not utilizing the information in the entire image. A consequence is that image noise is influencing the measurements, as seen from the error bars in the graphs shown in Figure 5, 6 and 7. We could utilize more of the image to obtain higher signal to noise ratios, for example by sampling more profiles or employing a 2D model.

The characterization is based on measurements of the subsurface scattering, so we would like to optimize the system to capture as much information about the subsurface scattering as possible. The parameters governing the measurements include the beam power and profile of the laser and the exposure time of the camera. A large proportion of the light reflected close to the center of the beam is a result of single scattering or diffuse reflection. Optimally the beam profile should be as small as possible, so our relatively large profile can make the result less precise.

The beam power and exposure time have similar effect, and a large power or long exposure results in a large saturation of the depicted laser spot. This gives a high signal to noise ratio, but at the cost of information at low intensities. Low beam power or exposure will provide this information, but with lower signal to noise ratio. This tradeoff between illumination and exposure time can be accounted for by using high dynamic range, where an image is composed of multiple exposures to obtain high signal to noise ratio in both the low and high intensity range. In this paper we chose a single exposure, and despite this we were able to distinguish small differences like homogenized vs. non-homogenized milk.

Many of the samples are distinguishable at one wavelength, but it is important to note that this is not known in advance. Consequently our SLS system allows us to select the wavelengths with highest discriminative power, and can this way aid in constructing an optimal food inspection system, for example based on less expensive hardware like laser diodes. As a result the reconfigurable nature of the SLS system has great potential in explorative food analysis, but also in more general material characterization.

5 Conclusion

We have addressed the problem of inferring properties of a material from measurements of subsurface light scattering. Our contributions are (*i*) a hyperspectral SLS (subsurface laser scattering) vision system, (*ii*) a procedure for characterizing the measured samples, and (*iii*) an experimental analysis of a number of dairy products. This explorative analysis shows a proof-of-principle of our hyperspectral SLS system for food characterization, and acts as a platform for future development.

Acknowledgements

This work was financed by the Centre for Imaging Food Quality project which is funded by the Danish Council for Strategic Research (contract no 09-067039) within the Program Commission on Health, Food and Welfare.

References

1. Carstensen, J.M., Møller, F.: Online monitoring of food processes using subsurface laser scattering. In: Advances in process analytics and control technologies APACT 2009, Glasgow, Scotland, (May 5-7, 2009)
2. Chen, Y.R., Chao, K., Kim, M.S.: Machine vision technology for agricultural applications. Computers and Electronics in Agriculture 36(173A/191) (2002)
3. Clemmensen, L.H., Hansen, M.E., Ersbøll, B.K., Frisvad, J.C.: A method for comparison of growth media in objective identification of penicillium based on multispectral imaging. Journal of Microbiological Methods 69, 249–255 (2007)
4. Dissing, B.S., Clemmesen, L.H., Lje, H., Ersbœll, B.K., Adler-Nissen, J.: Temporal reflectance changes in vegetables. In: 2009 IEEE 12th International Conference on Computer Vision Workshops (ICCV Workshops), pp. 1917–1922 (2010)
5. Fischer, P., Windhab, E.J.: Rheology of food materials. Current Opinion in Colloid & Interface Science (2010)
6. Gómez-Sanchís, J., Gómez-Chova, L., Aleixos, N., Camps-Valls, G., Montesinos-Herrero, C., Moltó, E., Blasco, J.: Hyperspectral system for early detection of rottenness caused by Penicillium digitatum in mandarins. Journal of Food Engineering 89(1), 80–86 (2008)

7. Gowen, A.A., O'Donnell, C.P., Cullen, P.J., Downey, G., Frias, J.M.: Hyperspectral imaging-an emerging process analytical tool for food quality and safety control. Trends in Food Science & Technology 18(12), 590–598 (2007)
8. Jensen, H.W., Marschner, S.R., Levoy, M., Hanrahan, P.: A practical model for subsurface light transport. In: Proceedings of the 28th Annual Conference on Computer Graphics and Interactive Techniques, pp. 511–518. ACM, New York (2001)
9. Joshi, N., Donner, C., Jensen, H.W.: Noninvasive measurement of scattering anisotropy in turbid materials by nonnormal incident illumination. Optics letters 31(7), 936–938 (2006)
10. Kim, M.S., Chen, Y.R., Mehl, P.M.: Hyperspectral reflectance and fluorescence imaging system for food quality and safety. Transactions of the ASAE 44(3), 721–729 (2001)
11. Nielsen, A.A.: Spectral mixture analysis: Linear and semi-parametric full and iterated partial unmixing in multi-and hyperspectral image data. Journal of Mathematical Imaging and Vision 15(1), 17–37 (2001)
12. Peng, Y., Lu, R.: An LCTF-based multispectral imaging system for estimation of apple fruit firmness. Part 2. Selection of optimal wavelengths and development of prediction models. Transactions of the ASAE 49(1), 269–275 (2006)
13. Peng, Y., Lu, R.: Analysis of spatially resolved hyperspectral scattering images for assessing apple fruit firmness and soluble solids content. Postharvest Biology and Technology 48(1), 52–62 (2008)
14. Sacoto, P., Lanza, F., Suarez, H., Garcia-Rubio, L.H.: A novel automatic dilution system for on-line particle size analysis. In: ACS Symposium Series, vol. 693, pp. 23–29. ACS Publications (1998)
15. Sun, D.W.: Hyperspectral imaging for food quality analysis and control. Academic Press, London (2010)
16. van der Meer, F.: Imaging spectrometry for geological remote sensing. Geologie en Mijnbouw 77(2), 137–151 (1998)
17. Wang, W., Paliwal, J.: Near-infrared spectroscopy and imaging in food quality and safety. Sensing and Instrumentation for Food Quality and Safety 1(4), 193–207 (2007)
18. Yasuma, F., Mitsunaga, T., Iso, D., Nayar, S.K.: Generalized Assorted Pixel Camera: Post-Capture Control of Resolution, Dynamic Range and Spectrum. Technical report (November 2008)

Real-Time Detection of Landscape Scenes

Sami Huttunen[1], Esa Rahtu[1], Iivari Kunttu[2], Juuso Gren[2], and Janne Heikkilä[1]

[1] Machine Vision Group, University of Oulu, Finland
firstname.lastname@ee.oulu.fi
http://www.cse.oulu.fi/MVG
[2] Nokia Corporation, Tampere, Finland
firstname.lastname@nokia.com

Abstract. In this paper we study different approaches that can be used in recognizing landscape scenes. The primary goal has been to find an accurate but still computationally light solution capable of real-time operation. Recognizing landscape images can be thought of a special case of scene classification. Even though there exist a number of different approaches concerning scene classification, there are no other previous works that try to classify images into such high level categories as landscape and non-landscape. This study shows that a global texture-based approach outperforms other more complex methods in the landscape image recognition problem. Furthermore, the results obtained indicate that the computational cost of the method relying on Local Binary Pattern representation is low enough for real-time systems.

Keywords: computational imaging, scene classification, image categorization.

1 Introduction

Knowledge of the scene type provides important information in a number of applications that deal with consumer photographs and digital cameras. Generally, determining the scene type is the starting point of further image analysis and search in large image collections [1,5]. On the other hand, it can already guide the online image capture process in a camera device [3,10].

In this paper we study different approaches that can be used in recognizing landscape scenes. The detection of landscape scenes is a difficult problem given the fact that several landscape scenes have similar objects as non-landscape scenes, and vice versa. Furthermore, illumination conditions are equally unpredictable for both cases. Due to the computational restrictions set by the target applications the primary goal of our work has been to find an accurate but still computationally light solution capable of real-time operation.

The results of our work can be utilized when developing a fast method for separating the landscape and non-landscape scenes. This kind of classification can serve as a preprocessing step for speeding-up image retrieval in large databases and improving accuracy, or for performing automatic image annotation [5]. In

A. Heyden and F. Kahl (Eds.): SCIA 2011, LNCS 6688, pp. 338–347, 2011.

Fig. 1. Example of landscape classification

addition to image retrieval applications, camera settings may be adjusted automatically depending on the scene type, so that the best possible representation can be achieved [3,10].

Definition of *landscape* and *non-landscape* images is not totally straightforward. In this work we assume that if there are no distinct and easily separable objects present in a natural scene, the image is classified as landscape. From the photographic point of view, this requirement would mean that as much of the scene as possible should be in focus. As a result of the aforementioned restrictions, the landscape category would contain sunset, beach, mountain, etc., subcategories. On the other hand, it is obvious that all the images taken indoors should be classified as non-landscape. In this case, the non-landscape branch would consist of indoor scenes and other images containing man-made objects at relatively close distance (Fig. 1).

Recognizing landscape images can be thought of a special case of scene classification which aims at labeling an image into a set of different semantic categories. Even though there exist a number of different approaches concerning scene classification, to the best of our knowledge, there are no any other works concentrating on classifying images into the *landscape* and *non-landscape* categories. The previous works differ by the number of the scene classes, the image representations, and the classification method. The most methods so far have aimed at classifying into a small number of scene categories, including indoor/outdoor [8,14,15,16], city/landscape [17], and subsets of urban and natural scenes [9,13,17]. It can be noticed that none of these categorizations is directly applicable in our problem.

A common approach in image categorization is to use local features [11,18] combined with the bag-of-words (BOW) representation [4] and the Support Vector Machine (SVM) classifier. In this approach the image is then expressed by a histogram of visual word occurrences which can be used in training a classifier.

Another common way to categorize images is to compute low-level features, such as color and texture, which are further processed with a classifier engine for inferring high-level information about the image. These methods assume that the type of scene can be directly described by the color or texture properties of the image. In fact it has been shown that low-level features can give very comparable results on many scene classification tasks [2,15,16]. The work done in [15] employs low-level color and texture features whereas [16] concatenates the histograms in the Ohta color space with texture and frequency features. Later [14] has introduced an indoor/outdoor classification technique based on edge analysis.

We show with extensive experiments that a global texture-based approach competes with or outperforms other more complex methods in the landscape image recognition problem. Especially the computational cost of the method relying on Local Binary Pattern [12] representation is minimal compared to the GIST [13] and BOW methods investigated in this paper.

The rest of the paper is organized as follows. Section 2 gives a detailed description of the different features and classifier used in this study. The experimental results are presented in Sect. 3. Finally, the conclusions are summarized in Sect. 4.

2 Methods for Landscape Scene Recognition

There are two main elements in a typical image classification system. The first one is responsible for the computation of the feature vector representing an image whereas the second part is the classifier, the algorithm that classifies an input image into one of the predefined categories based on the feature vector. In this section we describe two approaches for landscape/non-landscape image classification. We begin with the image representation models followed by the classifier engine.

2.1 Global Features

Here we present two different approaches based on global description of image content.

GIST. One of the most well known global approaches in scene categorization is the GIST descriptor that was initially proposed in [13]. The main idea of this approach is to develop a low dimensional representation of the scene, which does not require any form of segmentation. The authors propose a set of perceptual dimensions (naturalness, openness, roughness, expansion, ruggedness) that represent the dominant spatial structure of a scene. They show that these dimensions may be reliably estimated using spectral and coarsely localized information.

To compute the color GIST description, the image is first divided into a 4×4 grid on which orientation histograms are extracted. Most of the works using the GIST descriptor resize the image as a preliminary stage, producing a small square image whose width typically ranges from 32 to 256 pixels. In our work, the images are rescaled to 240×240 size irrespective of their original aspect ratio. This is sufficient due to the low dimensionality of the descriptor, in other words, it does not represent the details of an image.

Local Binary Pattern (LBP). The discrete occurrence histogram of the LBP patterns computed over an image or a region of image is shown to be a very

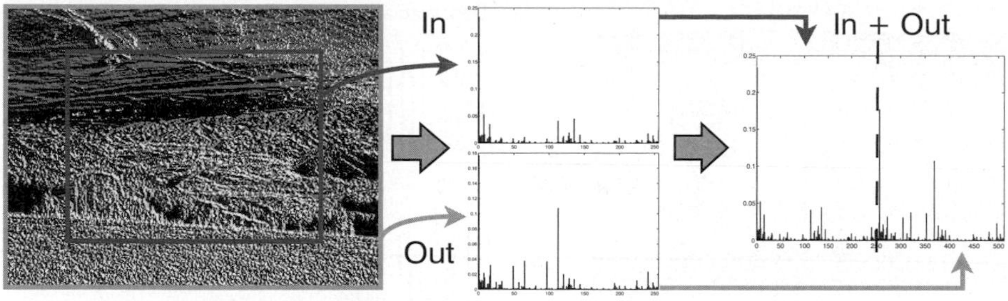

Fig. 2. The LBP histograms are computed in the center (*in*) and on the boundary areas (*out*) separately. The final image representation is then concatenation of these two histograms (*in+out*).

powerful texture feature. In LBP [12], the original 3×3 neighborhood is thresholded by the value of the center pixel. The values of the pixels in the thresholded neighborhood are multiplied by the weights given to the corresponding pixels. Finally, the values of the eight pixels are summed to obtain the number of a single texture unit.

When we think about landscape images depicting natural scenes usually the center of the image does not contain any distinctive objects. Therefore it is reasonable to utilize this information by computing the histograms in the center and on the boundary areas surrounding the center separately (Fig. 2). The final image representation is then concatenation of these two histograms providing us with a 512 bins long representation. From here onward it is referred as $\mathrm{LBP_{io}}$, and the basic version of the LBP is annotated by $\mathrm{LBP_b}$.

2.2 Local Features

A common approach in image categorization is to use some local features combined with the bag-of-words (BOW) representation which describes an image as an orderless collection of local features [4]. The basic idea of these approaches is that a set of local image patches is sampled either densely, randomly, or using a keypoint detector. After the sampling, a vector of visual descriptors is computed on each image patch independently (Fig. 3). There is a large number of different methods that can be used for describing the image patch content. One of the most popular approaches is to use SIFT-based descriptors [11,18] but also histograms or moments can be considered [18]. Regardless of the choice of the method, the resulting collection of descriptors is vector quantized and the global word histogram obtained is used as a characterization of the image.

In this study, the descriptors (see Table 1) were extracted using dense sampling with a step size of 10 pixels and default scale defined in the binary implementation [18]. For more information about the descriptors and their implementation details, please refer to [18]. The descriptor quantization was done by k-means clustering resulting in a vocabulary of 1000 words. To be independent of the

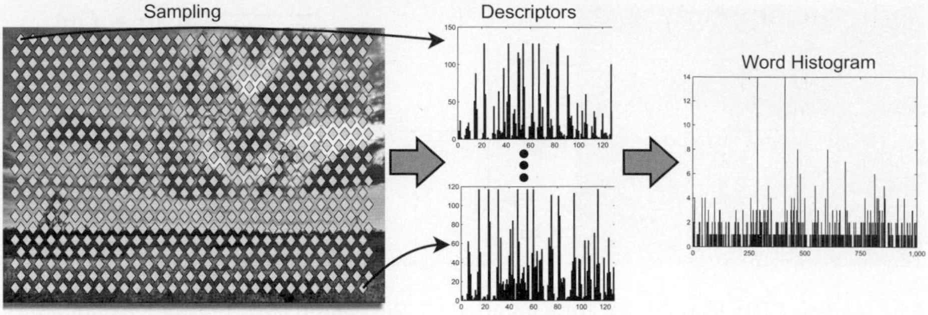

Fig. 3. The stages of the bag-of-words approach. First, the sample points are picked from the image. Then, for every point a color descriptor is computed over the area around that point. All the descriptors are subsequently vector quantized against a codebook of prototypical descriptors. This results in a fixed-length feature vector representing the image.

Table 1. Local descriptors[a]

Type	Descriptors	
SIFT	rgsift	csift
	opponentsift	rgbsift
	hsvsift	sift
	huesift	
Histogram	huehistogram	nrghistogram
	transformedcolorhistogram	opponenthistogram
	rgbhistogram	
Moment	colormomentinvariants	colormoments

[a] For details on the descriptors, see [18].

total number of descriptors in an image, the sum of the final feature vector was normalized to 1.

2.3 Classification

The Support Vector Machine (SVM) is widely used in scene classification and therefore it is selected as a classifier in this work. Even though the linear SVM is light in terms of computational burden, based on our preliminary evaluations we employ the Radial Basis Function (RBF) kernel in this study. In our application the classification step is carried out only once per image, thus its effect on overall time cost is minimal. When computing the kernels the distance function is Chi-squared with LBPs and local features whereas the GIST features are compared with the L2 norm.

3 Experimental Results

Comparative evaluation has been carried out between the methods described in Sect. 2. Combinations of the features were not considered because such kind of approaches would be too complex in view of the practical applications.

3.1 Image Sets

The images used for training and testing of the SVM classifier were downloaded from the PASCAL Visual Object Classes (VOC2007) database [6] and the Flickr site [7]. All the images mentioned below were manually labeled and resized to QVGA (320×240) resolution apart from the GIST, which uses 240×240 images.

Training dataset. The combined training and validation database contains 1115 landscape images and 2617 non-landscape images. Approximately 20 % of the training images were used for validation of the SVM classifier.

Testing dataset. Testing database contains 912 landscape images and 2140 non-landscape images. As with the training images, most of the landscape images come from the Flickr database and the non-landscape images originate mainly from the VOC2007 collection.

3.2 Evaluation Criteria

The classification task will be evaluated by the precision/recall curve, and the principal quantitative measure used is the average precision (AP). In addition, the performance will be evaluated by the Receiver Operating Characteristic (ROC) curve. In this case the measure used is the area under curve (AUC).

Furthermore we report the true positive and false positive rates (TPR and FPR, respectively) of the different approaches when the threshold for the SVM decision value is set to zero. In our case the definitions for the test images are as follows:

- False positive (FP): non-landscape classified as landscape
- True positive (TP): landscape classified as landscape

3.3 Results

The precision/recall and ROC curves are illustrated in Fig. 4. For clarity, only the best performing methods are included in the figures but Table 2 summarizes all the results in a numerical form. It can be seen that the LBP based approaches perform best both in terms of AUC and AP. It is worth noting that the LBP_{io} approach, which concatenates the histograms computed in the image center and boundary area, gives better performance than LBP_{b}.

Figure 5 contains a collection of sample images when using the LBP_{io} representation. When looking at the false positive images (Fig. 5c) it can be seen that most of the images contain smooth areas around some object.

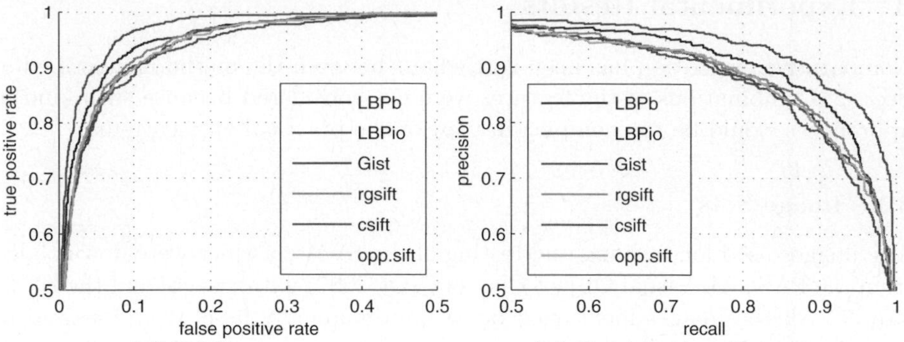

(a) ROC curves (b) Precision/recall curves

Fig. 4. Results of the best performing methods

Table 2. Summary of the results

		Classification				Execution time (s)	
		AUC	AP	TPR	FPR	Descriptor	Total
Global	LBP_{io}	0.982	0.958	0.882	0.040	0.001	0.005
	LBP_b	0.972	0.939	0.862	0.055	0.001	0.003
	GIST	0.963	0.924	0.809	0.050	NA	>0.029
Local descriptors + BOW	rgsift	0.969	0.934	0.814	0.045	0.340	2.699
	csift	0.966	0.926	0.825	0.052	0.350	2.712
	opponentsift	0.966	0.922	0.828	0.052	0.340	2.694
	rgbsift	0.960	0.918	0.804	0.047	0.330	2.744
	hsvsift	0.959	0.915	0.804	0.050	0.340	2.494
	sift	0.956	0.901	0.806	0.059	0.120	0.595
	huesift	0.954	0.902	0.791	0.067	0.290	1.046
	colormomentinvariants	0.926	0.857	0.737	0.067	1.410	1.444
	transformedcolorhistogram	0.924	0.851	0.692	0.061	0.100	0.147
	opponenthistogram	0.909	0.825	0.689	0.079	0.090	0.140
	rgbhistogram	0.903	0.805	0.683	0.087	0.070	0.118
	colormoments	0.897	0.811	0.697	0.084	1.340	1.376
	huehistogram	0.863	0.717	0.525	0.071	0.180	0.223
	nrghistogram	0.861	0.727	0.601	0.102	0.080	0.119

3.4 Computational Cost

In order to evaluate the computational cost of the different image representations the preliminary performance analysis was conducted on a regular Windows PC (Core 2 Duo 3.2GHz, 4GB RAM).

Our own LBP C code implementation was evaluated with Visual Studio 2010 Profiler whereas the execution times of the different color descriptors were obtained using the binaries publicly available [18]. The results are shown in Table 2

Fig. 5. Classification examples with LBP_{io} representation. (a) Landscape classified as landscape, (b) non-landscape classified as non-landscape, (c) non-landscape classified as landscape, and (d) landscape classified as non-landscape.

and they include the time spent on descriptor computation as well as the total time for SVM classification. It should be noted that the most time consuming part of the bag-of-words based methods is the word histogram computation.

Unfortunately the GIST descriptor codes [13] were available only for MATLAB and therefore its performance could not be studied thoroughly in these experiments. However, since the GIST descriptor is computed using several filters corresponding to different orientations and scales, its computational cost is likely to be higher than that of LBP.

3.5 Real-Time Implementation

Based on the results presented in Table 2, it is obvious that the LBP histogram is the best choice when building a real-time system. On the other hand, selection between the two different LBP representations depends mainly on the requirements set by the target platform. Our current real-time implementation coded in C relies on the basic LBP_b, which gives reasonable results with lower memory consumption.

Fig. 6. Video frames with the classification results. Green boundaries are used for the landscape and red boundaries for the non-landscape frames. If the boundary is black, selection between the classes cannot be done reliably.

When we take a closer look at the profiler results of the final system, the results indicate that most of the time is spent on the SVM classifier since LBP histogram computation takes only one third of the overall processing time. The total execution time for one QVGA frame is about 3 ms which guarantees real-time performance even on more constrained platforms.

Test videos. In order to evaluate the performance of the LBP_b approach in real-time scenarios we captured several video sequences with different cameras (Canon EOS 5D Mark II, Logitech QuickCam Fusion, Nokia N95). All the videos were resized to QVGA resolution but no other pre-processing steps were applied.

The results of the sequences are shown in Fig. 6. To illustrate how the detection of landscape scenes works with the given frames, we use green boundaries for the landscape and red boundaries for the non-landscape frames. If the boundary is black, the decision value of the classifier is close to zero and therefore selection between the classes cannot be done reliably.

4 Conclusion

In this paper we have studied different approaches that can be used in automatic landscape scene recognition. Due to the computational restrictions set by the target devices the primary goal of our work has been to find an accurate but still computationally light solution capable of real-time operation.

We have shown with extensive experiments that a global texture-based approach outperforms other more complex methods in the landscape image recognition problem. It appears that the local features are too distinctive for the given task. The results obtained clearly indicate that the computational cost of the method relying on the Local Binary Pattern (LBP) representation is low enough for real-time systems. It should be noted that the LBP operates on gray scale images, which means that the use of color information is not needed.

References

1. Bianco, S., Ciocca, G., Cusano, C., Schettini, R.: Improving color constancy using indoor–outdoor image classification. IEEE TIP 17(12), 2381–2392 (2008)
2. Bosch, A., Munoz, X., Marti, R.: Which is the best way to organize/classify images by content? Image and Vision Computing 25(6), 778–791 (2007)
3. Chung, D., Kim, S., Bae, J., Lee, S.: Photographic expert-like capturing by analyzing scenes with representative image set. In: Casasent, D.P., Hall, E.L., Röning, J. (eds.) Proc. SPIE, vol. 7252 (2009)
4. Csurka, G., Dance, C., Fan, L., Willamowski, J., Bray, C.: Visual categorization with bags of keypoints. In: Proc. Workshop on Statistical Learning in Computer Vision, ECCV, vol. 1, p. 22 (2004)
5. Datta, R., Joshi, D., Li, J., Wang, J.Z.: Image retrieval: Ideas, influences, and trends of the new age. ACM Computing Surveys 40(2), 5:1–5:60 (2008)
6. Everingham, M., Van Gool, L., Williams, C.K.I., Winn, J., Zisserman, A.: The PASCAL Visual Object Classes Challenge 2007 (VOC2007) Results (2007), `http://www.pascal-network.org/challenges/VOC/voc2007/workshop/`
7. Flickr: Flickr homepage (2010), `http://www.flickr.com/search/?q=landscape`
8. Kim, W., Park, J., Kim, C.: A novel method for efficient indoor-outdoor image classification. Journal of Signal Processing Systems 61, 251–258 (2010)
9. Lazebnik, S., Schmid, C., Ponce, J.: Beyond bags of features: Spatial pyramid matching for recognizing natural scene categories. Proc. IEEE CVPR 2, 2169–2178 (2006)
10. Lipowezky, U., Vol, I.: Indoor-outdoor detector for mobile phone cameras using gentle boosting. In: Proc. IEEE CVPR Workshops (CVPRW), pp. 31–38 (2010)
11. Lowe, D.: Distinctive image features from scale-invariant keypoints. IJCV 60(2), 91–110 (2004)
12. Ojala, T., Pietikäinen, M., Harwood, D.: A comparative study of texture measures with classification based on featured distributions. Pattern Recognition 29(1), 51–59 (1996)
13. Oliva, A., Torralba, A.: Modeling the shape of the scene: A holistic representation of the spatial envelope. IJCV 42(3), 145–175 (2001)
14. Payne, A., Singh, S.: Indoor vs. outdoor scene classification in digital photographs. Pattern Recognition 38(10), 1533–1545 (2005)
15. Serrano, N., Savakis, A., Luo, A.: A computationally efficient approach to indoor/outdoor scene classification. Proc. IEEE ICPR 4, 146–149 (2002)
16. Szummer, M., Picard, R.W.: Indoor-outdoor image classification. In: Proc. IEEE Workshop on Content-Based Access of Image and Video Database, pp. 42–51 (1998)
17. Vailaya, A., Figueiredo, M.A.T., Jain, A.K., Zhang, H.J.: Image classification for content-based indexing. IEEE TIP 10(1), 117–130 (2001)
18. van de Sande, K.E.A., Gevers, T., Snoek, C.G.M.: Evaluating color descriptors for object and scene recognition. IEEE TPAMI 32(9), 1582–1596 (2010)

Generic Object Class Detection Using Feature Maps

Oscar Danielsson and Stefan Carlsson

CVAP/CSC, KTH,
Teknikringen 14, S-100 44 Stockholm, Sweden
{osda02,stefanc}@csc.kth.se

Abstract. In this paper we describe an object class model and a detection scheme based on feature maps, i.e. binary images indicating occurrences of various local features. Any type of local feature and any number of features can be used to generate feature maps. The choice of which features to use can thus be adapted to the task at hand, without changing the general framework. An object class is represented by a boosted decision tree classifier (which may be cascaded) based on normalized distances to feature occurrences. The resulting object class model is essentially a linear combination of a set of flexible configurations of the features used. Within this framework we present an efficient detection scheme that uses a hierarchical search strategy. We demonstrate experimentally that this detection scheme yields a significant speedup compared to sliding window search. We evaluate the detection performance on a standard dataset [7], showing state of the art results. Features used in this paper include edges, corners, blobs and interest points.

Keywords: detector, AdaBoost, decision tree, distance transform, SIFT.

1 Introduction and Related Works

Object class modeling and detection is a difficult problem. Often the intra-class variation is significant and the background class is extremely large (i.e. all image patches not containing an object of the target class), so the decision boundary required to separate the positive and negative classes in feature space will generally be complex. To represent a complex decision boundary, we need a powerful classifier/model. However, such classifiers are in general expensive to evaluate. This is a problem because at the detection stage we will need to evaluate the classifier/model for a very large number of subregions of the test image.

To solve this problem Viola and Jones proposed using a cascade of increasingly complex AdaBoost classifiers [20]. The complex classifiers at the upper stages of the cascade are then only evaluated on a small subset of the patches in the test image. In addition they proposed integral images to make the computation of Haar features extremely efficient. They combined these two techniques to build an accurate, real-time face detector. However their method has a limited ability to handle intra-class variation, mainly due to the Haar features not being

A. Heyden and F. Kahl (Eds.): SCIA 2011, LNCS 6688, pp. 348–359, 2011.

robust to intra-class variation. Therefore Laptev exchange the Haar features for histogram features (which can be efficiently computed using integral histograms) and can thus handle more difficult classes than faces [14]. The reason being that the histogram features are more robust to intra-class variation and therefore the target class gets a more compact distribution in feature space. Felzenszwalb et. al. then take one step further and introduce deformable part models into the cascade to get an even more flexible classifier, which has shown good performance in the popular Pascal challenge [5,4].

We see that these methods handle increasingly difficult target classes by using features that are increasingly robust to intra-class variation, while maintaining computational efficiency. In the present paper we continue this line of research and propose a generic framework that takes feature maps as input. The number of feature maps and the methods used to generate them is not specified in the framework and can thus be adapted to the task at hand. We use an AdaBoost classifier (with decision trees as weak classifiers) that we cascade to minimize computations on obvious negatives. The basic image measurements used by our classifier are distances to feature occurrences. Therefore we can define an efficient hierarchical search that gives a significant speedup compared to the sliding window approach.

Hierarchical search schemes have been used previously minimize the Chamfer distance between a search template and a test image [1]. A very large number of templates are needed to represent an object class with significant intra-class variation. Gavrila has devised a search scheme that is hierarchical in both search space and in template space [11]. While the hierarchical search is a desirable property of the Chamfer matching methods, the template-based representation of an object class is not. The problem is that there is a big risk that even a very large set of templates does not represent the whole target class (overfitting). The use of a strong classifier is better in this sense, since most classifiers have been designed to have a good ability to generalize beyond the training set. For example, if weak classifiers can perform better than chance on every distribution over the training set, AdaBoost can provably achieve arbitrarily good generalization bound [8].

In summary our method (1) has good generalization properties (inherited from the AdaBoost procedure), (2) allows for a very fast hierarchical search and (3) allows the user to adapt the choice of image features to the task at hand.

The rest of the paper is organized as follows. In section 2 we describe how our method represents the object category and how this representation is learnt. In section 3 we describe the detection algorithm in detail. In section 4 we present experiments evaluating the detection performance and computational efficiency of our method. Finally, we conclude in section 5.

2 Object Class Model

In this section we describe how an object class is modeled and how the parameters of that model are learnt. The target object class is represented by a boosted decision tree classifier based on normalized distances to feature occurrences. The classifier can be visualized as a linear combination of flexible feature configurations, described in a normalized coordinate system.

We start by defining some notation. We then describe the classifier and how it is learnt in sections 2.1 to 2.4. Finally, we mention variations to the learning algorithm in section 2.5.

We assume that we have a set of features $\mathcal{K}$, for which we can compute feature maps, $\Phi_k(I, \mathbf{x}) \in \{0, 1\}$ that returns 1 if feature k occurs at location $\mathbf{x}$ in image I and 0 otherwise. We will also make use of distance transforms of feature maps: $d_k(I, \mathbf{x}) = \min_{\{\mathbf{x}' | \Phi_k(I, \mathbf{x}')=1\}} ||\mathbf{x} - \mathbf{x}'||$. Distance transforms can be computed efficiently [2].

The basic building blocks of the classifier are localized features $F = (k, \mathbf{p})$, defined by the feature index k and the location $\mathbf{p}$ in a normalized coordinate system. We also define the feature value, $f(I, \mathbf{t}, s) = d_k(I, s \cdot \mathbf{p} + \mathbf{t})/s$, which is obtained by translating ($\mathbf{t}$) and scaling (s) the normalized coordinate system into an image (I) and computing the normalized distance to the closest occurrence of the feature in the image. Note that the computation of the feature value essentially only involves a lookup into the distance transform table. All feature values are nonnegative.

We define a dictionary $\mathcal{F} = \{F_n | n = 1 \ldots N\} = \mathcal{K} \times \mathcal{P}$ of localized features, where $\mathcal{P}$ is a uniformly spaced grid in the normalized coordinate system. By concatenating the corresponding feature values, we get a feature vector $\mathbf{f}(I, \mathbf{t}, s) = [f_1(I, \mathbf{t}, s) \ldots f_N(I, \mathbf{t}, s)]^T$.

The training data consists of a set of images $\{I_j | j \in \mathcal{J}\}$ and a set of annotations $\{(\mathbf{t}_i, s_i, j_i) | i \in \mathcal{I}\}$, specifying the location, scale and image number of each instance of the target class in the image set.

2.1 Cascade

The cascade is not really a part of the object model, but rather a sequence of object models of increasing detail and specificity. However, it serves two important functions: (1) it minimizes the number of computations spent on obvious negatives at the detection stage and (2) it provides a mechanism for selecting hard negative examples at the training stage. The cascade is learnt according to Viola and Jones [20]. Each stage of the cascade contains an object model, which is learnt using all annotated instances of the target class as positive examples. We gather negative examples by running the current cascade on all training images and sample false positive detections. We then compute feature vectors for all (positive and negative) training examples and pass that to the strong learner, which will be described in the next section. The strong learner outputs a classification function H, that is thresholded to determined class membership. The threshold is typically selected to give a specific true positive rate on a validation set.

2.2 Strong Classifier

In this section we describe the strong classifier. The strong classifier is a linear combination of weak classifiers learnt using a variant of AdaBoost. We give a generalized description of the boosting algorithm, closely following Schapire and Singer [18], in listing 1. The input to the learner is a set of feature vectors $\{\mathbf{f}^m\}$, with target class $c_m \in \{-1, 1\}$. The classification function of the strong classifier, $H(\mathbf{f}) = \sum_{t=1}^{T} \alpha_t h_t(\mathbf{f})$, is a linear combination of the classification functions of the weak classifiers. The classification function is thresholded to determine class membership. We mention different alternatives for initializing and updating the weight distribution and for choosing the αs in section 2.5. In the next section, we describe the weak classifier.

Algorithm 1. Boosting

Require: $\{\mathbf{f}^m\}$, $c_m \in \{-1, 1\}$, T
  $\mathbf{d_1} \leftarrow$ initialize weight distribution
  for $t = 1$ to T **do**
    Train weak classifier $h_t : \mathbb{R}^{*N} \rightarrow \mathbb{R}$ using distribution $\mathbf{d_t}$
    Choose $\alpha_t \in \mathbb{R}$
    $\mathbf{d_{t+1}} \leftarrow$ update weight distribution
  end for
  return $\{\alpha_1, \ldots, \alpha_T\}$, $\{h_1, \ldots, h_T\}$

2.3 Weak Classifier

The weak classifier is a binary decision tree. The leaf nodes contain the outputs of the classifier and the internal nodes contain binary classifiers, which we will refer to as single feature classifiers (described in the next section). At the detection stage the output of the single feature classifier determines whether to visit the left or right subtree next; when a leaf node is reached, its output is returned.

A generalized description of the weak learner is given in listing 2. The input to the weak learner is a set of feature vectors $\{\mathbf{f}^m\}$, with target class $\{c_m\}$, and a weight distribution $\mathbf{d}$. The weak learner then computes the output of the current node and possibly constructs left and right subtrees recursively. We will mention different alternatives for computing the output of a node and for validating the split induced by a single feature classifier in section 2.5. In the next section we describe the single feature classifier.

2.4 Single Feature Classifier

A single feature classifier g consists of a single localized feature (selected from the dictionary) $F_n \in \mathcal{F}$, along with a distance threshold $t \in \mathbb{R}^+$ and its parity $p \in \{-1, 1\}$. The output of the single feature classifier is 1 if $p \cdot f_n \leq p \cdot t$ and -1 otherwise.

Algorithm 2. Weak learner

Require: $\{\mathbf{f}^m\}$, $\{c_m\}$, $\mathbf{d}$
Node.output $\leftarrow$ compute output using $\{c_m\}$ and $\mathbf{d}$
Train single feature classifier $g : \mathbb{R}^N \rightarrow \{-1, 1\}$ using $\{\mathbf{f}^m\}$, $\{c_m\}$ and $\mathbf{d}$
Compute split $\mathcal{M}_- = \{m|g(\mathbf{f}^m) = -1\}$ and $\mathcal{M}_+ = \{m|g(\mathbf{f}^m) = 1\}$
Stop $\leftarrow$ validate split using $\mathcal{M}_-$, $\mathcal{M}_+$,$\{c_m\}$ and $\mathbf{d}$
if Stop **then**
  return Node
end if
Node.left = Weak learner($\{\mathbf{f}^m|m \in \mathcal{M}_-\}, \{c_m|m \in \mathcal{M}_-\}, \mathbf{d}$)
Node.right = Weak learner($\{\mathbf{f}^m|m \in \mathcal{M}_+\}, \{c_m|m \in \mathcal{M}_+\}, \mathbf{d}$)
return Node

Learning a single feature classifier involves selecting a feature n, a threshold t and a parity p. A generalized procedure for learning a single feature classifier is given in listing 3. We have observed empirically that our feature values (being nonnegative) tend to be exponentially distributed. This suggests selecting the threshold t for a particular feature as the intersection of two exponential pdfs, where μ^+ is the (weighted) average of the feature values from the positive examples and μ^- is the (weighted) average from the negative examples (the parity is 1 if $\mu^+ \leq \mu^-$ and -1 otherwise):

$$t = \ln\left(\frac{\mu^-}{\mu^+}\right) \cdot \frac{\mu^-\mu^+}{\mu^- - \mu^+} \tag{1}$$

Thus each localized feature in the dictionary yields a single threshold and parity. The remaining task is to select the feature that minimizes the error function. We will mention different error functions in the following section.

Algorithm 3. Learn single feature classifier

Require: $\{\mathbf{f}^m\}$, $\{c_m\}$, $\mathbf{d}$
for $n = 1$ to N **do**
  $(t_n, p_n) \leftarrow$ select threshold and polarity using $\{f_n^m\}$, $\{c_m\}$ and $\mathbf{d}$
  $e_n \leftarrow$ compute error using $\{f_n^m\}$, $\{c_m\}$, $\mathbf{d}$ and (t_n, p_n)
end for
$n^* \leftarrow \arg\min_n e_n$
return (n^*, t_{n^*}, p_{n^*})

2.5 Variations

In the previous sections we have given a generalized description of the classifier and how to learn it. However, there are several ways in which this general scheme can be varied and in this section we mention the most interesting variations, which will also be compared experimentally in section 4.

Firstly, we have the choice of whether or not to use asymmetric weighting, as described in [19]. This choice affects the initialization and update of the weight distribution in the strong learner. Using asymmetric weighting requires setting a parameter k, specifying that false negatives cost k times more than false positives. We empirically found $k = 3n_-/n_+$ to be a reasonable choice in this case.

Secondly, we have the choice of whether to let the weak classifiers output binary or confidence rated predictions. This choice affects (1) the computation of the αs in the strong learner, (2) the computation of the output of a node in the weak learner and (3) the error that is minimized by the single feature learner. In the case of binary predictions we use the original AdaBoost algorithm of Freund and Schapire [8] to compute the αs. The output of a node is simply the weighted majority of the training examples and the error is the weighted training error. In the case of confidence rated predictions we follow Schapire and Singer's recipe for domain-partitioning hypotheses [18]. The αs are set to 1 in this case.

Finally, we can pose various constraints on the weak classifier. For example we can limit the depth of the decision tree to reduce the risk of over-fitting.

3 Detection

In this section we describe the detection procedure. It consists of three parts: (1) preprocessing, (2) scale space search and (3) aspect ratio estimation. The preprocessing is illustrated in figure 1 and entails computing feature maps and distance transforms for each feature. The scale space search can be done using a sliding window approach, however the features used in this paper allow a hierarchical search scheme with efficient search space culling to be defined. This is described in the next section. The scale space search yields the position and scale of detected objects. However, we want the bounding box, which also requires an aspect ratio. In section 3.2 we describe how to estimate the aspect ratio.

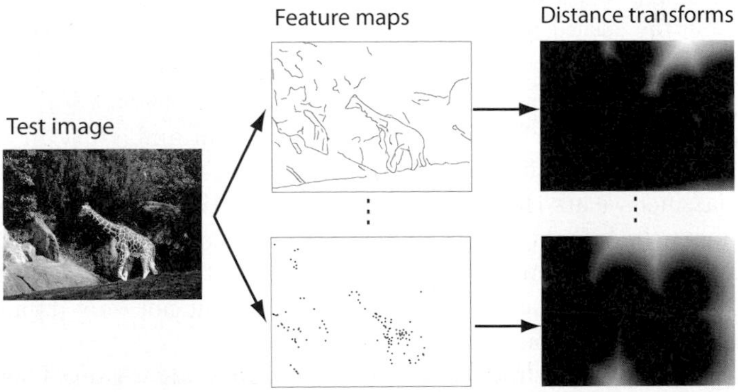

Fig. 1. Images are preprocessed by computing feature maps and the corresponding distance transforms for each feature

3.1 Hierarchical Search

In this section we describe the hierarchical search in scale space. The idea is that, given a region in search space, we can compute bounds on the value of all localized features and if none of the possible values would yield a detection, we can discard the whole region.

We have previously defined the value of a localized feature $F = (k, \mathbf{p})$ to be $f(I, \mathbf{t}, s) = d_k(I, s \cdot \mathbf{p} + \mathbf{t})/s$. Now, if we have a cuboid region, S, in search space, we can compute upper and lower bounds for the feature value; i.e. we can compute $f^{(u)}$ and $f^{(l)}$ such that $f^{(l)} \leq f(I, \mathbf{t}, s) \leq f^{(u)} \forall (\mathbf{t}, s) \in S$.

Let B contain the 8 corner points of S and let $(\mathbf{t}_0, s_0)$ be any point in S (for example the centroid). Then let $P' = \{s \cdot \mathbf{p} + \mathbf{t} | (\mathbf{t}, s) \in B\}$, $\mathbf{p}'_0 = s_0 \cdot \mathbf{p} + \mathbf{t}_0$ and $d_{\max} = \max_{\mathbf{p}' \in P'} \|\mathbf{p}'_0 - \mathbf{p}'\|$. We can now compute upper and lower bounds as follows: $f^{(u)} = (d_k(I, \mathbf{p}'_0) + d_{\max})/s_1$ and $f^{(l)} = \max((d_k(I, \mathbf{p}'_0) - d_{\max})/s_2, 0)$, where s_1 and s_2 are the minimum and maximum scales in S respectively.

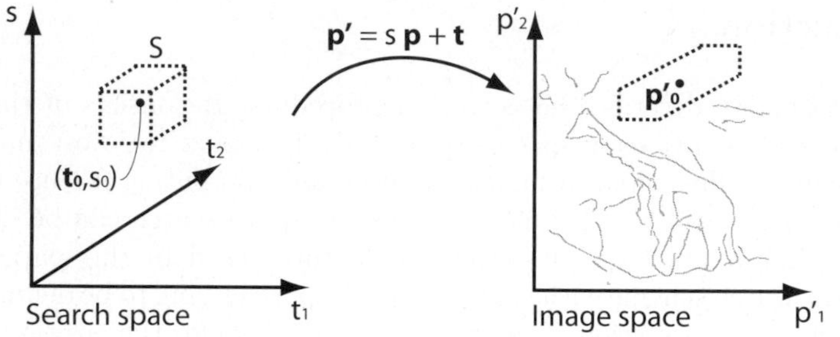

Fig. 2. If a localized feature has position $\mathbf{p}$ in normalized coordinates and the normalized frame is aligned with an image by translation $\mathbf{t_0}$ and scaling s_0, the position of the feature in the image is $\mathbf{p}' = s_0 \cdot \mathbf{p} + \mathbf{t_0}$. However, if we have a whole range S of possible translations and scalings, the position of the localized feature in the image can be anywhere in the dashed region in image space. We can easily compute bounds for the feature value given that the position of the localized feature is within that region.

The uncertainty in the feature value may yield an ambiguity in the output of the single feature classifier (i.e. it could be either 1 or -1). When evaluating the weak classifier we are then unable to decide whether to visit the left or right child node next. In such cases we pursue both paths and the output of the weak classifier is defined as the maximum of all leaf nodes that were reached. Thus we get an optimistic strong classifier that returns 1 if (but not only if) any point in the region, S, is a detection.

We are now ready to define the hierarchical search algorithm. The algorithm recursively partitions the search space into smaller regions, evaluating the classifier at each new region. If the classifier returns -1 for any region, that region is discarded. When the classifier returns 1, subdivision continues until the current region is small enough; then the classifier is evaluated at the centroid of that region. A more detailed description is given in listing 4.

Algorithm 4. Hierarchical search

```
Require: Classifier c, Search region S
  if S is sufficiently small then
    (t, s) ← centroid of S
    result ← evaluate classifier on (t, s)
    if result = 1 then
      return (t, s)
    else
      return ∅
    end if
  end if
  result ← evaluate classifier on S
  if result = -1 then
    return ∅
  end if
  [R_1, ..., R_l] ← split S into subregions
  initialize D ← ∅
  for all R_i do
    D ← D ∪ HierarchicalSearch(c, R_i)
  end for
  return D
```

3.2 Aspect Ratio Estimation

The detector scans the image over position and scale, but in order to produce a good estimate of the bounding box of a detected object we also need the aspect ratio (which typically varies significantly within an object class). We use regression to estimate the aspect ratio of a detected object. Specifically, we use gradient boosted regression trees [9]. The regressor is trained using set of feature vectors $\{\mathbf{f}^m\}$, with target aspect ratio a_m. We use the same training set for the aspect ratio estimator as for the detector (albeit the aspect ratio estimator only uses the positive examples). Each regression tree recursively splits the training examples in two and finally one estimate of the aspect ratio is assigned to each leaf node by optimizing some target function. Typically the target of the ensemble is to minimize the square norm of the residual and the target of each new regression tree is to correct the errors of the current ensemble.

At the detection stage the boosted regression trees are applied to the feature vector of each detected object to estimate its aspect ratio.

4 Experiments and Results

We have performed experiments on the ETHZ Shape Classes dataset [7]. This dataset is challenging due to large intra-class variation, clutter and varying scales. We used all images from the ETHZ dataset for testing only. Training images were downloaded from Google Images. These images contained a total of 106 applelogos, 128 bottles, 270 giraffes, 233 mugs and 165 swans. As in [6], a

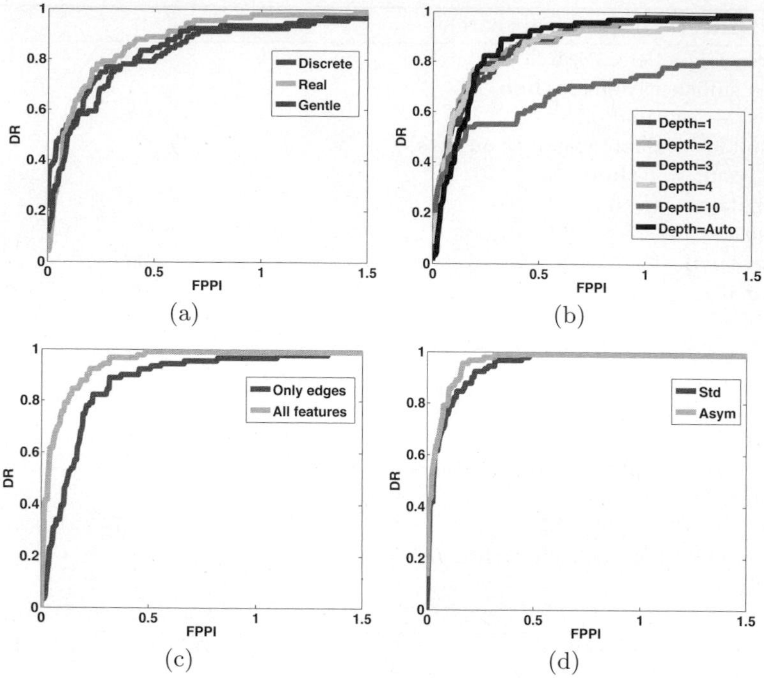

Fig. 3. Comparison of different variants of the algorithm. See text for details. Best viewed in color.

detection is counted as correct if the detected bounding box overlaps more than 20 % with the ground truth bounding box. Bounding box overlap is defined as the area of intersection divided by the area of union of the bounding boxes. Several other authors have evaluated their methods on this dataset and we let [17] represent state-of-the-art.

The goal of our first experiment was to compare the different variants of the algorithm, as described in section 2.5. We use the giraffes as the test class, because it is the class with the most intra-class variation and thus the most difficult and realistic class. The results are given in figure 3. We vary one property at a time, starting with the choice of boosting algorithm. We compare discrete AdaBoost [8], real AdaBoost [18] and gentle AdaBoost [10]. The results, shown in figure 3(a), indicate that real AdaBoost is the best choice. We then experiment with the depth setting of the decision tree weak learner (figure 3(b)). We compare different set depths and an automatic version, where we stop growing the tree when further growth does not improve the classification error on the training set. We see that we should either set the depth to some small value, like one or two, or use the automatic version (which typically outputs very shallow trees). Then we experiment with different image features, first using only oriented edges [3] and then using also corners [12], blobs [15] and interest points (figure 3(c)). Interest points were detected using the Kadir-Brady detector [13]. For each

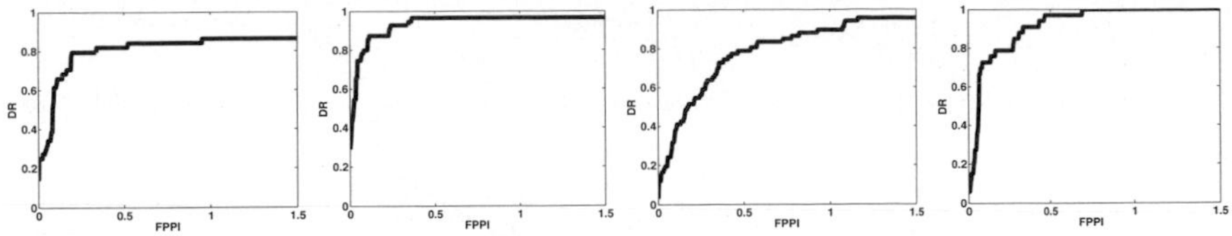

(a) Applelogos (b) Bottles (c) Mugs (d) Swans

Fig. 4. Detection rate (DR) plotted versus false positives per image (FPPI) for the remaining classes of the ETHZ dataset

Table 1. Comparison of detection performance. We state the detection rate at 0.4 FPPI. We compare to the systems of [6,17].

	A. logos	Bottles	Giraffes	Mugs	Swans
ours@0.4 FPPI:	81.8	**96.4**	**98.9**	74.2	**90.9**
[6]@0.4 FPPI:	83.2	83.2	58.6	83.6	75.4
[17]@0.4 FPPI:	**95.0**	**96.4**	89.6	**96.7**	88.2

interest point we compute the SIFT descriptor [16] and assign it to one out of eight different clusters which were computed using k-means on a set of interest points extracted from random background images. The interest points thus generate eight different feature maps - one for each cluster. We see that using more features improves the result. We finally tested the asymmetric weighting scheme [19], concluding that it improves the results (figure 3(d)).

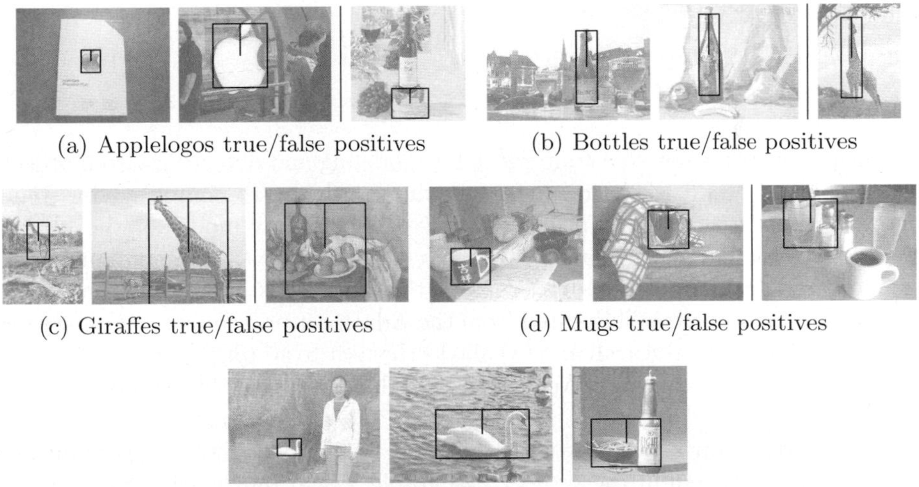

(a) Applelogos true/false positives (b) Bottles true/false positives

(c) Giraffes true/false positives (d) Mugs true/false positives

(e) Swans true/false positives

Fig. 5. Example detections (true and false positives) for each class

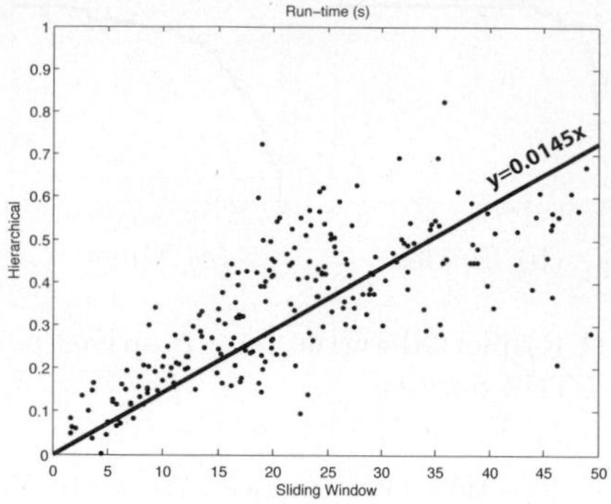

Fig. 6. Comparison of the runtimes of the hierarchical search (y-axis) and the sliding window search (x-axis). Each point represents one test image.

We also evaluated the performance of the detector, using the settings from the previous experiment (i.e. real AdaBoost, automatic depth determination, all features and asymmetric weighting), on all other classes in the ETHZ dataset. The results are plotted in figure 4 and in table 1 we compare our results to some previous methods. We also show some example detections in figure 5.

Finally, we compare the runtime of the hierarchical search with the sliding window approach. Here we again use the giraffe class. Each test image is represented by a point in the scatter plot shown in figure 6, with the sliding window runtime on the x-axis and the hierarchical runtime on the y-axis. We see that on average the hierarchical search yields a 70-fold speed-up. Both algorithms were implemented in MATLAB/mex and executed on a 2.8 GHz Pentium D desktop computer (using a single core).

5 Conclusion

In this paper we presented a framework for modeling and detecting visual object classes. The method is based on feature maps, which are computed by some external routine that is defined by the user. The learnt model of the object class is essentially a linear combination of a set of flexible spatial configurations of the input features. The advantages of the method is that it (1) has good generalization properties (inherited from the AdaBoost procedure), (2) allows for a very fast hierarchical search and (3) allows the user to adapt the choice of image features to the task at hand. We demonstrated these properties experimentally.

Acknowledgements. This work was supported by The Swedish Foundation for Strategic Research in the project "Wearable Visual Information Systems".

References

1. Borgefors, G.: Hierarchical chamfer matching: A parametric edge matching algorithm. IEEE Trans. Pattern Anal. Mach. Intell. 10(6), 849–865 (1988)
2. Breu, H., Gil, J., Kirkpatrick, D., Werman, M.: Linear time euclidean distance transform algorithms. IEEE Trans. Pattern Anal. and Mach. Intell. 17(5), 529–533 (1995)
3. Canny, J.: A computational approach to edge detection. IEEE Trans. Pattern Analysis and Machine Intelligence 8, 679–714 (1986)
4. Everingham, M., Van Gool, L., Williams, C.K.I., Winn, J., Zisserman, A.: The PASCAL Visual Object Classes Challenge (VOC 2009) Results (2009), `http://www.pascal-network.org/challenges/VOC/voc2009/workshop/index.html`
5. Felzenszwalb, P., Girshick, R., McAllester, D.: Cascade object detection with deformable part models. IEEE Computer Vision and Pattern Recognition (2010)
6. Ferrari, V., Jurie, F., Schmid, C.: Accurate object detection with deformable shape models learnt from images. IEEE Computer Vision and Pattern Recognition (2007)
7. Ferrari, V., Tuytelaars, T., Gool, L.V.: Object detection by contour segment networks. Proc. of the European Conference on Computer Vision (2006)
8. Freund, Y., Schapire, R.E.: A decision-theoretic generalization of on-line learning and an application to boosting. Journal of Computer Systems and Sciences 55, 119–139 (1997)
9. Friedman, J.H.: Greedy function approximation: A gradient boosting machine. The Annals of Statistics 29(5), 1189–1232 (2001)
10. Friedman, J., Hastie, T., Tibshirani, R.: Additive logistic regression: A statistical view of boosting. The Annals of Statistics 28(2), 337–374 (2000)
11. Gavrila, D.M.: A bayesian, exemplar-based approach to hierarchical shape matching. IEEE Transactions on Pattern Analysis and Machine Intelligence 29(8) (2007)
12. Harris, C., Stephens, M.: A combined corner and edge detector. In: Proc. of the 4th Alvey Vision Conference, pp. 147–151 (1988)
13. Kadir, T., Zisserman, A., Brady, M.: An affine invariant salient region detector. In: Proc. of the European Conference on Computer Vision (2004)
14. Laptev, I.: Improving object detection with boosted histograms. Image and Vision Computing 27, 535–544 (2009)
15. Lindeberg, T.: Feature detection with automatic scale selection. International Journal of Computer Vision 30(2), 77–116 (1998)
16. Lowe, D.G.: Distinctive image features from scale-invariant keypoints. International Journal of Computer Vision 60(2), 91–110 (2004)
17. Maji, S., Malik, J.: Object detection using a max-margin hough transform. In: Proc. of the IEEE Computer Vision and Pattern Recognition (2009)
18. Schapire, R.E., Singer, Y.: Improved boosting algorithms using confidence-rated predictions. Machine Learning 37, 297–336 (1999)
19. Viola, P.A., Jones, M.J.: Fast and robust classification using asymmetric adaboost and a detector cascade. In: Proc. of Neural Information Processing Systems (2001)
20. Viola, P.A., Jones, M.J.: Robust real-time face detection. International Journal of Computer Vision 57(2), 137–154 (2004)

Volume Local Phase Quantization for Blur-Insensitive Dynamic Texture Classification

Juhani Päivärinta, Esa Rahtu, and Janne Heikkilä

Machine Vision Group, Department of Electrical and Information Engineering, University of Oulu, P.O. Box 4500, 90014, Finland
{juhanipa,erahtu,jth}@ee.oulu.fi
http://www.ee.oulu.fi/mvg

Abstract. In this paper, we propose a blur-insensitive descriptor for dynamic textures. The Volume Local Phase Quantization (VLPQ) method introduced is based on binary encoding of the phase information of the local Fourier transform at low frequency points and is an extension to the LPQ operator used for spatial texture analysis. The local Fourier transform is computed efficiently using 1-D convolutions for each dimension in a 3-D volume. The data achieved is compressed to a smaller dimension before a scalar quantization procedure. Finally, a histogram of all binary codewords from dynamic texture is formed. The performance of VLPQ was evaluated both in the case of sharp dynamic textures and spatially blurred dynamic textures. Experiments on a dynamic texture database DynTex++ show that the new method tolerates more spatial blurring than LBP-TOP, which is a state-of-the-art descriptor, and its variant LPQ-TOP.

Keywords: Local Phase Quantization, Short-Term Fourier Transform, spatio-temporal domain, blur-insensitivity, dynamic texture.

1 Introduction

Dynamic textures can be seen as sequences of images of moving scenes that exhibit certain stationarity properties in time [1]. Some examples of dynamic textures in the real world are fire, moving clouds, a waving flag, and sea waves. Dynamic texture analysis is essential in many applications, such as facial expression recognition, action recognition, and background subtraction. Chetverikov and Péteri created a survey on the existing descriptors for dynamic texture recognition in [2] and divided the approaches into five classes: methods based on optical flow, methods computing geometric properties in the spatio-temporal domain, methods based on local spatio-temporal filtering, methods using global spatio-temporal transforms, and model-based methods that use estimated model parameters as features.

Among the most popular approaches for characterizing the local dynamics of dynamic texture are the methods based on optical flow. For example, in [3], Péteri et al. achieved promising results using normal flow features combined with periodicity features, and their features were translation invariant.

A. Heyden and F. Kahl (Eds.): SCIA 2011, LNCS 6688, pp. 360–369, 2011.

In [4], Zhao et al. introduced two methods based on Local Binary Patterns (LBP) [5]: Volume Local Binary Patterns (VLBP) and Local Binary Patterns from Three Orthogonal Planes (LBP-TOP). Of these two, LBP-TOP was shown to be the most efficient approach, and the results achieved were very promising. These methods are based on local characteristics, which is also our approach to dynamic texture classification.

One can also combine multiple descriptors. Recently, Ghanem et al. used Maximum Margin Distance Learning (MMDL) in [6] for dynamic texture recognition. They modeled the distance between two dynamic textures as a positively weighted sum of their elementary distances: spatial texture element, spatial texture layout, and dynamics. However, despite the comprehensiveness, their method is computationally very expensive, since it consists of computing multiple descriptors.

In some applications, there are degradation factors which complicate the actual recognition procedure. One common category of degradation is blur caused by e.g. atmospheric turbulence, motion, or out-of-focus. These blur types can be seen and considered as spatial blurring. To our knowledge, there are no dynamic texture descriptors that are claimed to be robust to spatial blurring. In [7], Ojansivu et al. proposed a method called Local Phase Quantization (LPQ) for blur-insensitive spatial texture analysis. LPQ can be also used for dynamic textures, e.g., when a straightforward generalization of LBP-TOP is made to form a method in which the LPQ descriptors are calculated from three orthogonal planes. For comparison, we have built a descriptor using this approach (LPQ-TOP), but we also propose a more elaborated approach.

In this paper, we introduce a novel method called Volume Local Phase Quantization (VLPQ), which is a dynamic texture descriptor insensitive to centrally symmetric spatial blurring. Our method is an extension to the original 2-D LPQ, and the characterization of dynamic texture is made using the quantized phase information of the Discrete Fourier Transform (DFT) computed in pixel volume neighborhoods. Our method uses Short-Term Fourier Transform (STFT) to evaluate the DFT, and we use the 13 low 3-D frequency points in the evaluation. The computational performance of our method is increased by calculating the STFT using 1-D convolutions for each dimension in a 3-D volume. In our method, dimension reduction is essential for the data before scalar quantization to achieve a reasonable sized binary codeword. After the quantization, a histogram of all codewords from a dynamic texture volume is formed.

2 Volume Local Phase Quantization

Dynamic texture is a sequence of spatial frames. Therefore, we can first consider spatial images suffering from blur. The discrete model for spatially invariant blurring of an original image $s(\mathbf{x})$ resulting in an observed image $g(\mathbf{x})$ can be expressed by a convolution, given by

$$g(\mathbf{x}) = (s * h)(\mathbf{x}) , \tag{1}$$

where $h(\mathbf{x})$ is the point spread function (PSF) of the blur, $*$ denotes 2-D convolution, and $\mathbf{x}$ is a vector of coordinates $[x, y]^T$. When (1) is taken to the Fourier domain, the convolution turns into a product. If we consider only the phase of the spectrum, we get

$$\angle G(\mathbf{u}) = \angle S(\mathbf{u}) + \angle H(\mathbf{u}) \; . \tag{2}$$

In the case of centrally symmetric PSFs, $H(\mathbf{u})$ is real valued, and the phase angle $\angle H(\mathbf{u})$ must equal 0 or π. For a typical PSF, the shape of $H(\mathbf{u})$ is similar to a low-pass filter. This often implies that at least the low frequency values of $H(\mathbf{u})$ are positive. At these frequencies, $\angle H(\mathbf{u}) = 0$, and hence $\angle S(\mathbf{u})$ is a blur-invariant property. [7]

In practice, the blur-invariance is partly disturbed because of the finite size of the observed images resulting to a loss of information at the borders. The convolution of the ideal image frame with the blur PSF extends beyond the borders of the observed image, and this results to a loss of information. When the Fourier transform is computed from local patches, this effect increases. However, the local computation allows the blur to vary within a single frame. Ojansivu et al. indicated in [7] that a highly blur-insensitive texture descriptor can be constructed by applying the aforementioned theory. The experiments in [7], [8], and [9] show clearly the blur-insensitive property. When we consider video sequences to consist of multiple spatial frames, this theory can also be extended to construct a blur-insensitive descriptor for dynamic textures. In the next sections, we propose a method for constructing VLPQ descriptor for dynamic textures.

2.1 Short-Term Fourier Transform in the Spatio-Temporal Domain

Dynamic texture consists of a video sequence of multiple frames spread over the time axis. Therefore, each position $\mathbf{x}$ in a sequence $f(\mathbf{x})$ can be expressed in 3-D coordinates, and every position in a sequence has a 3-D neighborhood. Since dynamic textures are textures in the spatio-temporal domain, dynamic texture is mainly a local property. Therefore, the Fourier transform estimation is performed locally using Short-Term Fourier Transform (STFT). STFT is computed over an M-by-M-by-N neighborhood $\mathcal{N}_{\mathbf{x}}$ centered at each position $\mathbf{x}$. M and N denote the size of the neighborhood in the spatial and the temporal domains, respectively. STFT of a sequence $f(\mathbf{x})$ can be defined by

$$F(\mathbf{u}, \mathbf{x}) = \sum_{\mathbf{y} \in \mathcal{N}_{\mathbf{x}}} f(\mathbf{x} - \mathbf{y}) e^{-j2\pi \mathbf{u}^T \mathbf{y}} \; , \tag{3}$$

where $\mathbf{u}$ is a 3-D frequency variable, and $j = \sqrt{-1}$. Using vector notation, we can rewrite (3) as

$$F(\mathbf{u}, \mathbf{x}) = \mathbf{w}_{\mathbf{u}}^T \mathbf{f}_{\mathbf{x}} \; , \tag{4}$$

where $\mathbf{w}_{\mathbf{u}}$ is the basis vector of the 3-D DFT at frequency $\mathbf{u}$, and $\mathbf{f}_{\mathbf{x}}$ is a vector containing all pixels from the neighborhood $\mathcal{N}_{\mathbf{x}}$. Because of the separability of the basis functions, the STFT can be efficiently evaluated for each pixel position using 1-D convolutions for each dimension. This increases the computational efficiency considerably.

As mentioned, the low frequency points are likely to satisfy $H(\mathbf{u}) > 0$. Therefore, we construct the descriptor using 13 lowest non-zero frequency points: $\mathbf{u}_1 = [\alpha, 0, 0]^T$, $\mathbf{u}_2 = [\alpha, 0, \beta]^T$, $\mathbf{u}_3 = [\alpha, 0, -\beta]^T$, $\mathbf{u}_4 = [0, \alpha, 0]^T$, $\mathbf{u}_5 = [0, \alpha, \beta]^T$, $\mathbf{u}_6 = [0, \alpha, -\beta]^T$, $\mathbf{u}_7 = [\alpha, \alpha, 0]^T$, $\mathbf{u}_8 = [\alpha, \alpha, \beta]^T$, $\mathbf{u}_9 = [\alpha, \alpha, -\beta]^T$, $\mathbf{u}_{10} = [\alpha, -\alpha, 0]^T$, $\mathbf{u}_{11} = [\alpha, -\alpha, \beta]^T$, $\mathbf{u}_{12} = [\alpha, -\alpha, -\beta]^T$, and $\mathbf{u}_{13} = [0, 0, \beta]^T$, where $\alpha = 1/M$ and $\beta = 1/N$. The selected frequency points are illustrated as closed circles in Fig. 1. The other frequency points illustrated in Fig. 1 are ignored, because they are the complex conjugates of the selected ones.

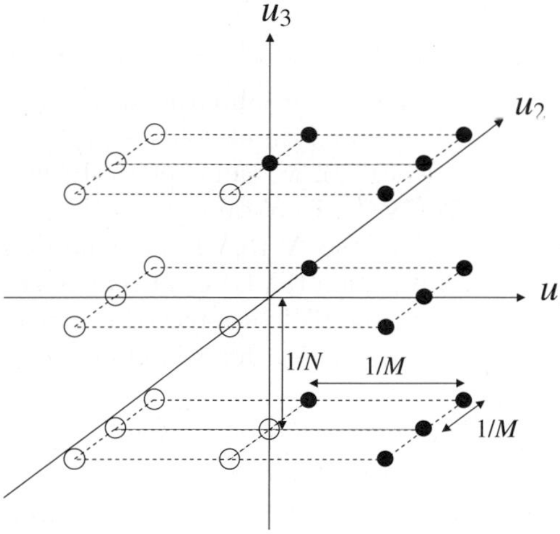

Fig. 1. Frequency points used to calculate STFT

At each position $\mathbf{x}$, after separating the real and imaginary parts of each component, we get a vector

$$\mathbf{F_x} = [\mathrm{Re}\{F(\mathbf{u}_1, \mathbf{x})\}, \mathrm{Im}\{F(\mathbf{u}_1, \mathbf{x})\}, \ldots, \mathrm{Re}\{F(\mathbf{u}_{13}, \mathbf{x})\}, \mathrm{Im}\{F(\mathbf{u}_{13}, \mathbf{x})\}]^T . \quad (5)$$

The corresponding 26-by-M^2N transform matrix can be written as

$$\mathbf{W} = [\mathrm{Re}\{\mathbf{w}_{\mathbf{u}_1}\}, \mathrm{Im}\{\mathbf{w}_{\mathbf{u}_1}\}, \ldots, \mathrm{Re}\{\mathbf{w}_{\mathbf{u}_{13}}\}, \mathrm{Im}\{\mathbf{w}_{\mathbf{u}_{13}}\}]^T . \quad (6)$$

Hence, the vector form of the STFT for all frequencies $\mathbf{u_1}$, ..., $\mathbf{u_{13}}$ can be written as

$$\mathbf{F_x} = \mathbf{W}\mathbf{f_x} . \quad (7)$$

2.2 Dimension Reduction

If we take into account all 13 frequency points and their real and imaginary parts, the length of the resulting descriptor at each position would be 26 real numbers.

Since this number of variables is excessive, dimension reduction is needed in order to compress the data. To do this, we first employ Principal Component Analysis (PCA) to transform the original, possibly correlated, set of variables to a smaller number of uncorrelated variables. For PCA, we use a correlation model with only two parameters. Finally, scalar quantization is performed for the uncorrelated samples.

We assume that the correlation coefficient between two adjacent pixels is ρ_s in the spatial domain, and ρ_t in the temporal domain. We also assume without loss of generality that the variance of each sample is $\sigma^2 = 1$. The covariance between two pixel values $f(\mathbf{x}_i)$ and $f(\mathbf{x}_j)$ can be written as

$$\sigma_{ij} = \rho_s^{d_{ij}^s} \rho_t^{d_{ij}^t} , \tag{8}$$

where $d_{ij}^s = \sqrt{\sum_{k=1}^{2} |\mathbf{x}_i(k) - \mathbf{x}_j(k)|^2}$ and $d_{ij}^t = |\mathbf{x}_i(3) - \mathbf{x}_j(3)|$. The covariance matrix of all M^2N pixel positions in a neighborhood $\mathcal{N}_\mathbf{x}$ can then be expressed as a M^2N-by-M^2N matrix $\mathbf{C}$, whose ijth element is σ_{ij}.

Based on the linear dependence (7), we can express the corresponding covariance matrix of $\mathbf{F_x}$ as $\mathbf{D} = \mathbf{W}\mathbf{C}\mathbf{W}^T$. To obtain uncorrelated sample vectors, we use a whitening transformation matrix $\mathbf{V}$ that is an orthonormal matrix derived from the singular value decomposition (SVD) of $\mathbf{D}$ that is $\mathbf{D} = \mathbf{U}\mathbf{\Sigma}\mathbf{V}^T$. Only L most important eigenvectors $\mathbf{v}$ from SVD are picked to calculate the whitening transformation. Hence, the final equation for whitening transformation can be defined as

$$\mathbf{G_x} = [\mathbf{v}_1, \mathbf{v}_2, \ldots, \mathbf{v}_L]^T \mathbf{F_x} . \tag{9}$$

In our method, the covariance matrix $\mathbf{C}$ is created using a correlation model that is based on assumptions on the correlation between pixel positions. However, these assumptions can be incorrect in the case of some blur PSFs that are not isotropic. Therefore, different correlation models could be used to form $\mathbf{C}$. One approach could also be to estimate $\mathbf{C}$ from the data.

2.3 Quantization

After calculation of the vector $\mathbf{G_x}$ for each volume position, quantization is performed. Since the samples to be quantized are now approximately uncorrelated, we use a simple scalar quantization method similar to the one used in [7]. The quantizer can be defined as

$$q_x(j) = \begin{cases} 1, & \text{if } g_x(j) \geq 0 \\ 0, & \text{otherwise} , \end{cases} \tag{10}$$

where $g_x(j)$ denotes the jth component of $\mathbf{G_x}$. The quantized coefficients are further represented as integer values, whose range depends on the number of eigenvectors L picked in the dimension reduction (9). The integer values can be formed using simple binary coding

$$b_x = \sum_{j=1}^{L} q_x(j) 2^{j-1} . \tag{11}$$

Finally, we form a histogram of the integer values obtained from all volume positions $\mathbf{x}$. This histogram is used as a 2^L dimensional feature vector.

3 Experiments

VLPQ algorithm was implemented using MATLAB. The algorithm computes the required STFTs using 1-D convolutions, and the convolutions are computed using only valid areas, i.e., areas that can be computed without zero-padding. The convolutions that occur multiple times in the process are calculated only once, and the results are stored for later usage in order to reduce the execution time. In the dimension reduction, L was selected to be 10. This results to a histogram of length $2^{10} = 1024$. The correlation coefficients used in the case of VLPQ were $\rho_s = 0.1$, and $\rho_t = 0.1$.

Also LPQ-TOP was implemented using MATLAB, and the algorithm calculates LPQ histograms from three orthogonal planes similar to LBP-TOP. The algorithm uses a correlation model with parameters $\rho_s = 0.1$, and $\rho_t = 0.1$. All the parameters were selected experimentally. The source codes for VLPQ and LPQ-TOP are available online[1].

The efficiency of VLPQ was experimented using a dynamic texture database DynTex++ [6], which is a new database compiled from the original DynTex database [10]. The performance was measured in the classification of sharp as well as spatially blurred dynamic textures. For comparison, we used LBP-TOP, which is a state-of-the-art method. Another reference method was our implementation of LPQ-TOP, which is a variant of LBP-TOP. These two methods are currently the best performing single descriptor methods and thus comparable to VLPQ.

DynTex++ database consists of 3600 dynamic textures of size $50 \times 50 \times 50$. The textures are divided into 36 classes, each holding 100 videos. Some example frames of the sequences used in our experiments are illustrated in Fig. 2. In our experiments, 50 % of each class was randomly selected to a training set, and the other 50 % to a test set. We used nearest neighbor method to classify the test set vectors. In classification, χ^2 distance was used as a measurement. Every test was repeated 20 times, and an average recognition rate was calculated.

3.1 Classification Tests

Classification accuracies of the methods used were measured in the case of sharp and spatially blurred dynamic textures. The blur was achieved by convolving the texture frames with spatial filters, and the training was done using the sharp textures. We used three different PSFs: circular blur of radii $\{0, 0.5, \ldots, 4\}$, Gaussian blur with standard deviations $\{0, 0.5, \ldots, 4\}$, and motion blur with lengths $\{0, 1, \ldots, 8\}$. Circular blur can be used to model out-of-focus blur, while Gaussian blur models atmospheric turbulence [11]. For motion blur, we used only horizontal direction.

[1] `http://www.cse.oulu.fi/Downloads/LPQMatlab/`

Fig. 2. Example frames from DynTex++ sequences: (a) frames from different classes, and (b) a circularly blurred frame, blurred using radii {0, 0.5, ..., 4}

In the case of blurred textures, the neighborhood size is a dominating factor in many cases. Usually, a small neighborhood works well at the low blur levels, but a larger neighborhood becomes more beneficial at the higher blur levels. Therefore, the experiment was performed using neighborhood sizes comparable to each other. In the case of dynamic textures, it is not usually reasonable to use similar number of neighboring points in the spatial domain and in the temporal domain [4]. However, the frame rate of DynTex++ sequences is high enough for using the same number of neighboring points in each direction. Fig. 3(a), Fig. 3(b), and Fig. 3(c) illustrate the achieved classification accuracies of VLPQ with $5 \times 5 \times 5$ neighborhood, LPQ-TOP with 5×5 neighborhood on each plane, and LBP-TOP with 8 samples and radii of 2 in each direction. These methods are denoted as $\text{VLPQ}_{5,5,5}$, $\text{LPQ-TOP}_{5,5,5}$, and $\text{LBP-TOP}_{8,8,8,2,2,2}$.

In addition, the performances of the methods were measured in the case of spatially and temporally varying blurring conditions. Each frame of the test sequences was divided into four regions of the same size. Each region of the first frame was blurred with different amount of blur. The blur was then linearly increased so that each region of the last frame suffered from similar amount of blur. The minimum blur levels of the three blur types were achieved using circular blur of radii {0, 1, 2, 3}, Gaussian blur with standard deviations {0, 1, 2, 3}, and motion blur with lengths {0, 2, 4, 6}. The maximum levels were the same as in the previous test. Fig. 3(d) illustrates the achieved accuracies.

From Fig. 3(a), Fig. 3(b), and Fig. 3(c) we can notice that $\text{VLPQ}_{5,5,5}$ is the best option in general. When no blur is present, the best accuracy (95 %) is achieved by $\text{LBP-TOP}_{8,8,8,2,2,2}$ followed by $\text{LPQ-TOP}_{5,5,5}$ and $\text{VLPQ}_{5,5,5}$. However, the differences are not significant, each accuracy being within 2 %. Each algorithm also achieved an accuracy higher than the one in [6]. When the blur becomes more eminent, the differences between the methods used become more considerable, and the high blur-insensitivity of $\text{VLPQ}_{5,5,5}$ becomes noticeable. In the case of circular or Gaussian blur, $\text{VLPQ}_{5,5,5}$ maintains its performance extremely well compared to the other methods, $\text{LPQ-TOP}_{5,5,5}$ being the second best solution.

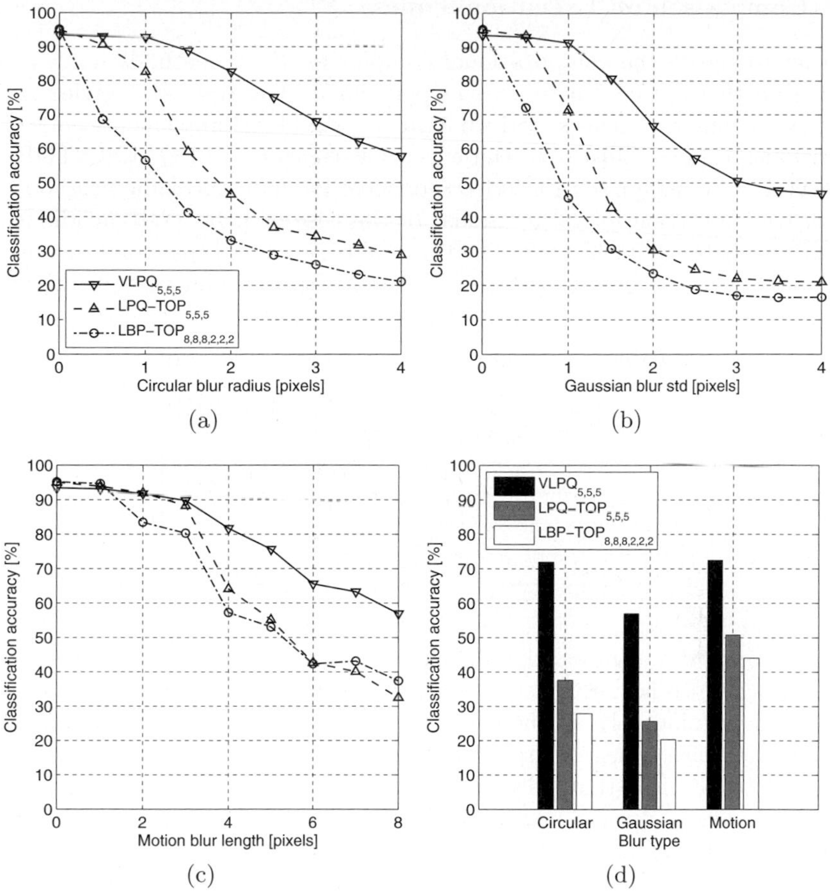

Fig. 3. Classification results in the case of different blur types: (a) circular blur, (b) Gaussian blur, (c) linear motion blur, and (d) varying blur

In the case of linear motion blur, the classification accuracies of the algorithms used are closer to each other than in the previous cases. This behavior can be understood knowing that the PSF of motion blur is not isotropic. Therefore, the correlation model of the LPQ-based methods is not as suitable as before. However, these methods perform well up to relatively high blur levels, $VLPQ_{5,5,5}$ once again being the best overall solution.

From Fig. 3(d) we can notice that in the case of varying blurring, $VLPQ_{5,5,5}$ outperforms the two other methods considerably. In all three cases, the classification accuracy of $VLPQ_{5,5,5}$ remains relatively high compared to the other methods even though the blurring conditions are now varying both spatially and temporally, and the classification is very challenging.

3.2 Comparison on Execution Times

In order to clarify the computational complexity of the methods used, a comparison on their execution times was performed. The test was carried out on DynTex++ video sequences, and we used the MATLAB implementations of the algorithms. Table 1 illustrates the execution times of VLPQ, LPQ-TOP, and LBP-TOP for one DynTex++ video sequence. We used the same neighborhood size in each direction for all methods. In the case of LBP-TOP, neighborhood size M equals to radii $(M\text{-}1)/2$. The times illustrated in Table 1 are mean times of 3600 sequences. Each algorithm was tested with the same configuration[2].

Table 1. Execution times of the methods used

Neighborhood size	VLPQ	LPQ-TOP	LBP-TOP
3	0.13 s	0.28 s	0.15 s
5	0.13 s	0.31 s	0.15 s
7	0.14 s	0.29 s	0.14 s
9	0.14 s	0.29 s	0.13 s
11	0.13 s	0.28 s	0.13 s

As we can notice, computationally the fastest algorithms are VLPQ and LBP-TOP. We can also notice that a larger neighborhood does not increase the execution time significantly. In the case of LBP-TOP, the execution time actually seems to decrease, when a larger neighborhood is used. This behavior can be explained by the fact that all of these algorithms use only the valid pixels of a video sequence. With a large neighborhood size, there are less valid neighborhoods, and a smaller part of a video volume can be used in calculation. DynTex++ sequences are small enough for this to have an effect on the execution time. It is also worth mentioning that the server used in the computation was variably stressed by other processes during the test. However, the relations between the execution times are valid.

4 Conclusions

In this paper, a novel dynamic texture descriptor VLPQ is proposed. VLPQ is a 3-D extension to the LPQ method, and it utilizes the Fourier transform phase information calculated locally at every texture volume position using 13 low nonzero frequency points. As a result of separating the real and imaginary parts of the Fourier transform, a vector of length 26 is formed. Dimension reduction is performed to achieve a codeword of a reasonable length, and a histogram is finally formed out of the results from all neighborhoods.

The performance of the method introduced was compared to a state-of-the-art method LBP-TOP and its variant LPQ-TOP. The results of the tests performed

[2] MATLAB R2010a on a 2.4 GHz, 96 GB Sunray server.

show that our method tolerates more centrally symmetric spatial blurring than the two aforementioned methods. It was also shown that VLPQ performs approximately equally compared to LPQ-TOP and LBP-TOP in the case of sharp dynamic textures.

Acknowledgments. This work was supported by the Academy of Finland (grant nos. 127702 and 128975).

References

1. Doretto, G., Chiuso, A., Wu, Y.N., Soatto, S.: Dynamic Textures. International Journal of Computer Vision 51(2), 91–109 (2003)
2. Chetverikov, D., Péteri, R.: A Brief Survey of Dynamic Texture Description and Recognition. In: International Conference on Computer Recognition Systems, pp. 17–26 (2005)
3. Péteri, R., Chetverikov, D.: Dynamic Texture Recognition Using Normal Flow and Texture Regularity. In: Marques, J.S., Pérez de la Blanca, N., Pina, P. (eds.) IbPRIA 2005. LNCS, vol. 3523, pp. 223–230. Springer, Heidelberg (2005)
4. Zhao, G., Pietikäinen, M.: Dynamic Texture Recognition Using Local Binary Patterns with an Application to Facial Expressions. IEEE Transactions on Pattern Analysis and Machine Intelligence (TPAMI 2007) 29(6), 915–928 (2007)
5. Ojala, T., Pietikäinen, M., Mäenpää, T.: Multiresolution Gray-Scale and Rotation Invariant Texture Classification with Local Binary Patterns. IEEE Transactions on Pattern Analysis and Machine Intelligence (TPAMI 2002) 24(7), 971–987 (2002)
6. Ghanem, B., Ahuja, N.: Maximum Margin Distance Learning for Dynamic Texture Recognition. In: Daniilidis, K., Maragos, P., Paragios, N. (eds.) ECCV 2010. LNCS, vol. 6312, pp. 223–236. Springer, Heidelberg (2010)
7. Ojansivu, V., Heikkilä, J.: Blur Insensitive Texture Classification Using Local Phase Quantization. In: Elmoataz, A., Lezoray, O., Nouboud, F., Mammass, D. (eds.) ICISP 2008. LNCS, vol. 5099, pp. 236–243. Springer, Heidelberg (2008)
8. Ojansivu, V., Rahtu, E., Heikkilä, J.: Rotation Invariant Local Phase Quantization for Blur Insensitive Texture Analysis. In: 19th International Conference on Pattern Recognition (ICPR 2008), pp. 1–4. Tampa, FL (2008)
9. Ahonen, T., Rahtu, E., Ojansivu, V., Heikkilä, J.: Recognition of Blurred Faces Using Local Phase Quantization. In: 19th International Conference on Pattern Recognition (ICPR 2008), pp. 1–4. Tampa, FL (2008)
10. Péteri, R., Fazekas, S., Huiskes, M.J.: DynTex: A Comprehensive Database of Dynamic Textures. Pattern Recognition Letters 31(12), 1627–1632 (2010), `http://www.cwi.nl/projects/dyntex/`
11. Banham, M.R., Katsaggelos, A.K.: Digital Image Restoration. IEEE Signal Processing Magazine 41(2), 24–41 (1997)

Optimal View Path Planning for Visual SLAM

Sebastian Haner and Anders Heyden

Centre for Mathematical Sciences
Lund University
{haner,heyden}@maths.lth.se
http://www.maths.lth.se

Abstract. In experimental design and 3D reconstruction it is desirable to minimize the number of observations required to reach a prescribed estimation accuracy. Many approaches in the literature attempt to find the next best view from which to measure, and iterate this procedure. This paper discusses a continuous optimization method for finding a whole set of future imaging locations which minimize the reconstruction error of observed geometry along with the distance traveled by the camera between these locations. A computationally efficient iterative algorithm targeted toward application within real-time SLAM systems is presented and tested on simulated data.

Keywords: Next best view planning, path optimization, SLAM.

1 Introduction

Visual simultaneous localization and mapping (SLAM) is the task of determining the position and orientation of a camera while concurrently building a map of the environment, using the camera images and possibly other sensors as input. It is a chicken-and-egg type problem; given the map, localization is relatively easy and given the camera positions, map triangulation is straightforward. Accomplishing both at once is at the heart of the SLAM problem, which has received a lot of attention in both the robotics and vision research communities. Much effort is spent improving the robustness and accuracy of algorithms, particularly with respect to error accumulation, drift and loop closing (see e.g. [1,2]). A less studied problem is how to make efficient use of the information collected in active SLAM systems, i.e. systems where the motion of the sensor can be controlled. This article considers the problem of maximizing the useful information gained from a fixed number of images by active planning of the vision sensor movement. Specifically, we consider the task of finding a camera trajectory between two predetermined locations such that the reconstruction accuracy of observed geometry is maximized while the path length is minimized. The envisioned application is robot path planning, where the accuracy usually is a secondary objective, so the focus is on providing the best reconstruction given time or distance constraints.

In this work we only consider the geometric aspects of the problem and do not account for availability of texture or object occlusion, which are of course issues in a real system relying on feature tracking. We further assume the following:

A. Heyden and F. Kahl (Eds.): SCIA 2011, LNCS 6688, pp. 370–380, 2011.

– An initial maximum likelihood estimate of the structure is available, based on observations up to that point.
– All cameras along the trajectory are oriented towards a particular point of interest, e.g. the centroid of the features to be estimated.
– The camera can be positioned with such relative accuracy that its pose and location is fully known at each observation.

These assumptions may be relaxed, as discussed in section 6.2. Finally, the robot path is represented by a sequence of camera locations, and the number of cameras on the path must be chosen in advance.

As an experimental design problem, so-called 'camera network design' has been studied extensively in the photogrammetry literature. The emphasis is on obtaining the most accurate reconstruction given a limited number of cameras, and time can be spent finding an optimal configuration. For example, in [14] a genetic optimization algorithm is used to search the high-dimensional parameter space of camera placements. Similar stochastic algorithms are usually employed since the problem is intrinsically multi-modal i.e. the objective function has many local minima, cf. [3]. In the context of 3D reconstruction in controlled environments, the task at hand is usually referred to as 'next best view planning', suggesting that given an approximate reconstruction we seek a single next view that will reduce the error the most. This is the case in [4] where the authors reconstruct objects using a camera mounted on a robotic arm. The object geometry is estimated using a Kalman filter, and the next imaging location is determined by searching a discrete parameter space and evaluating the expected information gain in the filter at each position. A different approach is taken in [5] where the next imaging location is decided based only on the single currently least well-determined feature, allowing a simple closed form solution. In the above problem formulations there are usually few or no constraints imposed on possible sensor configurations, computational complexity is less of an issue and the 'next best view' approaches do not consider more than one future observation. This work will show that given constraints on the camera positions, good solutions for many future observations can be found relatively quickly. For a recent general survey of the sensor planning field see the book by Chen et al. [6].

The work most similar in spirit to ours is [7] where the path of a robot moving in the plane is planned based on the expected reconstruction accuracy of an observed object. An approximation of the geometry is given and the expected information gain from observing the object from a particular vantage point is determined on a discrete grid of camera locations. Each grid cell is assigned a cost proportional to the inverse of the information gain, and a minimum cost path is found between the starting point and the global minimum grid cell. The algorithm does not take into account the new information gained after an actual observation is made, however, and becomes computationally expensive if we allow the camera to move in three dimensions. The minimum cost path formulation also restricts the choice of cost function. This work proposes an efficient continuous optimization approach to the problem of finding a short path with large information gain.

2 Problem Formulation

The planner takes as input an initial estimate of the structure, the current location of the sensor and the desired destination. The output is a path, represented by a discrete set of sensor locations, connecting these points. The number of locations on the path can be set explicitly or deduced from e.g. the robot's speed and sample rate and the distance to be travelled. For the experiments in this paper the sensor is assumed to be a single fully calibrated camera, although extension to stereo and multi-camera systems is straightforward. The standard pinhole camera model is used, so that the relation $\hat{x} = f(P, X)$ between a world point X and its projection $\hat{x}$ in homogeneous coordinates is given by

$$\lambda f(P, X) = KM \begin{pmatrix} X \\ 1 \end{pmatrix} = \begin{pmatrix} f_x & 0 & u_0 \\ 0 & f_y & v_0 \\ 0 & 0 & 1 \end{pmatrix} \begin{pmatrix} R \mid -Rt \end{pmatrix} \begin{pmatrix} X \\ 1 \end{pmatrix} \tag{1}$$

where R and t are the camera rotation and translation and K represents the known intrinsic calibration parameters. However, any differentiable projection function $f(P, X)$ may be substituted, e.g. to include radial distortion terms.

In the interest of reducing the parameter space dimension, each camera is parametrized only by its position and is automatically oriented toward a point of interest, typically chosen as the centroid of the structure under consideration. Features are deemed visible if they fall within the camera's field of view; possible occlusion by other objects is not considered. The measurement uncertainty of features is also considered fixed.

We define the optimization problem as follows:

Problem 1. Minimize the reconstruction uncertainty of observed geometry and the distance traveled by the sensor between imaging locations.

These are conflicting objectives, which are combined in a cost function defined below.

3 Cost Function

Lacking ground truth data or other *a priori* information, the quality of a reconstruction can only be judged by the statistical uncertainty of the estimate. Condensing a probability distribution into a scalar quality measure is not entirely straight-forward, however, and choices must be made depending on the intended application. Also, in most situations only estimates of the probability distribution are available, e.g. the mean and covariance. In the experimental design literature, many summary statistics have been proposed and are usually functions of the eigenvalues of the covariance matrix, e.g. the trace and determinant, cf. [8]. In the structure-from-motion problem, the eigenvalues have a direct geometric interpretation which we consider below.

If we assume the position and orientation of the camera is fully known when an observation is made, the structure estimates corresponding to individual features are independent of each other, and the covariance matrix is block diagonal with 3-by-3 blocks (assuming point features). The eigenvalues of each block correspond to the semi-axes of the ellipsoid representing the variance of the feature location. We would like these ellipsoids to be as small as possible, but in what sense? If we minimize the volume, i.e. the determinant, we admit solutions where a point may be very well-determined in two directions but with a large uncertainty in the third (typically the depth). Minimizing the determinant of the entire covariance matrix (the so-called D-optimality criterion) could favor solutions where one point is very well determined while others are much less certain. For navigation and mapping purposes, we would like all, or at least the majority of features to be reconstructed to reasonable accuracy. Minimizing the largest eigenvalue (E-optimality) would achieve this, but results in a non-smooth objective function. We choose to minimize the sum of the eigenvalues (A-optimality), i.e. the trace of the covariance matrix, which provides a good trade-off with the added computational benefit of not having to calculate individual eigenvalues.

Before introducing the cost function, we discuss how to compute the trace given a set of measurements.

3.1 Calculating Covariance

In many recent SLAM systems (e.g. [9,10,11]) maximum likelihood estimates obtained via bundle adjustment are available. We assume the structure estimate is optimal in the ML sense with respect to the observations; then the information matrix is given to first order by $I = J^\top R^{-1} J$ where J is the Jacobian of the reprojection error evaluated at the minimum, and R the measurement noise covariance [12]. Also, the (pseudo-)inverse of I gives an approximation of the covariance matrix. Since information is additive, including new observations in the estimate amounts to summing the individual information matrices. In other words, to calculate the effect of new observations on the structure estimate, we compute the Jacobian of each observation and add the corresponding information matrices to the initial one. New observations may of course shift the ML estimate, invalidating the approximation, but this is avoided in a natural way as discussed in section 4.

Given a world point X and a camera P, let x be the measured image coordinate, and $f(P, X)$ the projection function mapping X to the expected image coordinate $\hat{x}$. Define the re-projection error as $E_X(P, X, x) = f(P, X) - x$ with Jacobian

$$J_X = \frac{dE_X}{dX} = \begin{pmatrix} \frac{\partial f_1}{\partial X_1} & \frac{\partial f_1}{\partial X_2} & \frac{\partial f_1}{\partial X_3} \\ \frac{\partial f_2}{\partial X_1} & \frac{\partial f_2}{\partial X_2} & \frac{\partial f_2}{\partial X_3} \end{pmatrix} . \tag{2}$$

If several points $X^{1,\dots,N}$ are observed simultaneously, let

$$E(P, X^{1:N}, x^{1:N}) = \begin{pmatrix} E_{X^1} \\ \vdots \\ E_{X^N} \end{pmatrix} \tag{3}$$

with block diagonal Jacobian

$$J = \begin{pmatrix} J_{X^1} & & \mathbf{0} \\ & \ddots & \\ \mathbf{0} & & J_{X^N} \end{pmatrix} . \tag{4}$$

The information matrix for a single image is then given by

$$I(P, X^{1:N}) = \begin{pmatrix} J_{X^1}^\top R_1^{-1} J_{X^1} & & \mathbf{0} \\ & \ddots & \\ \mathbf{0} & & J_{X^N}^\top R_N^{-1} J_{X^N} \end{pmatrix} \tag{5}$$

where usually the $R_i = \left(\begin{smallmatrix} \sigma^2 & 0 \\ 0 & \sigma^2 \end{smallmatrix}\right)$.

The final information matrix given the initial information I_0 and images from camera positions $P^{1,\dots,M}$ is now

$$I_M = I_0 + \sum_{j=1}^{M} I(P^j, X^{1:N}) . \tag{6}$$

Note that the computation is linear in the number of observed features and the number of images, and that the covariance of the estimate is the inverse, $\Sigma_{P^{1:M}, X^{1:N}} = I_M^{-1}$. For notational convenience, from hereon let P denote the set $P^{1:M}$ of camera poses along a path, and $X = X^{1:N}$ the estimated structure.

3.2 Cost Function

We propose the following cost function:

$$\begin{aligned} C(P, X) &= \frac{1}{N}\mathrm{tr}(\Sigma_{P,X}) + \frac{\alpha}{(M-1)^{1-q}} \sum_{j=1}^{M-1} \|P_{\mathrm{pos}}^{j+1} - P_{\mathrm{pos}}^{j}\|^q \\ &= U(P, X) + \alpha D(P) , \end{aligned} \tag{7}$$

i.e. the uncertainty measure plus a function of the camera path, weighted by a constant factor $\alpha > 0$, where $q \geq 1$. The normalization constants N^{-1} and $(M-1)^{q-1}$ are designed to make the cost approximately invariant with respect to the number of observed features and camera positions on the path. Note that by choosing $q > 1$, $D(P)$ will favor solutions with equidistant spacing between the camera positions, and introducing an offset d, $D(P) = \sum_{j=1}^{M-1}(\|P_{\mathrm{pos}}^{j+1} - P_{\mathrm{pos}}^{j}\| - d)^q$, we can impose the soft constraint that the path length be $d(M-1)$, if desired.

3.3 Cost Function Properties

The multi-modality of the objective functions normally used in next best view planning makes optimization difficult. The proposed cost function is no exception, but due to the somewhat local nature of the sought solution there are obvious bounds on the cost and geometry of the path.

Proposition 1. *$U(P^{1:M}, X)$ is a non-negative decreasing function of the number of observations M.*

Proof. The information matrix I is positive semidefinite. Including a new observation amounts to adding another positive semidefinite matrix ΔI to I, and the result is again positive semidefinite. By the Courant-Fischer theorem, we know that the (sorted) eigenvalues satisfy $\lambda_i(I + \Delta I) \geq \lambda_i(I)$ for all $i = 1, \ldots, n$ and equivalently $\lambda_i(\Sigma_{\text{updated}}) = \lambda_i\big((I + \Delta I)^+\big) \leq \lambda_i(I^+) = \lambda_i(\Sigma_{\text{initial}})$. Evidently $\text{tr}(\Sigma_{\text{updated}}) \leq \text{tr}(\Sigma_{\text{initial}})$. □

Theorem 1. *The length of the path at the minimum P^* is bounded.*

Proof. Given any initial estimate $\hat{P}$ of the path, we have

$$\begin{aligned} \alpha D(P^*) &\leq U(\hat{P}, X) + \alpha D(\hat{P}) - U(P^*, X) \\ &\leq U(\hat{P}, X) + \alpha D(\hat{P}) \\ &\leq U_{\text{initial}} + \alpha D(\hat{P}) \end{aligned} \tag{8}$$

where $U_{\text{initial}} = \frac{1}{N}\text{tr}(\Sigma_0)$ and Σ_0 the covariance of the current structure estimate. Since $\|P^{j+1}_{\text{pos}} - P^j_{\text{pos}}\| < \|P^{j+1}_{\text{pos}} - P^j_{\text{pos}}\|^q + 1$, the length of P^* is bounded from above by $(M-1)^{1-q}\big(\alpha^{-1}U_{\text{initial}} + D(\hat{P})\big) + M - 1$. □

We see that the path must be contained inside an ellipsoid with foci at the (fixed) first and last camera positions, and that the bound can be computed easily in advance. As expected, the optimal path approaches the line segment between the foci as α grows.

This result suggests that we may attempt to find and compare several local minima by optimizing with varying initial paths sampled from within the feasible ellipsoid.

4 Proposed Algorithm

As noted in the introduction, the next best view problem is known to suffer from multiple local minima, cf. [3]; this is true for all reasonable choices of U. Finding the global minimum is a difficult problem, and the prevailing approach in the literature seems to be more or less exhaustive search over a discretized parameter space, [4,7], or stochastic optimization methods, [13,14]. In the interest of speed, however, we adopt a gradient based optimization scheme, using the well-known

Levenberg-Marquardt (LM) method. LM minimizes the 2-norm of a residual vector r, which we construct as

$$r = \left(\frac{\mathrm{tr}(\Sigma_{P,X^1})}{N}, \ldots, \frac{\mathrm{tr}(\Sigma_{P,X^N})}{N}, \frac{\alpha \| P^2_{\mathrm{pos}} - P^1_{\mathrm{pos}} \|^q}{(M-1)^{1-q}}, \ldots, \frac{\alpha \| P^M_{\mathrm{pos}} - P^{M-1}_{\mathrm{pos}} \|^q}{(M-1)^{1-q}} \right)^{\frac{1}{2}}$$

(the exponent indicates element-wise square root) so that $\|r\|^2 = C(P, X)$. The parameter space is the $M - 2$ intermediate camera positions; the camera orientation is determined by its position and the interest point.

The final hurdle is how to evaluate the cost function *before* any observations are made. The best we can do is predict what the camera will see at a particular location given the current best estimate of the structure. Assuming that measurements are corrupted with zero-mean noise, the expected observation is simply the projection $\hat{x} = f(P_i, X)$. Such an observation has zero reprojection error, and so does not affect the ML estimate.

The optimization is applied within the following framework:

1. Given an initial estimate of the structure, calculate its centroid and let this be the camera's point of interest. Select a target location for the camera, i.e. select the end point of the path.
2. Generate an initial path by linear interpolation between the first and last camera locations. The number of discrete camera locations along the path could be selected to match the image sampling rate and speed of the robot, but this would normally result in far too many locations and a very high-dimensional search space. However, it stands to reason that more images taken from approximately the same vantage point do not contribute qualitatively to the reconstruction, so a relatively sparse distribution of camera locations is sufficient.
3. Find a minimum of the cost function wrt. P using the LM algorithm.
4. Move the camera to the next location along the path and make an actual observation. Update the structure estimate with this new information, and update the camera interest point location and path end point, if needed.

Repeat steps 3 and 4, each time with one less camera location along the path and using the previous path estimate as an initial guess.

5 Experiments

We first apply the above algorithm to the scenario of a robot trying to pass through a doorway. The doorway is represented by a rectangular array of point features which are optimally triangulated from the first two views, see figure 1(a). In all experiments we assume an image measurement noise σ equivalent to about one pixel. The target location is placed in front of the doorway, and the path is discretized with four waypoints in between. The optimization is run until convergence and the robot is moved to the next prescribed location along the path, where a new image is acquired and the structure estimate is updated using bundle adjustment.

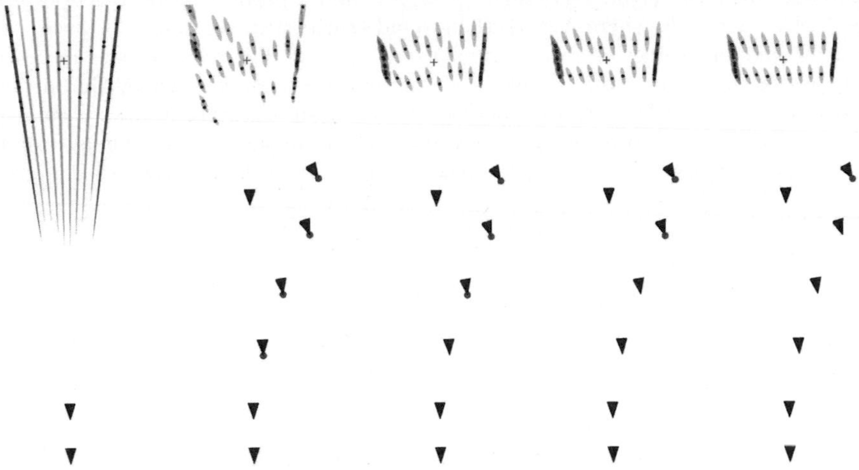

(a) (b) (c) (d) (e)

Fig. 1. Doorway scenario. The robot wishes to approach the passage while determining its geometry as accurately as possible. The first two cameras on the path represent the last two images the robot has acquired and provide the initial optimal triangulation of the geometry. Red dots indicate which cameras are free to move, the red cross is the point of interest. In this case subsequent observations do not visibly change the initially planned path. The uncertainty ellipsoids represent 5σ in (a) and 50σ in (b)-(e). Note that in the latter cases the *expected* uncertainties, given all observations along the path, are displayed. The values $q = 3$ and $\alpha = 4.5 \cdot 10^{-7}$ were used.

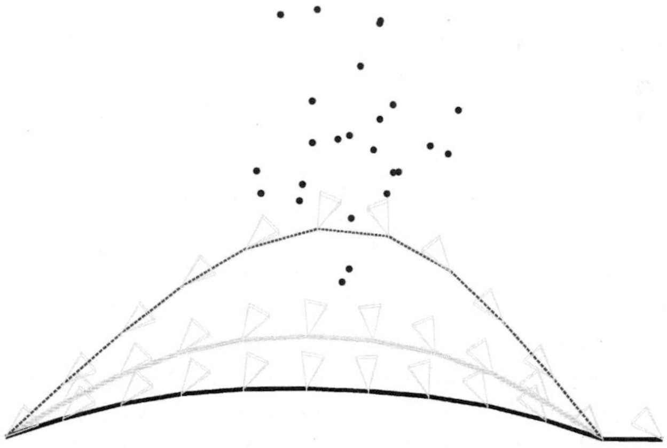

Fig. 2. Here the robot passes (from right to left) by a point cloud and makes a detour to get as close to the features as possible; this is natural, since the closer the feature, the higher its angular resolution. Three cases are plotted: $\alpha = 0.2 \cdot 10^{-7}$ (*red dashed*), $\alpha = 0.5 \cdot 10^{-7}$ (*green dotted*) and $\alpha = 10^{-6}$ (*black*).

Table 1. Relative error $U(P,X)/U(P^{1:2},X)$ and absolute reconstruction error $\frac{1}{N}\sum_{i=1}^{N}\|X^i - X^i_{\text{true}}\|$, where $X^{1:N}_{\text{true}}$ is the ground truth structure being observed, computed for different values of α in the scenario of figure 2. The relative error represents the expected decrease in uncertainty from the initial estimate given by the first two images, the reconstruction error the actual error after all observations have been made. As α is decreased, the optimized path deviates more from the straight line between the first and last camera position, and the reconstruction error is decreased.

	Optimized path		Straight path	
α	Rel. err.	Rec. err.	Rel. err	Rec. err
$1.0 \cdot 10^{-7}$	$1.64 \cdot 10^{-3}$	$8.32 \cdot 10^{-4}$	$2.02 \cdot 10^{-3}$	$1.03 \cdot 10^{-3}$
$0.5 \cdot 10^{-7}$	$1.25 \cdot 10^{-3}$	$7.15 \cdot 10^{-4}$	"	"
$0.2 \cdot 10^{-7}$	$5.36 \cdot 10^{-4}$	$4.53 \cdot 10^{-4}$	"	"

The influence of the parameter α is illustrated in figure 2 and table 1. The robot passes by a point cloud, and to get a closer look it must make a detour. A large α penalizes long paths at the expense of reconstruction accuracy.

6 Discussion

6.1 Computational Complexity

As noted in section 3.1, the cost function can be evaluated in $\mathcal{O}(MN)$ time. The LM algorithm requires the computation of the Jacobian of the residual vector r each iteration. The analytic expression may be very complicated and expensive to evaluate, so a finite difference approximation is preferred. The cost function must be differentiated with respect to $3(M-2)$ parameters, requiring $3(M-2)+1$ function evaluations to compute the Jacobian. But the covariance matrix is a function of a sum of individual information matrices, where only one term changes as the camera parameters are perturbed one at a time. By careful bookkeeping of the information matrices only 4 instances need to be computed for each camera instead of all $3(M-2)+1$ of a naïve implementation. This lowers the complexity of computing the Jacobian from $\mathcal{O}(M^2N)$ to $\mathcal{O}(MN)$. Nevertheless, in real-time applications computing the path should take a few seconds at most, and recent SLAM systems track hundreds or thousands of features. It may therefore be necessary to restrict attention to a subset of reconstructed features, e.g. those with the largest uncertainty, when evaluating the cost.

Furthermore, due to the iterative nature of the optimization, the path computation may be aborted before convergence but still yield a good approximation, depending on available time and computational resources.

6.2 Extensions

The assumptions in section 1 can of course be relaxed. If an initial ML structure estimate is not available, we can either choose to ignore any prior information and initialize the algorithm using optimal triangulation from the most recent images, or simply substitute a non-ML estimate (e.g. from an EKF). If the estimate is good enough, the inverse of the covariance matrix will still be a good approximation to the Fisher information. Even if it's a poor approximation we would expect the optimized paths to yield better reconstruction accuracy than a straight or random one.

The requirement that the camera be oriented toward a particular point is only intended to reduce the dimension of the parameter space. Optimization over the orientations, or other rules for selecting orientation based on camera position and estimated structure could easily be incorporated.

It is also assumed that the camera position and orientation are known to high accuracy when acquiring images. Obviously, this is rarely true in a practical SLAM system, where there may be considerable uncertainty in the robot location. However, the location is usually well-determined relative to nearby, recently observed features, so for short-term local path planning this is a fair approximation. Nevertheless, incorporating the camera uncertainty in the covariance estimation would be straightforward, but would also introduce correlations between features. The information and covariance matrices would no longer be block diagonal, raising the computational load considerably, and the cost function would possibly have to be modified to include the camera location uncertainty. The practical gain of incorporating such information is less clear.

The nature of the optimization scheme makes it easy to incorporate different constraints. For example, obstacles in the robot's path can be modeled as a potential field added to the cost function.

7 Conclusion

This paper has presented a continuous optimization approach to certain instances of the next best view planning problem, aimed toward application in SLAM systems. Unlike previous algorithms the next best view is chosen with consideration of several expected future observations. While the solutions are only locally optimal, experiments show that reconstruction accuracy is still much improved, at a computational cost linear in the number of cameras and features.

References

1. Botterill, T., Mills, S., Green, R.: Bag-of-words-driven, single-camera simultaneous localization and mapping. Journal of Field Robotics (2010)
2. Piniés, P., Paz, L.M., Gálvez-López, D., Tardós, J.D.: Ci-graph simultaneous localization and mapping for three-dimensional reconstruction of large and complex environments using a multicamera system. Journal of Field Robotics 27(5), 561–586 (2010)
3. Fraser, C.S.: Network design considerations for non-topographic photogrammetry. Photo Eng. and Remote Sensing 50(8), 1115–1126 (1984)

4. Wenhardt, S., Deutsch, B., Hornegger, J., Niemann, H., Denzler, J.: An information theoretic approach for next best view planning in 3-d reconstruction. In: Proc. International Conference on Pattern Recognition (ICPR 2006), vol. 1, pp. 103–106. IEEE Computer Society Press, Los Alamitos (2006)
5. Trummer, M., Munkelt, C., Denzler, J.: Online next-best-view planning for accuracy optimization using an extended e-criterion. In: Proc. International Conference on Pattern Recognition (ICPR 2010), pp. 1642–1645. IEEE Computer Society, Los Alamitos (2010)
6. Chen, S., Li, Y.F., Zhang, J., Wang, W.: Active Sensor Planning for Multiview Vision Tasks, 1st edn. Springer Publishing Company, Incorporated, Heidelberg (2008)
7. Dunn, E., van den Berg, J., Frahm, J.-M.: Developing visual sensing strategies through next best view planning. In: IEEE/RSJ International Conference on Intelligent Robots and Systems, IROS 2009, pp. 4001–4008 (October 2009)
8. Montgomery, D.C.: Design and Analysis of Experiments, 5th edn. John Wiley & Sons, Chichester (2000)
9. Klein, G., Murray, D.: Parallel tracking and mapping for small AR workspaces. In: Proc. Sixth IEEE and ACM International Symposium on Mixed and Augmented Reality (ISMAR 2007), Nara, Japan (November 2007)
10. Strasdat, H., Montiel, J.M.M., Davison, A.J.: Scale drift-aware large scale monocular slam. Proc. Robotics; Science and Systems (2010)
11. Mouragnon, E., Lhuillier, M., Dhome, M., Dekeyser, F., Sayd, P.: Generic and real-time structure from motion using local bundle adjustment. Image and Vision Computing 27(8), 1178–1193 (2009)
12. Hartley, R., Zisserman, A.: Multiple View Geometry. Cambridge University Press, Cambridge (2003)
13. Chen, S.Y., Li, Y.F.: Automatic sensor placement for model-based robot vision. IEEE Transactions on Systems, Man, and Cybernetics, Part B: Cybernetics 34(1), 393–408 (2004)
14. Dunn, E., Olague, G., Lutton, E.: Parisian camera placement for vision metrology. Pattern Recognition Letters 27(11), 1209 (2006)

Automatic Estimation of the Number of Deformation Modes in Non-rigid SfM with Missing Data*

Carme Julià[1], Marco Paladini[2], Ravi Garg[2], Domenec Puig[1], and Lourdes Agapito[2]

[1] Department of Computer Science and Mathematics
Universitat Rovira i Virgili, Tarragona, Spain
[2] School of Electronic Engineering and Computer Science
Queen Mary University of London, UK
{carme.julia,domenec.puig}@urv.cat,
{paladini,rgarg,lourdes}@dcs.qmul.ac.uk

Abstract. This paper proposes a new algorithm to estimate automatically the number of deformation modes needed to describe a non-rigid object with the well-known low-rank shape model, focusing on the missing data case. The 3D shape is assumed to deform as a linear combination of K rigid shape bases according to time varying coefficients. One of the requirements of this formulation is that the number of bases must be known in advance. Most non-rigid structure from motion (NRSfM) approaches based on this model determine the value of K empirically. Our proposed approach is based on the analysis of the frequency spectra of the x and y coordinates corresponding to the individual image trajectories, which are seen as 1D signals. The frequency content of the 2D trajectories is encoded using the modulus of the Discrete Cosine Transform (DCT) of the signals. Our hypothesis is that the value of K that gives the best prediction of the missing data also provides the best 3D reconstruction. Our proposed approach does not assume any prior knowledge and is independent of the 3D reconstruction algorithm used. We validate our approach with experiments on synthetic and real sequences.

Keywords: non-rigid SfM, Discrete Cosine Transform, frequency content.

1 Introduction

The Structure from Motion (SfM) problem is defined as the simultaneous estimation of the 3D coordinates of some scene points and the relative motion between the camera and the world purely from 2D trajectories of tracked features. Tomasi and Kanade [11] introduced the factorization technique to tackle the SfM problem in the case of rigid objects viewed by an orthographic camera

* This work was partially funded by the European Research Council under ERC Starting Grant agreement 204871-HUMANIS.

A. Heyden and F. Kahl (Eds.): SCIA 2011, LNCS 6688, pp. 381–392, 2011.

by imposing the rigidity constraint. This assumption was since relaxed to extend structure from motion algorithms to the non-rigid domain. Bregler et al. [4] were the first to propose a factorization approach based on a low-rank shape model to represent the deforming shape as a linear combination of K basis shapes which encode its main modes of deformation.

However, the non-rigid structure from motion problem (NRSfM) is severely under-constrained. Recent approaches to NRSfM have focused on the use of different optimization schemes and the definition of priors to overcome the problems caused by the inherent ambiguities and degeneracies [5,2,12,9]. The linear basis shape model has also allowed the formulation of closed form solutions both for the affine [14] and the perspective [15,13,6] cases. However, closed form solutions are known to be very sensitive to noise [3,12] and cannot deal with missing data.

Akhter et al. [1] depart from the low-rank shape model and instead describe the time varying 3D trajectories as a combination of trajectory bases for which they choose the Discrete Cosine Transform (DCT). The advantage of their approach is that the bases are generic and do not need to be estimated for each sequence.

So far there has been little work on the automatic estimation of the number of deformation modes needed to represent the time varying shape. Most of the aforementioned approaches estimate the number of deformation modes from the rank of the measurement matrix (e.g., [14]) or empirically (e.g., [12,9,1]). Roy-Chowdhury [10] introduces the *deformability index* (DI) to estimate the number of basis shapes by taking into account the statistics of the underlying noise in the shape sequence. However, this approach cannot deal with missing data. In their coarse-to-fine shape model, Bartoli et al. [2] use the Cross-Validation score to automatically decide when to stop adding modes of deformation to the model.

This paper addresses the automatic selection of the number of basis shapes needed to describe a non-rigid object represented using the well known low-rank shape model, focusing on the missing data case. The goal is to select the number of bases (K) that gives the best 3D reconstruction. Our hypothesis is that the value of K that gives the best prediction of the missing data also provides the best 3D reconstruction. The key point of our proposed approach is to consider the x and y coordinates of the 2D trajectories (the columns of the matrix of trajectories W) as 1D signals and to study their *frequency content*, which is assumed to be similar after filling the missing entries in W. The missing entries are filled with a NRSfM factorization technique, for different values of K. Then, a measure of goodness of the filled-in data based on the frequency content preservation is defined. The *modulus* of the Discrete Cosine Transform (DCT) is used to study the frequency content of the signals.

This paper is closely related to the work of Julià et al. ([7], [8]), where the goal was to estimate the rank of a missing data trajectory matrix in the case of multiple moving rigid objects using the FFT to describe the frequency content of the 2D trajectories. However, in this paper we focus on the more challenging case of non-rigid motion.

2 Deformable Low-Rank Shape Model

We use the low-rank shape model introduced by Bregler et al. [4] in which they describe the time varying 3D shape of a non-rigid object as a linear combination of some basis shapes B_1, B_2,..., B_K. Each basis shape B_K is a $3 \times p$ matrix describing the 3D coordinates of p points. The 3D points deform as a linear combination of the fixed basis set according to time varying coefficients: $S_i = \sum_{d=1}^{K} l_{id} B_d$, where the matrix $S_i = [\mathbf{S}_{i1}, ..., \mathbf{S}_{ip}]$ is the 3D shape of the object at frame i and l_{id} are the configuration weights. Under an orthographic projection model, the p points of S_i are projected onto 2D image points as:

$$W_i = R_i \Big(\sum_{d=1}^{K} l_{id} B_d \Big) + T_i \tag{1}$$

where R_i contains the first two rows of the full 3D camera rotation matrix and T_i is the camera translation, which can be eliminated by registering the origin of the image coordinate system to the centroid of the object. If we now consider all the frames, f, in the sequence, we can rewrite the linear combination in (1) as:

$$W = \begin{bmatrix} l_{11}R_1 & \dots & l_{1K}R_1 \\ \vdots & \ddots & \vdots \\ l_{f1}R_f & \dots & l_{fK}R_f \end{bmatrix} \begin{bmatrix} B_1 \\ \vdots \\ B_K \end{bmatrix} = \begin{bmatrix} M_1 \\ \vdots \\ M_f \end{bmatrix} \begin{bmatrix} B_1 \\ \vdots \\ B_K \end{bmatrix} = MS \tag{2}$$

Since M is a $2f \times 3K$ matrix and S is a $3K \times p$ matrix, the rank of W is constrained to be at most $3K$ and it can be factorized into two matrices: M contains the camera pose R_i and configurations weights l_{i1},...,l_{iK} for each frame i, while S contains the K basis shapes B_d.

3 Proposed Approach

This section describes our new algorithm to estimate the number of deformation modes K automatically in the NRSfM problem in the case of missing data.

Our goal is to select the value of K that yields the best 3D reconstruction of the deformable object. The missing data in the trajectory matrix W are filled with a NRSfM factorization technique, considering different values for K. Our hypothesis is that the value of K that best predicts the missing data also provides the best 3D reconstruction. Thus, the aim is to define a measure of goodness of the filled-in data, when different values of K are considered. One could consider using the *root mean square error* (*rms*):

$$rms = \|W - MS\|_F / \sqrt{n} \tag{3}$$

where $\|\cdot\|_F$ is the Frobenius norm and n is the number of known elements in W. However the *rms* error would only give information about how well the initially known entries are approximated. Alternatively, our proposed approach aims to define a measure of goodness of fitting for both the initially known data and the missing data. In this paper we propose to consider the x and y coordinates of each 2D trajectory (each column of W) as 1D signals and we define a measure of goodness based on the frequency content of these signals.

3.1 Frequency Content of 2D Trajectories

The proposed measure of goodness is based on the assumption that the frequency content of the signals (the 2D trajectories) should be preserved after filling-in the missing entries in W. The Discrete Cosine Transform (DCT) is used to study the frequency content of those 1D signals. More specifically, the *modulus* of the DCT coefficients, which encodes the amount of information (energy) of the signal contained at a given frequency, is used.

We propose to compare the energy of the original signals with the one obtained after filling in the missing entries considering different K values. The number of basis shapes K that gives the best frequency content preservation is then selected. Naturally, the problem is that the original signals are not full. This paper proposes a strategy to fill missing entries in the original signals, without assuming any K value, to give a full *reference trajectory matrix* (see details in Section 3.3). The frequency content of this *reference trajectory matrix* will then be compared with the one of the matrix filled-in using different values of K. It is therefore crucial that our *reference trajectory matrix* be a good approximation of the original, unknown, full matrix W.

To illustrate the key idea behind our approach, we consider one of the datasets used in Section 4 and we show the way in which the missing data in a single trajectory is recovered, assuming different values of K. It consists of a sequence of 37 3D points on a face tracked along 74 frames. A percentage of 30% missing data is randomly generated from the full matrix of original trajectories. Fig.1 shows the single trajectory studied in this section, when different values for K are considered. Specifically, the full trajectory (black line), the data filled-in with different values for K (red line) and the *reference* trajectory (blue-dashed line) are plotted. The corresponding x and y coordinates of this trajectory are plotted in Fig. 2 (a) and (b), respectively. In addition, the modulus of the DCT of each of the x and y signals for each K considered are plotted in Fig. 2 (c) and (d) respectively. The modulus of the DCT of the full signal (black line), the filled-in signal for different values of K (red line) and the *reference* signal (blue-dashed line) are shown. It can be seen that the *reference* matrix is a good approximation of the full data both in terms of the 2D image coordinates (see Fig. 2 (a) and (b)) and of the frequency content (see Fig. 2 (c) and (d)). Notice that most of the energy of the signal is contained in the lowest frequencies (left part of the frequency content plot). The proposed approach takes into account the frequencies containing about 99.99% of the energy of the signal. Fig. 2 (e) and (f) shows only the lowest frequencies corresponding to the current example.

Fig. 1 and Fig. 2 (a) and (b) show that the data are better filled when $K \geq 6$. Furthermore, the filled-in signal is most similar to the original one when $K \geq 6$

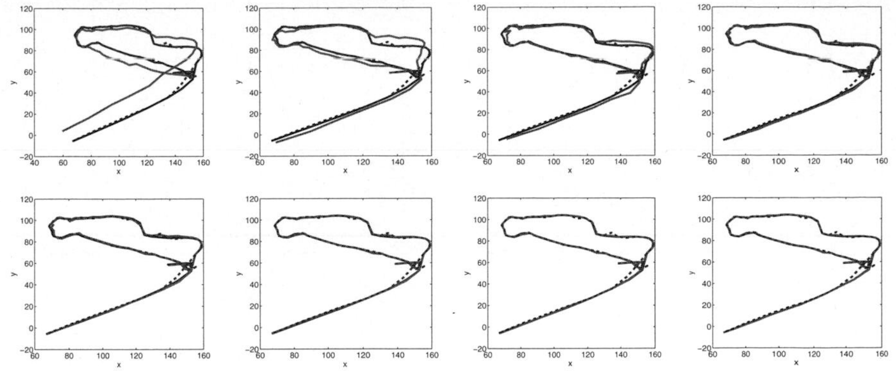

Fig. 1. Single trajectory plotted in the image plane: full data (black line), filled-in data with values of K ranging from 1 to 8 (red line) and *reference* data (blue-dashed line)

(see Fig. 2 (e) and (f)). In fact, the best 3D reconstruction is obtained for $K = 6$ in this example, as we will show later in Fig. 3 (b).

3.2 Algorithm

The proposed algorithm is based on the preservation of the frequency content (or energy) of the signals. First the *reference* matrix is built from the visible tracking data in W following the method described in Section 3.3. The missing data in W are then filled with a NRSfM factorization technique, considering different values of K. The modulus of the DCT of each filled-in matrix (referred to as DCT_K) is compared with the one given by the *reference trajectory* matrix (denoted as DCT_{ref}). In fact, only a small number of the lowest DCT frequencies, which contain about 99% of the energy of the signal, are considered. The proposed measure of goodness of fit compares the signals corresponding to the x and y coordinates separately and is defined as follows:

$$e_{DCT}(K) = e_x(K) + e_y(K) \tag{4}$$

where

$$e_x(K) = \|DCT_{ref|x} - DCT_{K|x}\|_F/\sqrt{l}, \tag{5}$$

$$e_y(K) = \|DCT_{ref|y} - DCT_{K|y}\|_F/\sqrt{l}, \tag{6}$$

l is the length of the signal and, $DCT_{ref|x}$ and $DCT_{ref|y}$ are the modulus of the DCT of the x and y coordinates of the *reference* matrix. At the same time, $DCT_{K|x}$ and $DCT_{K|y}$ are the modulus of the DCT of the x and y coordinates of the matrix filled for different values of K. Notice that the DCT is applied to the x and y coordinates of each individual trajectory (each column of the matrix). Therefore, l is the number of the lowest frequencies taken into account. We propose to stop increasing K when either e_{DCT} increases or when it decreases below a given threshold.

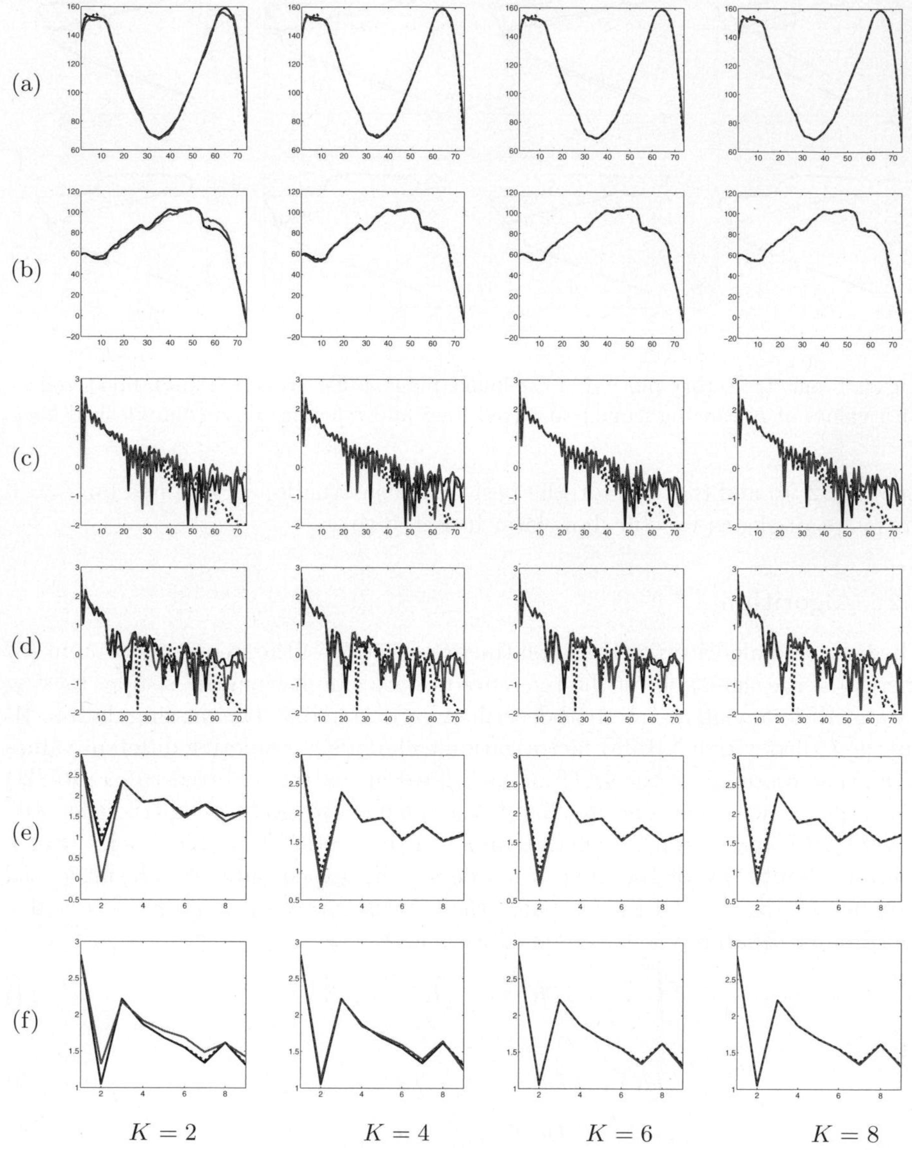

Fig. 2. (a) and (b): x and y coordinates of the studied trajectory; (c) and (d): modulus of the DCT (logarithmic scale) of the above signals; (e) and (f): modulus of the lowest frequencies of the DCT. Legend: full data (black line), filled-in data for different values of K (red line) and *reference* trajectories (blue-dashed line).

The proposed algorithm is summarized below:

Algorithm: Automatic estimation of the number of deformation modes in NRSfM with missing data

---

Input: A matrix of trajectories $W_{2f \times p}$ with missing data, where f is the number of frames and p the number of feature points.

1. Missing data entries of the original W are filled to obtain the *reference* matrix W_{ref} using the algorithm in Section 3.3.
2. Set $K = 1$ and the threshold τ. Compute $DCT_{ref|x}$ and $DCT_{ref|y}$ (modulus of the lowest frequencies of the DCT of W_{ref}).
3. Factorize the missing data matrix W into the structure and motion matrices using a non-rigid factorization technique: $\widetilde{W}_K = M_{2f \times 3K} S_{3K \times p}$.
4. Compute $DCT_{K|x}$ and $DCT_{K|y}$ (modulus of the lowest frequencies of the DCT of $\widetilde{W}_K$).
5. Compute the error value: $e_{DCT}(K) = e_x(K) + e_y(K)$,
6. Stop if $e_{DCT}(K) \geq e_{DCT}(K-1)$ or $(e_{DCT}(K-1) - e_{DCT}(K)) \leq \tau$. Otherwise, increase $K = K + 1$ and go back to step 3.

Solution: $K = K - 1$ is the estimated number of deformation modes.

Fig. 3 (a) and (b) show the proposed measure of goodness of fit (e_{DCT}) and the 3D error (rms_{3D}, defined in the next section) obtained for the current example (30% of missing data) for increasing values of K. If the proposed stopping criterion was used with $\tau = 0.09$, the selected number of deformation modes would be $K = 6$, which yields the best 3D reconstruction. Fig. 3 (c) shows the obtained rms. It would be more difficult to define a stopping criterion by studying the rms, since its value does not stabilize. The rms decreases as K increases, in general.

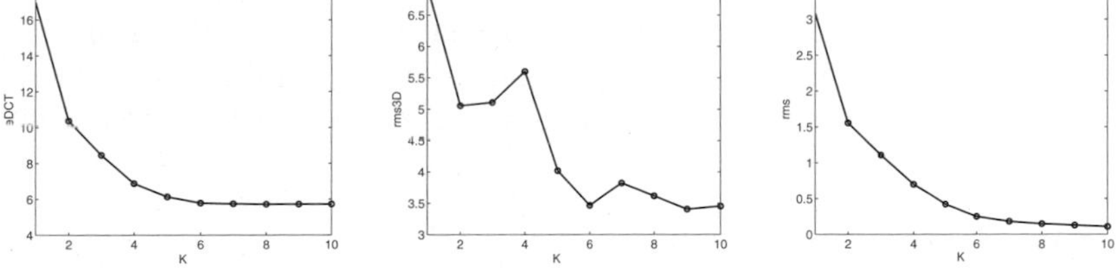

(a) (b) (c)

Fig. 3. (a) e_{DCT}; (b) rms_{3D}; (c) rms, all for different values of K (results correspond to the current example, 30% of missing data)

3.3 The *reference* Matrix

As mentioned above, missing data in the original matrix W should be filled in order to study the frequency content of the original signals. This section presents a strategy to obtain a full matrix that will be used as a *reference trajectory* matrix in the proposed algorithm. The main advantage of the proposed strategy is that it does not assume any K value. However, other *reference* matrices could be considered. In [7] and [8], for instance, the *reference* matrix was obtained by filling the missing entries with zeros. This paper proposes to express the original 1D signals using the DCT basis. That is, given the signal w_x^j (x coordinates of the jth-column of W), we express it as the following product:

$$w_x^j = \mathbf{\Phi}_{f \times d}\mathbf{x}_{d \times 1} \tag{7}$$

where $\mathbf{\Phi}$ contains a predefined set of d DCT basis vectors and $\mathbf{x}$ are the unknown coefficients. Specifically, each element in the matrix $\mathbf{\Phi}$ is the jth-frequency cosine term at time i:

$$\phi_{ij} = \frac{\sigma j}{\sqrt{f}} \cos\left(\frac{\pi(2i-1)(j-1)}{2f}\right) \tag{8}$$

with $\sigma_1 = 1$ and $\sigma_j = \sqrt{2}$, for $j \geq 2$, and f is the number of frames.

The following expression gives the solution to find the coefficients $\mathbf{x}$:

$$\mathbf{x} = (\mathbf{\Phi}^t\mathbf{\Phi})^{-1}(\mathbf{\Phi}^t w_x^j) \tag{9}$$

Once the coefficients $\mathbf{x}$ have been computed, the missing entries in w_x^j are filled with the product (7). It should be remarked that only the known entries in w_x^j and the corresponding rows in $\mathbf{\Phi}$ are used to compute $\mathbf{x}$. Due to that fact, the matrix $\mathbf{\Phi}$ may be close to singular when working with missing data and equation (9) may give incorrect results. In order to avoid this situation, we propose an incremental strategy to compute the DCT coefficients. In a first step, a small number of coefficients of the DCT basis are computed, by using only the initially known data in W. Then, missing entries in W are filled with the product (7). The following steps consist in computing a larger number of coefficients of the DCT basis by using the data filled in the previous step. This is repeated until the maximum number of coefficients is achieved (the number of frames). Therefore, we only work with missing data in the first step, where the number of DCT coefficients (that is, the number of unknowns in equation (9)) is very low.

4 Experiments

The goal of this section is to show that the proposed algorithm estimates the number of modes of deformation K that yields the best 3D reconstruction of the deformable object or a very close one. The algorithm is tested for different percentages of missing data in the initial matrix W—from 10% up to 40%. Missing entries are randomly generated, as in most of the works that deal with missing data (e.g., [12,2,9]). In order to obtain more robust results, 50 runs are carried out for each hypothesis. Although any NRSfM method can be used in step 3 of the proposed algorithm, in this paper we chose the EM algorithm proposed by Torresani et al. [12]. The quality of the 3D reconstruction (S) is measured, when the ground truth (S_{GT}) is available, by computing the rms_{3D} error:

$$rms_{3D} = \frac{\|S_{GT} - S\|_F}{\|S_{GT}\|_F} = \frac{\sqrt{\sum_{i,j} |(S_{GT})_{ij} - S_{ij}|^2}}{\|S_{GT}\|_F} \tag{10}$$

4.1 Synthetic Data

In our experiments with synthetic data, the 3D animation of a shark data-set, *Shark*, also tested in [12], is used. It consists of 91 3D points tracked along 240 frames and the orthographic projection is obtained by discarding the third coordinate of each 3D point. The object undergoes rigid motion and deformation corresponding to 2 basis shapes. Thus, $K = 3$ in our formulation. Two frames of the sequence are shown in Fig. 4 (a).

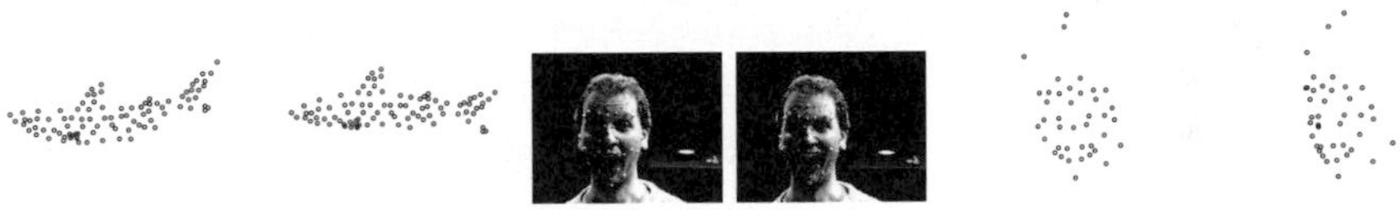

(a) (b) (c)

Fig. 4. Sequences: (a) *Shark* data-set: frames 1 and 50; (b) *Face1* data-set: frames 45 and 70. (c) *CMU face* data-set: frames 1 and 62.

Fig. 5 (a) and (b) shows the e_{DCT} and the rms_{3D} for different values of K and different percentages of missing data. In addition, the rms is plotted in Fig. 5 (c). In this synthetic example, the rms plot is similar to the one obtained with the proposed measure of goodness of fit. These plots correspond to a single run. Fig. 5 (a) shows that $e_{DCT}(4) > e_{DCT}(3)$, for any percentage of missing data. Therefore, the algorithm would stop at $K = 3$. The rms_{3D}, on the other hand, takes its minimum value at $K = 3$ in all the cases. The estimated value of K for 50 runs of the algorithm with different percentages of missing data are plotted in Fig. 6 (a). The threshold τ that defines the stopping criterion for K is empirically set to 0.09 in both synthetic and real data experiments and for all percentages of missing data. The number of deformation modes is correctly estimated ($K = 3$) for every percentage of missing data. Only a few outliers are obtained in the cases of 30% and 40% of missing data.

4.2 Real Data

Two different data-sets are used in the experiments with real data. The first data-set, *Face1*, is a motion capture sequence with 3D ground truth that is

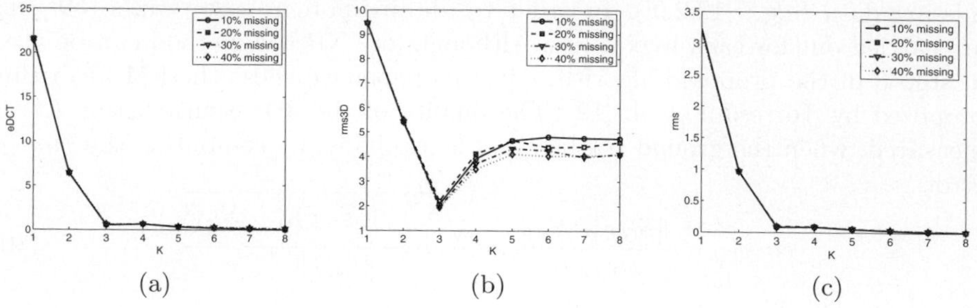

Fig. 5. *Shark* data-set: (a) e_{DCT}; (b) rms_{3D}; (b) rms, all for different K values and different percentages of missing data (single run)

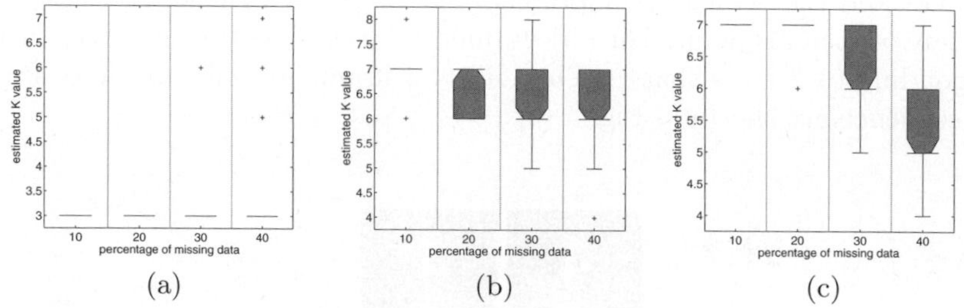

Fig. 6. Estimated K values for different percentages of missing data (50 runs): (a) *Shark* data-set; (b) *Face1* data-set; (c) *CMU face* data-set

also tested in [9] and has been used as an example in Section 3. It consists of 37 3D points on a face tracked with a motion capture system and projected synthetically onto a 74 frame long sequence using an orthographic camera model. Two frames of the sequence are shown in Fig. 4 (b). The second data-set, *CMU face*, also tested in [12], consists of 40 points tracked by a motion capture system along 316 frames. Data is obtained by orthographic projection. Fig. 4 (c) shows two frames of the sequence.

Fig. 7 (a) shows the e_{DCT} obtained with the *Face1* data-set for increasing values of K and different percentages of missing data (values are given for a single run of the algorithm). The e_{DCT} stabilizes at $K = 7$ for percentages of missing data below 20%. For percentages of missing data equal or higher than 20%, its value stabilizes at $K = 6$. Fig. 7 (b) shows that the rms_{3D} takes it minimum value at $K = 6$ for any percentage of missing data. It can be seen that the rms decreases for increasing values of K (see Fig. 7 (c)). Fig. 6 (b) shows the estimated K values with the defined threshold ($\tau = 0.09$) at the 50 runs and for different percentages of missing data. The median (horizontal line in the thinner region) of the estimated K is 7, for percentages of missing data below 30%. For percentages of missing data equal or higher than 30%, the median of the estimated K is 6. Therefore, the estimated K is equal or very close to the one

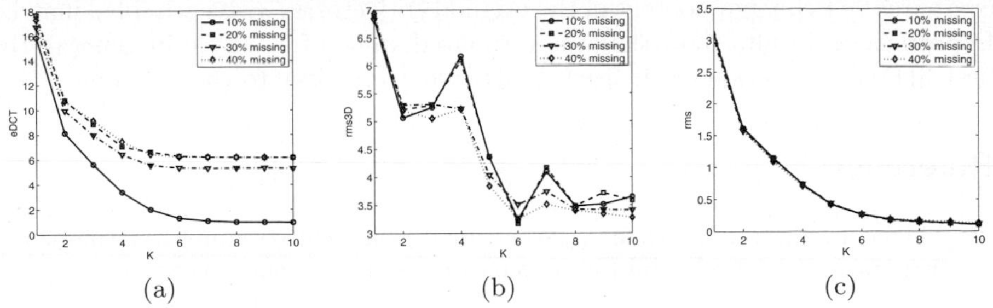

Fig. 7. *Face1* data-set: (a) e_{DCT}; (b) rms_{3D}; (c) rms, all for different K values and different percentages of missing data (single run)

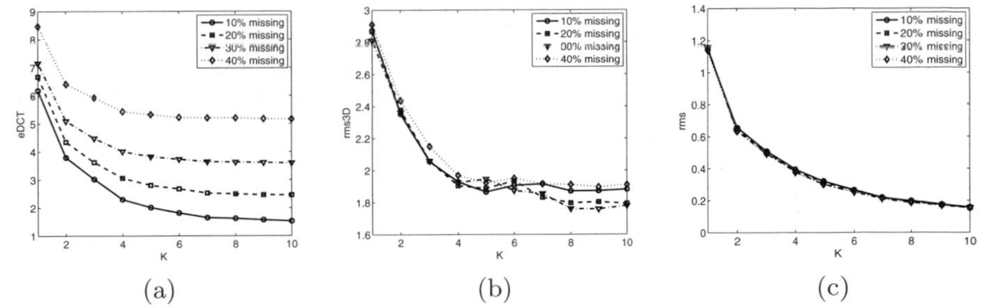

Fig. 8. *CMU face* data-set: (a) e_{DCT}; (b) rms_{3D}; (c) rms, all for different K values and different percentages of missing data (single run)

that gives the smallest 3D error reconstruction ($K = 6$) for any percentage of missing data (see Fig. 7 (b)).

Fig. 8 shows the results corresponding to the *CMU face* data-set. Fig. 8 (a) shows that the e_{DCT} stabilizes at $K = 7$ for percentages of missing data below 30%. For percentages of missing data equal or higher than 30%, the e_{DCT} stabilizes at $K = 6$. Notice in Fig. 8 (c) that the rms decreases as K increases. Fig. 6 (c) shows the estimated K values at the 50 runs, for different percentages of missing data. The median of the estimated K value is 7 for percentages of missing data below 30%. For percentages of missing data of 30% and 40% the median of the estimated K is 6 and 5, respectively. The estimated K for each percentage of missing data corresponds to the one that gives the smallest 3D reconstruction error, or an error very close to that (see Fig. 8 (b)).

5 Conclusions

This paper proposes an algorithm to estimate the number of deformation modes of a non-rigid shape K in the case of missing data entries in the matrix of trajectories W. The missing data are filled with a NRSfM algorithm for different values of K. The modulus of the Discrete Cosine Transform (DCT) is used to compare the frequency content of the original trajectories with each filled matrix. Experimental results show that the estimated value of K gives, in general, the best 3D reconstruction or, at least, a 3D error very close to the best one.

References

1. Akhter, I., Sheikh, Y., Khan, S., Kanade, T.: Nonrigid structure from motion in trajectory space. In: Neural Information Processing Systems (2008)
2. Bartoli, A., Gay-Bellile, V., Castellani, U., Peyras, J., Olsen, S., Sayd, P.: Coarse-to-fine low-rank structure-from-motion. In: CVPR (2008)
3. Brand, M.: A direct method for 3D factorization of nonrigid motion observed in 2D. In: CVPR, pp. 122–128 (2005)
4. Bregler, C., Hertzmann, A., Biermann, H.: Recovering non-rigid 3D shape from image streams. In: CVPR. pp. 690–696 (2000)
5. Del Bue, A., Lladó, X., Agapito, L.: Non-rigid metric shape and motion recovery from uncalibrated images using priors. In: CVPR, pp. 297–310 (2006)
6. Hartley, R., Vidal, R.: Perspective nonrigid shape and motion recovery. In: Forsyth, D., Torr, P., Zisserman, A. (eds.) ECCV 2008, Part I. LNCS, vol. 5302. Springer, Heidelberg (2008)
7. Julià, C., Sappa, A.D., Lumbreras, F., Serrat, J., López, A.: Rank estimation in 3D multibody motion segmentation. Electronics Letters 44(4) (2008)
8. Julià, C., Sappa, A.D., Lumbreras, F., Serrat, J., López, A.: Rank estimation in missing data problems. Journal of Mathematical Imaging and Vision 39, 140–160 (2010)
9. Paladini, M., Del Bue, A., Stošic, M., Dodig, M., Xavier, J., Agapito, L.: Factorization for non-rigid and articulated structure using metric projections. In: CVPR, pp. 2898–2905 (2009)
10. Roy-Chowdhury, A.K.: Towards a measure of deformability of shape sequences. Pattern Recognition Letters 28, 2164–2172 (2007)
11. Tomasi, C., Kanade, T.: Shape and motion from image streams under orthography: a factorization method. IJCV 9(2), 137–154 (1992)
12. Torresani, L., Hertzmann, A., Bregler, C.: Non-rigid structure-from-motion: Estimating shape and motion with hierarchical priors. IEEE Transactions on PAMI 30(5), 878–892 (2008)
13. Vidal, R., Abretske, D.: Nonrigid shape and motion from multiple perspective views. In: Leonardis, A., Bischof, H., Pinz, A. (eds.) ECCV 2006. LNCS, vol. 3952, pp. 205–218. Springer, Heidelberg (2006)
14. Xiao, J., Chai, J., Kanade, T.: A closed-form solution to non-rigid shape and motion recovery. In: IJCV, vol. 67(2) (2006)
15. Xiao, J., Kanade, T.: Uncalibrated perspective reconstruction of deformable structures. In: ICCV (2005)

Unsupervised Learning for Improving Efficiency of Dense Three-Dimensional Scene Recovery in Corridor Mapping

Thomas Warsop and Sameer Singh

Research School of Informatics, Holywell Park, Loughborough University, Leicestershire, UK, LE11 3TU
T.E.Warsop@lboro.ac.uk, S.Singh@lboro.ac.uk

Abstract. In this work, we perform three-dimensional scene recovery from image data capturing railway transportation corridors. Typical three-dimensional scene recovery methods initialise recovered feature positions by searching for correspondences between image frames. We intend to take advantage of a relationship between image data and recovered scene data to reduce the search space traversed when performing such correspondence matching. We build multi-dimensional Gaussian models of recurrent visual features associated with distributions representing recovery results from our own dense planar recovery method. Results show that such a scheme decreases the number of checks made per feature to 6% of a comparable exhaustive method, whilst unaffecting accuracy. Further, the proposed method performs competitively when compared with other methods presented in literature.

1 Introduction

The term *corridor* has been used to describe a linear, directional flowing, geographic band connecting two points of a transportation service ([20]). *Corridor mapping* is the process by which data is collected regarding such a transportation corridor for the creation of a virtual representation. The work presented in this paper is part of a larger project which is concerned with corridor mapping from a train mounted, forward-facing High-Definition video camera. The ultimate goal of this project is to perform line-of-sight analysis regarding railway assets, using recovered 3D scene data as input to a geometric analysis process. The work presented in this paper is only concerned with the 3D scene recovery from monocular video aspect of this project.

As pointed out by Favaro et al. [7], the majority of 3D scene recovery methods are based on the same principle of matching features between image frames and recovering 3D position using camera geometry. This can be achieved, for example, by tracking image features across image frames ([25, 16]). Typical features used in such scenarios include Harris corners ([13, 15, 6]), SIFT features ([27]) and more recently, SURF features ([1]). Detected feature points are then matched across images. For example, using template matching within a window of possible positions as described by Kanbard et al. [13].

A. Heyden and F. Kahl (Eds.): SCIA 2011, LNCS 6688, pp. 393–402, 2011.

However, these methods only considered 2D information present in the images processed when calculating feature correspondences. It is possible to integrate 3D information into this problem. Using stereo cameras, as can be seen in the work of Ogale et al. [22], Yun et al. [26] and Zhang et al. [29] (to name a few) this can be achieved by searching epipolar scanlines across left and right-hand images for matching feature correspondence, typically with a template matching scheme. It is possible to integrate these epipolar searching concepts into monocular camera configurations. For example, Klein et al. [14] presented a method named *Parallel Tracking and Mapping (PTAM)*. In which features are initialised with their 3D positions by searching along epipolar lines defined by depth between key frames of the image sequence. Davison et al. [4, 5] presented a similar idea. Along the depth-defined epipolar lines, regular intervals were considered and matched in subsequent frames by projecting them into the current frame, using normalised sum-of-square differences template matching.

The previous methods are only concerned with recovery of 3D points. However, it is possible to compute higher-order structures such as planes. In fact, doing so has the advantage that an infinite density of points can be described in only a few parameters. Whereas, with the previously discussed methods, increasing the number of feature points increases computation quadratically ([19]). Further, storing planes collapses state space reducing computation and improving scalability as well as giving a higher-level scene description ([11]). Also, memory requirements are reduced as many points are represented by a few parameters ([18]). There are different ways in which these planes can be computed. For example, Chekhlov et al. [2] and Gee et al. [11, 10] recover 3D points first and then fit planes to this information. Any new points that are subsequently recovered can be added to these created planes. Fraundorfer et al. [8] proposed a method in which initial planar *seed regions* were chosen from which the rest of the planar region could be grown. A different approach taken by Pollefeys et al. [23] tested a reduced set of planes, projecting image pixels onto the chosen planes, using image pixel value differences to select the best. Yet another type of method is presented by both Furukawa et al. [9] and Sinha et al. [24]. Sinha et al. [24] use sparse reconstructed point and line clouds to provide evidence for a set of candidate planes. Planar depth was then recovered for each image by assigning each pixel to one of the candidate planes.

In our application, the 3D scene recovery will be performed in an offline capacity. Thus allowing us to process image sequences in reverse chronological order - presenting two interesting properties. First, new scene elements appear at the image edge, allowing redundant information to be easily ignored. Secondly, image areas recovered in subsequent image frames exhibit similar 3D scene properties when they process similar image properties to those processed previously. This concept is highlighted in Figure 1. It may therefore be possible to exploit this information, using relationships between image features and recovered 3D scenes to reduce the size of the search spaces traversed when computing feature correspondences. Such a concept has not been proposed by previous methods

Fig. 1. When processing image sequences in reverse order, *new* scene elements entering at image edges exhibit similar image and 3D scene properties

and forms the main contribution of this work (named Temporal Search space Reduction, or TSR).

To further clarify the novelty of our proposal, most 3D scene recovery initialise new features by computing correspondences between image frames. Computing these correspondences requires searching a range of values in some capacity (for example, searching along epipolar scan lines for matches). This structure is shown in Figure 2(a). We propose the use of relationships learnt from previously processed image features to reduce the range traversed for correspondence computation. This is shown in Figure 2(b).

The structure of the remainder of this paper is as follows. Section 2 describes a simple, dense 3D scene recovery method and our novel method for learning recurring structures to reduce correspondence range traversal. Section 3 presents experimental results regarding our method. Finally, section 4 concludes this paper.

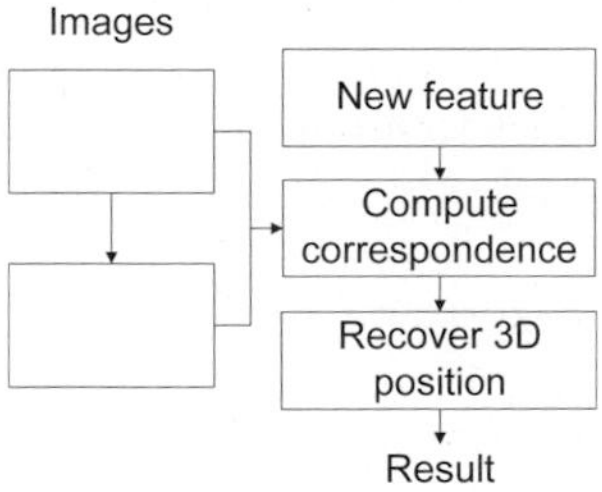

(a) The general structure of 3D scene recovery methods with regard to the recovery of individual features.

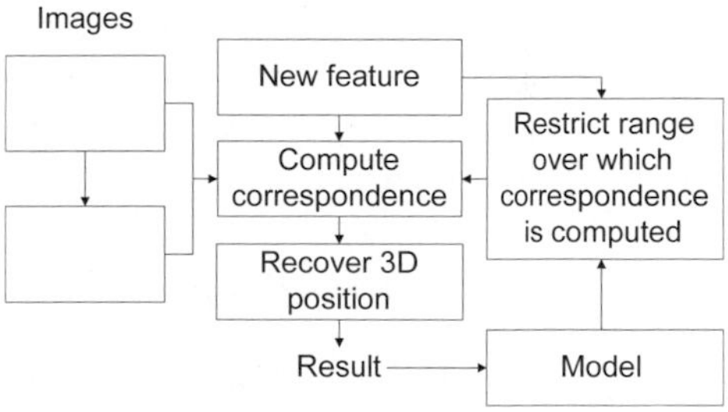

(b) Proposed extension to general 3D scene recovery methods, using previously processed results to reduce search space traversal when looking for correspondence, hence improving efficiency

Fig. 2. Comparison between general 3D scene recovery methods and that proposed by this work

2 Dense and Efficient 3D Scene Recovery

2.1 Recovering Planar Structures

Figure 1 shows typical images to be processed by our method. These images are typical in that they contain many planar structures to be recovered. For example, the flat ground and almost vertical dense vegetation. Therefore, we employ a method which searches for these planar structures directly.

Image Division into Quadrilaterals. First, each image considered for 3D scene recovery is divided into a set of quadrilaterals. Currently this is achieved by dividing the image into a regular grid and using the grid cells as quadrilaterals (more sophisticated methods could be employed in the future). Through experimentation we found the cell size of 64×64 provided the best trade off between execution time and accuracy.

Quadrilateral Recovery. Each quadrilateral is recovered by determining a plane (defined by a normal vector and an offset value) which gives the minimum difference between the original image area and that defined by the area of the plane reprojected into an adjacent image. The intersection of rays between between focal point, image quadrilateral and plane of best fit then provide the 3D coordinates of the recovered plane. This process is summarized in Figure 3.

If the image coordinates of a quadrilateral are denoted iq_0, iq_1, iq_2 and iq_3, the corresponding projected plane coordinates for a plane with normal n and focal point offset value V are computed as:

$$pq_i = F + \left(\frac{n \cdot ((F + nV) - F)}{n \cdot (iq_i - F)} \right) (iq_i + F) + C_x, \ \forall i \in \{0, 1, 2, 3\} \tag{1}$$

where, F is the cartesian coordinates of the focal point and C_x is a vector storing the central x-coordinate of the recovered scene space. Using the ego-motion between images, $pq_{0..3}$ are updated with respect to a new image in which they are likely to appear:

$$pq'_i = R \times pq_i + T, \ \forall i \in \{0, 1, 2, 3\} \tag{2}$$

where, R and T are rotation and translation matrices describing the ego-motion between frames. Note, ego-motion was detected using a similar method to Goecke et al. [12]. Projecting each pq'_i into the image space of this second image then provides coordinates of the updated quadrilateral with respect to the plane described by n and V.

Even though the initial quadrilateral dividing strategy produces squares, the previous will work for any shape quadrilateral (even if $iq_{0..3}$ represents a square, $iq'_{0..3}$ may not). Since we wish to compare the image information within these two quadrilaterals using a sum-of-absolute differences measure, for ease they are transformed into squares using a texture mapping procedure. If the two square

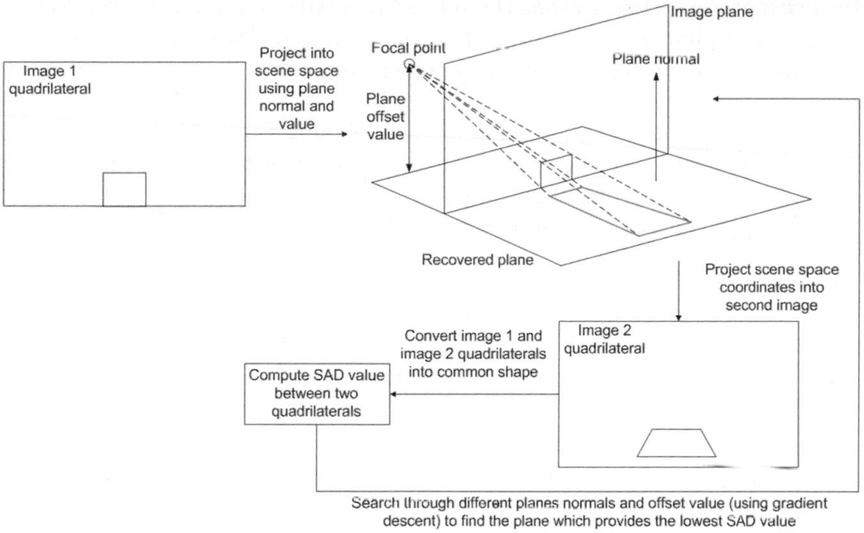

Fig. 3. 3D sequence recovery pipeline of the proposed dense, planar image quadrilateral recovery method

areas are denoted S_1 and S_2, they are then compared with a sum-of-absolute differences measure:

$$sad = \frac{\sum_{i=0}^{N-1} \sum_{j=0}^{N-1} \sum_{k=0}^{3} |S_1(i,j,k) - S_2(i,j,k)|}{N^2} \quad (3)$$

where, N is the length of one side of the squares and k iterates over the red, green and blue colour channels of the images.

Given the previously described method, the task of recovering the 3D coordinates of an image quadrilateral is now finding the plane normal vector and focal point offset which correspond to the lowest sum-of-absolute difference value for projection into a second image. For a single normal vector, we applied gradient descent for searching the possible values.

2.2 Unsupervised Learning for Temporal Search Space Reduction

As previously mentioned, the intention of TSR is to link image features with 3D scene recovery results. This is achieved by storing multi-dimensional Gaussians representing similar, recurring features. Each of these *feature* Gaussians is associated with one or more one-dimensional Gaussian distributions representing different focal offset values computed as part of the previous planar recovery method, when recovering quadrilaterals with corresponding image features. Further, each of these *value* distributions has an associated plane normal (as per the previous method).

In terms of image features for the image area within a quadrilateral, separate red, green and blue channel histograms are computed. From each histogram the mean, standard deviation, skewness, kurtosis and energy are computed, providing 15 image features in total.

For any new quadrilateral processed, each of these features are computed and the probability these 15 features (f) belong to any of the feature distributions currently stored in the model is computed:

$$p_{FD_i} = \frac{1}{\sqrt{2\pi\sigma^2_{FD_i}}} e^{\frac{-(f-\mu_{FD_i})^2}{2\sigma^2_{FD_i}}}, \forall i \in FD \tag{4}$$

where, FD is the set of feature distributions in the model, μ_{FD_i} and σ_{FD_i} are the mean and standard deviation respectively of feature distribution i. If no p_{FD_i} is greater than a chosen threshold (in experiments we used 0.6), f represents a new image structure. The corresponding quadrilateral is recovered by traversing all plane normals and offset values as previously described. A new feature distribution (FD_{new}) is created such the $\mu_{FD_{new}} = f$ and $\sigma_{FD_{new}}$ is set in each dimension to 20% of the possible range for the corresponding feature values. FD_{new} is associated with a new value distribution (VD_{new}) representing the results of the recovery. Specifically, $\mu_{VD_{new}}$ is the offset value of the best fitting plane. This new feature, value distribution are then added to the model.

However, if any p_{FD_i} are greater than the threshold, each associated value distribution is considered in turn and recovery proceeds using the plane normal associated with the value distribution and the value range defined by:

$$min_{VD_{i,j}} = \mu_{VD_{i,j}} - (D\sigma_{VD_{i,j}} \times (1 - p_{FD_i})) \tag{5}$$

$$max_{VD_{i,j}} = \mu_{VD_{i,j}} + (D\sigma_{VD_{i,j}} \times (1 - p_{FD_i})) \tag{6}$$

where, $VD_{i,j}$ represents the value distribution associated with FD_i currently considered, $\mu_{VD_{i,j}}$ and $\sigma_{VD_{i,j}}$ are the mean and standard deviation of the 3D values associated with each value distribution ($VD_{i,j}$) associated with FD_i and D is a scalar value (chosen in experimentation to be 3). If the sum-of-absolute difference value corresponding to the best fitting plane computed from these ranges is greater than a threshold, the values chosen are assumed to of been inappropriate and the quadrilateral is reprocessed using all possible plane normals and offset ranges (this has been done to prevent convergence). The results of which are used to create a new value distribution (as before) which is associated with the feature distribution with the highest p_{FD_i} value. Further, the mean and standard deviation of this best fitting feature distribution are updated using f.

Finally, if the sum-of-absolute difference value corresponding to the best fitting plane is less than the chosen threshold, the feature and value distribution corresponding to the best match are updated accordingly.

3 Experimental Results

The data used for experimentation consists of High-Definition (i.e. 1920 × 1080 pixels) image frames, captured from a front-forward facing camera mounted on a train. In total, 5 sequences totalling 520 image frames were used. Due to the restrictions of the railway environment, each image frame had to be ground truthed by hand - matching features between image pairs and using these correspondences to reconstruct the true 3D position of the feature manually. Approximately, 850 features were ground truthed in this manner in each image. Even though this was done as accurately as possible, this ground truthing will not be completely accurate and so will provide a source of error when comparing with the recovered scene. However, the difference between recovered and ground truth scene can still be used as an indicator of the performance of each method relative to each other.

Tables 1 and 2 provide the results for number of plane offset values checked (i.e. size of the search space traversed) and accuracy (which is measured in metres difference from the ground truth) respectively for an exhaustive method not using TSR and the described TSR method. Note, the table column heading SX refers to the sequence number corresponding to the results. These results show that the incorporation of the image, scene relationship used for reducing feature correspondence search ranges greatly reduces the number of checks made (and hence computation) whilst unaffecting accuracy.

Table 1. Average number of focal offset values checked per quadrilateral

Method	S1	S2	S3	S4	S5	Average
Exhaustive	335.16	288.62	345.46	314.04	340.39	324.73
TSR	20.32	16.97	22.64	17.00	21.18	19.62

Table 2. Average accuracy of recovered scenes (per image)

Method	S1	S2	S3	S4	S5	Average
Exhaustive	0.88	1.40	1.80	0.77	1.62	1.13
TSR	0.55	0.88	1.53	0.64	1.36	0.99

Table 3 compares this TSR method with others presented in literature. Where possible, authors implementations have been used. For fairness of comparison, all other methods for which results are presented, recovered the same image areas as the TSR method. These results show that with the data used in our application, the presented method provides the most accurate results in the least amount of time. For completeness, Figure 4 shows typical reconstruction results using the TSR method from parts of image sequences considered.

Table 3. Comparison results of the proposed method with others from literature

Method	Time (seconds)	Difference (m)
TSR	1.29	0.99
SIFT features ([17, 28])	2.6	4.09
ENFT ([27])	8.91	3.92
PTAM ([14])	9.77	1.43
MonoSLAM ([5])	13.03	1.19
Locally planar patches ([21])	11.41	1.08
Calway features ([3])	15.19	1.03

(a) Sequence image 0. (b) Sequence image 60. (c) Sequence image 119.

(d) Example recovered scene screen shot 1. (e) Example recovered scene screen shot 2. (f) Example recovered scene screen shot 3.

Fig. 4. Example 3D recovered sequence 1

4 Conclusions

In this work, we have presented a method for 3D scene recovery which explicitly stores relationships between recurring image features and recovered 3D information to reduce search spaces traversed when computing feature correspondences. Scenes were recovered in a railway corridor mapping context and results showed that storing and using such relationships can dramatically decrease the computation required to recover a scene. Further, the proposed planar recovery method used in conjunction with this TSR method performs competitively with other methods presented in literature. For future work, we intend to investigate the benefits of TSR-based methods as applied to data sets other than the specific one described in this work. That is, we believe there are other data sets to which the previously described TSR framework could be applied, and investigation of this would prove the ability of the presented approach to generlise to other cases.

References

[1] Bay, H., Ess, A., Tuytelaars, T., Van Gool, L.: Surf: Speeded up robust features. Computer Vision and Image Understanding (CVIU) 110(3), 346–359 (2008)
[2] Chekhlov, D., Gee, A.P., Calway, A., Mayol-Cuevas, W.: Ninja on a plane: Automatic discovery of physical planes for augmented reality using visual slam. In: International Symposium on Mixed and Augmented Reality, ISMAR (November 2007)
[3] Chekhlov, D., Mayol-Cuevas, W.: Appearance based indexing for relocalisation in real-time visual slam. In: 19th British Machine Vision Conference, pp. 363–372 (2008)
[4] Davison, A.J.: Real-time simulataneous localization and mapping with a single camera. In: Proc. International Conference on Computer Vision, pp. 1403–1411 (October 2003)
[5] Davison, A.J., Reid, I.D., Molton, N.D., Stasse, O.: Monoslam: Real-time single camera slam. IEEE Transactions on PAtterns Analysis and Machine Intelligence 29, 1–15 (2007)
[6] Engels, C., Fraundorfer, F., Nistér, D.: Integration of tracked and recognized features for locally and globally robust structure from motion. In: VISAPP International Workshop on Robotic Perception, VISAPP RoboPerc (January 2008)
[7] Favaro, P., Jin, H., Soatto, S.: A semi-direct approach to structure from motion. The Visual Computer 19, 377–384 (2003)
[8] Fraundorfer, F., Schindler, K., Bischof, H.: Piecewise planar scene reconstruction from sparse correspondences. In: Image and Vision Computing, vol. 24, pp. 395–406 (2006)
[9] Furukawa, Y., Curless, B., Seitz, S.M., Szeliski, R.: Manhattan-world stereo. In: CVPR, pp. 1422–1429. IEEE, Los Alamitos (2009)
[10] Gee, A.P., Chekhlov, D., Calway, A., Mayol-Cuevas, W.: Discovering higher level structure in visual slam. IEEE Transactions on Robotics 24, 980–990 (2008)
[11] Gee, A.P., Chekhlov, D., Mayol, W., Calway, A.: Discovering planes and collapsing the state space in visual slam. In: 18th British Machine Vision Conference (September 2007)
[12] Goecke, R., Asthana, A., Pettersson, N., Petersson, L.: Visual vehicle egomotion esitmation using the fourier-mellin transform. In: IEEE Intelligent Vehicles Symposium, pp. 450–455 (June 2007)
[13] Kanbara, M., Ukita, N., Kidode, M., Yokoya, N.: 3d scene reconstruction from reflection images in a sphereical mirror. In: The 18th International Conference on Pattern Recognition (ICPR 2006), pp. 874–879 (2006)
[14] Klein, G., Murray, D.: Parallel tracking and mapping for small ar workspaces. In: Proceedings and the Sixth IEEE and ACM International Symposium on Mixed and Augmented Reailty, ISMAR 2007 (2007)
[15] Li, P., Farin, D., Gunnewiek, R.K., de With, P.H.N.: On creating depth maps from monoscopic video using structure frm motion. In: 27th Symposium on Information Theory, pp. 508–515 (2006)
[16] Liu, G.-H., Feng, Q.-Y.: Recovering 3d shape and motion from image sequences using affine approximation. In: Second International Conference on Information and Computing Science, pp. 349–352 (2009)
[17] Lowe, D.G.: Distinctive image features from scale-invariant keypoints. International Journal of Computer Vision (2004)

[18] Martinez-Carranza, J., Calway, A.: Unifying planar and point mapping in monocular slam. In: British Machine Vision Conference, pp. 1–11 (September 2010)
[19] Martinez-Carranza, J., Calway, A.: Efficiently increasing map density in visual slam using planar features with adaptive measurements. In: British Machine Vision Conference, pp. 1–11 (September 2009)
[20] Metro Solutions (2006), http://metrosolutions.org/go/doc/1068/116948 (last accessed: July 25, 2010)
[21] Molton, N., Davidson, A., Reid, I.: Locally planar patch features for real-time structure from motion. In: Proc. British Machine Vision Conference, BMVC (September 2004)
[22] Ogale, A.S., Aloimonos, Y.: Shape and the stereo correspondence problem. International Journal of Computer Vision 65, 147–162 (December 2005)
[23] Pollefeys, M., Nister, D., Frahm, J.M., Akbarzadeh, A., Mordohai, P., Clipp, B., Engels, C., Gallup, D., Kim, S.J., Merrell, P., Salmi, C., Sinha, S.N., Talton, B., Wang, L., Yang, Q., Stewenius, H., Yang, R., Welch, G., Towles, H.: Detailed real-time urban 3d reconstruction from video. International Journal of Computer Vision, 143–167 (2008)
[24] Sinha, S.N., Steedly, D., Szeliski, R.: Piecewise planar stereo for image-based rendering. In: Twelth IEEE International Conference on Computer Vision, ICCV 2009 (2009)
[25] Tomasi, C., Kanade, T.: Shape and motion from image streams: a factorization method. Technical Report TR 92-1270, Carnegie Mellon (March 1992)
[26] Yun, S.U., Min, D., Sohn, K.: 3d scene reconstruction system with hand-held stereo cameras. In: 3DTV Conference, pp. 1–4 (2007)
[27] Zhang, G., Dong, Z., Jia, J., Wong, T.-T., Bao, H.: Efficient non-consecutive feature tracking for structure-from-motion. In: Daniilidis, K., Maragos, P., Paragios, N. (eds.) ECCV 2010. LNCS, vol. 6315, pp. 422–435. Springer, Heidelberg (2010)
[28] Zhang, G., Hua, W., Qin, X., Shao, Y., Bao, H.: Video stabilization based on a 3d perspective camera model. The Visual Computer 25, 997–1008 (2009)
[29] Zhang, G., Jia, J., Wong, T.-T., Bao, H.: Consistent depth maps recovery from a video sequence. IEEE Transactions on Pattern Analysis and Machine Intelligence 21, 974–988 (2009)

Catadioptric Silhouette-Based Pose Estimation from Learned Models

Christian Reinbacher, Markus Heber, Matthias Rüther, and Horst Bischof

Institute for Computer Graphics and Vision, Graz University of Technology,
Inffeldgasse 16/II, Graz, Austria
{reinbacher,mheber,ruether,bischof}@icg.tugraz.at
http://www.icg.tugraz.at

Abstract. The automated handling of objects requires the estimation of object position and rotation with respect to an actuator. We propose a system for silhouette-based pose estimation, which can be applied to a variety of objects, including untextured and slightly transparent objects. Pose estimation inevitably relies on previous knowledge of the object's 3D geometry. In contrast to traditional view-based approaches our system creates the required 3D model solely from the object silhouettes and abandons the need to obtain a model beforehand. It is sufficient to rotate the object in front of the catadioptric camera system. Experimental results show that the pose estimation accuracy drops only slightly compared to a highly accurate input model. The whole system utilizes the parallel processing power of graphics cards, to deliver an auto calibration in 20 s and reconstructions and pose estimations in 200 ms.

Keywords: pose estimation, model creation, shape from silhouette, catadioptric multi-view.

1 Introduction

Robotic pick & place deals with the problem of automated handling of objects. Typical tasks include sorting, packaging and automated manipulation. In order to correctly place an object, its position and orientation with respect to the actuator has to be known. In some scenarios the orientation is given by the way objects are produced, e.g. filled bottles moved on a conveyor belt, but typically the pose of the object has to be determined on the fly.

Vision-based pose estimation has become popular in industrial settings. Despite the vast amount of literature on various techniques, we limit ourselves to view-based approaches which were quite popular for a time and were recently revisited for industrial problems [1,2,3,16]. Here the object pose is determined by comparing the query image with precomputed 2D reference views of a known 3D model. Removing the translation by normalizing for the object location leads to three unknown degrees of freedom given by the possible rotations of the object. Hence, it is feasible to create reference views by placing a virtual camera on a sphere with the object in its center and later compare an acquired image to these

A. Heyden and F. Kahl (Eds.): SCIA 2011, LNCS 6688, pp. 403–413, 2011.

views. The accuracy of view-based approaches depends on the sampling density of the pose range, and the quality of the 3D model of the object.

Most state of the art methods are designed to work with man-made objects. These objects can be represented by a polyhedral 3D model, and typically resemble sharp edges, which are used as features for the pose estimation. However, there is a large class of objects which have an organic structure, lack edge features and are untextured or slightly transparent (e.g. organic moulding parts). The only remaining cue for them is the filled outline of the object, its silhouette. Using silhouettes, the pose estimation problem reduces to a 2D shape matching problem, where the best matching shape out of a database of precomputed views defines rotation and translation with respect to a camera.

A prerequisite for view-based methods are 3D models, which have to be created by either modeling them in CAD systems or by scanning the object. Reconstruction methods based on Structured Light [14,4] are able to produce very accurate reconstructions even from untextured objects. Shiny surfaces are difficult to handle for structured light methods. However, the object silhouette can also be used for 3D reconstruction.

Structure-from-Silhouette (SfS) methods use only a number of silhouettes to produce an approximation of the 3D object called the Visual Hull (VH), originally introduced in [9]. A visual hull is guaranteed to contain the object but it can be a coarse approximation depending on the number of cameras observing the object. SfS methods typically require a calibrated camera setup, which is able to capture the object from several defined viewpoints. A very elegant and at the same time inexpensive approach is to use a catadioptric system. Reflective surfaces like e.g. mirrors are placed in the field of view of a camera, to create additional views of a target object in a single image. Each mirror creates an additional virtual camera with viewpoint behind the mirror surface. Catadioptric camera setups have appealing advantages over conventional multi-view camera systems: a) they allow for a cheap and perfectly synchronized multi-view setup with a single camera and b) they reduce the number of camera parameters [5].

We propose to use a catadioptric camera system with planar mirrors for both, model learning and model-based pose estimation. The whole work flow of camera calibration, model creation and refinement, and finally pose estimation solely relies on the silhouettes of the objects. Our contributions are twofold: first, we propose to use a visual hull representation of an object as input to our model-based pose estimation. Second, we build an integrated system which can be used for pose estimation as well as model creation, needed by the pose estimation method.

Our experiments give evidence, that the proposed approach works for a variety of objects, where traditional approaches based on image features clearly fail.

2 Method

Our pose estimation method consists of four parts: a) silhouette extraction, b) system calibration, c) model creation, and d) pose estimation. In the following sections we will present the multi-view system, and how it is calibrated using silhouette information only. During this calibration a 3D model of the object is implicitly created. This model is further refined and subsequently used as input for our pose estimation method. All methods rely on one and the same hardware setup and do not require additional helper devices.

2.1 Silhouette Extraction

The accurate extraction of the object outline is crucial, since it directly influences the accuracy of all subsequent calibration and reconstruction steps. In this work we decided to adopt a recently proposed variational segmentation method introduced in [13]. Segmentation is performed by minimizing the energy:

$$\inf_{u} \left\{ \int_{\Omega} g \left| \nabla u \right| \mathrm{d}x + \lambda \int_{\Omega} u f \mathrm{d}x \right\}, \tag{1}$$

with $u : \Omega \to \{0, 1\}$. The function $g(x)$ is an edge indicator function which is low at a strong edge and high in homogeneous regions. The user-provided potential function f represents the likelihood of every pixel to belong to foreground or background, respectively.

We define $f = -\left| I - I_{\text{background}} \right|$ and $f = \infty$ at the image border, because both, background and foreground regions have to be given as input to the segmentation method. In contrast to background subtraction, we perform segmentation with an additional edge term and a powerful smoothing prior, which filters out segmentation errors caused by noise.

2.2 Catadioptric Camera Setup and Calibration

Our setup consists of a single camera, a light source, and n planar mirrors. Figure 1 shows a cross section of the camera setup. The robotic actuator moves the object between the radially arranged mirrors, such that the object is visible in every mirror.

It was shown by Hu et al. [8] and later by Heber et al. [6] that a catadioptric system with planar mirrors can be calibrated solely from outlines of objects within the mirror setup. The method requires an intrinsically calibrated camera $\mathbf{P_{real}}$ at the origin of the world coordinate frame.

The calibration of the catadioptric system results in a set of projectionmatrices

$$\mathbf{P_i} = \mathbf{P_{real}} \, \mathbf{D_i^T}, \tag{2}$$

where $\mathbf{D}_{4\times4}$ defines a reflection matrix, corresponding to a planar mirror in 3D space:

$$\mathbf{D} = \begin{bmatrix} \mathbf{I} - 2\mathbf{n}\mathbf{n}^T & \widetilde{\mathbf{c}} - 2d\mathbf{n} \\ 0 & 1 \end{bmatrix} = \begin{bmatrix} \mathbf{R} & \mathbf{t} \\ 0 & 1 \end{bmatrix} \quad . \tag{3}$$

Reflections in 3D space are Euclidean transformations, which additionally perform orientation changes. They depend on mirror plane normal $\mathbf{n}$, camera-mirror-distance d, and camera coordinate frame origin $\widetilde{\mathbf{c}}$ as proposed by Gluckman et al. [5]. For details on recovering plane normal and camera-mirror-distance we refer the reader to [6].

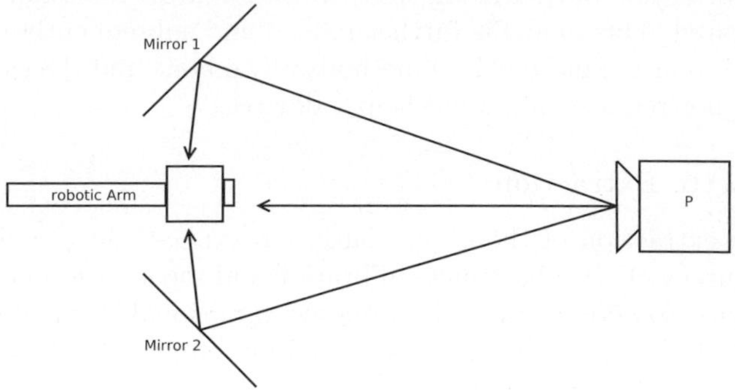

Fig. 1. Schematic of our catadioptric setup. The mirrors are arranged radially around the object.

Having these camera projection matrices along with a set of silhouettes, we are able to estimate a coarse approximation of the object by computing the visual hull. The visual hull is defined as the intersection of all viewing cones, that are generated via back projection of the 2D silhouettes into 3D space.

Figure 2 shows two visual hull 3D models of a toy figure, generated from 6 and 30 camera views, respectively. Obviously, increasing the number of views allows to reconstruct more details. However, accurate reconstructions of deep concavities are not feasible with a visual hull approach which poses no problem as our approach solely relies on object silhouettes.

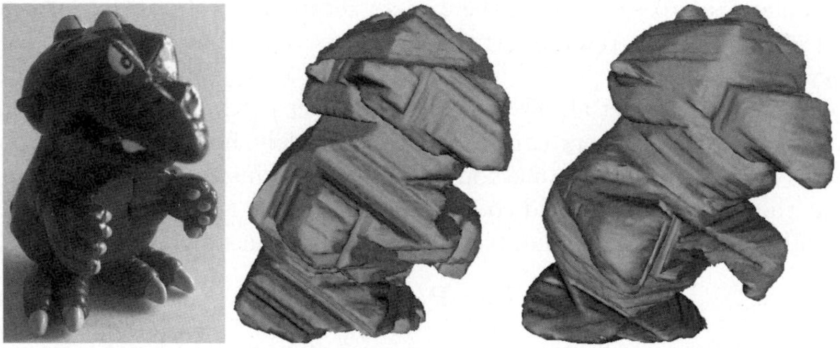

(a) (b) (c)

Fig. 2. Comparison of visual hull reconstructions of a toy figure from (b) 6 and (c) 30 camera views, respectively

2.3 Reconstruction Refinement

As shown in Section 2.2, the initial model can be refined by adding more views. A cheap way to add new views is given by moving either the object or the camera setup. In either way the relative orientations of all cameras have to be known. In our application, a robotic end effector anyway holds the object within the camera setup for further placement, so we rotate the object around the last joint in front of the camera. Each rotation introduces $n+1$ new virtual cameras. The motion of the new set of cameras with respect to the original ones is restricted to a circular motion around a common rotation axis. We consider this motion unknown and implicitly calibrate it during reconstruction.

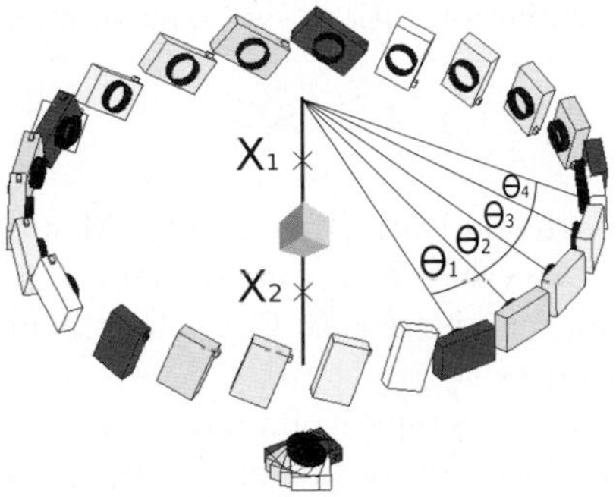

Fig. 3. Positions of the virtual cameras around the object and parametrization of the camera movements. Cameras of the same color belong to one turn of the object in front of the camera setup.

We parameterize the motion with $k+2$ parameters for k movements of the object: the rotation axis, defined by 2 points $\mathbf{x}_1, \mathbf{x}_2 \in \mathbb{R}^3$, and k angles $\theta_1 \dots \theta_k$ with respect to the original camera position. The coordinate system is defined, such that the real camera is located at the origin and the object at $[0,0,1]$. Without loss of generalization, we are able to reduce the dimensions of $\mathbf{x}_1, \mathbf{x}_2$ from $\mathbb{R}^3$ to $\mathbb{R}^2$ by fixing their z coordinate to lie on a plane in front of and behind the object, respectively. Since our fully calibrated $n+1$ camera setup is rigid, we can parameterize $(n+1)(k+1)$ cameras by only $k+2$ parameters.

A setup with $n=5$ mirrors and $k=4$ rotations yields a 30 camera multi-view system and can be parametrized by 6 parameters. This example can be seen in Fig. 3.

To automatically determine these parameters, the concept of silhouette consistency for auto-calibration was introduced in [7], which we will briefly discuss here. Given a set of silhouettes $\mathbf{S_i}, i \in [1,k]$ and its corresponding camera parameters $\mathbf{P_i}, i \in [1,k]$, the goal is to maximize the coherence of the measured silhouettes and the model projections. Every optic ray, defined by the camera center and a silhouette pixel in one view, must intersect the silhouette in any other view. This holds for perfect segmentation and camera calibration. Due to noise in both, segmentation and camera position, the above constraint will not hold for some rays.

Hernandez et al. proposed a simple metric to measure the degree of consistency for a set of $(\mathbf{S_i}, \mathbf{P_i})$ by simply counting the number of pixels, that do not comply to the consistency property. This metric can be computed by creating a visual hull, defined by the silhouettes and current projection matrices, back-projecting it into the camera images and comparing the two silhouettes. For a visual hull V defined by $(\mathbf{S_i}, \mathbf{P_i})$ and its projection into an image $\mathbf{S_i^V}$, we use the ratio of the areas between $\mathbf{S_i}$ and $\mathbf{S_i^V}$ as a consistency measure:

$$C(\mathbf{S_i}, \mathbf{S_i^V}) = \frac{\int (\mathbf{S_i} \cap \mathbf{S_i^V})}{\int \mathbf{S_i}} \quad . \tag{4}$$

In order to find optimal camera positions, we seek to maximize the total silhouette consistency

$$\sum_i C(\mathbf{S_i}, \mathbf{S_i^V}) \quad . \tag{5}$$

The problem is solved by the derivative-free Nelder-Mead algorithm [11]. During the optimization process, a visual hull approximation is being built implicitly. The evolution of the model can be seen in Fig. 2 for the initial camera setup and after 4 rotations of the object.

For the visual hull we use a simple volumetric space carving approach, originally proposed by [9]. Since the optimization procedure invokes the visual hull creation many times, we implemented a very efficient simple space carving method [15], that utilizes the parallelism of modern graphics cards. The resulting voxel model is then transformed into a triangulated mesh by applying a standard marching cubes algorithm proposed by [10].

2.4 Model-Based Pose Estimation

With a 3D model at hand, we seek to determine the rotation (roll, pitch, yaw) of an object with respect to the camera system. Seeing that we can only use the object boundaries as input we chose to extend the approach of [12] to a multi-view setup. There the authors did pose estimation by comparing the outline of an object to a database of reference views, created from a 3D model of the object. This potentially large database is indexed into a hierarchical structure by finding similar views, and by grouping them together in a bottom-up fashion. A rotation-invariant match to the database yielded pitch and yaw. The roll angle is determined by the matching procedure.

The original method was designed to be used in a single-view setting. To incorporate the remaining views created by the planar mirrors, we propose to apply the algorithm to only one silhouette. We use the other cameras for verification of the potential matches. Due to the fact, that the roll angle is determined during matching, the additional views can not be stored in the database, but have to be created on-the-fly from the 3D model.

In our setting, the silhouette produced by the real camera is always complete. The views from the virtual cameras may be partially occluded by the robotic end-effector. To cope with this, we propose a simple partial contour matching method. A closed contour from the database is given as a vector of points $\mathbf{C_{db}} = \langle \mathbf{p_1}, \cdots, \mathbf{p_n} \rangle$. The partial query contour is given by $\mathbf{C_q} = \langle \mathbf{q_1}, \cdots, \mathbf{q_k} \rangle$. In order to match them, we first perform a linear search, where we align $\mathbf{q}_1$ with every point of $\mathbf{C}_{\mathbf{db}}$, and measure the Euclidean distance of $\mathbf{q}_\mathbf{k}$ to the closest point in $\mathbf{C}_{\mathbf{db}}$. This pre-selection yields a set of possible start points for which the final error measure is obtained. The error is given by the sum of squared distances of the aligned $\mathbf{C}_\mathbf{q}$ to the closed contour $\mathbf{C}_{\mathbf{db}}$.

Out of a list of potential matches, the element of the database with the lowest error defines the rotational part of the object pose. The translation is restricted by the robotic end-effector. Remaining translation errors due to inaccuracies of the robot can be easily determined from the 2D input image.

3 Experiments

In our experiments we use a catadioptric system with 5 planar mirrors, which yields a 6-camera multi-view system. We first evaluate the accuracy of the proposed calibration and reconstruction method. In order to verify our claim that visual hull reconstructions can be used for pose estimation, we use synthetic images of previously scanned 3D models obtained by a laser scanner. Finally we apply our method to various real-world objects.

3.1 Calibration Accuracy

Intrinsic camera calibration is performed using the method proposed by Zhang [17]. The extrinsic parameters of the real and virtual cameras are obtained as described in Section 2.2. We evaluated the re-projection error of the calibration sphere center over 5 calibration runs with an average of 0.01 px, resulting in a geometric error of 2 μm at an object distance of 300 mm.

The optimization procedure converges after roughly 200 iterations. The total time for calibration, reconstruction and triangulation of the voxel representation is roughly 1 minute on a quad core PC with 4GB RAM and a NVidia GeForce GTX285. Due to the high repeatability in positioning of the robotic arm, the calibration has to be done only once. Consecutive reconstructions can be carried out in 100 ms for a voxel size of 512^3.

First, we evaluate the accuracy of the estimated rotation angles. The ground-truth is provided by a turn table with a precision of $1/77°$. The average deviation for several runs was $0.37°$.

Second, we evaluate the accuracy of the estimated rotation axis. To get a ground-truth, we let a sphere rotate off-axis, triangulate the center points and fit a plane through the reconstructed 3D points. The normal of the plane is defined as rotation axis. The average angular deviation for several runs was $0.34°$.

3.2 Pose Estimation with Synthetic Images

In the experiments so far we have focused on the quality of the calibration, which directly influences the quality of the reconstructed objects. Now, we want to

Table 1. Results of the synthetic view experiment. 800 synthetic contours generated from the ground-truth (GT) model are queried against differently detailed reconstructions, obtained from the real object. The table shows the mean deviation from the estimated viewpoint to the ground-truth.

Object	$\mathbf{VH_6}$ model			$\mathbf{VH_{30}}$ model			GT model		
	r [°]	p [°]	y [°]	r [°]	p [°]	y [°]	r [°]	p [°]	y [°]
Brick 1	11.28	10.79	7.85	8.52	8.26	5.86	4.57	4.08	2.52
Brick 2	6.74	6.44	4.31	5.03	5.21	3.23	2.44	2.78	1.88
Toy Figure	23.54	25.12	21.94	9.40	7.98	5.18	4.17	3.71	2.31

investigate how the reconstruction quality affects the pose estimation accuracy. In order to give a quantitative evaluation, we use two objects for which an accurate 3D model is given.

Each object is reconstructed with the methods presented in Sections 2.2 and 2.3, resulting in two models. The first model is a visual hull reconstruction with 5+1 camera views, the second model was created by turning the object $k = 4$ times, which equals a reconstruction from 30 camera views. Both models are converted into a triangulated mesh. One object used, a toy figure, is depicted in Fig. 4. (b) and (c) show a comparison between a visual hull reconstruction from 30 views and a scanned 3D model from roughly the same viewpoint.

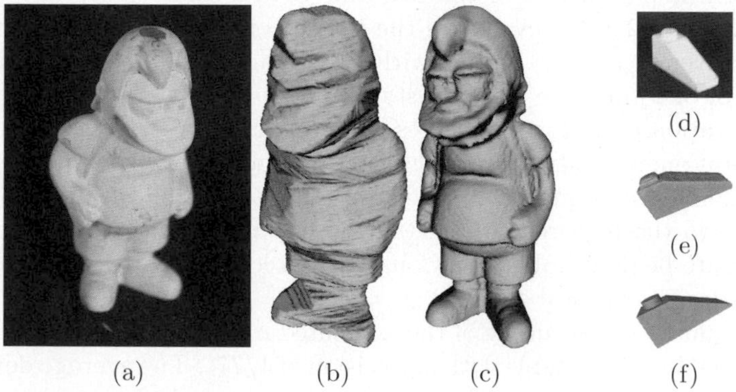

Fig. 4. Comparison of a model generated with our visual hull base reconstruction (b), (e) and a laser scanner (c),(f)

First, we use the ground-truth model to create artificial images of the object. The calibration parameters allow us to simulate the catadioptric camera system, whereas the 3D model gives us ground-truth poses. In our experiment we created 800 views of the object from random viewpoints. A viewpoint is defined by a point on a sphere with the object in its center and a roll angle along the camera's optical axis

$$\mathbf{V_l} = \langle \mathbf{p_l}, r_l \rangle, \mathbf{p_l} \in \mathbb{R}^2, r_l \in [0, 2\pi] \quad . \tag{6}$$

For each 3D model of the object a reference view database consisting of 1000 views is created with the method described in Section 2.4. Table 1 represents the results of this experiment in terms of mean deviation of the estimated pose to the ground-truth pose, in roll, pitch and yaw.

Clearly, a more detailed visual hull improves the accuracy of the estimated poses, bringing it very close to the results, that can be obtained by using a laser-scanned model. For the geometrically very complex toy figure, a visual hull obtained from a few camera views is not able to accurately represent the true object, resulting in pose deviations up to 25°. Adding additional views by turning the object in front of the camera improves the result to 8°.

Figure 5 depicts the number of correct pose estimations, given a maximum angular deviation for a simple and a complex object, respectively. The simple model can be approximated quite well even by a coarse visual hull reconstruction, whereas for the complex model the incorporation of more camera views leads to large improvements.

When allowing a maximal deviation from the true pose of 8° our method decreases by 5% for the brick with its simple geometry. For the more complex model, the accuracy decreases by 12%.

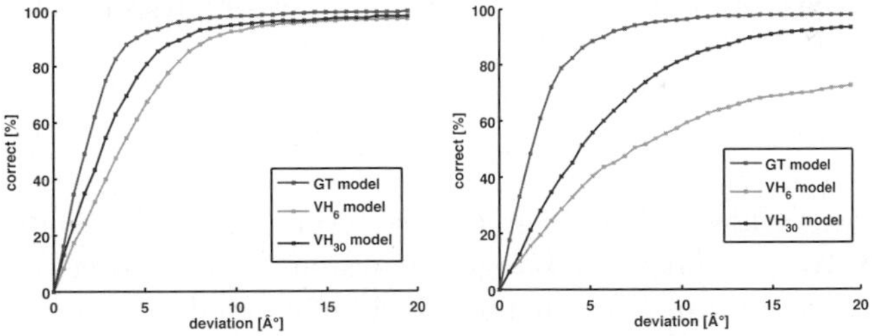

(a) (b)

Fig. 5. Results of our synthetic view experiment. The number of correct matches for a given maximum angular deviation is shown for three different 3D models: visual hull reconstructions from 6 and 30 views, respectively, and a laser scanned model. Two different objects were employed: (a) a brick with low complexity, and (b) a toy figure with rather high complexity

3.3 Pose Estimation with Real Images

We validated our approach for a variety of real world objects for which no 3D model was available. For this experiment we used a 2 MP FireWire camera and 5 planar standard mirrors. Figure 6 depicts those objects along with the obtained reconstructions and success rates. Since no ground-truth in terms of correct viewpoints is available, only qualitative results in terms of 'visually correct' or 'visually incorrect' are given. For every object, approximately one out of ten pose estimation was classified as incorrect, nevertheless the failure cases typically were near the correct solutions.

The objects resemble a variety of geometric complexities. They all share the property of being very low textured. The pose estimation results indicate, that our method can be used for almost any objects, as long as their outline can be extracted. A single pose estimation can be obtained in 200 milliseconds, including the time for segmentation, and pose estimation.

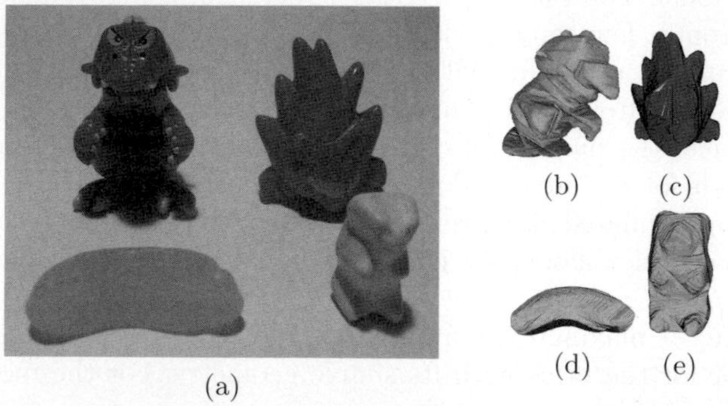

Fig. 6. Objects used for the experiments with real images. (b)-(e) show the obtained reconstructions using the method described in Section 2.3. The success rates of the pose estimation are (b) 83.3%, (c) 90%, (d) 92.8 % (e) 90% respectively.

4 Conclusion

In this work we tackled the problem of pose estimation in the context of robotic pick & place. We introduced an integrated system for model-based pose estimation, without the need of obtaining a model beforehand. Models of new objects are learned on the fly by placing them in front of the camera system. We presented a catadioptric multi-view system, which offers a cheap way of creating several viewpoints with a single camera. The whole process of camera calibration, 3D reconstruction, and pose estimation is solely based on outer contours of the objects. Those silhouettes can be extracted reliably for a variety of objects, making our method applicable to a wide range of products.

We have shown that the visual hull reconstruction can be used for accurate pose estimation, if enough camera views contributed to the reconstruction. Experiments with both synthetic and real objects prove, that the proposed system can be used for objects with arbitrary geometry and surface structure. The implementation of the core algorithm on modern graphics cards allows for pose estimations in 200 ms and system auto-calibration in less than 20 s without user interaction.

Future work may include the investigation of methods tolerant to segmentation errors in order to apply the method to applications with uncontrolled environment. Also the removal of the restriction on circular object movement to obtain a reconstruction refinement will be part of our future work.

Acknowledgments. We would like to thank the reviewers for their helpful and positive comments. This work was supported by the Austrian Research Promotion Agency (FFG) under the project SILHOUETTE (825843).

References

1. Byne, J., Anderson, J.: A CAD-based computer vision system. Image and Vision Computing 16(8), 533–539 (1998)
2. Costa, M.S., Shapiro, L.G.: 3D object recognition and pose with relational indexing. Computer Vision and Image Understanding 79(3), 364–407 (2000)
3. Cyr, C., Kimia, B.: 3D object recognition using shape similiarity-based aspect graph. In: ICCV, pp. 254–261 (2001)
4. Fofi, D., Sliwa, T., Voisin, Y.: A comparative survey on invisible structured light. In: SPIE, vol. 5303, pp. 90–98 (May 2004)
5. Gluckman, J., Nayar, S.K.: Catadioptric stereo using planar mirrors. IJCV 44 (2001)
6. Heber, M., Ruether, M., Bischof, H.: Catadioptric multiview pose estimation for robotic pick and place. In: VISAPP, vol. 1, pp. 423–426 (2010)
7. Hernandez, C., Schmitt, F., Cipolla, R.: Silhouette coherence for camera calibration under circular motion. PAMI 29(2), 343–349 (2007)
8. Hu, B., Brown, C., Nelson, R.: Multiple-view 3-D reconstruction using a mirror. Tech. rep., University of Rochester (May 2005)
9. Laurentini, A.: The visual hull concept for silhouette-based image understanding. PAMI 2 (1994)
10. Lorensen, W.E., Cline, H.E.: Marching cubes: A high resolution 3d surface construction algorithm. SIGGRAPH 21(4), 163–169 (1987)
11. Nelder, J.A., Mead, R.: A simplex method for function minimization. The Computer Journal 7(4), 308–313 (1965)
12. Reinbacher, C., Ruether, M., Bischof, H.: Pose estimation of known objects by efficient silhouette matching. In: ICPR (2010)
13. Santner, J., Unger, M., Pock, T., Leistner, C., Saffari, A., Bischof, H.: Interactive texture segmentation using random forests and total variation. In: BMVC, London, UK (September 2009)
14. Scharstein, D., Szeliski, R.: High-accuracy stereo depth maps using structured light. In: CVPR, vol. 1, pp. 195–202 (June 2003)
15. Szeliski, R.: Rapid octree construction from image sequences. In: CVGIP, vol. 58, pp. 23–32 (1993)
16. Ulrich, M., Wiedemann, C., Steger, C.: CAD-based recognition of 3D objects in monocular images. In: ICRA, pp. 1191–1198 (2009)
17. Zhang, Z.: Flexible camera calibration by viewing a plane from unknown orientations. In: ICCV, pp. 666–673 (1999)

Using the Local Phase of the Magnitude of the Local Structure Tensor for Image Registration

Anders Eklund[1,2], Daniel Forsberg[1,2,3],
Mats Andersson[1,2], and Hans Knutsson[1,2]

[1] Division of Medical Informatics, Department of Biomedical Engineering
[2] Center for Medical Image Science and Visualization (CMIV)
Linköping University, Linköping, Sweden
[3] Sectra Imtec, Linköping, Sweden

Abstract. The need of image registration is increasing, especially in the medical image domain. The simplest kind of image registration is to match two images that have similar intensity. More advanced cases include the problem of registering images of different intensity, for which phase based algorithms have proven to be superior. In some cases the phase based registration will fail as well, for instance when the images to be registered do not only differ in intensity but also in local phase. This is the case if a dark circle in the reference image is a bright circle in the source image. While rigid registration algorithms can use other parts of the image to calculate the global transformation, this problem is harder to solve for non-rigid registration. The solution that we propose in this work is to use the local phase of the magnitude of the local structure tensor, instead of the local phase of the image intensity. By doing this, we achieve invariance both to the image intensity and to the local phase and thereby only use the structural information, i.e. the shapes of the objects, for registration.

1 Introduction

Image registration is needed in a lot of applications. One example is medical imaging where image registration is necessary to for example be able to compare images of the brain before and after surgery. A problem with the image modalities used in medical imaging is that the images produced often differ significantly in intensity. The most common approach to register images of different intensity is to maximize the mutual information (MI) between the images [11,10]. While this approach is sufficient to handle many registration problems, it is not very hard to create a set of test images where the mutual information approach fails, such an example is given in Fig. 1.

The main problem with the mutual information approach, and many other similarity measures, is that they are based on the intensity of the image. A better approach is to use the local phase [8,9,1,4,2,13]. In this work we take the phase idea one step further and use the local phase of the magnitude of the local structure tensor, instead of the local phase of the image intensity. Local phase is commonly estimated by using quadrature filters [3].

A. Heyden and F. Kahl (Eds.): SCIA 2011, LNCS 6688, pp. 414–423, 2011.

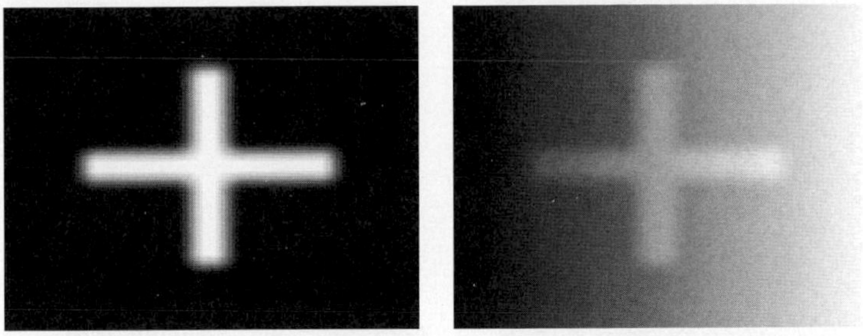

Fig. 1. Two simple test images for which intensity based registration algorithms fail

2 Methods

2.1 Quadrature Filters and Local Phase

A quadrature filter is a complex valued filter for combined edge and line detection. The real part of the filter, which is even, detects lines and the imaginary part, which is odd, detects edges. The magnitude of the complex filter response is an estimate of the phase invariant signal intensity and the phase determines whether there is an edge or a line and what kind of line or edge. We use log-normal quadrature filters Q, which in the Fourier domain are expressed as two polar separable functions R, and D.

$$Q_k(u) = R(||u||)D_k(u) \tag{1}$$

$$R(||u||) = e^{Cln^2\left(\frac{||(u)||}{u_0}\right)} \quad C = \frac{-4}{B^2 ln(2)} \tag{2}$$

Since the phase concept is only valid if we define a direction of the signal, we construct quadrature filters with different directions. The directions are defined such that

$$D_k(u) = \begin{cases} (u^T \hat{n}_k)^2 & u^T \hat{n}_k > 0 \\ 0 & \text{otherwise} \end{cases} \tag{3}$$

We use four quadrature filters with the directions, $\Psi_k \in \{0^0, 45^0, 90^0, 135^0\}$. The complex filter response q is an estimate of a bandpass filtered version of the analytical signal

$$q = A \cdot (cos(\phi) + i \cdot sin(\phi)) = A \cdot e^{i\phi} \tag{4}$$

with magnitude A and phase ϕ. For image registration applications, it is important that the filters have a nice and smooth phase. This can be obtained by optmizing the filters in the spatial domain and the frequency domain at the same time [7].

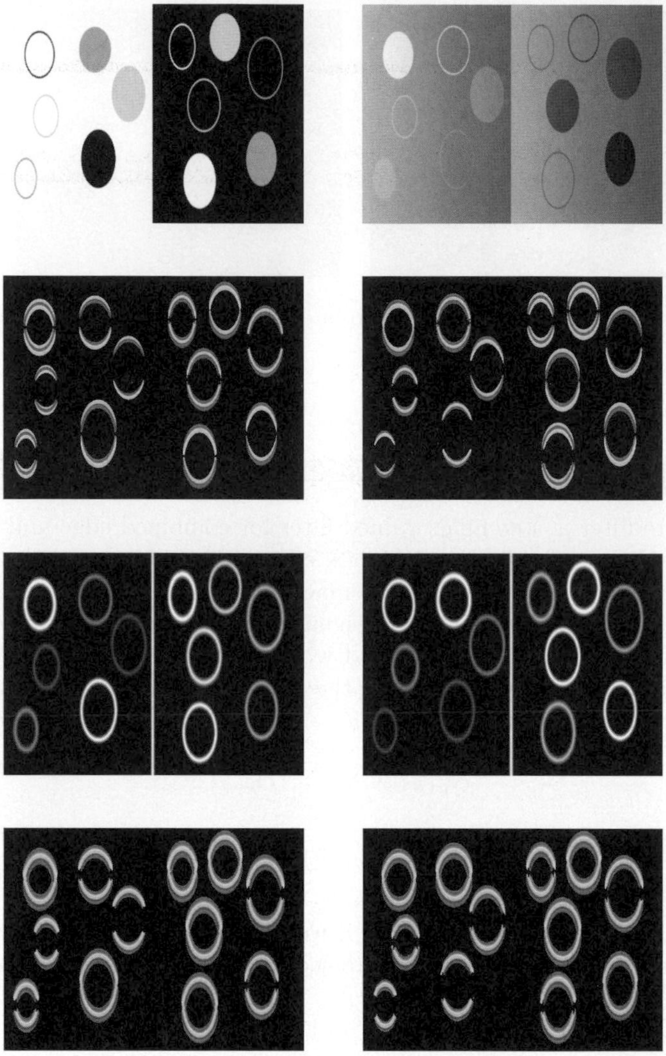

Fig. 2. First row left: A test image with all the kinds of phase for three different intensities. **First row right:** The test image with modified intensity and phase, a shading from right to left and noise. **Second row left:** The phase, in the y-direction, of the original test image. **Second row right:** The phase of the modified test image. The phase is only invariant to a change in intensity. **Third row left:** The tensor magnitude of the original test image. **Third row right:** The tensor magnitude of the modified test image. The tensor magnitude is only invariant to a change in phase. **Fourth row left:** The phase of the tensor magnitude, in the y-direction, of the original test image. **Fourth row right:** The phase of the tensor magnitude of the modified test image. The phase of the tensor magnitude is invariant both to change in intensity and to change in phase and thereby we can register the images by using the structural information only. Since quadrature filters are bandpass filters, they are robust to low frequencies, e.g. shadings, and high frequencies, e.g. noise.

2.2 The Local Structure Tensor

The local structure tensor was introduced by Knutsson [5] to represent the local structure in images and volumes. For an image it is a 2 x 2 matrix in each pixel. The structure tensor can for example be used for adaptive filtering, to steer the orientation of enhancement filters. The tensor can be constructed by using the complex valued filter responses q from quadrature filters. We sum over all filters k and multiply the magnitude of the filter response with the outer product N_k of the filter direction vector $\hat{n}_k$, I is the identity matrix.

$$T = \sum_k |q_k| \left(\frac{4}{3} N_k - \frac{1}{3} I \right), \quad T = \begin{pmatrix} t_1 \; t_2 \\ t_2 \; t_3 \end{pmatrix} \tag{5}$$

The magnitude of the tensor is given by

$$|T| = \sqrt{t_1^2 + 2t_2^2 + t_3^2} \tag{6}$$

2.3 Local Phase of the Magnitude of the Local Structure Tensor

The problem with using the local phase for image registration is that we might have structures in the images that are similar but have different phase, for example a white circle on a black background in one image and a black circle on a white background in another image. The mutual information of the phase can handle this, as long as the mappings are consistent, but not if we want to map a dark line to a bright line in one part of the image and to map a dark line to a dark edge in another part of the image. To fully take advantage of the structural information, a better approach is to use a signal representation that is invariant both to a change in intensity and to a change in the local phase. The magnitude of the local structure tensor is invariant to a change in phase, since the orientation for a line and an edge is the same, but not to a change in intensity. The local phase on the other hand is only invariant to a change in intensity. By using the local phase of the local structure tensor magnitude, we achieve a representation that is invariant both to a change in intensity and to a change in phase. An example of this is given in Fig. 2.

3 Results

We have made a comparison between mutual information of the intensity, mutual information of the phase of the intensity and mutual information of the phase of the tensor magnitude. One image was rotated between -30 degrees and 30 degrees while the other remained still. We divided the 60 degree interval into 101 evaluations. As test images, we used the synthetic test images shown in Fig. 2 and four MRI images, shown in Fig 3. These MRI images differ significantly

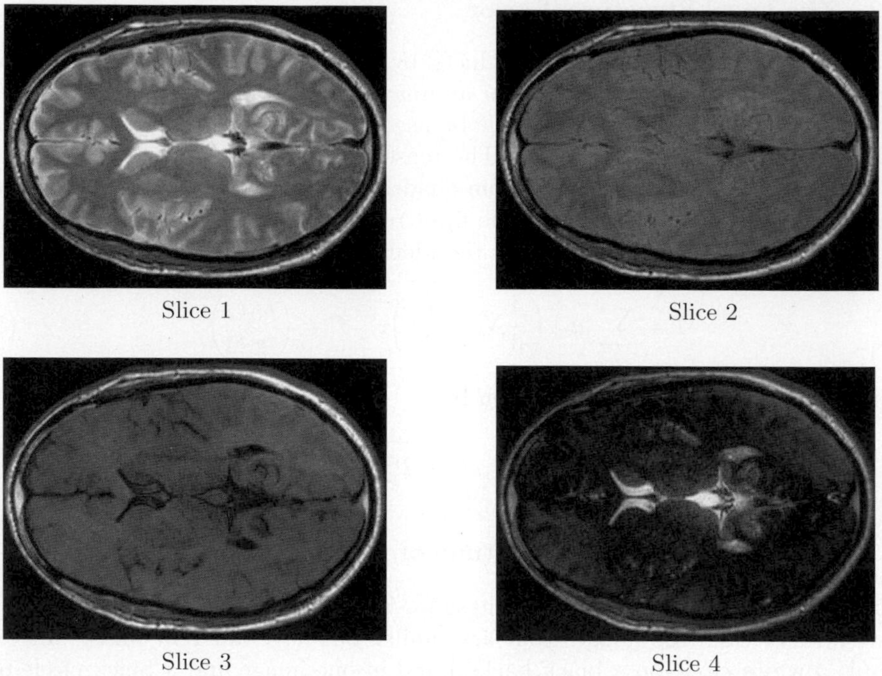

Fig. 3. Four MRI slices that are collected from the same location of one subject. The slices were acquired with a 1.5 T MR scanner. Different scanner settings were used to generate the different slices. The purpose of the image acquisition was pixel-wise quantification of physical parameters, based on signal intensity changes as a function of MR scanner settings. MRI quantification requires a motionless subject and image registration improves the result (courtesy of J.B.M. Warntjes, CMIV, Linköping, Sweden).

in intensity and for some parts of the image, but not all, the phase has been inverted. We normalized all similarity measures to have a maximum of 1, to easier compare the slopes. The resulting plots of the similarity measures as function of rotation are given in Fig. 4.

To show that the local phase of the tensor magnitude is better than the local phase of the image intensity for image registration, we performed non-rigid registration on the two synthetic test images given in Fig. 2 and on two of the MRI images given in Fig. 3. The MRI images are used for quantitative MRI, in order to measure physical properties [12]. To obtain good measurements it is important that the images are registered. The registration algorithm used is the Morphon [6], which is a phase based non-rigid registration algorithm.

The results of the registration of the synthetic test images are shown in Fig. 5. The results of the registration of the MRI images are shown in Fig. 6.

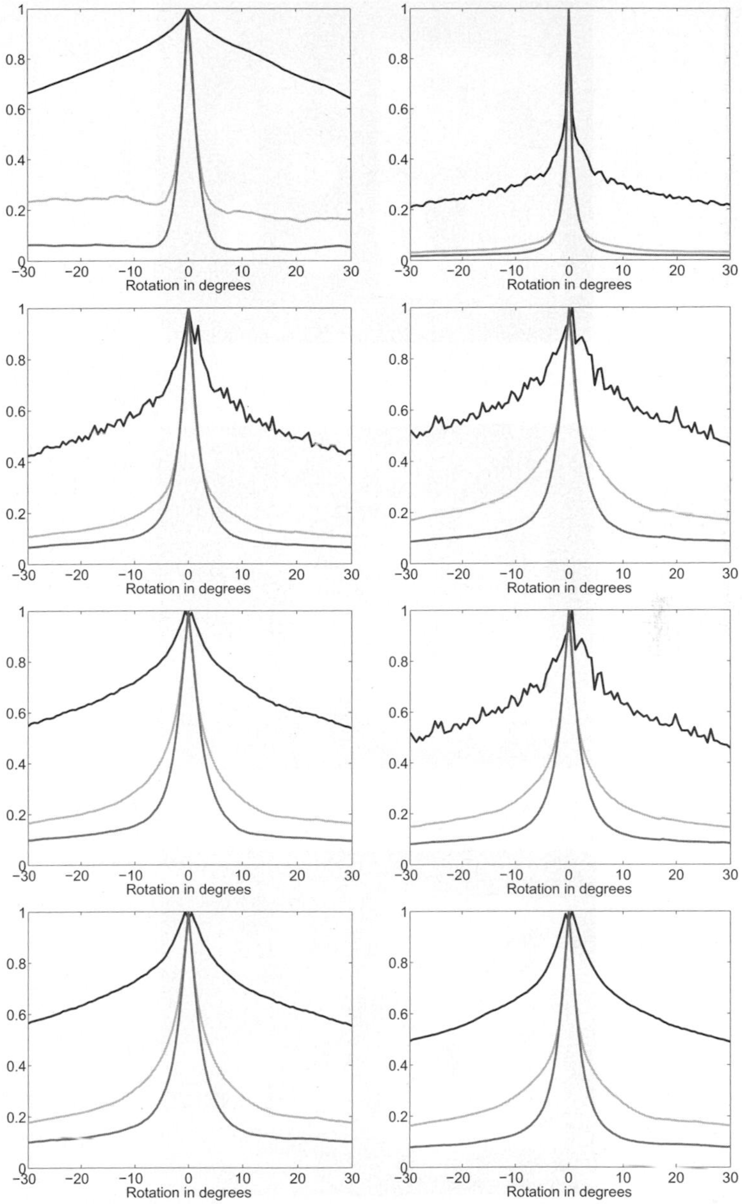

Fig. 4. Similarity measures as function of rotation between two images. The blue line is the mutual information of the intensity values, the green line is the mutual information of the phase of the intensity and the pink line is the mutual information of the phase of the tensor magnitude. **First row left:** Original test image and modified test image, from Fig. 2. **First row right:** Slice 1 and slice 1. **Second row left:** Slice 1 and slice 2. **Second row right:** Slice 1 and slice 3. **Third row left:** Slice 1 and slice 4. **Third row right:** Slice 2 and slice 3. **Fourth row left:** Slice 2 and slice 4. **Fourth row right:** Slice 3 and slice 4.

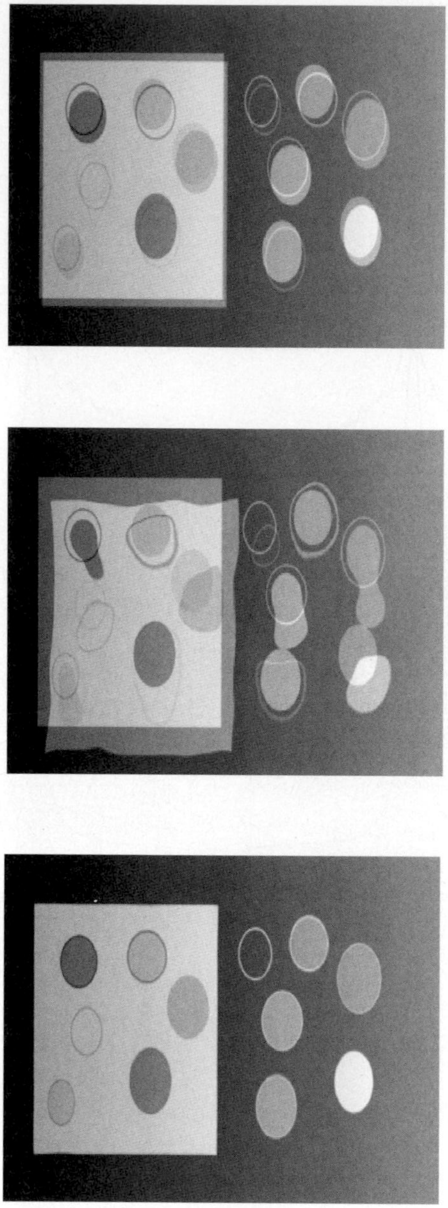

Fig. 5. Top: The original intensity difference between the original test image and the altered test image. The images have been shifted 3 pixels in the x-direction and 5 pixels in the y-direction. **Middle:** The intensity difference after the non-rigid registration with the phase of the intensity. The altered phases confuse the registration algorithm and the registration does not work at all. **Bottom:** The intensity difference after the non-rigid registration with the phase of the tensor magnitude. By using the phase of the tensor magnitude we achieve invariance both to the intensity and to the local phase and now the registration works correctly.

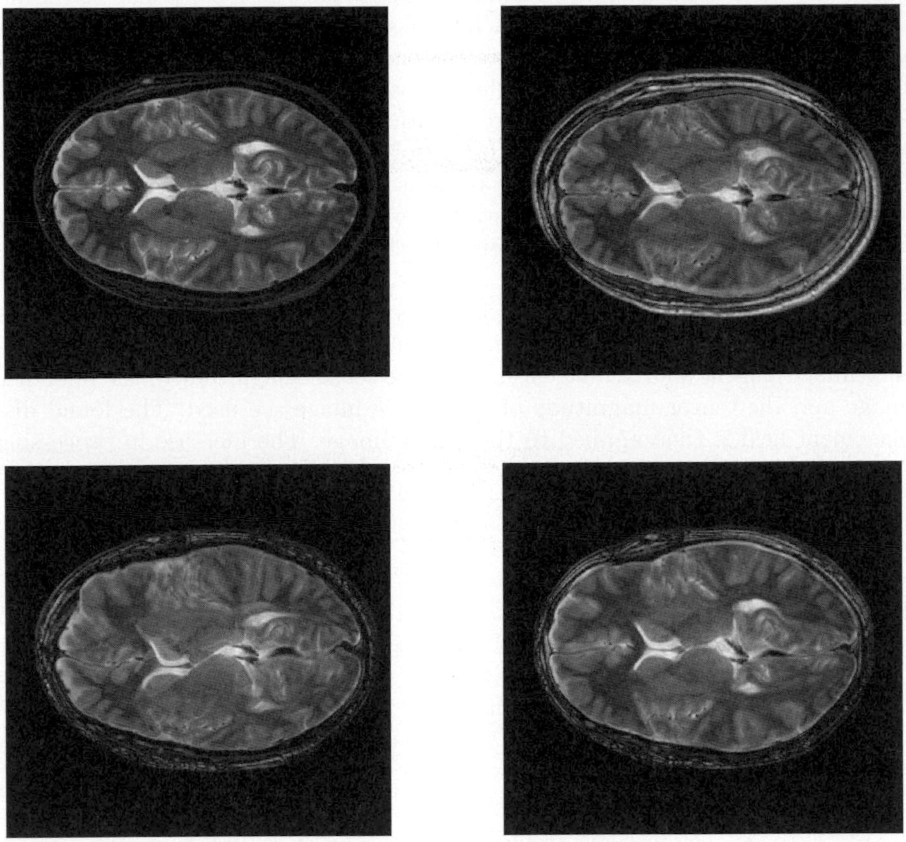

Fig. 6. Top left: The original absolute intensity difference between slice 3 and slice 1. **Top right:** The absolute intensity difference between slice 3 and slice 1 after shifting the images 6 pixels in the x-direction and 7 pixels in the y-direction. **Bottom left:** The absolute intensity difference after the non-rigid registration with the phase of the intensity. The registration works rather well for the fat border surrounding the brain but not at all for the ventricles, where the phase is inverted. **Bottom right:** The absolute intensity difference after the non-rigid registration with the phase of the tensor magnitude. Now the registration works for the ventricles as well.

4 Discussion

The similarity measure comparison in Fig. 4 clearly shows that our new similarity measure decays faster than the other similarity measures. The biggest difference is however between the intensity and the local phase.

As can be seen in Fig. 5, the local phase of the intensity does not work at all to register the synthetic test images. By instead using the local phase of the tensor magnitude we achieve invariance to the local phase and can use the structural information, i.e. the shape of the objects, for registration.

For the MRI images similar results are obtained, the local phase of the intensity works rather well for the fat border surrounding the brain, but it does not work at all for the ventricles since they are bright in one image and dark in the other. With the local phase of the tensor magnitude the registration works for the ventricles as well. For rigid registration, the local phase of the intensity works as well as the local phase of the tensor magnitude. The reason for this is that the fat border surrounding the brain is the same in all the images. If the fat border is removed, the rigid registration with the local phase of the intensity fails, while the registration works if the local phase of the tensor magnitude is used.

A major advantage with the presented approach is that existing image registration algorithms can be used without modification. Instead of using the reference image and the source image as inputs, the tensor magnitude of the reference image and the tensor magnitude of the source image are used. The found displacement field is then applied to the source image. The increase in processing time is thus rather small.

Acknowledgement

This work was supported by the Linnaeus center CADICS, funded by the Swedish research council.

We thank Marcel Warntjes et al. at CMIV for letting us use their MRI images to test our registration algorithm with.

References

1. Dalvi, R., Abugharbieh, R., Pickering, M., Scarvell, J., Smith, P.: Registration of 2D to 3D joint images using phase-based mutual information. In: Proceedings of SPIE (2007)
2. Eklund, A., Andersson, M., Knutsson, H.: Phase based volume registration using CUDA. In: IEEE International Conference on Acoustics, Speech and Signal Processing (ICASSP), pp. 658–661 (2010)
3. Granlund, G., Knutsson, H.: Signal Processing for Computer Vision. Kluwer Academic Publishers, Dordrecht (1995) ISBN 0-7923-9530-1
4. Hemmendorff, M., Andersson, M., Kronander, T., Knutsson, H.: Phase-based multidimensional volume registration. IEEE Transactions on Medical Imaging 21, 1536–1543 (2002)
5. Knutsson, H.: Representing local structure using tensors. In: Scandinavian Conference on Image Analysis (SCIA), pp. 244–251 (1989)
6. Knutsson, H., Andersson, M.: Morphons: Paint on priors and elastic canvas for segmentation and registration. In: Scandinavian Conference on Image Analysis (SCIA), Joensuu (2005)
7. Knutsson, H., Andersson, M., Wiklund, J.: Advanced filter design. In: Scandinavian Conference on Image Analysis, SCIA (1999)
8. Mellor, M., Brady, M.: Non-rigid multimodal image registration using local phase. In: Barillot, C., Haynor, D.R., Hellier, P. (eds.) MICCAI 2004. LNCS, vol. 3216, pp. 789–796. Springer, Heidelberg (2004)

9. Mellor, M., Brady, M.: Phase mutual information as similarity measure for registration. Medical Image Analysis 9, 330–343 (2005)
10. Pluim, J.P.W., Maintz, J.A., Viergever, M.A.: Mutual information based registration of medical images: a survey. IEEE Transactions on Medical Imaging 22, 986–1004 (2003)
11. Viola, P., Wells, W.: Alignment by maximization of mutual information. International Journal of Computer Vision 24, 137–154 (1997)
12. Warntjes, J., Dahlqvist, L., West, J., Lundberg, P.: Rapid magnetic resonance quantification on the brain: Optimization for clinical usage. Magnetic Resonance in Medicine 60, 320–329 (2008)
13. Wong, A., Fieguth, P.: Fast phase-based registration of multimodal data. Signal Processing 89, 724–737 (2008)

Coherence Probe Microscopy Imaging and Analysis for Fiber-Reinforced Polymers

Verena Schlager[1], Stefan E. Schausberger[2], David Stifter[2], and Bettina Heise[1,2]

Christian Doppler Laboratory for Microscopic and Spectroscopic Material Characterization,
[1] Department of Knowledge-Based Mathematical Systems, FLLL
[2] Center for Surface- and Nanoanalytics, ZONA
Johannes Kepler University Linz, A-4040 Linz, Austria
{bettina.heise,verena.schlager}@jku.at
http://www.jku.at

Abstract. The potential of full-field low coherence interferometric techniques for imaging internal structures, such as fibers, interfaces, or inclusions in technical materials is demonstrated by our coherence probe microscopy (CPM) setup. However, the huge amount of recorded data demand for an automatized enhancement and evaluation of the image data. We propose an automatic image analysis procedure adapted for full-field coherence probe microscopy, which we tested on fiber composite materials. The performed image enhancement and orientation analysis finally allow to cluster the internal fiber structures, to detect outliers and enable an improved characterization of investigated specimens supporting a sophisticated material design for the future.

Keywords: coherence probe microscopy, fiber composites, speckles, orientation, monogenic, clustering.

1 Introduction

The increasing demand of industry for new functional materials requires appropriate methods for material characterization and inspection. Aggregates and composite materials containing structures in the size range of few microns altering material behavior are of crucial interest in the field of material design. Microscopy techniques on micrograph sections provide excellent conditions for the analysis of internal microstructures for further material characterization. But, these methods are hampered by the destructive character of this investigation techniques. Hence, non-destructive imaging techniques in combination with an appropriate image analysis for deepening the knowledge about the material composition on a mesoscopic size scale are on the order of the day.

Computer tomography (CT) and ultrasound (US) imaging are well known non-destructive imaging techniques. However, they are restricted in their application due to the hazardous X-ray radiation and the achievable resolution limited by the relation to the sample dimensions, or as in case of US by requiring an

A. Heyden and F. Kahl (Eds.): SCIA 2011, LNCS 6688, pp. 424–434, 2011.

additional coupling medium. For investigation of translucent or scattering materials low coherence interferometry (LCI) techniques working in the near infrared wavelength range (NIR) can provide an alternative to CT methods. Their imaging capabilities can be tuned for the visualization of micro-structured materials. Especially the characterization of the internal structure of the specimen within semi-transparent scattering materials can be achieved by optical coherence tomography (OCT) techniques [1], having its origin in LCI techniques. Exploiting both intensity and run-time respectively phase information of the backscattered signal depth-resolved information about e.g. the matrix pattern, disturbances or inclusions inside the material can be obtained.

The combination of OCT techniques with microscopic methods and using 2D CCD or CMOS cameras instead of point detectors as imaging device results in full-field (FF) coherent probe microscopic (CPM) imaging [2], obtaining information about both axial and lateral sample structures, with decoupled depth and lateral resolutions.

Although OCT was originally developed for the biomedical diagnostics, recently, OCT techniques have shown their potential in the field of material research [3,5]. In a similar way, also for CPM as full-field imaging technique a comparable tendency focusing on material research can be noted [4]. Exploiting CPM imaging for micro-material inspection represents the aim in our experimental optical configuration. We describe the challenges for routinely evaluating measured CPM scans and suggest in the following a scheme for automated image analysis starting from the demodulation of the raw data, the enhancement of the resulting demodulated images, tested methods for orientation estimation of internal fiber structures, finally allowing a clustering of structures or image slices.

2 Methods

2.1 CPM Measurement Setup and Materials

A scheme of our CPM optical setup is shown in Fig. 1, depicted here in a Michelson configuration [2]. As low-coherence light source we apply likewise a superluminiscent diode (Superlum, central wavelength=850 nm, spectral bandwidth=50 nm) and a super-continuum light source (LEUKOS SM-30, central wavelength=825 nm, spectral bandwidth=350 nm), which provide an axial resolution of about 16 μm and 2 μm in air, respectively. The lateral resolution, determined by the focusing optical components totals about 3 μm. The achievable depth range for imaging yields about 200-500 μm dependent on the investigated material and the utilized wavelength range. Our conventional CPM system can be extended additionally by the possibilities as given in microscopy, e.g. by the modification of the applied imaging contrast [6]. In this paper we demonstrate an application for micro-material imaging using brightfield contrast.

In particular, polymers reinforced with fiber micro-structures are the technical materials in the scope of our interest. They contain internal (glass) fiber components, which may be randomly distributed, but which are often arranged

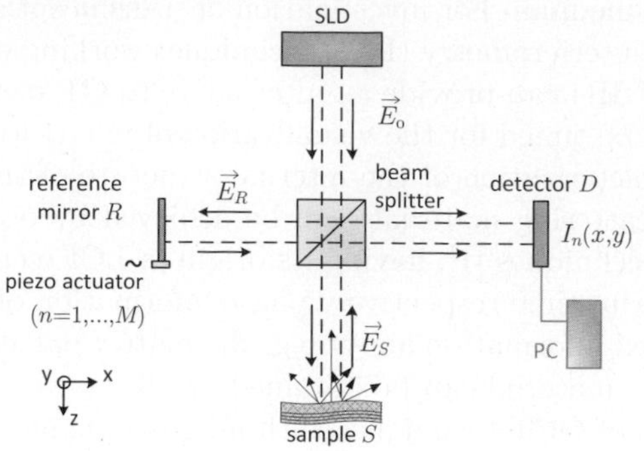

Fig. 1. Scheme of the Coherence Probe Microscopy optical setup, here illustrated in a Michelson configuration. The imaging lens systems are neglected in the drawing for sake of simplicity.

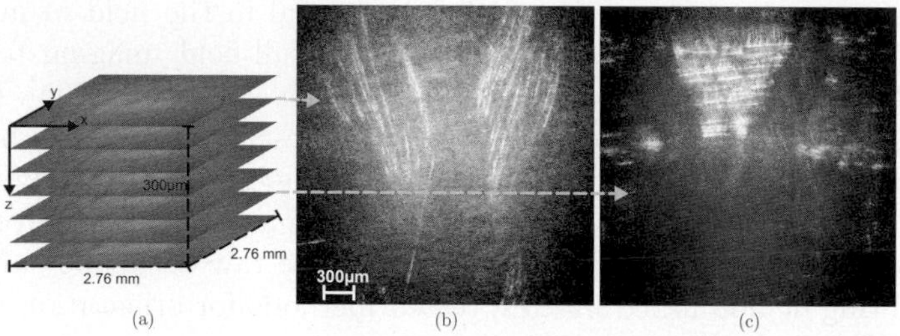

Fig. 2. Illustration for CPM imaging samples: (a) sketch of the CPM image stack taken as en-face scans (x, y) over depth z; (b) and (c) show two (already demodulated) CPM slices (amplitude images) recorded at different imaging depths, taken from fiber structures casted in a polymer matrix. The depth varying orientation of the fiber structures is clearly visible in this sample: the almost diagonal fiber structures in (b) change to horizontal internal structures in (c).

just as in a layered configuration. The fibers can be knitted or are appearing in a woven structure. Different fiber layers may be discerned over depth by their distinguished orientational characteristics of internal structures, as illustrated in Fig. 2. Additionally to the intended and designed fiber distribution the resulting CPM image stack may also contain scans showing typical artifacts, so called 'ghost-images'. These erroneous structures may occur due to multiple reflections at interfaces or are caused by the possible side-lobes of the autocorrelation function of the light source. These erroneous slices are representing outliers. As outliers complicate any analysis they should be automatically detected.

2.2 Image Demodulation

At each depth position z a sequence of interferometric images is taken in a phase-shifted way by equally-spaced phase steps $\phi_M(x, y)$ (in our case, with M up to

8 frames) between subsequent frames $I_M(x, y)$. These interferometric raw data images have to be demodulated, applying here a complex vector addition scheme [6]

$$I_C(x, y) = \sum_M I_M(x, y) exp(-i\phi_M(x, y)) \tag{1}$$

delivering the amplitude image $I(x, y) = abs(I_C(x, y))$ and the phase image $\phi(x, y) = arg(I_C(x, y))$. The thereby obtained amplitude images $I(x, y)$, as shown in Fig. 2, are used in the following for the demonstrated image analysis as they contain the structural information of interest. (It should be mentioned, that the amplitude information could be extended by analyzing the phase image too. However, these phase-based approaches require extended unwrapping procedure [7].)

The final sample images exhibit a field of view of 2.758×2.758 mm and the stepwidth into the depth is 3 μm. The example image stack counts 100 slices.

2.3 Image Enhancement

CPM scans, as taken by an interferometric imaging technique, are often highly disturbed by speckles. These speckles exhibit a two-fold nature: on one-hand they describe a noise component of the signal, but on the other hand they carry information about the internal structure. This ambiguity and the scattering behavior of the micro-structures result that the imaged features often appear in a patchy, non-continuous way, although the real structures are almost continuous. Furthermore, a non-uniform background illumination, fluctuations during the phase-stepping, and multiple scattering or reflections complicate an automatic analysis. Therefore, we have tested different denoising and background correction techniques to enhance the quality of the primary CPM-images.

Denoising. Discussing noise in the measured image $I_n(x, y)$, the speckle noise $n(x, y)$ has to be regarded as the dominant contribution, degrading the theoretical CPM image $I(x, y)$. Speckle noise (related to intensity) can be modeled in a multiplicative way. However, in the OCT community mostly a logarithm transform is applied on the image which converts the speckle noise into an additive component, $log(I_n(x, y)) = log(I(x, y)) + log(n(x, y))$. This logarithm scaled image is taken by us as basis for our further considerations.

As a well-established method for reducing speckle noise, different *adaptive median filtering* techniques are mentioned in literature [8]. Additionally, we have investigated a denoising approach based on the *curvelet transform* as introduced originally by Candes et. al. in [9]. For our application, it shows the advantage that the elongated fiber structure are taken into account. These fiber structures are then enhanced, whereas the randomly and isotropically distributed speckle noise is removed.

As third image enhancement technique tested a denoising based on the *á trous wavelet transform* [10] is performed. The á trous wavelet transform applies a, by a factor of 2, increasingly sized scaling function. At each scale the holes within the up-sampled scaling function are filled by zero values. It may be realized as a fast discrete wavelet transform by subsequently performing a low pass filtering in a convolutive way, being in particular of interest for the processing of the huge amount of data. In our case, we have taken a B_3-spline scaling function as convolution mask for our images.

Background Correction. Due to the collimated illumination the background exhibits a radial illumination profile which hampers the following analysis. Therefore, a further image enhancement step comprehends a correction for the non-uniformly shaped background. We have used both, a method based on a morphological opening approach, the well-established so-called *rolling ball algorithm* as introduced by Sternberg [11], and a method exploiting an (only) phase-based reconstruction scheme applying monogenic wavelets for an *equalization of brightness*, as recently suggested in [12].

2.4 Orientation Estimation

After preprocessing of the images with different enhancement techniques we are now able to analyze and to characterize the inner structure of the samples, where especially the fiber structure orientation indicating the different fiber layers, should be considered. We have focused on structure tensor methods and in addition on, complex wavelet-based methods as Gabor filtering and a monogenic wavelet-based orientation estimation.

Structure Tensor-based Orientation Estimation. As a first approach to get information about orientation and isotropy properties on internal fiber structures within the region of interest we have applied a *structure tensor-based orientation estimation*, which is based on the minimal deviation gradient direction [13]

$$\theta(\mathbf{x}_0) = \arg \max_{\theta \in [-\pi,\pi]} \int_{\mathbb{R}^2} w(\mathbf{x} - \mathbf{x}_0) |\nabla f(\mathbf{x})^T \bar{\mathbf{n}}|^2 d\mathbf{x}. \tag{2}$$

Here, $w(\mathbf{x}) \geq 0$ is a weighting function that specifies the area of interest and $\bar{\mathbf{n}}$ represents the local orientation $\bar{\mathbf{n}} = \left[\cos\theta \, \sin\theta\right]^T$. Rewriting the right-hand side of equation (2) a tensor form is given by

$$\int_{\mathbb{R}^2} w(\mathbf{x} - \mathbf{x}_0) |\nabla f(\mathbf{x})^T \bar{\mathbf{n}}|^2 d\mathbf{x} = \left[\cos\theta \, \sin\theta\right] \mathbf{J}(\mathbf{x}_0) \begin{bmatrix} \cos\theta \\ \sin\theta \end{bmatrix}. \tag{3}$$

With the help of the structure tensor $\mathbf{J} = \begin{pmatrix} J_{11} J_{12} \\ J_{12} J_{22} \end{pmatrix} = \langle \nabla f(\mathbf{x}) \otimes \nabla f(\mathbf{x}) \rangle_w$, determined by the weighted outer product $(\langle \otimes \rangle_w)$ of the image gradient $\nabla f(\mathbf{x}) = \nabla I(x, y)$, the orientation angle θ

$$\theta = \frac{1}{2} \arctan \left(\frac{2(J_{12})}{(J_{22}) - (J_{11})} \right), \tag{4}$$

the coherence χ, as measure for the isotropy of the pattern in the local neighborhood,

$$\chi = \frac{\sqrt{((J_{22}) - (J_{11}))^2 + 4(J_{12})^2}}{(J_{11}) + (J_{22})}, \tag{5}$$

and the energy E, as measure for significance,

$$E = trace(\mathbf{J}) = (J_{11}) + (J_{22}), \tag{6}$$

can be defined.

Orientation Estimation by the Gabor Wavelet Transform. In contrast to the structure tensor approach, the *Gabor wavelet transform* [14] as a linear filter, may be described by its complex-valued filter function $g(x, y) = w_r(x, y) \cdot s(x, y)$, being a 2D Gaussian kernel function $w_r(x, y)$ modulated by a complex exponential plane wave $s(x, y)$. The filter applied in different orientations θ gives highest response in the orientation best fitting to the inner structure of the image.

Monogenic Wavelet-based Orientation Estimation. As a third approach for the local orientation estimation of internal structures we tested a *monogenic wavelet-based* method for the structure tensor following an approach as described in [15]. In analogy to equation (2), by replacing the directional derivative with the directional Hilbert operator $\mathcal{H}_\theta$ and the gradient by the Riesz operator $\mathcal{R}$, as defined in [15,16], now the function

$$\theta(\mathbf{x}_0) = \arg \max_{\theta \in [-\pi, \pi]} \int_{\mathbb{R}^2} w(\mathbf{x} - \mathbf{x}_0) |\mathcal{H}_\theta f(\mathbf{x})|^2 d\mathbf{x} \tag{7}$$

is maximized over a local neighborhood specified by the weighting function $w(\mathbf{x}) = w(-\mathbf{x}) \geq 0$. The right-hand side of equation (7) can be rewritten in tensor form by

$$\int_{\mathbb{R}^2} w(\mathbf{x} - \mathbf{x}_0) |\mathcal{H}_\theta f(\mathbf{x})|^2 d\mathbf{x} = \begin{bmatrix} \cos\theta \; \sin\theta \end{bmatrix} \mathbf{J}(\mathbf{x}_0) \begin{bmatrix} \cos\theta \\ \sin\theta \end{bmatrix}, \tag{8}$$

where $\mathbf{J}(\mathbf{x}_0)$ now contains the directional Hilbert transforms (HT) of $f(\mathbf{x})$ as components similar to equation (3). Additionally, this optimization is performed on different scalings, given by Laplacian like spline wavelet basis. At scale i a wavelet-based structure tensor is expressed by

$$[\mathbf{J}_i(\mathbf{k})]_{mn} = \sum_{\mathbf{l} \in \mathbb{Z}^2} w[\mathbf{l} - \mathbf{k}] r_{m,i}[\mathbf{l}] r_{n,i}[\mathbf{l}], \tag{9}$$

with $m, n \in \{1, 2\}$, for a given weighting sequence $w[\mathbf{l}] \geq 0$. The term $r_{1,i}[\mathbf{l}]$ represents the real and $r_{2,i}[\mathbf{l}]$ the imaginary part of the complex-valued wavelet coefficients at scale i in a monogenic wavelet basis, obtained by applying the Riesz resp. directional HT on an isotropic wavelet basis, as suggested in [15].

3 Results

3.1 Image Enhancement

We have exemplified the described image analysis procedure on several fiber-reinforced polymer samples investigated by our CPM optical setup. The polymer matrix of these samples consisted of either epoxy resine, poly-propylene or poly-ethylene material, whereas the reinforcement mainly was given by glass-fibers, included in preferred directions or in a random manner within the polymer material. We show our results for one typical representative of these glass-fiber reinforced polymer samples, containing glass-fibers embedded in an epoxy resin with different orientation layers. The radial background illumination can clearly be recognized in Fig. 3 (a) and is emphasized in the corresponding binary version (b). As shown in Fig. 3 (c) and (d), the background is sufficiently removed by the morphological correction, whereas the correction given by equalization of brightness is depicted in Fig. 3 (e) and (f). For our purposes morphological background correction proves most suitable, as so-called ghost structures (multi-reflections) are better suppressed. The different denoising results are illustrated in Fig. 4. Whereas median filtering gives insufficient results, as visible in Fig. 4 (a) and (b), the curvelet-based denoising fits well for the fiber structures, as shown Fig. 4 (c) and (d). Here, the á trous wavelet-based method is combined with a corresponding masking and segmentation, as depicted in Fig. 4 (e) and (f).

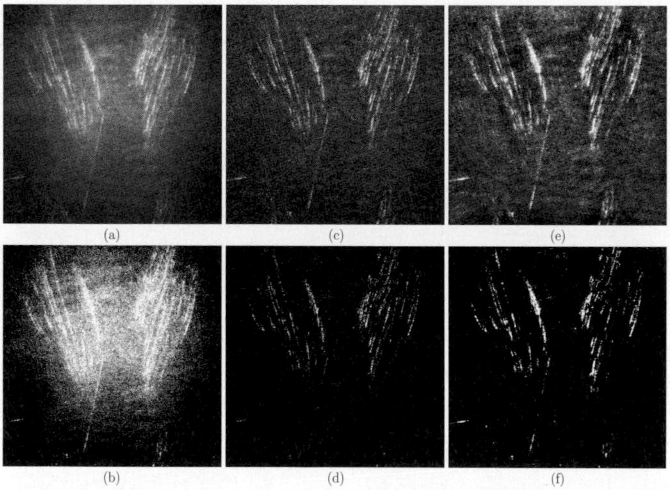

Fig. 3. Background correction exemplified on the fiber-reinforced polymer: (a) the demodulated amplitude image as used for analysis, applying in (c) the morphological correction method and (e) the monogenic wavelet-based equalization of brightness approach [12]. The corresponding binary versions are shown in (b), (d), and (f). As clearly recognizable, the originally radial illumination profile could be removed.

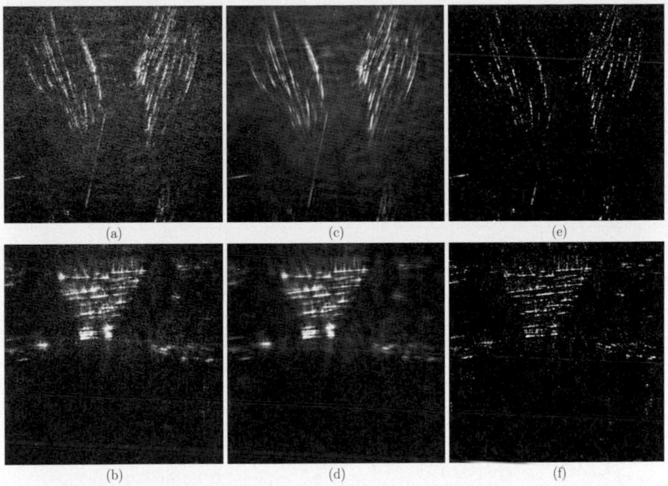

Fig. 4. Denoising illustrated for the CPM slices as depicted in Fig. 2 (b) and (c): applying (a) and (b) median filtering, (c) and (d) curvelet-based denoising, (e) and (f) á trous wavelet-based denoising method

3.2 Orientation Estimation

The local orientation values for fiber structures given by the different estimation methods are comparatively depicted in Fig. 5, where the original image is enhanced by the median denoising method and the rolling ball background correction. The conventional structure tensor-based orientation estimation (a) is clearly outperformed by both the Gabor wavelet (b) and the monogenic wavelet-based method (c). The latter has shown to be more robust to noisy structures due to its multi-scale character, partly allowing to skip an extensive denoising before. Also the entropy of the orienation in Fig. 5 (b) is smaller than the one of (a). Therefore, we have performed our cluster analysis, on features obtained by this monogenic wavelet-based estimation scheme.

Having evaluated the different pre-processing and orientation estimation methods on the investigated polymer samples and additionally validated by simulations we finally suggest the following processing scheme: A) Background estimation by the rolling ball algorithm, B) Denoising by the median filter (or can be ommitted), and C) Orientation estimation by the monogenic wavelet-based method.

3.3 Clustering

As final step towards an automatic classification k-means clustering has been performed. First, the clustering is applied on a data set of feature vectors, having the computed local orientation, coherency, and energy, defined in each pixel, as their entries. Here, the initial clustering is used for classifying the internal fiber

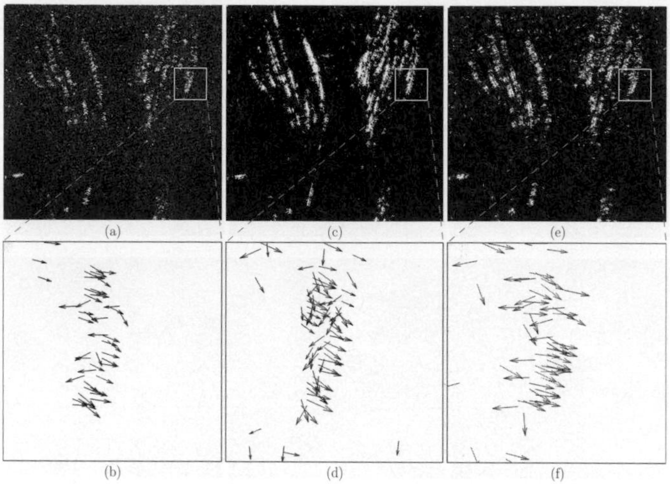

Fig. 5. Local orientation estimation for the enhanced internal fiber structures, performed in (a) and (b) with the conventional structure tensor approach, in (c) and (d) with a Gabor filter-based method, (e) and (f) with a modified structure tensor approach exploiting monogenic wavelets. The usual HSV representation (with hue: orientation, saturation: coherency, brightness: energy according to equations (4),(5) and (6)), is replaced here by a vector plot for a better visibility in gray-scale coding.

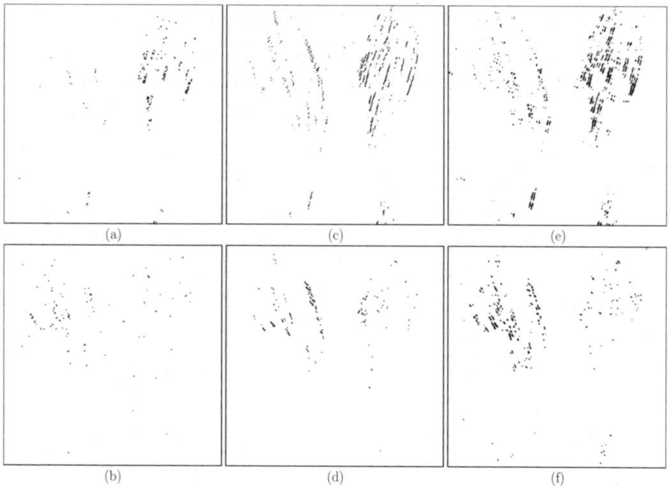

Fig. 6. Clustering of the internal fiber structures within a single slice (here into three classes: The black area in the images shows the pixels belonging to a class. The top images (a), (c) and (e) are showing the first class, the bottom images (b), (d) and (f) are showing the second class. The third class are the remaining pixel points, the background. The k-means clustering was applied on data (features concerned: local orientation, coherency, and energy) obtained by: (a) and (b) the (conventional) structure tensor-based estimation, (c) and (d) the Gabor wavelet-based method, (e) and (f) the monogenic wavelet-based method, [15].

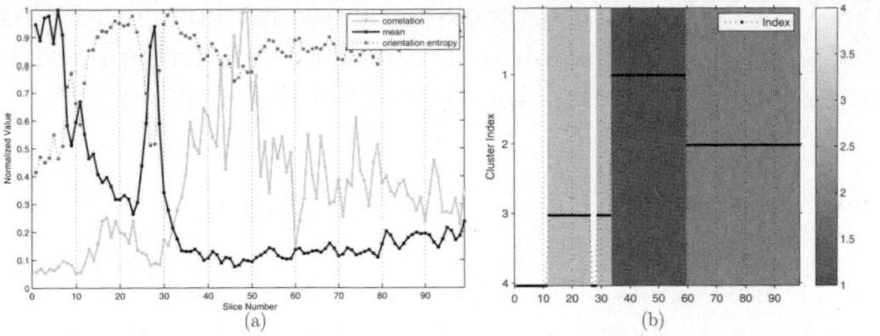

(a) (b)

Fig. 7. Clustering of slices within the whole CPM data stack: (a) representation of slice-related normalized features (cross-correlation (gray), mean intensity value (black), entropy of the orientation distribution (dotted)) over depth, (b) resulting clusters, where surface/outliers (white), diagonal (lightgray) and horizontal (darkgray) fiber slices, and fiber layer blendings (medium gray) are automatically discernible

structures within a single slice into three classes, as depicted in Fig. 6. The visibility of the results was improved by a median filter and an morphologic open operation.

Additionally, a second clustering is realized over the whole CPM data stack for classifying all slices into four different categories: slices containing fiber layers of distinguished principal orientations, into surface region, and into erroneous 'ghost images'. In contrast to Fig. 6, which is a pixel based clustering, the clustering in Fig 7 is performed slicewise. The normalized cross-correlation between subsequent scans, the mean value, and entropy of the orientation distribution, defined for each slice, give the entries for the feature vector here. These features calculated for each slice, as depicted in Fig. 7 (a), were taken for the clustering. The resulting clusters, into which the subsequent slices may by grouped, are depicted in Fig. 7 (b). Clearly recognizable in the clustering are the distinguished fiber orientations layers (light and dark gray), the outliers and the surface (white both, as outliers are weak repetitions of the surface here), and the deeper bulk material, where no sufficient information can be gained (medium gray).

4 Conclusions

Summarizing we have shown a complete imaging and image analysis procedure suitable for the investigation of fiber-reinforced polymers. In conclusion, we have demonstrated the capability of our established CPM setup and the potential, which can be achieved in combination with image processing tools for a better visualization, analysis and classification of the internal fiber structures within technical materials, finally enabling an automatized evaluation of CPM image data.

Acknowledgments. The financial support by the Federal Ministry of Economy, Family and Youth and the National Foundation for Research, Technology and Development is gratefully acknowledged. Furthermore, we thank Katja Schladitz at the Fraunhofer Institute ITWM, Kaiserslautern for fruitful discussions and providing the MAVI 3D image processing software. For computing the monogenic orientation and equalization of brightness we have applied both wavelet toolboxes: MonogenicJ [15] and Monogenic Wavelet Toolbox [12].

References

1. Drexler, W., Fujimoto, J.G.: Optical coherence tomography. Springer, Berlin (2008)
2. Dubois, A., Vabre, L., Boccara, A., Beaurepaire, E.: High-resolution full-field optical coherence tomography with a Linnik microscope. Appl. Opt. 41, 805–812 (2002)
3. Stifter, D.: Beyond biomedicine: a review of alternative applications and developments for optical coherence tomography. Appl. Phys. 88, 337–357 (2007)
4. Latour, G., Echard, J.P., Soulier, B., Emond, I., Vaiedelich, S., Elias, M.: Structural and optical properties of wood and wood finishes studied using optical coherence tomography. Appl. Optics 48, 6485–6491 (2009)
5. Wiesauer, K., Pircher, M., Gotzinger, E., Hitzenberger, C.K., Engelke, R., Ahrens, G., Gruetzner, G., Stifter, D.: Transversal ultrahigh-resolution polarization-sensitive optical coherence tomography for strain mapping in materials. Optics Express 14, 5945–5953 (2006)
6. Schausberger, S.E., Heise, B., Maurer, C., Bernet, S., Ritsch-Marte, M., Stifter, D.: Flexible contrast for low-coherence interference microscopy by Fourier-plane filtering with a SLM. Opt. Lett. 35, 4154–4156 (2010)
7. Stifter, D., Leiss-Holzinger, E., Major, Z., Baumann, B., Pircher, M., Götzinger, E., Hitzenberger, C.K., Heise, B.: Dynamic optical studies in materials testing with spectral-domain polarization-sensitive OCT. Opt. Express 18, 25712–25725 (2010)
8. Gallagher, N.C., Wise, G.L.: Median filters: a tutorial. In: Proc. IEEE ISCAS, vol. 88, pp. 1737–1744 (1988)
9. Candes, E.J., Demanet, L., Donoho, D.L., Ying, L.: Fast Discrete Curvelet Transform (2005)
10. Shensa, M.J.: The discrete wavelet transform: Wedding the Á trous and Mallat algorithms. IEEE Trans. Signal Proc. 40, 2464–2482 (1992)
11. Sternberg, S.R.: Biomedical image processing. Computer 16, 22–34 (1983)
12. Held, S., Storath, M., Massopust, P., Forster, B.: Steerable wavelet frames based on the Riesz transform. IEEE Trans. Image Proc. 19, 653–667 (2010); Monogenic wavelet toolbox, `http://www.mamebia.de/Software`
13. Jähne, B.: Digital Image Processing. Springer, Heidelberg (2002)
14. Movellan, J.R.: Tutorial on Gabor Filters
15. Unser, M., Sage, D., Ville, D.V.D.: Multiresolution monogenic signal analysis using the Riesz-Laplace wavelet transform. IEEE Trans. Image Proc. 18, 2402–2418 (2009); MonogenicJ toolbox, `http://bigwww.epfl.ch/demo/monogenic/`
16. Felsberg, M., Sommer, G.: The monogenic signal. IEEE Trans. Image Proc. 49, 3136–3144 (2001)

Automatic Segmentation of Veterinary Infrared Images with the Active Shape Approach

Tom Wirthgen[1], Stephan Zipser[1], Ulrike Franze[2], Steffi Geidel[2], Franz Dietel[3], and Theophile Alary[4]

[1] Fraunhofer Institute for Transportation and Infrastructure Systems, Zeunerstr. 38, 01069 Dresden, Germany
{tom.wirthgen,stephan.zipser}@ivi.fraunhofer.de
www.ivi.fraunhofer.de

[2] HTW Dresden, Pillnitzer Platz 2, 01326 Dresden, Germany
franze@htw-dresden.de, geidel@pillnitz.htw-dresden.de
www.htw-dresden.de

[3] HTWK Leipzig, Postfach 30 11 66, 04251 Leipzig, Germany
dietel@ftz.htwk-leipzig.de
www.htwk-leipzig.de

[4] Universite de technologie de Troyes, France
theophile.alary@utt.fr
www.utt.fr

Abstract. Modern livestock farming follows a trend to higher automation and monitoring standards. Novel systems for a health monitoring of animals like dairy cows are under development. The application of infrared thermography (IRT) for medical diagnostics was suggested long ago, but the lack of suitable technical solutions still prevents an efficient use. Within the R&D project VIONA new solutions are developed to provide veterinary IRT based diagnostic procedures with precise absolute temperature values of the animal surface. Amongst others this requires a reliable object detection and segmentation of the IR images. Due to the significant shape variation of interest objects advanced segmentation methods are necessary. The "active shape" approach introduced by Cootes and Taylor [7] is applied to veterinary IR images for the first time. The special features of the thermal infrared spectrum require a comprehensive adaptation of this approach. The modified algorithm and first results of the successful application on approximately two million IR images of dairy cows are presented.

Keywords: active shape segmentation, infrared imaging, precise temperature measurements, veterinary diagnostics.

1 Motivation and State of the Art

The trend to higher automation and monitoring standards in modern livestock production as well as more restrictive legal requirements for animal welfare support the development of novel systems for an automatic health monitoring of

A. Heyden and F. Kahl (Eds.): SCIA 2011, LNCS 6688, pp. 435–446, 2011.

livestock [4]. For the health monitoring of animals, like the dairy cows discussed here, infrared thermography (IRT) can be used. The use of IRT for medical diagnostic has already been suggested in 1956 [13] by Lawson. But in spite of many investigations IRT is still rarely applied in veterinary.

Actually the value of veterinary IRT is discussed controversy. A short application orientated survey gives Knizkova [12]. In case of the IRT diagnostic of dairy cows Barth [1] concludes that IRT is not suitable for the early detection of subclinical udder infections. But Colak et al. [6] showed that all kinds of udder infections (clinical as well as subclinical) can be recognised with IRT. Similar results found Berry et al. [3]. In contrast to human medicine, were measurement and diagnostic standards where established in the last years [9,16], the present veterinary IRT still suffer from following disadvantages:

1. The lack of technical defined standards (required thermal resolution, maximal measurement uncertainty etc.) and procedural standards (camera pose, ambient conditions etc.) for the IRT measurement.
2. The elaborate determination of temperature values. The infrared (IR) image analysis is often performed on basis of a computer aided calculation of temperature values of regions of interest (ROI), e.g. the average temperature of udder quarters. Therefore first the two ROI left and right udder quarter must be localised and marked in the IR image. This take place by a fault-prone and time consuming manual segmentation. As a consequence only a few IR images per animals can be analysed.
3. The diagnosis, i.e. the veterinary interpretation of the temperature values, strongly depends on the individual experience and cognitive skills.

Therefore the interdisciplinary R&D project VIONA was established whereat scientific and industrial partners are developing and evaluating a novel system for an automatic infrared based health monitoring. The focus is on monitoring

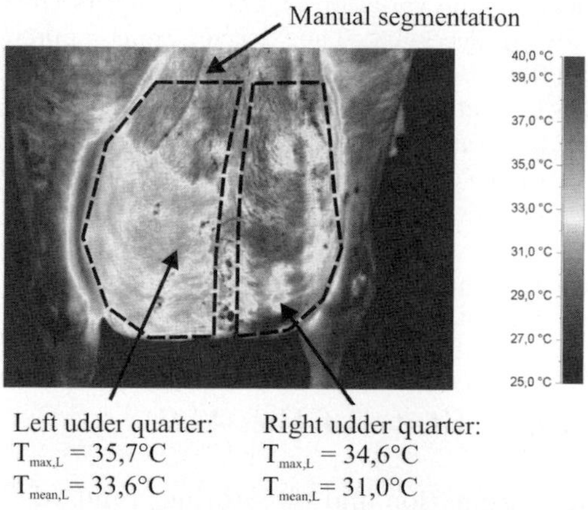

Fig. 1. Manual segmentation and feature extraction of an IR image of an udder

of dairy cows under typical farming conditions like moving animals as well as varying ambient conditions. The paper discusses the objective precise IRT based temperature measurement. The main focus is the automatic extraction of precise temperature values, the basis of the veterinary diagnostic algorithms, Fig. 1.

2 Image Acquisition and IR Temperature Calculation

Within the VIONA project many IRT measurements are realised with the configuration shown in Fig. 2. Two IR cameras[1] are used in combination with a reference body of known temperature and emissivity. This generates referenciated IR images sequences from dairy cows on a milking carousel. The ambient conditions are recorded and an identification refers the IR images to the individual animal. In the following the images from the rear IR camera are considered.

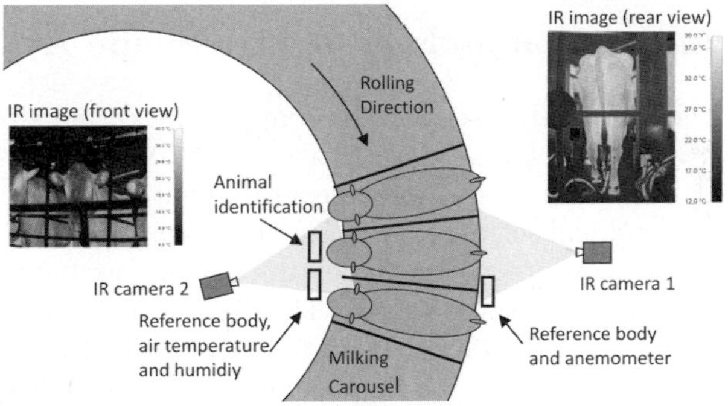

Fig. 2. IRT measurement of dairy cows on a milking carousel

Veterinary diagnostics require a "precise" temperature determination. Relevant are temperature differences of about 0.3 K, [15]. From the measurement point of view this implies first that the IRT measurement has to provide IR images with a low temperature uncertainty. Second an accurate image segmentation is necessary to calculate the diagnostic temperature values based on the "correct" ROI. Obviously both process steps influence the resulting temperature "precision".

State of the art IR cameras provide a temperature resolution of about 0.1 K. A common mistake is the assumption that this high resolution is also valid for comparative analysis between different IR images, e.g. time series of images. The measuring uncertainty is ignored in nearly all veterinaty studies. An analysis of temperature measurement uncertainty according to the procedure defined by the industry measurement standard DIN1319 [14] shows, that primary due to sensor drift the resulting temperature uncertainty lies at about ±2.2K even if the

[1] DIAS Infrared: PYROVIEW 640L, 640×480 pixels, spectral range 8-14 μm, measurement uncertainty $\pm 2.0\ K$, temperature resolution $< 0.1K$.

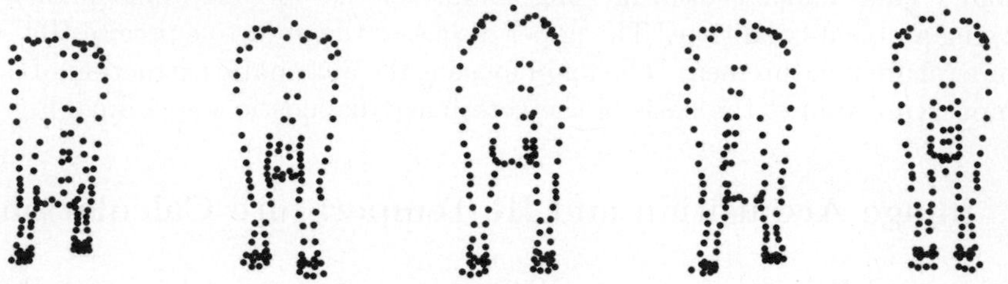

Fig. 3. Exemplary landmarks of "training shapes" for the dairy cow shape model

conventional radiant temperature correction [2] is performed. With the help of a model based temperature correction in combination with a reference bodies of exactly known emission properties leads to a temperature uncertainty of about $\pm 0.4\,\mathrm{K}$, [18].

3 IRT Segmentation and the Active Shape Approach

To investigate the potential of segmentation approaches fixed shape model approaches were evaluated in former investigations [17]. Within this investigation a set of models could be found that provide a satisfying segmentation compared to the results of an manual segmentation. The used image resolution of 320×240 pixels shows some disadvantages for the feature extraction due to the fact that some anatomic structures are very small. Therefore a high resolution IR camera of 640×480 pixels (DIAS Infrared: PYROVIEW 640L) is used for further investigations. As a consequence the shape and pattern are depicted much more detailed. This variety could not be governed by a fixed model approach.

Based on the surveys of model based matching algorithms [5,11] a promising approach was chosen – the Active-Shape-Models (ASM), introduced by Cootes and Taylor[8]. This approach involves three separated parts that can be optimized individually:

1. The shape representation as a parametric statistical model.
2. The statistical grey value model for the landmarks[2].
3. The search algorithm using both models.

The shape is represented by a vector $\boldsymbol{x} = (x_1, y_1, \ldots, x_m, y_m)^T$ including the m landmarks of the shape (Fig. 3). Based on a manually labelled set of "training shapes" the shape model is statistically derived. The parametric model consisting of the mean shape $\bar{\boldsymbol{x}}$ and a deviation term:

$$\boldsymbol{x} = \bar{\boldsymbol{x}} + P\boldsymbol{b}. \tag{1}$$

The dimension of the deviation term is reduced by a principle component analysis (PCA) and leads to the compact deviation term P. The limitation of the

[2] Landmarks are characteristic points of the object, in most cases they are equally spaced along borders and at junctions.

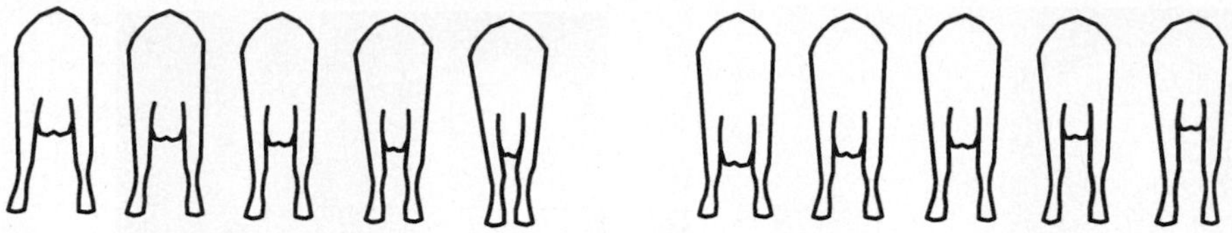

Fig. 4. Visualisation of the modelled shape variation $\boldsymbol{x}(\boldsymbol{b})$
left: parameter $b_1 = \{-2; -1; 0; 1; 2\}$ – right: parameter $b_2 = \{-2; -1; 0; 1; 2\}$

parameters $\boldsymbol{b}$ ensure that the model represents valid shapes and allows the coverage of shapes not included in the training set. Fig. 4 shows exemplary the shape variation due to the first two components (modes) of the model parameter vector $\boldsymbol{b}$. The parameters in general effect the whole shape, but some mainly effect specific characteristic, e.g. the second parameter b_2 mainly influence the height of the udder.

The grey value model describes the appearance of each landmark (LM). The model uses a normalised grey value profile $\boldsymbol{g_n}$ in a line-shaped surrounding j of a LM, giving the grey value vector $\boldsymbol{g}$ for each landmark:

$$\boldsymbol{g_n} = \frac{1}{\sum_{(j)} g_j} \boldsymbol{g} . \tag{2}$$

Using this normalized grey value profile for each image in the training set the mean profile $\bar{\boldsymbol{g}}_n$ and the covariance matrix C_g are generated for each LM.

Finally both models are joined by a search algorithm performing an iterative fitting process repeating the following steps:

1. Projecting the shape in the image.
2. Search best fitting landmarks in the shape points environment, by minimising the weighted distance between the model $\bar{\boldsymbol{g}}_n$ and the image grey $\boldsymbol{g}_{n,i}$

$$D^2 = \left(\boldsymbol{g}_{n,i} - \bar{\boldsymbol{g}}_n\right)^T C_g \left(\boldsymbol{g}_{n,i} - \bar{\boldsymbol{g}}_n\right) . \tag{3}$$

3. Calculate the shape parameters using the fitted landmarks.
4. Normalisation of the shape by parameter limitation.

The use of ASM approach according to the configuration of [7] optimised for image of visible spectal range leads to a poor segmentation quality in case of veterinary IR images. An analysis shows following reasons:

- The image contrast is dominated by the ambient temperature, see Fig. 5. This makes normalised derivative landmarks inadequate.
- Parts of the shape model have great variance in shape or align and lead to undesirable feedback to other body parts in the model.
- Textured objects show unspecific grey value profiles due to the influence of view angle, environmental conditions, coat structure or dirt, see Fig. 5.

To achieve improved segmentation results the known ASM approach was adapted to the specific features of images from the thermal infrared spectrum.

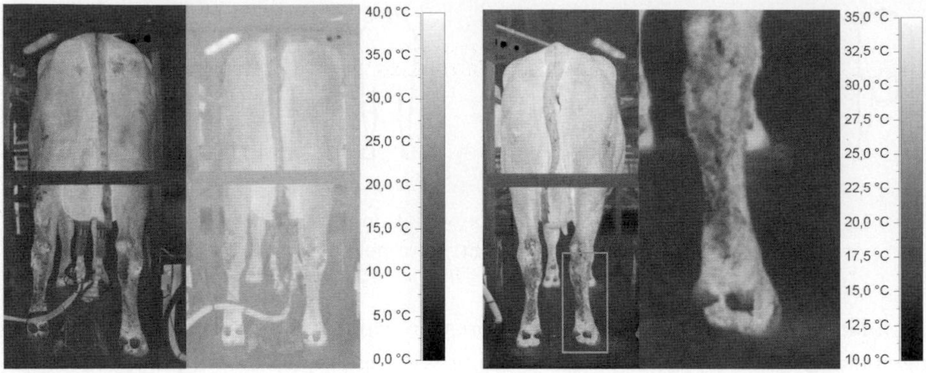

Fig. 5. Properties of IR images– *left:* influence of the ambient temperature (left: 9 °C, right: 27 °C) to IR image contrast – *right:* texture disturbance due to coat

4 Choice of Segmentation Criterion

For the evaluation of the segmentation algorithm an objective criterion is necessary. The common mean point displacement [8] (for the m landmarks of the fitted shapes $\boldsymbol{x}_f$ against the training shapes $\boldsymbol{x}_t$ over n images):

$$\delta = \frac{1}{mn} \sum_{i=1}^{n} \sqrt{\left(\boldsymbol{x}_{f,i} - \boldsymbol{x}_{t,i}\right)^T \left(\boldsymbol{x}_{f,i} - \boldsymbol{x}_{t,i}\right)} \tag{4}$$

is not suitable as segmentation quality criterion. A point displacement is not always leads to a change in segmentation (see Fig. 6). Therefore a different criterion describing the enclosed area calculated with the segmentation area of the training set a_t and the fitted model a_f is suggested:

$$A = \frac{\bigcap (a_f, a_t)}{\bigcup (a_f, a_t)}. \tag{5}$$

This criterion is sensitive to segmentation differences and insensitive to point displacements along the segmentation borders, Fig. 6.

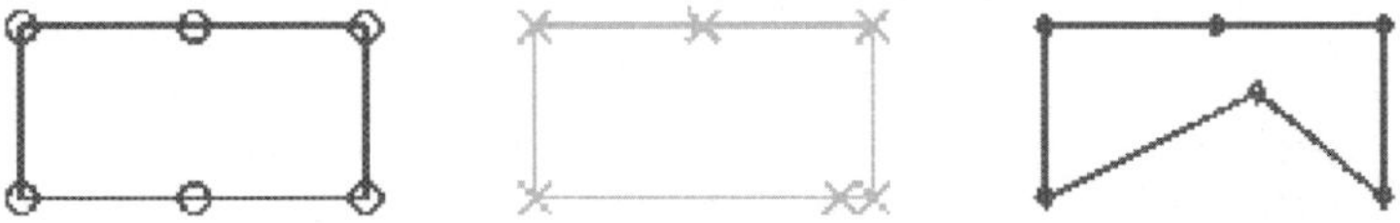

Fig. 6. Evaluation of the Segmentation: training shape (left), "correct" segmentation (mid, criterion $A = 1,0$), and "incorrect" segmentation (right, criterion $A = 0,69$)

For applications the finding rate R_α

$$R_\alpha = \frac{1}{n} \sum S(A, \alpha) \quad \text{where } S(A, \alpha) = \begin{cases} 1, & A > \alpha \\ 0, & \text{otherwise} \end{cases} \tag{6}$$

is calculated. The finding rate R_α describes, how many "correct" segmentations were found for a set of n test images.

5 Specific Modifications of the ASM Segmentation

Following steps of the ASM approach were modified for IR image segmentation:

1. Image preprocessing,
2. Landmark representation,
3. Landmark selection for shape creation and initialisation.

5.1 Image Preprocessing

The first modification addresses the disturbing effect of the ambient temperature on the image contrast. To "normalise" the IR images following preprocessing approaches were evaluated:

- Scaling to ambient temperature based interval (SAT),
- SAT and edge filter (Canny, Sobel, gradient),
- SAT and smoothing filter (mean, gauss and median), and
- Local histogram equalisation (LHE) [10].

Where the first three options gives negligible improvements the LHE shows good results, Fig. 7. The ambient temperature influence is reduced significantly and the landmark representations are much more stable. Even if the influence is not fully compensated, the grey value normalization Equ. (2) becomes obsolete.

5.2 Landmark Representation

As mentioned above, especially for body parts with coat the images show unspecific grey value profiles for the landmarks, see Fig. 5. The disturbing effect can be reduced by applying e.g. median filters. More efficient is the use of two dimensional temperature patterns instead of the conventional profile lines for landmark description.Investigation showed that 2D patterns have a generalising effect over textured landmark surroundings.

5.3 Shape Creation and Initialisation

During the investigation of the ASM approach it was noticed that certain body parts (e.g. the legs and the tail) show a significant different scale of variation. This is critical for the creation of proper shape models because within the model

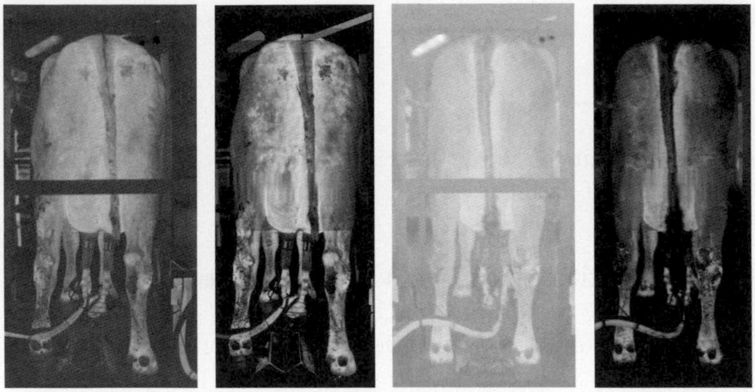

Orig. image A Prefilt. image A Orig. image B Prefilt. image B

Fig. 7. Preprocessing for IR images of different ambient temperatures; *Remark: the horizontal bar is removed by interpolation; image A: 9° C, image B: 27° C*

reduction step, the PCA "prefers" great form variations. This implies unintended couplings and the rejection of small varying body parts.

A possibility to handle this is the use of non equidistant aligned landmarks to equal the body parts weight in the model. In combination with the exclusion of body parts with high variance (e.g. the tail, which appears to be of no diagnostic interest) this algorithm shows good segmentation results.

The shape initialisation has a great impact on convergence and segmentation quality due to the fact that the ASM is a local search algorithm. For this reason an adapted pre-fitting for the shape was developed. Table 1 shows that the segmentation with the adapted initialisation is better than a segmentation using more pyramidal levels (which is equivalent to a great search space) and leads with $A > 0.7$ for the claw and $A > 0.8$ for the udder to a high segmentation quality.

All these modifications make a parameter set optimisation for the ASM search algorithm necessary. Therefore parameters as the size and alignment of the search area profile, the size of the grey value model pattern and the method of shape model parameter limitation were examined and adopted. The results of this optimisation are not discussed in detail, but the landmark pattern size optimisation will be exemplified. The criteria introduced above are calculated for different

Table 1. Influence of the initialisation and different number of pyramid levels, basis is a test set of 101 images and a shape model of 68 landmarks

Adapted Initialisation	Pyramidal Levels	Segmentation Criterion		
		A "Udder"	A "Right claw"	A "Left claw"
no	$[\frac{1}{2}; 1]$	0.68	0.41	0.37
no	$[\frac{1}{4}; \frac{1}{2}; 1]$	0.74	0.71	0.58
yes	$[\frac{1}{2}; 1]$	0.84	0.76	0.71

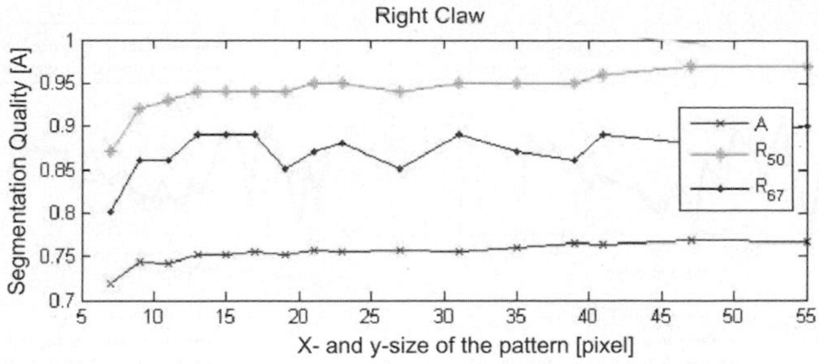

Fig. 8. Influence of landmark pattern size on segmentation quality

pattern sizes and test regions. Fig. 8 shows the results for the ROI "right claw". Summarised larger patterns show better segmentation quality, but require higher computational power.

6 Application Results

The ASM was successfully applied for the segmentation of more than two million IR images. The shape model was used as a framework to define veterinary ROI for objects like the right and the left quarter of the udder automatically. Based on the determined ROI for every IR image about 30 IR features, especially temperature values, were calculated for the development of the veterinary diagnostic approaches.

Table 2. Correlation coefficients between the IR features calculated from manually and automatically generated ROI

IR feature	claw ROI variant 1	claw ROI variant 2	claw ROI variant 3	udder	rear section
T_{mean}	0.84	0.82	0.85	0.66	0.93
T_{max}	0.89	0.88	0.88	0.76	0.85
			...		

For the evaluation of the automatic image analyse a manually labelled test set of about 11000 images each with 7 ROI was created. The automatically created IR features show a high correlation to those calculated from manually segmented images (Tab. 2). Fig. 9 confirms this showing four time series of a cow over 34 days. The IR features T_{mean} as well as the T_{max} are nearly equal for manually and automatically generated ROI.

For the modified ASM approach in most cases a fast convergence is observed, typical are less then 15 iterations. The Fig.10 depicts the first four steps of a fitting process. The sidewards shift in an image sequence due to the milking

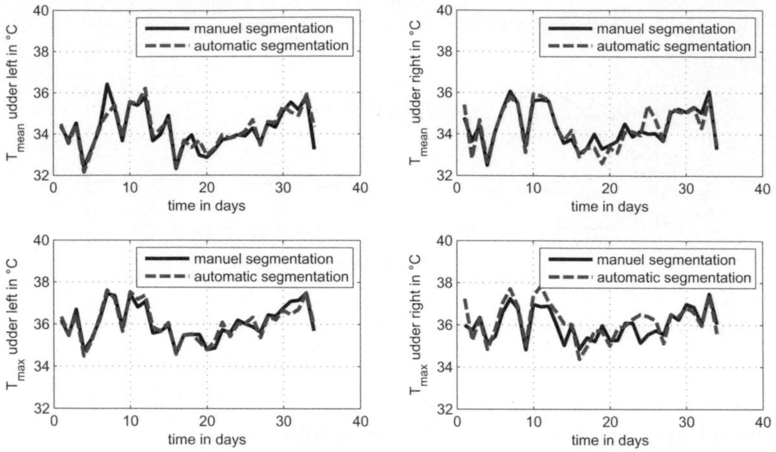

Fig. 9. IR feature T_{mean} and T_{max} time series for the ROI "udder left" and "udder right" of one cow (comparison of manually and automatically created ROI)

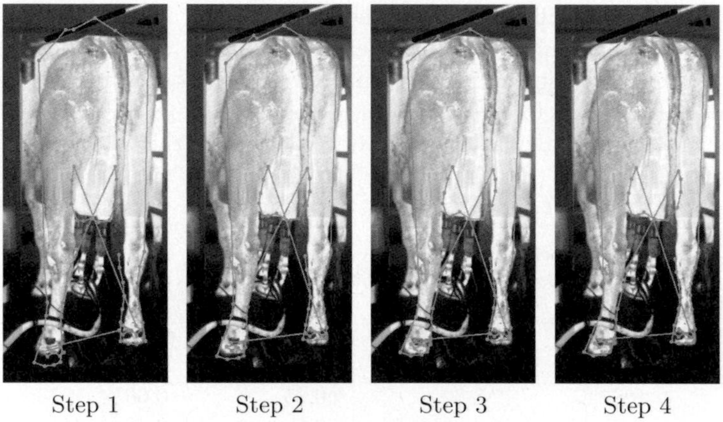

Fig. 10. Fitting progress for an IR image

carousel movement refits the algorithm quickly. The main drawbacks for the veterinary IRT application have been solved by an adoption of the ASM algorithm.

The modification of the ASM approach for veterinary IR images could be summarised as follows:

- The specific features of IR images require an adapted preprocessing, best results were found for a combination of normalisation on ambient temperature (SAT) and local histogram equalisation (LHE).
- For the landmark model "large" 2D-patterns are suggested, which are much more robust than line profiles.

– The suggested segmentation criterion is appropriate for numerical evaluation and also conform to a manual review.

The finding rate R_α could be increased from up to 60% for the fix model approach to more than 80% for the ASM segmentation. The image processing is implemented in the HALCON software and runs on standard computer hardware. The current processing capacity is approximately three images per second.

7 Conclusions and Future Work

The evaluation of the potential of veterinary IRT requires a precise IR temperature features based on a reliable automatic image segmentation. Due to the significant varying object shapes an advanced ASM approach was chosen and adapted to the specific properties of thermal IR images.

The approach was successfully tested on two million IR images. Further investigations face the development of a benchmark for the segmentation and runtime optimisation as well as an adaption to more distinct animal movements, maybe even "walking" animals. Moreover suitable segmentations criteria without a ground truth to detect incorrect segmentations (Fig. 11) has to be developed.

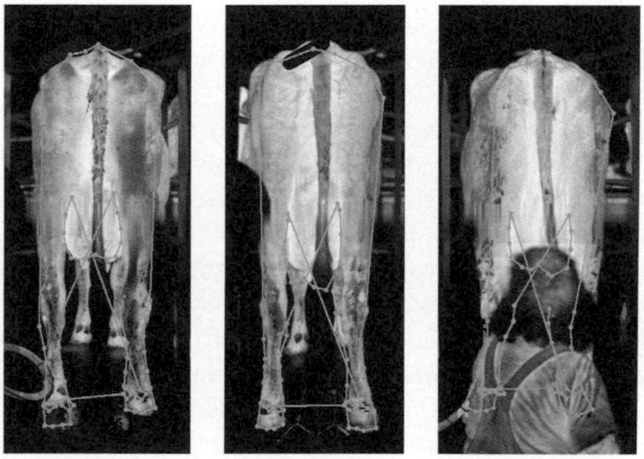

Missed left claw Missed udder Occluding person

Fig. 11. Examples for missed shape model fits

Acknowledgement

This investigations are done within the scope of the interdisciplinary VIONA project (www.viona-system.net) financed by the German Federal Ministry of Education and Research (BMBF, ID 03WKP04B). The authors are grateful to the industry partners of the project DIAS Infrared, Ralle Landmaschinen, and Yoo as well as the hosting farm Methauer Agro AG.

References

1. Barth, K.: Basic investigations to evaluate a highly sensitive infraredthermograph-technique to detect udder inflammation in cows. Milchwissenschaft 55(4), 607–609 (2000)
2. Bernhard, F.: Technische Temperaturmessung. In: VDI-Buch. Springer, Berlin (2004)
3. Berry, R., Kennedy, A., et al.: Daily variation in the udder surface temperature of dairy cows measured by infrared thermography: Potential for mastitis detection. Can. Journal of Animal Science 83(4), 687–693 (2003)
4. Büscher, W.: Current developments in livestock farming technology. Yearbook Agricultural Engineering 2011 23, 7–15 (2011)
5. Cheung, K.W., Yeung, D.Y., Chin, R.T.: On deformable models for visual pattern recognition. Pattern Rec. 35(7), 1507–1526 (2002)
6. Colak, A., Polat, B., et al.: Short Communication: Early Detection of Mastitis Using Infrared Thermography in Dairy Cows. J. Dairy Sci. 91(4), 4244–4248 (2008)
7. Cootes, T.: Model-Based Methods in Analysis of Biomedical Images. In: Image Processing and Analysis, pp. 223–248. Oxford University Press, Oxford (2000)
8. Cootes, T., Taylor, C.: Active shape model search using local grey-level models: A quantitative evaluation. In: Illingworth, J. (ed.) British Machine Vision Conference, pp. 639–648. BMVA Press (1993)
9. Diakides, N., Bronzino, J.: Medical infrared imaging. CRC Press, Boca Raton (2008)
10. Jähne, B.: Digital Image Processing. Springer, Weinheim (1997)
11. Jain, A.K., Zhong, Y., Dubuisson-Jolly, M.P.: Deformable template models: A review. Signal Processing 71(2), 109–129 (1998)
12. Knizkova, I., Kung, P.: Applications of infrared thermography in animal production. J. of Agric. Faculty of Ondokuz Mayis University 22(3), 329–336 (2007)
13. Lawson, R.: Implications of surface temperatures in the diagnosis of breast cancer. Canadian Medical Association Journal 75(4), 309 (1956)
14. Fundamentals of metrology: evaluation of measurements; uncertainty of measurement. DIN1319-4. Beuth Verlag, berlin (February 1999)
15. Clinical thermometers - part 5: Performance of infra-red ear thermometers (with maximum device). DIN EN 12470-5. Beuth Verlag, berlin (September 2003)
16. Ring, E.F.J., McEvoy, H., et al.: New standards for devices used for the measurement of human body temperature. J. Med. Eng. Technol. 34(4), 249–253 (2010)
17. Wirthgen, T.: Entwicklung und Berechnung IR-basierter Kenngrößen zur Analyse des Gesundheitszustandes von Kühen. diplom thesis, TU Dresden (2007)
18. Wirthgen, T., Zipser, S., et al.: Precise ir-based temperature measuring - a case study for the automatic health monitoring of dairy cows. In: SENSOR+TEST Conference - IRS^2, (2011) (accepted paper)

Using the Skeleton for 3D Object Decomposition

Luca Serino, Gabriella Sanniti di Baja, and Carlo Arcelli

Istituto di Cibernetica "E.Caianiello", CNR
Pozzuoli, Naples, Italy
{l.serino,g.sannitidibaja,c.arcelli}@cib.na.cnr.it

Abstract. An object decomposition method is presented, which is guided by a suitable partition of the skeleton. The method is easy to implement, has a limited computational cost and produces results in agreement with human intuition.

1 Introduction

Object decomposition is of interest in the framework of the structural approach to description and recognition to reduce the complexity of the task. In fact, as discussed in [1-4], the human visual system may represent objects with complex shape in terms of simpler parts, by decomposing the objects into parts and by organizing object representation in terms of the parts and of their spatial relationships. The main advantage of such a structured representation is a greater robustness under changes in viewing conditions.

Since the appearance of the above papers, several methods have been proposed for object decomposition. For example, decomposition has been guided by skeleton partition [5-8], distance information [9,10], diffusion distance [11], spectral clustering [12], modal analysis [13], and classification within triangle mesh object representation [14,15].

Decomposition guided by skeleton partition has been followed particularly for objects than can be perceived as articulated in parts with tubular shape, where a one-to-one correspondence exists between the individual curves composing the skeleton and the individual parts of the object. In this case, it is convenient to associate the points of the skeleton with their distance from the complement of the object. Then, the union of the balls centered on the points of a given curve of the skeleton and with radii equal to the associated distances identifies a perceptually significant object part. In turn, when the object also consists of parts that cannot be interpreted as 3D generalized cylinders or cones, individual skeleton curves do not necessarily correspond to perceptually significant object parts. Thus, some clever grouping of skeleton curves is necessary to generate a skeleton partition where each partition component corresponds to a perceptually meaningful object part.

We also note that the partition of the skeleton into its constituting individual curves may result in a decomposition where the separation between adjacent parts does not occur in correspondence of significant curvature changes along the boundary of the object. This problem is due to the fact that the skeleton of an object that is not articulated into generalized cylinders or cones actually represents a rather sketched version of the object where large parts of the original object are not recovered by the union of

A. Heyden and F. Kahl (Eds.): SCIA 2011, LNCS 6688, pp. 447–456, 2011.

the balls associated with the skeleton points. As a consequence, in the obtained object decomposition the separation between adjacent parts is in correspondence with the curvature changes along the boundary of the sketched version of the object, rather than along the boundary of the original object.

In [8] we introduced a criterion to decompose a 3D object by suitably partitioning the skeleton. Here, we present an improved method whose strategy is as follows. A partition of the skeleton in three different kinds of subsets is performed by taking into account the notion of *zone of influence*. Then, the components of the partition are used to build object's parts. Since pairs of adjacent parts may be separated by non-planar surfaces, a concavity filling procedure is employed to redistribute voxels in each pair of adjacent parts in such a way to obtain an almost planar separation. Finally, a merging process is accomplished to obtain a decomposition of the object into a smaller number of perceptually significant parts.

The main differences with respect to the work in [8] regard: i) the way in which the partition of the skeleton is performed (two kinds of skeleton partition components were considered before), ii) the introduction of suitable criteria to manage cases in which an individual part may result as split into sub-parts, and iii) the suggestion of a more powerful merging strategy to reduce the number of parts to the most significant ones.

2 Preliminaries

We refer to solid objects, i.e., rid of cavities, in binary voxel images in cubic grids. The object is the set of 1's and the background is the set of 0's. We use the 26-connectedness for the object and the 6-connectedness for the background.

For an object voxel p, the 3×3×3 neighborhood N(p) includes the six face-, the twelve edge- and the eight vertex-neighbors of p.

Given two voxels p and q, their distance is measured as the length of a minimal discrete path linking p to q. We use the weights w_f=3, w_e=4 and w_v=5, as suggested in [16], to measure moves from a voxel towards its face-, edge- and vertex-neighbors along the path, respectively. This choice of weights is motivated by the fact that the <3,4,5> weighted distance provides a reasonable approximation to the Euclidean distance.

The skeleton is a subset of the object consisting of curves symmetrically placed within the object, with the same topology of the object, and such that each point of the skeleton is associated with the value of its distance from the background, i.e., the radius of a ball that, centered on the point, is tangent to the object's boundary and is included in the object. Skeletonization has been influenced by the notion of medial axis transform introduced by Blum [17], and a number of papers dealing with the computation of the skeleton can be found in the literature (e.g., see [18] and the references quoted therein). In this work, we use the skeletonization algorithm suggested in [19] to guide object's decomposition. Skeletonization aims at the inclusion in the skeleton of the centers of maximal balls of the object, i.e., the voxels whose associated balls are included in the object but are not completely included by any other single ball in the object. In fact, inclusion of all centers of maximal balls, CMB, guarantees that the object can be fully recovered by applying to the skeleton the reverse distance transformation [16]. However, for 3D objects the CMB generally concentrate along symmetry planes and axes, so that not all CMB of the object can be kept as skeleton points.

The ball associated to a distance labeled voxel p is obtained by applying to p the reverse distance transformation. Balls associated to a set of possibly sparse voxels may overlap and merge into connected components. Each group of balls forming a connected component is called zone of influence of the set of distance labeled voxels it includes. Distance labeled voxels that are neighbors of each other or are closer to each other than the sum of the corresponding radii are included in the same zone of influence.

A voxel p of the skeleton is an end point when it has only one neighboring skeleton voxel in N(p).

A voxel p of the skeleton is a branch point when it has more than two neighboring skeleton voxels in N(p). The zones of influence obtained by applying the reverse distance transformation to the branch points will be used in this paper.

Concavity filling is a process that identifies voxels of the background placed in local concavities of the object and adds them to the object. Concavity filling can be iterated as far as local concavities are detected. The concavity filling algorithm used in this paper is based on the use of 3×3×3 operations [20].

3 Object Decomposition

Our method provides a one-to-one correspondence between skeleton subsets and object parts. It includes the following tasks: i) skeleton partition into three types of subsets, called *simple curves*, *complex sets*, and *single points*; ii) recovery of object parts associated to simple curves, single points and complex sets, respectively called *simple regions*, *bumps and kernels*, where the latter regions constitute a sort of main bodies of the object, from which simple regions and bumps protrude; iii) making planar the separating surface between adjacent recovered parts; iv) managing the case of parts resulting erroneously split into sub-parts; and v) expanding simple regions, bumps and kernels.

To describe our procedure, let us consider the example shown in Fig.1.

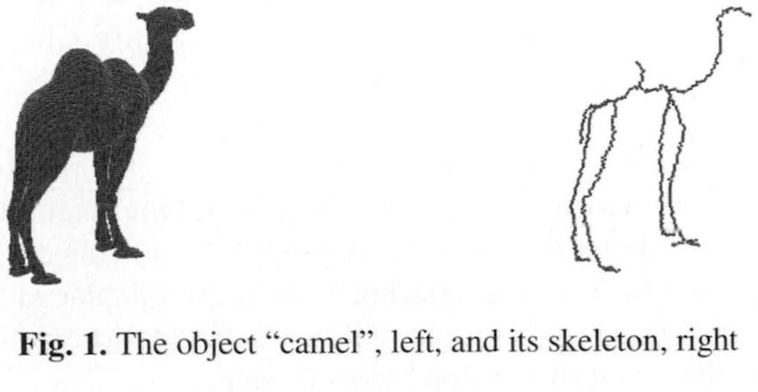

Fig. 1. The object "camel", left, and its skeleton, right

3.1 Skeleton Partition

We apply the reverse distance transformation to the branch points (see Fig. 2 left). Then, as said in the previous section, a number of connected components, i.e., the zones of influence of the branch points, is obtained which is smaller than or equal to the number of branch points. The zones of influence are used to partition the skeleton into simple curves, complex sets, and single points. A simple curve is a connected component of skeleton voxels that are not included in any zone of influence. As regards skeleton voxels included in zones of influence, we distinguish two cases. When end points are not included in a zone of influence, all skeleton voxels included therein constitute a complex set (see the paws "camel"). In turn, if end points are included in a zone of influence, the end points themselves constitute single point partition components, while the remaining skeleton voxels in the zone of influence constitute a complex set (see the body of "camel"). In Fig. 2 right, the three types of partition components are shown in different colors (green for simple curves, gray for complex sets, and red for single points).

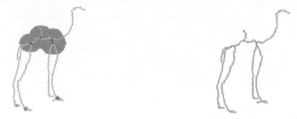

Fig. 2. The zones of influence, shown in gray, obtained by applying the reverse distance transformation to the branch points, left, and the three types of partition components, right

Each partition component is assigned an identity label that accounts for the component type and distinguishes the components of the same type.

3.2 Recovery of Simple Regions, Bumps and Kernels

The reverse distance transformation is applied to the individual partition components, and the identity label ascribed to the partition component is, in principle, assigned to the object voxels recovered by that component. Actually, individually recovered parts partially overlap, so that more than one identity label is possible for some recovered voxels. Thus, to have a decomposition into disjoint parts, we identify the connected components of recovered voxels with more than one identity label and ascribe to the voxels in each of these components the identity label pertaining to the kernel that overlaps the component itself.

Note that for a complex set with end points taken as single points, we do not apply the reverse distance transformation to voxels that, in the skeleton, linked the end points to the remaining skeleton voxels of the complex set. This choice avoids that the surfaces separating bumps from the adjacent kernels are misplaced with respect to the intuitively expected positions. This topic will be treated in more detail in Section 5.

Fig.3 left shows the result of the first recovery step.

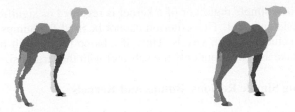

Fig. 3. Simple regions, bumps and kernels after the first recovery step, left. Decomposition of "camel" where each skeleton partition component is associated with an individual object part, right.

3.3 Improving the Separation between Parts

The surface separating a bump or a simple region from an adjacent kernel may be not planar. An example is shown in Fig. 4 left, where a simple region of "camel" (the head-neck region) is shown.

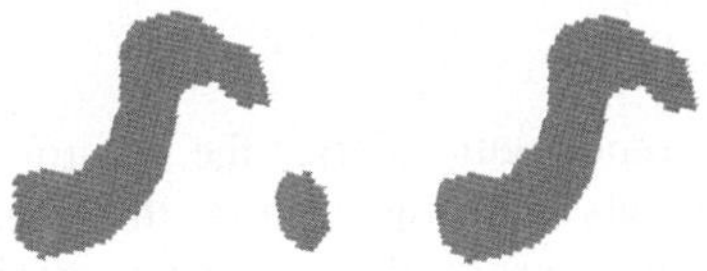

Fig. 4. A simple region before, left, and after, right, concavity filling. Voxels shown in the middle are the voxels removed from the adjacent kernel and added to the simple region to make planar the separating surface.

Concavity filling is employed to assign to a bump or to a simple region the voxels placed in local concavities of that region and belonging to an adjacent kernel. By iterating concavity filling as far as local concavities are detected, the surface separating the region from the adjacent kernel becomes almost planar. Since concavity filling uses 3×3×3 operations that are able to derive curvature information from a 5×5×5 neighborhood [20], the separating surfaces reasonably well approximate planar surfaces.

As an example of the effect of concavity filling see Fig. 4 right.

3.4 Removal of Sub-parts

We note that a part with a given identity label may result as divided into sub-parts, due to i) the criterion described in Section 3.2 to manage overlapping among regions, and ii) to the re-assignment of identity label during concavity filling. We want that only one connected part is associated a given identity label, so that a one-to-one correspondence exists between partition components and object parts. To this purpose, whenever sub-parts with the same identity label are detected, we discriminate them into significant sub-parts and non-significant sub-parts. Only significant sub-parts are preserved, while non-significant sub-parts are set to the background value zero.

A sub-part of a simple region or of a kernel is regarded as significant if it includes at least one skeleton voxel. This criterion cannot be used for bumps, since they definitely do not include skeleton voxels. Thus, if a bump results split into sub-parts, the criterion is to take as significant only the sub-part with the largest size.

3.5 Expanding Simple Regions, Bumps and Kernels

As already pointed out, the original object cannot be completely recovered starting from the skeleton, so that bumps, simple regions and kernels obtained so far are parts of a sketched version of the input object, rather than of the whole original object.

To decompose the input object, expansion of bumps, simple regions and kernels is performed over the voxels of the input object that were not recovered from the skeleton. Object voxels reached by the expansion process are assigned the identity label of the part they are closer to. Voxels at the same distance from more than one part are assigned the label of the part where they have the largest number of neighbors. The resulting decomposition for "camel" is shown in Fig. 3 right.

4 Merging

Though the obtained decomposition satisfies the one-to-one correspondence between skeleton partition components and object parts, the number of parts may be not in accordance with human intuition, so that merging criteria to reduce the number of parts to the perceptually most relevant ones should be devised.

Since we regard kernels as constituting the main bodies of the object, we aim at merging to kernels suitable bumps and simple regions protruding from them.

We distinguish simple regions into peripheral regions, i.e., adjacent to one kernel only, and non-peripheral regions, i.e., delimited by two kernels.

We first candidate to merging only non-peripheral simple regions. To decide whether any such a region should be merged into a unique object part together with the two delimiting kernels, we use the following visibility criterion.

For the current simple region we consider its surface, which consists of the voxels having a face-neighbor in either the background or any of the delimiting kernels. The total area of the surface is given by the number of faces of the surface voxels of the simple region that are 6-adjacent to the complement of the simple region. The surface is interpreted as consisting of two portions: a visible portion and a non-visible portion. The area of the visible portion, A_v, consists of the number of faces that are 6-adjacent to the background. The area of the non-visible portion, A_{nv}, is given by the number of faces 6-adjacent to the delimiting kernels.

If the ratio A_v/A_{nv} is smaller than an a priori fixed threshold θ, the simple region is regarded as scarcely visible and is merged with the adjacent kernels into a unique component. In this paper, θ has been set to 2 by considering a continuous cylinder with height *h*, for which it is $A_v/A_{nv}= 2\pi rh/2\pi r^2$, as scarcely visible if *h* is smaller than the diameter *2r*. To appreciate the effect of merging, see Fig. 5, where the object "horse", its skeleton, the decomposition before merging non-peripheral simple regions, and the result after merging are shown.

Fig. 5. From left to right, the object "horse", its skeleton, the obtained decomposition before merging non-peripheral simple regions, and the final result

For complex objects, a kernel may be adjacent to more than one non-peripheral simple region. If the visibility criterion is satisfied for all simple regions adjacent to such a kernel, an excessive merging may originate. To solve this problem, we use the following strategy. We associate a multiplicity degree *m* to each kernel, by counting the number of adjacent non-peripheral simple regions satisfying the visibility criterion. If a non-peripheral simple region S_j satisfying the visibility criterion is delimited by kernels having both m=1, the three regions are merged. The identity label of the kernel with the largest volume is ascribed to the obtained merged region.

If for S_j one delimiting kernel has m=1 while the second delimiting kernel has m>1, we first merge S_j with the delimiting kernel with m=1. S_j is ascribed the identity label of that kernel. Once merging involving all kernels with m=1 has been accomplished, kernels with m>1 are considered. If for the inspected kernel K_i the *m* adjacent regions that could undergo merging already carry an identity label typical of kernels, K_i is assigned to the adjacent region with which it shares the largest portion of its surface. As an example see Fig. 6, showing the object "cow", its skeleton, and the decomposition before and after merging. For "cow", one kernel with m=2 (shown in black in the decomposition before merging) and two kernels with m=1 (shown in red and pink in the decomposition before merging) exist. Both non-peripheral simple regions adjacent to the kernel with m=2 satisfy the visibility criterion and are accordingly merged with their second delimiting kernels with m=1. Then, the kernel with m=2 is merged as described above.

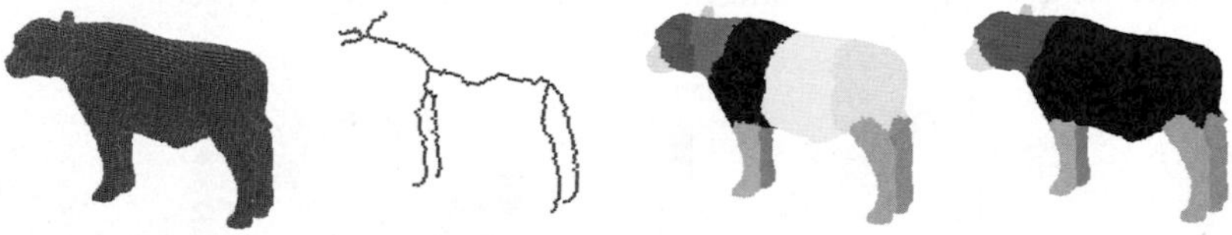

Fig. 6. From left to right, the object "cow", its skeleton, the decomposition before merging (where the kernel shown in black has m=2), and the result after merging

As concerns merging of peripheral regions, which can be bumps or simple regions, the visibility criterion is integrated by a further condition taking into account the volume of the object parts. Let S_j be a peripheral region satisfying the visibility criterion and let K_i be the adjacent kernel. Merging is accomplished if the ratio between the volume (measured as number of voxels) of the region union of S_j and K_i, and the volume of K_i is smaller than an a priori fixed threshold τ (set to 1.2 in this work). Using

Fig. 7. From left to right, the object "prism", its skeleton, the decomposition before merging peripheral regions, and the result after merging

the visibility criterion also when dealing with peripheral regions is done to avoid merging elongated and narrow regions that satisfy the condition on volume.

The result of merging peripheral regions is shown in Fig. 7 for the object "prism".

5 Discussion and Conclusion

We have tested our decomposition procedure on a number of 3D objects taken from publicly available databases [21,22]. A small set of test objects is shown in Fig. 8 together with the corresponding skeletons.

Fig. 8. Test objects and corresponding skeletons

The resulting decompositions before and after merging are shown in Fig.9. The same values for the thresholds θ and τ have been used for all test objects.

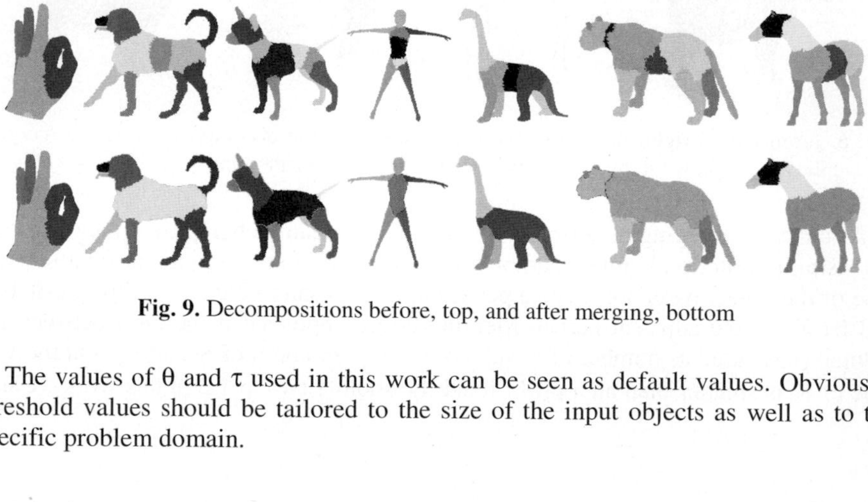

Fig. 9. Decompositions before, top, and after merging, bottom

The values of θ and τ used in this work can be seen as default values. Obviously, threshold values should be tailored to the size of the input objects as well as to the specific problem domain.

We note that if an object is provided in different poses or scales, whichever skeltonization algorithm is used, the skeleton is not guaranteed to have in all cases exactly the same number of branches. Thus, a slightly different partition and, hence, a slightly different decomposition is likely to be obtained. Moreover, we point out that the perceptual significance of the obtained decomposition parts strongly depends on the way skeleton partition has been carried on. In this respect, one could argue that a straightforward partition of the skeleton could be used, where only two types of components are taken into account, namely components consisting of branch points and components consisting of simple curves constituted by the remaining skeleton voxels. However, if this partition is used as input to the recovery process, a perceptual dominance of the regions recovered by the simple curves is obtained at the expenses of the regions reconstructed by the branch points. As a result, the surfaces separating adjacent parts do not cut the object in correspondence with the main concavities along the boundary of the object, but intrude significantly in the object. See Fig. 10 showing the two decompositions obtained for the object "hand", when starting from the above straightforward skeleton partition and from our partition.

Fig. 10. From left to right, the object "hand", its skeleton, the decomposition obtained by a straightforward skeleton partition, and the decomposition originated by our skeleton partition

The introduction of the notion of complex sets in the skeleton partition plays a crucial role in obtaining a perceptually significant decomposition. In fact, the kernels are not just coinciding with the union of the balls associated with the branch points, but are obtained by applying the reverse distance transformation to the skeletal voxels included in the zones of influence of the branch points. Thus, kernels are significantly larger than the union of the balls associated only to the branch points and, due to the criterion adopted to manage overlapping, the separations between kernels and the adjacent simple regions are not biased towards the innermost part of the object.

Another important feature of our partition scheme is the fact that some skeleton subsets belonging to a complex set do not participate in the recovery of the corresponding kernel. Each of these subsets is constituted by the voxels linking an end point, taken as single point in the partition, to a branch point. If the linking voxels participate to the recovery of the kernel, the bump generated by the corresponding single point would be a part characterized by a very small volume so that the perceptual relevance of the bump would not be enhanced. In turn, if the linking voxels are removed from the complex set, but are taken together with the end point to constitute a peripheral simple curve, the same problem illustrated in the example in Fig. 10 would occur. Thus, we keep the linking voxels in the complex set, but do not allow them to participate to the recovery process.

The method is easy to implement, has a limited computational cost and produces results in agreement with human intuition.

References

1. Palmer, S.E.: Hierarchical structure in perceptual representation. Cognitive Psychology 9, 441–474 (1977)
2. Marr, D., Nishihara, H.K.: Representation and recognition of three-dimensional shapes. Proc. Royal Society of London: Series B 200, 269–294 (1978)
3. Hoffman, D.D., Richards, W.A.: Parts of recognition. Cognition 18, 65–96 (1984)
4. Biederman, I.: Recognition-by-components: A theory of human image understanding. Psychological Review 94, 115–147 (1987)
5. Cornea, N.D., Silver, D., Yuan, X., Balasubramanian, R.: Computing hierarchical curve-skeletons of 3D objects. The Visual Computer 21(11), 945–955 (2005)
6. Lien, J.-M., Geyser, J., Amato, N.M.: Simultaneous shape decomposition and skeletonization. In: Proc. 2006 ACM Symposium on Solid and Physical Modeling, pp. 219–228 (2006)
7. Reniers, D., Telea, A.: Skeleton-based hierarchical shape segmentation. In: Proc. IEEE Int. Conf. on Shape Modeling and Applications, pp. 179–188 (2007)
8. Serino, L., Sanniti di Baja, G., Arcelli, C.: Object decomposition via curvilinear skeleton partition. In: Proc. ICPR 2010, pp. 4081–4084. IEEE, Los Alamitos (2010)
9. Svensson, S., Sanniti di Baja, G.: Using distance transforms to decompose 3D discrete objects. Image and Vision Computing 20, 529–540 (2002)
10. Zhang, X., Liu, J., Jaeger, M., Li, Z.: Volume decomposition for hierarchical skeletonization. Int. J. Virtual Reality 8(1), 89–97 (2009)
11. de Goes, F., Goldenstein, S., Velho, L.: A hierarchical segmentation of articulated bodies. Computer Graphics Forum 27(5), 1349–1356 (2008)
12. Liu, R., Zhang, H.: Segmentation of 3D meshes through spectral clustering. In: Proc. 12th Pacific Conf. on Computer Graphics and Applications, pp. 298–305 (2004)
13. Huang, Q.-X., Wicke, M., Adams, B., Guibas, L.: Shape decomposition using modal analysis. Computer Graphics Forum 28(2), 407–416 (2009)
14. Bischoff, S., Kobbelt, L.: Ellipsoid decomposition of 3D models. In: Proc. Int. Symp. 3D Data Processing Visualization and Transmission, pp. 480–488 (2002)
15. Mortara, M., Patanè, G., Spagnuolo, M., Falcidieno, B., Rossignac, J.: Plumber: a method for a multi-scale decomposition of 3D shapes into tubular primitives and bodies. In: Proc. 9th ACM Symp. on Solid Modeling and Applications, pp. 339–344 (2004)
16. Borgefors, G.: On digital distance transform in three dimensions. CVIU 64(3), 368–376 (1996)
17. Blum, H.: Biological shape and visual science. J. Theor. Biol. 38, 205–287 (1973)
18. Siddiqi, K., Pizer, S.M. (eds.): Medial Representations: Mathematics, Algorithms and Applications. Springer, Heidelberg (2008)
19. Arcelli, C., Sanniti di Baja, G., Serino, L.: Distance driven skeletonization in voxel images. IEEE Trans. PAMI, `http://doi.ieeecomputersociety.org/10.1109/TPAMI.2010.140`
20. Borgefors, G., Sanniti di Baja, G.: Analyzing non-convex 2D and 3D patterns. CVIU 63(1), 145–157 (1996)
21. AIM@SHAPE Shape Repository, `http://shapes.aimatshape.net/viewmodels.php`
22. Shilane, P., Min, P., Kazhdan, M., Funkhouser, T.: The Princeton Shape Benchmark. Shape Modeling International, Genova, Italy (June 2004)

A Three-Dimensional Shape Description Algorithm Based on Polar-Fourier Transform for 3D Model Retrieval

Dariusz Frejlichowski

West Pomeranian University of Technology, Szczecin,
Faculty of Computer Science and Information Technology,
Zolnierska 49, 71-210, Szczecin, Poland
dfrejlichowski@wi.zut.edu.pl

Abstract. In the paper a new 3D shape representation algorithm is proposed — the *Polar-Fourier 3D Shape Descriptor*. Similarly to the *Light Field Descriptor*, the proposed method is based on rendering several two-dimensional projections of a 3D model, taken from various points of view. However, the proposed descriptor uses the *2D Polar-Fourier transform* for obtained projections This enables the new descriptor to be more efficient in the recognition or retrieval of 3D models. In order to evaluate the performance of the algorithm, it was experimentally compared with four other popular approaches — the *Extended Gaussian Image*, *Shape Distributions*, *Shape Histogram* and *Light Field Descriptor* — in the problem of 3D shape retrieval. The achieved results have shown that the new method outperforms the other four explored ones. The presented 3D shape descriptor can be used in representation, recognition and retrieval of 3D models.

Keywords: 3D model retrieval, 3D shape description, Polar-Fourier transform.

1 Introduction

The problem of 3D model representation, recognition and retrieval is more popular nowadays than for example ten or twenty years ago. It is mainly caused by the recent development in computer hardware and software and possibility of efficient and fast computation of large multimedia data. Thanks to this many new applications of 3D models have appeared. One of them, especially arising lately, is the 3D model retrieval, which is a special case of Content-Based Information Retrieval problem of retrieving data from usually large multimedia collections. Nevertheless, from the historical point of view the first popular application of 3D models was the Computer Aided Design, CAD ([1]). However, some other exemplary applications can be easily found. For example, the entertainment application became more common lately ([2]) — in virtual reality, games, movies. Another example is the three-dimensional biometrics, mainly the 3D face recognition ([3]). Finally, the incorporation of a 3D shape description method in the

A. Heyden and F. Kahl (Eds.): SCIA 2011, LNCS 6688, pp. 457–466, 2011.

MPEG-7 standard for multimedia content description has to be mentioned ([4]). In spite of the increasing popularity of 3D model processing the number of algorithms developed for the representation of 3D shapes is still definitely smaller than for the planar (two-dimensional) ones. However, there have been several approaches developed and explored so far. They can be divided into four main groups: geometrical, structural, symmetrical and local. The approaches based on geometrical information about a model are the oldest and most widely used ones and hence may be easily enumerated. They include the *Extended Gaussian Image, EGI* ([5]), its modified version — *Complex Extended Gaussian Image, CEGI* ([6]), *3D moments* ([7]), *Shape Histograms* ([8]), *Shape Distributions* ([9]) and *spherical harmonics* ([10]). The *Multiresolutional Reeb Graph* ([11]) is an exemplary algorithm from the second group. The *Reflective Symmetry Descriptor* ([12]) belongs to the third one. Finally, the method based on *canonical geometric scale-space analysis* ([13]) is an example of the local approaches.

In the paper new algorithm is proposed. The general idea applied here is close to the approach used in the *Light Field Descriptor* ([14]). Namely, twenty two-dimensional projections for a 3D model are obtained, with cameras placed in the vertices of dodecahedron enclosing the object. However this is the only similarity, because for the achieved projected planar shape another approach for its description is used. This time the *2D Polar-Fourier transform* is applied, which is very efficient in the problem of planar shape recognition.

The proposed *Polar-Fourier 3D Shape Descriptor* was experimentally compared with results provided by four other 3D shape descriptors — the *Extended Gaussian Image* ([5]), *Shape Distributions* ([9]), *Shape Histograms* ([8]) and *Light Field Descriptor* ([14]). These algorithms selected for comparison were previously analysed in [15]. For the problem of 3D object retrieval the models taken from *The Princeton Shape Benchmark* database ([16]) were applied.

The remaining part of the paper is organized as follows. Section 2 presents the proposed *Polar-Fourier 3D Shape Descriptor*. Section 3 describes briefly approaches selected for the experimental comparison with the proposed algorithm. Section 4 provides a detailed description of the conditions and results of the performed experiments. Finally, the last section concludes the paper and provides some suggestions for further research directions.

2 Description of the Polar-Fourier 3D Shape Descriptor

As it has been stated in the introductory part of this paper, the motivation underlying the construction of a new 3D shape descriptor was the good result of the *Light Filed Descriptor* in the 3D model retrieval. The idea is based on the use of another planar shape descriptor for the projected 2D shapes. Hence, the beginning of the proposed algorithm is similar to the previous one.

The *Polar-Fourier 3D Shape Descriptor* starts with the calculation of the centroid L of a three-dimensional object:

$$L = (L_x, L_y, L_z) = (\frac{1}{n}\sum_{i=1}^{n} x_i, \frac{1}{n}\sum_{i=1}^{n} y_i, \frac{1}{n}\sum_{i=1}^{n} z_i), \tag{1}$$

where:
(x_i, y_i, z_i) — a vertex of an object,
n — number of vertices for particular 3D shape.

Later, all vertices are translated in order to move the centroid into the origin of the co-ordinate system. For a vertex P it can be formulated as follows:

$$P_i = (x_i, y_i, z_i) = (x_i - L_x, y_i - L_y, z_i - L_z), \tag{2}$$

where: $i = 1, 2, \ldots, n$.

The normalisation of co-ordinates according to the maximal distance from the centre of gravity is then performed. Thanks to this we can achieve the unitary maximal distance:

$$M = \max_i \{\|P_i - L\|\}, \tag{3}$$

where: $i = 1, 2, \ldots, n$.

And:

$$P_i = (\frac{x_i}{M}, \frac{y_i}{M}, \frac{z_i}{M}). \tag{4}$$

Later, the projections are obtained from 20 various angles. It results from the assumption that cameras are placed in the vertices of the dodecahedron enclosing the object. Each time the camera is directed into the origin of the co-ordinate system. The projections are stored in bitmaps. For each shape from them polar co-ordinates are calculated for a contour. Firstly, the centroid for the planar shape is derived (notice that the centroid L of the 3D shape is not equivalent to the centoid O, which is calculated for each planar shape separately):

$$O = (O_p, O_q) = (\frac{1}{s}\sum_{i=1}^{s} p_i, \frac{1}{s}\sum_{i=1}^{s} q_i). \tag{5}$$

where:
s — number of points in a contour of a planar shape,
p_i, q_i — Cartesian coordinates of the i-th point of the projected shape.

By means of the centre of an object O we can calculate the polar co-ordinates — Θ^i for angles and P^i for radii:

$$\rho_i = \sqrt{(p_i - O_p)^2 + (q_i - O_q)^2}, \tag{6}$$

$$\theta_i = atan(\frac{q_i - O_q}{p_i - O_p}). \tag{7}$$

The achieved points are put into the matrix, providing as a result a two-dimensional representation. This enables us to apply the *2D Fourier transform* to it. Usually for the shape representation, the absolute spectrum is used. Its values are derived by means of the following equation ([17]):

$$C(k,l) = \frac{1}{HW}\left|\sum_{h=1}^{H}\sum_{w=1}^{W} R(h,w)\cdot e^{(-i\frac{2\pi}{H}(k-1)(h-1))}\cdot e^{(-i\frac{2\pi}{W}(l-1)(w-1))}\right|, \quad (8)$$

where:
H, W — height and width of the image in pixels,
k — sampling rate in vertical direction ($k \geq 1$ and $k \leq H$),
l — sampling rate in horizontal direction ($l \geq 1$ and $l \leq W$),
$C(k,l)$ — value of the coefficient of discrete Fourier transform in the coefficient matrix in k row and l column,
$R(h,w)$ — value in the image plane with coordinates h, w.

From the obtained absolute spectrum square subpart with a side equal to 10 elements is selected and concatenated into the vector. It represents a planar projection of a 3D model. For matching any similarity or dissimilarity measure may be applied, e.g. the *Euclidean distance.*

3 Brief Description of the Algorithms Selected for the Comparison with the Proposed Method

As it has already been mentioned in the first section, the proposed algorithm for the 3D shape representation was compared with the results of four other algorithms — *Extended Gaussian Image* ([5]), *Shape Distributions* ([9]), *Shape Histograms* ([8]) and *Light Field Descriptor* ([14]), provided in [15]. In this section each of them is shortly described.

The *Extended Gaussian Image* (*EGI*, [5]) is one of the oldest and most popular techniques for the description of 3D models. In this approach the Gaussian image is obtained through the association of the point on the Gaussian sphere with each point on object's surface with the same surface orientation.

Each point belonging to a patch on the object (denoted as δJ) corresponds to a point on the Gaussian sphere (denoted as δS). The Gaussian curvature can be defined as being equal to the limit of the ratio of the two areas as they tend to zero ([5]):

$$K = \lim_{\delta J \to 0} \frac{\delta S}{\delta J} = \frac{\mathrm{d}S}{\mathrm{d}J}. \quad (9)$$

Assuming S — the area of the corresponding patch on the Gaussian sphere, having in mind the previous equation, one can derive the formula ([5]):

$$\iint_J K\mathrm{d}J = \iint_S \mathrm{d}S = S. \quad (10)$$

For J denoting the corresponding patch on the object the above formula can be rewritten as ([5]):

$$\iint_S \frac{1}{K}\mathrm{d}S = \iint_J \mathrm{d}J = J. \quad (11)$$

The inverse of the Gaussian curvature in the formulation of the EGI descriptor can be applied thanks to the above relationship ([5]). That gives the possibility of a mapping that associates the inverse of the Gaussian curvature for a point on the surface with a corresponding point on the Gaussian sphere. The *EGI* can be defined in the following way ([5]):

$$G(\zeta, \eta) = \frac{1}{K(\mu, \nu)}, \tag{12}$$

where point with the coordinates $(\zeta,\ \eta)$ lies on the Gaussian sphere and has the same normal as point with the coordinates $(\mu,\ \nu)$ on the original surface.

The *Shape Distribution* ([9]) was the second approach compared with the proposed algorithm. In this method a function representing a model is firstly selected. It may be of any type, however the authors have proposed a few ones: the angle between three random points on the object's surface (**A3**), the distance between a centroid and a random point on the surface (**D1**), the distance between a pair of random points (**D2**), the square root of the area of the triangle lying between three random points on the surface (**D3**), and the cube root of the volume of the tetrahedron between four random points on the surface (**D4**).

For a function N samples are evaluated and using them a histogram is constructed, containing the information on how many of the samples fall into B bins. From the histogram a piecewise linear function is derived, with V equally spaced vertices, $V \leq B$, e.g. $N = 1024^2$ samples, $B = 1024$, and $V = 64$ vertices ([9]).

All polygons of the 3D object are split into triangles in order to obtain the samples. For each triangle its area is calculated and stored along with the cumulative area of all previously considered triangles. Later, a triangle with a probability proportional to its area is selected. This task is performed through the generation of a random number between 0 and the total cumulative area and performing a binary search on the array of cumulative areas. For each of thus obtained triangles a point P on its surface is derived, applying two random numbers r_1 and r_2 ranged from 0 to 1 ([9]):

$$P = (1 - \sqrt{r_1})A + \sqrt{r_1}(1 - r_2)B + \sqrt{r_1}r_2C, \tag{13}$$

where A, B and C — the vertices of the selected triangle.

The third approach was the *Shape Histograms* ([8]). The general idea of the algorithm is based on the process of partitioning of the space, where a 3D object is placed. Using the particular obtained cells the histogram is built. The method of the decomposition of the space can be chosen freely. However, the authors of the approach have proposed three ones — a shell model, a sector model, and a spider-web model (see Fig. 1 for illustration).

The *Light Field Descriptor* (*LFD*, [14]) was the last method, which has been compared with the proposed algorithm. In fact its main idea was the basis for the algorithm proposed in this paper — the rendering of several two-dimensional projections of a 3D object (see Fig. 2). Those projections are compared in order to indicate the similar objects. Obviously, this task is performed for various points of view.

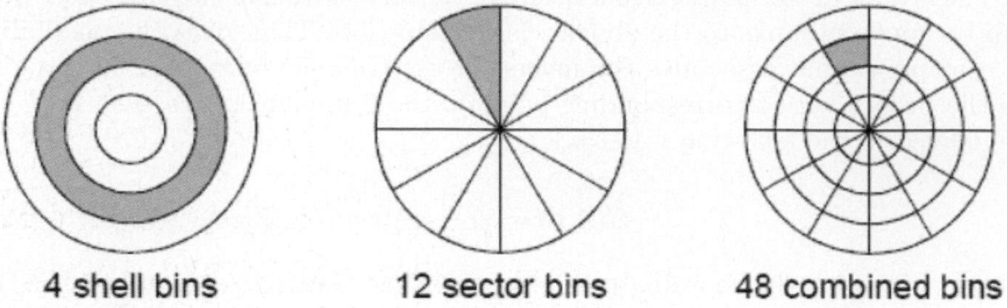

Fig. 1. Three exemplary methods of space decomposition for shape histograms ([8])

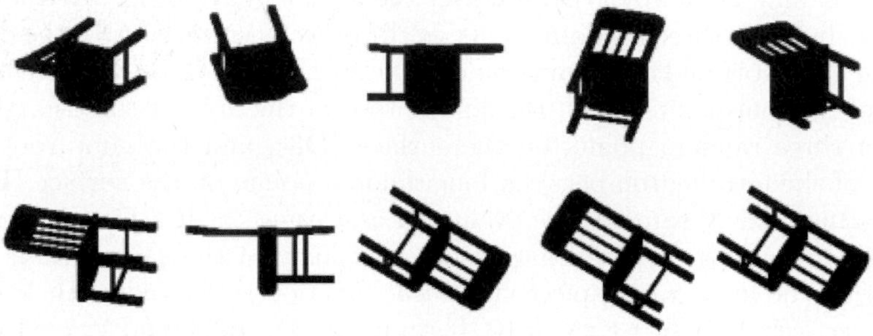

Fig. 2. Exemplary projections obtained for the representation of a model by means of the Light Field Descriptor ([14])

The algorithm for obtaining the *LFD* 3D shape description starts with the shifting of the object's vertices into the origin of the Cartesian co-ordinates system. The second step is the normalization of the co-ordinates according to the maximal one. Later, the crucial stage starts — for 20 various angles (the cameras are placed in the vertices of dodecahedron enclosing the model) the rendered planar projections are obtained ([14]). The obtained planar projections of 3D object are stored in bitmaps, and they are the representations of the model. Hence, the similarity between two objects is calculated by means of matching between their projections.

4 Experimental Conditions and Results

All five 3D shape description algorithms presented in this paper — the proposed *Polar-Fourier 3D Shape Descriptor* as well as the four approaches selected for the comparison — were experimentally evaluated by means of the *Princeton Shape Benchmark* ([16]). It is a free database made by *Princeton University*, created to help in performing the benchmark of different algorithms. This database is very popular in evaluating the 3D shape descriptors (see for example [18] and [19]).

During the experiments 312 objects belonging to 13 different classes were used (see Fig. 3). The idea of the experiment was simple. The retrieval was

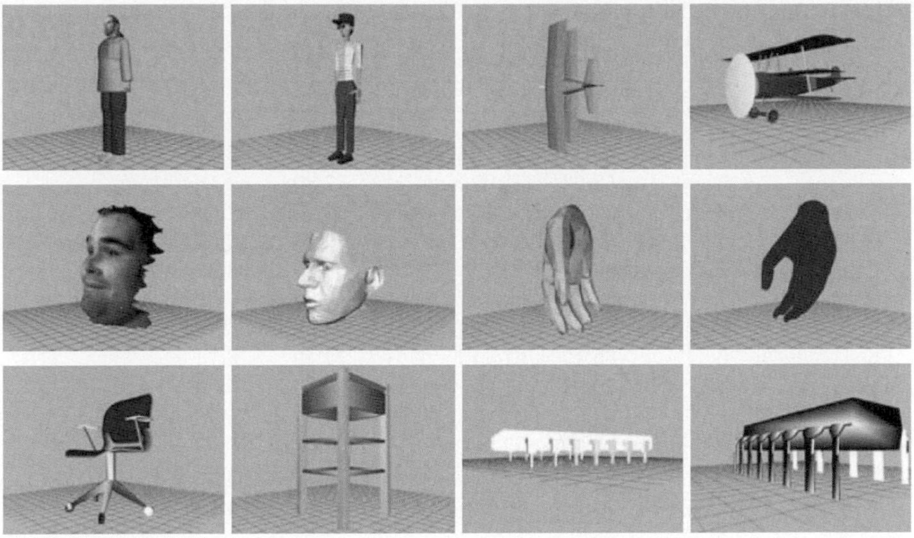

Fig. 3. Examples of the 3D models used in the experiment, taken from the *Princeton Shape Benchmark* database ([16])

successful if the *Euclidean distance* between a represented using a descriptor test and template was the smallest for objects belonging to the same class. Obviously, the template models did not perform the role of the test ones. The precise results of the retrieval obtained for investigated algorithms are provided in Table 1.

The results provided in Table 1 prove that the proposed algorithm outperforms the other explored 3D shape description techniques. Its average recognition rate (RR) is close to 75%. This result is more than 5% better than in the case of the second best descriptor — *Light Field Descriptor*.

Although the average result of the *Polar-Fourier 3D Shape Descriptor* is significantly the highest in some cases other methods have performed better. For example, *EGI* achieved 80% for class number 5, while the *P-F 3D* was two times worse. Similarly, for class no. 12 *EGI* achieved 50%, while the proposed method gave 37.5%. The highest difference is visible in the case of class no. 13. *EGI* descriptor worked in that case really well, while *P-F 3D* achieved only a 33.33% retrieval rate. On the other hand, for the rest of the classes the proposed approach has performed better.

Shape Distributions proved better than the *Polar-Fourier 3D* only in one case. For class no. 3 the SD achieved 84.21% and the *P-F 3D* — 63.16%. The *Light Field Descriptor* has also appeared better only once. Its RR for class no. 6 was equal to 88.89%, while the *P-F 3D* was slightly worse and achieved 83.33%. *Shape Histograms* turned out the worst during the test and never gave a result better than the proposed approach.

Table 1. Results of the experiments — percentage of the successful retrieval (retrieval rate) for particular 3D shape descriptors

Class no.	EGI	SH	SD	LFD	P-F 3D
1.	57.75	29.58	78.87	78.87	83.10
2.	65.71	48.57	57.14	85.71	85.71
3.	52.63	21.05	84.21	57.89	63.16
4.	53.13	56.25	34.38	56.25	62.50
5.	80.00	20.00	30.00	10.00	40.00
6.	50.00	44.44	72.22	88.89	83.33
7.	66.67	33.33	50.00	50.00	66.67
8.	66.67	0.00	0.00	33.33	66.67
9.	65.12	67.44	27.91	74.42	76.74
10.	70.00	10.00	60.00	60.00	70.00
11.	60.61	9.09	54.55	66.67	75.76
12.	50.00	12.50	12.50	25.00	37.50
13.	100.00	16.67	50.00	16.67	33.33
Overall	**60.26**	**36.86**	**56.09**	**68.91**	**74.68**

The result of the *Polar-Fourier 3D Shape Descriptor* seems to be far from the ideal; however, the problem of 3D model retrieval is very difficult. This is illustrated in Fig. 4, where some examples of the objects from the same class are presented — they sometimes look very dissimilar.

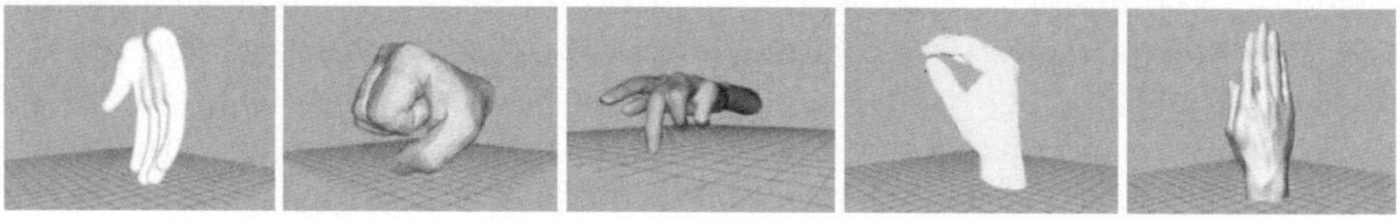

Fig. 4. Illustration of the difficulty involved with 3D-model retrieval — examples of 3D shapes belonging to the same class, yet very different in appearance ([16])

5 Conclusions and Future Plans

In the paper a new algorithm for the description of three-dimensional shapes has been presented and experimentally compared with four popular methods — *Extended Gaussian Image* (*EGI*, [5]), *Shape Distributions* ([9]), *Shape Histograms* ([8]) and *Light Field Descriptor* (*LFD*, [14]). The problem of 3D object retrieval has been analysed. For this purpose the models from the *Princeton Shape Benchmark* ([16]) were used. The achieved average retrieval rates have indicated that the proposed method works better in the problem than the other approaches. *The Polar-Fourier 3D Shape Descriptor* achieved almost a 75% retrieval rate. This result can be considered as satisfactory, because in many cases the objects within a class display strong differences (see Fig. 4 for an example).

The other algorithms achieved a retrieval rate equal to: 69% (*Light Field Descriptor*), 60% (*Extended Gaussian Image*), 56% (*Shape Distributions*), and 37% (*Shape Histograms*).

The obtained experimental results have confirmed the high efficiency of the approach proposed in *Light Field Descriptor* ([14]), namely rendering 2D projections of a 3D model, taken from various points of view. The improvement applied in the new descriptor is based on the usage of *polar-Fourier transform* for the achieved planar shapes. In the future, some other 2D shape descriptors will be verified by means of the same method. It is possible that thanks to them the retrieval results will be even better.

References

1. Ikeuchi, K.: Generating an interpretation tree from a CAD model for 3D-object recognition in bin-picking tasks. International Journal of Computer Vision 1(2), 145–165 (1987)
2. Lengyel, E.: Mathematics for 3D Game Programming and Computer Graphics, 2nd edn. Charles River Media (2003)
3. Bronstein, A.M., Bronstein, M.M., Kimmel, R.: Expression-Invariant 3D Face Recognition. LNCS, vol. 2688, pp. 62–70 (2003)
4. Bober, M.: MPEG-7 Visual Shape Descriptors. IEEE Trans. on Circuits and Systems for Video Technology 11(6), 716–719 (2001)
5. Horn, B.: Extended Gaussian Images. Proc. of the IEEE A.I. Memo, no. 740 72(12), 1671–1686 (1984)
6. Kang, S., Ikeuchi, K.: Determining 3-D Object Pose Using the Complex Extended Guassian Image. In: Proc. of the CVPR, pp. 580–585 (1991)
7. Novotni, M., Klein, R.: Shape Retrieval Using 3D Zernike Descriptors. Computer-Aided Design 36(11), 1047–1062 (2004)
8. Ankerst, M., Kastenmuller, G., Kriegel, H., Seidl, T.: 3D Shape Histograms for Similarity Search and Classification in Spatial Databases. In: Proc. of the 6th Int. Symp. on Spatial Databases, pp. 207–226 (1999)
9. Osada, R., Funkhouser, T., Chazelle, B., Dobkin, D.: Matching 3D Models with Shape Distributions. In: Proc. of Int. Conf. SMI 2008, pp. 154–166 (2001)
10. Mousa, M.-H., Chaine, R., Akkouche, S., Galin, E.: Toward an Efficient Triangle-Based Spherical Harmonics Representation of 3D Objects. Computer Aided Geometric Design 25(8), 561–575 (2008)
11. Hilaga, M., Shinagawa, Y., Kohmura, T., Kunii, T.L.: Topology Matching for Fully Automatic Similarity Estimation of 3D Shapes. In: Proc. of the 28th Conference on Computer Graphics and Interactive Techniques, pp. 203–212 (2001)
12. Kazhdan, M., Chazelle, B., Dobkin, D., Funkhouser, T., Rusinkiewicz, S.: A Reflective Symmetry Descriptor for 3D Models. Algorithmica 38, 201–225 (2003)
13. Novatnack, J., Nishino, K.: Scale-Dependent/Invariant Local 3D Shape Descriptors for Fully Automatic Registration of Multiple Sets of Range Images. In: Forsyth, D., Torr, P., Zisserman, A. (eds.) ECCV 2008, Part III. LNCS, vol. 5304, pp. 440–453. Springer, Heidelberg (2008)
14. Chen, D.-Y., Ouhyoung, M., Tian, X.-P., Shen, Y.-T.: On visual similarity based 3D model retrieval. Computer Graphics Forum, 223–232 (2003)

15. Frejlichowski, D.: 3D Shape Description Algorithms Applied to the Problem of Model Retrieval. Central European Journal of Engineering 1(1), 117–121 (2011)
16. Shilane, P., Min, P., Kazhdan, M. M., Funkhouser, T.A.: The Princeton Shape Benchmark. In: Proc. of the SMI 2004, Genova, Italy, pp. 145–156 (2004)
17. Kukharev, G., Kuzminski, A.: Biometric Techniques Part I - Face Recognition Methods. Szczecin University of Technology Press, Szczecin (2003) (in polish)
18. Min, P., Kazhdan, M., Funkhouser, T.: A Comparison of Text and Shape Matching for Retrieval of Online 3D Models. In: Heery, R., Lyon, L. (eds.) ECDL 2004. LNCS, vol. 3232, pp. 209–220. Springer, Heidelberg (2004)
19. Grana, C., Davolio, M., Cucchiara, R.: Similarity-Based Retrieval with MPEG-7 3D Descriptors: Performance Evaluation on the Princeton Shape Benchmark. In: Thanos, C., Borri, F., Candela, L. (eds.) Digital Libraries: Research and Development. LNCS, vol. 4877, pp. 308–317. Springer, Heidelberg (2007)

Combining Stereo and Time-of-Flight Images with Application to Automatic Plant Phenotyping

Yu Song[1], Chris A. Glasbey[1], Gerie W.A.M. van der Heijden[2], Gerrit Polder[2], and J. Anja Dieleman[3]

[1] Biomathematics and Statistics Scotland, The King's Buildings, Edinburgh, EH9 3JZ, UK
{yu,chris}@bioss.ac.uk

[2] Biometris, Wageningen UR, PO Box 100, 6700 AC Wageningen, Netherlands
{gerie.vanderheijden,gerrit.polder}@wur.nl

[3] Wageningen UR Greenhouse Horticulture, P.O. Box 644, 6700 AP Wageningen, Netherlands
anja.dieleman@wur.nl

Abstract. This paper shows how stereo and Time-of-Flight (ToF) images can be combined to estimate dense depth maps in order to automate plant phenotyping. We focus on some challenging plant images captured in a glasshouse environment, and show that even the state-of-the-art stereo methods produce unsatisfactory results. By developing a geometric approach which transforms depth information in a ToF image to a localised search range for dense stereo, a global optimisation strategy is adopted for producing smooth and discontinuity-preserving results. Since pixel-by-pixel depth data are unavailable for our images and many other applications, a quantitative method accounting for the surface smoothness and the edge sharpness to evaluate estimation results is proposed. We compare our method with and without ToF against other state-of-the-art stereo methods, and demonstrate that combining stereo and ToF images gives superior results.

1 Introduction

In our post-genomic world, where ever increasing volumes of genetic information are obtained at great speed and little cost, the collection of phenotypic information is often a bottleneck to scientific progress. A phenotype is any observable characteristic of an organism such as its shape and height. In stark contrast to genotyping, phenotyping is slow, and expensive in human time. Moreover, measurements are affected by the varying perception and interpretation of different observers. Image analysis has the potential to overcome these problems, but automatic interpretation of images of plants and animals remains very difficult. For example, Figures 1(a) and 1(b) show a stereo pair of images of pepper plants, from which we wish to estimate phenotypic characteristics such as leaf area, stem length or fruit size. This is a challenging task, as surfaces are of complex shape,

A. Heyden and F. Kahl (Eds.): SCIA 2011, LNCS 6688, pp. 467–478, 2011.

Fig. 1. Plant images: (a) and (b) show a stereo pair of images of pepper plants, (c) is the matching ToF image, which is at much coarser resolution and has been scaled to match (a) and (b)

and there are multiple depths, linear features and occlusions. Further, shadows are inconsistent between images because a flash light attached to the camera was used to offset ambient lighting.

These images were collected as part of an EU-funded FP7 project, SPICY (Smart tools for Prediction and Improvement of Crop Yield). The plant breeding industry has contributed greatly to the increased quality and yield of plant products over recent decades. However, to sustain and accelerate this progress, the relationship between genotype and phenotype needs to be better understood. For example, yield is a result of the interaction of many genetic factors, and is also subject to large, extraneous variation. The approach taken in SPICY is to use crop growth models to predict the phenotypic response, with genotype encapsulated in model parameters. Our component of the project is the development of image analysis tools to replace hand measurements for phenotyping over a large range of genotypes in a practical environment, with the first step being recovery of dense depth information from image pairs such as Figures 1(a) and 1(b). This is usually seemingly-effortless for the human eye and brain, but unfortunately still not so for computers!

One approach to dense stereo is via robust point correspondence methods using local feature descriptors such as SIFT [12], followed by methods such as DAISY [17] and SIFTflow [11]. However, no convincing result addressing the issue of preserving discontinuity was produced in [11,17] for complex real world scenes. Global optimisation methods such as graph cuts [3] can produce edge-preserving results on the Middlebury dataset [15], but challenges in the Middlebury dataset are different to these images in our work. Ogale and Aloimonos [13] proposed to use shape in establishing edge-preserving dense correspondence, but their images were mostly planar surfaces.

Recently the use of low-resolution range cameras based on the Time-of-Flight (ToF) principle has received increasing attention. A ToF range camera is an active image sensor using infrared illumination, and distance measure in cm is calculated from the time the light has used for travelling to the object and back. Kolb *et. al.* [9] gave an overview on techniques and applications of ToF images, and these provide an option for improving recovery of depth information by augmenting stereo pairs with partial, coarse resolution, ToF images as in Fig. 1(c). Given the availabilities of high-resolution stereo images taken close to the viewpoint of the ToF sensor, it is natural to combine ToF and stereo results and develop statistical relations between them. In the direction of combining ToF and stereo, Gudmundsson *et. al.* [6] transformed ToF points into colour images by rectification homographies, and then fed them into a hierarchical stereo matching algorithm. Hahne and Alexa [7] demonstrated the combined ToF and stereo method can enhance the depth estimation even without accurate extrinsic calibration. Zhu *et. al.* [18] developed a weighting method combining stereo and ToF data by fixed values, and then used belief propagation to optimise the data. Motivated by this research, we first present a geometric approach to transform points from ToF image coordinates to colour image coordinates, and then derive a localised search range for stereo matching. Despite the simplicity of the ToF transformation, we demonstrate that a global stereo strategy can then be applied and does improve results and preserve discontinuity. Compared with above works [6,7,18], challenging low-resolution ToF images 48×64 were used in this work. Beder *et. al.* [1] also developed a fusion scheme using ToF images in the same resolution as ours, but their images were planar surfaces while ours are more complicated.

Current ToF and stereo fusion work (e.g. [1,6,7,10]) lack quantitative results on preserving depth-discontinuity, and most results were qualitative (except [18] which used another 3D scanner to produce pixel-by-pixel depth data). This is partly due to the fact that it is impossible to collect pixel-by-pixel depth data for ground truth. Our images were collected inside a glasshouse unlike the work by Zhu *et. al.* [18] which was done in an indoor lab environment, and the use of a ToF camera can become obsolete given the readily available and accurate depth data. In the situation without pixel-by-pixel depth data, we propose a method to quantify how much depth-discontinuity has been preserved and evaluate the quality of depth estimation for our approach as well as other state-of-the-art stereo methods.

In addition to address challenges raised from our applications, the technical contributions of this paper are: a simple yet effective geometric approach transforming ToF points and producing a localised search range for dense stereo; a global graph-cut strategy using the localised search range with an emphasis on preserving discontinuity; an evaluation method to determine the quality of estimation without pixel-by-pixel depth data. After describing our contributions, this paper presents comparison results on some challenging pepper plant images.

2 Methods

2.1 Setup and Calibration

The camera rig consisted of a colour camera and a ToF camera. The ToF camera is a RF modulated camera with phase shift detectors (IFM O3D201 PMD camera), with a resolution of 64×48 pixels, while the colour camera has a resolution of 480×1280. The rig known as Spy-See [14] moved in a straight line on top of rigid heating pipes in the glasshouse and captured overlapping images at a fixed interval. The baseline between images was 5 cm, and objects of interest (e.g. leaves) were located between 55 cm and 120 cm away from the camera. Fig. 1(a)-(c) show a pair of stereo colour images and the corresponding ToF image.

Given a rigid and fixed camera setup described above, a two-layer board shown in Fig. 2(a) was used for calibration at different distances from the camera. The front layer moved from 40 cm to 120 cm away from the camera in 5 cm steps, and we used a simple pinhole camera model for the colour camera. Denote s as the baseline distance between images measured in cm and f' as the focal length for the colour camera, and the relationship between the disparity d and the depth z is,

$$d = s\, f' / z \tag{1}$$

Given multiple depth measurements $\mathbf{z}$ (e.g. 40 cm to 120 cm in this work) and correspondences in each view to compute $\mathbf{d}$, $\hat{f}'$ can be obtained by applying the least squares fitting technique:

$$\hat{f}' = \arg\min_{f'} ||\mathbf{d} - (s\, f' / \mathbf{z})||^2 \tag{2}$$

The centre of the square seen in Fig. 2(a) is used to compute $\mathbf{d}$, and $\mathbf{z}$ is known for each image. Fig. 2(b) presents the relationship in (1) and plots $\mathbf{d}$ against $\mathbf{z}$.

2.2 Dense Stereo Methods

Dense stereo methods can estimate disparity d for every pixel given a pair of stereo images. However, the pixel consistency assumption is often made for building the correspondence between two images. In our application, we have found that pixel values were not reliable for matching due to changes of perspective, lighting, and noise. To address this issue, the SIFTflow [11] method was chosen, which uses pixel-wise SIFT features between two images instead of pixel values for matching. Complex image pairs across different scenes and object appearances have been shown robustly matched in [11].

For our application, discontinuity preserving results are highly desirable. The pepper plant images shown in Figures 1(a) and 1(b) have very sharp depth edges, and we have observed step changes over 50 pixels between neighbourhood pixels. Although Liu *et. al.* used a simple synthetic image in [11] to demonstrate that the dense SIFT features contain sharp edges with respect to the sharp edges in the original image, there is no close-up on complex scenes to prove that the

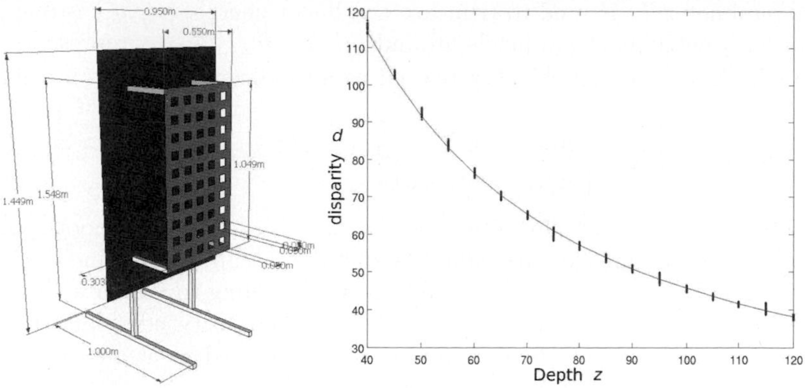

(a) (b)

Fig. 2. Calibration: (a) diagram of calibration board, (b) plot of the relationship between depth z in cm and disparities d in pixels for colour camera. Blue dots were disparity measurements d for each z, and the red line was the fit by (2).

SIFTflow method can preserve discontinuity. Ogale and Aloimonos [13] examined the implications of shape on the process of finding dense correspondence, and attempted to produce disparities in the form of a piecewise continuous function consistent with the stereo images. Using piecewise constant and piecewise linear shape models, they have presented results on images with slanted planar surfaces as well as a pair of stereo images on some branches of a tree, but no results on curved or nonrigid surfaces common in the pepper plant images have been shown.

Global optimisation methods such as graph cuts and belief propagation have been shown producing satisfactory discontinuity-preserving results on the Middlebury dataset [15]. Since global stereo methods produce better results compared with local stereo methods for combining with ToF information [18], we chose the alpha expansion technique applied in a graph-based energy minimisation framework [3]. The energy cost E given a pixel disparity d is defined as:

$$E(d) = \sum D(d_{(x',y')}) + \sum_{q \in N} V(d_{(x',y')}, d_{(x'_q,y'_q)}) \tag{3}$$

where N denotes the first-order neighbourhood pixels. For the data term cost D,

$$D(d_{(x',y')}) = \min \left\{ \frac{1}{3} \sum_{c=\{R,G,B\}} \left| I^{(c)}_{(x',y')} - I'^{(c)}_{(x'+d_{(x',y')},y')} \right|, T_d \right\} \tag{4}$$

where I and I' represent the intensity value in the pair of colour images. T_d is a truncation constant, and $D(d_{(x',y')})$ is computed for all the possible disparities. For the smoothness term cost V,

$$V(d_{(x',y')}, d_{(x'_q,y'_q)}) = u_{(x',y',x'_q,y'_q)} \min \left\{ \left| d_{(x',y')} - d_{(x'_q,y'_q)} \right|, T_k \right\} \tag{5}$$

where parameter T_k is used to truncate the linear energy. (x'_q, y'_q) is one of the first-order 4-neighbourhood pixels around (x', y'). $u_{(x',y',x'_q,y'_q)}$ represents static cues in Boykov *et. al.* [3], which was used as an indicator function in this work as:

$$u_{(x',y',x'_q,y'_q)} = \begin{cases} \alpha_v & \text{if } \sum_{c=\{R,G,B\}} \left| I^{(c)}_{(x',y')} - I'^{(c)}_{(x'_q,y'_q)} \right| > 25 \\ n_v\, \alpha_v & \text{otherwise} \end{cases} \quad (6)$$

α_v is the smoothness cost for intensity edges, and $n_v\, \alpha_v$ is the smoothness cost for surfaces. The thresholding value 25 was empirically determined from our experiments. Both α_v and $n_v\, \alpha_v$ should be set according to the data cost values in (4). (6) gives more smoothness if there is no intensity edge, and therefore achieves edge-preservation by encouraging changes at edges at a cost of α_v and limiting changes on the surface by $n_v\, \alpha_v$.

2.3 Localised Search Range from ToF Image

Given the complexity associated with the pepper plant images for dense stereo methods, a localised search range derived from the corresponding ToF depth image should improve the estimation accuracy. First of all, a transformation should be established for points in colour image and ToF image. In our experiments, a near-linear relationship between ToF depth measurements z'' and z was observed as in [18]. We used the same procedure for $\hat{f}'$ to obtain $\hat{f}''$ for the ToF camera, and developed ToF transformation methods in (7)-(10) to tolerate errors in ToF camera. For further information on ToF camera calibration, Kolb *et. al.* [9] briefly discussed error sources and challenges, and Beder and Koch [2] developed a checkerboard method and calibration software. Since the ToF image is much coarser in resolution compared to the colour image, the transformation from ToF image coordinates to colour image coordinates alone would only give isolated point depth measurements in the colour image. We therefore treat each ToF pixel as a patch centring around the pixel, and then transform all points in the patch to the colour image (see Fig. 3 for an example). In effect, this transformation is one of the up-scaling techniques as discussed by Lindner *et. al.* [10] and they provided a biquadratic scheme for this purpose.

Due to different viewing positions of ToF and RGB cameras, there are n ToF measurements for z $(n \geq 0)$ at location (x', y'). If multiple depths were found at (x', y'), the minimum value would be chosen, which represents the closest point to the camera. If no measurement of z is available for (x', y'), this would be treated as a missing value. To produce a localised search range $[d_{min}, d_{max}]$ for stereo matching, we used a patch centring around every pixel in the colour image to compute the minimum and maximum depth values. Denote (x', y', z) as $z_{(x',y')}$ and the patch as $z_{(\mathbf{m},\mathbf{n})}$,

$$|\mathbf{m} - x'| \leq r \quad (7)$$

$$|\mathbf{n} - y'| \leq r \quad (8)$$

In effect, this allows mis-alignment up to r pixels when transforming the ToF image to the colour image. The maximum and minimum depths ($\max\{z_{(\mathbf{m},\mathbf{n})}\}$ and $\min\{z_{(\mathbf{m},\mathbf{n})}\}$) are then converted into disparities as,

$$d_{min(x',y')} = s\,f'/\max\{z_{(\mathbf{m},\mathbf{n})}\} - k \tag{9}$$

$$d_{max(x',y')} = s\,f'/\min\{z_{(\mathbf{m},\mathbf{n})}\} + k \tag{10}$$

The search range is expanded by k pixels (normally $0 \leq k \leq 3$) at each direction to allow for the noise in the ToF estimates.

Given a localised search range $[d_{min}, d_{max}]$ for every pixel, a stereo method can then be used to find correspondences between images. To incorporate the localised search range in a graph-based energy minimisation framework, for the data term cost D in (4), if $d_{(x',y')}$ is outside the search range $[d_{min}, d_{max}]$ or $d_{(x',y')}$ is linked to a pixel outside the image, $D(d_{(x',y')})$ is set to the maximum pixel difference value T_d. If the localised search range $[d_{min}, d_{max}]$ is missing, $D(d_{(x',y')})$ is computed for all the possible disparities same as a dense stereo method.

2.4 Quality Quantification

From Fig. 1(a) and 1(b), we see a few foreground leaves with depth edges present along the leaf boundary. Although pixel-by-pixel depth data were not available, we can label depth edges to quantify how well the result has preserved depth edges. The Canny filter was used to detect intensity edges, and these edges were then manually refined for leaf boundaries (see Fig. 4). Note that we only performed this manual edge refinement at this evaluation stage to produce ground truth for depth edges, and neither the ToF transformation nor the stereo method required any intervention after calibration. The area within the leaf boundaries was considered a leaf surface, and the final output was a binary image with surface pixels located at (x'_s, y'_s) and edge pixels located at (x'_e, y'_e). To compute the smoothness of the surface and sharpness of the depth edges, we applied 3×3 Sobel operators in both horizontal and vertical directions, and surface smoothness penalty P_s was calculated as,

$$P_s = \overline{M_{(x'_s,y'_s)}} \tag{11}$$

where M is the edge magnitude by the Sobel operators. Edge sharpness score S_e was calculated as,

$$S_e = \overline{g_{(x'_e,y'_e)}} \tag{12}$$

where g denotes the edge magnitude M convoluted with a Gaussian filter in order to deal with thin and sharp depth edges. In this work, we set the neighbourhood size of the Gaussian filter to 15 and the standard deviation to 5. A quality score S accounting for the surface smoothness P_s and the edge sharpness S_e was therefore computed as below,

$$S = S_e - P_s \tag{13}$$

The score S penalises displacement between defined depth edges and depth edges produced by a dense method while requiring the surface to be smooth.

3 Results

This section compares three dense stereo algorithms with our method on some challenging pepper plant images. Let SIFTflow, Shape and GC represent methods by Liu *et. al.* [11], Ogale and Aloimonos [13] and Boykov *et. al.* [3] respectively. GC refers to the graph cut method without using ToF, and GC+ToF is the method we propose in this paper. Parameters for all the methods were optimised by running the particular method for several iterations through all parameters with different testing orders, and both qualitative and quantitative results were taken into account. For all our experiments, SIFTflow was configured with a 5-level pyramid, 5×5 window, $\alpha = 1$ and $\gamma = 0.001$. The α in the Shape method was set to 2. Parameters T_d, α_v, n_v, T_k for GC were set as $20, 4, 4, 6$. For GC+ToF, the same parameters for GC were used for dense stereo and ToF parameters r and k were set to 10 and 1 respectively. Since these methods are established, readers can see the effects of these parameters by following [11,13,3] for SIFTflow, Shape and GC respectively.

Fig. 3 shows an example of qualitative stereo results produced by the four methods. Methods GC and GC+ToF produced results with leaves recognisable from the background. SIFTflow produced smooth results but did not preserve discontinuity, while Shape was opposite. This can be further examined in Fig. 4, which shows effects of (11) and (12) on a close-up of a leaf (Leaf 1) by the four methods. The edge magnitude was weak for SIFTflow, although the surface was the most smooth. Method Shape suffered from noises on the surface, and GC failed to produce some depth edges. In comparison, GC+ToF produced best qualitative results among the four methods, and this was verified by two more examples in Fig. 5 (Leaf 2 and Leaf 3).

A summary of quantitative results (S_e, P_s, S) for all three leaves is shown in Table 1. Similar to the findings in the qualitative results above, we see that GC+ToF produced sharp depth edges represented by a high S_e score especially for Leaf 1 and Leaf 2. The ranking of methods produced by the score S is also consistent with the qualitative results for the two leaves. Leaf 3 is in front of another leaf, and the magnitude of depth edges is therefore not strong as those in Leaf 1 and Leaf 2. GC+ToF still produced the best scores S_e and S among the four methods.

This section has shown results on one example of stereo images (Pepper 1), and two more qualitative results (Pepper 2 and Pepper 3) have been made available[1]. Table 2 presents $\sum S$ for all three results. By using ToF as a localised search range, the estimation results were improved by at least 16% measured by the score $\sum S$.

[1] `http://www.bioss.ac.uk/staff/yu/tof`

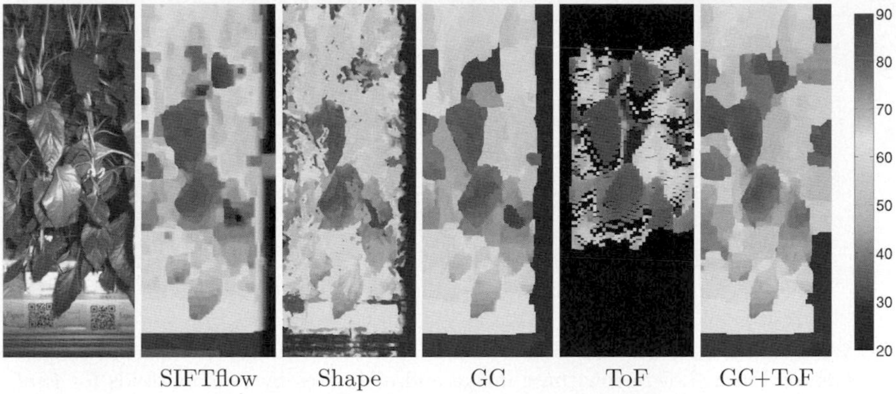

Fig. 3. Disparity results on the 'Pepper 1'. ToF shows transformed points in colour image coordinates and the black pixels indicate missing ToF information.

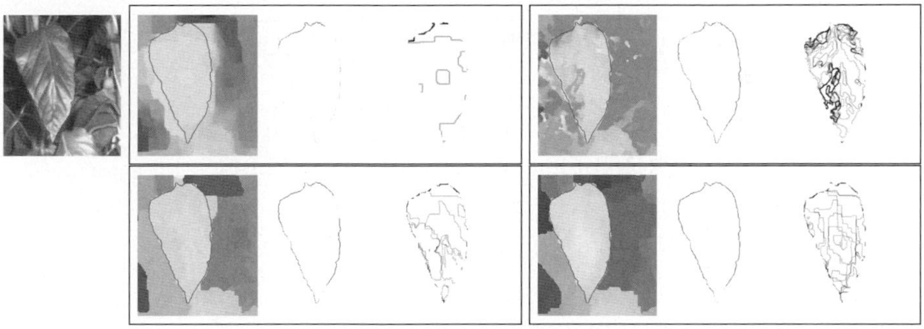

Fig. 4. Quality evaluation for Leaf 1. In every panel, the grey values represent the disparity (left), S_e (middle) and P_s (right) respectively. All four disparity maps use a common scale shown in Fig. 5. Also the S_e and P_s images use a common scale. Left column: base colour image with depth edges plotted in red. Middle column: results by SIFTflow (upper) GC (lower). Right column: results by Shape (upper) GC+ToF (lower).

Table 1. Numerical summary of quality evaluation for Leaf 1, Leaf 2 and Leaf 3. S_e refers to edge sharpness, P_s refers to surface smoothness and S is the quality score.

	Leaf 1			Leaf 2			Leaf 3		
	S_e	P_s	S	S_e	P_s	S	S_e	P_s	S
SIFTflow	4.55	0.81	3.74	9.35	5.04	4.30	3.56	0.94	2.62
Shape	12.66	4.09	8.56	12.81	8.79	4.02	6.52	1.90	4.61
GC	14.27	1.66	12.61	7.80	3.86	3.94	4.76	0.93	3.83
GC+ToF	20.89	2.76	18.13	20.76	6.20	14.56	7.20	1.65	5.54

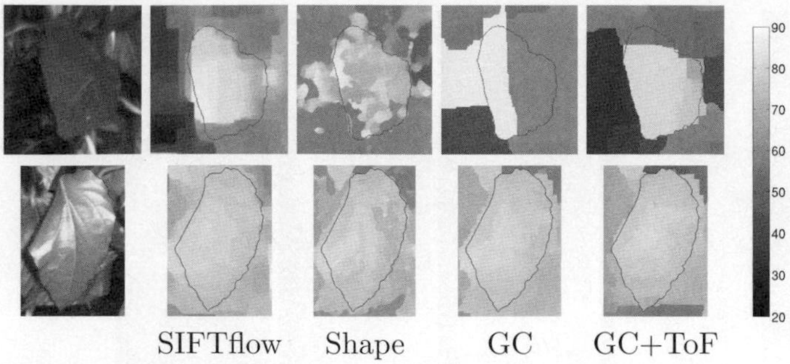

Fig. 5. Results for Leaf 2 and Leaf 3. Upper row: base image and estimates by four methods for leaf 2. Lower row: base image and estimates by four methods for Leaf 3. Depth edges are plotted in red.

Table 2. Quantitative summary of quality evaluation for three image examples. Figures shown here are total quality scores for all leaves in a image, $\sum S$.

	Pepper 1	Pepper 2	Pepper 3
SIFTflow	10.65	3.21	7.80
Shape	17.19	22.65	9.66
GC	20.37	21.03	10.50
GC+ToF	38.22	31.38	12.21

4 Discussion

This paper shows that dense stereo matching is not a trivial task for the pepper plant images collected inside a glasshouse. All three state-of-the-art methods produced unsatisfactory results, but a simple yet effective geometric approach to transform coarse-resolution ToF image together with a global graph-cut strategy can produce smooth results and preserve discontinuity. We have provided both visual and numerical results to demonstrate this. Fig. 6 presents a surface reconstruction for Leaf 1 using depth estimates by the proposed method combining stereo and ToF results, and depths have been recovered for such a complex surface. Although the quality score can quantify the quality of estimation without pixel-by-pixel depth data as shown in the results section, it only considers the surface smoothness and the edge sharpness without comparing the depth values. This was our first attempt on quality quantification that is different to those in [15,18], and we would like to draw the community's attentions on evaluation methods producing quantitative results of depth-discontinuity preservation.

Combining ToF and stereo offers two main advantages. For occlusions and areas affected by unpredictable illumination, the data term in a global stereo framework (i.e. D in (4)) produces inaccurate energy costs since corresponding pixels are either unavailable or difficult to be matched. Using ToF in these situations provided an estimate and reduced ambiguities. Another advantage is that

Fig. 6. Surface reconstruction for Leaf 1 using depth estimates by the GC+ToF method combining stereo and ToF results

dense stereo can be a super resolution technique for ToF images as discussed by [4,16], and we have presented discontinuity preserving results by combining ToF and stereo (e.g. Fig. 4). We have not considered environmental effects or measurement uncertainties related to the ToF camera as in [5,9] (e.g. the reflection issue in a cluttered environment and the influence of intensity on depth), which are beyond the scope of this paper.

Although we presented the method for one pair of stereo and one ToF images, it is in principle rather straightforward to apply it to multiple colour images and one ToF image, or even to multiple colour and ToF images. As Kim *et. al.* [8] have shown some promising results on this subject, we hope to build on the work in this paper for combining multiple colour and ToF images. Problems faced by stereo methods would be easier given multiple views, and the baseline would also be increased allowing more accurate depth estimation. We will then consider how to deal with occlusion and visibility issues within a multiple-view framework.

Acknowledgements

This work is part of the Smart tools for Prediction and Improvement of Crop Yield (SPICY) project supported by the European Community and funded by the KBBE FP7 programme. (Grant agreement number KBBE-2008-211347)

References

1. Beder, C., Bartczak, B., Koch, R.: A combined approach for estimating patchlets from PMD depth images and stereo intensity images. In: Hamprecht, F.A., Schnörr, C., Jahne, B. (eds.) DAGM 2007. LNCS, vol. 4713, pp. 11–20. Springer, Heidelberg (2007)
2. Beder, C., Koch, R.: Calibration of focal length and 3d pose based on the reflectance and depth image of a planar object. International Journal of Intelligent Systems Technologies and Applications 5, 285–294 (2008)

3. Boykov, Y., Veksler, O., Zabih, R.: Fast approximate energy minimization via graph cuts. IEEE Transactions on Pattern Analysis and Machine Intelligence 23, 1222–1239 (2001)
4. Diebel, J., Thrun, S.: An application of markov random fields to range sensing. In: Proceedings of Conference on Neural Information Processing Systems (NIPS). MIT Press, Cambridge (2005)
5. Gudmundsson, S.A., Aanæs, H., Larsen, R.: Environmental effects on measurement uncertainties of time-of-flight cameras. In: International Symposium on Signals Circuits and Systems (2007)
6. Gudmundsson, S.A., Aanaes, H., Larsen, R.: Fusion of stereo vision and time-of-flight imaging for improved 3d estimation. International Journal of Intelligent Systems Technologies and Applications 5(3/4), 425–433 (2008)
7. Hahne, U., Alexa, M.: Combining time-of-flight depth and stereo images without accurate extrinsic calibration. International Journal of Intelligent Systems Technologies and Applications 5(3/4), 325–333 (2008)
8. Kim, Y., Theobalt, C., Diebel, J., Kosecka, J., Micusik, B., Thrun, S.: Multi-view image and tof sensor fusion for dense 3d reconstruction. In: Proceedings of the 3DIM 2009 (2009)
9. Kolb, A., Barth, E., Koch, R., Larsen, R.: Time-of-Flight Sensors in Computer Graphics. In: Pauly, M., Greiner, G. (eds.) Eurographics 2009 - State of the Art Reports Eurographics, pp. 119–134. (2009)
10. Lindner, M., Lambers, M., Kolb, A.: Sub-pixel data fusion and edge-enhanced distance refinement for 2d/3d images. International Journal of Intelligent Systems Technologies and Applications 5, 344–354 (2008)
11. Liu, C., Yuen, J., Torralba, A.: Sift flow: Dense correspondence across scenes and its applications. IEEE Transactions on Pattern Analysis and Machine Intelligence (2010)
12. Lowe, D.: Object recognition from local scale-invariant features. In: Proceedings of the Seventh IEEE International Conference on Computer Vision, vol. 2, pp. 1150–1157 (1999)
13. Ogale, A.S., Aloimonos, Y.: Shape and the stereo correspondence problem. International Journal of Computer Vision 65, 147–162 (2005)
14. Polder, G., van der Heijden, G.W.A.M., Glasbey, C.A., Song, Y., Dieleman, J.A.: Spy-See - Advanced vision system for phenotyping in greenhouses. In: Proceedings of the MINET Conference: Measurement, Sensation and Cognition. National Physical Laboratory, pp. 115–117 (2009)
15. Scharstein, D., Szeliski, R.: A taxonomy and evaluation of dense two-frame stereo correspondence algorithms. International Journal of Computer Vision 47(1-3), 7–42 (2002)
16. Schuon, S., Theobalt, C., Davis, J., Thrun, S.: Lidarboost: Depth superresolution for tof 3d shape scanning. In: Proceedings of the IEEE CVPR 2009 (2009)
17. Tola, E., Lepetit, V., Fua, P.: Daisy: an efficient dense descriptor applied to wide baseline stereo. IEEE Transactions on Pattern Analysis and Machine Intelligence 32(5), 815–830 (2010)
18. Zhu, J., Wang, L., Yang, R., Davis, J.: Fusion of time-of-flight depth and stereo for high accuracy depth maps. In: Proceedings of the IEEE CVPR 2008 (2008)

Iterative Reconstruction for Quantitative Tissue Decomposition in Dual-Energy CT

Maria Magnusson[1,2,3], Alexandr Malusek[2,3,4], Arif Muhammad[2], and Gudrun Alm Carlsson[2,3]

[1] Dept. of Electrical Engineering,
[2] Dept. of Medical and Health Sciences, Radiation Physics,
[3] Center for Medical Image Science and Visualization (CMIV),
Linköping University, SE-581 83 Linköping, Sweden
[4] Dept. of Radiation Dosimetry, Nuclear Physics Institute AS CR, v.v.i.,
Na Truhlarce 39/64, 180 86 Praha 8, Czech Republic
{maria.magnusson,alexandr.malusek,gudrun.alm.carlsson}@liu.se,
muhammad_arif57@hotmail.com

Abstract. Quantitative tissue classification using dual-energy CT has the potential to improve accuracy in radiation therapy dose planning as it provides more information about material composition of scanned objects than the currently used methods based on single-energy CT. One problem that hinders successful application of both single- and dual-energy CT is the presence of beam hardening and scatter artifacts in reconstructed data. Current pre- and post-correction methods used for image reconstruction often bias CT numbers and thus limit their applicability for quantitative tissue classification.

Here we demonstrate simulation studies with a novel iterative algorithm that decomposes every soft tissue voxel into three base materials: water, protein and adipose. The results demonstrate that beam hardening artifacts can effectively be removed and accurate estimation of mass fractions of all base materials can be achieved.

In the future, the algorithm may be developed further to include segmentation of soft and bone tissue and subsequent bone decomposition, extension from 2-D to 3-D and scatter correction.

Keywords: Iterative reconstruction, Dual energy CT, Tissue classification, Tissue composition, Tissue decomposition.

1 Introduction

1.1 Information Attainable from CT Imaging

Computed tomography (CT) measures spatial distribution of the linear attenuation coefficient, $\mu(x, y, z)$, [1]. The reconstructed μ-values are affected by quantum noise, scatter, and beam hardening. Scatter and beam hardening lead to cupping and streak artifacts in reconstructed images. Pre-processing with a water beam hardening correction algorithm [1] is used in practice. For head imaging,

A. Heyden and F. Kahl (Eds.): SCIA 2011, LNCS 6688, pp. 479–488, 2011.

post-processing to remove severe streaks and cupping caused by beam hardening in bone is performed. In this case, however, the received μ-values for bone are inaccurate. It is generally accepted that a more complete suppression of scatter and beam hardening artifacts can only be achieved by iterative image reconstruction algorithms.

1.2 Recent Technical Developments in CT Imaging

CT techniques have developed rapidly in recent years. To speed up image acquisition, spiral and multi-slice imaging techniques are used. Helical scanning with multi-row detectors increases the speed even further and provides reconstructed volumes, see for example [2].

Dual Energy CT (DECT) with two rotating X-ray tubes was introduced by Siemens for heart scanning. Later, by using two different tube voltages, it was used to improve segmentation of anatomical structures with tissue compositions too close to be discriminated with conventional CT scanners [3].

1.3 Tissue Classification Using Single-Energy CT Scans

In single-energy CT, the historically first tissue classification method was performed by assigning the linear attenuation coefficient values into groups (for instance bone, soft tissue, etc.) delimited by threshold values. A more elaborate method currently used in clinical practice was developed by [4]. They assumed that each tissue was a mixture of two base materials and derived formulas for the determination of weight fractions of these two materials. The authors suggested that all soft tissues could be expressed as a weighted mixture of three materials (water, protein and adipose) but their single-energy technique did not allow tissues to be expressed as a combination of three materials.

1.4 Tissue Classification Using Dual-Energy CT Scans

In [5], it was demonstrated that DECT can be used to determine electron densities and effective atomic numbers. In [6] it was showed that DECT can be used to quantify mass fractions of three materials (water, hydroxyapatite and aqueous iron nitrate). In [7] the method was applied for the determination of (i) iron content in liver composed of soft tissue, fat, and iron, and (ii) bone-mineral density in a trabecular bone composed of calcium hydroxyappitite (CaHA), yellow- and red-marrow. All these applications may help in non-invasive medical diagnostic methods. None of the DECT applications suggested so far, however, has considered to use the data about quantitative tissue classification for the suppression of beam hardening and scatter artifacts. In this respect, our approach is novel.

2 Methods

2.1 Filtered Backprojection Reconstruction in CT

The most common reconstruction method in CT is filtered backprojection. There exist different variants for parallel and fanbeam projection geometries, see for

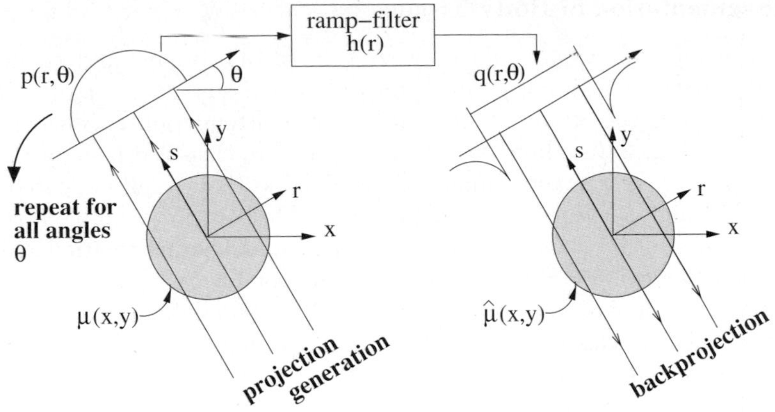

Fig. 1. Parallel computed tomography illustrated

example [1], as well as for helical geometry, see for example [2]. It is also possible to obtain parallel projections by rebinning fanbeam projections (a resorting and interpolation process). Here we describe parallel filtered backprojection, see Fig. 1. The *projection generation* is performed by the CT scanner and subsequent rebinning. The actual *filtered backprojection* reconstruction consists of *ramp-filtering* and *backprojection*. The measured attenuation coefficient data is denoted $\mu(x, y)$ and the reconstructed object is denoted $\hat{\mu}(x, y)$.

Projection generation is described by

$$p(r, \theta) = \int_{-\infty}^{\infty} \mu(x, y)\, ds\ , \quad \text{where} \quad \begin{pmatrix} x \\ y \end{pmatrix} = \begin{pmatrix} \cos\theta & -\sin\theta \\ \sin\theta & \cos\theta \end{pmatrix} \begin{pmatrix} r \\ s \end{pmatrix} . \tag{1}$$

The ramp-filter is applied according to

$$q(r, \theta) = \mathcal{F}_r^{-1}\Big[\mathcal{F}_r[p(r, \theta)] \cdot \mathcal{F}_r[h(r)]\Big]\ , \tag{2}$$

where $\mathcal{F}_r$ denotes the Fourier transform in the r-direction, $\mathcal{F}_r^{-1}$ denotes the inverse Fourier transform, and

$$\mathcal{F}[h(r)] = H(\rho) = \begin{cases} |\rho|, \text{ if} |\rho| \leq \rho_{max}\ , \\ 0, \quad \text{elsewhere}\ . \end{cases} \tag{3}$$

Then back-projection is applied, which means smearing of filtered projection data over the image plane according to

$$\hat{\mu}(x, y) = \int_0^{\pi} q(x\cos\theta + y\sin\theta, \theta)\, d\theta\ . \tag{4}$$

Note that projection and backprojection must be repeated for all angles θ in the interval $0 \leq \theta < \pi$.

2.2 Segmentation of Body Tissues

A CT scan of a body part can only contain certain organs and tissues. The linear attenuation coefficient $\mu[cm^{-1}]$ for different tissues can be plotted for two X-ray tube voltages, 80 and 140kV, in a linear attenuation coefficient (LAC) diagram, see Fig. 2. In a first step, these tissues are classified using a threshold classification to for instance lung, soft, and bone tissues, as indicated in the figure. This might, however, not be sufficient. There is, for example a risk that bone marrow will be classified as soft tissue. Topologic information may then be taken under consideration, e.g. a procedure of *image segmentation*. In the current work, however, only soft tissues were considered. In the second step, the soft tissues are classified using the three-material decomposition method as described in the next section.

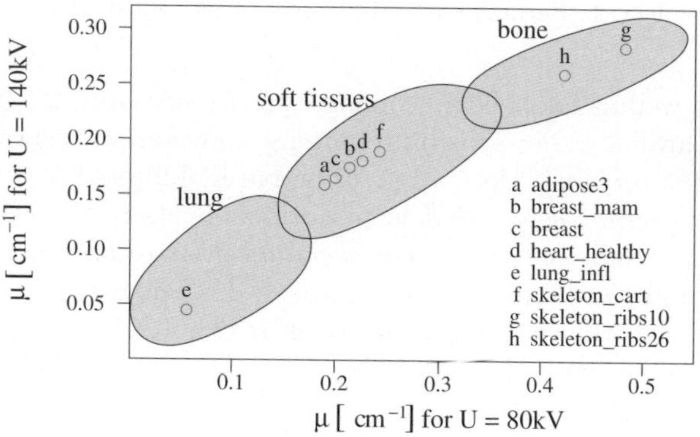

Fig. 2. Threshold classification in the LAC diagram separates lung, soft, and bone tissues. Attenuation coefficients for selected tissues defined in ICRU44 [8].

2.3 The Three Material Decomposition method

We extended the method by Schneider [4] to dual-energy CT (DECT) as the three-material decomposition method. It is important to choose a proper set of base materials. For our case with soft tissue decomposition we chose water, protein and adipose. Assume that the tissue consists of a mixture of these base materials with mass fractions w_1, w_2 and w_3, where

$$w_1 + w_2 + w_3 = 1 . \tag{5}$$

If the volume of the mixture is the sum of the volumes of individual components, then the density ρ of the three-material mixture in a volume V [m^3] with mass m [kg] can be written

$$\rho = \frac{m}{V} = \frac{m}{\frac{m_1}{\rho_1} + \frac{m_2}{\rho_2} + \frac{m_3}{\rho_3}} = \frac{1}{\frac{w_1}{\rho_1} + \frac{w_2}{\rho_2} + \frac{1-w_1-w_2}{\rho_3}} . \tag{6}$$

The linear attenuation coefficient for the mixture of materials depends on the volume fractions of the three materials as

$$\mu = w_1 \frac{\rho}{\rho_1}\mu_1 + w_2 \frac{\rho}{\rho_2}\mu_2 + w_3 \frac{\rho}{\rho_3}\mu_3 = \frac{V_1}{V}\mu_1 + \frac{V_2}{V}\mu_2 + \frac{V_3}{V}\mu_3 , \tag{7}$$

where we have utilized the mixture rule and the fact that

$$\frac{V_1}{V} = \frac{m_1 \rho}{\rho_1 m} = \frac{w_1 \rho}{\rho_1} , \tag{8}$$

and similarly for V_2 and V_3. Using (7) and (5), $\mu(E_1)$ and $\mu(E_2)$ for energies E_1 and E_2 can be written

$$\begin{cases} \mu(E_1) = \rho\left(w_1 \frac{\mu_1(E_1)}{\rho_1} + w_2 \frac{\mu_2(E_1)}{\rho_2} + (1 - w_1 - w_2)\frac{\mu_3(E_1)}{\rho_3}\right) , \\ \mu(E_2) = \rho\left(w_1 \frac{\mu_1(E_2)}{\rho_1} + w_2 \frac{\mu_2(E_2)}{\rho_2} + (1 - w_1 - w_2)\frac{\mu_3(E_2)}{\rho_3}\right) . \end{cases} \tag{9}$$

The mass attenuation coefficient is defined as μ/ρ. Using the vector notation $\bar{M} = (\mu(E_1)/\rho, \mu(E_2)/\rho)^T$ for a mixture of interest (and similarly for base materials $\bar{M}_1$, $\bar{M}_2$, and $\bar{M}_3$), equation (9) can be written

$$\bar{M} = w_1(\bar{M}_1 - \bar{M}_3) + w_2(\bar{M}_2 - \bar{M}_3) + \bar{M}_3 . \tag{10}$$

This equation is illustated in Fig. 3.

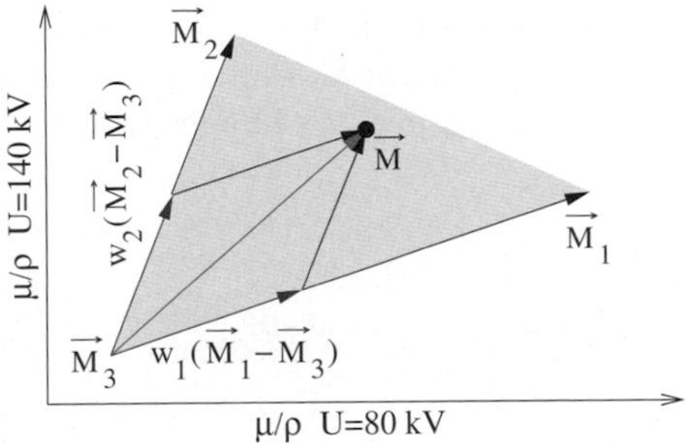

Fig. 3. Vector diagram for the three-material decomposition method

Now by combining equations (6) and (9), we get a system of linear equations,

$$\begin{pmatrix} \frac{\mu(E_1)-\mu_3(E_1)}{\rho_3} \\ \frac{\mu(E_2)-\mu_3(E_2)}{\rho_3} \end{pmatrix} + \mathbf{M}\begin{pmatrix} w_1 \\ w_2 \end{pmatrix} = \begin{pmatrix} 0 \\ 0 \end{pmatrix} , \tag{11}$$

where

$$\mathbf{M} = \begin{bmatrix} \frac{\mu(E_1)-\mu_1(E_1)}{\rho_1} - \frac{\mu(E_1)-\mu_3(E_1)}{\rho_3} & \frac{\mu(E_1)-\mu_2(E_1)}{\rho_2} - \frac{\mu(E_1)-\mu_3(E_1)}{\rho_3} \\ \frac{\mu(E_2)-\mu_1(E_2)}{\rho_1} - \frac{\mu(E_2)-\mu_3(E_2)}{\rho_3} & \frac{\mu(E_2)-\mu_2(E_2)}{\rho_2} - \frac{\mu(E_2)-\mu_3(E_2)}{\rho_3} \end{bmatrix} . \tag{12}$$

The solutions to (11) are the weight fractions w_1 and w_2 of the first two materials. The third weight fraction w_3 is obtained from (5).

2.4 The Iterative Reconstruction Algorithm

The iterative reconstruction algorithm is illustrated in Fig. 4. As indicated in the figure, the iterative loop consists of two parts, one for each energy. Fuchs used a somewhat similar iterative reconstruction algorithm, which was only in one part, however. It is described and referenced in [9]. Note that the projections are reconstructed with a full *ramp-filtered* backprojection.

- Two sets of projections denoted $\mathbf{P_{M,U1}}$ and $\mathbf{P_{M,U2}}$ are measured by the CT scanner for two different X-ray spectra corresponding to x-ray tube voltages of U_1 and U_2. All other data are initialized to 0.
- The measured projections are submitted to the filtered backprojection algorithm which computes the reconstructed images $\mu_\mathbf{1}$ and $\mu_\mathbf{2}$ with attenuation coefficients corresponding approximately to the effective energies E_1 and E_2 of the X-ray spectra U_1 and U_2.
- Our tissue classification method described in sections 2.2 and 2.3 (the tissue in a voxel is a mixture of three basic tissues) gives the classified reconstructed image $\mu_\mathbf{C}$.
- Then monoenergetic projections $\mathbf{P_{E1}}$ and $\mathbf{P_{E2}}$ at energies E_1 and E_2, and polyenergetic projections $\mathbf{P_{U1}}$ and $\mathbf{P_{U2}}$ for spectra U_1 and U_2 are calculated.
- The polyenergetic projections are then subtracted from the measured projections, giving a (small) error term. The error term is added to the monoenergetic projections and the result is submitted to the next iteration.

The error term will diminish with each iteration. The final result is the reconstructed images $\mu_\mathbf{1}$ and $\mu_\mathbf{2}$ for energies E_1 and E_2 and the $\mu_\mathbf{C}$ image containing classified tissue voxels. The $\mu_\mathbf{1}$, $\mu_\mathbf{2}$ and $\mu_\mathbf{C}$ images will be free from beam hardening distortions.

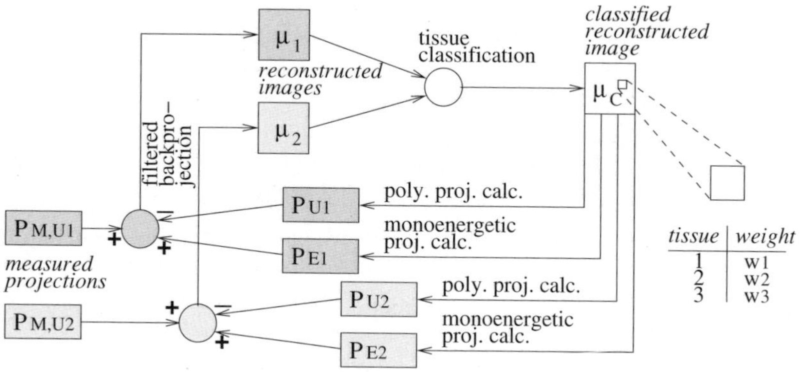

Fig. 4. Our iterative reconstruction algorithm. After a certain number of iterations, the μ_1 and μ_2 images will contain reconstructions corresponding to energies E_1 and E_2, respectively, and the μ_C image will contain classified tissue voxels. The three images will be free from beam hardening distortions.

3 Experiments

3.1 Considerations for the Iterative Reconstruction Algorithm

For simulation of measured X-ray projections the MATLAB/C program *take* was used [10]. In the simulation, a fan-beam CT geometry with flat detector, 280 projections per rotations, 256 detector elements, and a fan-beam angle of 13° was used. The source-to-isocenter distance was 1m. The fan-beam projections were rebinned to parallel projections before they were used in the iterative loop. The energy spectra were produced by x-ray tube voltages of 80kV and 140kV (the latter voltage was used in combination with an additional Sn filter) provided by Siemens under a non-disclosure agreement. Their principal appearances are shown in Fig. 5. The calculation of projections on the classified reconstructed image was performed using the method in [11].

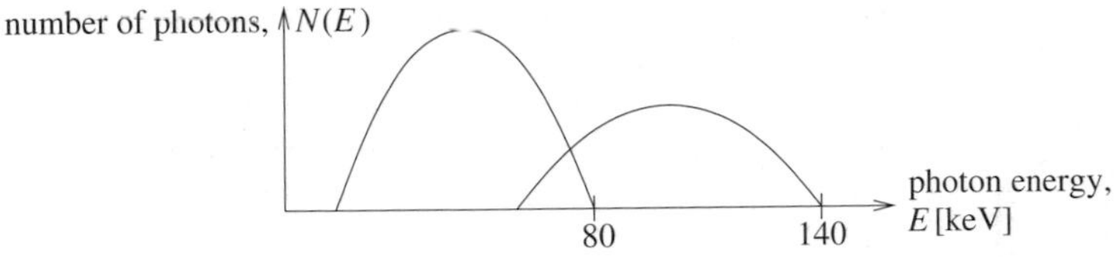

Fig. 5. The principal appearances of two spectra, a 80kV and a 140kV with Sn filter

3.2 The Mathematical Phantom

A mathematical phantom was used in the experiment. It consisted of a large circular water disc R_0 of diameter 40cm, with five small circular regions R_1 to R_5 of size 5cm, numbered from top-to-bottom and from left-to-right, see Fig. 6. The regions were composed of three base materials: water, protein and adipose and their mixtures with known mass fractions as given in Table 1.

Table 1. Base materials mass fractions in different regions of the phantom

R_0	R_1	R_2	R_3	R_4	R_5
100% Water	100% Protein	25% Protein 75% Adipose	40% Protein 30% Adipose 30% Water	75% Protein 25% Adipose	100% Adipose

3.3 Linear Attenuation Coefficients and Effective Energies

To generate projections through the mathematical phantom, the X-ray attenuation values of each material were calculated by using linear attenuation coefficients $\mu(E) = \rho[\sigma_{Co}(E)+\sigma_{In}(E)+\sigma_{Ph}(E)]$, where $\rho[g/cm^3]$ is the density of the material and $\sigma[cm^2/g]$ is the mass attenuation coefficient of the coherent scattering (Rayleigh scattering), incoherent scattering (Compton scattering) and the photoelectric effect, respectively, see e.g. [10]. The mass attenuation coefficients for water, protein and adipose were obtained from [12]. The effective attenuation coefficient μ_{mE} [m^{-1}] for water was calculated as energy-fluence weighted linear attenuation coefficient for water,

$$\mu_{mE} = (\int_0^{E_{max}} E\, N(E)\, \mu(E)\, dE)/(\int_0^{E_{max}} E\, N(E)\, dE)\,. \tag{13}$$

Then, using the $\mu(E)$-curve for water, the energy value corresponding to μ_{mE} for water, was taken as the effective energy E_{eff}. Then the effective attenuation coefficients for adipose and protein were taken as $\mu(E_{eff})$ in the attenuation curves for adipose and protein, respectively, see Table 2.

Table 2. Effective energies and linear attenuation coefficients for the two spectra

X-ray spectrum	Effective energies, E_{eff} [keV]	μ_{mE}[1/m] for Water	μ_{mE}[1/m] for Protein	μ_{mE}[1/m] for Adipose
80 kV	49.9	22.69	28.15	20.79
140 kV + Sn	88.5	17.73	22.70	16.93

Table 3. Quantitative evaluation of weight fractions measured in %

	True values			After 0 iter.			After 7 iter.		
Region	Water	Protein	Adipose	Water	Protein	Adipose	Water	Protein	Adipose
R_0	100	0	0	-6.7	11.2	94.0	97.3	0.4	2.5
R_1	0	100	0	-58.8	104.1	56.3	-1.4	100.0	1.5
R_2	0	25	75	-45.5	27.8	119.2	1.6	25.0	73.5
R_3	30	40	30	-64.9	46.4	118.0	31.9	39.9	28.2
R_4	0	75	25	-54.4	78.9	77.9	1.7	74.9	23.4
R_5	0	0	100	-41.3	2.9	139.1	-2.4	0.5	101.7

3.4 Results

The reconstruction results for the 0th iteration (i.e. plain reconstruction without iterations) and the 7th iteration are given in Fig. 6. For comparison, the plain reconstructions from monoenergetic effective energies, 49,9kV and 88.5kV, are also shown in the figure. Note that the results after 0 iterations are affected by beam hardening artifacts, whereas the results after 7 iterations are very similar to the monoenergetic reconstructions. The material decomposition results for the 0th iteration and the 7th iteration are given in Fig. 7 and Table 3 show mean values measured in a surrounding of each region. Note that the weight fractions are unaccepable after 0 iterations and sufficiently accurate after 7 iterations.

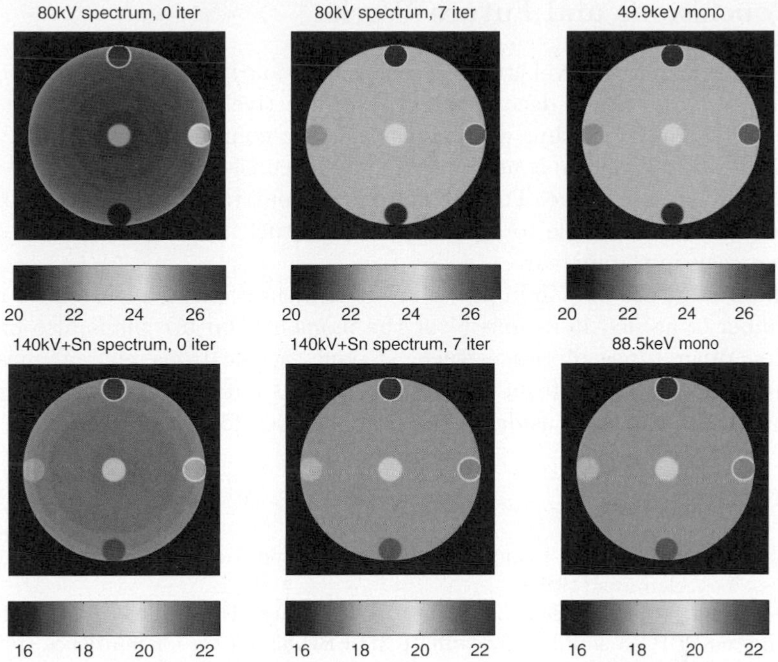

Fig. 6. Reconstruction results after 0 (left) and 7 (middle) iterations corresponding to 80kV (up) and 140kV+Sn (down) spectrum. Right: Reconstruction results for monoenergetic effective energies, 49,9kV (up) and 88.5kV (down).

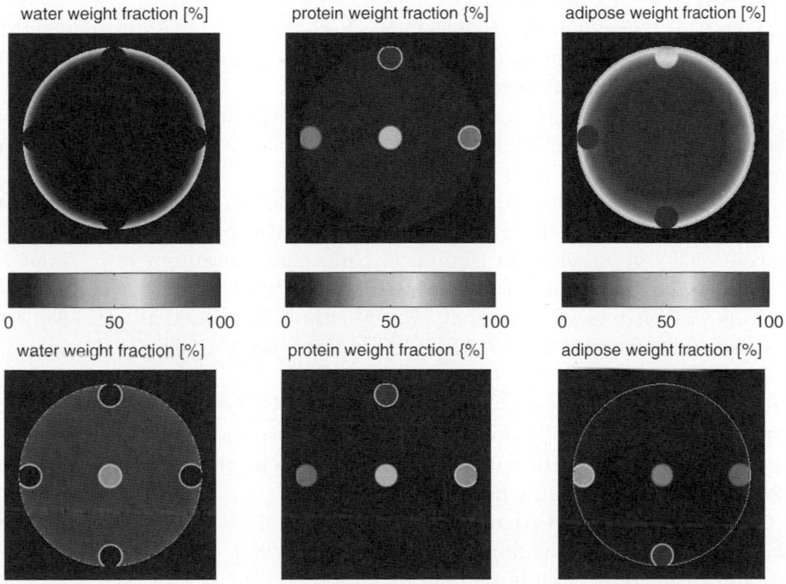

Fig. 7. Weight fractions for water, protein, adipose after 0 (up) and 7 (down) iterations

4 Conclusions and Future Work

We have presented a novel iterative reconstruction algorithm for dual-energy CT that performs tissue decomposition and effectively removes beam hardening artifacts. The algorithm was evaluated using computer simulations with a cylindrical water phantom containing rod inserts consisting of mixtures of water, protein, and adipose tissue. The simulations demonstrated that the proposed iterative algorithm was able to accurately reconstruct mass fraction values of all base materials in the mixture.

In the near future we will improve our implementation with the aim to reduce the number of needed iterations (7 at the moment). Future plans also involves including other types of tissue, such as bone, applications on real measured CT data, and extension from 2-D images to 3-D data sets. Also, scatter and statistical noise will be considered and compensated for.

References

1. Kak, A.C., Slaney, M.: Principles of Computerized Tomographic Imaging. IEEE Press, Los Alamitos (1988)
2. Stierstorfer, K., Rauscher, A., Boese, J., Bruder, H., Schaller, S., Flohr, T.: Weighted FBP - a simple approximate 3D FBP algorithm for multislice spiral CT with good dose usage for arbitrary pitch. Phys. Med. Biol. 49, 2209–2218 (2004)
3. Persson, A., Jackowski, C., Engström, E., Zachrisson, H.: Advances of dual source, dual-energy imaging in postmortem CT. Eur. J. Radiol. 68, 446–455 (2008)
4. Schneider, W., Bortfeld, T., Schlegel, W.: Correlation between CT numbers and tissue parameters needed for Monte Carlo simulations of clinical dose distributions. Phys. Med. Biol. 45, 459–478 (2000)
5. Bazalova, M., Beaulieu, L., Palefsky, S., Verhaegen, F.: Tissue segmentation in Monte Carlo treatment planning: a simulation study using dual-energy CT images. Radiother Oncol. 86, 93–98 (2007)
6. Liu, X., Yu, L., Primak, A.N., McCollough, C.H.: Quantitative imaging of element composition and mass fraction using dual-energy CT: Three-material decomposition. Med. Phys. 36(5), 1602–1609 (2009)
7. Yu, L., Liu, X., McCollough, C.H.: Pre-reconstruction three-material decomposition in dual-energy CT. In: Proc. of SPIE, vol. 7258, pp. 72583V–1 (2009)
8. International Commission on Radiation Units and Measurements: Tissue Substitutes in Radiation Dosimetry and Measurement, ICRU Report No. 44 (1989)
9. De Man, B., Nuyts, J., Dupont, P., Marchal, G., Suetens, P.: An Iterative Maximum-Likelihood Polychromatic Algorithm for CT. IEEE Trans. on Med. Imaging 20(10) (2001)
10. Seger, O., Magnusson Seger, M.: The MATLAB/C program take - a program for simulation of X-ray projections from 3D volume data. Demonstration of beam-hardening artifacts in subsequent CT reconstruction, Technical Report LiTH-ISY-R-2682 (2005), `http://liu.diva-portal.org`
11. Joseph, P.: An Improved Algorithm for reprojectiong Rays Through Pixel Images. IEEE Trans. on Med. Imaging 1(3), 1992–1996 (1982)
12. National Institute of Standards and Technology, `http://physics.nist.gov/PhysRefData/XrayMassCoef/cover.html`

An Automated System for the Detection and Diagnosis of Kidney Lesions in Children from Scintigraphy Images

Matilda Landgren[1,2], Karl Sjöstrand[1,3], Mattias Ohlsson[1,4], Daniel Ståhl[1,2], Niels Christian Overgaard[2], Kalle Åström[2], Rune Sixt[5], and Lars Edenbrandt[1]

[1] EXINI Diagnostics AB, Lund, Sweden
{karl.sjostrand,mattias.ohlsson,lars.edenbrandt}@exini.com
[2] Centre for Mathematical Sciences, Lund University, Lund, Sweden
{nco,kalle}@maths.lth.se
[3] Department of Informatics and Mathematical Modelling, Technical University of Denmark, Kgs. Lyngby, Denmark
[4] Department of Theoretical Physics, Lund University, Lund, Sweden
[5] Queen Silvia Children's Hospital, Göteborg, Sweden

Abstract. Designing a system for computer aided diagnosis is a complex procedure requiring an understanding of the biology of the disease, insight into hospital workflow and awareness of available technical solutions. This paper aims to show that a valuable system can be designed for diagnosing kidney lesions in children and adolescents from ^{99m}Tc-DMSA scintigraphy images. We present the chain of analysis and provide a discussion of its performance. On a per-lesion basis, the classification reached an ROC-curve area of 0.96 (sensitivity/specificity e.g. 97%/85%) measured using an independent test group consisting of 56 patients with 730 candidate lesions. We conclude that the presented system for diagnostic support has the potential of increasing the quality of care regarding this type of examination.

Keywords: Computer Aided Diagnosis, Nuclear Imaging, Active Shape Models, Artificial Neural Networks.

1 Introduction

Proper medical treatment begins with a correct diagnosis. Medical imaging systems provide a wealth of information which provide possibilities as well as challenges for the interpreting physician. The processing of this information is a complex procedure, where collective knowledge in the field, familiarity with the specific examination procedure and technical equipment, patient history, and common sense come together in the formation of a diagnosis. Creating a fully automated system for processing information of this diversity is difficult; however there are situations where a computerized system can provide valuable *diagnostic support*. Computers excel at keeping track of large amounts of data and at

A. Heyden and F. Kahl (Eds.): SCIA 2011, LNCS 6688, pp. 489–500, 2011.

performing time-consuming and tedious tasks quickly. The combination of a human interpreter and a computerized system can therefore improve diagnostic accuracy [1]. The main contribution of such a system is to improve sensitivity, i.e. avoiding oversight. This paper presents a fully automated system for detecting and diagnosing kidney lesions from 2D scintigraphy images. There are two main contributions of this system. First, it eliminates time-consuming manual procedures in currently used systems such as the delineation of the kidneys. Second, it provides objective diagnostic support on a per-lesion basis to physicians with limited experience with this type of examination.

1.1 Clinical Background

One of the most common bacterial infections among children is urinary tract infection, caused by bacterial growth. This condition may develop into pyelonephritis[1] which, left untreated, may cause scars in the parenchyma of the kidneys (cf. Figure 1(a) for anatomical terms). Among the possible consequences of such lesions are future renal hypertension (high blood pressure) and renal failure [2]. Children with recurring infections are investigated for possible kidney lesions using an imaging method where a harmless agent known as dimercaptosuccinic acid (DMSA) is injected into the blood. DMSA accumulates in the kidneys and the local accumulation is proportional to the density of functional kidney cells [3,4]. Low accumulation is therefore indicative of locally reduced kidney function. To make it possible to image the amount of accumulation, DMSA is combined with a radioactive molecule, ^{99m}Tc, a weak gamma radiation emitter. A planar gamma detector is used to measure the amount of radiation emitted from the kidneys, thus forming an image of the renal function. The distribution of ^{99m}Tc-DMSA in the kidneys are normally homogeneous. When a patient has had repeated urinary tract infections with lowered kidney function as a result, this can be seen as wedge-shaped areas of locally reduced intensity in the scintigraphy image [4], cf. Figure 1(b).

1.2 Related Work

A segmentation method, specific to renal scintigraphy, is proposed in [5]. An automatic thresholding algorithm is used to segment each kidney. To avoid under-segmentation, pixels in an area around the initial boundary are classified as kidney pixels or background. This method does, however, not consider the fact that diseased kidneys may show lower uptake in wedge-shaped areas around its boundary. The paper also proposes a system for diagnosing the entire kidney as normal or abnormal based on a boundary curvature measure. The sensitivity and specificity of this method was 88% and 96 % respectively.

A commercial ^{99m}Tc-DMSA analysis program is available from Hermes Medical Solutions [6]. This software presents various kidney-specific measurements and presents a statistical map of uptake deviations.

[1] Inflammation in the renal pelvis.

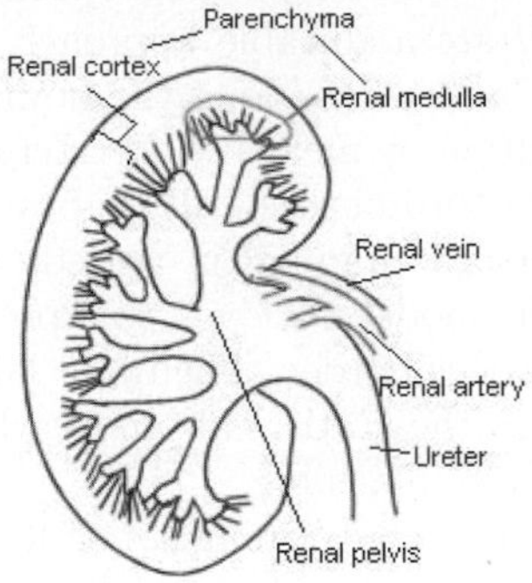

(a) A schematic image of the basic anatomy of the kidney.

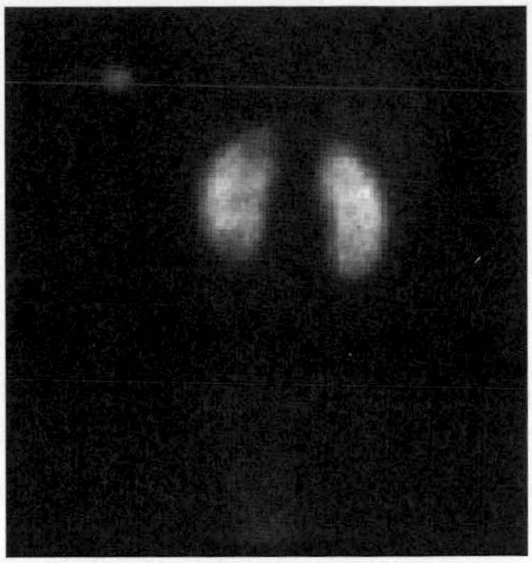

(b) A renal scintigraphy image where lesions are present in the upper and lower part of the left kidney, and the right kidney is normal. The image size is 128 × 128 pixels and the side of a pixel is 2.26 mm.

Fig. 1.

2 Methods

An overview of our system can be seen in Figure 2 and the different steps are explained in more detail below.

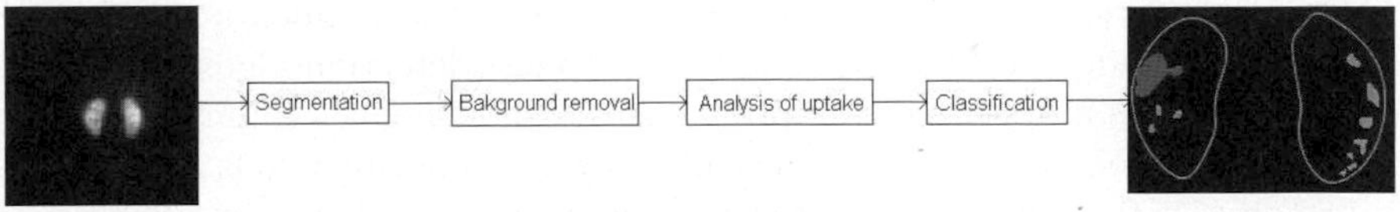

Fig. 2. An overview of the system components, from input image to a lesion-based classification

2.1 Kidney Segmentation

To segment and classify lesions we require some knowledge of relevant kidney anatomy; for instance we wish to build a map of normal ^{99m}Tc-DMSA uptake and to measure the size of a lesion relative to the entire kidney. As is evident from Figure 1(b), delineating the outer borders of the kidneys is a relatively easy task, the kidneys are mostly of high intensity while the background is considerably darker. However, lesions commonly distribute along the border, creating wedge-like regions of low intensity. To recover a plausible kidney border in such areas, strong prior information on the kidney shape must be incorporated. We believe that Active Shape Models (ASMs) [7] are a suitable approach for this purpose. An ASM models the distribution of landmarks along the boundary of a structure as a multivariate Gaussian distribution by means of a principal component analysis on the concatenated x- and y-coordinates of all shapes. Tuning the parameters of this model to fit an object in a given image is carried out in an alternating fashion. First, each landmark of the model is moved to a position in its vicinity which most likely represents the object border. Then, the landmark configuration is relaxed using information from the statistical landmark model to ensure that the resulting shape is anatomically plausible.

To create the statistical model of kidney anatomy, a training set of 40 kidneys were annotated with 14 landmarks along the boundary. The model is of a right kidney; left kidneys were mirrored to be incorporated in the model. By mirroring the model, we obtain a segmentation tool which can be used on both kidneys under the assumption of no consistent difference between left and right kidneys [5]. The resulting shape model uses 10 principal axes which captures 95 % of the training set variation.

Successful delineation of a kidney using the ASM scheme requires an initial estimate of the segmentation which is reasonably close to the actual structure. A bounding box containing the kidney to segment is easily obtained from the marginal image histograms. The position, size and rotation of this kidney is then estimated by computing the centroid and principal axes for the coordinates corresponding to pixels above a foreground intensity threshold. Using this information, the mean shape is translated such that its centroid coincides with the estimated kidney centroid. The shape is then rotated according to the principal axes. Finally, the shape is scaled in the directions of the principal axes according to the variance explained along each axis. Results of this initialization can be seen in the upper row of Figure 3.

The ASM search for an improved fit from the initial segmentation guess is based on image edge information. Applying an edge detection algorithm on the raw image data is unwise; scintigraphy images exhibit uneven intensities due to the underlying Poisson process of nuclear decay. Neighboring pixels representing the same tissue type may display vastly different intensity levels just by chance. To reduce this effect while preserving more global edge structures we apply a bilateral image filter [8]. Bilateral filters are similar to standard Gaussian blurring with the modification that the Gaussian bell is weighted in each position by the photometric distance between the central pixel and its neighbors. This has the effect of smoothing homogenous regions while preserving structure. As a final preparatory image modification, we encourage the ASM to disregard edges enclosed in bright areas to some extent by taking the square root of all intensity values, thus focusing more on the background/foreground edges of interest.

When moving a landmark to a new position, we search among 30 samples along profiles perpendicular to the shape as suggested in [7]. From these candidate positions, we select the one which maximizes the difference between the mean of inside samples and the mean of outside samples. An advantage of this

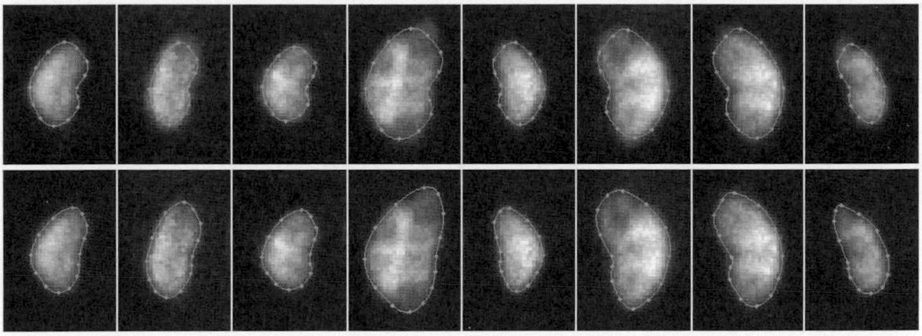

Fig. 3. Example of segmentations with the initialization in the upper row and the final segmentation in the lower row. In the fourth example from the left it can be seen that the segmentation algorithm recovers the low-intensity upper and lower kidney poles.

formulation is that it considers edges with background on the outside and foreground on the inside of the shape model, rather than any image edges. The algorithm is run until the landmark difference between iterations is sufficiently low. The second row of Figure 3 shows examples of resulting segmentations.

2.2 Boundary Representation

As stated above, the kidney shape model consists of 14 landmarks placed along the kidney image boundary. This results in a rather course representation of the outline. However, a larger number of landmarks is difficult to achieve since the kidney exhibits few distinctive anatomical points of reference as projected in ^{99m}Tc-DMSA images. Instead, we rely on a suitable interpolation technique to connect the landmarks accurately. The boundary is represented by a simple closed curve, making the use of Fourier descriptors [9] suitable. This boundary representation uses a combination of the discrete Fourier transform and Fourier series to calculate the Fourier coefficients c_k and to recover a continuous boundary curve representation $f(t)$ respectively,

$$c_k = \frac{1}{n} \sum_{j=0}^{n-1} e^{-2\pi ijk/n} f_j, \quad f(t) = \sum_{k=-n/2}^{n/2} c_k e^{ikt}.$$

Here $n = 14$ is the number of landmarks, $f_j = x_j + iy_j$, $j = 0 \dots n-1$ represents the set of input landmarks, and i is the complex unit. The complex boundary function $f(t)$, here sampled at 200 points, is a sum of harmonics of differing phase and frequency which leads to a globally smooth boundary suitable for describing the kidney boundary. Further, there exists convenient analytical expressions for the area and the centroid of the resulting shape [9]. The outlines in Figure 3 are interpolated using this technique; note how it better handles the curvedness of the outline than line segments would.

2.3 Background Removal

The background radiation present in the ^{99m}Tc-DMSA kidney images is due to partial uptake in the blood and other organs. This also occurs behind and in front of the kidneys, as viewed from the gamma detector. This effect can be substantial and must be taken into account for accurate estimation of the kidney-specific ^{99m}Tc-DMSA uptake. Our approach is to create a smooth surface representing how the background radiation varies over the kidney, based on background samples outside, but close to, the kidney. We then subtract the intensities implied by this surface from the kidney area and a result of this can be seen in the top row of Figure 5.

To represent a smoothly varying surface without sudden kinks or excessive bending, we use a smoothing thin-plate spline [10]. To obtain a smooth estimate of the background uptake, and avoid fitting the surface to noise, we choose to regularize the thin-plate spline rather than smoothing the image background samples. The resulting surface solves

$$\arg\min_f \sum_{i=1}^{n} (z_i - f(x_i, y_i))^2 + \lambda \iint \left[\left(\frac{\partial^2 f}{\partial x^2} \right)^2 + 2 \left(\frac{\partial^2 f}{\partial x \partial y} \right)^2 + \left(\frac{\partial^2 f}{\partial y^2} \right)^2 \right] \mathrm{d}x \, \mathrm{d}y,$$

where $\{z\}$ is the set of background samples outside the kidney, $\{x, y\}$ is the set of image coordinates of these samples, $f(x, y)$ is the thin-plate spline approximant and $\lambda \in [0, \infty)$ determines the stiffness of the plate. There exists a closed-form solution for solving this problem via a linear system of equations [10].

2.4 Candidate Lesion Segmentation

The most distinctive image feature of kidney lesions is reduced uptake of ^{99m}Tc-DMSA. We therefore base our lesion segmentation approach on a pixel-wise statistical map of uptake in healthy kidneys and classify areas of a kidney as candidate lesions which exhibit significantly lowered uptake, measured on the 5% level. In order to create a map of normal uptake, we created a database of normal kidneys; six patients where both kidneys are considered normal, eleven patients with normal left kidneys, and 17 patients with normal right kidneys — a total of 40 samples. Since kidneys have different shapes and sizes they must be transformed to a common frame of reference where we obtain an approximate pixel-wise anatomical correspondence. We use thin-plate spline interpolation of the 14 corresponding outline landmarks to this end where each warp is represented by a pair of thin-plate splines taking care of landmark deflections in the x and y directions respectively.

Besides this spatial normalization the images also require photometric normalization by an unknown multiplicative factor. This is a general challenge in many investigations in nuclear medicine as absolute uptake depends on many unknown biological and technical parameters. Our normalization approach matches image A to image B by multiplying A by a factor such that the median of regions of A with high intensities (almost certainly healthy) matches the median of the

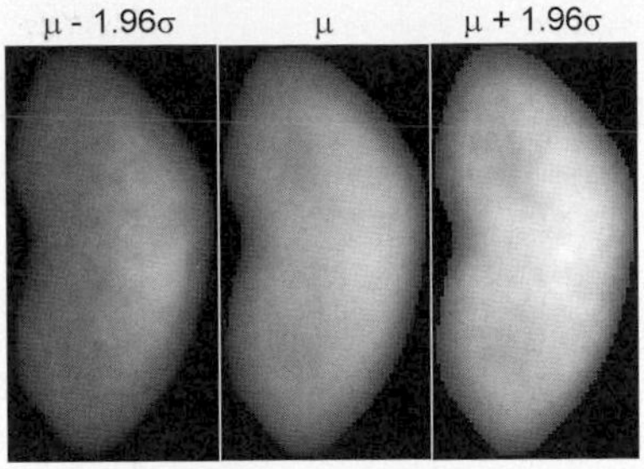

Fig. 4. The middle image shows the mean uptake of ^{99m}Tc-DMSA and the two outer images shows the uptake at the borders of the confidence interval

corresponding regions in B. In the normal database, all samples are normalized with respect to an arbitrarily chosen normal sample.

Empirical experience shows that a normal distribution is sufficiently accurate to describe the distribution of intensities. The parameters of these pixel-wise distributions are estimated by computing the mean and standard deviation of all normalized normal samples. Figure 4 shows the mean uptake and its 95% confidence interval. The middle row of Figure 5 shows the resulting statistical maps of z-values where tones of yellow towards red indicate regions lower than -2 standard deviations (-2z).

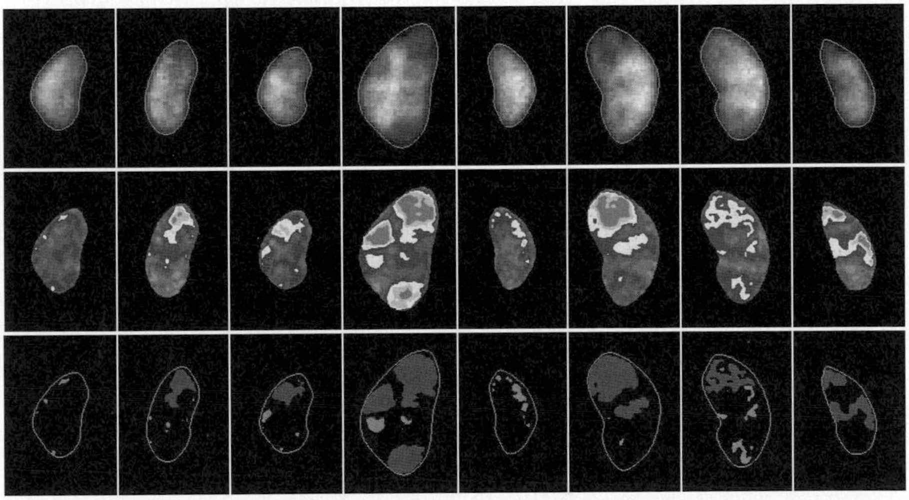

Fig. 5. Top row shows the resulting intensities when the background radiation has been subtracted. In the middle row a statistical maps of z-values for the selection of samples can be seen. Yellow towards red indicate areas lower than -2z. Bottom row shows example of classification with LDA, the red areas are classified as scars and the blue ones are classified as healthy.

2.5 Classification

The essence of a system for computer aided diagnosis (CAD) is a classification into normal or abnormal, or gradings thereof, either on a per-lesion basis or regarding the patient as a whole. Here, we classify each lesion as either normal (blue) or abnormal (red). Typically, such systems are tuned such that very few actual lesions are classified as normal (high sensitivity). This gives the interpreting physician the possibility to focus on lesion candidates classified as abnormal, thus streamlining the work and reducing the risk of oversight.

We conducted experiments with three classifiers, two relatively simple baseline classifiers and one state-of-the-art approach. For baseline experiments, we used linear and quadratic discriminant analysis (LDA, QDA), and the more advanced approach is represented by an artificial neural network (ANN). A set of features is calculated from each potential lesion in order to perform the classification. These relate both to the lesion shape and texture, as well as to the kidney and patient as a whole. The following set of features were used here:

Lesion edge closeness. This feature measures the distance from the lesion to the kidney edge. For each pixel position along the contour of the lesion, the distance to the closest point on the continuous kidney perimeter is found using numerical optimization. The smallest such distance, measured in millimeters, is returned.

Lesion major and minor axis length. Length in millimeters of the principal axes of the ellipse with the same second moments as the lesion.

Relative lesion area. The area of the lesion divided by the kidney area.

Lesion sum of z-scores. The sum of the z-values within a lesion. The z-values are obtained by subtracting the lesion normal database mean image and dividing by the database standard deviation image, making each lesion pixel $\mathcal{N}(0,1)$-distributed.

Lesion relative sum of z-scores. The sum of lesion z-values divided by the area of the lesion. Measured in z-scores per square millimeter.

Lesion localization. These two features measure the position of the lesion centroid relative to its bounding box in the x- and y-directions. Since the scars are often located at the lateral wall of the kidney this measure can be an important addition to lesion edge closeness. Measures range from 0 to 1 with 1 corresponding to the most lateral/caudal positions and 0 corresponding to the most medial/cranial positions.

Lesion eccentricity. This feature measures the elongation of the lesion as the eccentricity of the ellipse with the same second moments as the lesion. Values range from 0 to 1, where 0 represents a circle and 1 represents a line segment.

Lesion rate of extreme database deviation. This feature measures the proportion of the lesion which falls under 4 standard deviations when compared to the normal database.

Kidney separate function. This important measure quantifies the functional relation between the two kidneys of a patient. With equally functioning kidneys, this measure is at 50%. Lower numbers indicate loss of kidney function.

Kidney length. This feature is of importance since partially damaged kidneys are likely to suffer from impaired growth. Measured in millimeters.

Kidney area. Another way of measuring kidney growth. Measured in square millimeters.

Patient age. Age can be an important factor to control for as kidneys develop much during childhood.

To train the classifiers we created a training set consisting of 36 patients with a total of 483 candidate lesions. These lesions were classified as normal or abnormal by a leading specialist on interpreting ^{99m}Tc-DMSA renal scintigraphy images. The prevalence of lesions was 12%. Separate from this training set, we created a test set from 56 patients with a total of 730 candidate lesions. The prevalence in the test set was 8%.

Under the assumption that the vector of features for a patient follows a multi-dimensional Gaussian distribution, LDA and QDA provide optimal classification in terms of minimizing error rate [11]. Further, LDA assumes that normal and abnormal candidate features share the same covariance matrix while QDA allow for different such matrices. LDA and QDA assign a candidate lesion to the class k that maximizes

$$\delta_k = x^T \mathbf{\Sigma}^{-1} \mu_k - \frac{1}{2} \mu_k^T \mathbf{\Sigma}^{-1} \mu_k + \log \pi_k, \quad \text{and} \tag{1}$$

$$\delta_k = -\frac{1}{2} \log |\mathbf{\Sigma}_k| - \frac{1}{2} (x - \mu_k)^T \mathbf{\Sigma}_k^{-1} (x - \mu_k) + \log \pi_k \tag{2}$$

respectively, where $k \in \{\text{normal, abnormal}\}$, x represents the input feature vector to test for, $\mathbf{\Sigma}$ represents a covariance matrix, μ_k is the mean feature vector for class k, and π_k is the prior probability for class k.

The ANN classification model was implemented as an ensemble of multi-layer perceptrons (MLP), where each MLP consisted of one hidden layer (7 nodes). Training was carried out by minimizing a cross-entropy error with an additional weight elimination term [12] to allow for a possible regularization of the ensemble. Four-fold cross validation was used during the model selection phase and the final ensemble model used on the test set was created using 3-fold cross splitting, repeated 10 times, resulting in an ensemble of size 30. The average output of the MLPs was used as the ensemble prediction.

Examples of lesions classified by LDA can be seen in the bottom row of Figure 5.

3 Results

The segmentation works well both on kidneys with normal ^{99m}Tc-DMSA uptake and on kidneys with lower uptake, cf. Figure 3. The shape model also makes sure that the shape of a kidney is maintained. The segmentation has been evaluated on 40 kidneys and the rate of acceptable segmentations is around 95 %. Most of the unacceptable segmentations have minor errors; most common is an unsatisfying segmentation of the upper and lower pole of the kidney.

Table 1. Classification results as measured on the test set of 730 candidate lesions

	LDA	QDA	ANN
Area under ROC curve (AUC)	0.964	0.935	0.960
Sensitivity (%)	96.5	96.5	96.5
Specificity (%)	84.8	61.2	83.4
Positive Predictive value (%)	35.0	17.4	32.9
Negative Predictive value (%)	99.7	99.5	99.6
Mis-classification rate (%)	14.2	36.0	15.6

The lesion segmentation algorithm based on the database of normal uptake detected 100% of diagnosed lesions in the training and test data sets. We did not have the opportunity to assess the accuracy of candidate lesion geometry.

The classification was validated on a test set of 730 possible lesions and the performance of the different classifiers can be seen in Table 1. We fixed the sensitivity at a high value, here 96.5%, since this lessens the risk of classifying an actual lesion as normal while maintaining reasonable specificity. LDA and ANN show similar performance with high specificity and negative predictive value. QDA has notably lower specificity and positive predictive value as well as a larger misclassification rate. Receiver Operating Characteristic (ROC) curves for each classifier can be seen in Figure 6.

The program has been developed using MATLAB. The computation time for the analysis of one patient ranged from 5-9 seconds when running on a 2.2 GHz Windows PC with 1.5 Mb of RAM.

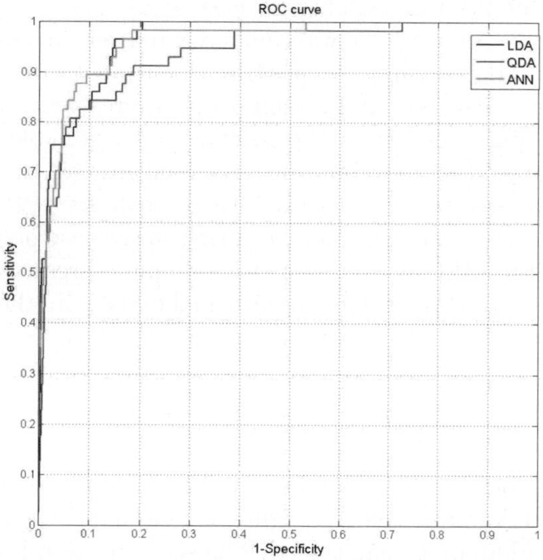

Fig. 6. ROC curves for LDA (blue), QDA (red), and ANN (green). LDA and ANN perform similarly while QDA does slightly worse.

4 Discussion

We have shown that an accurate system for the diagnosis of kidney lesions can be created. Similar systems have previously been shown to increase diagnostic accuracy in practice, particularly by increasing sensitivity [1]. This means that physicians are less likely to miss non-conspicuous lesions. In contrary to many presently used systems, our approach is fully automatic and quick. This has the potential of increasing care effectiveness and relieving the interpretation from some of its inherent subjectiveness.

In our classification experiments, linear discriminant analysis performed at least as good as the more flexible alternatives. Cross-validation results for the artificial neural network approach was significantly better than those of LDA and QDA, but performance dropped when measured on the independent test set. LDA did not suffer from this effect. This is most likely due to the rigid nature of LDA, rather than that the assumptions of LDA are fulfilled by the data [11]. It also seems as if the classification problem is rather linear in nature, in fact, one can obtain a reasonably good system (95% AUC) using relative lesion area as a single feature. Fair comparisons with CAD systems for other diagnoses are difficult, but it is interesting to note that positive predictive values of typical mammography systems are 2-3% [13]. Here, we reach 35%.

The lesion detection system detected 730 lesions in the test material — 8% of these represented actual lesions. This stresses the importance of offering classification of detected findings. The work involved in classifying 730 findings from scratch is far greater than reviewing around 60 candidates classified as abnormal paired with a quick review of remaining lesions.

In this paper, we have used data from a single hospital. In future work we will evaluate the method on material from more centers and a bigger variety of cameras. Further, we wish to develop the user interface to better fit typical hospital workflow, including integration with image storage and retrieval systems, and to provide a system for (semi-)automatic reporting. One may also consider providing a diagnosis for the patient as a whole, based on the diagnoses of the individual lesions, in order to quantify the risk of future renal malfunction.

References

1. Sadik, M., Suurkula, M., Höglund, P., Järund, A., Edenbrandt, L.: Improved classifications of planar whole-body bone scans using a computer-assisted diagnosis system: a multicenter, multiple-reader, multiple-case study. J. Nucl. Med. 50(3), 368–375 (2009)
2. Fotter, R.: Pediatric Uroradiology. Springer, Heidelberg (2008)
3. Piepsz, A., Colarinha, P., Gordon, I., Hahn, K., Olivier, P., Roca, I., Sixt, R., van Velzen, J.: Guidelines on 99^mTc-DMSA scintigraphy in children. Eur. J. Nucl. Med. 28(3), 37–41 (2001)
4. Jonson, B., Wollmer, P.: Klinisk Fysiologi. Liber AB (2005) (in swedish)
5. Marcuzzo, M., Masiero, P.R., Scharcanski, J.: Quantitative Parameters for the Assessment of Renal Scintigraphic Images. In: 29th Annual International Conference of the IEEE Engineering in Medicine and Biology Society, pp. 3438–3441 (2007)

6. Hermes Medical Solutions, `http://www.hermesmedical.com/index.lasso?id=128`
7. Cootes, T.F., Taylor, C.J., Cooper, D.H., Graham, J.: Active Shape Models – their training and application. Computer Vision and Image Understanding 61(1), 38–59 (1995)
8. Tomasi, C., Manduchi, R.: Bilateral Filtering for Gray and Color Images. In: Proceedings of the 1998 IEEE International Conference on Computer Vision, India (1998)
9. Sjostrand, K., Ericsson, A., Larsen, R.: On the Alignment of Shapes Represented by Fourier Descriptors. In: SPIE International Symposium on Medical Imaging, USA (2006)
10. Bookstein, F.L.: Principal Warps: Thin-Plate Splines and the Decomposition of Deformations. IEEE Transactions on Pattern Analysis and Machine Intelligence 11(6), 567–585 (1989)
11. Hastie, T., Tibshirani, R., Friedman, J.: The Elements of Statistical Learning. Springer, Heidelberg (2008)
12. Hanson, S.J., Pratt, L.Y.: Comparing biases for minimal network construction with back-propagation. In: Touretzky, D.S. (ed.) Advances in Neural Information Processing Systems, pp. 177–185 (1989)
13. Freer, T.W., Ulissey, M.J.: Screening Mammography with Computer-aided Detection: Prospective Study of 12,860 Patients in a Community Breast Center. Radiology 220, 781–786 (2001)

Automatic Segmentation of Abdominal Adipose Tissue in MRI

Thomas Hammershaimb Mosbech[1], Kasper Pilgaard[2], Allan Vaag[2], and Rasmus Larsen[1]

[1] Technical University of Denmark, DTU Informatics, Richard Petersens Plads, Building 321, DK-2800 Lyngby, Denmark
{tm,rl}@imm.dtu.dk
[2] Steno Diabetes Center, Niels Steensens Vej 2, DK-2820 Gentofte, Denmark

Abstract. This paper presents a method for automatically segmenting abdominal adipose tissue from 3-dimensional magnetic resonance images. We distinguish between three types of adipose tissue; visceral, deep subcutaneous and superficial subcutaneous. Images are pre-processed to remove the bias field effect of intensity in-homogeneities. This effect is estimated by a thin plate spline extended to fit two classes of automatically sampled intensity points in 3D. Adipose tissue pixels are labelled with fuzzy c-means clustering and locally determined thresholds. The visceral and subcutaneous adipose tissue are separated using deformable models, incorporating information from the clustering. The subcutaneous adipose tissue is subdivided into a deep and superficial part by means of dynamic programming applied to a spatial transformation of the image data. Regression analysis shows good correspondences between our results and total abdominal adipose tissue percentages assessed by dual-emission X-ray absorptiometry ($R^2 = 0.86$).

Keywords: Image processing, MRI, Abdominal adipose tissue, Bias field correction, Tissue classification.

1 Introduction

It has been estimated that 171 million people worldwide had diabetes in the year 2000 and that this would increase to 366 million by 2030 [19]. If untreated, diabetes can cause complications such as blindness, amputation and kidney failure. This stresses the importance of methods for screening and early detection.

A measure related to type 2 diabetes is insulin resistance (IR). The gold standard for measuring IR is the hyperinsulinemic euglycemic clamp. However, this method is invasive, expensive and labour intensive – therefore impractical for clinical practice.

Abdominal obesity has a well established association with increased risk of IR and type 2 diabetes. In the assessment of abdominal adipose tissue (AT), it is relevant to distinguish between subcutaneous (SAT) and visceral (VAT), since a strong association between the quantity of VAT and IR is well proven [1].

A. Heyden and F. Kahl (Eds.): SCIA 2011, LNCS 6688, pp. 501–511, 2011.

Various methods exist for assessing body fat, such as body mass index (BMI), waist size related measures (WS), skin fold callipers, dual-emission X-ray absorptiometry (DXA), X-ray computed tomography (CT) and magnetic resonance imaging (MRI). BMI, WS and callipers only offer crude general approximations, and they (along with DXA) are unable to distinguish between different types of AT, although correlation has been reported [15]. CT can give very detailed information of both quantity and spatial distribution by means of the Hounsfield scale, but the acquisition entails a radiation hazard to the subject. On the other hand, MRI is attractive, as it is a safe modality, also providing visualisations suitable for accurate identification of different AT types.

However, in MRI there is no direct correspondence between intensities and tissue type, and MRI often suffers from problems related to image quality and artefacts. This can call for cumbersome manual or semi-automatic segmentation performed by trained experts. A robust automated assessment from MRI would therefore be highly beneficial in clinics.

A common artefact in MRI is the hardware related *bias field*; a non-anatomic variability within same-tissue intensity values over the image domain. The inhomogeneity is spatially smooth, with a reported level of variation reaching up to 20% [18].

One way of correcting the effect is by means of extra images of a uniform phantom acquired in connection with each scan session [11]. However, this increases the total scanning time and cost. Instead, we present a method for estimating the effect and correcting the images retrospectively based solely on the MRI of the subject.

Methods from unsupervised learning have successfully been applied for labelling AT by intensity thresholding in MRI. [7] demonstrated the suitability of fuzzy c-means clustering (FCM) for this purpose.

For partitioning the abdomen into the regions containing SAT and VAT, [12] used dynamic programming (DP) coupled with an active shape model, trained on a set of manual segmentations. In [2] a region growing algorithm was used to isolate the VAT. For the same task, a deformable model based on concepts of active contours was applied by [17]. Leinhard et al. [16] used atlas-based segmentation, registering a manually segmented prototype to each target image. In our work we combine FCM, DP and active contours in an automatic segmentation method requiring no training data.

It has been suggested to subdivide SAT into superficial SAT (sSAT) and deep SAT (dSAT), anatomically partitioned by Scarpa's fascia (SF) – a thin layer of connective tissue in the abdominal wall. In [14] both dSAT and VAT were found to be strongly associated to IR, whereas sSAT only had a weak relation. Differing from previous methods, we adopt this strategy for our segmentation algorithm, and automatically assess three different types of AT.

2 Data

The participants in the study were 40 young healthy twins; 23 men and 17 women, age 18 to 21 years, characterised as ranging from very lean to slightly obese with BMI between 14.7 and 21.0. Multi-slice T1 weighted MRI was acquired with a 3T Philips Achieva whole body scanner. For each subject, between 15 and 26 slices were used to cover the abdominal region bounded by L1 and L4. Slices with resolution 512×512 pixels, size 0.8984×0.8984 mm^2, thickness 7 mm and gap 1 mm. For the same region, the total fat percentage was also assessed with DXA.

3 Methodology

Our method consists of three parts; a preprocessing step to remove the spatial inhomogeneity of the bias field, a pixel-wise classification identifying AT, and a separation of regions to distinguish between the three types of AT.

3.1 Bias Field Correction

A commonly used model for the bias field effect on a voxel with acquired intensity y_{observed} is the multiplicative link [10]

$$y_{\text{observed}} = y_{\text{true}} \cdot y_{\text{bias}} \Leftrightarrow \tag{1}$$

$$\log(y_{\text{true}}) = \log(y_{\text{observed}}) - \log(y_{\text{bias}}), \tag{2}$$

where y_{true} is the true intensity, and y_{bias} is the bias field effect. With this formulation we can remove the field from an acquired image by subtraction – if the effect is known.

Our method exploits the slow spatial variation and estimates the bias field effect by a smooth function in three dimensions, with parameters obtained through regression.

The regression is based on a set of spatially dense reference voxel points with intensities holding information about the bias field effect. [12] proposed a method based on automatically sampled points corresponding to adipose tissue and the assumption, that these intensities would be similar across the entire image – if not corrupted by the bias field.

However, given the lean nature of the subjects in this study, this method results in too few points, especially from VAT. In order to cover the entire abdomen, we extend the method by regarding two classes of reference points; AT and tissue of high water content.

For each slice, points are sampled automatically across the abdomen as local intensity minima (high water content) and maxima (AT). Under the assumption of a spatially smooth effect, we use 12×9 rectangles overlapping 10 pixels to subdivide the abdomen. For each rectangle we trim the two point sets to only contain points with intensities within 15% of each rectangle-minimum and maximum, respectively. To avoid clusters of points, the points are spatially trimmed by 10×10 non-overlapping rectangles, only keeping the single points in each rectangle with highest and lowest intensity.

Different values around the chosen, were tested for both the number of rectangles and the percentage thresholds. It was found that they yielded more or less the same sets of points.

After the trimming, the sampled points are gathered from all slices to form a three dimensional point set; N observations $\mathbf{s} \in \mathbb{R}^3$, with coordinates $[s_1\ s_2\ s_3]^T$, log-transformed intensity y and a class-indicator c

$$c(\mathbf{s}) = \begin{cases} 0 & \text{for } \mathbf{s} \text{ high water content} \\ 1 & \text{for } \mathbf{s} \text{ adipose tissue} \end{cases} \tag{3}$$

Supported by the assumption of smooth variation, we use a thin plate spline (TPS) [6] to model the bias field. Estimating this smoothing TPS is formulated as the minimisation a penalised sum of squared differences S subject to the function f

$$S(f) = \sum_{i}^{N} \{y_i - f(\mathbf{s}_i)\}^2 + \alpha J(f), \tag{4}$$

where $J(f)$ is the curvature. The parameter α controls the amount of smoothness enforced, our selection of a proper value is described later.

For fitting the two classes of observations, we extend the standard formulation of f presented in [8] and [9]

$$f(\mathbf{s}) = \beta_0 + \beta_1^T \mathbf{s} + \gamma c(\mathbf{s}) + \sum_{j}^{n} \delta_j h_j(\mathbf{s}). \tag{5}$$

This way, γ is a constant difference between intensities of the two classes.

The basis-functions $h_j(\mathbf{s})$ are defined by means of cubed distances from the observation points to n knots $\mathbf{t}$ with coordinates $[t_1\ t_2\ t_3]^T$, located on a regular grid covered by the points.

$$h_j(\mathbf{s}_i) = \|\mathbf{s}_i - \mathbf{t}_j\|^3. \tag{6}$$

We formulate (4) as a set of linear equations. The knots and data points are gathered in two coordinate matrices

$$\mathbf{T}_k = \begin{bmatrix} 1 & \cdots & 1 \\ \mathbf{t}_1 & \cdots & \mathbf{t}_n \end{bmatrix}_{[4\times n]}, \quad \mathbf{T}_d = \begin{bmatrix} 1 & \cdots & 1 \\ \mathbf{s}_1 & \cdots & \mathbf{s}_N \end{bmatrix}_{[4\times N]} \tag{7}$$

The corresponding data values and class-indicators are gathered in two $N \times 1$ vectors $\mathbf{Y}$ and $\mathbf{C}$.

Matrices forming the basis functions of f in (5) are arranged as $\mathbf{E}_k$ and $\mathbf{E}_d$, with elements computed as

$$\{\mathbf{E}_k\}_{ij} = h_j(\mathbf{t}_i), \text{ with } i, j = 1, \cdots, n \tag{8}$$

$$\{\mathbf{E}_d\}_{ij} = h_j(\mathbf{s}_i), \text{ with } i = 1, \cdots, N \text{ and } j = 1, \cdots, n \tag{9}$$

Equation (5) can then be written in matrix form

$$\mathbf{F} = \mathbf{E}_d\delta + \mathbf{T}_d^T\beta + \mathbf{C}\gamma = \left[\mathbf{E}_d\ \mathbf{T}_d^T\ \mathbf{C}\right]\begin{bmatrix}\delta\\ \beta\\ \gamma\end{bmatrix} \tag{10}$$

where the vector $\mathbf{F}$ consists of N elements $\{\mathbf{F}\}_i = f(\mathbf{s}_i)$, and $\beta = [\beta_0\beta_1]_{[4\times 1]}$.

Gathering the coefficients δ_j in a $n \times 1$ vector δ, we can write the curvature function $J(f)$ as

$$J(f) = \delta^T\mathbf{E}_k\delta. \tag{11}$$

We add a set of linear constraints on the basis function coefficients δ_j

$$\sum_{j=1}^{n}\delta_j = \sum_{j=1}^{n}\delta_j t_{j1} = \sum_{j=1}^{n}\delta_j t_{j2} = \sum_{j=1}^{n}\delta_j t_{j3} = 0. \tag{12}$$

They can be incorporated in the linear system of equations as $\mathbf{T}_k\delta = \mathbf{0}$ and a 4×1 Lagrange multiplier vector λ.

With this setup (4) can be written as:

$$\begin{aligned}S(f) = &\left[\mathbf{Y} - \mathbf{E}_d\delta - \mathbf{T}_d^T\beta - \mathbf{C}\gamma\right]^T\left[\mathbf{Y} - \mathbf{E}_d\delta - \mathbf{T}_d^T\beta - \mathbf{C}\gamma\right]\\ &+\alpha\delta\mathbf{E}_k\delta + \lambda^T\mathbf{T}_k\delta.\end{aligned} \tag{13}$$

We estimate the TPS as the least squares solution to the system of equations, composed by $\frac{\partial S}{\partial\delta} = \frac{\partial S}{\partial\beta} = \frac{\partial S}{\partial\gamma} = \frac{\partial S}{\partial\lambda} = 0$,

$$\begin{bmatrix}\mathbf{E}_d^T\mathbf{E}_d + \alpha\mathbf{E}_k & \mathbf{E}_d^T\mathbf{T}_d^T & \mathbf{E}_d^T\mathbf{C}^T & \mathbf{T}_k^T\\ \mathbf{T}_d\mathbf{E}_d & \mathbf{T}_d\mathbf{T}_d^T & \mathbf{T}_d\mathbf{C}^T & \mathbf{0}\\ \mathbf{C}\mathbf{E}_d & \mathbf{C}\mathbf{T}_d^T & \mathbf{C}\mathbf{C}^T & \mathbf{0}\\ \mathbf{T}_k & \mathbf{0} & \mathbf{0} & \mathbf{0}\end{bmatrix}\begin{bmatrix}\delta\\ \beta\\ \gamma\\ \lambda\end{bmatrix} = \begin{bmatrix}\mathbf{E}_d^T\mathbf{Y}^T\\ \mathbf{T}_d\mathbf{Y}^T\\ \mathbf{C}\mathbf{Y}^T\\ \mathbf{0}\end{bmatrix} \tag{14}$$

From parameter estimates $\hat{\delta}$ and $\hat{\beta}$, the effect $\hat{f}$ can be computed for voxel positions $\mathbf{x}$ gathered in a matrix $\mathbf{T}_x$. With a basis function matrix $\mathbf{E}_x$ set up as in (9), a vector of the estimated effect $\hat{\mathbf{Y}}_x$ with elements $\{\hat{\mathbf{Y}}_x\}_i = \hat{f}(\mathbf{x}_i)$ is

$$\hat{\mathbf{Y}}_x = \left[\mathbf{E}_x\ \mathbf{T}_x^T\right]\begin{bmatrix}\hat{\delta}\\ \hat{\beta}\end{bmatrix} \tag{15}$$

The effect of a given α to control the rigidity of the TPS varies when fitting to different observation sets. In order to get a consistent estimate across subjects, we adapt a measure of effective degrees of freedom, df_α [9]. With this, specifying $df_\alpha = 5$ leads to the least squares fitting hyperplane, while $df_\alpha = n$ leads to an interpolating fit.

For the TPS estimation a regular grid of $11 \times 7 \times 5$ knots is used. We find, that a value of $df_\alpha = 80$ provides a good overall trade off; fitting the intensity variation caused by the bias field while remaining robust towards noise. While increasing the value to $df_\alpha = 120$ does not seem to improve the fit, a choice of $df_\alpha = 50$ yields a too rigid hypersurface. Figure 1 illustrates the bias field correction.

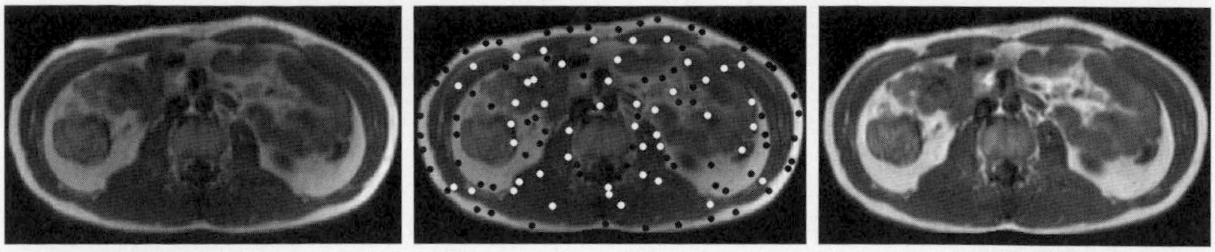

Fig. 1. Bias field correction. Left; the original image. Middle; the two classes of sampled points (black and white are intensity maxima and minima, respectively). Right; the corrected image.

3.2 Identifying Adipose Tissue

We label the volume in an unsupervised manner using FCM with random seeds [5], automatically distinguishing between voxels of the two classes by intensity based thresholding.

For a voxel j the FCM algorithm yields membership values $0 \leq u_{jk} \leq 1$, with $k = 1, 2$ and $u_{j1} + u_{j2} = 1$, reflecting the degrees of membership to the two clusters. These membership values form a reference between intensity and tissue type comparable between subjects. This way overall determined thresholds on the membership values can adapt to the intensity characteristics in each individual subject. A threshold of $\varepsilon = 0.5$, corresponds to labelling as the most likely tissue type.

3.3 Identifying Regions

We automatically divide the abdomen into the anatomically defined regions containing dSAT, sSAT and VAT. The region identification is performed slice-by-slice.

Active Contours. The SAT is characterized as a ring of homogeneous high intensity located under the skin. The shape of the layer is generally smooth.

The boundary between the SAT layer and the region containing the VAT is located using a variant of the active contours algorithm [13,20]. The method is based on spatially evolving a closed curve in 2-dimensions $\mathbf{X}(s) = (X(s), Y(s))$, with parameterisation $s \in [0, 1]$. For simplicity, we omit s in the following.

The evolution is driven to minimise the curve energy. By treating the curve $\mathbf{X}$ as a function of time t this corresponds to a dynamic formulation

$$\gamma \frac{\partial \mathbf{X}}{\partial t} = \mathbf{F}_{\text{int}}(\mathbf{X}) + \mathbf{F}_{\text{ext}}(\mathbf{X}). \tag{16}$$

The internal force component $\mathbf{F}_{\text{int}}$ should govern the smoothness of the curve during the evolution and make the segmentation robust e.g. towards discontinuities in the image structures of interst. The external force $\mathbf{F}_{\text{ext}}$ should incorporate image information related to the segmentation task. γ merely makes the units on both sides consistent.

The internal force is written as

$$\mathbf{F}_{\text{int}}(\mathbf{X}) = \frac{\partial}{\partial s}\left(\alpha \frac{\partial \mathbf{X}}{\partial s}\right) - \frac{\partial^2}{\partial s^2}\left(\beta \frac{\partial^2 \mathbf{X}}{\partial s^2}\right), \tag{17}$$

where $\frac{\partial \mathbf{X}}{\partial s}$ is the degree of stretching, while $\frac{\partial^2 \mathbf{X}}{\partial s^2}$ is the curvature. The contributions of the two are controlled by weights α and β.

We use a *balloon* model [3], forming the external force by two terms

$$\mathbf{F}_{\text{ext}}(\mathbf{X}) = \mathbf{F}_{\text{def}}(\mathbf{X}) + \mathbf{F}_{\text{imp}}(\mathbf{X}), \tag{18}$$

where $\mathbf{F}_{\text{def}}$ is a *deflation* force, and $\mathbf{F}_{\text{imp}}$ is an *impurity* force.

The deflation force for a point $\mathbf{X}$ on the curve is defined as

$$\mathbf{F}_{\text{def}}(\mathbf{X}) = w_{\text{def}} \mathbf{N}(\mathbf{X}), \tag{19}$$

where $w_{\text{def}} > 0$ is a weighting parameter, and $\mathbf{N}(\mathbf{X})$ is the inward unit normal for the curve at the point. A deformation using $\mathbf{F}_{\text{def}}$ alone would cause the curve to contract – like a deflating balloon.

The second force term of (18), $\mathbf{F}_{\text{imp}}$, is directed opposite of $\mathbf{F}_{\text{def}}$, and should neutralise the deformation by means of image information.

In the formulation of $\mathbf{F}_{\text{imp}}$, we rely on the assumption of distinct homogeneous high intensities in the SAT layer. At a given time in the deformation, the force magnitude is defined by the content of the region enclosed by the initial and current curve.

The magnitude is zero for a *pure* area, and is designed to grow proportional to the share of *impure* intensity covered. For a point $\mathbf{X}$ on the curve, we write

$$\mathbf{F}_{\text{imp}}(\mathbf{X}) = -w_{\text{imp}} \mathbf{N}(\mathbf{X}) \int_0^1 H(\Theta - I(\mathbf{X}_z))dz, \tag{20}$$

with weight $w_{\text{imp}} > 0$. H is a Heaviside step function based on a threshold Θ and image value I at the location $\mathbf{X}_z = (1 - z)\mathbf{X}_{\text{init}} + z\mathbf{X}$. That is, the line integral between the point position on the initial and current curve.

To define Θ in a generic fashion across subjects, we base the segmentation on the AT-class membership values provided by the FCM algorithm. This way the intuitive choice $\Theta = 0.5$, gives good results.

The method is first used for segmenting the outer boundary of the SAT layer; initialised as a circle around the abdomen, with impurity based on non-AT. This is then used to initialise the inner boundary segmentation. Figure 2 shows an example of the SAT-layer segmentation.

Dynamic Programming. We partition the SAT layer into a deep and a superficial part by identifying SF. On the MRI, SF appears as a smooth low intensity line on the high intensity AT. The shape generally follows the outline of the abdomen. We make use of these properties in the segmentation; spatially transforming the image and applying dynamic programming (DP) [4,5].

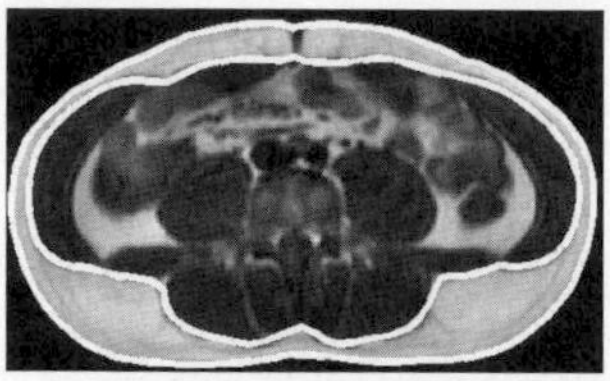

Fig. 2. SAT-layer segmentation by active contours

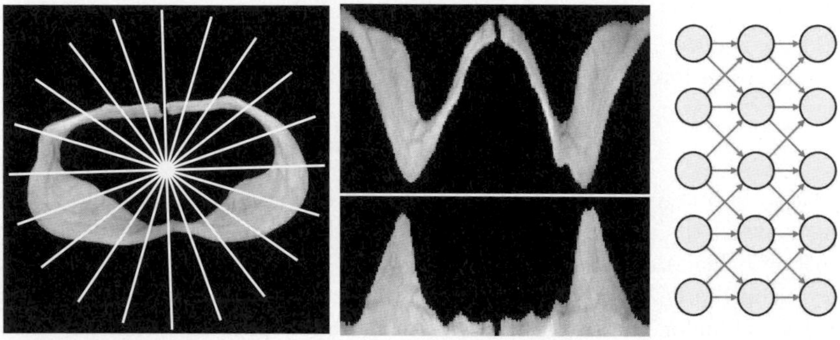

Fig. 3. The spatial transformation of the SAT layer. Left; 20 profiles illustrating the resampling concept. Middle; the resampled image using 200 profiles and the *flat* transformed image. Right; directed acyclic graph illustrating the edge structure.

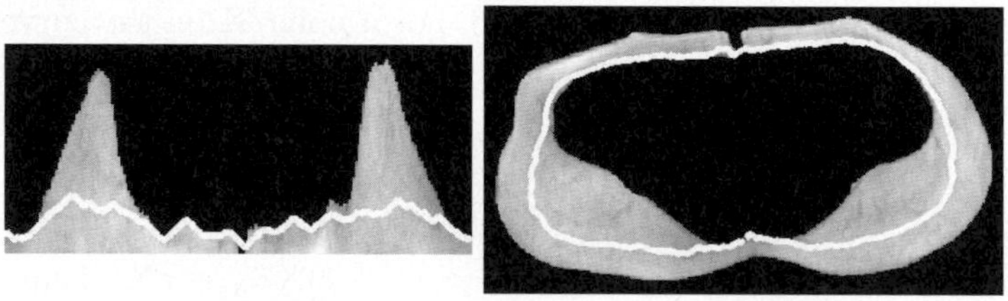

Fig. 4. Partitioning of the SAT layer by DP. Left; transformed image. Right; original set-up.

We apply a polar transformation of the SAT layer; resampling along profiles from the centre. Furthermore, to make SF appear straighter, the resampled image is *flattened* removing all zero-intensity pixels outside the SAT-layer. Figure 3 illustrates the resampling steps.

In the transformed image, SF runs approximately straight across the image. We utilise this, and regard the image as a directed acyclic graph; pixels are vertices weighted by their intensity with connecting directed edges as illustrated on the rightmost drawing on Fig. 3.

This way, we can identify SF as the shortest path from a vertex in the leftmost column to one in the rightmost. The edge structure chosen is suitable, as it enforces smoothness on the path. Figure 4 shows the resuling path on both the transformed image and the original set-up – after transforming it back.

4 Results

The clustering and the identified regions are combined to form the final segmented volume. We observe a slight difference in the characteristics of VAT and SAT, as the MRI generally exhibit less contrast for the latter, due to the partial volume effect. We handle this by means of locally defined thresholds; $\varepsilon = 0.85$ for VAT and $\varepsilon = 0.50$ in the SAT layer. Figure 5 shows an example of the final segmentation.

The segmented volumes were subject to a visual inspection by medical experts. On slices, where blurry artefacts in the anterior part were caused by insufficient breath-holding during image acquisition, the SAT layer identification generally proved robust.

Most subjects featured very little anterior SAT. A decision was therefore made to only consider the subdivision in the posterior. On slices with little SAT, SF coincides with the inner SAT layer boundary (e.g. Fig. 1). Here, the DP scheme classified the entire layer as sSAT.

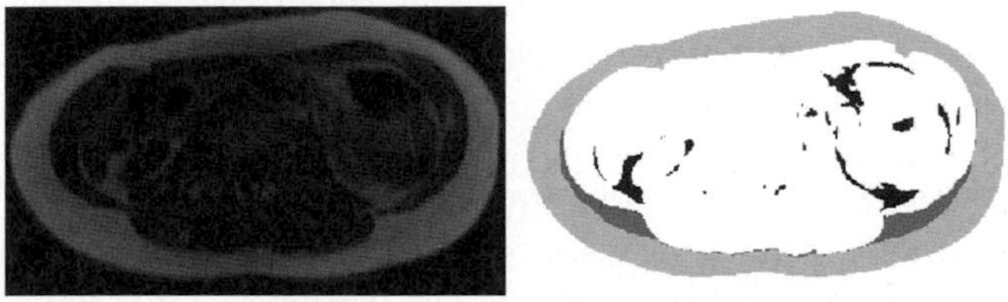

Fig. 5. Final AT segmentation. Light grey; sSAT. Dark grey; dSAT. Black; VAT.

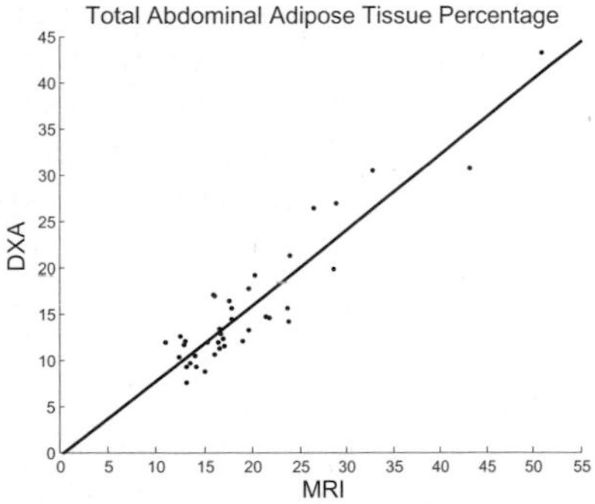

Fig. 6. Corresponding percentages of total abdominal adipose tissue; computed with our MRI-based method and assessed by DXA. The line shows the linear regression fit $y = -0.3975 + 0.8169x$ with $R^2 = 0.86$.

As a quantitative assessment, the obesity was reported as three volume percentages for each subject; sums of voxels in each AT-class relative to the total sum of voxels in the abdomen.

Figure 6 shows a comparison of our total AT percentage with a corresponding measure assessed by DXA. A linear regression analysis showed good a fit between the two ($y = -0.3975 + 0.8169x$, $R^2 = 0.86$). Our method seems to produce slightly higher values in comparison to DXA-measurements. This supports our choice of applying a stricter threshold for VAT, as this over-estimation would have been more distinct.

5 Conclusion

This work presents a method for fully automated segmentation of VAT, dSAT and sSAT in abdominal MRI.

The method automatically performs a three-dimensional correction of the MRI to remove the hardware-related bias field effect, enabling intensity based tissue classification.

The unsupervised classification scheme, allows us to use structures in intensity distributions related to the two classes. Furthermore, we can distinguish between characteristics of VAT and SAT.

The deformable model identifying the SAT layer proved to handle discontinuities and artefacts well without a training set. Our inclusion of image information uses results from the tissue classification, adapting to the individual subjects to makie the segmentations more robust.

Considering that both quantities of VAT and dSAT have a reported connection to IR, our partitioning into sSAT and dSAT has an advantage over VAT due to the degree of partial volume effect present in the VAT on the MRI used in this study. Where the appearance of SF generally is well-defined; either clearly visible on the SAT layer or coinciding with the interior SAT boundary.

The segmentations were visually validated by medical experts. Furthermore, to evaluate the tissue classification, total percentages of AT measured by our method was compared to similar measures obtained from DXA of the same abdominal region. A linear regression showed good correspondence ($R^2 = 0.86$).

The developed automated segmentation method proved suitable for distinguishing between three types of abdominal AT from MRI. In comparison to manual and semi-automatic segmentations, our method enables a much larger throughput and eliminates intra- and interobserver variability.

References

1. Abate, N., Garg, A., Peshock, R.M., Stray-Gundersen, J., Grundy, S.M.: Relationships of generalized and regional adiposity to insulin sensitivity in men. Journal of Clinical Investigation 96(1), 88 (1995)

2. Armao, D., Guyon, J.P., Firat, Z., Brown, M.A., Semelka, R.C.: Accurate quantification of visceral adipose tissue (VAT) using water-saturation MRI and computer segmentation: Preliminary results. Journal of Magnetic Resonance Imaging 23(5), 736–741 (2006)
3. Cohen, L.D.: On active contour models and balloons. CVGIP: Image Understanding 53(2), 211–218 (1991)
4. Cormen, T.H., Leiserson, C.E., Rivest, R.L., Stein, C.: Introduction to Algorithms, 2nd edn. MIT Press, Cambridge (2001)
5. Dawant, B.M., Zijdenbos, A.P.: Handbook of Medical Imaging. Medical Image Processing and Analysis, ch.2, vol. 2. SPIE Press, Bellingham (2000)
6. Duchon, J.: Interpolation of functions of two variables following the principle of the bending of thin plates. Revue Francaise d'Automatique Informatique Recherche Operationnelle 10, 5–12 (1976)
7. Engholm, R., Dubinskiy, A., Larsen, R., Hanson, L.G., Christoffersen, B.Ø.: An adipose segmentation and quantification scheme for the abdominal region in minipigs. In: International Symposium on Medical Imaging 2006, The International Society for Optical Engineering. SPIE, San Diego (February 2006)
8. Green, P.J., Silverman, B.W.: Nonparametric Regression and Generalized Linear Models: A Roughness Penalty Approach. Chapman and Hall, Boca Raton (1994)
9. Hastie, T., Tibshirani, R., Friedman, J.H.: The Elements of Statistical Learning. Springer, Heidelberg (2001)
10. Hou, Z.: A review on MR image intensity inhomogeneity correction. International Journal of Biomedical Imaging 2006, 1–11 (2006)
11. Ji, Q., Glass, J.O., Reddick, W.E.: A novel, fast entropy-minimization algorithm for bias field correction in mr images. Magnetic Resonance Imaging 25, 259–264 (2007)
12. Jørgensen, P.S., Larsen, R., Wraae, K.: Unsupervised assessment of subcutaneous and visceral fat by MRI. In: Salberg, A.-B., Hardeberg, J.Y., Jenssen, R. (eds.) SCIA 2009. LNCS, vol. 5575, pp. 179–188. Springer, Heidelberg (2009)
13. Kass, M., Witkin, A., Terzopoulos, D.: Snakes: Active contour models. International Journal of Computer Vision 1(4), 321–331 (1988)
14. Kelley, D.E., Thaete, F.L., Troost, F., Huwe, T., Goodpaster, B.H.: Subdivisions of subcutaneous abdominal adipose tissue and insulin resistance. The American Journal of Physiology - Endocrinology and Metabolism 278, E941-E948 (2000)
15. Kullberg, J., Von Below, C., Lönn, L., Lind, L., Ahlström, H., Johansson, L.: Practical approach for estimation of subcutaneous and visceral adipose tissue. Clinical Physiology and Functional Imaging 27(3), 148–153 (2007)
16. Leinhard, O.D., Johansson, A., Rydell, J., Smedby, Ö., Nyström, F., Lundberg, P., Borga, M.: Quantitative abdominal fat estimation using mri. In: 19th International Conference on Pattern Recognition, ICPR 2008, pp. 1–4 (December 2008)
17. Positano, V., Gastaldelli, A., Sironi, A., Santarelli, M.F., Lombardi, M., Landini, L.: An accurate and robust method for unsupervised assessment of abdominal fat by MRI. Journal of Magnetic Resonance Imaging 20(4), 684–689 (2004)
18. Sled, J.G., Zijdenbos, A.P., Evans, A.C.: A nonparametric method for automatic correction of intensitynonuniformity in MRI data. IEEE Transactions on Medical Imaging 17, 87–97 (1998)
19. Wild, S., Roglic, G., Green, A., Sicree, R., King, H.: Global prevalence of diabetes. Diabetes Care 27(5), 1047 (2004)
20. Xu, C., Pham, D.L., Prince, J.L.: Handbook of Medical Imaging. Medical Image Processing and Analysis, ch. 3, vol. 2. SPIE Press, Bellingham (2000)

Fully Automatic Liver Volumetry Using 3D Level Set Segmentation for Differentiated Liver Tissue Types in Multiple Contrast MR Datasets

Oliver Gloger[1], Klaus Toennies[2], and Jens-Peter Kuehn[3]

[1] Ernst Moritz Arndt University of Greifswald, Institute for Community Medicine, Walther-Rathenau-Str.48. 17475 Greifswald, Germany
gloger@uni-greifswald.de

[2] Otto-von-Guericke University of Magdeburg, Institute for Simulation and Graphics, Universitaetsplatz 2, 39106 Magdeburg, Germany
klaus@isg.uni-magdeburg.de

[3] Ernst Moritz Arndt University of Greifswald, Institute for Diagnostic Radiology and Neuroradiology, Ferdinand-Sauerbruch-Strasse, 17475 Greifswald, Germany
kuehn@uni-greifswald.de

Abstract. Modern epidemiological studies analyze a high amount of magnetic resonance imaging (MRI) data, which requires fully automatic segmentation methods to assist in organ volumetry. We propose a fully automatic two-step 3D level set algorithm for liver segmentation in MRI data that delineates liver tissue on liver probability maps and uses a distance transform based segmentation refinement method to improve segmentation results. MR intensity distributions in test subjects are extracted in a training phase to obtain prior information on liver, kidney and background tissue types. Probability maps are generated by using linear discriminant analysis and Bayesian methods. The algorithm is able to differentiate between normal liver tissue and fatty liver tissue and generates probability maps for both tissues to improve the segmentation results. The algorithm is embedded in a volumetry framework and yields sufficiently good results for use in epidemiological studies.

Keywords: Level Set Segmentation, Distance Transformation, Linear Discriminant Analysis, Bayes' Theorem.

1 Introduction

Advances in medical imaging techniques have substantially increased the demand on medical image segmentation. Besides being used as a tool in routine clinical practise, medical image segmentation can be very helpful for analyzing certain health-related properties in populations in modern epidemiological science. Organ volumetry is an important part of this. Epidemiological studies often analyze enormous amounts of data from participants, which would make manual segmentation very time-consuming and exhaustive and, consequently, prone to intra- and interreader bias.

A. Heyden and F. Kahl (Eds.): SCIA 2011, LNCS 6688, pp. 512–523, 2011.

Automatic image segmentation is preferred but is difficult because understanding the complexity of medical images requires radiologists with special training and skills. Automatic liver segmentation is particularly challenging since the properties of hepatic tissue are similar to those of adjacent organs and tissues. Consequently, state-of-the-art segmentation techniques can lead to oversegmentations with liver segments including adjacent organs such as the kidney, pancreas, spleen, and stomach. Conversely, some diseases such as cirrhosis, fatty liver, or tumors can show heterogeneous tissue properties inside the liver, which can lead to undersegmentation.

This work sets out to assist medical experts in analyzing MR datasets in the setting of epidemiological studies investigating large populations of different subjects. MR datasets typically show lower contrast and smaller edge magnitudes than CT datasets. Further challenges of tissue delineation in MR datasets are motion and pulsation artifacts as well as partial volume effects. All of these drawbacks require robust segmentation techniques especially designed for MR datasets and incorporating flexibilities for identifying oversegmentation in the setting of automatic volumetry. The approach presented here uses flexible level set segmentation including the ability of recognizing and reducing oversegmentation. Liver MR signal intensity patterns of multiple contrast datasets differ strongly between normal and fatty livers. The method proposed here differs from existing approaches for MR image segmentation in that it differentiates between fat liver and normal liver, enabling successful segmentation for both kinds of liver tissues.

2 Related Work

Literature research shows that numerous approaches for liver segmentation in CT datasets exist, while only a few methods have been proposed for MR datasets. CT segmentation approaches cover a wider spectrum of different methods ranging from fundamental concepts (like histogram analysis, morphological operations, threshold techniques, and region growing) [1, 2] to deformable models [3, 4, 5], atlas-based concepts [6, 7, 8, 9], classification methods [10, 11, 12], and graph-cut techniques [13, 14]. There exist a fast liver segmentation method [15] especially for contrast enhanced MR images using a partitioned probabilistic model. However, only few approaches are available for native MR datasets using level set segmentation techniques [16, 17, 18] or fast marching and improved fuzzy cluster methods [19].

Although MR acquisition usually produces multiple contrast datasets, existing analysis approaches to the segmentation of MR datasets do not apply image information from all weighting available. Variations in appearance resulting from liver disease or the presence of different types of liver tissue are not accounted for. Twenty percent of the subjects in our study have fatty livers [20]. Fatty livers have different tissue properties than nonfatty livers and therefore have different MR signal intensities. Automatic methods should recognize fatty livers and segment them as well as nonfatty livers. Hence, we developed a fully automatic liver segmentation framework that can differentiate between fatty livers and nonfatty livers and segments both types of tissue by using class-specific prior knowledge about MR signal intensities. We use 3D geodesic active contours and extend and accelerate the work of [21] for segmentation of liver-specific probability maps by calculating improved stopping terms in a two-step segmentation approach. The drawbacks of existing approaches discussed above are overcome by the approach we are presenting here.

3 Data Acquisition

The study is based on images taken from participants of the population-based Study of Health in Pomerania (SHIP). All abdominal MR datasets were acquired on a 1.5 Tesla MR scanner (Magnetom Avanto; Siemens Medical Systems, Erlangen, Germany). Subjects were placed in the supine position, and two phased-array surface coils were placed over the abdomen and pelvis. The spinal coil was embedded in the scanner table. Two trained technicians performed all examinations in a standardized way. Four different datasets were created using the VIBE sequence (Fig. 1). The T1-weighted gradient-echo sequence in two-point Dixon technique [22] provides in- and out-phase as well as water- and fat-saturated images. Images were acquired with TR = 7.5 (ms) and multimodal TE = 2.4/4.8 (ms) and a flip angle of 10. The voxel size was 1.64 x 1.64 x 4.0 mm, and 64 slices were acquired in 19 s. The image resolution used is common for diagnosis in clinical routine although it is relatively coarse. It was used in SHIP in order to avoid long image acquisition times. The Dixon technique ensures that the four different datasets are sufficiently well registrated for the subsequent methods that are used in our liver volumetry framework.

4 Description of the Method

4.1 Denoising of MR Datasets

Edge-preserving anisotropic diffusion [23] is used to homogenize the MR intensities inside the different tissue types and to preserve edge magnitudes that are important for distinguishing liver tissue from adjacent tissues. We applied this denoising method over 50 iterations by using time steps of 0.0625.

4.2 Training Phase

A training phase is mandatory for supervised probability map generation techniques. Thus, for training purposes, binary masks of 20 livers from different subjects were segmented manually and saved. Manual segmentation was performed by medical experts. The binary masks served to obtain prior knowledge of MR signal intensity distributions and can be used for later probablity map generation. Since many subjects in SHIP have fatty livers, we determined MR signal intensities separately for fatty liver and nonfatty livers. As biopsy results

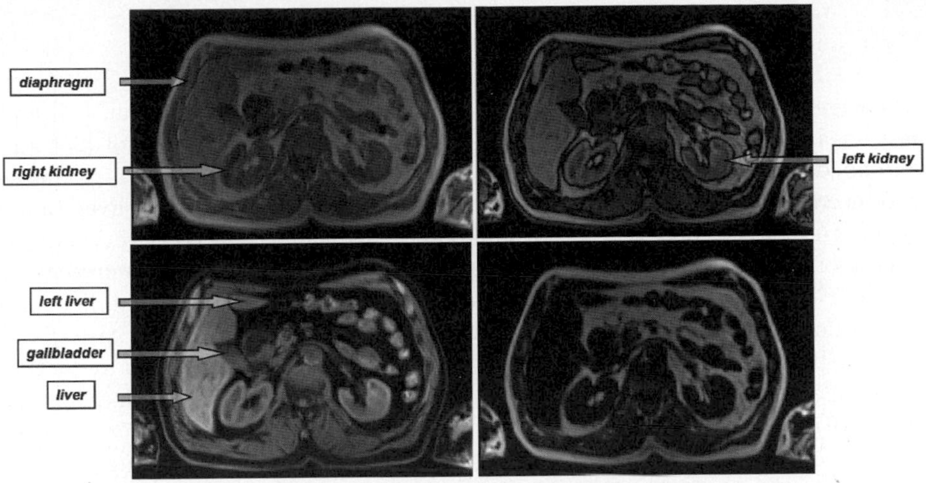

Fig. 1. Original MR images taken from a transverse slice of the VIBE sequence. In-phase weighting (upper left), opposed-phase weighting (upper right), fat-saturated weighting (lower left), water-saturated weighting (lower right). Frequently mentioned organs and tissue types in this work are labeled on the images for better orientation.

are available for some SHIP subjects, we selected MR datasets of 10 subjects with nonfatty livers (< 5 % fat) and 10 subjects with fatty livers (25% - 64% fat) for this purpose. For our supervised recognition technique, we aim to enhance the transition region between liver and kidney and therefore we have to assign three tissue types (liver, kidney, and background). Hence, binary masks of the 20 selected subjects' right kidneys were segmented manually by medical experts and saved separately. Finally, an overlap region, which is contained in all 20 binary masks of the segmented livers, was determined. We call this region the "reliable common liver" (rcl) region because it is most likely contained in all liver regions of the SHIP subjects.

4.3 Probability Map Generation

MR signal intensity distributions for liver and surrounding tissues are estimated from the training data. Since intensity distributions in the MR images vary for fatty and nonfatty livers, two distributions in the rcl region are estimated. Likelihoods for the two tissue types can be determined with the MR intensity distributions of the two types of trained binary masks. Thus, for every tissue type, we can calculate their mean (μ_f, μ_{nf}) and covariance matrices (Σ_f, Σ_{nf}) and estimate their multivariate normal distributions (P_f, P_{nf}). We extract all N test subjects' MR signal intensity samples $(V = \{\overrightarrow{X}_i \| \overrightarrow{X_i} \in rcl, i = 1..N\})$ inside the rcl region and assign the liver tissue type according to the maximum likelihood classification by using the calculated log-likelihoods:

$$\max\{\sum_{i=1}^{N} \ln P_{nf}(\overrightarrow{X_i}\|\mu_{nf}, \Sigma_{nf}), \ln P_f(\overrightarrow{X_i}\|\mu_f, \Sigma_f)\} \tag{1}$$

For generating probability maps we apply the work of Gloger et.al. [24] and use linear discriminant reduction techniques based upon the work of [25] and extended by [26] for multiple distribution classes. By using the binary masks produced during the training phase, MR distributions for the two liver tissue types, the kidney, and the background can easily be estimated. Every sample vector of the collected MR distributions consists of four elements representing the four different MR weightings. We distinguish two types of probability map generation: the two-class case (liver, background) and the three-class case (liver, kidney, background). For each case, we perform linear discriminant reduction (LDA)[25] and determine the axis that serves as optimal projection axis for the data to reduce class overlaps after projection. LDA reduces the dimensionality of the samples from n=4 to n=1 in a linear manner by preserving as much discriminant information between the given class distributions as possible. By projecting the sample vectors of every class onto the projection axis we obtain one-dimensional probability distributions for every class. The distributions are generated using a kernel density estimator on the histogram. We used a value of $\sigma = 2.0$ as standard deviation in the gaussian kernel. Additionally, we incorporate the information of the trained positions in the given binary masks of the three classes as independent probabilities into the likelihoods. In the case of three classes this results in:

$$P(L|\overrightarrow{V}) = \frac{P(\overrightarrow{V}|L)P_{xyz}(L)}{P(\overrightarrow{V}|L)P_{xyz}(L) + P(\overrightarrow{V}|K)P_{xyz}(K) + P(\overrightarrow{V}|B)P_{xyz}(B)} \tag{2}$$

$$P_{xyz}(L) = P_{xyz}(L|x, y, z) = P(L|x)P(L|y)P(L|z) \tag{3}$$

for the liver class. Here $V = V(x, y, z)$ represents a voxel with its MR dataset coordinate and L, K, B represent the 3 classes of liver, kidney, and background, respectively. Liver pobability map generation for the two-class case is defined straight-forward in the same manner as (2) and (3), treating kidney samples and kidney locations as part of the background class information. In this approach we do not differentiate between the class occurrences and set the a priori probabilities of every class to 1. For every test subject we calculate the liver probability maps for the three-class case and the two-class case, depending on which liver tissue type is present. The segmentation is performed in the liver probability map of the two-class case, incorporating liver probability maps of the three-class case for refinement purposes (Fig. 2).

4.4 3D Level Set Segmentation

Instead of using original MR datasets, we perform level set segmentation on the calculated probability maps. We use the liver probability map of the two-class case calculated as described in the previous section. In the liver probability

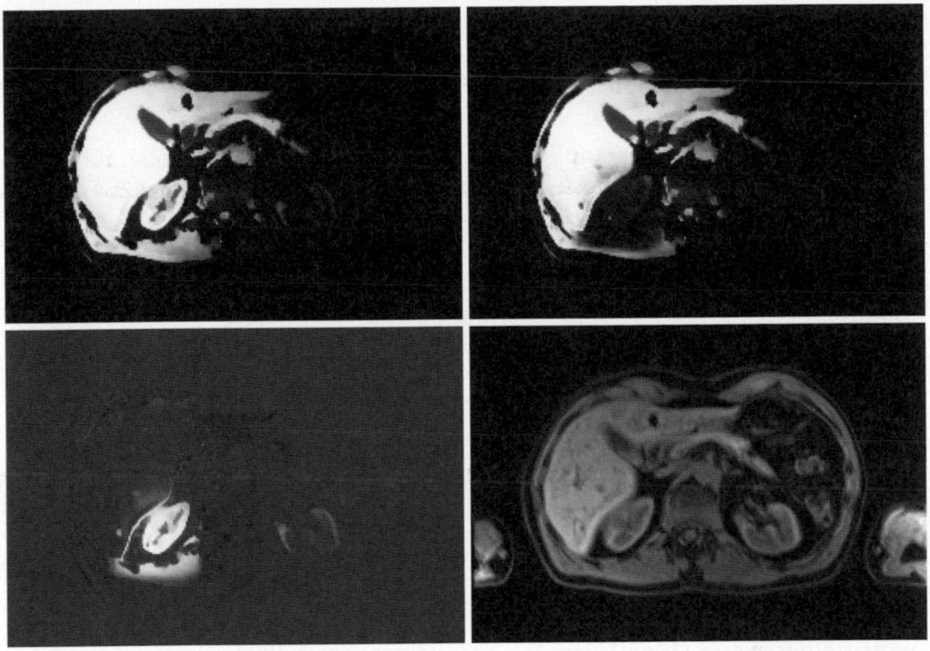

Fig. 2. Two-class liver probability map (upper left) and three-class liver probability map with kidney significantly suppressed (upper right). Difference image enhances transition region between liver and kidney (lower left). Original fat-saturated image (lower right).

map, the most probable liver tissue is enhanced based on liver- specific MR signal intensity distributions and MR dataset locations. A further advantage is that we can use the maximum value of the probability map as the starting point for 3D level set segmentation. During the test phase of our method, we observed that the maximum value is always located inside the liver. As possible MR artifacts or liver disease may show different probability values, we use the Geodesic Active Contour approach of Caselles et.al. [21]. Consequently, we use the flexibility of the level sets to perform topological changes for our segmentation purpose. A drawback of the level set method is its time-consuming propagation process. Hence, we perform the segmentation in two steps: a fast and coarse segmentation step on lower resolved probability maps and a fine segmentation step in the probablity maps with original resolution. Fine segmentation is initiated with the coarse segmentation result that is scaled up to the original matrix resolution. Level set propagation is steered by the following partial diffential equation:

$$\frac{\partial \phi}{\partial t} = g(pm)(a + b\kappa)|\nabla \phi| + \nabla g(pm)\nabla \phi \tag{4}$$

Here, ϕ represents the signed distance function depending on the segmenting surface, κ is the mean curvature, $pm = pm(x, y, z)$ represents the probability map values at the MR dataset positions, and a, b are weighting parameters for propagation speed and level set mean curvature weighting. As stopping function we chose:

$$g(pm) = \frac{1}{1 + |\nabla pm|^2} \tag{5}$$

The stopping effect of g is influenced by the strength of the probability map gradients. To accelerate level set propagation we suppress the influence of lower probability map gradients. Instead of using a threshold to remove low gradients we use a sigmoid function to transform the gradient values to the relevant range of gradients to ensure faster propagation. We focus on a particular set of gradient values and progressively attenuate values outside that range:

$$S(|\nabla pm|) = (\max(|\nabla pm|) - \min(|\nabla pm|)) \frac{1}{1 + \exp(-\frac{|\nabla pm| - \beta}{\alpha})} + \min(|\nabla pm|) \tag{6}$$

For the sigmoid transformation we apply the following values for the parameters: $\alpha = 10$ and $\beta = \frac{\max(|\nabla pm|)}{3}$.

4.5 Distance Transform Based Segmentation Refinement

Due to adjacent tissue with similar appearance overspills can occur. Some of those overspills could be avoided by penalizing the curvature term during level set propagation. However, it was crucial to find a representative weighting parameter for penalizing the curvature term for all the variously shaped livers having different curvature properties. In case of strong curvature penalizations, elongated and tapered liver parts are excluded during segmentation. Interior liver parts having low probability values (i.e. vasular structures or the hepatic portal vein) have to be overcome by topological changes. This is not possible, if high curvatures are necessary to overcome those inner structures. Since, higher penalization of the curvature term produces undersegmentations we used curvature weightings, which in fact can produce overspills but includes all liver parts.

Then we applied a new method to remove those overspills, which are recognized and removed in a postprocessing step where we assume that regions erroneously connected to the liver are touching the liver only in a small region. By eroding the liver boundary such regions should be found since erosion should split the segment at those sites. Hence we erode the liver segment, remove erroneously included segment parts and use the remaining, eroded part to predict the correct liver boundary at sites of overspill. We use the distance transform that has been generated by the level set segmentation to guide this erosion process. During level set propagation we have assigned positive distance values inside the liver and negative ones outside the liver. Hence, the positive part represents a distance transform of the segmentation result (SR) and we determine an initial 3D label (SR label) constructed by all positive distance values. Now we iteratively subtract a distance value (we chose 1 mm) from the signed distance map, which leads to a subsequent inwards shrinkage of the zero level set. If the segment is split in a shrinkage step, then we continue with the segment that contains the

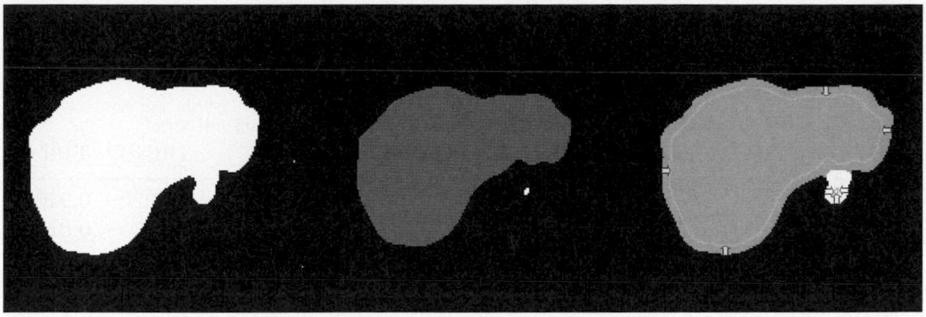

Fig. 3. Slice of 3D label resulting from level set segmentation (left). Same slice following label separation as a result of the shrinkage method (middle). Voxels contained in level set segmentation result and not contained in one of the separated 3D labels are assigned to the 3D labels according to their minimal euclidean distance. The borders of the shrinked 3D labels (middle) are depicted in green with arrows indicating the shrinkage direction (right).

starting point of the level set propagation. Voxels removed by the actual shrinkage step get segment labels assigned according to their euclidean distance to the nearest segment. We construct a new signed distance map depending on the liver-representing label surface. Thus, we remove all labels which we regard as overspills (Fig. 3).

Given the high liver shape variability and the fact that livers consist of left and right liver parts we aim to avoid label separations inside the liver. Livers can show concave surface regions, which can lead to separations inside the liver when this method is used. We found that most overspills are detected in the first shrinkage steps; hence, we use an upper shrinkage frontier (20 mm) to avoid removal of liver parts. However, parts of the kidney region may not be removable by this technique since the kidney has similar tissue properties, and there is a higher degree of surface contact between liver and kidney. Overspill into kidney regions can be removed if we perform shrinkage beyond 20 mm but only at sites where label separations occur inside the transition region between liver and kidney. This transition region can be determined by subtracting the liver probability map of the two-class case from the liver probability map of the three-class case (Fig. 2, lower left). We threshold this difference dataset by choosing the half of the probability map maximum (0.5 in case of probability values of [0;1]).

5 Results

We tested our method on 40 MR datasets from different subjects, which are not contained in the training set. 20 Twenty of the MR datasets contained livers with normal tissue and 20 MR datasets showed livers with fatty tissue. Result quality was different depending on whether fatty livers or nonfatty livers were

Table 1. Mean (Mean) and standard deviations (Std) of segmentation quality measures for evaluating liver segmentation with the new method proposed here. Segmentation quality differs for nonfatty livers (left) versus fatty livers (right).

	Nonfatty livers				Fatty livers			
	VE	OE	DICE	TPF	VE	OE	DICE	TPF
Mean	0.047	0.129	0.944	0.881	0.120	0.206	0.892	0.940
Std	0.031	0.028	0.020	0.052	0.078	0.082	0.057	0.017

segmented. Hence, we evaluate and present the results for fatty and nonfatty livers separately (Tab. 1).

We used three segmentation quality measures for result evaluation. We calculate the volume error (with V_T, V_S representing the training and segmented volume respectively)

$$VE = \frac{V_T - V_S}{V_T} \tag{7}$$

and overlap error according to:

$$OE = \frac{N(|M_T - M_S|)}{N(M_T)} \tag{8}$$

with M_T, M_S representing the binary masks of trained and segmented dataset respectively. $N()$ represents the number of voxels. Furthermore, we calculated the true positive fraction according to:

$$TPF = \frac{N(M_T \cap M_S)}{N(M_T)} \tag{9}$$

Finally, we determined the DICE coefficient, which has been established as a reliable measure for segmentation quality in large-scale studies [27]:

$$DICE = \frac{2N(M_T \cap M_S)}{N(M_T) + N(M_S)} \tag{10}$$

Our method performs better when used to segment nonfatty livers. All quality measures are superior for nonfatty livers compared with fatty livers. A comparison with existing approaches to liver segmentation in CT and MR datasets is difficult due to inconsistently used quality measures. Unfortunately, reliable data on the quality of MR segmentation is scarce. Although comparing quality measures between different imaging modalilities is precarious, we compare our results with the few results published on CT datasets. In [5] the authors report overlap errors of 12.2, which is nearly the same as our results for nonfatty livers. The authors in [28] achieved a mean value of 0.91 for the Dice coefficient, which is worse than our results for nonfatty livers. The only reliable information about quality measures for MR liver segmentation is given in [18]: our results for the

TPF measures are with a mean value of 0.94 nearly as good as their TPF results of 0.95. However, our method is fully automatic and takes different tissue types into account, which is not possible by applying the method described by Chen et al. Result analysis with visualization techniques in our volumetry framework shows that probability maps of nonfatty livers are less susceptible to overspill. Furthermore, overspills from probability maps of nonfatty livers are easier to remove. With the upper border for the maximum shrinkage distance we used during the distance-based refinement phase, some overspills are not removed from fatty liver probability maps.

6 Discussion

We developed a fully automatic 3D volumetry framework, which uses and extends an existing edge-based level set approach to segment livers in MR datasets. Previously, we tested also a well-known region-based level set approach [29] delivering worse results than our extended edge-based level set approach. A two-step level set segmentation is performed in liver probability maps produced by combining methods of linear discriminant analysis with a Bayesian formulation. We filter relevant liver edges from liver probability maps by using sigmoid functions which generates adapted stopping functions to improve and accelerate level set propagations. Prior knowledge about liver-specific MR intensity distributions is collected during a primary training phase, which is used for probability map generation. Thus, no user-interaction is required. Our method differentiates between fatty liver tissue and non-fatty liver tissue and generates tissue-specific probability maps automatically. Consequently, our method performs liver sgementation for both tissue types, which is very helpful for applications in epidemiological studies.

We tested our method for 40 probands of an epidemiological study and achieved good results. Comparisons show that our results for non-fatty livers are in the same quality range as results from existing approaches for liver segmentation of CT and MR datasets. Our method outperforms several approaches for CT datasets. A volume error of less than 5% for non-fatty livers is already appropriate for fully automatic non-fatty liver volumetry in large-scale studies.

The segmentation results for fatty livers should be improved to be used for epidemiological studies. Fatty liver tissue shows more similarity to adjacent tissue types, which reduces the probability map quality for the application of edge-based level set segmentation techniques. Due to higher tissue similarity, overspill into adjacent tissue is more probable on fatty liver probability maps. In future work we aim to improve the segmentation quality especially for fatty livers by using more relevant liver features in order to reduce the volume error below 10%. Although livers show high shape variabilities, we will incorporate prior shape information to improve the results for fatty livers.

References

[1] Gao, L., Heath, D., Kuszyk, B., Fishman, E.: Automatic liver segmentation technique for three-dimensional visualization of CT data. Radiology 201(2), 359–364 (1996)

[2] Seo, K.S.: Improved Fully Automatic Liver Segmentation Using Histogram Tail Threshold Algorithms. In: International Conference on Computational Science, pp. 822–825 (2005)

[3] Evans, A., Lambrou, T., Linnery, A., Todd-Pokroped, A.: Automatic Segmentation of Liver Using a Toplogy Adaptive Snake. In: International Conference on Biomedical Engineering, pp. 205–208 (2004)

[4] Schenk, A., Prause, G.P.M., Peitgen, H.O.: Efficient semiautomatic segmentation of 3d objects in medical images. In: Medical Image Computing and Computer-Assisted Intervention, pp. 186–195 (2001)

[5] Daisuke, F., Akinobu, S., Hidefumi, K.: Automatic Liver Segmentation Method based on Maximum A Posterior Probability Estimation and LevelSet Method. In: Medical Image Computing and Computer Assisted Intervention, pp. 117–124 (2007)

[6] Lamecker, H., Lange, T., Seebass, M.: A Statistical Shape Model for the Liver. In: Dohi, T., Kikinis, R. (eds.) MICCAI 2002. LNCS, vol. 2489, pp. 421–427. Springer, Heidelberg (2002)

[7] Ling, H., Zhou, S.K., Zheng, Y., Georgescu, B., Suehling, M., Comaniciu, D.: Hierarchical, learning-based automatic liver segmentation. In: IEEE Conf. on Computer Vision and Pattern Recognition (CVPR 2008). IEEE Computer Society, Anchorage (2008)

[8] Soler, L., Delingette, H., Malandain, G., Montagnat, J., Ayache, N., Koehle, C., Dourthe, O., Malassagne, B., Smith, M., Mutter, D., et al.: Fully Automatic Anatomical, Pathological, and Functional Segmentation from CT Scans for Hepatic Surgery. In: Hanson, K.M. (ed.), February 14, pp. 246–255. SPIE, San Diego (2000)

[9] Heimann, T., Wolf, I., Meinzer, H.-P.: Active shape models for a fully automated 3D segmentation of the liver – an evaluation on clinical data. In: Larsen, R., Nielsen, M., Sporring, J. (eds.) MICCAI 2006. LNCS, vol. 4191, pp. 41–48. Springer, Heidelberg (2006)

[10] Li, M., Yang, L.: Liver Segmentation Based on Expectation Maximization and Morphological Filters in CT Images. In: Bioinformatics and Biomedical Engineering (ICBBE 2007). IEEE, Wuhan (2007)

[11] Freiman, M., Eliassaf, O., Taieb, Y., Joskowicz, L., Azraq, Y., Sosna, J.: An iterative Bayesian approach for nearly automatic liver segmentation: algorithm and validation. International Journal of Computer Assisted Radiology and Surgery 3(5), 439–446 (2008)

[12] Sosna, J., Berman, P., Azraq, Y., Libson, E.: Liver segmentation and volume calculation from MDCT using Bayesian likelihood maximization technique: comparison with manual tracing technique. RSNA, Chicago (2006)

[13] Massoptier, L., Casciaro, S.: Fully automatic liver segmentation through graph-cut technique. In: Rousseau, J., Delhomme, G., Akay, M. (eds.), Lyon, France, August 22-26, pp. 5243–5246. IEEE, Los Alamitos (2007)

[14] Beichel, R., Bauer, C., Bornik, A., Sorantin, E., Bischof, H.: Liver Segmentation in CT Data: A Segmentation Refinement Approach. In: Ayache, N., Ourselin, S., Maeder, A. (eds.), Brisbane, Australia, pp. 235–245. Springer, Heidelberg (October 29, 2007)

[15] Rusko, L., Bekes, G.: Liver segmentation for contrast-enhanced MR images using partitioned probabilistic model. International Journal of Computer Assisted Radiology and Surgery 6(1), 13–20 (2010)
[16] Platero, C., Gonzalez, M., Tobar, M.C., Poncela, J.M., Sanguino, J., Asensio, G., Santos, E.: Automatic method to segment the liver on multi-phase MRI. In: Jover, J.H. (ed.), Barcelona, Spain, June 25-28 (2008)
[17] Cheng, K., Gu, L., Xu, J.: A novel shape prior based level set method for liver segmentation from MR Images, Shenzhen, China, May 30-31, pp. 144–147 (2008)
[18] Chen, G., Gu, L., Qian, L., Xu, J.: An Improved Level Set for Liver Segmentation and Perfusion Analysis in MRIs. IEEE Transactions on Information Technology in Biomedicine 3(1), 94–103 (2009)
[19] Yuan, Z., Wang, Y., Yang, J., Liu, Y.: A novel automatic liver segmentation technique for MR images. In: Image and Signal Processing (CISP), Yantai, pp. 1282–1286 (2010)
[20] Baumeister, S.E., Voelzke, H., Marschall, P., John, U., Schmidt, C.O., Flessa, S., Alte, D.: Impact of Fatty Liver Disease on Health Care Utilization and Costs in a General Population: A 5-Year Observation. Gastroenterology 134(1), 85–94 (2008)
[21] Caselles, V., Kimmel, R., Sapiro, G.: Geodesic active contours. In: International Conference on Computer Vision (ICCV 1995). IEEE Computer Society, Massachusetts (1995)
[22] Hussain, H.K., Chenevert, T.L., Londy, F.J., Gulani, V., Swanson, S.D., McKenna, B.J., Appelman, H.D., Adusumilli, S., Greenson, J.K., Conjeevaram, H.: Hepatic fat fraction: MR imaging for quantitative measurement and display early experience. Radiology 237, 1048–1055 (2005)
[23] Whitaker, R.T., Xue, X.: Variable-conductance, Level-Set Curvature for Image Denoising, Thessaloniki, Greece, pp. 142–145 (2001)
[24] Gloger, O., Kuehn, J., Stanski, A., Voelzke, H., Puls, R.: A fully automatic three-step liver segmentation method on LDA-based probability maps for multiple contrast MR images. Magnetic Resonance Imaging 28(6), 882–897 (2010)
[25] Fisher, R.: The statistical utilization of multiple measurements. Ann. Eugenics 8, 376–386 (1938)
[26] Rao, C.: The utilization of multiple measurements in problems of biological classification. Journal of the Royal Statistical Society 10, 159–203 (1948)
[27] Crum, W.R., Camara, O., Hill, D.L.G.: Generalized Overlap Measures for Evalution and Validation in Medical Image Analysis. IEEE Transactions on Medical Imaging 25(11), 1451–1458 (2006)
[28] Maier, F., Wimmer, A., Soza, G., Kaftan, J.N., Fritz, D., Dillmann, R.: Automatic Liver Segmentation Using the Random Walker Algorithm. Bildverarbeitung fuer die Medizin, pp. 65–61 (2008)
[29] Chan, T.F., Vese, L.A.: Active contours without edges. IEEE Transactions on Image Processing 10(2), 266–277 (2001)

Stable Structure from Motion for Unordered Image Collections

Carl Olsson and Olof Enqvist

Centre for Mathematical Sciences, Lund University, Sweden

Abstract. We present a non-incremental approach to structure from motion. Our solution is based on robustly computing global rotations from relative geometries and feeding these into the known-rotation framework to create an initial solution for bundle adjustment. To increase robustness we present a new method for constructing reliable point tracks from pairwise matches. We show that our method can be seen as maximizing the reliability of a point track if the quality of the weakest link in the track is used to evaluate reliability. To estimate the final geometry we alternate between bundle adjustment and a robust version of the known-rotation formulation. The ability to compute both structure and camera translations independent of initialization makes our algorithm insensitive to degenerate epipolar geometries. We demonstrate the performance of our system on a number of image collections.[1]

1 Introduction

Structure from motion is by now becoming a well studied problem [25]. The dominant approaches are the incremental or sequential reconstruction algorithms [6,24]. Typically these algorithms are initialized using a minimal solver, solving for either two or three views. Additional points are then triangulated and added to the reconstruction. Once this is done new cameras viewing the reconstructed points can be added. By alternating triangulation and resectioning the full reconstruction is computed an incremental way. The downside of this approach is that it is highly dependent on the initial configuration and sensitive to degenerate configurations. Indeed, if the baseline is small it is easy to see that it is not possible to determine the depth of the structure. Since these methods rely on a well estimated structure for adding new cameras, degenerate geometries may cause them to fail. To avoid this [6,24] removes configurations where the data can be well fitted to a homography. Furthermore, due to their sequential nature these methods suffer from drift (error accumulation) [7], rather than distributing the error evenly throughout the sequence. This is addressed in [26] where a heuristic approach based on covariance estimation of the structure and the CIRC criterion [27] is presented. A method for determining a reliable initial pair is proposed in [4].

Another approach to structure from motion that is less sensitive to drift are the so called hierarchical methods [11,19,23,12]. Here the images are organized in a hierarchical cluster tree, and the reconstruction proceeds from the root to the leafs. Still

[1] Code and data sets can be downloaded from http://www.maths.lth.se/matematiklth/personal/calle/

A. Heyden and F. Kahl (Eds.): SCIA 2011, LNCS 6688, pp. 524–535, 2011.

degenerate geometries have to be avoided since the structure is used for reconstruction. As noted in [19] the loss of feature points and the necessity of a reasonable baseline creates a trade-off. That is, there is a sweet spot in terms of view separation, where calculation of multi view geometries is best performed.

A third option, which we follow in this paper, was investigated in [17,10]. Here rotations are first estimated separately using two-view geometries. Then these rotations are fed into the L_∞ framework [15] which solves for structure and camera translations simultaneously without the need for any initial solution. We solve a robust version of the known-rotation problem [22] that is also able to remove outliers. As shown in [10] this approach is not sensitive to degenerate configurations. Even though the geometry is degenerate if the baseline is zero the rotation is not. In fact, the rotation estimation will be accurate when the baseline is small, since in this case the number of matches is usually large. Furthermore, with this approach one does not have to estimate the scale of the two-view reconstructions since the only information that is used from the two-view estimations are the rotations, and they are independent of the scale.

2 System Overview

In this section we present the basic design of our structure from motion system. Figure 1 shows an overview of the system. The first step is pairwise matching of images. We run matching using Lowe's implementation of SIFT [16] for each pair of images. At present, this is by far the most computationally demanding step of the algorithm. For the cathedral data set (cf. Section 3) with 480 images of size 1936×1296 pixels this takes more than one week. On the other hand there are more efficient implementations of SIFT and moreover, this step could easily be parallelized since the different pairs are

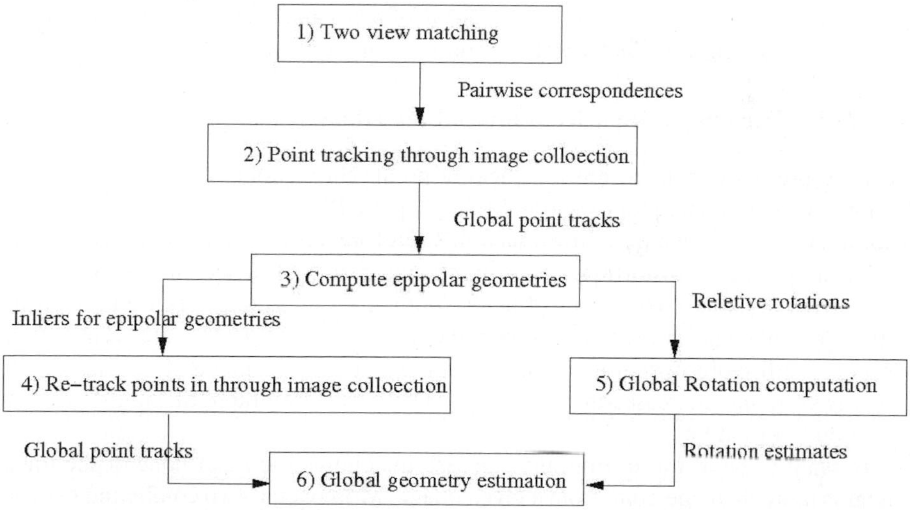

Fig. 1. System overview. The various stages and the data structures passed between them.

independent. For certain scenes the number of pairs could probably be reduced by first using vocabulary trees [21,2], however this has not been implemented here.

The detected correspondences are passed on to the next step which creates global point tracks throughout the unordered image collection. Section 2.1 presents a graph-based algorithm for creating consistent point tracks and show that this can be seen as trying to maximize the reliability of a point track, where the reliability is defined as the weakest connection in the track.

In the next step, point tracks are used to compute epipolar geometries for all image pairs seeing the same points. We use the five-point algorithm [20] since we assume calibrated cameras. The point tracks are constructed before computing geometries since this increases the number of pairs where a useful geometry can be computed. This also increases the redundancy in the camera graph making it easier to detect incorrect geometries.

The points that have been deemed inliers to the pairwise geometries are used to create new global point tracks using the same method as before; see Section 2.1. The relative rotations are used in a rotation averaging approach to compute camera orientations in the global coordinate system; see Section 2.2.

The point tracks and the global rotations are then fed into the final step where the global geometry is computed. To compute the geometry we alternate between a robust version of the known-rotation problem [9,22] and bundle adjustment [28]; see Section 2.3. Since we use the known-rotation formulation all that is needed for a starting solution is the rotations. Furthermore, since we only use the rotations from the pairwise geometries our system is not sensitive to degenerate geometries (small baseline). As is shown in [10] the rotations are still well defined. Finally we remove all 3D-points that have an uncertain depth. Note that we use as many points as possible, even those that are only seen by two nearby cameras. The depth of such points may be difficult to estimate however they still help constrain the rotations and should therefore not be removed until the geometry has been computed; see Section 2.3. Note that in an incremental system such points can be damaging, since the addition of new cameras rely on a well estimated structure. This is however not a problem for our non sequential approach.

2.1 Point Tracking in Unordered Image Collections

Next we present our algorithm for tracking points throughout unordered image collections. Feature descriptors such as SIFT [16], SURF [3], GLOH [18] etc. are not invariant to a full projective transformation. Therefore it is difficult to match points if a significant projective distortion is present, making matches between images with large baseline less reliable. Note that, in principle, our algorithm would work well even using only pairs with small baselines. However, the positions of points that are seen in many views are still more certain than those seen only in a few cameras. Furthermore, the tracking of points increases the redundancy in the camera graph, making it easier to detect outlier rotations.

We want to build tracks from the pairwise matchings such that none of the tracks contains more than one point from a given image. Moreover, if two conflicting matches exist, we want to pick the one from the most reliable view pair. As a measure of this reliability, we use the number of SIFT correspondences obtained in that pair, but the algorithm works with other measures as well. Let i_k denote image point k in image i. We build an undirected graph $\mathcal{G} = (\mathcal{V}, \mathcal{E})$, where the nodes $\mathcal{V}$ are the detected image points from all images. We assume that we have matched all or a subset of the image pairs. These matchings induce an edge set $\mathcal{E}$ where $(i_m, j_n) \in \mathcal{E}$ if the image point corresponding to node i_m has been matched to j_n. Furthermore we have an edge weight function $w : \mathcal{E} \mapsto \mathbb{R}_+$, representing the reliability of the match. We will use the number of matchings between two views to measure the reliability, but other choices are possible. Note that the weight of an edge between points k, l in images i, j only depends on the images. Hence we denote it $w_{i,j}$.

We assume that the graph is connected, otherwise we consider a subgraph. We want to form tracks such that the selected correspondences are as reliable as possible. If we use the sum of edge weights for measuring this reliability, a track consisting of two edges and one weak edge might still be considered very strong. Therefore we use the minimum edge weight instead. Hence, our goal is to maximize the minimal edge weights in the edge set representing a track. The quality of the track is basically the quality of the weakest link. Formally we define the reliability of a path P as

$$\mathcal{R}(P) = \min_{(i_m, j_n) \in P} w_{i,j}. \tag{1}$$

We will use Algorithm 1 to optimize reliability. The algorithm has certain similiarities to Prim's algorithm for computing a maximum spanning tree; see [5]. We start with one initial point track, $T(i_m)$ for each image point, i_m in each image, i. As the algorithm proceeds, tracks with corresponding image points are merged. To start the algorithm we pick an arbitrary image i and look for another image j such that the weight $w_{i,j}$ is maximized. This image pair will correspond to a lot of point-to-point correspondences, $(i_m, j_n) \in \mathcal{E}$. We go through all of these and merge tracks $T(i_m)$ and $T(j_n)$ unless this leads to an inconsistency.

Algorithm 1.

input : $(\mathcal{V}, \mathcal{E})$
output: Tracks $T(i_m)$
begin
  Let $\mathcal{E}_\mathcal{I} := \{(i,j) : w_{i,j} \neq 0\}$;
  For each image point i_k in each image i, init $T(i_k) = \{i_k\}$;
  Select an image i randomly and set $I = \{i\}$;
  while $\mathcal{E}_\mathcal{I} \neq \emptyset$ **do**
    Find a pair $(i,j) \in \mathcal{E}_\mathcal{I}$ such that $i \in I$ and $w_{i,j}$ is maximized ;
    for *each* (m,n) *such that* $(i_m, j_n) \in \mathcal{E}$ **do**
      if $T(i_m) \bigcup T(j_n)$ *has* $\leq$ *one point from each image* **then**
        Merge $T(i_m)$ with $T(j_n)$
    $\mathcal{E}_\mathcal{I} := \mathcal{E}_\mathcal{I} \setminus \{(i,j)\}$;
end

Definition 1. *A path in the correspondence graph is accepted by Algorithm 1 if its endpoints end up in the same track.*

Definition 2. *An inconsistent path in the correspondence graph is a path from an image point i_a in image i to another image point i_b in the same image. A simple inconsistent path is an inconsistent path such that image i is the only image visited twice.*

The constraint that we only merge tracks $T(i_m) \bigcup T(j_n)$ has no more than one point from each image, ensures that the final tracks contain no inconsistent paths. Moreover, the following theorem shows that no matches are removed unless there is an inconsistent path.

Theorem 1. *If a path P is not accepted by Algorithm 1 then some edge $(i_a, j_b) \in P$ is the weakest edge in a simple inconsistent path and all the other edges in that path are accepted.*

Proof. Clearly some $(i_a, j_b) \in P$ was not accepted. Consider the step when this edge was considered by Algorithm 1 . Let $T_1 = T(i_a)$ and $T_2 = T(i_b)$ at this time. If (i_a, j_b) was not accepted we know that T_1 and T_2 were not merged and hence that $T_1 \bigcup T_2$ contains two points from the same image. We denote this k_a and k_b. Since a track is connected there is a path $P_1 \subset T_1$ connecting i_a and k_a and a path $P_2 \subset T_2$ connecting j_b and k_b. Together with the edge (i_a, j_b) these paths form a simple inconsistent path and all edges of this path apart from (i_a, j_b) have already been accepted. It remains to show that (i_a, j_b) is the weakest edge in this path.

To do so, we consider the order in which the edges of this inconsistent path has been considered in Algorithm 1. Some image visited by the path must have been the first that was added to I (see Algorithm 1). After that, until all but one edge is considered there is always at least two different edges in the path that could be added and the algorithm will pick that with the highest weight. But this won't be the weakest edge and hence the weakest edge is considered last. Since we know that (i_a, j_b) was considered last it is the weakest edge.

To gain some intuition around this result, let a and b be the endpoints of a path P. Clearly this path indicates that a and b are projections of the same 3D point. Now, with notation from the proof, we can also find a path P_a from a to k_a (via i_a) and a path P_b from b to k_b (via i_b). Together these paths indicate that a and b are in fact projections of different 3D points. Hence, if P is not accepted then

$$\mathcal{R}(P) \leq \min\{\mathcal{R}(P_a), \mathcal{R}(P_b)\}. \tag{2}$$

One way to view this is that P as well as (P_a, P_b) yield hypotheses concerning a and b. Theorem 1 shows that Algorithm 1 chooses the hypothesis having highest reliability.

Figures 2 and 3 shows examples of the result of the algorithm. In Figure 2 two images from the sequence is matched directly. This results in 20 matches. Figure 3 shows the result of the tracking algorithm. Here we obtain 48 matches. In addition we show the adjacency matrix for the camera graphs. In this case the camera graphs have an edge between i and j if there are more than 20 matches between images i and j. There are 1116 edges in the one computed from the direct matches, and 1436 in the one obtained from the tracks.

Fig. 2. Image nr 1 and 12 in the Vercingetorix sequence and matches when only matching the images directly. There are 20 matches (and it can be seen that at least two are incorrect). To the right is the adjacency matrix for the camera graph thresholded at 20 matches.

Fig. 3. Image nr 1 and 12 in the Vercingetorix sequence after running the tracking algorithm. There are 48 matches. To the right is the adjacency matrix for the camera graph thresholded at 20 matches.

Remark. The point tracking algorithm is used twice in our structure from motion framework. The first time all correspondences from the SIFT matching are used and the weight $w_{i,j}$ is simply the total number of correspondences between image i and image j. The second time, only the inliers from the epipolar geometries are used and $w_{i,j}$ is the number of inliers of the best epipolar geometry estimated from views i and j.

2.2 Robust Global Rotation Computation

The most common approach to rotation averaging are variants of [13], where a relaxation of the maximum likelihood estimator is solved. However, it has recently been shown [8] that this approach may fail if there is a camera loop where the total rotation is 360 degrees. Furthermore, it does not handle outlier rotations. Zach et al. [29] use cycles in the camera graph and a Bayesian framework to detect incorrect pairwise rotations. This leads to an intractable problem so they have to limit the length of the cycles to 6 edges.

In contrast, we employ a simple RANSAC approach, similar to [14], for finding a set of rotations consistent with as many of the relative rotations as possible. Given relative rotations $R_{i,j}$, in each RANSAC iteration, we want to compute a set of rotations R_k (in the global coordinate framework) such that

$$R_i = R_{i,j} R_j \tag{3}$$

roughly holds for as many relative rotations as possible. To achieve robustness to noise we allow a small error in (3). The global rotations are computed by randomly selecting a spanning tree in the camera graph. The rotations can then be computed by simple (linear) elimination along the edges of the tree. Once this is done we evaluate how well the remaining equations are fulfilled. We say that $R_{i,j}$ is an inlier rotation if the angle of rotation of the $R_i^T R_{i,j} R_j$ is less than 1 degree.

In contrast to [14] which uses an unweighted graph, we select each rotation with a probability proportional to the total number of matchings, to achieve efficiency. This introduces a bias towards selecting rotations from geometries with small baselines. At first this might seem like a serious problem as relative orientation estimation gets unstable for short baselines. However, it is shown in [10] that this instability does not affect the rotation estimates. Hence, even with short baseline or no baseline at all, the relative rotation can be accurately estimated, using e.g. [20].

2.3 Global Geometry Estimation

The final step of our framework is to estimate the full structure and motion in the global coordinate frame. The input is the global point tracks and the global rotation estimates. Even though the point tracks have been constructed from points that have been deemed inliers in the pairwise geometries, there will still be a portion of outliers when considering the entire tracks. Therefore we employ a robust version of the known-rotation formulation [22], which we briefly outline.

Estimating structure, camera positions and outliers. If the camera matrix is $P = [R\, t]$ then the (squared) reprojection error can be written

$$E_i(X, R, t) = \left|\left|\left(x_1^i - \frac{R_1X + t_1}{R_3X + t_3}, x_2^i - \frac{R_2X + t_2}{R_3X + t_3}\right)\right|\right|^2, \tag{4}$$

where R_j and t_j denotes the j'th row of R and t respectively. If $R_3X + t_3 > 0$, that is, if visible points are located in front of the camera, we may write the condition that the reprojection error is less than γ, $E_i(X, R, t) \leq \gamma^2$ as

$$\left|\left|\left((x_1^i R_3 - R_1)X + x_1^i t_3 - t_1, (x_2^i R_3 - R_2)X + x_2^i t_3 - t_2\right)\right|\right| \leq \gamma(R_3X + t_3) \tag{5}$$

If either X or R is known then (5) is a convex constraint. The known-rotation problem (see [15]) is another example where the 3D-points and the positions of the cameras are allowed to vary simultaneously.

Now, assume that we define an outlier-free solution to be a solution where all errors are less than γ. Since the intersection of convex sets is convex it is possible to test, using convex programming, whether a solution is free from outliers. To be able to remove potential outliers we add a non negative slack variable s_i to (5), giving

$$\left|\left|\left((x_1^i R_3 - R_1)X + x_1^i t_3 - t_1, (x_2^i R_3 - R_2)X + x_2^i t_3 - t_2\right)\right|\right| \leq \gamma(R_3X + t_3) + s_i. \tag{6}$$

Now, minimizing the number of outliers means minimizing the number of nonzero slack variables subject to the constraint (6). If we do this and remove the residuals for which

s_i is non-zero, we will get an high-quality, outlier-free solution. However, minimizing the number of non-zero s_i's is difficult so we consider the relaxation

$$\min \sum_i s_i, \tag{7}$$

instead. Details can be found in [22].

Bundle adjustment. The method outlined in the previous section, computes structure and camera translations independently of the initialization. This gives us the advantage that we do not need to estimate the scale factors needed to fuse the pairwise geometries. This is particularly difficult when the baseline is small, since in that case the structure is very uncertain. On the other hand the rotation estimates are more certain for a small baseline, so we want to use these geometries as well.

Still, the rotations from the rotation averaging step may not be optimally aligned and may need to be reestimated as well. Therefore we propose an alternating scheme. Given the rotations we estimate an inlier set that is as large as possible using the known-rotation framework. In a second step, we update the structure and motion using bundle adjustment [28] based on the current inlier set. These steps are iterated until the number of outliers has stabilized. Usually two iterations is sufficient.

Finally, we remove all the 3D points that have an uncertain depth estimate. This is determined by considering the second derivative of the reprojection error, in the direction of the camera center. Points having a very small second derivative are discarded.

3 Results and Conclusions

This section presents the results of our structure from motion system for a number of image collections. The implementation is mainly Matlab-based[2]. For the the SIFT descriptors we use the implementation from [16]. And for solving the known-rotation problem we use MOSEK [1]. For increased computational efficiency, we use linear programming instead of second order programming when solving the known-rotation formulation; cf. [22].

Figures 4-9 shows the results of running our algorithm on the various image collections. The tables show the execution times of the various steps of the algorithm; see Figure 1. The computationally most demanding step is matching SIFT features between views. For the datasets with repeated textures the number of outliers are higher, e.g. the dome of the Pantheon. This is because the tracking algorithm can merge these if one false correspondence survives the RANSAC step. Since the known-rotation framework cannot split tracks into smaller pieces it instead finds the largest consistent subtrack and classifies the rest of the image points as outliers. The number of outliers is reduced if the merging of tracks $(T(i_m) \bigcup T(j_n))$ is turned off. On the other hand this reduces the size of the tracks. Another way to reduce the number of outliers is to split the track at the weakest link if an outlier in the track is detected. This is easily done by searching the tree constructed in Section 2.1.

[2] Code and data sets can be downloaded from http://www.maths.lth.se/matematiklth/personal/calle/

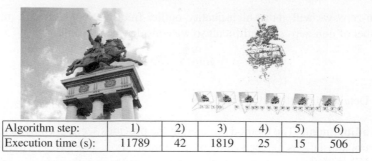

Algorithm step:	1)	2)	3)	4)	5)	6)
Execution time (s):	11789	42	1819	25	15	506

Fig. 4. The statue of Vercingetorix. The image set consists of 69 cameras. The algorithm creates 41274 tracks which are projected into 107078 image points, and 2869 of these are deemed outliers in the geometry estimation step.

Algorithm step:	1)	2)	3)	4)	5)	6)
Execution time (s):	17233	58	2911	11	34	2362

Fig. 5. The city hall of Stockholm. The image set consists of 43 cameras. The algorithm creates 47833 tracks which are projected into 266517 image points, and 3440 of these are deemed outliers in the geometry estimation step.

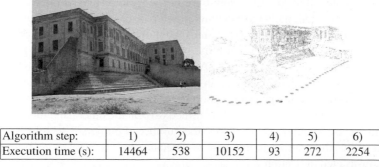

Algorithm step:	1)	2)	3)	4)	5)	6)
Execution time (s):	14464	538	10152	93	272	2254

Fig. 6. Alcatraz courtyard. The image set consists of 133 cameras. The algorithm creates 41173 tracks which are projected into 342658 image points, and 12247 of these are deemed outliers in the geometry estimation step.

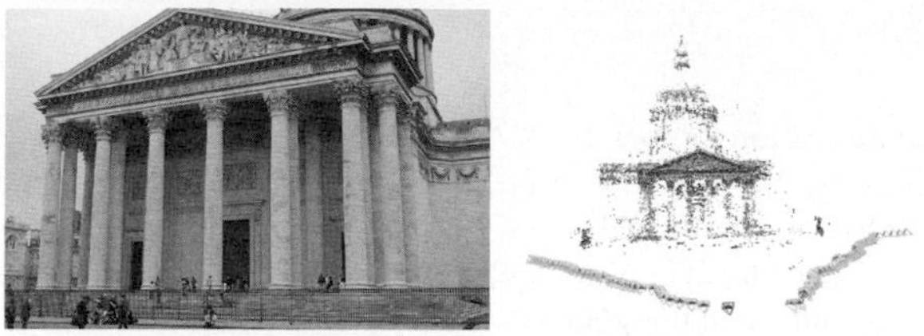

Algorithm step:	1)	2)	3)	4)	5)	6)
Execution time (s):	41883	1364	17664	186	541	2977

Fig. 7. Pantheon Paris. The image set consists of 182 cameras. The algorithm creates 59724 tracks which are projected into 415498 image points, and 59066 of these are deemed outliers in the geometry estimation step.

Algorithm step:	1)	2)	3)	4)	5)	6)
Execution time (s):	28540	952	14558	174	380	3259

Fig. 8. Arc de Triomphe, Paris. The image set consists of 173 cameras. The algorithm creates 56655 tracks which are projected into 387651 image points, and 27674 of these are deemed outliers in the geometry estimation step.

Algorithm step:	1)	2)	3)	4)	5)	6)
Execution time (s):	947450	22081	102150	1134	11425	24636

Fig. 9. The Cathedral of Lund. The image set consists of 480 cameras. The algorithm creates 77182 tracks which are projected into 1044574 image points, and 4520 of these are deemed outliers in the geometry estimation step.

References

1. The MOSEK optimization toolbox for MATLAB manual, 531
2. Agarwal, S., Snavely, N., Simon, I., Sietz, S., Szeliski, R.: Building rome in a day. In: Int. Conf. Computer Vision (2010), 526
3. Bay, H., Ess, A., Tuytelaars, T., Van Gool, L.: Surf: Speeded up robust features. Computer Vision and Image Understanding (2008), 526
4. Beder, C., Steffen, R.: Determining an initial image pair for fixing the scale of a 3D reconstruction from an image sequence. In: Franke, K., Müller, K.-R., Nickolay, B., Schäfer, R. (eds.) DAGM 2006. LNCS, vol. 4174, pp. 657–666. Springer, Heidelberg (2006), 524
5. Bondy, J.A., Murty, U.S.R.: Graph Theory. Springer, Heidelberg (2008), 527
6. Brown, M., Lowe, D.: Unsupervised 3d object recognition and reconstruction in unordered datasets. In: Conf. 3-D Digital Imaging and Modeling (2005), 524
7. Cornelis, K., Verbiest, F., Van Gool, L.: Drift detection and removal for sequential structure from motion algorithms. Trans. Pattern Analysis and Machine Intelligence (2004), 524
8. Dai, Y., Trumpf, J., Li, H., Barnes, N., Hartley, R.: Rotation averaging with application to camera-rig calibration. In: Asian Conf. on Computer Vision (2009), 529
9. Dalalyan, A., Keriven, R.: L1-penalized robust estimation for a class of inverse problems arising in multiview geometry. Neural Information Processing Systems (2009), 526
10. Enqvist, O., Kahl, F., Olsson, C.: Stable structure from motion using rotational consistency. Technical report, Centre for Mathematical Sciences, Lund University (2010), 525, 526, 530
11. Fitzgibbon, A., Zisserman, A.: Automatic camera recovery for closed or open image sequences. In: Eur. Conf. Computer Vision (1998), 524
12. Gherardi, R., Farenzena, M., Fusiello, A.: Improving the efficiency of hierarchical structure-and-motion. In: Conf. Computer Vision and Pattern Recognition (2010), 524
13. Govindu, V.: Combining two-view constraints for motion estimation. In: Conf. Computer Vision and Pattern Recognition (2001), 529
14. Govindu, V.: Robustness in motion averaging. In: Eur. Conf. Computer Vision (2006), 529, 530
15. Kahl, F., Hartley, R.: Multiple view geometry under the L_∞-norm. Trans. Pattern Analysis and Machine Intelligence (2008), 525, 530
16. Lowe, D.: Distinctive image features from scale-invariant keypoints. Int. Journal of Computer Vision (2004), 525, 526, 531
17. Martinec, D., Pajdla, T.: Robust rotation and translation estimation in multiview reconstruction. In: Conf. Computer Vision and Pattern Recognition (2007), 525
18. Mikolajczyk, K., Schmid, C.: A performance evaluation of local descriptors. Trans. Pattern Analysis and Machine Intelligence (2005), 526
19. Nistér, D.: Reconstruction from uncalibrated sequences with a hierarchy of trifocal tensors. In: Eur. Conf. Computer Vision (2000), 524, 525
20. Nistér, D.: An efficient solution to the five-point relative pose problem. Trans. Pattern Analysis and Machine Intelligence (2004), 526, 530
21. Nistér, D., Stewénius, H.: Scalable recognition with a vocabulary tree. In: Conf. Computer Vision and Pattern Recognition (2006), 526
22. Olsson, C., Hartley, I., Eriksson, A.: Outlier removal using duality. In: Conf. Computer Vision and Pattern Recognition (2010), 525, 526, 530, 531
23. Schaffalitzky, F., Zisserman, A.: Multi-view matching for unordered image sets, or How do I organize my holiday snaps?. In: Eur. Conf. Computer Vision (2002), 524

24. Snavely, N., Seitz, S.M., Szeliski, R.: Modeling the world from Internet photo collections. Int. Journal on Computer Vision 80(2), 189–210 (2008), 524
25. Szeliski, R.: Computer Vision: Algorithms and Applications. Springer, Heidelberg (2010), 524
26. Thormaehlen, T., Broszio, H., Weissenfeld, A.: Keyframe selection for camera motion and structure estimation from multiple views. In: Eur. Conf. Computer Vision (2004), 524
27. Torr, P., Fitzgibbon, A., Zisserman, A.: The problem of degeneracy in structure and motion recovery from uncalibrated image sequences. Int. Journal on Computer Vision (1999), 524
28. Triggs, B., McLauchlan, P., Hartley, R., Fitzgibbon, A.: Bundle adjustment - a modern synthesis. In: Int. Conf. Computer Vision (1999), 526, 531
29. Zach, C., Klopschitz, M., Pollefeys, M.: Disambiguating visual relations using loop constraints. In: Conf. Computer Vision and Pattern Recognition (2010), 529

Projector Calibration by "Inverse Camera Calibration"

Ivan Martynov, Joni-Kristian Kamarainen, and Lasse Lensu

Machine Vision and Pattern Recognition Laboratory (Kouvola Unit)
Lappeenranta University of Technology, Finland
http://www2.it.lut.fi/mvpr

Abstract. The accuracy of 3-D reconstructions depends substantially on the accuracy of active vision system calibration. In this work, the problem of video projector calibration is solved by inverting the standard camera calibration work flow. The calibration procedure requires a single camera, which does not need to be calibrated and which is used as the sensor whether projected dots and calibration pattern landmarks, such as the checkerboard corners, coincide. The method iteratively adjusts the projected dots to coincide with the landmarks and the final coordinates are used as inputs to a camera calibration method. The otherwise slow iterative adjustment is accelerated by estimating a plane homography between the detected landmarks and the projected dots, which makes the calibration method fast.

1 Introduction

In the recent years, video projectors have become the devices of choice for computer vision systems of active scene exploration and reconstruction. A camera-projector pair alleviates the difficult task of establishing correspondences between the views, and therefore, systems like Structured Light [10] can provide accurate 3-D reconstructions. Lately, projector-camera pairs have also become increasingly popular in modern game controllers such as Kinect (XBox). However, even if active systems alleviate the matching problem, calibrated video projectors are still required.

The camera calibration problem, i.e., the estimation of camera intrinsic and extrinsic parameters, has been studied for a particularly long time and the existing state-of-the-art techniques including [14,15,6,4] can be used for accurate calibration [12]. The basic working flow is the following: i) a set of images of a known calibration pattern are captured from various camera poses, ii) pixel coordinates of the calibration pattern "landmarks", such as the corners of a printed checkerboard pattern, are located, and iii) the camera parameters are non-linearly estimated based on correspondence of the located 2-D image coordinates and the known 3-D landmark coordinates under the selected camera model. The video projector projection is usually modelled as the inverse projection of a pin-hole camera, and therefore, it is treated as perspective projection

A. Heyden and F. Kahl (Eds.): SCIA 2011, LNCS 6688, pp. 536–544, 2011.

similar to the camera models. Therefore, if correspondences between the projector pixels and the calibration landmarks can be established, the standard camera calibration methods can be adopted for the video projector calibration as well.

This work is based on the popular camera calibration technique implemented in Bouguet's Camera Calibration Toolbox for Matlab [2]. The technique is extended for fast video projector calibration by adopting the inverted camera calibration procedure based on an iterative search of 2-D projector coordinates coinciding with the calibration pattern landmarks. The calibration results are reported for several real settings.

1.1 Related Work

During the last few years, the interest to use inexpensive off-the-shelf cameras and video projectors for active and computer vision has increased considerably. Camera and projector calibration are the necessary steps, and therefore, various approaches and methods have been proposed to calibrate video projectors. The idea of "inverting" the camera calibration is not new, and it has been exemplified by several authors [9,7]. However, their formulations are different to the ones presented here: they project a calibration pattern onto a plane, "the wall", capture it by a camera, and then utilise the standard calibration work flow. The main disadvantage of this approach is that it requires a calibrated camera and, moreover, errors from the camera calibration are transferred to the projector.

One class of the calibration methods utilise known relations of the camera, and the wall or the projector [11,13]. This makes the methods accurate and the problem easier to formulate, but also less flexible than those requiring a calibrated camera. These methods can be used for fixed industrial camera-projector systems, but not in the general case where configurations and poses are unknown.

Another important class of the methods includes those referred to as auto-calibration methods. These methods do not require a physical calibration target. Most auto-calibration methods work only for the extrinsic parameters [8] or require a calibrated camera [7], but lately even more automatic methods have been proposed. For example, the method by Draneni et al. [3] assumes a plane projection geometry, "the wall", and that one of the projector poses is "roughly frontal". These methods are attractive choices due to their automatic processing, but there always exists the need for very accurate calibration in the structured light and active vision systems. The extrinsic parameters can be solved by the auto-calibration methods, but the intrinsic parameters should be solved by the inverted camera approach utilising a physical calibration target since this is accurate and needs to be done only once.

2 Projector Calibration

2.1 Camera Calibration

The main objective of camera calibration is to solve camera's intrinsic parameters (focal length, lens aberration model parameters, etc.). Similarly, also the extrinsic parameters (location and pose) are accurately found by the same optimisation process. Typically, the intrinsic parameters do not change when the camera is moved and camera's optics is not touched, and therefore, solving the extrinsics with known intrinsics is considered as its own problem, e.g. [1]. The standard camera calibration methods aim to solve the parameters as accurately as possible, and therefore, they typically use a physical calibration pattern, such as a printed planar checkerboard pattern. Images from the pattern are captured from different camera poses, and the camera model parameters are optimised to match the 2-D image coordinates and the known 3-D coordinates of the pattern. The most popular methods with their implementations available are Tsai's [14], Zhang's [15] and Heikkilä's [6] methods. The methods mainly differ by the camera model parameters and how they utilise the calibration pattern landmarks.

For our study, the Matlab toolbox implementation by Bouguet [2] was chosen. The toolbox makes use of Zhang's method and a planar checkerboard as the calibration pattern. The method requires the user to capture a sufficient number of images with the same camera in different locations. Then the toolbox provides functions to detect the pattern cross points which is done separately for all the images. The detection is semi-automatic as the first four corners need to be annotated manually (see the left image in Fig. 1) and then the algorithm computes the remaining corners automatically (see the right image in Fig. 1). The four corners help to initiate the locations of the other cross points, and then the algorithm searches for the accurate corner coordinates within some predefined window whose default size is 11x11 pixels. To achieve sub-pixel accuracy, the Harris corner detection is applied.

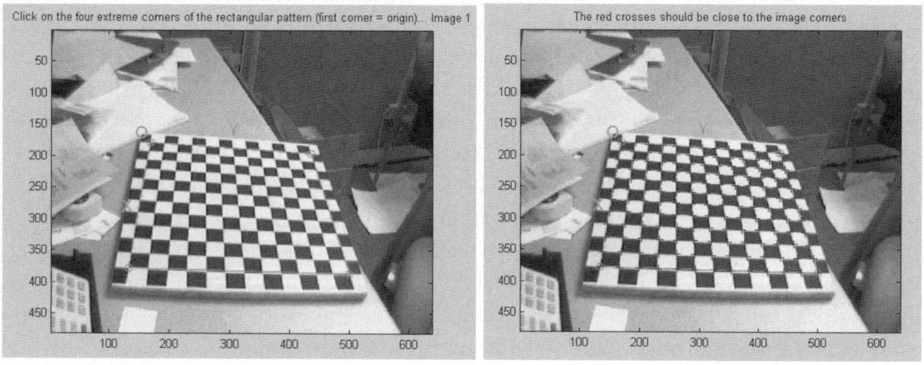

Fig. 1. Semi-automatic location of the checkerboard corners in Camera Calibration Toolbox [2]

If the corner detection fails, the toolbox allows to adjust the detection parameters, such as the size and number of the squares in the checkerboard pattern, a visually estimated distortion factor, etc. For the most cameras, the detection works out-of-the-box, and therefore, it is utilised in our projector calibration.

The next step is to calculate the intrinsic parameters of the camera (focal length, principal point, skew, radial and tangential distortions) using the detected corners. This is done by the main calibration function. After the optimisation process, the toolbox outputs the estimated parameters and the pixel errors. Again, these values can be adjusted and the calibration re-run. It is worth to remark that the detection of corners can be done without knowing the intrinsics, apparently.

2.2 Inverting Camera Calibration

For calibrating the projector, the same checkerboard pattern is used as for the camera calibration. The main problem is to define the grid of cross points in the projector plane which project exactly onto the grid of the real pattern. This task is solved with the help of an uncalibrated camera. The camera can be used to capture the pattern and projected points. The points can be projected with a distinguishable colour which is easy to detect. Again, the detection of the cross points can be achieved with the same semi-automatic method of the toolbox. The projector grid points can be projected onto the same view, captured by the camera and detected in the camera view, i.e., in camera pixel coordinates. The both detected sets of points can be compared, and if the distance between any of them is larger than a specified threshold, the points in the projector plane are moved towards the corners points of the pattern in the camera view. Fig. 2 illustrates this procedure to automatically find the correspondence of the calibration pattern corners (the checkerboard cross points) and the projected grid. In this figure, four steps are shown and it can be seen that the difference between the third and fourth steps is very small (the two bottom images).

After the iterative search, the coordinates in the projector "view" are known and it is possible to directly apply the toolbox functions to compute the intrinsics and extrinsics of the projector. Corresponding to the camera calibration, the projector needs to be put in different locations where the corner detection procedure is repeated. When all corner points in the projector plane are computed for all locations, the main toolbox optimisation process can be started.

2.3 Proposed Calibration Method

For the method, it needs to be decided how to detect the corner points of the calibration pattern in the projector plane. First of all, the relation between the camera and projector points is defined as the projective homography. This relation helps to make an accurate initial estimation of the corners in the projector plane and speed up the iterative search in the next stage. For the homography estimation the direct linear transform (DLT) [5] is used.

To compute the projective homography, at least four points are needed, but the DLT is fast for even hundreds of points. In the current implementation, four points are used in a rectangular configuration in the projector plane and they are projected on the wall. The wall here denotes any planar background. The points are coloured and, therefore, easy to distinguish and detect. The only

Fig. 2. Example of automatic adjustment of the projected dots to the calibration pattern corners (from the up left to the bottom right)

consideration is that the points are visible to the camera, i.e., not outside its view. Homography from the camera coordinates to the projector coordinates is computed using the DLT method.

Using the computed homography, all the detected calibration pattern corner points on the camera plane are transformed into the corresponding points on the projector plane. These points can now be projected and their location verified by using the camera. The verification is again achieved by locating the points with the camera and comparing their camera coordinates to the calibration pattern coordinates. The DLT estimated points do not exactly match due to the non-linearity in the projector intrinsics and since the DLT camera model is linear. However, the points are close to the correct locations and can be iteratively adjusted by a re-projection and re-capturing loop.

After the adjusted corner points on the projector plane are computed, the calibration routines of the toolbox are used. The algorithm for the described inverted camera projection method is given in Alg. 1.

It should be noted that if the location of the camera does not change while the projector is moved, the corner detection of the calibration pattern needs to be done only once. Generally, there is a need to recompute the corners' locations of the checkerboard pattern in the camera plane only if the location of the camera has changed. Algorithm 1 is executed for each different location of the projector and all coordinate sets are the input to the toolbox calibration function.

Algorithm 1. Inverted camera calibration for video projector calibration.

1. Project four or more points which are visible to the camera.
2. Capture an image and detect the projected points.
3. Compute homography $\boldsymbol{H}$ from the camera points to the projector points (DLT).
4. Capture an image and detect the corners of the checkerboard pattern.
5. Transform the detected corner points to the projector points using $\boldsymbol{H}$.
6. **for all** corner points **do**
7. Project the projector plane points in the neighbourhood of the transformed corner point.
8. Capture an image and detect the point's coordinates
9. Select the one closest to the detected corner.
10. **end for**

3 Experiments

The proposed algorithm was applied to a camera-projector system. The used camera was Unibrain Fire-i BCL 1.2 with the native resolution of 640×480, and the video projector was ViewSonic DLP projector with the resolution of 800×600. These can be considered as inexpensive commodity hardware.

In the experimental setup, the camera and projector were put in locations where that the angle between the views of the devices was roughly 30 degrees. During the experiments, the location of the projector was changed several times, thus, the angle between the camera and projector varied from 10 to 60 degrees. The configuration is demonstrated in Fig. 3.

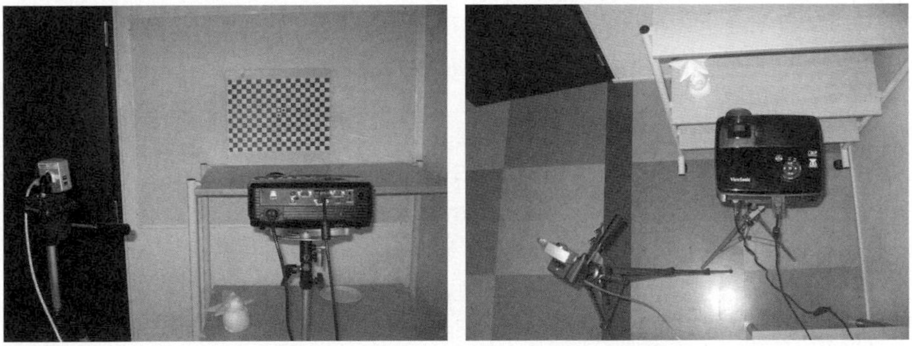

Fig. 3. The used camera-projector system

The main factor affecting the calibration accuracy are the camera properties, mainly the resolution, and the location of the camera from the projection plane. The resolution was kept fixed, but the effect of the camera distance was studied. The two distances used were approximately 60 and 120 cm from the wall. Example images captured from these two distances are shown in Fig. 4. In the both cases, the viewing angle remained approximately the same.

(a) 60 cm (b) 120 cm

Fig. 4. The two camera configurations investigated

The projector location was changed 8 times, i.e., Algorithm 1 was executed for nine different images. These points were the input to the calibration procedure. The estimated intrinsic parameters are shown in Table 1 and the extrinsic parameters for a roughly similar view in Table 3. For the accuracy evaluation, the reprojection error was used (the last line in the tables). The reprojection error was computed by using the estimated intrinsic and extrinsic values and by projecting the projector plane coordinates on the wall and measuring the standard deviation of the distances to the detected calibration pattern coordinates. From the errors in Table 1 we see that the distance change results to the error increase of 20-30% for the double distance. Note that the error numbers are given in pixel coordinates and are, therefore, affected by the projector resolution.

Table 1. Calibration results for the intrinsics

Param	*60 cm*	*120 cm*
Focal Length:	fc = [1301.9; 1289.2]	fc = [1317.6; 1314.0]
Principal point:	cc = [360.5; 718.8]	cc = [347.4; 719.3]
Skew:	alpha = -0.00785	alpha = -0.00960
Distortion:	kc = [-0.145; 0.177; -0.004; -0.010; 0.000]	kc = [-0.109; 0.211; 0.008; -0.013; 0.000]
Pixel error:	err = [1.051; 1.045]	err = [1.369; 1.240]

In order to see how the distance affects the accuracy, it was necessary to investigate the change of the focal length error because it is less affected by larger errors in a few single pixels than the reprojection error. Several tests were carried out and it was noticed that a degrade of approximately of 25% in the accuracy occurs. In other words, if the distance from the camera to the wall is doubled then the reprojection error becomes roughly one fourth bigger. Table 2 presents the errors in the focal length estimation from the same images.

Table 2. Focal length estimation error from the both distances

Param	*60 cm*	*120 cm*
Focal length error:	err = [41.79; 40.40]	err = [57.03; 55.11]

The comparison of the extrinsic parameters for the two sets is rather useless since the projector location was different. However, this can be solved by using the same image as an evaluation image. The results for this experiment, the reprojection pixel deviations for the one view, are shown in Table 3. The chosen evaluation view was from the second test where the distance from the camera to the wall was approximately 120 centimetres. Again, the error increased by approximately 17%.

Table 3. Calibration results for the extrinsic parameters of the last location of the projector

Param	*60 cm*	*120 cm*
Pixel error:	err = [1.539; 1.156]	err = [1.541; 1.160]

The last experiment was the estimation of a sufficient number of images for the calibration of the projector. This means that the algorithm was run with 2 to 9 images. The error is affected by the location of the projector. When the projector is located with a wider angle with respect to the camera, the reprojection error is somewhat larger. However, if the computation of the focal length is considered, the error of the computation of the focal length tends to decrease as the number of planes increases. From Fig. 5 it can be seen that 5 images are sufficient in the sense that the error does not decrease significantly as the number of images further increases. Also, this experiment demonstrates that the computation of the focal length, and the intrinsics in general, are not seriously affected by larger errors in a few single points.

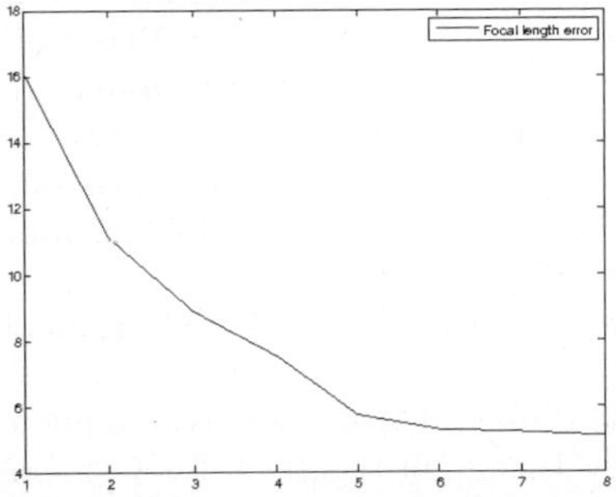

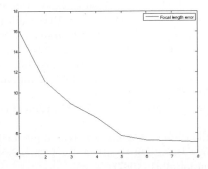

Fig. 5. Focal length error (in pixels) depending on the number of planes

4 Conclusion

In this work, a method to calibrate a video projector by inverting the work flow of camera calibration is proposed. The method is based on the existing popular camera calibration tool, and by integrating the method to the tool, it can be used to accurately calibrate any camera-projector or single projector system without the need to first calibrate the camera.

At the core of the method is the iterative search of projector plane points which correspond to the points in the calibration pattern. This otherwise slow search is enhanced by introducing good initialisation by plane homography estimation. All code will be made publicly available.

References

1. Ansar, A., Daniilidis, K.: Linear pose estimation from points or lines. IEEE PAMI 25(5) (2003)
2. Bouguet, J.Y.: Camera calibration toolbox for Matlab, `http://www.vision.caltech.edu/bouguetj/calib_doc/`
3. Drareni, J., Roy, S., Sturm, P.: Geometric video projector auto-calibration. In: CVPR Workshop on Projector-Camera Systems (2009)
4. Furukawa, Y., Ponce, J.: Accurate camera calibration from multi-view stereo and bundle adjustment. Int. J. Comput. Vis. 84, 257–268 (2009)
5. Hartley, R., Zisserman, A.: Multiple View Geometry in computer vision. Cambridge Press, Cambridge (2003)
6. Heikkilä, J.: Geometric camera calibration using circular control points. IEEE PAMI 22(10) (2000)
7. Kimura, M., Mochimary, M., Kanade, T.: Projector calibration using arbitrary planes and calibrated camera. In: CVPR (2007)
8. Okatani, T., Deguchi, K.: Autocalibration of a projector-camera system. IEEE PAMI 27(12) (2005)
9. Sadlo, F., Weyrich, T., Peikert, R., Gross, M.: A practical structured light acquisition system for point-based geometry and texture. In: Eurographics Symposium of Point-Based Graphics (2005)
10. Salvi, J., Fernandez, S., Pribanic, T., Llado, X.: A state of the art in structured light patterns for surface profilometry. Pattern Recognition 43, 2666–2680 (2010)
11. Shen, T.-S., Menq, C.-H.: Digital projector calibration for 3-D active vision systems. J. Manuf. Sci. Eng. 124(1) (2002)
12. Sun, W., Cooperstock, J.R.: An empirical evaluation of factors influencing camera calibration accuracy using three publicly available techniques. Machine Vision and Applications 17(1), 51–67 (2006)
13. Tao, J.: Slide projector calibration based on calibration of digital camera. In: SPIE, vol. 6788 (2007)
14. Tsai, R.Y.: A Versatile Camera Calibration Technique for High-Accuracy 3D Machine Vision Metrology Using Off-the-Shelf TV Cameras and Lenses. IEEE J. of Robotics and Automation 3(4) (1987)
15. Zhang, Z.: Flexible camera calibration by viewing a plane from unknown orientations. In: ICCV (1999)

Representing Local Structure Using Tensors II

Hans Knutsson[1,2], Carl-Fredrik Westin[1,3], and Mats Andersson[1,2]

[1] Department of Biomedical Engineering, Linköping University, Sweden
[2] Center for Medical Image Science and Visualization (CMIV), Linköping, Sweden
[3] Laboratory of Mathematics in Imaging, Brigham and Women's Hospital, Harvard Medical School, Boston, MA

knutte@imt.liu.se

Abstract. Estimation of local spatial structure has a long history and numerous analysis tools have been developed. A concept that is widely recognized as fundamental in the analysis is the *structure tensor*. However, precisely what it is taken to mean varies within the research community. We present a new method for structure tensor estimation which is a generalization of many of it's predecessors. The method uses filter sets having Fourier directional responses being monomials of the normalized frequency vector, one odd order sub-set and one even order sub-set. It is shown that such filter sets allow for a particularly simple way of attaining phase invariant, positive semi-definite, local structure tensor estimates. We continue to compare a number of known structure tensor algorithms by formulating them in monomial filter set terms. In conclusion we show how higher order tensors can be estimated using a generalization of the same simple formulation.

Keywords: structure tensor, higher order, quadrature, monomial filter.

1 Introduction

Many of the popular image analysis concepts of today have roots that can be traced to early work in signal processing and optics, e.g. Riesz transforms,[1], Zernike moments, [2], and Gabor signals,[3]. The first steps towards analysis of digital images were taken more then four decades ago [4]. From the very start detecting edges and lines in images was considered a fundamental operation [5]. Since these early days new and more advanced schemes for analysis of local image structure has been suggested in a seemingly never ending stream. Papers having a particular relevance in the present context can be found in, for example [6] - [33]. Local image orientation, scale, frequency, phase, motion and locality of estimates are prominent examples of features that have been considered central in the analysis.

The main force driving the research has been the need for an efficient and useful analysis of data produced by increasingly capable imaging devices. Both the outer and the inner dimensionality is commonly high, e.g. volume sequence data and tensor field data respectively. Regardless of this development the first stages in the analysis remain the same. In most cases the processing starts by

A. Heyden and F. Kahl (Eds.): SCIA 2011, LNCS 6688, pp. 545–556, 2011.

performing local linear combinations of image values, e.g. convolution operators. The output from these convolutions are then usually combined in a non-linear fashion to produce local feature descriptors.

We will focus on developments regarding a particular instance of such algorithms, local structure tensor estimation. We start by presenting a general estimation scheme using monomial filter sets.

2 Monomial Filters

The monomial filters are spherically separable, i.e. defined as a product of one radial and one directional part:

$$F(\hat{\boldsymbol{\mu}}) = R(\rho)\, D(\hat{\boldsymbol{\mu}}) \tag{1}$$

where $\boldsymbol{\mu}$ defines the Fourier domain (FD) coordinates and $\rho = \|\boldsymbol{\mu}\|$. The radial part, $R(\rho)$, is a band-pass or high-pass filter ($R(0) = 0$) and a typical choice is the lognormal function [9].

Directional part - The directional part consists of monomials i.e. products of positive integer powers of the components of $\hat{\boldsymbol{\mu}}$. Performing n repeated outer products of $\hat{\boldsymbol{\mu}}$ will contain all order n component products.

$$\hat{\boldsymbol{\mu}}^{\otimes n} = \underbrace{\hat{\boldsymbol{\mu}} \otimes \hat{\boldsymbol{\mu}} \ldots \otimes \hat{\boldsymbol{\mu}}}_{n \text{ entities}} \tag{2}$$

For convenience we rearrange the terms such that the directional part, $\boldsymbol{D}_n(\hat{\boldsymbol{\mu}})$, becomes a matrix:

$$\boldsymbol{D}_n(\hat{\boldsymbol{\mu}}) = \hat{\boldsymbol{\mu}} \lfloor \hat{\boldsymbol{\mu}}^{\otimes(n-1)} \rfloor^T \tag{3}$$

Here the " $\lfloor \ \rfloor$ " notation implies a *lineup* operation which arrange the elements of a multi dimensional array into a lexicographic ordered column vector. The motivation for introducing this notation is that letting $\boldsymbol{D}_n$ contain the elements of $\hat{\boldsymbol{\mu}}^{\otimes n}$ arranged as a matrix greatly simplifies the equations needed in the following analysis.

To handle the special cases of $n = 0$ and $n = 1$ we introduce the following definitions:

$$\hat{\boldsymbol{\mu}} \lfloor \hat{\boldsymbol{\mu}}^{\otimes(-1)} \rfloor \equiv \hat{\boldsymbol{\mu}}^{\otimes 0} \equiv \mathbf{I} \tag{4}$$

where $\mathbf{I}$ is an identity matrix scaled to have a unity frobenius norm. The need to introduce these definitions correspond to the fact that order 0 implies a scalar entity that does not carry orientation information and thus constitutes a special case.

It is also worth noting here that the odd part of $\boldsymbol{D}_1(\hat{\boldsymbol{\mu}})$ corresponds to the Hilbert transform in the 1-dimensional case and the Riesz transform for higher dimensions, [1].

The monomial filter matrix - For each order n a *monomial filter matrix* is defined as:

$$\boldsymbol{F}_n = R(\rho)\ \boldsymbol{D}_n(\hat{\boldsymbol{\mu}}) \tag{5}$$

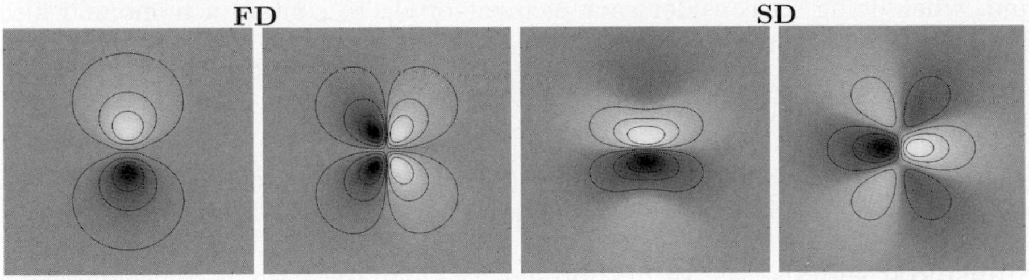

Fig. 1. Left: Fourier domain images of $F_3(1,1)$ and $F_3(1,2)$, see eq. (6). High values are bright and low values are dark. Green indicates positive real values and red indicates negative real values. Right: Spatial domain images of $\mathrm{F}_3(1,1)$ and $\mathrm{F}_3(1,2)$. Yellow indicates positive imaginary values and blue indicates negative imaginary values. The black contours are iso-level lines. The remaining filters in the set are 90 deg rotated copies of the shown filters.

As an example consider the monomial filter matrix of order three in 2D. Using the notation $\hat{\boldsymbol{\mu}} = (\mu,\, \nu)^T$ the monomial filter matrix is computed as:

$$\begin{aligned} \boldsymbol{F}_3 &= R(\rho) \begin{pmatrix} \mu \\ \nu \end{pmatrix} \left\lfloor \begin{matrix} \mu^2 & \mu\nu \\ \mu\nu & \nu^2 \end{matrix} \right\rfloor^T \\ &= R(\rho) \begin{pmatrix} \mu \\ \nu \end{pmatrix} \begin{pmatrix} \mu^2 & \mu\nu & \mu\nu\, \nu^2 \end{pmatrix} \\ &= R(\rho) \begin{pmatrix} \mu^3 & \mu^2\nu & \mu^2\nu & \mu\nu^2 \\ \mu^2\nu & \mu\nu^2 & \mu\nu^2 & \nu^3 \end{pmatrix} \end{aligned} \tag{6}$$

For clarity of the presentation most examples in this paper are given in 2D. The proposed concept is, however, valid for any signal dimensions.

Monomial filter responses - Now let the spatial domain (SD) correspondence of the monomial filter matrix $\boldsymbol{F}_n$ be denoted $\mathbf{F}_n$. Each element of $\mathbf{F}_n$ consequently contains the convolution kernel of the corresponding FD filter function in $\boldsymbol{F}_n$. If the multi dimensional signal is denoted $\mathsf{s}(\mathbf{x})$ where $\mathbf{x}$ denotes the SD coordinates the *monomial filter response matrix*, $\mathbf{Q}_n(\mathbf{x})$, is defined as:

$$\mathbf{Q}_n(\mathbf{x}) = \mathbf{F}_n(\mathbf{x}) * \mathsf{s}(\mathbf{x}) \tag{7}$$

Denoting the Fourier transform of s around $\mathbf{x}$ by $\mathsf{S}_\mathbf{x}$ the same relation is, in the Fourier domain, expressed as:

$$\mathbf{Q}_n(\mathbf{x}) = \int \boldsymbol{F}_n(\boldsymbol{\mu})\ \mathsf{S}_\mathbf{x}(\boldsymbol{\mu})\, d\boldsymbol{\mu} \tag{8}$$

In this general description each element of $\mathbf{Q}_n(\mathbf{x})$ contains the monomial filter responses for the entire signal. Since all filtering operations in this paper are shift invariant we may from now on sometimes omit the spatial coordinate vector $\mathbf{x}$

and, when doing so, consider each element of $\mathbf{Q}_n$ to contain a monomial filter responses for any given spatial coordinate.

3 Signal Classes

It is useful in the following to define different classes of signals. We will here define three different signal classes: Sinusoidal, Simple and Rank d signals.

Sinusoidal signals - We first present the simplest case, a sinusoidal signal with amplitude a, spatial frequency $\boldsymbol{u}$, and phase θ. For this case the monomial filter response matrix can be described in FD terms as:

$$\mathsf{s}(\mathbf{x}) = \mathsf{a}\cos(\boldsymbol{u}^T\mathbf{x} + \theta) \tag{9}$$

both even and odd order filters will respond and we get:

$$\mathbf{Q}_n = \begin{cases} \mathsf{a}\cos(\theta)\, R(\rho)\, \boldsymbol{D}_n(\hat{\boldsymbol{u}}) & \text{for even } n \\ -i\mathsf{a}\sin(\theta)\, R(\rho)\, \boldsymbol{D}_n(\hat{\boldsymbol{u}}) & \text{for odd } n \end{cases} \tag{10}$$

Simple signals - Following [18] we define signals that can be expressed by equation (11) to be termed simple signals.

$$\mathsf{s}(\mathbf{x}) = \mathsf{g}(\hat{\boldsymbol{u}}^T\mathbf{x}) \tag{11}$$

Here $\mathsf{g}(\mathrm{x})$ is any real, one variable, function and $\mathrm{x} = \hat{\boldsymbol{u}}^T\mathbf{x}$. $\hat{\boldsymbol{u}}$ is a unit vector giving the orientation of the signal. For this case the monomial filter response matrix can be described in FD terms as:

$$\begin{aligned} \mathbf{Q}_n(\hat{\boldsymbol{u}}) &= \mathsf{A}_n\, \boldsymbol{D}_n(\hat{\boldsymbol{u}}) \\ &= \mathsf{A}_n\, \hat{\boldsymbol{u}}\, \lfloor \hat{\boldsymbol{u}}^{\otimes(n-1)} \rfloor^T \end{aligned} \tag{12}$$

The local orientation invariant filter factor, A_n, is a function of the radial filter function, $R(\rho)$, and the signal generating function, $\mathsf{g}(\mathrm{x})$. The fact that the Fourier transform of a simple signal is non-zero only on a line through the origin makes for a simple solution. Denoting the Fourier transform of $\mathsf{g}(\mathrm{x})$ by $\mathsf{G}(u)$ we find the filter response amplitude as:

$$\begin{cases} \mathsf{A}_n = \mathsf{A}_\mathsf{e} = \int R(|u|)\, \mathsf{G}(u)\, du & \text{for even } n \\ \mathsf{A}_n = \mathsf{A}_\mathsf{o} = \int R(|u|)\, \mathsf{G}(u)\, \mathrm{sign}(u)\, du & \text{for odd } n \end{cases} \tag{13}$$

Unless explicitly mentioned all signals will in the following be regarded simple.

Rank d signals - Although not directly used here, it is worth noting that it is straight forward to classify more complex signals in a similar manner. Let $\hat{\boldsymbol{U}}$ be a projection operator of rank d and g be a real function of d variables, then

$$\mathsf{s}(\mathbf{x}) = \mathsf{g}(\hat{\boldsymbol{U}}\mathbf{x}) \tag{14}$$

is a rank d signal. Thus, a simple signal is a rank one signal. A full rank signal corresponds to $\hat{\boldsymbol{U}} = \hat{\boldsymbol{I}}$. In the following we will only distinguish between sinusoidal, simple and non-simple signals.

4 Second Order Structure Tensors

The next step towards obtaining a structure tensor is to compute the outer product of the filter matrix.

$$\mathbf{T}_n^2 = \mathbf{Q}_n \, \mathbf{Q}_n^T \tag{15}$$

where " T " denotes complex conjugate transpose.

We will present the case where the local neighborhood of the image consists of a simple signal with direction $\hat{\boldsymbol{u}}$. As a simple introductory example we consider 2-dimensional monomial filters of order three.

$$\mathbf{Q}_3 = \mathsf{A}_\mathsf{o} \begin{pmatrix} u^3 & u^2v & u^2v & uv^2 \\ u^2v & uv^2 & uv^2 & v^3 \end{pmatrix} \tag{16}$$

Carrying out the sums we get:

$$\begin{aligned} \mathbf{T}_3 &= \mathbf{Q}_3 \, \mathbf{Q}_3^T \\ &= \mathsf{A}_\mathsf{o}\mathsf{A}_\mathsf{o}^* \begin{pmatrix} u^3 & u^2v & u^2v & uv^2 \\ u^2v & uv^2 & uv^2 & v^3 \end{pmatrix} \begin{pmatrix} u^3 & u^2v \\ u^2v & uv^2 \\ u^2v & uv^2 \\ uv^2 & v^3 \end{pmatrix} \\ &= |\mathsf{A}_\mathsf{o}|^2 \underbrace{(u^2+v^2)^2}_{=1} \begin{pmatrix} u^2 & uv \\ uv & v^2 \end{pmatrix} \\ &= |\mathsf{A}_\mathsf{o}|^2 \begin{pmatrix} u^2 & uv \\ uv & v^2 \end{pmatrix} \end{aligned} \tag{17}$$

In general the matrix product of equation (15) becomes:

$$\begin{aligned} \mathbf{T}_n^2 &= \underbrace{\mathsf{A}_n \; \hat{\boldsymbol{u}} \, \lfloor \hat{\boldsymbol{u}}^{\otimes(n-1)} \rfloor^T}_{\mathbf{Q}_n} \; \underbrace{\lfloor \hat{\boldsymbol{u}}^{\otimes(n-1)} \rfloor \, \hat{\boldsymbol{u}}^T \, \mathsf{A}_n^*}_{\mathbf{Q}_n^T} \\ &= \mathsf{A}_n \; \hat{\boldsymbol{u}} \; \underbrace{\lfloor \hat{\boldsymbol{u}}^{\otimes(n-1)} \rfloor^T \lfloor \hat{\boldsymbol{u}}^{\otimes(n-1)} \rfloor}_{\text{inner product}} \; \hat{\boldsymbol{u}}^T \, \mathsf{A}_n^* \end{aligned} \tag{18}$$

The inner product of the lined up outer products above can be performed in reversed order. Then, for $n > 0$, equation (18) simplifies to:

$$\mathbf{T}_n^2 = \mathsf{A}_n \; \hat{\boldsymbol{u}} \; \underbrace{(\hat{\boldsymbol{u}}^T \hat{\boldsymbol{u}})^{(n-1)}}_{=1} \; \hat{\boldsymbol{u}}^T \, \mathsf{A}_n^* \tag{19}$$

By definition $\hat{\boldsymbol{u}}^T \hat{\boldsymbol{u}}$ is equal to one. It follows that the under-braced term also equals one and we have the desired result:

$$\mathbf{T}_n^2 = |\mathsf{A}_n|^2 \, \hat{\boldsymbol{u}} \, \hat{\boldsymbol{u}}^T \quad ; \qquad n > 0 \tag{20}$$

For $n = 0$ we have a special case since the filter is isotropic, $\boldsymbol{D}_n = 1$, and $\mathbf{T}_0^2 = \mathbf{Q}_0 \, \mathbf{Q}_0^T = |\mathsf{A}_\mathsf{e}|^2 \, \mathbf{I}$.

Monomial quadrature - As stated in equation (13) even and odd filters will have different local magnitudes.

$$\mathbf{T}_n^2 = \begin{cases} \mathsf{A}_\mathsf{e}^2 \;\hat{\boldsymbol{u}}\,\hat{\boldsymbol{u}}^T & \text{for even } n \\ |\mathsf{A}_\mathsf{o}|^2 \;\hat{\boldsymbol{u}}\,\hat{\boldsymbol{u}}^T & \text{for odd } n \end{cases} \tag{21}$$

A phase invariant monomial quadrature tensor can now be computed as the sum of one even index tensor and odd index tensor. Letting n be even and m odd we obtain:

$$\begin{aligned} \mathbf{T}_{nm}^2 &= \mathbf{T}_n^2 + \mathbf{T}_m^2 \\ &= \mathbf{Q}_n \mathbf{Q}_n^T + \mathbf{Q}_m \mathbf{Q}_m^T \\ &= |\,\mathsf{A}_\mathsf{e} + \mathsf{A}_\mathsf{o}\,|^2 \;\hat{\boldsymbol{u}}\,\hat{\boldsymbol{u}}^T \\ &= \mathsf{q}^2 \;\hat{\boldsymbol{u}}\,\hat{\boldsymbol{u}}^T \end{aligned} \tag{22}$$

Note that the tensor magnitude, q, will be the same regardless of the order of the filters used.

Tensor positivity - A more compact expression of the monomial quadrature tensor can be attained by concatenating the even and the odd filter response matrices to a single matrix. The " , " notation implies concatenation of the arguments left to right.

$$\mathbf{Q}_{nm} = (\mathbf{Q}_n \,,\, \mathbf{Q}_m) \tag{23}$$

and compute the monomial quadrature tensor of origin (m, n) as

$$\mathbf{T}_{nm}^2 = \mathbf{Q}_{nm}\, \mathbf{Q}_{nm}^T \tag{24}$$

As the monomial quadrature tensor is computed from products of filter response matrices

$$\mathbf{T}_{nm}^2 = \mathbf{Q}_{nm} \mathbf{Q}_{nm}^T = \sum_k \lambda_k \,\hat{\mathbf{e}}_k \hat{\mathbf{e}}_k^T \tag{25}$$

it follows that all $\lambda_k \geq 0$ which allows for robust certainty estimates for the local structure estimation.

5 Structure Tensor Estimation Variations

Local structure analysis algorithms are quite complex and involve a lot more than the filters used. This makes comparisons difficult to interpret from a filter point of view. There are, however, a number of interesting similarities between different suggested algorithms. A few previous comparisons can be found in [21] and [26]. In the following we point out the relation to the monomial approach for a number of well known approaches to structure tensor estimation. We show that nearly all variants can be formulated as special or modified versions of the monomial approach.

The structure tensor, T - The first publications mentioning tensors as a representation for local orientation and structure is due to Knutsson, [12,16]. Similar to the earlier developed vector representation, [9,11], the construction is based on a set of quadrature filters oriented in a number of fixed orientations, q_k, k indicating the orientation. The structure tensor is obtained as:

$$\mathsf{T} = \sum_k \sqrt{\mathsf{q}_k \mathsf{q}_k^*}\, \mathbf{T}_k \tag{26}$$

The vector variant works for two dimensional signals but for three dimension, or more, the tensor formulation is necessary. The loglet based structure tensor estimation suggested in [22] also uses this weighted 'basis tensor' approach but involve a different set of filters allowing higher order orientations components to be incorporated.

Unlike the methods discussed below these method for structure tensor construction are not possible to describe as a special or modified case of the monomial approach.

The gradient tensor, T_G - The simplest way to obtain a matrix describing local orientation is exemplified by Bigun-Granlund's inertia matrix [13] and Förstners corner detector [15]. This matrix is constructed as the outer product of the local gradient and is, in the notation introduced above and Q defined by equation(7), given by:

$$\begin{aligned} \mathsf{T}_\mathsf{G} &= \mathsf{T}_1 \\ &= \mathsf{Q}_1\, \mathsf{Q}_1^T \end{aligned} \tag{27}$$

Although the authors never mention tensors in the original work this outer product matrix estimate is often referred to as the gradient tensor or the structure tensor.

Since only a single order, i.e. order one, is used this tensor is not phase invariant. Another drawback is that the frequency bandwidth of the estimate can become twice that of the original signal which may cause significant aliasing artifacts. Both these shortcomings are in practice, to some extent, remedied by the use of an averaging filter performing a weighted summation of local outer products. On the other hand this decreases the spatial resolution of the estimate, [24].

The boundary tensor, T_B - The boundary tensor originally suggested by Köthe, [23], uses orders one and two and constitutes a special case of the monomial quadrature tensor.

$$\begin{aligned} \mathsf{T}_\mathsf{B} &= \mathsf{T}_{12} \\ &= \mathsf{Q}_{12}\, \mathsf{Q}_{12}^T \end{aligned} \tag{28}$$

The energy tensor, T_E - The energy tensor, suggested by Felsberg, [28], is a variant where filters of different orders are involved in the computed products.

The energy tensor uses an isotropically bandpass filter signal, it's gradient and it's Hessian. It can in monomial terms be expressed as:

$$\begin{aligned} \mathsf{T}_{\mathsf{E}} &= \mathsf{T}_1 + \mathsf{T}_{(0,2)} \\ &= \mathsf{Q}_1\mathsf{Q}_1^T + \mathsf{q}_0\mathsf{Q}_2 \end{aligned} \tag{29}$$

Note that the filter response matrices here have different radial frequency response and the mixing of different order terms will not give a positive semi-definite tensor for all image neighborhoods.

Gradient energy tensor, T_{GE} - The gradient energy tensor (GET) suggested in [29] can be said to use the same formula as the energy tensor with the input signal replaced by it's gradient. In monomial terms the result can be expressed:

$$\mathsf{T}_{\mathsf{GE}} = \mathsf{Q}_2\,\mathsf{Q}_2^T + \frac{1}{2}\left(\mathsf{Q}_1\,\mathsf{Q}_3^T + \mathsf{Q}_3\,\mathsf{Q}_1^T\right) \tag{30}$$

Note that also in this case the filter response matrices here have different radial frequency response and that the mixing of different order terms will not give a positive semi-definite tensor for all image neighborhoods.

Spatial 2:nd order polynomial tensor, T_{SP} - The 2:nd order polymer tensor suggested by Farnebäck in [19] is a sum of outer products of 1:st and 2:nd order monomial filters. The difference from the monomial approach is that the filters are designed as windowed 1:st and 2:nd order polynomials in the spatial domain.

$$\begin{aligned} \mathsf{T}_{\mathsf{SP}} &= \mathsf{T}_1 + \mathsf{T}_2 \\ &= \mathsf{Q}_1\mathsf{Q}_1^T + \mathsf{Q}_2\mathsf{Q}_2^T \end{aligned} \tag{31}$$

This spatial design results in 1:st and 2:nd order filter that have different radial functions in the frequency domain. For this reason the result is not in general phase invariant i.e components are not in quadrature. However, since it is a sum of squares, the result is always positive semi-definite.

Spherical harmonics, T_{SH} - A somewhat different way to estimate a local structure tensor is suggested in [24]. This approach is based on sums of products of spherically separable filters. The filter have the same radial function and the directional functions are spherical harmonic functions. The structure tensor carries information about 0:th and 2:nd order variations in orientation. A product between an order j filter and an order k filter will contain signal components of orders $j - k$ and $j + k$. By an appropriate weighted summation of a number of filter products it is possible to retain only order 0 and order 2 in the correct proportion while canceling out all other orders: i.e:

$$\mathsf{T}_{\mathsf{SH}} = \sum_{jk} w_{jk}\mathsf{H}_j\mathsf{H}_k \tag{32}$$

This is a very general approach and, since spherical harmonic filter sets of orders 1 to N span the same function space as monomial filter sets of orders 1 to N, all monomial tensor variations can also be expressed in this way. With proper weights the result can also be made phase-invariant.

Sum of monomial tensors - Even more careful weighting of spherical harmonic filter products will give positive semi-definite tensors, in this case the result will be equivalent to a sum of tensor estimates over different order, $n \geq 0$ (even and odd), monomial filter matrices, $\mathbf{Q}_n$.

$$\mathbf{T}_{\mathbf{SM}} = \sum_n w_n \mathbf{Q}_n \mathbf{Q}_n^T \tag{33}$$

6 Higher Order Structure Tensors

In equation (18) the filter matrix is constructed to produce a 2:nd order tensor. However, a simple rearrangement of the order n filter matrix components will allow tensors of order $2p$ to be estimated.

$$\begin{aligned}\mathbf{T}^2_{\mathbf{2p},n} &= \underbrace{\mathsf{A}_n \ \lfloor \hat{\boldsymbol{u}}^{\otimes p} \rfloor \lfloor \hat{\boldsymbol{u}}^{\otimes (n-p)} \rfloor^T}_{\mathbf{Q}_{(p)n}} \ \underbrace{\lfloor \hat{\boldsymbol{u}}^{\otimes (n-p)} \rfloor \lfloor \ \hat{\boldsymbol{u}}^{\otimes p} \rfloor^T \mathsf{A}_n}_{\mathbf{Q}^T_{(p)n}} \\ &= \mathsf{A}_n \ \lfloor \hat{\boldsymbol{u}}^{\otimes p} \rfloor \ \underbrace{\lfloor \hat{\boldsymbol{u}}^{\otimes (n-p)} \rfloor^T \lfloor \hat{\boldsymbol{u}}^{\otimes (n-p)} \rfloor}_{\text{inner product}} \ \lfloor \ \hat{\boldsymbol{u}}^{\otimes p} \rfloor^T \mathsf{A}_n\end{aligned} \tag{34}$$

As before the inner product of the *lined up* outer products above can be performed in reversed order. Then, for $n \geq p \geq 0$, equation (18) simplifies to:

$$\mathbf{T}^2_{\mathbf{2p},n} = \mathsf{A}_n \ \lfloor \ \hat{\boldsymbol{u}}^{\otimes p} \rfloor \ \underbrace{(\hat{\boldsymbol{u}}^T \hat{\boldsymbol{u}})^{(n-p)}}_{=1} \ \ \lfloor \ \hat{\boldsymbol{u}}^{\otimes p} \rfloor^T \mathsf{A}_n \tag{35}$$

By definition $\hat{\boldsymbol{u}}^T \hat{\boldsymbol{u}}$ is equal to one. It follows that the under-braced term also equals one which gives:

$$\mathbf{T}^2_{\mathbf{2p},n} \ = \ |\mathsf{A}_n|^2 \ \lfloor \hat{\boldsymbol{u}}^{\otimes p} \rfloor \lfloor \ \hat{\boldsymbol{u}}^{\otimes p} \rfloor^T \ ; \qquad n \geq p \geq 0 \tag{36}$$

The result now holds the components of a tensor of order $2p$. However, due to the use of the *lineup* operator, the components are stored in matrix form and they need to be re-organized in order to obtain the result as a proper tensor $\boldsymbol{\Upsilon}$ of order $2p$.

$$\boldsymbol{\Upsilon}_{\mathbf{2p},n} \ = \ \lceil \ \mathbf{T}^2_{\mathbf{2p},n} \rceil \tag{37}$$

The " $\lceil \ \rceil$ " notation used here indicates a reshape operation that restores the proper structure of the data, i.e. the result is a tensor having $2p$ indexes.

As 2:nd order tensors are naturally represented as matrices the *lineup* operator greatly simplifies the notation. For higher order tensors, however, the use of standard tensor notation may be preferred by some readers. Equations (36) and (37) can then be jointly expressed as:

$$\Upsilon_{\mathsf{n}}{}^{\mathsf{a}_1 \dots \mathsf{a}_\mathsf{p}}_{\mathsf{b}_1 \dots \mathsf{b}_\mathsf{p}} \ = \ |\mathsf{A}_\mathsf{n}|^2 \ \mathsf{u}^{\mathsf{a}_1 \ \dots \ \mathsf{a}_\mathsf{p}}_{\mathsf{a}_{\mathsf{p}+1} \dots \mathsf{a}_\mathsf{n}} \ \mathsf{u}^{\mathsf{a}_{\mathsf{p}+1} \dots \mathsf{a}_\mathsf{n}}_{\mathsf{b}_1 \ \dots \ \mathsf{b}_\mathsf{p}} \tag{38}$$

According to the Einstein convention a summation is performed over equal indexes and equation 38 clearly shows that the difference between tensors of different order is how many indexes are summed over (contracted). Letting $p = 0$ means summing over all indexes and the result is a scalar representing the local energy. For $p = 1$ we obtain the standard structure tensor. For $p > 1$ we obtain higher order tensors having the power to represent more complex local structure.

Non-simple signals - For such non-simple signals equation (38) is no longer applicable since there is no unique local orientation, $\boldsymbol{u}$. Directly expressed as a sum of filter products, corresponding to a generalization of the monomial filter response matrix product in equation (15), we obtain an order $2p$ structure tensor as:

$$\Upsilon_{n}{}^{a_1 \ldots a_p}_{b_1 \ldots b_p} = q^{a_1 \ \ldots \ a_p}_{a_{p+1} \ldots a_n} \, q^{a_{p+1} \ldots a_n}_{b_1 \ \ldots \ b_p} \tag{39}$$

Tensors of order four have been used to analyze situations with two orientations present, e.g. [25,31,33]. Applications where tensors of order higher than four have been used are so far not known to the authors but can be expected to prove a powerful tool when more that two orientation are present.

To produce quadrature type tensors we still need to add a tensor from odd order filter sets and a tensor from even order filter sets. In the most general case we can express the estimation of local structure tensors of order $2p$ as a weighted summation of order $2p$ tensors, here of order $\binom{p}{p}$, from monomial filter sets of different orders, i.e:

$$\Upsilon^{a_1 \ldots a_p}_{b_1 \ldots b_p} = \sum_{n} w_n \, q^{a_1 \ \ldots \ a_p}_{a_{p+1} \ldots a_n} \, q^{a_{p+1} \ldots a_n}_{b_1 \ \ldots \ b_p} \tag{40}$$

7 Conclusion

Research concerning 2:nd order structure tensor estimation is still continuing after more than two decades. The higher order tensor estimates produced by equation (40) contains a much richer representation of the local structure and we expect that the future will hold considerable effort towards fully understanding these new higher order constructs.

Acknowledgment

The Swedish Research Council and Linköpings Universitet are gratefully acknowledged for supporting this work.

References

1. Riesz, M.: Sur les fonctions conjuge'es. Math. Zeit. 27, 218–244 (1927)
2. Zernike, F.: Diffraction theory of the cut procedure and its improved form, the phase contrast method. Physica 1, 689–704 (1934)

3. Gabor, D.: Theory of communication. J. Inst. Elec. Eng. 93(26), 429–457 (1946)
4. Hu, M.K.: Visual pattern recognition by moment invariants. IRE Transactions on Information Theory, IT-8(2), 179–187 (1962)
5. Roberts, L.G.: Machine Perception of three-dimensional Solid. In: Tippell, J.T. (ed.) Optical and Electro-Optical Information Processing, pp. 159–197. MIT Press, Cambridge (1965)
6. Granlund, G.H.: In search of a general picture processing operator. Computer Graphics and Image Processing 8(2), 155–178 (1978)
7. Danielsson, P.E.: Rotation invariant operators with directional response. In: Proceedings 5'th Int. Conf. on Pattern Recognition, Miami Beach, Florida (1980)
8. Knutsson, H., Wilson, R.G., Granlund, G.H.: Anisotropic filtering operations for image enhancement and their relation to the visual system. In: IEEE Computer Society Conference on Pattern Recognition and Image Processing, Dallas, Texas (August 1981)
9. Knutsson, H.: Filtering and Reconstruction in Image Processing. PhD thesis, Linköping University, Sweden, Diss. No. 88 (1982)
10. Knutsson, H., Granlund, G.H.: Texture analysis using two-dimensional quadrature filters. In: IEEE Computer Society Workshop on Computer Architecture for Pattern Analysis and Image Database Management - CAPAIDM, Pasadena (October 1983)
11. Knutsson, H.: Producing a continuous and distance preserving 5-D vector representation of 3-D orientation. In: IEEE Computer Society Workshop on Computer Architecture for Pattern Analysis and Image Database Management - CAPAIDM, pp. 175–182, Miami Beach, Florida, November 1985. IEEE. Report LiTH–ISY–I–0843, Linköping University, Sweden (1986)
12. Knutsson, H.: A tensor representation of 3-D structures. In: 5th IEEE-ASSP and EURASIP Workshop on Multidimensional Signal Processing, Noordwijkerhout, The Netherlands (September 1987), poster presentation
13. Bigün, J., Granlund, G.H.: Optimal orientation detection of linear symmetry. In: IEEE First International Conference on Computer Vision, London, Great Britain, pp. 433–438 (June 1987)
14. Lenz, R.: Rotation-invariant operators and scale space filtering. Pattern Recognition Letters 6, 151–154 (1987)
15. Forstner, W., Gulch, E.: A fast operator for detection and precise location of distinct points, corners and centres of circular features. In: ISPRS Intercommission Conference on Fast Processing of Photogrammetric Data, pp. 281–305 (1987)
16. Knutsson, H.: Representing local structure using tensors. In: The 6th Scandinavian Conference on Image Analysis, Oulu, Finland, pp. 244–251, (June 1989); Report LiTH–ISY–I–1019, Computer Vision Laboratory, Linköping University, Sweden
17. Knutsson, H., Bårman, H., Haglund, L.: Robust orientation estimation in 2D, 3D and 4D using tensors. In: Proceedings of Second International Conference on Automation, Robotics and Computer Vision, ICARCV 1992, Singapore (September 1992)
18. Granlund, G.H., Knutsson, H.: Signal Processing for Computer Vision. Kluwer Academic Publishers, Dordrecht (1995) ISBN 0-7923-9530-1
19. Farnebäck, G.: Fast and accurate motion estimation using orientation tensors and parametric motion models. In: Proceedings of 15th International Conference on Pattern Recognition, vol. 1, pp. 135–139. IAPR, Barcelona (2000)
20. Felsberg, M., Sommer, G.: The monogenic signal. IEEE Transactions on Signal Processing 49(12), 3136–3144 (2001)

21. Johansson, B., Farnebäck, G.: A theoretical comparison of different orientation tensors. In: Proceedings SSAB 2002 Symposium on Image Analysis, pp. 69–73. SSAB, Lund (2002)
22. Knutsson, H., Andersson, M.: Loglets: Generalized quadrature and phase for local spatio-temporal structure estimation. In: Proceedings of the Scandinavian Conference on Image Analysis (SCIA) (June 2003)
23. Köthe, U.: Inegrated edge and junction detection with the boundary tensor. In: Proceedings of Ninth IEEE International Conference on Computer Vision, ICCV (2003)
24. Knutsson, H., Andersson, M.: Implications of invariance and uncertainty for local structure analysis filter sets. Signal Processing: Image Communications 20(6), 569–581 (2005)
25. Nordberg, K.: A fourth order tensor for representation of orientation and position of oriented segments. Other academic, Linköping University, Department of Electrical Engineering, Sweden, diva2:288343 (2004)
26. Nordberg, K., Farnebäck, G.: Estimation of orientation tensors for simple signals by means of second-order filters. Signal Processing: Image Communication 20(6), 582–594 (2005)
27. Köthe, U., Felsberg, M.: Riesz-transforms versus derivatives: On the relationship between the boundary tensor and the energy tensor. In: Kimmel, R., Sochen, N.A., Weickert, J. (eds.) Scale-Space 2005. LNCS, vol. 3459, pp. 179–191. Springer, Heidelberg (2005)
28. Felsberg, M., Jonsson, E.: Energy tensors: Quadratic, phase invariant image operators. In: Kropatsch, W.G., Sablatnig, R., Hanbury, A. (eds.) DAGM 2005. LNCS, vol. 3663, pp. 493–500. Springer, Heidelberg (2005)
29. Felsberg, M., Köthe, U.: GET: The Connection Between Monogenic Scale-Space and Gaussian Derivatives. In: Kimmel, R., Sochen, N.A., Weickert, J. (eds.) Scale-Space 2005. LNCS, vol. 3459, pp. 192–203. Springer, Heidelberg (2005)
30. Herberthson, M., Brun, A., Knutsson, H.: Representing pairs of orientations in the plane. In: Ersbøll, B.K., Pedersen, K.S. (eds.) SCIA 2007. LNCS, vol. 4522, pp. 661–670. Springer, Heidelberg (2007)
31. Barmpoutis, A., Vemuri, B.C., Forder, J.R.: Registration of high angular resolution diffusion MRI images using 4 order tensors. In: Ayache, N., Ourselin, S., Maeder, A. (eds.) MICCAI 2007, Part I. LNCS, vol. 4791, pp. 908–915. Springer, Heidelberg (2007)
32. Wang, Q., Ronneberger, O., Burkhardt, H.: Fourier analysis in polar and spherical coordinates. Technical Report Internal Report 1/08, IIF-LMB, Computer Science Department, University of Freiburg (2008)
33. Westin, C.-F., Knutsson, H.: Representation and Estimation of Tensors-Pairs. In: Visualization and Processing of Tensor Fields: Proceedings of the Dagstuhl Workshop (2010) submitted

Automatic Compartment Modelling and Segmentation for Dynamical Renal Scintigraphies

Daniel Ståhl[1,2], Kalle Åström[1], Niels Christian Overgaard[1], Matilda Landgren[1,2], Karl Sjöstrand[2,3], and Lars Edenbrandt[2]

[1] Centre for Mathematical Sciences, Lund University, Lund, Sweden
{kalle,nco}@maths.lth.se
[2] Exini Diagnostics AB, Lund, Sweden
{karl.sjostrand,lars.edenbrandt}@exini.com
[3] Department of Informatics and Mathematical Modelling, Technical University of Denmark, Kgs. Lyngby, Denmark

Abstract. Time-resolved medical data has important applications in a large variety of medical applications. In this paper we study automatic analysis of dynamical renal scintigraphies. The traditional analysis pipeline for dynamical renal scintigraphies is to use manual or semiautomatic methods for segmentation of pixels into physical compartments, extract their corresponding time-activity curves and then compute the parameters that are relevant for medical assessment. In this paper we present a fully automatic system that incorporates spatial smoothing constraints, compartment modelling and positivity constraints to produce an interpretation of the full time-resolved data. The method has been tested on renal dynamical scintigraphies with promising results. It is shown that the method indeed produces more compact representations, while keeping the residual of fit low. The parameters of the time activity curve, such as peak-time and time for half activity from peak, are compared between the previous semiautomatic method and the method presented in this paper. It is also shown how to obtain new and clinically relevant features using our novel system.

Keywords: Medical image analysis, time-resolved, compartment modelling, dynamical renal scintigraphies, segmentation.

1 Introduction

Dynamical renal scintigraphy, or simply *Renography*, is a method used by medical doctors to assess the renal function of a patient. It exploits the mechanisms of the *homeostasis* - preservation of an optimal extracellular fluid volume and the ability to either remove or restore ions and chemical compounds produced as a result of the metabolism. Since these abilities heavily rely on the complex structure of the kidney any impairments, such as kidney stones, cancer or obstructions, on the kidneys' anatomy and physiology lead to decreased renal function. If this is suspected by the medical doctor, then renography is performed. The procedure of the examination is that the patient is excessively hydrated to build up the

A. Heyden and F. Kahl (Eds.): SCIA 2011, LNCS 6688, pp. 557–568, 2011.

urine production. The patient is then given an injection of a *tracer* consisting of a radioactive isotope, ^{99m}Tc, that is attached to a molecule specifically designed to be removed by the kidneys. The progression of this tracer is then recorded by a gamma camera to form a time-resolved image sequence that is used in the further analysis.

The acquired sequence holds the accumulated counts between time points $t - \Delta t$ and t for each detector on location (x, y) in the frame corresponding to time t. The data that is used in this paper was retrieved from *Skånes universitetssjukhus*, SUS, where they record this progression with a 128-by-128 detector grid and with uniform time sampling, $\Delta t = 15$. This provides a resulting image sequence which consists of $n_p = 80$ frames. In Figure 1 a summarized image sequence is displayed.

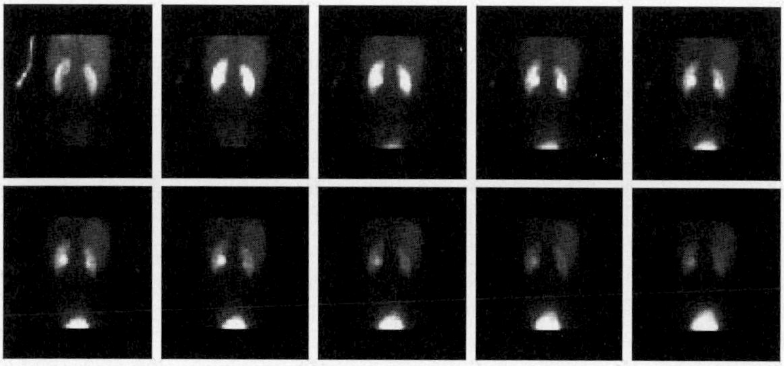

Fig. 1. A summarized image sequence from dynamical renal scintigraphies, the images show the accumulated counts every second minute

The traditional analysis pipeline then is to use manual and/or semi-automatic methods for segmenting the data into pixels, which correspond to the different physical compartments, to estimate the corresponding time-activity curves for the different compartments by summing the pixels in each compartment and to estimate parameters or make classification based on such curves. Two problems arise from the above, (a) manual methods are often time-consuming and different operators may obtain slightly different results and (b) each pixel contains an unknown mixture from the different compartments which is interfering the results. Especially interesting is the way to obtain the *Renogram*, the TAC which describes the uptake and washout from the kidney and is the primary result of renography studies. In a publication from 2010 Piepsz et al. [2] states "The way of handling a renogram remains extremely variable from country to country and even from department to department. Part of these divergences is obviously related to the use of obsolete software available on most of the gamma camera systems". The result of the previously mentioned problems is the huge variety of renal software packages currently used by practitioners, where many of them are developed to fit local fashion e.g. [3] or the one found at SUS. There also exists software from commercial actors trying to bridge the gap [4]. Common for these applications is their manual or semi-automatic approach to obtain the parameters [5].

The aim of this paper is thus to address the problems stated above, (a) and (b), and construct an automatic method to assess the renal function by exploiting the fact that each pixel contains a mixture of contributions from a few types of tissue and organs, in this paper denoted as compartments, which can be identified and used to obtain the structure of tissue and organs that is present in the image sequence. This corresponds to finding the compartments, their time-activity curves and the composition of compartments in each pixel. The result includes data about (i) for each pixel (x,y), the weight $c_k(x, y)$ representing the contribution from each compartment k in the pixel, (ii) the time-dependence $b_k(t)$ of each compartment and (iii) system identification of the underlying compartment model. We will do this in the setting of positivity and spatial smoothness constraints applied on c_k and b_k. With this information an analysis of the renal function is performed.

Many articles have been published on how to obtain the image sequence, the renogram and which parameters that can be used for the medical assessment. One way of exploiting information in the data is to use *Proper Orthogonal Decomposition*, POD, where it was shown by Veltri et al. [1] that a few modes generated from it were sufficient to distinguish different parts of the anatomy of the healthy kidney as well as pathological areas in the pathological kidney. At ISCORN[1] 2010 Richard Lawson presented a summary of the methodologies used when performing an analysis of the kidney and the extraction of the renogram [6]. In his presentation he primarily focused on two strategies for counteracting the accumulated counts from background tissue - the Patlak plot and the deconvolution analysis. Whereas the mathematical model behind the Patlak plot relies on the assumption of constant infusion of tracer, deconvolution analysis models the kidneys' impulse response function from an injection from the blood, cf. [7,8]. Other approaches to extract the renogram are also introduced in [9,5]. Compartmental modelling has also drawn some attention, in the mid-nineties Fine et al. developed a model for parametric deconvolution analysis [10]. Other attempts include the use of concepts from *pharmacokinetics* e.g. Meng et al. propose a 2-compartmental model approach to reconstruct the renogram and estimate physical parameters [11]. Drainage and flow rate parameters between different compartments can also be estimated using compartment models [12].

2 Methods

Our proposed system is built up by several modules further explained in this section. At first we present a brief introduction to the *Singular Value Decomposition*,

[1] XIV International Symposium on Radionuclides in Nephrourology.

SVD, which is used as a reference method. Later in this section our method for estimating the weights $c_k(x, y)$, the bases $b_k(t)$ and the compartmental models are introduced.

Our assumption is that the data $D(x, y, t)$ can be approximated well as a linear combination of these components according to

$$D(x, y, t) \approx \tilde{D}_{c,b}(x, y, t) = \sum_{k=1}^{K} c_k(x, y) b_k(t), \quad (1)$$

where K is the number of compartments, in our experiments $K = 5$, and $\mathbf{c}$ and $\mathbf{b}$ denotes the sets of weights and bases that is reconstructing D. Since the image sequence is a recording of the accumulated counts it is further assumed that each element in D can be regarded as generated from a counting process e.g. Poisson process with intensity λ. However, if the accumulated counts are large it could as well be approximated by a normal distribution. It should also be outlined that scattering and attenuation effects introduces noise in each element of D.

2.1 Using SVD to Approximate the Data

A common approach to reduce the dimensionality of the data and its noise is to use SVD. The data sequence can then be optimally reconstructed in a least squares sense [13], i.e. the approximation $\tilde{D}_{c,b}$ that minimizes

$$\min_{\mathbf{c},\mathbf{b}} \sum_x \sum_y \sum_t |D(x, y, t) - \tilde{D}_{c,b}(x, y, t)|^2 \quad (2)$$

is found by (i) rearranging the data D in a matrix M so that each time point t in D forms a column in M and (ii) performing a singular value decomposition of M, $M = USV^T$. In the case of 5 compartments and 5 basis functions, the first 5 columns of V gives the optimal basis functions and the first 5 columns of US gives the optimal weights c_k after rearrangement of the columns back to matrix form again. An illustration of the output is shown in Figure 2.

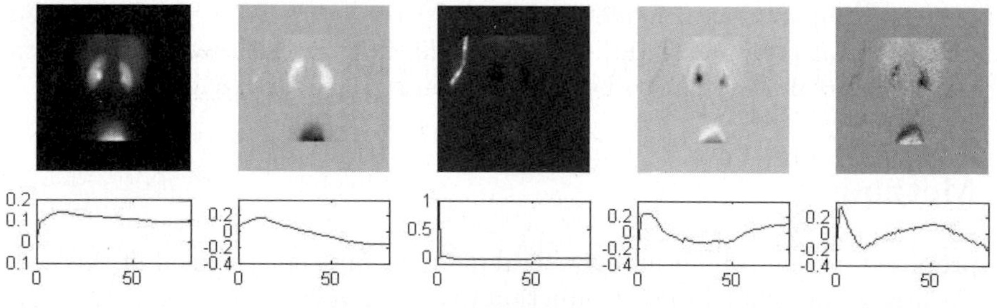

Fig. 2. The first five modes generated by SVD from left to right. The lower row holds the bases and the upper row holds the scores.

SVD provides the optimal L^2 fit, but ignores constraints such as sparsity, spatial continuity and positivity. The weights $c_k(x, y)$ is also expected to assume both positive and negative parts where most of them will be nonzero. Although no particular spatial continuity constraints are assumed, the weights might still be relatively smooth due to the structure of the data. Note also that the generated bases b_k does not in general provide any physiological information about compartment k due to the orthogonality of the bases and that the concentration of tracer only can assume positive values. Hence, the bases are not expected to give an expression of a possible underlying compartment model.

2.2 Using Classification to Approximate the Data

An alternative method is to enforce sparsity by using machine learning techniques. In this method we exploit basis functions that are extracted from data from four healthy patients after manual segmentation of the image into four parts (i) injection site, (ii) blood and surrounding tissue, (iii) kidney and (iv) bladder. For a novel data set we first remove pixels (x, y) for which the time series measurements contain insufficient data to be able to classify reliably. For the remaining pixels an over-segmentation is performed. Each individual segment is then classified into in one of the four classes above. Finally the left and right kidney is automatically separated using a horizontal histogram function of the segmented kidney class. Since the left and right kidney by nature is well-separated it is therefore straightforward to segment them. Prior to the kidney separation a morphological operator is used to obtain a homogenous classification, see Figure 3. The spatial location of the clusters then indicates the possibility of having non-zero weights of the particular bases, these areas are denoted as the *support* $m_k(x, y)$ of compartment k. An estimate of $c_k(x, y)$ are then obtained from Equation 2. In figure 4 the estimated compartments after classification is displayed.

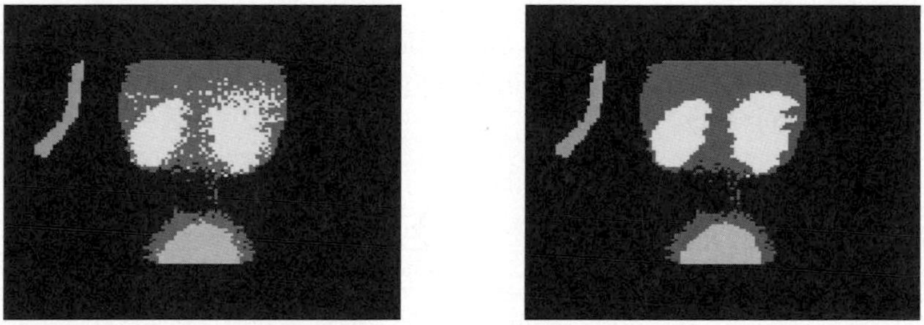

Fig. 3. A figure displaying the classification of pixels into the four classes (left) and the adjusted classification using a morphological operator (right). Legend: Black - pixels not classified due to poor SNR. Green: pixels classified as injection site. Red: pixels classified as blood/tissue. Yellow: pixels classified as kidney. Cyan: pixels classified as bladder.

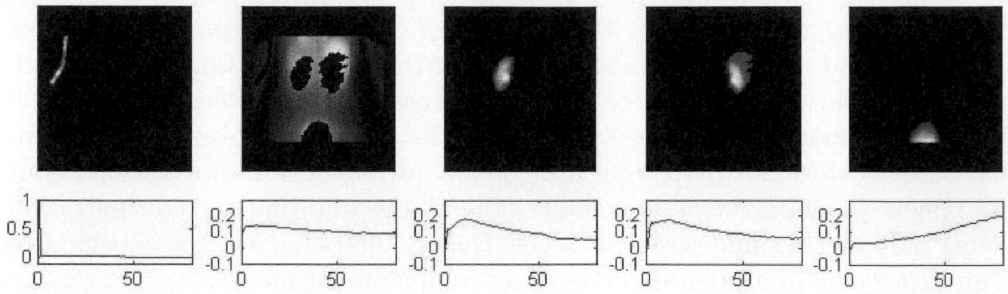

Fig. 4. The compartments generated from classification from left to right (Injection, blood/tissue, left kidney, right kidney, bladder). The lower row holds the bases and the upper row holds the scores. Note the similarity between blood/tissue, left and right kidney TACs, suggesting that the mixture of them has to be estimated.

2.3 Estimation of b_k

The composition of each pixel is described by $\mathbf{c}$ and can be used to reduce the influence of one compartment in other compartments and their associated $b_k(t)$. The b_ks can be estimated using least squares, let $D_k(x, y, t)$ denote the data subtracted by the other compartments except for the one to be estimated, k, then $b_k(t) \mid c_k(x, y)$ is estimated as

$$\widehat{b}_k(t) = \min_{b_k(t)} \sum_{t=1}^{n_t} \sum \left(D_k(x, y, t) - b_k(t) c_k(x, y)\right)^2 . \tag{3}$$

2.4 Estimation of c_k Using Positivity Constraints and Spatial Smoothness Priors

Once estimates of $b_k(t)$ and $m_k(x, y)$ are given for compartment k it is possible to estimate $c_k(x, y)$ using positivity constraints and spatial smoothness priors. If no spatial smoothing is applied, estimation of $c_k(x, y)$ becomes independent for each pixel (x, y). If such, the estimation problem becomes $n_x n_y$ non-negative least squares problems,

$$\min_{c_k(x,y)} \sum_{t=1}^{n_t} \left(D(x, y, t) - \sum_{(x,y) \in m_k(x,y)} b_k(t) c_k(x, y) \right)^2 , \tag{4}$$

of size $n_t n_c$, where n_x and n_y are 128, n_t for our data is 80 and n_c is the number of relevant compartments acting on the pixel, in our experiments 1 or 2. To decrease the computational demand two methods of introducing spatial regularization is considered in this paper. The first is based on linear parametrization of c_k so as to enforce spatial smoothness and the other is based on penalizing the second derivatives of c_k.

For the linear parametrization, each weight $c_k(x, y)$ is parameterized linearly with much fewer parameters or *control points*. This makes the minimization problem for different pixels connected and the independent pixel problem can instead be written as a large nonlinear least squares problem of the form $d = Mc$, where d is a vector of length $n_x n_y n_t$ (for our data 1310720) and M is a sparse matrix of size $n_x n_y n_t \times n_x n_y K$, (1310720×81920), where K denotes the number of compartments. The parametrization of c_k can now be seen as a linear mapping $c_k = Rx$, where x denotes the control points. x is then estimated by solving $d = MRx$ in a non-negative least squares manner. This problem is efficiently solved by sparse numerical linear algebra routines since the relevant Fischer matrix $R^T M^T MR$ is relatively small and has sparse band-diagonal structures.

The first regularization implies smoothing in the neighborhood around the control points. However, the estimation problem is still independent between control points, the second way of regularization connects the control points to enforce spatial smoothing between these as well. To penalize the second derivatives the laplacian of the weights c_k is calculated and added into the estimation problem with a proportionality constant $C > 0$, i.e. we wish to minimize $|MRx - d|^2 + C|Lx|^2$, where the parameter C controls the amount of global regularization applied. The higher C is the smoother the c_ks get. In our experiments the selection of C was obtained by manual determination about whether the computed c_ks reflected the actual compartment well or not e.g. it is expected that the blood/tissue distribution covers the whole body and have high weights where there is a high concentration of blood.

2.5 Compartment Modelling

Given the estimated bases and weights for each compartment and prior knowledge of the interaction between them, the compartment modelling can be performed with the deconvolution analysis approach in mind. With the assumption that the interactions between compartments is linear they can be characterized with an impulse response between the systems' input and output i.e $b_j(t) = (h * b_k)(t)$. In matrix notation this can be formulated as $B_j = HB_k$ where B_j is the complete time series of $b_j(t)$ $(n_j = 80)$, B_k is $b_k(t)$'s $(n_k = n_j)$ ditto and H is a circulant matrix $(H \in \mathbb{R}_{n_k \times n_k})$. By rearranging the right hand side $HB_k = Xh$, where X is a left triangular matrix containing elements from B_k and h is the impulse response function, h can now be estimated in non-negative least squares sense. To reduce the computational effort regularization using control points is used, similar to the first type introduced in section 2.4, to estimate smooth impulse response functions.

2.6 Incorporating All Constraint Modalities

The algorithm of the complete system, incorporating all constraint modalities, can be outlined in two steps - First classification of each pixel is performed to obtain preliminary bases and their support in the image domain. Then an iterative scheme for estimation of **b** and **c** is performed according to the description in

Section 2.3, 2.4 and 2.5. The output now consists of the estimated compartments and a compartment model describing their interaction.

3 Experimental Validation

In this section the experimental results, validation and a presentation of new features are presented. At first, the experimental results addresses the problem of sparsity, positivity and residual patterns for our data set. The proposed method for c_k estimation is also compared to *thin plate splines interpolation* [14]. Secondly, we use the extracted information from our algorithm to generate the renogram and the parameters computed by the software currently used at SUS and compare the results of the two systems on two healthy patients. At last, a review of possible features using our algorithm is presented.

As mentioned earlier the goal was to come up with an algorithm providing reasonable estimates which fulfills the constraints on positivity, sparseness and spatial smoothness in comparison with the optimal case found by SVD, the SVD results are found in Figure 2. With the introduction of machine learning techniques, the dense c_k matrix is reduced to a sparse equivalent containing

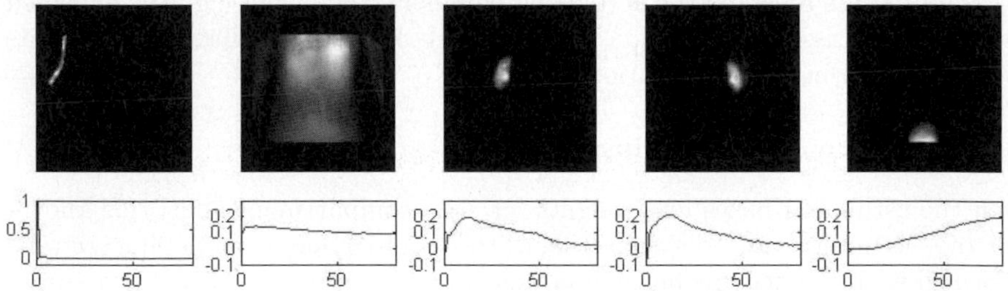

Fig. 5. The injection, blood/tissue, left kidney, right kidney and bladder compartments after *thin plate splines interpolation*. The lower row holds the bases and the upper row holds the scores.

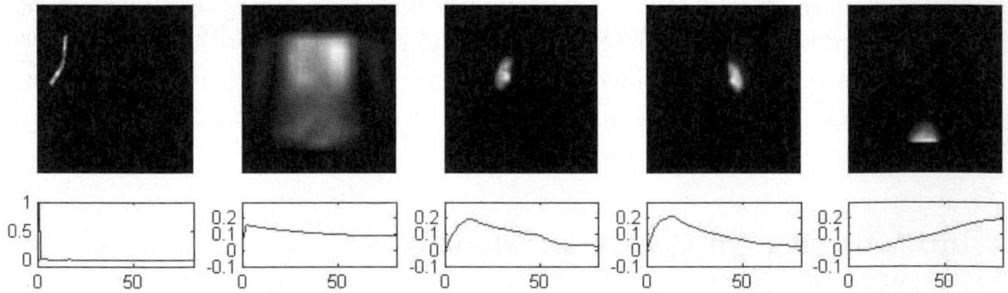

Fig. 6. The injection, blood/tissue, left kidney, right kidney and bladder compartments after the iterative scheme proposed in 2.6. The lower row holds the bases and the upper row holds the scores.

Table 1. A summary of the results of the algorithm. The system tends to produce sparse weights containing only positive elements and bases also containing only positive elements. The residuals drop a bit as the iteration goes on.

Step #	% $c_k(x,y) \neq 0$	% $c_k(x,y) > 0$	% $b_k(t) > 0$	Residual error
PCA	100	63.87	57.50	27.61
Classification	20.00	100.00	100.00	34.26
TPS	23.14	100.00	95.75	33.71
Iteration #1	24.31	100.00	100.00	36.86
Iteration #2	24.33	100.00	100.00	36.23
Iteration #3	24.34	100.00	100.00	36.19

Table 2. A comparison between our system (left) and the current one used at SUS (right). In the renograms (top left and top right) it is seen that our system is able to extract the same shape of the curve.

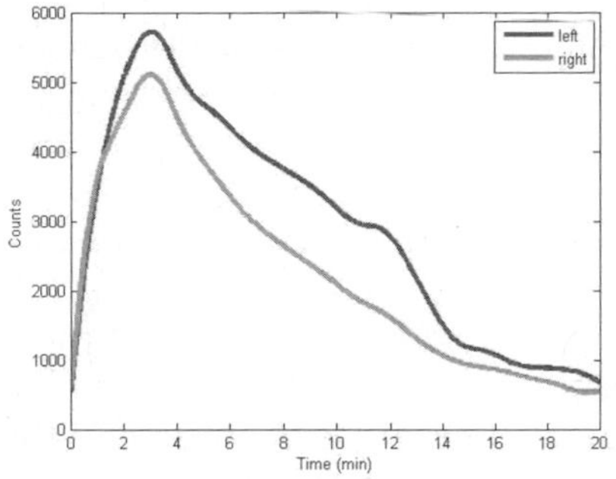

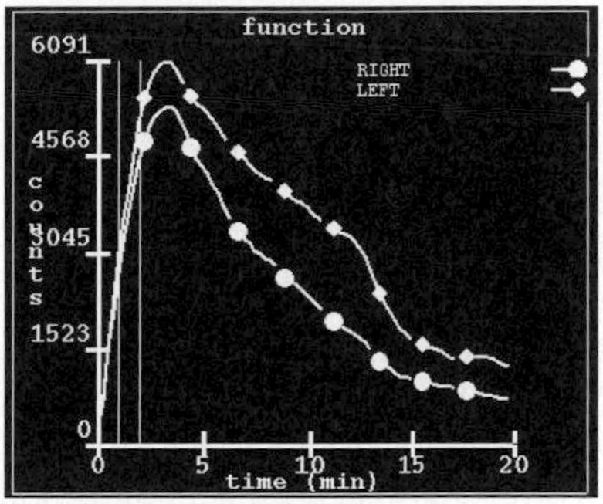

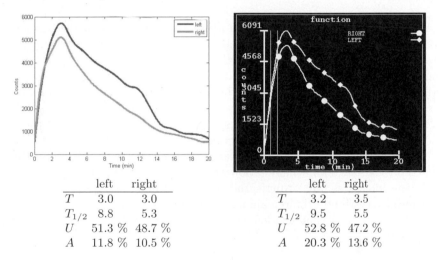

	left	right
T	3.0	3.0
$T_{1/2}$	8.8	5.3
U	51.3 %	48.7 %
A	11.8 %	10.5 %

	left	right
T	3.2	3.5
$T_{1/2}$	9.5	5.5
U	52.8 %	47.2 %
A	20.3 %	13.6 %

only a fifth of the original non-zero elements, it also produces weights that are non-negative, see Figure 4. The bases are all positive but holds a mixture of information from other compartments as well e.g. the kidney bases are strongly influenced by over- and underlying tissue.

By estimating the influence of other compartments in one compartment a new estimate of c_k and b_k is obtained. On our data, the thin plate spline interpolation should provide an estimate of tissue in the injection site, kidneys and bladder, see Figure 5. A possible risk by doing this is that to much tissue correction can produce artifacts such as negative elements in b_k. The interpolation also adds elements to c_k, which results in denser c_ks. With the introduction of positivity and spatial smoothness constraints and three iterations of weights and basis estimation, the b_ks have converged to bases that have been reduced from influence from other compartments, see Figure 6. The c_k is still sparse and the non-zero elements are positive as well. A summary of the results is obtained in Table 1.

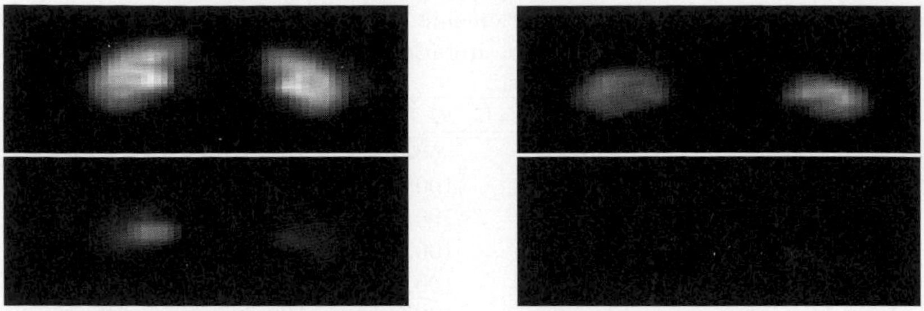

Fig. 7. The coordinate images of the kidney compartment (upper) and bladder compartment (lower) of two healthy subjects (left respective right). There should not be any tracer accumulation if the kidneys are normal, as can be seen in the subject on the right hand side. The left subject's left pelvis accumulates tracer.

A verification study was performed against a program using the manual approach to obtain the renogram. The parameters to test are those currently measured at SUS; Time in minutes to peak of the renogram T, time in minutes to reach half peak activity $T_{1/2}$, relative uptake by the two kidneys U and residue activity at the end of study A. It can be seen in Table 2 that our system is able to reproduce similar results.

By introducing the concept of compartments and the estimation of these our system is able to distinguish non-functional regions of the kidney from normal regions in the particular case of tracer accumulation. Since the bladder compartment represents such an accumulation we can estimate the level of accumulation inside the kidney as we estimate the coordinate image $c_{bladder} \in m_{kidney}$. In return we also estimate the remaining function in the functional regions. In Figure 7 it can be seen that the left subject's left renal pelvis suffers a bit from accumulation.

4 Discussion and Conclusions

The novel system was tested against a reference system at SUS, using the parameters which is currently used at SUS for assessing the renal function. The results from this comparison study show that our system is able to produce similar results as the present software. However, it needs further development in order to handle pathological kidneys. Since the algorithm just decomposes data in to several compartments it is not sure whether the weights coincides with the true compartments e.g. this can be displayed as an erroneous shape of the kidney if there is no outflow of urine. Validation studies using pathological kidneys therefore have to be performed in the future.

The novel system introduces a new feature - the level of tracer accumulation in the kidney. Since the algorithm outlined in the methods section is able to distinguish the mixture of compartments in each pixel, one could estimate e.g. bladder characteristics inside the kidney. If the kidneys suffer from tracer accumulation or obstruction the algorithm induce the presence of bladder inside the kidney. If the generated $c_{bladder} \in m_{kidney}$ is compared against a normal database it should be possible to find regions that significantly differs from healthy kidneys. Further studies have to be undertaken to determine whether this feature are relevant for medical assessment or not and how it could be implemented in renography.

All in all, the novel system is successful in automatically retrieving the compartments and use this information to evaluate the composition of compartments in each pixel. With this information it is possible to evaluate characteristics and produce similar results as the present software. Practically, an automated software based on this approach would extract more information and provide better background subtraction since the composition of compartments can be determined. Meanwhile, it reduces the time spent on outlining the different compartments.

The sparseness introduced in this paper is introduced to achieve a compact representation of data. With this representation, spatial smoothness priors can be used in the estimation of the compartments. The implication is that the computational complexity of the method is reduced due to the fact that less pixels is involved in the proposed nonlinear least squares problem.

Recall that the residuals of the least squares estimate should be independent and identically distributed for it to be a valid estimator. However, typical estimates are assumed to attain real numbers whereas counting processes only generate integers. A loss function that penalizes the likelihood for the estimate to come from a counting process could then be considered. However, in our works we keep the estimation with subject to the L^2-norm.

References

1. Veltri, P., Vecchio, A., Carbone, V.: Proper orthogonal decomposition analysis of spatio-temporal behavior of renal scintigraphies. Physica Medica 26, 57–70 (2010)
2. Piepsz, A., Sixt, R., Gordon, I.: Performing renography in children with antenatally detected pelvi-ureteric junction stenosis: errors, pitfalls, controversies. The Quarterly Journal of Nuclear Medicine and Molecular Imaging (August 2010)
3. Lawson, R.: Renogram Processing - The Manchester Method. In: XIV. International Symposium on Radionuclides in Nephrourology, Mikulov, Czech Republic, May 11-14 (2010)
4. Hermes Medical Solutions, `http://www.hermesmedical.com/index.lasso?id=128`
5. Prigent, A., Cosgriff, P., Gates, G.F., Granerus, G., Fine, E.J., Itoh, K., Peters, M., Piepsz, A., Rehling, M., Rutland, M., Taylor Jr, A.: Consensus Report on Quality Control of Quantitative Measurements of Renal Function Obtained From the Renogram: International Consensus Committee From the Scientific committee of Radionuclides in Nephrourology. Seminars in Nucl. Med. 29, 146–159 (1999)
6. Lawson, R.: Quantitative Methods in Renography. In: XIV. International Symposium on Radionuclides in Nephrourology, Mikulov, Czech Republic, May 11-14 (2010)
7. Rutland, M.D.: A comprehensive analysis of renal DTPA studies. Theory and normal values. Nuc. Med. Comm. 6, 11–20 (1985)

8. Durand, E., Blaufox, M.D., Britton, K.E., Carlsen, O., Cosgriff, P., Fine, E., Fleming, J., Nimmon, C., Piepsz, A., Prigent, A., Samal, M.: International Scientific Committee of Radionuclides in Nephrourology (ISCORN) Consensus on Renal Transit Time Measurement. Semin. Nucl. Med. 38, 82–102 (2008)
9. Moonen, M.: Gamma Camera Renography with 99mTc-DTPA; Assessment of Total and Split Renal Function, Gothenburg (1994)
10. Fine, D.R., Lurie, R.E., Candy, G.P.: An anatomical and physiological model of the renal parenchyma - model development and parametric identification. Physiol. Meas. 15, 407–428 (1994)
11. Meng, L.K., Ng, D., Ghista, D.N., Rudolph, H.: Quantitation of Renal Function based on Two-Compartmental Modeling Renal Pelvis. In: Proceedings of the 2005 IEEE Engineering in Medicine and Biology 27th Annual Conference, Shanghai, China, September 1-4 (2005)
12. Coffey, J.P.: Analysis of compartmental models of type 4 nuclear renograms with calculation of flow rate parameters and instantaneous drainage rates. In: BJU International, vol. 92, pp. 85–91 (2003)
13. Golub, G.H., van Loan, C.F.: Matrix Computations. The Johns Hopkins University Press (1996)
14. Bookstein, F.L.: Principal Warps: Thin Plate Splines and the Decomposition of Deformations. IEEE Transactions on Pattern Analysis and Machine Intelligence 11(6) (June 1989)
15. Hastie, T., Tibshirani, R., Friedman, J.: Elements of Statistical Learning. Springer, New York (2008)

Expression Recognition in Videos Using a Weighted Component-Based Feature Descriptor

Xiaohua Huang[1,2], Guoying Zhao[1], Matti Pietikäinen[1], and Wenming Zheng[2]

[1] Machine Vision Group, Department of Electrical and Information Engineering, University of Oulu, Finland

[2] Research Center for Learning Science, Southeast University, China

{huang.xiaohua,gyzhao,mkp}@ee.oulu.fi,
wenming_zheng@seu.edu.cn
http://www.ee.oulu.fi/mvg

Abstract. In this paper, we propose a weighted component based feature descriptor for expression recognition in video sequences. Firstly, we extract the texture features and structural shape features in three facial regions: mouth, cheeks and eyes of each face image. Then, we combine these extracted feature sets using confidence level strategy. Noting that for different facial components, the contributions to the expression recognition are different, we propose a method for automatically learning different weights to components via the multiple kernel learning. Experimental results on the Extended Cohn-Kanade database show that our approach combining component-based spatiotemporal features descriptor and weight learning strategy achieves better recognition performance than the state of the art methods.

Keywords: Spatiotemporal features, LBP-TOP, EdgeMap, Information fusion, Multiple kernel learning, Facial expression recognition.

1 Introduction

A goal of automatic facial expression analysis is to determine the emotional state, e.g., happiness, sadness, surprise, neutral, anger, fear, and disgust, of human beings based on facial images, regardless of the identity of the face. To date, there have been some surveys describing the state-of-the-art techniques of facial expression recognition, based on static images or video sequences [4,23]. The surveys show that dynamic features from video sequences can provide more accurate and robust information than the static features from images.

Feature representation is very important for automatic facial expression analysis. Methods combining geometric and appearance features have been considered earlier [23]. For example, Tian et.al [22] proposed to use facial component shapes and transient features like crow-feet wrinkles and nasal-labial furrows. A framework of combining facial appearance (Scale-invariant feature transform) and shape information (Pyramid histogram of orientated gradient) was proposed for facial expression recognition [15]. Both similarity-normalized shape (SPTS) and canonical appearance (CAPP) were derived from the active appearance models (AAM) to interpret the face images [16]. It is

A. Heyden and F. Kahl (Eds.): SCIA 2011, LNCS 6688, pp. 569–578, 2011.

observed that the combination of geometric and appearance information can describe the face in a better way. But most of approaches used complicated geometric information like shapes and the trasient feature [16,22]. Furthermore some researches [8,10,15,20] cropped the facial image into some sub-regions or components, and then extracted the appearance features from those components. Researches [8,10] have shown that component-based approach is robust in some cases against pose motion or partial occlusion. But the features in the earlier component-based methods were only extracted from static images, even though some of them [20,24] use Hidden Markov Models (HMMs) or Dynamic Bayesian Networks (DBNs) to integrate the static information with time development.

In facial expression recognition, it is notable that the facial components take distinct effect on different expressions [13,19,21]. Hence, another major task in this paper is to select the most relevant features among the multiple feature sets extracted from the different facial regions. Using boosting algorithm or just simply assign the weight parameters to the corresponding face components [21,28] would be feasible. Recently, the multiple kernels learning (MKL) in support vector machines (SVM) has been introduced to combine heterogeneous sources of information for decision fusion in computer vision. In addition, recent studies in [3,7] have shown that the MKL method achieves decent performance in applications of object/image recognition.

In this paper, we focus on combining dynamic texture features and structural features of facial components for describing facial movement. In order to reduce the complexity, we develop a method for fusing multiple feature representations. Motivated by the aforementioned MKL method, we aim to learn weights for multiple feature sets in facial components. We test our approache on the Extended Cohn-Kanade Database which contains 97 subjects with seven emotions. Our person-independent experiment shows that the weighted component-based approach performs better than other approaches. The contributions of this paper include: 1) we applied the dynamic texture and structural shape features [5,27] from facial components to represent facial dynamic sequences; 2) we developed the framework of feature fusion via confidence level method, and 3) weight learning by MKL was presented.

2 Component-Based Feature Descriptor

Concerning pose variation and partial occlusion, component-based features [8,10,15] are more effective for representing facial expressions. Three facial components: mouth, cheeks and eyes are considered in our method and shown in Figure 1(c). Facial points, shown in Figure 1(a) in each frame can be obtained by AAM [2]. Then eyes, nose and mouth areas are determined by the detected 62 facial points. Please note that because eyebrows are also important in expression, the eyes component is extended from the blue dashed rectangle to blue solid rectangle, as shown in Figure 1(b). In order to extract micro-information from components, each component is further divided into a couple of blocks, as shown in Figure 2(b). In this paper, we use CFD (Component-based Feature Descriptor) as the abbreviation of the proposed framework.

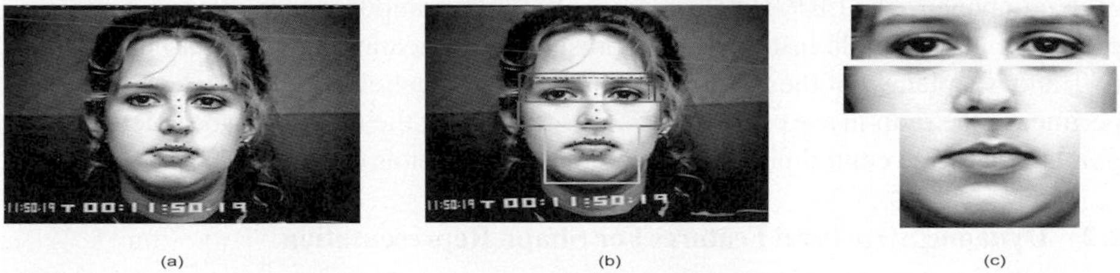

Fig. 1. (a) 62 facial points detected by AAM [2,16] (b) Rectangles for eyes, nose, mouth determined by detected facial points (c) Three components cropped from the facial image-eyes, nose and mouth

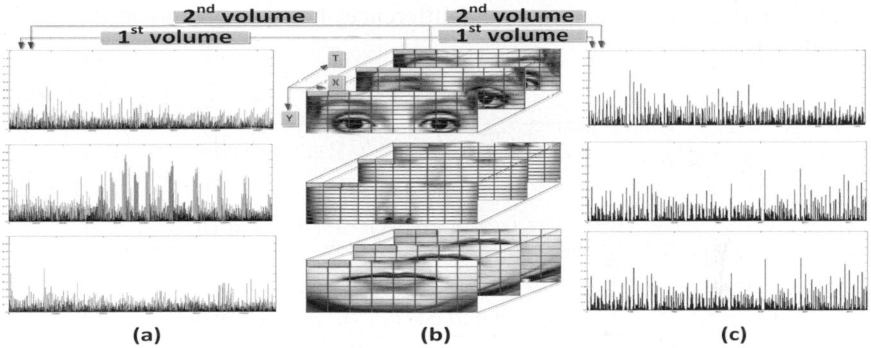

Fig. 2. Framework of component-based feature descriptor. (a) Dynamic appearance representation by LBP-TOP; (b) Three components (eyes, nose, mouth); (c) Dynamic shape representation by EdgeMap.

2.1 Dynamic Texture Features For Appearance Representation

The local binary pattern (LBP) operator is a gray-scale invariant texture primitive statistic, which has shown excellent performance in the classification of various kinds of textures [18]. And LBP operator is defined as:

$$LBP_{S,R} = \sum_{s=0}^{S-1} f(g_s - g_c)2^s, \tag{1}$$

where

$$f(g_s - g_c) = \begin{cases} 1, g_s - g_c \geq 0 \\ 0, g_s - g_c < 0 \end{cases},$$

and g_c is the gray value of the center pixel, g_s is the gray values of S equally spaced pixels on a circle of radius R at this center pixel.

LBP-TOP has been recently proposed for motion analysis and shown excellent performance in the classification of expression [28] and lip-reading [25]. Features extracted by this method effectively describe the appearance, horizontal motion and vertical motion from the image sequence. We extend to use LBP-TOP to describe the spatiotemporal features (XY, XT, and YT planes) of three components. That is to say, after detecting each component, the LBP-TOP histograms for each component are computed and concatenated into a single histogram to represent the appearance (XY plane) and motion (XT and YT planes) of the facial expression sequence, shown in Figure 2(a). In our experiments, the radii in axes X, Y and T are set as three; the number of local neighboring points around the central pixel for all three planes is set as eight.

2.2 Dynamic Structural Features For Shape Representation

Edge map (EdgeMap) features were recently proposed to describe the edge orientation of the pixel for detecting facial landmarks [5] and also utilized as describing structural features together with LBP (only in XT and YT planes) for speaker identification from lipreading [26]. Given a smoothed image from one video with a set of 16 kernels, the whole set of 16 kernels results from the differences between two oriented Gaussians with shifted kernel:

$$G_{\theta_t} = \frac{G^-_{\theta_t} - G^+_{\theta_t}}{\sum_{u,v}[(G^-_{\theta_t} - G^+_{\theta_t}) \cdot h(G^-_{\theta_t} - G^+_{\theta_t})]}, \tag{2}$$

where

$$G^-_{\theta_t} = \frac{1}{2\pi\sigma^2}\exp(-\frac{(u - \sigma\cos\theta_t)^2 + (v - \sigma\sin\theta_t)^2}{2\sigma^2}), \tag{3}$$

$$G^+_{\theta_t} = \frac{1}{2\pi\sigma^2}\exp(-\frac{(u + \sigma\cos\theta_t)^2 + (v + \sigma\sin\theta_t)^2}{2\sigma^2}), \tag{4}$$

$$h(G^-_{\theta_t} - G^+_{\theta_t}) = \begin{cases} 1, G^-_{\theta_t} - G^+_{\theta_t} > 0 \\ 0, G^-_{\theta_t} - G^+_{\theta_t} \leqslant 0 \end{cases}, \tag{5}$$

and σ is a root mean square deviation of the Gaussian distribution, θ_t is angle of the Gaussian rotation, $\theta_t = 22.5 \times t, t = 0, \cdots, 15$; $u, v = -3, -2, -1, 0, 1, 2, 3$.

In our paper, same to [5], 10 kernels ($t = 2, 3, 4, 5, 6, 10, 11, 12, 13, 14$) is used to define the contrast magnitude of a local edge at pixel (p, q). The orientation of a kernel that gave the maximum response is estimated by the orientation of a local edge:

$$\vartheta_{p,q,\theta_t} = \sum_{c,d} g_{p-u,q-v} G_{\theta_t}, \tag{6}$$

where $g_{p,q}$ denotes the gray level of the image at pixel (p, q); $p = 0, \cdots, W - 1$, $q = 0, \cdots, H - 1$; W and H are the width and height of the image, respectively.

After getting the edge orientation for each pixel, a histogram is created to collect up the occurrences of different orientations. Studies in [6,26] used EdgeMap to describe the structural features in XY plane of a video sequence. Inspired by them, the EdgeMap histograms from XY plane in block volumes (Figure 2(b)) are concatenated into a single histogram for representing structural features, shown in Figure 2(c). But different from [26], in which they only considered LBP texture features in XT and YT planes, in our approach, LBP operation in XY plane is still utilized to describe appearance features and then concatenated into a single histogram together with those from XT and YT planes, shown in Figure 2(a), in order to avoid the loss of appearance feature.

3 Multiple Feature Fusion

As shown in Figure 2, we extract component-based feature sets, which represents texture features from LBP-TOP operation or structural features from EdgeMap in each component. In studies on various feature extraction approaches, it has been suggested that different feature sets could offer complementary information. A fusion scheme that harnesses various representations is likely to improve the overall performance. The outputs of various feature extractors can be fused to obtain decisions that are more accurate than the decisions made by any individual feature representation. As shown in Figure 3, each feature set of LBP-TOP or EdgeMap is the input of one matching module and the model of weight learning.

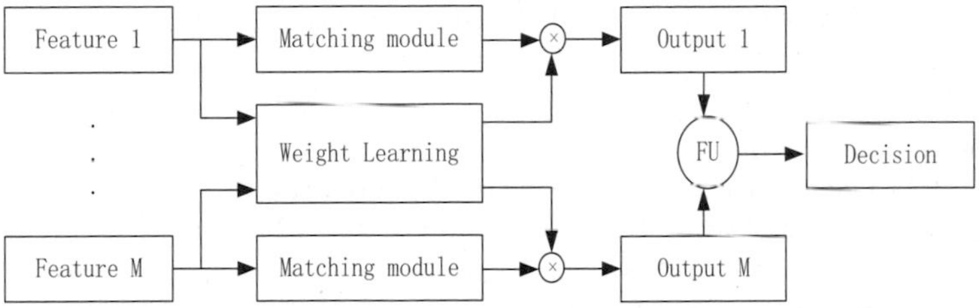

Fig. 3. Framework of multiple feature fusion, FU: Fusion Module

3.1 The Weight Learning Framework

The MKL approach [3,7,14] is used to combine or select relevant representations. The multiple kernel learning tasks in our approach are viewed as an efficient way to learn weights that are optimal for several feature sets. Suppose we have M feature sets $\{\boldsymbol{\Omega}_m\}_{m=1}^M$, each of them has N samples $\{\overrightarrow{x}_{i,m}\}_{i=1}^N$, and the corresponding class label of $\overrightarrow{x}_{i,m}$ is y_i, where $y_i \in \{+1, -1\}$. Thus, the kernel function of MKL is defined as

$$k_{i,j} = \sum_{m=1}^{M} \beta_m k(\overrightarrow{x}_{i,m}, \overrightarrow{x}_{j,m}), \tag{7}$$

s.t. $\beta_m \geq 0$ and $\sum_{m=1}^M \beta_m = 1$, where β_m is the weight of m-th feature set $\boldsymbol{\Omega}_m$, $k(\overrightarrow{x}_{i,m}, \overrightarrow{x}_{j,m})$ is the base kernel of $\overrightarrow{x}_{i,m}$ and $\overrightarrow{x}_{j,m}$ from $\boldsymbol{\Omega}_m$. Here, all kernel matrices of feature sets have been normalized to unit trace.

The MKL task, which is based on the framework of SVM, is considered as a way of optimizing the kernel weights. When a kernel machine for multiple feature sets is used, the dual problem of MKL is defined as

$$\max \sum_{i=1}^{N} \alpha_i - \frac{1}{2} \sum_{i=1}^{N} \sum_{j=1}^{N} \alpha_i \alpha_j y_i y_j \sum_{m=1}^{M} \beta_m k(\overrightarrow{x}_{i,m}, \overrightarrow{x}_{j,m}), \tag{8}$$

s.t. $\sum_{i=1}^N y_i \alpha_i = 0, 0 \leq \alpha_i \leq \varepsilon$ and $\beta_m \geq 0, \sum_{m=1}^M \beta_m = 1$, where, α_i is the Lagrange coefficient, and the regularization ε determines the trade-off between the margin and the error on training data.

Optimizing over both the Lagrange coefficient α_i and the weights for m-th feature set β_m is one particular form of semidefinite programming (SDP). MKL algorithm is terminated when a stopping criterion is met. The stop criterion in our implementation is based on the variation of coefficients β_m between two consecutive steps. In order to compute the weights for different feature sets from specific expression, we should consider an approach that divides multi-class problem into some **one-vs-rest** classification problems. Finally, this framework will generate the weight of m-th feature set under c-th class, i.e. $\beta_{c,m}$. In our case, we use MKL-WL (MKL for Weight Learning) for abbreviation, which is summarized in Algorithm 1.

Algorithm 1. MKL-WL on expression recognition

input : M feature sets $\{\boldsymbol{\Omega}_m\}_{m=1}^{M}$ with N samples, C classes
output: $\{\beta_{c,m}\}_{c=1,\ldots,C;m=1,\ldots,M}$

for $c \leftarrow 1$ **to** C **do**
  for $m \leftarrow 1$ **to** M **do**
    Generate Positive Set $\boldsymbol{\Omega}_m^+ \leftarrow$ Find the data from $\boldsymbol{\Omega}_m \in c$;
    Generate Negative Set $\boldsymbol{\Omega}_m^- \leftarrow$ Find the data from $\boldsymbol{\Omega}_m \notin c$;
    Form $K_m \leftarrow \boldsymbol{\Omega}_m^+$ and $\boldsymbol{\Omega}_m^-$;
  Unit trace normalization of $\{K_m\}_{m=1}^{M}$;
  $\{\beta_{c,m}\}_{m=1,\ldots,M}$ by optmizing Equation(8);

3.2 The Fusion Module Framework

For exploiting the complementary information among all feature sets, we investigated one decision rule, i.e. mean rule. Detailed derivation of decision rules can be found e.g. in [12]. Assume that all feature sets are generally statistically independent, and the priori probability of occurrence for c-th class model are under assumption of equal priors, the fusion rule of multiple feature sets [9] is described as:

Assign $\overrightarrow{x} \rightarrow \mu$ if

$$P(c=\mu|\overrightarrow{\boldsymbol{x}}, \boldsymbol{\Omega}_1, \ldots, \boldsymbol{\Omega}_M) = \max_{c\in\{1,\ldots,C\}} [\boldsymbol{Q}(\{P(c|\boldsymbol{\Omega}_1)\beta_{c,1}, \ldots, P(c|\boldsymbol{\Omega}_M)\beta_{c,M}\})]$$
$$= \max_{c\in\{1,\ldots,C\}} \frac{\sum\{P(c|\boldsymbol{\Omega}_1)\beta_{c,1}, \ldots, P(c|\boldsymbol{\Omega}_M)\beta_{c,M}\}}{M} \quad (9)$$

where $\overrightarrow{x}$ and μ represents the testing sample and the corresponding class, respectively.

In our framework, LIBSVM [1] is used for modeling matching module and generating voting numbers or probabilities.

4 Experiments

The proposed approach was evaluated on the Extended Cohn-Kanade facial expression database (CK+) [16]. The orginal Cohn-Kanade database [11] includes 486 FACS-coded sequences from 97 subjects for six basic expressions: happiness, sadness, surprise, anger, disgust and fear. For CK+ distribution, it has been further augmented to include 593 sequences from 123 subjects for seven expressions (additional 107 sequences,

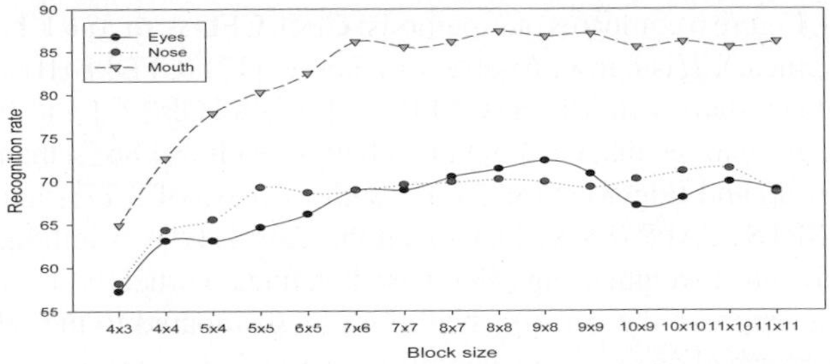

Fig. 4. Performance of three components with different block sizes

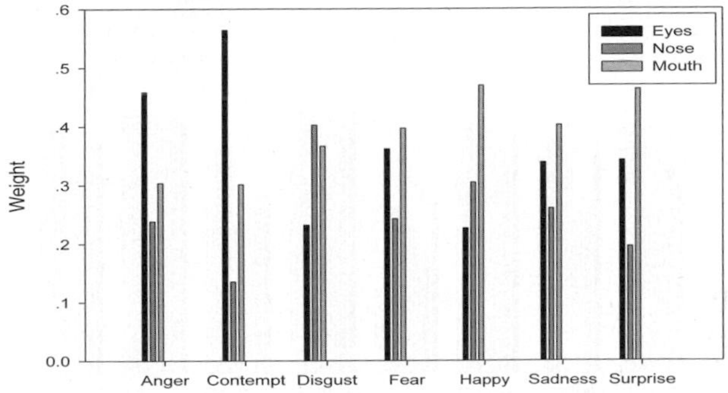

Fig. 5. Average weights for three components based on three kernels

26 subjects and contempt expression), which makes it more challenging than the original database. In our experiments, 325 sequences from 118 subjects were selected from the database for seven basic expression recognition. **Leave-one-subject-out** method was used in the whole scenario.

In our approach, three components are cropped as shown in Figure 1. However, the size of each facial component is so large that more than one block is needed to describe its local spatiotemporal information. Moreover, as observed from Figure 1(c), the areas of different parts are different. This means that using the same number of blocks for all components is not reasonable [27]. Thus, different number of blocks is used for three components. Figure 4 shows the performance of using different block numbers of eyes, nose, and mouth. As observed from Figure 4, the highest recognition rate is achieved when the block size is 9×8, 11×10, 8×8, for eyes, nose and mouth, respectively. Based on the results in Figure 4, 9×8, 11×10, 8×8 block sizes are used in eyes, nose and mouth, respectively.

In Section 3.1, we proposed dynamic weight learning by using MKL. In order to figure out the importance of the components to different expressions, the weights on three components are shown in Figure 5. In this figure, these weights clearly show: (1) both eyes and mouth components play important roles in fear and sadness; (2) both mouth and nose components contribute to disgust and happiness; (3) anger and contempt, mostly depend on eyes; (4) mouth component determines surprise.

Below, we give brief comparison with the state-of-the-art works [16,27] for expression recognition. Figure 6 compares our methods: CFD, CFD with <u>M</u>KL based on linear kernel (CFDM-Linear), <u>H</u>istogram <u>I</u>ntersection kernel [17] (CFDM-HI), and Gaussian kernel (CFDM-Gaussian), with SPTS+CAPP [16], LBP-TOP [27] and EdgeMap [6]. From this figure, we can see that CFD obtained better result (89.85%) than block-based LBP-TOP (87.07%) and EdgeMap (82.77%), with increase of 2.77% and 7.08%, and also better than SPTS+CAPP (88.38%), with an increase 1.47%. Additionally, it is very interesting that dynamic weight using MKL based on linear kernel (93.23%) and HI kernel (93.85%) can improve the performance of CFD. Compared to the other methods, CFDM-HI outperformed on average recognition rate and all expressions except anger.

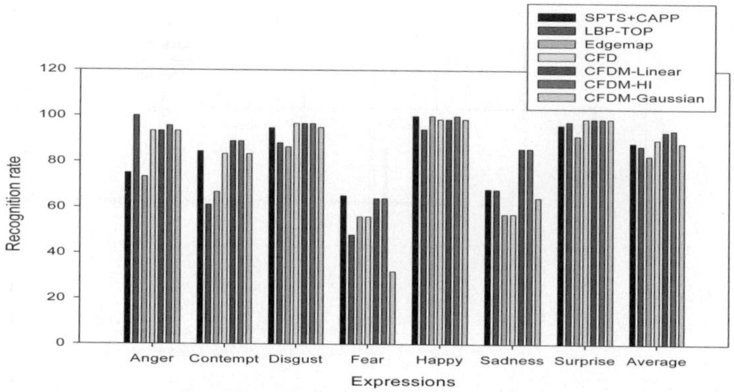

Fig. 6. Performance comparison (%) with different approaches

5 Conclusion

In order to boost facial expression recognition, we propose a component-based feature descriptor to describe facial expressions from video sequences. In our approach, three components (eyes, nose and mouth) are cropped from facial image according to automatically detected facial points, and dynamic texture and shape features are extracted by LBP-TOP and EdgeMap, respectively. Then multiple feature sets are combined by fusion strategy. Furthermore, for boosting CFD, we proposed an approach for learning weights for multiple feature sets.

In experiments on the CK+ Database, we discussed the roles and significance of components with respect to expressions, through analyzing the weights computed by MKL-WL algorithm. Besides, we also have demonstrated that the CFDM-Linear, CFDM-HI lead to a promising improvement in facial expression classification, comparing with previous works. In future work we plan to explore how our approach could be adopted to the very challenging problems including view variation and partial occlusion.

Acknowledgement

The financial support provided by the Academy of Finland is gratefully acknowledged. The first author is funded by China Scholarship Council of Chinese government. This work was partly supported by Natural Science Foundations of China under Grant 61073137, and partly by the Jiangsu Natural Science Foundations under Grant BK2010243. The authors would like to thank the anonymous reviewers for their constructive advice.

References

1. Chang, C., Lin, C.: Libsvm: a library for support vector machines, Software available as `http://www.csie.ntu.edu/tw/~cjlin/libsvm`
2. Cootes, T., Edwards, G., Taylor, C.: Active appearance models. IEEE Transactions on Pattern Analysis and Machine Intelligence 23(6), 681–685 (2001)
3. Dileep, A., Sekhar, C.: Representation and feature selection using multiple kernel learning. In: International Joint Conference on Neural Networks, pp. 717–722. IEEE Press, New York (2009)
4. Fasel, B., Luettin, J.: Automatic facial expression analysis: a survey. Pattern Recognition 36, 259–275 (2003)
5. Gizatdinova, Y., Surakka, V.: Feature-based detection of facial landmarks from neutral and expressive facial images. IEEE Transactions on Pattern Analysis and Machine Intelligence 28(1), 135–139 (2006)
6. Gizatdinova, Y., Surakka, V., Zhao, G., Makinen, E., Raisamo, R.: Facial expression classification based on local spatiotemporal edge and texture descriptor. In: 7th International Conference on Methods and Techniques in Behavioral Research Measuring (2010)
7. Goene, M., Alpaydin, E.: Localized multiple kernel machines for image recognition. In: NIPS 2009 Workshop on Understanding Multiple Kernel Learning Methods. MIT Press, Cambridge (2009)
8. Heisele, B., Koshizen, B.: Components for face recognition. In: IEEE International Conference on Automatic Face and Gesture Recognition, pp. 153–158. IEEE Press, New York (2004)
9. Huang, X., Zhao, G., Pietikäinen, M., Zheng, W.: Dynamic facial expression recognition using boosted component-based spatiotemporal features and multi-classifier fusion. In: Blanc-Talon, J., Bone, D., Philips, W., Popescu, D., Scheunders, P. (eds.) ACIVS 2010, Part II. LNCS, vol. 6475, pp. 312–322. Springer, Heidelberg (2010)
10. Ivanov, Y., Heisele, B., Serre, T.: Using component features for face recognition. In: IEEE International Conference on Automatic Face and Gesture Recognition, pp. 421–426. IEEE Press, New York (2004)
11. Kanade, T., Cohn, J., Tian, Y.: Comprehensive database for facial expression analysis. In: IEEE International Conference on Automatic Face and Gesture Recognition, pp. 46–53. IEEE Press, New York (2000)
12. Kittler, J., Hatef, M., Duin, R., Matas, J.: On combining classifiers. IEEE Transactions on Pattern Analysis and Machine Intelligence 20(3), 226–239 (1998)
13. Kotsia, I., Buciu, I., Pitas, I.: An analysis of facial expression recognition under partial facial image occlusion. Image and Vision Computing 26(7), 1052–1067 (2008)
14. Lanckriet, G., Cristianini, N., Bartlett, P., Ghaoui, L., Jordan, M.: Learning the kernel matrix with semidefinite programming. Journal of Machine Learning Research 5, 27–72 (2004)
15. Li, Z., Imai, J., Kaneko, M.: Facial-component-based bag of words and phog descriptor for facial expression recognition. In: IEEE International Conference on Systems, Man, and Cybernetics, pp. 1353–1358. IEEE Press, New York (2009)

16. Lucey, P., Cohn, J., Kanade, T., Saragih, J., Ambadar, Z.: The extended cohn-kanade dataset (ck+): a complete dataset for action unit and emotion-specified expression. In: IEEE Conference on Computer Vision and Pattern Recognition Workshops, pp. 94–101. IEEE Press, New York (2010)
17. Maji, S., Berg, A., Malik, J.: Classification using intersection kernel support vector machines is efficient. In: IEEE Conference on Computer Vision and Pattern Recognition. IEEE Press, New York (2008)
18. Ojala, T., Pietikäinen, M., Maenpaa, T.: Multiresolution gray-scale and rotation invariant texture classification with local binary patterns. IEEE Transactions on Pattern Analysis and Machine Intelligence 24(7), 971–987 (2002)
19. Pantic, M., Rothkrantz, L.: Expert system for automatic analysis of facial expressions. Image and Vision Computing 18(11), 881–905 (2000)
20. Sun, Y., Yin, L.: Evaluation of spatio-temporal regional features for 3D face analysis. In: IEEE Computer Vision and Pattern Recognition Workshop, pp. 13–19. IEEE Press, New York (2009)
21. Taini, M., Zhao, G., Pietikäinen, M.: Weight-based facial expression recognition from near-infrared video sequences. In: 16th Scandinavian Conference on Image Analysis, pp. 239–248. Springer, Heidelberg (2009)
22. Tian, Y., Kanade, T., Cohn, J.: Facial expression analysis. In: Li, S.Z., Jain, A.K. (eds.) Handbook of Face Recognition, pp. 247–276. Springer, Heidelberg (2005)
23. Zeng, Z., Pantic, M., Roisman, G., Huang, T.: A survey of affective recognition methods: Audio, visual and spontaneous expression. IEEE Transactions on Pattern Analysis and Machine Intelligence 31(1), 39–58 (2009)
24. Zhang, Y., Ji, Q.: Active and dynamic information fusion for facial expression understanding from image sequences. IEEE Transactions on Pattern Analysis and Machine Intelligence 27(5), 699–714 (2005)
25. Zhao, G., Barnard, M., Pietikäinen, M.: Lipreading with local spatiotemporal descriptors. IEEE Transaction on Multimedia 11(7), 1254–1265 (2009)
26. Zhao, G., Huang, X., Gizadinova, Y., Pietikäinen, M.: Combining dynamic texture and structural features for speaker identification. In: ACM Multimedia 2010 Workshop on Multimedia in Forensics, Security and Intelligence. ACM, New York (2010)
27. Zhao, G., Pietikäinen, M.: Dynamic texture recognition using local binary pattern with an application to facial expressions. IEEE Transactions on Pattern Analysis and Machine Intelligence 29(6), 915–928 (2007)
28. Zhao, G., Pietikäinen, M.: Boosted multi-resolution spatio temporal descriptors for facial expression recognition. Pattern Recognition Letters 30, 1117–1127 (2009)

Spatio-chromatic Image Content Descriptors and Their Analysis Using Extreme Value Theory*

Vasileios Zografos and Reiner Lenz

Computer Vision Laboratory, Linköping University, Sweden
zografos@isy.liu.se, reile@itn.liu.se

Abstract. We use the theory of group representations to construct very fast image descriptors that split the vector space of local RGB distributions into small group-invariant subspaces. These descriptors are group theoretical generalizations of the Fourier Transform and can be computed with algorithms similar to the FFT. Because of their computational efficiency they are especially suitable for retrieval, recognition and classification in very large image datasets. We also show that the statistical properties of these descriptors are governed by the principles of the Extreme Value Theory (EVT). This enables us to work directly with parametric probability distribution models, which offer a much lower dimensionality and higher resolution and flexibility than histogram representations. We explore the connection to EVT and analyse the characteristics of these descriptors from a probabilistic viewpoint with the help of large image databases.

1 Introduction

With the considerable increase in online visual content, there has been a great demand for tools to handle efficiently, large and dense collections of image data. Furthermore, online images exhibit a large variation in content, appearance and quality. An automated image search engine must therefore be able to process quickly such large datasets and accurately recover a selection of images that fit a user's query. As a result, many sophisticated feature descriptors [1], are not capable of dealing with image databases comprised of many million samples, in a reasonable time frame.

Motivated by these observations, we suggest a novel spatio-chromatic image descriptor and an associated model selection method that are well suited for very fast search over very large image databases. These descriptors (or filters) are designed to preserve important image information (e.g. colour edges and line features), while being invariant under certain spatio-chromatic changes. Such characteristics can be useful in tasks of object recognition, image retrieval and classification. In this paper, we explore the visual significance of these descriptors and demonstrate that they form effective tools, which may be used to investigate the internal structure of the image databases.

* Funded by the EU FP7/2007-2013 programme, under grant agreement No 247947 GARNICS.

A. Heyden and F. Kahl (Eds.): SCIA 2011, LNCS 6688, pp. 579–591, 2011.

In the rest of this paper, we briefly introduce the theory behind the construction of our descriptors in Sec. 2. In Sec. 3 we review the main properties of EVT and explain how it is connected to the descriptors. In Sec. 4 we propose a simple approach for EVT model estimation and selection. We continue with experiments and their analysis on public image datasets in Sec. 5. Finally, we conclude with a succinct summary discussion in Sec. 6.

2 Spatio-chromatic Descriptors

In this work, we propose a number of spatio-chromatic descriptors that have been constructed using the representation theory of finite groups (see [2]). The groups used are the dihedral groups D(3) and D(4). The dihedral group D(n) is defined as the group of all geometry preserving transformations (rotations and reflections) of the regular n-sided polygon, in this case the triangle and the square. The group D(4) exploits the square grid structure of most modern image sensors. The details of the usage of D(4) are described in [3]. The usage of D(3) is based on the observation that in a statistical sense, the three color channels R,G,B are interchangeable. This statistical permutation property suggests the usage of the permutation group S(3) of three elements, which is identical to the group D(3). For an intuitive understanding it might be helpful to identify the three channels R,G and B as corners of the regular triangle. For additional details see [4].

For the descriptor construction, we use only RGB vectors on 4×4 neighborhoods around a pixel. These vectors are all located in a 48-dimensional space. The tools of representation theory are applied to split this space into its smallest subspaces that are invariant under all spatial and RGB transformations in D(4) and D(3). The result is that the RGB space is first transformed into the 1-dimensional R+G+B (intensity) component and the 2-dimensional color opponent space given by the combinations RG=R-G and YB=R+G-2B. This is then followed by a combination with the spatial D(4) filters. The final result is a decomposition of the original 48d space into 24 subspaces of dimensions 1, 2 and 4. The first 12 are spatial filters operating on the intensity component R+G+B whereas the other 12 filters operate on the two-dimensional opponent color space (RG,YB). This decomposition is implemented by an orthonormal transformation and so the norms of the vectors in the subspaces are preserved under the spatial and color operations in D(4) and D(3). To summarize: the original image is first filtered with 48 filters, then the magnitudes of 24 collections of filter results, are computed and the produced images $r_1, ..., r_{24}$ with non-negative pixel/magnitude values provide the spatio-spectral descriptors of the original image. Figure 1 gives an illustration of the relation between the original image and the 24 computed descriptor images. A computer implementation of the filtering process is available from [5].

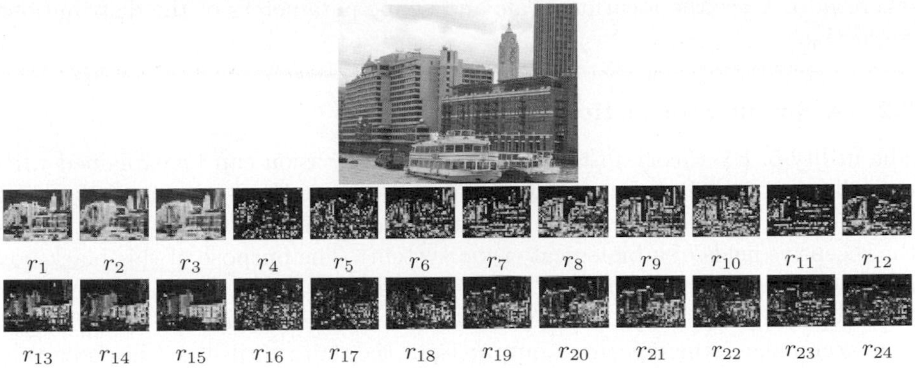

Fig. 1. The intensity (middle row) and colour (lower row) filter results from a typical image. Note that the first three filters represent averaging of pixel values.

3 Extreme Value Theory

Extreme Value Theory (EVT) deals with the behaviour of the extrema (minima and maxima), of a probability distribution. EVT has been applied to many natural processes and also in biological and computer vision. In this paper, we suggest a connection between filtered image data and EVT, and we have used the latter to model and analyse the distribution of the former. In the next chapter, we will show experimental results, which demonstrate that the vast majority of examined filtered images follow the EVT model.

3.1 The Basics of Univariate EVT

EV theory, similarly to the central limit theorem, states that the non-degenerate asymptotic distributions of the sample extremum of a process, must belong to one of just three possible general families regardless of the original distribution function F. Furthermore, it is not necessary to know the detailed nature of F or which limiting form (if any) it gives rise to. As a matter of fact, we just need to know the behaviour of the tails of $F(x)$ for large x, so that a good deal may be said about the asymptotic properties of the extremum.

More formally, suppose that we have an i.i.d. sequence of random variables X_N whose common distribution is $F(x)$=$\Pr\{X_i \leq x\}$. Also let s_n=$\text{Max}^{(n)}(X_N)$ denote the n_{th} sample maximum of the process. Then $\Pr\{s_n \leq x\}$=$F(x)^n$. For non-trivial limit results, and suitable normalising constants a_n>0, b_n, the previous equation converges to $\Pr\{a_n(s_n - b_n) \leq x\}$= $F(a_n^{-1}x + b_n)$→$H(x)$. In [6] it is shown that the possible non-degenerate limiting forms of H are:

$$\begin{array}{lll} H(x) = \exp\left(-\exp(\frac{\mu - x}{\sigma})\right) & ,\forall x & \text{Gumbell} \\ H(x) = 1 - \exp\left(-\left(\frac{x-\mu}{\sigma}\right)^k\right) & ,x > \mu & \text{Weibull} \\ H(x) = \exp\left(-\left(\frac{x-\mu}{\sigma}\right)^{-k}\right) & ,x > \mu & \text{Fréchet} \end{array} \quad (1)$$

where μ, σ, k are the location, scale and shape parameters of the distributions respectively.

3.2 A Simple Stochastic Model

The utility of EV theory in the study of low-level vision can be explained with the following simple model: consider a black-box unit U with input X the pixel values from a finite window in a digital image (a similar analogy can be applied to the receptive fields of a biological vision system). The purpose of this black-box is to measure the amount of some non-negative quantity, $X(t)$ that changes over time. We write $u(t)=U(X(t))$. We also define an accumulator $s(n)=\int_0^n u(t)dt$ that accumulates the measured output from the unit, until it reaches a certain threshold $s(n)=\text{Max}^{(n)}(X)$ or a certain period of time, above which the accumulator is reset to zero and the process is restarted. If we consider $u(t)$, $s(n)$ as stochastic processes and select a finite number N of random samples $u_1,...u_N$, then their joint distribution $J(u_1,...,u_N)$ and the distribution $Y(s_N)$ of s_N, depend on the underlying original distribution $F(X_N)$. At this point we may pose two questions:

1. When $N \to \infty$ is there a limiting form of $Y(s) \to \Phi(s)$?
2. If there exists such a limit distribution what are the properties of the black-box unit U and of $J(u_1,...,u_N)$ that determines the form of $\Phi(s)$?

In [7] the authors have demonstrated that under certain conditions on $Y(s)$ the possible limiting forms of $\Phi(s)$ are the familiar forms in (1) and depend on the tail behaviour of $F(X)$ at large X. In our particular case, we use as units U the black-box that computes the absolute value of the filter result vectors from the irreducible representations of the dihedral groups. The filter vectors not associated with the trivial representation, are of the form $s=\sum(x_i\text{-}x_j)$ where x_i, x_j are pixel values. We can therefore expect that these filter values are usually very small and that high values will appear very seldom. In addition, these sums are calculated over a small, finite neighbourhood, and for this reason, the random variables are highly correlated. In short, the output for each filter has a form similar to the sums described in [7], and so it should be possible to use the EVT to model their distribution. As we will show experimentally later, the EVT models in (1) provide a good fit to our filtered data, which is a strong indication that the requirements for EVT equivalence from [7] generally hold. We also note, that since we are always dealing with positive quantities (norms of sums) that have a strictly positive support, we do not use the Gumbel model, which is unbounded, but only the Weibull and Fréchet models.

4 Proposed Approach

In the previous section, we have discussed the connection between our proposed filters and the EVT models. In this section, we suggest a simple approach for estimating the parameters of these models, using maximum likelihood, and then selecting the model that has the best fit using a residual analysis approach.

Distribution parameter estimation: We begin with a log-likelihood function $\Lambda(\theta)$ that expresses the conditional probability of realising the data sample given the model parameters $\theta=(\mu, \sigma, k)$, and then try to determine the choice of parameters (ML estimates) that maximise the likelihood for the available data. Since the 3-parameter Weibull and Fréchet distributions, do not have closed form expressions of the ML estimates, we need to apply an iterative method, such as the Newton-Rhapson approach. The iteration step, which usually is executed until convergence, is given by $\hat{\theta}_{t+1}=\hat{\theta}_t+p_t$, for t=0,1,2..., where p_t=-$\nabla^2 f_t^{-1} \nabla f_t$ is a search (descend) direction on the log-likelihood function. As such, we need expressions for the gradient ∇f_t and Hessian $\nabla^2 f_t$ of the Weibull and Fréchet distributions. For the Weibull, the gradient $\nabla f_t = \left[\frac{\partial \Lambda(\theta)}{\partial \theta}\right]$ is given by:

$$\begin{aligned}
\frac{\partial \Lambda(\theta)}{\partial \mu} &= -(k-1)\sum \tfrac{1}{x_i-\mu} + \tfrac{k}{\sigma}\sum \left(\tfrac{x_i-\mu}{\sigma}\right)^{k-1}, \\
\frac{\partial \Lambda(\theta)}{\partial \sigma} &= \tfrac{k}{\sigma}\left[-n + \sum \left(\tfrac{x_i-\mu}{\sigma}\right)^{k}\right], \\
\frac{\partial \Lambda(\theta)}{\partial k} &= \tfrac{n}{k} - n\log\sigma + \sum \log(x_i-\mu) - \sum \left(\tfrac{x_i-\mu}{\sigma}\right)^{k} \log\left(\tfrac{x_i-\mu}{\sigma}\right),
\end{aligned} \tag{2}$$

and the Hessian $\nabla^2 f_t = \left[\frac{\partial^2 \Lambda(\theta)}{\partial\theta\partial\theta'}\right]$ by:

$$\begin{aligned}
\frac{\partial^2 \Lambda(\theta)}{\partial \mu^2} &= -(k-1)\left[\sum \left(\tfrac{1}{x_i-\mu}\right)^2 + \tfrac{k}{\sigma^2}\sum \left(\tfrac{x_i-\mu}{\sigma}\right)^{k-2}\right], \\
\frac{\partial^2 \Lambda(\theta)}{\partial \mu\,\partial \sigma} &= \frac{\partial^2 \Lambda(\theta)}{\partial \sigma\,\partial \mu} = -\left(\tfrac{k}{\sigma}\right)^2 \sum \left(\tfrac{x_i-\mu}{\sigma}\right)^{k-1}, \\
\frac{\partial^2 \Lambda(\theta)}{\partial \mu\,\partial k} &= \frac{\partial^2 \Lambda(\theta)}{\partial k\,\partial \mu} = -\sum \tfrac{1}{x_i-\mu} + \tfrac{k}{\sigma}\sum \left(\tfrac{x_i-\mu}{\sigma}\right)^{k-1} \log\left(\tfrac{x_i-\mu}{\sigma}\right) + \tfrac{1}{\sigma}\sum \left(\tfrac{x_i-\mu}{\sigma}\right)^{k-1}, \\
\frac{\partial^2 \Lambda(\theta)}{\partial \sigma^2} &= \tfrac{k}{\sigma^2}\left[n - (k-1)\sum \left(\tfrac{x_i-\mu}{\sigma}\right)^{k}\right], \\
\frac{\partial^2 \Lambda(\theta)}{\partial \sigma\,\partial k} &= \frac{\partial^2 \Lambda(\theta)}{\partial k\,\partial \sigma} = -\tfrac{1}{\sigma}\left[n - \sum \left(\tfrac{x_i-\mu}{\sigma}\right)^{k} - k\sum \left(\tfrac{x_i-\mu}{\sigma}\right)^{k} \log\left(\tfrac{x_i-\mu}{\sigma}\right)\right], \\
\frac{\partial^2 \Lambda(\theta)}{\partial k^2} &= -\tfrac{n}{k^2} - \sum \left(\tfrac{x_i-\mu}{\sigma}\right)^{k} \left[\log\left(\tfrac{x_i-\mu}{\sigma}\right)\right]^2.
\end{aligned} \tag{3}$$

Similarly for the Fréchet:

$$\begin{aligned}
\frac{\partial \Lambda(\theta)}{\partial \mu} &= (k+1)\sum \tfrac{1}{x_i-\mu} - \tfrac{k}{\sigma}\sum \left(\tfrac{x_i-\mu}{\sigma}\right)^{-1-k}, \\
\frac{\partial \Lambda(\theta)}{\partial \sigma} &= \tfrac{k}{\sigma}\left[n - \sum \left(\tfrac{x_i-\mu}{\sigma}\right)^{-k}\right], \\
\frac{\partial \Lambda(\theta)}{\partial k} &= \tfrac{n}{k} + n\log\sigma - \sum \log(x_i-\mu) + \sum \left(\tfrac{x_i-\mu}{\sigma}\right)^{-k} \log\left(\tfrac{x_i-\mu}{\sigma}\right),
\end{aligned} \tag{4}$$

$$\begin{aligned}
\frac{\partial^2 \Lambda(\theta)}{\partial \mu^2} &= (k+1)\left[\sum \left(\tfrac{1}{x_i-\mu}\right)^2 - \tfrac{k}{\sigma^2}\sum \left(\tfrac{x_i-\mu}{\sigma}\right)^{-k-2}\right], \\
\frac{\partial^2 \Lambda(\theta)}{\partial \mu\,\partial \sigma} &= \frac{\partial^2 \Lambda(\theta)}{\partial \sigma\,\partial \mu} = -\left(\tfrac{k}{\sigma}\right)^2 \sum \left(\tfrac{x_i-\mu}{\sigma}\right)^{-1-k}, \\
\frac{\partial^2 \Lambda(\theta)}{\partial \mu\,\partial k} &= \frac{\partial^2 \Lambda(\theta)}{\partial k\,\partial \mu} = \sum \tfrac{1}{x_i-\mu} + \tfrac{k}{\sigma}\sum \left(\tfrac{x_i-\mu}{\sigma}\right)^{-k-1} \log\left(\tfrac{x_i-\mu}{\sigma}\right) - \tfrac{1}{\sigma}\sum \left(\tfrac{x_i-\mu}{\sigma}\right)^{-k-1}, \\
\frac{\partial^2 \Lambda(\theta)}{\partial \sigma^2} &= -\tfrac{k}{\sigma^2}\left[n - (1-k)\sum \left(\tfrac{x_i-\mu}{\sigma}\right)^{-k}\right], \\
\frac{\partial^2 \Lambda(\theta)}{\partial \sigma\,\partial k} &= \frac{\partial^2 \Lambda(\theta)}{\partial k\,\partial \sigma} = \tfrac{1}{\sigma}\left[n - \sum \left(\tfrac{x_i-\mu}{\sigma}\right)^{-k} + k\sum \left(\tfrac{x_i-\mu}{\sigma}\right)^{-k} \log\left(\tfrac{x_i-\mu}{\sigma}\right)\right], \\
\frac{\partial^2 \Lambda(\theta)}{\partial k^2} &= -\tfrac{n}{k^2} - \sum \left(\tfrac{x_i-\mu}{\sigma}\right)^{-k} \left[\log\left(\tfrac{x_i-\mu}{\sigma}\right)\right]^2.
\end{aligned} \tag{5}$$

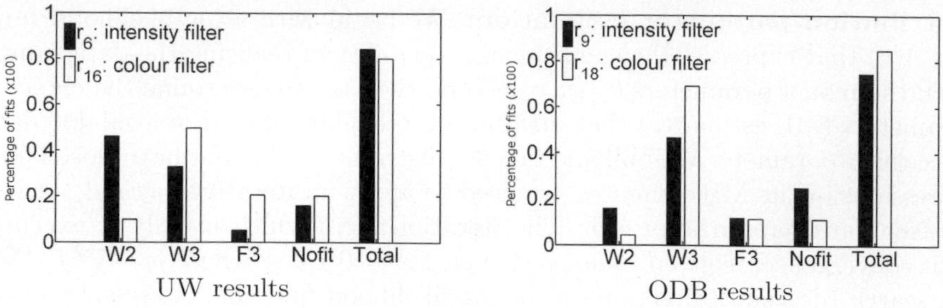

Fig. 2. Typical EVT model fitting results from the two databases using the R^2 g.o.f. statistic. Note that the numbers are comparable to those in Table 1.

For a discussion on more advanced iterative ML estimators and appropriate initial estimates for $\hat{\theta}_0$ we refer to the excellent book by [8] on the Weibull distribution. Similar techniques apply for the Fréchet.

Model selection: Once we have fitted the two models by ML, we can choose the most appropriate of the two, using a goodness-of-fit (g.o.f.) criterion. This criterion is chosen as the deviation between each of the fitted distributions and the data. Given the empirical cumulative distribution function (cdf) $\hat{\Delta}_n$ of the data sample $(x_1, ..., x_n)$ [9], and cdf F_n (evaluated at the same points as the data sample) from the Weibull and Fréchet distributions separately (equations in (1)), then the g.o.f. measure, called the *coefficient of determination*, is defined as:

$$R^2 = 1 - \frac{(n-1)\sum_{i=1}^{n}(\hat{\Delta}_n - F_n)^2}{(n-\zeta)\sum_{i=1}^{n}(\hat{\Delta}_n - \bar{\Delta}_n)^2}, \text{ with } \zeta = 3 \text{ the model degrees of freedom.} \tag{6}$$

We choose the model with the maximum R^2 value. If in addition we wish to reject a sample ("no-fit"), we can impose a lower threshold on R^2.

5 Experiments

We have used two datasets for our experiments and subsequent analysis. The first is the **UW** database [10], which consists 1109 colour photos of various vacation locations and natural, outdoor scenes e.g. "Barcelona", "Iceland" etc. The images have been obtained by different cameras and resolutions, but most of them are 756×504 pixels. The second dataset, **ODB** [11], contains 30000 thumbnail images (reduced in size so that the maximum size in one direction is 128 pixels), across 15 object categories. These images were automatically crawled from public web pages using a variety of textual keywords.

5.1 Statistical Analysis: Goodness of Fit

In this section, we show experimentally the following:

I) the R^2 g.o.f. test is more reliable and robust than common statistical g.o.f. tests for model selection.

II) the 3-parameter Weibull-Fréchet models provide a good fit to the distribution of filtered natural images across different datasets.

III) The 3-parameter Weibull-Fréchet models are more flexible and can describe a larger portion of the data, than the 2-parameter Weibull model alone can.

We demonstrate I) on synthetic data, where the ground truth is known, and compare 4 different approaches: the two sample Kolmogorov-Smirnov test, the χ^2 and g-test and the R^2 test from (6). In total, we carried out 6000 tests, with 500 samples drawn from various distributions (2 and 3-param. Weibull "**W2**", "**W3**"; 3-param. Fréchet "**F3**"; and a 2-param. Lognormal, used here as a "**no-fit**" sample), with realistic parameter settings, that is, ones that we are likely to observe in natural images. The results are shown in Table 1. We can see that the R^2 is the only test that performs consistently well along the different samples even for the "hard" W3 and F3 cases (these are samples with parameter choices that lead to problematic ML surfaces). For this reason, we have decided to use the R^2 test in the remainder of our analysis.

II) and III) are demonstrated on the UW and ODB databases. We applied the filters, selected the appropriate model and rejected any fits with a low R^2 value. The results are shown in Fig. 2. Due to space limitations, we have only included 2 filters (one intensity and one colour), but all the other filters exhibit the same typical behaviour. In particular, for the intensity filters, W2 fits a much larger percentage of data than in the colour case (sometimes the W2 model dominates in the intensity filters), with the F3 being the least contributing sub-model. The former is in line with the findings of [12] when intensity gradient filters are used as image patch descriptors (our descriptors are essentially localised gradient filters). Note however, that by combining all the EVT sub-models we can describe well in excess of 80% of the data. This is something that the W2 alone cannot do. This observation becomes more pronounced for the colour filters, where W3 and F3 have a more prominent role, with W3 alone modelling between 50-70% of the data. In this case, W2 is limited to around 10% and thus the approach of [12] cannot be used to model colour edges, unless one applies W2 to each colour channel separately [13].

We note here that around 15-20% of the fits have been rejected. The no-fit portion includes outliers (i.e. non-natural images, trivial filter results etc) and data where the ML estimation did not converge. These numbers are similar to the no-fit results we have observed in the synthetic tests in Table 1, and are therefore related to the characteristics of the algorithm as well as the data.

Table 1. Goodness-of-fit comparative results (as percentage of correct classifications)

	F3	W3	W2	no-fit	hard F3	hard W3
Kolmogorov-Smirnov	80.3%	23%	**99.2%**	25%	**93.1%**	1.1%
g-test	0.81%	16%	66.1%	92.4%	19.4%	4%
χ^2	12.4%	31.6%	88%	**98.8%**	0%	0%
R^2	**99.5%**	**88.7%**	89.7%	87.9%	85.5%	**77.3%**

In conclusion, these experiments indicate that the EVT may be considered as a viable hypothesis for modelling the distribution of our descriptors (or similar types of intensity and colour gradient filters). Moreover, the additional modelling capacity of W3 and F3, relative to W2 alone, has also been demonstrated.

5.2 Further Analysis: The σ, k-Space

We continue with an analysis of the types of images that are assigned to each submodel (W2, W3 and F3) for a specific filter (r_9) and the image position in the σ, k parameter space. For economy of space, we only demonstrate a single filter on the UW dataset, but the results generalise to all filters and different datasets. We omit the μ parameter since for these datasets it exhibits very little variation and the most important behaviour is observed in the other two parameters. First of all, if we look at Fig. 4 we see a correlated dispersion in the two axes, with the F3 images spanning only a very small region of the space at low σ, k, and well separated from W2 and W3. Also notice how the F3 set typically includes images with near-uniform coloured regions with smooth transitions between them, or alternatively very coarse-textured, homogeneous regions with sharp boundaries. High frequency textures seem to be relatively absent from F3, and on average the image intensities seem to be lower in F3 than in W2 and W3.

On the other hand, the W2 and W3 clusters are intermixed, with W2 mostly restricted to the lower portion of the space. For smaller σ, k values, the W2 images exhibit coarser textures, with the latter becoming more fine-grained as σ, k increase in tandem. Also, there seems to be a shift from low exposure, low contrast images with shadows (small σ, k), to high contrast, more illumination, less shadows when σ, k become large. Furthermore, W2 shows a preference for sharp linear edges associated with urban scenes, whereas W3 mostly captures the "fractal"-type edges, common in nature images.

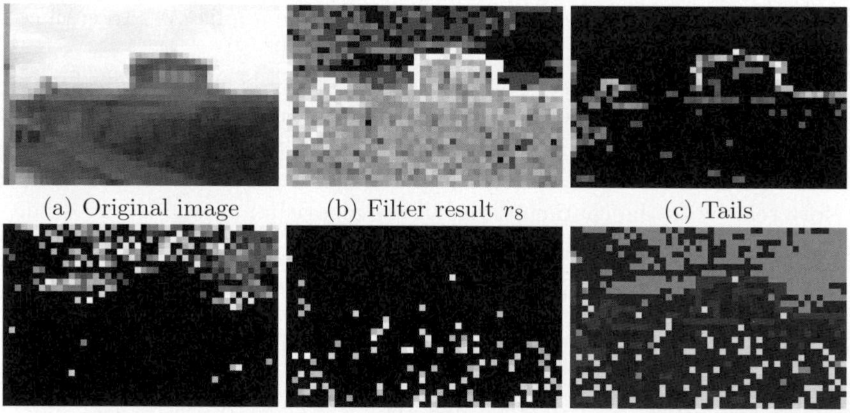

(a) Original image (b) Filter result r_8 (c) Tails

(d) Mode (e) Median (f) Synthesis

Fig. 3. A comparison between the extrema and other regions of a filtered image

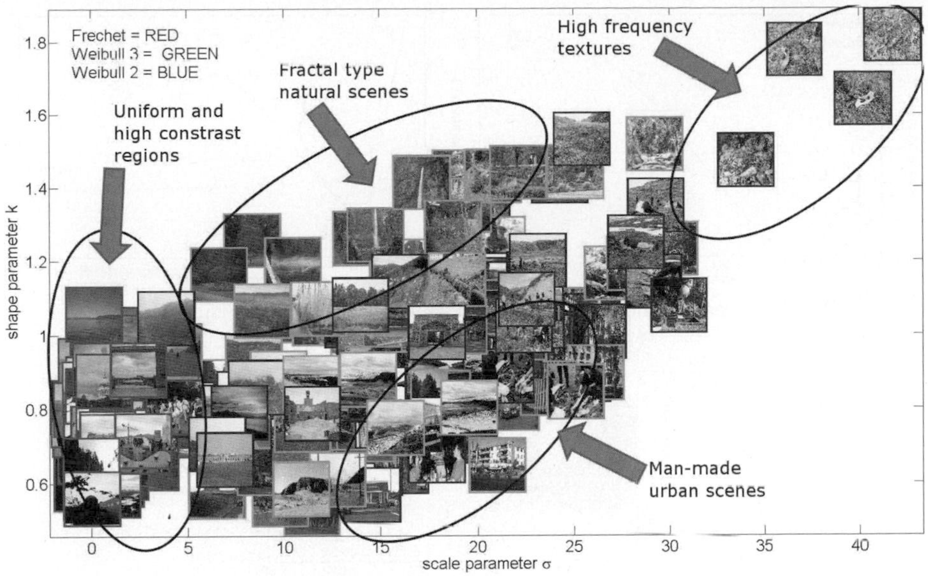

Fig. 4. Image type and model distribution in σ, k-space

These observations become more apparent when looking at Fig. 5(a) and (b). In these experiments, we took one (grayscaled) image from the database, and introduced different amounts of noise and smoothing to simulate high and low frequency texture components (Fig. 5(a)) and also linear and nonlinear intensity changes, in order to simulate variations in the amount of illumination (Fig. 5(b)). The image was filtered and the distribution parameters fitted at each instance are shown as trajectories in the σ, k-space. As we have already seen, the images shift to the upper right corner of the space as higher frequency components are added, and for the opposite (smoothing of textures) the images will move towards areas of lower σ and gradually increase in k as the texture homogeneity is increased. For textures that have an approximate constant colour (e.g. sky) the images will cluster on the upper left corner of the space. The UW dataset does not contain such images, and so that space in Fig. 4 remains empty.

If we now look at intensity variations, we see that an increase in gain will move the image toward the upper right corner where all the well-illuminated images lie. When the gain is decreased, we will move towards the upper left corner where the very dark (almost constant) images are. If we now increase the bias, then we see that mostly the k parameter increases (note that the two parameters do not have the same units). Similarly, a decrease in bias will cause a similar decrease in k, while leaving σ relatively intact. Finally, we examine nonlinear changes in intensity (gamma correction). A decrease in gamma value, first reduces the σ parameter only (unlike the bias) and then for additional decreases, the k values start to increase when all the pixels take the same very low (dark) values. Note however, that in this case, the increase in k is much slower and converges to

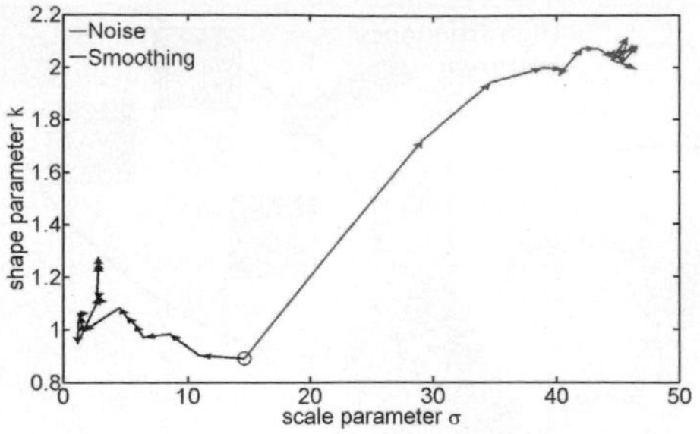

(a) Noise and smoothing.

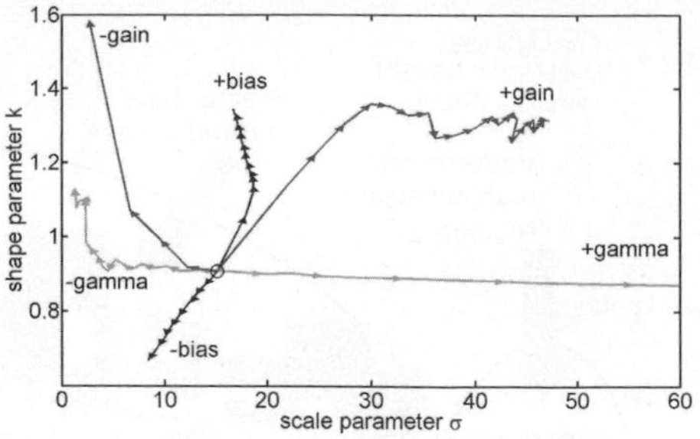

(b) Image intensity changes.

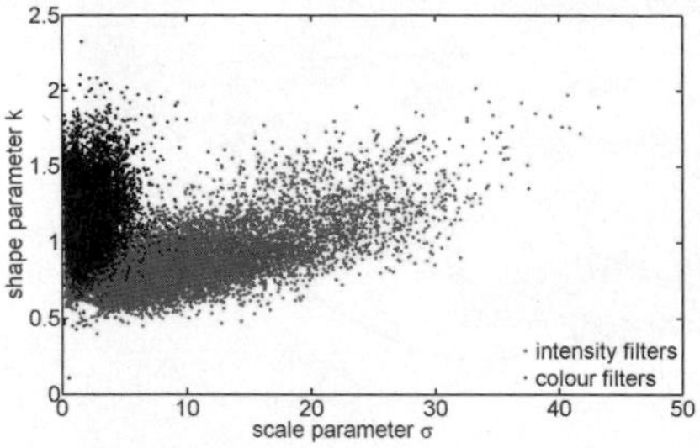

(c) Intensity and colour filter scatter plot.

Fig. 5. The behaviour of filtered images in σ, k-space

a much lower k, than when the gain was decreased. On the other hand, if we increase the gamma without re-normalising the pixel values between [0,255], then we see a shift towards the lower right corner of the space (increase of σ without increase of k). This region of the σ, k-space is usually empty, but when it is not (depending on the data) it mostly occupied by simple pictorial images such as graphics, designs and logotypes on white background.

In Fig. 5(c) we see a scatter plot for all the images in UW using all the filters (except r_1,...,r_3). We see two very distinct clusters, one for the intensity filters that is spread along a σ, k diagonal (as in Fig. 4), and one for the colour filters spread mainly along the k-axis. In conclusion, all the above properties of the σ, k-space are only applicable due to the EV theory and cannot be exploited with histogram representations. The fact that the images exhibit clear clusters and predictable variation in that space, is a good indication of the utility of the EVT framework for retrieval and classification tasks.

Finally, we illustrate the importance of the data at the extrema of a filtered image, as described by the EVT. In Fig. 3(a) we show an image from UW (rescaled for comparison) and its filtered result using r_8 in Fig. 3(b). This is essentially a gradient filter in the x- and y-directions. Next is Fig. 3(c) that shows the response at the tails of the fitted distribution. It it immediately obvious that the tails contain all the important edges and boundary outlines that abstract the main objects in the image (house, roof, horizon, diagonal road). These are the salient features that a human observer will focus on, or that a computer vision system might extract for object recognition or navigation. We also show the regions near the mode in Fig. 3(d). We see that much of it contains small magnitude edges and noise from the almost uniform sky texture. Although this is part of the scene, it has very little significance when one is trying to classify or recognise objects in an image. A similar observation holds for the grass area, which although contains stronger edges than the sky and is distributed near the median (Fig. 3(e)), it is still not as important (magnitude-wise and semantically) as the edges in the tails are. Finally, Fig. 3(f) shows how all the components put together, can describe different regions in the image: the salient object edges in the tails (red); the average response, discounting extreme outliers, (median) in yellow; the most common response in light blue (mode); and the remaining superfluous data in between (dark blue). This is exactly the type of semantic behaviour that the EVT models can isolate with their location, scale and shape parameters, something which is not immediately possible when using histograms.

5.3 Classification and Retrieval

We also include a a basic example on how our descriptors may be used, in principle, for classification and retrieval tasks. For this example, we have isolated 4 classes from the ODB dataset, with tags "Andy Warhol", "Claude Monet", "beach" and "garden", each containing 1000 images. After filtering with r_{21} and model selection, we used 75% of the images to train an SVM (with standard settings), and classified the remaining 25%. For the SVM input, we generated 1000 samples from the probability density function of the model chosen for each image.

The overall classification score was 40.5% with the random baseline at 25%. This result is satisfactory considering the many outliers and high variation in the data (due to the automated text-based harvesting) and the lack of specificity in the 4 categories. The 10 top ranked images in each category (one-to-all retrieval) are shown in Fig. 6. The goal here, just like in online image search, is not to retrieve the most representative images for each class (means of the clusters) but the ones that are the furthest away from the SVM decision boundaries (cluster

Fig. 6. 4 class image retrieval from the ODB dataset using r_{21} with an SVM

extrema). Therefore, a perfect classification score in CBIR is not as important as fast and accurate retrieval of very few, relevant samples.

Observe in Fig. 6, the differences between the vivid, near-constant colours and sharp edges in the "Warhol" set and the less saturated, softer tones and faint edges of the "Monet" set. In the same way, the "garden" images contain very high frequency natural textures and the "beach" images more homogeneous regions with similarly coloured boundaries. These characteristics are the exact information captured by the filters and the EVT models and which can be used very effectively for image classification and retrieval purposes.

6 Conclusion

In this work, we have presented a set of spatio-chromatic, image content descriptors that are inspired by the theory of group representations. We have demonstrated that by using the EVT to model the output distribution of the descriptors, we can take advantage of specific parametric distribution models that offer a more flexible representation than histograms. Furthermore, additional important characteristics of large image datasets only become visible inside this parametric probability space. These descriptors, combined with the EVT models, offer themselves for very efficient and effective tools for content-based retrieval and classification of image data.

We would like to explain here that the EVT is not the only model one may use to describe similar image properties. In fact [14] have used fragmentation theory to describe the apparent Weibull distribution of gradient-filtered grayscale images. Despite this, our experiments have shown that EVT is more *flexible*, since [14] advocate a very restrictive fragmentation schedule that might not always apply in practice; more *descriptive*, since EVT has 3 submodels instead of 1 as in [14]; and finally EVT is easily applied to *colour* filters as well.

References

1. Everingham, M., Van Gool, L., Williams, C.K.I., Winn, J., Zisserman, A.: The Pascal visual object classes (voc) challenge. IJCV 88, 303–338 (2010)
2. Fässler, A., Stiefel, E.L.: Group theoretical methods and their applications. Birkhäuser, Boston (1992)
3. Lenz, R.: Investigation of receptive fields using representations of dihedral groups. Journal of Visual Communication and Image Representation 6, 209–227 (1995)
4. Lenz, R., Bui, T.H., Takase, K.: A group theoretical toolbox for color image operators. In: ICIP, vol. 3, pp. 557–560 (2005)
5. `http://people.isy.liu.se/en/cvl/zografos/CBIR`
6. Gumbel, E.J.: Statistics of Extremes. Columbia University Press, New York (1958)
7. Bertin, E., Clusel, M.: Generalised extreme value statistics and sum of correlated variables. Journal of Physics A: Mathematical and General 39 (2006)
8. Rinne, H.: The Weibull Distribution: A Handbook. CRC Press, Boca Raton (2008)
9. Kaplan, E.L., Meier, P.: Nonparametric estimation from incomplete observations. J. Amer. Statist. Assn. 53, 457–481 (1958)

10. Li, Y., Shapiro, L., Bilmes, J.: A generative/discriminative learning algorithm for image classification. In: ICCV, vol. 2, pp. 1605–1612 (2005)
11. Solli, M., Lenz, R.: Emotion related structures in large image databases. In: ACM CIVR, pp. 398–405 (2010)
12. Yanulevskaya, V., Geusebroek, J.M.: Significance of the Weibull distribution and its sub-models in natural image statistics. In: VISAPP, vol. 1, pp. 355–362 (2009)
13. Gijsenij, A., Gevers, T.: Color constancy using natural image statistics and scene semantics. IEEE PAMI 99 (2010)
14. Geusebroek, J.-M., Smeulders, A.W.M.: Fragmentation in the vision of scenes. In: ICCV, pp. 130–135 (2003)

Model-Based Transfer Functions for Efficient Visualization of Medical Image Volumes

Daniel Forsberg[1,2,3], Claes Lundström[2,3], Mats Andersson[1,2], and Hans Knutsson[1,2]

[1] Department of Biomedical Engineering, Linköping University, Sweden
[2] Center for Medical Image Science and Visualization (CMIV), Linköping University, Sweden
[3] Sectra Imtec, Linköping, Sweden

Abstract. The visualization of images with a large dynamic range is a difficult task and this is especially the case for gray-level images. In radiology departments, this will force radiologists to review medical images several times, since the images need to be visualized with several different contrast windows (transfer functions) in order for the full information content of each image to be seen. Previously suggested methods for handling this situation include various approaches using histogram equalization and other methods for processing the image data. However, none of these utilize the underlying human anatomy in the images to control the visualization and the fact that different transfer functions are often only relevant for disjoint anatomical regions.

In this paper, we propose a method for using model-based local transfer functions. It allows the reviewing radiologist to apply multiple transfer functions simultaneously to a medical image volume. This provides the radiologist with a tool for making the review process more efficient, by allowing him/her to review more of the information in a medical image volume with a single visualization. The transfer functions are automatically assigned to different anatomically relevant regions, based upon a model registered to the volume to be visualized. The transfer functions can be either pre-defined or interactively changed by the radiologist during the review process. All of this is achieved without adding any unfamiliar aspects to the radiologist's normal work-flow, when reviewing medical image volumes.

1 Introduction

The visualization of images with a large dynamic range, i.e. images that have a large value range, is a difficult task and is common in many imaging applications. This also applies to gray-level images, since the human eye has a limited ability to discern different gray-levels and since many display devices are incapable of properly displaying a large number of gray-levels, i.e. there is a limited display range.

A radiology department is a high-pace work environment, where radiologists are under constant pressure to review a never-ending stream of images, and in

This work was funded by the Swedish Research Council, grant 2007-4786.

A. Heyden and F. Kahl (Eds.): SCIA 2011, LNCS 6688, pp. 592–603, 2011.

which it is especially important to handle the problem of visualizing gray-level images with a large dynamic range. Despite the digitalization that the whole work-flow has undergone in radiology departments, the review process of the images still remains the same to a large extent, i.e. images are reviewed as gray-level images on an image by image basis. This means that the review process for a whole body CT scan, which can easily generate thousands of images, will require a considerable amount of time.

The issue of a large dynamic range is usually handled by providing the radiologist with functionality that allows him/her to interactively change, what is know as, the contrast window (or the window/level) of the displayed images; hereafter referred to as applying a transfer function. A contrast window is defined as a linear mapping of the pixel values in a certain value range to a given display range. The value range is either determined by a min and a max value or by a width and a center value. This allows him/her to adjust the contrast and the brightness of the visualized images in accordance with either some pre-defined settings or based upon experience. However, when visualizing images, the radiologist often employs several transfer functions. In the case of a CT chest scan, this can mean that he/she first scrolls through the image stack with a soft tissue contrast window applied, then with a bone window, and finally with a lung window, see Fig. 1. Thus, the radiologist has to scroll through the stack several times, despite the fact that the different windows are often only relevant to disjoint regions of the body.

The problem of having too large a dynamic range to display is a well-known problem within the medical imaging community [11], and for which a number of different solutions have been proposed. Many of these suggestions are based on histogram equalization and include adaptive histogram equalization (AHE) [12], contrast limiting adaptive histogram equalization (CLAHE) [13] and multi-scale adaptive histogram equalization (MAHE) [6]. Although they enable the radiologist to see more, they are limited in the sense that they rely on a pre-processing step. Unsatisfactory pre-processing might force the radiologist to manually find an optimal set of parameters for each medical image volume in order to produce satisfactory images. Since parameters such as tile size, number of bins and clip limit are unfamiliar to the radiologist and also difficult to master, in practice the only tool for changing the visualization of an image still is a global min-max windowing. See Fig. 2 for an example using CLAHE with different parameter sets.

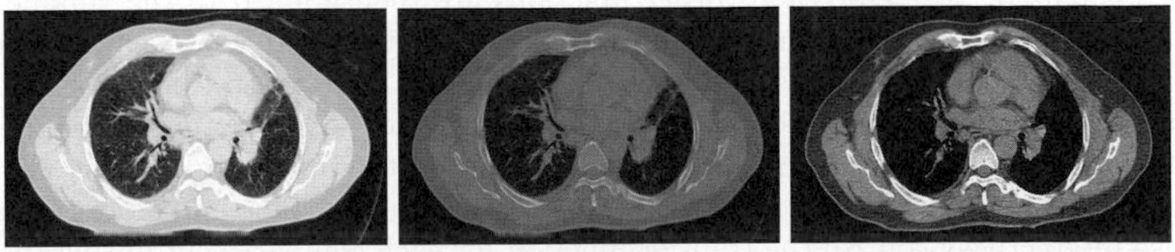

Fig. 1. An example from a CT chest scan displaying the use of different transfer functions. **From left**: Lung window, bone window and mediastinum window.

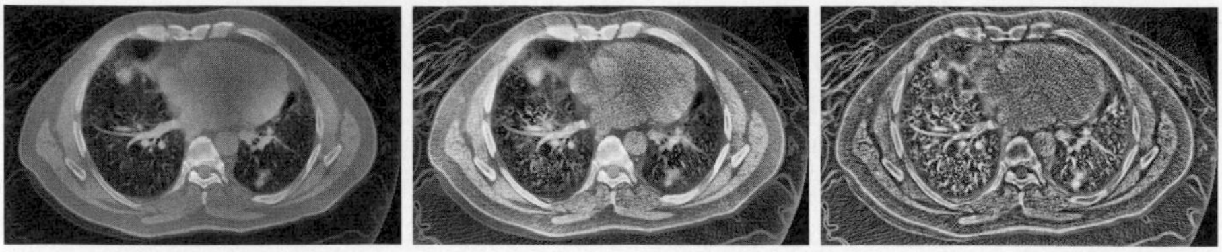

Fig. 2. An image from a CT chest scan displaying the use of CLAHE (adapthisteq in MATLAB) with various parameter settings

There are other approaches for handling this problem that do not include histogram equalization. In [7] it is suggested that the use of a bi-linear transfer function will improve the visualization. Another approach, presented in [4], is where multiple transfer functions are applied separately and then combined using weighted averaging. In a US patent application, [2], yet a third alternative is presented, where a single transfer function is applied first and later, two other transfer functions are applied to the values that were clipped due to the first transfer function. This approach resembles a functionality, known as dual window, that used to be available on some modality workstations. Dual window functionality allowed the radiologist to apply a contrast window within an already applied contrast window. However, a common limitation of these three suggestions is that they fail to make use of the fact that different transfer functions are often only relevant to disjoint regions.

In this paper, we present a method for the utilization of local transfer functions for visualization of medical image volumes based upon deformable models. The aim of this suggestion is to enable the radiologist to view images with multiple local transfer function applied simultaneously to the volume, instead of just one global transfer function. The transfer functions are automatically assigned to different anatomically relevant regions in the volume to be visualized and they can either be pre-defined or interactively changed by the radiologist during the visualization.

2 Model-Based Local Transfer Function

The basic idea behind the proposed method consists of an anatomical model that is deformed, with the aid of non-rigid registration, to fit the data volume to be visualized. Voxel-specific transfer functions are then applied to the volume, where the transfer functions are derived from the deformed model. This will enable the radiologist to review images while applying multiple transfer functions simultaneously. The applied model can be more or less complex depending on the number of segmented tissues (compartments) in the model, in which a predefined transfer function is linked to each compartment. The radiologist can also interactively control the transfer function for each compartment during the review process. See Fig. 3 for a graphical overview of the proposed method.

The following sections will in more detail describe the different aspects of the proposed method.

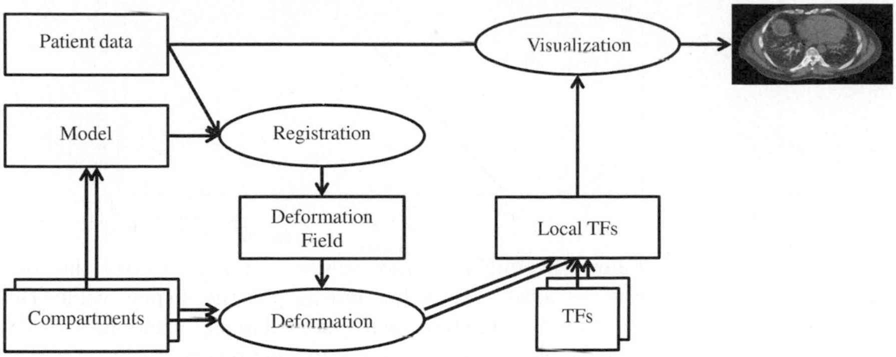

Fig. 3. Method overview

2.1 Model

The model I_M consists of a body with N compartments, where $I_{C_i}(\boldsymbol{x})$ describes the probability $[0, 1]$ of tissue i in $\boldsymbol{x}$. The different compartments are combined to create the model according to:

$$I_M = \sum_{i=1}^{N} a_i I_{C_i} \tag{1}$$

Where $\sum_{i=1}^{N} I_{C_i}(\boldsymbol{x}) = 1$ and where a_i are values used to combine the different compartments I_{C_i} in order to create a model suitable for image registration. How to select a_i depends on which registration method that is used in the subsequent step, e.g. an intensity-based method would require that the voxel values of the model are similar to the voxel values of the volume to visualize whereas a phase-based method would require that the boundaries between the different compartments in the model have the same sign as in the volume to visualize. A min and max value (α_i and β_i) are assigned to each compartment. These values are used to control the transfer functions, see Fig. 4.

2.2 Registration

A segmentation and registration algorithm known as the Morphon is employed to register the model with the data set to be visualized. The Morphon is a phase-based algorithm where a source image $I_S(\boldsymbol{x})$, in our case $I_S = I_M$, is iteratively deformed, $I_D(\boldsymbol{x}) = I_S(\boldsymbol{x} + \boldsymbol{d}(\boldsymbol{x}))$, until it is sufficiently similar to a target image I_T. This process is performed over multiple scales starting on coarse scales to register large global displacements and moving on to finer scales to register smaller local deformations. For a more detailed review of the algorithm, the reader is referred to [8].

When the registration process is completed, the estimated deformation field is applied to all the compartments of the model using linear interpolation.

$$\tilde{I}_{C_i}(\boldsymbol{x}) = I_{C_i}(\boldsymbol{x} + \boldsymbol{d}(\boldsymbol{x})) \tag{2}$$

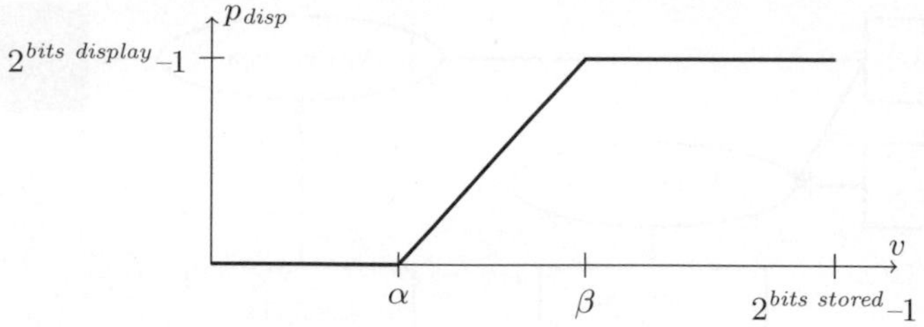

Fig. 4. An illustration of how the min and max values α and β control the local transfer function, where v is the local voxel value and p_{disp} is the display value. Bits stored denotes the number of bits used to store each voxel value and where bits display denotes the number of bits available for display in the display device

2.3 Visualization Based Upon Local Transfer Functions

The next step is to define the voxel-specific transfer functions, which are defined by a min and max value for each voxel, $I_\alpha(\boldsymbol{x})$ and $I_\beta(\boldsymbol{x})$. The deformed compartments $\tilde{I}_{C_i}$ are combined for both the min and max values (α_i and β_i) to create $I_\alpha(\boldsymbol{x})$ and $I_\beta(\boldsymbol{x})$.

$$I_\alpha(\boldsymbol{x}) = \frac{\sum_{i=1}^{N} \alpha_i \tilde{I}_{C_i}(\boldsymbol{x})}{\sum_{i=1}^{N} \tilde{I}_{C_i}(\boldsymbol{x})} \tag{3}$$

$$I_\beta(\boldsymbol{x}) = \frac{\sum_{i=1}^{N} \beta_i \tilde{I}_{C_i}(\boldsymbol{x})}{\sum_{i=1}^{N} \tilde{I}_{C_i}(\boldsymbol{x})} \tag{4}$$

The data set to be visualized, I, is then transformed according to the voxel-specific transfer functions to form I_{disp}, which then is used for visualization.

$$I_{slope} = \frac{2^{\text{bits display}} - 1}{I_\beta - I_\alpha} \tag{5}$$

$$\tilde{I} = \min\left(\max\left(I, I_\alpha\right), I_\beta\right) \tag{6}$$

$$I_{disp} = I_{slope}\left(\tilde{I} - I_\alpha\right) \tag{7}$$

2.4 Smooth Transition Regions between Transfer Functions

An important issue to consider and to handle correctly is that of the transition regions between the compartments, i.e. how to handle the transition between different transfer functions. This is important since no registration algorithm can produce perfect results and since the borders between different tissues are rarely binary. Thus, it is important to have a transition that does not introduce any new features that are disturbing to the radiologist reviewing the images.

A first step which handles the transition regions is already incorporated into the model, since the compartments are described with a continuous probability between [0, 1] instead of with a binary model. The effect of this on the transfer functions in the transitions regions can be seen in Fig. 5 and the effect on the final visualization result can be seen in Fig. 6.

Another approach is to provide the radiologist with a tool for controlling the transition regions. A simple but effective tool is to include averaging of the transition regions, in which the radiologist can select which averaging filter to apply and the size of the applied filter.

Other approaches for handling the transition regions were tested, including different non-linear mappings of the probability functions describing the compartments and different non-linear combinations of the transfer functions in the transition region. However, none of them added any significant improvements than the already described continuous model and the user-controlled averaging of the transition regions.

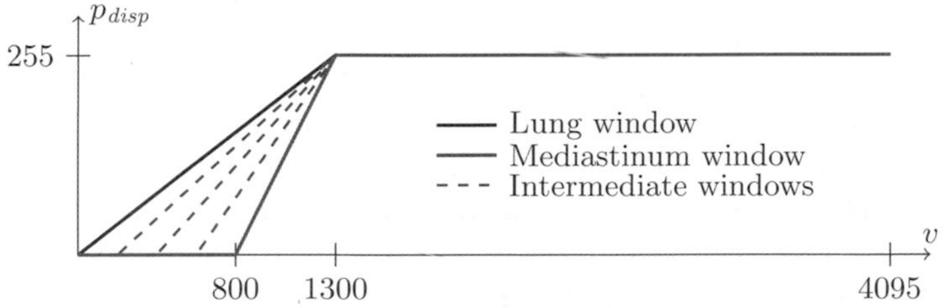

Fig. 5. An example to demonstrate how the transfer functions varies in the transition region between two different transfer functions

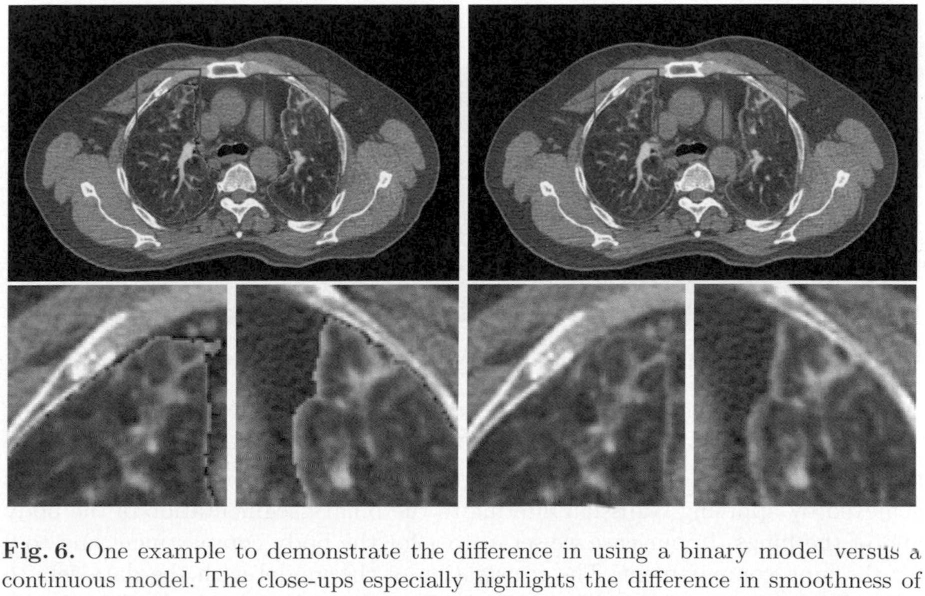

Fig. 6. One example to demonstrate the difference in using a binary model versus a continuous model. The close-ups especially highlights the difference in smoothness of the features introduced in the transition regions. **Left side**: Binary model, **Right side**: Continuous model.

3 Evaluation

To evaluate the usefulness of the proposed method we have tested it on a number of clinical data sets and allowed three clinicians to evaluate the proposed method based upon the visualized images. The evaluation was based upon the following questions:

- What are the possibilities of the proposed method?
- What are the limitations of the proposed method?
- What is important to consider when handling transition regions, i.e. the region between two different transfer functions?
- Would it be possible to use the proposed method to make the review process of large medical image volumes more efficient?

4 Implementation

The proposed method was evaluated using data sets made available by [1] at *http://www.dir-lab.com/*. The data sets consist of 4D CT thoracic data from patients with esophageal cancer. Each 3D data set, in the 4D data sets, has a size of 512x512x128 and a spatial resolution of 0.97x0.97x2.5 mm. Using one of the patients, a model was created consisting of two compartments, see Fig. 7. The model was then registered with two different data sets from the same patient but from different exhale/inhale phases. Each of the estimated deformation fields was applied to the model, which was then used to visualize the data sets using multiple transfer functions.

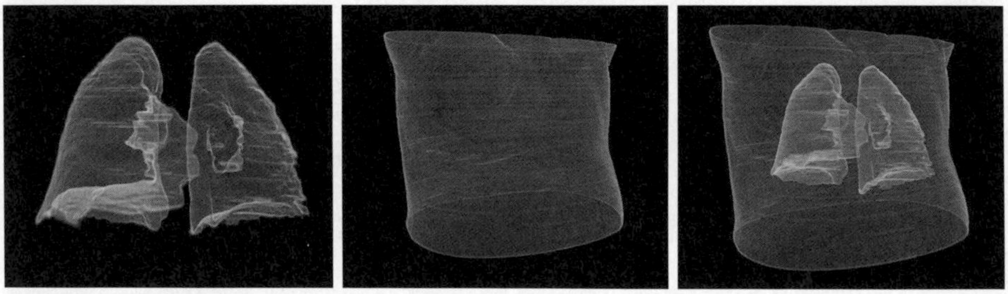

Fig. 7. Two different compartments (lung and body) combined to form the model

The model was created using MIPAV 5.0.0 and a semi-automated method to segment the contour of the body and of the lungs. A continuous model was achieved by applying Gaussian filtering to the binary segmentation of the body and of the lungs. In our case we set a_i to 1 for the body compartment and to 0 for the lung compartment. The registration of the model with the data sets to be visualized was performed in MATLAB R2010a with the aid of a GPU-based implementation of the Morphon, implemented with CUDA 3.0. Due to memory constraints on the graphics card the data sets were downsampled to 256x256x128 before registering the model with the data sets.

The deformation of the model and the visualization were performed in MeVisLab 4.6.2. Two different transfer functions were applied, one lung contrast window (min-max equal to 0 – 1300) and one mediastinum contrast window (min-max equal to 800 – 1300). The display range for the visualized images was limited to eight bits, i.e. 256 gray-levels, since this is the commonly used display range when reviewing medical gray-level images.

5 Results

5.1 Results from the Evaluation

All three radiologists acknowledged the potential in the proposed method, in terms of making the review process more efficient by avoiding the need to

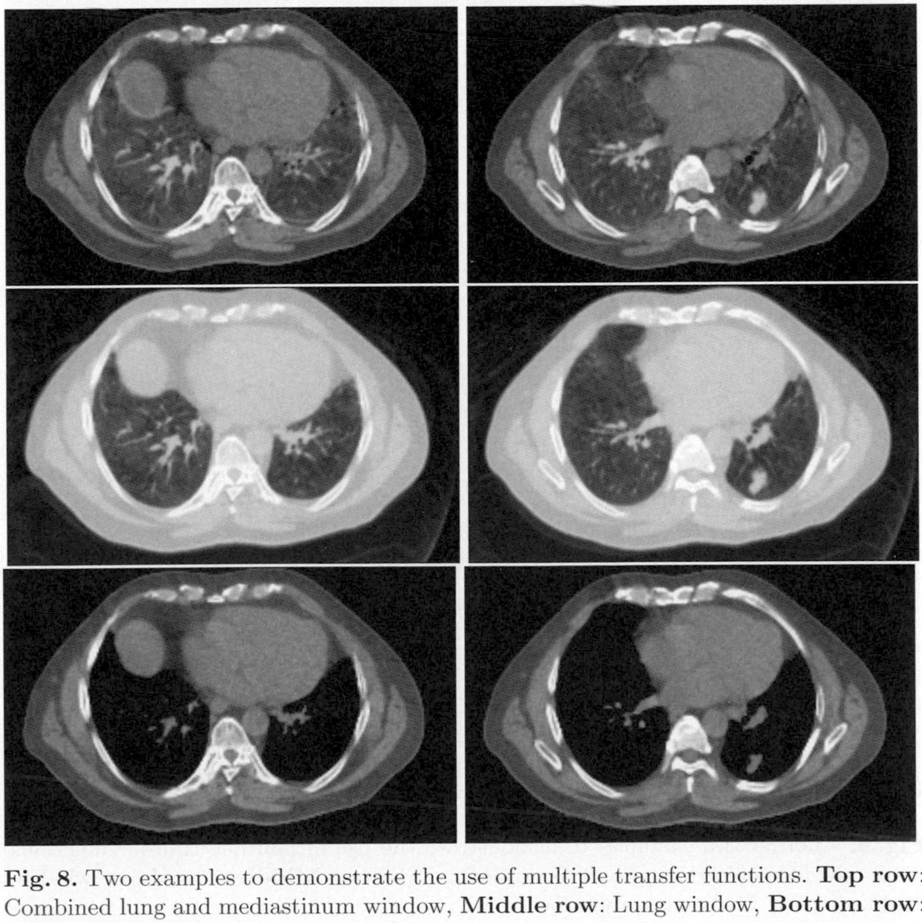

Fig. 8. Two examples to demonstrate the use of multiple transfer functions. **Top row**: Combined lung and mediastinum window, **Middle row**: Lung window, **Bottom row**: Mediastinum window.

scroll through an image stack multiple times. They predicted that the method would have the greatest potential when working with images that display tissues/compartments where the visually important information is located within the tissues and not on the border between the tissues. Another type of relevant images would be those where there is a large difference between the applied transfer functions, e.g. transfer functions for air, soft tissues and/or bone. Another comment was that this method would be useful when there is a need for a quick overview, e.g. when the reason for the examination is vague or in trauma cases.

On the other hand, the radiologists found little or no potential in the proposed method, when reviewing images with small structures or where the borders between the different tissues/compartments contain vital information or when the applied transfer functions are very similar.

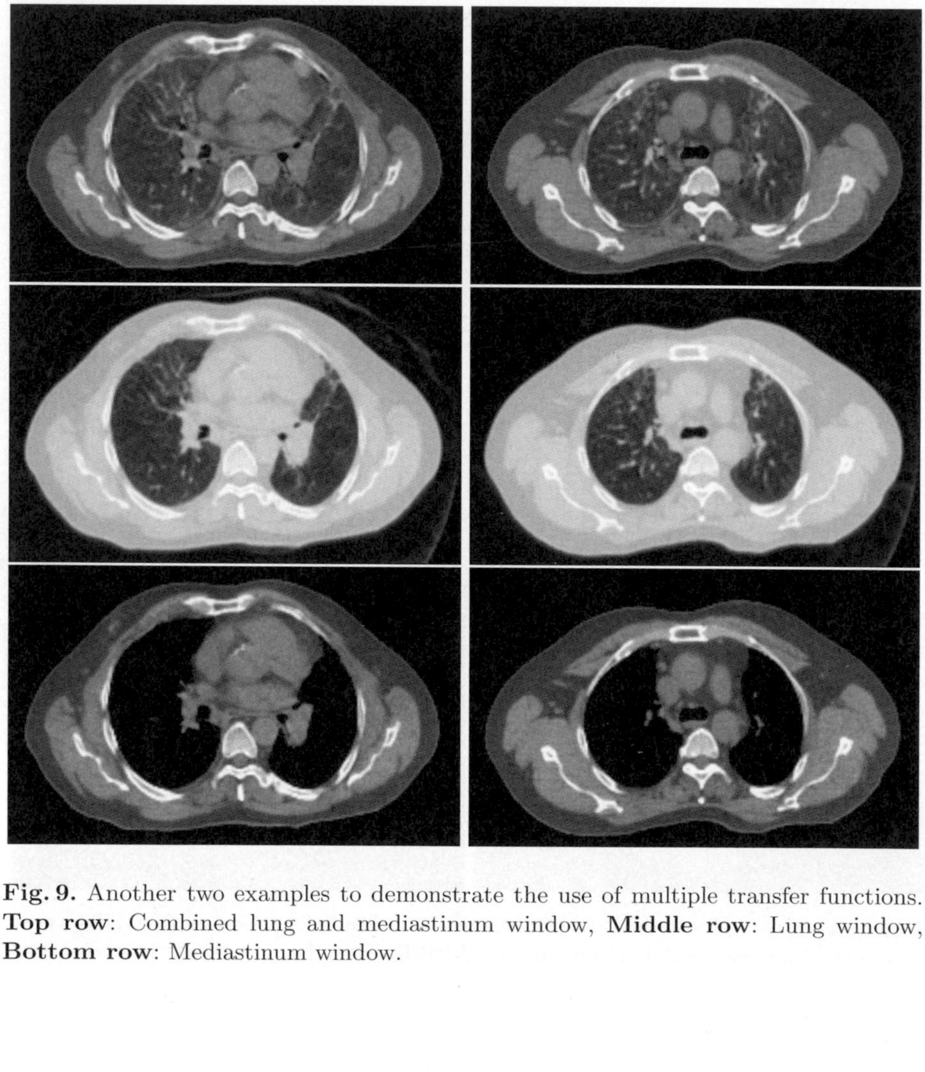

Fig. 9. Another two examples to demonstrate the use of multiple transfer functions. **Top row**: Combined lung and mediastinum window, **Middle row**: Lung window, **Bottom row**: Mediastinum window.

Another important comment from the radiologists, was that the images appeared familiar, albeit the simultaneous use of multiple transfer functions. Also the fact that the visualization was controlled using the familiar parameters of a contrast window, was highly appreciated.

The comments regarding how to handle the transition regions differed. One radiologist appreciated the smooth transition between the different transfer regions, because it did not visually disturb him as much as a sharp transition would, whereas the other two radiologists appreciated the sharp transition since it reminded them about the fact that multiple transfer functions where applied simultaneously.

5.2 Results from the Implementation

Results from the implementation of the proposed method can be seen in Figs. 8 and 9.

6 Discussion

In this paper, we have presented a method for applying multiple transfer functions for visualizing gray-level images with a large dynamic range. This is possible since different transfer functions are often only relevant to disjoint anatomical regions, when radiologists review medical image volumes. To apply multiple transfer functions we have used a model, registered to the data set to be visualized, to control the local transfer function applied in each voxel.

The results presented, clearly indicate the usefulness of the proposed method, both in terms of its use of multiple transfer functions and its use of a registered model to control the applied transfer functions, in order to make the review process more efficient.

Two important features of the proposed method are that it does not introduce any new and unfamiliar parameters for the radiologists to work with and that, even though multiple transfer functions are applied simultaneously, voxels belonging to the same anatomical region are mapped with a single linear transfer function. The fact that these features are important and relevant to a radiologist was confirmed in the results from the evaluation in Sec. 5.1. This separates our method from the methods described in Sec. 1, where either both or one of these features are missing. For instance the histogram-based methods introduce an unfamiliar parameter set to work with and a non-linear mapping of the voxel values. The non-linear mapping of the voxel values is also introduced by the methods that attempts to visualize more by adapting the transfer functions.

However, there are a few aspects of the proposed method which can be commented upon. First, the method presented is dependent upon a successful registration of the model with the medical image volume to be visualized and especially that the deformation field, estimated by the registration process, is smooth. Thus, it is important to use registration methods that are diffeomorphic and that allows incorporation of prior knowledge to control the deformation field in order to improve the registration result, something which can be done using the

Morphon, [3,5]. Second, the reason for registering the model and not the actual patient data, upon which the model is based, is to avoid the risk of allowing details in the image volume to control the registration. Because of this, it was also natural to use the Morphon algorithm for the registration process, since, unlike other methods, it is phase-based and not intensity-based.

As previously described, we used a continuous probability of the different compartments in the model, in order to achieve a smooth transition region between different transfer functions, see Fig. 6, which would not introduce visually disturbing features to the radiologist whilst reviewing images. However, the results from the evaluation show, that there appears to exist a difference in opinion regarding how to handle the transitions regions. An individual accommodation to this, could easily be obtained by using the suggestion in Sec. 2.4, i.e. providing the user with functionality for smoothing the boundaries between the different compartments. Despite the use of a continuous model and various other attempts, new features were introduced in the transition regions, something which was difficult to completely avoid. However, this can be avoided if the voxel-specific transfer functions combined together form a global monotonically increasing transfer function. Since this would limit the contrast for each applied transfer function, it was not deemed relevant.

One of the key features of the proposed method is the use of local transfer functions, which has not been previously utilized in visualization of gray-level images. However, the notion of local or spatially dependent transfer functions is not entirely new. For instance, both [9,10] make use of spatially dependent transfer functions for direct volume rendering. A major difference, however, is that they use local histograms to control the local transfer functions instead of using a model which is registered to the volume to be visualized.

Future work includes creating more complex anatomical models and to evaluate examinations that include blood vessels with contrast, hip implants, trauma cases and brain scans. Furthermore, the proposed method needs to be evaluated in a user study involving a larger number of radiologists. Another future development would be to extend the method to incorporate transfer functions used in direct volume rendering.

References

1. Castillo, R., Castillo, E., Guerra, R., Johnson, V.E., McPhail, T., Garg, A.K., Guerrero, T.: A framework for evaluation of deformable image registration spatial accuracy using large landmark point sets. Physics in Medicine and Biology 54(7), 1849–1870 (2009)
2. Choi, R.J., F.L.R.: Multi-grayscale overlay window. US Patent Application Appl. No.: 12/175,308 (January 2010)
3. Forsberg, D., Andersson, M., Knutsson, H.: Adaptive anisotropic regularization of deformation fields for non-rigid registration using the morphon framework. In: ICASSP, Dallas, USA (March 2010)
4. Hidajat, N., Schroeder, R.J., Cordes, M., Felix, R.: Simultaneous presentation of soft tissue and bone tissue in computed tomography with combined window. Computers in Biology and Medicine 37(11), 1629–1636 (2007)

5. Janssens, G., Jacques, L., de Xivry, J.O., Geets, X., Macq, B.: Diffeomorphic registration of images with variable contrast enhancement. International Journal of Biomedical Imaging (2010)
6. Jin, Y., Fayad, L.M., Laine, A.F.: Contrast enhancement by multiscale adaptive histogram equalization. Presented at the Society of Photo-Optical Instrumentation Engineers (SPIE) Conference.SPIE, vol. 4478, pp. 206–213 (December 2001)
7. John, A., Huda, W., Scalzetti, E.M., Ogden, K.M., Roskopf, M.L.: Performance of a single lookup table (LUT) for displaying chest CT images. Academic Radiology 11(6), 609–616 (2004)
8. Knutsson, H., Andersson, M.: Morphons: Paint on priors and elastic canvas for segmentation and registration, Joensuu (June 2005)
9. Lindholm, S., Ljung, P., Lundström, C., Persson, A., Ynnerman, A.: Spatial conditioning of transfer functions using local material distributions. IEEE Transactions on Visualization and Computer Graphics 16(6), 1301–1310 (2010)
10. Lundström, C., Ljung, P., Ynnerman, A.: Local histograms for design of transfer functions in direct volume rendering. IEEE Transactions on Visualization and Computer Graphics 12(6), 1570–1579 (2006)
11. Pizer, S.M.: Intensity mappings to linearize display devices. Computer Graphics and Image Processing 17(3), 262–268 (1981)
12. Pizer, S.M., Amburn, E.P., Austin, J.D., Cromartie, R., Geselowitz, A., Greer, T., Romeny, B.T.H., Zimmerman, J.B.: Adaptive histogram equalization and its variations. Comput. Vision Graph. Image Process 39, 355–368 (1987)
13. Zuiderveld, K.: Contrast limited adaptive histogram equalization, pp. 474–485. Academic Press Professional, London (1994)

Anatomical Landmark Tracking for the Analysis of Animal Locomotion in X-ray Videos Using Active Appearance Models

Daniel Haase and Joachim Denzler

Friedrich Schiller University of Jena, Chair for Computer Vision
Ernst-Abbe-Platz 2, 07743 Jena, Germany
{daniel.haase,joachim.denzler}@uni-jena.de
http://www.inf-cv.uni-jena.de/

Abstract. X-ray videography is one of the most important techniques for the locomotion analysis of animals in biology, motion science and robotics. Unfortunately, the evaluation of vast amounts of acquired data is a tedious and time-consuming task. Until today, the anatomical landmarks of interest have to be located manually in hundreds of images for each image sequence. Therefore, an automatization of this task is highly desirable. The main difficulties for the automated tracking of these landmarks are the numerous occlusions due to the movement of the animal and the low contrast in the x-ray images. For this reason, standard tracking approaches fail in this setting. To overcome this limitation, we analyze the application of *Active Appearance Models* for this task. Based on real data, we show that these models are capable of effectively dealing with occurring occlusions and low contrast and can provide sound tracking results.

Keywords: Active Appearance Models, X-ray Videography, Landmark Tracking, Locomotion Analysis.

1 Introduction

An important field of ongoing research in biology, motion science and robotics is concerned with the analysis of how the morphology of animals constrains their locomotion. Discovering the underlying relations means not only obtaining a better understanding of common principles of locomotion, but also learning about the adaptivity of the locomotor system to certain circumstances or gaining a more precise knowledge of evolution [8]. It also provides deep insight into the mechanical properties and self-stabilization techniques of animals, which is, for instance, of great interest for the construction of walking robots.

To enable reliable conclusions regarding these open questions, extensive studies have to be carried out on many specimens across different species. These studies are focused on analyzing the movement of the locomotor system. For the case of bipedal terrestrial locomotion, the parts of interest are mainly the

A. Heyden and F. Kahl (Eds.): SCIA 2011, LNCS 6688, pp. 604–615, 2011.

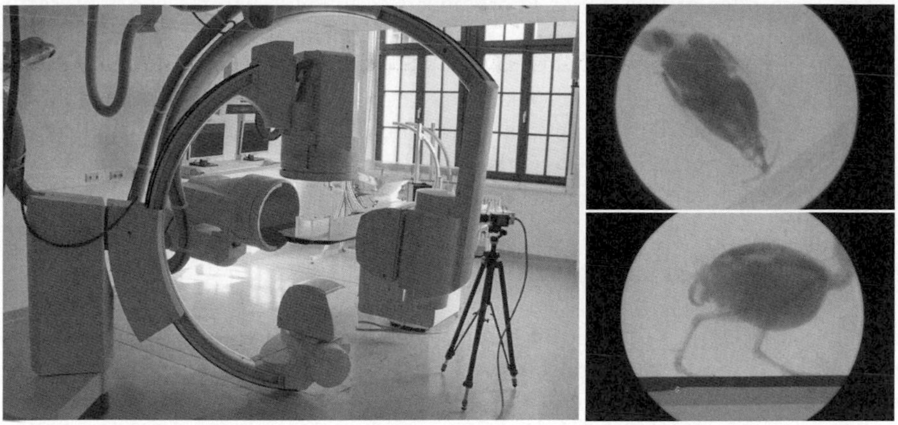

(a) Acquisition System (b) Example Images

Fig. 1. (a) Biplanar high-speed x-ray acquisition system (Neurostar®, Siemens AG). (b) Two example images of a quail (*Coturnix coturnix*) for the dorsoventral (*top row*) and lateral (*bottom row*) camera view acquired with this system.

pelvis, the *femur* and joints like the hip and knee joints [8]. X-ray videography has gained large popularity for this sort of locomotion analysis over the past decades, as it allows for a relatively unobstructed observation compared to external marker based videography [4,8]. A typical state-of-the-art x-ray acquisition system is shown in Fig. 1a. Two C-arms allow biplanar recordings at 1000 Hz with a resolution of 1536 × 1024 pixels. For locomotion analysis, a treadmill is placed on the table to enable recordings of walking animals. Two example images of the dorsoventral (top row) and lateral (bottom row) view obtained with this system are given in Fig. 1b. The images show the locomotion of a quail (*Coturnix coturnix*).

The evaluation of the recorded data is based on anatomical landmarks which have to be located in each image of the sequence. The amount of landmarks differs from sequence to sequence, but common values range from ten to thirty per image. To this day, the labeling task mainly has to be carried out by the human expert, because common tracking algorithms fail due to the overlaps and the low contrast present in the x-ray projections (see Fig. 1b). To speed up the tedious task of manual labeling and to enable the evaluation of large amounts of data, an automatic tracking approach for anatomical landmarks is necessary. The goal of this work is to develop a method which can deal with the problem of overlapping body parts and low contrast x-ray images, and which allows to substantially reduce the human effort spent on manual landmark labeling. In the following we propose the application of Active Appearance Models [5,7,6]. The primary reason for the choice of Active Appearance Models is that relationships between landmarks and gray values are modeled in the context of the entire image (*i.e.* globally) and not just locally, which is a promising way of dealing with the problems stated above.

The remainder of this paper is organized as follows. After a short literature review and a motivation for the use of Active Appearance Models in Sect. 2, we will give a brief introduction to these models in Sect. 3. In Sect. 4 we will discuss general aspects and specific properties of Active Appearance Models applied to the scenario of anatomical landmark tracking. The results of our experiments are presented in Sect. 5. At the end we will summarize our findings and discuss future work.

2 Related Work and Motivation

Tracking is an important field of computer vision and a subject of research for many years. It can be distinguished between data-driven and model-based tracking approaches. For the former, prominent representatives are optical-flow-based tracking [10], the "KLT tracker" [1], region-based tracking [9,11] or trackers based on SIFT descriptors [14]. All these approaches use local image features and allow for a tracking solely based on the given data. The local treatment is the main weakness for the present case, as occlusions in the x-ray images can often only be resolved by using global context information.

Model-based approaches, on the contrary, try to explain the given data by using an underlying model. In the field of medical x-ray analysis, for instance, target regions are tracked by registering a 2D image sequence to a previously recorded 3D computer tomography dataset [15]. In the biological context, this approach is also known as *X-ray Reconstruction of Moving Morphology* (XROMM) [2,3]. However, this approach is very demanding and complex in our scenario, as not only a full-body computer tomography scan, but also a skeletal model for each specimen need to be provided for each tracking task.

For our application, Active Appearance Models [5,7,6] combine the advantages of both tracking principles. On the one hand, training is based on the image sequence and given landmarks, and no explicit model information is necessary in advance. Instead, a combined model of shape and texture is learnt automatically based on the training data. This model describes landmarks and gray values within a combined global framework. Active Appearance Models have been applied to numerous tasks, the most prominent being face modelling and tracking [7,19] and medical applications (*e.g.* [16]). A non-exhaustive overview of example applications is given by Stegmann [17]. Important extensions of Active Appearance Models for our application are for instance presented by Walker *et al.* [19], who make use of the sequential nature of their data or by Lelieveldt *et al.* [12], who extend Active Appearance Models to multiple camera views.

3 Active Appearance Models

Active Appearance Models [5,7,6] are generative statistical models which jointly describe the shape (represented by landmarks) and the appearance (represented by gray values) of non-rigid objects pictured in digital images. The application of such models generally involves two steps, namely the training and the fitting step. For training, annotated images showing an instance of the object to be modeled are needed. The annotations only consist of landmarks, *i.e.* 2D points which define the shape of the object instance in the according image. In our case, these landmarks consist of parts of the locomotor system (*e.g.* joints) and the torso. Once trained, an Active Appearance Model can be fit to new images in an easy and quick manner. The following two subsections give a brief overview of the basics of Active Appearance Models.

3.1 Training Step

Given the N training images $\boldsymbol{I}_n \in \mathbb{R}^{Y \times X}$, $1 \leq n \leq N$ and their corresponding M landmarks $\boldsymbol{l}_n = (x_{n,1}, \ldots, x_{n,M}, y_{n,1}, \ldots, y_{n,M})^{\mathrm{T}} \in \mathbb{R}^{2M}$, Active Appearance Models are trained in three sub-steps: the creation of a statistical shape model, a texture model and a combined model. The next passage will give a short overview of these three steps.

Shape Model. At first, the combined variation of the landmarks over the training set is analyzed. The goal is to reveal how the position of each landmark correlates with the positions of the other landmarks in order to obtain a specific description of the object's shape. After removing the effects of rotation, scaling and shifting, principal component analysis (PCA) is applied on the centered and aligned landmarks. The result of the PCA is the matrix $\boldsymbol{P}_{\mathrm{L}}$ of shape eigenvectors, which can be used to represent each shape $\boldsymbol{l}'$ via

$$\boldsymbol{l}' = \boldsymbol{l}_0 + \boldsymbol{P}_{\mathrm{L}} \boldsymbol{b}_{\mathrm{L}}, \tag{1}$$

where $\boldsymbol{l}_0$ is referred to as the *mean shape*. The elements of the vector $\boldsymbol{b}_{\mathrm{L}} = \boldsymbol{P}_{\mathrm{L}}^{\mathrm{T}}(\boldsymbol{l}' - \boldsymbol{l}_0)$ are the *shape parameters* of $\boldsymbol{l}'$.

Texture Model. The second step is to build a statistical model of the image gray values given in the training data. The approach is very similar to the previous step. The gray values of every training image $\boldsymbol{I}_n$ are warped into a common reference shape. The remaining actions for the texture model follow those from the shape model. Again, PCA is applied and each texture vector $\boldsymbol{g}'$ in the given reference shape can be represented via

$$\boldsymbol{g}' = \boldsymbol{g}_0 + \boldsymbol{P}_{\mathrm{G}} \boldsymbol{b}_{\mathrm{G}}, \tag{2}$$

where $\boldsymbol{g}_0$ is the *mean texture*, $\boldsymbol{P}_{\mathrm{G}}$ are the texture eigenvectors and $\boldsymbol{b}_{\mathrm{G}} = \boldsymbol{P}_{\mathrm{G}}^{\mathrm{T}}(\boldsymbol{g}' - \boldsymbol{g}_0)$ are the *texture parameters* of $\boldsymbol{g}'$.

Combined Model. To model the dependencies between shape and texture, an additional PCA is applied on the vectors $\boldsymbol{c}_n = (w\boldsymbol{b}_{\mathrm{L,n}}^{\mathrm{T}}, \boldsymbol{b}_{\mathrm{G,n}}^{\mathrm{T}})^{\mathrm{T}}$, where $\boldsymbol{b}_{\mathrm{L,n}}$ and $\boldsymbol{b}_{\mathrm{G,n}}$ are the shape and texture parameters for the nth training example and $w \in \mathbb{R}$ is a scaling factor (to account for the different units of shape and texture). In the end, each object instance with the concatenated parameters $\boldsymbol{c}'$ can be represented by

$$\boldsymbol{c}' = \boldsymbol{P}_{\mathrm{C}} \boldsymbol{b}_{\mathrm{C}}. \tag{3}$$

Here, $\boldsymbol{b}_{\mathrm{C}}$ are the *combined parameters* or *appearance parameters* and the matrix $\boldsymbol{P}_{\mathrm{C}}$ are the combined eigenvectors. If this matrix is restricted on the first eigenvectors which explain a certain amount of model variance, a vast dimension reduction can be achieved. This typically leads to statistical combined models which are capable of explaining the appearance of an object with a very compact set of appearance parameters.

3.2 Model Fitting

Model fitting describes the process of finding suitable appearance parameters for a given model such that the model instance fits a previously unseen image. As every Active Appearance Model describes one specific object, it can be assumed that all fitting tasks are similar. Therefore, we do not need to carry out a separate time-consuming optimization each time we see a new image, but instead can learn the solution for these similar tasks in an offline step. This is achieved by using multivariate regression where parameter changes are predicted based on the texture difference between the model and the real image. The necessary training data is obtained by systematically displacing known model instances from the training set. Once learnt, this relationship is used to iteratively fit a model instance to a given image in a quick and easy way.

4 Application to X-ray Locomotion Landmark Tracking

The general application of Active Appearance Models for tracking tasks in video sequences is straightforward and has been widely discussed in the literature, however mainly under the aspect of face tracking [7,19]. For the application to high-speed x-ray locomotion sequences, there are two important differences compared to the case of usual tracking. First of all does the training data not consist of miscellaneous instances of the object to be modeled (*e.g.* a face database for face tracking), but rather of images taken from the sequence to be tracked itself. The reason for this approach is that often only one sequence per species is available or that available sequences differ considerably, either in their visual appearance or in the labeled landmarks.

The second specific characteristic compared to usual Active Appearance Model tracking is the property which is characterized by the shape model. Instead of the variation of landmarks between static instances of an object, the shape model describes the *dynamic* variation of landmarks during the locomotion of one specific specimen. Therefore, the shape model becomes actually a very basic locomotion model. An example for this effect can be seen in Fig. 2. It shows the first two eigenmodes of the statistical shape model for the trunk and *femora* (thighs) landmarks of a quail trained on the lateral view of the dataset shown in Fig. 1b. The first eigenmode explains 85% of the total shape variation, and it can be

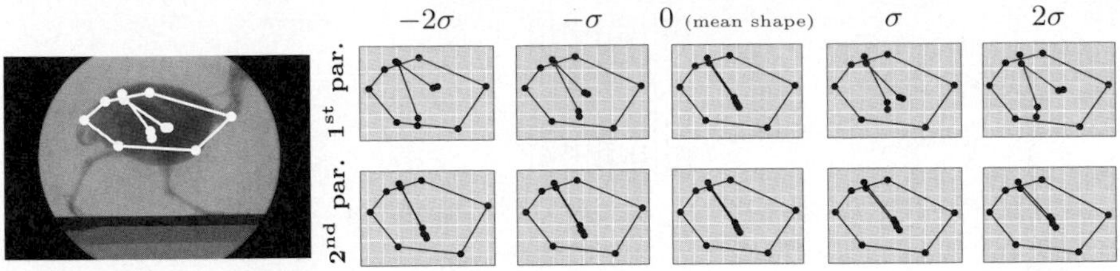

(a) Real Landmarks (b) Shape Variance of the Active Appearance Model

Fig. 2. Shape variance of the trunk and *femora* landmarks for the lateral view of the dataset shown in Fig 1b. The first and second shape parameters explain 85% and 11% of the total variance of the landmarks, respectively. Due to the specific application, the statistical shape model actually characterizes a very basic locomotion model.

seen that it mainly expresses the forward and backward *femora* movement during the locomotion. Therefore, the first eigenmode of the shape model roughly corresponds to the angle which is spanned between the two projections of the *femora*. The second eigenmode shows a large movement of the rightmost landmark relative to the rest of the trunk. As this particular landmark corresponds to the quail's 5th *vertebra*, the second eigenmode models the typical cervical movement of a quail while walking.

5 Experiments and Results

The experiments presented in the following were performed on the quail dataset as shown in Fig. 1b. The sequence has a total length of 2.245 s (2245 images) and covers $5^1/_2$ walking periods (about 11 strides) at a resolution of 1536×1024 pixels. Because the labeling for all sequences was done by human experts so far, plenty of groundtruth data is available. For this data set, the groundtruth data consists of 10 and 12 anatomical landmarks for the dorsoventral and the lateral view in 68 and 81 images of the sequence, respectively. Approximately every 20th image was labeled. The landmarks of interest cover the 5th *vertebra* (neck), the *pelvis*, the *acetabula* (hip joints), the *pygostyle* (pearson's nose), the *caudal carina* (rear breastbone), the *furcula* (wishbone) and the knee joints. The most part of the tracking relevant occlusions occur in the region of the knee joints.

In our experiments, we wish to investigate the following issues:

(1) Are Active Appearance Models suitable for this kind of tracking task?
(2) Does the global modeling lead to better results compared to local methods?
(3) How do image size and preprocessing influence the tracking quality?
(4) Which and how many images of a sequence are best suited for training?

Based on the *point to point error* [17], which is the Euclidian distance between tracking result and groundtruth landmark position, we examine general suitability, the *generalization ability* and the *model accurateness* for various scenarios.

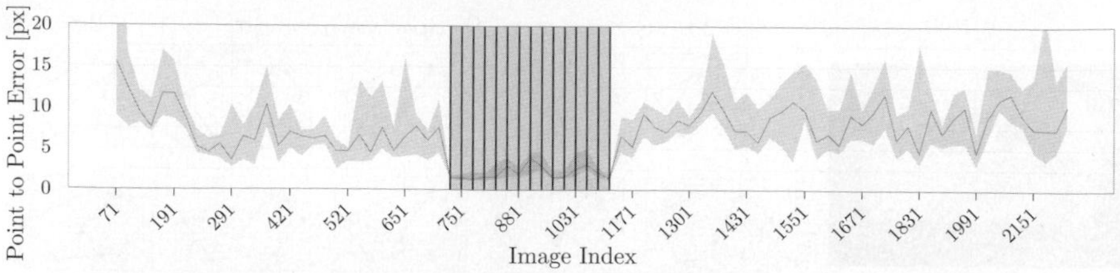

(a) Point to Point Errors

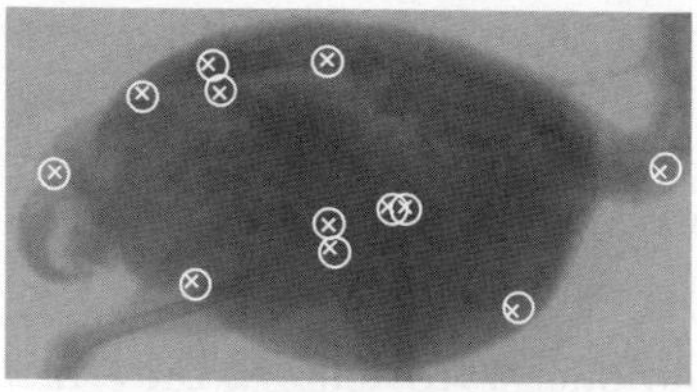

(b) Result for Image 261

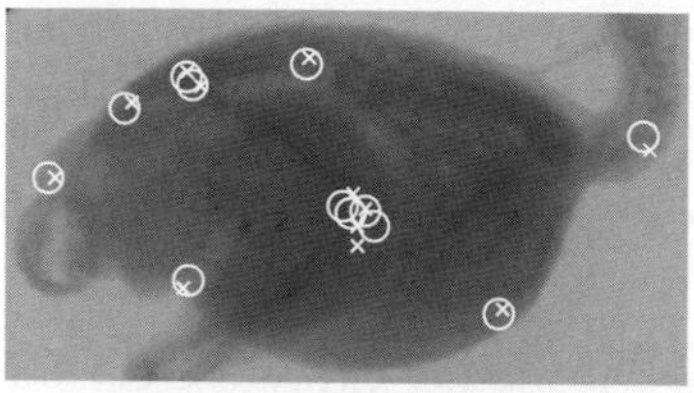

(c) Result for Image 1361

Fig. 3. (a) Point to point errors of the tracked landmarks of the lateral view using a basic Active Appearance Model compared to the groundtruth landmark positions. For each image index, the median error as well as the first and third quartiles of the landmark errors are shown. The training images are selected from equally spaced frames (indicated by vertical lines) of the walking period marked with a shaded background. Subfig. (b) and (c) show the tracking results for the images 261 and 1361 in detail, where crosses and circles denote tracked and groundtruth landmarks.

5.1 General Suitability

Proof-of-Concept. As a general proof-of-concept for the application of Active Appearance Models to this kind of tracking task, we trained a basic model on the given dataset. As training set we chose 15 images evenly spread over one walking period in the middle of the sequence. After a coarse initialization of the landmark positions for the first image of the sequence, the landmarks were tracked solely based on the trained model and without any further user interaction. To ensure temporal consistency, we used the result of frame t as initial solution for frame $t+1$. Fig. 3a shows the point to point errors of the tracked landmarks for each image having groundtruth data available. For each image index, the median error and the first and third quartiles of the landmark errors are shown as a measure of accuracy and precision, respectively. The images used for training are indicated by vertical lines and the according walking period is marked with a gray background.

First of all, the difference between the results on the training and non-training images is clearly visible. Both accuracy and precision are about two to four times larger in the previously unseen images compared to the training images. However, median errors of ten pixels for the non-training images are a promising result, taking the image resolution of 1536×1024 pixels into account. To support this claim, Fig. 3b and 3c show the detailed tracking result for the images

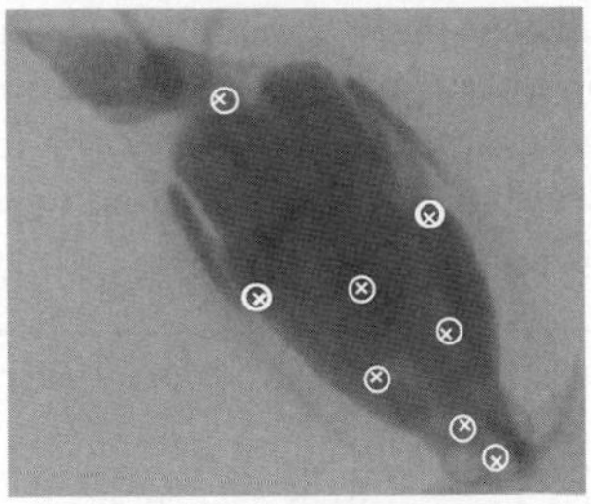

(a) Result for Image 1231

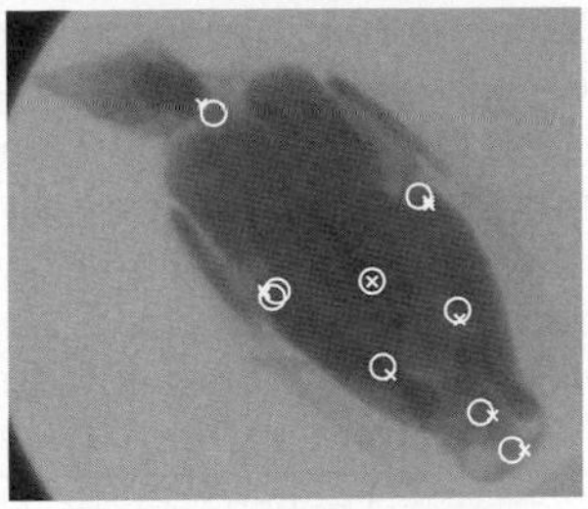

(b) Result for Image 161

Fig. 4. Tracking results for the images (a) 1231 and (b) 161 of the dorsoventral camera view. Image 1231 has one of the best and image 161 has one of the worst tracking results on the non-training images of the sequence.

261 and 1361, where crosses and circles denote tracked and groundtruth landmarks, respectively. From Fig. 3a it can be seen that image 261 has one of the best tracking results amongst the non-training images. This observation can be verified by Fig. 3b. Image 1361, on the contrary, has one of the worst performances of the tracked sequence according to the point to point error. This result is also visible in Fig. 3c, where especially the knee joint landmarks are imprecise. One reason for the different tracking qualities of these two images is probably the amount of relevant occlusions (*i.e.* occlusions of the *femora*, hip joints and knee joints), which differs substantially in the two images.

Nevertheless, above results show that Active Appearance Models are capable of dealing with the difficulties of the given data. Despite the considerable occlusions, no landmark is completely lost. In contrast to the human expert, no temporal model or anatomical knowledge was exploited. However, the tracking accuracy is promising for real applications, and it has to be considered that even the hand-labeled groundtruth landmarks may deviate from their true anatomical positions by several pixels.

For the dorsoventral view, the results are closely related to those from the lateral view. For a similar training set, the point to point error curve is akin to the one of the lateral view as shown in Fig 3a. In Fig. 4a and 4b, examples for one of the best and worst tracking results of the dorsoventral sequence are shown in detail. Again, both results demonstrate that Active Appearance Models can handle the existent difficulties of the data very well.

Comparison to Local Approaches. In contrast to global approaches like the Active Appearance Models, local tracking methods are likely to fail in this setting. To verify this claim, we tested the Horn-Schunck optical flow tracking method [10] on the same dataset. As expected, the results show that indeed this method is adequate to track landmarks which are not subject to occlusions, like the 5th *vertebra*, the *pelvis* or the *pygostyle*. The other landmarks, however, were irretrievably lost as soon as occlusions occurred in the x-ray projections due to the locomotion of the quail. This result underlines another advantage of

Table 1. Computational considerations for identical models trained on various image scales of the quail dataset. Training was performed on 15 images taken from one walking period. The tracking was performed on the entire sequence of 2245 images. The landmark errors were calculated on the non-training images of the sequence only. All error values refer to the original image size of 1536 × 1024 pixels.

Image Size	**Texture Size**	**Computing Time**		**Error Quartiles**		
		Training	*Tracking*	1st	2nd	3rd
100.0%	146,055 px	95.4 min	362.4 min	3.43 px	6.45 px	10.73 px
50.0%	36,432 px	29.2 min	82.7 min	3.39 px	6.45 px	10.93 px
25.0%	9,068 px	6.2 min	19.8 min	3.52 px	6.81 px	10.96 px
12.5%	2,257 px	1.7 min	4.6 min	4.09 px	7.33 px	12.16 px

Active Appearance Models for this tracking task, which can usually recover after suboptimal model fits in the image sequence.

5.2 Impact of Image Resolution and Preprocessing

Image Resolution. For 15 training images, the learning and tracking step of an Active Appearance Model took about 7.63 h on a modern desktop PC (Intel® Core™ i5 CPU 760 @ 2.80 GHz). We therefore examined the performances of Active Appearance Models for several resolutions of the input data in order to find out whether full resolution images are necessary. The experiments were made for image scales of 100% (1536 × 1024), 50% (768 × 512), 25% (384 × 256) and 12.5% (192 × 128). The results of these experiments are listed in Tab. 1. It can be seen, that despite the enormous differences in the training and tracking time, the results for image scales of 100%, 50% and 25% do not deviate substantially. For a scale of 12.5%, however, the loss of quality due to the resolution reduction becomes apparent.

Preprocessing. Another important aspect we analyzed was how sensitive Active Appearance Models react on different methods of preprocessing of the input data. We compared the performance of Active Appearance Models applied to (1) the original data with background-subtracted and contrast scaled images, (2) images sharpened based on the Laplacian operator and (3) gradient images. All three methods have their justification, as the first two improve the contrast in the images and reveal faint structures, whereas the latter emphasizes the anatomical structures of interest, such as the *femur*. The results, as listed in Tab. 2, however, show that only the first two methods benefit the tracking performance, while the gradient approach even worsens the result. This result suggests that homogeneous areas in the image (like certain organs) are important for the fitting process. Based on these findings, we used background-subtracted and contrast scaled images for the majority of the conducted experiments.

Table 2. Influence of different preprocessing methods on the tracking performance

Preprocessing	Error Quartiles		
	1st	2nd	3rd
Original (no preprocessing)	3.77 px	7.40 px	11.85 px
Background subtraction & contrast stretching	3.52 px	6.81 px	10.96 px
Laplace-based enhancement	3.45 px	6.44 px	10.99 px
Gradient image (Sobel)	4.03 px	8.59 px	15.77 px

5.3 Selection of Training Images

For real applications, the amount of human effort spent in landmark labeling to create training data is the main limiting factor for data evaluation. Our goal is to achieve the desired tracking quality with as much as necessary, but as little as possible human interaction. Therefore, two very important questions about the given training data arise. The first one is how much training images are actually necessary to achieve the desired tracking quality, and the second question is which images of the given sequence are most suitable as training images. To answer these questions, we trained several Active Appearance Models with varying sizes of the training set and selection schemes. In the first case we started with images entirely taken from one walking period. Then, we successively added new images, one walking period at a time. In the end, the training size ranged from 3 images (1/5 walking period) to 58 images (4 walking periods). In the other case, the same image amounts were used, but the images were selected from equally spaced images of the entire sequence.

We evaluated the experiments in two different ways. In one case we only used the unseen images of the series for testing, which gives the generalization ability of the according models. In the second case, only the errors made on the training set were evaluated, giving an estimation for the model accurateness. The evaluations for both cases are shown in Fig. 5a and 5b. It can be noticed that the results for both selection methods differ substantially. Considering both the generalization ability and the model accurateness, the period-based method seems to be the better choice for few training examples, whereas the equally spaced selection gives better results for many training images. In both cases, the turning point is located around 15 images, which is the maximum amount of images taken from one period. That is, as long as images from one period are to be used for training, the period-based method is to be preferred. As soon as images from more than one walking period should be used, the equally spaced selection is more advantageous. The reason for this result is quite clear: few equally spaced images will generally not cover all parts of a walking period, which is a disadvantage compared to period-based selection. For many images, equally spaced methods will perform better because they cover all walking periods of the sequence in contrast to the period-based selection.

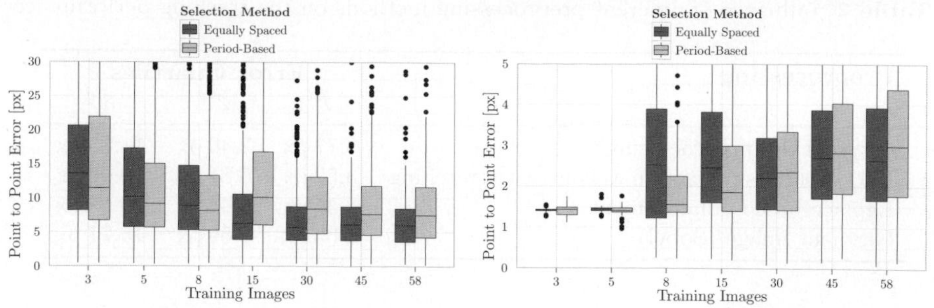

(a) Errors on Non-Training Images (b) Errors on Training Images

Fig. 5. Tracking errors on (a) non-training images (generalization ability) and (b) on training images (model accurateness) for varying sizes and selection schemes of the training set. For few training examples, the period-based selection appears to be more advantageous.

6 Conclusions and Further Work

We analyzed the application of Active Appearance Models for anatomical landmark tracking in x-ray videos of animal locomotion. As landmarks and gray values are modeled in a global manner, these models are well suited to deal with occlusions and low contrast in images. We showed that the Active Appearance Model based approach performed substantially better than local approaches on real data. We also studied the effect of different preprocessing and image selection methods on the performance and generalization ability of the models.

Further work should focus on the combined modelling of both camera views (for instance based on [12]) to improve the performance for frames with high occlusion and thus uncertainty. Additionally, the knowledge that the training data is actually a sequence and not just a set of images should be exploited. For the reduction of user interaction, bootstrapping methods for Active Appearance Models based on [18,13] could be utilized. Another important issue will be to derive a confidence value from the texture error of the Active Appearance Models to automatically detect ill-fitted frames.

Acknowledgements

The authors would like to especially thank John Nyakatura and Alexander Stößel from the Institute of Systematic Zoology and Evolutionary Biology with Phyletic Museum at the Friedrich Schiller University of Jena for the valuable comments and for providing the labeled quail dataset.

This research was supported by grant DE 735/8-1 of the German Research Foundation (DFG).

References

1. Baker, S., Matthews, I.: Lucas-kanade 20 years on: A unifying framework. Int. J. Comput. Vision 56(3), 221–255 (2004)
2. Bey, M.J., Zauel, R., Brock, S.K., Tashman, S.: Validation of a new model-based tracking technique for measuring three-dimensional, in vivo glenohumeral joint kinematics. J. Biomech. Eng. 128, 604–609 (2006)
3. Brainerd, E.L., Gatesy, S.M., Baier, D.B., Hedrick, T.L.: A method for accurate 3D reconstruction of skeletal morphology and movement with CTX imaging. Comp. Biochem. Physiol. 146, 119 (2007)
4. Brainerd, E.L., Baier, D.B., Gatesy, S.M., Hedrick, T.L., Metzger, K.A., Gilbert, S.L., Crisco, J.J.: X-ray reconstruction of moving morphology (XROMM): Precision, accuracy and applications in comparative biomechanics research. J. Exp. Zool. A 313A(5), 262–279 (2010)
5. Cootes, T.F., Edwards, G.J., Taylor, C.J.: Active appearance models. In: Burkhardt, H., Neumann, B. (eds.) ECCV 1998. LNCS, vol. 1407, pp. 484–498. Springer, Heidelberg (1998)
6. Cootes, T.F., Edwards, G.J., Taylor, C.J.: Active appearance models. IEEE T. Pattern Anal. 23(6), 681–685 (2001)
7. Edwards, G.J., Cootes, T.F., Taylor, C.J.: Face recognition using active appearance models. In: Burkhardt, H., Neumann, B. (eds.) ECCV 1998. LNCS, vol. 1407, pp. 581–595. Springer, Heidelberg (1998)
8. Gatesy, S.M.: Guineafowl hind limb function. I: Cineradiographic analysis and speed effects. J. Morphol. 240(2), 1097–4687 (1999)
9. Hager, G.D., Belhumeur, P.N.: Efficient region tracking with parametric models of geometry and illumination. IEEE T. Pattern Anal. 20(10), 1025–1039 (1998)
10. Horn, B.K.P., Schunck, B.G.: Determining optical flow. Artif. Intell. 17(1-3), 185–203 (1981)
11. Jurie, F., Dhome, M.: Hyperplane approximation for template matching. IEEE T. Pattern Anal. 24(7), 996–1000 (2002)
12. Lelieveldt, B., Üzümcü, M., van der Geest, R., Reiber, J., Sonka, M.: Multi-view active appearance models for consistent segmentation of multiple standard views. International Congress Series 1256, 1141–1146 (2003)
13. Liu, X.: Video-based face model fitting using adaptive active appearance model. Image Vision Comput. 28(7), 1162–1172 (2010)
14. Lowe, D.G.: Distinctive image features from scale-invariant keypoints. Int. J. Comput. Vision 60(2), 91–110 (2004)
15. Rohlfing, T., Denzler, J., Gräßl, C., Russakoff, D.B., Maurer Jr, C.R.: Markerless real-time 3-d target region tracking by motion backprojection from projection images. IEEE T. Med. Imaging 24(11), 1455–1468 (2005)
16. Roussos, A., Katsamanis, A., Maragos, P.: Tongue tracking in ultrasound images with active appearance models. In: Proceedings of the IEEE International Conference on Image Processing, pp. 1733–1736 (2009)
17. Stegmann, M.B.: Active Appearance Models: Theory, Extensions and Cases. Master's thesis, Informatics and Mathematical Modelling, Technical University of Denmark, DTU, Richard Petersens Plads, Building 321, DK-2800 Kgs. Lyngby (2000)
18. Sung, J., Kim, D.: Adaptive active appearance model with incremental learning. Pattern Recogn. Lett. 30(4), 359–367 (2009)
19. Walker, K.N., Cootes, T.F., Taylor, C.J.: Automatically building appearance models from images sequences using salient features. In: Proceedings of the British Machine Vision Conference, British Machine Vision Association (1999)

Image Foresting Transform: On-the-Fly Computation of Segmentation Boundaries

Filip Malmberg

Centre for Image Analysis,
Uppsala University, Sweden
filip.malmberg@cb.uu.se
http://www.cb.uu.se

Abstract. The Image Foresting Transform (IFT) is a framework for seeded image segmentation, based on the computation of minimal cost paths in a discrete representation of an image. In two recent publications, we have shown that the segmentations obtained by the IFT may be improved by refining the segmentation locally around the boundaries between segmented regions. Since these methods operate on a small subset of the image elements only, they may be implemented efficiently if the set of boundary elements is known. Here, we show that this set may be obtained on-the-fly, at virtually no additional cost, as a by-product of the IFT algorithm.

Keywords: Interactive Image Segmentation, Image Foresting Transform.

1 Introduction

Image segmentation, the process of identifying and separating relevant objects and structures in an image, is a fundamental problem in image analysis. Accurate segmentation of objects of interest is often required before further processing and analysis can be performed. Despite years of active research, fully automatic segmentation of arbitrary images remains an unsolved problem.

Seeded segmentation methods attempt to solve the segmentation problem in the presence of prior knowledge in the form of a partial segmentation. Given an image where a small subset of the image elements (called *seed-points*) have been assigned correct segmentation labels (e.g., object or background), an automatic algorithm completes the labeling for all image elements. The seed-points may be provided either by some automatic pre-processing algorithm, or by a human user in an interactive setting. Many different algorithms for seeded segmentation have been proposed ranging from classical seeded region growing [1,11], through to the more recent minimal graph cuts [3], random walks [7], and image foresting transform (IFT) [6] approaches. Here, we focus on the IFT approach.

In the IFT, the image is represented by an edge-weighted graph. Each image element corresponds to a node in the graph, and adjacent image elements are connected by graph edges. Segmentation is performed by assigning to each node

A. Heyden and F. Kahl (Eds.): SCIA 2011, LNCS 6688, pp. 616–624, 2011.

the label of the closest seed-point, as determined by the *minimum cost path* from the node to the set of seed-points.

The IFT can be computed using Dijkstra's algorithm [4], slightly modified to allow multiple seed-points [6]. An efficient implementation of Dijkstra's algorithm, and so of the IFT, requires $\mathcal{O}(|\mathcal{I}|)$ operations, where $|\mathcal{I}|$ is the number of image elements, for a sparse graph with bounded integer path costs.

In interactive segmentation applications, a user often adds or removes seed-points to refine an existing segmentation. In [5], it was shown that seed-points can be added to, or removed from, an existing IFT solution, without recomputing the entire solution. This modified algorithm, called the differential IFT (DIFT), gives a significant reduction of the total time required for interactive segmentation. In a differential implementation, the computation time required for each editing operation is proportional to the number of image elements that are modified by the operation. This number is usually much smaller than $|\mathcal{I}|$. For typical segmentation scenarios, the DIFT reduces the computation time required for editing operations by a factor between 10 and 20, compared to the IFT [5]. The DIFT is described in detail in Section 3.

In two recent publications [9,10], we show that the segmentations obtained by the IFT may be improved by performing local operations around the boundaries of the segmented regions. These methods are reviewed, and examples of their application are given, in Section 4.

The boundary of a segmentation is here defined as the set of image elements adjacent to at least one element with a different label. This set is usually much smaller than the set of image elements. Since the methods proposed in [9] and [10] operate only in a small region around the boundary, they may be computed efficiently if the set of boundary elements is known.

For any given image element, it is easy to check if the element is part of the segmentation boundary by comparing the label of the element to the labels of its neighbors. Thus, a trivial algorithm for obtaining the boundary is to iterate over all image elements and check if the element is on the boundary. This however, requires $\mathcal{O}(|\mathcal{I}|)$ operations, and thus the advantage of the differential implementation is lost. Here, we show that the set of boundary elements may be computed on the fly, at virtually no additional cost, as a by-product of the DIFT algorithm[1]. This makes it possible to implement the methods proposed in [9,10] efficiently in conjunction with the DIFT, thereby making them more attractive for interactive segmentation.

2 Background

2.1 Images and Graphs

An *image* $\mathbf{I}$ is a pair $(\mathcal{I}, I)$ consisting of a set $\mathcal{I}$ of image elements and a mapping I that assigns to each image element $p \in \mathcal{I}$ an element in some arbitrary set,

[1] We note that the concept of extracting segmentation boundaries while computing the DIFT was previously investigated by Audigier et al. [2], for the purpose of visualizing the segmentation results.

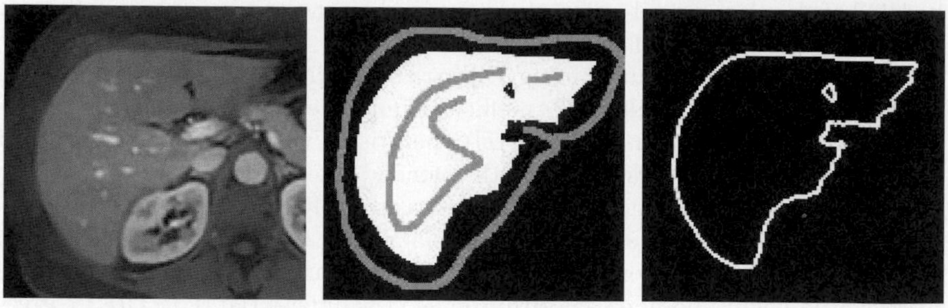

Fig. 1. Segmentation of the liver in a slice from an MR volume image. (Left) Original image. (Middle) Segmentation obtained with the IFT, from user defined seed-points shown in gray. (Right) Boundary of the segmentation, computed on-the-fly as a by-product of the IFT algorithm.

typically a subset of $\mathbb{Z}^n$ or $\mathbb{R}^n$ (e.g., $\mathcal{I} \subset \mathbb{Z}^n$ and $I : \mathcal{I} \rightarrow [0, 255]$). We associate an image with an *adjacency function* $\mathcal{N}$ that maps each image element $p \in \mathcal{I}$ to a set $\mathcal{N}(p) \subseteq \mathcal{I}$ of *adjacent* image elements. We require the adjacency function to be symmetric, so that $p \in \mathcal{N}(q) \iff q \in \mathcal{N}(p)$ for all $p, q \in \mathcal{I}$. An image, together with an adjacency function, may be interpreted as a graph, whose nodes are the image elements and whose edges are all ordered pairs of image elements $p, q \in \mathcal{I}$ such that $q \in \mathcal{N}(p)$.

For each ordered pair of adjacent image elements p and q, we assign a real valued, non-negative, *edge weight* $w(p, q)$. The edge weights represent local *dissimilarity,* i.e., p and q are strongly connected if $w(p, q)$ is close to 0. Typically, edge weights are computed from local image features such as intensity or gradient magnitude.

2.2 Paths and Path Costs

A *path* $\pi = \langle p_1, p_2, \ldots, p_k \rangle$ of length $|\pi| = k - 1$ is a sequence $p_1, p_2, \ldots, p_k$ of image elements such that $p_{i+1} \in \mathcal{N}(p_i)$. We denote the *origin* p_1 and the *destination* p_k of π by $org(\pi)$ and $dst(\pi)$, respectively. If π and τ are paths such that $dst(\pi) = org(\tau)$, we denote by $\pi \cdot \tau$ the concatenation of the two paths.

The *cost* of a path is denoted $f(\pi)$. This cost is typically a function of the edge weights along the path, e.g., the sum of all the edge weights along the path or the maximum edge weight along the path. The maximum possible cost of a path is denoted $+\infty$.

A path π is a *minimum cost path* if $f(\pi) \leq f(\tau)$ for any other path τ with $org(\tau) = org(\pi)$ and $dst(\tau) = dst(\pi)$. In general, a minimum cost path is not unique. The set of minimum cost paths between two image elements p and q is denoted $\pi_{min}(p, q)$.

The definition of a minimum cost path between two sets of image elements is analogous. For two sets $A \subseteq \mathcal{I}$ and $B \subseteq \mathcal{I}$, π is a path between A and B if $org(\pi) \in A$ and $dst(\pi) \in B$. If $f(\pi) \leq f(\tau)$ for any other path τ between A and

B, then π is a minimum cost path between A and B. The set of minimum cost paths between A and B is denoted $\pi_{min}(A, B)$.

2.3 Spanning Forests

A *predecessor map* is a mapping P that assigns to each image element $p \in \mathcal{I}$ either an element $q \in \mathcal{N}(p)$, or $\emptyset$. For any $p \in \mathcal{I}$, a predecessor map P defines a path $P^*(p)$ recursively as

$$P^*(p) = \begin{cases} \langle p \rangle & \text{if } P(p) = \emptyset \\ P^*(P(p)) \cdot \langle P(p), p \rangle & \text{otherwise} \end{cases} .$$

We denote by $P^0(p)$ the first element of $P^*(p)$. A *spanning forest* is a predecessor map that contains no cycles, i.e., $|P^*(p)|$ is finite for all $p \in \mathcal{I}$. If $P^*(p) = \emptyset$, then p is a *root* of P.

2.4 Image Segmentation

A *segmentation* of an image $\mathbf{I}$ is a mapping $\mathcal{L}$ that assigns to each image element $p \in \mathcal{I}$ an element in some arbitrary set of *labels*, e.g., $\mathcal{L} : \mathcal{I} \to \{object, background\}$. The *boundary* $\partial\mathcal{L} \subseteq \mathcal{I}$ of a segmentation is defined as

$$\partial\mathcal{L} = \mathcal{I} \setminus \{p \mid \mathcal{L}(p) = \mathcal{L}(q) \text{ for all } q \in \mathcal{N}(p)\} ,$$

i.e., an image element belongs to the boundary if at least one of its neighbors has a different label.

2.5 The Image Foresting Transform

Given an image $\mathbf{I}$, a path cost function f, an adjacency function $\mathcal{N}$ and a set of seed-points $S \in \mathcal{I}$ with corresponding labels, the IFT computes a spanning forest P such that $P^*(p) \in \pi_{min}(p, S)$ for all image elements $p \in \mathcal{I}$. During this process, a *cost map* C and a segmentation $\mathcal{L}$ are built, such that $C(p) = f(\pi_{min}(p, S))$ and $\mathcal{L}(p) = \mathcal{L}(P^0(p))$. A triple $(P, C, \mathcal{L})$ that satisfies these properties is a *solution* of the IFT with respect to S.

3 The Differential Image Foresting Transform

The DIFT allows seed-points to be added to, or removed from, an existing IFT solution in an efficient way. Given a solution of the IFT with respect to a set of seed-points S, the DIFT algorithm computes a solution with respect to another set of seed-points S'. The difference between S and S' can be written in terms of the following two sets: $S^+ = S' \setminus S$ and $S^- = S \setminus S'$. It holds that $S' = (S \setminus S^-) \cup S^+$, i.e., S' can be obtained from S by adding all elements in S^+ and removing all elements in S^-.

Algorithm 1. DIFT

Input: Image **I**, adjacency function $\mathcal{N}$, path cost function f, solution $\{C, P, \mathcal{L}\}$, set S of old seed-points, and set S' of new seed-points.
Output: C, $\mathcal{L}$, P, and B.
Auxiliary: Three sets of image elements Q, T, and V.

1 Update the labels of all elements in S', according to the user input;
2 **foreach** $p \in S^+$ **do**
3     $C(p) \leftarrow 0$, $P(p) \leftarrow \emptyset$;
4 $(C, P, F) \leftarrow$ `RemoveSeeds`$(C, P, \mathcal{N}, S^-)$;
5 $Q \leftarrow F \cup S^+$, $T \leftarrow \emptyset$, $V \leftarrow \emptyset$;
6 **while** $Q \neq \emptyset$ **do**
7   Remove p from Q such that $C(p)$ is minimum;
8     $B \leftarrow B \setminus \{p\}$, $V \leftarrow V \cup \{p\}$, $T \leftarrow T \setminus \{p\}$;
9   **foreach** $q \in \mathcal{N}(p)$ **do**
10         $cost \leftarrow f(P^*(p) \cdot \langle p, q \rangle)$;
11   **if** $q \notin V$ **then**
12             $T \leftarrow T \cup q$;
13   **if** $q \in V$ *and* $\mathcal{L}(p) \neq \mathcal{L}(q)$ **then**
14             $B \leftarrow B \cup \{p, q\}$;
15   **if** $cost < C(q)$ *or* $P(q) = p$ **then**
16             $Q \leftarrow Q \cup \{q\}$;
17             $P(q) \leftarrow \{p\}$, $\mathcal{L}(q) \leftarrow \mathcal{L}(p)$, and $C(q) \leftarrow cost$;
18 **foreach** $p \in T$ **do**
19     $B \leftarrow B \setminus \{p\}$;
20   **foreach** $q \in \mathcal{N}(p)$ **do**
21   **if** $\mathcal{L}(p) \neq \mathcal{L}(q)$ **then**
22             $B \leftarrow B \cup \{p, q\}$;

The procedure for computing the DIFT is given in Algorithm 1. This algorithm is essentially the same as that presented in [5]. However, in addition to the solution $(C, P, \mathcal{L})$, Algorithm 1 computes a set B (for *boundary*) such that $B = \partial\mathcal{L}$. See Figure 1. To see that B, as computed by Algorithm 1, equals the boundary of $\mathcal{L}$, we observe that if a node is not inserted into Q during Algorithm 1, then the label of that node is not changed. Thus, to compute the correct boundary, we only need to update the nodes that pass through Q during the algorithm, and their neighbors.

Each node is inserted into and removed from Q at most once. Thus, when a node is removed from Q, it has already been given its final label. The set V (for *visited*) is used to keep track of this – each time a node is removed from Q, it is inserted into V. On line 13, it holds that $p \in V$. Thus, if $q \in V$, we can safely compare $\mathcal{L}(p)$ and $\mathcal{L}(q)$ to check if p and q belong to the boundary.

The set T (for *touched*) is used to keep track of elements that are adjacent to at least one element is V, but are not in V themselves. All nodes that remain in

Procedure `RemoveSeeds`

Input: Cost map C, predecessor map P, adjacency function $\mathcal{N}$, and set S^- of seed-points to be removed.
Output: C,P, and set F of frontier image elements.
Auxiliary: FIFO queue U, and set W of visited elements.

```
F ← ∅, W ← ∅;
foreach p ∈ S⁻ do
    Insert p in U;
while U is not empty do
    Remove p from U;
    C(p) ← +∞, P(p) ← ∅;
    W ← W ∪ {p}, F ← F \ {p};
    foreach q ∈ N(p) do
        if q ∉ W then
            F ← F ∪ {q};
        if P(q) = p then
            Insert q in U;
```

T after the termination of the *while*-loop on lines 6-17 also need to be checked for possible inclusion in B, as is done on lines 18-22.

4 Applications

In this section, we review the methods presented in [9] and [10]. Both these methods improve the segmentations obtained by the IFT by performing operations locally around the segmentation boundary. Thus, the methods benefit from the on-the-fly approach presented here.

4.1 Sub-pixel Segmentation with the IFT

The original IFT produces *crisp* segmentations, i.e., each image element is assigned the label of exactly one seed-point. However, due to the finite resolution of digital images, an image element may be partially covered by more than one (continuous) object. By allowing mixed labels, it is possible to obtain segmentations with sub-pixel precision. Numerous studies have confirmed that *pixel coverage segmentation* [14] outperforms crisp segmentation for subsequent measuring of object properties such as length/surface area and area/volume, see, e.g., [13,12].

In [9], we presented a method, called the *sub-pixel IFT*, for approximating pixel coverage segmentation within the IFT framework, by computing mixed labels at the segmentation boundaries. Experiments, reported in [9], indicate that the sub-pixel IFT is less sensitive to small variations in seed-point placement than the crisp IFT. A segmentation result obtained with the sub-pixel IFT is shown in Figure 2.

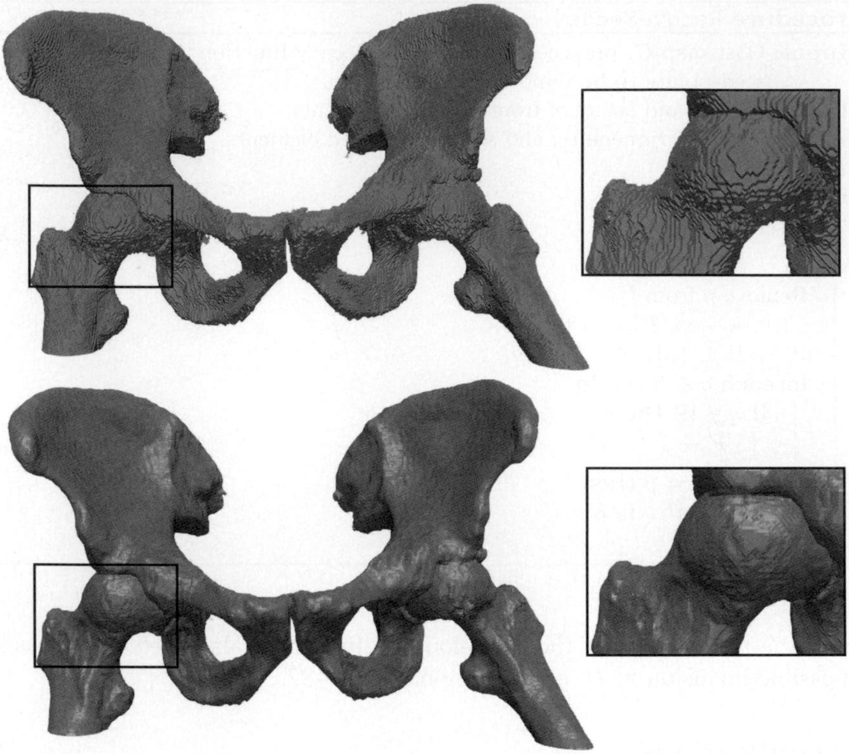

Fig. 2. Hip bones of a human, segmented from a CT volume image. The segmentation was obtained using the IFT, with seed-points selected interactively by a human user. A polygonal surface was extracted from the segmented volume using the Marching Cubes algorithm [8], which takes sub-pixel information into account when available. (Top) Segmentation obtained by the IFT. (Bottom) Segmentation obtained by the sub-pixel IFT proposed in [9].

4.2 The Relaxed IFT

Numerous studies have shown that the IFT, and similar methods based on minimal cost paths, are capable of producing high quality segmentations in a wide range of contexts. However, in images with weak or missing boundaries the IFT tends to produce irregular segmentation boundaries. An explanation for this is that the IFT propagates information from the seed-points only along minimum cost paths. Since two adjacent image elements may receive their information from different seed-points, regularity of the segmentation boundary is not enforced.

In [10], we address this weakness of the IFT by proposing the *relaxed IFT* (RIFT). This modified version of the IFT features an additional parameter that controls the smoothness of the segmentation boundary, thereby making the results more predictable in the presence of noise and weak edges. The method works by applying an iterated relaxation procedure to the segmentation labels, in a narrow band around the segmentation boundary. The effect of the relaxation

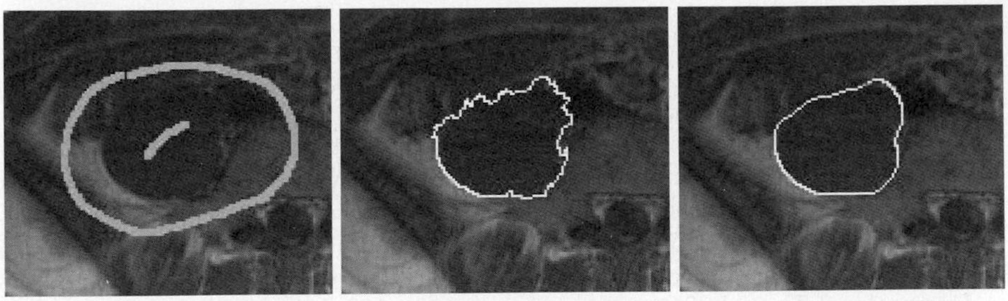

Fig. 3. Segmentation of a muscle in a slice from an MR volume image. (Left) Original image with seed-points representing muscle and background. (Middle) Segmentation result obtained by the IFT. (Right) Segmentation result obtained after 30 iterations of the relaxation procedure proposed in [10].

procedure is illustrated in Figure 3. In [10], the RIFT was used to refine manual segmentations of a thoracolumbar muscle in MR images. The manual segmentations, segmentations obtained with the IFT, and segmentations obtained with the RIFT, were graded by 12 observers. The segmentations obtained by the RIFT were preferred over the segmentations obtained by the IFT without relaxation. Additionally, the segmentations obtained by the RIFT were found to be qualitatively comparable to the manual segmentations, while intra-user variations were reduced by more than 50%.

5 Conclusion

We have shown that the boundary of the segmentations obtained by the IFT may be computed on-the-fly, as a by-product of the DIFT algorithm. This allows the sub-pixel IFT and the RIFT to be implemented efficiently in conjunction with the DIFT.

As mentioned in Section 2.2, the minimum cost path between two image elements may not be unique. Therefore, a strategy is needed for assigning labels in ambiguous cases. In previous literature on the IFT, such a strategy is usually referred to as a *tie-breaking policy* [5]. In Algorithm 1, a *first-in-first-out* (FIFO) policy is assumed. However, extensions to other tie-breaking policies (e.g., the mean tie-breaking policy proposed in [9]) should be straightforward.

Acknowledgments

Ingela Nyström and Ewert Bengtsson at the Centre for Image Analysis, Uppsala University, are acknowledged for scientific support.

References

1. Adams, R., Bischof, L.: Seeded region growing. IEEE Transactions on Pattern Analysis and Machine Intelligence 16(6), 641–647 (1994)
2. Audigier, R., Lotufo, R., Falcão, A.: On integrating iterative segmentation by watershed with tridimensional visualization of MRIs. In: Proceedings of the Computer Graphics and Image Processing, XVII Brazilian Symposium, pp. 130–137. IEEE Computer Society, Los Alamitos (2004)
3. Boykov, Y., Funka-Lea, G.: Graph cuts and efficient N-D image segmentation. International Journal of Computer Vision 70(2), 109–131 (2006)
4. Dijkstra, E.W.: A note on two problems in connexion with graphs. Numerische Mathematik 1, 269–271 (1959)
5. Falcão, A.X., Bergo, F.P.: Interactive volume segmentation with differential image foresting transforms. IEEE Transactions on Medical Imaging 23(9), 1100–1108 (2004)
6. Falcão, A.X., Stolfi, J., Lotufo, R.A.: The image foresting transform: Theory, algorithms, and applications. IEEE Transactions on Pattern Analysis and Machine Intelligence 26(1), 19–29 (2004)
7. Grady, L.: Random walks for image segmentation. IEEE Transactions on Pattern Analysis and Machine Intelligence 28(11), 1768–1783 (2006)
8. Lorensen, W.E.: Marching cubes: A high resolution 3D surface construction algorithm. Computer Graphics 21(4), 163–169 (1987)
9. Malmberg, F., Lindblad, J., Nyström, I.: Sub-pixel segmentation with the image foresting transform. In: Wiederhold, P., Barneva, R.P. (eds.) IWCIA 2009. LNCS, vol. 5852, pp. 201–211. Springer, Heidelberg (2009)
10. Malmberg, F., Nyström, I., Mehnert, A., Engstrom, C., Bengtsson, E.: Relaxed image foresting transforms for interactive volume image segmentation. In: Dawant, B.M., Haynor, D.R. (eds.) Proceedings of SPIE Medical Imaging, vol. 7623. SPIE, San Jose (2010)
11. Mehnert, A.J.H., Jackway, P.T.: An improved seeded region growing algorithm. Pattern Recognition Letters 18, 1065–1071 (1997)
12. Sladoje, N., Lindblad, J.: Estimation of moments of digitized objects with fuzzy borders. In: Roli, F., Vitulano, S. (eds.) ICIAP 2005. LNCS, vol. 3617, pp. 188–195. Springer, Heidelberg (2005)
13. Sladoje, N., Lindblad, J.: High-precision boundary length estimation by utilizing gray-level information. IEEE Transactions on Pattern Analysis and Machine Intelligence 31(2), 357–363 (2009)
14. Sladoje, N., Lindblad, J.: Pixel coverage segmentation for improved feature estimation. In: Foggia, P., Sansone, C., Vento, M. (eds.) ICIAP 2009. LNCS, vol. 5716, pp. 929–938. Springer, Heidelberg (2009)

Scale Space Smoothing, Image Feature Extraction and Bessel Filters

Sasan Mahmoodi and Steve Gunn

School of Electronics and Computer Science, Building 1, Southampton University, Southampton, SO17 1BJ, UK
{sm3,srg}@ecs.soton.ac.uk

Abstract. The Green function of Mumford-Shah functional in the absence of discontinuities is known to be a modified Bessel function of the second kind and zero degree. Such a Bessel function is regularized here and used as a filter for feature extraction. It is demonstrated in this paper that a Bessel filter does not follow the scale space smoothing property of bounded linear filters such as Gaussian filters. The features extracted by the Bessel filter are therefore scale invariant. Edges, blobs, and junctions are features considered here to show that the extracted features remain unchanged by varying the scale of a Bessel filter. The scale invariance property of Bessel filters for edges is analytically proved here. We conjecture that Bessel filters also enjoy this scale invariance property for other kinds of features. The experimental results presented here confirm our conjecture of the scale invariance property of the Bessel filters.

Keywords: Scale Space, Linear Filtering, Bessel Filter, Feature Extraction.

1 Introduction

Scale space theory has been established based on the application of a series of bounded linear filters such as a Gaussian filter on images. In a scale space setting, it is observed that the features extracted from an image may change if the scale of a Gaussian filter varies. This phenomenon is known as scale space smoothing. Such an observation has led to the scale space theory to propose a framework to select the "most important" scale in which a feature should be extracted [1],[2]. Bounded linear filters usually demonstrate scale space smoothing. However, in this paper, we demonstrate that a Bessel filter which is unbounded at the center does not show any property associated with the scale space smoothing when it is used to extract features such as edges, ridges, blobs, and corners. Such an unbounded filter is numerically intractable. We therefore propose a method here to regularize the filter. The rest of the paper is structured as follows. Section 2 introduces the Bessel filter and the theory behind it and a regularization method for implementations is presented in section 3. Section 4 deals with the numerical results. The paper concludes in section 5.

A. Heyden and F. Kahl (Eds.): SCIA 2011, LNCS 6688, pp. 625–634, 2011.

2 Theory

The Green function associated with the Mumford-Shah functional for the whole plane, in the absence of boundaries, is a modified Bessel function of the second kind and zero degree [3]. A closed form of this Green function is written as:

$$h(x, y; v, w)) = K_0\left(\sqrt{\frac{\left|(x-v)^2 + (y-w)^2\right|}{\mu}}\right) \tag{1}$$

where $K_0(.)$ is the modified Bessel function of the second kind and zero degree and $(x, y), (v, w) \in R^2$.

A three dimensional view of Green function (1) for $(u, w) = (0,0)$is shown in figure (1-a). The cross-section of this Green function is also depicted in figure (1-b). As shown in figure (1), Bessel function (1) is singular at the centre which is not numerically tractable for implementation. It is therefore important for numerical purposes to regularize function h.

In this paper, we suggest the following regularized and normalized function named as *Bessel* filter.

$$h_\varepsilon(r) = \begin{cases} \dfrac{K_0(\frac{|r|}{\sqrt{\mu}})}{K_0(\frac{\varepsilon}{2\sqrt{\mu}})} & |r| > \dfrac{\varepsilon}{2} \\ 1 & |r| \le \dfrac{\varepsilon}{2} \end{cases} \tag{2}$$

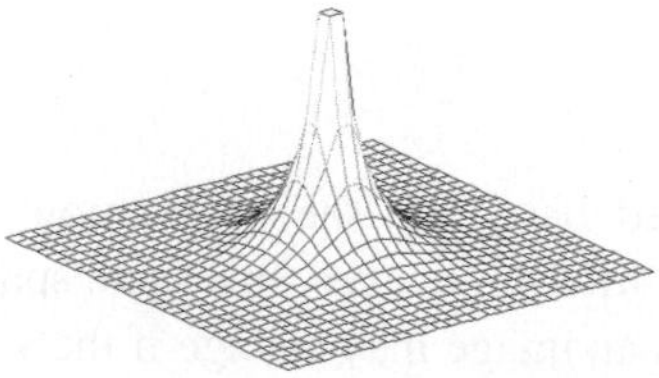

(a)

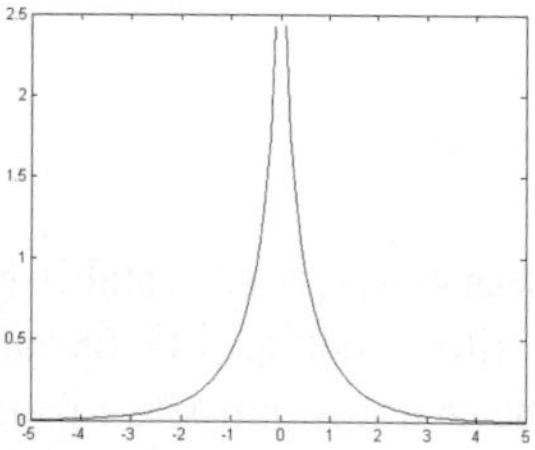

(b)

Fig. 1. The M-S Green function for $\mu = 10$: a) 3D view b) a cross-section

The construction of the filter proposed in equation (2) is explained in more details in section 3 and figure (3). We are here inspired by the following theorem proved for an edge detection algorithm based on the Bessel filter [4].

Theorem: *The gradient magnitude of the convolved image* $u: R^2 \to R^+$ *calculated in* $u = h_\varepsilon * g$ *has local maxima on discontinuities of a given piecewise-constant image* $g: \Omega \to R^+$ *as* $\varepsilon \to 0$.

The above theorem implies that scale-space smoothing is not applicable to Green function (2) when it is used for edge detection. In fact, there is a family of filters which are scale invariant for edge detection. The Bessel filter investigated in this paper is a member of this family. Another example in such a family is also designed and analyzed in [5]. We conjecture in this paper that Green function (1) does not demonstrate any property associated with the scale space smoothing for the detection of any feature, i.e. features extracted by the Bessel filter investigated here are scale invariant. The numerical results presented in section 4 of this paper support such a conjecture.

3 Implementation Issues

The convolution of the function h in (1) with the original input image g is calculated as the first step for feature extraction to calculate the convolved image u. Then an appropriate differential entity of u is examined to find regions for which this differential entity is maximum.

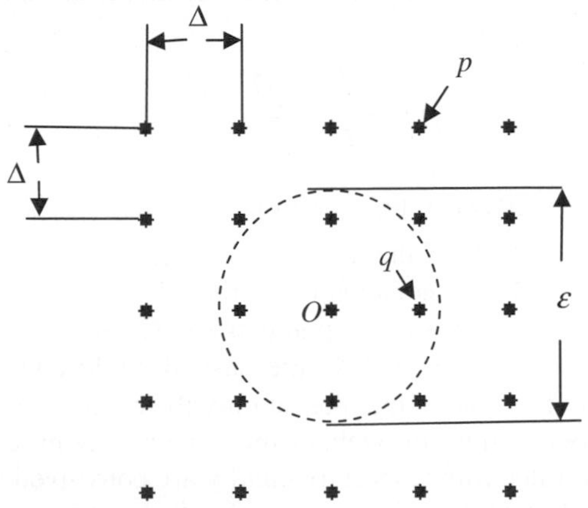

Fig. 2. A 5 x 5 grid used for the construction of a Bessel filter proposed in equation (2) for the case of $2<\frac{\varepsilon}{\Delta}<3$

The algorithm proposed here is implemented in Matlab 7.3 environment. We have exploited the built in *besselk* function in Matlab to construct the Bessel filter. Figure (2) helps us understand how the regularized Bessel filter proposed in (2) can be constructed. A 5 x 5 window forming the window grids of the filter is shown in this figure. It is noted that Δ and ε in the figure are the sampling distance and regularizing parameter respectively. The dashed line circle in figure (2) represents the circle with a radius given in (3).

$$|r|=\frac{\varepsilon}{2} \tag{3}$$

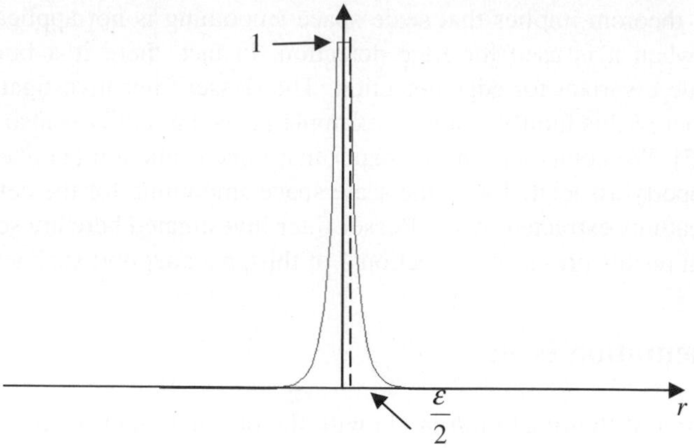

Fig. 3. The cross section of the regularized filter proposed in (2)

According to equation (2), the values of the filter in all points inside this circle should be unity and the filter values in all points outside of this circle should be set to the following value:

$$h_\varepsilon(r) = \frac{K_0(\frac{|r|}{\sqrt{\mu}})}{K_0(\frac{\varepsilon}{2\sqrt{\mu}})} \tag{4}$$

where $|r|$ is the distance between the central point O and the point outside of the circle. If the point is the outside of the dashed line circle (such as point p shown in the figure), then the value given in equation (4) is therefore assigned to the filter at point p. For a point inside the circle (such as points q and O), unity is assigned to the filter at this point. For the case when $\varepsilon < \Delta$, the dashed circle contains only the central point O and therefore the value of the filter at only the central point O is set to unity.

We consider Δ being unity throughout this paper. Having constructed the filter, the derivatives of the filter with respect to x and y are convolved with the original image to compute the derivatives of the image. Such derivatives can then be used in various differentials entities for image feature extraction. A cross section of constructed regularized Bessel filter is also depicted in figure (3). Finally we need to determine the window size according to which the Bessel filter defined in (2) is truncated, since this filter in spatial domain is not band limited. Therefore we define the truncated filter as:

$$h_\varepsilon(r,d) = \begin{cases} 1 & 0 \le r < \frac{\varepsilon}{2} \\ \dfrac{K_0(\frac{r}{\sqrt{\mu}})}{K_0(\frac{\varepsilon}{\sqrt{\mu}})} & \frac{\varepsilon}{2} < r \le d \\ 0 & r > d \end{cases}$$

We use the term defined in (5) to determine a filter size for the Bessel filter with respect to μ.

$$E(d) = \sum_r \left| h_\varepsilon(r) - h_\varepsilon(r,d) \right| \tag{5}$$

We notice that for, $d = 5\sqrt{\mu}$ E becomes negligible ($E = 0.0045$) in comparison with the total area under the filter $h_\varepsilon(r)$, i.e.,

$$E(d = 5\sqrt{\mu}) << \sum_r h_\varepsilon(r)$$

Therefore, in this paper the window size of the filter proposed here is set to $W = (10\sqrt{\mu} + 1) \times (10\sqrt{\mu} + 1)$. It is clear that if we choose larger window sizes than this, the algorithm becomes numerically more expensive with almost the same accuracy. In summary, once the Bessel filter is constructed, its derivatives with respect to x and y directions are numerically calculated and then these derivatives are convolved with an input image to compute the derivatives of the image in x and y directions. The various differential entities investigated in this paper are finally computed to extract appropriate features for image analysis by detecting the local maxima of the corresponding differential entities.

4 Numerical Results

Let us start this section by presenting our numerical results on edge detection. It is customary in literature (see e.g. [6]) to convolve an image with a filter and then find the maxima of the absolute value of the gradient of the convolved image to detect edges, i.e., the maxima of the following differential entity correspond to the edges of image I.

$$\Upsilon = \left| \nabla u \right| \tag{6}$$

where $u = h * I$ and h is the filter. The image of figure (4-a) is examined for edge detection. Gaussian and Bessel filters with size 41 are employed for edge detection to produce the results in figures (4-b and c).

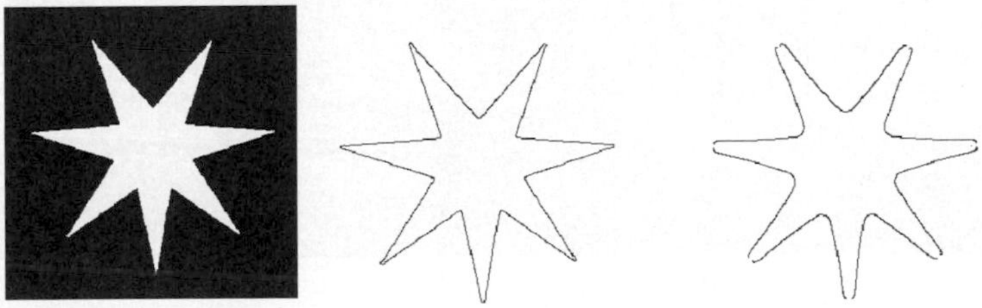

(a) (b) (c)

Fig. 4. Edge detection with two filters with the size 41, a) Original image b) Edge map produced by Bessel filter($\varepsilon = 0.1$) c) Edge map produced by Gaussian filter

As shown in figure (4), the corners in the edge map produced by a Gaussian filter, become distorted when the filter size (and hence scale) is considerably high. This phenomenon is known as scale space smoothing. The corners in the edge map produced by the Bessel filter however do not show any distortion as the filter size (scale) increases. We note that the filter parameters such as the standard deviation ($\sigma = \frac{filter\ \ size}{6}$) of the Gaussian filter and μ for Bessel filter are calculated according to the filter size. Figure (5-a) shows a real world image whose edge maps are detected by the Bessel and Gaussian filters. This figure depicts another example for edge detection showing that the Bessel filter can extract same features regardless of the scale. However some features are distorted in some scales when a Gaussian filter is used for edge detection. Same filter size (size =9) is used for both filters. As shown in this figure, some letters (such as "t", "f", "a", "m" and so on) even in lower scales are detected with better accuracy by the Bessel filter. A noisy synthetic image is also shown in figure (6-a). In order to remove the noise, the filter size 13 is chosen for both filters. More details are extracted in the edge map produced by the Bessel filter. According to the theorem presented in section 2, as $\varepsilon \to 0$ higher accuracy in edge detection is achieved by the Bessel filter. The parameter ε however is set to unity for the purpose of noise removal in this example. As can be seen from this figure, a better accuracy in edge detection is achieved by the Bessel filter.

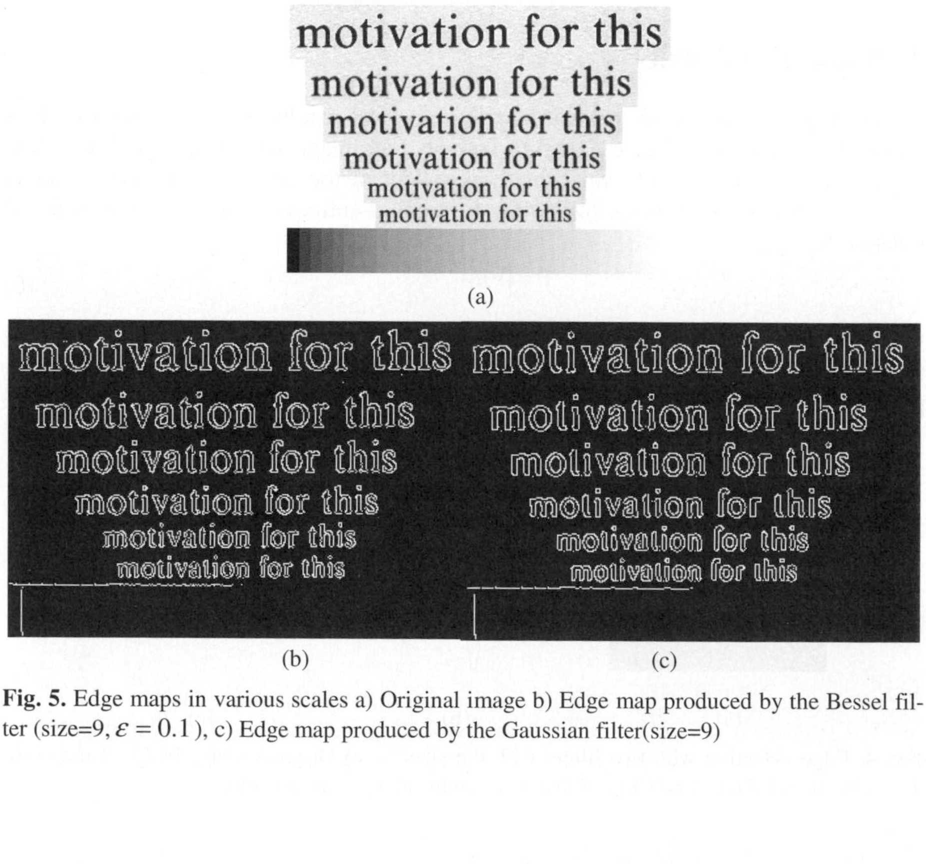

(a)

(b) (c)

Fig. 5. Edge maps in various scales a) Original image b) Edge map produced by the Bessel filter (size=9, $\varepsilon = 0.1$), c) Edge map produced by the Gaussian filter(size=9)

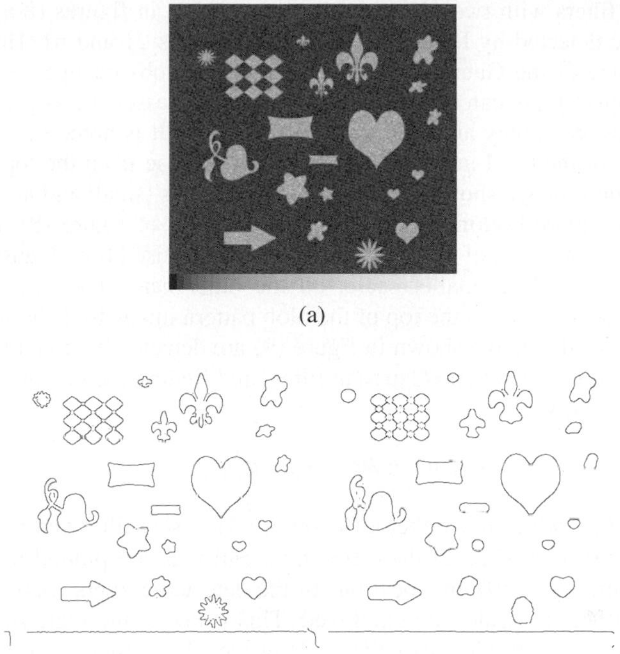

(a) (b) (c)

Fig. 6. Edge maps of a noisy image produced by the Gaussian and Bessel filters (size=13) a) Original noisy image b) Edge map produced by the Bessel filter ($\varepsilon = 1$) c) Edge map produced by the Gaussian filter

In both figures (5) and (6), a stair case strip of logarithmically increasing grey scales is added at the bottom of the original images to ensure that the equivalent values for thresholds are used in both algorithms.

Figure (7-a) shows a Gaussian circle. Bessel filters with size 9 and 301 are applied to this Gaussian circle to detect edges as shown in figures (7-b and c). Gaussian filters with the same sizes are applied to the Gaussian circle to produce edge maps shown in figures (7-d and e).

As shown in figure (7), the edge map of the Gaussian circle significantly changes when the filter size (and consequently the scale) of the Gaussian filter increases from 9 to 301. However a slight change in edge maps is observed when the Bessel filter with two different sizes are used. The reason for the slight change in the edge maps is that it is not numerically tractable to set ε to zero. Analytically it can be proved, as $\varepsilon \to 0$ the edge maps produced by the Bessel filter will be unchanged, regardless of the filter size (the proof will be similar to the proofs of the theorems presented in [4]).

For blob detection, the maxima of the following differential entity are detected.

$$\Gamma = -\nabla^2 u$$

where $u = h * I$ in which h is either a Bessel or a Gaussian filter and I is the input image. Figure (8) shows the first 11 maxima of Γ for blob detection using the Bessel and Gaussian filters with two different sizes. As shown in figures (8-a and b), lower scale blobs are detected by Bessel filters with both sizes 21 and 61. However, by increasing the size of the Gaussian filter, the detected blobs change significantly (see figures (8-c and d)). As can be seen from figure (8), Bessel filters produce scale invariant features when they are used for blob detection. It is noted that for Bessel filters the values of the local maxima of Γ always decrease from the top to the bottom of the blob pattern image shown in figure (8) in all scales (small and large scales).

However the more bottom the blob is in the image of figure (8), the higher the value of the local maxima of Γ is, when a large scale is used for a Gaussian filter. For a Gaussian filter with a smaller scale, on the other hand, the values of the local maxima of Γ decrease from the top of the blob pattern image to its bottom.

The corners of the image shown in figure (9) are detected by convolving the original image with both Bessel and Gaussian filters and finding the maxima of the following differential entity:

$$\Xi = u_y^2 u_{xx} - 2u_x u_y u_{xy} + u_x^2 u_{yy}$$

where $u = h * I$ in which h is either a Bessel or a Gaussian filter and I is the input image. The first seven maxima of the differential entity Ξ are plotted in figure (9). As can be seen from figure (9), the locations of the detected corners change, when Gaussian filters with higher scales are employed. This is due to the scale space smoothing property associated with Gaussian filters. However the corner locations detected by the Bessel filters with various sizes remain unchanged.

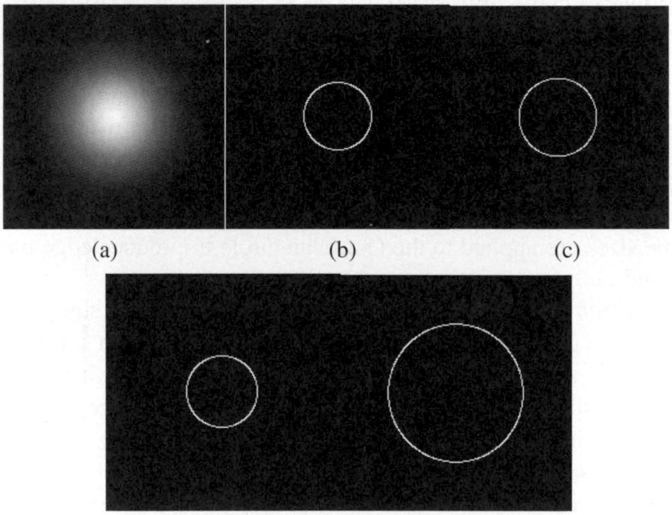

(a) (b) (c)

(d) (e)

Fig. 7. The effect of scale space smoothing on the edge maps of a Gaussian circle a) Original image b) edge map produced by the Bessel filter with size=9 c) edge map produced by the Bessel filter with size=301 d) edge map produced by the Gaussian filter with size=9 e) edge map produced by the Gaussian filter with size=301

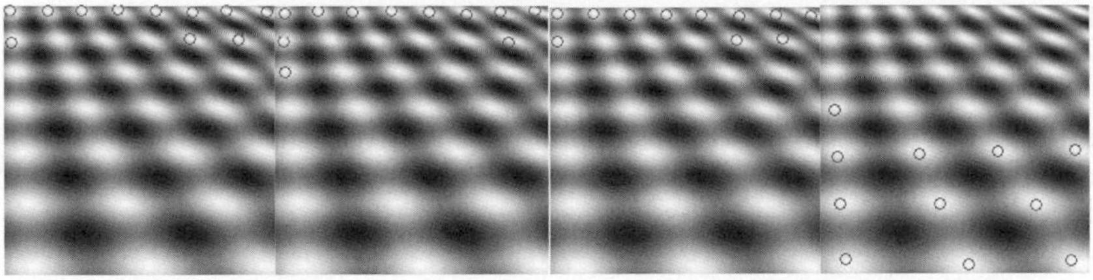

(a) (b) (c) (d)

Fig. 8. The first 11 blobs detected by using Bessel and Gaussian filters with two different filter sizes a) Bessel filter with size=21($\varepsilon = 0.1$) b) Bessel filter with size=61($\varepsilon = 0.1$) c)Gaussian filter with size 21 and d) Gaussian filter with size 61

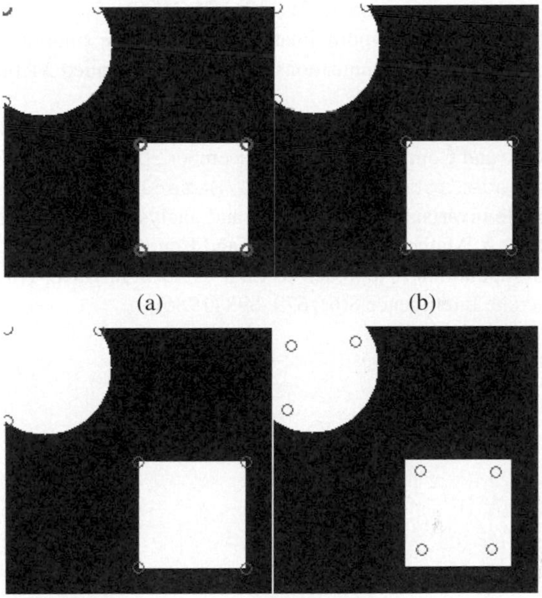

(a) (b) (c) (d)

Fig. 9. The first seven most important corners detected by Bessel and Gaussian filters a) Bessel filter with size=9 ($\varepsilon = 1$) b) Bessel filter with size=201 ($\varepsilon = 1$) c) Gaussian filter with size=9, d) Gaussian filter with size=201

5 Conclusion

The Green function associated with the Mumford-Shah functional in the absence of discontinuities is considered in this paper for feature extraction. A regularization method is presented here to introduce a Bessel filter. It is analytically proved in this work that Bessel filters produce scale invariant features for edge detection. It is therefore conjectured here that Bessel filters always produce scale invariant features for the detection of other features. Numerical results for Gaussian edges, blobs, corners as well as edges presented in this paper support such a conjecture. The features extracted by Bessel filters are invariant to the scale (size) of the filter.

Acknowledgments. This work was supported in part by the IST program of the European Community, under the PASCAL2 Network of Excellence, the IST-2007-216886 and PinView project with grant number 216529.

References

1. Lindeberg, T.: Feature Detection with Automatic Scale Selection. International Journal of Computer Vision 30(2), 79–116 (1998)
2. Lindeberg, T.: Edge Detection and Ridge Detection with Automatic Scale Selection. International Journal of Computer Vision 30(2), 117–154 (1998)
3. Mumford, D., Shah, J.: Optimal approximations by piecewise smooth functions and associated variational problems. Communications on Pure and Applied Mathematics 42(4), 577–688 (1989)
4. Mahmoodi, S.: Technical Report 1: Bessel Filter Analysis, University of Southampton, School of Electronic and Computer Science (December 2010), `http://users.ecs.soton.ac.uk/sm3/BesselFilterTheorems.pdf`
5. Mahmoodi, S.: Scale invariant filtering design and analysis for edge detection. Proceedings of the Royal Society A: Mathematical, Physical and Engineering Sciences (in press)
6. Canny, J.F.: A Computational Approach to Edge Detection. IEEE Transactions on Pattern Analysis and Machine Intelligence 8(6), 679–698 (1986)

A Free-Viewpoint Virtual Mirror with Marker-Less User Interaction

Matthias Straka, Stefan Hauswiesner, Matthias Rüther, and Horst Bischof

Institute for Computer Graphics and Vision,
Graz University of Technology,
Inffeldgasse 16/II, Graz, Austria
{straka,hauswiesner,ruether,bischof}@icg.tugraz.at

Abstract. We present a Virtual Mirror system which is able to simulate a physically correct full-body mirror on a monitor. In addition, users can freely rotate the mirror image which allows them to look at themselves from the side or from the back, for example. This is achieved through a multiple camera system and visual hull based rendering. A real-time 3D reconstruction and rendering pipeline enables us to create a virtual mirror image at 15 frames per second on a single computer. Moreover, it is possible to extract a three dimensional skeleton of the user which is the basis for marker-less interaction with the system.

Keywords: Virtual Mirror, Shape-from-Silhouette, CUDA, Markerless User-Interaction, Free-Viewpoint Video.

1 Introduction

A virtual mirror is an Augmented Reality (AR) system which renders an image of the user from a virtual viewpoint and creates the illusion of a mirror image. In addition to that, it allows to add virtual objects and to modify the image in a way that is not possible with physical mirrors. In this paper, we propose a physically correct simulation of a full-body mirror using a multi-camera system and a single monitor. We also extend its viewing capabilities by allowing users to rotate their mirror image using solely natural hand gestures. This is beneficial, for example, in dressing rooms where users want to see how they look from the side or from behind in new clothes.

The concept of a virtual mirror is not new in the area of computer vision and AR [5,6,8]. One common property of existing virtual mirror systems is that they consist of a single camera with a fixed position where the horizontally flipped video stream is shown to the user on a monitor. However, such systems generally do not allow one to simulate a correct mirror because video devices are only able to capture a projected image and not the reflection of the user from his viewpoint. Free viewpoint video systems on the other hand are able to render an arbitrary view of a person by combining images from multiple fixed cameras [3,9,18]. This allows for the accurate simulation of optical effects, including rendering of a reflection image. Due to the amount of image data,

A. Heyden and F. Kahl (Eds.): SCIA 2011, LNCS 6688, pp. 635–645, 2011.

processing of the camera input often can not be performed in real-time on a single computer. Only recent developments in GPU computing have made it possible to render virtual viewpoints at interactive frame rates. We provide a more detailed review of the current literature in Sect. 2.

Our contribution is a novel virtual mirror system which combines a multi-camera capture system with real-time free-viewpoint video. We equip a room with several cameras (see Sect. 3) and use a virtual camera to render an artificial mirror image which we display on a large monitor. Even though such a design incurs additional hardware compared to a single camera system, it adds several benefits. Due to the fact that the virtual camera has no restrictions on its position and parameters, we can generate an optically correct mirror effect. In Sect. 4 we describe how we determine and adapt the camera parameters when the user moves in front of the monitor. The capabilities of a multi-view camera system reach far beyond basic mirror simulations. We are able to not only show the frontal view of the user but rotate the virtual camera in a 360° fashion around her. So far, our system is the only virtual mirror which provides such possibilities. The user can control this rotation by means of hand-gestures which we detect in a skeletal representation of the body. In Sect. 5 we show that we are able to achieve real-time processing of the camera images using only a single computer. We evaluate the robustness of user input detection and present a qualitative evaluation of the mirror image. Finally, Sect. 6 provides conclusions and a comparison to existing virtual mirror systems as well as suggestions for future enhancements of the proposed system.

2 Related Work

In this section we will give an overview of previous work concerning virtual mirrors and free-viewpoint video. Virtual mirrors have gained huge interest in recent years in the area of computer vision and augmented reality. For example, in [6] a camera is attached to a portable flat screen in order to simulate a hand-held mirror. Other virtual mirrors are able to display augmented objects or completely altered appearances instead of the true mirror image [2,5,17]. In fashion stores, people will use a mirror for looking at themselves in new clothes or with gadgets. This leads to the idea of using virtual mirrors for augmenting clothes [8] or shoes [4] onto the mirror image of a person without the need to actually wear them. Recently, commercial websites such as [11] have started to offer web cam applications which for example show an augmented mirror image of users with virtual sunglasses on their face. All these systems share the restriction of a single view-point: they only allow a frontal view of the user.

In contrast, free viewpoint video systems are able to render arbitrary views of an object by using images from multiple fixed cameras. There exist two major forms of object representation in such systems. Polygon based models [3,14] explicitly reconstruct the object as a triangle-mesh and use texture mapping to overlay the current video stream on the object. While such methods allow high quality outputs, they are only suitable for off-line processing due to the

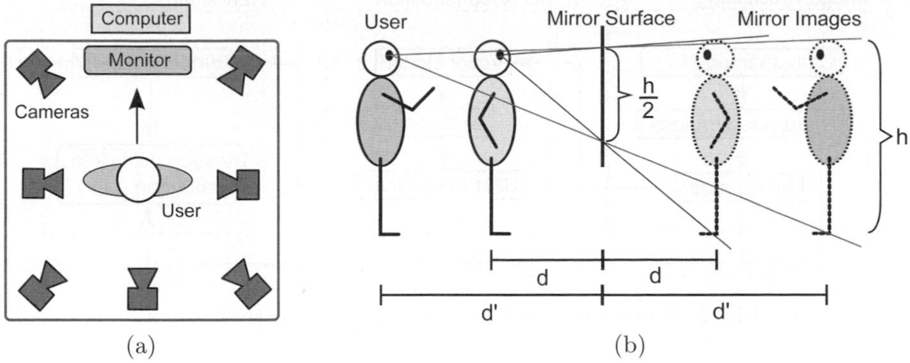

Fig. 1. (a) Top-view of the camera and virtual mirror setup: The user is surrounded by multiple cameras and sees an artificial mirror image of himself or herself on the display. (b) Illustration of the mirror effect: When the user has a distance d from the mirror, the mirror image appears at the same distance behind the mirror. The height of the mirror image on the mirror surface always is half the height h of the user and does not depend on the distance d.

computationally intensive reconstruction. Visual-hull based rendering [1,9] requires only depth information obtained through processing of camera images with background segmentation (silhouette) in order to synthesize a new viewpoint. However, true real-time processing of such data is still a challenging task. Only recent developments in GPU computing have made it possible to render virtual viewpoints at interactive frame rates [18], but often exceed the computational power of one computer [16].

3 System Design

Our virtual mirror system requires three components: multiple cameras to capture images of the user, a computer to process the data and a monitor to show the mirror image. Figure 1a sketches the setup and shows the positions of the user, the mirror display and the multi-view camera system.

3.1 Geometric Considerations for the Mirror

A virtual mirror needs to simulate the properties of a real mirror as accurate as possible. When standing in front of a mirror at a distance d, the mirror image of oneself appears exactly at the same distance but behind the mirror. However, even though this distance can change, the size of the user in the mirror image when projected on the mirror surface stays constant at half the height h of the user. This is illustrated in Fig. 1b. We take advantage of this observation in order to choose an appropriate monitor for our mirror. A 47 inch Full-HD television mounted in portrait mode has a height of 104 cm and therefore can display the

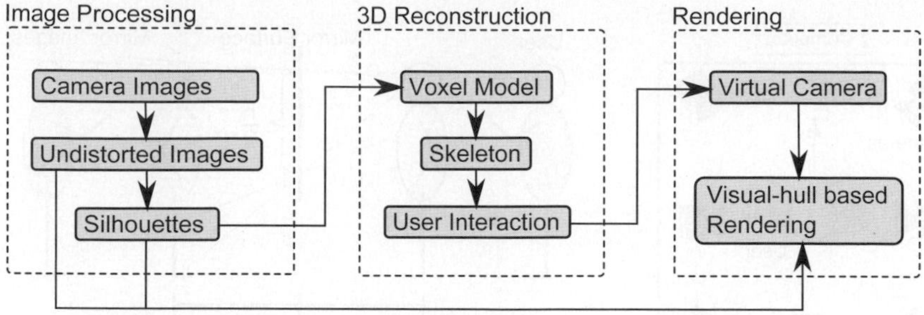

Fig. 2. Processing pipeline for the Virtual Mirror System

full-body mirror image of users up to 2 meters in height, which includes 99 percent of all people according to [15].

3.2 System Architecture

The complete setup is required to fit into a small room of 3×2 meters, which is equipped with ten synchronized color cameras connected to a single computer via three FireWire buses. Due to the space limitations, the viewing frustums of all cameras are focused on an area approximately 1.5 meters in front of the monitor, so the user is only allowed to move within a small area. The cameras deliver 640×480 pixel images at 15 frames per second. In order to process the amount of input data produced by our setup (around 100 MB/s), we exploit the computational power of a CUDA enabled NVIDIA GTX 480 graphics card. Developing algorithms that execute on the GPU enables high performance in applications with many parallel tasks [10] such as pixel-wise image processing (e.g. image undistortion and silhouette extraction). Due to these hardware components, we are able to process the camera images and display an output on the virtual mirror at 15 frames per second using only a single computer.

4 Methodology

Our Virtual Mirror system uses a series of processing steps which extract the required information from the input images. We illustrate the pipeline that performs our reconstruction and rendering process in Fig. 2. In the first stage, we acquire a live stream of multiple synchronized camera images. Each image is then undistorted using radial distortion parameters determined during camera calibration. A subsequent silhouette extraction step segments the user from the background in all images. We employ a luminance insensitive background subtraction method in order to cope with shadows caused by the user. Silhouette data is used to generate a low-resolution voxel model and extract a skeleton which we use to implement marker-less user interaction. In the mirror simulation mode of our system, a virtual camera is controlled by the 3D position of the user's head which we determine in voxel space. An alternative mode of operation

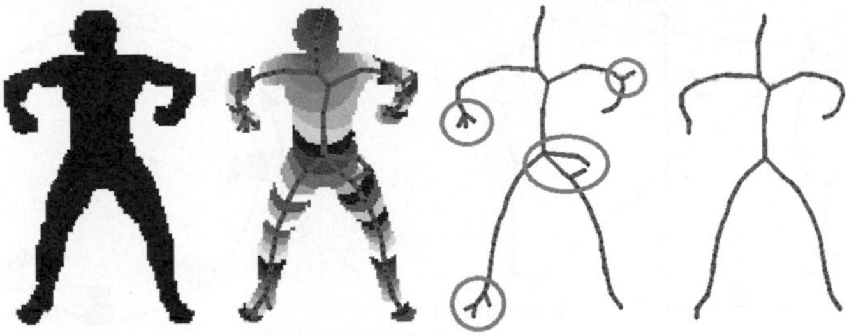

Fig. 3. Voxel scooping demonstrated on a 2D silhouette (in 3D the silhouette corresponds to object voxels): (a) Silhouette image. (b) Scooped levels and the resulting graph. (c) Graph with markings for some scooping errors. (d) pruned skeleton graph.

allows the user to rotate the camera around him- or herself by hand gestures. Finally, we use an image based visual hull (IBVH) technique to render the image of the user using the virtual camera. The remainder of this section describes important components of our system in more detail.

4.1 3D Reconstruction and Robust Skeleton Estimation

In our system, we use a 3D model to determine the position of the head and hands of the user. We use a fast space carving approach on the GPU [13] to obtain a discrete voxel grid V with a resolution of k^3 voxels ($k = 64$). Once the voxel model has been obtained, we need to perform a hierarchical segmentation into head, body and limbs. In the recent years it has become popular to build a so-called Reeb graph [19] to represent the topology of arbitrary multidimensional structures. A Reeb graph is generated by extracting level sets from such structures and keeping track of critical points where a level set becomes disconnected. When applied to the human body, an optimal Reeb graph has a tree structure with branches for head, arms and legs.

In this work, we utilize a fast and robust method called *Voxel Scooping* [12] for extracting the Reeb graph of the human body. While the algorithm was originally intended for tracing centerlines of neurons in medical data, we show that it can be easily applied to volumetric body scans such as obtained from our shape-from-silhouette approach. Starting with the node at a seeding point, each node in the graph spherically expands in voxel space with a locally adaptive radius (hence the name scooping). Based on this expansion, a new node is created and the process is repeated until there are no more voxels left to scoop. When the expanded voxels of a single node no longer form a connected component, a branching node is created and each branch is processed individually. In the final Reeb graph there will be artifacts in the form of short branches (see Fig. 3c). A final pruning step removes branches that only consist of two or less nodes in order to obtain a clean graph with only six arcs corresponding to head, body and limbs (as in Fig. 3d). We propose to use the top of the head as the seeding

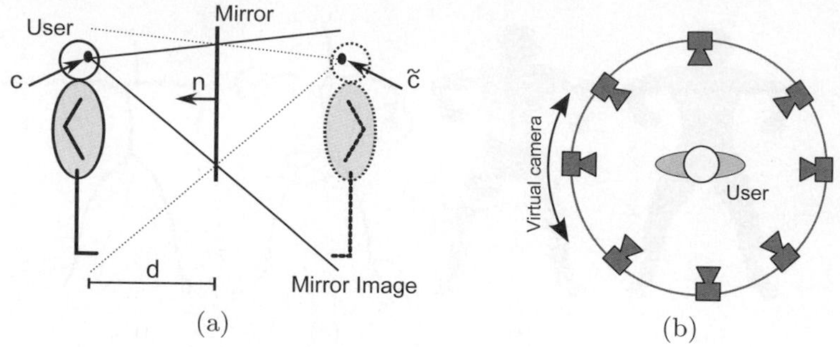

Fig. 4. (a) Illustration of the mirror effect with the position of the eyes $\mathbf{c}$, the position of the virtual camera $\tilde{\mathbf{c}}$ as well as the distance d between the user and the mirror surface plus the mirror normal $\mathbf{n}$. (b) shows how the virtual camera is rotated around the user in free-viewpoint mode.

point for voxel scooping, which will always produce a tree structure similar to the human skeleton as in Fig. 3b. The position of the head is determined when the user steps into the system and is further tracked in voxel space.

4.2 Hand Position Estimation

For user interaction we use the position of the hands of the user, which we detect in the skeletal Reeb graph. The detection must work independently from the current body pose while being robust towards graph artifacts that cannot be removed using our length based graph pruning alone. Therefore, we propose to use the geodesic distance between leaf nodes as a pose-invariant feature to detect hands in the graph. Suppose there are N_E leaf nodes in the graph, then $pd(n)|_{n=1\ldots N_E}$ is the shortest path-distance from node n to the root of the graph (which is the head). In order to classify a leaf node as a hand, we compare each $pd(n)$ to the expected geodesic distance between the head and hands which is approximately 0.6 times the body height. During voxel scooping, geodesic distances between all nodes and the root are calculated automatically, therefore no further processing is required (such as building shock graphs). Note that the graph will not completely represent the full human body topology in the general case. For example, arms will not be distinguishable from the upper body in the voxel model when they are close to the body. However, for user-interaction we are only interested in hands that are stretched away from the body and therefore we can ignore hands in undetectable poses.

4.3 Virtual Mirror Camera

A mirror image as seen by the user depends on two factors: the position of the eyes $\mathbf{c} \in \mathbb{R}^3$ and the mirror plane $\pi \in \mathbb{R}^4$. While the mirror plane is fixed and configured once, the position of the eyes changes when users move. For an authentic mirror simulation, it is sufficient to approximate the position of the eyes by adding a constant offset to the top of the skeletal graph in every frame. The mirror plane π, which is the surface of the monitor in our system, can be expressed using a homogeneous notation which satisfies $\pi^T \mathbf{X} = 0$ for every 3D point $\mathbf{X}$ that lies on the plane. The first three components of π correspond to the plane normal

$$\mathbf{n} = [\pi^{(1)}, \pi^{(2)}, \pi^{(3)}]^T \qquad \|\mathbf{n}\| = 1 \tag{1}$$

of the mirror while the fourth component $\pi^{(4)}$ describes the distance of the plane from the origin as determined in the configuration step. The orthogonal distance d between $\mathbf{c}$ and the mirror surface can be calculated as follows:

$$d = \pi^T \begin{bmatrix} \mathbf{c} \\ 1 \end{bmatrix} . \tag{2}$$

The 3×4 camera matrix $\tilde{\mathbf{P}} = \tilde{\mathbf{K}}[\tilde{\mathbf{R}}|\tilde{\mathbf{t}}]$ producing an optically correct mirror image from the user's view on the monitor can be calculated from the position of eyes $\mathbf{c}$, the distance d and the normal $\mathbf{n}$ of the mirror plane (see Fig. 4a). The rotation $\tilde{\mathbf{R}}_{[3\times 3]}$ of the virtual camera is defined so that the camera looks along the normal $\mathbf{n}$ of the mirror surface with an up-vector ($\mathbf{up} = [0, 0, 1]^T$):

$$\tilde{\mathbf{R}} = \begin{bmatrix} \mathbf{r}_x{}^T \\ (\mathbf{r}_x \times \mathbf{n})^T \\ \mathbf{n}^T \end{bmatrix} \quad \text{with} \quad \mathbf{r}_x = \mathbf{n} \times \mathbf{up} . \tag{3}$$

Note that the gazing direction of the user does not affect the mirror image and therefore does not need to be considered. The position $\tilde{\mathbf{c}}$ of the virtual camera is simply a mirrored version of the position of the eyes $\mathbf{c}$ which yields the translation vector $\tilde{\mathbf{t}}$ for the virtual projection matrix $\tilde{\mathbf{P}}$:

$$\tilde{\mathbf{t}} = -\tilde{\mathbf{R}} \cdot \tilde{\mathbf{c}} \qquad \text{with} \quad \tilde{\mathbf{c}} = \mathbf{c} - 2 \cdot d \cdot \mathbf{n} . \tag{4}$$

The last component of the camera matrix $\tilde{\mathbf{P}}$ is the intrinsic matrix $\tilde{\mathbf{K}}$ which mirrors and projects the scene onto the monitor's surface:

$$\tilde{\mathbf{K}} = \begin{bmatrix} -f & 0 & p_x \\ 0 & -f & p_y \\ 0 & 0 & 1 \end{bmatrix} \qquad \text{with} \quad f = 2 \cdot d . \tag{5}$$

The focal length f of the camera is equal to the distance between the virtual camera and the user, which is twice the user-mirror distance d. This can be explained by the observation that the size of oneself's image on the mirror surface is constant and independent from d and the focal length of the eyes (see Fig. 1b). In the general case, the mirror image will be an off-center projection with the principal point offsets p_x and p_y shifted depending on the eye position $\mathbf{c}$, the size of the monitor and its resolution in pixels as well as the position of the application window on the monitor.

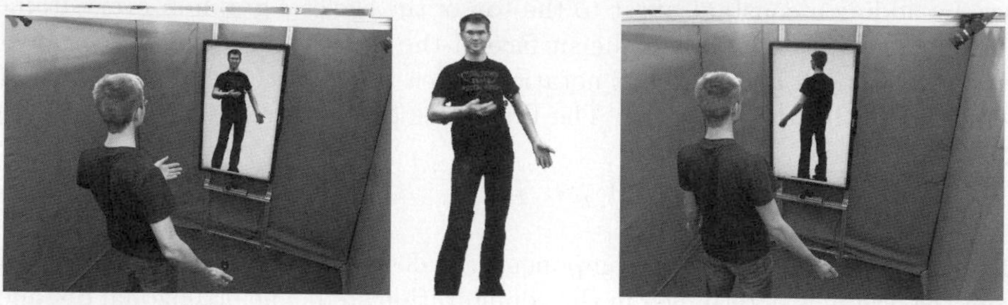

(a) (b) (c)

Fig. 5. (a) Simulation of a mirror with the generated mirror image in (b). (c) The user is looking at his own back.

4.4 User Interaction

Apart from the mirror simulation, our system supports a full 360° view of the user by rotating the virtual mirror camera around the body as seen in Fig. 4b. We propose a simple and intuitive way of controlling this view through hand gestures. The user can trigger a clockwise or counterclockwise rotation of the mirror image by stretching his left or right hand away from his body, respectively. Stretching out both hands resets the rotation and sets the camera back to the normal mirror mode. Such input can be implemented by detecting hand positions as described in Sect. 4.2 and does not require visible markers attached to the human body. In order to minimize unintentional user inputs, we require the user to maintain a certain pose for a short amount of time (e.g. one second) before an action is triggered.

4.5 Image-Based Visual Hull Rendering

For mirror image rendering, our system uses an efficient implementation of the image-based visual hull (IBVH) algorithm by Matusik et al. [9] which only needs to calculate those parts of the visual hull that appear in the rendered image. Similar to [18], it is entirely implemented on the GPU but offers a set of additional features: our algorithm can process images from cameras that do not see the entire body of the user. Moreover, we implemented a view-dependent texture mapping scheme including a visibility check and stereo matching which allow us to improve the visual quality of the output. Implementation details about this rendering module can be found in [7].

5 Experiments

In this section we evaluate our virtual mirror system in terms of visual quality, robustness and run-time. Figure 5a shows an example of an user interacting with the system. As soon as the user steps in front of the monitor, a virtual mirror

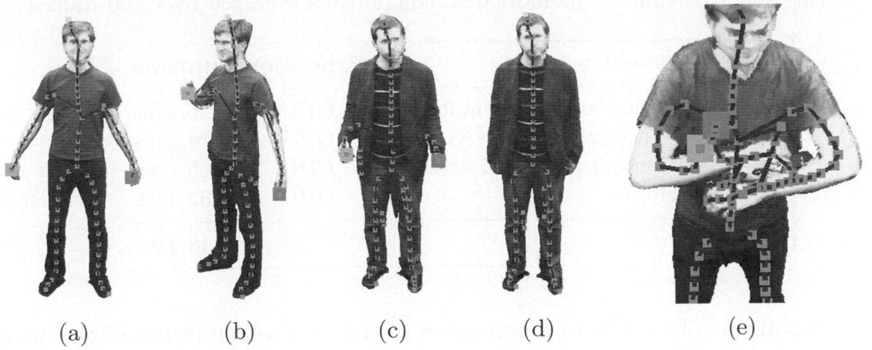

Fig. 6. Evaluation of skeleton extraction by voxel scooping and hand detection on different poses. (a) to (c) show correct skeleton and hand detection. In (d) the arms are merged with the body and no hands are detected. (e) shows wrong hand detections due to errors in the voxel model and skeleton.

image such as in Fig. 5b is shown on the screen. We obtain an appealing artificial mirror image at a resolution of 540×960 pixels, from any virtual camera position such as in Fig. 5c which shows a user looking at his own back.

5.1 User Interaction

In our system, we implement marker-less user interaction through hand gestures. As we rely only on a very simplistic model of the human body (it must contain a head and arms) we can robustly detect the hands when they are represented correctly in the underlying skeletal graph. This is shown in Fig. 6 (a) to (c). When the arms are too close to the body, they cannot be distinctively detected in the skeletal graph anymore (Figure 6d). Similarly, when the arms have multiple connections to the body in voxel space (as in Fig. 6e), the skeleton reconstruction fails and wrong detections can occur. However, such errors will only appear when the hands are close to the body. As we react to user input only when hands are distinctly away from the body, we can ignore these errors.

5.2 Run-Time Evaluation

For an interactive system, fast processing and a low latency between user input (or movement) and graphical output is desirable. A balanced use of graphics hardware and CPU processing allows us to achieve real-time execution for the whole system. We are able to render an output mirror image at 15 frames per second and display it to the user less than 100 ms after camera image acquisition. A detailed evaluation of the average run-time of individual components can be found in Table 1 where the total runtime of all components is below 1/15 s or 66 ms. In contrast to other systems such as [1,16], we require only a single computer for processing the camera images. Also, we do not need to process a

Table 1. Run-time of the individual components averaged over 100 frames

Component	Processor	Runtime
Undistortion and Segmentation	GPU	6.1 ms
Voxel Space-carving (64^3 voxels)	GPU	4.2 ms
Skeletal graph and hand detection	CPU	5.7 ms
Rendering	GPU	32.4 ms
Total		48.4 ms

high resolution volumetric representation of the user as rendering of the output is performed on an image-based visual hull. For Reeb graph generation and hand detection, a 64^3 voxel model is sufficient.

6 Conclusions and Discussions

We have presented a system which displays a convincingly and optically correct mirror image of the user who is standing in front of a large monitor. This has been achieved through a free-viewpoint video system and visual hull based rendering. In order to interact with the system, around 15 frames per second and low latencies are desirable which we are able to achieve on a single computer using simple image features (silhouettes) and high performance processors (GPU). The key benefit in using the GPU is the parallelization of image processing and rendering tasks, which account for more than 80 percent of our computing workload. Besides the simulation of a real mirror, we allow the user to look at him- or herself from an arbitrary viewpoint and control this behavior through hand gestures.We realize this through a skeleton like representation of the user in which we detect the hands robustly without the need for visual markers.

To our knowledge, our system is the first virtual mirror that accurately simulates a real mirror. The best existing mirror simulation so far is [6] where the facial image of a single fixed camera is transformed and displayed by assuming the face lies on a plane parallel to the monitor. Our system does not require any transformations in image space, which facilitates integration of artificial objects that do not lie on the facial plane but can be placed anywhere in space. While all existing virtual mirror systems allow real-time operation by processing 2D images, we produce a similar output but from a full 3D representation of the user within the same time constraints. Unlike marker based systems such as [5], users do not have to wear or carry objects in order to interact with our system. We allow user interaction in 3D space using no more than their hands.

The current implementation is limited to displaying only the user as seen by the cameras from an arbitrary viewpoint. In future work we will integrate artificial objects such as virtual clothes into the mirror image and let users interact with them. Also, our multi-view camera system allows for generation of high quality 3D scans and motion capture.

Acknowledgements. This work was supported by the Austrian Research Promotion Agency (FFG) under the BRIDGE program, project #822702.

References

1. Allard, J., Franco, J.S., Ménier, C., Boyer, E., Raffin, B.: The GrImage Platform: A Mixed Reality Environment for Interactions. In: Proc. of the International Conference on Computer Vision Systems (2006)
2. Darrell, T., Gordon, G., Woodfill, J., Harville, M.: A virtual mirror interface using real-time robust face tracking. In: Proc. of the International Conference on Automatic Face and Gesture Recognition (1998)
3. De Aguiar, E., Stoll, C., Theobalt, C., Ahmed, N., Seidel, H.P., Thrun, S.: Performance capture from sparse multi-view video. In: Proc. of ACM SIGGRAPH (2008)
4. Eisert, P., Rurainsky, J., Fechteler, P.: Virtual mirror: Real-time tracking of shoes in augmented reality environments. In: Proc. of the ICIP (2007)
5. Fiala, M.: Magic mirror system with hand-held and wearable augmentations. In: Proc. of the IEEE Virtual Reality Conference, pp. 251–254 (2007)
6. François, A.R., Kang, E.: A handheld mirror simulation. In: Proc. of the International Conference on Multimedia and Expo., vol. 2, pp. 745–748 (2003)
7. Hauswiesner, S., Straka, M., Reitmayr, G.: Coherent image-based rendering of real-world objects. In: Proc. of the Symposium on Interactive 3D Graphics (2011)
8. Hilsmann, A., Eisert, P.: Realistic cloth augmentation in single view video. In: Proc. of Vison, Modelling, and Visualization Workshop, pp. 55–62 (2009)
9. Matusik, W., Buehler, C., Raskar, R., Gortler, S., McMillan, L.: Image-based visual hulls. In: Proc. of ACM SIGGRAPH, pp. 369–374 (2000)
10. Nickolls, J., Dally, W.: The GPU computing era. IEEE Micro 30(2), 56–69 (2010), doi:10.1109/MM.2010.41
11. Ray-Ban Sunglasses: Virtual mirror, from `http://www.ray-ban.com/usa/science/virtual-mirror` (retrieved March 14, 2011)
12. Rodriguez, A., Ehlenberger, D., Hof, P., Wearne, S.L.: Three-dimensional neuron tracing by voxel scooping. Journal of Neuroscience Methods 184(1), 169–175 (2009), doi:10.1016/j.jneumeth.2009.07.021
13. Schick, A., Stiefelhagen, R.: Real-time GPU-based voxel carving with systematic occlusion handling. In: Denzler, J., Notni, G., Süße, H. (eds.) Pattern Recognition. LNCS, vol. 5748, pp. 372–381. Springer, Heidelberg (2009)
14. Starck, J., Hilton, A.: Surface capture for performance based animation. IEEE Computer Graphics and Applications 27(3), 21–31 (2007)
15. Tilley, A.R., Dreyfuss, H.: The Measure of Man & Woman. John Wiley & Sons, Chichester (2002)
16. Tzevanidis, K., Zabulis, X., Sarmis, T., Koutlemanis, P., Kyriazis, N., Argyros, A.: From multiple views to textured 3D meshes: a GPU-powered approach. In: Proc. of the Computer Vision on GPUs Workshop, CVGPU (2010)
17. del Valle, A.C.A., Opalach, A.: Enhanced reflection to encourage healthy living. In: Proc. of UbiComp Workshop: Monitoring, Measuring, and Motivating (2005)
18. Waizenegger, W., Feldmann, I., Eisert, P., Kauff, P.: Parallel high resolution real-time visual hull on GPU. In: Proc. of ICIP (2009)
19. Werghi, N., Xiao, Y., Siebert, J.P.: A functional-based segmentation of human body scans in arbitrary postures. IEEE Transactions on Systems, Man and Cybernetic 26(1), 153–165 (2006)

Wood Detection and Tracking in Videos of Rivers

Imtiaz Ali[1,2], Julien Mille[1,3], and Laure Tougne[1,2]

[1] Université de Lyon, CNRS
[2] Université Lyon 2, LIRIS, UMR5205, F-69676, France
[3] Université Lyon 1, LIRIS, UMR5205, F-69622, France

Abstract. Rivers during floods bring a lot of fallen trees and debris. Video surveillance systems are installed on strategically important places on the rivers. To protect these places from destructions due to accumulation of wood, such systems must be able to automatically detect wood. Image segmentation is performed to separate wood and other moving elements from the rest of the water. Moving objects are detected with respect to brightness and temporal variation features. The floating wood is then tracked in the sequence of frames by temporal linking of the segments generated in the detection step. Our algorithm is tested on multiple videos of floods and the results are evaluated both qualitatively and quantitatively.

1 Introduction

Video monitoring systems installed on rivers record videos throughout the year. During floods, rivers carry many fallen trees, bushes, branches of fallen trees and other small pieces of wood. Automatic detection and counting of these fallen trees and other wooden pieces will help to protect infrastructures like bridges and dams from hazardous accumulation of trees. This automation will also decrease the manual efforts involved in supervised surveillance. In this paper, automatic wood detection in the river is performed by image segmentation and motion tracking. Dynamic nature of such application implies many constraints and limitations.

This paper is organized as follows. Section 2 presents a review of relevant works. Section 3 summarizes observations and assumptions made on available videos. The image segmentation method is presented in 4. Moving objects are related within successive frames thanks to a temporal linking method, which is described in section 5. This section also presents the method for counting wood pieces in the river. The experimental results, including comparison with ground truth data are presented in section 6. Section 7 concludes and presents perspectives to video analysis in outdoor scenarios.

2 Related Works

Wood detection and tracking in rivers is an example of moving object detection within moving background. There are two major theories for object recognition

A. Heyden and F. Kahl (Eds.): SCIA 2011, LNCS 6688, pp. 646–655, 2011.

in fixed camera videos [1]. In the first approach, the moving object is identified first and then the motion it performs in the image sequence is sought (*e.g.* background subtraction methods). In the second approach, the motion information is used directly to recognize moving objects (*e.g.* optical flow based techniques). For moving object detection, the adaptive background model was proposed for non-stationary backgrounds by [2]. It is constructed by adapting the changes during the training period. Gaussian Mixture Model (GMM) method is used by many researchers [3,4], where one or more Gaussian(s) are used to represent a pixel-wise background model. The Gaussian model parameters are recursively updated in order to follow the gradual background changes. The Weiner filter is used by [5] to learn and predict color changes in each background pixel. In [6] a spatio-temporal filtering method is proposed for compensation of the limitations of region-based image blocks, applied in an aquatic context. A filtering method based on spatial features with spectral features is also presented in [7].

Unlike previously discussed methods, optical flow-based methods proposed by [8] directly detect moving objects from their motion information. [9] used the estimation of the consistency of the optical flow over a short duration of time.

3 Limitation of Existing Methods in Our Case

Available videos of wood imply many constraints and difficulties which are summarized. Fig. 1 represents a few images extracted from the videos. The presence of bridge (top left corner of images), moving branches of tree in front of the camera (right middle portions of images) and the shadows of surrounding trees over the river are evident from these images. The detection of wood depends on the intensity difference between wood and water. But water waves in the presence of sunshine resemble wood pieces as shown in Fig. 2. The distinction between waves and floating wood must be made for correct wood detection and tracking. Waves and wood move at similar speed and hence cannot be distinguished with respect to motion dissimilarity criterion. The motion of wood is not purely translational. Finally, due to remote location of the monitoring scene and the limitations of transfer rate of data networks, the frame rate in the video is very low (~4 fps). Consequently, the object displacement is large between consecutive frames of videos as shown in Fig. 6.

Due to above properties of videos, existing methods may suffer from several limitations. The GMM method may lead to misclassification when the

(a) (b) (c) (d)

Fig. 1. Few original images of, (a) a wood piece under the shadows of surrounding trees, (b) surrounding building cast shadows over water, (c) a fallen tree in the cloudy weather and (d) a wood piece having reflection of sun shine from the surface of water background scene is complex [10]. For tracking objects in consecutive frames, the consistency of differential optical flow methods require small object displacements, which is not the case in current videos. Larger water waves have strong consistent movements in multiple frames. Moreover the object shape also play an important role in such methods, but in our case there is no specific shape or size of wood objects. Consequently, due to the complex nature of our application, we chose not to construct a background model. As a matter of fact the background is dynamic with water waves and wood in motion with the same speed.

4 Segmentation of Floating Wood

This paper is an improvement of our previous work [11]. We have developed the mathematical modelization of the problem. The intensity based segmentation method described in this new paper gives better results. Automatic detection of wood begins with the image segmentation step, which is a pixel-based probabilistic approach based on intensity and its temporal variation. We take as an input a sequence of T frames $\{I(.,t)\}_{1\leq t\leq T}$. Basically, we rely on two observations: wood is darker than water and undergoes permanent motion. The intensity probability map P_i contains the likeliness of pixels to be wood with respect to their brightness, whereas the temporal probability map P_t contains this information with respect to the brightness temporal variations at each pixel level.

4.1 Intensity Probability Map

The brightness of floating wood pieces is lower than water, even under the shadows of surrounding trees. Moreover, it does not change significantly in the presence of sunlight. Fig. 5 shows intensity histograms of wood pieces as an example. It seems relevant to approximate the intensity distribution of wood by Gaussian distribution with fixed mean and variance. The input grayscale value of each pixel $\mathbf{x}$ at time t being denoted by $I(\mathbf{x},t)$, the probability of the current pixel to belong to wood is

$$P_i(\mathbf{x},t) = g_{\mu,\sigma^2}(\mathbf{x},t) \quad \text{and} \quad g_{\mu,\sigma^2}(\mathbf{x},t) = \frac{1}{\sigma\sqrt{2\pi}} \exp\left(-\frac{(I(\mathbf{x},t)-\mu)^2}{2\sigma^2}\right)$$

where g is a Gaussian probability density function. To find μ and σ^2, we led experiments on different wood pieces under various lighting conditions. Selection of mean and variance is discussed in section 4.4. Fig. 4(b) shows an example

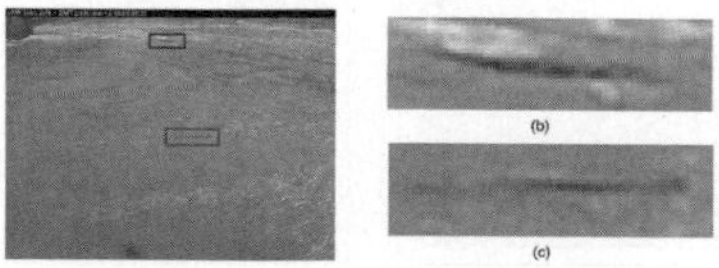

Fig. 2. An image with water wave and wood piece are highlighted, (b) upper portion of image is zoomed to show shape and color intensity of wave, (c) part of image is zoomed to show shape and color intensity of wood piece

of P_i for a wood piece. In the presence of cast shadows of surrounding tree, the intensity probability map P_i has higher value in wood regions but also at undesirable shadowed regions.

4.2 Temporal Probability Map

Wood cannot be extracted relying solely on intensity considerations. Indeed, some objects like bridge pillars or cast shadows of surrounding trees have the same intensity as wood. To remove these static objects, we rely on pixel-wise temporal variations. The temporal probability is partially based on the normalized inter-frame difference $\Delta_t I$:

$$\Delta_t I(\mathbf{x}, t) = \frac{I(\mathbf{x}, t) - I(\mathbf{x}, t-1)}{255} \tag{1}$$

which takes its values within range $[-1, 1]$. Hard thresholding the absolute interframe difference $|\Delta_t I|$ has been extensively tested for object detection. By nature, this technique only detects new object pixels and inevitably removes object areas that overlap in time. This is the case here with big wood pieces. Our temporal probability P_t is defined in order to avoid this drawback. We design it according to the observation that, when wood passes through a given pixel, $\Delta_t I$ dips to a negative value and then to a positive value afterwards. Moreover, P_t should naturally remain constant if $\Delta_t I = 0$. This is achieved using a recursive definition in time:

$$P_t(\mathbf{x}, t) = P_t(\mathbf{x}, t-1) + H(\Delta_t I(\mathbf{x}, t)) \tag{2}$$

where $H \in [-1, 1]$ is an updating function, mapping the inter-frame difference to the amount of changes in the temporal probability. We express it in accordance with the considerations previously addressed. To handle noise and ignore insignificant intensity variations due to the non-uniformity of wood or water, $H(\Delta_t I)$ should be null for relatively small values of $|\Delta_t I|$. It allows to handle slow illumination variations as well. Beyond certain threshold value, H should increase or decrease as $\Delta_t I$ gets significantly negative or positive, respectively. Instead of using hard thresholding which would cause H to jump suddenly from 0 to 1 or -1, we use a soft approach less critical with respect to the choice of threshold parameters leading to the following piecewise linear definition:

$$H(\Delta_t I) = \begin{cases} 1 & \text{if } \Delta_t I \in [-1, -\tau - \frac{B}{2}] \\ \alpha \Delta_t I + \beta & \text{if } \Delta_t I \in [-\tau - \frac{B}{2}, -\tau + \frac{B}{2}] \\ 0 & \text{if } \Delta_t I \in [-\tau + \frac{B}{2}, \tau - \frac{B}{2}] \\ \alpha \Delta_t I - \beta & \text{if } \Delta_t I \in [\tau - \frac{B}{2}, \tau + \frac{B}{2}] \\ -1 & \text{if } \Delta_t I \in [\tau + \frac{B}{2}, 1] \end{cases} \tag{3}$$

where $\alpha = \frac{-1}{B}$ and $\beta = \frac{1}{2} - \frac{\tau}{B}$. Fig. 3 plots H versus $\Delta_t I$. Variation of H in turns requires a threshold τ and transition length B. The probability of a wood pixel must have higher value than surrounding. It should be noted that $P_t(\mathbf{x}, t)$ in Eq. (2) is truncated between 0 and 1 afterwards to remain a probability. In

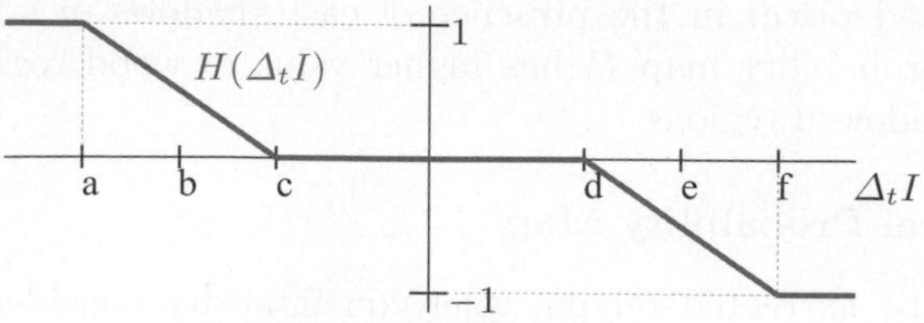

Fig. 3. Representation of updating function $H(\Delta_t I)$

the first frame, we set $P_t(\mathbf{x}, 1)$ to 0 everywhere, as it is very unlikely that wood pieces appear at initial time. Temporal probability P_t is non-null only if temporal brightness variation is negative enough, *i.e.* if a pixel gets significantly darker or has the same brightness as it had in the previous frame. It helps in removing stationary objects in the scene (*e.g.* pillars of bridge). Fig. 4(c) highlights the fact that P_t has higher values for a wood piece than water and static areas.

4.3 Combination of Intensity and Temporal Probability Maps

Since we expect wood to be simultaneously dark and under motion, wood pixels should have both high intensity and temporal probabilities, hence it is relevant to multiply the two probability maps. The product yields the joint probability P_{global}, representing the likelihood of a given pixel to be wood with respect to its intensity and corresponding variation: $P_{global}(\mathbf{x}, t) = P_i(\mathbf{x}, t)P_t(\mathbf{x}, t)$. The foreground image is obtained by simple thresholding of the joint probability map:

$$FG(\mathbf{x}, t) = \begin{cases} 1 & \text{if} \quad P_{global}(\mathbf{x}, t) \geq G_{Th} \\ 0 & \quad \text{otherwise} \end{cases} \tag{4}$$

The joint probability P_{global} is high for wood pixels but also unfortunately for pixels located on dark waves. Hence, global threshold G_{Th} should be chosen in order to limit the number of false detections without removing significant parts of real wood pieces (choice of G_{Th} is discussed in section 4.4). An example of final foreground image is shown in Fig. 4(d), which clearly indicates that the algorithm can detect moving wood pieces under difficult weather conditions. Also, we have evaluated the segmentation results with ground truth images in section 6.

4.4 Selection of Parameters

In previous sections, we introduced some parameters which need to be investigated thoroughly. For this purpose, we extracted small and large wood pieces under different weather conditions. An example of floating wood along with three portions highlighted in different colors is shown in Fig. 5. We fix $\mu = 55$ and $\sigma^2 = 225$. Computation of the temporal probability involves threshold τ and its transition length B, whereas extraction of the final foreground image requires global threshold G_{Th}. Parameter tuning was performed through a brute-force

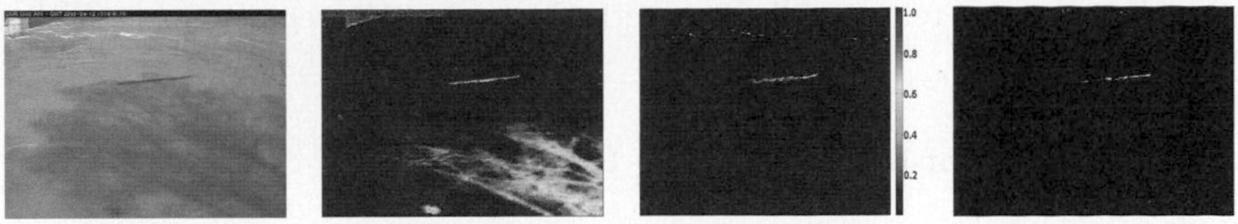

(a) (b) (c) (d)

Fig. 4. (a) An example of wood piece under sunlight with corresponding, (b) intensity probability map P_i, (c) temporal probability map P_t and (d) resulting FG after thresholding

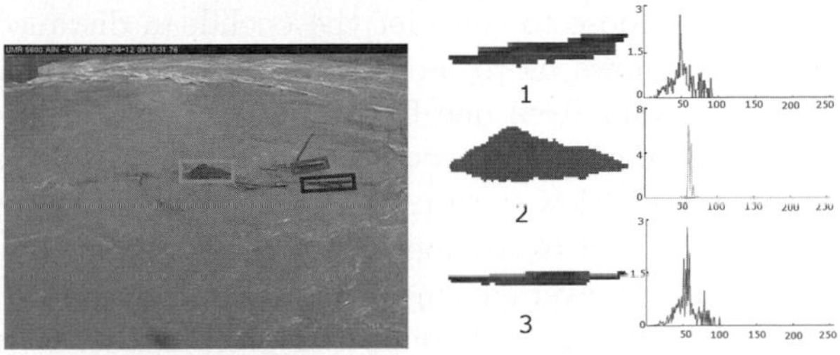

Fig. 5. Floating wood piece; (1) Zoomed portion of wood pixels and corresponding intensity histogram highlighted by red, (2) green and (3) blue rectangle

approach, by maximizing the overlap between the foreground image generated with current parameter values on one hand and ground truth segmentations on the other hand, on a training dataset. The overlap was measured using the Dice coefficient, which is a commonly used measure of segmentation quality (see for example [12]). It is expressed as $S = \frac{2|X \cap Y|}{|X|+|Y|}$ where X is the result of image segmentation and Y is the corresponding ground truth image. S is equal to 1 when the segmented region and the ground truth region perfectly overlap, and 0 when they are disjoint. Firstly, for each parameter, the range of values giving satisfactory results was coarsely located by successive attempts. We determined that the triplet (τ, B, G_{Th}) leading to the best segmentation was located in range $[0.1, 0.4] \times [0.1, 0.4] \times [0.01, 0.2]$. Then, all parameter values within these ranges were tested, with respective steps 0.05, 0.05 and 0.02.

The optimal values for these parameters for which S values are maximum for both small and big wood pieces are $\tau = 0.3$,$B = 0.3$ and $G_{Th} = 0.05$. For big wood pieces, S average value obtained is 0.8, with a maximum value equals to 0.9 and a minimum value equals to 0.71. For small wood pieces, average S is 0.71 with a maximum value equals to 0.8 and a minimum value equals to 0.6.

5 Tracking of Floating Wood

During flood water waves and turbulences are prominent. As shown in Fig. 2 waves and wood resemble and therefore, the distinction should be made between them. We propose a temporal linking method based on the segmentation method for this purpose.

5.1 Extraction of Representative Points

The size, shape and orientation of the floating wood do not remain the same in consecutive frames. Moreover, submergence causes partial occlusions resulting in variable number of connected components, which is shown in Fig. 6. In order to group several connected components which may correspond to the same object, we first rely on centroids. The centroid c_{R_i} of a given component R_i is taken as the representative of R_i. To evaluate the closeness between two connected components R_1 and R_2, we choose to consider the euclidean distance between $\boldsymbol{c}_{R_1}$ and $\boldsymbol{c}_{R_2}$. This distance allows us to label the connected components of same object even if their size vary from one frame to another due to occlusion. We perform hierarchical grouping of connected components as long as the distance between their centroids is below a threshold s. At each step, the two closest connected components R_a and R_b are merged in a new region whose representative center is assigned to the average $(\boldsymbol{c}_{R_a} + \boldsymbol{c}_{R_b})/2$, until $\|\boldsymbol{c}_{R_a} - \boldsymbol{c}_{R_b}\| < s$. Let $R = \{R_i\}_{i=1...n}$ be a set of gathered connected components. Its representative center $\boldsymbol{c}_R$ is the average of centroids $\boldsymbol{c}_{R_i}$, and the following relation is verified:

$$R = \{R_1, ..., R_i, ...R_n\} \Rightarrow \boldsymbol{c}_R = \frac{1}{n}\sum_{i=1}^{n} \boldsymbol{c}_{R_i} \quad \text{and} \quad \|\boldsymbol{c}_{R_i} - \boldsymbol{c}_R\| < s \quad \forall i \in 1...n$$

This method is robust to partial occlusion of wood in water. Hence, every object in the frame is localized by a representative point, which is linked to its corresponding point in the next frame.

5.2 Temporal Linking of Floating Wood

Let $\boldsymbol{c}_R(t)$ and $\boldsymbol{c}_R(t+1)$ be representative points of object R matched in two consecutive frames. This is actually verified if their distance is below δ:

$$\|\boldsymbol{c}_R(t) - \boldsymbol{c}_R(t+1)\| \leq \delta \tag{5}$$

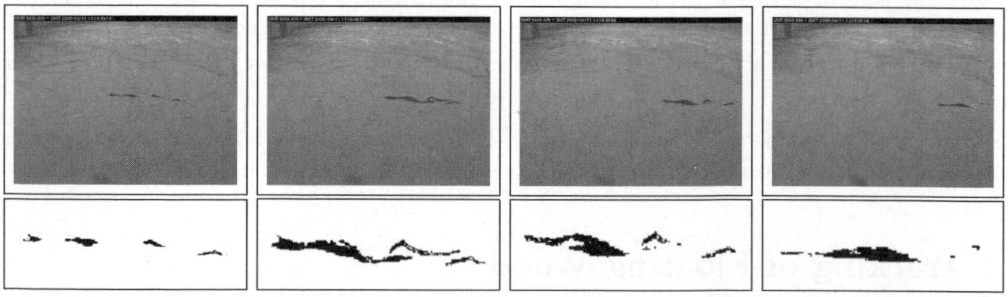

Fig. 6. Four consecutive frames of a moving wood object, zoomed resulting segmented object regions show the appearance of floating wood in the images

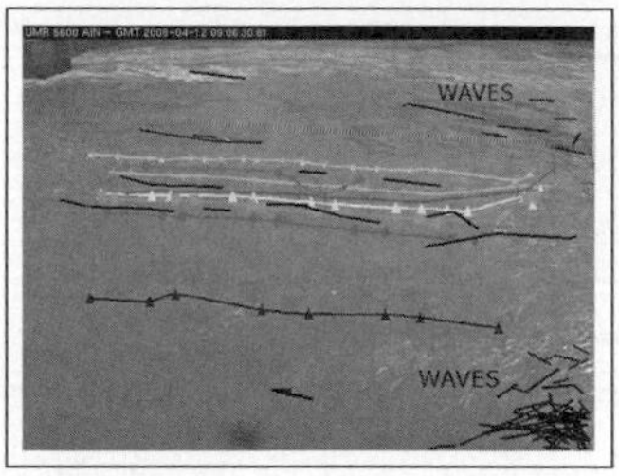

Fig. 7. A summary of small video portion represents wood (in different colors) and water waves (black color) trajectories

where $\delta = 100$ pixels, which is the maximal displacement of wood pieces we learned after experimentally testing on different videos. Incidentally, it allows us to give a lower bound of threshold s. If s is lower than δ, objects may be mismatched in consecutive frames. A component of an object may be mistakenly matched with another component of the same object, which does not happen if $s > \delta$. Similarly two objects moving simultaneously can be counted separately.

The positions of the representative point of an object in consecutive frames can be linked by line segments, which yields a trace in the *summary image*. Such an image is a graphical representation of trajectories during a given duration, an example is shown in Fig. 7. We can notice from the summary image that wood objects make longer traces than waves. The summary image also exhibits that water waves disappear after some frames. This property is used in the following to distinguish wood pieces from waves.

5.3 Counting Wood Pieces

For each object R, we determine the number of consecutive frames in which it appears. We obtain a sequence of n representative points $\{\boldsymbol{c}_R(t), \boldsymbol{c}_R(t+1), ..., \boldsymbol{c}_R(t+n-1)\}$ in which each couple $(\boldsymbol{c}_R(t+i), \boldsymbol{c}_R(t+i+1))$ verifies Eq. 5. Wood pieces and water waves are separated from one another according to their persistence in the consecutive frames. Hence, the chosen criterion to consider R as a wood piece is $n \geq K$. If a wood piece is not totally submerged, its representative point at different times should all be linked two by two. Unlike wood pieces, waves generally disappear after three or four frames. Hence, floating wood is counted on this basis. The relevancy of this limit is evaluated in section 6.

6 Experimental Results

The studied videos were generated by a monitoring system set up on the river Ain in France. Notice that even if all our videos come from a unique camera, weather conditions vary a lot. No assumption is made about the wood position in the water or according to static parts such as bridge. Consequently our method could be used with another camera in a likewise scene. We tested our algorithm of wood counting on five videos of 1500 frames each, for which we had ground truth

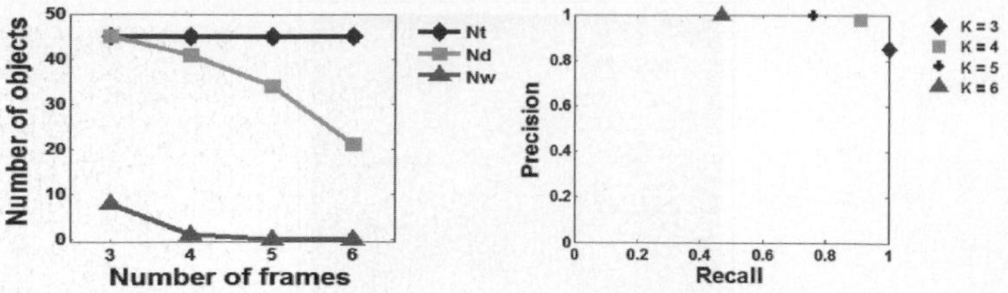

Fig. 8. (*on the left*) Quantitative comparison of selection the number of consecutive frames for wood attribution for a video (*on the right*) precision and recall for video evaluated for $K = 3,4,5$ and 6 consecutive frames

Table 1. Quantitative evaluation of wood counting and segmentation in videos

	Wood counting				Wood segmentation
Video	N_t	N_d(%)	N_{pd}(%)	N_w(%)	Overlap ratio(%)
1	41	91	9	1	79
2	37	90	10	0	76
3	47	90	10	0	81
4	80	92	8	3	83
5	85	93	7	4	80

data for validation. Frames have size 640×480 and are extracted from MPEG4-compressed streams tested on an Intel Core2 Duo 2.66GHz with 4GB RAM running C code. Average computation time per frame is 210 ms and it can be used smoothly in the on-line scenario. In section 5.3, we introduced the minimal number of consecutive frames K during which wood pieces should appear and to be counted as wood. This number is evaluated in Fig. 8. Qualitative evaluation is given by precision Pr and recall Re, defined as:

$$Pr = \frac{N_d}{N_d + N_w} \quad ; \quad Re = \frac{N_d}{N_t}$$

where N_d is the number of detected wood pieces by algorithm, N_w is the number of waves detected as wood and N_t is the total number of wood objects *i.e.* ($N_t = N_d + N_{pd}$) where N_{pd} number of non detected wood pieces. We can see that the best trade-off between false positive and negative detections is obtained with $K = 4$. Successful wood counting is validated manually by visual inspection frame per frame. Results are summarized in Table 1. Moreover, we randomly selected a wood piece per video and compute the overlap ratio of segmented wood object with ground truth.

After visual inspection, it turns out that undetected wood pieces correspond to very small parts, which are not critical with respect to the application. These small pieces are often totally submerged in some frames.

7 Concluding Remarks

In this paper we presented an automatic method for detecting and counting the floating wood in rivers. Intensity and temporal probability maps are computed for every incoming frame. These two probability maps are combined and resulting image is segmented by selecting a threshold. The resulting segmented image contains wood pieces along with some water waves. Water waves are separated from wood pieces by temporal linking method. Due to outdoor environment there are many constraints in our case. The experimental results are evaluated on every step. This algorithm could be extended to any object detection within multiple motions in background. Future work will be dedicated to the incorporation of prior object motion knowledge in both segmentation and tracking processes to reduce again omissions and false detections.

References

1. Shah, M.: Motion-based recognition: A survey. Image and Vision Computing 13, 129–155 (1995)
2. Li, L., Huang, W.M., Gu, I.Y.H., Tian, Q.: Statistical modeling of complex background for foreground object detection. IEEE Trans. on Image Processing 13(11), 1459–1472 (2004)
3. Stauffer, C., Grimson, W.: Learning patterns of activity using real-time tracking. IEEE Trans. Pattern Anal Machine Intell. 22(8), 747–757 (2000)
4. Wren, C., Azarbayejani, A., Darrell, T., Pentland, A.: Pfinder: realtime tracking of the human body. IEEE Trans. on Pattern Anal. Machine Intell. 19(7), 780–785 (1997)
5. Toyama, K., Krumm, J., Brumitt, B., Meyers, B.: Wallflower: principles and practices of background maintenance. In: IEEE Int. Conf. Computer Vision (ICCV), pp. 255–261 (1999)
6. Eng, H.L., Wang, J., Wah, A.H.K.S., Yau, W.Y.: Robust human detection within a highly dynamic aquatic environment in real time. IEEE Trans. on Image Processing 15(6), 1583–1600 (2006)
7. Mittal, A., Paragios, N.: Motion-based background subtraction using adaptive kernel density estimation. In: IEEE Conf. Comp. Vision and Pattern Recog. (CVPR), pp. 302–309 (2004)
8. Horn, B.K.P., Schunck, B.G.: Determining optical flow. Artificial Intelligence 17, 185–203 (1981)
9. Wixson, L.: Detecting salient motion by accumulating directionally-consistent flow. IEEE Trans. Pattern Anal Machine Intell. 22(8), 774–780 (2000)
10. Gao, X., Boult, T., Coetzee, F., Ramesh, V.: Error analysis of background adoption. In: IEEE Conf. Comp. Vision and Pattern Recog. (CVPR), pp. 503–510 (June 2000)
11. Ali, I., Tougne, L.: Unsupervised video analysis for counting of wood in river during floods. In: Bebis, G., Boyle, R., Parvin, B., Koracin, D., Kuno, Y., Wang, J., Pajarola, R., Lindstrom, P., Hinkenjann, A., Encarnação, M.L., Silva, C.T., Coming, D. (eds.) ISVC 2009. LNCS, vol. 5876, pp. 578–587. Springer, Heidelberg (2009)
12. Cárdenes, R., Bach, M., Chi, Y., Marras, I., de Luis, R., Anderson, M., Cashman, P., Bultelle, M.: Multimodal evaluation for medical image segmentation. In: Kropatsch, W.G., Kampel, M., Hanbury, A. (eds.) CAIP 2007. LNCS, vol. 4673, pp. 229–236. Springer, Heidelberg (2007)

Interactive Image Segmentation Using Level Sets and Dempster-Shafer Theory of Evidence*

Björn Scheuermann and Bodo Rosenhahn

Leibniz Universität Hannover, Germany
{scheuermann,rosenhahn}@tnt.uni-hannover.de

Abstract. Variational frameworks based on level set methods are popular for the general problem of image segmentation. They combine different feature channels in an energy minimization approach. In contrast to other popular segmentation frameworks, e.g. the graph cut framework, current level set formulations do not allow much user interaction. Except for selecting the initial boundary, the user is barely able to guide or correct the boundary propagation. Based on Dempster-Shafer theory of evidence we propose a segmentation framework which integrates user interaction in a novel way. Given the input image, the proposed algorithm determines the best segmentation allowing the user to take global influence on the boundary propagation.

1 Introduction

Mumford and Shah [13] formalized the problem of image segmentation as the minimization of an error functional. Independent of each other, Chan and Vese [3] and Tsai et al. [21] proposed level set implementations of the Mumford-Shah functional. The boundary between object and background is represented by the zero-level set of a signed distance function $\varphi : \Omega \rightarrow \mathbb{R}$ [15]. The boundary evolution is modeled by a partial differential equation coming from the corresponding Euler-Lagrange equation. In contrast to the frameworks propagating explicit boundary points [9], the implicit level set representation has several well known properties, e.g. it can handle topological changes elegantly and it can easily be extended to higher dimensions.

Due to their popularity, region-based segmentation frameworks have been refined continuously [11,2,18,14,5,22,17,6] to increase the number of scenes, where this framework can succeed. E.g. authors proposed statistical modeling of regions [22], additional feature channels like texture [17] or shape priors [6].

Yet, most existing level set methods are not qualified as an interactive segmentation tool. The corresponding initial value problem propagates the region boundary to a local minimum of the energy function without allowing the user to correct the final segmentation result. In contrast to the variational approaches, discrete energy minimization segmentation frameworks such as graph cut approaches [20,1,16] provide an elegant way to treat user interaction to guide or correct the segmentation process.

* This work is partially funded by the German Research Foundation (RO 2497/6-1).

A. Heyden and F. Kahl (Eds.): SCIA 2011, LNCS 6688, pp. 656–665, 2011.

Fig. 1. Segmentation results using the proposed user-interactive segmentation framework. The left example is a James Bond photo from the internet and the right one is from the Berkeley Segmentation Database.

A simple rule-based reasoning is usually used to integrate user interaction into the segmentation process: if the user marks a pixel as an object, then it is forced to be object, on the contrary a pixel is background if the user marks it as background. These so-called hard constraints can also be found in [1,16,4]

Level set methods for interactive segmentation have been proposed earlier by Cremers et al. [4]. They developed a statistical framework integrating user interaction. In addition to an initial boundary they provide a framework, where the user is able to mark object and background regions in terms similar to a shape prior. Thus the user can indicate which areas are likely to be part of the object or the background. In contrast, the key contribution of our paper is to develop a framework based on Dempster-Shafer theory of evidence which actually also uses the intensity information contained in the user defined regions. Thus, the evolving boundary is directly driven by the following three terms:

- the intensity information contained in the image [22],
- the user labeling in terms similar to a shape prior [4] and
- the intensity information of the user labeling (**our contribution**).

The proposed contribution results in global influence of the user defined regions, while other frameworks only allow local refinement of the segmentation (e.g. [4,1]). The different features contained in the image and the user defined regions are combined according to Dempster's rule of combination.

We continue with a review of the variational approach for image segmentation, which is the basis of our segmentation framework. Section 3 introduces the proposed segmentation method which integrates the user interactivity and the final workflow of the segmentation is recapitulated. Experimental results in Section 4 demonstrate the advantages of the proposed method in comparison to other state-of-the-art segmentation methods. Section 5 concludes the paper.

2 Level Set Segmentation with Evidence Theory

The variational approach for image segmentation used in our framework is based on the works of [3,5,22]. An extension of these works introducing the Dempster-Shafer theory of evidence is presented in [19]. In this section we will shortly review this framework and the key advantages of using evidence theory for level set based segmentation methods instead of the traditional Bayesian framework.

The key idea, which makes it different from other Bayesian segmentation frameworks, is the use of Dempster's rule of combination to fuse informations arising from different feature channels [7]. This framework is often described as a generalization of the Bayesian theory to represent inaccuracy and uncertainty at the same time. With the Bayesian theory, feature channels with low support have a high influence on the decision. In contrast, with Dempster-Shafer theory of evidence feature channels with high support for a specific region have a higher influence on the evolving boundary [19]. We make use of these two properties to introduce the proposed user interactivity.

The basis for our segmentation method is the following energy-functional:

$$E(\varphi) = \underbrace{-\int_{\Omega} H(\varphi) \log m_{im}(\Omega_1)\, d\Omega - \int_{\Omega} (1 - H(\varphi)) \log m_{im}(\Omega_2)\, d\Omega}_{\text{data term}} + \lambda_1 \underbrace{\int_{\Omega} |\nabla H(\varphi)|\, d\Omega}_{\text{curve constraint}}, \tag{1}$$

where λ_1 is a weighting parameter between the given constraints, $H(s)$ is a regularized Heaviside function and $m_{im} : \wp(\Omega) \to [0, 1]$ is the mass function defined over the hypothesis set $\Omega = \{\Omega_1, \Omega_2\}$. In this context the region Ω_1 denotes the object region and Ω_2 the background. The mass function m_{im}, fuses k feature channels with Dempster's rule of combination:

$$m_{im} = m_1 \otimes m_2 \otimes \ldots \otimes m_k\,, \tag{2}$$

where the single mass functions m_j are defined by probability densities for background and object. Dempster's rule of combination is given by

$$m(A) = m_1(A) \otimes m_2(A) = \frac{\sum_{B \cap C = A} m_1(B) m_2(C)}{1 - \sum_{B \cap C = \emptyset} m_1(B) m_2(C)}\,. \tag{3}$$

The probability densities are computed by a histogram analysis for each region. They are defined by

$$\begin{aligned} &m_j(\Omega_1) = p_{1,j}(I(x)), \quad m_j(\Omega_2) = p_{2,j}(I(x))\,, \\ &m_j(\emptyset) = 0\,, \quad m_j(\Omega) = 1 - (p_{1,j}(I(x))) + p_{2,j}(I(x)))\,, \end{aligned} \tag{4}$$

for $j \in \{1, \ldots, k\}$. For the quality of the segmentation process, it is very important how the probability densities for each region are modeled. In this paper we restrict to the nonparametric Parzen density estimates [10]. Using discrete histograms this approach comes down smoothing the histograms computed for each region i and channel j by a Gaussian kernel. Other cues and models that can be integrated in such a framework are texture information [17] and shape priors [11].

Minimizing the energy (1) with respect to φ using variational methods and gradient descent leads to the following partial differential equation:

$$\frac{\partial \varphi}{\partial t} = \delta(\varphi)\left(\log \frac{m_{im}(\Omega_1)}{m_{im}(\Omega_2)} + \lambda_1 \operatorname{div}\left(\frac{\nabla \varphi}{|\nabla \varphi|}\right)\right). \tag{5}$$

Thus the segmentation process works according to the well known expectation-maximation principle [8] with an initial partitioning (Ω_1, Ω_2).

3 Interactive Variational Image Segmentation

Analogue to Cremers et al. [4] we assume a given image $I : \Omega \to \mathbb{R}$ and a user input L marking certain image locations as object or background regions.

$$L : \Omega \to \{-1, 0, 1\}, \tag{6}$$

where the label values reflect the user input:

$$L(x) = \begin{cases} 1, & x \text{ marked as object,} \\ -1, & x \text{ marked as background,} \\ 0, & x \text{ not marked.} \end{cases} \tag{7}$$

Using the user-defined labeling $L(x)$ and defining a new segmentation constraint on this leads to the proposed energy function:

$$E(\varphi) = E_{im}(\varphi) + \lambda_1 E_{curve}(\varphi) + \underbrace{E_{user}(\varphi)}_{new} \tag{8}$$

where $E_{user} = \nu \cdot E_{user-shape} + E_{user-image}$. The first term of the *user-defined* energy function is defined according to [4] by

$$E_{user-shape} = -\frac{1}{2}\int_{\Omega} L_{\sigma}(x)\operatorname{sign}(\varphi(x))\, d\Omega\,, \tag{9}$$

with a Gaussian-smoothed label function

$$L_{\sigma}(x) = \int_{\Omega} L(x) k_{\sigma}(x)\, d\Omega \tag{10}$$

and the Gaussian kernel function $k_{\sigma}(x)$.

This model has two free parameters ν and σ which can be interpreted as follows. The parameter ν provides the overall weight of the user interaction and determine how strongly the user input will affect the segmentation. The parameter σ defines the spatial range within which a point labeled as object or background will affect the segmentation. It can therefore be interpreted as a *brush size*.

The novel second term $E_{user-image}$ of E_{user} is inspired by the image energy E_{image} and is defined as follows:

$$\begin{aligned} E_{user-image} = & \int_{\Omega} H(\varphi) \log m_{user}(\Omega_1)\, d\Omega \\ & - \int_{\Omega} (1 - H(\varphi)) \log m_{user}(\Omega_2)\, d\Omega\,. \end{aligned} \tag{11}$$

The mass function m_{user} is, in contrast to the mass function m_{image}, defined by the marked regions while the function m_{image} is defined by the image regions divided by the curve.

$E_{user-shape}$ can be interpreted as a user-defined shape prior, while $E_{user-image}$ takes the image information on the marked regions into account and can therefor be interpreted as an indicator for the appearance of a region.

Fusing the mass functions m_{im} and m_{user} contained in E_{image} and $E_{user-image}$ respectively, with Dempster's rule of combination we obtain an energy-functional of the form:

$$\begin{aligned} E(\varphi) = & \underbrace{-\int_{\Omega} H(\varphi) \log m(\Omega_1)\, d\Omega - \int_{\Omega} (1 - H(\varphi)) \log m(\Omega_2)\, d\Omega}_{\text{data term + user defined term}} \\ & + \lambda_1 \underbrace{\int_{\Omega} |\nabla H(\varphi)|\, d\Omega}_{\text{curve constraint}} - \lambda_2 \nu \underbrace{\int_{\Omega} L_{\sigma} H(\varphi)\, d\Omega}_{\text{user-shape}}\,, \end{aligned} \tag{12}$$

where the mass function $m = m_{im} \otimes m_{user}$ fuses the image data given by m_{im} and the user data given by m_{user} according to Dempster's rule of combination. Minimizing (12) using variational methods and gradient descent leads to the following partial differential equation:

$$\frac{\partial \varphi}{\partial t} = \delta(\varphi) \left[\log \frac{m(\Omega_1)}{m(\Omega_2)} + \lambda_1 \mathrm{div} \left(\frac{\nabla \varphi}{|\nabla \varphi|} \right) + \lambda_2 \left(\nu L_{\sigma} \right) \right]. \tag{13}$$

The Dempster-Shafer theory of evidence is used to fuse the information because feature channels with low support have a lower influence on the evolving boundary as shown in [19]. This is helpful because the user-defined regions can be very sparse, which means that the resulting channel-histograms can have regions where neither the object nor the background region is supported. Using the Bayesian framework for fusing this information would lead to small probabilities for both regions, ignoring all other feature channels, especially the image feature channels. With the proposed framework based on Dempster's rule of combination, this would be interpreted as uncertainty meaning that the other feature channels are not affected by this feature.

In contrast to the work of Cremers et al. [4] the proposed framework not merely provides an indication in terms of a shape prior for the segmentation,

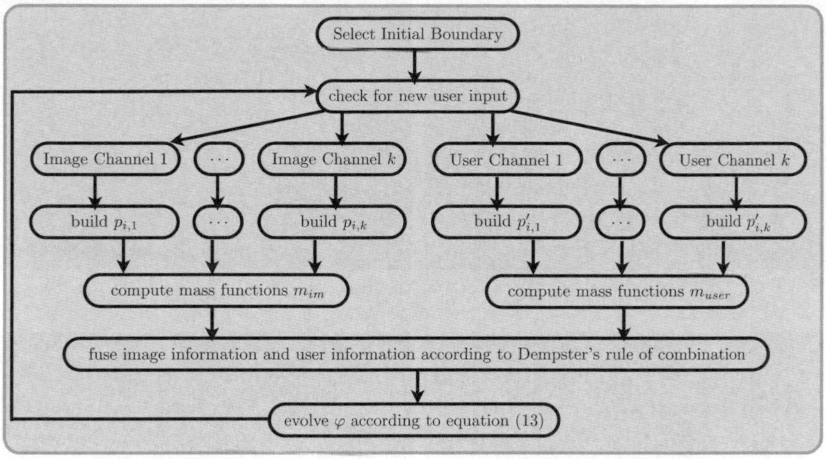

Fig. 2. General workflow of the proposed variational, user interactive segmentation framework

but actually uses the intensity information given by the user labeling. This information is further combined with Dempster's rule of combination, instead of multiplying the different probabilities, to represent inaccuracy and uncertainty. While the user labels in [4] have only local support to the evolving boundary and thus to the final segmentation, our framework allows global support for user defined regions. Figure 2 shows the proposed general interactive segmentation workflow.

4 Experiments

In this section we test the proposed user-interactive segmentation framework experimentally. Several results are shown in Figures 1 and 3 and compared to the graph cut framework by Boykov et al. [1]. The images used for the experiments are natural images taken from the berkley segmentation dataset [12]. Furthermore we compared the proposed framework with the user-interactive framework in [4]. While user-interaction only has local influence on the final segmentation in the framework proposed by Cremers et al., our framework allows global influence on the segmentation result with a small stroke, e.g. the global influence of the small foreground stroke in Figure 3.

We also performed a user study, where six persons segmented five real images with the proposed framework and the graph cut segmentation tool. In these moderately difficult examples (e.g. the soldier in Figure 4) the proposed framework needed significantly fewer user-interactions while the mean F_1 measure over all segmented images is comparable. The result of our user study is shown in Table 1. Figure 4 shows some of the segmented images. We have to distinguish that users tend to make longer strokes using graph cuts. Especially the two initial strokes are very large (see Figure 3 and 4) compared to the small strokes in our

initialization (2 clicks)
initialization (5 strokes)
segmentation result
segmentation result
user interactivity (4 additional strokes)
user interactivity (9 additional strokes)
Final segmentation result after user refinement (Initialization (2 clicks, 1 foreground and 3 background strokes)
Segmentation result after user refinement (11 foreground- and 3 background strokes)

Fig. 3. Segmentation results using the proposed interactive segmentation framework (left) and graph cut (right). The proposed segmentation algorithm needs significant fewer user interactions (red and blue strokes) to produce a slightly better result.

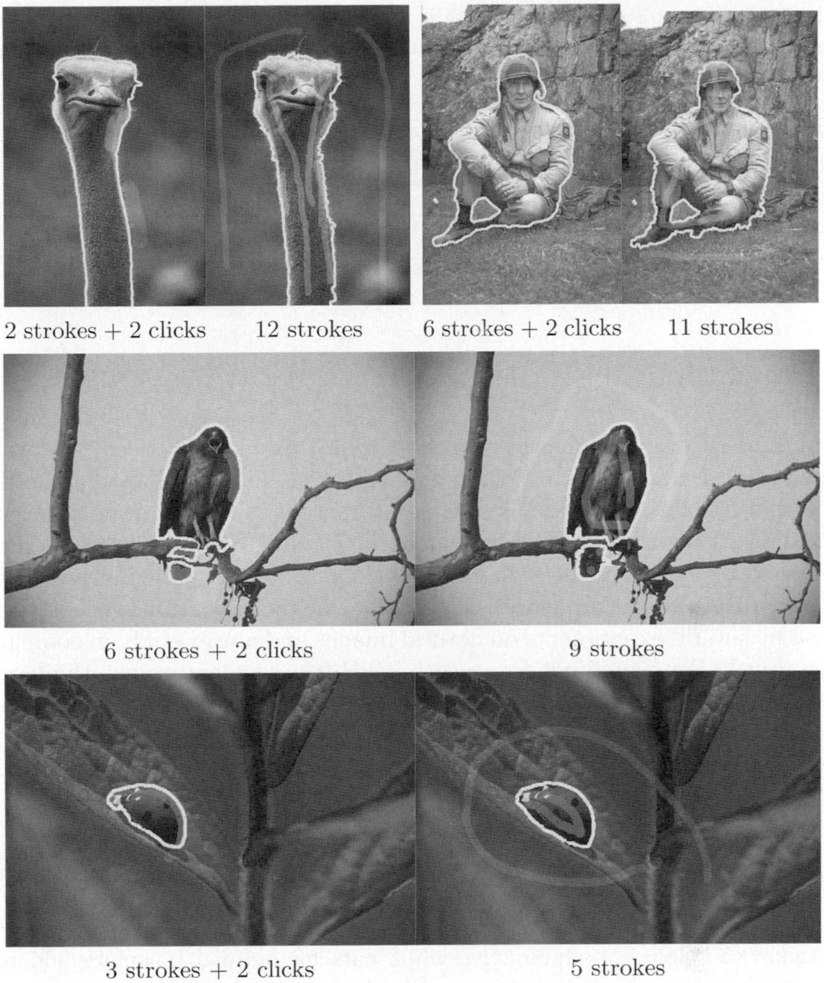

Fig. 4. Segmentation results using the proposed variational framework (left) and GraphCut (right). The yellow curves describe the segmentation boundaries, while the blue and red strokes mark the user defined regions.

framework. The average stroke size with the proposed method is approximately half of the stroke size with graph cuts. Although the proposed method is not implemented on the GPU, the total time for segmenting the images was almost the same for both methods. In addition the users are able to guide the evolving boundary instead of changing the final segmentation.

We have to mention that we did not test other segmentation frameworks like e.g. GrabCut [16], but the results presented in [16] are very close to what we and the users have achieved in our study.

Table 1. Results of our user study. While the mean F_1-measure is comparable for all methods, the proposed method needed significantly fewer user interactions, comparing the average number of strokes.

Image	Graph Cuts	F_1	[4]	F_1	proposed Method	F_1
Lady Bug	4.33 str.	0.9366	1.3 str. + 2 klicks	0.8943	1.3 str. + 2 klicks	0.9011
Eagle	9.33 str.	0.9676	7 str. + 2 klicks	0.9265	5.5 str. + 2 klicks	0.9472
Bird	7.83 str.	0.9610	2.3 str. + 2 klicks	0.9541	1.83str. + 2 klicks	0.9624
Flowers	7.17 str.	0.9808	6.6 str. + 2 klicks	0.9891	4 str. + 2 klicks	0.9892
Soldier	9.33 str.	0.9654	10.3 str. + 2 klicks	0.9814	7.33 str. + 2 klicks	0.9736

5 Conclusion

We presented a new framework for foreground extraction based on level set methods and Dempster-Shafer theory of evidence. The framework extends the traditional framework by means of user-interactivity to allow more precise segmentations. The user-interactivity (strokes) is integrated into the traditional framework by a user-defined shape prior (local influence) and by user-defined image features (global influence). The impact of the new framework is demonstrated by several experiments on natural images and a user study in comparison to the well known graph cut framework. With the new extensions the level set based segmentation framework allows small user interactions having global influence on the evolving boundary. In comparison to graph cut, the presented framework needs significantly fewer user interactions to produce high-quality segmentations.

References

1. Boykov, Y., Jolly, M.: Interactive graph cuts for optimal boundary and region segmentation of objects in nd images. In: International Conference on Computer Vision, vol. 1, pp. 105–112 (2001)
2. Caselles, V., Kimmel, R., Sapiro, G.: Geodesic active contours. International Journal of Computer Vision 22(1), 61–79 (1997)
3. Chan, T., Vese, L.: Active contours without edges. IEEE Transactions on Image Processing 10(2), 266–277 (2001)
4. Cremers, D., Fluck, O., Rousson, M., Aharon, S.: A probabilistic level set formulation for interactive organ segmentation. In: Proc. of the SPIE Medical Imaging, San Diego, USA (2007)
5. Cremers, D., Rousson, M., Deriche, R.: A review of statistical approaches to level set segmentation: integrating color, texture, motion and shape. International Journal of Computer Vision 72(2), 195–215 (2007)
6. Cremers, D., Schnörr, C., Weickert, J.: Diffusion Snakes: Combining statistical shape knowledge and image information in a variational framework. In: Paragios, N. (ed.) IEEE First Int. Workshop on Variational and Level Set Methods, Vancouver, pp. 137–144 (2001)

7. Dempster, A.P.: A generalization of bayesian inference. Journal of the Royal Statistical Society. Series B (Methodological) 30(2), 205–247 (1968)
8. Dempster, A., Laird, N., Rubin, D., et al.: Maximum likelihood from incomplete data via the em algorithm. Journal of the Royal Statistical Society. Series B (Methodological) 39(1), 1–38 (1977)
9. Kass, M., Witkin, A., Terzopoulos, D.: Snakes: Active Contour models. International Journal of Computer Vision 1(4), 321–331 (1988)
10. Kim, J., Fisher III, J., Yezzi Jr., A., Cetin, M., Willsky, A.: Nonparametric methods for image segmentation using information theory and curve evolution. In: IEEE International Conference on Image Processing (ICIP), pp. 797–800 (2002)
11. Malladi, R., Sethian, J.A., Vemuri, B.C.: Shape modeling with front propagation: A level set approach. IEEE Transactions on Pattern Analysis and Machine Intelligence 17, 158–175 (1995)
12. Martin, D., Fowlkes, C., Tal, D., Malik, J.: A database of human segmented natural images and its application to evaluating segmentation algorithms and measuring ecological statistics. In: Proc. 8th Int'l Conf. Computer Vision, vol. 2, pp. 416–423 (2001)
13. Mumford, D., Shah, J.: Boundary detection by minimizing functionals. In: IEEE Computer Society Conference on Computer Vision and Pattern Recognition, pp. 22–26. IEEE Computer Society Press, Springer, San Francisco, CA (1985)
14. Osher, S., Paragios, N.: Geometric level set method in imaging, vision, and graphics. Springer, Heidelberg (2003)
15. Osher, S., Sethian, J.: Fronts propagating with curvature dependent speed: Algorithm based on hamilton-jacobi formulation. Journal of Computational Physics 79, 12–49 (1988)
16. Rother, C., Kolmogorov, V., Blake, A.: Grabcut: Interactive foreground extraction using iterated graph cuts. In: ACM SIGGRAPH 2004 Papers, p. 314. ACM, New York (2004)
17. Rousson, M., Brox, T., Deriche, R.: Active unsupervised texture segmentation on a diffusion based feature space. In: IEEE Computer Society Conference on Computer Vision and Pattern Recognition, Madison, WI, pp. 699–704 (2003)
18. Rousson, M., Paragios, N.: Shape priors for level set representations. In: Heyden, A., Sparr, G., Nielsen, M., Johansen, P. (eds.) ECCV 2002. LNCS, vol. 2351, pp. 78–92. Springer, Heidelberg (2002)
19. Scheuermann, B., Rosenhahn, B.: Feature quarrels: The dempster-shafer evidence theory for image segmentation using a variational framework. In: Kimmel, R., Klette, R., Sugimoto, A. (eds.) ACCV 2010, Part II. LNCS, vol. 6493, pp. 426–439. Springer, Heidelberg (2011)
20. Shi, J., Malik, J.: Normalized cuts and image segmentation. IEEE Transactions on Pattern Analysis and Machine Intelligence 22(8), 888–905 (2000)
21. Tsai, A., Yezzi Jr., A., Wells III, W., Tempany, C., Tucker, D., Fan, A., Grimson, W., Willsky, A.: Model-based curve evolution technique for image segmentation. In: Proceedings of the 2001 IEEE Computer Society Conference on Computer Vision and Pattern Recognition, vol. 1, pp. 463–468 (2001)
22. Zhu, S.C., Yuille, A.: Region competition: unifying snakes, region growing, and bayes/mdl for multiband image segmentation. IEEE Transaction on Pattern Analysis and Machine Intelligence 18(9), 884–900 (1996)

Fast and Efficient Saliency Detection Using Sparse Sampling and Kernel Density Estimation

Hamed Rezazadegan Tavakoli, Esa Rahtu, and Janne Heikkilä

Machine Vision Group, Department of Electrical and Information Engineering,
University of Oulu, Finland
{hamed.rezazadegan,esa.rahtu,janne.heikkila}@ee.oulu.fi
http://www.ee.oulu.fi/mvg

Abstract. Salient region detection has gained a great deal of attention in computer vision. It is useful for applications such as adaptive video/image compression, image segmentation, anomaly detection, image retrieval, etc. In this paper, we study saliency detection using a center-surround approach. The proposed method is based on estimating saliency of local feature contrast in a Bayesian framework. The distributions needed are estimated particularly using sparse sampling and kernel density estimation. Furthermore, the nature of method implicitly considers what refereed to as center bias in literature. Proposed method was evaluated on a publicly available data set which contains human eye fixation as ground-truth. The results indicate more than 5% improvement over state-of-the-art methods. Moreover, the method is fast enough to run in real-time.

Keywords: Saliency detection, discriminant center-surround, eye-fixation.

1 Introduction

Saliency detection in images and videos was introduced to computer vision in late 90s. One of the classical, most well-known papers is the one published by Itti et al. [1] in 1998. Their approach is based on extracting early visual features (e.g. colors, orientations, edges, ...) and fusing them into a saliency map in a three-step process.

Saliency detection has two key aspects: biological and computational. From the biological point of view, we can categorize saliency detection methods into top-down, bottom-up, and hybrid classes. In the top-down approach, it is assumed that the process of finding salient regions is controlled by high-level intelligence in brain. The main idea of bottom-up approach is that the process of saliency detection is an uncontrolled action on the shoulder of eye's receptors. Hybrid aspect believes in parallel and complementary role of top-down and bottom-up approaches.

Considering the computational view, we grouped saliency detection into different paradigms. One well-known class of algorithms is the center-surround technique. In this paradigm, the hypothesis is that there exists a local window divided into a center and a surround; and the center contains an object. Figure 1

A. Heyden and F. Kahl (Eds.): SCIA 2011, LNCS 6688, pp. 666–675, 2011.

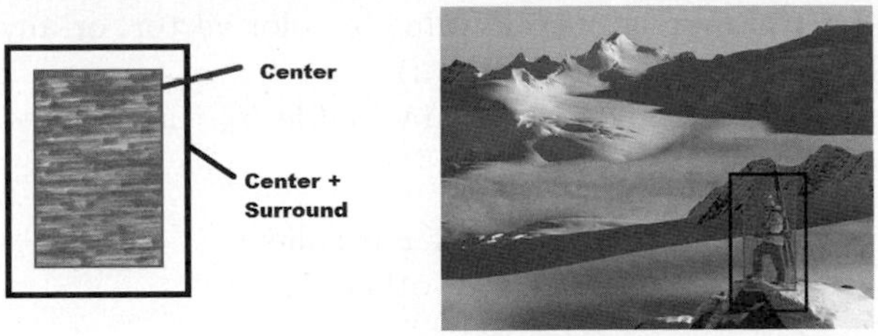

(a) (b)

Fig. 1. An example showing center surround concept

shows this concept. Achanta et al. [2] provides us such a sample. They measured the color difference of a center pixel and average color in its immediate surrounding. Seo and Milanfar [3] used Local Steering Kernel (LSK) response as a feature and applied Parzen window density estimation to estimate the probability of having an object in each local window. Rahtu et al. [4] employed histogram estimation over contrast features in a window.

Frequency domain methods can be considered another category. Examples of such techniques can be found in [5,6,7]. Hou and Zhang [6] proposed a method based on relating extracted spectral residual features of an image in the spectral domain to the spatial domain. In [5] phase spectrum of quaternion Fourier transform is utilized to compute saliency. Achanta et al. [7] introduced a technique which relies on reinforcement of regions with more information.

Another class of algorithms relies on information theory concepts. In [8] a technique based on self-information is introduced to compute the likelihood of having a salient region. Lin et al. [9] employed local entropy to detect a salient region of an image. Mahadevan and Vasconcelos [10] utilized Kullback-Leibler divergence to measure mutual information to compute saliency.

In this paper, we introduce a method which belongs to the center-surround category. The major difference between the proposed technique and other similar methods is that it uses sparse sampling and kernel density estimation to build the saliency map. Also, proposed method's nature implicitly includes center bias. The method is tested on a publicly available data set. Finally, it is shown that the proposed method is fast and accurate.

2 Saliency Measurement

In this section, general Bayesian framework toward a center-surround approach is initially discussed. Afterwards, basics of proposed method are explained. It is followed by introducing the multi-scale extension. Finally, a brief explanation about implementation and algorithm parameters is provided.

2.1 Bayesian Center-Surround

Let us assume that we have an image I. We define each pixel as $x = (\bar{x}, f)$ where $\bar{x}$ is the coordinate of pixel x in image I, and f is a feature vector for each coordinate. So, f can be a gray-scale value, a color vector, or any other desired feature (e.g., LBP, Gabor, SIFT, LSK, ...).

Suppose, there exists a binary random variable H_x that defines pixel saliency. It is defined as follows:

$$H_x = \begin{cases} 1, & \text{if } x \text{ is salient} \\ 0, & \text{otherwise.} \end{cases} \tag{1}$$

The saliency of pixel x can be computed using $P(H_x = 1|f) = P(1|f)$. It can be expanded using the Bayes rule as follows:

$$\frac{P(f|1)P(1)}{P(f|1)P(1) + P(f|0)P(0)}. \tag{2}$$

In the center-surround approach, we have a window W divided into a surround B and center K where the hypothesis is that K contains an object. In fact, pixels in K contribute to $P(f|1)$, and pixels in B contribute to $P(f|0)$. Having a sliding window W, we can sweep the whole image and calculate the saliency value locally.

The difference between center-surround methods is the way they deal with $P(1|f)$. For instance, Rahtu et al. [11] estimate (2), by approximating both $P(f|1)$ and $P(f|0)$ using histogram approximation over pixels' color values. Moreover, they assume $P(0)$ and $P(1)$ are constant. Seo and Milanfar [3] suppose $P(1|f) \propto P(f|1)$ and apply Parzen window estimation over LSK features to approximate $P(f|1)$.

2.2 Defining Saliency Measure

We define saliency measure for x belonging to center utilizing $P(1|f, \bar{x})$. Applying Bayes' theorem, we can write:

$$P(1|f, \bar{x}) = \frac{P(f|\bar{x}, 1)P(1|\bar{x})}{P(f|\bar{x})}. \tag{3}$$

This can be further expanded to:

$$P(1|f, \bar{x}) = \frac{P(f|\bar{x}, 1)P(1|\bar{x})}{P(f|\bar{x}, 1)P(1|\bar{x}) + P(f|\bar{x}, 0)P(0|\bar{x})}. \tag{4}$$

Computing (4) require the estimation of $P(f|\bar{x}, 1)$ and $P(f|\bar{x}, 0)$, which can be done in several ways. For instance in order to estimate $P(f|1)$ and $P(f|0)$, in [12,13,14] a generalized Gaussian model is used, in [3] Parzen window estimation was adapted, and Histogram estimation is applied in [11]. We adapt kernel density estimation method to compute feature distribution. As a result, we can write:

$$P(1|f, \bar{x}) = \frac{\frac{1}{m}\sum_{i=1}^{m} \mathcal{G}\left(f - f_{\bar{x}Ki}\right) P(1|\bar{x})}{\frac{1}{m}\sum_{i=1}^{m} \mathcal{G}\left(f - f_{\bar{x}Ki}\right) P(1|\bar{x}) + \frac{1}{n}\sum_{i=1}^{n} \mathcal{G}\left(f - f_{\bar{x}Bi}\right) P(0|\bar{x})}, \tag{5}$$

where n and m are the number of samples, $x_{Bi} = (\bar{x}_{Bi}, f_{\bar{x}_{Bi}})$ is the i_{th} sample belonging to B and $x_{Ki} = (\bar{x}_{Ki}, f_{\bar{x}_{Ki}})$ is the i_{th} sample belonging to K, and $\mathcal{G}(.)$ is a Gaussian kernel.

Since we plan to compute saliency of pixel x belonging to center, (5) can be simplified by selecting K as small as a pixel. In that case, we have

$$\mathcal{G}(f - f_{\bar{x}_{Ki}}) = \frac{1}{\sqrt{2\pi}\sigma_1} exp(-\frac{\|f - f\|^2}{2\sigma_1^2}) = \frac{1}{\sqrt{2\pi}\sigma_1}, \tag{6}$$

where σ_1 is standard deviation. Afterwards, we assume that only a few samples from B, which are scattered uniformly on a hypothetical circle with radius r contribute to $P(f|\bar{x}, 0)$. In fact, by substituting (6) into (5) and knowing the fact that $P(0|\bar{x}) + P(1|\bar{x}) = 1$, we can write:

$$P_r^n(1|f, \bar{x}) = 1 \Bigg/ \left(1 + \frac{\sigma_1(1 - P(1|\bar{x}))}{n\sigma_0 P(1|\bar{x})} \sum_{i=1}^{n} exp\left(\frac{\|f - f_{\bar{x}_{Bi,r}}\|^2}{2\sigma_0^2}\right)\right), \tag{7}$$

where σ_1 and σ_0 are standard deviations, n is the number of samples form B and r shows the radius at which samples will be taken. Figure 2 illustrates an example of such a central pixel and sample pixels around it. This sparse sampling reduces the number of operations required to estimate $P(f|\bar{x}, 0)$ and increases computation speed.

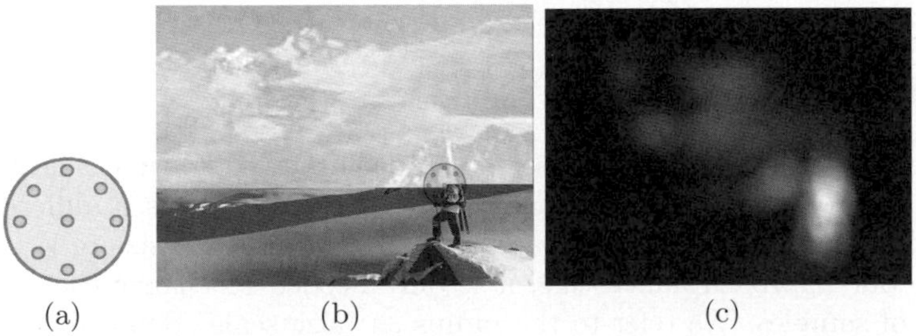

Fig. 2. (a) A pixel and its selected surrounding samples in a window, (b) Procedure of applying a window, (c) A sample saliency map obtained, using proposed method

In order to approximate the distribution $P(1|\bar{x})$, we compute average fixation map over a training set. Also, to avoid zero value we biased the obtained probability by adding $b = 0.1$. We further smooth the estimated distribution using a Gaussian kernel of size 30×30 and $\sigma = 20$. Figure 3 shows the probability obtained.

We define saliency in terms of sampling circle radius and number of samples as follows:

$$S_r^n(x) = \mathcal{A}_c * [P_r^n(1|f, \bar{x})]^\alpha, \tag{8}$$

where $\mathcal{A}_c$ is a circular averaging filter, $*$ is convolution operator, $P_r^n(1|f, \bar{x})$ is calculated using (7), and $\alpha \geq 1$ is an attenuation factor which emphasizes the effect of high probability areas.

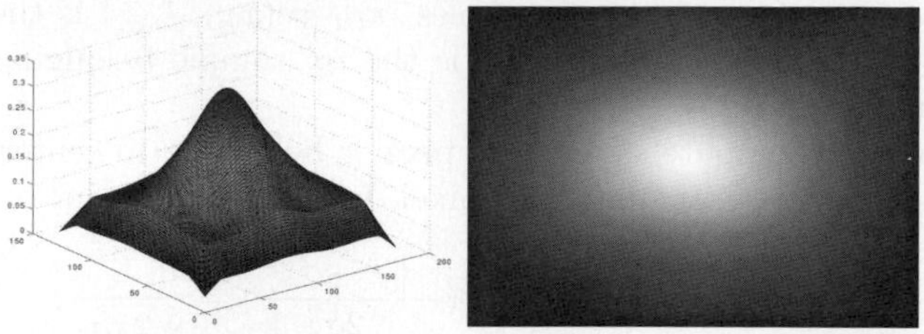

Fig. 3. Estimated $P(1|\bar{x})$. It is generated by low pass filtering an average fixation map obtained from several fixation maps.

Center bias. There exists evidence that human eyes fixates mostly on the center of image [15]. This is because most of the human taken photos are taken in such a way to have the subject in the center of the image. This knowledge can be used to improve saliency detection performance. Saliency detection benefits from center bias by giving more weight to the center. For instance, Judd et al. [15] applied an arbitrary Gaussian blob on the center of the image to centrally bias their technique. Yang et al. [14] learned the central bias by learning a normal Bivariate Gaussian over the eye fixation distribution.

In our method $P(1|\bar{x})$ gives weight to the positions more probable to observe an object. However, since we learn it from human taken photos, it can be considered equivalent to center bias in this case. Studying figure 3 conveys the same concept.

2.3 Multi-scale Measure

Many techniques apply the multi-scale approach toward saliency. The reason for such an approach is that each image may consist of objects of different sizes. Generally multi-scale property is achieved by changing the size of W. In order to make our approach multi-scale, it is only needed to change the radius and number of samples. We refer to the radius as "size scale" denoted by r and to the number of samples as "precision scale" denoted by n. Computing saliency of a pixel at different scales we take the average over all scales:

$$S(x) = \frac{1}{M} \sum_{i=1}^{M} S_{r_i}^{n_i}(x), \tag{9}$$

where M is the number of scales, $S_{r_i}^{n_i}(x)$ is the i_{th} saliency map calculated at a different scale using (8).

2.4 Implementation

In our implementation, we used CIELab color vector as feature. So for any pixel $x = (\bar{x}, f)$, we have $f = [L(\bar{x}), a(\bar{x}), b(\bar{x})]$ where $L(\bar{x})$, $a(\bar{x})$ and $b(\bar{x})$ are CIELab values at $\bar{x}$. In order to reduce the effect of noise, we employed a low-pass filter. For this purpose, we used a Gaussian kernel of size 9×9 with standard deviation

$\sigma = 0.5$. We also normalized all the images to 171×128 to make easier the process of images with different sizes.

We applied three different size scales with fixed precision scales. The parameters were $r = [13, 25, 38]$, $n = [8, 8, 8]$, $\sigma_1 = [1, 1, 1]$, and $\sigma_0 = [10, 10, 10]$. The attenuation parameter α was set to 25, and an averaging disk filter of radius 10 was applied. All the tests were performed by means of MATLAB R 2010a on a machine with Intel 6600 CPU running at 2.4 GHz clock, and 2GB RAM.

3 Experiments

This section is dedicated to the evaluation of proposed saliency detection technique. We compare proposed technique with Achanta et al. [7], Achanta et al. [2], Zhang et al.[1] [13], Seo and Milanfar[2] [3], Goferman et al.[3] [16], Rahtu et al.[4] [11], Bruce and Tsotsos[5][8], and Hou et al.[6] [6]. We use available public codes for all the methods except for [2,7]. The parameters used for each algorithm are the same as reported in the original paper. We provide qualitative and quantitative tests to show the pros and cons of each technique. Also, we evaluate running time of each method.

We used data set released by Bruce and Tsotsos in [8]. The data set consists of 120 images of size 681×511 and eye fixation maps. Almost all of images are composed of everyday life situations which makes the data set a difficult one. We divide the data set into the train and test sets containing 80 and 40 images, respectively. $P(1|\bar{x})$ was obtained using the training set.

3.1 Quantitative Analysis

Receiver Operating Characteristic (ROC) curve is a method of evaluating saliency maps using eye fixation density maps [8,15,14]. In this method, a threshold is varied over saliency map; and number of fixated and non-fixated points are counted at each threshold value. Amount of true positive rate and false positive rate are obtained by comparing the results with a reference saliency map. These values will build the ROC curve.

In order to perform quantitative analysis, we use a similar approach as in [8]. In fact, we moved the threshold value from zero to maximum pixel value, and computed true positive and false positive values. Eventually, reported the average value over all images. Figure 4 depicts the resulting curves. Table 1 reports the Area Under the ROC (AUC). As it can be seen from both Figure 4 and Table 1, proposed method outperforms all the other methods with a considerable margin.

---

1 http://cseweb.ucsd.edu/~l6zhang/

2 http://users.soe.ucsc.edu/~rokaf/SaliencyDetection.html

3 http://webee.technion.ac.il/labs/cgm/Computer-Graphics-Multimedia/Software/Saliency/Saliency.html

4 http://www.ee.oulu.fi/mvg/page/saliency

5 www.cse.yorku.ca/~neil

6 http://www.its.caltech.edu/~xhou/projects/spectralResidual/spectralresidual.html

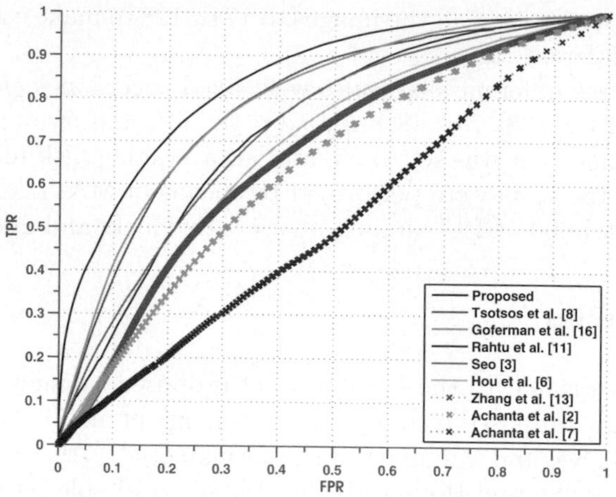

Fig. 4. Comparing the performance of proposed method and other state-of-the-art techniques in terms of Receiver Operating Characteristic (ROC) curve

Table 1. Comparison of different methods in terms of Area Under the Curve (AUC). Mean ± standard deviation is reported.

Algorithm	AUC
Achanta et al. [7]	0.5024 ± 0.1216
Achanta et al. [2]	0.6447 ± 0.1067
Zhang et al. [13]	0.6719 ± 0.0874
Hou et al. [6]	0.6863 ± 0.1117
Seo and Milanfar [3]	0.7292 ± 0.0972
Rahtu et al. [11]	0.7495 ± 0.0624
Goferman et al. [16]	0.8022 ± 0.0844
Bruce and Tsotsos [8]	0.7971 ± 0.0691
Proposed	0.8614 ± 0.0648

Table 2. Comparison of different methods in terms of running time

Algorithm	**Timing**(msec/pixel)
Achanta et al. [7]	1.25e-3
Achanta et al. [2]	3.71e-3
Zhang et al. [13]	0.20
Hou et al. [6]	6e-3
Seo and Milanfar [3]	0.58
Rahtu et al. [11]	6.5e-2
Goferman et al. [16]	1.43
Bruce and Tsotsos [8]	8.7e-2
Proposed	7.6e-3

Table 2 summarizes the measured running time per pixel. Although the proposed method is not the fastest method in the list, it is the fastest among high-performance methods.

Fig. 5. An example showing saliency maps produced using different techniques. The leftmost column shows the original image and its fixation map. On the right side from left to right and top to bottom results from Achanta et al. [7], Achanta et al. [2], Zhang et al. [13], Seo and Milanfar [3], Goferman et al. [16], Rahtu et al. [11], Bruce and Tsotsos [8], Hou et al. [6], and Proposed method are depicted.

3.2 Qualitative Assessment

In order to have better conception, we provide some sample images. Figure 5 shows saliency maps produced by several methods. The Human eye fixation map of each image is also provided for comparison.

4 Conclusion

In this paper, We introduced a new saliency technique based on center-surround approach. We showed that the proposed method can effectively compute the amount of saliency in images. It is fast in comparison to other similar approaches.

We introduced a method which utilizes $P(1|f, \bar{x})$ to measure saliency. We used sparse sampling and kernel density estimation to build the saliency map. The proposed method's nature implicitly includes center bias.

We compared the proposed method with eight state-of-the-art algorithms. We considered running time, and area under the curve in evaluation of methods. The method is the best technique in terms of AUC. Also, it is the fastest accurate method in comparison to other techniques.

References

1. Itti, L., Koch, C., Niebur, E.: A model of saliency-based visual attention for rapid scene analysis. IEEE Transactions on Pattern Analysis and Machine Intelligence 20, 1254–1259 (1998)
2. Achanta, R., Estrada, F.J., Wils, P., Süsstrunk, S.: Salient region detection and segmentation. In: Gasteratos, A., Vincze, M., Tsotsos, J.K. (eds.) ICVS 2008. LNCS, vol. 5008, pp. 66–75. Springer, Heidelberg (2008), `http://icvs2008.info/index.htm`
3. Seo, H.J., Milanfar, P.: Training-free, generic object detection using locally adaptive regression kernels. IEEE Transactions on Pattern Analysis and Machine Intelligence 32, 1688–1704 (2010)
4. Rahtu, E., Heikkilä, J.: A simple and efficient saliency detector for background subtraction. In: Proc. the 9th IEEE International Workshop on Visual Surveillance (VS 2009), Kyoto, Japan, pp. 1137–1144 (2009), `http://www.ee.oulu.fi/mvg/page/saliency`
5. Guo, C., Ma, Q., Zhang, L.: Spatio-temporal saliency detection using phase spectrum of quaternion fourier transform. In: IEEE Conference on Computer Vision and Pattern Recognition, CVPR 2008, pp. 1–8 (2008), doi:10.1109/CVPR.2008.4587715
6. Hou, X., Zhang, L.: Saliency detection: A spectral residual approach. In: IEEE Conference on Computer Vision and Pattern Recognition, CVPR 2007, pp. 1–8 (2007), doi:10.1109/CVPR.2007.383267
7. Achanta, R., Hemami, S., Estrada, F., Süsstrunk, S.: Frequency-tuned Salient Region Detection. In: IEEE International Conference on Computer Vision and Pattern Recognition (CVPR), Miami Beach, Florida (2009), `http://www.cvpr2009.org/`

8. Tsotsos, J.K., Bruce, N.D.B.: Saliency based on information maximization. In: Weiss, Y., Schölkopf, B., Platt, J. (eds.) Advances in Neural Information Processing Systems 18, pp. 155–162. MIT Press, Cambridge (2006)
9. Lin, Y., Fang, B., Tang, Y.: A computational model for saliency maps by using local entropy. In: AAAI Conference on Artificial Intelligence (2010)
10. Mahadevan, V., Vasconcelos, N.: Spatiotemporal saliency in dynamic scenes. IEEE Transactions on Pattern Analysis and Machine Intelligence 32, 171–177 (2010)
11. Rahtu, E., Kannala, J., Salo, M., Heikkilä, J.: Segmenting salient objects from images and videos. In: Daniilidis, K., Maragos, P., Paragios, N. (eds.) ECCV 2010. LNCS, vol. 6315, pp. 366–379. Springer, Heidelberg (2010), `http://www.ee.oulu.fi/mvg/page/saliency`
12. Gao, D., Mahadevan, V., Vasconcelos, N.: On the plausibility of the discriminant center-surround hypothesis for visual saliency. Journal of Vision 8(7) (2008), `http://www.journalofvision.org/content/8/7/13.abstract`, doi:10.1167/8.7.13
13. Zhang, L., Tong, M.H., Marks, T.K., Shan, H., Cottrell, G.W.: Sun: A bayesian framework for saliency using natural statistics. Journal of Vision 8(7) (2008), `http://www.journalofvision.org/content/8/7/32.abstract`, doi:10.1167/8.7.32
14. Yang, Y., Song, M., Li, N., Bu, J., Chen, C.: What is the chance of happening: A new way to predict where people look. In: Daniilidis, K., Maragos, P., Paragios, N. (eds.) ECCV 2010. LNCS, vol. 6315, pp. 631–643. Springer, Heidelberg (2010), `http://dx.doi.org/10.1007/978-3-642-15555-0_46`
15. Judd, T., Ehinger, K., Durand, F., Torralba, A.: Learning to predict where humans look. In: IEEE International Conference on Computer Vision, ICCV (2009)
16. Goferman, S., Zelnik-Manor, L., Tal, A.: Context-aware saliency detection. In: 2010 IEEE Conference on Computer Vision and Pattern Recognition (CVPR), pp. 2376–2383 (2010), doi:10.1109/CVPR.2010.5539929

Combining Contrast Information and Local Binary Patterns for Gender Classification

Juha Ylioinas, Abdenour Hadid, and Matti Pietikäinen

Machine Vision Group, P.O. Box 4500,
FI-90014 University of Oulu, Finland
{juyl,hadid,mkp}@ee.oulu.fi

Abstract. Recent developments in face analysis showed that local binary patterns (LBP) provide excellent results in representing faces. LBP is by definition a purely gray-scale invariant texture operator, codifying only the facial patterns while ignoring the magnitude of gray level differences (i.e. contrast). However, pattern information is independent of the gray scale, whereas contrast is not. On the other hand, contrast is not affected by rotation, but patterns are, by default. So, these two measures can supplement each other. This paper addresses how well facial images can be described by means of both contrast information and local binary patterns. We investigate a new facial representation which combines both measures and extensively evaluate the proposed representation on the gender classification problem, showing interesting results. Furthermore, we compare our results against those of using Haar-like features and AdaBoost learning, demonstrating improvements with a significant margin.

Keywords: Texture Features, Local Binary Patterns, Contrast, Gender Classification.

1 Introduction

Recent developments in face analysis showed that local binary patterns (LBP) [1] provide excellent results in representing faces [2,3]. For instance, it has been successfully applied to face detection [4], face recognition [2], facial expression recognition [5], gender classification [6] etc. LBP is a gray-scale invariant texture operator which labels the pixels of an image by thresholding the neighborhood of each pixel with the value of the center pixel and considers the result as a binary number. LBP labels can be regarded as local primitives such as curved edges, spots, flat areas etc. The histogram of the labels can be then used as a face descriptor. Due to its discriminative power and computational simplicity, the LBP methodology has already attained an established position in face analysis research[1].

LBP is by definition a purely gray-scale invariant texture operator, codifying only the facial patterns while ignoring the magnitude of gray level differences (i.e.

[1] See LBP bibliography at http://www.cse.oulu.fi/MVG/LBP_Bibliography

A. Heyden and F. Kahl (Eds.): SCIA 2011, LNCS 6688, pp. 676–686, 2011.

contrast). However, texture can be regarded as a two-dimensional phenomenon characterized by two orthogonal properties: spatial structure (patterns) and contrast (the strength of the patterns). Pattern information is independent of the gray scale, whereas contrast is not. On the other hand, contrast is not affected by rotation, but patterns are, by default. These two measures supplement each other in a very useful way. The question which arises then is how well facial images can be described by means of both contrast information and local binary patterns? In other words, could contrast information enhance the effectiveness of the popular LBP-based facial representation? If so, how the two measures could optimally be combined? This paper addresses these issues by proposing and investigating a new facial representation which combines contrast information and local binary patterns. We extensively evaluate the proposed facial representation on the gender classification problem, although other face related tasks such as face detection, facial expression recognition or face authentication could also be considered.

Gender classification from facial information consists of determining whether the person whose face is in the given image or video is a man or a woman. This is a two-class pattern recognition task which is very useful in many applications such as more affective Human-Computer Interaction (HCI), audience measurement and reporting, consumer behavior analysis and marketing, content-based image and video retrieval, restricting access to certain areas based on gender, and so on. The main challenges in gender classification from facial images are due to geometrical non-uniformity, make-up and occlusions, pose and illumination variations, and image degradations e.g. caused by blur and noise. These factors are unfortunately often present in real-world face images captured in unconstrained environments.

First attempts of using computer vision based techniques to gender classification started in early 1990s. Since then, a significant progress has been made and several approaches have been reported in literature. Fundamentally, the proposed techniques differ in (i) the choice of the facial representation, ranging from the use of simple raw pixels to more complex features such as Gabor responses, and in (ii) the design of the classifier, ranging from the use of nearest neighbor (NN) and fisher linear discriminant (FLD) classifiers to artificial neural networks (ANN), support vector machines (SVM) and boosting schemes. For instance, Moghaddam and Yang [7] used raw pixels as inputs to SVMs while Baluja and Rowley [8] adopted AdaBoost to combine weak classifiers, constructed using simple pixel comparisons, into single strong classifier. Both systems showed good classification rates. A comparative analysis on gender classification approaches can be found in [9].

The rest of this paper is organized as follows. Section 2 briefly describes the popular LBP methodology for representing face images. Our proposed facial representation that combines contrast information and local binary patterns is then presented in Section 3. Section 4 considers the gender classification problem and provide extensive experiments and analysis on the effectiveness of using contrast information to supplement local binary patterns. The section also analyzes the effects of illumination normalization, the generalization ability and the real-time implementation of the proposed gender classification method. A conclusion is drawn in Section 5.

2 Face Representation Using Local Binary Patterns

The LBP texture analysis operator, introduced by Ojala et al. [1], is defined as a gray-scale invariant texture measure, derived from a general definition of texture in a local neighborhood. It is a powerful means of texture description and among its properties in real-world applications are its discriminative power, computational simplicity and tolerance against monotonic gray-scale changes.

The original LBP operator forms labels for the image pixels by thresholding the 3×3 neighborhood of each pixel with the center value and considering the result as a binary number. Fig. 1 shows an example of an LBP calculation. The histogram of these $2^8 = 256$ different labels can then be used as a texture descriptor.

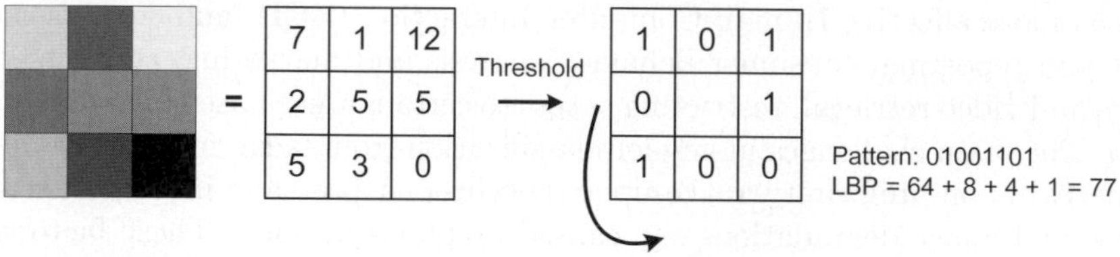

Fig. 1. The basic LBP operator

The operator has been extended to use neighborhoods of different sizes. Using a circular neighborhood and bilinearly interpolating values at non-integer pixel coordinates allow any radius and number of pixels in the neighborhood. The notation (P, R) is generally used for pixel neighborhoods to refer to P sampling points on a circle of radius R. The calculation of the LBP codes can be easily done in a single scan through the image. The value of the LBP code of a pixel (x_c, y_c) is given by:

$$\mathrm{LBP}_{P,R} = \sum_{p=0}^{P-1} s(g_p - g_c)2^p, \tag{1}$$

where g_c corresponds to the gray value of the center pixel (x_c, y_c), g_p refers to gray values of P equally spaced pixels on a circle of radius R, and s defines a thresholding function as follows:

$$s(x) = \begin{cases} 1, \text{ if } x \geq 0; \\ 0, \text{ otherwise.} \end{cases} \tag{2}$$

Another extension to the original operator is the definition of so called *uniform patterns*. This extension was inspired by the fact that some binary patterns occur more commonly in texture images than others. A local binary pattern is called uniform if the binary pattern contains at most two bitwise transitions from 0 to 1 or vice versa when the bit pattern is traversed circularly. In the computation of the LBP labels, uniform patterns are used so that there is a separate label for each uniform pattern and all the non-uniform patterns are labeled with a single label. This yields to the following notation for the LBP operator: $\mathrm{LBP}^{u2}_{P,R}$. The subscript represents using the operator in a (P, R) neighborhood. Superscript $u2$ stands for using only uniform patterns and labeling all remaining patterns with a single label.

Each LBP label (or code) can be regarded as a micro-texton. Local primitives which are codified by these labels include different types of curved edges, spots, flat areas etc. The occurrences of the LBP codes in the image are collected into a histogram. The classification is then performed by computing histogram similarities. For an efficient representation, facial images are first divided into several local regions from which LBP histograms are extracted and concatenated into an enhanced feature histogram.

3 Face Representation Using LBP and Contrast

LBP operator by itself totally ignores the contrast information which is a property of texture usually regarded as a very important cue for our vision system. In many applications, a purely gray-scale invariant texture operator like LBP may waste useful information, and adding gray-scale dependent information like contrast may enhance the accuracy of the method. This observation is behind our idea of combining contrast information and local binary patterns for facial representation.

We measure the rotation invariant local contrast in a circularly symmetric neighbor set just like the LBP:

$$\mathrm{VAR}_{P,R} = \frac{1}{P}\sum_{p=0}^{P-1}(g_p - \mu)^2 \ , \quad \text{where} \quad \mu = \frac{1}{P}\sum_{p=0}^{P-1} g_p \ . \tag{3}$$

$\mathrm{VAR}_{P,R}$ is, by definition, invariant against shifts in the gray scale. Since contrast is measured locally, the measure can resist even intra-image illumination variation as long as the absolute gray value differences are not badly affected.

Like in LBP methodology, the contrast measures could be collected into a histogram and used as a contrast descriptor of the face. However, variance measure has a continuous-valued output; hence, quantization of its feature space is needed before computing the histograms. We therefore perform the quantization by adding together feature distributions for every single model image in a total distribution, which is then divided into B bins having an equal number of entries, thus obtaining the cut values of the bins of the histograms. In our experiments, we have set the value of B to 8. Fig. 2 shows some examples of contrast images after quantization.

After quantization, we collect the contrast measures into a histogram as follows: we first divide the face into blocks and then extract a contrast histogram

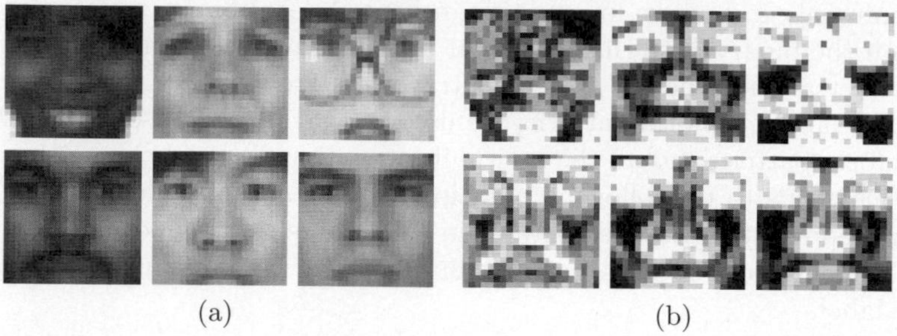

Fig. 2. Examples of contrast images using VAR operator. (a) Original training samples and (b) corresponding contrast images using $VAR_{8,1}$ operator and B=8 level of quantization.

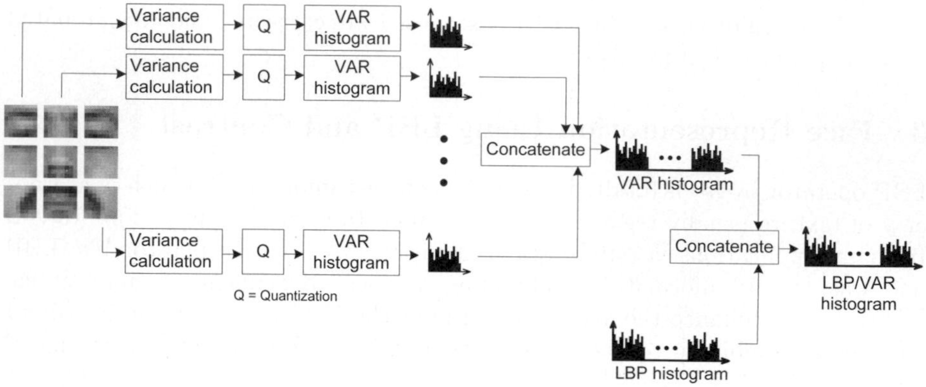

Fig. 3. Proposed facial representation combining contrast information and local binary patterns

from each block and concatenate them into a single histogram that is used as a contrast descriptor of the face.

Hence, given a facial image, our proposed representation for describing both facial texture patterns (LBP) and their strength (i.e. contrast) consists of (i) dividing the face into local blocks; (ii) extracting local LBP histograms and concatenating them into a single LBP histogram; (iii) extracting local contrast histograms and concatenating them into a single contrast histogram; and (iv) concatenating the LBP and contrast histograms to obtain spatially enhanced histogram denoted as LBP/VAR histogram. The procedure of extracting the LBP/VAR histogram is illustrated in Fig. 3.

4 Experiments on Gender Classification

To assess the effectiveness of combining contrast information and local binary patterns, we considered the gender classification problem and conducted extensive experiments evaluating the performance of the proposed facial representation and comparing the results against those of using only LBP (i.e. without contrast).

4.1 Experimental Data

For experiments we considered three publicly available face databases namely FRGC 2.0 [10], FERET [11], and XM2VTS [12]. The databases encompass variations in illumination, expressions, pose angles, age of the subjecs, ethnicity etc. We randomly divided the datasets into training and testing sets as described in Table 1.

Table 1. The division of the data into training and testing sets

Database	Training			Testing		
	Males	Females	Total	Males	Females	Total
FRGC 2.0	13,565	10,518	24,083	2,050	2,050	4,100
FERET	1,801	1,039	2,840	260	260	520
XM2VTS	1,092	962	2,054	130	130	230

4.2 Settings

We first normalized the training face samples to 24×24 pixels using the eye coordinates that are supplied with the datasets. Figure 4 illustrates some examples from the training samples.

Our proposed facial representation involves the following free parameters to be fixed: the number and size of blocks when dividing the face images, the radius and number of neighbors for the LBP operator, the radius and number of neighbors for the contrast operator (VAR) and the quantization level.

Regarding the division of the faces into blocks and given the relatively small size of the training face images (24×24 pixels), we divided the images into 3×3 equally sized rectangular regions as shown in Figure 3. We considered both overlapping (using 3 pixels both horizontally and vertically) and non-overlapping

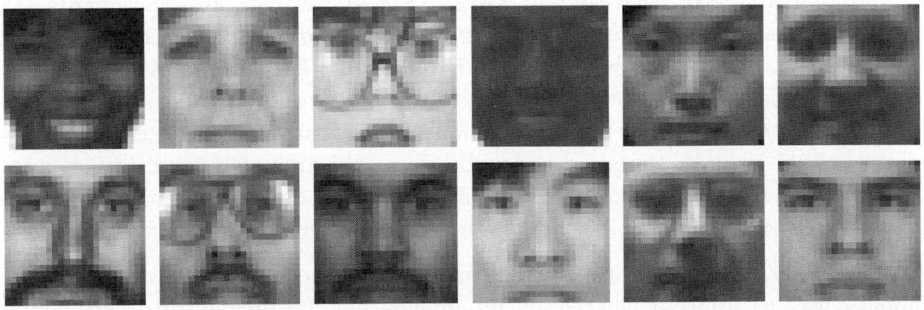

Fig. 4. Sample images from the training set

divisions, yielding block sizes of 10×10 pixels for overlapped blocks and 8×8 pixels for non-overlapping blocks.

When looking for the optimal LBP operator, we noticed that LBP representation is quite robust with respect to the selection of P and R parameters. Changes in these parameters may cause big differences in the length of the feature vector, but the overall performance is not necessarily affected significantly. Hence, we selected the $\text{LBP}_{8,1}^{u2}$ operator since it is a good trade-off between discriminative power and feature vector length.

For contrast calculation, we used the rotation invariant variance $\text{VAR}_{P,R}$ operator with 8 neighbors (P=8) in radius of 1 (R=1). Given the continuous-valued nature of the contrast measures, quantization is then needed before computing the histograms. We first computed a total contrast distribution from all our training samples by adding together feature distributions from each sample. We then performed quantization by thresholding the total distribution into 8 sections having an equal number of entries. Hence, we determined the threshold values that are later used for quantizing the contrast measures for the test samples. Therefore, in most experiments $\text{LBP}_{8,1}^{u2}$ and $\text{VAR}_{8,1}$ operators are used for computing the histograms.

For determining the gender of a person in a given test image, we used the extracted facial representations as inputs to an SVM classifier with a non-linear RBF kernel. The choice of SVM is motivated by its proven performance in various object detection and recognition tasks in computer vision. The parameters of the SVM classifier were determined using grid search and five-fold cross validation. For SVM implementation, we used the publically available LIBSVM library [13].

For the purpose of analyzing the effects of illumination variations, we also considered an illumination normalization procedure using Tan and Triggs' method [14].

4.3 Results and Analysis

We conducted extensive experiments in 9 different configurations. Tables 2 and 3 describe the considered parameters in each configuration. In the first seven experiments (#1 till #7), we trained the classifier using only training samples from FRGC 2.0 database and evaluated the performance on the rest of the data including FRGC 2.0, FERET and XM2VTS test samples. In experiments #8 and #9, the system was trained using training samples from FRGC 2.0 and FERET databases, and evaluated on FRGC 2.0, FERET and XM2VTS test data. Training the system on one or more databases and then doing evaluation on other (different) databases is important for gaining insight into the generalization ability of the proposed method under different and unknown conditions.

The average classification rates in each configuration are summarized in the last columns of Tables 2 and 3, whereas more detailed results are given in Table 4.

(A) Importance of contrast information: The primary goal of the experiments was to analyze whether facial images can be efficiently described by means of both contrast information and local binary patterns. In other terms, could contrast information enhance the effectiveness of the popular LBP-based

Table 2. Experiments conducted using FRGC 2.0 training samples

Exp. (#)	Method	Window size	Overlap	Illumination normalization	Quantization levels	Avg. classification rate (%)
1	$LBP_{4,1}$	10×10	3	-	-	87.34
2	$LBP^{u2}_{8,1}$	8×8	-	-	-	91.53
3	$LBP^{u2}_{8,1}$	10×10	3	-	-	91.93
4	$LBP^{u2}_{8,1}$	8×8	-	applied	-	92.13
5	$LBP^{u2}_{8,1}$	10×10	3	applied	-	91.69
6	$LBP^{u2}_{8,1}/VAR_{8,1}$	8×8	-	-	8	**94.53**
7	$LBP^{u2}_{8,1}/VAR_{8,1}$	10×10	3	-	8	93.73

Table 3. Experiments conducted using FRGC 2.0 and FERET training samples

Exp. (#)	Method	Window size	Overlap	Illumination normalization	Quantization levels	Avg. classification rate (%)
8	$LBP^{u2}_{8,1}$	10×10	3	-	-	92.31
9	$LBP^{u2}_{8,1}/VAR_{8,1}$	10×10	3	-	8	**96.33**

facial representation? The obtained results comparing LBP versus LBP/VAR (see Exps. #2 versus #6, #3 versus #7, and #8 versus #9) clearly indicate that combining contrast information and local binary patterns does enhance the gender classification performance in all configurations. The performance gain was around 3%.

(B) Effects of illumination normalization: To gain insight into the sensitivity of the proposed facial representations against illumination variations, we considered and experimented with an illumination normalization procedure proposed by Tan and Triggs [14]. It consists of pre-processing the facial images by applying Gamma correction, difference of Gaussian (DoG) filtering, masking and equalization. The experiments (see Exps. #2 versus #4 and #3 versus #5) showed no significant improvements using illumination normalization, hence pointing out the relative robustness of our proposed approach against illumination variations.

(C) Generalization ability of the system: To gain insight into the generalization ability of the system under different and unknown conditions, we considered experiments in which training and test samples are taken from different databases. As expected, the results showed performance degradation when evaluating the system on different and unknown conditions. This problem can be alleviated by training the system on larger and different databases. For instance, training the system using samples from only FRGC database yielded classification rate of 93.73% while using training samples from both FRGC and FERET databases improved the performance, reaching 96.33%.

(D) Comparison to other methods: We compared our results against those of one of the state-of-the-art methods using Haar-like features and AdaBoost learning for gender classification. The obtained results, shown in Table 5, clearly

Table 4. Comparison of gender classification results of several approaches on three different test sets

Exp. (#)	Method	Gender Classification Rate (%)					
		FRGC 2.0		FERET		XM2VTS	
		Males	Females	Males	Females	Males	Females
1	$\text{LBP}_{4,1}$	91.95	89.22	73.46	71.46	82.31	56.15
2	$\text{LBP}^{u2}_{8,1}$	94.63	93.17	88.46	73.08	90.77	60.77
3	$\text{LBP}^{u2}_{8,1}$	95.51	93.22	85.38	74.62	86.15	68.46
4	$\text{LBP}^{u2}_{8,1}$	95.80	93.37	90.77	70.77	83.85	68.43
5	$\text{LBP}^{u2}_{8,1}$	95.29	93.71	88.08	66.15	83.58	70.00
6	$\text{LBP}^{u2}_{8,1}/\text{VAR}_{8,1}$	98.00	96.97	87.69	73.46	92.31	59.23
7	$\text{LBP}^{u2}_{8,1}/\text{VAR}_{8,1}$	98.78	94.39	89.62	68.46	93.08	63.08
8	$\text{LBP}^{u2}_{8,1}$	92.98	94.44	88.38	84.62	89.23	74.62
9	$\text{LBP}^{u2}_{8,1}/\text{VAR}_{8,1}$	98.24	96.98	95.38	87.69	90.77	80.77

Table 5. Comparison between our proposed method and Haar-classifier based on AdaBoost learning

Method	Gender Classification Rate (%)									
	FRGC 2.0			FERET			XM2VTS			All
	M	F	Avg.	M	F	Avg.	M	F	Avg.	Avg.
$\text{LBP}^{u2}_{8,1}/\text{VAR}_{8,1}$ + SVM (Exp. #9)	98.24	96.98	97.61	95.38	87.69	91.54	90.77	80.77	85.77	**96.33**
Haar-like features + AdaBoost	79.71	82.93	81.32	86.92	76.15	81.54	76.15	77.69	76.92	**81.10**

assess the effectiveness of our proposed approach as it outperforms the method using Haar-like features and AdaBoost with a significant margin (96.33% versus 81.10%).

(E) Real-time implementation: Among the advantages of using LBP-like facial representation is the computational simplicity of the LBP operator. We built a real-time demonstration using the LBP representation and SVM for gender classification in real-world scenarios. Including face and eye detection modules, the framework runs at more than 17 frames per second on a 3 GHz Intel Core 2 Duo computer and successfully recognizes the gender of the users in most cases.

5 Conclusion

From the observation that LBP approach codifies only the facial patterns while ignoring their strength, we proposed a novel facial representation combining LBP and contrast information. The extensive experiments on the gender classification problem showed significant performance enhancement compared to popular methods such as basic LBP method or using Haar-like features with AdaBoost learning. Pre-processing the facial images using illumination normalizations seemed to not enhance the performance, hence pointing out the relative robustness of our proposed approach against illumination variations. To gain insight into the generalization ability of the proposed approach, we considered experiments in which training and test samples are taken from different databases. The results suggested using larger and different databases to alleviate the generalization problem. Exploiting the computational simplicity of the LBP-like facial representations, we also built a real time demonstration for real-world applications.

Analyzing the misclassification errors made by the system, we noticed that female's faces are harder to classify than male's ones. Perhaps, this could be explained by the fact that when only facial areas are used for gender classification, the presence of moustaches and beards helps more the classification of male's images. However, one can expect better classification of female's images when external features such as hair are also included. This issue will be further investigated in our future work.

To further assess the effectiveness of combining contrast information and local binary patterns for face representation, we also plan to extend the evaluation of our methodology on other face-related tasks including age estimation and ethnicity classification especially from real-life faces acquired in unconstrained conditions using, for instance, the recently built database called the Labeled Faces in the Wild (LFW) [15].

Acknowledgment

This work has been partially performed within two EU funded projects called MOBIO (contract number: IST-214324) and TABULA RASA (grant agreement number: 257289). These projects are within the 7th Framework Research Programme of the European Union (EU).

References

1. Ojala, T., Pietikäinen, M., Mäenpää, T.: Multiresolution gray-scale and rotation invariant texture classification with local binary patterns. IEEE Transactions on Pattern Analysis and Machine Intelligence 24(7), 971–987 (2002)
2. Ahonen, T., Hadid, A., Pietikäinen, M.: Face description with local binary patterns: Application to face recognition. IEEE Transactions on Pattern Analysis and Machine Intelligence 28(12), 2037–2041 (2006)
3. Hadid, A., Zhao, G., Ahonen, T., Pietikäinen, M.: Face analysis using local binary patterns. In: Mirmehdi, M., Xie, X., Suri, J. (eds.) Handbook of Texture Analysis, pp. 347–373. Imperial College Press, London
4. Hadid, A., Pietikäinen, M., Ahonen, T.: A discriminative feature space for detecting and recognizing faces. In: IEEE Conference on Computer Vision and Pattern Recognition, vol. II, pp. 797–804 (2004)
5. Shan, C., Gong, S., McOwan, P.: Facial expression recognition based on local binary patterns:a comprehensive study. Image and Vision Computing 27(6), 803–816 (2009)
6. Yang, Z., Ai, H.: Demographic classification with local binary patterns. In: International Conference on Biometrics, pp. 464–473 (2007)

7. Moghaddam, B., Yang, M.H.: Learning gender with support faces. IEEE Transactions on Pattern Analysis and Machine Intelligence 24(5), 707–711 (2002)
8. Baluja, S., Rowley, H.: Boosting sex identification performance. International Journal of Computer Vision 71, 111–119 (2007)
9. Mäkinen, E., Raisamo, R.: Evaluation of gender classification methods with automatically detected and aligned faces. IEEE Transactions on Pattern Analysis and Machine Intelligence 30(3), 541–547 (2008)
10. Phillips, P.J., Flynn, P.J., Scruggs, T., Bowyer, K.W., Chang, J., Hoffman, K., Marques, J., Min, J., Worek, W.: Overview of the face recognition grand challenge. In: IEEE Computer Society Conference on Computer Vision and Pattern Recognition 2005 (CVPR 2005), pp. 947–954 (2005)
11. Phillips, P.J., Wechsler, H., Huang, J., Rauss, P.: The FERET database and evaluation procedure for face recognition algorithms. Image and Vision Computing 16(10), 295–306 (1998)
12. Messer, K., Matas, J., Kittler, J., Luettin, J., Maitre, G.: XM2VTSDB: The extended M2VTS database. In: Second International Conference on Audio- and Video-based Biometric Person Authentication 1999 (AVBPA 1999), pp. 72–77 (1999)
13. Chang, C.-C., Lin, C.-J.: LIBSVM: a library for support vector machines (2001), Software, available at `http://www.csie.ntu.edu.tw/~cjlin/libsvm`
14. Tan, X., Triggs, B.: Enhanced local texture feature sets for face recognition under difficult lighting conditions. IEEE Transactions on Image Processing 19(6), 1635–1650 (2010)
15. Huang, G.B., Ramesh, M., Berg, T., Learned-Miller, E.: Labeled Faces in the Wild: A Database for Studying Face Recognition in Unconstrained Environments. University of Massachusetts, Amherst, Technical Report 07-49 (2007)

Indexing Tree Structures through Caterpillar Decomposition

Fadi Yilmaz and M. Fatih Demirci

TOBB University of Economics and Technology,
Computer Engineering Department,
Sogutozu Cad. No:43 , 06560 Ankara, Turkey
{fhyilmaz,mfdemirci}@etu.edu.tr

Abstract. Graphs provide effective data structures modeling complex relations and schemaless data such as images, XML documents, circuits, compounds, and proteins. Given a query graph, efficiently finding all database graphs in which the query is a subgraph is an important problem raising in different domains. In this paper, we propose a new method for indexing tree structures based on a graph-theoretic concept called caterpillar decomposition and discuss its advantages over two previous indexing algorithms. Experimental evaluation of the proposed framework including the comparison with the previous approaches demonstrates the efficacy of the overall approach.

Keywords: shape retrieval, indexing, caterpillar decomposition.

1 Introduction

One of the highly active research areas within the field of multimedia systems is multimedia retrieval. With the increasing availability of multimedia collections due to various digital storage devices, an efficient retrieval of similar multimedia items for a given query from a large database is essential. Since images form the base for other multimedia types such as video and animation, we present an efficient graph-based image retrieval system in this paper.

Graphs provide an effective data structure modeling complex relations such as organization of entities in images, XML documents, compounds, and proteins. A critical and common retrieval problem exists in many graph-based applications. Given a query graph q and database $D = \{g_1, g_2, \ldots, g_n\}$, this problem is stated as efficiently finding all graphs in which q is a subgraph. Since checking whether a pair of graphs is isomorphic to each other is computationally expensive, sequential search of the database for this problem is impractical.

A number of indexing approaches have been proposed in the past to address this problem. Generally, these approaches use some graph attributes such as maximum, minimum, average node degrees, path lengths, and node adjacency to locate database graphs with similar attributes. One such approach presented in the literature is path-based approach [8,7,2], which utilizes graph paths for indexing. In particular, this algorithm first extracts paths from each database

A. Heyden and F. Kahl (Eds.): SCIA 2011, LNCS 6688, pp. 687–696, 2011.

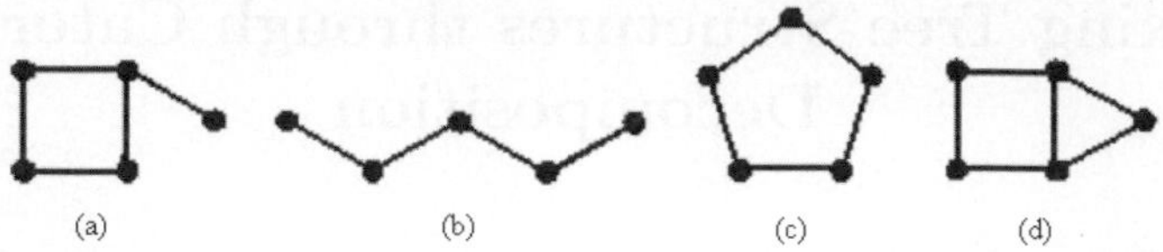

Fig. 1. Limitations of the path-based approach. Although the query shown in part (a) appears as a subgraph in part (d) only, the path-based approach retrieves all graphs in parts (b)-(d)

graph up to same maximum length. Given a query graph, it then locates a database graph, which contains all paths that exist in the query. Although one can easily index a query graph into the database using the path-based approach, this indexing algorithm has an important drawback: paths of a graph do not carry sufficient information regarding its structure, resulting in a number of false positive retrievals. Figure 1 presents an example, where query and three database graphs are shown in parts (a)-(d), respectively. One may notice that the only graph in part (d) includes the query as a subgraph. However, since all database graphs contain a path up to length four, they are all retrieved as the result of this indexing algorithm. This shows that the path-based approach is not suitable for applications where graphs in the system contain too many paths.

To decrease the number of false positive retrievals, an indexing algorithm should take into consideration graph's structure. gIndex [11] is an example of this type of indexing. This algorithm extracts frequent subgraphs from the database and uses discriminative ones for indexing. Here, a subgraph is called frequent if it is included by a large number of database graphs. Each frequent and discriminative substructures form the feature set. Once the feature set is computed, features are translated into sequences and a prefix tree is constructed to store and retrieve them efficiently. For a given query, all its substructures up to some maximum size is generated and the prefix tree is used to search for database graphs which consists of the same substructures.

In this paper, we propose a new method for indexing tree structures. Our algorithm is based on a graph-theoretic concept named caterpillar decomposition (CD), which is the collection of edge-disjoint, root-leaf paths. Computing the CD for a tree enables us to represent it as a vector in the geometric space. After representing the query in the same fashion, we perform a range search around the query to retrieve similar database trees efficiently. The proposed algorithm uses tree structures for indexing rather then path lengths alone and it does not require an extra step to determine frequent substructures unlike path-based and gIndex approaches. Experimental evaluation of the proposed approach shows the improved retrieval performance over these two algorithms. Figure 2 presents an overview of the proposed framework.

Indexing tree structures has been proposed before by Shokoufandeh et al. [10]. In that work, the sum of the largest eigenvalues of the tree's adjacency matrix for the root is used to represent it in the geometric space. After performing the same process for the query, similar database trees is retrieved by means

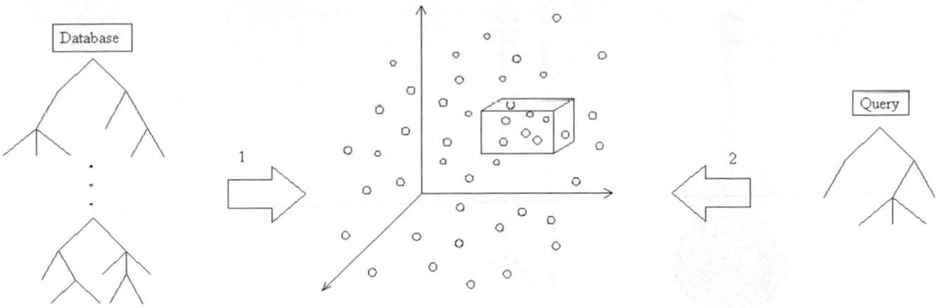

Fig. 2. Overview of the proposed algorithm. Each database tree is represented as a set of points in the geometric space using its caterpillar decomposition (transition 1). After representing query in the same fashion (transition 2), trees with the same substructures are retrieved by means of an efficient k-nearest neighbor search algorithm.

of an efficient nearest neighbor search around the query vector. To account for local deformation and substructure, this approach also represents the root of each subtree as such a vector. Eigenvalues of graph's laplacian matrices has also been used for indexing in the literature [3]. The motivation for choosing laplacian matrix over adjacency matrix comes from studies showing that the laplacian matrix is more informative and more representative in terms of creating fewer number of co-spectral graphs. Given a graph, this approach computes its signature using the sorted eigenvalues of laplacian matrix. For a query graph and a large database, the indexing amounts to a nearest neighbor search in the model database. Similar to the work presented in [10], the authors compute the vectors for each subgraph in the system. Borrowing the same ideas, we compute the CD for each subtree to represent the local structure and thus to retrieve graphs with the same substructures.

The rest of the paper is organized as follows. After providing a brief review of some concepts in Section 2, we describe our indexing approach in Section 3. We present the experiments including the comparison of our approach with path-based and gIndex algorithms in the domain of shape retrieval in Section 4. Finally, we finish the paper with the conclusion in Section 5.

2 Preliminaries

In this section, we provide definitions of some concepts which we use in our framework. A graph G is a pair (V, E), where V is a finite set of vertices (nodes) and E is a set of edges between the vertices. An edge $e = (u, v)$ connects two vertices such that $u, v \in V$. Two vertices are adjacent, if there exists an edge between them. $|G|$ denotes the size of graph G and it is defined by the number of vertices. A tree is a graph without cycles. A pair of vertices in the tree is, thus, connected by one simple path.

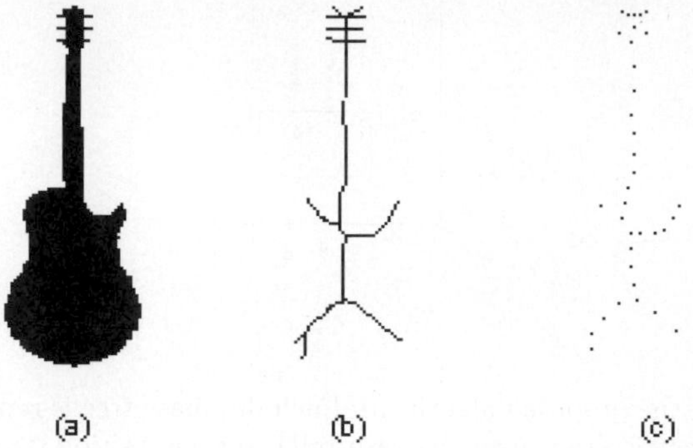

Fig. 3. Skeleton points of the silhouette image in part (a) is shown in part (b). After applying k-means algorithm, the representative points are shown in part (c). The minimum spanning tree is computed using the representative points.

Two graphs G_1 and G_2 share substructures if there exists two subgraphs $g_1 \in G_1$ and $g_2 \in G_2$ which are isomorphic to each other. Two graphs $H = (V_H, E_H)$ and $G = (V_G, E_G)$ are said to be isomorphic if there is a bijection between their vertex sets, $f : V_H \rightarrow V_G$ such that any pair of vertices u and v of G are adjacent if and only if $f(u)$ and $f(v)$ are adjacent in H.

Since the proposed indexing framework is designed especially for trees, our algorithm starts by representing input images as trees through skeleton points. A skeleton point (or, shock point) is defined in [4] as the dynamic view of the medial axis where the propagation of waves from the shape boundary results in the formation of singularities. In [1] medial axis is described as the locus of centers of circles inside the region which are bitangent to the boundary in at least two places. Each skeleton point p is associated with a 3-dimensional vector $v(p) = (x, y, r)$, where (x, y) are the Euclidean coordinates of the point and r is the radius of the maximal bi-tangent circle centered at the point. Each shock point represented as a vertex in the skeleton graph, which takes over significant role especially on structural and statistical pattern recognition. Each pair of skeleton points in the graph is connected by an edge whose weight reflects the Euclidean distance between them. We convert the graph to a tree by computing its minimum spanning tree. As a result, nodes correspond to skeleton points, and edges connect nearby skeleton points. The root of the tree is the node that minimizes the sum of the shortest path distances to all other nodes.

The number of the skeleton points is proportional to size of the image. As a result, the large number of points make the overall process slower. To reduce the number of these points, we use k-means algorithm, which clusters the skeleton points and returns one representative for each cluster. The minimum spanning tree is then computed using the k-representatives. Figure 3 illustrates this process. The skeleton points of a silhouette image shown in part (a) appear in part (b). Part (c) shows the k-means cluster representatives computed using these points.

3 Indexing Tree Structures through Caterpillar Decomposition

Given a query and a large database represented as tree structures, the objective of our indexing algorithm is efficient retrieval of database trees, which share substructures with the query. Our algorithm is based on a graph-theoretical concept named caterpillar decomposition (CD), which captures the topological structure of the tree. This concept has been used in [5,6] for embedding the tree nodes into low dimensional Euclidean spaces such that the distances between the vertices are realized by the Euclidean distances between the embedded points. In this paper, we use the CD to represent the root of each input tree as a vector. Once each tree is represented as such a vector, performing a nearest neighbor search around the query allows us to retrieve trees consisting of the same substructures.

The concept of the CD is described in a sample tree shown in Figure 4. The three paths between a and e, a and j, a and h are called level 1 paths and represent first three paths in caterpillar decomposition. If we remove these three level 1 paths from the tree, we are left with the 2 edge-disjoint paths. These are the paths between c and k, and b and l, called level 2 paths, which represent the other two paths in caterpillar decomposition. If removing the level 2 paths had left additional connected components, the process would be repeated until all the edges in the tree had been removed. The union of the paths is called the caterpillar decomposition of the tree. The total number of paths in the CD specifies the dimensionality of the geometric space into which the root of the tree is embedded.

To compute the coordinate of the root in the geometric space, we begin by finding the unique path from each leaf lying on the first level. The weight of a root-leaf path determines the value of its corresponding coordinate. Once the weight of each path on the first level is computed, we repeat this process with the leaves on the second level, etc., until all leaves of the tree have been considered. In this procedure, the order in which the paths appear in CT changes the position of the root in the geometric space. To be consistent, we select the paths by their

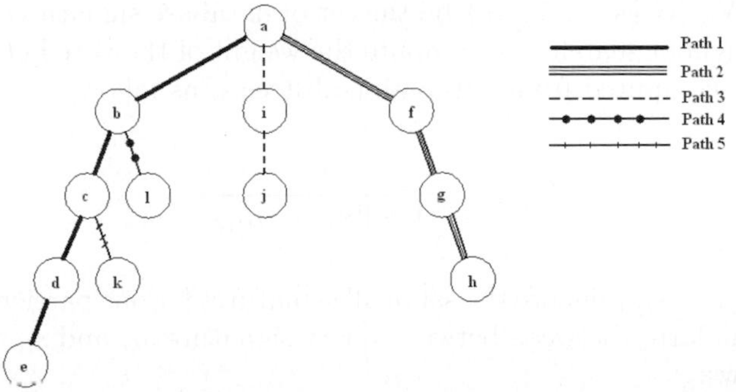

Fig. 4. Caterpillar decomposition of a rooted tree. Root-leaf paths are extracted from the tree by their levels and weights.

levels and their weights. To illustrate this algorithm, we turn back to Figure 4 in which the root of the tree is embedded into a 5-dimensional space. Assuming that each edge in the tree has a uniform weight, the value of the first coordinate is determined by the weight between a and e, which is 4 in this case. The value of the second and the third coordinates are also defined by the paths from the leaves on the first level, namely h and j, respectively. Repeating the same process for the level 2 paths, we obtain the coordinates of the root, $(4, 3, 2, 3, 2)$.

It is important to note that using the above procedure, trees are represented into geometric spaces of different dimensions. Therefore, we first have to perform a registration step whose objective is to represent the trees in the same space. To do this, we bring up lower dimensional signatures to higher dimensions by padding them with zeros. Let p_m denote the maximum number of paths in a database tree. Suppose that tree T_1 has p_1 paths and $p_1 \leq p_m$. By adding $p_m - p_1$ 0-valued coordinates, we make the dimensions of the tree signatures equal. In case that the number of paths in the CD of the query is greater than p_m, we reduce its dimension using a dimensionality reduction technique, e.g., Principal Component Analysis.

Having equalized the dimensionality of the trees and represented them in the same space, we can now proceed with performing a nearest neighbor search around the query. Unfortunately, the indexing formulation given above cannot support local structures: two trees may share the same structures up to only some level. Although adding or removing tree structure changes the coordinates of the root, the position for the root of each subtree that survives such alteration will not be affected. Therefore, the proposed indexing mechanism cannot depend on the vector (or, signature) of the whole tree only. As done in previous indexing algorithms [10,3], we compute the signature of each subtree in the database and represent each signature in the geometric space using the same fashion.

Applying the same process to the given query results in a set of vectors corresponding to the tree and subtrees of the query. We then perform a nearest neighbor search around each vector and combine their retrieval results in a weighted schema such that database trees with bigger size and closer distance to the query vectors gets higher weights then others. More specifically, let $S_Q = \{s_{q1}, \ldots, s_{qm}\}$ be the set of query signatures extracted from query Q. For a particular signature $s_{qi} \in S_Q$, let $N_{s_{qi}} = \{s_{t1}, \ldots, s_{tk}\}$ be the set of database signatures returned by the nearest neighbor search. We compute the weight of the vote between s_{qi} and a signature s_{ti} computed from database (sub)tree t_i as follows:

$$\psi_{s_{qi}, s_{ti}} = \frac{|t_i|}{1 + ||s_{qi} - s_{ti}||_2} \tag{1}$$

Let $S_T = \{s_{t1}, \ldots, s_{tp}\}$ denote the set of all signatures for one particular database tree T. The similarity between between query signature s_{qi} and $s_{tl} \in S_T$ is computed as follows:

$$w_{s_{qi}, s_{tl}} = \begin{cases} \psi_{s_{qi}, s_{tl}} & \text{if } s_{tl} \in N_{s_{qi}}, \\ 0 & \text{otherwise.} \end{cases} \tag{2}$$

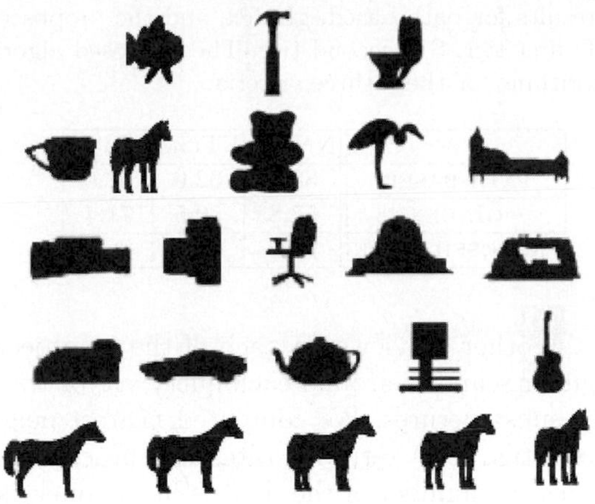

Fig. 5. The top four row presents sample silhouettes from the dataset, while the bottom row shows some sample views for the same object class

Given a query Q and database tree T along with their signature sets $S_Q = \{s_{q1}, \ldots, s_{qm}\}$ and $S_T = \{s_{t1}, \ldots, s_{tp}\}$ computed from Q and T, respectively, the final similarity between Q and T is then obtained as:

$$W_{Q,T} = \sum_{u=1}^{m} \sum_{v=1}^{p} w_{s_{qu} s_{tv}}. \tag{3}$$

This formulation ensures that database trees which frequently appear in the nearest neighbor lists of the query get higher similarity scores than others.

Revisiting the key features of the proposed algorithm, encoding of a tree's structure captures its local topology, thus allowing for its use to retrieve database trees with the same substructures. The signature of a tree is invariant under the reorderings of its branches. This, in turn, allows us to compare the signatures of a pair of trees without solving the corresponding problem. In addition, the algorithm sorts the database trees by similarity to the given query without requiring an extra step to determine the frequent substructures.

4 Experiments

In this section we evaluate the proposed approach in the context of a shape recognition experiment. We use a silhouette dataset, consisting of 18 different objects with 72 views for each. The top four rows of Figure 5 presents sample silhouettes, while the bottom row shows some sample views for the same object. Each silhouette in the dataset is represented as a rooted undirected skeleton tree using the method described in Section 2.

To test the proposed approach on the database, we removed 36 of the 72 views of each object (every other view) and used these as queries to the remaining

Table 1. Retrieval results for path-based, gIndex, and the proposed algorithms. NN: nearest neighbor, FT: first tier, ST: second tier. The proposed algorithm outperforms the two previous algorithms for these three criteria.

	NN(%)	FT(%)	ST(%)
PATH-BASED	38.9	32.6	61.6
GINDEX	57.8	50.5	71.4
PROPOSED WORK	91.2	66.7	88.3

database, which is the other 36 views for each of the 18 objects. We then performed nearest neighbor searches around each query vector to retrieve database trees with the same substructures. We computed nearest neighbor (NN), first tier (FT), and second tier (ST) retrieval rates for the experiments. Here, the first tier rate measures the number of the models in the query's class appearing within the top $K-1$ retrievals, where K denotes the size of the query's class [9]. Similarly, the second tier considers the top $2K-1$ retrievals for measuring the same rate. For comparison purposes, we also computed the retrieval rates of both path-based and gIndex approaches on the same database.

The results are shown in Table 1 and reveal that the proposed framework and gIndex algorithm are more effective than the path-based approach for all three retrieval rates. This shows the importance of encoding structural information for retrieval rather than using the path lengths only. One may notice that the proposed framework also outperforms the gIndex algorithm considering all three retrieval criteria. Although both approaches take into consideration tree structures, the gIndex algorithm look for exact patterns that exist in the query. In case a minor topological change to a tree happens, e.g., slightly changing the edge weights or adding/removing a leaf, exact patterns may not appear in close structures. On the other hand, these small changes make the coordinate for the root of the resulting tree close to its original position using our algorithm. As a result, representing substructures by computing the CD for each subtree in the system enables the proposed approach to retrieve trees with similar substructures effectively.

To test the sensitivity of the proposed indexing algorithm to perturbation of the query, we perturbed each query by deleting a randomly selected connected subset of its skeleton points whose size was around 15% of the total number of skeleton points. The average nearest neighbor, first tier, and second tier retrieval rates were recorded as 85.7%, 60.8%, 83.3%, respectively. This reflects the algorithm's stability to missing data. Although not a true occlusion experiment, these results present the algorithm's ability to match local structure.

We should note that many of the objects in the database are symmetric. If a query has an identical view elsewhere on the object, that view might be retrieved as its nearest neighbor and scored as an error. Thus, the nearest neighbor rates, in these experiments, should be considered as worst-case. In addition, by improving the sampling resolutions of the viewing sphere, we expect that retrieval rates would increase for all three algorithms.

5 Conclusions

Graph indexing is an important problem facing researchers in different domains. In this paper, we have proposed a new technique for indexing tree structures using a graph-theoretical concept, named caterpillar decomposition, which is defined as the collection of edge-disjoint, root-leaf paths. Our algorithm starts by representing each database tree along with its subtrees as a point in the geometric space based on its caterpillar decomposition. After representing the query in the same fashion, an efficient retrieval of trees with the same substructures is performed by means of a nearest neighbor search. Experimental evaluation of the framework, including a comparison with the two previous approaches demonstrates the efficacy of the overall algorithm. Performing a more comprehensive experimental test using a larger dataset with different image formats and applying our framework to different domains are our future plans.

Acknowledgements

Fatih Demirci gratefully acknowledges the support of TÜBİTAK Career grant 109E183.

References

1. Blum, H.: Biological shape and visual science (part i). Journal of Theoretical Biology 38(2), 205–287 (1973)
2. Chen, Q., Lim, A., Ong, K.: D(k)-index: an adaptive structural summary for graph-structured data. In: Proceedings of the 2003 ACM SIGMOD International Conference on Management of Data, pp. 134–144. ACM, New York (2003)
3. Demirci, M.F., van Leuken, R.H., Veltkamp, R.C.: Indexing through laplacian spectra. Computer Vision Image Understanding 110(3), 312–325 (2008)
4. Giblin, P., Kimia, B.: On the local form and transitions of symmetry sets, medial axes, and shocks. International Journal of Computer Vision 54(1-3), 143–156 (2003)
5. Gupta, A.: Embedding tree metrics into low dimensional euclidean spaces. In: Proceedings of the Thirty-First Annual ACM Symposium on Theory of Computing, pp. 694–700. ACM, New York (1999)
6. Matousek, J.: On embedding trees into uniformly convex banach spaces. Israel Journal of Mathematics 237, 221–237 (1999)
7. Min, J., Chung, C., Shim, K.: An adaptive path index for xml data using the query workload. Information Systems 30(6), 467–487 (2005)
8. Shasha, D., Wang, J., Giugno, R.: Algorithmics and applications of tree and graph searching. In: Proceedings of the 21st ACM SIGMOD-SIGACT-SIGART Symposium on Principles of Database Systems, Madison, Wisconsin, pp. 39–52. ACM, New York (2002)
9. Shilane, P., Min, P., Kazhdan, M., Funkhouser, T.: The princeton shape benchmark. In: Proceedings of the Shape Modeling International, pp. 167–178. IEEE Computer Society, Washington, DC, USA (2004)

10. Shokoufandeh, A., Macrini, D., Dickinson, S., Siddiqi, K., Zucker, S.W.: Indexing hierarchical structures using graph spectra. IEEE Transactions on Pattern Analysis and Machine Intelligence 27(7), 1125–1140 (2005)
11. Yan, X., Yu, P., Han, J.: Graph indexing: a frequent structure-based approach. In: Proceedings of the 2004 ACM SIGMOD International Conference on Management of Data, Paris, France, pp. 335–346. ACM, New York (2004)

Recovering Missing Data on Satellite Images

Isabelle Herlin[1,2], Dominique Béréziat[3], and Nicolas Mercier[1,2]

[1] INRIA
[2] CEREA, Join Laboratory ENPC–EDF R&D – Université Paris-Est
[3] Université Pierre et Marie Curie – LIP6

Abstract. Data Assimilation is commonly used in environmental sciences to improve forecasts, obtained by meteorological, oceanographic or air quality simulation models, with observation data. It aims to solve an evolution equation, describing the dynamics, and an observation equation, measuring the misfit between the state vector and the observations, to get a better knowledge of the actual system's state, named the reference. In this article, we describe how to use this technique to recover missing data and reduce noise on satellite images. The recovering process is based on assumptions on the underlying dynamics displayed by the sequence of images. This is a promising alternative to methods such as space-time interpolation. In order to better evaluate our approach, results are first quantified for an artificial noise applied on the acquisitions and then displayed for real data.

1 Introduction

Satellite acquisitions are commonly contaminated during the acquisition process: images display noise of various extent. Moreover, part of the data are covered by clouds. These structures are considered as occlusions in case of ocean images. The issue of recovering noisy and missing data has been extensively studied by the scientific community, in order to allow a better visualization and understanding of the information. A first class of methods groups the interpolation techniques [1,8]. Interpolation is used to convert data acquired on an irregular grid to a regular one. B-splines are frequently chosen as they allow a good compromise between the adequacy to input data and the regularity of the result. If interpolation is applied to the issue of recovering missing data, regions can be recovered with multi-scale B-splines [10]. Another possibility is to use a normalized convolution [9] applying only on valid pixels. The kernel convolution, usually chosen Gaussian, can be driven by the local image gradient orientation [12]. However, if the surface of missing data is too large, these techniques become insufficient. A second class of methods concerns the so-called "inpainting" approaches, which make use of oriented diffusion processes. Using the local orientation of image gradient, it becomes possible to close interrupted lines [6], and even, to recover large regions by diffusing the image texture in the direction of the image gradient [4,5,7,11,14]. However, these methods are either spatial or space-time techniques, with time only considered as an additional dimension:

A. Heyden and F. Kahl (Eds.): SCIA 2011, LNCS 6688, pp. 697–707, 2011.

they do not use any knowledge on the underlying dynamics that is visualized by the image sequence. In this paper, we propose an alternative and design a new data assimilation method to recover missing data, based on assumptions over the dynamics.

Section 2 briefly summarizes the weak formulation of variational data assimilation, that is applied in the paper. Section 3 describes its application to the issue of recovering missing data while Section 4 displays results and quantifies them on artificial data.

2 Variational Data Assimilation

Let us first summarize the principles of variational data assimilation.

2.1 Mathematical Setting

Let $\mathbf{X}$ being a state vector depending on the spatial location $\mathbf{x}$ ($\mathbf{x} = (x, y)$ for 2D images) and time t. $\mathbf{X}$ is defined on $A = \Omega \times [0, \mathbf{T}]$, Ω being the bounded spatial domain and $[0, \mathbf{T}]$ the temporal domain.

We assume $\mathbf{X}$ is evolving in time according to:

$$\frac{\partial \mathbf{X}}{\partial t}(\mathbf{x}, t) + \mathbb{M}(\mathbf{X})(\mathbf{x}, t) = \mathcal{E}_m(\mathbf{x}, t) \tag{1}$$

$\mathbb{M}$, named *evolution model*, is supposed differentiable. As $\mathbb{M}$ describes approximately the effective evolution of the state vector, based on assumptions, a *model error* $\mathcal{E}_m$ is introduced to quantify the deviation in space and time.

Observations $\mathbf{Y}(\mathbf{x}, t)$, which are satellite image acquisitions in this paper, are available at location $\mathbf{x}$ and date t and linked to the state vector through an observation equation:

$$\mathbf{Y}(\mathbf{x}, t) = \mathbb{H}(\mathbf{X}(\mathbf{x}, t)) + \mathcal{E}_O(\mathbf{x}, t) \tag{2}$$

The *observation error* $\mathcal{E}_O$ simultaneously represents the imperfection of the observation operator $\mathbb{H}$ and the measurement errors.

We consider having some knowledge on the initial condition of the state vector at $t = 0$:

$$\mathbf{X}(\mathbf{x}, 0) = \mathbf{X}_b(\mathbf{x}) + \mathcal{E}_b(\mathbf{x}) \tag{3}$$

with $\mathbf{X}_b$ named the *background value* and $\mathcal{E}_b$ the *background error*.

$\mathcal{E}_m$, $\mathcal{E}_O$ and $\mathcal{E}_b$ are assumed to be Gaussian and characterized by their covariance matrices Q, R and B [13].

2.2 Variational Formulation

In order to solve the system (1), (2), (3) with respect to $\mathbf{X}$ having a maximal a posteriori probability given the observations, the functional (4) is defined and has to be minimized. This is called "weak formulation" of 4D-Var, because the first term corresponds to a non perfect model.

$$\begin{aligned}E(\mathbf{X}) =& \frac{1}{2}\int_A \left(\frac{\partial \mathbf{X}}{\partial t} + \mathbb{M}(\mathbf{X})\right)^T (\mathbf{x},t) Q^{-1}(\mathbf{x},t) \left(\frac{\partial \mathbf{X}}{\partial t} + \mathbb{M}(\mathbf{X})\right)(\mathbf{x},t) d\mathbf{x}dt \\ &+ \int_A (\mathbf{Y} - \mathbb{H}(\mathbf{X}))^T (\mathbf{x},t) R^{-1}(\mathbf{x},t) (\mathbf{Y} - \mathbb{H}(\mathbf{X}))(\mathbf{x},t) d\mathbf{x}dt \\ &+ \int_\Omega \left(\mathbf{X}(\mathbf{x},0) - \mathbf{X}_b(\mathbf{x})\right)^T B^{-1}(\mathbf{x}) \left(\mathbf{X}(\mathbf{x},0) - \mathbf{X}_b(\mathbf{x})\right) d\mathbf{x}\end{aligned} \tag{4}$$

$\mathcal{E}_m$, $\mathcal{E}_O$ and $\mathcal{E}_b$ are assumed to be independent with no correlation between two space-time location and the functional E represents the log-density of the joint probability law [2]. The minimization is carried out by solving the associated Euler-Lagrange equation with an auxiliary variable λ, named *adjoint variable*:

$$\lambda(\mathbf{x}, \mathbf{T}) = 0 \tag{5}$$

$$-\frac{\partial \lambda}{\partial t} + \left(\frac{\partial \mathbb{M}}{\partial \mathbf{X}}\right)^* \lambda = \left(\frac{\partial \mathbb{H}}{\partial \mathbf{X}}\right)^* (\mathbf{x},t) R^{-1} (\mathbf{Y} - \mathbb{H}(\mathbf{X}))(\mathbf{x},t) \tag{6}$$

$$\mathbf{X}(\mathbf{x},0) = B\lambda(\mathbf{x},0) + \mathbf{X}_b(\mathbf{x}) \tag{7}$$

$$\frac{\partial \mathbf{X}}{\partial t} + \mathbb{M}(\mathbf{X}) = Q\lambda(\mathbf{x},t) \tag{8}$$

As the initial condition for λ is given at time $\mathbf{T}$ (Equation (5)), λ is computed backward in time using (6). Equation (6) makes use of two *adjoint operators* denoted by $\left(\frac{\partial \mathbb{M}}{\partial \mathbf{X}}\right)^*$ and $\left(\frac{\partial \mathbb{H}}{\partial \mathbf{X}}\right)^*$ that are formally the dual operators of $\frac{\partial \mathbb{M}}{\partial \mathbf{X}}$ and $\frac{\partial \mathbb{H}}{\partial \mathbf{X}}$. Solving Equations (5–8), also named the Optimality System, is however not straightforward: the state vector is determined from Equations (7) and (8) using the adjoint variable and the adjoint variable is determined from Equations (5) and (6) using the state vector. To break this deadlock, an incremental method is applied, that is fully described in [3].

3 Recovering of Missing Data

To recover the missing data, we define the quantities described in Section 2.1 in the following way. $\mathbf{X}$ is defined as $(\mathbf{W} \quad \mathbf{q})^T$: $\mathbf{W} = (\mathbf{u} \quad \mathbf{v})^T$ is the motion vector, and $\mathbf{q}$ is a tracer that is compared to the image observations during the assimilation phase.

In Equation (1), $\mathbb{M}$ is equal to $(\mathbb{M}_\mathbf{W} \quad \mathbb{M}_\mathbf{q})^T$, with $\mathbb{M}_\mathbf{W}$ and $\mathbb{M}_\mathbf{q}$, respectively, the evolution models of $\mathbf{W}$ and $\mathbf{q}$. A stationary assumption is used for the velocities and $\mathbb{M}_\mathbf{W}$ reduces to 0. This simple heuristics is acceptable for a large range of marine processes if the velocity is less than 0.1 to 0.5 meters per second. The evolution of $\mathbf{q}$ is modeled with its transport by the velocity $\mathbf{W}$ and $\mathbb{M}_\mathbf{q} = \nabla \mathbf{q}^T \mathbf{W}$. Moreover, we assume that $\mathcal{E}_m$ reduces to its component on the evolution of $\mathbf{q}$.

As the quantity $\mathbf{q}$, which is compared to the image data, is one component of $\mathbf{X}$, $\mathbb{H}$ is a projection and Equation (2) reduces to:

$$I(\mathbf{x}, t) = \mathbf{q}(\mathbf{x}, t) + \mathcal{E}_O \tag{9}$$

The variance R of the Gaussian noise $\mathcal{E}_O$ is chosen so that $R^{-1}(\mathbf{x}, t)$ (used in Equation (2)) is almost infinitesimal, on noisy pixels. These are then discarded from the computation.

The background value $\mathbf{X}_b$ depends on the available knowledge. A null value is given for the background of motion $\mathbf{W}_b$ and the first observation is taken as background of the tracer $\mathbf{q}_b$.

4 Results

The approach, described in Section 3, is applied on satellite acquisitions and compared with state-of-the-art methods. First, an artificial noise is added to the original data, in order to quantify results. Second, our approach is used on a sequence displaying missing data, in order to illustrate its potential to recover information on satellite acquisitions.

4.1 Artificial Noise

A sequence of satellite Sea Surface Temperature (SST) images has been acquired by NOAA-AVHRR over the Black Sea in July 2005[1] (see Fig. 1).

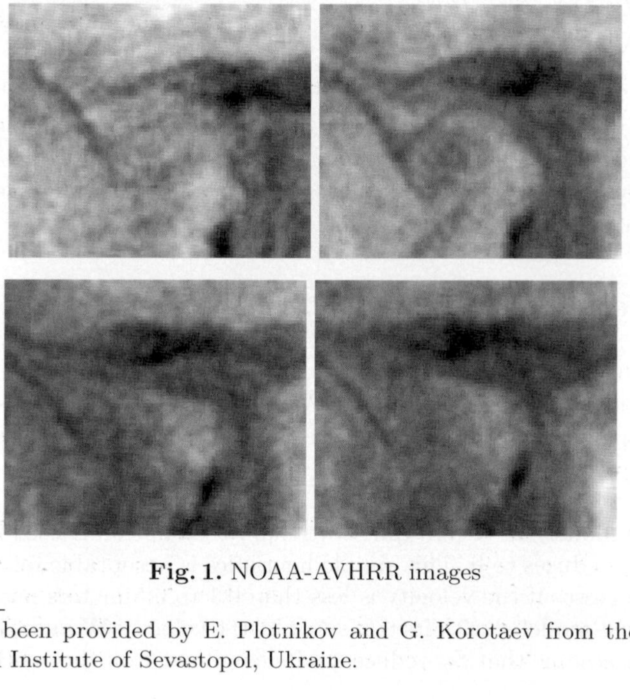

Fig. 1. NOAA-AVHRR images

[1] Data have been provided by E. Plotnikov and G. Korotaev from the Marine Hydrophysical Institute of Sevastopol, Ukraine.

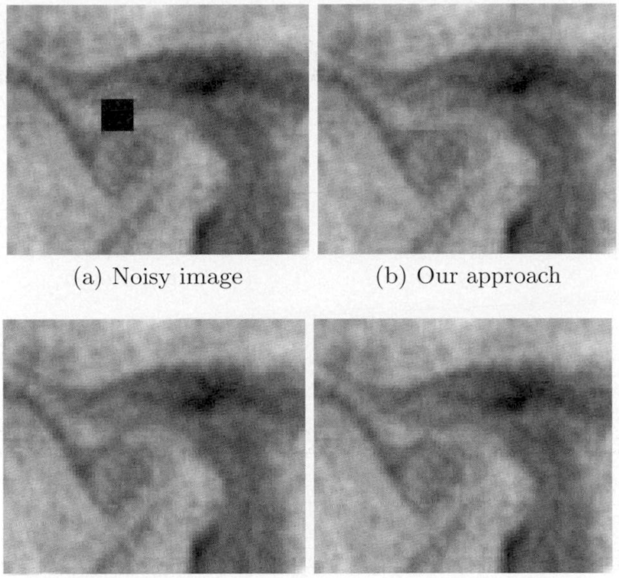

(a) Noisy image (b) Our approach

(c) Bertalmio *et al* (d) Tschumperlé *et al*

Fig. 2. Recovering of the noisy data

In a first experiment, a noise has been added to the second image as a black square (10×10) (see Fig. 2). Data assimilation is then applied as explained in Section 3. Bertalmio *et al* [4] and Tschumperlé *et al* [14] are also used on the same data. Results are displayed on Fig. 2. Their quality is quantified, in Table 1, by the mean, minimum and maximum of the difference between the recovered image and the original image whose grey level values over the whole sequence range from 23.428595 to 25.71952.

In a second experiment, the noise is a 50×50 square added to the second image (see Fig. 3). The same methods are again applied and results are displayed on

Table 1. Statistics on the recovered images

Method	Mean	Min	Max
Our approach	-0.001010	-0.215643	0.382748
Bertalmio *et al*	-0.004595	-0.254509	0.145491
Tschumperlé *et al*	-0.000339	-0.299999	0.299999

Table 2. Statistics on the recovered images

Method	Mean	Min	Max	Correlation
Our approach	0.008273	-0.543972	0.769663	0.702
Bertalmio *et al*	0.023610	-0.867842	0.950588	0.482
Tschumperlé *et al*	0.026362	-0.799999	1.000000	0.572

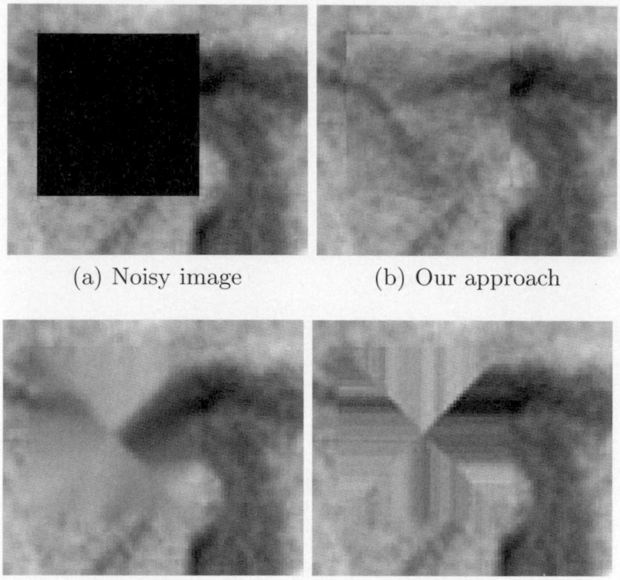

(a) Noisy image (b) Our approach

(c) Bertalmio *et al* (d) Tschumperlé *et al*

Fig. 3. Recovering of the noisy data

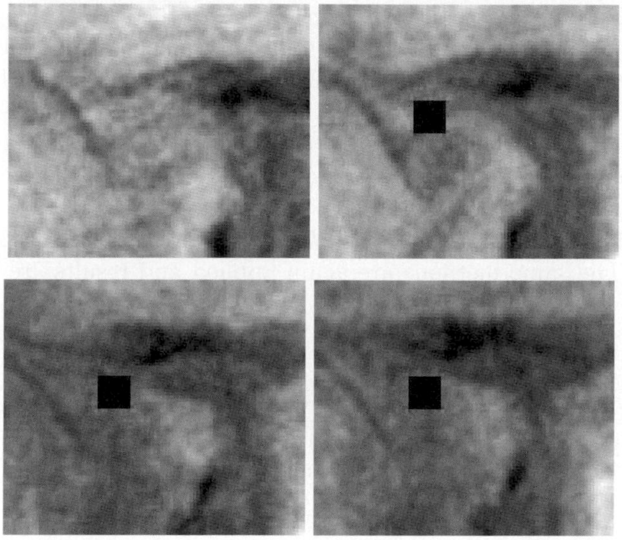

Fig. 4. Noisy sequence (squares are 10×10)

Fig. 3. Statistics are given in Table 2. We also provide the correlation value between recovered and real data.

These experiments demonstrate that our approach is ahead of state-of-the art techniques as the size of the noisy region increases. First order statistics, correlation

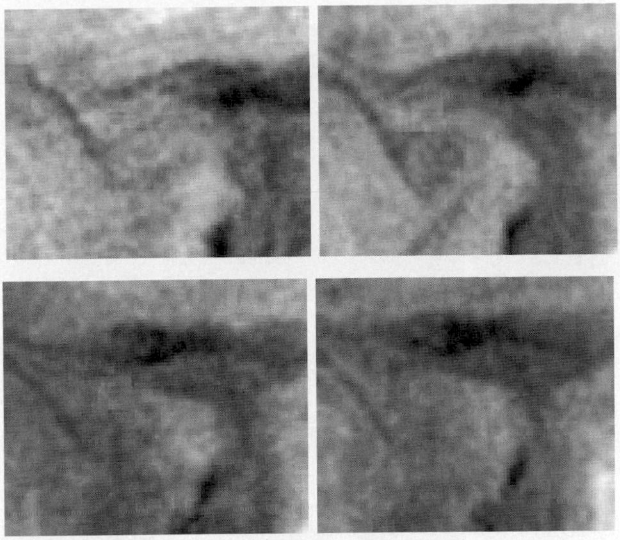

Fig. 5. Recovering of the noisy data

and visual results are much more better with our approach in the case of the 50×50 square. This demonstrates the usefulness of dynamics information in the process.

In a third experiment, noise is added on all images, except the first one (see Fig. 4). Our approach is applied and results are displayed on Fig. 5. Table 3 provides statistics (Mean, Min, Max) of the three corrupted frames, over the 10×10 squares, for the original, result and difference data.

Table 3. Error statistics

Frame	Stat.	Original	Result	Difference
2	Mean	24.652100	24.563805	-0.001706
	Min	23.415665	23.415922	-0.482744
	Max	25.715666	25.716354	0.220243
3	Mean	24.652100	24.652100	0.001935
	Min	23.642063	23.642063	-0.461876
	Max	26.042063	26.042063	0.151356
4	Mean	24.652100	24.652100	-0.00124
	Min	23.543968	23.543968	-0.361067
	Max	26.143969	26.143969	0.250856

These three experiments demonstrate that our approach successfully recover missing or noisy data of limited extension.

4.2 Real Noise

A sequence of six SST acquisitions acquired by NOAA-AVHRR over the Black Sea in May 2005 is displayed on Fig. 6. Noise is mainly due to clouds. Using

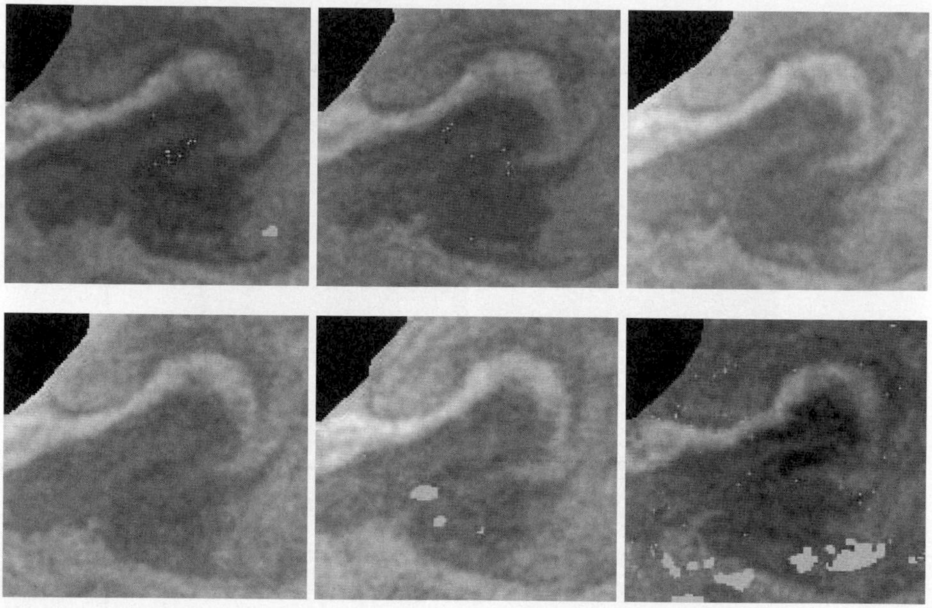

Fig. 6. Satellite acquisitions

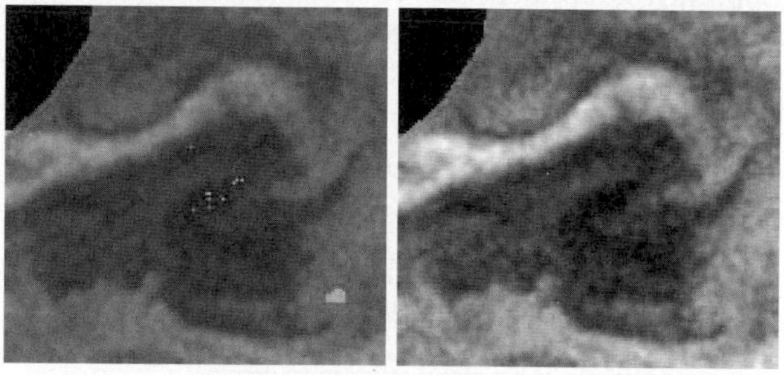

Fig. 7. First frame: original data and result of preprocessing

metadata linked to the image, a null radiometric value is given to these noisy pixels that are displayed in cyan. A specific value is given to ground pixels, which are displayed in black. This is the case for region at the left corner.

Using Bertalmio *et al* [4], a pre-processing is applied on the first image (see Fig. 7) in order to fill in the missing data (excepted ground pixels).

Our approach is applied. The comparison between the original and result data is displayed on Fig. 8. This demonstrates the potential of our approach.

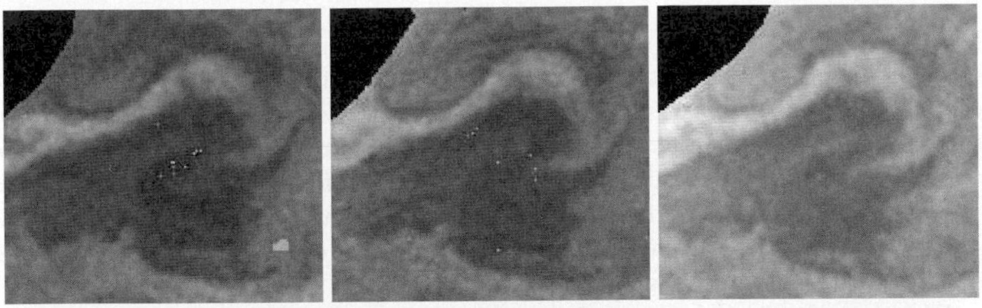

(a) Observations: frames 1, 2 and 3

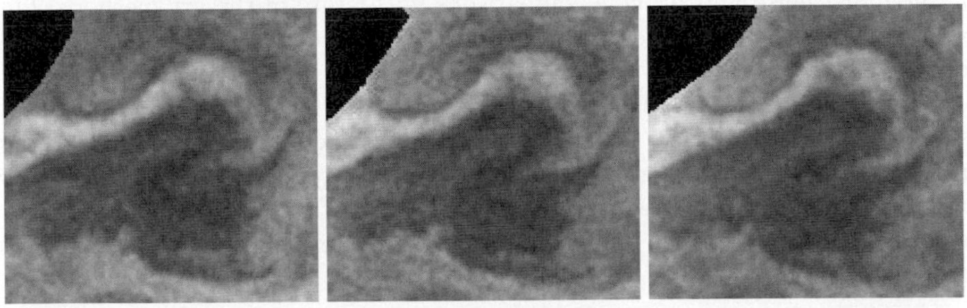

(b) Results: frames 1, 2 and 3

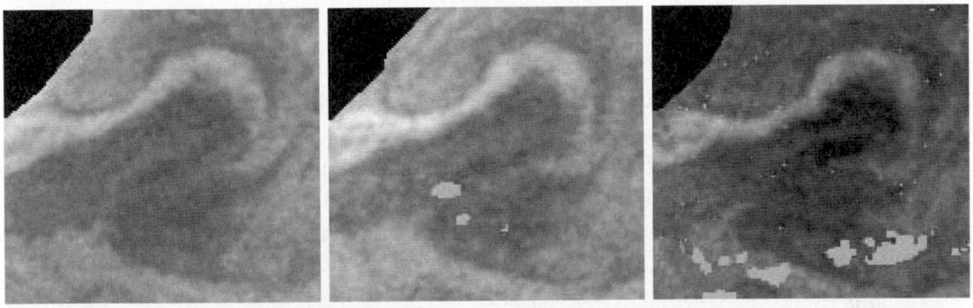

(c) Observations: frames 4, 5 and 6

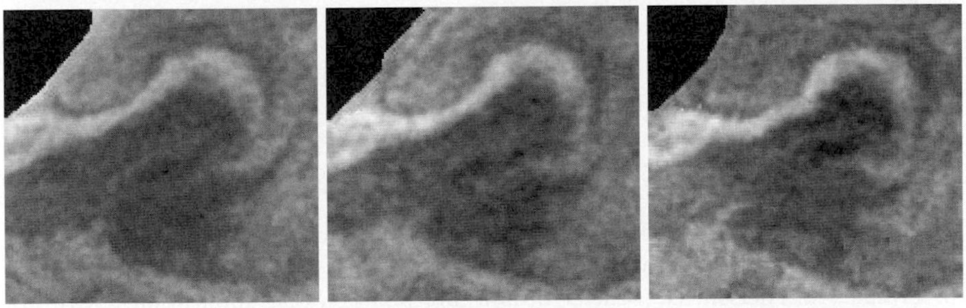

(d) Results: frames 4, 5 and 6

Fig. 8. Observations and results

5 Conclusion

In this paper, we describe an approach to recover missing data on a sequence of satellite images, based on the underlying dynamics. This is an alternative to the use of spatial properties as commonly done in the state-of-the-art. The method relies on an evolution equation, describing the dynamics, and a variational data assimilation algorithm that solves the evolution equation with constraints from the observations. Given an image sequence, the data assimilation method computes a tracer $\mathbf{q}$ and a velocity field $\mathbf{W}$ on the space-time domain. The resulting $\mathbf{q}(\mathbf{x}, t)$ is the recovered image value.

We quantify the relevance of our approach on satellite data, corrupted by an artificial noise and provide comparisons with state-of-the-art methods. Our approach has also been tested on satellite images displaying natural missing data.

In order to improve the quality of results, alternative evolution equations should be considered. For instance, shallow water equations are known to correctly describe the surface velocity of SST acquisitions. Their use should allow a better recovering process. Moreover, the illumination change, due to various acquisition times over the sequence, should be better modeled in the evolution equation.

References

1. Amidor, I.: Scattered data interpolation for electronic imaging systems: a survey. Journal of Electronic Imaging 11(2), 157–176 (2002)
2. Apte, A., Jones, C.K.R.T., Stuart, A.M., Voss, J.: Data assimilation: Mathematical and statistical perspectives. Int. J. Numer. Meth. Fluids 56, 1033–1046 (2008)
3. Béréziat, D., Herlin, I.: Solving ill-posed image processing problems using data assimilation. Numerical Algorithms 52(2), 219–252 (2011)
4. Bertalmio, M., Bertozzi, A., Sapiro, G.: Navier-Stokes, Fluids Dynamics, and Image and Video Inpainting. In: Proceedings of International Conference on Computer Vision, pp. 1335–1362 (2001)
5. Bertalmío, M., Sapiro, G., Caselles, V., Ballester, C.: Image Inpainting. In: Proceedings of the International Conference on Computer Graphics and Interactive Techniques (SIGGRAPH), New Orleans, Luisiana, USA, July 23-28, pp. 417–424 (2000)
6. Breuß, M., Burgeth, B., Weickert, J.: Anisotropic continuous-scale morphology. Lecture Notes on Computer Sciences, Part II, pp. 515–522 (2007)
7. Criminisi, A., Pérez, P., Toyama, K.: Region filling and object removal by exemplar-based inpainting. Transactions on Image Processing 13(9), 1200–1212 (2004)
8. Franke, R., Nielson, G.: Scattered data interpolation and applications: A tutorial and survey. In: Geometric Modelling: Methods and Their Application, pp. 131–169. Springer, Heidelberg (1991)
9. Knutsson, H., Westin, C.-F.: Normalized and differential convolution: Methods for interpolation and filtering of incomplete and uncertain data. In: Proceedings of Conference on Computer Vision and Pattern Recognition, pp. 515–523 (1993)

10. Lee, S., Wolberg, G., Shin, S.Y.: Scattered data interpolation with multilevel B-splines. IEEE Transactions on Visualization and Computer Graphics 3(3), 228–244 (1997)
11. Masnou, S.: Disocclusion: a variational approach using level lines. Transactions on Image Processing 11(2), 68–76 (2002)
12. Pham, T.Q., van Vliet, L.J., Schutte, K.: Robust fusion of irregularly sampled data using adaptive normalized convolution. Journal on Applied Signal Processing, 1–12 (2006)
13. Tarantola, A.: Inverse Problem Theory and Methods for Model Parameter Estimation. Society for Industrial and Applied Mathematics, Philadelphia (2005)
14. Tschumperlé, D., Deriche, R.: Vector-Valued Image Regularization with PDE's: A Common Framework for Different Applications. In: Proceedings of Conference on Computer Vision and Pattern Recognition, pp. 651–659 (2003)

Target Segmentation in Scenes with Diverse Background

Christina Grönwall and Gustav Tolt

Division of Information Systems, FOI (Swedish Defence Research Agency),
P.O. Box 1165, SE-58111 Linköping, Sweden
{christina.gronwall,gustav.tolt}@foi.se
http://www.foi.se

Abstract. We propose a target segmentation approach based on sensor data fusion that can deal with the problem of a diverse background. Features from sensor images, including data from a laser scanner and passive sensors (cameras), are analyzed using Gaussian mixture estimation. The approach tackles some of the difficulties with Gaussian mixtures, e.g., selecting the number of initial components and a good description of data in terms of the number of Gaussian components, and determining the relevant features for the current data set. The feature selection quality is analyzed on-line. We propose a criterion that determines the quality of the resulting clusters in terms of their respective spatial distribution. The output from the analysis is used for object-background segmentation. Segmentation examples of surface-laid mines in outdoor scenes are shown.

Keywords: Feature selection, segmentation, Gaussian mixture, mine detection, cluster selection.

1 Introduction

Detection of small targets in complex and changing environments is a challenging problem due to factors like varying lighting conditions, shadowing effects, different physical properties of the targets, varying aspect angles of the sensors, occlusion, etc. The complex and changing background in which the targets are placed can often be described by a mixture model, but the model parameters have to be estimated from data to give a meaningful representation. Without a priori information of the most informative sensor data in a particular case, measurements of several physical phenomena are desired. As a consequence, we need a signal processing framework that can extract information from multi-faceted data and has the flexibility to handle new terrain types and a diversity of target signatures. The application in mind is detection of surface-laid land-mines in vegetation areas. The scene in Fig. 1a contains several mines of different models, and although no mines are buried they are not that easy to find.

In this paper a segmentation method based on *Gaussian mixture models* is proposed. It addresses some of the difficulties with Gaussian mixtures; selecting

A. Heyden and F. Kahl (Eds.): SCIA 2011, LNCS 6688, pp. 708–718, 2011.

the number of initial components and a good description of the data set and determining relevant features for the current data set. Assuming that data are samples from mixtures of Gaussian distributions reduces the problem partly to a "missing parameter problem". Several features are computed and evaluated to determine what combination gives the best results, using measures in the feature domain as well as estimates of the physical size of the segments. The only exploited a priori knowledge is the approximate target dimensions. Due to the complexity of the background, we propose *on-line* selection of both the number of components and features. We add one feature at a time and need dynamic ranking of the features and the possibility to vary the order that features are added.

Mixture models constitute a widely used approach for unsupervised learning problems. Selecting the number of components is discussed in [5,10,11], where [5] proposes the *Minimum Message Length* (MML) for component number selection and [10,11] combine component and feature selection in a Bayesian framework. Bali [8] proposes a joint solution for the number of features and selection of number of components problem, taking into account both the spatial and spectral structures in data. Fauvel et al. [13] tackles the problem by fusing morphological information (spatial data properties) and the original hyperspectral data using support vector machines. Feature selection is also discussed in [4,12], where [12] uses the *Principal Component Analysis* (PCA) for feature selection. The drawbacks of PCA and other measures with unclear physical interpretation are discussed in [8]. Jimenez [9] describes a preprocessing step for reducing the number of features. Two criteria for feature selection are discussed in [4]: the scatter separability (SS) criteria and the *Maximum Likelihood* (ML).

Our work is inspired by [4] and [5], but we use histogram peak detection to guide the initial number of components instead of starting with several components and then reducing them. We use the MML criterion [5] to select the proper number of components. We incorporate feature selection in the component estimation and analyze the quality of the current feature selection on-line. We also propose an complement to the normalized SS measure that is based on analyzing the spatial distribution of the resulting clusters. High-dimensional mixture modeling is common for segmentation of hyper spectral images [8,9,13]. We fuse features originating from image data of various resolution (laser scanner and passive sensors). Sensor data are co-registered to pixel-correspondence. Earlier work of this approach has been reported in [7,6]. Our segmentation approach is described in Section 2. Examples on real data and analysis results are shown in Section 3. The work is discussed and concluded in Section 4.

2 Clustering of Object and Background Data

The main problems associated with the proposed clustering method are to a) determine the best clustering given a certain set of features, b) determine whether the addition of another feature improves the result and c) specify the order in which the features should be added. Below, we describe the basic building blocks of the method and how we address the problems.

2.1 Gaussian Mixture Model

We start by recalling that the probability density function (pdf) for a Gaussian mixture can be written as

$$
\begin{aligned}
P(\mathbf{y}|\Theta) &= \sum_{m=1}^{k} \alpha_m p(\mathbf{y}|\theta_m) \qquad (1)\\
\theta_m &\equiv [\mu_m, \sigma_m] \\
\Theta &\equiv [\theta_1, \ldots, \theta_k, \alpha_1, \ldots, \alpha_k] \\
p(\mathbf{y}|\theta_m) &\in N\left(\mu_m, \sigma_m^2\right) \\
\alpha_m \geq 0, &\qquad m = 1, \ldots, k, \qquad \sum\nolimits_{m=1}^{k} \alpha_m = 1,
\end{aligned}
$$

where $\mathbf{y} = [y_1, \ldots, y_n]^T$ is the given feature vector with n samples, k is the number of Gaussian components, $p(\cdot|\cdot)$ is the Gaussian probability function, α_m is the relative weight between each Gaussian, θ_m contains the mean, μ_m, and standard deviation, σ_m, for each component m.

2.2 The Minimum Message Length Criterion

When estimating the parameters with the EM algorithm it is required that the number of components is known, which is not the case for unsupervised methods. For this purpose, we use the Minimum Message Length (MML) criterion and choose the optimal number of components as the one that minimizes the MML. The underlying idea of the MML criterion is that if a short code can be built for the data, the data generation model is good [3,5]. In the unsupervised case the MML criterion is formulated as [5]

$$
\begin{aligned}
L(\Theta, Y) = \frac{D}{2} &\sum_{m:\alpha_m>0} \log\left(\frac{n\alpha_m}{12}\right) + \\
&\frac{k}{2}\log\frac{n}{12} + \frac{k(D+1)}{2} - \log p(Y|\Theta), \qquad (2)
\end{aligned}
$$

where D is the number of parameters specifying each component, k the total number of components and n the number of samples/observations.

2.3 The EM-MML Algorithm and Initialization

The MML criterion is added to the EM algorithm and we further on refer to the EM-MML algorithm. In order to preserve small clusters, a local maximum-based initialization was chosen over other techniques, such as random initialization or initialization based on principal directions. In order to avoid finding local maxima in a high-dimension feature space, we start with a 1D clustering problem and then add features sequentially until the best segmentation is obtained. The feature sorting procedure is described in Sec. 2.6.

To initialize the 1D clustering, a smoothed 1D histogram of a feature vector Y is created and the location of the top k local maxima in the histogram are chosen as start values for μ_m. The weights α_m are distributed equally between the start components and the standard deviations are given a small constant value.

Starting from an initialization with k Gaussian components, an EM estimation is made for each $m = k, ..., 1$. A threshold τ is set that removes model components whose weights (α's) are too small between each estimation, to avoid the problem with a singular covariance matrix. If none of the weights are close to zero, the two components with the shortest Euclidean distance are selected and of those two, the component with the smallest weight is removed. After one component has been removed, the clustering continues with the remaining ones. The clustering result giving the lowest MML value is then selected as the optimal one.

The parameters of a current d-dimensional model are used to initialize a higher dimension ($d+1$) model. This is done by extending the d-dimensional model with the parameters from the 1-D analysis of the feature to be added. For example, assume that the current 1-D model contains three components and that a second feature containing four components is added. The 2-D model is then initialized with 12 components.

2.4 The Normalized Scatter Separability Criterion

The SS criterion [4] is a measure of how separated the clusters are and how compact each cluster is, the assumption being that the more separated the clusters, the better the segmentation. The SS criterion is defined as

$$SS = trace\left(S_w^{-1} S_b\right), \tag{3}$$

where S_w is a sum of the weighted covariances and S_b is the sum of the weighted sample variance. A high value of SS equals a maximization of the between-class scatter matrix, S_b, and a minimization of the within-class scatter matrix, S_w.

To compare SS criteria for two set-ups with different number of features, the criterion is normalized with respect to dimension [4]:

$$\overline{SS}\left(s_j, C_j\right) = SS\left(s_j, C_j\right) \cdot SS\left(s_{j+1}, C_j\right), \tag{4}$$

where $s_j = [\mathbf{y_1}, \ldots, \mathbf{y_j}] \in Y$, where $j = 2, \ldots, d-1$, C_j is the number of components after estimation of s_j.

2.5 The Spatial Scatter Criterion

When judging whether the EM-MML clustering has successfully divided the data into object and background, existing application-specific knowledge about the expected targets should be used. The target size is known to lie within a certain interval. Ideally the background would be random and would then result in segments consisting of samples that are uniformly distributed across the scene, while segments that form some sort of spatially concentrated cluster can correspond to targets. Therefore, we propose a spatial scatter criterion (SC), defined as the mean distance from the segment centroid to the samples in the segments. Let $\mathcal{I}_m$ represent the indices of all samples x_i belonging to cluster m, such that

$$\mathcal{I}_m = \{i : p(\mathbf{y}_i|\theta_m) = arg \max_{l=1,\ldots,k} p(\mathbf{y}_i|\theta_l)\}. \quad (5)$$

Then the *spatial scatter* measure for cluster m, SC_m, can be written as

$$SC_m = \frac{1}{n_m} \sum_{i \in \mathcal{I}_m} \|x_i - \bar{x}_m\|, \quad (6)$$

where $\|\cdot\|$ is the Euclidean distance in the real world coordinate system and $\bar{x}_m$ is the centroid coordinates of cluster m.

2.6 Feature Sorting

As the clustering result depends on the order in which the features are added, they have to be sorted wisely prior to the main segmentation. To solve this, every feature is subject to one-dimensional EM-MML clustering. The comparison between features is first done by sorting the corresponding clustering results according to ascending SS measure and then selecting features giving clusters of acceptable SC measures first (if any). As a result, we give priority to features that produce clusters of acceptable physical size that are also well separated in the feature space.

3 Examples

The proposed method is tested on real data from field trials. The analysis is based on optical sensors, which implies that the mines should be (partly) visible, i.e., surface laid mines. In Fig. 1 the features for one of targets are shown and the segmentation is shown in Fig. 2. In this case the target data is segmented into two parts (blue and green) and the background into one segment (red). Fig. 3 shows another example, where the result obtained with highest-ranked feature is improved as more features are added.

3.1 Sensor Data and Data Registration

Data was collected at different field trials [1,2] where images were captured in a forward-looking view. Three sensors were used: a scanning 3D-imaging laser radar, a passive IR camera collecting data in four SWIR/MWIR spectral bands (1.5-5.2 μm), and a high-resolution camera operating in the visual range. The spatial resolution of the laser scanner and the visual range camera was in the order of 1 cm per point/pixel on the ground, while the resolution of the SWIR/MWIR sensor was about 2.5 cm/pixel.

To fuse data on the pixel level, sensor data was registered [2], i.e., transformed to a reference coordinate system (here, the local coordinate system of the laser scanner). Using the range information from the laser sensor, 3D points can readily be projected onto an image plane to support the image matching in

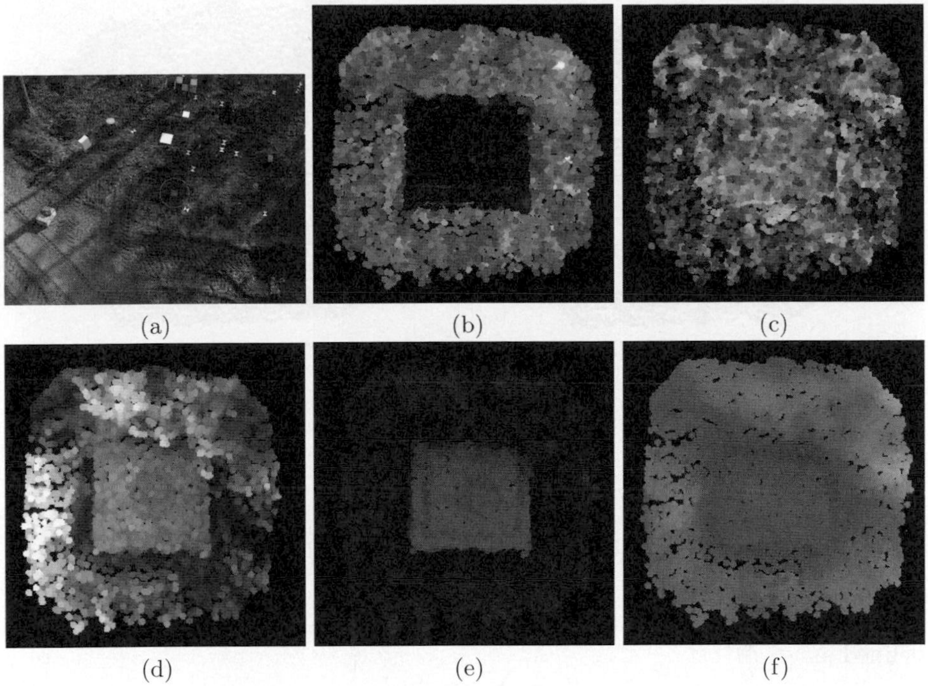

Fig. 1. (a) A forest scene, with the target under study marked with a red circle. (b) Laser intensity. (c) Surface score. (d) Height above local ground plane. (e) RGB data. (f) Three Mid-wave IR bands pseudo-colored as RGB values.

complex scenes. All objects were placed on a quite flat ground surface and an ordinary image matching approach produced results at par with the 3D based registration. A visual inspection was made to verify the overlap of the data after the transformation, although an offset of a few centimeters is possible. For the sets that contained mine data and other objects of interest ground truth target masks were created to support the evaluation of the resulting segmentation.

3.2 Features

Three features were generated from the laser radar images: the laser return intensity, height above the ground plane (calculated by rotation of the 3D point cloud) and a surface score. From the passive sensors (IR and visual cameras) the spectral bands (four IR bands and the color channels R, G, and B) were used as features. Each sample is associated with a d-dimensional feature vector and the complete data set could then be viewed as a $n \times d$ feature matrix.

The height above the ground plane and the surface score are spatial features, included to support segmentation when the spectral contrast is poor. We assume that targets consist of relatively smooth surface patches which make them different from the background. The *surface score* (S_x) is used to represent the degree

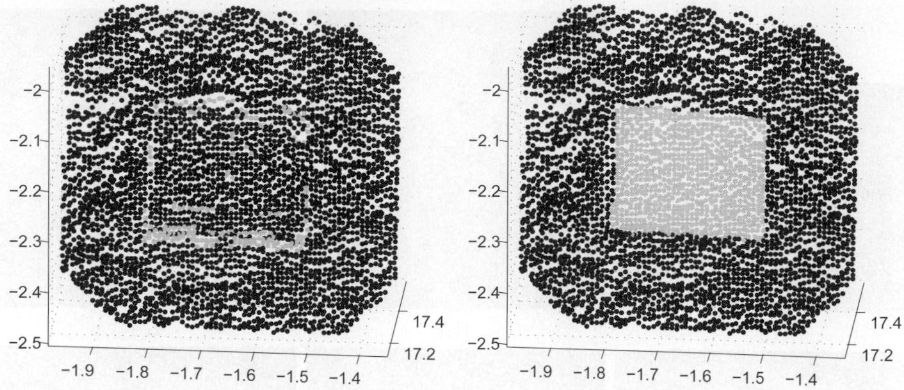

Fig. 2. Left: Segmentation result for the object shown in 1, consisting of three segments. Right: Ground truth.

to which each laser point belongs to a smooth surface patch. This measure is obtained through fitting of a local parabolic surface to each laser 3D sample and its neighbors. It is defined in terms of residual distance between the points and the surface and the normal direction similarity. For a particular sample x, S_x is defined as

$$S_x = \sum_{i \in \mathcal{N}_x} \langle \mathbf{n}_x, \mathbf{n}_i \rangle s_i, \tag{7}$$

where $\mathcal{N}_x$ defines the neighborhood of x, $\langle \hat{\mathbf{n}}_x, \mathbf{n}_i \rangle$ denotes the scalar product between the estimated normal at x_i and the normal at a sample on the surface, and s_i denotes the proximity between x_i and the surface. s_i equals 1 when the distance is zero and decreases for increasing distances and equals 0 beyond a distance threshold ρ. Hence, only points close to the surface and with normals similar to $\mathbf{n}_x$ contribute significantly to the surface score.

3.3 Parameter Settings

Throughout the examples, the following parameter settings were used. We set $k = 5$ for all scenes. The final number of clusters, obtained after fusion of several features, was not limited. The threshold for removing low-weighted Gaussian functions was set to $\tau = 0.01$. Assumptions of target dimensions resulted in 0.02 m $\leq SC \leq$ 0.12 m. The distance threshold for SC was set to $\rho = 0.04$ m, based on a priori knowledge of the range uncertainty of the laser scanner.

4 Results

The proposed method was applied on data from five scenes, where the mines were placed in forest, grass fields or on gravel road. There were a total of 126 targets of various sizes, from small anti-personnel mines (diameter 6-7 cm) to large anti-tank mines (about 30 cm). The weighted average of the feature order for

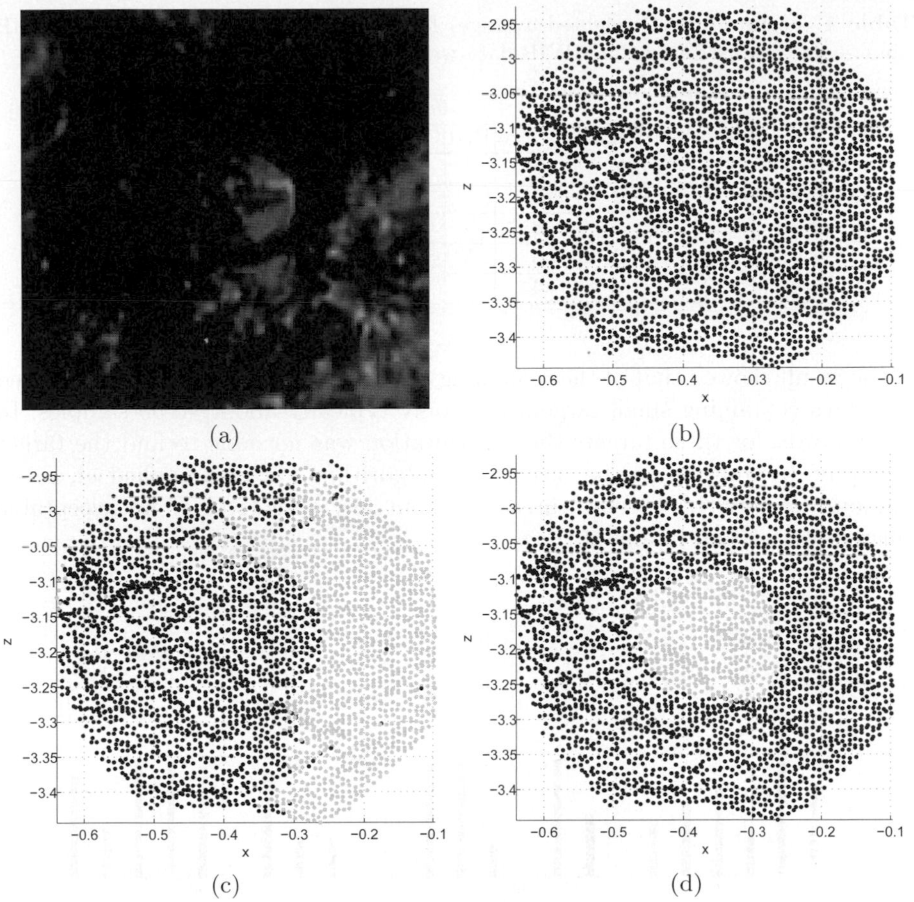

Fig. 3. (a) Image of a mine. (b) Segmentation result with the proposed method, based on the highest ranked feature (Intensity). (c) Final segmentation result with the proposed method (with four features: Intensity, Green, Height and Red). (d) Ground truth.

the five scenes is shown in Table 1. For scene five the RGB camera was not used and the MWIR data was preprocessed with the RX algorithm to one feature [6]. The feature order varies between the scenes, but features originating from laser scanner data get high ranking for all scenes. In the final segmentation result, all extracted segments of acceptable physical size were compared to ground truth data and the number of true target and non-target points, respectively, were counted. A total of 114 segments were found, of which 72 contained a majority of true target points. Detection statistics for scene 1 is shown in Fig. 4. If there are more than 100 samples on the mine we get good performance. If there are less than 100 samples on the mine (mine 10-20), the segmentation sometimes fails in producing a good target-background segmentation. A closer inspection

Table 1. Feature order (weighted average) for the five scenes. For scene 5 the RGB camera was not used and the MWIR data was preprocessed to one feature.

Scene	Features									
	Intensity	Height	Surface	Red	Green	Blue	MW1	MW2	MW3	MW4
1 (forest)	1	2	5	6	4	3	10	7	9	8
2 (forest)	1	2	4	5	6	3	9	7	8	10
3 (road)	2	1	8	5	6	4	9	10	7	3
4 (grass)	1	3	6	5	4	2	7	8	10	9
5 (forest)	2	3	4	-	-	-	1	1	1	1

of the result showed that of the remaining 42 segments, all but five corresponded to scenes containing small targets with only typically about 40-50 samples. In other words, for these targets the segmentation was not able to find the target correctly. In addition to the targets, the algorithm was also applied on seven randomly chosen background areas (without any targets) and no acceptable clusters were found in any of them.

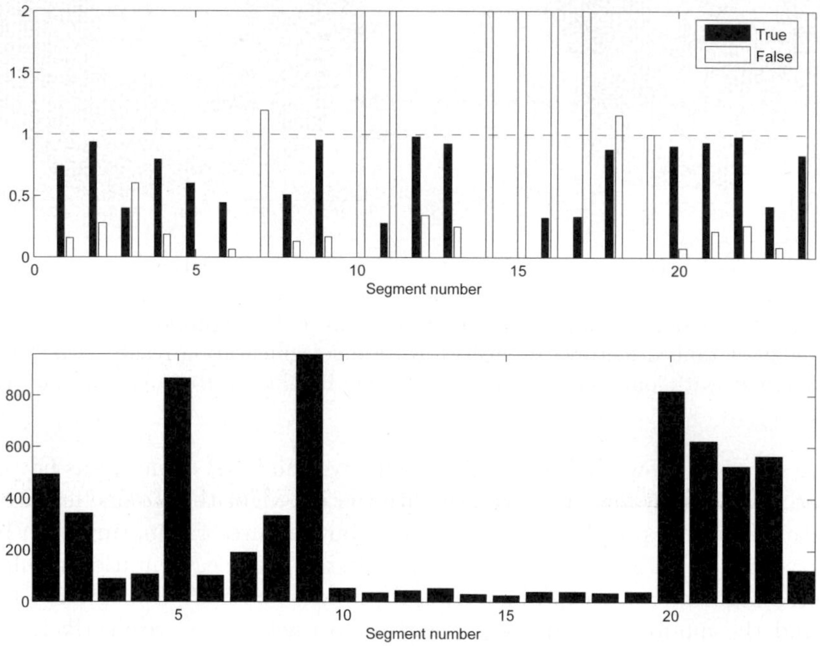

Fig. 4. Detection results for scene 1. Top: The number of true detections (black) and false detections (white) relative to the number of ground truth samples. For visualization purposes the scale has been truncated, and hence false detection values equal to two indicate that segments with at least twice the number of ground truth samples were found. Below: The number of ground truth samples for the targets in the scene.

5 Conclusions and Future Work

In this paper, an approach to target-background segmentation based on fusion of optical sensor data is presented. The underlying source of the sensor data was assumed to be a mixture of Gaussians. The expectation maximization algorithm was used to estimate the parameters of the mixtures. Since the "true" number of mixtures is not known a priori, the minimum message length criterion was utilized to determine which of the Gaussian mixture estimations to use as a representation of the original data. Two criteria for quantifying clustering performance were investigated: a spatial scatter criterion and the normalized scatter separability criterion.

The method was tested on five scenes containing a total of 114 targets of which 72 were correctly segmented. The missed targets were mainly anti-personnel mines with a diameter smaller than 10 cm. This implies that the segmentation method as such works quite well, but that there are data quality issues associated with small objects in cluttered environments. Not only are registration and ground truth errors more significant for smaller targets, but smaller objects tended to be more occluded than larger ones when placed in a cluttered environments (grass, sprigs, etc). Since the laser scanner has an inherent limitation to resolve multiple surfaces within the path of one laser pulse, noisy range readings are introduced for objects occluded by grass. Further, the range noise of the laser sensor is in the order of about $\sigma = 1$ cm, which makes it difficult to accurately perform local spatial analysis for small objects, e.g. compute normal directions and the surface score measure.

Currently we use a fixed size of the neighborhood, chosen small to avoid smoothing effects for small objects, but a possible future improvement would be to perform a multi-scale spatial analysis or to adapt the size of the neighborhood according to the local statistics. Using a laser radar sensor with higher precision would most likely also improve the discrimitive power of the surface score.

It should be pointed out that the proposed method is a segmentation technique rather than a dedicated mine detector. In fact, the size of the segments (here measured in terms of a spatial scatter measure) is the only exploited target property. This means that as expected the method sometimes finds segments not corresponding to targets, but twigs, tufts of grass, etc. Including other properties of the targets, e.g. the fact that they are solid bodies, would most likely improve the results further. Further work will focus on how range data filtering approaches such as the ones presented in [14] could be incorporated in the process.

Currently, the clustering is performed in the feature space and the spatial distribution of points is used only for verification of the clustering results. A possible improvement would be to integrate the spatial relations between points into the clustering process itself. This could serve as a complement to the verification of cluster size that was proposed in this paper.

References

1. Letalick, D., et al.: MOMS - Analysis and evaluation of experimental data, Tech. Rep., FOI, FOI-R–2012-SE (2006)
2. Letalick, D., et al.: MOMS - Progress report 2008, Tech. Rep., FOI, FOI-R–2622-SE (2008)
3. Oliver, J., Baxter, R., Wallace, C.: Unsupervised Learning Using MML. In: 13th International Conference on Machine Learning, pp. 364–372 (1996)
4. Dy, J.G., Brodley, C.E.: Feature Selection for Unsupervised Learning. Journal of Machine Learning Research 5, 845–889 (2004)
5. Figueiredo, M.A.T., Jain, A.K.: Unsupervised Learning of Finite Mixture Models. IEEE Trans. Pattern Analysis and Machine Intelligence 24(3), 381–396 (2002)
6. Tolt, G., Westberg, D., Grönwall, C.: A sensor fusion method for detection of surface laid mines. In: Swedish Symposium on Image Analysis, pp. 1–4 (2008)
7. Linderhed, A., Sjökvist, S., Nyberg, S., Uppsäll, M., Grönwall, C., Andersson, P., Letalick, D.: Temporal analysis for land mine detection. In: International Symposium on Image and Signal Processing and Analysis (ISPA), pp. 389–394 (2005)
8. Bali, N., Mohammad-Djafari, A.: Bayesian approach with hidden markov modeling and mean field approximation for hyperspectral data analysis. IEEE Trans. Image Processing 17, 217–225 (2008)
9. Jimenez, L.O., Landgrebe, D.A.: Hyperspectral data analysis and supervised feature reduction via projection pursuit. IEEE Trans. Geoscience and Remote Sensing 37, 2653–2667 (1999)
10. Constantinopoulos, C., Titsias, M.K., Likas, A.: Bayesian feature and model selection for Gaussian mixture models. IEEE Trans. Pattern Analysis and Machine Intelligence 28, 1013–1018 (2006)
11. Law, M.H.C., Figueiredo, M.A.T., Jain, A.K.: Simultaneous feature selection and clustering using mixture models. IEEE Trans. Pattern Analysis and Machine Intelligence 26, 1154–1166 (2004)
12. Mao, K.Z.: Identifying critical variables of principal components using unsupervised feature selection. IEEE Trans. Systems, Man and Cybernetics 35, 339–344 (2005)
13. Fauvel, M., Benediktsson, J.A., Chanussot, J., Sveinsson, J.R.: Spectral and Aptial classification of hyperspectral data using SVMs and morphological profiles. IEEE Trans. Geoscience and Remote Sensing 46, 3804–3814 (2008)
14. Grönwall, C., Tolt, G., Chevalier, T., Larsson, H.: Spatial filtering for detection of partly occluded targets. To be published in Optical Engineering, 50 (2011)

A Hybrid Approach to Brain Extraction from Premature Infant MRI

Michèle Péporté[1], Dana E. Ilea Ghita[1], Eilish Twomey[2], and Paul F. Whelan[1]

[1] Centre for Image Processing and Analysis, Dublin City University, Ireland
[2] Department of Radiology, Childrens University Hospital, Dublin, Ireland
michele.peporte2@mail.dcu.ie, danailea@eeng.dcu.ie,
eilish.twomey@cuh.ie, paul.whelan@dcu.ie

Abstract. This paper describes a novel automatic skull-stripping method for premature infant data. A skull-stripping approach involves the removal of non-brain tissue from medical brain images. The new method reduces the image artefacts, generates binary masks and multiple thresholds, and extracts the region of interest. To define the outer boundary of the brain tissue, a binary mask is generated using morphological operators, followed by region growing and edge detection. For a better accuracy, a threshold for each slice in the volume is calculated using k-means clustering. The segmentation of the brain tissue is achieved by applying a region growing and finalized with a local edge refinement. This technique has been tested and compared to manually segmented data and to four well-established state of the art brain extraction methods.

Keywords: Skull Stripping, Newborns MRI, Brain Segmentation.

1 Introduction

In this study, we focus on Magnetic Resonance Imaging (MRI) brain segmentation from premature infants. Premature birth is associated with a high risk of an injury in white matter. This brain injury can cause the development of cerebral palsy [12] [26]. Therefore, the segmentation of newborn brain MRI is an important task for the study and diagnosis of neurodevelopment disorders at an early stage. The first stage of brain segmentation involves the extraction of the entire region of interest (ROI) which consists of the brain tissue such as cortical grey matter (GM), white matter (WM), deep grey matter, and cerebellum. This procedure is called skull-stripping and requires removing the skull, fat and cerebrospinal fluid (CSF) parts. Skull-stripping is a difficult task on adult brain MRI. However, it is more challenging using premature infant brain MRI because infants are still in an early development stage of the brain structure. Harnsberger et al. [8] provides an useful insight into the development of the newborn brain MRI and the undergoing changes in the brain structure during the first years of age.

Over the past years, various techniques have been proposed for unsupervised skull stripping such as histogram-based [2] [20], region-based [7] [22] , boundary-based [23] , graph-cut based [18], fuzzy-based [9] or hybrid approaches [4] [19].

A. Heyden and F. Kahl (Eds.): SCIA 2011, LNCS 6688, pp. 719–730, 2011.

Some of the methods have been embedded in software tools such as BrainSuite [21], SPM8 [25], MRIcroN [17] or FMRIB Software Library (FSL) [5] [24]. Brain Surface Extraction (BSE) [22] is one of the well-established Brain Extraction Algorithms (BEA). BSE is an edge based method which uses an anisotropic diffusion filter, followed by a Marr and Hildreth edge detector. The final segmentation is obtained by applying morphological operators on the edge map to enable the removal of the non-brain tissue. The second well-established BEA is called Brain Extraction Tool (BET) [23]. This method is based on estimating the intensity threshold of the brain and non-brain regions, and then determines the centre of gravity of the brain volume, followed by defining the initial sphere which is based on the previous calculated centre of gravity. Finally, the technique deforms the initial sphere outwards to the brain tissue boundaries. The third well-known brain segmentation approach is called Statistical Parametric Mapping (SPM) [6] which consists of realigning, normalizing and segmenting steps. Realigning and normalizing were performed to transform the volume into the Talairach space. The segmentation generates GM, WM and CSF areas.

Only a few methods have been developed with the main focus on brain extraction from MRI data from infants. One of these approaches was proposed by Chiverton et al. [4]. Their technique first removes the background using region growing, then uses parameter estimation to fit an intensity Gaussian mixture model to a predefined histogram. A 2D mask is created by segmentation using thresholding and region growing. The final segmentation is achieved using simple 3D morphological operators. Another approach based on infant brain MRI was proposed by Kobashi et al. [9]. This technique uses fuzzy rule-based active surface models. The images were segmented using thresholding and morphological operations. A surface model was achieved using connected triangles which allow the surface to be deformed by moving them around. The positions of the triangles were defined using fuzzy IF-THEN rules.

The aim of this paper is to present a novel skull-stripping method called Hybrid Skull-Stripping (HSS) which removes all non-brain tissue in brain MRIs using premature infant data. At this stage, the region of interest is composed of cortical grey matter, deep grey matter, white matter and the cerebellum. The removal parts are skull, fat, fluid, eyes and body parts. According to our knowledge, BET and BSE have been used by the majority of the previous developed skull-stripping approaches for comparison purposes. In this paper, we use BET, BSE and SPM to compare with the new method.

2 Proposed Method

2.1 Overview

Figure 1 presents an overview on the structure of the HSS algorithm proposed in this paper. The pre-processing step deals with the improvement of the image quality. This step is divided in two parts, first the image is smoothed to reduce noise and the second part implicates intensity adjustment to remove the intensity shifts between slices throughout the volume. The next step comprises the

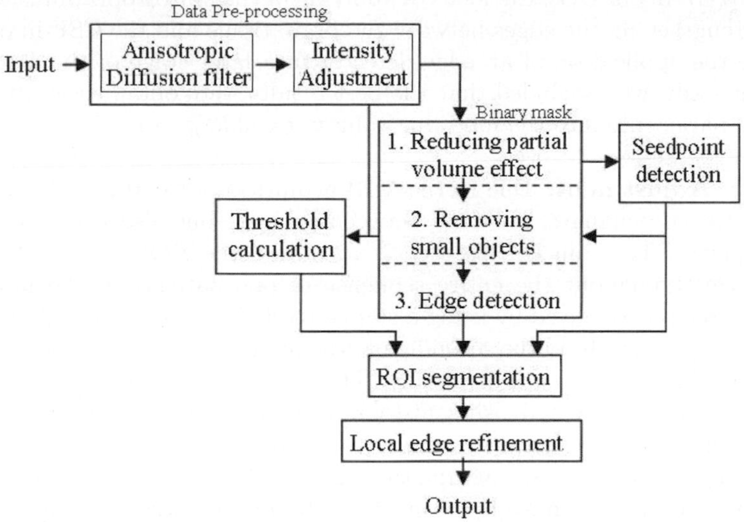

Fig. 1. Overview of the proposed skull stripping technique

generation of a binary mask. The mask is created within three steps, first reducing the partial volume effect, second removing small objects and finally detecting the outer boundaries of the brain tissues. Before the ROI can be segmented, a seed point is automatically defined and a threshold for each image in the volume is calculated. The final step refines the outer edges.

2.2 Data Pre-processing

One challenge in medical images is generated by the inconsitencies appearing in the images between patients and throughout the patient volumes. In order to address this issue we propose to apply a two-step procedure. The first step addresses the noise reduction in the images while preserving the edges, while the second step deals with the adjustment of intensity changes in all slices of the dataset.

Anisotropic diffusion filter. The Coherence Enhancing Diffusion Filter (CED) from Weickert [27] allows us to smooth the image and strengthen the edges. In previous skull stripping approaches [22] [28], a similar anisotropic diffusion filter [13] has been used to strengthen the edges between each region. This allows a more precise removal of the non-brain tissue and it facilitates the separation of each region of interest such as WM and GM. This works well on adult MRIs. However, when using infant brain MRIs especially preterm children, this task is more complicated and this is caused by a higher quantity of Partial Volume

Effect (PVE). In our case, the focus of applying of the anisotropic diffusion filter lies in strengthening the edges between the brain tissue and the CSF in order to facilitate the application of an edge detector in a later stage of the algorithm. Experimentally, we concluded that the best results were obtained when setting the CED paramenters to the following values: $\sigma = 0.5$, $\rho = 4$.

Intensity Adjustment. Due to the MRI acquisition procedure, MRIs images include intensity changes, not only between patients but also within the same data sequence. The aim of this step is to adjust the ROI intensity into the same range throughout the entire sequence of one patient. In the first part, the background is removed by using a simple tresholding procedure that sets all background pixels to 0. In the second part, the intensity of the foreground region is adjusted in each image individually. The approximate ROI which includes all brain tissue is detected using histogram analysis. In each histogram, one local maximum and two local minima of the ROI are detected. By knowing the location of the ROI in the histogram, the region is shifted into the same intensity range for each image. To avoid a cut-off in the bright intensity, that area will be stretched out, so a smooth transition is still maintained. Figure 2 presents an example of an image taken before and after the intensity adjustment and its corresponding histogram. The approximate ROI which lies between two local minimums is clearly visible in the histogram. The pixels with intensities smaller than 1×10^4 in the histogram belong to the background. The adjustment of the intensity does not mean that each region has the same intensity throughout the volume but implies that each region can be found in a certain range. The problem which remains to be addressed is that the GM and WM still overlap in their intensity range.

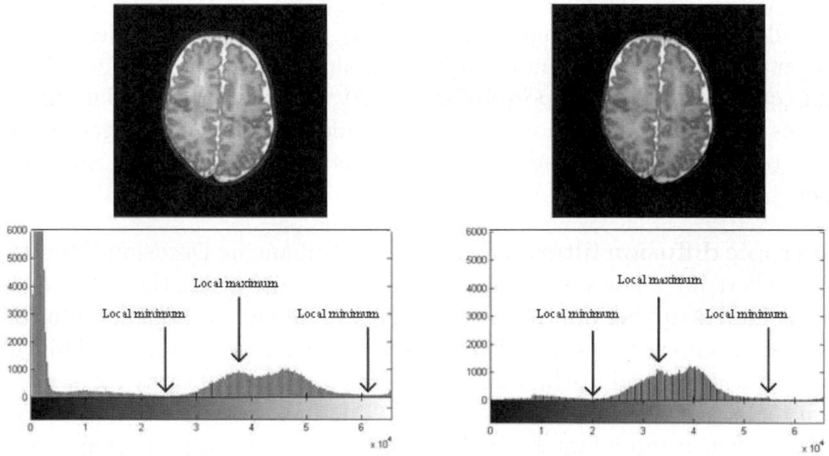

Fig. 2. Left: an sample and its associated histogram before applying the intensity adjustment; right: same sample after the intensity adjument was applied

2.3 Creating Mask

In the first stage, a primary mask of the main brain region is constructed with the intention of reducing the PVE. This is provided by bringing the ROI into the foreground and the other region into the background using once the erosion and dilation operators. In the resulting image, the foreground region will be defined by a different intensity value when compared to the background region.

In the second step, a fast binary region growing is used to check the connectivity of the main brain region. Additionally this enables us to remove regions that are not connected such as the eyes. The automated seedpoint detection for this step is explained in the next sub-section.

To generate the final mask, the Marr and Hildreth edge detector [11] is applied on the second mask that was modified by projecting the intensities on the ROI. The Marr and Hildreth edge detector first runs a Gaussian low-pass filter followed by detecting the boundaries using the Laplacian edge operator. The best results have been obtained using a Gaussian kernel of 5×5 and a variance σ of 2. The purpose of this final step is to remove the large fluid areas on the outside of the brain region. Due to partial volume effect, in some cases the edge detector does not find enclosed boundaries. Morphological operators have been applied on the edge map to connect loose ends of edges. The images corresponding to each mask generation step are given in Figure 3. In the proposed HSS algorithm, the generation of the binary mask is essential, as it will be used as boundary stopping condition in a later procedure.

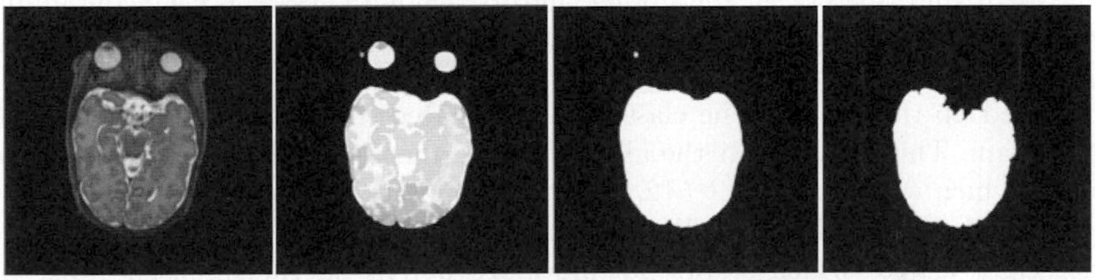

Fig. 3. Displays each mask step, starting with the original image, followed by first mask, then second mask and finish with the final mask. The small bright part visible in the third image is a leftover of the lacrimal glands.

2.4 Automatic Seedpoint Detection

The seedpoint is the starting point for the region growing algorithm used in HSS. During the intensity adjustment, the seedpoint in the z direction is determined by selecting the image with the largest connected region of brain tissue. Within the image of seedpoint z, the x and y coordinates are obtained by extracting the largest connected region associated with the dominant intensity. The dominant intensity in ROI is retrieved as a local maximum in the histogram. One pixel will be taken from the extracted region and defined as seedpoint with the coordinate (x,y,z).

2.5 ROI Segmentation

To extract the ROI, a region growing algorithm is applied on the MRI sequence. Pohle et al. [14] proposed an adaptive region growing to segment regions in medical images using two runs of the region growing. However, if conditions such as shape differences or intensity changes within the region of interest are not well defined then the method does not work well. Li et al. [10] propose a different region growing method to address this problem. This has been done by using an adaptive threshold based on the mean value and standard deviation of the region of interest to define the grey value range of the current pixel.

We tried different thresholds such as the adaptive threshold proposed by Li et al. and we tried to use the difference of the current value and a fixed value. In our trials these thresholds have generated erroneous segmentation in several volumes. Therefore, we decided that the use of one threshold for the entire volume is not as efficient as calculating thresholds for each slice individually. The range of the intensity values in the ROI is still very large. By using a threshold for each image, we can define a more precise threshold for different parts of the volume. The idea on how to calculate the threshold came from the K-means clustering algorithm, where the clustering process is defined as follows:

$$J = \sum_{j=1}^{K} \sum_{n \in S_j} |x_n - \mu_j|^2 \quad (1)$$

The algorithm clusters the data points into K disjoint classes S_j each containing n_j data points, where x_n is an observation and μ_j is the geometric centroid of the data points in cluster S_j. Each cluster was initialised with a predefined value. To speed up the process, the classes are calculated from the grey values of the histogram. This means that the algorithm does not need to run over the entire image which would be 512×512. Instead the classes can be calculated from an array of the size of 1×126. For each image, the intensity range is partitioned into eight classes which allows putting more weight on the intensity range of the ROI. The eight classes are presented in an array which is used as threshold in the ROI segmentation. During the extraction procedure, the class to which the current voxel will be assigned to, will define the voxel as brain or non-brain tissue.

Region Growing. A region growing algorithm is used to extract the brain tissue. This algorithm considers two thresholds as a stopping condition. The first threshold is used for the identification of the outer boundaries between ROI and CSF in which case we applied the final binary mask. As soon as the algorithm hits a boundary pixel, the region growing stops. The second threshold is used to differentiate the ROI and non-brain tissue within the volume in this case the previous calculated array threshold is applied. To assign the current voxel to a class in that array, the smallest distance between the current voxel and the class centroids is used. In a post-processing step, a local edge refinement has been applied which uses the gradient magnitude to refine the outer border pixel. A few automated segmented samples are shown in Figure 4 (top row).

3 Evaluation

3.1 Data Aquisition

T2 brain volume MRIs (TR: 2660; TE: 142.7; DFOV: 16×16cm) of premature infants have been imaged at full term equivalent in the Children's University Hospital, Dublin, Ireland. Each slice has a thickness of 1 mm and a dimension of 512 × 512 pixels. Our database consists of MRI volumes from five patients. The data of Patient 1 includes 170 images, Patient 2 has 178 images, Patient 3 consists of 186 images, Patient 4 consists of 172 images and the fifth patient includes 88 images. The dataset is composed of a total of 794 images. The first four patients have a slice spacing of 0.5 mm and the fifth patient has a slice spacing of 1 mm. In order to perform a comprehensive quantitative evaluation of the proposed HSS, the entire database was manually segmented. The manually segmented data has been marked in conjunction with a clinical expert from the Children's University Hospital, Dublin, Ireland.

3.2 Visual Examination

Figure 4 (top row) shows automated segmented images sampled from one patient volume. A visual examination of our results indicates the accuracy of the

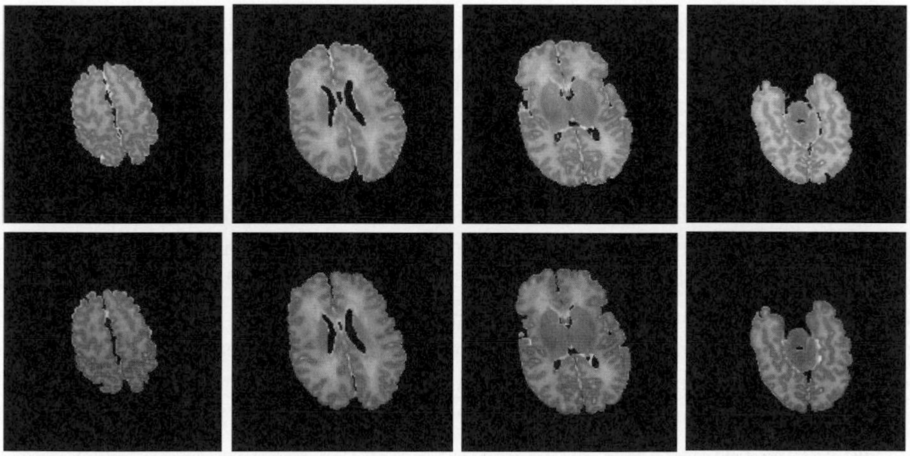

Fig. 4. Top row: result images of the automated skull-stripping segmentation; bottom row: images manually annotated by a clinical expert. The intensity difference between the top and bottom row images is caused by an automatic intensity adjustment in the display of the top row images by Matlab.

proposed HSS and in order to emphasis this, we have performed a quantitative evaluation when our method is compared against the manually segmented data. During the post-processing step, only the outer boundaries of the ROI were refined but not inside the ROI. Consequently, on some images small parts of CSF can remain. To get a clear opinion on the efficiency of the proposed segmentation method, the results of HSS were compared against the manually segmented data and against four state of the art BEA tools. Each tool, BrainSuite [21], FSL [5] [24], SPM8 [25] and MRIcroN [17], are freely available on the internet, and use one of the three well-established BEA. BrainSuite has embedded BSE and allows the application in a stepwise manner so that the parameters can be adjusted for each step. The only parameter we need to optimize is the size of the structuring element employed in the erosion algorithm in the final step. BET is embedded in two software tools we used. MRIcroN applies BET (version 1) and FSL applies BET2 (version 2). The best results of both tools were obtained using their default values with a fractional intensity threshold of 0.5. Applying SPM8, the best results were provided by adjusting the bias regularisation to a value of 0.1 and using the native space for the generation of GM, WM and CSF.

3.3 Similarity Metrics and Numerical Evaluation

1. The first set of tests is done by using the Dice Similarity Metric (DSM) which describes the amount of overlap voxels between the manual segmented data and the automated segmented data. The mathematical formula to calculate the metric is described as follow: $DSM = \frac{2|M_1 \cap M_2|}{|M_1|+|M_2|}$, where M1 is the automated segmented volume and M2 is the manual segmented volume. The dice similarity metric is a very popular comparison metric used for evaluations in many MRI segmentation approaches [1] [3] [15] [18] [22].
2. The Jaccard metric (JS) measures the similarity between two volumes and has been used as a comparison in previous brain segmentation techniques [16] [18] [19] [22]. This is done by dividing the size of the intersection and the size of the union of the two datasets. The mathematical formula to calculate the Jaccard similarity is described as follow: $JS = \frac{|M_1 \cap M_2|}{|M_1| \cup |M_2|}$
3. Over-segmentation can be calculated using the false positive. This formula calculates the percentage of the amount of voxels which remains in the volume as a part of the ROI but do not belong to the ROI. The false positive was calculated as follow: $FP = \frac{|M_1 - M_2|}{|M_2|}$
4. Under-segmentation can be calculated using the false negative. This formula calculates the percentage of the amount of voxels which have been removed from the ROI but would belong to the ROI. The false negative was calculated as follow: $FN = \frac{|M_2 - M_1|}{|M_2|}$

All the comparison results are shown in Table 1.

Table 1. Quantitative performance evaluation when the proposed skull-stripping method (HSS) is compared against four state of the art implementations. Best results are highlighted in bold.

	Methodology	DSM	JS	FP(%)	FN(%)
Patient 1	HSS	**0.9586**	**0.9249**	**4.3435**	3.9532
	FSL	0.8800	0.7858	26.8620	**0.3171**
	BrainSuite	0.9065	0.8290	18.2950	1.9336
	MRIcroN	0.7840	0.6448	38.3500	10.7870
	SPM8	0.9076	0.8308	16.1460	3.5014
Patient 2	HSS	**0.9462**	**0.8979**	7.0101	3.9170
	FSL	0.8793	0.7846	26.5170	**0.7418**
	BrainSuite	0.9029	0.8229	**1.0563**	16.8360
	MRIcroN	0.8547	0.7463	30.7940	2.3911
	SPM8	0.9187	0.8496	12.5900	4.3385
Patient 3	HSS	**0.9607**	**0.9245**	**3.7178**	4.1182
	FSL	0.8838	0.7918	26.2120	**0.1605**
	BrainSuite	0.7437	0.5919	24.6060	26.2380
	MRIcroN	0.7097	0.5501	45.0090	20.2370
	SPM8	0.8386	0.7220	27.651	7.8324
Patient 4	HSS	**0.9586**	**0.9205**	4.5710	3.7439
	FSL	0.8586	0.7522	32.9050	**0.0275**
	BrainSuite	0.9044	0.8255	**0.3393**	17.1720
	MRIcroN	0.8144	0.6869	38.3750	49.4460
	SPM8	0.8733	0.7751	27.8950	0.8640
Patient 5	HSS	**0.9475**	**0.9004**	**3.6053**	6.7189
	FSL	0.8955	0.8107	22.4920	**0.6913**
	BrainSuite	0.9262	0.8626	12.6160	2.8591
	MRIcroN	0.8714	0.7721	25.2660	3.2830
	SPM8	0.8529	0.7436	15.5720	14.0590

4 Discussion

The quantitative results displayed in Table 1 indicate that HSS returns accurate results when applied to skull stripping on brain MRI data of premature infants. Table 2 reveals the accuracy of each analysed technique in comparison with the other brain extraction methods by observing the average results of each test. HSS provides the overall best results in the dice similarity, Jaccard similarity and false positive results. The average similarity values are: 95% for the Dice calculation and 91% for the Jaccard calculation. There is an average of misclassified voxels of less than 5% which is a satisfactory result.

Every approach has its strong and weak points which is reflected in the results values in Table 1 and Table 2. HSS has two main weak points which have to be addressed in future work. First, due to the partial volume effect, the boundaries between the lacrimal glands (tear glands) and the ROI are not always visible on the MRI of premature infant. As a consequence, the region growing algorithm will continue to grow in the region instead of excluding it. A second weak point

Table 2. Average values over the entire database of the results from each comparison test

Methodology	DSM	JS	FP(%)	FN(%)
HSS	**0.9543**	**0.9127**	**4.6495**	4.4902
FSL	0.8794	0.7850	26.9976	**0.3876**
BrainSuite	0.8767	0.7863	11.3825	13.0077
MRIcroN	0.8068	0.6800	35.5588	17.2288
SPM8	0.8782	0.7842	19.9708	6.1191

consists in the presence of CSF boundaries inside the brain volume. During the pre-processing step only outer boundaries have been refined and for that reason small parts of fluid can remain inside the ROI.

The comparison evaluation revealed that FSL returned the smallest percentage in false negatives but a higher percentage in false positives. This occurs because FSL leaves the CSF in the image and therefore it is less likely to have removed too much of the brain tissue. On the other hand, the higher rate of false positives is caused by the remaining CSF. FSL removes the skull and the fat and only in a few places small parts of the skull can be observed. This technique seems to be a good solution for the removal of skull and fat. In brain MRIs of premature children at the age of a few weeks, the brain structure has not been fully developed. The challenge of early brain development is mainly caused by the fact that the infant brain contains less white matter myelin then the adult brain which results in less defined edges between different regions. Looking at the results generated by BrainSuite and FSL, we observed that they are simular. The major differences can be found in the over segmentation and under segmentation. BrainSuite has average error rates of 11% for FP and 13% for FN and this might be caused by the edge detection that BSE is based on and the partial volume effect that prevents the edge detection to find the correct boundaries. The problem of PVE has been solved in HSS by using morphological operators to reduce the PVE and by combining the edge detection with morphological operators to enclose the main edges between fluid and brain tissue. MRIcroN uses the first version of BET technique. Same as FSL, MRIcroN does not take the fluid inside the brain volume into consideration. For example, when applying MRIcroN, within an image, on one half CSF and sometimes skull and fat tissue remains and on the other half the CSF is removed but often some of the brain tissue is removed as well. This leads to high error rates. The differences on the results compared to FSL show us that the second version of BET comprise significant improvement. SPM8 is the only technique of these four which was not developed for skull stripping in the first place. The result is presented in three different volumes where each volume represents a different region such as GM, WM or CSF. The similarity and comparison results were calculated by combining the GM and WM images. SPM8 results lie within the same accuracy of FSL and BrainSuite. It has not been stated but in our opinion, SPM8 has been developed to be used on clear structured adult brain MRI and not on children brain MRI with the age of under two years.

5 Conclusion

The purpose of this paper is to introduce an automatic algorithm for the brain extraction from infant MRI data. The developed algorithm is based on a hybrid approach that embeds a suite of image processing tools that include a reduction of artefacts, generation of a binary mask and the application of a region growing for the extraction of the main brain region. One of the advantages of the proposed approach consists in the reduction of PVE, and the numerical results indicate higher performance of the proposed algorithm when compared to state of the art implementations.

Acknowledgment. This study was funded by the Children's University Hospital, Dublin, Ireland. We wish to thank our colleagues for providing us with the medical insight and for expert visual assessment of MRI scans.

References

1. Babalola, K.O., Patenaude, B., Aljabar, P., Schnabel, J., Kennedy, D., Crum, W., Smith, S., Cootes, T., Jenkinson, M., Rueckert, D.: An evaluation of four automatic methods of segmenting the subcortical structures in the brain. NeuroImage 47, 1435–1447 (2009)
2. Balan, A.G.R., Traina, A.J.M., Ribeiro, M.X., Marques, P.M.A., Traina Jr., C.: Head: The Human Encephalon Automatic Delimiter. In: CBMS 2007: Proceedings of the Twentieth IEEE International Symposium on Computer-Based Medical Systems, pp. 171–176. IEEE Computer Society Press, Washington, DC, USA (2007)
3. Boesen, K., Rehm, K., Shaper, K., Stoltzner, S., Lueders, E., Rottenberg, D.: Quantitative comparison of four brain extraction algorithms. NeuroImage 22, 1255–1261 (2004)
4. Chiverton, J., Wells, K., Lewis, E., Chen, C., Podda, B., Johnson, D.: Statistical morphological skull stripping of adult and infant MRI data. Computers in Biology and Medicine 37, 342–357 (2007)
5. Crum, W.R., Rueckert, D., Jenkinson, M., Kennedy, D., Smith, S.M.: A framework for detailed objective comparison of non-rigid registration algorithms in neuroimaging. In: Barillot, C., Haynor, D.R., Hellier, P. (eds.) MICCAI 2004. LNCS, vol. 3216, pp. 679–686. Springer, Heidelberg (2004)
6. Friston, K.J., Penny, W.: Posterior probability maps and SPMs. NeuroImage 19, 1240–1249 (2003)
7. Hahn, H.K., Peitgen, H.-O.: The skull stripping problem in MRI solved by a single 3D watershed transform. In: Delp, S.L., DiGoia, A.M., Jaramaz, B. (eds.) MICCAI 2000. LNCS, vol. 1935, pp. 134–143. Springer, Heidelberg (2000)
8. Harnsberger, H.R., Osborn, A.G., Ross, J., Macdonald, A.: Diagnostic and Surgical Imaging Anatomy: Brain, Head and Neck, Spine. Amirsys Inc. (2006)
9. Kobashi, S., Fujimoto, Y., Ogawa, M., Ando, K., Ishikura, R., Kondo, K., Hirota, S., Hata, Y.: Fuzzy-ASM Based Automated Skull Stripping Method from Infantile Brain MR Images. In: IEEE International Conference on Granular Computing, pp. 632–635 (2007)
10. Li, X.: CI, L., Wang, R., Li, J.: A Region Growing Method Based on Fuzzy Connectedness. In: ICALIP, pp. 993–997 (2008)

11. Marr, D., Hildreth, E.: Theory of edge detection. Proceedings of Royal Society of London 207(B), 187–217 (1980)
12. Mathur, A.M., Neil, J.J., Inder, T.E.: Understanding Brain Injury and Neurodevelopment Disabilities in the Premature Infant: The Evolving Role of Advanced Magnetic Resonance Imagine. Seminar in Perinatology 34, 57–66 (2010)
13. Perona, P., Malik, J.: Scale-Spacing and Edge Detection Using Anisotropic Diffusion. IEEE Transactions on Pattern Analysis and Machine Intelligence 12(7), 629–639 (1990)
14. Pohle, R., Toennies, K.D.: Segmentation of medical images using adaptive region growing. Proceedings of SPIE 4322, 1337–1346 (2001)
15. Prastawa, M., Gilmore, J.H., Lin, W., Gerig, G.: Automatic segmentation of MR image of the developing newborn brain. Medical Image Analysis 9, 457–466 (2005)
16. Rehm, K., Schaper, K., Anderson, J., Woods, R.: Putting our heads together: a consensus approach to brain/non–brian segmentation in T1–weighted MR volumes. NeuroImage 22, 1262–1270 (2004)
17. Rorden, C., Brett, M.: Stereotaxic display of brain lessions. Behavioural Neurology 12, 191–200 (2000)
18. Sadananthan, S.A., Zheng, W., Chee, M.W., Zagorodnov, V.: Skull stripping using graph cuts. NeuroImage 49, 225–239 (2010)
19. Segonne, F., Dale, A.M., Busa, E., Glessner, M., Salat, D., Hahn, H.K., Fischl, B.: A hybrid approach to the skull stripping problem in MRI. NeuroImage 22, 1060–1075 (2004)
20. Shanthi, K., Sasi Kumar, M.: Skull stripping and automatic segmentation of brain MRI using seed growth and threshold techniques. In: International Conference on Intelligent and Advanced Systems, ICIAS 2007, November 25-28, pp. 422–426. IEEE Computer Society, Los Alamitos (2007)
21. Shattuck, D.W., Leathy, R.M.: BrainSuite: An automated cortical surface identification tool. Medical Image Analysis 6, 129–142 (2002)
22. Shattuck, D.W., Sandor-Leathy, S.R., Shaper, K.A., Rottenberg, D.A., Leathy, R.M.: Magnetic Resonance Image Tissue Classification Using a Partial Volume Model. NeuroImage 13, 856–876 (2001)
23. Smith, S.M.: Fast robust automated brain extraction. Human Brain Mapping 17, 143–155 (2002)
24. Smith, S., Jenkinson, M., Woolrich, M., Beckmann, C., Behrens, T., Johansen-Berg, H., Bannister, P., Luca, M.D., Drobnjak, I., Flitney, D., Niazy, R., Saunders, J., Vickers, J., Zhang, Y., Stefano, N.D., Brady, J., Matthews, P.: Advances in functional and structural MR image analysis and implementation as FSL. NeuroImage 23(S1), 208–219 (2004)
25. SPM8: This software is available at the web address, `http://www.fil.ion.ucl.ac.uk/spm/`
26. Tzaroushi, L.C., Astrakas, L.G., Zikou, A., Xydis, V., Kosta, P., Andronikou, S., Argyropoulou, M.I.: Preventricular leukomalacia in preterm children: assessment of grey and white matter and cerebrospinal fluid changes by MRI. Pediatric Radiology 39, 1327–1332 (2009)
27. Weickert, J.: Coherence–Enhancing Diffusion Filtering. Internation Journal of Computer Vision 31(2/3), 111–127 (1999)
28. Zhao, W., Xie, M., Gao, J., Li, T.: A Modified Skull-Stripping Method Based on Morphological Processing. In: ICCMS 2010: Second International Conference on Computer Modeling and Simulation, vol. 1, pp. 159–163 (2010)

Adaptive Classification of Dirt Particles in Papermaking Process

Nataliya Strokina, Tuomas Eerola, Lasse Lensu, and Heikki Kälviäinen

Machine Vision and Pattern Recognition Laboratory (MVPR)
Department of Information Technology
Lappeenranta University of Technology (LUT)
P.O. Box 20, FI-53851 Lappeenranta, Finland
firstname.surname@lut.fi
http://www2.it.lut.fi/mvpr

Abstract. In pulping and papermaking, dirt particles significantly affect the quality of paper. Knowledge of the dirt type helps to track the sources of the impurities which would considerably improve the paper making process. Dirt particle classification designed for this purpose should be adaptable because the dirt types are specific to the different processes of paper mills. This paper introduces a general approach for the adaptable classification system. The attention is paid to feature extraction and evaluation, in order to determine a suboptimal set of features for a certain data. The performance of standard classifiers on the provided data is presented, considering how the dirt particles or different types are classified. The effect of dirt particle grouping according to the particle size on the results of classification and feature evaluation is discussed. It is shown that the representative features of dirt particles from different size groups are different, which has an effect on the classification.

Keywords: machine vision, particle segmentation, dirt particle classification, feature extraction, pulping, papermaking, image processing and analysis.

1 Introduction

Recently the papermaking industry has been focusing on process optimization and has become more interested in machine vision methods. Dirt particles affect considerably the formation of paper, impairing the printing properties. Tracking the amount and type of dirt in pulp enables to use the materials and energy more efficiently. Additionally, knowing the type of the particles it is easier to determine the source of dirt and to eliminate the problem of dirt particles. Manual dirt counting is a time-consuming process, involving human for analysis and evaluation. In this case the human factor affects significantly the results of evaluation. A human is not able to keep the same level of concentration and attention during the whole period of work, and the decisions might be subjective depending on a researcher. The process of dirt counting might be automated so that

A. Heyden and F. Kahl (Eds.): SCIA 2011, LNCS 6688, pp. 731–741, 2011.

the tedious work is performed by a machine and a human has only to analyze the results.

The machine vision approach in the paper quality control consists of acquisition of digital images of the paper samples and the analysis of the digitized samples using computational methods. The idea of such systems is described in [1,2,3] where not only off-line but also on-line methods for paper evaluation are presented. The off-line methods for dirt detection consider scanned images of the paper sheets. The system evaluates the mean intensity of the pixels and according to the local threshold segments the impurities. In [2] a threshold is determined manually, in the other cases there is an opportunity of automatic calculation of the threshold. On-line systems usually adapt to the intensity automatically and determine the threshold. The classification of particles is not done or only dirt clustering according to the shape is performed, e.g., in [6].

This study focuses on the development of the approach for adaptive classification of the dirt particles. The approach should use a standard classification method to be capable of adapting for the specific data. Types of dirt features and their evaluation are paid a special attention. The particles are divided into subgroups according to their size and the results of classification for the subgroups are compared to the results without the division. Section 2 provides the description of the approach and the method proposed. In Section 3 the results of feature extraction and classification are discussed. The conclusions are drawn in Section 4.

2 Classification of Dirt Particles

2.1 Problem Statement

Objectives. The aim of the presented research is to develop a method for adaptive classification of dirt particles in dry pulp sheets. Feature selection should be automated. State-of-art generic classification methods are used so that the classification was not related to any data. It is important since the system should handle adding new dirt types. Additionally, it is needed to study how the division of dirt particles according to their size can affect the classification results.

Restrictions. The research is based only on the provided data, which includes dry pulp sheets with dirt particles of four dirt types: bark, sand, plastic, and shives. The provided data does not introduce all the possible variations of pulp and dirt.

Test samples. Each test sample contains dirt of a single type. The samples were scanned, and the examples of test samples are presented in Figure 1.

2.2 General Workflow

Algorithm 1 introduces the main steps of the adaptive classification. After dirt particle segmentation the grouping of the whole set based on the area is performed.

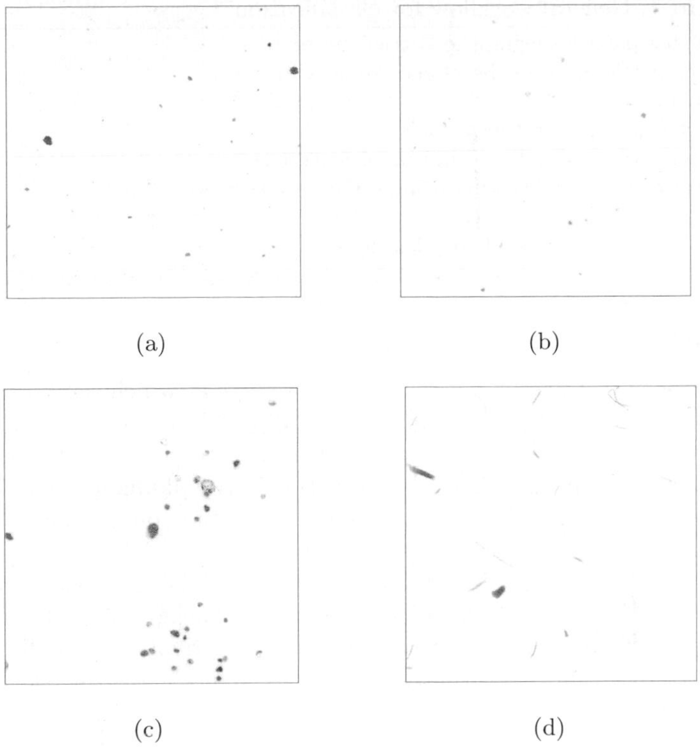

Fig. 1. Pulp sheets: (a) Bark; (b) Plastic; (c) Sand; (d) Shive

In the case of multiple subsets the features should be evaluated separately for each subset since for dirt particles of different size different characteristics can be significant. It is worth mentioning that the classification method should not be related to the specific data set since the available data does not represent all the possible dirt particles and pulp types. For these reasons the performance of several standard classifier is evaluated.

2.3 Grouping of Dirt Particles Based on a Size

The experiments have revealed that dirt particles of different size might have different features that count. Varying significantly within one class some features cause problems in classification because of considerable overlapping of the classes in feature space. A number of grounds might be found to figure out groups of particles within one class. For example, based on the area histogram one could divide one class into several depending on histogram bins. In the this work ISO 5350-1:2006 [13] is employed for group categorization.

Algorithm 1. General workflow for classification

```
Segment dirt particles using the Kittler method [7]
Divide the particles into subsets according to the size
for each subset do
  Extract features from the particles
  Determine the optimal or suboptimal feature set
  Perform training and testing using different classifiers
end for
Evaluate the performance of the classifiers
```

2.4 Segmentation

Segmentation of dirt particles is an important stage at which small low contrast areas should be detected in an image. According to the survey [10], there is a number of methods to use but none of them can be universally used for any segmentation problem. In this study the Kittler thresholding method [7] is used. The choice of the method is based on the previous study on automated counting and characterization of dirt particles in pulp [4].

Grayscale images are considered for segmentation. The images are divided into foreground which consists of the dirt particles and background. The foreground and background are modeled as a mixture of two Gaussians [7]. The threshold can be calculated by optimizing the cost function based on the Bayesian classification rule.

2.5 Feature Extraction

The features can be divided into two categories: geometric features and color features. Geometric features include characteristics of shape, form, and uniformity of a dirt particle. Color features include, for example, mean color, variation of color, and intensity. The calculated features are presented in Table 1.

Table 1. Feature set

Maximum diameter	Extent		Elongation	Eq. (6)
Minimum diameter	Fiber length	Eq. (1)	Curl	Eq. (7)
Solidity	Fiber width	Eq. (2)	Mean intensity	
Eccentricity	Form factor	Eq. (3)	Mean color	
Convex area	Roundness	Eq. (4)	Area	
Perimeter	Aspect ratio	Eq. (5)	Coarseness	Eq. (8)
Std of color				

For each dirt particle a bounding box is determined which is the smallest rectangle enclosing the dirt particle. The Solidity specifies the proportion of the pixels in the convex hull that are also in the region. The Eccentricity specifies the eccentricity of the ellipse that contains the same second-moments as the region. Convex area is the number of pixels in the convex hull of a dirt particle.

Extent specifies the ratio of pixels in the region to pixels in the total bounding box. Mean color and mean intensity are calculated as the mean hue value and the mean intensity over a dirt particle area. Std of color describes the standard deviation of color within the area of a dirt particle.

Other geometric features are calculated according to the following formulas:

$$Fiberlength = 0.25 \cdot (Perimeter - (\sqrt{|Perimeter^2 - 16 \cdot Area|})) \tag{1}$$

$$FiberWidth = \frac{Area}{FiberLength} \tag{2}$$

$$FormFactor = \frac{4 \cdot \pi \cdot Area}{Perimeter^2} \tag{3}$$

$$Roundness = \frac{4 \cdot Area}{\pi \cdot MaxDiameter^2} \tag{4}$$

$$AspectRatio = \frac{MaxDiameter}{MinDiameter} \tag{5}$$

$$Elongation = \left| \frac{FiberLength}{FiberWidth} \right| \tag{6}$$

$$Curl = \left| \frac{MaxDiameter}{FiberLength} \right| \tag{7}$$

$$Coarseness = \frac{Perimeter^2}{4 \cdot \pi \cdot Area} \tag{8}$$

2.6 Feature Evaluation

Feature evaluation is performed to determine the set of features that should be used to classify the dirt particles. The evaluation function is determined by the Linear Discriminant Analysis (LDA) [5] that is used for data classification and the reduction of feature space dimensions.

The goal of the LDA method is to maximize the separability of data classes, which implies the maximization of the ratio

$$r = tr\left(\frac{|S_b|}{|S_w|}\right). \tag{9}$$

Within the class scatter matrix

$$S_w = \sum_{i=1}^{C} \sum_{j=1}^{N_i} (x_j - mean_i) \tag{10}$$

where C is the number of classes, N_i is the number of samples in class i, x_j is the j-th element of class i, and $mean_i$ is the mean value of class i, determines the variance of values within one class.

Between the class scatter matrix

$$S_b = \sum_{i=1}^{C}(mean_i - mean) \tag{11}$$

where $mean$ is the mean of the means of all the classes, evaluates the variance of feature values within one class.

To find the space where the current features might be distinguishable in the most efficient way one should maximize the criterion

$$cr = tr(S_w^{-1} \cdot S_b) \tag{12}$$

which means that the eigenvectors of the criterion matrix should be calculated. The matrix of eigenvectors describes the transformation to the new feature space. The sample vectors from all the classes should be transferred to that space and using one or several thresholds might be distinguishable.

In order to decrease the computational time suboptimal algorithms are usually employed. An algorithm should be developed specifically for a certain task. A sequential approach for feature selection is presented in Algorithm 2. In this case the ratio is calculated for different combinations of features, consisting of one, two, and three items. If the optimal combination consists of three features, the values of ratio for the combinations consisting of the optimal set and one new feature is calculated. If the current ratio is more than the maximum, one should continue adding features until the calculated ratio is less than the maximum. As an output the algorithm provides the suboptimal feature set and the ratio value for it.

Algorithm 2. Feature selection

```
Calculate the ratio values for all combinations consisting of one, two, and three
features
Find the list of features feat_list corresponding to the maximum ratio max_ratio 9
if length(feat_list)==3 then
  while curr_max_ratio > max_ratio do
    for all unused features do
      Add the current feature to the optimal set
      Calculate the ratio for the new combinations
    end for
    Find the maximum of the calculated values of ratio
    Update the maximum ratio max_ratio and the optimal list features feat_list
  end while
end if
```

2.7 Classification

The classifiers used in the study are listed in Table 2. State-of-the-art generic classification methods as well as the well-known structural approaches are used in order not to be related to the specific data. K-NN is used with a neighborhood of 1, 3, and 5 samples. LDA is based on the transformation described in

Section 2, where the linearizing transformation is described. GMM classifier is used with expectation maximization (GMMem) and Figueiredo-Jain (GMMfj) criteria [8]. SVM is used with a second order polynomial kernel. In the case of expectation maximization criterion 4 components were used to model the data. For Figueiredo-Jain criterion the maximum number of components was 10. The Adaboost method introduces a set of weak classifiers, represented as a separate feature, to create a strong classifier. In the case of the Adaboost classification all the features are employed.

Table 2. List of classifiers

K-Nearest Neighborhood (k-NN)	[9]	Gaussian Mixture Model (GMM)	[11]
Naive Bayesian Classifier (Bayes)	[9]	Support Vector Machine (SVM)	[11]
Linear Discriminant Analysis (LDA)	[11]	AdaBoost	[12]

3 Experiments and Discussion

3.1 Test Samples and Experiments

The samples for experiments are prepared by papermaking specialists of LUT FiberLaboratory. Based on the expert choice the selected types of particles are plastic, bark, sand, and shive. The samples have been scanned with reflective light. The examples of dirt particles used in the experiments are presented in Figure 1. The examples of the separate dirt particles are presented in Figure 2.

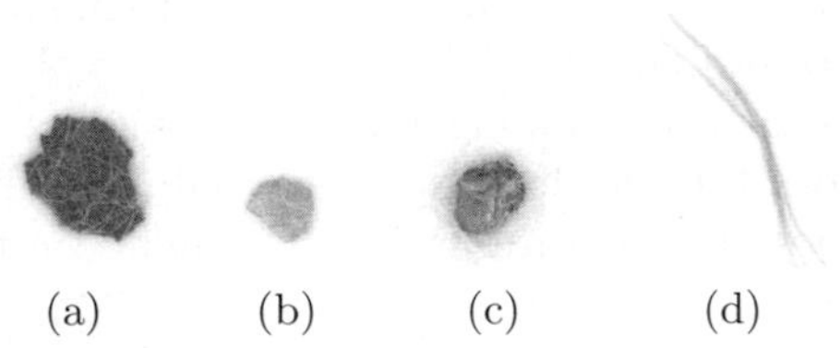

Fig. 2. Dirt particles: (a) Bark; (b) Plastic; (c) Sand; (d) Shive

The dirt particles were segmented and features were computed using Algorithm 2. Since the amount of dirt particles was restricted two middle size groups were combined into one. The suboptimal feature sets for each size group are described in Table 3.

From the results it can be seen that the color is more important for bigger particles, since the color of smaller ones is not saturated. Standard deviation of color also becomes a more effective when the area of particles is large enough to estimate the feature. At the same time coarseness is considered to be a significant feature for the smaller groups. It is interesting to notice, that for the whole set of

Table 3. Suboptimal feature sets for each size group

Group	Feature set
0.04-0.15 mm^2	Form factor + Coarseness
0.15-1.00 mm^2	StdColor + Coarseness
1.00-5.00 mm^2	Mean color + Std of color
The whole set	Mean color + Std of color

particles, without division into groups, the most effective features are the mean color and the standard deviation of color as for the biggest particles.

Two experiments were carried out. In the first experiment the whole data set was considered and the classification was performed on the training set, on the separate test set and using leave-one-out validation. In the second experiment the dirt particles were divided into the size groups. The classification was performed for all subsets separately. Table 5 shows the amount of particles in the train and the test sets for each dirt type for the whole set and for the size groups. The particles for training and testing were selected independently for the size groups and for the whole set. The amount of the dirt particles in the test set was restricted by the total amount of dirt.

3.2 Classification on the Whole Set

The classification results can be found in Table 4. The numbers represen the percentage of correctly classified dirt particles. For better representation the highest results are set in bold. One can notice that it is possible to divide the classifiers into two groups according to their performance. The first group with the best performance includes nearest neighborhood methods, SVM, and Gaussian mixture model classifiers producing approximately the same result. The poor performance of LDA and Adaboost can be explained by the fact that the classes are significantly overlapping in the feature space. From the results one can conclude that both the choice of an appropriate classifier and the selection of the optimal or suboptimal features lead to the sufficient classification results.

3.3 Classification Using Subsets

The results of classification have been averaged for the size groups and can be found in Table 6. The numbers represent the percentage of correctly classified dirt particles.

The result of classification for size groups are slightly worse than for the whole set which can be conditioned by the lack of samples in each of the groups. Here the same tendency among classification methods can be noticed as in the experiment with the whole set. The classifiers giving the best results are the Gaussian mixture model approach and the nearest neighborhood classifiers. However, the Adaboost, SVM and LDA classifiers have better performance than in the case of the whole set, which means that the size groups of particles are less overlapping in the feature space than the whole set.

Table 4. Classification results for the whole set

Classifier	Train set	Leave-one-out	Test set				
			Bark	Plastic	Sand	Shive	Average
1-NN	-	**98.3%**	87.6%	97.5%	88.7%	64.4%	**83.3%**
3-NN	98.0%	97.6%	86.7%	96.8%	84.4%	55.9%	82.1%
5-NN	**98.9%**	96.6%	**95.2%**	**98.2%**	54.6%	51.7%	82.4%
Bayes	87.0%	85.3%	74.5%	81.2%	29.7%	65.2%	68.8%
LDA	68.3%	67.0%	92.1%	51.6%	79.4%	66.1%	59.8%
GMMfj	97.3%	93.7%	84.5%	96.0%	85.1%	45.5%	78.8%
GMMem	98.5%	96.0%	83.8%	95.5%	51.1%	45.0%	77.3%
SVM	81.3%	78.5%	82.2%	84.7%	**97.3%**	40.0%	76.1%
AdaBoost	73.3%	69.5 %	54.6%	82.6%	57.6%	**79.4%**	68.8%

Table 5. Amount of particles for each dirt type

Size group	Train set				Test set			
	Bark	Plastic	Sand	Shive	Bark	Plastic	Sand	Shive
0.04-0.15 mm^2	50	50	50	50	609	89	29	22
0.15-1.00 mm^2	20	20	20	20	342	184	9	55
1.00-5.00 mm^2	40	40	40	40	20	24	24	101
The whole set	100	100	100	100	981	307	72	188

Table 6. Classification results for the size groups

Classifier	Train set	Leave-one-out	Test set				
			Bark	Plastic	Sand	Shive	Average
1-NN	-	75.5%	68.8%	59.3%	61.5%	59.2%	62.2%
3-NN	88.4%	80.3%	76.6%	55.2%	60.7%	63.5%	64.0%
5-NN	85.5%	77.8%	76.3%	52.9%	57.5%	67.8%	63.6%
Bayes	83.9%	79.2%	90.9%	50.0%	58.1%	62.2%	65.3%
LDA	65.6%	64.8%	84.2%	42.3%	70.9%	61.6%	64.8%
GMMfj	**95.1%**	83.0%	77.5%	68.8%	64.3%	64.0%	68.7%
GMMem	89.5%	**86.3%**	**94.5%**	70.1%	49.1%	64.5%	**69.5%**
SVM	67.8%	64.3%	75.6%	**73.3%**	52.1%	41.1%	60.5%
AdaBoost	71.2%	69.8%	58.7%	56.3%	**71.7%**	**87.3%**	68.5%

In the future work, it will be useful to obtain more samples with dirt in order to perform classification of size groups on bigger sets. Besides that, if there is a need, particle texture can be studied to discover new features. Low performance of some classifiers has to be also addressed: either those classifiers should not be used or their parameters must be tuned. Some prior information from the experts might be obtained concerning the frequency of occurrence of the specific dirt types.

4 Conclusion

The present study focuses on the problem of the adaptive classification of dirt particles. An approach for feature selection is described, and relevant features are extracted for classification. The experiments were performed on the whole set and for the size groups of the particles.

It was discovered that for different size groups of dirt different features count. The satisfactory results of classification were obtained for the whole data set. Although the results were slightly worse for size groups, it was shown that the size groups of classes are less overlapping in the feature space. The results show that the critical task is to select the appropriate features. The final tuning for an application can be made by selecting a specific classifier from the best ones and with enough tuning possibilities.

Acknowledgements

The research was carried out in the "PulpVision" project (TEKES project 70010/10) funded by the European Union and the participating companies. The authors wish to acknowledge the FiberLaboratory in LUT, TEKES, and the companies for their support and collaboration.

References

1. Duarte, F., Araujo, H., Dourado, A.: An Automatic System for Dirt in Pulp Inspection Using Hierarchical Image Segmentation. Computers & Industrial Engineering 37, 343–346 (1999)
2. Jones, S., Thomas, R., Awcock, G., Humphrey, K.: Machine vision techniques for ink particle analysis within the paper recycling process. In: Fifth International Conference on Image Processing and its Applications, pp. 682–686 (1995)
3. Parker, S., Chan, J.R.: Dirt Counting in Pulp: An Approach Using Image Analysis Methods. In: Proceedings of the IASTED International Conference on Signal and Image Processing, SIP (2002)
4. Fouladgaran, M., Mankki, A., Lensu, L., Käyhkö, J., Kälviäinen, H.: Automated Counting and Characterization of Dirt Particles in Pulp. In: Bolc, L., Tadeusiewicz, R., Chmielewski, L.J., Wojciechowski, K. (eds.) ICCVG 2010. LNCS, vol. 6375, pp. 166–174. Springer, Heidelberg (2010)
5. Fukunaga, K.: Introduction to Statistical Pattern Recognition. Academic Press, San Diego (1990)
6. The Verity IA Color Image Analysis software. Dirt Counter, `http://www.verityia.com/stripscanner.php`
7. Kittler, J., Illingworth, J.: On threshold selection using clustering criteria. IEEE Transactions on System, Man, and Cybernetics 12, 652–655 (1985)
8. Figueiredo, M.A.T., Jain, A.K.: Unsupervised learning of finite mixture models. IEEE Transactions on Pattern Analysis and Machine Intelligence 24(3), 381–396 (2002)
9. Theodoridis, S., Koutroumbas, K.: Pattern Recognition. Academic Press, London (1999)

10. Sezgin, M., Sankur, B.: Survey over image thresholding techniques and quantitative performance evaluation. Journal of Electronic Imaging 13(1), 146–165 (2004)
11. Duda, R.O., Hart, P.E., Stork, D.G.: Pattern Classification. Wiley, Chichester (2001)
12. Freund, Y.: Boosting a weak learning algorithm by majority. Information and Computation 121(2), 256–285 (1995)
13. Pulps – Estimation of dirt and shives – Part 1: Inspection of laboratory sheets by transmitted light. ISO 5350-1:2006

Text Extraction Using Component Analysis and Neuro-fuzzy Classification on Complex Backgrounds

Michael Makridis[1], Nikolaos E. Mitrakis[2],
Nikolaos Nikolaou[1], and Nikolaos Papamarkos[1]

[1] Image Processing and Multimedia Laboratory, Department of Electrical & Computer Engineering, Democritus University of Thrace, 67100 Xanthi, Greece
[2] European Commission, Joint Research Centre, Institute for Protection and Security of the Citizen, Maritime Affairs Unit G.04, TP 051, 21027 Ispra (VA), Italy
{mmakridi,papamark,nnikol}@ee.duth.gr,
nikolaos.mitrakis@jrc.ec.europa.eu

Abstract. This paper proposes a new technique for text extraction on complex color documents and cover books. The novelty of the proposed technique is that contrary to many existing techniques, it has been designed to deal successfully with documents having complex background, character size variations and different fonts. The number of colors of each document image is reduced automatically into a relative small number (usually below ten colors) and each document is divided into binary images. Then, connected component analysis is performed and homogenous groups of connected components (CCs) are created. A set of features is extracted for each group of CCs. Finally each group is classified into text or non-text classes using a neuro-fuzzy classifier. The proposed technique can be summarized into four consequent stages. In the first stage, a pre-processing algorithm filters noisy CCs. Afterwards, CC grouping is performed. Then, a set of nine local and global features is extracted for each group and finally a classification procedure detects document's text regions. Experimental results prove the efficiency of the proposed technique, which can be further extended to deal with even more complex text extraction problems.

Keywords: Text extraction, Color reduction, Connected component analysis, Adaptive run length smoothing, Pattern classification, Neuro-fuzzy classifier.

1 Introduction

This paper proposes a technique for text extraction in complex color documents and cover books. Interest about exploiting text information in images and video has grown notably during the past years. Text can provide powerful description of the image content and it reasonably attracts the research interest.

A main categorization of text extraction methods include texture based techniques [1]-[4] and connected components (CCs) based techniques [5]-[9].

Texture based methods use the observation that text in images has distinct textural properties that distinguish them from the background. They are mainly used in video text based applications [10]-[12]. On the other hand, CCs based techniques are fast

A. Heyden and F. Kahl (Eds.): SCIA 2011, LNCS 6688, pp. 742–751, 2011.

and relatively simple in implementation and exploit the fact that characters are segmented. The proposed approach belongs to this specific category of text information extraction techniques.

The proposed technique performs color reduction to limit document's colors and divides each document into a set of binary documents, one for every color. Then, it performs connected component (CC) analysis and creates groups of components. For each group, a set of features is extracted and finally the classification process, based on a neuro-fuzzy system, detects those groups that correspond to text regions.

Most text extraction techniques focus on data sets of documents with certain specifications such as:

- Documents pixel depth is 8-bit gray-scale
- Documents have low character size variations
- Text gray values are greater than background values
- Documents have uniform background without contrast variations

The novelty of the proposed paper is that overcomes the specifications mentioned above and deals successfully with complex text extraction problems.

2 Description of the Technique

The technique proposed in this paper is based on an iterative procedure of four stages. A document image is the input of the technique. The number of its colors is decreased (usually in less than ten colors) according to a color reduction technique [7]. After color reduction, the initial document can be represented by a set of binary images, one for each color, which we call color planes. Then, an iterative procedure is applied to each color plane. Generally, the proposed technique can be summarized into four stages:

Stage 1. Pre-processing: CC analysis is performed to each color plane. Color reduction process usually creates noisy, superfluous CCs. Most of these CCs, though, can be easily recognized and removed during this stage.
Stage 2. Page segmentation: CCs of each color plane are grouped according to an adaptive run length smoothing algorithm (ARLSA) [16].
Stage 3. Feature extraction: Each group of CCs is considered as a pattern. For each pattern, a set of nine local run length and spatial features is extracted.
Stage 4. Classification using Adaptive Neuro-Fuzzy Interference System (ANFIS) [14]. A subset of patterns is first used to train the classifier.

A block diagram of the proposed technique is shown in Fig. 1. In the rest of this section a brief description of color reduction [7] and ARLSA [13] algorithms is given.

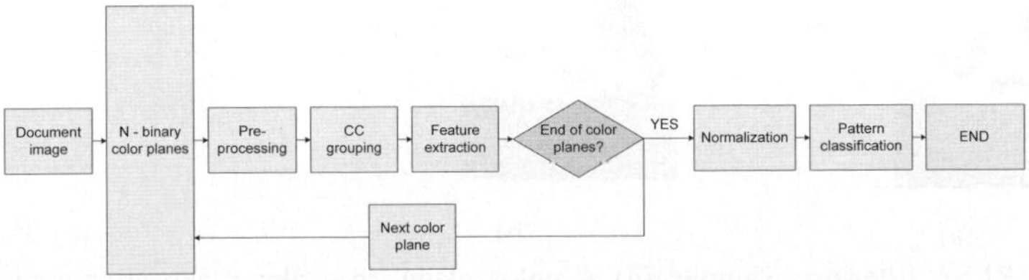

Fig. 1. The block diagram of the proposed technique

2.1 Color Reduction

A color document or a cover book has millions of different color values. In order to apply CC analysis, we have to limit the total number of colors. To achieve that, we use an unsupervised clustering algorithm to find clusters of similar colors, originally proposed by Sobottka et al. [7]. We chose to implement this color reduction technique for three basic reasons:

- Simplicity of the algorithm
- Very low computational cost
- Text objects (CCs) are coherent and final color distribution inside the document image is homogenous.

2.2 Adaptive Run Length Smoothing Algorithm

Adaptive run length smoothing algorithm (ARLSA) [13] is a modified version of RLSA [15], a common algorithm, that it is used in page layout analysis and segmentation techniques. Generally, ARLSA is applied on CCs of binary images.

$$\begin{aligned} L(CC_i, CC_j) < T_l \\ H_R(CC_i, CC_j) < T_h \\ O_R(CC_i, CC_j) < T_o \end{aligned} \tag{1}$$

The novelty of ARLSA is, that it applies run length at a certain direction only between pixels of different CCs and only if these CCs fulfill certain specifications. In the proposed technique, ARLSA is applied in the horizontal direction.

Let p_i and p_j be two pixels that belong to CCs CC_i and CC_j and $CC_j\,(i \neq j)$. The connection between p_i and p_j is made only if the following specifications are fulfilled:

where $L(CC_i, CC_j)$ is the Euclidean distance between the bounding boxes of CC_i and CC_j, $H_R(CC_i, CC_j)$ is the height ratio between CC_i and CC_j and $O_R(CC_i, CC_j)$ is the overlapping ratio between CC_i and CC_j. Furthermore, H_R can be defined as:

$$H_R(CC_i, CC_j) = \min(H_{CC_i}, H_{CC_j}) / \max(H_{CC_i}, H_{CC_j}) \tag{2}$$

Where H_{CC_i} and H_{CC_j} the heights of CC_i and CC_j.

Finally, O_R is defined as the overlapping ratio between two components.

(a) (b) (c)

Fig. 2. ARLSA filtering example: (a) A color plane, (b) color plane after application of ARLSA, (c) filtered color plane

3 Image Pre-processing

The purpose of this stage is to remove small noisy connected components and large background or graphic components. Pre-processing filtering is applied in two separate steps:

First, noisy elements are filtered out based on three characteristics of the connected components and their corresponding bounding boxes. For a connected component CC_i these characteristics are:

The height of the bounding box of the CC_i, H_{CC_i}

The elongation $E(CC_i) = \dfrac{\min\{H_{CC_i}, W_{CC_i}\}}{\max\{H_{CC_i}, W_{CC_i}\}}$

The density $D(CC_i) = \dfrac{P_{num}(CC_i)}{BB_{size}(CC_i)}$,

which is the ratio of the number of foreground pixels $P_{num}(CC_i)$ to the total number of pixels in the bounding box $BB_{size}(CC_i) = H(CC_i) \cdot W(CC_i)$.

Connected components with $H(CC_i) < AH/3$, or $D(CC_i) < 0.08$, or $E(CC_i) < 0.08$ are considered as noisy elements and they are eliminated, where AH is the average height of all CC of the color plane. These values have been selected very carefully, so no character elements will be eliminated.

The second type of filtering removes large background and graphic components. It is based on the comparison of the connected components from two images, the initial binary document image and the resulted image after the application of the ARLSA. Let I_1 be the original image (see Fig. 2(a)), I_2 the image after the application of the ARLSA (see Fig. 2(b)). The number of pixels P_{I_2} of each connected component $CC_i \in I_2$ is calculated, that is the number of the black pixels. In the defined area of each $CC_i \in I_2$, the sum P_{I_1} of the corresponding black pixels of I_1 is also calculated.

The ratio of these two sums is taken into account as in the following equation:

$$P_R = \frac{P_{I_2}}{P_{I_1}} \leq T_R \tag{3}$$

As it is mentioned above, ARLSA connects only similar neighbor components. In this case, graphic components of Fig. 2(a) are isolated and the application of ARLSA does not link them with other components. Therefore, their pixel size remains almost the same and P_R has a value near to one. Components, which correspond to pixel size ratio smaller than T_R (Eq. 3), are removed and a new image I_3 (see Fig. 2(c)) is produced. The parameters used in ARLSA are those parameters proposed as optimal by the authors.

4 Document Segmentation

Document page segmentation is very important for successful classification. During this stage, CCs of color planes are grouped to form a pattern for the classification procedure. False grouping will have as a result unreliable feature values and furthermore classification failure. Therefore, we need a reliable technique that groups CCs of the same class (text or non-text).

To perform successful grouping, we use ARLSA. ARLSA groups only similar CCs as far as height and overlapping is concerned.

The choice of ARLSA is based on the following reasons:

- Characters are in most cases CCs of similar height in a certain direction (in most cases horizontal). Furthermore, the height ratio between two characters of the same font size (in the same sentence) is less than 2.
- Graphics consist of CCs that have great variation in height. Furthermore, graphic CCs do not have a defined arrangement in space and therefore overlapping measure in a certain direction is very low.
- Background CCs are large isolated CCs.

Because of the above reasons, text CCs group together in most cases, while non-text CCs form small groups. Each group is considered as a pattern for the feature extraction and classification stages.

5 Feature Extraction

In this stage, we form a set of nine features for each pattern (group of CCs) of each binary color plane. Feature selection has been made carefully, in order to distinguish text from non-text patterns as much as possible.

Mean Elongation: Elongation feature has been introduced in Section 3. Each pattern after CC grouping is formed by a set of CCs. The value of this feature is the mean elongation of a pattern's CCs. The idea of choosing mean elongation is that usually, character CCs have similar width to height ratio. On the other hand, lines and big graphic CCs can have either too small or too big width to height ratio.

Mean Density: Density feature has been also introduced in Section 3. The value of this feature is the mean density of a pattern's CCs. The idea of choosing mean density is that most graphic CCs have many holes and therefore their density values are smaller than character CCs.

Mean pixel size: This feature represents the mean pixel size of the CCs of each pattern.

Local Connectivity: This feature measures the coherence of a pattern. For each pixel $p_{i,j}$ of a pattern, the number of neighbor pattern pixels, within a 3x3 neighborhood, is counted. The total number of neighbor pattern pixels is divided by the pixel size of the pattern for normalization reasons. This feature takes large values for coherent CCs, while it takes small values for thin CCs or CCs with many holes. It can be expressed as follows:

$$lc_l = \frac{\sum_{k=1}^{PS_l} \sum_{m=i-1}^{i+1} \sum_{n=j-1}^{j+1} p_{l,i,j}}{PS_l} \tag{4}$$

Where $p_{l,i,j}$ a pixel of a pattern l and PS_l the total number of pixels of the pattern, which is pixel size of pattern l.

Run length mean and Run length variance features: For each pattern, we calculate the mean run length value at a certain direction that we call it G_d (group direction). Each pattern is a group of CCs, as it is mentioned in Section 4. The center points of these CCs define a least squares line. The gradient of this line, we call it G_d. Least squares line is represented by the following equation:

$$y = a + bx \tag{5}$$

We are interested in the direction of this line, which is defined as:

$$b = \frac{n\sum_{l=1}^{n} Xc_l Yc_l - (\sum_{l=1}^{n} Xc_l)(\sum_{l=1}^{n} Yc_l)}{n\sum_{l=1}^{n} Xc_l^2 - (\sum_{l=1}^{n} Xc_l)^2} \tag{6}$$

Where n is the number of a pattern's CCs and $\{(Xc_0 Yc_0),...,(Xc_n Yc_n)\}$ are their center points.

Run length mean and variance features are extracted from the run length histogram of each pattern.

Group direction mean feature: For each pair of CCs of a pattern $.CC_i$. and CC_j, we compute the corresponding gradient $G_{d,i,j}$. Group direction mean feature is the mean value of all $G_{d,i,j}$.

Mean Overlapping feature: As it is mentioned above, the center points of the CCs of a pattern define a group direction G_d. For each pair of CCs of a pattern CC_i and CC_j, we compute the corresponding overlap measure in the direction of G_d. The mean overlapping feature is the mean overlapping value of a pattern.

Fig. 3 illustrates an example of this feature. Suppose that the word "Example" is a pattern that consists of seven CCs, we calculate the overlap between letters-CCs "E" and "X" in the group direction. This feature is similar to the overlap feature that we introduced in Section 2.2 in the horizontal direction, but now overlapping is calculated in the direction of G_d

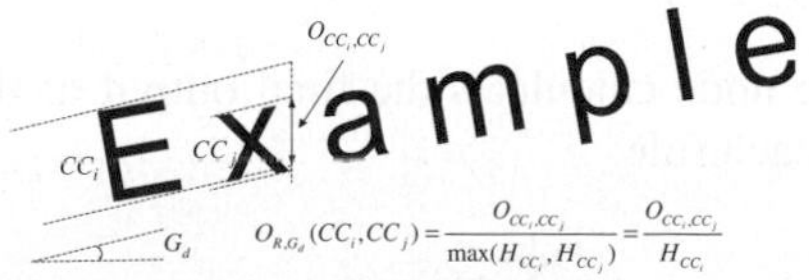

Fig. 3. Overlapping feature for CCs "E" and "x" in the direction of G_d

Black and white alterations: This feature is calculated by the total number of alterations between pattern and non-pattern pixels in the group direction, G_d. The number of black and white alteration is divided by the width of the pattern for normalization.

6 Pattern Classification Using ANFIS

ANFIS (Adaptive-Network-based Fuzzy Interference System) [14] is a neuro-fuzzy multilayered architecture, which was first introduced by Jang, well known for dealing with complex nonlinear modeling or classification problems. ANFIS main advantage is that it combines the strong descriptive characteristics of fuzzy logic with the learning capabilities of neural networks.

ANFIS consists of 6 layers which are described below:

Layer 1: The nodes of this layer carry the inputs of the network to the next layer.

Layer 2: Each node of this layer implements a fuzzy membership function that describes a fuzzy set of each input (linguistic nodes). The proposed implementation uses Gaussian membership functions which are described by the following equation:

$$\mu_{A_j}^{i}(x_j) = e^{\frac{-(x_j-\sigma_j^i)^2}{2\sigma_j^{i2}}}, \quad j = 1,\ldots,m, \qquad i = 1,\ldots,k_j \tag{7}$$

The output of this layer reveals the membership degree of feature x_j to fuzzy set A_j^i, where j stands for the input and i for the fuzzy set defined in input j. The fuzzy input partition has been implemented through subtractive clustering [16].

Layer 3: The nodes of this layer are called rule nodes. The output of each node represents the degree that satisfies the hypothesis of a rule. The number of nodes of this layer is equal to the number of the rules, that is $n = k_1 \times \cdots \times k_m$. The degree of fulfillment of each rule can be calculated by the following:

$$\mu_i(\boldsymbol{x}) = \prod_{j=1}^{m} \mu_{A_j}^{i}(x_j), \text{ i} = 1,\ldots \text{n} \tag{8}$$

Layer 4: In this layer, the normalized fulfillment of each rule is calculated:

$$\overline{\mu}_i(\boldsymbol{x}) = \frac{\mu_i(\boldsymbol{x})}{\sum_{i=1}^{n} \mu_i(\boldsymbol{x})}, \text{ i} = 1,\ldots \text{n} \tag{9}$$

Layer 5: The nodes of this layer calculate the output of each rule:

$$y(i) = \overline{\mu}_i(\boldsymbol{x}) \times w_i, \text{ i} = 1,\ldots \text{n} \tag{10}$$

Layer 6: In this layer the node calculates the final output of the model by summarizing the partial output of each rule:

$$y = \sum_{i=1}^{n} y(i) \tag{11}$$

Fuzzy input partition has been implemented via subtractive clustering [16], while hybrid batch learning algorithm [15] is used to calculate the parameters of the network.

7 Experimental Results

In order to achieve objective experimental results, we created a dataset with document and ground truth images for evaluation purpose. Document dataset consists of 50 color cover books and documents with complex background, various font colors, sizes and types. Ground truth binary images were created for all 50 documents manually, using commercial image processing software. The proposed technique can identify text areas with skew up to 45 degrees. The documents are all taken from the internet, while their resolution is at least 200 dpi.

Due to space limitations, we present in Fig. 4 two characteristic results that they should be discussed. These examples reveal some of the advantages and disadvantages of the proposed technique.

Fig. 4 (b) shows a successful result. The cover book has non-uniform background and fonts of different sizes and colors. Main contribution to the successful result has the great resolution and successful color reduction that leads to coherent CCs.

Fig. 4 (c) shows a movie poster with uniform background and a large graph. Text areas, which include fonts of different color, type and size, have been successfully detected. However, some graph patterns in the middle of the Fig. 4 (d) have wrongly classified as text. These patterns have common text characteristics, such as elongation, density, run length variation and overlapping, which lead to classification error.

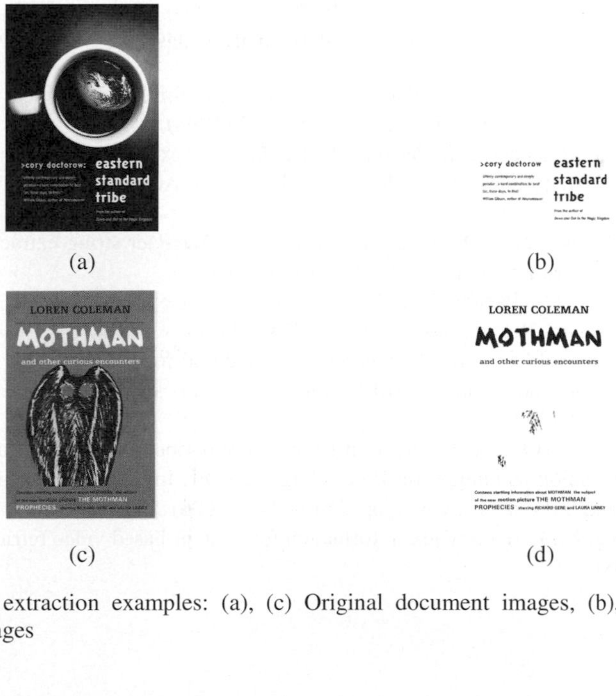

Fig. 4. Text extraction examples: (a), (c) Original document images, (b), (d), resulted document images

8 Conclusions

We have presented a new technique for text extraction on complex color documents. In this type of documents, text and graphics are highly mixed with the background and therefore color reduction, page segmentation and furthermore text extraction is a challenging task. Experiments have been performed and presented to test the effectiveness of the proposed technique.

The main advantage of the presented technique lies on the fact that although it deals with complex documents, it performs high successful rates and a reliable result for further processing. Pattern extraction based on connected component analysis and classification using ANFIS seem to work fine, even under extreme circumstances. Additionally, ARLSA provides very useful information about text patters. However, we intend to perform more research in the field of color reduction (extraction of color planes) and pattern extraction.

References

1. Jain, A.K., Zhong, Y.: Page Segmentation Using Texture Analysis. Pattern Recognition 29, 743–770 (1996)
2. Wu, V., Manmatha, R.: TextFinder: an automatic system to detect and recognize text in images. IEEE Trans. on Pattern Analysis and Machine Intelligence 21, 1224–1229 (1999)
3. Deng, S., Latifi, S., Regentova, S.: Document segmentation using polynomial spline wavelets. Pattern Recognition 34, 2533–2545 (2001)
4. Wang, B., Li, X., Liu, F., Hu, F.: Color text image binarization based on binary texture analysis. Pattern Recognition Letters 26, 1650–1657 (2005)
5. Fletcher, L., Kasturi, R.: A robust algorithm for text string separation from mixed text/graphics images. IEEE Trans. on Pattern Analysis and Machine Intelligence 10, 910–918 (1988)
6. Chen, W.Y., Chen, S.Y.: Adaptive page segmentation for color technical journals' cover images. Image and Vision Computing 16, 855–877 (1998)
7. Sobottka, K., Kronenberg, H., Perroud, T., Bunke, H.: Text Extraction from Colored Book and Journal Covers. International Journal on Document Analysis and Recognition 2, 163–176 (2000)
8. Hase, H., Shinokawa, T., Yoneda, M., Suen, C.Y.: Character string extraction from color documents. Pattern Recognition 34, 1349–1365 (2001)
9. Strouthopoulos, C., Papamarkos, N., Atsalakis, A.: Text extraction in complex color documents. Pattern Recognition 35, 1743–1758 (2002)
10. Lyu, M.R., Song, J., Cai, M.: A comprehensive method for multilingual video text detection, localization, and extraction. IEEE Trans. on Circuits and Systems for Video Technology 15, 243–255 (2005)
11. Chen, Y.L., Wu, B.F.: Text extraction from complex document images using the multiplane segmentation technique. In: Proceedings of IEEE International Conference on Systems, Man and Cybernetics, vol. 4, pp. 3540–3547 (2006)
12. Xu, L., Wang, K.: Extracting text information for content-based video retrieval. LNCS, pp. 58–69 (2008)

13. Nikolaou, N., Makridis, M., Gatos, B., Stamatopoulos, N., Papamarkos, N.: Segmentation of Historical Machine-Printed Documents Using Adaptive Run Length Smoothing and Skeleton Segmentation Paths. Image and Vision Computing (2009)
14. Jang, J.-S.R.: ANFIS: adaptive-network-based fuzzy inference system. IEEE Transactions on Systems, Man, and Cybernetics 23, 665–685 (1993)
15. Wahl, F.M., Wong, K.Y., Casey, R.G.: Block Segmentation and Text Extraction in Mixed Text/Image Documents. Computer Graphics and Image Processing 20, 375–390 (1982)
16. Chiu, S.: Fuzzy Model Identification Based on Cluster Estimation. Journal of Intelligent & Fuzzy Systems 2, 267–278 (1994)

Using Active Illumination for Accurate Variational Space-Time Stereo

Sergey Kosov, Thorsten Thormählen, and Hans-Peter Seidel

Max-Planck-Institut Informatik (MPII), Saarbrücken, Germany

Abstract. This paper addresses the problem of space-time stereo with active illumination and presents a formulation of this problem in the variational framework. Variational problems of this scale are computationally expensive to solve directly. We overcome this challenge by showing that speed-improving techniques, as the full-multi-grid and the multi-level-adaptation techniques, can be applied. We evaluate the performance of our method on 3 ground-truth datasets. The experimental results for synthetic and real datasets show that the combination of active illumination and variational space-time stereo improves the quality of the reconstruction on average by up to 3.1 times compared to a reconstruction from a single passive stereo image pair without active illumination.

1 Introduction

A classical problem in computer vision is the reconstruction of disparity field between several stereo images. The task is to find those corresponding pixels in the stereo images that are the projections of the same 3D point. The collection of displacement values for all pixels of an image forms a dense disparity map.

Algorithms for dense disparity map reconstruction are often a basic building block of more complicated systems for automatic 3D scene analysis, event detection, or object recognition. These systems are applied, for example, in machine vision, robotics, or medical applications. Furthermore, the recent development in cinematography, where more movies are shot in stereo, has sparked a new interest in the topic of stereo estimation in academia as well as in the post-production and home-entertainment industry.

A number of researchers have worked on fast and accurate stereo estimation (e.g., [1,2,3]). Nowadays, variational methods are among the best techniques for optic flow reconstruction, which is very related to disparity estimation, e.g. Mémin and Pérez [4] and Brox et al. [5]. These methods minimize an energy functional by solving the corresponding Euler-Lagrange equation. In order to solve this equation numerically, it is represented as a system of parabolic partial differential equations in finite differences. To optimize the energy functional, iterative solvers, like the Jacobi and Gauss-Seidel methods, are used. In 2006, Bruhn et al. [6] presented a real-time implementation of a variational solver for optic flow reconstruction, based on the multigrid method [7]. Recently, Valgaerts et al. [8] have presented an approach that allows to incorporate both

A. Heyden and F. Kahl (Eds.): SCIA 2011, LNCS 6688, pp. 752–763, 2011.

spatial and temporal information (from two subsequent image pairs) for optic flow reconstruction. A real-time variational solver for disparity reconstruction was demonstrated [9]. The real-time performance has been achieved by a combination of the full-multi-grid (FMG) method, the multi-level adaptation technique (MLAT) [10], and adaptive parameter techniques.

Classical stereo vision algorithms process the stereo image pairs of different points in time independently. However, better results can be obtained by considering the problem not only in space but also in time. In 2003, Zhang et al. [11] showed that the space-time approach gives better results for disparity estimation. They suggested that each classical stereo algorithm can be extended to the spatio-temporal domain. In this paper we follow their suggestion and show how a variational solver can be used for space-time disparity estimation.

Nevertheless, though space-time approaches can improve disparity estimation results, almost all disparity estimation methods need local textures to compute dense disparity maps. Therefore, the algorithms lose their accuracy in homogeneous image regions. Additional texture can be generated when active illumination is applied [12]. In this paper it will be argued that projected vertical color strip pattern are very well suited to be used in combination with the variational method. Furthermore, infrared light can be used in order to project patterns that are not visible to the human eyes [13].

In this paper, we present a combination of structured light and fast variational space-time stereo. To the best of our knowledge, this paper is the first to perform space-time disparity estimation with active illumination in the variational framework. However, we are of course not the first to combine active illumination and space-time stereo. The benefit of additional spatio-temporal information for stereo vision has been shown before, e.g., by Zhang et al. [11]. The advantage of the variational framework is the high reconstruction accuracy. The disadvantage of variational solvers is that they tend to become slow, if they are applied on large equation systems. This is especially a problem as the number of equations is increased by adding information from different points in time. In this paper, we show that speed-improving techniques, like FMG and MLAT, can still be applied. The approach is evaluated with 3 ground-truth datasets.

2 The Space-Time Variational Method

Currently, almost all stereo vision algorithms analyze and process stereo image sequences in pairs of a left and a right frame. Processing the stereo pairs separately from the whole sequence leads to the loss of the dynamics occurring in this image sequence [14]. However, these dynamics (such as displacement between two frames, or occluded/exposed areas) contain vital information and can be used to achieve a better convergence rate for the variational method and to enhance the accuracy. We address this issue by extending the variational approach to the spatiotemporal domain, as described in the following subsections.

Problem formulation. Given a rectified stereo sequence consisting of individual sequences for the left and right camera, each scalar-valued image sequence

$I(x,y,t)$ is stored in a pixel matrix and $(x,y,t)^\top$ is the space-time coordinate of a voxel within the three-dimensional spatio-temporal domain $\bar{\Omega} = \Omega \times T$. For every voxel of the left sequence $I_l(x,y,t)$, we now try to estimate the disparity value $u(x,y,t)$, which is the offset of the x-coordinate of the voxel position, in order to match the corresponding voxel from the right sequence $I_r(x,y,t)$:

$$I_r(x,y,t) - I_l(x + u(x,y,t), y, t) = 0 \quad . \tag{1}$$

Since we are dealing with continuous real-world data, the disparities are not necessarily integer values. This is taken into account by employing different linearization techniques while solving Eq. (1). In our case, we use a linear interpolation approach [9] for the linearization.

An energy functional is constructed that consists of two terms: a data term that imposes the constancy assumption on the grey values, and a smoothness term that regularizes the local and often non-unique solution for the data term by an additional smoothness assumption.

Data term. In a real-world recording, we have to deal with occlusions and non-lambertian surfaces in the scene. Therefore, the left-hand side of Eq. (1) is usually not exactly zero. However, it should be as close to zero as possible. Therefore, we minimize the corresponding energy functional

$$E(u(x,y,t)) = \iiint_{\bar{\Omega}} \|I_r(x,y,t) - I_l(x + u(x,y,t), y, t)\|^2 \, dx\, dy\, dt \quad . \tag{2}$$

Smoothness term. The smoothness term is based on the assumption that neighboring space-time regions belong to the same object and, thus, have similar disparities. The main role of the smoothness term is the redistribution of the computed information and the elimination of local disparity outliers. If reliable information from the data term is not available, the smoothness term helps to fill the problematic region with disparities calculated from neighboring regions and from previous and future points in time.

In our work, we use 3 different regularizers: Tichonov, Charbonnier, and Perona-Malik regularization. Tichonov regularization assumes overall smoothness and does not adapt to semantically important image or disparity field structures (Horn and Schunck [15]). Charbonnier's and Perona-Malik's disparity-driven regularizations assume piecewise smoothness and respect discontinuities in the disparity field (see, e.g., [16,17]).

For all three regularizers, the smoothness term in general form is expressed as $\Psi(|\nabla_3 u(x,y,t)|^2)$. The energy functional from Eq. (2) extended by the smoothness term takes the following form:

$$E(u) = \iiint_{\bar{\Omega}} \|I_r(x,y,t) - I_l(x + u, y, t)\|^2 + \varphi \cdot \Psi(|\nabla_3 u|^2) \, dx\, dy\, dt \quad , \tag{3}$$

where φ is the weight of the smoothness term.

Euler-Lagrange equation. The goal of the variational method is to find a function $u(x, y, t)$, which minimizes the energy functional $E(u(x, y, t))$. Once we have constructed the energy functional, we need to find a solution, i.e., disparity field, which minimizes the functional. If the functional is constructed over a strict convexity requirement, the problem of minimization can be simplified, since there exists only one unique solution.

The Euler-Lagrange equation is an equation that is satisfied by the unknown function $u(x, y, t)$, which minimizes the functional

$$E(u)) = \iiint_{\bar{\Omega}} F(x, y, t, u, u_x, u_y, u_t) \, dx \, dy \, dt \quad , \tag{4}$$

where $u_x = \frac{\partial u}{\partial x}$, $u_y = \frac{\partial u}{\partial y}$, $u_t = \frac{\partial u}{\partial t}$ and F is a given function that has continuous first order partial derivatives. The Euler-Lagrange equation then is the partial differential equation:

$$F_u - \frac{\partial}{\partial x} F_{u_x} - \frac{\partial}{\partial y} F_{u_y} - \frac{\partial}{\partial t} F_{u_t} = 0 \quad . \tag{5}$$

For the energy functional from Eq. (3) the Euler-Lagrange equation for each voxel $(x, y, t)^\top$ is given by

$$I_{lx}(x + u, y, t)(I_r(x, y, t) - I_l(x + u, y, t)) + \varphi \cdot \mathrm{div}(\Psi'(|\nabla_3 u|^2) \cdot \nabla_3 u) = 0 \quad . \tag{6}$$

In order to minimize the energy functional, we solve the resulting system of differential equations with homogeneous Neumann boundary conditions [18]. This step is done via discrete numerical schemes. The Euler-Lagrange equations are discretized, linearized, and approximated via finite-differences schemes. In the end, we arrive at a linear (in case of Tichonov regularizer) or non-linear (in case of Charbonnier or Perona-Malik regularizers) system of equations.

Discretization. In order to discretize Eq. (6), we use linear interpolation for the data term and standard discretization for the diffusion filters [19]. For the space-time variational method we use a 6-voxel stencil (see Fig. 1, left) for the computation of the smoothness term (instead of a 4-pixel stencil as is used by classical variational approaches that do not smooth in time dimension). The discretized smoothness term can be written as $\Psi'(|\nabla_3 u(i\Delta x, j\Delta y, k\Delta t)|^2) \equiv$

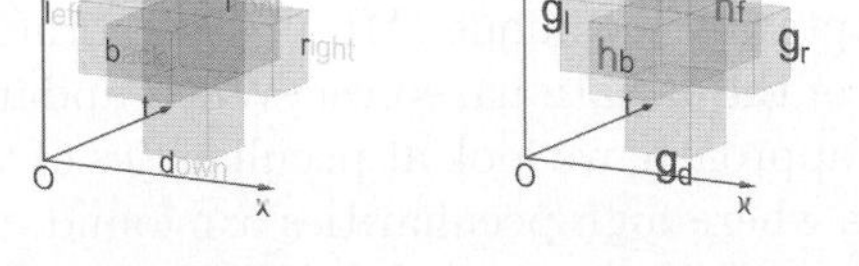

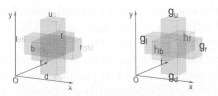

Fig. 1. 3D stencil for the smoothness term discretization: **left:** labeling of weighting coefficients; **right:** splitted stencil for different space and time regularization

$g_{i,j,k}$. We also introduce the following substitutions (cf. Fig. 1): $g_{i+1,j,k}+g_{i,j,k} \equiv g_r$, $g_{i-1,j,k}+g_{i,j,k} \equiv g_l$, $g_{i,j+1,k}+g_{i,j,k} \equiv g_u$, $g_{i,j-1,k}+g_{i,j,k} \equiv g_d$, $g_{i,j,k+1}+g_{i,j,k} \equiv g_f$, $g_{i,j,k-1} + g_{i,j,k} \equiv g_b$ and $\sum_{o\in\{l,r,u,d,f,b\}} g_o \equiv g_c$. Then the smoothness term takes the following expression:

$$\begin{aligned}\varphi \cdot [\ g_r \cdot u(x+1,y,t) + g_l \cdot u(x-1,y,t) + g_u \cdot u(x,y+1,t) \\ + g_d \cdot u(x,y-1,t) + g_f \cdot u(x,y,t+1) + g_b \cdot u(x,y,t-1) \\ - g_c \cdot u(x,y,t)] \quad .\end{aligned} \tag{7}$$

Since *space* and *time* are incommensurable concepts in mathematics, we may want to penalize the solution in space and time differently (e.g., the Charbonnier regularizer for space, and the Tichonov regularizer for time). For that purpose we modify the standard discretization scheme and introduce the alternative function $h_{i,j,k}$, and parameter ϕ to function $g_{i,j,k}$ and parameter φ, respectively. Eq. 7 can be rewritten as

$$\begin{aligned}\varphi \cdot [\ g_r \cdot u(x+1,y,t) + g_l \cdot u(x-1,y,t) + g_u \cdot u(x,y+1,t) \\ + g_d \cdot u(x,y-1,t) - g'_c \cdot u(x,y,t)] \\ +\phi \cdot [\ h_f \cdot u(x,y,t+1) + h_b \cdot u(x,y,t-1) - h'_c \cdot u(x,y,t)] \quad ,\end{aligned} \tag{8}$$

where $g'_c \equiv \sum_{o\in\{l,r,u,d\}} g_o$ and $h'_c \equiv \sum_{o\in\{f,b\}} h_o$.

Note that Eq. (8) will be identical to Eq. (7) for $h_{i,j,k} \equiv g_{i,j,k}$ and $\phi = \varphi$. Therefore Eq. (8) describes the more general case and provides the additional flexibility. In addition, for $\phi = 0$, we end up with the classical variational approach for disparity reconstruction.

Space-time FMG and MLAT. The multigrid method implies the usage of coarser grids, i.e., a pyramid of scaled versions of the initial images. Classical multigrids methods use the factor of two as a scale factor. So the maximal reasonable number of levels we can express are: #levels $\leq log_2 \min\{X, Y, T\}$.

Usually, the time dimension is much smaller than the space dimensions: $T << \min\{X, Y\}$, e.g., if we have video at 25 fps and want to process several blocks per second, we could use for example around 10 frames in a space-time block. On the other hand, the image spatial resolution measures in hundreds of pixels. Therefore, the number of coarse grids will be too small for effective application. As a consequence, we have reverted to the solution to use the full-multi-grid approach only in the spatial directions for each time slice independently. Thus, for each frame, we use the same number of pyramid levels. Implementation details about the of the FMG approach in the variational framework are given in [9].

The multi-level adaptation technique (MLAT) is another technique to reduce the computation time of the variational solver. When updating from a coarser to finer grid in the FMG approach, we look at peculiarities of the solution, and only refine the grid in areas where high peculiarities are found. This results in a non-regular grid structure on the finest level. During space-time stereo processing it can be assumed that the solution is changing very smoothly with time: $u_t \to 0$. Thus, in order to apply the MLAT in the space-time framework, we can use the classical MLAT approach for calculating the adapted grid once per currently processed space-time block. As the structure is the same for all frames of the block, the neighbouring voxels in time have the same spatial resolution, and thus can be directly used to perform the iterative variational optimization steps with the described 6-voxel stencil.

3 Active Illumination

In most stereo matching algorithms, the inherent ambiguity of image values in homogeneous image regions leads to a loss of accuracy in the computation of dense disparity maps. A possible solution to this problem is the introduction of artificial texture into the scene, e.g., by the projection of intensity coded light [12]. These stereo setups with active illumination benefit from improved local scene texture – hence better correspondences – and therefore allow the reconstruction of more accurate dense disparity maps.

Our setup consists of a Point Grey Bumblebee® XB3 camera synchronized with a projector casting a structured light pattern onto the scene (see Fig. 2). We projected patterns in the visible light spectrum but projecting infra-red patterns, which are not visible to the human eye, is possible as well.

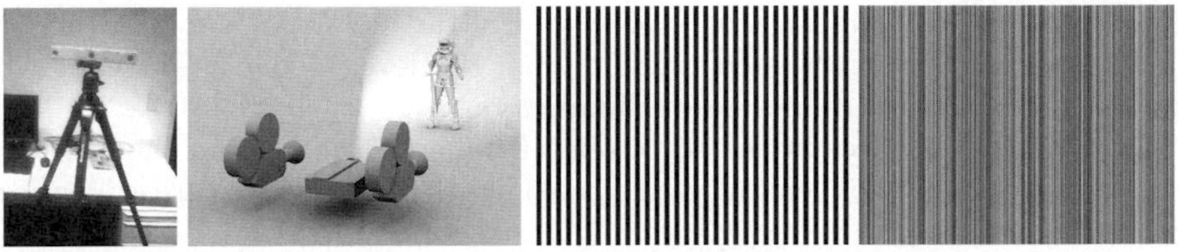

Fig. 2. Our stereo setup and examples of projected patterns: (from left to right: Point Grey Bumblebee® XB3 camera; principle of a stereo system using active illumination; binary pattern; random color pattern

The question is now what is the best suited projection pattern for the scene and for our reconstruction method. A number of researchers have worked on optimizing the employed patterns that are mostly based on vertical stripes [20,21]. The main idea of these works is to adapt the pattern in such a way, that interference by the scene is minimized. Using a graph-cuts approach, the algorithm identifies the pattern and reconstructs the disparity map. Thereby, a combination of geometric coding, color coding and tracking over time is used.

Using with the variational method and a stereo camera, we do not need to identify the pattern during the reconstruction process. That gives us the following advantages: 1.) we do not need to know the exact position of the projector and 2.) we do not need prior knowledge about the structure of the projected light. Let $I(x, y, t)$ be an image of a scene without active illumination used (only with ambient illumination), and $I^C(x, y, t)$ will be the image of the scene with active illumination used (plus the same ambient illumination) and taken from the same position as $I(x,y,t)$. Then the $C(x,y,t) = I^C(x,y,t) - I(x,y,t)$ will be the visible color pattern.

The data term of the Euler-Lagrange equation (6), which we solve to estimate the disparity map, has the following form: $I_{lx}(I_r - I_l)$. In order to achieve accurate results, we need to make this term as informative as possible (for details, please refer to [9]). Using structured light, we can express this demand as follows: $\frac{\partial I^C}{\partial x} >> 0$, or

$$\arg\max_C \frac{\partial I^C}{\partial x} = \arg\max_C \frac{\partial (I+C)}{\partial x} = I_x + \arg\max_C C_x \quad , \tag{9}$$

i.e. the optimal structured pattern for the variational approach is such a pattern, where the horizontal derivative is maximal. Thus, vertical black-and-white stripes (see Fig. 2) without any adaptation to $I_x(x,y,t)$ or to the observed scene are best suited to achieve highest accuracy. This conclusion agrees with the work of Horn and Kiryati [22]. However, such a pattern has some important disadvantages. If the scene lacks texture, after illuminating it with the black and white stripes pattern, we get the same uncertainty, because of the repeating structure of the pattern. Moreover, using multi-grids, the variational method needs to have a set of coarser copies of the input images, and using the black-and-white stripes with geometric coding could cause ambiguities on some coarse levels. As a solution, we propose a random generated, high-contrast color pattern (see Fig. 2). Since this pattern is generated randomly, all the levels (coarse and fine) will contain random vertical lines based illumination.

Assuming all surfaces in the scene obey Lambertian reflection, the reflected light resulting from the blending of projected light and object texture is identical in both images [23].

4 Evaluation

In this section we show results for the presented space-time variational method with active illumination for disparity estimation. The results are also presented in the supplemental video. The method was implemented, using single-threaded C++ code, and all the experiments were made on a Intel Core 2 Quad Processor 2,83GHz with 8GB DDR2 RAM. To evaluate our novel method, we use three different data sets with ground-truth disparity and occlusion maps. We evaluate the results with the percentage of "bad" voxels (which have a disparity error larger than one or two pixels, see [24] for more details).

Dynamic scene without active illumination. As a first example, we use the data set *Gargoyle* from York University [25], with a resolution of 640x480x40 voxels. The results for one of the frames from the sequence for the classical variational single frame processing (SFP) and novel variational space-time processing (STP) approaches can be found in Fig. 3. For both approaches, the number of iterations at the finest level is 10, and the parameter λ of the non-linear

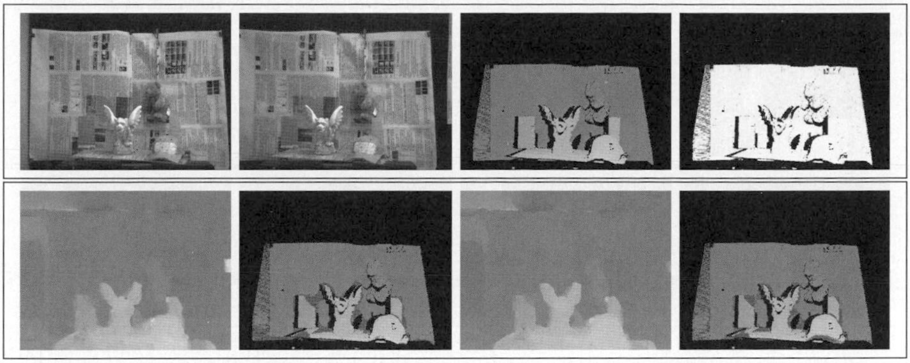

Fig. 3. Gargoyle scene: **top row** (from left to right): left and right images of the 27th stereo pair from the sequence, the corresponding ground truth disparity and occlusion map; **bottom row:** (from left to right) solution and bad pixels map (9.69%) for the SFP approach, solution and bad pixels map (7.99%) for the STP approach (error threshold = 2 pixels) (red pixels = bad pixels).

Charbonnier regularizer is $\lambda = 0.03$. The only difference are the smoothness parameters, which are $\varphi = 2500$ for SFP, and $\varphi = 2300$ and $\psi = 100$ for STP.

The calculation time for the whole space-time block containing all 40 frames is 114 seconds. For the 27th stereo frame, we can observe an improvement from 9.69% for SFP to 7.99% for STP. Fig. 5 shows the percentage of bad pixels for the whole sequence. The STP curve is smoother than the SFP curve and on average we gain about 1.3% improvement (SFP: 10.42%; STP: 9.16%).

Static scene with active illumination. In a second experiment, we use the dataset *Ship*, with a resolution of 600x400x10 voxels. The scene was shot with a point Grey Bumblebee® XB3 camera and the ground truth was obtained with a Konika Minolta 3D laser scanner. In Fig. 4, the results for the classical SFP and novel STP are shown. For both approaches we set the number of iterations to 25, and used the linear Tichonov penalizer for time dimension and the non-linear Charbonnier and Perrona-Malik penalizers with $\lambda = 0.01$ and $\lambda = 0.3$, respectively, for space dimensions. The SFP approach is applied with smoothness parameter $\varphi = 5000$ and STP with $\varphi = 1000$ and $\psi = 1000$. The calculation time for this scene is 55 seconds.

For the first stereo frame, we can observe a large improvement from 14.74% for SFP to 10.41% for STP. This is because in static scenes the solution is the same for all the frames of the input sequence, and therefore the algorithm can rely strongly on the temporal regularizer and we can use a very sharp penalizer for the space dimensions. As a result, we gain more accurate edges and less noise in the background of the reconstructed disparity map. Fig. 5(right) shows the percentage of bad pixels for the whole sequence. We can observe that the STP curve is almost constant and concurs with the average value of bad voxels. In contrast, SFP curve is not smooth and on average we gain an improvement of about 4% (SFP: 14.56%; STP: 10.54%).

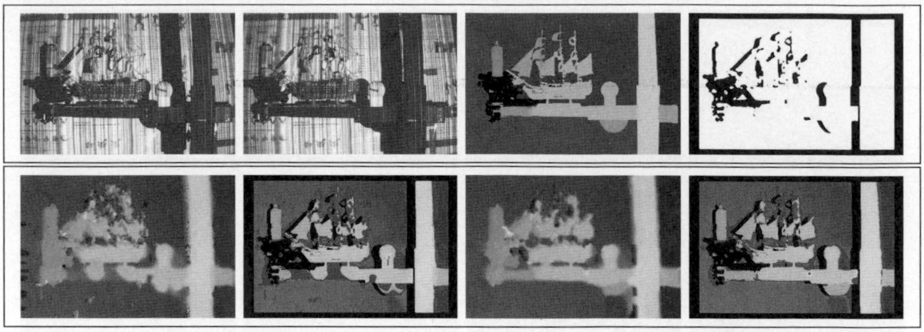

Fig. 4. Ship scene: **top row** (from left to right): left and right images of the first stereo pair from the sequence, the ground-truth disparity and occlusion map; **bottom row:** (from left to right) solution and bad pixels map (14.74%) for the SFP approach, and solution and bad pixels map (10.41%) for the STP approach (error threshold = 2 pixels) (red pixels = bad pixels).

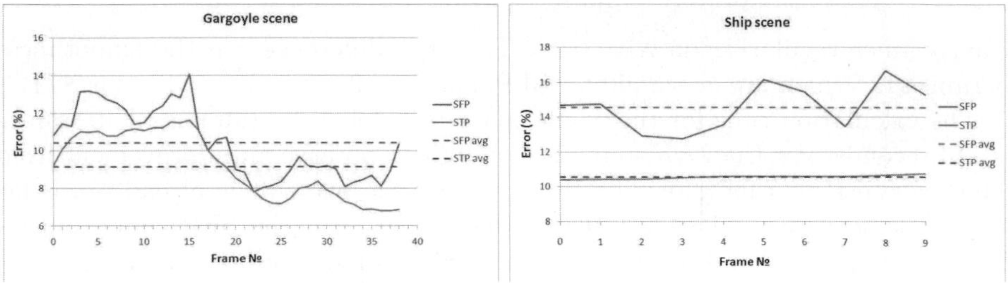

Fig. 5. Comparison of the reconstruction accuracy for SFP and STP (error threshold = 2 pixels). **left:** Gargoyle scene: Average values: SFP: (10.42%); STP: (9.16%); **right:** Ship scene: Average values: SFP: (14.56%); STP: (10.54%).

Dynamic scene with active illumination. The last dataset is the synthetic scene *Knight*, with a resolution of 640x360x18 voxels. The 3D scene and ground truth data are generated in manually in a 3D modeling package. The scene has a static background and a rotating knight shell. The maximal disparity in the scene is 16 pixels. In Fig. 6 the results for the novel STP approach with and without active illumination is shown. For both cases we used 15 iterations on the finest level and non-linear Charbonnier and Perrona-Malik penalizers with $\lambda = 0.01$ and $\lambda = 0.3$ for time and space dimensions, respectively. The smoothness parameters are $\varphi = 2500$ and $\psi = 1100$.

For the 7th stereo frame (shown in Fig. 6), we can observe more than two times improvement, from 4.46% of bad pixels without active illumination to 2.13% with active illumination. As we can see from the Fig. 6, with active illumination and space-time processing it became possible to completely get rid of bad pixels in the static background, and significantly reduce the amount of bad pixels at the edges of the moving objects due to the application of the non-linear regularization in the time dimension. The processing of the whole scene took 58 seconds. The

Fig. 6. Knight scene: **top row** (from left to right): left images of the 7th stereo pair from the sequence (without active illumination (AI) and with AI), the ground truth, and occlusion map; **bottom row:** (from left to right) solution and bad pixels map (4.46%) for STP approach without AI, and solution and bad pixels map (2.13%) for STP with AI (error threshold = 1 pixel) (red pixels = bad pixels)

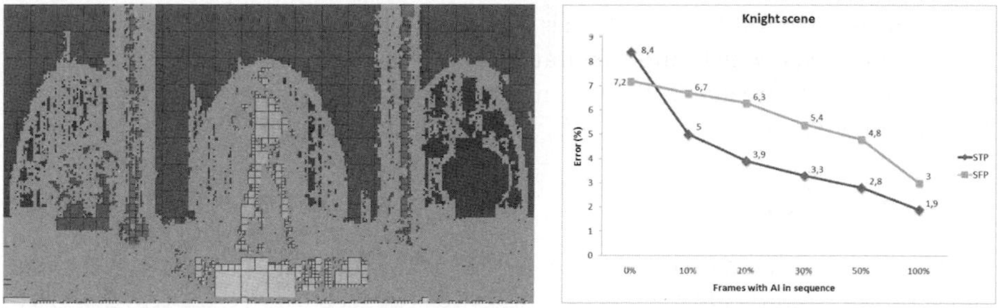

Fig. 7. **left:** The finest MLAT grid for the *Knight* scene; **right:** Emitting active illumination color pattern each i-th frame (error threshold = 1 pixel)

finest grid, calculated by MLAT and used for all 18 frames of the sequence is depicted in Fig. 7(left).

We further evaluated the approach by applying active illumination not all the time, but only each i-th frame. This can significantly reduce the energy consumption for an LED-structured light projector in real-life applications without losing too much accuracy in reconstructed disparity maps. The results of this experiment are shown in Fig. 7(right). We used the following parameters: number of iterations is 20, non-linear Charbonnier and Perrona-Malik penalizers with $\lambda = 0.01$ and $\lambda = 0.3$ for time and space dimensions, respectively, and smoothness parameters $\varphi = 2300$ and $\psi = 1500$.

From the diagrams in Fig. 7(right) we can observe that if there are no frames with active illumination used in the sequence, the SFP approach gives better results than STP. That is because we used the same parameters for the whole experiment, and these parameter must be a trade-off between processing scenes with active illumination and without. In our case, STP gives worse results, because of too strong smoothness of the solution in time direction, which resulted in a too strong blurring of the disparity map around the moving objects in scene. On the other hand, we can observe that already with 20% frames with active

Table 1. Comparison of the average percentage of bad pixels for the *Knight* scene (error threshold = 1 pixel). Improvement ratio are given in brackets.

	without AI		with AI	
	SFP	STP	SFP	STP
Variational method	5.9%	5.2% (1.1x)	3% (**2**x)	1.9% (**3.1**x)
Expansion method	2.9%	3.7% (0.8x)	2.4% (1.2x)	2.2% (1.3x)
Belief propagation	3.1%	2.9% (1.1x)	1.9% (1.6x)	1.4% (2.2x)
Swap method	10.3%	8.8% (1.2x)	7.2% (1.4x)	4% (2.6x)
Infection method	16.3%	16.2% (1.0x)	9.1% (1.8x)	8.9% (1.8x)
TRW method	3.6%	2.4% (**1.5**x)	2.4% (1.5x)	1.3% (2.8x)

illumination used in the sequence we observe two times better accuracy than with SFP.

In the Tab. 1 we show the best results that are gained with different combinations of the proposed variational methods in the top row of the table. The worst case is the processing of each frame separately and without active illumination. The best result was achieved for the space-time approach with active illumination with 1.9% of bad voxels. The other rows of Tab. 1 show results for classical methods, which implementations are available online[1]. The STP results of these methods are generated by smoothing the SFP results over time with the Tichonov regularizer.

5 Conclusion

We have shown that processing time-space blocks instead of single stereo image pairs provides significantly higher accuracy for the disparity reconstruction. Processing the time-space blocks within the variational method and the combination with active illumination has shown to be an effective approach. The accuracy of static scenes with different randomly generated color patterns increases the accuracy of reconstruction. A comparison on datasets with a classical variational disparity estimator, which processes only a single frame, shows that our implementation of the extended variational approach outperforms the current state-of-the-art. Furthermore, we showed how speed-improving techniques, like the full-multi-grid technique and the multi-level-adaptation technique, can be applied in the space-time stereo variational framework.

References

1. Ross, W.P.: A practical stereo vision system. In: IEEE Conference on Computer Vision and Pattern Recognition, pp. 148–153 (1993)
2. Kolmogorov, V., Zabih, R.: Computing visual correspondence with occlusions via graph cuts. In: International Conference on Computer Vision, pp. 508–515 (2001)
3. Scharstein, D., Szeliski, R.: High-accuracy stereo depth maps using structured light. In: Proc. Computer Vision and Pattern Recognition, vol. I, pp. 195–202 (2003), `http://vision.middlebury.edu/stereo/`
4. Mémin, E., Pérez, P.: Dense estimation & object-based segmentation of the optical flow with robust techniques. IEEE Trans. on Image Processing 7, 703–719 (1998)

[1] Middlebury stereo evaluation web-site: http://vision.middlebury.edu/stereo/

5. Brox, T., Bruhn, A., Papenberg, N., Weickert, J.: High accuracy optical flow estimation based on a theory for warping. In: Pajdla, T., Matas, J(G.) (eds.) ECCV 2004. LNCS, vol. 3024, pp. 25–36. Springer, Heidelberg (2004)
6. Bruhn, A., Weickert, J., Kohlberger, T., Schnörr, C.: A multigrid platform for real-time motion computation with discontinuity-preserving variational methods. Int. J. Comput. Vision 70, 257–277 (2006)
7. Fedorenko, R.: Relaxation method for solving elliptic differential equations. Journal of Computational Mathematics and Mathematical Phisics 1, 922–927 (1961)
8. Valgaerts, L., Bruhn, A., Zimmer, H., Weickert, J., Stoll, C., Theobalt, C.: Joint estimation of motion, structure and geometry from stereo sequences. In: Daniilidis, K., Maragos, P., Paragios, N. (eds.) ECCV 2010. LNCS, vol. 6314, pp. 568–581. Springer, Heidelberg (2010)
9. Kosov, S., Thormählen, T., Seidel, H.-P.: Accurate real-time disparity estimation with variational methods. In: Bebis, G., Boyle, R., Parvin, B., Koracin, D., Kuno, Y., Wang, J., Wang, J.-X., Wang, J., Pajarola, R., Lindstrom, P., Hinkenjann, A., Encarnação, M.L., Silva, C.T., Coming, D. (eds.) ISVC 2009. LNCS, vol. 5875, pp. 796–807. Springer, Heidelberg (2009)
10. Brandt, A.: Multi-level adaptive technique (MLAT) for fast numerical solution to boundary value problems. Lecture Notes in Physics 18, 82–89 (1973)
11. Zhang, L., Curless, B., Seitz, S.: Spacetime stereo: Shape recovery for dynamic scenes. In: IEEE Conf. on Comp. Vision and Pattern Recognition, pp. 367–374 (2003)
12. Kang, S.B., Webb, J., Zitnick, C., Kanade, T.: A multibaseline stereo system with active illumination and real-time image acquisition. In: Proceedings of the Fifth International Conference on Computer Vision (ICCV 1995), pp. 88–93 (1995)
13. Frueh, C., Zakhor, A.: Capturing $2\frac{1}{2}$d depth and texture of time-varying scenes using structured infrared light. In: Proc. 3DIM, pp. 318–325 (2005)
14. Ristivojevic, M., Konrad, J.: Space-time image sequence analysis: Object tunnels and occlusion volumes. IEEE Transactions on Image Processing 15, 364–376 (2006)
15. Horn, B.K.P., Schunck, B.G.: Determining optical flow. Artificial Intelligence 17, 185–203 (1981)
16. Charbonnier, P., Aubert, G., Blanc-Ferraud, M., Barlaud, M.: Two deterministic half-quadratic regularization algorithms for computed imaging. In: International Conference on Image Processing, vol. 2, pp. 168–172 (1994)
17. Cohen, I.: Nonlinear variational method for optical flow computation. In: Eighth Scandinavian Conference on Image Analysis, vol. 1, pp. 523–530 (1993)
18. Cheng, A., Cheng, D.T.: Heritage and early history of the boundary element method. Engineering Analysis with Boundary Elements 29, 268–302 (2005)
19. Kosov, S.: 3D map reconstruction with variational methods. Master thesis, Saarland University (2008)
20. Blake, A., McCowen, D., Lo, H.R., Lindsey, P.J.: Trinocular active range-sensing. IEEE Trans. Pattern Anal. Mach. Intell. 15, 477–483 (1993)
21. Koninckx, T., Gool, L.V.: Real-time range acquisition by adaptive structured light. IEEE Transac. on Pattern Analysis & Machine Intelligence 28, 432–445 (2006)
22. Horn, E., Kiryati, N.: Toward optimal structured light patterns. In: Proc. 3DIM, p. 28. IEEE Computer Society, Washington, DC, USA (1997)
23. Koschan, A., Rodehorst, V., Spiller, K.: Color stereo vision using hierarchical block matching and active color illumination. In: ICPR 1996, vol. I, pp. 835–839 (1996)
24. Scharstein, D., Szeliski, R.: A taxonomy and evaluation of dense stereo correspondence algorithms. International Journal of Computer Vision 47, 7–42 (2001)
25. Sizintsev, M., Wildes, R.P.: Spatiotemporal stereo via spatiotemporal quadric element (stequel) matching. In: CVPR, pp. 493–500 (2009)

Kernel Fisher Discriminant and Elliptic Shape Model for Automatic Measurement of Allergic Reactions

Heikki Huttunen[1], Jari-Pekka Ryynänen[1], Heikki Forsvik[1], Ville Voipio[1], and Hisakazu Kikuchi[2]

[1] Department of Signal Processing, Tampere University of Technology, Finland
[2] Graduate School of Science and Technology, Niigata University, Japan

Abstract. A semiautomatic segmentation method for images of allergic reactions in skin prick test is proposed. The method is based on elliptic model for the shape of the wheal, and it uses the kernel Fisher discriminant for grayscale projection and for measuring the separability of the object and the background areas. Experiments indicate that the method is robust and the results are close to those obtained manually.

Keywords: Allergy Test, Kernel Fisher Discriminant, Elliptic Shape Model.

1 Introduction

The skin prick test is a standard allergy diagnosis method. Compared to its alternatives, e.g., measuring the antibody levels in the blood, it is simpler and the results are available immediately. In a typical skin prick test, multiple allergens are tested at the same time by placing drops of allergen extracts on the patient's skin (usually on the forearm) and piercing the skin with a small metal lancet. A positive reaction induces a raised itchy area, a *wheal*, whose size is used for estimating the sensitivity to certain allergen. Traditionally, a medical doctor uses a ruler to manually measure the size of the wheal. The test procedure assumes an elliptic shape, with possible elongated branches (called *pseudopodia*) disregarded and the result of the measurement is the mean of the major and minor axes of the imaginary ellipse [10]. An illustration of the measurement is in Figure 1. As can be seen, most practitioners apply pressure to improve the visibility.

Problems with the traditional method are that the measurement result is subjective and only one measurement can be taken at a single time instant (so all wheals are not measured simultaneously). The wheal growth speed may also have some clinical importance, which can not be exploited today. Additionally, no documentation is left from the reaction (besides the possibly biased measurements). Thus, automation of allergy test using image analysis is of interest.

Several approaches using digital photography and subsequent image analysis for skin erythema detection and melanoma detection have been proposed. There exists a lot of literature on melanoma segmentation [2,4,5], but only a few studies

A. Heyden and F. Kahl (Eds.): SCIA 2011, LNCS 6688, pp. 764–773, 2011.

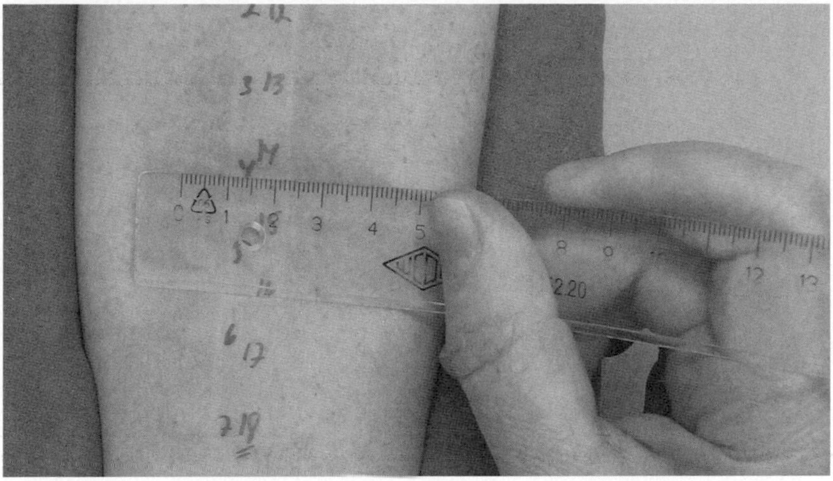

Fig. 1. Manual allergy measurement

of measurement of allergic reactions from 2D pictures [8,9], 3D profiles [10] or other specialized imaging hardware [13]. Our concern is in low-cost 2D digital color photography. Among these, Roullot *et al.* [9] considers seven well known color spaces and compares the separability of the reaction from the background using a training database. As a result, they discover that the optimal dimension among the color spaces is the a^*-component of the $L^*a^*b^*$ color space. Using the extracted a^*-component, they use simple thresholding for segmenting the wheal.

Nischik *et al.* [8] also discover the $L^*a^*b^*$ color space most suitable for the wheal segmentation and use the standard deviations of the L^* and a^* components as the features for classification. The classifier is trained to separate between foreground (the wheal) and the background (healthy skin) using manually generated training data. The classifier output determines directly the boundary between the two regions.

Recent work by Celebi *et al.* consider finding optimal color transformation for extracting the foreground [2]. Although the paper concentrates on melanoma segmentation, the principle is applicable for other skin diseases, as well. The paper searches for optimal linear combination of the RGB-components, such that the output maximizes the separability of the foreground and background. The foreground and background are determined in each iteration using Otsu thresholding. Thus, the algorithm iterates all projections defined on a finite grid, and tests their performance by measuring the Fisher ratio of the foreground and background (which are determined using Otsu thresholding).

The method of [2] is an unsupervised method, which attempts to find the best projection without any user manual assistance. However, in our work we study the case, in which the user points the approximate center of the wheal. From the practical point of view this is acceptable, because it requires less work than the manual measurement. However, we plan to automate the detection of the wheal location in the future. Note also that in the temporal direction, clicking

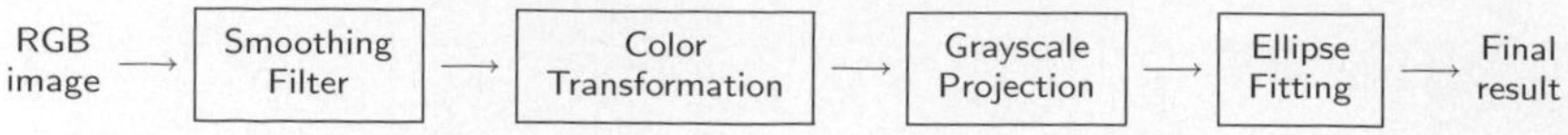

Fig. 2. Proposed wheal detection framework

the last image in the time series is enough for determining the wheal location in all pictures, if temporal motion compensation is used.

The method proposed in this paper consists of the steps in the block diagram of Figure 2 and are described in the paper as follows. In Section 2, the optimal grayscale projection is stated in terms of the Fisher Discriminant (FD). Section 2 also considers the Kernel Fisher Discriminant (KFD), which generalizes the FD using the kernel trick. After describing the optimal grayscale mapping, we define an elliptical shape model for the wheal in Section 3. Finally, in Section 4 we present experimental results and conclude with discussion in Section 5.

2 Grayscale Projection

The key problem when searching the borders of the wheal is the poor contrast between the wheal and skin. An example of a wheal is illustrated in Figure 3 (a). Although the wheal borders are barely visible, the shape becomes highlighted when mapped into grayscale in a suitable manner. Well known mappings for skin color processing include the hue component of the HSV color space (Figure 3 (b)) and the a^* component of the $L^*a^*b^*$ color space (Figure 3 (c)). In all projections, we have smoothed the RGB image by convolution with a disc shaped window of radius 5. However, these are more or less arbitrary, and variability in skin color and allergic reaction strength may decrease their applicability. Instead, training based projections may improve the separation further, and make it more invariant for all patients. An unsupervised method for finding a well-separating projection in terms of the Fisher criterion was proposed by Celebi *et al.* [2], whose result is shown in Figure 3 (d). In this case the coefficients are 1, -0.1 and -0.3 for red, green and blue channels, respectively.

Optimality of the grayscale projection can be studied assuming that we know the approximate location of the wheal. This way we can construct training sets consisting of the wheal area and the surrounding healthy skin, denoted by $\mathcal{S}_1$ and $\mathcal{S}_0$, respectively. With the training sets we can seek for optimal separation in the RGB space in a supervised fashion.

The training set is acquired as follows. When the user has pointed the approximate location of the center of the wheal, a set of RGB values is obtained from the neighborhood. In our experiments, the training set of the wheal ($\mathcal{S}_1$) is obtained inside the circular neighborhood with the radius of 10 pixels. The training set of the healthy skin ($\mathcal{S}_0$) is acquired from pixels that are far away from the center. In our experiments this is done by taking all pixels located at a radius between 45 and 50 pixels from the center, as illustrated in Figure 3 (h).

The natural tool for optimally projecting the three-dimensions to grayscale is the *Fisher Discriminant*, [3]. Fisher discriminant finds the projection dimension

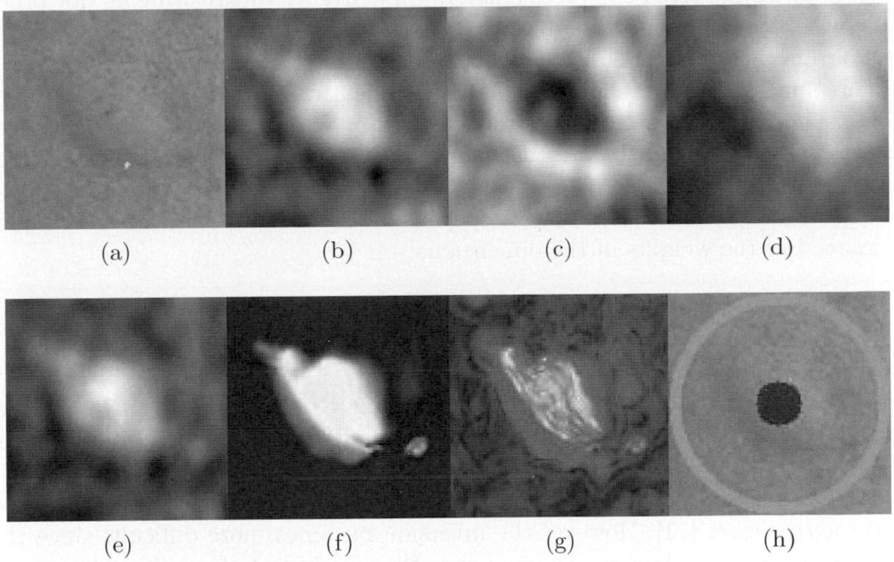

Fig. 3. The projection of the wheal in RGB color space. The original RGB image is shown in Figure (a), and (b) shows the hue component, (c) the a^* component of the $L^*a^*b^*$ color space and (d) is the projection proposed in [2]. Optimal Fisher discriminant projection is shown in Figure (e), and the results of its kernelized version are shown in figures (f) and (g) using RBF kernel with bandwidth σ selected using Silverman rule of thumb and with fixed $\sigma = 0.5$. The training sets are obtained from areas shown in (h), where the blue center is the foreground sample region and the green circle is the background sample region.

$\mathbf{w}$ that maximizes the separability of the classes in terms of the ratio of the between-class-variance and within-class-variance; i.e., the so called Fisher ratio:

$$J(\mathbf{w}) = \frac{\mathbf{w}^T \mathbf{S}_B \mathbf{w}}{\mathbf{w}^T \mathbf{S}_W \mathbf{w}}, \tag{1}$$

where $\mathbf{S}_W \in \mathbf{R}^{3\times3}$ and $\mathbf{S}_B \in \mathbf{R}^{3\times3}$ are the within-class and between-class scatter matrices, respectively. It can be shown that the optimal direction $\mathbf{w}$ is given by

$$\mathbf{w} = \mathbf{S}_W^{-1}(\boldsymbol{\mu}_1 - \boldsymbol{\mu}_0), \tag{2}$$

where $\boldsymbol{\mu}_1 \in \mathbf{R}^3$ and $\boldsymbol{\mu}_0 \in \mathbf{R}^3$ are the sample means of $\mathcal{S}_1$ and $\mathcal{S}_0$. An example of the result of the Fisher discriminant projection is shown in Figure 3 (e).

The FD is a special case of so called *Kernel Fisher Discriminant* (KFD) [7,11], which is a kernelized version of the standard FD. As all kernel methods, the KFD implicitly maps the original data into a high-dimensional feature space and finds the optimally separating manifold there. Using the implicit mapping via the *kernel trick*, the explicit mapping can be avoided, which allows calculating the FD even in an infinite-dimensional space.

In practice the KFD can be calculated implicitly by substituting all dot products with a kernel function $\kappa(\cdot,\cdot)$. It can be shown, that all positive definite kernel functions correspond to a dot product after transforming the data to a feature space $\mathcal{H}$ with mapping $\mathbf{\Phi}(\cdot)$ [11]. The feature space $\mathcal{H}$ can be very high dimensional, and the use of the projection vector $\mathbf{w}$ directly may be impractical or impossible. Instead, the famous *Representer theorem* guarantees that the solution can be represented as a linear combination of the mapped samples [11]. Thus, the Fisher ratio in the feature space is based on the weights of the samples $\boldsymbol{\alpha}$ instead of the weights of the dimensions:

$$J(\boldsymbol{\alpha}) = \frac{\boldsymbol{\alpha}^T \mathbf{Q}^T \mathbf{S}_B^{\mathbf{\Phi}} \mathbf{Q} \boldsymbol{\alpha}}{\boldsymbol{\alpha}^T \mathbf{Q}^T \mathbf{S}_W^{\mathbf{\Phi}} \mathbf{Q} \boldsymbol{\alpha}}, \tag{3}$$

where $\boldsymbol{\alpha} \in \mathbf{R}^N = (\alpha_1, \alpha_2, \ldots, \alpha_N)^T$ is the weight vector for the mapped training samples in the matrix $\mathbf{Q} = [\mathbf{\Phi}(\mathbf{x}_1), ..., \mathbf{\Phi}(\mathbf{x}_N)]$, and $\mathbf{S}_B^{\mathbf{\Phi}}$ and $\mathbf{S}_W^{\mathbf{\Phi}}$ are the between-class and within-class scatter matrices in the feature space $\mathcal{H}$, respectively.

Similar solution as the one for the Fisher discriminant in Eq. (2) can be found also for this case, [11]. However the inversion becomes more difficult, since the dimension of the weight vector $\boldsymbol{\alpha}$ is now the number of the collected training samples. Therefore, we need a regularization term $\lambda\mathbf{I}$, where λ is a small positive scalar and $\mathbf{I}$ is the $N \times N$ identity matrix. In our notation this yields the solution

$$\boldsymbol{\alpha} = (\mathbf{Q}^T \mathbf{S}_W^{\mathbf{\Phi}} \mathbf{Q} + \lambda \mathbf{I})^{-1} \mathbf{Q}^T (\boldsymbol{\mu}_1^{\mathbf{\Phi}} - \boldsymbol{\mu}_0^{\mathbf{\Phi}}), \tag{4}$$

where $\boldsymbol{\mu}_1^{\mathbf{\Phi}} \in \mathcal{H}$ and $\boldsymbol{\mu}_0^{\mathbf{\Phi}} \in \mathcal{H}$ are the sample means of the mapped wheal and skin samples, respectively. It is straightforward to show, that Eq. (4) can be expressed in terms of dot products and thus the kernel trick, [7,11]. Also the actual projection of a test sample $\mathbf{x} \in \mathbf{R}^3$ can be expressed through the kernel as $y = \boldsymbol{\alpha}^T \mathbf{Q}^T \mathbf{\Phi}(\mathbf{x}) = \sum_{i=1}^{N} \alpha_i \kappa(\mathbf{x}_i, \mathbf{x})$.

There are various alternatives for the kernel function $\kappa(\cdot,\cdot)$, among which the most widely used are the polynomial kernels and the Radial Basis Function (RBF) kernel. We experimented with various kernels, and found out that the polynomial kernels do not increase the separation significantly when compared with the linear kernel, which is equivalent to the traditional FD. In other words, all low-order polynomial kernels produce a projection very similar to the first order kernel, shown in Figure 3 (e). However, the separation seems to improve with the RBF kernel

$$\kappa(\mathbf{u}, \mathbf{v}) = \exp\left(-\frac{||\mathbf{u} - \mathbf{v}||^2}{2\sigma^2}\right). \tag{5}$$

There are two parameters in the KFD projection with RBF kernel: The regularization parameter λ and the kernel width σ^2. Since there exists a lot of training data in our case, it seems to be less sensitive to the regularization parameter λ than the width σ^2. In our experiments we set the value of $\lambda = 10^{-5}$, and if the condition number of the matrix in Eq. (4) indicates that the matrix is close to singular, the value of λ is increased ten-fold until the inversion succeeds.

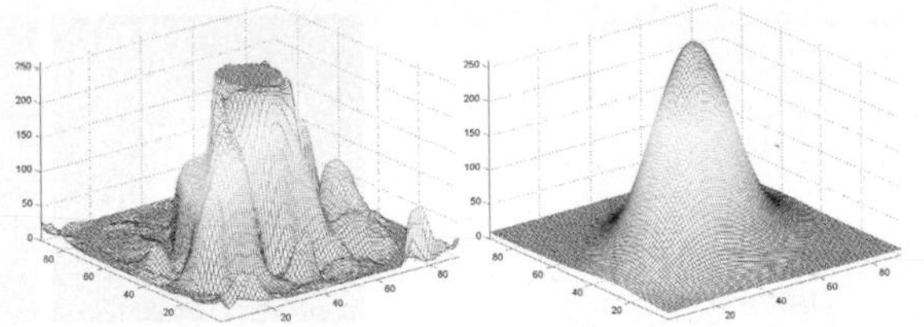

Fig. 4. Left: The grayscale projection data of the wheal in Figure 3 using KFD projection with RBF kernel and $\sigma = 1$. Right: The final result after nonlinear LS fit.

Figures 3 (f-g) illustrate the effect of the bandwidth parameter σ^2. Figure 3 (f) uses the bandwidth selected using so called Silverman's rule of thumb [12], widely used in kernel density estimation and defined by $\hat{\sigma}_{\text{rot}} = 1.06\hat{\sigma}_x N^{-\frac{1}{5}}$, where $\hat{\sigma_x}$ is the sample standard deviation of the data and N is the data length. In the example in Figure 3 (f) the rule of thumb gives $\sigma_{\text{rot}} = 1.37$. Figure 3 (g) on the other hand illustrates the result with fixed $\sigma = 0.5$.

3 Elliptic Shape Model

The transition from the background (the healthy skin) to the foreground (the wheal) can be quite smooth, and the KFD-projected image may contain several individual foreground regions although the image has only one wheal. This is mostly due to the noise in the data, whose effect is greatly emphasized by the grayscale projection. Therefore, simple thresholding results in ragged boundaries, and unrealistic wheal size estimates. In order to increase the robustness of the segmentation, we fit a shape model for the appearance of the wheal. Since the manual measurement assumes that the wheals are ellipses, an elliptic shape model seems reasonable. Thus, the problem is to find an ellipse that divides the image into two maximally inhomogeneous areas.

Since there are an infinite amount of ellipses, we have to limit the search space somehow. This can be done by fitting a model to the grayscale projection and considering only the isosurfaces of the model. Based on Figure 3, the Gaussian surface seems an appropriate model for the spatial grayscale distribution in this case. Moreover, it suits our assumption of elliptic wheals, because the isosurfaces of the two-dimensional Gaussian are ellipses.

More specifically, the Gaussian model is defined by

$$f(\mathbf{x}; c, \mathbf{x}_0, \mathbf{\Sigma}) = c \cdot \exp\left(-(\mathbf{x} - \mathbf{x}_0)^T \mathbf{\Sigma} (\mathbf{x} - \mathbf{x}_0)\right), \tag{6}$$

where $c \in \mathbf{R}_+$ defines the scale of the Gaussian, $\mathbf{x} = (x, y)^T$ denotes the image coordinates where the the model is fitted, $\mathbf{x}_0 = (x_0, y_0)^T$ denotes the location of the peak of the Gaussian and $\mathbf{\Sigma} \in \mathbf{R}^{2\times 2}$ is a symmetric coefficient matrix.

The least squares (LS) fit to the grayscale image data is defined by

$$\min_{c, \mathbf{\Sigma}, \mathbf{x}_0} \sum_{k=0}^{N} (z_k - f(\mathbf{x}_k; c, \mathbf{x}_0, \mathbf{\Sigma}))^2, \tag{7}$$

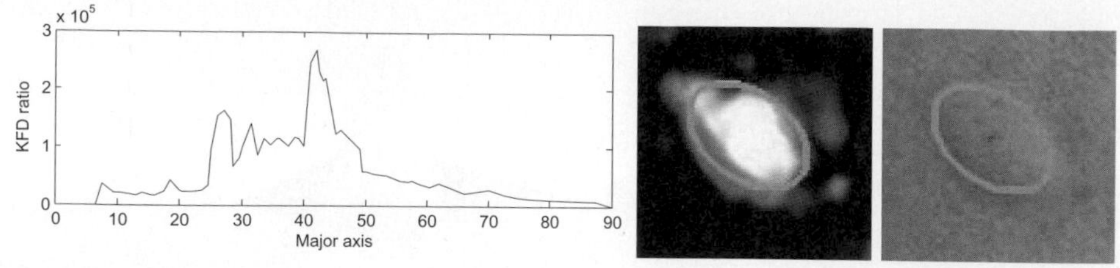

Fig. 5. Left: The KFDR as a function of the ellipse size. Center: The maximally separating ellipse overlaid on top of the corresponding KFD projection. Right: The maximally separating ellipse overlaid on top of original RGB data.

where z_k denotes the grayscale value at image position $\mathbf{x}_k$. Note that the data has to be preprocessed by subtracting the minimum of z_k, $k = 0, \ldots, N$, in order to avoid a constant offset term in the model.

Fitting the Gaussian is a nontrivial problem, although lot of literature on the topic exists (e.g., [1]). However, the easiest approach is to use software packages such as Matlab Optimization toolbox to find the optimal parameters. In order to avoid local minima, we initialized the iterative search with the parameters obtained from a logarithmic transformation of the model and the data. This makes the problem linear least squares, and provides a good starting point. Figure 4 shows the original grayscale data on the left, the result of logarithmic fitting in the center and the result of nonlinear iterative fitting on the right.

The isosurfaces of the Gaussian fit can be used as candidates for elliptic segmentation. As noted earlier, all the isosurfaces are cross-sections of a paraboloid and thus ellipses. Moreover, due to fitting, they most likely have the correct orientation and correct ratio of major and minor axis lengths. Thus, our next goal is to seek for the best elliptic isosurface among them all.

The definition of a good ellipse among the candidates needs some measure of separation between the segmented areas. Recent work by Harchaoui *et al.* [6] considers using the Kernel Fisher Discriminant Ratio (KFDR) for testing the homogeneity between two sets, which coincides well with our use of KFD for grayscale projection in Section 2.

In other words, we test all ellipses that are cross sections of the fitted Gaussian and attempt to maximize the KFDR of Eq. (3) with respect to training sets defined by the ellipse. The situation is similar to the grayscale projection, but now we are not looking for a good classifier for the RGB data, but only assessing how well the data *could be classified*. Unlike Section 2, the choice of the training samples is now based on the boundaries of the ellipse to be tested. Note that this is not equivalent to calculating the variances directly from the projections of Figure 3, because the projection is calculated separately for the training sets determined by each ellipse candidate.

Sometimes the KFDR separability criterion results in very small ellipses, because a small foreground training set tends to be well separable. As an extreme example, an ellipse containing only a single pixel has extremely good separability assuming no other pixel has exactly the same RGB value. Thus, we decided to modify the criterion by multiplying it with the cardinality of the smaller training set. Alternatively, we could set a minimum size restriction for the ellipse.

An example of the separability test is shown in Figure 5. The figure shows the KFDR between the "inside" class and the "outside" class for ellipses with different radius. It can be seen that the maximal separation is obtained at radius 42, and the corresponding ellipse is illustrated in Figure 5, as well.

4 Experimental Results

The results from the described method are compared to manual wheal segmentations (made by a non-medical expert). The similarity measure used by Celebi et al. [2] compares the *areas* of the segmentations. For our purposes, this is not an appropriate criterion, since ultimately we are interested in the major and minor axes of the wheal. The error in areas increases quadratically with respect to the axes, which is not desirable. Instead, we used the following error criterion between the computer segmentation A and the manual ground truth B:

$$E(A,B) = \frac{\sqrt{\text{Area}(\text{OR}(A,B))} - \sqrt{\text{Area}(\text{AND}(A,B))}}{\sqrt{\text{Area}(B)}}, \qquad (8)$$

where $\text{OR}(A,B)$ consists of pixels segmented as foreground in A or B, and $\text{AND}(A,B)$ of foreground pixels in both A and B. Moreover, $\text{Area}(A)$ is the number of foreground pixels in A. The favourable property of Eq. (8) is that it increases linearly with respect to the error in major and minor axes. For example, it can be shown that the error measure for concentric circles with radii $r+a$ and $r-a$ are equal if the true radius is r. This is not the case with the error of [2].

Examples of segmentation results are illustrated in Figure 6. The figure shows the result of manual segmentation (red) compared with the result of the proposed

Table 1. The comparison of automated wheal measurement methods in terms of the error of Eq. (8). Each row defines an initial color space, each column corresponds to a grayscale transformation. The last column corresponds to a manually designed transformation based on what looks good. In the RGB case, the *Ad Hoc* transformation is the difference $G-B$, in the $L^*a^*b^*$ case it is the a^* component, and in the HSV case the H component.

		Gaussian ($\sigma = 0.5$)	*Gaussian* ($\sigma = 1$)	*Gaussian* ($\sigma = \sigma_{\text{rot}}$)	*Linear kernel*	*2. order kernel*	*Celebi method*	*Ad hoc*
With shape model	*RGB*	0.3283	0.2152	0.2331	0.4008	0.2119	1.5159	0.2552
	$L^*a^*b^*$	0.2120	0.2296	0.2141	0.1853	0.2154	1.4405	0.9945
	HSV	0.2501	0.2225	0.1951	0.4922	0.3948	1.2466	0.6302
Without shape model	*RGB*	0.4850	0.2327	0.1871	0.2602	0.2170	1.1963	0.2799
	$L^*a^*b^*$	0.2274	0.1866	0.3017	0.2403	0.2190	1.0266	1.4060
	HSV	0.2218	0.2219	0.5129	0.3932	0.3435	1.0099	0.4573

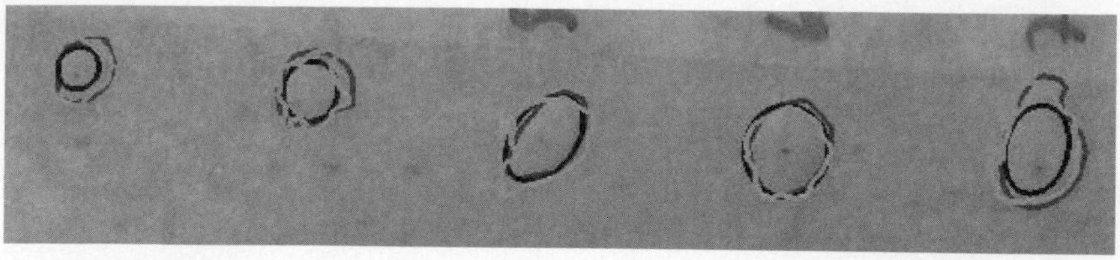

Fig. 6. An example of segmentation result. The red boundary is the result of manual segmentation, while blue and green boundaries represent the result of our method with and without the elliptic shape model, respectively. The errors (with / without shape model) for the five wheals are as follows (from left to right): 0.3144/0.2157, 0.2284/0.1562, 0.1130/0.2336, 0.1233/0.1269, 0.2457/0.1212.

method with (blue) and without (green) the shape model. Table 1 represents the average errors with different grayscale transformations. The test data consists of seven wheals including those shown in Figure 6. The five first columns represent different KFD projections designed using training data, while in the last two columns the projection is designed in an unsupervised or *ad hoc* manner.

From the results one can clearly see that the KFD projections have the smallest errors. The errors are many times larger in the last two columns. On the other hand, the best performing projections (e.g., the Gaussian kernel) seems to make the elliptic shape model unnecessary. On the other hand, this is rather obvious when looking at, e.g., the result in Figure 3(f), where the separation between foreground and background is very clear.

Another reason for a worse than expected performance of the shape model is seen in Figure 6. The manually segmented wheals are not ellipses, so the elliptic model can not reach zero error even in theory. The best cases are the ones where the true wheal is ellipse-shaped with no elongated pseudopodia, i.e., 3rd and 4th wheals from the left. In all other cases the wheal shape is more irregular, and the shape model results in the largest inscribed ellipse. However, there is some randomness in the results due to the small N. We plan to study the performance with larger N and compare them with the manual results of a trained physician.

5 Conclusions

In this paper we proposed a method for automatic segmentation of allergic reactions. The method combines an optimal grayscale transformation with an elliptic shape model for the allergic reactions. Experiments show that the method can efficiently quantify the size of the wheal. The experiments also indicate that the grayscale transformation is sometimes powerful enough to render the elliptic shape mode unnecessary. However, the shape model results may be in coherence with medical doctor's measurements, since they also disregard the pseudopodia.

We plan to continue the development of the algorithm into several directions. One is to consider a recently introduced method of *graph cuts* with shape priors. It will also be interesting to compare the results with those of a medical doctor, together with larger population of test persons. Also the robustness of the method to, e.g., the starting point pointed by the user is an important topic for practical applicability. Additional topics of future work include automatic wheal detection and extension of the method to time series measured from video.

References

1. Brändle, N., Chen, H., Bischof, H., Lapp, H.: Robust parametric and semi-parametric spot fitting for spot array images. In: 8th Intl. Conf. on Intell. Syst. for Mol. Biol., ISMB 2000, pp. 1–12 (2000)
2. Celebi, M., Iyatomi, H., Schaefer, G.: Contrast enhancement in dermoscopy images by maximizing a histogram bimodality measure. In: 16th IEEE Int. Conf. on Image Proc. (ICIP), pp. 2601–2604 (2009)
3. Fisher, R.: The use of multiple measurements in taxonomic problems. Annals of Eugenics 7, 179–188 (1936)
4. Gomez, D.D., Clemmensen, L.H., Ersbøll, B.K., Carstensen, J.M.: Precise acquisition and unsupervised segmentation of multi-spectral images. Comp. Vis. and Image Understanding 106(2-3), 183–193 (2007)
5. Gomez, D., Butakoff, C., Ersboll, B., Stoecker, W.: Independent histogram pursuit for segmentation of skin lesions. IEEE Trans. Biomed. Eng. 55(1), 157–161 (2008)
6. Harchaoui, Z., Bach, F., Eric, M.: Testing for homogeneity with kernel fisher discriminant analysis. In: Adv. in Neural Inf. Proc. Syst. 20, pp. 609–616. MIT Press, Cambridge (2008)
7. Mika, S., Ratsch, G., Weston, J., Scholkopf, B., Mullers, K.: Fisher discriminant analysis with kernels. In: Proc. IEEE Neural Netw. for Signal Process. IX, pp. 41–48 (1999)
8. Nischik, M., Forster, C.: Analysis of skin erythema using true-color images. IEEE Trans. Med. Imag. 16(6), 711–716 (1997)
9. Roullot, E., Autegarden, J.-E., Devriendt, P., Leynadier, F.: Segmentation of erythema from skin photographs for assisted diagnosis in allergology. In: Singh, S., Singh, M., Apte, C., Perner, P. (eds.) ICAPR 2005. LNCS, vol. 3687, pp. 754–763. Springer, Heidelberg (2005)
10. Santos, R., Mlynek, A., Lima, H., Martus, P., Maurer, M.: Beyond flat weals: validation of a three-dimensional imaging technology that will improve skin allergy research. Clin. Exp. Dermatol. 33(6), 772–775 (2008)
11. Schölkopf, B., Smola, A.J.: Learning with Kernels: Support Vector Machines, Regularization, Optimization, and Beyond, 1st edn. MIT Press, Cambridge (2001)
12. Silverman, B.: Density Estimation for Statistics and Data Analysis. Chapman-Hall, Boca Raton (1986)
13. Wöhrl, S., Vigl, K., Binder, M., Stingl, G., Prinz, M.: Automated measurement of skin prick tests: an advance towards exact calculation of wheal size. Experimental Dermatology 15(2), 119–124 (2006)

Continuous Orientation Representation for Arbitrary Dimensions – A Generalized Knutsson Mapping

Bernd Rieger*, Lucas J. van Vliet, and Piet W. Verbeek

Quantitative Imaging Group,
Delft University of Technology,
Lorentzweg 1, 2628 CJ Delft, The Netherlands
{b.rieger,l.j.vanvliet,p.w.verbeek}@tudelft.nl

Abstract. In this paper we present a framework to construct a continuous orientation representation in arbitrary dimensions. Existing methods for 2D (doubling the angle) and 3D (Knutsson mapping) were found ad hoc. We show how they can be put in a general framework to derive suitable representations for filtering in spaces of arbitrary dimension. The dimensionality of the derived representation is shown to be minimal. Connections with the gradient structure tensor and Knutsson mapping are shown, like the fact that angle doubling works in each pair-cone of the Knutsson mapping. Finally, using projection operators we show how angles between vectors in the base space are related to vectors in the mapped spaces and in particular how to achieve preservation of isotropy.

Keywords: orientation representation, angle doubling, projection operators.

1 Introduction

The representation of directional information such that filtering can be applied without discontinuities has received considerable attention in the early days of image analysis for two-dimensional images [1,2,3,4]. Later representations for 3-dimensional images have been found [5,6]. Most notably are here the contributions of Knutsson [4,5], who found a 5D minimal representation for 3D data and Granlund who found the angle doubling for 2D data [1].

The important role of directional information comes from the need to characterize simple neighborhoods - the local structure - in images. They are the basic building blocks of images. Simple neighborhoods are commonly referred to as shift invariant in at least one direction and not shift invariant in at least one other direction[2,3,7]. First order intensity variations are described by gradients and a collection of local gradients is needed to compute a dominant orientation. A vector has direction but locally only the orientation is needed. Representing orientation by angles (direction information) is troublesome, in the sense that it

* Corresponding author.

A. Heyden and F. Kahl (Eds.): SCIA 2011, LNCS 6688, pp. 774–783, 2011.

is discontinuous. E.g. representing a line in 2D by its angle $[0, 2\pi]$ with respect to a fixed coordinate axis is not suitable. More general, vectors v and $-v$ have the same orientation but point in opposite directions.

Averaging operations on directional representation by standard filtering in order to reduce noise produce artifacts at the discontinuities given by e.g. the angle representation. Standard filtering requires a continuous orientation representation, i.e. to compute the local dominant orientation. A well-known tool to analyze one-dimensional neighborhoods from gradients is the Gradient Structure Tensor (GST) [2,3,8,9,10]. It is defined as the dyadic product of the image gradients

$$\overline{G} := \overline{\nabla I \nabla I^t} \text{ and } G := \nabla I \nabla I^t \,, \tag{1}$$

where I is a nD grey-value image and the over-lining stands for averaging the tensor elements inside a local neighborhood. This smoothing scale is typically 3 to 10 times larger than the scale at which the (regularized) gradients are computed. This suppresses gradient orientation contributions due to noise and yields a smooth, robust orientation output. Interpretation of the filtering is done via an eigenvalue analysis of G and the ratio of the eigenvalues describe the local structure. Other applications that require continuous orientation representations include the estimation of curvature (i.e. the rate of change of local orientation) [11,12] and block matching in MRI diffusion tensor imaging [13]. Also the widely used Hough transform for detecting straight lines benefits from a continuous parameter representation [14,15].

For locally multi-directional neighborhoods more complex approaches are needed. Structure such as crossing fibers or corners in images have locally more than one dominant orientation. The eigenvalue analysis of e.g. the structure tensor cannot handle that and standard smoothing of the representation will not return any of the dominant orientations, but a weighted average. A variety of different approaches have been developed that can deal with these neighborhoods [16,17,18,19].

In 1989 Knutsson [5] introduced the following mapping $M : \mathbb{R}^n \to \mathbb{R}^{n \times n}$ to map discontinuous to continuous representations that allow further processing

$$M(v) = \frac{vv^t}{\|v\|} \,, v \in \mathbb{R}^n \,. \tag{2}$$

Here the vector v is generally the image gradient. From the construction it is clear that M is symmetric and has only $n(n+1)/2$ independent components. The mapping is slightly different from the structure tensor G. Both mappings treat antipodal vectors the same by mapping them onto the same tensor $M(v) = M(-v)$. They have a rotation invariant norm, i.e. the information carried by the magnitude is not mixed with information carried by the angle (polar separability). However, eq. 2 differs from the GST in that it preserves distances between the input and output space (uniform stretch), i.e. $\|\delta M(v)\| = c\|\delta v\|$ for $\|v\| = const.$ whereas $\|\delta G(v)\| = c\|\delta v\|\|v\|$. The uniform stretch property allows to compute curvature of lines and surfaces in nD by applying derivative filters to M and to interpret the outcome [11,12]. Without distance preservation the outcome of derivative filters on the mapped representation cannot be interpreted in the same way as in the base space.

The property of a rotation invariant norm of eq. 2 leads to another restriction on the mapping in the form of $trace(M) = const.$. Therefore the dimensionality of the mapping proposed in eq. 2 can be further reduced [6], i.e. in addition to omitting the non-unique terms. Applying this dimensionality reduction to the 2D case of eq. 2 in polar form leads to the double angle method of Granlund $r(\cos 2\varphi, \sin 2\varphi)$ [2,7,6]. Already in 1985 Knutsson presented the solution for the 3D case [4] ad hoc. Later it turned out that his solution can also be directly obtained from eq. 2 by applying dimensionality reduction and reverting to polar coordinates [6].

2 Construction of the General Knutsson Mapping

The construction of the mapping with minimal dimensions from eq. 2 for the n-dimensional case has remained unclear. In [6] we already observed that the dimensionality reduction of eq. 2 led to the angular harmonics in 2D and the spherical harmonics in 3D. The construction, however, of an orthonormal basis for higher dimensional spherical harmonics is not straight-forward [20].

Here we present a concept to iteratively construct an orthonormal basis to represent orientation in nD. We put the dimensionality reduction into a framework that allows intuitive construction. Let the diagonal elements $\{M_{ii}\}, i = 1, \ldots n$ of eq. 2 span a nD space where M_{ii} is one basis vector $(0, \ldots, \overset{i\downarrow}{1}, 0, \ldots, 0)$. As the trace must be constant, i.e. $\sum M_{ii} = const.$, we rotate the basis such that one new axis is aligned with $\mathbf{1} = (1, \ldots 1)$ and the rest are orthogonal to it (orthonormality can always be achieved later if necessary by normalization). The off-diagonal elements of eq. 2 remain untouched, they comprise already a minimal set, and will flow into the mapping as is.

2.1 The 2D Case in the General Framework

We now apply a (unknown) rotation matrix $\mathbf{R_2}$ to the standard basis $\mathbf{I}$ in 2D such that $\mathbf{R_2 I} = \mathbf{D_2}$ produces a matrix $\mathbf{D_2}$ in which the last column is a vector with only ones $\mathbf{1} = (1, 1)$. For the 2D case this recipe looks for a rotation matrix $\mathbf{R_2}$:

$$\mathbf{R_2} \begin{pmatrix} 1 & 0 \\ 0 & 1 \end{pmatrix} = \begin{pmatrix} a_1 & 1 \\ a_2 & 1 \end{pmatrix} = \mathbf{D_2} \tag{3}$$

such that the inner product of vector a and $\mathbf{1}$ is zero, i.e. $(a, \mathbf{1}) = (a_1, a_2) \cdot (1, 1) = 0 \Rightarrow a_1 = -a_2$. Up to a scaling factor the matrix $\mathbf{D_2}$ is again a rotation matrix. Let us choose $a_1 = 1$ and apply $\mathbf{D_2}$ to the diagonal elements of $M(v) = (v_1^2, v_2^2)$ for $\|v\| = r = 1$ and we obtain $v^T \boldsymbol{D}_2 = (v_1^2 - v_2^2, v_1^2 + v_2^2 = const.) = (\cos 2\varphi, const.)$. Together with the off-diagonal terms $2v_1v_2 = \sin 2\varphi$ and normalization with $\|v\| = r$ this gives indeed the well-known double angle representation [1,2]. The connection between the tensor representation of eq. 2 and the double angle method has already been pointed out and made explicit in [7, Chapter 9].

2.2 The 3D Case in the General Framework

Going to 3D we can use the 2D result if we rotate only in subspaces orthogonal to the ones constructed for 2D. This way we construct $\mathbf{D_3}$

$$\mathbf{R_3}\begin{pmatrix}1\,0\,0\\0\,1\,0\\0\,0\,1\end{pmatrix}=\begin{pmatrix}1\;b_1\;1\\-1\;b_2\;1\\0\;b_3\;1\end{pmatrix}=\mathbf{D_3} \tag{4}$$

such that $b \perp \mathbf{1} \perp (1,-1,0)$. This orthogonality gives two equations for the components of vector b

$$b_1 - b_2 = 0 \tag{5}$$

$$b_1 + b_2 + b_3 = 0\,. \tag{6}$$

Let us choose $b_1 = -1 \Rightarrow b_2 = -1, b_3 = 2$. This choice yields the mapping Knutsson found intuitively [4]. Applying this choice of $\mathbf{D_3}$ to the diagonal elements of $M(v) = (v_1^2, v_2^2, v_3^2)$ for $\|v\| = 1$ we obtain $v^T\mathbf{D_3} = (v_1^2 - v_2^2, 2v_3^2 - v_1^2 - v_2^2, v_1^2 + v_2^2 + v_3^2 = const.)$. In polar form this reads $(\sin^2\vartheta\cos 2\phi, \sqrt{3}(\cos^2\vartheta - \frac{1}{3}), const.)$. Putting these terms together with the off-diagonal elements (v_1v_2, v_1v_3, v_2v_3) of eq. 2 we arrive at the original description by Knutsson [6].

2.3 The *n*D Case in the General Framework

We notice that there was a choice in one of the components of the vector a and b to fulfill the requirements of orthogonality. This implies of course that the mappings are not unique in terms of scaling (of an axis) as long as we do not require orthonormality. We will also see that the implicit historic choices for a and b do not generalize well to nD. For a systematic iterative construction let us chose $a_1 = -1 \Rightarrow a_2 = 1$, or

$$\mathbf{D_2} = \begin{pmatrix}1\;1\\-1\;1\end{pmatrix} \tag{7}$$

and for 3D we use the earlier $b_1 = -1 \Rightarrow b_2 = -1, b_3 = 2$, or

$$\mathbf{D_3} = \begin{pmatrix}-1 & -1 & 1\\1 & -1 & 1\\0 & 2 & 1\end{pmatrix}. \tag{8}$$

From this we can continue the construction for nD as follows

$$\mathbf{D_n} = \begin{pmatrix}-1 & -1 & -1 & \cdots & 1\\1 & -1 & -1 & \cdots & 1\\0 & 2 & -1 & \cdots & 1\\0 & 0 & 3 & \cdots & 1\\ & & & & \\0 & 0 & 0 & \ddots & 1\\0 & 0 & 0 & n-1 & 1\end{pmatrix}. \tag{9}$$

The last column vector is **1** and the i-th vector is $(\overbrace{-1,\ldots,-1}^{i \text{ times}}, i, 0, \ldots)$. It is apparent from this iterative construction that all properties for each subspace are preserved. That is, the lower dimensional mappings are embedded in the higher dimensional representation. For example application of $\mathbf{D_4}$ to the diagonal elements of $M(v)$ in 4D reduces the set as follows: $(v_1^2, v_2^2, v_3^2, v_4^2) \to (-v_1^2 + v_2^2, -v_1^2 - v_2^2 + 2v_3^2, -v_1^2 - v_2^2 - v_3^2 + 3v_4^2, const.)$. Orthonormality can always be imposed if desired.

3 Alternative Mapping Based on Projection Operators and Angles between Vectors in Mapped Space

We shall now give an alternative mapping based on projection operators of the form $I - P_I$. This mapping gives the same angles between mapped vectors and therefore must be equivalent to the reduced mappings (angle doubling, [4, Eq. 50] and the general mapping implied by eq. 9), i.e. equal up to a global rotation in mapped space. This rotation implicit in the former mappings brings the identity matrix along one of the axes (the last variable indicated as *const.*). In the alternative presented here we just project it away.

A projection of a vector w onto a vector v is given by $P_v w = \frac{(v,w)}{(v,v)} v$, with $v, w, \in \mathbb{R}^n$. P_v is idempotent and we have $(I - P_v)P_v = P_v(I - P_v) = 0$. Using this property the inner product of two vectors v, w can be split into $(v, w) = (P_a v, P_a w) + ((I - P_a)v, (I - P_a)w)$ by projection onto an arbitrary vector $a \in \mathbb{R}^n$. The projection onto $I - P_a$ is to be interpreted as the projection onto the $n - 1$ dimensional hyperplane with normal a.

The angle between two vectors in mapped space by projections (from eq. 2) is in operator notation $\cos \angle(P_v, P_w) = (P_v, P_w) = \cos^2 \angle(v, w) = \frac{1}{2} + \frac{1}{2}\cos(2\angle(v, w))$. This result was already found in [6, Eq. 21].

We now propose the following equivalent alternative mapping to the iterative construction of eq. 9

$$v \to (I - P_I)P_v \,. \tag{10}$$

To deduce the angle between the projection operators $(I - P_I)P_v$ and $(I - P_I)P_w$ we use eq. 24 from the appendix

$$\cos \angle((I - P_I)P_v, (I - P_I)P_w) = \frac{\cos \angle(P_v, P_w) - n^{-1}}{1 - n^{-1}} \tag{11}$$

$$= \frac{1 - 2n^{-1}}{2 - 2n^{-1}} + \frac{\cos(2\angle(v, w))}{2 - 2n^{-1}} \tag{12}$$

where we have used

$$\cos \angle(I, P_v) = \frac{(I, P_v)}{\|I\| \|P_v\|} = \frac{1}{\sqrt{n}} \,. \tag{13}$$

If we make this relation explicit for $n = 2, 3, 4$ we get for eq. 12

$$\begin{aligned} n = 2: &\quad 0 + \cos(2\angle(v,w))\,, \\ n = 3: &\quad \tfrac{1}{4} + \tfrac{3}{4}\cos(2\angle(v,w))\,, \\ n = 4: &\quad \tfrac{1}{3} + \tfrac{2}{3}\cos(2\angle(v,w))\,. \end{aligned}$$

The case $n = 2$ was already long known as doubling of the angle and gives the same relation as eq. 3. The case $n = 3$ gives the same relation as the mapping of Knutsson as in [4, Eq. 50] or of course as eq. 8. For all higher dimensional mappings generated by eq. 9 the angles in mapped space are to be computed by eq. 12. For example for $n = 3$ we get for the diagonal elements by eq. 8 $(-v_1^2 + v_2^2, -v_1^2 - v_2^2 + 2v_3^2, v_1^2 + v_2^2 + v_3^2 = const.)$ (up to scaling) and using the projection of eq. 10 we get $\frac{1}{3}(2v_1^2 - v_2^3 - v_3^2, -v_1^2 + 2v_2^2 - v_3^2, -v_1^2 - v_2^2 + 2v_3^2)$. See also the appendix for a comparison of the mappings.

From eq. 13 we see that $1/n$ can be interpreted as the average cosine angle between two vectors in the mapped space M or

$$\langle \cos\angle(P_v, P_w)\rangle = \left\langle \cos^2\angle(v,w)\right\rangle = \frac{1}{n}\,. \tag{14}$$

In this average, the vector v is fixed and the set $\{w\}$ has uniform distribution over the $n-1$ dimensional solid angle.

From here it is not yet clear what the advantage is to use $v \to (I - P_I)P_v$ instead of the approach $v \to P_v$ of eq. 2, however, in the following we will see that if we want the mapping to preserve the isotropy then it is indeed useful. Eq. 9 is also shown to preserve isotropy and reduces the components of the mapping to be computed by one compared to eq. 2 or eq. 10.

4 Preserving Isotropy in Mapped Space

Summarizing the relations between angles in mapped space and original space (eq. 11 and 13) we get

$$\cos\angle((I - P_I)P_v, (I - P_I)P_w) = \frac{\cos\angle(P_v, P_w) - \langle\cos\angle(P_v, P_w)\rangle}{1 - \langle\cos\angle(P_v, P_w)\rangle} \tag{15}$$

$$= \frac{\cos(2\angle(v,w)) - \langle\cos(2\angle(v,w))\rangle}{1 - \langle\cos(2\angle(v,w))\rangle}\,. \tag{16}$$

Now we see that the average cosine angle of this expression is zero, i.e. $\langle\cos\angle((I - P_I)P_v, (I - P_I)P_w)\rangle = 0$, just as is the case for the average angle $\langle\cos\angle(v,w)\rangle$. Using the operator $(I - P_I)P_v$ produces a representation that preserves isotropy.

The angle between operators does not change when they are multiplied by a positive scalar $\angle(P'_v, P'_w) = \angle(P_v, P_w)$ with $P'_v = f(v)P_v$. Moreover, if $f(v)$ does not depend on the direction of v, preservation of isotropy (the zero average of eq. 15) also holds for P' instead of P. Now we can characterize Knutsson's mapping and our iterative construction scheme as follows: i) [4, Eq. 18-22] for 3D is equivalent to isotropy preservation of $\|v\|(I-P_I)P_v$, ii) [5, Eq. 4] (or eq. 2) for nD is equivalent to $\|v\|P_v$ and iii) the iterative construction for nD of eq. 9 is equivalent to isotropy preserving $\|v\|(I-P_I)P_v$.

Please note, that Knutsson always used $f(v) = \|v\|$. We remark that mappings with different choices of $f(v)$ could be studied, e.g. $f(v) = \|v\|^p$. In particular $p = 0$ and $p = 2$ look interesting, with $D_v = \|v\|^2 P_v$ being the dyadic product of v and v applied in the gradient structure tensor.

5 Doubling the Angle – Knutsson Cones in Higher Dimensions

The angle between two mapped vectors has been investigated by Knutsson with special attention to the case of a 2D Euclidean subspace (plane) in 3D [4]. He found that each halfplane in his 5D reduced mapping is mapped onto a 2D manifold in a separated 3D subspace where the manifold is the surface of a cone. Note that doubling of the half-plane angle occurs in mapping the half-plane onto the surface of a cone. That is due to the fact that the iterative construction of the generalized mapping for arbitrary dimensions embeds all lower dimensional mappings with their properties among which the angle doubling that was found in 2D.

In generalizing from 2D to nD one might hope for generalization of the cone to a hypercone. That appears to be impossible. Each pair of axes in nD forms a 2D subspace with a corresponding cone. The extra dimension of a cone represents at once both off-diagonal elements in the symmetric matrix. In nD the number of off-diagonal element pairs can only be represented by one extra dimension for each 2D subspace and this is what one cone per 2D subspace amounts to. In Fig. 1 and Fig. 2 we visualize the cases for $n = 2$ and $n = 3$; below we formalize our reasoning.

Let us consider now for sake of simplicity, but without loss of generality a normal vector $v = (c_1, c_2, c_3) \in \mathbb{R}^3$ with $\|v\| = 1$, where c_i represents the

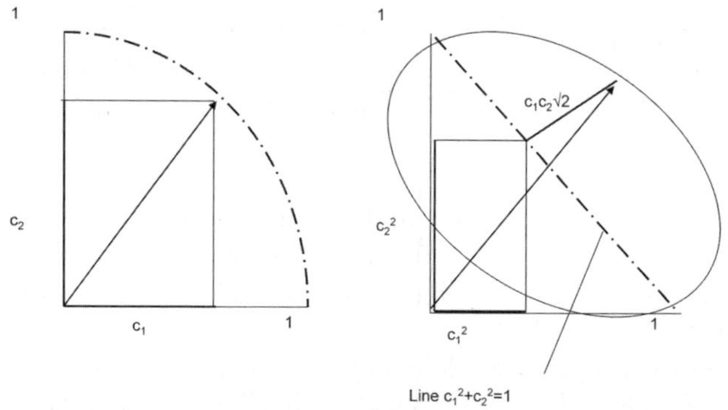

Fig. 1. For the case $n = 2$ we draw the relation between the diagonal elements c_1^2, c_2^2 and the off-diagonal element $\sqrt{2}c_1c_2$ and how this pair forms a cone

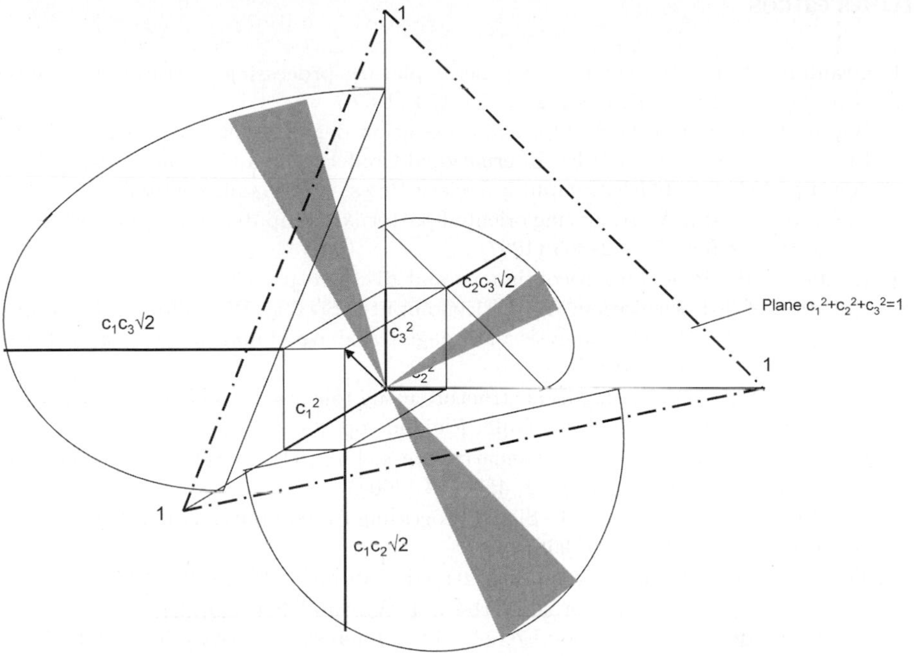

Fig. 2. Knutsson cones in higher dimensions. In the general case each pair of c_i, c_j gives one extra dimension and one guiding cone. The extra dimension of a cone represents at once both off-diagonal elements in the symmetric matrix.

direction cosine. For the diagonal components of $M(c)$ is it clear that they stay in the subspace $c_1^2+c_2^2+c_3^2 = 1$. The non-diagonal elements c_1c_2, c_1c_3, c_2c_3 follow the respective guiding cones, i.e. the angle doubling works per pair-cone. Also in higher dimensions only pairs operate in 2D. For the cones we must check the norms such that everything adds up to one. This will give a scaling factor of $\sqrt{2}$ for the $n(n+1)/2$-dimensional mapping M

$$c_1^2 + c_2^2 + c_3^2 = 1 \tag{17}$$

$$(c_1^2)^2 + (c_2^2)^2 + (c_3^2)^2 + (\sqrt{2}c_1c_2)^2 + (\sqrt{2}c_1c_3)^2 + (\sqrt{2}c_2c_3)^2 = 1\,. \tag{18}$$

6 Conclusion

This paper presents a generalized framework for the construction of a continuous orientation representation in arbitrary dimensions. The mappings for all dimensions lower than the current one are embedded and hence its properties hold as well. We introduced projection operators as an alternative to construct isotropy preserving mappings. The ad hoc constructions of Granlund and Knutsson are now explicit and available for arbitrary dimensional spaces. The well-known angle doubling works in each pair-cone of the Knutsson mapping.

References

1. Granlund, G.H.: In search of a general picture processing operator. Computer Graphics and Image Processing 8, 155–173 (1978)
2. Bigün, J., Granlund, G.H.: Optimal orientation detection of linear symmetry. In: Proceedings of the First IEEE International Conference on Computer Vision, London, pp. 433–438. IEEE Computer Society Press, Los Alamitos (1987)
3. Kass, M., Witkin, A.: Analyzing oriented patterns. Computer Vision, Graphics and Image Processing 37, 362–385 (1987)
4. Knutsson, H.: Producing a continuous and distance preserving 5-d vector representation of 3-d orientation. In: IEEE Computer Society Workshop on Computer Architecture for Pattern Analysis and Image Database Management, Miami Beach, Florida, pp. 175–182 (1985)
5. Knutsson, H.: Representing local structure using tensors. In: The 6th Scandinavian Conference on Image Analysis, Oulu, Finland, pp. 244–251 (1989)
6. Rieger, B., van Vliet, L.J.: A systematic approach to nD orientation representation. Image and Vision Computing 22, 453–459 (2004)
7. Granlund, G.H., Knutsson, H.: Signal processing for computer vision. Kluwer Academic Publishers, Boston (1995)
8. Jähne, B.: Digital Image Processing, 4th edn. Springer, Berlin (1997)
9. van Ginkel, M., van de Weijer, J., Verbeek, P.W., van Vliet, L.J.: Curvature estimation from orientation fields. In: Ersboll, B.K., Johansen, P. (eds.) SCIA 1999, Proc. 11th Scandinavian Conference on Image Analysis, Kangerlussuaq, Greenland, pp. 545–551. Pattern Recognition Society of Denmark, Lyngby (1999)
10. Bigün, J., Granlund, G.H., Wiklund, J.: Multidimensional orientation estimation with applications to texture analysis and optical flow. IEEE Transactions on Pattern Analysis and Machine Intelligence 13, 775–790 (1991)
11. Rieger, B., van Vliet, L.J.: Curvature of n-dimensional space curves in grey-value images. IEEE Transactions on Image Processing 11, 738–745 (2002)
12. Rieger, B., van Vliet, L.J., Verbeek, P.W.: Estimation of curvature based shape properties of surfaces in 3D grey-value images. In: Bigun, J., Gustavsson, T. (eds.) SCIA 2003. LNCS, vol. 2749, pp. 262–267. Springer, Heidelberg (2003)
13. van Noorden, S., Caan, M.W.A., van der Graaf, M., van Vliet, L.J., Vos, F.M.: A comparison of the cingulum tract in ALS-B patients and controls using kernel matching. In: Jiang, T., Navab, N., Pluim, J.P.W., Viergever, M.A. (eds.) MICCAI 2010. LNCS, vol. 6362, pp. 249–256. Springer, Heidelberg (2010)
14. Westin, C.-F., Knutsson, H.: The Möbius strip parameterization for line extraction. In: Sandini, G. (ed.) ECCV 1992. LNCS, vol. 588, pp. 33–38. Springer, Heidelberg (1992)
15. Westin, C.F.: A Tensor Framework for Multidimensional Signal Processing. PhD thesis, Linköping University, Linköping, Sweden (1994)
16. Mühlich, M., Aach, T.: Analysis of multiple orientations. IEEE Transactions on Image Processing 18, 1424–1437 (2009)
17. Franken, E.M., Duits, R., Haar Romenij, B.M.: Nonlinear diffusion on the 2D euclidean motion group. In: Sgallari, F., Murli, A., Paragios, N. (eds.) SSVM 2007. LNCS, vol. 4485, pp. 461–472. Springer, Heidelberg (2007)
18. Faas, F.G.A., van Vliet, L.J.: 3D-orientation space; filters and sampling. In: Bigun, J., Gustavsson, T. (eds.) SCIA 2003. LNCS, vol. 2749, pp. 36–42. Springer, Heidelberg (2003)

19. Herberthsson, M., Brun, A., Knutsson, H.: Pairs of orientation in the plane. In: Proceedings of the SSBA Symposium on Image Analysis. SSBA (2006)
20. Stein, E., Stein, E.M., Weiss, G.: Introduction to Fourier Analysis on Euclidean Spaces. Princeton University Press, Princeton (1971)

Appendix

Projection Operator Properties

Let us consider the angle between $P_a v$ and $P_a w$ and $(I - P_a)v$ and $(I - P_a)w$, but first we compute the required inner products

$$(P_a v, P_a w) = \left(\frac{(a,v)}{(a,a)}a, \frac{(a,w)}{(a,a)}a\right) \tag{19}$$
$$= (a,v)(a,w)(a,a) \tag{20}$$
$$= \|v\|\|w\| \cos\angle(a,w)\cos\angle(a,v)\,, \tag{21}$$

$$((I - P_a)v, (I - P_a)w) = (v,w) - (P_a v, P_a w) \tag{22}$$
$$= \|v\|\|w\| \left(\cos\angle(v,w) - \cos\angle(a,w)\cos\angle(a,v)\right) . \tag{23}$$

For $v = w$ we get $((I - P_a)v, (I - P_a)v) = \|v\||\sin\angle(a,v)|$. Finally we arrive at

$$\cos\angle((I - P_a)v, (I - P_a)w) = \cos\angle(w,v) - \frac{\cos\angle(a,v)\cos\angle(a,w)}{|\sin\angle(a,v)||\sin\angle(a,w)|}\,, \tag{24}$$

$$\cos\angle(P_a v, P_a w) = \cos\angle(a,v)\cos\angle(a,w)\,. \tag{25}$$

Eqs. 19 to 25 are also valid for the mapped vectors of a, v, w.

Relation between Iterative (eq. 9) and Alternative Mapping (eq. 10)

Let the symmetric matrices span the space $\mathcal{S}$ of dimensionality $n + (n^2 - n)/2$. Further the off-diagonal symmetric matrices the $(n^2 - n)/2$-dimensional space $\mathcal{N}$ and the diagonal matrices the n-dimensional space $\mathcal{D}$, where $\mathcal{N}$ and $\mathcal{D}$ are orthogonal. $\mathcal{D}$ consists of the unit matrix $\mathbf{I}$ and its orthogonal complement, the space $\mathcal{T}$, of traceless matrices. The difference between eq. 9 and eq. 10 is the treatment of the unit matrix $\mathbf{I}$. In both cases $v \in \mathbb{R}^n$ is mapped to $\mathcal{S}$ by projection on $\mathcal{S}$ of $v^T v$ (or a scaled version of it with $f(v)$). The projection onto $\mathcal{N}$ is also the same, just copying the matrix elements $v_i v_j$ for $i < j$. The projection onto $\mathcal{D}$ is different. Eq. 9 constructs an orthogonal basis in $\mathcal{D}$ consisting of $\mathbf{I}$ and a basis of $\mathcal{T}$ consisting out of matrices orthogonal to $\mathbf{I}$. Then it is projected onto this basis in $\mathcal{D}$ and the projection onto $\mathbf{I}$ can be omitted as it is irrelevant for the goal of the mapping. Eq. 10 also copies the matrix elements $v_i v_i$ but eliminates the projection onto $\mathbf{I}$.

Eq. 10 uses n components with condition that the sum over all components must be zero, where eq. 9. uses the condition that the last component must be constant.

Real-Time Line Detection Using Accelerated High-Resolution Hough Transform

Radovan Jošth, Markéta Dubská, Adam Herout, and Jiří Havel

Graph@FIT
Brno University of Technology, Faculty of Information Technology
Brno, Czech Republic
{ijosth,idubska,herout,ihavel}@fit.vutbr.cz
http://www.fit.vutbr.cz/research/groups/graph/

Abstract. Hough transform is a well-known and popular algorithm for detecting lines in raster images. The standard Hough transform is rather slow to be usable in real-time, so different accelerated and approximated algorithms exist. This paper proposes a modified accumulation scheme for the Hough transform, which makes it suitable for computer systems with small but fast read-write memory – such as the today's GPUs. The proposed algorithm is evaluated both on synthetic binary images and on complex high resolution real-world photos. The results show that using today's commodity graphics chips, the Hough transform can be computed at interactive frame rates even with a high resolution of the Hough space and with the Hough transform fully computed.

Keywords: Line Detection, Hough-Transform, Real-Time, GPU, CUDA.

1 Introduction

The Hough transform is a well-known tool for detecting shapes and objects in raster images. Originally, Hough [6] defined the transformation for detecting lines; later it was extended for more complex shapes, such as circles, ellipses, etc., and even generalized for arbitrary patterns [1].

When used for detecting lines in 2D raster images, the Hough transform is defined by a *parameterization* of lines: each line is described by two parameters. The input image is preprocessed and for each pixel which is likely to belong to a line, voting accumulators corresponding to lines which could be coincident with the pixel are increased. Next, the accumulators in the parameter space are searched for local maxima above a given threshold, which correspond to likely lines in the original image. The Hough transform was formalized by Princen et al. [14] and described as an *hypothesis testing* process.

Hough [6] parameterized the lines by their *slope* and y-axis *intercept*. A very popular parameterization introduced by Duda and Hart [3] is denoted as θ-ϱ; it is important for its inherently bounded parameter space. It is based on a line equation in the normal form: $y \sin\theta + x \cos\theta = \varrho$. Parameter θ represents the

A. Heyden and F. Kahl (Eds.): SCIA 2011, LNCS 6688, pp. 784–793, 2011.

angle of inclination and ϱ is the length of the shortest chord between the line and the origin of the image coordinate system. There exist several other bounded parameterizations, mainly based on intersections of lines with image's bounding box [18][11][4]. Different properties of these intersects are used as parameters.

The majority of currently used implementations seems to be using the θ-ϱ parameterization – for example the OpenCV library implements several variants of line detectors based on the θ-ϱ parameterization and none other. It is mainly because the parameterization uses a very straightforward transformation from the image space to one bounded space of parameters and because of its uniform distribution of the discretization error across the Hough space.

Several research groups invested effort to deal with computational complexity of the Hough transform based on the θ-ϱ parameterization. Different methods focus on special data structures, non-uniform resolution of the accumulation array or special rules for picking points from the input image.

O'Rourke and Sloan developed two special data structures: *dynamically quantized spaces* (DQS) [13] and *dynamically quantized pyramid* (DQP) [17]. Both these methods use splitting and merging cells of the space represented as a binary tree, or possibly a quadtree. After processing the whole image, each cell contains approximately the same number of votes; that leads to a higher resolution of the Hough space of accumulators at locations around the peaks.

A typical method using special picking rules is the Randomized Hough Transform (RHT) [19]. This method is based on the idea, that each point in an n-dimensional Hough space of parameters can be exactly defined by an n-tuple of points from the input raster image. Instead of accumulation of a hypersurface in the Hough space for each point, n points are randomly picked and the corresponding accumulator in the parameter space is increased. Advantages of this approach are mostly in rapid speed-up and small storage. Unfortunately, when detecting lines in a noisy input image, the probability of picking two points from same line is small, decreasing the probability of finding the true line.

Another approach based on repartitioning the Hough space is represented by the Fast Hough Transform (FHT) [8]. The algorithm assumes that each edge point in the input image defines a hyperplane in the parameter space. These hyperplanes recursively divide the space into hypercubes and perform the Hough transform only on the hypercubes with votes exceeding a selected threshold. This approach reduces both the computational load and the storage requirements.

Using principal axis analysis for line detection was discussed by Rau and Chen [15]. Using this method for line detection, the parameters are first transferred to a one-dimensional angle-count histogram. After transformation, the dominant distribution of image features is analyzed, with searching priority in peak detection set according to the principal axis. There exist many other accelerated algorithms, more or less based on the above mentioned approaches; e.g. HT based on eliminating of particle swarm [2] or some specialized tasks like iterative RHT [9] for incomplete ellipses and N-Point Hough transform for line detection [10]. For more information about different existing modifications of Hough transform, please see [7].

This paper presents an algorithm for real-time detection of lines based on the standard Hough transform using the θ-ϱ parameterization. The classical Hough transform has some advantages over the accelerated and approximated methods (it does not introduce any further detection error and it has a low number of parameters and therefore usually requires less detailed application-specific fine-tuning). That makes the real-time implementation of the Hough transform desirable. The algorithm uses a modified strategy for accumulating the votes in the array of accumulators in the Hough space. The strategy was designed to meet the nature of today's graphics chips (GPUs). The modified algorithm is presented in Section 2 of the paper. Section 3 presents the experiments comparing the commonly used variant of Hough transform with the implementation of the algorithm run on a GPU. The results show that the GPU implementation achieves such performance which allows running the Hough transform with a high-resolution accumulator space in real time. Section 4 concludes the paper and proposes directions for future work.

2 Real-Time Hough Transform Algorithm

Before discussing the new real-time Hough transform algorithm, let us review the "classical" Hough transform procedure based on the θ-ϱ parameterization in Algorithm 1 (the θ-ϱ parameterization itself is depicted by Figure 1).

Algorithm 1. HT for detecting lines based on the θ-ϱ parameterization.

Input: Input image I with dimensions I_w, I_h, Hough space dimensions H_ϱ, H_θ
Output: Detected lines $L = \{(\theta_1, \varrho_1), \ldots\}$
1: $H(\bar{\varrho}, \bar{\theta}) \leftarrow 0, \forall \bar{\varrho} \in \{1, \ldots, H_\varrho\}, \bar{\theta} \in \{1, \ldots, H_\theta\}$
2: **for all** $x \in \{1, \ldots, I_w\}, y \in \{1, \ldots, I_h\}$ **do**
3:   **if** $I(x, y)$ **is edge then**
4:     **increment** $H\big(\bar{\varrho}(\bar{\theta}, x, y), \bar{\theta}\big), \forall \bar{\theta} \in \{1, \ldots, H_\theta\}$
5:   **end if**
6: **end for**
7: $L = \{(\theta(\bar{\theta}), \varrho(\bar{\varrho})) | \bar{\varrho} \in \{1, \ldots, H_\varrho\} \wedge \bar{\theta} \in \{1, \ldots H_\theta\} \wedge$ at $(\bar{\varrho}, \bar{\theta})$ is a high max. in $H\}$

Points in the input image I with dimensions I_w and I_h are classified with a binary decision on line 3 (e.g. by an edge detector and thresholding). Lines 2–6 accumulate curves into the Hough space. Function $\bar{\varrho}(\bar{\theta}, x, y)$ computes the corresponding $\bar{\varrho}$ for each line passing through point (x, y) at angle $\bar{\theta}$:

$$\bar{\varrho}(\bar{\theta}, x, y) = \left[\frac{H_\varrho \big((y - \frac{I_h}{2}) \sin(\frac{\pi}{H_\theta} \bar{\theta}) + (x - \frac{I_w}{2}) \cos(\frac{\pi}{H_\theta} \bar{\theta}) \big)}{\sqrt{I_w^2 + I_h^2}} + \frac{H_\varrho}{2} \right]. \tag{1}$$

Line 7 detects above-threshold local maxima in the accumulated space and transforms the discretized Hough space coordinates $\bar{\varrho}$ and $\bar{\theta}$ to ϱ and θ by the following functions:

$$\varrho(\bar{\varrho}) = \frac{\sqrt{I_w^2 + I_h^2}}{H_\varrho} \left(\bar{\varrho} - \frac{H_\varrho}{2} \right), \qquad \theta(\bar{\theta}) = \frac{\pi}{H_\theta} \bar{\theta}. \tag{2}$$

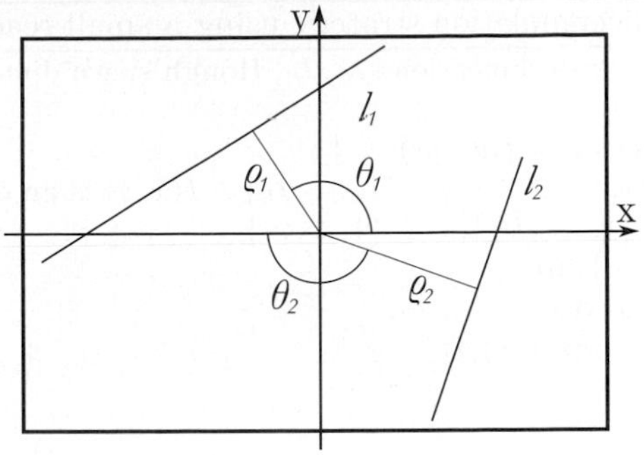

Fig. 1. The θ-ϱ parameterization of lines in a coordinate system with origin in the center of the input image.

Usually, a small neighborhood (3×3 in OpenCV, 5×5 or 7×7 in cases of high resolution of the Hough space) is used for detecting the local maxima by line 7. The accumulator value must be above a given threshold to be considered for a "high local maxima". The threshold is another input parameter of the algorithm, but since it does not influence the algorithm's structure, it is used silently by line 7 for simplicity of the algorithmic notation.

The key characteristic of this algorithm is rasterization of the sinus curve and incrementation the corresponding accumulators in the Hough space. On some systems, this might be expensive or even not available at all.

2.1 Hough Transform on a Small Read-Write Memory of Accumulators

The classical Hough transform accesses sparsely a relatively large amount of memory. This behavior can diminish the effect of caching. On CUDA and similar architectures, this effect is even more significant, as the global memory is not cached. To achieve real-time performance, the memory requirements must be limited to the *shared memory* of a multiprocessor (typically 16 kB).

Algorithm 2 shows the modified Hough transform accumulation procedure. The key difference from Algorithm 1 is the actual size of the Hough space. The new algorithm stores only $H_\varrho \times n$ accumulators, where n is the neighborhood size required for the maxima detection. Functions $\bar{\varrho}, \theta, \varrho$, and the edge and maxima detection are identical to Algorithm 1. First, the detected edges are stored in a set P (line 1). Then, first n rows of the Hough space are computed by lines 2–7. The memory necessary for containing the n lines is all the memory required by the algorithm and even for high resolutions of the Hough space, the buffer of n lines fits easily in the *shared memory* of the GPU multiprocessors.

In the main loop (lines 9–18), for every row of the Hough space, the maxima are detected (line 10), the accumulated neighborhood is shifted by one row (lines 11–13) and a new row is accumulated (lines 14–17); please refer to Figure 2 for an illustration of the algorithm. Thus, only the buffer of n lines is being

Algorithm 2. HT accumulation strategy using a small read-write memory.

Input: Input image I with dimensions I_w, I_h, Hough space dimensions H_ϱ, H_θ, neighborhood size n
Output: Detected lines $L = \{(\theta_1, \varrho_1), \ldots\}$

1: $P \leftarrow \{(x,y) | x \in \{1,\ldots,I_w\} \wedge y \in \{1,\ldots,I_h\} \wedge I(x,y)$ is an edge$\}$
2: $H(\bar{\varrho}, i) \leftarrow 0, \forall \bar{\varrho} \in \{1,\ldots,H_\rho\}, \forall i \in \{1,\ldots.n\}$
3: **for all** $i \in \{1,\ldots,n\}$ **do**
4:   **for all** $(x,y) \in P$ **do**
5:     **increment** $H(\bar{\varrho}(i,x,y), i)$
6:   **end for**
7: **end for**
8: $L \leftarrow \{\}$
9: **for** $\bar{\theta} = \lceil \frac{n}{2} \rceil$ **to** $H_\theta - \lfloor \frac{n}{2} \rfloor$ **do**
10:   $L \leftarrow L \cup \{(\theta(\bar{\theta}), \varrho(\bar{\varrho})) | \bar{\varrho} \in \{1,\ldots H_\varrho\} \wedge (\bar{\varrho}, \lceil \frac{n}{2} \rceil)$ is a high local max. in $H\}$
11:   **for** $i = 1$ **to** $n-1$ **do**
12:     $H(\bar{\varrho}, i) \leftarrow H(\bar{\varrho}, i+1), \forall \bar{\varrho} \in \{1,\ldots,H_\varrho\}$
13:   **end for**
14:   $H(\bar{\varrho}, n) \leftarrow 0, \forall \bar{\varrho} \in \{1,\ldots,H_\varrho\}$
15:   **for all** $(x,y) \in P$ **do**
16:     **increment** $H(\bar{\varrho}(\bar{\theta} + \lceil \frac{n}{2} \rceil, x, y), n)$
17:   **end for**
18: **end for**

reused. The memory shift can be implemented using a circular buffer of lines to avoid data copying.

In the pseudocode, maxima are not detected at the edges of the Hough space. Eventual handling of the maxima detection at the edge of the Hough space does not change the algorithm structure, but it would unnecessarily complicate the pseudocode. Two solutions exist – either copying the border data or rasterizing necessary parts of the curves outside of the Hough space. Both approaches perform similarly and their implementation is straightforward.

On CUDA, the threads in a block can be used for processing the set of edges P (lines 15–17 and 4–6) in parallel, using an atomic increment of the shared memory to avoid read-write collisions. In order to use all multiprocessors of the GPU, the loop on line 9 is broken to a number (e.g. 90 is suitable for current NVIDIA GeForce graphics chips) of sub-loops processed by individual blocks of threads.

The algorithm as described above uses exactly $H_\varrho \times n$ memory cells, typically 16-bit integer values. In the case when the runtime system has more fast random-access read-write memory, this memory can be used fully, and instead of accumulating one line of the Hough space (lines 15–17 of the algorithm), several lines are accumulated and then scanned for maxima. This leads to further speedup by reducing the number of steps carried out by the loop over $\bar{\theta}$ (line 9).

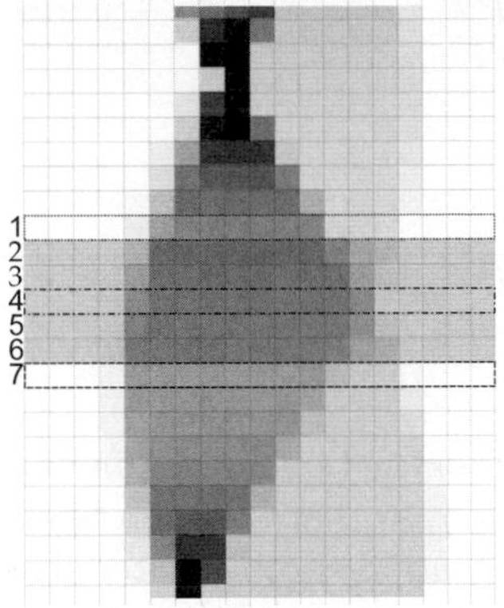

Fig. 2. Illustration of Algorithm 2. The gray rectangle represents the buffer of n lines. For row 4, the above-threshold maxima are detected in each step within the buffer. Then, the row 7 values are accumulated into the buffer, using the space of row 2, which will not be needed in future processing.

2.2 Harnessing the Edge Orientation

In 1976 O'Gorman and Clowes came with the idea not to accumulate values for each θ but just one value instead [12]. The appropriate θ for a point can be obtained from the gradient of the detected edge which contains this point [16]. One common way to calculate the local gradient direction of the image intensity is using the Sobel operator. Sobel detector uses two kernels, each approximates the derivation in horizontal (G_x), respectively vertical (G_y) direction. Using these two values, the gradient's direction can be obtained as $\theta = \arctan(\frac{G_y}{G_x})$. To avoid errors caused by noise and rasterization, accumulators within several degrees around the calculated angle are also incremented. From experimental testing, the interval's radius equal to 20° seems suitable. This approach reduces the computation time and highlights the maxima peaks. A disadvantage of this method is its dependency of the results on another user parameter – the radius. Small radius of the incremented interval of θ can lead into discarding some maxima due to inaccurate θ location. On the other hand, a too high radius can diminish the performance benefits of the method.

This approach to utilizing the detected gradient can be incorporated to the new accumulation scheme presented in the previous section. When extracting the "edge points" for which the sinusoids are accumulated in the Hough space (line 1 in Algorithm 2), also the edge inclination is extracted:

1: $P \leftarrow \{(\alpha, x, y) | x \in \{1, \ldots, I_w\} \wedge y \in \{1, \ldots, I_h\}$
$\wedge\ I(x, y)$ is an edge with orientation $\alpha\}$.

Then, instead of accumulating all points from set P (lines 4–6), only those points which fall into the interval with radius w around currently processed θ are accumulated into the buffer of n lines:

4: **for all** $(\alpha, x, y) \in P \wedge\ i - w < \bar{\alpha} < i + w$ **do**
5: **increment** $H(\bar{\varrho}(i, x, y), i + \lfloor \frac{n}{2} \rfloor)$
6: **end for**

and similarly for lines 15–17:

16: **for all** $(\alpha, x, y) \in P \wedge\ \bar{\theta} + \lfloor \frac{n}{2} \rfloor - w < \bar{\alpha} < \bar{\theta} + \lfloor \frac{n}{2} \rfloor + w$ **do**
17: **increment** $H(\bar{\varrho}(\bar{\theta} + \lfloor \frac{n}{2} \rfloor, x, y), n)$
18: **end for**.

Please, note that the edge extraction phase (line 1) can sort the detected edges by their gradient inclination α, so that loops on lines 15–17 and 4–6 do not visit all edges, but only edges potentially accumulated, based on the current $\bar{\theta}$ (line 9 of Algorithm 2). For (partial) sorting of the edges on GPU, an efficient prefix sum can be used [5].

3 Experimental Results

This section evaluates the speed of the newly presented line-detection algorithm. Two groups of experiments were made: the first one is focused on the speedup in the case when ϱ is calculated for each θ (Section 2.1, Algorithm 2); the second test evaluates the situation when the Sobel operator is used for detection of edge orientation and only an interval of the sinusoid curves is accumulated to the Hough space (Section 2.2).

Each test compares the computation time of 4 implementations: new algorithm running on (i) ASUS nVIDIA GTX480 graphics card (1.5GB GDDR5 RAM) and (ii) ASUS nVIDIA GTX280 graphics card (1GB GDDR3 RAM), (iii) an OpenMP parallel CPU implementation of the presented algorithm (Intel Core i7-920, 6GB 3×DDR3-1066(533MHz) RAM – the same machine was used for evaluating the GPU variants), (iv) and an OpenMP parallel "standard" implementation running on the same machine. As the "standard" implementation, the code based on OpenCV functions was used and optimized by parallelization.

3.1 Performance Evaluation on Synthetic Binary Images

As the dataset for this experiment we used automatically generated black-and-white images. The generator randomly places L white lines and then inverts pixels on P different positions in the image. The evaluation is done on 36 images (resolution 1600×1200): images 1–6, 7–12, 13–18, 19–24, 25–30, 31-36 are generated with $L = 1, 30, 60, 90, 120, 150$ respectively, with increasing $P = 1, 3000, 6000, 9000, 12000, 15000$ for each L. The suitable parameters for images of these properties were $H_\varrho = 960$ and $H_\theta = 1170$ (resolution of the Hough space) and the threshold for accumulators in the Hough space was 400.

Figure 3 reports the results of the four implementations. Note, please, that the CUDA version is several times faster than the commonly used OpenCV implementation and achieves real-time or nearly real-time speeds.

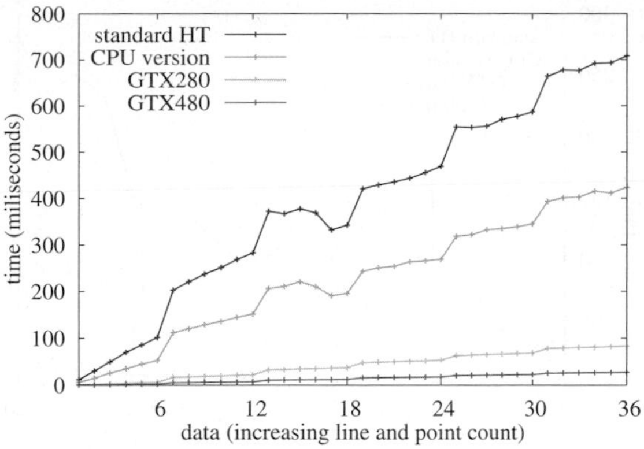

Fig. 3. Performance evaluation on synthetic binary images. Red: GTX480, Orange: GTX280, Green: Striped algorithm on the CPU, Blue: Standard HT accumulation.

3.2 Performance Evaluation on Real-Life Images

The images used in this test were real-world images (see Figure 4). For possibility of comparison with previous test, resolution of Hough space was same; i.e. $H_\varrho = 960$ and $H_\theta = 1170$; the threshold for accumulators in the Hough space was dependant on the input image resolution (one fourth of the diagonal; this corresponds to the shortest possible line detected by Hough transform); the radius of the accumulated interval (refer to Section 2.2) was 20°.

Figure 5 contains the measured results. They indicate that even for complex real-world images the proposed algorithm implemented on commodity graphics hardware can detect lines at interactive frame rates. Contrary to the version that

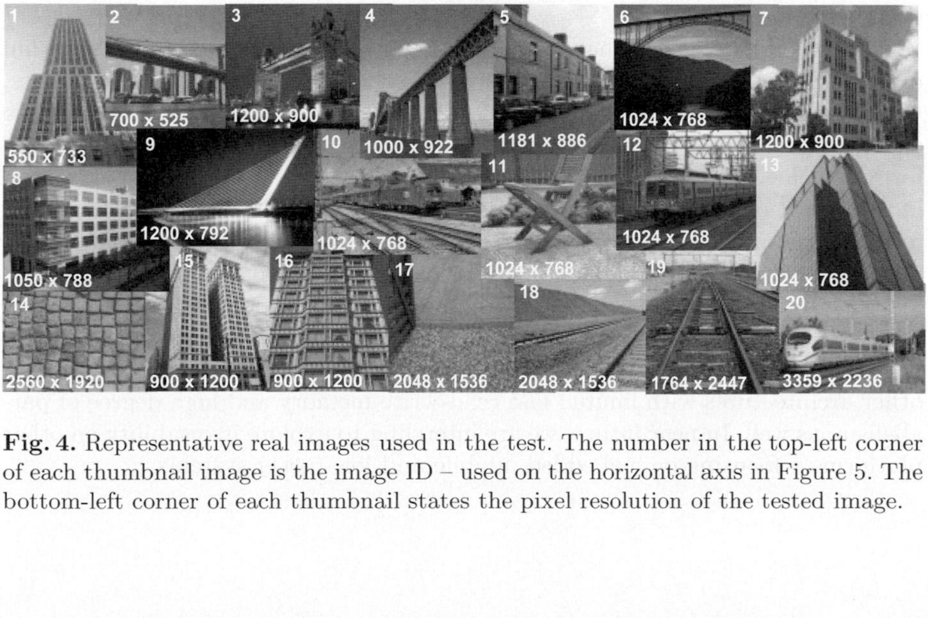

Fig. 4. Representative real images used in the test. The number in the top-left corner of each thumbnail image is the image ID – used on the horizontal axis in Figure 5. The bottom-left corner of each thumbnail states the pixel resolution of the tested image.

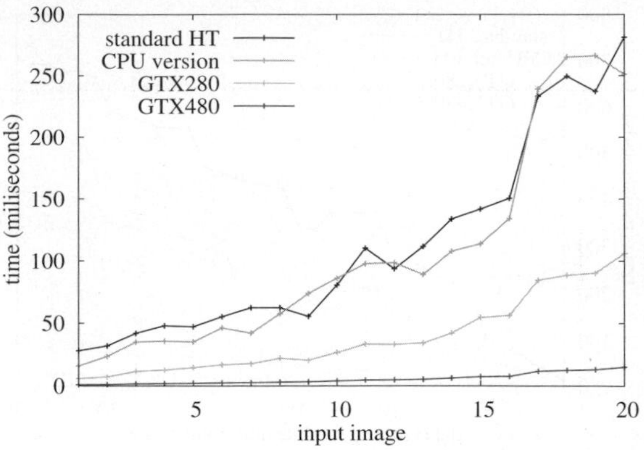

Fig. 5. Performance evaluation on real-world images (see Figure 4) using the Sobel operator and only accumulating intervals of the sinusoids. Red: GTX480, Orange: GTX280, Green: Striped algorithm on the CPU, Blue: Standard HT accumulation.

works with the whole sinusoids in the Hough space (Section 3.1), the speed of the CPU implementation of the presented algorithm is about as fast as the standard CPU version. This can be explained by better cache coherency when only fractions of the sinusoids are rasterized. However, for efficient implementation on CUDA and similar architectures, the presented algorithm is required.

4 Conclusions

This paper presents a modified algorithm for line detection using the Hough transform based on θ-ϱ parameterization. The algorithm was designed to fully using of small read-write memory; that makes it suitable for execution on recent graphics processors.

The experiments show that on commodity graphics hardware, the algorithm can operate at interactive frame rates even on high-resolution real-life images, while accumulating to a high-resolution Hough space to achieve accurate line detections. This real-time processing speed is achieved for the plain Hough transform, which – contrary to the acceleration and approximation mechanisms used in the literature – does not require many application-specific parameters. Therefore, its use in applications is more straightforward and does not require complicated human-assisted parameter tweaking. While the algorithm was designed for GPU processing, it outperforms the standard HT implementation even on the CPU, thanks to better cache usage of the new accumulation scheme.

The algorithm is very suitable for recent GPUs; however, it can be used on other architectures with limited fast read-write memory and high degree of parallelism, as well. In near future, we are intending to explore its usability on other platforms – focusing on embedded, mobile and low-power systems.

Acknowledgements. This work was partially supported by the BUT FIT grant FIT-10-S-2, by the research plan MSM0021630528, by the research program LC-06008 (Center for Computer Graphics), and by the FP7-ARTEMIS project no. 100230 SMECY.

References

1. Ballard, D.H.: Generalizing the Hough Transform to Detect Arbitrary Shapes, pp. 714–725 (1987)
2. Cheng, H.D., Guo, Y., Zhang, Y.: A novel hough transform based on eliminating particle swarm optimization and its applications. Pattern Recogn. 42, 1959–1969 (2009)
3. Duda, R.O., Hart, P.E.: Use of the Hough transformation to detect lines and curves in pictures. Commun. ACM 15(1), 11–15 (1972)
4. Eckhardt, U., Maderlechner, G.: Application of the projected Hough transform in picture processing. In: Proceedings of the 4th International Conference on Pattern Recognition, pp. 370–379. Springer, London (1988)
5. Harris, M.: GPU Gems 3. In: Parallel Prefix Sum (Scan) with CUDA, ch. 39, pp. 851–876. Addison-Wesley, Reading (2007)
6. Hough, P.V.C.: Method and means for recognizing complex patterns, u.S. Patent 3,069,654 (December 1962)
7. Illingworth, J., Kittler, J.: A survey of the Hough transform. Comput. Vision Graph. Image Process. 44(1), 87–116 (1988)
8. Li, H., Lavin, M.A., Le Master, R.J.: Fast Hough transform: A hierarchical approach. Comput. Vision Graph. Image Process. 36, 139–161 (1986)
9. Lu, W., Tan, J.: Detection of incomplete ellipse in images with strong noise by iterative randomized hough transform. Pattern Recogn. 41, 1268–1279 (2008)
10. Mochizuki, Y., Torii, A., Imiya, A.: N-point hough transform for line detection. J. Vis. Comun. Image Represent. 20, 242–253 (2009)
11. Natterer, F.: The mathematics of computerized tomography. Wiley, John & Sons, Incorporated, Chichester (1986) ISBN 9780471909590
12. O'Gorman, F., Clowes, M.B.: Finding picture edges through collinearity of feature points. IEEE Trans. Computers 25(4), 449–456 (1976)
13. O'Rourke, J.: Dynamically quantized spaces for focusing the Hough transform. In: Proceedings of the 7th International Joint Conference on Artificial Intelligence, vol. 2, pp. 737–739. Morgan Kaufmann Publ. Inc., San Francisco (1981)
14. Princen, J., Illingowrth, J., Kittler, J.: Hypothesis testing: A framework for analyzing and optimizing Hough transform performance. IEEE Trans. Pattern Anal. Mach. Intell. 16(4), 329–341 (1994)
15. Rau, J.Y., Chen, L.C.: Fast straight lines detection using Hough transform with principal axis analysis. J. Photogrammetry and Remote Sensing 8, 15–34 (2003)
16. Shapiro, L.G., Stockman, G.C.: Computer Vision. Tom Robbins (2001)
17. Sloan, K.R.: Dynamically quantized pyramids. In: Proc. International Joint Conference on Artificial Intelligence (IJCAI), pp. 734–736. Morgan Kaufmann, San Francisco (1981)
18. Wallace, R.: A modified Hough transform for lines. In: Proceedings of CVPR 1985, pp. 665–667 (1985)
19. Xu, L., Oja, E., Kultanen, P.: A new curve detection method: Randomized Hough Transform (RHT). Pattern Recognition Letters 11, 331–338 (1990)

Decomposition of a Curve into Arcs and Line Segments Based on Dominant Point Detection

Thanh Phuong Nguyen and Isabelle Debled-Rennesson

ADAGIo Team, LORIA, UMR 7503, Nancy University
Campus Scientifique - BP 239
54506 Vandoeuvre-ls-Nancy Cedex, France
{nguyentp,debled}@loria.fr

Abstract. A new solution is proposed to decompose a curve into arcs and straight line segments in $O(n \log n)$ time. It is a combined solution based on arc detection [1] and dominant point detection [2] to strengthen the quality of the segmentation results. Experimental results show the fastness of the proposed method.

1 Introduction

An important problem in computer vision is the extraction of meaningful features from image contour for constructing high level descriptors of images. Many existing methods use critical points or straight segments as meaningful features to construct the descriptors. Arc and straight segments are basic objects that appear often in images, specially in graphic document images. A combination of arcs and straight segments is a good solution that avoids the problem in which an arc is approximated by many straight segments or critical points.

Many methods have been proposed for decomposition of a planar curve into arcs and line segments. Rosin et al. [3] constructed firstly a polygonal description and detected fitting arcs by grouping connected lines. Chen et al. [4] proposed a method for segmenting a digital curve into lines and arcs in which the number of primitives is given. This procedure has two stages. The first stage, based on the detection of significant changes on curvature profile, is to obtain a starting set of break points and determine an initial approximation by arcs and lines based on this set of break points. The second stage is an optimization phase that adjusts the break points until the error norm is locally minimized. Horng et al. [5] introduced a curve-fitting method to approximate digital planar curves using lines and arcs based on an approach of dynamic programming. After that, Horng [6] proposed an adaptive smoothing approach for decomposition of a digital curve into arcs and lines. Firstly, a curvature profile is determined by using a Gaussian filter. Then, it is smoothed by using an adaptive smoothing technique. Finally, the input curve is segmented by arcs and lines based on the smoothed curvature representation. Similarly, Salmon et al. [7] proposed a method for decomposition of a curve into arcs and segments based on curvature profile. They used a notion of discrete curvature based on arithmetic discrete

A. Heyden and F. Kahl (Eds.): SCIA 2011, LNCS 6688, pp. 794–805, 2011.

lines and blurred segments. The main idea is to construct the curvature profile of the curve and use the extracted key points for reconstruction. Tortorella [8] et al. introduced a method to approximate a curve by arcs and straight segments based on an approach of dynamic programming. This method works in a transformed domain, called the turning function (see Arkin [9]). Bodansky [10] presented a method for the approximation of a polyline with straight segments, circular arcs and free curves. It contains two steps. The first step is the segmentation of polygonal lines into fragments (short polygonal lines) and the second step is the approximation of the fragments by geometric primitives. If some fragments can not be approximated by geometric primitives with acceptable precision, they are recognized as free curves.

In this paper, we present a novel method for decomposition of a curve into arcs and lines. It is based on a new method for circle detection [1] and dominant point detection [2]. Dominant point detection [2] is used as a preliminary step to extract the critical points of the curve. It has a complexity in $O(n \log n)$ time. So, it possesses a low processing cost. In addition, it is easy and simple to implement. The rest of this paper is organized as follows. The next section recalls a method for dominant point detection. Section 3 presents a method for circle detection. In section 4, we propose a method to split a curve into arcs and straight line segments. Section 5 presents some experimentations and applications to vectorization based on curve reconstruction.

2 Dominant Point Detection

Dominant points (DP) are local maximum curvature points on a curve that have a rich information content and are sufficient to characterize this curve. We recall hereafter a method of dominant point detection [2] based on an approach of discrete geometry.

2.1 Blurred Segment

The notion of blurred segment [11] was introduced from the notion of an arithmetical discrete line. An ***arithmetical discrete line***, noted $D(a, b, \mu, \omega)$, $(a, b, \mu, \omega) \in \mathbb{Z}^4, gcd(a, b) = 1$, is a set of points $(x, y) \in \mathbb{Z}^2$ that satisfies: $\mu \leq ax - by < \mu + \omega$. A ***blurred segment*** (BS) [11] with a main vector (b, a), lower bound μ and thickness ω is a set of integer points (x, y) that is optimally bounded (see [11] for more detail) by a discrete line $D(a, b, \mu, \omega)$. The value $\nu = \frac{\omega-1}{max(|a|,|b|)}$ is called the width of this BS. Figure 1.a shows a blurred segment (the sequence of gray points) whose the optimal bounding line is $\mathcal{D}(5, 8, -8, 11)$, the vertical distance is 1.25. Nguyen et al. proposed in [12] the notion of maximal blurred segment. A ***maximal blurred segment of width*** ν (MBS) (see figure 1.b) is a width ν blurred segment that can not be extended to the left and the right sides of a given curve. A linear recognition algorithm of width ν blurred segments is described in [11].

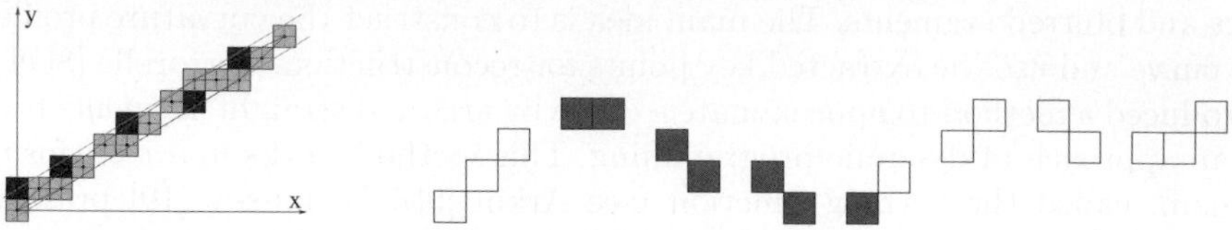

(a) A blurred segment

(b) A maximal blurred segment of width 1 (in dark gray points).

Fig. 1. Blurred segments of width ν

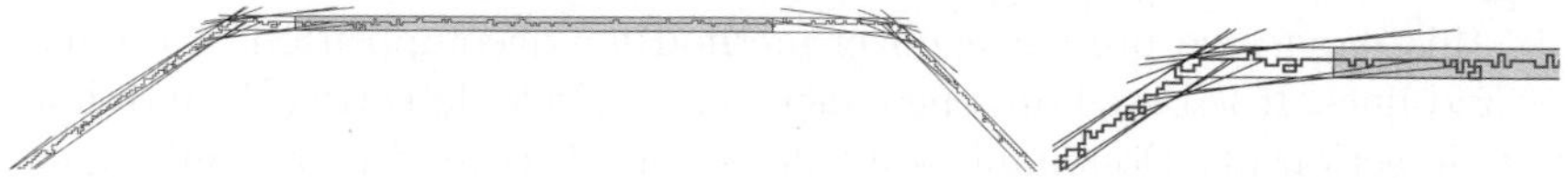

(a) Set of maximal blurred segments on a curve

(b) Zoom of (a)

Fig. 2. Gray zone is not a common zone of successive maximal blurred segments

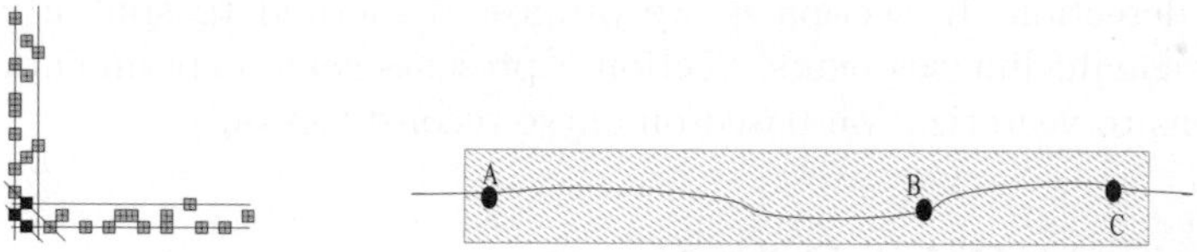

(a) Common zone in black

(b) a MBS contains at most 2 candidates as DP

Fig. 3. MBS and dominant point

2.2 A Method for Dominant Point Detection

Nguyen et al. introduced some propositions utilized in [2] to locate and eliminate weak candidates as dominant points (DP). Considering a given width ν, we have:

Proposition 1. *A DP must be in a common zone of successive maximal blurred segments (see figure 2).*

Proposition 2. *The smallest common zone of successive maximal blurred segments whose slopes are monotone contains a candidate of DP (see figure 3.a).*

Proposition 3. *A maximal blurred segment contains a maximum of 2 DP candidates (see figure 3.b).*

Heuristic strategy: *In each smallest zone of successive maximal blurred segments whose slopes are increasing or decreasing, the candidate as dominant point is detected as the middle point of this zone.*

Based on the above study, Nguyen et al. proposed a method for the dominant point detection (see algorithm 1).

Algorithm 1. Dominant point detection [2].

Data: C discrete curve of n points, ν width of the segmentation
Result: D set of extracted dominant points
begin
  Build $MBS_\nu = \{MBS(B_i, E_i, \nu)\}_{i=1}^m$, $\{slope_i\}_{i=1}^m$;
  $m = |MBS_\nu|$; $p = 1$; $q = 1$; $D = \emptyset$;
  while $p \leq m$ **do**
    while $E_q > B_p$ **do** $p++$;
    Add $(q, p-1)$ to stack;
    q=p-1;
  while $stack \neq \emptyset$ **do**
    Take (q, p) from stack;
    Decompose $\{slope_q, slope_{q+1}, ..., slope_p\}$ into monotone sequences;
    Determine the last monotone sequence $\{slope_r, ..., slope_p\}$;
    Determine the middle point DP of the last monotone sequence $\{slope_r, ..., slope_p\}$;
    $D = \{D \cup DP\}$;
end

3 Arc Detection

In this section, we recall a linear method [1] for the detection of digital arcs. Nguyen and Debled proposed in [1] some properties of arcs in tangent space representation that are inspired from Arkin [9] and Latecki [13].

3.1 Tangent Space Representation

Let $C = \{C_i\}_{i=0}^n$ be a polygon, l_i - length of segment C_iC_{i+1} and $\alpha_i = \angle(\overrightarrow{C_{i-1}C_i}, \overrightarrow{C_iC_{i+1}})$. If C_{i+1} is on the right of $\overrightarrow{C_{i-1}C_i}$ then $\alpha_i > 0$, otherwise $\alpha_i < 0$.

Let us consider the transformation that associates a polygon C of $\mathbb{Z}^2$ to a polygon of $\mathbb{R}^2$ constituted by segments $T_{i2}T_{(i+1)1}, T_{(i+1)1}T_{(i+1)2}$, $0 \leq i < n$ (see figure 4) with:

$T_{02} = (0, 0)$,
$T_{i1} = (T_{(i-1)2}.x + l_{i-1}, T_{(i-1)2}.y)$, i from 1 to n,
$T_{i2} = (T_{i1}.x, T_{i1}.y + \alpha_i)$, i from 1 to $n-1$.

3.2 Properties of Arc in the Tangent Space

Nguyen et al. also proposed in [1] some properties of a set of sequential chords of a circle in the tangent space. They are resumed by proposition 4 (see also figure 5).

Proposition 4. *[1] Let $C = \{C_i\}_{i=0}^n$ be a polygon, $\alpha_i = \angle(\overrightarrow{C_{i-1}C_i}, \overrightarrow{C_iC_{i+1}})$ such that $\alpha_i \leq \alpha_{max} \leq \frac{\pi}{4}$. The length of C_iC_{i+1} is l_i, for $i \in \{1, \ldots, n\}$. We consider the polygon $T(C)$, that corresponds to its representation in the modified tangent space, constituted by the segments $T_{i2}T_{(i+1)1}, T_{(i+1)1}T_{(i+1)2}$ for i from*

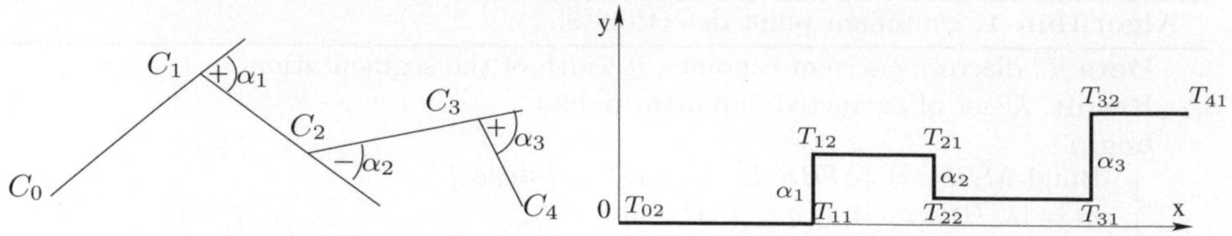

(a) Input polygonal curve (b) Tangent space representation

Fig. 4. Tangent space representation

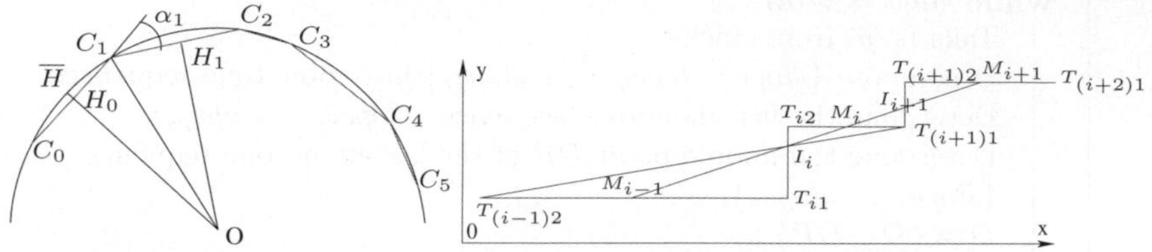

(a) A set of sequential chords of an arc. (b) Its property in tangent space representation.

Fig. 5. The chords in tangent space

0 to $n-1$. $MpC = \{M_i\}_{i=0}^{n-1}$ is the midpoint set of $\{T_{i2}T_{(i+1)1}\}_{i=0}^{n-1}$. So, C is a polygon whose vertices are on a real arc only if $MpC = \{M_i\}_{i=0}^{n-1}$ is a set of quasi collinear points.

From now on, MpC is called the midpoint curve.

3.3 Algorithm for Arc (Circle) Detection

Thanks to proposition 4, Nguyen et al. proposed a linear algorithm in [1] (see algo. 2) for the arc/circle detection.

4 Curve Decomposition into Arcs and Lines

Algorithm 2 allows to recognize a digital circle by detecting straight line segment in the tangent space. The parameter α_{max} is used to assure that the hypothesis of theorem 4 is valid. We have the definition below.

Definition 1. *In the curve of midpoints in the tangent space,* **an isolated point** *is a midpoint satisfying that the differences of ordinate values between it and one of its 2 neighboring midpoints on this curve is higher than the threshold α_{max}. If this condition is satisfied with all 2 neighboring midpoints, it is called* **a full isolated point**

Algorithm 2. Detection of a digital arc/circle [1].

Data: $C = \{C_i\}_{i=0}^{n}$ digital curve, α_{max} - maximal admissible angle, ν- width of blurred segment
Result: ARC if C is an arc, CIRCLE if C is a circle, FALSE otherwise.
begin
    Use [11] to decompose C with blurred segments of width 1: $P = \{P\}_{i=0}^{m}$;
    Represent P in the modified tangent space by $T(P)$ (see section 3.1);
    if *there exists i such that* $T_{i2}.y - T_{i1}.y > \alpha_{max}$ **then return** FALSE;
    Determine the midpoint set $MpC = \{M_i\}_{i=0}^{m-1}$ of $\{T_{i2}T_{(i+1)1}\}_{i=0}^{m-1}$;
    Use the algorithm in [11] to verify if MpC is a blurred segment of width ν;
    if MpC *is a straight line segment* **then**
        if $|M_{m-1}.y - M_0.y| \simeq 2 * \pi$ **then**
            return CIRCLE;
        else return ARC;
    else return FALSE;
end

4.1 Main Idea of the Proposed Method

We present in this section a new method for curve decomposition into arcs and straight line segments. Our principal idea is to apply a dominant point detector [2] as preprocessing step to enhance the segmentation quality. We assume that the extremities between an arc and a straight segment, or among 2 arcs, or among 2 straight line segments are also dominant points. It is true for almost all cases. Therefore, we detect firstly the dominant points on the input curve C. These points are considered as candidates for extremities between the arcs and the straight line segments in a decomposition of C. In the next step, we will group the points if they constitute an arc. The detection of an arc [1] is based on theorem 4 by using algo. 2. Thanks to this algorithm, an arc corresponds to a straight segment on the curve of midpoints (MpC) such that the difference of ordinate values among 2 successive midpoints is less than a threshold α_{max}. The isolated points correspond to straight line segments. This process is done in the tangent space representation of the polygon that is constructed from detected dominant points.

4.2 Analysis of Configurations

Let us consider figure 6. In this example, there are all basic configurations among the primitive arc and line: arc-arc, arc-line and line-line. Figure 7 presents these configurations in detail in the tangent space. Concerning the midpoint curve (MpC) in the tangent space, we have several remarks below.

- An isolated point in MpC corresponds to an extremity among two adjacent primitives in C.
- A full isolated point in MpC corresponds to an line segment in C.
- An isolated point in MpC can be co-linear with a set of co-linear points that corresponds to an arc.

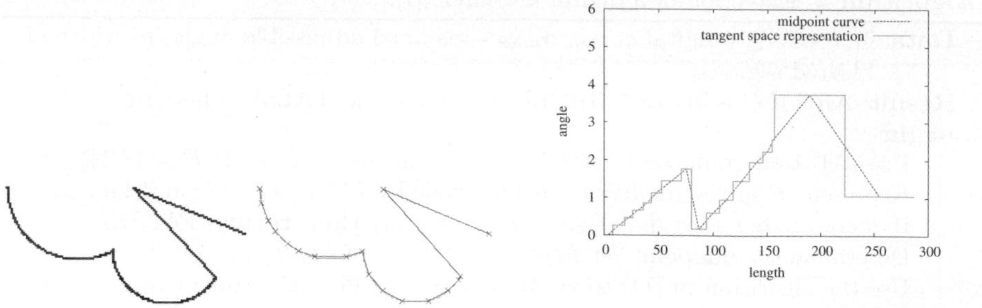

(a) Input curve (b) DP detection (c) Representation in the tangent space

Fig. 6. An example of curve

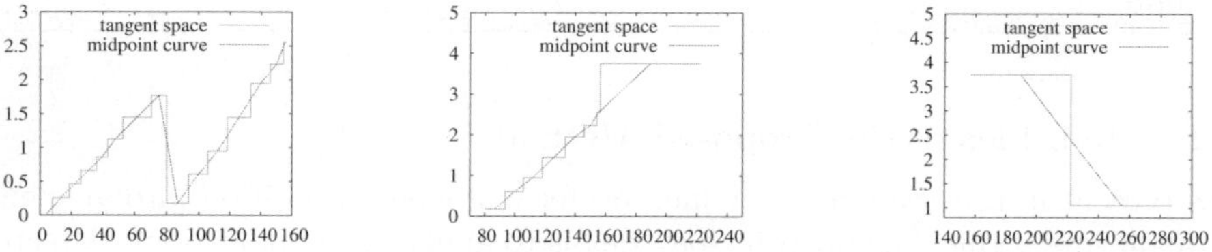

(a) arc-arc (b) arc-line (c) line-line

Fig. 7. Configurations on tangent space

Due to the second remark, it is not appropriate to apply directly a polygonalization on the midpoint curve to extract arcs from the input curve.

4.3 Proposed Algorithm

Thanks to the above remarks, we present hereafter an algorithm (see algo. 3) to decompose a curve C into arcs and straight line segments. First, the sequence of dominant points (DpC) of C is computed. DpC is then transformed in the tangent space and the MpC curve is constructed. An incremental process is then used and each point of MpC is tested: if it is not an isolated point (in this case, it corresponds to a segment in C), the blurred segment recognition algorithm [11] permits to test if it can be added to the current blurred segment (which corresponds to an arc in C). If it is not possible, a new blurred segment starts with this point.

Complexity: As shown in [2], the detection of dominant points can be done in $O(n \log n)$ time. The transform to the tangent space is done in linear time. The recognition process in MpC is also done in linear time [11]. So, the proposed method is done in $O(n \log n)$ time.

[1] By default, $\alpha_{max} = \frac{\pi}{4}$, $\nu = 0.2$ (see algo. 3).

Algorithm 3. Curve decomposition into arcs and lines

Data: $C = \{C_1, \ldots, C_n\}$-a digital curve, α_{max}- maximal angle, ν-width of blurred segments [1]
Result: $ARCs$- set of arcs, $LINEs$- set of lines
begin
  Use [2] to detect the set of dominant points: $DpC = \{D_0, \ldots, D_m\}$; $BS = \emptyset$;
  Transform DpC in the tangent space and construct the midpoint curve $MpC = \{M_i\}_{i=0}^{m-1}$;
  for i=0 **to** m-1 **do**
    $C_{b_i}C_{e_i} = \{C_i\}_{b_i}^{e_i}$- part of C wich corresponds to M_i;
    if $\Big((|M_i.y - M_{i-1}.y| > \alpha_{max})\&\&(|M_i.y - M_{i+1}.y| > \alpha_{max})\Big)$ **then**
      Push $C_{b_i}C_{e_i}$ to $LINEs$;
    else
      if $BS \cup M_i$ *is a blurred segment of width* ν *[11]* **then**
        $BS = BS \cup M_i$;
      else
        C' - part of C corresponding to BS;Push C' to $ARCs$;
        if $\Big((|M_i.y - M_{i-1}.y| > \alpha_{max})||(|M_i.y - M_{i+1}.y| > \alpha_{max})\Big)$ **then**
          Push $C_{b_i}C_{e_i}$ to $LINEs$;$BS = \emptyset$;
        else
          $BS = \{M_i\}$;
end

5 Experimentations

5.1 Experimental Results and Comparisons

This method is rapid and simple to implement. Figures 8, 9 and 10 show some experimental results of the proposed methods.

Moreover, figures 11, 12 and table 1 show some comparisons with other methods [7,5,6]. Salmon et al. [7] proposed a method for the same purpose based on

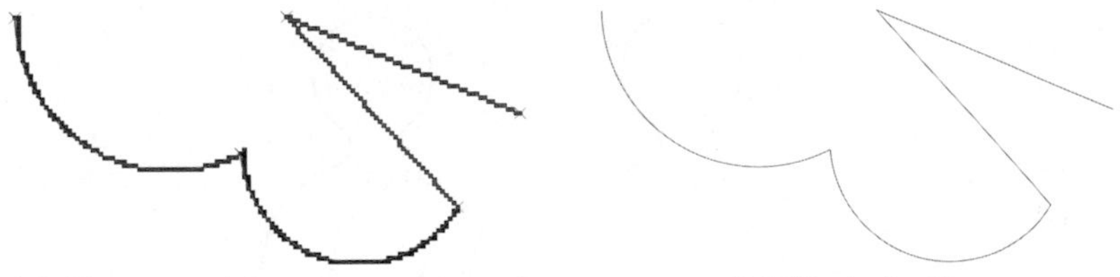

(a) Decomposition into arcs and lines

(b) Vectorization

Fig. 8. Test on the curve in figure 6. Parameters: $\alpha_{max} = \frac{\pi}{4}$, $\nu = 0.2$

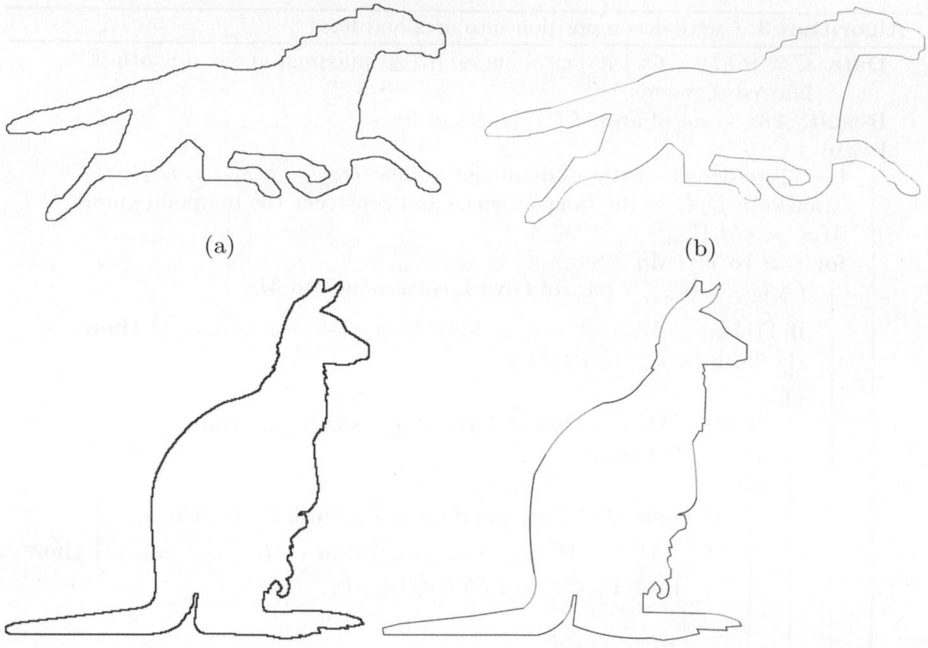

(a) (b) (c) (d)

Fig. 9. Curve reconstruction by using the proposed method. (a) (resp. (c)): Input curve, (b) (resp. (d)): Reconstructed curve. Parameters: $\alpha_{max} = \frac{\pi}{4}$, $\nu = 0.2$.

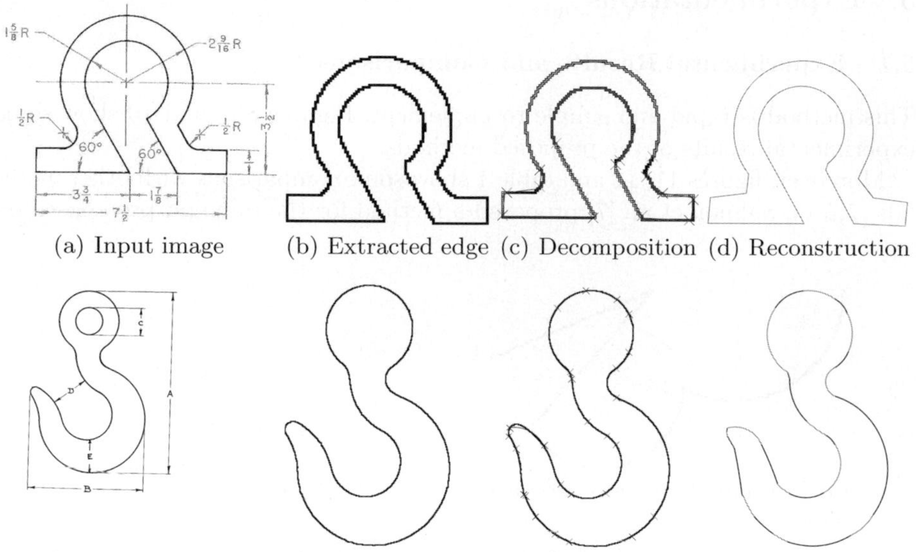

(a) Input image (b) Extracted edge (c) Decomposition (d) Reconstruction

(e) Input image (f) Extracted contour (g) Decomposition (h) Reconstruction

Fig. 10. Test on technical images. Parameters: $\alpha_{max} = \frac{\pi}{4}$, $\nu = 0.2$.

Table 1. Comparison with others methods: Horng et al. [5] and Horng [6]

Curve	No of point	Method	No of primitives	ISE	CR	FOM	CPU Time (s)
Fig. 12.b	605	Proposed	22	449.828	27	0.060	0.05
		Horng et al.	15	489.7	40.333	0.0824	1274.75
		Horng	29	329.9	20.862	0.0632	3.23
Fig. 12.c	413	Proposed	22	139.746	22	0.1288	0.03
		Horng et al.	13	175.4	31.769	0.1811	511.77
		Horng	26	107.7	15.885	0.1475	0.94

curvature profile that is constructed by using the determination of left and right blurred segment at each point in $O(n^2)$ time. So, this method is less efficient than our method. Moreover, the use of filtering and least square fitting methods on the curvature profile cause a distortion in the results of reconstruction. On the contrary, our method is based on a dominant point detector, so the extremities among sequential primitives are well located. Table 1 compares qualitatively the proposed method with other methods. We adapt the criterion of Sarkar [14] that is used in polygonal approximation to calculate the quality of each method. CR is the compression ratio between the number of points and the number of extracted primitives, ISE is the integral square error between the curve and the reconstructed curve and FOM is the ratio between CR and ISE to balance these two aspects. The proposed method is a little less efficient than Horng et al. [5], Horng [6] but it is more rapid than these ones.

5.2 Application to Vectorization

Thanks to this method, figure 8.b presents the reconstruction of the curve based on extracted arcs and lines. That is also the main idea for an application to vectorization of a curve based on the reconstruction of the curve from extracted arcs and lines. An arc is constructed simply based on 2 extremities and the middle point of the digital arc. Figure 10.d and figure 9.b, d show some examples of vectorization by using the proposed method with other curves.

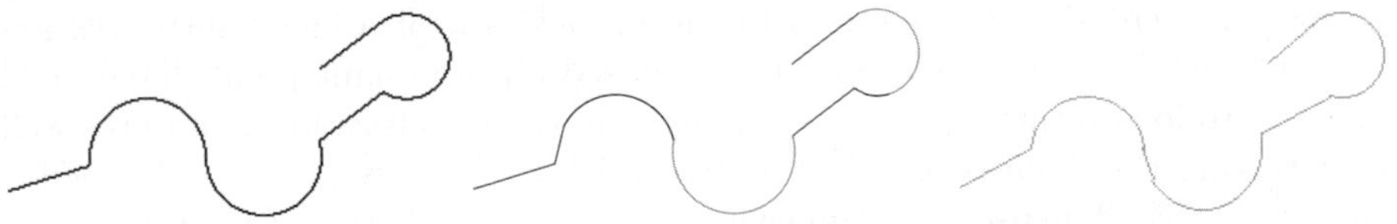

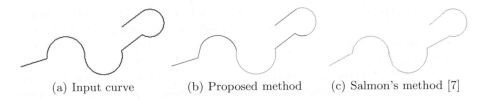

(a) Input curve (b) Proposed method (c) Salmon's method [7]

Fig. 11. Comparison with Salmon et al. [7]

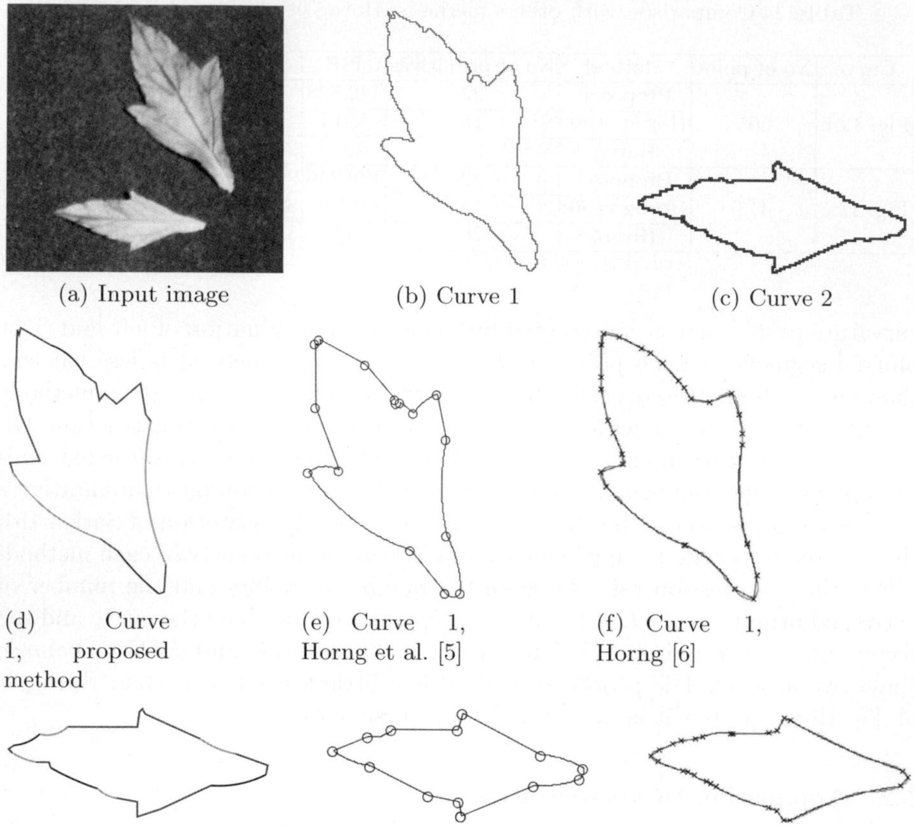

(a) Input image (b) Curve 1 (c) Curve 2 (d) Curve 1, proposed method (e) Curve 1, Horng et al. [5] (f) Curve 1, Horng [6] (g) Curve 2, proposed method (h) Curve 2, Horng et al. [5] (i) Curve 2, Horng [6]

Fig. 12. Comparison with Horng et al. [5] and Horng [6]. Parameters: $\alpha_{max} = \frac{\pi}{4}$, $\nu = 0.2$.

6 Conclusion

We have presented a new method for decomposition of a curve into arcs and lines in $O(n \log n)$ time. A preprocessing based on dominant point detector [2] allows us to locate the extremities among primitives such as lines and arcs well. By detecting the *isolated points*, the arc and line primitives can be located in the input curve. The use of 2 primitives (arc and line) allows us to obtain a good description of curves in relation with other techniques based on corner points and polygonalization.

References

1. Nguyen, T.P., Debled-Rennesson, I.: A linear method for curves segmentation into digital arcs. Technical report, LORIA, Nancy university (2010), http://www.loria.fr/~nguyentp/pubs/arcSegmentation.pdf
2. Nguyen, T.P., Debled-Rennesson, I.: A discrete geometry approach for dominant point detection. Pattern Recognition 44(1), 32–44 (2011)
3. Rosin, P.L., West, G.A.W.: Segmentation of edges into lines and arcs. Image Vision Comput. 7(2), 109–114 (1989)
4. Chen, J.-M., Ventura, J.A., Wu, C.H.: Segmentation of planar curves into circular and line segments. Image Vision and Computing 14, 71–83 (1996)
5. Horng, J.H., Li, J.T.: A dynamic programming approach for fitting digital planar curves with line segments and circular arcs. Pattern Recognition Letters 22(2), 183–197 (2001)
6. Horng, J.H.: An adaptive smoothing approach for fitting digital planar curves with line segments and circular arcs. Pattern Recognition Letters 24(1-3), 565–577 (2003)
7. Salmon, J.P., Debled-Rennesson, I., Wendling, L.: A new method to detect arcs and segments from curvature profiles. In: ICPR, vol. 3, pp. 387–390 (2006)
8. Tortorella, F., Patraccone, R., Molinara, M.: A dynamic programming approach for segmenting digital planar curves into line segments and circular arcs. In: ICPR, pp. 1–4 (2008)
9. Arkin, E.M., Chew, L.P., Huttenlocher, D.P., Kedem, K., Mitchell, J.S.B.: An efficiently computable metric for comparing polygonal shapes. PAMI 13(3), 209–216 (1991), doi:10.1109/34.75509
10. Bodansky, E., Gribov, A.: Approximation of a polyline with a sequence of geometric primitives. In: Campilho, A., Kamel, M.S. (eds.) ICIAR 2006. LNCS, vol. 4142, pp. 468–478. Springer, Heidelberg (2006)
11. Debled-Rennesson, I., Feschet, F., Rouyer-Degli, J.: Optimal blurred segments decomposition of noisy shapes in linear time. Computers & Graphics 30(1), 30–36 (2006)
12. Nguyen, T.P., Debled-Rennesson, I.: Curvature estimation in noisy curves. In: Kropatsch, W.G., Kampel, M., Hanbury, A. (eds.) CAIP 2007. LNCS, vol. 4673, pp. 474–481. Springer, Heidelberg (2007)
13. Latecki, L., Lakamper, R.: Shape similarity measure based on correspondence of visual parts. PAMI 22(10), 1185–1190 (2000), doi:10.1109/34.879802
14. Sarkar, D.: A simple algorithm for detection of significant vertices for polygonal approximation of chain-coded curves. Pattern Recognition Letters 14(12), 959–964 (1993)

Author Index

Printing: Mercedes-Druck, Berlin
Binding: Stein+Lehmann, Berlin